The United States
D. VAN NOSTRAND CO., NEW YORK

Australia and New Zealand
WILLIAM HEINEMANN LTD., MELBOURNE

Canada
THE MACMILLAN COMPANY OF CANADA, TORONTO

South Africa
THE OXFORD UNIVERSITY PRESS, CAPE TOWN

India and Burma
ALLIED PUBLISHERS LIMITED
BOMBAY   CALCUTTA   NEW DELHI

THE CONSTITUTIONAL HISTORY
OF MEDIEVAL ENGLAND

Uniform with this volume

THE CONSTITUTIONAL HISTORY
OF MODERN BRITAIN
1485–1951
by
SIR DAVID LINDSAY KEIR, M.A., LL.D.
MASTER OF BALLIOL COLLEGE, OXFORD

FIFTH EDITION

THE CONSTITUTIONAL HISTORY
OF
MEDIEVAL ENGLAND

FROM THE ENGLISH SETTLEMENT TO 1485

by

J. E. A. JOLLIFFE, M.A.
FELLOW AND SUB-WARDEN OF KEBLE COLLEGE, OXFORD
LECTURER IN MEDIEVAL ENGLISH HISTORY
IN THE UNIVERSITY OF OXFORD

THIRD EDITION

LONDON
ADAM AND CHARLES BLACK
1954

A. AND C. BLACK LIMITED
4, 5 AND 6 SOHO SQUARE LONDON W.I

FIRST PUBLISHED 1937
SECOND EDITION 1947
REPRINTED 1948
THIRD EDITION 1954

MADE IN GREAT BRITAIN
PRINTED BY R. AND R. CLARK, LTD., EDINBURGH

CONTENTS

I

FROM THE ENGLISH SETTLEMENT TO THE REIGN OF ÆLFRED

II

FROM THE REIGN OF ÆLFRED TO THE NORMAN CONQUEST

III

FROM THE NORMAN CONQUEST TO THE REIGN OF HENRY III

IV

1272–1377

V

1377–1485

THE CONSTITUTIONAL HISTORY
OF MEDIEVAL ENGLAND

I

FROM THE ENGLISH SETTLEMENT TO THE
REIGN OF ÆLFRED

i

THE FOLK ORGANIZED BY KINDRED AND LORDSHIP

A CONSTITUTIONAL history of England may properly begin with Introduc-
the English settlement. Whatever the degree of Romanization of *tory*
the British Province, no trace of Latin influence upon the English
peoples has been or is likely to be detected before the Gregorian
mission introduced an ecclesiastical strand into the land law of
the seventh century. There are some obvious survivals from the
past in Northumbria and in the extreme west of the Midlands;
but they are Celtic, and testify rather to the failure of Rome to
change the essentials of life in the remoter parts of the island than
to any permanent influence of Latin political or social forms. On
the other hand, the customs of the various invading races, coming,
as most of them did, from the most primitive north-western extensions of Germany, preserve in a very perfect form the principles
of Germanic society. They share with all the northern peoples the
essential ideas of the joint responsibility of kindreds before the
law, the blood-feud and its compositions, and a primitive classification of society into the noble, the free, and the half-free, which
is the outward manifestation of the predominance of the tie of
blood and inheritance. This primitive phase of social organization
gives its character to the centuries during which the English
were building up the Heptarchy, and constitutes a defined epoch
sharply distinguished from the age of feudalism which followed

it. It can only be understood in the terms which the Anglo-Saxons themselves used in codes and charters and in their courts, and by way of their own preconceptions as to the nature of their political and social system.

The nation   The most primitive idea as to the nation is that it is a kindred, enlarged past all rememberable degrees of relationship, but holding to a tradition of common ancestry, human or divine. Nations speak of themselves as Angel*cynn*,[1] Iutna*cynn*, and among many of the northern races a royal stock transmits the blood of the founder, bears his name, and embodies the legendary unity of the nation in the person of a king. So the oldest Danish dynasty are Ynglingas from the divine hero Yngvi, while in Britain the West Saxons call themselves Gewissae and trace the descent of the house of Cerdic from Gewiss.[2] Such groups, ideally kindred grown to nations, in practice political communities, are spoken of as late as the Alfredian chronicles and translations as *maegths*,[3] groups united by one blood and custom. This sense of common blood is carried deeply into the structure of the nation. The rank, status, and privilege of each man are his birthright. They are only valid if he can establish their inheritance from four generations and point to a full kindred extending through four degrees of descent. It is not until the requisite generations have inherited his freedom, and a free kin has been built upon an original act of emancipation, that his descendants will grow into their full right in the folk,[4] and what is true of the passage from slavery to freedom is said also to have been true of that from freedom to nobility. Only at the fourth generation does rank become heritable and carry with it its full privilege.[5]

The kindred   A full kindred is essential to the enjoyment of folkright for very practical reasons. Early law cannot and will not deal with the individual. The actions of every man involve his kinsmen, and they share his responsibility. The most striking instance of

[1] Anglo-Saxon Chronicle, 449A.
[2] Grimm, *Teutonic Mythology*, i. 354.
[3] Prologue to Wihtraed's Laws—cantwara *maegð*. Maegth = kindred.
[4] *Ibid.* 8. The man freed at the altar has no wergeld or inheritance.
[5] Norð Leoda Laga, 11. But it is doubtful whether the Anglo-Saxons recognized the possibility of transition from one to the other of their primitive birth-grades. The text cited is a late one and shows marked Celtic influence.

this is in the feud. In slaying or injuring another the offender not
only brings upon himself the enmity of his victim's kin, but
involves his own. By the act of the individual the families of both
parties—to seven or nine degrees according to usage—are legally
open to vengeance or committed to taking it, though they may,
if they like, pay the heavy blood-price or *wergeld* to "buy off the
spear".[1] It is not until the reign of Eadmund that a man's kin can
lawfully disclaim revenge and leave him to bear the feud alone.[2]
The feud, moreover, is only the most striking and not the most
important function of the blood-group, which is, in fact, fundamental to early English society. A man's whole citizenship depends
upon his being backed by an adequate kindred. The law will not
deal with individuals, will not admit them into its courts, or listen
to their oaths, or accord them any sort of protection, unless they
are vouched for by guarantors—*borh* is the term used—who
originally should be their blood-relations. If a man is to be treated
as a member of the moot, with the legal rights of a freeman, there
must be someone who will guarantee that he will behave lawfully, stand to justice if called upon, fulfil any judgment the court
may put upon him, pay any damages which he may have incurred
towards others.[3] Increasingly, as time goes on, lords will be
required to take upon them this responsibility of borh towards
their men ; but the natural and original warrantors of any man
are his own kin,[4] his *maegburg*,[5] and only as a known resident
with an adequate maegth can he be received as a responsible
and lawful man who can sue and be sued, and whose oath is
valid in law. The kindred is said to "domicile its members to
folkright",[6] and the man who has no kin and can find no
lord is outlaw, *caput gerit lupinum*.[7] Further, within the court
itself, accepted and given legal standing there, he still cannot act
alone. Stage by stage, in any cause he pleads, his own oath will
not carry him; his kin must swear with him, twelve or more,[8]
according to the cause, must offer themselves with him as oath-

---

[1] Ælfred, 27; I Cnut, 5, 2b. *Mid his magum, þae fehþe moton mid beran, oððe
forebetan*: with his kin who must bear the feud with him or buy it off.

[2] II Eadmund, 1.   [3] Æthelbert, 23.

[4] II Æthelstan, 1. 3; 6. 1; III Æthelstan, 7. 2.   [5] Ine, 74. 1.

[6] II Æthelstan, 2.   [7] A twelfth century phrase.

[8] Ine, 21. 1; II Æthelstan, 11; VIII Æthelred, 23; Northumbrian Priest's
Law, 51.

helpers, and thus, as by a combined act of the kin, a valid oath can be achieved. Thus, the individual as a person in law cannot act in isolation. His status is incomplete in itself, and his right is effective only as a member of the group with which he is joined by descent. As such it is known as his *maegth-law*,[1] and this, in turn, can be destroyed by outlawry, so that the outlaw's kin is loosed from all obligation.[2]

One form of the predominance of the blood-tie was lacking with the English and, indeed, with all Teutonic peoples. By the period of their appearance in history they had abandoned the joint family holding of land which seems to have been common to all the primitive peoples of the North and which survived in Wales into the Middle Ages.[3] Even so, the practice of equal partition at each generation was common in many parts of England,[4] and shows the right of birth into the stock of descent still resisting the disintegrating forces of free economy and individual ownership. But, this apart, the Saxon freeman was involved in relationships natural or contracted, bound either by the ties of blood or by the conventionally idealized ties of lordship, which, as we shall see, were thought of as extensions of them. All that came of this heightened sense of kinship, the feud and its composition, surety-ship, compurgation, and the validity of legal standing and the power to offer oath—law-worthiness and oath-worthiness—is the mainspring of contemporary life, and makes up almost the whole equipment of ideas about law and social relations which the age needs or can conceive. It is natural, therefore, for the nation to be determined by race and descent, since it is the aggregate of the interrelated kindreds of its members, the common maegth of the Mercians or Kentings. So organized, society throws the weight of habit against the forces of free economy and individualism, and thinks less of land or other wealth as a criterion of rank or author-ity. Not until the exclusive reverence for descent has been sapped

[1] I Cnut, 5. 2d. The novice monk is said to "come out of his *maegthlage* when he enters his rule-law".

[2] III Eadgar, 7. 2.

[3] The right of pasture in a common waste used in many parts of Britain is another matter from the common right of property.

[4] Probably much more commonly than is yet realized. It was predominant in Kent as *gavelkind*, but it was also common in East Anglia and may be found in Dorset. The Lombards broke up their joint holdings by the practice of adfratellamentum-fictitious brotherhood.

by centuries of economic and political experience is the way clear for the rudiments of feudalism and the territorial state.[1]

From the imagined community of descent a common inherit- *The law* ance of law was deduced. Law was an attribute of the stock, and *and the* every member of it was born into folkright, a complex of privi- *individual* lege, status, and obligation coming to him with his father's blood and his material inheritance of land and goods. Such a man was said to be folk-free. There were slaves—*theows*—rightless men who had sold themselves into slavery, or incurred it by their failure to carry through the right expiation of some breach of custom, but they had no place in kin [2] or community. Ideally, in the rule of society held by the northern world as a whole, folkright endowed the individual with all that was necessary for the completeness of life—a sufficiency of land equal in amount among equals in rank, and the status of his immediate ancestors, noble, free, or half-free. An equal law gave him a sure process of defence in folkmoots, where his landright and his person were defended by common right and by judgment of his neighbours. His life was defended by the blood-price or wergeld, by which his paternal and maternal kindred would be appeased for his death; lesser prices, elaborately graded according to the importance of the injured member, pro- tected him limb by limb from maiming, and as the head of a household he possessed over his house and dependants a peace of which the King's Peace of later days was only one survival. The fence about his house was a sacred mark in law; crimes done within it bore a double and treble penalty, and with some nations incurred the rarely inflicted judgment of death. Ideally, then, to be born into the folk was to inherit full folkright, to take an equal place in public assemblies, to possess a full right of inheritance, and to come under the common burden of the folk, service in war and suit and judgment in the courts. It is best to retain for this social organization the name it gave itself—the *folk*; for democracy, popular self-government, and so on, are phrases drawn from entirely different political conditions. They are terms of politics

[1] This element in English history is best described in F. Seebohm, *Tribal Custom in Anglo-Saxon Law.*   [2] II Eadward, 6.

and the early English peoples were primarily communities of law. How far these half-barbarous peoples observed their own principles is, of course, now past determining.

The grades of the folk   It may be that in some earlier phase of their history the German nations were societies of equals, neither noble nor half-free, free tribesmen of equal rank. Many savage races are. By the beginning of history they have developed a system of castes, most possessing a nobility, and many a caste of half-free cultivators. These castes do not anticipate feudal serfdom or the nobility of feudalism with its dominion by tenure. The two systems have scarcely anything in common. In no case is the oldest nobility of the North an outcome of tenure or property. Either it arises out of the primitive structure of the folk, as with the Bavarians, or, as among the Celts of Wales, nobility comes by office—the service of the king may be the sole source of nobility. Such lordship need not convey power over other freemen and has no necessary connection with land. It is a personal nobility by blood, office, or service. Quite literally, it enhances the value of its possessor, doubling, trebling, even raising sixfold the money value of the wergeld, of the compositions for bodily injuries, and of the price of the house-peace, making the noble's oath outweigh those of many commoners swearing together. But it is a privilege of the person simply. No more than the privilege of the common freeman is it, of itself, lordship of lands or men. The caste of freemen is, as it were, duplicated upon a higher standard of personal worth. The noble is said to be "dearer born"[1] than the freeman, and that is all.

To these two castes free and noble, many nations added a third identical in principle with the others. The *lazzi, liberti, leysings*, of certain German and Scandinavian peoples, the *taeogs* of Wales, lay below the other classes, enjoying point by point the same privilege, but at a lower price, half a freeman's wergeld, sometimes more than half, but throughout the scale at a lower value than the free. They were as a rule members of the community and shared its privileges and obligations: the Saxon *litus* sued and was judged in the public courts, and was represented in the annual assembly of the Marklo,[2] while the Lex Frisionum shows the Frisian *liti* accorded that right of making judicial oath which is the hall-mark of membership of the folk.[3] It is this which is the impassable line between

[1] Ine, 34. 1.   [2] Stubbs, *Constitutional History*, I, § 22.
[3] Lex Frisionum, iii. 4.

membership and non-membership of the community; the slave has no oath and no legal personality apart from his master. Thus in all civil right the *litus* stands with the free and even with the noble. The full member of the folk, folk-free, and an inheritor of law and estate, is, therefore, the type of the barbarian community, and, though above and below him lie the ranks of the noble and the half-free, their privilege is only the freeman's enhanced or diminished. Together these orders make up the folk, and their privilege and obligation is the sum of folkright. Here are rank, order, and degree, but not the *dominium*, vassalage, and customary servitude which come with feudal law.

Since blood-relationship was accepted as the bond of society, the *folc* was nominally equalitarian in its public life, equal, that is to say, within each of the birth-grades of which the folk was composed. This found expression in the law, in the courts in which it was administered, in their composition and procedure, in the rights and duties of the individual. The oldest sections of the Germanic codes [1] are lists of the rights that all freemen have by birth into the *folc*, the landshare in the paternal *alod*,[2] the peace upon the land and the homestead, the blood-prices for death, for an eye, for a limb: all these, material and immaterial, were thought of as one undifferentiated birthright. The right of all free individuals of the race, and—upon the level of dearer birth—that of all nobles, was identical, a common racial inheritance. Handed down by tradition, or committed without conscious analysis to writing, it was the law of the Ripuarians, the Law of the Kentings, Mercnalage. The law-courts, therefore, deal with the adjustment of rights between individuals and kindreds. They do not, or at the beginning of our history they are only just beginning to conceive of the community as something more than the aggregate of its

The Law and the Community

[1] *E.g.* the primitive sections of the Ripuarian and Salian codes.

[2] Alod, *alodium*, is the term used by many continental nations for the original nucleus of the freeman's paternal inheritance, in some cases the *sors* or lot received at the settlement. It is not used in England until the eleventh century, when its meaning was extended to cover all land freely held, but the Saxon *eðel* may be equivalent. Alod is common enough as a term of legal science to be used in speaking of English institutions without any suggestion that the Saxons themselves employed it.

individuals and kindreds. A "breach of the peace" in itself means nothing,[1] for there is no general peace of the community, but only the thousands of islands of peace which surround the roof-tree of every householder, noble and simple, *eorl* and *ceorl*. The king's peace itself covers only his hall and his immediate presence. It is the dearest of peaces, but it concerns no one but himself. For this reason, there is no punishment, or at least only for offences against nature. Acts of violence are civil wrongs done to the individual. They may still be wiped out by the feud, but commonly they will be compensated for by the *bot*, or payment of damages, appropriate to the injury done. Violence, therefore, will not appear as a crime, nor as an offence against king or state. Its effects are exhausted in the injury done to the offended party, and are fully atoned for if he and his kindred are satisfied by the bot.[2]

In all this there is little scope for interpretation since the law expresses the simple facts of life adequately and with the sanctity of race heritage; equally little for authority since the state is not a party to any cause. There are thus at first no royally made judges. Our oldest law, like that of the Germans and Celts, is one in which the appropriate maxim is on every man's lips as soon as the facts of any case have been determined. From this it follows that the court is a meeting of common men, neighbours, a folk-moot. Freed from questionings about law, since it has the acknowledged rules of folkright to apply, it expends its full force upon establishing the efficacy and integrity of its means of arriving at

The oath right judgment. As the basis of its system it has established a conception of far-reaching importance, that of the " lawful man ", the man not only credible upon oath, but whose oath has in itself the decisive effect of proof. This conception is at once rational and religious. The lawful man is the man of standing in the community, of full and free kindred, of known residence and good repute. Such men, irrespective of wealth or influence, are "oath-

---

[1] The use of the word *fredum* for a fraction of the compensation for violence among the Franks used to be thought to prove an early notion of folk-peace or *landfried*. It is not found among the Saxons.

[2] The *wite* of Frisian and English law comes later to be used as a penalty, but in origin it may be a payment to the court for its work of umpirage, being derived from *witan*, to know or take cognizance of—or possibly a payment to the king's officer for arresting the culprit. Cf. p. 45 n. 1 *infra*.

worthy".[1] But in the act of swearing they achieve something
more than credibility, and their oath as it is spoken takes a power
over them and over their cause which is other than their own. It
is in ritual form. Taking to witness at first the pagan and later the
Christian divinities, and incorporating their names, it is at once an
affirmation, an ordeal, and a doom.[2] For certain favoured classes
and certain kinds of process the successful accomplishment of the
oath is a final judgment; the priest swearing at the altar,[3] the king's
thegn,[4] and the foreigner,[5] the man who has a royal charter for
his land,[6] can put an end to any process against himself or his landright by the swearing of a clean oath of defence.

The oath is, therefore, a vital sanction of Saxon public life. At *Oath-*
the head of all his law Ælfred places this command: "I will that *helping*
every man look well to his oath". The man who once foreswears
himself is never again oathworthy and is refused Christian burial.[7]
In ordinary processes the oath of one party may be countered by
that of the other—in the event of a deadlock the solution is the
ordeal of fire or water—and more than the single oath of principals
is needed. The normal member of society, oathworthy and worthy
of folkright though he may be, cannot of himself bring the oath
into being in its full efficacy. He must be backed by associates,
many or few according to the nature of the cause, who will swear
to their belief in the honesty and truth of his oath: "by the Lord
God, this oath that N. has sworn is clean and without guile".[8]
Only with such support can a true oath, with its power to rebut
accusations and establish right, be achieved. In the earliest law it is
the kindred group which must come into court and swear with
their kinsman,[9] and, no doubt, the whole system of compurgation

---

1 I Edw. 3. Men who are notorious false swearers . . . shall never again be
oathworthy, but only ordeal-worthy.

2 Leis Willelme, 21. 5: "According to English procedure a man's oath, once
adjudged valid, cannot be set aside".

3 Wihtraed, 18. *Preost hine claensie sylfaes soþe*: a priest may clear himself
with his unsupported oath.   4 *Ibid.* 20.   5 *Ibid.* 20.

6 *English Historical Review*, vol. l, p. 1.

7 II Æthelstan, 26. Let him never be oathworthy again.

8 Swerian, 6.

9 Ine, 21. 1. In the proportion of two-thirds of the paternal kin and one-third
of the maternal kin as in payment of wergelds. II Æthelstan, 11. The requirement of an oath by the kindred in answer to such charges of violence as gave
ground to the feud (the oldest branch of Teutonic law), lasted long after an
oath by neighbours or friends had superseded it for other kinds of cause. In

finds its origin in the solidarity of the kin. Those who pay and receive the bot with their kinsman, the *maegburg*,[1] are the warrantors of his oathworthiness.

These practices and the theory which inspires them are the background of constitutional history. One of the decisive points of English history was that when the Christian church, having destroyed the authority of the old gods and with it the religious character of oath and ordeal and the validity of every process of law, took the law under its own sanction, lent the name of the Christian god to the formulae of oath, and devised a ceremony of ordeal with masses and the cleansing of the elements of iron and water. This was the bridge by which the pagan world carried its law unchanged into the Christian dispensation. Other changes came with time, more slowly, but everywhere the essentials remained. The neighbourhood replaced the family, but it took on the same duty of mutual warranty, and upon it fell the obliga-

The Folk- tion of witness and oath. The folkmoot continued to be the centre
moot of provincial life. Its elaborate procedure, moving from stage to stage by the oath of kinsmen, or neighbours in later times, setting and overseeing the mutual surety of its constituent townships to the peace, multiplying as time went on its devices of pledge, security, warranty, and witness, necessitated an open court free to all but the slave. Its assumption of the lawfulness of the common man, and its safeguards that he should be so, maintained a legally active community to serve it, and made its name of folkmoot a reality. The use of representation and the emergence of aristocratic leadership characterized its later phases; but its basis was popular, and, as feudalism began to take over this or that area from its jurisdiction, they passed into lordship with the forms and habits of action which the folkmoot had given them. From such courts came all those elements in the English polity which did not come from the Crown. They were the centres of our earliest political divisions, whether under such general names as the *provinciae* of Bede and the maegths of his ninth-century translator, or under the local forms of the *lathe* in Kent, the *rape* in Sussex, and the *scirs* of

the eleventh century even the priest was still required to rebut a charge of homicide by an oath of his kin. VIII Æthelred, 23. I Cnut, 5. 2b. "Let him swear himself clean with those relatives who would have to bear the feud with him."

[1] Ine, 74. 1.

the North and West. All English courts, shire and hundred, borough, wapentake, soke, and, in procedure at least, manor, were in origin and essence folkmoots, and the establishment of this organization of life on a personal basis, and its conversion in the tenth and eleventh centuries into a territorial community, are the contribution of the Anglo-Saxons to English history. With them, indeed, the essential qualities of English political life are established.

Such general principles govern all the English settlements, but *The Kent-* each of the political groups into which they fall has its own setting *ings* of the general theme. The earliest law of Kent, that of Æthelbert, shows a society of three ranks, eorls, ceorls, and *laets*, primitive folk-grades, rigid and determined by ancient racial rule. The nobility is *eorlcund*,[1] noble by blood and descent, and not by service of the king. It has a wergeld of three hundred gold shillings, three times that of the ceorls. Those who are not wholly free do not owe their inferiority to dependence on any lord, but to status. They form a caste, the laets, below, but only slightly below, the free ceorl in their blood-price, and, though no English record describes their custom, their possession of a substantial wergeld[2] makes it almost certain that they enjoyed the rights of the Saxon *liti*, attending folkmoots with the right of making oath there. Thus, the Kentings of the beginning of the seventh century were a perfect example of the folk in practice, since nobility and the semi-free status were merely special grades of a folk of which the common man was the type. These freemen themselves, the ceorls, had the personal peace or *mund* which is the common mark of Germanic freedom, and the eorl's *mundbyrd* or compensation for its violation, was, again, only three times the mundbyrd of the ceorl.[3] The principle of the kindred asserted itself strongly in the land-law. Every freeman of the stock was born into a full birthright of land which expressed itself in the equal partition of inheritance between all the sons at the father's death, and which

---

[1] Æthelbert, 13, 14, 75; Hlothaere and Eadric, 1.
[2] Æthelbert, 26. "If any one slays a laet, one of the highest class, he shall compound for him with eighty shillings." The right to a wergeld and the right of legal action in the moot go together. He who has them is called "worthy of folkright".
[3] *Ibid.* 13-16; Hlothaere and Eadric, 1.

preserved a universal peasant freehold into the Middle Ages.[1] In the seventh century and till modern times the kindred of a dead ceorl, and no lord, was guardian of his heirs and lands.[2] This was the custom of gavelkind, which Angevin judges called the Common Law of Kent, and throughout the county it took the place of villeinage.

The West Saxons   The codes of the late seventh century tell us little more of the basic rules of the folk, but in the laws of Ine (*circa* 690) they give us our first glimpse of the constitution of the West Saxons. Here, in contrast with Kent, we find three fully free classes, distinguished by wergelds of two hundred, six hundred, and twelve hundred silver shillings,[3] and the lowest class, the laets, is not mentioned. There has been no word of the Kentish laets since the beginning of the century, and it would be rash to assume that they did not originally form a fourth class of the West Saxon community also, since we have no West Saxon code of the age of Æthelbert. With the Old Saxons of the Continent, the nearest to our island Saxon stock, the laets persisted as one of the principle grades of the nation. However that may be, the ceorl is presented as the lowest free rank of the West Saxon community, possessed of the normal marks of membership of the folk, a wergeld of two hundred shillings,[4] a legal personality which can be brought to judgment in the courts, and the right to make oath there[5] and offer ordeal.[6] Conversely, he is burdened with the duty of service in the *fyrd*, or national host, in war.[7] He has a mund or peace over his house, protected, like that of the Kenting, by a penalty for its breach,[8] and the breaking of his enclosure is an offence which, though vastly less costly, is of the same quality as the breaking of the defences of the king's *burh*.[9] Again, as with the Kenting, the inheritance of the Wessex ceorl and the wardship of his children lies with the kin,[10] and vouches for a heritable landright. Later the ceorls come under lordship, but, convenient as it would be to

---

[1] Cf. the *Consuetudines Kancie* printed in Lambarde's *Perambulation of Kent*.

[2] Hlothaere and Eadric, 6. The family of a serf, even that of a freedman, were in the lord's mund after his death, and the lord took the wergeld. *Consuetudines Kancie*: cf. Lambarde's *Perambulation of Kent*.

[3] Ine, 70.   [4] Ælfred, 25.   [5] Ine, 30.

[6] *Ibid*. 37.   [7] *Ibid*. 51.   [8] *Ibid*. 6. 3.

[9] Ælfred, 40. The burh is the boundary dyke surrounding some privileged mansion or settlement.

[10] Ine, 38. Clause 57 suggests the widow's dower of a third part of the inheritance.

derive them from the laets of old Saxony, their wergeld of a sixth part of the noble's is that of the Saxon freeman on both sides of the North Sea, and their treatment as the basic freemen of the folk forbids this simplification of history. As to the origin of the classes of the West Saxons whose wergelds stood at six hundred and twelve hundred shillings we know nothing. They seem to have derived their rank from birth, for, as contemporaries put it, they were "dearer born" than the ceorls,[1] and the phrase "eorl and ceorl", surviving as a comprehensive description of society, seems to set them upon the same footing as the Kentish eorlcund men. But their most common title, *twelfhynd* and *sixhynd*, tells us nothing, for it denotes the number of shillings in the wer. Of the other English races we know almost nothing, save that the Mercians divided their folk into blood-grades like those of the Saxons, while the Northumbrians knew no nobility but that of office.

Written law gives us a distorted picture of the seventh century. The main stream of custom was never put into writing. The whole land-law, the rules which governed kinship, and in general the accustomed ways of life, were the habit of the community, and passed from generation to generation by unwritten tradition. Thus it is that, while the codes reveal the solid and ancient structure by kin and descent implicitly and by oblique reference, they are directly concerned with what is new or exceptional. Consequently, the earlier Kentish codes were largely concerned with the incorporation of the foreign Christian clergy into the folk by means of analogy and legal fiction,[2] extending the king's mundbyrd to cover the peace of the Church,[3] and that of the folkmoot to protect the places of worship,[4] placing theft from a priest under the same penalty as theft from the king,[5] and making robbery from a common clerk equal to that from a ceorl.[6] Towards the end

---

1 *Ibid.* 34. 1.

2 In later days this was described as the "setting of Holy Church to world-law", and was considered a great feat of legal wisdom. Griδ, 24. So also in Cristne Saga, viii. 11: "Christendom was taken into the law of Iceland".

3 Ethelbert, 1.   4 *Loc. cit.*   5 *Ibid.* 1 and 4.

6 The expedient of grading the clergy according to the secular orders finally brought the priest to be classed as a thegn with the title of mass-thegn (Be Mirciscan Aδe. 2).

of the seventh century the dooms became full of a similar problem, voluntarily accepted lordship, divorced in principle from the old nobility by blood, and abundantly illustrated in records of custom because the legists were labouring to bring it under rule and control by much the same methods that they had applied to the Church. While the old eorlcund rank was a passive privilege of blood and rank conferring authority of no kind over other men, this, the second phase of class distinction among the English, was *Lordship* lordship as we understand it in later times, the patronage of one man over another. It had its own terms; not the eorl, but in Kent the *dryhten* and in Wessex the *hlaford*, were the types of the magnates by lordship.

This conventional relation is created by the client taking his patron to *hlaford and to mundbora*, and in this phrase the full facts of lordship, both economic and legal, are expressed. The lord as hlaford [1] is the master of a plentiful household, from which he maintains those who seek him as his guests or dependants. As society becomes more wealthy the hlaford's benefits become less simple. The king or the noble becomes generous not so much. in the mere elements of life as in gold and silver, gilded swords, and rings.[2] He is no longer only the *hlafweard* but the *goldweard*, the gold-giver,[3] the lord of gold.[4] Of this relation, half self-interest, half devotion, we hear much in law and poetry. At least by the seventh century, probably much earlier, there were many men, especially young men of ambition, who had left their kindred and attached themselves to the households of kings and nobles. Such men were called *gesiths*, companions of the prince, and we hear of young men of royal birth who were content to serve as gesiths to leaders of established fame,[5] and of young nobles bred up with king's sons to become their war-band.[6] This is the social and

---

1 Hlaford, i.e. hlafweard, bread-ward, or bread-giver.
2 Beowulf, 1. 921: *Beahhorda weard.*
3 *Ibid.* 1. 2652: *Goldgiefa.*
4 *Goldwine.*
5 J. M. Kemble, *Codex Diplomaticus*, 80: *Ego Æthelric subregulus atque comes* (gesith) *gloriosissimi principis Ethilbaldi*: I Æthelric, underking and gesith of the most glorious prince Æthelbald.
6 Earle and Plummer, *Two Saxon Chronicles*, i. 47. Military attendance upon the king and monastic vows seem to have been the only two careers for the young Northumbrian noble in the seventh century. Eddius, *Vita Wilfridi*, xxi.

economic aspect of primitive lordship, that maintenance of which Ælfred speaks in his testament—"the men who now follow me and whose vails I pay at Eastertide".[1] The client takes his patron "to hlaford", "to mundbora"—protector and warrantor of legal standing—"mund" is protection. The latter is the vital fact in law, that which brings the institution of lordship within the rules of folkright. The gesith or *gesithcundman*, the *geneat*, the cleric, and the stranger, tend to receive similar treatment in law, and to find their place in closely related clauses in the codes,[2] since they have all left their kin and so divorced themselves from the normal safe-guards,[3] or have impaired their standing with their kindred by entering into artificial ties with a lord. In an age of war and chivalry many of the gesiths were strangers, attracted by the reputation of a foreign court for leadership or generosity.[4] To such men the lord became the protector and warrantor in law,[5] taking them into his mund or peace. By having found such a warrantor the man recovers the legal standing which he can no longer derive from a kindred. With his lord as mundbora he may sue or be sued in the courts and offer oath and ordeal. Injuries against him will be visited by the payment of the mundbyrd of the lord whose protection has been violated. If he evades justice his lord must make his offence good,[6] and he may assume the legal personality of his man, and plead his cause if he is indicted before king or ealdorman.[7] Thus he stands towards his gesith

---

[1] J. M. Kemble, *Codex Diplomaticus*, 314.   [2] Ine, 19-27.

[3] So the monk is said to "come out of his maegthlaw". VIII Æthelred, 25.

[4] Bede, *Historia Ecclesiastica*, iii. 14: *Undique ad eius* (Oswin of Northumbria) *ministerium de cunctis prope provinciis viri etiam nobilissimi concurrerunt*: from all the neighbouring nations the most noble men came to be his gesiths. Cf. Beowulf, ll. 199-258.

[5] Beowulf, l. 1480. Beowulf begs that Hrothgar will take his place as mundbora to his thegns after his death.

[6] Ine, 22; Ælfred, 21.

[7] Ine, 50: "If a gesithcund man acts as advocate for his household dependants with (*Thingiath with*) the king or a king's ealdorman or with his lord. . . ." This has been taken to imply private justice, of which there is no other trace in this age. It seems, however, to be no more than the common German and Scandinavian practice by which a man of influence or legal knowledge would take the case of another less favourably placed upon his shoulders and argue it as his own. Thus (W. de Gray Birch, *Cartularium Saxonicum*, 591) an anonymous magnate writes to King Eadward telling him how Helmstan, being accused of theft, came to him to seek his help as "fore-speaker" or advocate, and how the writer agreed *and thingade him to Ælfrede cinge*. The reputation of Gunnar of Lith

instead of kindred, and can legalize his status in the same manner as they. To the stranger and ecclesiastic the king is mundbora, and the relation, akin to the tie of family,[1] honours lord and man alike. "No kin is dearer to a man than his lord."[2]

Lordship and the folk

However ancient, even primitive, this kind of lordship may be, in the codes of Ine and Wihtraed it is in process of being reconciled with the basic law. The folk, which is fundamentally a pattern woven upon the threads of kindred, is being distorted by individual power. But, while we recognize this, we must also recognize that the folk's reaction was that of a vigorous body, which could make its own terms with the future. Basically it had been informed by loyalty of blood-relationship, it was now to incorporate the motive of loyalty between lord and man, but it did so in its own fashion, by extending its own principles, not by abandoning them. There can, indeed, be no question of conscious conflict between the principle of kinship and the principle of lordship. Both were relationships natural to a community where economic life was non-competitive and action was governed by personal associations and loyalties. As natural they were accepted, and were favoured and advanced by the impersonal reaction of law and the conscious policy of the crown. The manner of this was characteristic, though to us unfamiliar. It would, perhaps, be rash to say that the tie of lord and man was regarded by way of conscious fiction as analogous to blood-relationship, but it was treated in practice as if it were, and the man was in effect taken into his lord's *familia*. It was one of a group of relationships of which the more intimate blend imperceptibly into physical kinship, and which tend to find similar treatment in law; foreign residence,[3] hospitality,[4] vassalage, fosterage, the tie of the godson

End was founded upon such advocacies, in which the advocate really constitutes himself a principal in the cause in his client's stead. So the reeve Abba asks that successive abbots of St. Augustine's shall be to him and to his heirs *forespreoca and mundbora*, so that "they be in the abbot's *hlaforddome*" (*ibid.* 412, A.D. 833). The case of the gesith who intercedes with his own lord for his man may be that of one who secures his lord's aid as forespeaker in a public court. The term has less precise applications in other contexts. The whole clause may be compared with Ine. 76. 2.

1 Eadward and Guthrum, 12. For the stranger and the cleric the king and the bishop shall be *maeg and mundbora*. So Beowulf speaks of his gesiths as his "brother thegns" (Beowulf, 1480).

2 Anglo-Saxon Chronicle, 755A.

3 Hlothaere and Eadric, 15; Ine, 20 and 21.

4 Leges Edwardi Confessoris, 23. 1.

and his sponsors,[1] all are treated as in one degree or another parallel with the tie of kinship. The mund of lordship, originating in the peace of the house-father over his sons and men, spreads itself over that wider family of protected and commended dependants to whom the mundbora is not father but lord. *Mundbyrdnis* is, therefore, the term for lordship.

The process is the same which we have seen in the reception of the Church and clergy in Ethelbert's code, an incorporation of vassalage into the law of the folk, determined by the precedents of folkright and of the law of kindred, and extending to it many of the latter's incidents. The mund is transferred from the kindred to the lord, the lord replaces the kin as surety,[2] like the kin, he can swear against the slayer for his man's death,[3] the *mægbot*, amendment for loss of honour by insult to a kinsman, is reproduced in a *manbot* or lordship-price,[4] the *heriot*, or manly equipment of arms and horses, once the privilege of the eldest male of a dead man's kin, is now reserved for the lord.[5] Lord and man may wage the blood-feud for each other,[6] and for a kinless man the lord may take or pay the *wer*.[7]

Lordship and vassalage did not yet go to the root of social relations. They could not alter a man's grade in the folk by changing his birth-price. But they did convey valuable privileges, and these privileges were in the end to become the basis of a new grouping of society. Clientage might be no more than a temporary relation, honourable while it lasted, but making no permanent change in a man's status. In many cases, however, it was clearly a lifelong tie, and then its effects went deep. There is nothing in Wihtraed's laws or Ine's to prove that a caste of lords or a caste of vassals had yet come to be recognized. The gesith, apparently,

Lordship and new classes

---

[1] Ine, 76; Lege Henrici Primi, 79.

[2] Ine, 22 and 50.   [3] *Ibid.* 21 and 21. 1.

[4] *Ibid.* 76: "Let the maegbot and the manbot be alike and increase in proportion to the wer". Cf. *ibid.* 70.

[5] *Harvard Essays in Anglo-Saxon Law*, p. 136. In later days the heriot of the West Saxon thegn was equated with the *halsfang*, or portion of the wer allotted to the immediate kin. Leges Henrici I, 14, 3.

[6] Alfred, 42. 5.

[7] Ine, 23. 1. The same is true of the foreigner, to whom the king is mundbora, and the monk. *Ibid.* 23. 2; Ælfred, 21.

remained twyhynd, sixhynd, or twelfhynd, according to his birth-right, in spite of his relation to the king.[1] But, beside the blood-price and its analogues, which continued to depend upon birth as long as the true traditions of the folk were in vigour, there are other money compensations defending the honour, prestige, and peace of individuals, and these are determined by official rank or proximity to the king. Such are the *bohrbryce* or amendment for breach of the protection extended to a dependant, the *burgbryce*, or compensation for violence done within the fortified enclosure of a notable, and the *oferhyrnes*, or that for disobedience or contempt of an order which he is qualified to give by virtue of his office or status. Such privileges are more elastic than the older bots, and increase with the status of the individual whatever his birth. Ealdor-men, bishops, gesiths, and thegns are entitled to such privilege in a rising scale according to their office and irrespective of their birth-price,[2] and they play an important part in the building of a new nobility by service, for the greater the lord the greater the man, whose service could enhance his privilege, though it could not alter his basic rank in the folk by kin and descent. The status of the individual is beginning to be affected by that of his mund-bora, though not yet in essentials. To be in the mund of a common man cannot improve the dependant's standing and may impair it. To be in that of a bishop or ealdorman or their like is a distinction. But to be in that of the king already confers privileges and marks of rank. The king's gesith has a higher burgbryce and a higher defence of his peace.[3] In its upper degrees, therefore, service is an active rival to blood as a determinant of social status.

The gesithcund class   In a rudimentary way it is also coming to be associated with land. By the end of the seventh century the king's benefactions to his *comites* were usually completed by cessions of estates, and such benefactions were clearly held to be in the public interest and to be essential to the gesith's function. The defence of the kingdom rested upon the fyrd in part, but also upon the many gesiths and

[1] Ine, 30: "The gesithman shall pay according to his wer"; *ibid.* 19: "The King's geneat if his wer is twelve hundred shillings. . . ."

[2] *Ibid.* 45. Cf. Leges Hen. I, 68. 3: *Omnis presbyter . . . in seculari dignitate thaini legem habeat, si tamen occidatur . . . secundum natale suum reddetur:* every priest enjoys a thegn's privilege in secular right . . . but if he is slain he is to be paid for according to his birth-price. Cf. Cnut, 6. 2a.

[3] Ine, 45.

men of noble rank who had been given land to equip them as
military leaders. A career as a landed gesith for their sons was
coming to be regarded by the nobility almost as a right, and such
of the younger men as could get no hold upon the land at home
were apt to carry their services abroad. The Northumbria of
Bede's day was, indeed, losing its military strength because its
kings preferred to use the available land to enrich the Church.
Even the clergy who profited by it recognized the danger of this
abuse.[1] Nothing was more likely to establish the gesithcundmen *The*
as a permanent class than the association of their rank with land- *gesith and*
holding, but the endowment of the gesiths did not come to them *the land*
in full right of property. It would seem that in taking to the land
they carried with them something of that relation of lord and man
to which they owed their status. Their landright, as seen in the
laws of Ine, is not unrestricted property. The gesithcund land-
holder is privileged in contrast to his landless equal in status. His
estate is normally between three and twenty hides in extent,[2] he
has a moated burh, and a burhbryce only less than that of a king's
thegn.[3] But the land and its cultivators are not given over to his
discretion. Three-fifths of it must be kept in peasant occupation,[4]
and the relation between this peasantry and the gesith must follow
certain rules. From land, rent only may be exacted. The bodily
labour which comes to be characteristic of the Midland *villanus* of
later days can only be imposed if a homestead—and probably
farming stock also—are provided by the gesith; that is to say, if
there is an additional private bargain and a consequent advantage
to the ceorl.[5] Again, if sentence of outlawry delivers the gesith to
the feud, its executors must confine themselves to driving the
outlaw himself from his capital messuage: they cannot touch his

[1] Bede, *Epistola ad Ecgbertum.* Bede complained of the cession of lands to
monasteries instead of to gesiths. The point is almost certainly that grants to
thegns would be by way of laen or temporary grant, those to the Church in
perpetuity, and so permanently lost to the fisc. The same objection to grant
other than by laen was felt in later days in the case of the Church.

[2] Ine, 64-66.

[3] *Ibid.* 45: "Burgbryce shall be paid for a king's thegn sixty shillings, for a
gesithcund man who has land thirty-five shillings". (The landless gesith would
obviously have no burh.)

[4] *Ibid.* 64-66: "He who has twenty hides shall show twelve hides in occupation" (*xii hida gesettes landes*).

[5] *Ibid.* 67.

dependent cultivators.[1] Similarly, if the gesith gives up his estate voluntarily, he must not impair its settlement. He may take his personal servants with him. The cultivators he must leave upon the land.[2] From these restrictions it is clear that the king's benefactions to his military followers were not gifts and did not constitute property nor confer heritable right. They bear some marks of the conditional grant of *laen* which was to play a great part throughout the history of Saxon land-law. They would, no doubt, like the laens, be granted for a term of years, for life, or for a short term of lives, and the fact that the gesiths as a class faded out of history from the eighth century onwards is amply explained by their failure to establish themselves in an hereditary grasp upon the soil.

Gesith and ceorl But, though they had a comparatively short history themselves, the gesithcund land-holders left a permanent mark upon the peasantry. The major portion of the gesith's estate was *gesettland*, *i.e.* land peopled with cultivators. Presumably they with their land were under the mundbyrdnis, the lordship. There were several ways in which they may have entered into such dependence. The gesith's land was assessed in hides like the rest of the peopled land of England, and the hides and their fractions, the yardlands, were units of assessment for royal rents and public services such as were borne by the community at large. The first assumption must be that the greater number of the gesiths' dependants were ceorls of common standing who were required henceforth to pay to a lord what they had once paid to a king, the *gafol*,[3] or rent, and the *feorm*, or fixed renders of corn, meat, bread, and other provender. The profit of the gesiths may sometimes have consisted not in bringing landless men on to land of their own but in taking up the king's dues in rent and kind over ceorls on the king's land. Their service may have lain, for the most part, in arming and leading their dependants to the host. They could not strip the land of its

[1] *Ibid.* 68. A similar principle guaranteed the return of laenland to its grantor when the holder suffered forfeiture for wrong done. A clause to secure this was inserted in many charters of laenland, for example, those of Bishop Oswald.

[2] *Ibid.* 63.

[3] Gafol was a royal rent of a penny or twopence upon the *sulung* (double hide) in Kent, and the twyhynd commoner of Wessex is called indifferently ceorl and *gafolgelda*. Ine, 6. 3, and Ælfred and Guthrum's Peace, 2: ðam ceorle ðe on gafollande sit. That the West Saxon kings granted away farm-rents to religious houses is proved by Ælfred, 2, and it is likely that the gesiths shared the same kind of grants.

men, and the latter's occupancy was secured to them in the event of their lord's outlawry. On the other hand, though the farming of the king's dues may have brought many ceorls under a shadow of lordship, there were others who took voluntarily to a lord. These entered into a contractual dependence. Two forms of contract existed in seventh-century Wessex by which the landless ceorl could obtain a holding and a lord. By one the land only was received in return for gafol, and by the other a homestead and, perhaps, farming stock with it, were included in the grant, and were paid for by peasant labour upon the lord's own fields.[1] In the example set by such indentured dependence we may see an outstanding factor in the decline of the common freeman of the Midlands towards the villeinage which bound his remote descendants under the Normans. Already in the code of Ine the class of ceorls was in process of fissure. There were gafolgeldas, those who now payed the ancient royal rents to a king's follower,[2] and geburs, who, in the language of the eleventh century as of the seventh, were propertyless contractors for land and stock. For them labour extended to three or even more days a week, with additional service in ploughing time and harvest,[3] and in them many types of villein find their prototypes. Such agrarian indentures did not at once debase the individuals who entered into them. Clearly, they did not impair the ceorls' standing in the folk for they retained their ceorl's wergeld,[4] their freemen's duty in the fyrd,[5] and their right of oath and ordeal.[6] If a proportion of them were transferred in the eleventh century to courts of franchise, not

---

[1] Ine, 67: "If a man take a yardland at an agreed gafol and plough it, and the lord later wishes to establish an obligation of labour as well as gafol, that man need not submit unless his lord has provided him with a homestead as well as the land".

[2] *Ibid*. 6. 3. The ceorlish class divided into gafolgeldas or geburs.

[3] Rectitudines Singularum Personarum (*circa* A.D. 1025), cap. 4: "Gebures riht. On some estates he must do two days of week-work of any work set him, and during Lent three days week-work, and from Candlemass to Easter three days, etc. And where such is the custom it is the gebur's right to be given two oxen, a cow, and six sheep to set him up on the land, and seven acres of his yardland ready sown." It can hardly be doubted that this gebur's right of the eleventh century is substantially that referred to in Ine 67; it is also typical of the villein right of middle England.

[4] Ælfred and Guthrum's Peace, 2.   [5] Ine, 51.

[6] Ælfred, 4. 2. Where the standard of the oath of the ceorl is set for certain causes.

private courts, they were courts which administered folkright by the universal procedure. Only as the sense of hereditary status died, and was replaced by the notion that personal freedom and the tenure of free land were part and parcel of each other, would freedom of person without free landright pass into quasi-servitude.

Growth of lordship   We happen to hear of these contractual relations in connection with the gesiths, but there is no reason to suppose that they were not being entered into between all grades of landed proprietors and those freemen who had no land or needed more. A slow change may have been going on at all levels. Though the lord who is a gesith takes the foremost place in the codes because his lordship has been imposed upon the peasantry by the king, the gesiths can have been only a minority of those who held lordship. There was already much "seeking to lordship" by lesser men. But we must not read into the mundbyrdnis and *hlafordscipe* of the eighth century more than a tithe of the *dominium* of the twelfth. The terms of lordship take new meanings as the centuries pass, and in the age of Ine and for some generations the thing itself has no roots in the soil. It is everywhere, but it is revocable, with less lasting effects and fewer implications in law than feudal lordship. Ideally, it can still be a natural relation, holding the affection and devotion which were to inspire feudal vassalage, and not perhaps yet altogether stultified by legal materialism. Such poetical or descriptive accounts as we have, the story of Cynewulf's thegns,[1] Beowulf, or the lament for Eadgar,[2] have the freshness of human feeling. At least lordship could be used to fortify all kinds of institutions without dishonour. The monastery sought a secular magnate as lord and the priest could call himself a mass-thegn. As yet its own traditions were in the making and it drew its law from that of the kindred, borrowing the various peaces, bots, and protections which surrounded the freeman's hearth and bound together his kin; in the seventh century it had not yet conquered the whole of life. There is no sound evidence that it gave a right of justice over those within its ambit,[3] it had only the most accidental relation to land, nor did it change the law of persons. The old system of courts, pleas, and procedure persists, together with the full public status of all members of the com-

---

[1] Anglo-Saxon Chronicle, 755E.   [2] *Ibid.* 975E.
[3] Cf. p. 64, *infra*.

munity. The folk community finds itself faced with an alien relation, analogous to, but distinct from, the blood-tie, and it treats it on that analogy, absorbing it without any deep change in its theory or practice. The structure of society is altering, but the community interprets those changes according to its ancient law. It is always to alter itself thus by interpretation and slow change, keeping the spirit and letting the letter go. It is this power of absorption, displayed in the seventh, and again and again in later centuries, which brings the English state system through feudalism, enriched and elaborated, but essentially intact.

In the seventh century the distinction which we are used to *Society* drawing between public and private institutions was as yet not *and the* conceived of. "Constitutional principles" were merely special *state* manifestations, to us the most striking manifestations, of a general life-habit, arrived at for the most part unconsciously, but rising logically from the basis of the folk and the kindred. Thus, while it is convenient to isolate one aspect of early English life as the sphere of public action—assemblies, circumscriptions of government, officials, and so on—the division is really an anachronism. To contemporaries all these things were part of one folkright with the law of land and persons. Therefore, in so far as a theory of government existed in the three centuries after the settlement, it was the application upon a grand scale of those rules of personal association which we have just been considering. All that part of government which is not royal, was, indeed, in origin no more than the simple form of assembly necessary to secure impartial umpirage under an immutable law, and the minimum of officialdom necessary to enforce it. For the economist and the legal historian each of the Heptarchic nations has its distinctive customs, but their simple economy has a certain sameness in the factors of value which they will hand on to the West Saxon supremacy and to the later history of England. All proceed from the basic conception of the folk of lawful men as the inheritors and judges of their law. All deduce from that concept the law-worthiness and legal responsibility of all freemen, and give play to it either directly in folkmoots which all freemen attend, or indirectly through the vaguely conceived representative quality of notables, *sapientes*, *witan*. However it finds utterance, the law remains the domain of the community.

The king must not lay down the law unsupported, not because his folk are jealous, but because it is not in him so to do. Law is not in the king's mouth, but so surely in the voice of the nation that it matters little how it finds utterance. There is a deep conservatism in the procedure of the moots. Even the amendment of law is thought of as judgment, a speaking out of that element of law hitherto unrevealed, an act of judgment of the folk through its witan, and this, too, does not radically impair the equality of public life. Where every phase of judgment, oath, and ordeal reflects in word and gesture the principle from which it proceeds, the individuals who bear the moot's person are not jealously determined. The court speaks through them, "*dicit hundredum*", "*teste tota scira*", "*this is Angolcynnes witenes geraednes*".[1] This legal popularism, elastic, practical, tolerant as to the composition of its assemblies, yet unyielding in its demand that lawful men shall pronounce right law, is the first and most far-reaching rule which united England inherited from the embryo states of the Heptarchy. It remained the prevailing current of life, strong, deep, for the most part invisible, but determining the range within which executive power could be exerted, and in the end forcing it into avowed conformity with itself.

Provinces of the folk　　Almost automatically, then, the unwieldy masses of the nations fall into legal provinces not too large to make use of a single place of assembly, yet large enough to provide the knowledge and authority of a folkmoot. The ninth-century translator of Bede, when writing of the Midlands, called such subdivisions of the nation maegths, kindreds. We are suspicious of any suggestion of blood-relationship upon a provincial scale, but we have only to study the web of interrelationship which riddled the peasant tenure of any of the Kentish lathes in the Middle Ages, to see that it must have been very easy for such neighbourhoods to think of themselves as large and loosely related families. Allowing for a measure of sentiment and unreality in this, the basis of the provinces of the seventh-century kingdoms was in fact personal rather than territorial. In many parts of England they took their names from their communities, the "Men of the River Meon" (*Meonwara*), the "Men of the Chester" or "the Burh" (*Ceasterwara* of Rochester, and *Burhwara* of Canterbury), the "Settlers on the

---

[1] The hundred testifies. By the witness of the whole shire. This is the agreed edict of the witan of the English.

River Arrow" (*Arosetna*), the "Marshmen" (*Merscwara*), and the sense of this community forced a political framework into being to embody it. In this sense, also, as the nature of law and social relations would lead us to expect, the basis of public life was popular, and was not created by a scheme imposed from above.

Folkright made the common law-courts folkmoots, but the *Principle function of judgment often fell to men of reputation who were of witan seniores* or witan, as being wise in law. The popular principle in the moots was satisfied either when they embodied the folk directly or by delegation of function to those who were representative of the legal wisdom of the community,[1] and this made it possible for the judgments and political decisions of a nation to be made by a few of its wise men in council, the *witenagemot, consilium sapientum*.[2] The council of a great nation could not be a universal assembly, but the Kentings or Gewissae were thought to speak as fully through their *seniores* as in the open forum of their local moots. Although circumstances imposed a different composition upon the witenagemot, the scir-witan, and the hundred-witan, and required the former to act at times in what we have come to regard as matters of state, contemporaries had little inclination to draw such distinctions, or to invent constitutional rules on any ground of difference of function. Any alteration of custom would naturally affect the whole race, and so the central assembly was the authority for general codes, while the local moots were confined to judgment, but the witan of the English were not essentially different from those of the smallest folkmoot in the eyes of Saxon England. The lesser kingdoms used very full assemblies in their earlier days,[3] because it was practicable so to do, but as the kingdoms grew in size the witan came to be of greater distinction

---

[1] Anglo-Saxon Chronicle, 995F. The principle of the witan is exemplified by the choice by Archbishop Ælfric of "all the wisest men that he knew anywhere. . . . Such as most surely knew how all things stood in the land in their forefathers' days . . . and many ancient men told how the law was laid down soon after Augustine's day."

[2] Nom. sing., *wita*, a wise man; nom. plur., *witan*; gen. plur., *witena*; and so *witena gemot*, the assembly of wise men or notables.

[3] Æthelbert, 2: "If the King call his folk to him . . ."; Wihtraed, Prologue: "Every order of the Church and the loyal laity". So as late as Æthelstan the folk of the countryside intervene: "*tota populi generalitate ovanti*". (J. M. Kemble, *Codex Diplomaticus*, 364.)

and fewer. An original record of the Council of London of 811[1] professes to give the actual composition of a Mercian witenagemot. There were present King Coenwulf, the Queen, Sigered, king of Essex, the Archbishop, the bishops of Rochester, Worcester, and Selsey, three principes, four duces (these titles being apparently variants of the Mercian title of *heretoga*), Coenwald the king's nephew, and Cyneberht another relative, Æthelheah *pedes sessor*, two abbesses, and Cuthred the priest. Though smaller than many, this was by no means exceptional in its composition, but to the end the king and witan were at times afforced by a wider popular element, and they continued by their style to assert their claim to stand for the nation.[2] The witenagemot has no fixed composition. Wisdom, wealth, prestige make it inevitable that certain great men shall find a place there—"the most eminent of my people" is Ine's phrase—but there is no status of *wita, consiliarius*, no formal qualification or disqualification for attendance. The councils contain both clerical and lay notables,[3] "all orders of the Church" attend, ordinances both spiritual and secular are issued, and the king or the archbishop seems at any time after the seventh century to preside indifferently.

Witan and King   As between two authorities, king and witan, each felt deeply if obscurely to bear the person of the race, there should be no conflict of powers. Where the first function of both is not to make law but to apply an unchanging custom, neither king nor witan has reason to assert a superiority over the other, and we cannot force upon these primitive assemblies the monarchy, aristocracy, or democracy of which it is so hard to rid our minds. For this reason our authorities show neither king nor witan superior in making dooms or decisions of policy, or in executive enactments. As the authority of the code of Wihtraed we have the prologue's dating "Wihtraed the most merciful king of the Kentings then ruling", but we are told almost immediately that the "magnates

1 W. de Gray Birch, *Cartularium Saxonicum*, 335: *Concilium pergrande collectum habebatur in quo videlicet ipse rex Coenwulf . . . atque majores natu quorum nomina infra caraxantur*: A great council was held, in which (were) King Coenwulf himself . . . and the notables whose names are written below (in the test).

2 Dunsaete, Prologue, Angelcynnes witan; V Æthelred, Inscr. Angolwitena.

3 W. de Gray Birch, *Cartularium Saxonicum*, 386: "There was a synodical gemot at . . . Clovesho, and there were the said King Beornwulf, and his bishops and ealdormen, and all the witan of this people".

brought them in with the agreement of all". Ine's code was conceived "with the counsel and wisdom . . . of all my ealdormen,
and the chief witan of my people". Ælfred claims that his dooms
are his own gathering from past law, but they have been shown to
his witan, and "they all liked them well to hold". At times the
form of the laws purports to record king and witan speaking with
one voice,[1] while at others our idea of their functions is reversed,
and it is the king who convenes and the witan who enact: "first
they decree as to holy orders", says the oldest text of Eadmund's
synod, and it is the notables, lay or clerical, who are thus made to
speak.[2]

The distinction between the grouped dooms of a code and the
single doom of an act of judgment is, of course, a modern one,
and in this too the king will have no distinctive power. At the
Clovesho synod or witenagemot of 825 a claim for right of pasture
was made by the bishop of Worcester against the reeve of Sutton,
and was judged by the Archbishop and "all the witan", although
the king was there.[3] Æthelstan of Sunbury had claim to an estate.
He came to King Eadgar, and "bade a doom of him": "then the
Mercian witan doomed him the land".[4] Again, Dunstan petitions
Eadgar on behalf of a widow whose husband Ecgferth has been
forfeit for theft, and who is in his mund; but the king has to
answer, "my witan has declared all Ecgferth's wealth forfeit".[5]
The king's interest may be overridden. A Mercian suit of the year
840 shows the bishop of Worcester successfully reclaiming land
which King Berhtwulf had taken from his church and given to
his personal followers. The bishop challenged his action at the
Easter witenagemot at Tamworth, and, in Berhtwulf's presence,
the witan judged that he had been unjustly dispoiled. Berhtwulf
returned the lands, and gave gifts to the church in reparation.[6]

---

1 Ælfred and Guthrum's Peace, 5: *And ealle we cwaedon.*
2 I Eadmund. London Synod, 1.
3 W. de Gray Birch, *Cartularium Saxonicum*, 386.
4 *Ibid.* 1063.
5 *Ibid.* 1063 and 1064.
6 J. M. Kemble, *Codex Diplomaticus*, 245: *Contigit autem quod Berhtwulf rex
Merciorum tolleret a nobis . . . terram nostram . . . rex praefatus suis propriis
hominibus condonavit, sicut se inimici homines docuerunt. Et ibi (ad Tomworthie)
ante regem suosque proceres fuerunt allecta (libertates et cartulae) et ibi Merciorum
optimates dejudicaverunt illi, ut male et injuste dispoliati essent:* it happened that
Berhtwulf, King of the Mercians, took away our land from us and made it

Individually, these tales may be no more than memories, but they vouch for a traditional belief as to the function of the Saxon king that carries conviction. It is uniformly held to and it is that of the feudal king after him. Land which lapses to the king through failure of heirs or forfeiture, or folkland which is granted to the king in the freer law of bookright, he must obtain by the judgment of his witan.[1] We must, however, be on our guard against giving a wrong interpretation of this. It is a practical application of the supremacy of law, and reflects no constitutional subordination of the king to the witan. Where his personal concern does not make his participation an obvious injustice, the king's is among the voices which pronounce judgment, and, if his character deserves it, it may be the leading one. Echoes of decisive sentences of Offa have come down to us,[2] and Ælfred clearly made himself the centre of English legal wisdom and its most trusted interpreter.[3] The judgment which deposed Archbishop Wulfred from his see was made in a witenagemot at London, but was clearly prompted by the Mercian king Coenwulf.[4] That of his milder successor Beornwulf, restoring him to his lands and honours, was equally clearly popular, and was made "with one mind and with common consent".[5] Thus, circumstances and the play of personality thrust

over to his own men as certain enemies of ours had advised. But then at Tamworth our liberties and charters were adduced and the witan of the Mercians gave judgment to the king (that they had been wrongly taken away?). There is a break in the construction at this point.

[1] W. de Gray Birch, *Cartularium Saxonicum*, 390 (A.D. 825): *Optimorum meorum decreto adjudicante*: by the judgment of my notables. J. M. Kemble, *Codex Diplomaticus*, 1019.

[2] W. de Gray Birch, *Cartularium Saxonicum*, 293.

[3] Asser, De Rebus Gestis, 106. Yet Ælfred placed himself upon the judgment of the witan as to whether his action under his father's will had been in conformity with folkright. J. M. Kemble, *Codex Diplomaticus*, 314.

[4] *Ibid.* 220 (A.D. 825): *Rex Coenwulfus cum suis sapientibus ad regalem villam Lundoniae perveniens ad hoc eodemque concilio illum archiepiscopum . . . invitabat. Tunc in eodem concilio cum maxima districtione illo episcopo mandavit . . . disspoliatus debuisset fieri, omnique de patria ista esse profugus*: King Coenwulf came to the royal town of London with his witan and summoned the archbishop to the moot. Then in the said moot he ordained to the bishop by most strict judgment that he should be despoiled and outlawed from the whole realm.

[5] *Loc. cit. Tunc vero omnis ille synodus ad aequitatem invenerunt huncque judicium unanimo consensu constituerunt*: then the whole synod deemed right and made this judgment by unanimous consent.

An instance of criminal judgment by the witan upon a great layman is that of the witan at Cirencester upon Ælfric Cild, Ealdorman of Mercia, for

to the fore now one element and now another. It is the indivisible law which speaks through king and witan, and for them the divided and often antagonistic functions and rights of more advanced political theory have no meaning.

The most characteristic function of the witenagemot, that from which it took its name, was the giving of judgment, deeming of dooms[1] as *sapientes*, and it is of this function that we have most record. Of the same order of activity, according to the thought of the day, was the general scrutiny of the law and its working, the placing and keeping of men in their rank and due, and the safeguarding and amending of secular and spiritual custom. Of legislation, as we understand it, there was, of course, almost nothing. "To look to the needs of God's churches and the right keeping of monastic rule, and to take counsel for the stability of the secular state", is the account given of its own purpose by the Council of Clovesho of 825, and, as a means to that end, it set out to enquire "what men had been maintained in justice and equity, and who had been defrauded by violence and injustice, or dispoiled".[2] Evidence for such care is plentiful from the reign of Eadward the Elder to that of the Confessor, during which time the nation was building a new system of law and administration under the leadership of its kings. With nothing but the Ælfredian Chronicle to go upon, we can say little of it before the tenth century, and hardly more of the witan's part in affairs of state and executive government. What little is recorded shows the usual lack of precision as to the power that acts, for there is a prevailing confusion of the functions of the crown with those of the national council. We see Ecgfrith of Northumbria preparing to defend his people against Wulfhere *consilio senum*,[3] and the Mercian witan joining with their king to put themselves under Æthelwulf's leadership against the Danes in 853.[4] Oswiu consults his *sapientes* one by one as to the

Function of the witan (margin note)

treason in 985, *quando ad synodale concilium ad Cyrneceaster universi optimates simul in unum convenerunt et eundem Ælfricum maiestatis reum de hac patria profugum expulerunt* (J. M. Kemble, *Codex Diplomaticus*, 1312).

1 W. de Gray Birch, *Cartularium Saxonicum*, 115. The bishop of London describes a joint witenagemot of the kingdoms of Wessex and Essex, which met at Brentford in October, 705, as *reges ambarum partium, episcopi et abbates, judicesque reliqui*, i.e other doomsmen.

2 W. de Gray Birch, *Cartularium Saxonicum*, 384.

3 Eddius, *Vita Wilfridi*, xx. (Rolls Series.)

4 Anglo-Saxon Chronicle, 853A.

fitness of Wilfred for the Northumbrian see,[1] and Bede records a similar procedure when Northumbria receives Christianity.[2] *Haec est voluntas regis et principum ejus.*[3] Under Offa the Lichfield archbishopric is created in the Synod of Chelsea,[4] but its first archbishop, Higbert, is recorded as chosen by the king.[5]

Succession and deposition of kings

To say without qualification that the witenagemot could elect and depose kings would be to ignore the changing value of terms. We have seen what power inherited place in the blood-grades of the folk had to determine status and right. The potentiality of kingship inhered in the highest kin of all, the *cynecynn*,[6] and was transmitted to all its members, together with the aetheling's wer,[7] and other marks of preëminence. From the cynecynn the choice of king must be made, for it only was royal. A ruler taken from a lesser stock was *dubius*,[8] *ungecynd*,[9] and, though the disorders ot the eighth century produced some such monarchs, they were ill looked upon by responsible opinion.[10] But within the cynecynn —perhaps the kin within nine generations of descent—choice should in theory have been free, and seems often to have been so. Egbert, though of the "right kin that goeth unto Cerdic", was divided from the main line of descent from Coenred by five generations.

Within the covering principle of kinship, ability, family arrangement, and popularity produced a different solution at every vacancy of the throne. Ælfred was called to the crown over the heads of his elder brother's sons, and Asser tells us that, as the noblest of his family, he might have preceded his senior Æthelred,

---

[1] Eddius, *Vita Wilfridi*, xi.　　　　[2] Bede, *Historia Ecclesiastica*, ii. 13.

[3] Eddius, *Vita Wilfridi*, lx.

[4] Anglo-Saxon Chronicle, 785A.

[5] *Loc. cit.*

[6] *Ibid.* 1067D: *Eadgar was Eadreding and swa forþ on þonne cynecynn. Ibid.* 449E, 547A.

[7] Ælfred translates Bede's *nobiles et regii viri*, in the account of the baptism of Eadwin's household, as *æðelingas þæs cynecynes. Historia Ecclesiastica*, ii. 14. According to the North People's Law (clause 1) the wer of the royal kin was uniform at 15,000 thrymsas, including the king himself.

[8] Bede, *Historia Ecclesiastica*, iv. 26. *Reges dubii vel extranei.*

[9] Anglo-Saxon Chronicle, 867E. The Northumbrians had deposed their king Osbryht and *ungecyndne cyning underfengon Ællan.*

[10] Asser, *De Rebus Gestis*, 27: *Tyrannus quidam, Aella nomine, non de regali prosapia progenitus, super regni apicem constituerant*: a certain tyrant, Ælla, not of the royal kin. . . .

had he been so minded, and reigned with general approval. Where there was no fixed rule of succession, the favour of the people must have kept its importance, and the witan's action in election, as in other matters, was then an act of the nation. Alcuin writes to the *nobiles et populus laudabilis, et regnum imperiale Cantuariorum* during the native Kentish régime which followed Offa's death and exhorts them *rectores vobis praeponite nobilitate claros*. The address is characteristic both in the width of its appeal to the Kentish nation as the basis of authority and in its lack of precision as to the allocation of constituent power. On the other hand, this same lack of rule must have given play to other than popular forces, to the exceptional power of individual claimants, or the policy of the throne's holder. The practice of naming a successor as *secundarius* during the reigning king's lifetime was not uncommon. Ecgfrith was king of the Mercians before Offa died, Æthelbald divided the kingdom with his father Æthelwulf, and Ælfred was *secundarius* under Æthelred. Æthelwulf's reign, indeed, is an example of how diverse considerations could affect the throne almost contemporaneously. Two years before his death the authority of the witan[1] carried through a partition of the kingdom between himself and his eldest son, but his will embodied a disposition of the crown between Æthelbald and Æthelbert, which was in fact carried into effect. Deposition was uncommon as long as the old national dynasties were able to produce suitable candidates, but we have an example in Sigebert, from whom "Cynewulf and the witan of the West Saxons took his realm for ill conduct",[2] and Æthelred, king of the Northumbrians, was deposed, thrown into prison, and restored at the end of the eighth century.[3] Instances both of election and deposition persist throughout the Saxon period,[4] but it is difficult to feel that they represent

[1] Asser, *De Rebus Gestis*, 12: *Omnium astipulatione nobilium*: with the assent of all the magnates.

[2] Anglo-Saxon Chronicle, 755A.

[3] Alcuin. Letter to Joseph. Haddan and Stubbs. *Councils*, iii. 495.

[4] Cf. the election of Eadred (J. M. Kemble, *Codex Diplomaticus*, 411), and of Eadward the Martyr (*Ibid.*, 1312), *omnes utriusque ordinis optimates . . . fratrem meum Eaduuarduum unanimiter elegerunt*: all the witan both spiritual and secular unanimously elected Edward my brother as king.

Anglo-Saxon Chronicle, 1016E: *Ealle þa witan þe on Lundene waron and se burhwaru gecuron Eadmund to cynge*: all the witan at London and the men of the borough chose Eadmund as king. *Ibid.* 1036, 1041.

a settled constitutional rule. Rather they are the result of social habit in the interplay of the principles of kinship within the royal house and of the folk principle throughout the whole community, finding their highest expression through the magnates in the witenagemot of the nation. These principles, though they cannot defeat the ambition of a Cnut or a Harold, suffice in the main to keep the throne within the cynecynn yet tolerably popular, but they are automatic responses to underlying social beliefs[1] rather than rules of the constitution.

Government, as we have described it so far, is in basis popular, either through the folk in council or through the "wise men". With no more than the rudimentary equipment of moots and some device of elective ealdormanry or moot presidency, great branches of the Northern races have made shift to maintain a stable government. The Icelandic settlements of the tenth century, and the Old Saxons, the Germanic stock nearest in custom to the West Saxons of Britain, had no non-popular executive until it was imposed upon the latter from without by Charlemagne. It is, perhaps, remarkable that all the large national units of the Anglo-Saxons maintained monarchies from the earliest times of their history, though several of them preserved the tradition that their founders were not kings, and only the house of Offa[2] claimed that its ancestors of the fourth century reigned in Germany. As a consequence of monarchy, from the earliest time of which we have any knowledge, lathe, scir, and rape were also the frames of *Provincial* an administration whose officers were the king's. He was the pro-*govern-* tector and executant, though not the fountain, of their law. They *ment* were heavily interlaced with the demesne lands and interests of the crown, and taxed to support it upon an assessment by townships and hamlets or ploughgangs in the North, and by hides or sulungs in the South. It is this phase of the provinces' functions which has found its way into record, and if we wish to describe them in detail we can only do so in so far as they are units in the king's fiscal and judicial administration. Even so, our knowledge is very

---

[1] In Kent there is some tendency for the crown to conform to the custom of gavelkind and to be departed between coheirs in each generation.
[2] Cf. H. M. Chadwick, *Origins of the English Nation*, chap. vi.

partial. We know something of the Anglo-Celtic administrations[1] of the North, and also of the lathe of the Jutish South-East, for they survived into the early Middle Ages, and we may suspect—without at present a shadow of proof—that East Anglia and Essex may have lain under a somewhat similar system. We know practically nothing as to Wessex or Mercia, but the few facts that we do know about those kingdoms suggest that their early administration developed along different lines from that of the others.

In Northumbria the Anglian king's state is roughly that of a *North-* Celtic prince, and the Northumbrian *scirs* of the twelfth century *umbria* and the princely estates of medieval Wales are hardly to be distinguished. A central court—often adopted as the hundred court in the Middle Ages—serves the whole area, a capital township, *cinges tun,* or *urbs regis,* is the administrative seat of a reeve. A scattering of hamlets of *terra regis,* or demesne of some immunist, owner of liberty of court and administration, form, as it were, the agrarian nucleus of the scir; there is a common waste or shire-moor, and the folk of the countryside, holding by a custom called husbandry or bondage,[2] live in independent settlements or "bondage townships". Such hamlets contribute to general dues assessed on the scir, pasture rents like *cornage* and *neatgeld,* and the cattle rents of *vacca de metreth, cugeld,* or *beltancu,* of which the metreth is the *treth calan Mai* of Wales. They are under an obligation to provide house-room and provender for the king's servants going about their administrative duties. In Latin, these duties appear as *putura serjeantium,* or *forestariorum,* but the Welsh *cylch*[3] survives as far north and east as Staffordshire.[4] Besides this, there is the sending of labourers into the demesne harvest, keeping the hall and buildings of the demesne in repair, feeding, and training the lord's horses, hawks, and hounds, carting, errand-riding, and other various and variable services. These simple agrarian communities, which are the basis of the Anglian-Celtic folk, are politically quite unspecialized. To the modern mind it is impossible to decide where private life ends and public life begins. The demesne interest of the king or immunist generates no separate

[1] *English Historical Review,* vol. xli. p. 1.
[2] Cf. the term boneddig for the free Welsh cultivator.
[3] Cf. Cylch hebbogyddion, or puture of foresters.
[4] Public Record Office. *Calendar of Inquisitions Post Mortem,* iii. 536.

officialdom. The reeve of the moots is also the bailiff of the king's lands. As he exacts the work of the men of the townships in his lord's harvest, or collects their renders of cattle, it is impossible to say whether he is more the steward or the tax-gatherer. The rudiments of taxation lie in these rustic dues of the homesteads and the fields. All the primitive crown can exact is that it shall live on the countryside, and that the men of the countryside shall come to the help of its great household of servants and officials with the work of their hands, and pass the king's officers freely fed and housed about their business. This is the king's revenue of the day, and exhausts the fiscal resources of the state. It is probably as contributing to such renders that the common folk of the North are spoken of in the eighth century as *tributarii*.

Monarchical influence is equally strong in the higher ranges of Northumbrian society. The governors of the subordinate national units within Northumbria are deputies of the crown—under-kings —and, as was usual in the Celtic kingdoms, nobility by office seems to have taken the place of the Germanic blood nobility. In Eddius and Bede it is the reeves who fill the foreground of Northern history. They are *heah-gerefan*, high reeves, and are the mainstay of the nobility, lying between the under-kings—whom the Saxon Chronicle calls ealdormen—on the one side, and the gesiths and king's thegns on the other. When Wilfred summoned the magnates of the North to the consecration of Ripon, it was in the persons of the two kings, Ecgfrith and Ælwin, and of "their abbots, reeves, and under-kings".[1] Bede, in arraigning the greed of the Northumbrian nobles, again, treats the reeves as the type of secular power: "there is scarce one of the reeves of that nation who in his term of office has not bought himself a house of religion . . . and, so far has the abuse been carried, that even the king's thegns and his domestics have been busy to imitate them".[2] Such men were clearly above the king's thegns, attended the witenagemot—one of them pronounced the witan's sentence upon Wilfred[3]—and attained to great wealth on the profits of

---

[1] Eddius, *Vita Wilfridi*, xvi.

[2] Bede, *Epistola ad Ecgbertum*, 13. So also the Anglo-Saxon Chronicle records (under ann. 779E) that the "high reeves of Northumbria" murdered ealdorman Beorn. The term seems here almost equivalent to magnates or *nobiles*.

[3] Eddius, *Vita Wilfridi*, lx.

their charge. It is not surprising, therefore, to find one of them described as *secundus a rege* and to hear that the conversion of the Lindiswaras turned upon that of Blaecca the reeve of Lincoln. Other than this officialdom, there seems, indeed, to have been no Northumbrian nobility. The Northern social ranks, unlike those of any other English people, are reckoned for wergeld according to official standing and not by the ancient blood-grades. The high-reeves of the North Peoples Law[1] have a wergeld of twice the value of the thegn's, and the latter derives his worth not from birth but from his thegnage. It is the Celtic social grading, as we see it in the Laws of Hoel Dda, strongly official in character and the antithesis of English usage.[2] Thus, Northumbria represents a growth of monarchical institutions more precocious than was usual with the Anglo-Saxons, and there is little doubt that the line of Ida took over the framework of a British kingship which was already highly developed. To this may be attributed the success of the Celtic missions in the North, while the absence of the normal tribal sanction in the crown may have had much to do with the instability of Northumbrian monarchy in the seventh and eighth centuries.

A very similar system is found in the independent kingdom of Kent, and, almost certainly, in Sussex and eastern Surrey. The social and administrative unit of the lathe can be carried back into the early eighth century of Kentish history.[3] The rape is obliquely but clearly referred to in a Surrey charter of 947,[4] and the Sussex rapes, though they do not appear *eo nomine* until the Contessor's reign, leave the mark of their general agrarian type in charters from the eighth century onwards. The remains of provincial organization surviving into the Middle Ages make their antiquity almost certain. This provincial organization is more clearly marked as we move eastwards towards its political centre in Kent, but it must have had a wider extension before the West Saxon conquest impaired the independence of the south-eastern kingdoms, and it has a strong hold upon the Jutish provinces of South Hampshire, the New Forest—Florence of Worcester's Ytene—and the

---

1 Liebermann, *Gesetze der Angelsachsen*, p. 460.
2 Bede, *Historia Ecclesiastica*, ii. 16.
3 J. E. A. Jolliffe, *Pre-Feudal England: the Jutes.*
4 W. de Gray Birch, *Cartularium Saxonicum*, 820.

Meonwara.[1] The structure of lathe and rape hardly differed from that of the northern scir in the essentials which concern the constitution. A central *villa regis*, a king's reeve, a court, a population of *tributarii*,[2] or gavelkinders, a provincial waste of forest, the wealds in Andred which were apportioned to each rape or lathe. The main difference is one of social habit, a stronger birthright bringing into being in Kent a peasant freehold with partition of inheritance between co-heirs. The dues of the crown differ in detail rather than in principle. The puture of the serjeants and foresters, which comes from the Celtic strain in the North, is absent in the South-East, and in Kent and part of east Sussex there is a money rent of gafol. Otherwise the occasional service on the demesne, and the work upon the king's hall and outbuildings, are much the same, as natural in the simple relation of a primitive kingship to the folk which maintains it in southern as in northern Britain. Scir, rape, lathe, are, indeed, natural outcomes of the phase of society they govern, and such variety as they display is the outcome of differences in private law and administrative history.

Wessex   It is remarkable that we know less of the early administration of Wessex, from which country the laws of Ine and Ælfred survive, together with some early charters, than we do of that of Northumbria, which has given us few public records from before the eleventh century. We know, in fact, almost nothing. The ealdorman had his scir, but there is nothing to show whether it was the large shire like the modern county of the South-West, or some smaller unit. The practice of Kent and Northumbria would lead us to expect that early Wessex should have been governed, not by the dual system of shire and hundred which was used by the English kingdom of the tenth century, but by a single system of provinces of manageable size, perhaps larger than the later hundred, and smaller than the county, which is inconveniently large for the meetings of a folkmoot. After the hundred was adopted in the tenth century many hundreds were annexed to royal townships, bore their name, and came under the jurisdiction of the reeve of the king's town, as were the scirs of Northumbria. Of sixty estates bequeathed by Ælfred in his will, twenty-nine have

---

[1] J. E. A. Jolliffe, *Pre-Feudal England*, p. 89.
[2] W. de Gray Birch, *Cartularium Saxonicum*, 50, 64, 144, 145, 198, 212, 262.

given their names to hundreds of later days.[1] In this one feature, therefore, we have a possible Saxon parallel to the scir, the rape, and the lathe. The primitive unit of Wessex cannot have been the hundred, for that was a growth of the tenth century; on the other hand, many of the royal manors of Wessex were the capitals of large areas. In Cornwall the three medieval hundreds of Stratton, Lesnewth, and Trigg seem to have been formed from the older unit of Triggshire, or Triconscire, one of the *septem parvae scirae* into which ancient Cornwall was divided. Here we have in outline the Celtic scir as it was in Northumbria, and where, in Wessex proper, "the pleas of Cicemantone and Sutlesberg hundreds belong to the farm of Malmesbury",[2] or "the soke of two hundreds lies in King's Somborne",[3] it may well be that the West Saxons of the tenth century, in the process of creating a uniform English administration, broke down an earlier scir system, carving out hundreds within the boundaries of the scirs, but retaining the capital authority of the older *cynges tuns*. In so treating their own system they would have been doing no more than they had done in Kent and Cornwall.[4] This admitted, however, we should still be far from an identity of the Wessex scir with its Anglian-Celtic namesake, or with the lathe. There is an agrarian, social, and fiscal unity about these latter which is lacking in the greater part of Wessex. The hold of the king's vills of Wessex upon the hundreds is, as a rule, purely judicial and administrative, and before the reign of Ælfred there is no text to tell us that the reeves had a place in the folkmoots. There is no proof that the king's vills were the sites of courts, while, if the Saxon king drew his rents and services from them, as the Kentish king drew his gafol from the lathe, or as Celtic or English princes received the cornage and cattle rents of Northumbria and North Wales, or the *berbagium* of South Wales and Cornwall, we have yet to prove it. Nor is

[1] For what follows, Miss H. M. Cam's article, "Manerium cum Hundredo" (*English Historical Review*, xlvii.), from which facts and references have been taken, should be consulted.

[2] Domesday Book, i. 64b.

[3] *Ibid.* i. 39b.

[4] The most plausible instance of the survival of a primitive West Saxon scir is that of Wincelcumbscira (W. de Gray Birch, *Cartularium Saxonicum*, 309, A.D. 803), which Miss Cam considers may have included six or eight of the hundreds of Gloucestershire, with Winchcombe as capital (*Historical Essays in Honour of James Tait*, p. 18).

there, as a rule, that agrarian community of the whole province which is expressed in the wealds, or common woods, of the rapes and lathes, and the shire-moors[1] of the North. Such differences may well be accounted for by primitive social differences, such as the contrast between the close agrarian unity of the Midlands village and the looser organization of the North, the East, and the West, and if so the political system of the West Saxons may have had peculiarities which were not shared by their Anglo-Celtic and Jutish neighbours, and which are not to be explained away.

In fact, the administration of Wessex and Mercia seems to have been less monarchical than that of their neighbours. In early days it rests not upon the king's reeve but the ealdorman, and the ealdorman has the best claim of any Saxon official to an origin independent of the crown. *Heretoga*, the Mercian name for the office,[2] "leader of the host", carries us back to the time when there was no king as war-lord, and one may speculate on its relation to the *princeps* of Tacitus, or, with more reason, to those *satrapae* of the Old Saxons, who in Bede's day still cast lots for leadership on the outbreak of war.[3] An old document, known as the Tribal Hidage,[4] shows the Midlands divided into many units like the *provinciae* or maegths of Bede and his translator, and, as no king of Mercia is known before the seventh century, it may be that Penda's kingship was built upon a confederacy of such maegths and their "satraps".[5] But, outside Mercia there is less to suggest it. At least some of the lesser dynasties seem to have exchanged their royal for ducal rank, and so to have continued under their conquerors. Such was Ealdwulf, *rex*[6] or *dux* of the South Saxons. Here[7] "the relation of the ealdorman to the King has probably been created by commendation . . . and the hereditary descent of the office is only occasionally interfered with by royal nomina-

---

[1] Apparently the forest system of Wiltshire and south Somerset has points of similarity with that of the scir, but it is exceptional in Wessex.

[2] J. M. Kemble, *Codex Diplomaticus*, 557, etc. The word was still used in its literal sense as "leaders of the host", not ealdorman, in tenth-century Mercia, as in the Chronicles E and F, which have Mercian affinities, under 794, 993.

[3] Bede, *Historia Ecclesiastica*, v. 10.

[4] W. de Gray Birch, *Cartularium Saxonicum*, 297.

[5] Bede, *Historia Ecclesiastica*, iii. 24. Penda took thirty duces (Anglo-Saxon translation, *ealdormen and heretogena*) into battle at Winwaed.

[6] W. de Gray Birch, *Cartularium Saxonicum*, 197, 261.

[7] Stubbs, *Constitutional History*, i. 177.

tion". It is, of course, possible that the ealdormen of Wessex also may stand for some forgotten native rulers of the Sumorsaetas or Wilsaetas, but, on the whole, it is difficult to find reasons for believing that popular institutions were carried so far even among the West Saxons. We first meet with their ealdormen at a time when the crown was already head of an executive. Their position seems to have been that of royal governors and their full title "king's ealdormen".[1] The absence, in contrast with Northumbrian usage, of any distinctive ealdorman's wer, proves that they did not derive their status from any primitive standing by blood and descent, and their privileges are like those of the king's thegns, calculated to fortify their office, a higher mundbryce and burhbryce,[2] which in Ine's law are said to be that of "any other eminent counsellor".[3] The burhbryce is lower than that of a bishop and only a little higher than that of a king's thegn.[4] They may forfeit their office for default of duty.[5] These are the marks of a *ministerium* rather than of an innate rank in the folk. The West Saxon ealdorman seems, however, to have been a public official as well as a king's reeve, his function centred upon a folkmoot rather than upon the *terra regis*, and he presided there upon occasion, having custody of prisoners,[6] enforcing the attendance of parties,[7] and guaranteeing the order of his court by his own mund.[8] He seems to have been responsible for the general government of the scir, for those domiciled within it could not leave his jurisdiction without his discharge.[9] It is probable, therefore, that we should be right in looking for more than one origin of the ealdormanry in different parts of England. That of Wessex is, perhaps, an officialdom nominated by the crown. Its status was markedly enhanced during the eighth and ninth centuries, for Ælfred's ealdormen have come to be of equal rank with bishops,[10] and their mundbyrd has been doubled.[11] But, outside Wessex, the Mercian heretogas, such as the ealdorman of the Gwrvas,[12] or of the Gaini,[13] may have begun as

1 Ine, 50. 2 *Ibid.* 45. 3 *Ibid.* 6. 2.
4 *Ibid.* 45. 5 *Ibid.* 36. 1. 6 *Ibid.* 36. 1.
7 Ælfred, 42. 3. 8 *Ibid.* 3. 38. 9 *Ibid.* 37.
10 *Ibid.* 15. In Ine's code, the ealdorman ranks below the bishop.
11 *Ibid.* 3.
12 Bede, *Historia Ecclesiastica*, iv. 19.
13 W. de Gray Birch, *Cartularium Saxonicum*, 571. The charter is spurious, but the title is vouched for by Asser.

the heads of semi-independent maegths, and those of Sussex, Kent, and the Hwiccan as *sub-reguli*. Thus, the West Saxon ealdormen, who were upon the up-grade before the reign of Ælfred, joined with those representatives of the old royal stocks who were losing their royalty to form that class of great provincial governors of the tenth century of whom Æthelstan Half-King is the type.

Summary   It will be seen that many factors, racial custom derived from the common Germanic stock, contact with or borrowing from indigenous Celtic usages, the varied influences of social and economic change, have worked, with effects which we can only determine imperfectly, to preserve or weaken the distinctions between the several English settlements in Britain. Nearest, perhaps, to the equality of freedom which underlies, however remotely, all primitive life, are the Kentings in whom a free peasantry enjoys what is surely the most primitive of English customs, and where the reeves are confined to their fiscal and administrative functions and to the management of the *terra regis*. A somewhat similar system prevails in Northumbria, but the influence of monarchy is more strongly marked by the recognition of the high-reeves as a rank of the folk and the consequent obliteration of the primitive ranks of the noble and the free by blood. As to Wessex we may be more doubtful. The Wessex ceorl has become involved in a more definite economic dependence than have those of other nations. Lordship is perhaps more commonly associated with the possession if not the ownership of land. The village type of settlement of the Midlands is more favourable to the consolidation of lordship than are those of the hamlet and the small township. Even here we may doubt whether the freedom of the ealdormen from reeveship, domestic ministry of the king, may not be the mark of an older elective status. In all the Heptarchic states, not only in the earliest phase of their development, but in later centuries, when political and social change has widened the gulf between the king, the aristocracy and the common freeman, the structure of law and the theory from which its procedure arises preserve traditions of an originally free community. The ceorl retains his public standing whether in the fyrd or the moot, the process of the courts by oath and ordeal assumes the essential equality of all, however much that equality may be obscured by the duties laid upon lords and their right to act through and plead for their men. Less evidently, in politics, but still without possibility of misunderstanding, the general theory of the folk informs those institutions which are less judicial and provincial than general and of the nation. The theory of witan gives a representative value to the deliberations of national assemblies, which is no less real because it is not created by election or formal commission. Monarchy itself is still an ideal personification of racial unity and common descent. These survive as ideas rather than as explicit maxims expressed in positive institutions, but they are, nevertheless, constantly operative. The governing preconceptions of any age, feudalism, democracy, or, as here, the principles of the folk, are seldom susceptible of precise definition or uniform in their effects, but they set the limits within which institutions may evolve, and they are a constant check upon rapid change. These general habits of mind and action, arising in the last analysis from their root in the folk united by kin and descent, and as late as the ninth century essentially unimpaired, will be seen to extend their influence into that most decisively formative period, the age of Ælfred's successors. Much of the work of that great succession of kings lay in the piecemeal amendment of law in the light of a new and more practical view of social relations and in the creation of a monarchy which could rise above racial loyalties, but the process of their work was slow and in part unconscious, the past was never broken with, and much, almost everything that was of value in the freedom and integrity of racial institutions was carried forward to the account of the English state.

ii

THE EARLY KINGSHIPS

Except in Northumbria, where it borrowed Celtic forms, and in Kent, where Frankish precedents were available, the resources of English monarchy may be traced in process of evolution from very simple beginnings. Ideas which form the background of Anglo-Saxon thought about kingship may be found elsewhere in the common German and Scandinavian tradition. The law does

Pagan kingship

not originally come from the king, he has no subjects as the modern state understands them, and few vassals such as he will come to have under feudalism, though he already holds the centre of the stage, having to the casual view much the same universality of relationship to the community and much the same ceremonial primacy, attracting the same semi-religious awe. His most essential quality to his people is something more subtle than executive power. In all ages and countries the king is representative. There are times when the nation must think as one, feel as one, and find issue for its common emotion in symbolic act. At such moments the king is the supreme individual of the race, incarnating its will in ritual act, giving to its ideal the coherence and endurance of personality. Just within the shadow at which the records of English history fail stands the sacrificial king. The three high feasts of English heathendom were Winter's Day (November 7), Mid-winter's Day (December 25), and Summer's Day (May 7). Under the Christian dispensation "thrice a year the king wore his crown. At Easter he wore it at Winchester, at Pentecost at Westminster, and at Midwinter at Gloucester", and there was feasting and entertainment of the king's faithful men—his *hyred* or great household.[1] These, in the pagan North, were the great ceremonial feasts when the king sacrificed for the people, on Winter's Day for a good year, at Midwinter for good crops, and on Summer's Day for victory in battle. That is the first and oldest function of the Germanic king. As the representative of the nation, the descendant of the gods, and their most acceptable votary, he "made the year".

The magical elements in kingship were slowly exorcized by Christianity, but the king remained the focus of emotions which were fundamentally pagan, and in his person the proper virtues of a barbaric folk were seen to be exemplified and ennobled. In this also the king was the type of his people, that he drew to a head the warlike prowess in which the race felt itself to live most keenly. Courage was less a quality of the individual king than a function of the crown, and its wealth was a trust for the endowment of war. The king was the gold-giver,[2] the treasurer of heroes,[3] the

[1] Anglo-Saxon Chronicle, 1086E.
[2] Beowulf, 1170. Goldwine gumena.
[3] *Ibid.* 1047. Hordweard hœleþa.

patron of warriors.[1] To this contrast between the pagan and Christian ideals of kingship we must attribute the violent fluctuations of conduct and fortune which came upon the first Christian kings. For the weak, the conflict was too great. Under an apostate king the gods were estranged, every man's virtue was affronted, and the very course of nature turned unkind. Some, like Redwald of East Anglia,[2] sacrificed after their conversion as before. Many gave up the struggle and became Christian monks, or vanished upon pilgrimage. Some were killed by their subjects, like that Sigebert of the East Saxons whom his kindred slew "because he forgave his enemies".[3] As conversion became real, this religious and representative quality was Christianized, and remained a principal justification of kingship. Alcuin, writing at the end of the eighth century, could still say, "in the king's righteousness is the common weal, victory in war, mildness of the seasons, abundance of crops, freedom from pestilence. It is for the king to atone with God for his whole people."[4] Christianity, indeed, brought with it a tradition of sympathy of church and crown, in which the latter also was a divinely given authority. Gregory put before Æthelbert the example of Constantine,[5] and Vitalian saw Oswy's kingship as the pledge of his people's conversion.[6] However imperfectly such theories were understood, they foreshadowed a new relation between king and folk, and one which might come to transcend the small patriotism of the races. On the whole, however, the first effect of Christianity was to impoverish the prestige of the barbarian thrones, and it was slow to confer upon them any countervailing lustre. Prayers *pro regibus ac ducibus* were introduced only by the Council of Clovesho of 747, and after protest against the clergy's indifference to secular welfare.[7] The bishops pursued a sectional ecclesiastical interest, and some-

Christian kingship

---

1 Beowulf, 1960. Wigendra hleo.
2 Bede, *Historia Ecclesiastica*, ii. 15. 3 *Ibid.* iii. 22.
4 Alcuin, Letter to King Æthelred, A.D. 793: *Pro totius gentis prosperitate Deum deprecari debet*: it is for him to beseech God for the welfare of the whole people. The Swedes sacrificed their king, Olaf, to Odin when his own sacrifices had failed, blaming him for a succession of years of bad harvest: Ynglinga Saga, xlvii.
5 Bede, *Historia Ecclesiastica*, i. 32.
6 *Ibid.* iii. 29: *Dedi te in foedus populi etc.*: I have given thee as a pledge to the people.
7 Haddan and Stubbs, *Councils*, iii. 375.

times tried to stand neutral in national quarrels.[1] Throughout the seventh century no English king ventured to style himself *rex Dei gratia* in public documents,[2] and Theodore, himself archbishop "by Divine favour", withheld that title from the kings to whom he wrote.[3] It cannot have been easy to accord, or, indeed, to accept. The claim of royalty rested so plainly upon divine and racial descent. Nine generations carried the royal kin to Woden or Saxneat, and Bishop Daniel recalls how the English clung to their divine genealogies in the face of reason, and how much of their sense of the antiquity and legitimacy of their state was bound up with them.[4] Alcuin attributed the chaos into which the kingly power had fallen in his day to their disrepute: "scarce one of the ancient royal kindreds survives, and by as much as their lineage is uncertain, by so much is their power enfeebled".[5]

Limited scope of kingship
To be king, then, meant, first and above all, to embody religion and racial pride, to lead the nation in war and bear its person in peace. To turn from the king as representative to the theory and practice of government, which came in later times to be his proper function, is to find him a vastly shrunken figure. Hardly more than a first estate of the folk, he reproduced upon a higher level the status of the noble. His family had special standing as the cynecynn, and he, at its head, had mund and wer at a higher value than the eorl. We cannot say that there were no powers of kingship, but they were few, and thrust upon him by necessity. Acts which we should accept as proper to the crown the seventh-century king did as if unconscious of their implication, and explained them as outcomes of his personal rank and privilege. Subjects, for their part, sought his protection not because of his

---

[1] So the Bishop of London writes to Archbishop Berctwald in 705 regretting the war between Essex and Wessex on the ground that "ecclesiastics who live under the two governments become involved willingly or unwillingly in their dissensions".

[2] Ine, in the prologue to his laws, is made to speak *Dei gratia*, but the text is of Ælfred's day. In genuine charters no West Saxon or Kentish king made the claim before Egbert, and in Mercia it did not become usual until the middle of the eighth century.   [3] Eddius, *Vita Wilfridi*, xliii.

[4] Daniel's letter to Boniface, A.D. 719–722. Haddan and Stubbs, *Councils*, i. 304.

[5] Alcuin, letter to Eanbald: *tanto incertiores sunt originis, quanto minores sunt fortitudinis.*

royal authority, but because his mund was more dangerous to break, and his protection stronger than that of any noble. Essentially they were not different. The law was not the king's law, but the folk's—folkright. It was administered in district courts which were folkmoots, and where the judges were the men of the countryside. Neither the king nor his officers had the power of deeming dooms, judgment, nor were the acts of violence which we count as crimes and punish as offences against the state— against the king—then so regarded. To kill a man, or to wound him, were primarily acts of private wrong. If the killer suffered death, it was at the hands of his victim's kin, by feud and not in punishment. If he preferred to pay, it was by way of ransom, to wipe out the wrong done, and to appease his enemies. The king's part in law was to follow up the breach of folkright, to pursue outlawry, and to put down violence when it became too strong for the neighbourhoods and kindreds to resist. It was an extra-judicial authority. As with some other Germanic peoples, there was a money payment for the king to take, the wite, but it was insignificant beside the bot or composition for blood, and its origin was certainly not penal.[1] Neither in theory nor in practice did the king judge. The peace, again, was not the king's. During their sessions the courts lay under their own peace, *methel-frith* or *moot-frith*,[2] and this is as near as we get to any public peace in

[1] There seem to have been three ways of regarding these public payments which accompanied the bot. The Franks exacted a sum (five-sixteenths of the blood-price) *pro fredo*, "for the frith", and may possibly have regarded it as compensation for breach of a national peace. No such notion prevailed in England. The Old Saxons exacted a sum *pro wargida*, a payment to the freemen of the court for their services as judges, and a second sum, *pro destrictione*, if they had to take action to enforce the court's judgment. After the Frankish conquest, however, the latter payment lapsed to the king if the action took place before a royal *missus* (Capitulare Saxonicum, 4). With the Welsh also the king took a third of every blood-price "because it is for him to enforce judgment where a kindred is too weak" (Laws of Howel the Good, v. 20b, 14. A: Ed. Wade-Evans). With the Bavarians (Lex Baiuwariorum. Textus Primus. ii. 15), the *judex* took a ninth from every composition for his services. From one of these principles the English wite must be derived, and not from any theory of punishment. If the term comes from the root of "witan", to know, to be wise (in law), and, therefore, capable of giving judgment, it was originally a perquisite of the freemen as judges. The choice of origin lies between the wargida and the mulct *pro districtione* of the Old Saxons. In either case it had lapsed to the king by the period of record.

[2] Æthelbert, 6.

early England. The country was full of legal sanctuaries, but they were the preserves of individuals. The king's peace was like other men's. It lay upon his palace, it was over his household, he could extend it to his friends, servants, and messengers.[1] A man in the safe-conduct of the king is said to bear the king's *hand-grith*.[2] We shall find the king's mund extended by analogy and fiction in later days, but in this first age its use is almost wholly private, and confined to its avowed purpose. Even this personal peace is extinguished when the king enters a subject's house. The guest, king though he be, has come under his host's mund, and the relation of subject to sovereign is reversed.[3]

Functions of the crown

If we seek for any foreshadowing of what the crown will come to be, it must be in such rough essays in action as the titular head of a nation and its strongest member will do inevitably at any time or place. He is the nation's and the law's defender and has often been chosen as the most warlike of his kin. His household of gesiths is a natural rallying point. He is the spokesman of his people, though he speaks with and from among the notables, who embody the wisdom of the folk, and who are called the wise men, the *seniores*, the witan. Crises of war and peace, the reception of the Christian faith, the choice between the Scottish and Roman communions, may turn largely on his word. Force was sometimes too strong for local power, and then the king must intervene. It was a threat held *in terrorem*, hardly more than a corollary of the king's headship in war.[4] These may seem substantial functions. They were enough to make the throne the focus of history. But there was lacking almost everything of that power of later monarchy which rests upon law and lawful obedience. If the king acted it was to impose a sentence which was not his own. The life of the countryside in its villages and halls went on without the king. He did not make its law, he was only remotely its protector. What stability it had, came from its own specific gravity, the

---

[1] Pax (Liebermann, *Gesetze*, p. 390). Thus far shall be the king's grith from his burh-gate where he resides, in all four directions: three miles and three furlongs and three lineal acres and nine feet and nine inches and nine barleycorns.

[2] Eadweard and Guthrum, i.   [3] Æthelbert, 3.

[4] Ælfred, 42. 3. If he has sufficient force a man must bring one who has wronged him to court himself; if he has not, he may appeal to the ealdorman, and, if he will not act, to the king.

weight of innumerable immunities of ceorl and eorl guarded by peace which custom held inviolate. No tie bound the multitude of individuals to their king: rather, they were tied in the network of natural kinship and the loyalties and legal obligations of neighbourhood. Indeed, here lay such strength as the barbarian throne possessed, for upon it were projected the loyalties which made the common life stable. Bound in kindred, the folk saw in their king the purest and most jealously recorded ancestry of their race. Religious in every act of life, they had in him the eldest descendant of the gods. Warlike by instinct, they looked to him to exemplify and sustain the prowess of the nation. In its infancy as a principle of state, the throne yet answered to the religious and emotional needs of the community.

Such kingship could be strong, and the earliest dynasties seem to have maintained an unbroken succession. But its weakness was that it rested on the past, upon paganism and the tribal community. It was hard to extend these kingdoms which had their roots in heathendom. The racial state was their natural scope, and rule over an alien kin could only be maintained by force.[1] The folkright of one nation was invalid with the others.[2] Æthelbert, Eadwin, and a few more, acquired a passing supremacy, and were called Bretwealdas, perhaps with some memory of Rome, but such power lasted only so long as they were victorious. The first monarchy to outgrow racialism to some degree arose in Mercia. Æthelbald in 716 succeeded to some sort of hegemony based upon the military strength of Penda and Wulfhere, and, in spite of defeats at the hands of Wessex, he and his successors maintained it, and gave it a fuller meaning. Æthelbald is not only the first king to incorporate the lordship of alien races into his title, claiming to be king "not only of the Mercians, but of those neighbouring peoples over whom God has set me",[3] but he is also the first to

Growth of theory and title of kingship

[1] Cf. the story of the monks of Bardney, who refused to give burial to the body of Oswald of Northumbria "although they knew him to be a saint, because he, though of another nation by birth, had acquired the kingdom over them. So they pursued him even after his death with lasting hate" (Bede, *Historia Ecclesiastica*, iii. 11).

[2] Thus the oath, the crux of every legal suit, was invalid as between Welsh and English except by agreement. Ordinance Respecting the Dunsœtas, 2. 1.

[3] W. de Gray Birch, *Cartularium Saxonicum*, 181 (A.D. 755-757).

sign "by divine dispensation": he claims an *imperium divino suffragio fultus*, and once writes himself *rex Brittaniae.*[1] Æthelbald's was a new dynasty, not descended from Penda, and Bede, writing in 731, shows him established over all England south of the Humber except Kent, and of part of Wales. Such a leadership, almost a century old at his death, needed a fuller title than king of the Mercians. Intermittently Offa used the new titles, and added a further definition of what was coming to be a stable supremacy. He is the first to sink the identities of the southern English in a common *Regnum Anglorum.*[2] In the year 774, when, at Otford, he had subdued the Kentings, his charters adopt a form which must have been designed to exalt the Christian right of conquest over the right of native kings.[3] To the Pope and the Emperor he is preëminently *Rex Anglorum*, and to his own people *rex et decus Britanniae.*[4]

Offa   It is with Offa that the change in claim and title is first translated into a measure of fact. The Bretwealdarship was being outgrown. In the past the component peoples of that vague supremacy had kept their native dynasties and broken away when it suited them to do so. Offa was clearly driving towards a lasting kingdom of the English. The kings of the Hwiccas had already become *reguli* under Æthelbald.[5] Offa killed or dethroned those of the East Angles and Kentings, and absorbed their peoples into his own kingdom. The native dynasty of the South Saxons disappeared at this time also. Where he did not govern he interfered with government. The under-kings accepted the position of gesiths under him,[6] and he denied them the right of granting land by charter without his sanction,[7] while he himself used that right as a means to further Mercian influence and distributed the lands of Kent and the Mercians at his will. The halving of the see of Canterbury, and the

---

[1] W. de Gray Birch, *Cartularium Saxonicum*, 155.

[2] *Ibid.* 213 (A.D. 774) and 265 (A.D. 793).

[3] *Ibid.* 213, 214 (A.D. 774): *In nomine Jhesu Christi . . . per quem reges regnunt et dividunt regna terrarum. Sicut dispensator universae terrae mihi distribuit . . . ego Offa Rex Anglorum dabo et concedo*: in the name of Christ Jesus . . . through Whom Kings rule and divide the nations of the world. As the Bestower of all lands has given to me . . . so I, Offa King of the Angles, give and grant.

[4] J. M. Kemble, *Codex Diplomaticus*, 1020.

[5] *Ibid.* 154: *Ic Aldred Wigracestres undercining*; cf. also Alcuin's letter to Offa.

[6] This link had already been forged under Æthelbald. J. M. Kemble, *Codex Diplomaticus*, 80.   [7] *Ibid.* 93, 97, 125.

establishment of a Mercian archbishopric of Lichfield, was not only an act of Mercian patriotism but a crippling blow to the Augustinian tradition upon which the sanctity of the heptarchic crowns had come to rest.[1] How great had been the power behind this breach with the old order the Pope's fear of dethronement through the influence of Offa[2] is witness, and in his successor's reign the prestige of Canterbury was so far impaired as to make a central see of London a conceivable alternative.[3]

The death of Offa stopped that normal development of a general English crown and title in which enlightened contemporaries had placed their faith.[4] Wessex had never lost her kingship, and Offa's successors sign as kings of the Mercians and Kentings, or maintain a Kentish kingdom for a Mercian prince until they lose their power at Ellendune. Thenceforward, they sign as kings of Mercia only, though Essex seems to have remained within their system. The conquests of Egbert were only effective south of the Thames, and, though he seems to have revived the *Regnum Anglorum* of Offa in his last years[5] after his nominal conquest of the North, his successors ruled only in the South, and, like the Mercians, made Kent an autonomous appanage of the Saxon house.[6] For the time being, indeed, the rise of Wessex hardened the political distinctions between the three principal states. What consolidation there was took place within the southern kingdom,[7] where the East Saxons, Kentings, South Saxons, and Surrey were thrown to-

Rise of West Saxon monarchy

[1] The target which Offa was attacking appears in Alcuin's letter to the Kentings (A.D. 797): *vos vero principium salutis Anglorum, initium prosperitatis, portus intrantium, triumphi laus, sapientiæ origo, et a vobis Imperii potestas prius processit, et fidei catholicæ origo exorta est*: for you are the source of the salvation of the Angles, the spring of their prosperity, a gateway for those who would enter, their boast, and the beginning of wisdom. From you their empire first came and the Catholic faith had birth.

[2] Haddan and Stubbs, *Councils and Ecclesiastical Documents*, iii. 440: letter of Adrian I to Charles.

[3] *Ibid.* iii. 521-525: letter of Cenwulf to Leo III.

[4] Cf. Alcuin's letter to Ecgfrith, Offa's destined successor, foretelling his reign *cunctis Anglorum populis prodesse in prosperitate*: to be for the prosperity of all the peoples of the Angles.

[5] J. M. Kemble, *Codex Diplomaticus*, 223.

[6] *Ibid.* 269.

[7] *Ibid.* 241: *Æthelwulf rex Occidentalium Saxonum, Centuriorum, nec non cunctibus (aus)trali populi*: Æthelwulf, king of the West Saxons, the Kentings, and of all the southern peoples. *Ibid.* 254: *Æðelwulf rex Australium populorum*: Æthelwulf, king of the southern peoples.

gether into a composite kingdom, which had a fleeting existence as the Eastrige,[1] served for a throne for the heir of Wessex until his succession, and may have done something to extinguish the sparks of Kentish and East Saxon nationalism. With the conquests of Ælfred's later years, we come to a revival of the English title, which, after various experiments, *Rex Saxonum*, *Rex Anglorum*, *Rex Anglorum et Saxonum*,[2] and the like, expands into the imperial roll of titles of his successors, kings of Britain.

Ælfred   The reign of Ælfred may be taken as a stage upon the path of kingship which now rose again after the eclipse of Mercia. It is the last reign of that tetrarchy which had grown out of the ruin of Offa's *Regnum Anglorum*, but its later years developed a power which was to carry Ælfred's successors to a general monarchy of Britain, and to a kingship new in kind. Perhaps no stronger than Offa's Bretwealdership, it had a greater grace and legitimacy. In the strength of Offa there was a relic of pagan violence.[3] He was a robber of monasteries, and popular belief canonized his victims.[4] In Ælfred the ideal of Christian kingship reached its fullness. Under him the most deeply felt attributes of the folk, their law and their descent, sought to justify themselves to the Christian world. Ælfred's laws are prefaced by the Mosaic law of Exodus, so that English custom, abandoning its barbarian tradition, may claim a place as a local variant of a law of Christendom. The genealogy of the royal kin,[5] though still advanced to prove the right of a king "whose fathers' kin goeth unto Cerdic", is Christianized. Woden, now no more than a royal ancestor, descends from Geat, "who some say was born in the Ark", and so, through the nine patriarchs, from Adam. The Ælfredian genealogies of the Chronicle and of Asser's Life are still apologies for the crown's right, and now borrow the ancestry of the Danish Scyldings to attract the loyalty of the Danes, but their pagan element is consciously rejected. They are the logical conclusion of the claim of English kings to rule "by Divine permission", and to stand in the

[1] Anglo-Saxon Chronicle, 836A.

[2] J. M. Kemble, *Codex Diplomaticus*, 324, 1069, etc. The charters of this reign are rarely of the first authority.

[3] Letter of Alcuin to Osbert: *pro confirmatione regni multum sanguinem effudit*: he shed much blood to fortify his kingdom.

[4] As it did Æthelbert of East Anglia, whom he had executed.

[5] Anglo-Saxon Chronicle, 855A.

succession of Old Testament kingship. Such changes in style and title, and in the historical origin which the crown imagined for itself, point to new claims made by the king upon the people. Kingship has found its place in the Christian hierarchy, a temporal vicariate of God, and imposes ties and loyalties stronger and more precise than those of paganism.

The feeling that the king was natural lord of all Englishmen *The king* was of slow growth in England, and before the Norman Conquest *as lord* not deeply held. Many had sought the king's mund, but great subjects might rival him in this. King Ecgfrith's quarrel with Wilfred was in part due to his jealousy of the bishop's following,[1] which was greater than his own. It is true that from the eighth century certain official relations have a colour of vassalage. Offa treated his under-kings as his *comites*. But this may have been by commendation, and the Ælfredian Chronicle is the first document which identifies the preëminence of the king with that of a lord over the men within his mund. Under the year 823 it is said that, for fear of the Mercians, the East Anglian king and his people sought King Egbert "to frith and to mundbora", and, whatever we may make of this cast backward over seventy years of tradition, the phrase was used of the king's power in Ælfred's own day, and in those of his successors.[2]

How far the lordship of the king over all the folk can be pressed is doubtful. The most generalized expression of a relation which depended upon interest and inclination as much as upon formal undertaking, it was, for that very reason, the least real, and might be forgotten in the special loyalty which bound the commended men to their lords. It was a natural term for the king's preëminence in an age which knew only the tie of blood and the tie of lordship, but where the hold-oath was widely sworn to the king it was by

---

[1] Eddius, *Vita Wilfridi*, xxiv.
[2] Asser, *De Rebus Gestis*, 80: *Reges Gwent . . . suapte eundem expetivere regem, ut dominum et defensionem ab eo pro inimicis suis haberent*: the kings of Gwent of their own free will sought the king as lord and mundbora against their enemies. So, Anglo-Saxon Chronicle, 774E. The Northumbrians dethrone Ælfred and take Æthelred, son of Moll, *to hlaforde*. Æthelred, who was more than ealdorman and less than king of Mercia, calls himself *Mircena hlaforde* (J. M. Kemble, *Codex Diplomaticus*, 339).

the massed assembly of the moots, and it might be a feeble counter to the personal contract between individual lord and man. Perhaps a half-century after Ælfred's death, words are ascribed to a king which show that the lordship of the crown had not yet created a community of unquestioning subjects: "think, ye who are my men, how unfitting it were if I should have the name of king and not the power: or what shall a man desire for his lord if not due authority?"[1]

Though the material strength of Offa's reign was regained by Ælfred, the functions of the crown were still few and unspecialized. The king summoned and dismissed the fyrd and such a king as Ælfred was the driving force of national defence. The *trinoda necessitas*—fyrd-service, burh- and bridge-building—though an ancient duty of all freemen, was at his disposal, and in and after his day a period of constant war exposed the local authorities to closer control in such matters than they had experienced before.[2]

Resources of the crown

But the activity even of an Ælfred was limited not only by habit but by lack of resources. There was as yet no taxation, and, unlike some other nations, Wessex may have left its kings entirely to the renders of royal estates and the profits of the courts.[3] Minor members of the royal family were ready to pool their lands and forgo their immediate inheritance in the interest of the ruling head of the house,[4] but, beyond narrow limits, the revenue was inexpansive, and yet Ælfred's use of it shows that it was more than sufficient for the range of function that he could conceive as natural to the crown. Yearly, half the king's revenue went to "God and the Church", and of this a quarter was given to the poor in alms, another quarter to his two foundations of Athelney and Shaftsbury, and the same as gifts to the king's school and to monasteries throughout his kingdom and abroad. The half kept

1 Appendix to Ælfred and Guthrum's Peace (A.D. 940–956?).

2 Asser, *De Rebus Gestis*, 91.

3 Maitland's attempt (*Domesday Book and Beyond*, pp. 235–239) to prove that the West Saxon kings had a right of farm over their subjects' lands as well as their own turns mainly upon an interpretation of II Cnut, 69. 1 (wrongly quoted as II Cnut, 62), which seems unjustified. Such a right existed in Mercia. W. de Gray Birch, *Cartularium Saxonicum*, 366. Further enquiry may reveal it in Wessex, but it has not done so at present.

4 Cf. Ælfred's own account of his and his brothers' resignation of their inheritance in favour of King Æthelbert (J. M. Kemble, *Codex Diplomaticus*, 314).

for secular purposes was divided equally between the pay and upkeep of his military attendants and thegns, the pay of native and foreign craftsmen, and gifts to foreign guests.[1] Charity, hospitality, the reconstruction of the various *cynges tuns*, and their rebuilding in more suitable sites, exhausted the practical ends of royal expenditure. Ælfred appears less as a king than as a great country gentleman, drawing his rents from his estates and spending them magnificently upon good works and a great household.

This is, perhaps, the most simple proof of the extent to which the latent potentialities of kingship remained unrealized at the end of the ninth century, and a like unconsciousness kept the crown from intervening directly in law. The king is claiming to be mundbora to his folk. In so far as this is more than a phrase, it means that he will see that they are not denied the justice that is due to them, that folkright shall prevail over force and fraud. As mundbora the king will intervene when a plaintiff has been denied justice three times at home, and will deal with unjust reeves, and put down overmighty kindreds who deny right to their neighbours. On the basis of this mundbyrdnis the crown will intervene more and more during the next 150 years in the detailed working of law, will put an increasing number of offences under its personal ban and make them pleas of the king, and will lend its personal guarantee to the peace of the realm. But in the time of Ælfred these practical applications were not yet envisaged. Such legal authority as Ælfred has still comes from his private estate even though in the earliest records the privilege to which it gave rise was tentatively applied to public ends by the use of the "king's wite". The highest wite for any offence which did not touch the king's person was sixty shillings (the "full wite" of Ine, 43), while any cause which did incurred the special king's wite of a hundred and twenty shillings.[2] This wite is variously explained. Originally his mundbryce,[3] incurred only by fighting in his presence or attacking persons in his special peace,[4] it defended no more than his private quality. Progress towards a fuller concept was made by the gradual realization of new

The king and the law

---

1 Asser, *De Rebus Gestis*, 102.
2 VIII Æthelred, 5. 1.
3 Æthelbert, 3. The fifty-shilling king's mundbryce of Kent is the equivalent of the hundred-and-twenty-shilling wite of Wessex.
4 Ine, 45.

matters in which the king's direct concern might be presumed, and where aggression might be said to violate his mund. The latter came to be extended over the church and churchmen. The bishop has the king's mundbryce,[1] fighting in a minster and false oath before a bishop come to bear the hundred-and-twenty-shilling wite.[2] The application of the mund to secular affairs may, perhaps, be seen in the burh-bryce for violence done within a king's burh,[3] in the fyrd-wite of a hundred and twenty shillings,[4] and—the furthest extension of the mund in Ine's reign —the same fine for gathering a host for unlawful purposes.[5] This principle was recognized in Ælfred's laws, but with little development. The greatest change was the increase from a hundred and twenty to three hundred Wessex shillings for the king's mundbryce.[6] But the king's protection was extended to no new field of law. There had been little progress. In one clause only do we see a new application of the king's responsibility for public order: fighting in the moot is construed as a violation of the king's mund.

Summary   A summary of the position of monarchy in the reign of Ælfred would show it balanced between two ages. It is thoroughly Christianized and can claim obedience as the temporal vicariate of God. It has extended beyond its racial home in Wessex, and there is no great likelihood of the revival of Mercia or the smaller kingdoms of the South. It is making some claim to a lordship over its subjects akin to that of a lord over his commended men. In law the king is thought of as mundbora of the nation, and, as such, charged to see that no man's rights are infringed and that the presiding officers of the moots know the law and interpret it justly. All this constitutes a great advance upon the limited, tribal, and half-pagan monarchy of the seventh century, and is a sufficient achievement for two hundred years, but it is rather the theory and potentiality of a new monarchy than its realization. Particularly is this so in law. The mundbora is the advocate of his men and will see that they are accorded their full legal right, but only in the last recourse.[7] There is as yet little notion of going beyond this to a special king's law to cover the more dangerous offences, and

[1] Wihtraed, 2.   [2] Ine, 13.   [3] *Ibid.* 45.
[4] *Ibid.* 51.   [5] *Ibid.* 14.   [6] Ælfred, 3.
[7] *Ibid.* 42. In the first instance the plaintiff is expected to besiege his adversary in his house and bring him to court. If his strength is insufficient he may appeal to the ealdorman to do so. If he fails him the king will act.

there are, perhaps, no true king's pleas. The mundbora will protect the individual's peace if it is infringed and he can get no redress, but there is no peace of the realm. The king cannot tax or legislate, he has no feudal right in the soil, no standing army. Under his mundbyrdnis the provinces live by their own custom in their own moots, members of the law of the West Saxons or Mercians far more truly than they are subjects of an English king. The creation of an English nation, of a crown and subjects, of a general peace, of a king's law, is a work of Ælfred's successors of which his own reign gives only the promise and which even they did not bring to completion.

II

FROM THE REIGN OF ÆLFRED TO THE NORMAN CONQUEST

i

THE FOLK ORGANIZED BY TERRITORIAL NEIGHBOURHOOD AND LORDSHIP

Introduc-
tory
WE may characterize the phase of English society seen in the codes of the seventh century as that in which the primitive organization of the folk is in process of invasion by the forces of lordship and Christianity, but has already shown that it will succeed in incorporating them both upon its own terms and will hand on its own essential principles unchanged. Of the two centuries from the reign of Ine to that of Ælfred little is known. The code of Offa has been lost, the church has declined from that power of orderly thinking which produced the Penitentials of Theodore and Bede, and we have only about fifty charters, genuine or in plausible copies. But from the time of Ælfred there begins a richer documentation, and almost every reign has left legal matter of importance. When we examine the first great document presented to us after the two centuries which alone deserve the name of the Dark Ages, we are conscious that the eclipse of learning has had a conservative effect. It is in the days of Ælfred's descendants that the great changes begin, for his own code repeats much of the code of Ine or supplements it with matter of the same archaic type.[1] There is no conscious remodelling of institutions such as was made by Charlemagne, and what change in private relations there has been has taken place unrecognized by, and here and there in avowed conflict with, public law. We know from other sources that society was in rapid evolution, and that Wessex was in the first

[1] Ælfred, Prologue: "I did not dare to set much of my own in writing . . . but what I found of Ine my kinsman, or of Offa the Mercian king's, or of Æthelbert's . . . of that I gathered such as seemed most just".

stages of advance towards vital change. There, and apparently in Mercia also, the position of the common freeman had been decisively worsened, for, while dependence had been sporadic under Ine, it had come to be the rule under Ælfred, and in social estimation the ceorl was now no more than equivalent with the Danish freedman.[1] His legal status was, however, still that of the free twyhynd ceorl of the past[2] and he retained his legal safeguards[3] and took an active part in the moots. Written law, and the law practised in the courts, still assumed the old dualism of eorl and ceorl, and continued to do so for another century. It would, indeed, be difficult to point to any section of the law in which, after a lapse of two centuries, the newer tendencies of Ine's reign were explicitly advanced by Ælfred, save for a sharpening of the sanctity of lordship and of the heinousness of conspiracy against it.[4] Public law still conformed to the original structure of the folk.

In spite of this legal conservatism in the Ælfredian code, the country was upon the verge of one of the most profoundly re-volutionary periods of its history, that in which the essentials of the territorial state were laid down and kingship first realized its trust of government and began to equip itself with powers to carry it out. Among these vital changes which were to occupy the years between 900 and 1066, the most profound of all, one whose effects are even now not exhausted, was the conversion of the older organization by kindreds into that matrix of the medieval and modern society, the territorial community.

The territorializing of all relations of life, beginning in the *Terri-* sphere of private law and spreading outwards to all the institutions *torializing* of state, is first to be traced in the procedure of the courts, and in *of legal* the rights and obligations of the individual. The kindred did three *process* things for its members. It made them oath-worthy and law-worthy: it made their oath valid by swearing a confirmatory oath: it acted as bohr or surety that they should stand to judgment. All

---

[1] Ælfred and Guthrum's Peace, 2.

[2] Ælfred, 39, 40, 44-77. The twyhynd man is still the typical freeman of the community.

[3] *Ibid.* 10, 11, 18. 1, 26, 29, 35, 39.

[4] The compassing of a lord's death is punished by death and forfeiture upon the analogy that homicide within the kin is unamendable.

three of these sanctions were needed in combination to achieve a legal standing for the individual and to constitute the multitude of individuals into a society. It is for this reason, because the legal virtue and status of each of its members was a creation of the solidarity of the kindred, that we say that English society was in the beginning based upon the tie of blood. But, with the lapse of time, mainly during the two centuries with which we have now to deal, each of these functions was transferred from the kindred of the individual to his neighbours, at first to those who in a general way lived near and knew him, and later to organized neighbourhoods, townships, titheings, and hundreds, which arose in response to the new stress laid upon the tie of vicinity and the need to give it territorial definition. This revolution of the tenth and eleventh centuries, silent and unconscious, was perhaps the most deeply formative change of life that the English people ever experienced, for upon the community which it brought into being arose the national state.

Terri-
torializing
of compur-
gation
Compurgation, arising in the oldest stratum of Teutonic law, that dealing with bodily wrongs such as led to the feud, was designed to force upon a kindred which was jointly responsible with its offending member the choice of telling the truth or affronting the gods, and so the principal's relations were made his oath-helpers with intention. But this is an archaic notion. In the laws of Ine there is already a hint of a more sceptical purpose, that of securing an oath which shall be independent of bias. A king's thegn is to be included among the oath-helpers of a man rebutting a charge of homicide.[1] The rise of other fields of law by the side of this primitive law of violence, creating new offences and calling for new expedients, strengthened this new demand, and the law of theft—at least in the elaborate form it took in the tenth century a new law—opened the way for new kinds of oath. Theft, a lonely and secret business, might take a man beyond the knowledge of his family;[2] it did not arouse the feud; and upon charges of theft the oath of the kindred, if it ever had been exacted, was then no longer enforced. It sufficed if the accused could induce men of his village to swear with him.[3] By the reign of Eadward the Elder a further step has been taken towards independent testimony. On a charge of theft a man may be forced to put himself

[1] Ine, 54.   [2] *Ibid.* 7. 1.   [3] I Eadward, 1. 4.

on the oath of compurgators nominated for him by the court from among his fellow villagers[1] or from within the administration in which he dwells.[2] No doubt by attraction, procedure in actions for property is moving in the same direction. By I Eadward, 1. 3 a man who defends his property may find his own oath-helpers if he can: in the next reign he must defend it by independent men chosen for him.[3] The crown also, with its absorbing preoccupation with the problem of the peace, uses this procedure in offences against the king's *grith*,[4] and for greater certainty a register of all lawful men is set up and from these the parties must choose their oath-helpers.[5] At last, accused of default from fyrd and borough service, a man clears himself by compurgation of his titheing.[6] The oath of defence of the Northumbrian thegn of the tenth century is an epitome of all the stages through which the practice of compurgation has passed.[7] He must clear himself with three groups of twelve, one of his own kindred, one chosen by himself from the open court, one chosen by the court for him. In this last stage of its evolution the oath of independent men must have given the same general safeguard of impartiality as the verdict of a jury, though it was still sworn to afforce the oath of the principal, and not to specific fact. In the eleventh century the notion of peerage, which is to play so great a part in the evolution of the jury, has already made its appearance. The landowner, the cleric, and the ceorl, will alike be required, perhaps will demand, to clear themselves by the oath of their equals, and the Norman will speak, in a parallel though distinct sense, of peers of a tenure.[8]

The kindred also ceases to be the sanction by which the mere *Territorializing of warranty* capacity to enjoy the protection or share in the processes of the law is obtained. A full kindred once made a man oath-worthy and law-worthy. The lord as mundbora was allowed to replace the deficiency of the kin, and in Æthelred's reign he was still guarantor

---

1 The *gecorene að*, or oath chosen by the court.
2 II Cnut, 22. 3 II Æthelstan, 9.
4 An oath of 36 compurgators, "and the reeve shall choose the oath". III Æthelred, 13.
5 V Æthelstan, 1. 5.
6 Consiliatio Cnuti, ii. 19. 2A: *Et si negat . . . ex propria sua decimatione secum juraturos assumet.*
7 Northumbrian Priest's Law, 51.
8 Domesday Book, i. 374A: *Willelmus de Perci advocat pares suos in testimonium quod . . . fuit ipse saisitus de Boditone.*

of his men's lawfulness.[1] But in the reign of Cnut that function also is found to have been placed upon the same territorial basis as compurgation. To "be worthy of his law and his wer", to have the right to make oath with legal effect, and receive compensation if successful, every freeman over twelve years of age must be "brought into hundred and into titheing", that is to say, he must be sworn a member of the titheing or township in which he lives;[2] the right of legal action and status has come to depend upon settlement. There has been much debate as to how far this responsibility of the titheing was carried. It appears first in the reign of Æthelstan as a voluntary association for legal help, but already territorialized.[3] By the reign of Henry I it has come to be responsible for the *frith-borh* or frankpledge, a mutual obligation of neighbours which bound the township to report to the hundred court all crime within its bounds, and to produce the criminal for judgment, in short, to act in that capacity of pledge or bohr in which lords had been allowed to act in the past, and for which men of doubtful reputation could once produce *festermen* or sworn sureties from among their neighbours.[4] It has been doubted whether the titheing was charged with the frankpledge before the Conquest, and there can be no certain answer. There was, no doubt, a period of transition during which all freemen derived their lawfulness from their titheing membership, yet had to provide a further guarantee of good behaviour by inducing a lord to stand pledge for them, or by arranging mutual surety privately with their neighbours. It is a question whether the transition was already completed by the reign of Cnut,[5] but the distinction is a very fine

---

[1] I Æthelred, 1. 2-4.   [2] II Cnut, 20.
[3] VI Æthelstan.   [4] Northumbrian Priest's Law, 2. 3.
[5] The problem turns upon a phrase of Cnut's ordinance (II Cnut, 20), which is and must remain ambiguous. Men are to be "brought into titheing and hundred", if they wish to be oath-worthy and law-worthy, but also in the following clause they are to be "brought into hundred and into bohr". Is it intended that, having made their legal standing valid by membership of a titheing, they are further to be placed in pledge by some lord or man of standing, or is the repetition no more than a pleonasm, bohr amplifying titheing and explaining its function? The Instituta Cnuti of the early twelfth century, translating this passage, assumes the latter, and thus betrays its opinion that the frankpledge was already the business of the titheings in the reign of Cnut. Lords of franchises of the thirteenth century occasionally claim that they hold the right of view of frankpledge *ex conquestu Angliae*. Cf. *Placita de Quo Warranto*, pp. 254, 721, etc.

one. The step from being guarantor of a man's legal standing to being responsible for the use he makes of it is easily taken: we know that lords had the option of forcing their men to find themselves sureties from among their fellows, and we must suppose that the hundred reeves might do the same. With the authorities, royal and private, imposing mutual surety upon a populace which was already organized by titheings, the titheing would soon become the normal form of frith-borh without any positive enactment. In making itself guarantor for the lawfulness of its members, the titheing had made it certain that it would become the vehicle of the frankpledge. The change from personal to territorial organization was already irrevocably made.

In all this we see the kindred organization of the past melting as law grows more elaborate and develops new needs and force and fraud come to be recognized as dangers to the community at large. The neighbourhood takes over the task of restraining them in hundred and titheing, in part at its own will and in part by national enactment. The principals in court actions now establish their oath not by the warranty of their kin, but by the impartial voice of the countryside. But the composition of the courts was affected only slowly by these changes. They remained folkmoots. The countrysides flocked into them as before, though now in their territorial grouping of the titheings where before they stood in their kindreds. The virtue and obligations of the individual juridically regarded, the *legalis homo*, were unchanged. The procedure moved through the same routine of oath and ordeal and exacted the same standard of integrity, though neighbourhood was now its basis. In short the English legal system had been individualized and territorialized, had taken the great step from the maegth to the community of the land, but had retained the vitality of its principles and continued to place the same political and judicial requirements upon its folk. In this sense, and it is the deepest sense of all, the community of medieval and modern England draws its tradition from a Saxon past.

But, though these essentials remained, there had been a subtle but radical change in the theory of legal administration, and this came in time to be reflected in the structure and practice of the

Effect upon the composition of moots

courts. As long as their sole duty was to set hostile kindreds at one, the impulse was towards full courts to which all freemen came. The kindreds with all their members were the natural components of the moots. But as these faded out of procedure the way was open to adjustments which might lessen the burden of attendance and make for efficiency. The courts were now dealing with individuals, and with titheings or townships which lent themselves to representation. Moreover, as we shall see later, though the old justice of tort between parties was still being judged, it had been supplemented by a new field of law which was not tied by the old rules. In this fresh matter the crown was asserting responsibility with an especial interest in the peace and in those kinds of theft which were in themselves violent or gave rise to disorder. In this the crown's interest was to secure intelligent and impartial witness, and its instinct was to deal not with masses but with selected individuals. Thus, though the theory and basis of the courts remained popular, their practice tended to become less so, and active participation was not so

Aristo- cracy in the moots

universal as it had been in the past. In time a legal aristocracy emerged and partially monopolized the active work of judgment and witness. Asser could still refer to the "judgment of eorl and ceorl" in the folkmoots, but by the Confessor's reign the latter's voice was of doubtful value.[1] We have seen how the courts of Æthelstan were constrained to confine the function of witness to a panel of "unlying men", and throughout the ensuing century the references to these legal worthies thicken. The *seniores*, the senior men of the court, the senior thegns,[2] are clearly coming to be relied upon for all processes of court where independence of word and judgment is needed. Æthelred, if I read the text rightly, takes an oath of twelve thegns to pledge a whole moot to just judgment.[3] Judgment by twelve judices seems to have been wide-

[1] William de Chernet claims this land . . . and adduces witness from among the wisest and most substantial (*de melioribus et antiquis*) men of the whole county and hundred. And Picot brings against them testimony from the villeins and obscure people and reeves (*de villanis et vili plebe et de prepositis*) who offer to make proof by oath or ordeal (*per sacramentum aut per dei judicium*): Domesday Book, i. 44B.

[2] III Æthelred, 3. 1.

[3] *Loc. cit.* Reading, 3. 1. with the previous clauses, this now seems to me the best explanation of the yldestan XII pegnas. It is, of course, true that the enactment is for a Danish administration where one might expect to find lawmen.

spread in Northumbria and in certain borough courts. The thegns of the county have by the time of the Conquest come to be synonymous with the county court in many Wessex shires.[1]

Later evidence, moreover, leads us to suspect that the number of suitors to the moots was in process of reduction not because of any shadow upon the free right of the countryside, but because a more complex law, and perhaps a denser population, was making necessary a kind of court less unwieldy than the old folkmoot. The shiremoot met twice a year in the tenth century,[2] the hundred every month.[3] By the twelfth century a readjustment has taken place, which, while it does not impair the standing of the common folk in the courts, yet relieves them of the burden of constant attendance. Twice a year courts are held to which the suit of all freemen is obligatory[4]—and in this sense those whom the law calls villeins are free—but they are courts of administration and not of judgment. In them the view of frankpledge is held, new members are sworn into titheing, the hundred hears any charge the sheriff's officers may have in hand from the king, and in later days swears fealty if ordered so to do. These biennial courts are called Lawdays of the Hundred, and attendance is said to be *per omnia capita*.[4] The London lawday appears as early as the reign of Henry I, and its name of Folkmoot points to its descent from the old full court of Saxon times. After the rise of the lawdays, judgment, on the contrary, no longer involves the common suit of the countryside. It is done not monthly, but in courts meeting, at intervals which have given their name to the jurisdiction, *De Tribus Septimanis in Tres Septimanas*, and to them the obligation of common suit is recognized, but exercised by representation only. The titheings appear by their headmen and four companions,[5] who present all causes within the jurisdiction of the court, and produce accused persons, and by this suit their constituents of the titheings are free, except such as are principals or witnesses in any suit. This is the basis of the legal system of the Middle Ages in shire and hundred, and though, as with the frankpledge itself, we may question whether the adjustment was made in Saxon or in

Narrowing of suit to shire and hundred

---

1 J. M. Kemble, *Codex Diplomaticus*, 755, gives a good account of the leaders of the shiremoot of Hereford in Cnut's reign.

2 III Edgar, 5. 1.

3 I Edgar, 1.

4 Leges Henrici Primi, 8.

5 *Ibid.* 7. 7.

Norman times, the distinction is academic rather than historical. The institution of the titheing, not the refinement of its use, marks the territorializing of English country life.

Franchise jurisdiction The Saxon king had no jurisdiction like that of the feudal lord to give his men. He could give his wites and withdraw his reeve, and nothing more. Even direct loss of legal administration, the passing of the men of the folkmoots into franchise courts, can be proved to have been in progress no earlier than the eleventh century and may fairly be conjectured of the tenth; before that it cannot be proved, nor is it, indeed, probable.

Clause 50 of Ine's code, which speaks of the gesith who "acts as intermediary for his man with—*þingað wið*—the king or a king's ealdorman or with his own lord", and, in so doing, loses his claim to the wite which will follow a condemnation, has been believed to refer to private jurisdiction. The lord in question, it has been thought, must have a court, since he is in a position to accord or withhold the profits of judgment. It is certain, however, that no unequivocal proof can be extracted from this provision.

Seventh-century evidence The subject of the clause may be representing his dependant's innocence through his own lord, obtaining the latter's support in a court of king or ealdorman where all three, the gesith, his lord, and his man, are justiciable. The practice described—*þingan for his man*—is that of adopting the cause of a dependant as one's own and pleading it *in propria persona* in the courts,[1] of becoming his *forespreoca*, a general obligation of lordship throughout the Teutonic and Scandinavian North, and one which might easily be transferred from the gesith to a noble even better skilled and of greater influence to secure the small man's right than would be the gesith himself. On the other hand, the clause shows that the practice of according to a lord the profits of the justice done upon his men already prevails. The ground of this resignation of the wite to the lord is not entirely clear. In all probability it is done on the assumption that he produces his man for judgment, and so relieves the king and his reeves of that function by which the monarch earns the profits of justice, the function which is the justification of all money penalties in this age when the theory of crime does not yet exist. The gesith probably loses these wites because by his office he is, like the thegn of later days, under a

[1] Cf. p. 15 *supra*, note 7.

special obligation to the king to maintain order within his sphere of influence. He is the king's minister and representative. The wites are part of the privilege granted by charter from a very early date, and are especially freely conferred in the eighth century, where they appear as wites,[1] or *witerædden*[2]—the same term as is used in clause 50 of Ine—or in some less direct formula. There is, however, no single phrase or charter which explicitly grants jurisdiction as well as wites; on the contrary one latinization of the privilege describes it as the *vindicta popularium conciliorum*,[3] the "wites of the folkmoots", as though to leave no doubt that the immunist was empowered to collect the profits of judgment which took place in the courts of the community, but had neither need nor licence to hold his own. It is curious that the very charters which have been put forward as proving the existence of private courts at a slightly later date—in the ninth century—tell, with the exception of one formula of most dubious interpretation, against it. Upon Maitland's reading of these charters, and particularly *Weakness* upon that of two of them,[4] his argument for the existence of *of evidence for* private justice in the eighth and ninth centuries largely rests, and *it in the* in order to show its weakness we must commit ourselves to the *ninth* examination of an involved and difficult text. The charters in *century* question define the privilege of certain great churches as being that of clearing "the men of God's church", *i.e.* the commended men of the abbey, by the unsupported oath of the reeve or abbot, if they can conscientiously do so. The privilege is that defined in Wihtraed, 22-24, and so far the case is simple. But the charters go on to state what will happen if the reeve is uncertain of the man's innocence and will not venture upon the oath, and unfortunately do so in Latin which varies as between two texts,[4] and is too corrupt to admit of word-for-word translation: *sin autem ut recipiat alienam* (J. M. Kemble, *Codex Diplomaticus*, 236, ibid. 214 reading *aliam*) *justiciam huius vicissitudinis condicionem praefatum delictum cum simplo praetio componat. De illa autem tribulatione que witereden nominatur sit libera.* It would be natural to take the reading *alienam*, and—remembering that the act of exculpation by the sole oath of

---

[1] J. M. Kemble, *Codex Diplomaticus*, 206 (A.D. 814); ibid. 313: *And noht ut to wite.*

[2] Ibid. 1063: *Libera . . . a taxationibus quod dicimus wite redenne.*

[3] Ibid. 116.

[4] Ibid.,214 and 236. They are of doubtful authenticity.

an ecclesiastical person was regarded as a completed act of judgment, a self-doom—to construe the sentence as follows: "But if he accepts alien or independent judgment (*i.e.* in preference to the self judgment of the reeve), he must compound for the offence by damages (*singulare pretium*, *angyld*, to the plaintiff), but of the liability which is called *witereden* (the church) shall be free". The purpose of the clause seems, therefore, to be not to grant jurisdiction but to acknowledge the church's claim to the wite which the king may fairly grant since it is his own, and at the same time to secure that the plaintiff's damages (*simplex pretium*) shall not be drawn into the immunity also and lost to him.[1]

---

1 Maitland's interpretation of these charters (*Domesday Book and Beyond*, p. 292) involves somewhat violent treatment of their texts, and the explanation of some of their terms in senses strange to the ninth century. His case really rests upon the formula used in J. M. Kemble, *Codex Diplomaticus*, 214 and 236, and specifically on the phrase *sin autem ut recipiat alienam* (*ibid.* 214 has *aliam*) *justiciam huius vicissitudinis condicionem praefatum delictum cum simplo praetio componat*. He explains it (very tentatively, "our best guess as to its meaning is this") as follows: If the reeve dare not make the sole oath, he may pay the damages claimed, and by performing this *condition* he may obtain a transfer (*vicissitudo*) of the cause and do what other justice remains to be done, *i.e.* he may exact the wite. "In guessing that *vicissitudo* points to a transfer of a suit, we have in mind the manner in which the Leges Henrici, 9, § 4, speak of the 'transition' of causes from court to court." The objections to this reading are very strong. In the first place, the reading *alienam justiciam* suits the case excellently. It is the external, alien judgment of the folkmoot where the defendant will be tried if his ecclesiastical lord and reeve dare not pronounce favourable judgment upon him by the sole oath. Maitland takes the weaker *aliam justiciam* of J. M. Kemble, *Codex Diplomaticus*, 214, and translates, "he may do what other justice remains to be done"; but there is no question of *other* justice; it is an alternative between the judgment by oath of the reeve or the judgment of the folkmoot, very aptly described as *aliena*.

Exception must again be taken to the reading of the words *vicissitudinis* and *condicionem*. The Latin of this hopelessly corrupt sentence is a debased example of charters in which *condicio* is used in the sense of "terms" or "obligations" of land-holding. Thus J. M. Kemble's *Codex Diplomaticus*, 199, has: *et ab universis etiam terrenis difficultatibus notis et ignotis condicionibus ac tributis . . . libera*, and *ibid.* 253 has: *ut regalium tributorum et principali dominatione, et in coacta operatione et poenalium conditionum*. *Vicissitudo* is probably no more than another of the exaggerated synonyms used for *onera*, of which *difficultas, obstaculum, gravitas, tribulatio, impedimentum, gravidinis, lesio*, and *molestia* are others. The *vicissitudinis condicio* of *ibid.* 214 and 236 is, indeed, a fairly evident synonym, slightly more rhetorical, for the *pœnalium conditiones* of its contemporary (*ibid.* 253).

Remembering the base and florid Latin of the day, and the law that underlies it, the following reading may be suggested as sounder, though less spectacular, than Maitland's: "Let him compound for his man's liabilities (*hujus vicissitudinis condicionem*) and for the aforesaid crime (*praefatum delictum*) by paying the angyld". This reading conforms to the legal terminology of the early ninth

Only Maitland's treatment of these clauses justifies their detailed examination, for they are dubiously authentic, of doubtful meaning, and are slight evidence to base a theory which would impose franchise of justice upon the ninth century. However, some charters of this age have their place in the general narrative of events, because, so far from proving the existence of franchise jurisdiction from the earliest times, they may be used to give us a date, and a comparatively late one, before which it is almost certain that such jurisdiction did not exist. These rare charters of the eighth and ninth centuries[1] contain clauses which, in addition to the ordinary promises of immunity from witeraeden and the like, tell us the conditions under which this immunity from wites is held. The immunist is to pay angyld, or *singulare pretium*, to the party against whom his vassal has done injury. Only on this condition, that the legitimate interest of the plaintiff shall be secured by the payment of the value of the property stolen from him, or the wergeld, or other bot, as the case may be, does the king promise that he will exact no wite, or, as more probably would happen, let it fall to the lord of the convicted man. It is evident that if the immunist possessed a court of his own, he would be able to exact his own wites there, and that these scrupulously worded and evidently coveted grants of the "wites of the folkmoots"[2] show that his men were, on the contrary, still justiciable by the public courts.

The charters which we have been discussing convey further *Privilege* privileges which tend to confirm this impression.[3] The grantee, in *of self-* this case the abbot of Abingdon, may, if he believes in his man's *oath*

century in a way that Maitland's does not. It also places the immunity in an intelligible light, whereas Maitland has apparently failed to envisage fully the situation to which his suggestion might give rise, that the reeve, having refused to take the sole oath, and chosen the alternative of paying the angyld and claiming the case for his supposed court, might then on trial find the accused to be innocent. If we take the translation as suggested, we shall avoid fastening such an absurdity upon that very wideawake person the clerical immunist as the payment of damages against one of his men who was as yet untried. An immunity by which the king relieves the lord of the royal wites on condition that he indemnifies the injured party is a reasonable one and borne out by interpretation of the text of the charters in contemporary terms.

[1] J. M. Kemble, *Codex Diplomaticus*, 116, 117, 206, 214, 215, 216, 227, 236, 253, 262, 277, 313, 1068.
[2] *Ibid.* 116: *Vindicta popularium conciliorum.*
[3] *Ibid.* 214 and 236.

innocence, swear him clean of the charge by his unsupported oath, and by so swearing release him from all challenge by oath or ordeal. This privilege, which, as we have already had to consider, is not, as Maitland assumed it to be, the forerunner of the claiming of court of the Middle Ages,[1] by which the lord of an immunity could claim his men and their causes and have them transferred from the public courts to his own. That was a feudal usage, this is of the older world of the folkmoots, one more example of a rule of old standing, by which certain classes of persons to whose character or position the common process of oath-helping was unsuitable, were released from the obligation to find oath-helpers, and allowed to clear themselves by an unsupported or *self-oath*[2] taken at the altar, no doubt that of the church in which the ordeals of the folkmoot were sanctified. By the time of Wihtraed this privilege was shared by the king's thegn, the foreigner, priests, deacons, and the heads of monasteries,[3] and had been extended to cover the unfree servants of religious communities,[4] and kings' reeves and bishops' reeves as their deputies were able to swear away the guilt of their lords' servants by the same self-oath.[4] Now this process, so far from being a claiming of court, is a completed trial in the public court; the self-oath is itself the process and the judgment: in Icelandic law it would be said to be a *self-doom*. That the folkmoot was the place of trial is proved by the laws of Wihtraed. If the lord or his reeve will not venture on the oath, the accused is not remitted for trial to some private court, such as Maitland assumes to lie in the background, but is dealt with at once in the folkmoot and by the ordinary penalty of the unfree; his lord must deliver him to the lash.[4] The affinities of the Abingdon liberty are, therefore, not with immunity of court. They have their root in the age before feudalism in the archaic procedure of folk-justice.

Judicial powers by royal grant   Turning to the surer ground of later record, it seems that when judicial immunities arose they were not feudal in origin, that is to say, they could not be assumed in virtue of the mere fact of holding land or of having received the fealty of commended men and with it a claim upon their forfeitures. They were, as the lawyers of Edward I maintained, the effect of explicit royal grants. The later

---

[1] F. W. Maitland, *Domesday Book and Beyond*, p. 282.
[2] Wihtraed, 20. *Gest hine clænsie sylfes aþe on wifode.*
[3] *Ibid.* 17 18, 20.   [4] *Ibid.* 23.

Saxon kings were making such grants under two forms. By one, mainly, perhaps only, for the benefit of religious houses, they were granting the full administrative rights of the hundred. Hundreds so given were thenceforth governed by the reeves of bishop or abbot, and the hundred court became the court of an ecclesiastical immunity. The same pleas were tried there as before, the same suit was due, the same profits of jurisdiction were exacted, but now to the profit of the saint. How old such grants may be we cannot tell. Eadward the Confessor gave "the soke of the eight *Immunity* and a half hundreds of Thinghowe" to Saint Edmund,[1] and "the *of the* soke within Bichamdik" to Saint Benet of Ramsey,[2] and ordered *hundred* the shire of Norfolk to support the Abbot ad justiciam if necessary. Not long after the Conquest Ramsey was claiming hundred there over "all men that are moot-worthy, fyrd-worthy, and fold-worthy";[3] but records of such gifts are rare even in Eadward's reign. If we believed that there were no grants of this kind other than those for which genuine charters and writs have survived, we should find it hard to account for the very general possession of hundredal rights by the medieval churches and for the tradition which attributes to them a very great antiquity. We need not, indeed, accept the bishop of Salisbury's claim to the hundred of Ramsbury by grant of Offa, but such immunities as the three Worcester hundreds of Oswaldslaw coincide so clearly with the outline of the see of Worcester's lands in the tenth century that it is difficult to dissociate their origin from grants either of land and jurisdiction together, or of hundredal rights over land already held, and made in the tenth century as the church claimed. The Domesday hundreds of Kent are in their outline an epitome of the growth in landed estate of the archbishopric, the priory of Christchurch, and the abbey of Saint Augustine during the tenth and eleventh centuries. There seems no reason either in reliable tradition or record to carry back these ecclesiastical hundreds behind the reign of Eadgar [4]—the hundred itself was not much

---

[1] F. E. Harmer, *Anglo-Saxon Writs*, No. 9.   [2] *Ibid*. No. 60.

[3] *Ibid*. No. 61.

[4] J. M. Kemble, *Codex Diplomaticus*, 600. Eadgar's gift of a hundred hides at Taunton to Winchester, though it is silent as to jurisdiction, is a case in point, for the bishopric held the hundred court in the Confessor's reign. On the other hand, the Confessor's grant of Pershore to Westminster (F. E. Harmer, *Anglo-*

older—nor to extend the enjoyment of hundredal grants to the laity, but they have a large place in English life at the moment of the Conquest, and by the thirteenth century something like a quarter of the English hundreds must have come, some in fee, but more by lease in farm, into the hands of great feudatories.

Sake and soke

A second form of private justice, though still justice by royal grant, may be traced in record to Cnut. This is the grant of sake and soke, together with the special justice over thieves caught red-handed known as *infangentheof*, which may itself have been new in the tenth century. Cnut has convicted himself of conferring rights of justice upon his subjects, for his ordinances tell us that he will rarely give the highest of pleas to any subject, except to do him special honour.[1] Soke or *socn* means suit, among other things suit of court, but also suit in other matters. There is *fyrd-socn* and *ship-socn*, *fold-socn*, and so on, and the sense seems to be that of rendering any custom to the centre to which it is due. It is, no doubt, this soke of customs which we find at the beginning of the eleventh century.[2] Sake, on the other hand, is the Germanic *sache*, a cause or plea, and definitely confers jurisdiction when granted, and the right to hold a court.[3] What that jurisdiction was we are never told directly; perhaps all causes pertaining to wer and wite, which, in turn, should mean the old law of personal violence, such as gave rise to the feud, including theft, but often without the newer categories of justice, which were construed as touching the king and withheld as *cynges gerihta*. It was probably felt that such matters as were emendable by compensation between kindreds scarcely touched the common interest or the king's, and might be left to be settled within the lordship. Justice in actions for landed property, which the immunity of sake and soke un-doubtedly carried, would no doubt come under the same principle for it was a maxim of eleventh-century law that matters concern-ing the custom of any district should be judged by the peers of that custom and not by strangers. But though the social outlook of the day may have made such rights unobjectionable, there is

Saxon Writs, Nos. 99-101), at least as the monks saw it, seems to have treated jurisdiction as a separate privilege.   [1] II Cnut, 12.

[2] *E.g.* in Wulfric's will. D. Whitelock, *Anglo-Saxon Wills*, xvii. A.D. 1002-1004.

[3] F. E. Harmer, *Anglo-Saxon Writs*, No. 28. Ðæt he beo his saca ond socne wyðre ond griðbryces ond hamsocne ond forstealles on infangenes þeofes ond flymena fyrmðe.

no reason to suppose that they could be assumed as the prerogative of lordship or without royal license.

How soon the royal grants began we cannot say, though we have given reason to think that they are not older than the tenth century. Before the reign of the Confessor sake and soke was given by writ only, and not by charter, and our oldest writs are those of Cnut.[1] Nor can we be sure how completely a grant of soke freed the land and the men upon it from suit and other obligations of shire and hundred, and specifically from that obligation of frankpledge which, at some period or other of the eleventh century, was coming into being, and was closely associated with private justice. On the whole, Domesday suggests that a man under the soke of a lord was freed from suit to the hundred, and several of the Confessor's grants of sake and soke are accompanied by quittance *de hundredis et schiris*,[2] which must surely mean freedom from external suit. The commonest immunity of the medieval manor was that of holding a private view of frankpledge, and when the proctors of the crown examined the counties in the inquiries *De Quo Warranto* of the first three Edwards, there were many landholders who based their claim to the view upon their right of sake and soke,[3] or on such quittances from shire and hundred as were given by the Confessor.[4] Of the franchises of immunity from the view which riddled England in the Middle Ages, a great number are known to have been created by post-Conquest charters, and some arose by the neglect of the sheriff to exercise his right of view; but if frankpledge was already existing in the reigns of Cnut and the Confessor, we need not dismiss the possibility that it was a corollary of sake and soke, and part of a substantial growth of immunity, both judicial and administrative, in the last half-century of Saxon history.[5]

Thus aristocracy and franchise are increasingly the marks of

[1] The earliest being by Cnut to Archbishop Æthelnoth. F. E. Harmer, *Anglo-Saxon Writs*, No. 28. One possibly authentic writ of Æthelred survives.

[2] *Ibid.* No. 76.

[3] *Placita de Quo Warranto*, pp. 211, 244. The king's proctors denied this on occasion. [4] *Ibid.* 290.

[5] As in Essex, where certain tenants "were so free that they could sell their land where they would, and the soke and sake with it" (Domesday Book, ii. 59A).

later Saxon history, and, while the common freeman is not disfranchised, he is thrust into the background, required to act by representatives, and often subjected to the court of an immunity. He attends the folkmoots when the law needs him, or when he is specially concerned. Nevertheless, this growth of the aristocratic principle in the courts is compatible with conservatism in many spheres of the law, and apparently has little tendency to bring England into line with the movement towards feudalism which was developing in the empire of the Franks. More than any other side of English life, the growth of the English land system from Ælfred to the Conquest leaves the impression of a very remarkable blend of insularity and adaptability. In common with many of the Germanic codes the laws of the English contain no complete *Growth of* statement of the custom of landright. It was known to all, needed *land-law* no written record, and was spoken by verbal memory in the courts. What we know of it comes from charters which record only specialized forms of land-holding, and from the few records of sale and formulae of pleading which have survived, and from Domesday Book. Bearing in mind the nature of the feudal practice which is to be grafted upon England after the Conquest, the distinctive fact of Saxon custom is that it is governed by the notion not of *dominium* but of property,[1] and almost entirely by the right of individuals. In some remote past the English may have shared with their German cousins a system of joint family holding of land, related groups maintaining an undivided birthright and cultivating the soil coöperatively. If so, the joint family must have lost its unity long before the migration. In Britain the only limit upon individual property is the rule of equal partition among heirs, which preserves the joint birthright of the stock of descent but expresses it in every generation by allotting an equal part of the inheritance to each of the heirs, with right to give, sell, and bequeath. Sometimes under the name of gavelkind, sometimes passing unnamed as local custom, this archaic rule was universal in Kent, common in East Anglia, and sporadic in part of the East Midlands, the West, Essex, and Sussex. The Borough English of the south-coast

---

[1] More properly, a presumptive right in the possessor (F. Pollock and F. W. Maitland, *History of English Law*, i. 57), for which "property" is used in this section.

manors may have been a debased form of gavelkind,[1] but it is unlikely that gavelkind ever predominated in the purely Mercian and West Saxon settlement of the Midlands—it may well have reflected a difference of race—and there impartible descent may have been the rule from the earliest times. However that may be, landright everywhere seems to have shared the free right of alienation which prevailed in gavelkind if we may trust the few instances of gift in the spoken forms of ancient custom which have been recorded for us.[2] By the tenth century all Saxon landright seems to have been unbound by entail, except where a special deed of limitation had determined its descent, or where, as upon certain parts of the church lands, a customary prohibition against alienation was observed. Whether partible or impartible, all land held *Folk-land* by the ancient rules of inheritance was subject to action and defended in the folkmoots by the process of oath and ordeal, which was in itself part of landright. The property held in it, the right of inheritance, of gift and so forth, together with the forms of pleading appropriate to it, were that part of folkright which related to land. At least over a period of years at the end of the ninth and the beginning of the tenth centuries, land held in folkright seems to have been known as *folk-land*.[3]

This main stock of English land-law came, no doubt, from *Book-land* Germanic custom, and the greater part of the land was held in folkright, though, since *ex hypothesi* it passed by verbal transfer, we know little of it. But, imposed upon this Germanic foundation, was a foreign landright of Latin and clerical origin, which made land the subject of gift by *boc* or charter. At the time when charter grants were first made, perhaps in the age of Theodore, perhaps from the time of the conversion, the choice of written gift may in part have been dictated by the fact that it conveyed *perpetua et libera haereditas*, by which was meant—rather oddly— the right to give, sell, or devise, but this motive can only have

---

[1] It preserved the gavelkind rule of reserving the house and hearth to the eldest son, and in many cases enjoyed the security of *gavelate*, and gave the kin the prior right of purchase which is known as *retrait lignager*. J. E. A. Jolliffe, *Pre-Feudal England*, pp. 79 *et seq.*

[2] Cf. the Peterborough gifts and sales made in the hundred court with verbal guarantee (*festermen*) and witness, but without charter: W. de Gray Birch, *Cartularium Saxonicum*, 1128, 1130. They are of the late tenth century.

[3] Cf. F. W. Maitland, *Domesday Book and Beyond*, pp. 244-258.

been operative if, at that early period, rights of kindred and binding rules of descent hampered the free alienation of the paternal inheritance. In later days the charter usually gave rights of legal immunity, but in the early grants it is rare that more than simple landright should be conveyed. Certainly the most distinctive quality of book-land, chartered land, was that it was especially under the protection of the king, the witan, and the church, that the charter promised damnation to those who broke its terms, and that it could not be called in question in any lower court than the witenagemot.[1] Folkright in the folkmoots, bookright in the witenagemot before the king and the bishops, whose authority had instituted it, seems to have been the rule of law, and, when challenged, the holder by book had the supreme advantage that the production of his charter, backed by a competent oath, was sufficient to nullify all further question. The two forms of property, therefore, were distinguished from each other only by differences of authority, or of procedure, sanction, and venue, and holders by charter clung to their bookright century by century mainly because of the strong legal defence that it afforded them. In historical times the holder of folk-land seems to have been no less free to dispose of it, possessed of no less absolute property, than he who held book-land. We are brought, therefore, to conclude that in the tenth and eleventh centuries the Saxon land-holder was free both from customary rules such as may have prevailed in a remote past, and from the manifold restrictions upon tenant right and lord's right which were the essence of feudal *dominium*. The Saxon's right was, in short, not tenure but property.[2]

The free right of book-land and folk-land had, no doubt, its

[1] J. E. A. Jolliffe, "English Book-right", *English Historical Review*, vol. l.

[2] Norman scribes, faced with the contrast between the *feudum* and English book-land, imported for the latter the Continental term *alod*. This was used more loosely in the eleventh century, but had originally denoted the paternal inheritance of the freeman, the German *frei eigen* as opposed to *beneficium*, or even to land acquired by gift. In equating *alod* with book-land the Continentals were, no doubt, seizing upon the phrase *in aeternam haereditatem* in *bocs*. So, in the Norman translations known as the Instituta Cnuti, we have *Carta alodii ad aeternam haereditatem* (Instituta Cnuti, iii. 46), and *si liberalis homo, quem Angli thegen vocant, habet in alodio (id est bocland) suo ecclesiam* (I Cnut, 11). Cf. also II Cnut, 13. 1. In Domesday in the south-eastern counties, though not

advantages. It had, however, one serious drawback: gifts had to *Draw-* be made outright, and therefore without conditions. The lord who *backs of* wished to reward his man or retain a material pledge of his faith- *absolute right of* fulness could only do so by creating a right of property in the *property* donee as free as his own. This fact the formula of the charters reflects accurately by specifying that the land transferred has been given not on condition of future service but in reward for past service done. The *feudum*, the quintessential achievement of feudalism, provided a *via media* by which the giver could set up a dependent and heritable *dominium* in the donee, while himself retaining a parallel *dominium* in himself and his heirs. This bound the heirs of both parties to behave towards each other as lord and man in perpetuity, and at once rewarded the servant and secured the service and fealty of his descendants. The device of the fee the Saxons had not, nor by the date of the Norman Conquest is there any sign that they were on the way to acquiring it; nevertheless from very early times precisely the difficulty that the *feudum* was designed to solve was felt in England. If our estimate of the land-right of the gesiths of Ine is correct, they passed out of history because they had no property or inheritance in their lands, and their lords would not, or would but rarely, accord it them. Bede tells us how they tried to get book-land in perpetuity, posing as founders of monasteries, begging land from the king for that purpose, and if the abuse had not been checked the recurrent demands of generations of landless warriors exacting estates from the *terra regis* would have left the fisc bankrupt.

The case of that equally great landlord, the church, was even more difficult. Over a large portion of their lands, bishops, abbots, and monks had not the same right of free alienation as the layman. Every see had its permanent endowment *de episcopatu*, every monastery its lands *de abbatia, de victu*, or *de vestitu monachorum*, or the like,[1] and these were often ancient bequests, which by convention or rule could not be broken away from their sacred pur-

---

consistently, perhaps, *alodium* is used to denote the free English land-holding. It also occurs in certain charters conveying the dependence of thegns to the churches of Canterbury, *thegen* being Latinized *alodiarius*, no doubt as one who often held land in bookright.

[1] Domesday Book, i. 65B: *Haec sunt de victu monachorum . . . qui tenuerunt T.R.E. non poterant ab ecclesia separari. Ibid.* i. 135A: *Hoc manerium tenuerunt iii teigni . . . et vendere potuerunt. Hoc manerium non est de episcopatu.*

pose.[1] They formed the *firma* or consolidated fund of land for the up-keep of the necessary services of the community or see.[2] Moreover the great church estates were larger than most others, and might reach the dimensions of a province. They needed the services of laymen as administrators and protectors. Like others, they needed ready money, but they could not, as did the king and the magnates, reward the services of laymen by an outright gift of land. With perhaps the greatest need of all to render their resources liquid, they alone were restricted in their right to alienate. Consequently, we find them testing the resources of the law, seeking to render more elastic the rigid property of their lands, and producing a variety of experimental relations which keep the letter of inalienability, but approach, though they never realize, the device of the *feudum*.

The laen   The laen, or *praestitum*, the outstanding example of this, was arrived at at the latest very early in the ninth century,[3] when the see of Worcester, and, no doubt other religious houses, was making use of it. It was precisely what its name implies, a loan of land, usually for a term of three lives. Since it did not give property it could be granted on condition of service. At the end of the tenth century Bishop Oswald of Worcester was making loans of from one to five hides for three or five lives in return for an oath of general obedience,[4] and service of acting as bishop's messenger and travel-ling escort which he called *lex equitandi*, "riding custom", and which probably gave the name *radknight* to the recipients. These loans could not be construed as alienation, a strict check was kept on their terms of lives, and Oswald informed the king of their terms in a well-known letter,[5] so that Eadgar as patron of the church might know that no improper alienation was taking place. So, during the two hundred and fifty years through which we can trace it, the loan shows no sign of becoming hereditary: the

---

[1] Thus, Coenwulf of Mercia, in endowing Winchcombe, ordained that no grant for more than one life should be made from the monastery lands. J. M. Kemble, *Codex Diplomaticus*, 323.

[2] Domesday Book, i. 67B: *De eadem terra tenuit Aluric . . . unam hidam . . . ea conditione ut post mortem ejus rediret ad aecclesiam quia de dominica firma erat.*

[3] J. M. Kemble, *Codex Diplomaticus*, 279, 303, 315.

[4] *Ibid.* 1287: *Quamdiu ipsas terras tenent in mandatis pontificis humiliter . . . perseverare*: to observe the commands of the bishop with humility as long as they shall hold the said lands. This is not the hold-oath of a vassal, but an official's oath of obedience in his office.

[5] *Loc. cit.*

Domesday survey records the dependent estates of Worcester still carefully denoted as *praestita* not to be renewed without the bishop's leave.[1] One modification alone shows that it was a form of holding hardly secure enough to attract the type of men the churches desired, and this came to fill a useful niche in English land-law. Bishop Oswald himself made general the practice—he did not invent it—of giving greater stability to the laen by granting the recipient a book, while still preserving the reversion of the land to the see at the end of the allotted term of lives. To this end he issued charters converting *laen-land* into *book-land* for a period only,[2] borrowing the literal form of the diploma of gift, and creating a legal chimaera which, as he himself puts it, conveyed "eternal inheritance for three lives".[3] This did, in fact, produce a kind of holding which might carry a condition of service, lodged an effective right in the holder, gave him the paramount advantage of pleading by bookright, and yet secured ultimate reversion and avoided alienation. Thus, by a roundabout way, some of the advantages of the *feudum* were secured and the see was enabled to carry out something which had roughly the effect of an enfeoff-ment. The device was a clumsy one, but it had great success in the absence of a purer legal concept. The pretence of "eternal inherit-ance" being soon dropped,[4] other churches and even the king are found making gifts by book for a term of lives even up to the Conquest.[5] Such holdings, no doubt, underlie many of the un-explained restrictions upon those Domesday land-holders of King

Gifts for term of lives

---

[1] Domesday Book, i. 172B.

[2] F. W. Maitland, *Domesday Book and Beyond*, pp. 310-318, considered that the laen was the natural forerunner of the *feudum* and formed a link between a rudimentary English feudalism and that of the Normans. This was not so, for up to 1066 the laen showed no sign of becoming hereditary, did not necessarily create a lord and man relation (cf. note 5 *infra*), showed, in general, no sign of developing along the lines of the *feudum*.

[3] J. M. Kemble, *Codex Diplomaticus*, 617: *Oswald . . . bocath Eadrice his thegne . . . swa swa he aer haefde to lanlande.* Cf. also *ibid.* 651.

[4] *Ibid.* 586: *Perpetua largitus sum haereditate, et post vitae suae terminum duobus tantum heredibus immunem derelinquat*: I have granted in eternal inheritance and after his life he may leave it freely to two heirs only. This curious form persisted in the leases being made by Burton Abbey until well into the twelfth century.

[5] Domesday Book, i. 72A: *Toti emit eam T.R.E. de aecclesia Malmesburiensi ad etatem trium hominum, et infra hunc terminum poterat ire cum ea ad quem vellet dominum*: Tofi bought from the church of Malmesbury for a term of three lives in King Eadward's day. Within that term he could go with it to any lord he liked.

Eadward's day[1] who could not "go with their land",[2] though others were by the clear terms of the grant free to go. They are a striking proof of the incapacity of the English to develop the theory and practice of feudalism, since, advancing from the same point—the *praestitum*—which was the origin of the Frankish *feudum*, the English made scarcely any progress at all, and had to be contented with producing an illogical and contradictory blend of the laen and the alod, the conflicting elements of which were never properly reconciled, and certainly never acquired the clarity of feudal tenure.

Absence of feudalism in England   If, therefore, we are concerned with the technical form of law, we can say that England had not arrived at the *feudum* by 1066; if it be thought that this is a fact of antiquarian rather than historical interest, it must be answered that, because the English had not the fee, they also had not feudalism. There seem to have been three principal ways of land-holding in England of the eleventh century, by bookright, by folkright, and by laen.[3] Of these three ways of land-holding not one could create a permanent link between the component parts of any accumulation of property such as made the Norman honour indissoluble, nor bind the heirs of any lord and those of his vassal to each other through an indefinite future. In English law, unless there was specific limitation by will, no inheritance bound the inheritor,[4] whether in land or in lordship. Though Domesday speaks of the *Honour* of Bristric, the *Honour* of Wisgar, it is a misuse of terms, for the Norman honour had per-

[1] J. M. Kemble, *Codex Diplomaticus*, 1170, 1231.

[2] Domesday Book, i. 66B: *Tres hidas vendiderat abbas cuidam taino T.R.E. ad etatem trium hominum, . . . et postea debebat redire ad dominum*: the abbot sold three hides to a thegn for three lives in King Eadward's day . . . and after that term it ought to return to the original lord.

[3] *Ibid.* i. 257A: *Edricus tenuit de Episcopo et non poterat ab eo divertere quia de victu suo erat et ei prestiterat tantum in vita sua*: Eadric held it of the bishop and could not depart from him because it was *de victu suo* and he had loaned it to him for his life only.

[4] The generation of Ælfred tried to do something to remedy this defect by giving a right to entail book-land. Ælfred legislated with that intention (Ælfred, 41), and took advantage of the law in his will (J. M. Kemble, *Codex Diplomaticus*, 314), and his contemporary, Burhred of Mercia, adopted the same practice (*ibid.* 299), but the right was never reasserted in later reigns and seems to have fallen into desuetude.

manent existence, and the lands of any Saxon, however great, were no more than a casual grouping, inherited, bought, given by the king or others, commended to him by his followers at their own will and pleasure. Not only might they be dispersed within the owner's lifetime or by his testament, but they habitually were. The Englishman was, therefore, devoid of that dynastic sense which drove the feudatories of later days to project their ambitions into the future, scheming always to safeguard a dynastic estate and to augment it. The Saxon land-holder bestowed his lands at death not as a dynast, but so as to complete his own life, save his own soul, and satisfy his love for those whom he had known in his lifetime. There was no leaning towards primogeniture in bequest, for there was no enduring unity, and no law which bound the future. Great accumulations of land and lordship rose and were dispersed within a lifetime, as was that of Wulfric, "thegn and dear to the heart of King Eadred", whose great estate of lands in Berkshire, Sussex, and Wiltshire were so broken after his death that they were in twenty-eight different hands in the days of the Confessor, or that of the Lady Æflaed, who willed her lands to the king and to nine different religious communities.

Because of this brittleness and impermanence in the higher strata of Saxon land-holding, no typically feudal policy develops, no leagues of nobles, no specifically feudal reaction against the crown. Throughout the whole Saxon period there is nothing that we can call a feudal rising. So the omission of four words —*in feodo et haereditate*—from the formulary of English land-law went far to determine the whole history of the later Saxon age.

The form taken by the English law of property was, therefore, the greatest factor in determining the evolution of social relations. It is directly reflected in the relation of lord and man. In the absence of dependent tenure, lordship was not feudal. There was, of course, no homage, that is to say, no oath or ceremony acknowledging dependent tenure and promising faith and service as from a given tenement and in virtue of it. A form described as "bowing"[1] to the lord, the *commendatio* of Domesday, was gone through and an oath

Lordship without feudalism

---

[1] *Mid þaem monnum ðe him to gebugon.* Anglo-Saxon Chronicle, 901A.
Ic wille ðat Ælfrich Modercope mot bugan to ðo tweyen abboten at seynt Eadmunde and at sancte Ætheldrede. F. E. Harmer, *Anglo-Saxon Writs*, No. 21.

was sworn to be in general faithful or *hold*, from which comes the common term *hold-oath*[1] for what was later called the oath of fealty. The characteristic phrase of the formula is the promise to "be hold and true to N., loving all that he loves and shunning all that he shuns". The hold-oath does not create the dependent tenure of feudal land. The advantage to the man was still, of course, the acquiring for himself and his property and dependents of the protection of the lord's mund,[2] and his maintenance in the courts. The lord could take his man's cause upon himself and plead it in the courts in his own person,[3] and there are many signs in the codes that lords were ready and able to save their men by force and guile from due process of law.[4] Such advantages were, of course, mutual. We are apt to think that a lord's one motive to increase his following must be economic, to establish a title to other men's lands, to get more rent and agrarian service. That is not so in the eleventh century. With many impalpable advantages of social prestige and security which we can no longer fully appreciate, man and lord could be of very solid use to each other at law. Maintenance, later the object of many denunciatory statutes, was still a motive force in legal procedure. The family had "maintained" its kinsmen by oath, warranty, and witness, and, as the family's obligation in such matters declined, the individual found himself still dependent upon the opinion of a court of neighbours. A trial which point by point judged by the public estimate of the parties, and required them to be backed by men

---

[1] Swerian, 1: *Ðus man shall swerigean hyldaðas.*

[2] D. Whitelock, *Anglo-Saxon Wills*, xvii. Wulfric (circa 1006) requests that Ælfhelm shall be mund to his daughter and to the land he leaves her. Domesday Book, i. 32B: *Potuit ire quo voluit sed per defensionem sub abbatia se misit*: he could go where he would, but for his defence he put himself under the abbey. Leges Henrici Primi, 61. 17. D.B. i. 137B: *Postea ad Wigotum se vertit pro protectione*: afterwards he commended himself to Wigot for the mund. *Ibid.* i. 58A: *Potuit ire quo voluit sed pro sua defensione se commisit Hermanno Episcopo*: he could go where he would but commended himself to Bishop Herman for his defence. *Mundbyrdnis* is still the term for lordship in the late eleventh century, F. E. Harmer, *Anglo-Saxon Writs*, Nos. 99-101.

[3] For all capital causes a man might claim stay of process until his lord could appear on his behalf.

[4] Cf. Domesday Book, ii. 401B. Brungar was under the jurisdiction of the abbot of Ely, but was the man of Robert fitz Wymarc. Stolen horses were found in Brungar's possession, but Robert conferred with the abbot and no charge was made.

who were willing to swear to their right, put a premium upon good neighbourship, and still more upon good lordship and faithful vassalage.[1] It was for this that in even later generations the greatest men of the realm bound their men to legal maintenance in the charters of their tenures.[2]

The incurable Gallicism of Domesday is such as at first sight to give the impression that conditional tenure existed in the days of King Eadward. The jurors were required to give an account of the state of vassalage and lordship. Whether the phrase was put into their mouths by their inquisitors or occurred to them spontaneously, they tell us that a vast number of Englishmen held *de* or *sub*[3] *Rege Edwardo*, and that an almost equal number held *of* bishops, earls, and lesser men whom we can often identify as king's thegns. In Norman legal speech the *tenet de* should denote tenure and point to a joint tenant's and lord's *dominium* in the soil,[4] and probably when used of the tenant of William's day it usually does so, but a very little examination of Eadward's men will show that, used of the vassals of his day, it stood for a less real and more personal tie, that of commendation by the hold-oath. We find that there are a vast number of men in the South-West and East[5] who hold *de Rege*,[6] or *de* or *sub* some lesser magnate, and yet are so free that they "can sell their land where they will", or "go with their land where they will", are *liberi homines*,[7] or "can become any man's

Dependent tenure not recorded in Domesday

---

[1] J. M. Kemble, *Codex Diplomaticus*, 328; II Cnut, 30. 1.

[2] *Cartularium Monasterii de Rameseia*, iii. 260: *Tali pacto, quod tam ipse, quam heres suus . . . totam terram Sancti Benedicti, pro posse suo, in omnibus defendat placitis, ubicunque opus fuerit*: on these terms, that he and his heir shall defend the whole land of St. Benet with all his power in every plea.

[3] To hold *sub* or *de* seem to be equivalent, the former being a variant expression in the East Midlands, Hertfordshire, Buckinghamshire, and East Anglia.

[4] *Cartularium Monasterii de Rameseia*, i. 141: *Et eadem terra est de feudo abbatis Ramesiae et Stephani Deseschalers, qui de abbate eam tenet* (T.R. Henry I).

[5] The tie of lordship is rarely recorded in Northumbria. It is likely that the West Saxon kings had little lordship there, for even in the South commendation to the king, not as monarch but as lord, was, of course, voluntary. Thus Swegen, though a subject, came to Eadward, and "promised that he would be his man" (Anglo-Saxon Chronicle, 1049C).

[6] Domesday Book, i. 144A: *Hoc manerium tenuerunt duo fratres, unus homo Ulfi et alter homo Eddevae. Potuerunt dare et vendere cui voluerint. Ibid.* i. 170A: *Clifton tenuit Seuuinus . . . de Rege Edwardo et poterat ire cum hac terra quo volebat.*

[7] This seems to be the meaning of *fuit liber homo* or *tenuit libere*, at least in the South and Midlands. *Ibid.* i. 248B: three men held Little Sandon, *duo eorum*

man",[1] according to the formula used in the county in question. They are commended, but can undo the act of commendation.[2] Occasionally the record is more explicit, and we can see how tenuous is the tie of lordship, and how easily loosed at the vassal's will: "Alric holds half a hide now. His father held it of King Eadward, but Alric himself has not sought the King."[3] The son has not felt the bond worth renewing and has let it drop, but he still holds the land. Another has taken the contrary course: "Tori's father held the land T.R.E. and could go where he would, but to get protection"—*pro sua defensione*—the old *to hlaford and to mundbora*—"he commended himself to Bishop Herman, and Tori has done the same to Bishop Osmund".[4] Sometimes we can see the owner exercising the right of alienation which such formulae imply: "Bolle held Windrush and could go with the land where he would, and he gave it to the abbey".[5]

Prevalence of free landright   Not to have the right to dispose of land is comparatively very uncommon. Buckinghamshire, for instance, is almost entirely under ecclesiastics and lay magnates, or under their *homines*, and, almost without exception, the latter can sell their lands where they will. Staffordshire, similarly, is monopolized by freemen who can sell their lands. In Cheshire they are largely preponderant, and in Sussex there are only a sprinkling of instances to the contrary. Moreover, familiarity with Domesday leads one to suppose that where it is silent we have to deal with some king's thegn or other notable whose freedom is too well known to need comment, often the general antecessor of the Norman tenant-in-chief. Usually we can assume that freedom to alienate was possessed unless there is

---

liberi fuerunt. Wicstui cum terra discedere non poterat. Domesday Book, i. 31A; Bromley: *Quattuor ex his hidis fuerunt liberorum hominum qui de Alnod secedere potuerunt.* There are exceptions, usually in East Anglia and near by, but there the notion of "freedom" is confused by that of freedom from certain customs such as foldsoke, and by the need of drawing a contrast with the prevalent holding in socage. Cf. *Ibid.* ii. 59B.

[1] *Ibid.* ii. 119A, Thetford: *Alii omnes poterant esse homines cujuslibet.*

[2] *Ibid.* ii. 47B: *Quidam liber homo erat commendatus Roberto . . . et poterat ire quo vellet.* It would seem that to contract a new vassalage a man would have to get his late lord's clearance of good-conduct (II Edward, 7), but III Æthelstan, 4 shows that the lord could not refuse it without convincing cause.

[3] *Ibid.* i. 50B. Sometimes the son had forgotten, or never known, to whom his father had been commended, so purely formal might its nature be in some instances.

[4] *Ibid.* i. 58A.   [5] *Ibid.* 165B.

explicit record to the contrary.[1] To be tied in landright to a lord was, therefore, an exception, though one shared by perhaps five per cent of the manorial land-holders of England, of whom Domesday records *non potuit vendere, non potuit recedere*, and the whole trend of the Survey suggests that these tied estates were not dependent tenures held in perpetuity after the manner of the *feudum*, but land not really in the ownership of the immediate occupier, being granted to him for a period or for life only,[2] as farm from clerk to layman, by some special contract, or, most commonly of all, by laen or gift for a fixed term of lives.[3] Such holdings are found, for the most part, about the demesnes of the church and the great units of *terra regis*, or great lay manors.

Thus, Old English land-law governs the custom of lordship, starving it of the soil of feudalism and confining it to a purely personal basis. That rigidity which provided no other alternative to the lord but the giving of land outright or the granting of temporary possession, prevents the assimilation of the tie of lord and man to that of *dominus* and *tenens*, and especially of that form of it in which a parallel *dominium* in the soil is held by both lord and tenant in a perpetuity of interdependence. In short, it bars the way to tenurial feudalism.

If we try to pierce below the stratum of the substantial land- *Lordship* holders we can say little with certainty. Beneath the uniformity of *over* bookright there are many Englands, for each of the old kingdoms *ceorls* has maintained its ceorlish custom. It is virtually impossible to answer the old question as to the freedom or unfreedom of the eleventh-century peasant. There can be no one touchstone of freedom, such as the Angevin courts applied, to which Deira,

[1] No details of lordship are given in Yorkshire and Lincolnshire, but wills show the right of free alienation by gift or exchange. D. Whitelock, *Anglo-Saxon Wills*, p. 95.

[2] Domesday Book, i. 136B: *Hanc terram tenuit Godwinus de Ecclesia Sancti Petri. Non potuit vendere, sed post mortem ejus debebat ad ecclesiam redire.* Sometimes they were held by manorial servants. *Ibid.* i. 47A: *Wenesi tenuit de Rege Edwardo . . . sicut antecessor ejus tenuit qui fuit mediator caprorum. Non potuit se vertere ad alium dominum. Ibid.* ii. 41B: *Unam hidam quam tenuerunt ii servientes Wisgari. . . Nec poterant abire sine jussu domini sui.*

[3] *Ibid.* i. 257A: *Non potuit ab eo (Episcopo) divertere quia de victu suo erat et ei præstiterat tantum in vita sua.*

Bernicia, Mercia, East Anglia, Essex, Kent, and Wessex, will react alike. One thing only is clear, that the English peasantry moved across the line of the Conquest in every variety of dependence and independence, status, and relation to the state. Constitutional history can do no more than take note of this variety as the basis of its treatment of law and administration. Lordship over peasants settled upon the land of great men had by the tenth century some quality which made it different in kind from normal lordship, more real and enduring. In relation to the men upon his estate the lord was already the *land-rica*.[1] Both the name and the institution of the manor are lacking, but the law of the estate is coming to be thought of as something different from folkright.[2] Even by the reign of Ælfred, the ceorls of Wessex could be given no higher status than the Danish freedmen when a common standard between the ranks of the two peoples was sought,[3] and in the Midlands the manorial records of the Middle Ages reveal a considerable proportion of villages whose cultivators have no landright apart from their lord, who cannot leave the estate, and whom the law reckons as unfree. The persistence with which such masses of landright preserved their unity, and were transferred from owner to owner unbroken, suggests that even in the Saxon age the Midland cultivators were involved in a lordship which could not be shaken off, and perhaps had forgotten that the possibility had ever existed.

Decline of the ceorl   We need not think that the Saxon lord enjoyed a feudal right over his peasants which in his own acres and for his commended men was not yet imagined. There were principles in English law which would in themselves suffice to keep the men of the townships immobile, though such principles had yet to be fused into a conscious rule of servile tenure. Precisely in that part of England, Mercia, and central Wessex, where villeinage was the rule in later days, the open fields, the interlocked tenements of the village, and the common ploughs, made the agricultural community almost indissoluble, and the greater number of such communities were under a single lord who was also its greatest proprietor. So early

---

1 IV Eadgar, 8. 1; VIII Æthelred, 8.
2 Gerefa, 1: *Se gerefa sceal aegðaer witan ge hlafordes landriht ge folces gerihtu*: a reeve must know both the custom of his lord's land and folkright.
3 Ælfred and Guthrum's Peace, 3.

as the seventh century we know that the ceorl who had no land, but settled upon a gesith's land as a gebur, was a common social type,[1] and a document of the eleventh century [2] shows the geburs as one of the two principal classes of the cultivators, still without landright of their own, and paying for a lord's loan of land and stock by labour. It would be rash to say that all those manors whose courts in the Middle Ages denied a heritable right to their villeins derived their custom from the geburs of Saxon England, but they were fewer than is commonly supposed, even in the servile Midlands, and the strength of peasant right of inheritance in such widely scattered lands as those of the churches of Winchester shows that the West Saxon ceorl had much of freedom to bequeath to his villein descendants. Continuity of lordship and commendation from generation to generation is likely to have been most common with the peasantry. It was perhaps almost universal in the Midlands, and might easily harden into an obligation where the lordship sought was that of the one man of standing, whose landright was the greatest in the community, and whose power was an ever-present reality. Fealty sworn generation by generation would easily become a necessity and a rule. A twofold origin, in grants made to landless men, and in commendation by ceorls who had landed right and inheritance but needed protection, may well be a sound analysis of the lordship of the land-rica over his peasantry, if we allow for that loss of the fine edge of definition which may come to unwritten right transmitted by memory and exercised in community under the shadow of social and material power.

The Domesday term *villanus*, which the surveyors scattered far *The vil-* and wide over the peasantry of England, seems to have borne *lanus of* little or no relation to its use in the courts of the thirteenth century. *Domesday* It is applied equally to the men of Kent, where villeinage was non-existent, to the bondagers of the North with their heritable Tenant Right, to many of the comparatively free peasantry of East Anglia and Essex, and to every variety of customary holding in Wessex and Mercia. It ignores the nature of the landright and of the service due from the holding. In so far as it was applied consistently, it seems to have been a simple borrowing of the Saxon term *tunesman*, and to have denoted a holder of land which could not be

1 *Ante*, p. 20.   2 *Rectitudines Singularum Personarum*, 4.

detached from the manor, and whose holder appeared before the law as a member of the township for which the manor answered, or of which it formed a part. As with the more considerable land-owners, so with the cultivators, the crown is primarily interested in determining the outlines of the estates, whether this or that man can or cannot "go with his land where he will", and we are again brought back to the condition of the *villanus* as bound to the soil on which he lives and to its lord. This, no doubt, was a limitation far more widely spread than heavy service of labour or precarious landright, and would justify in a large measure the Domesday extension of the villeins. There is no doubt that Saxon England had come to treat the cultivators of each estate as a unit for administration where such estates were compact areas. In part, this practice was, perhaps, due to the emergence of the township as the primary unit of administration in the tenth century, but, in addition, there are factors in the custom of lordship which may explain this restriction upon the mobility of the ceorl without appeal to any doctrine of servile tenure. Commendation was free to all and as free to be renounced as to be incurred, as far as the law went, but it had been hedged about with safeguards. From the time of Ælfred, it had had to be made publicly, and in a public court. A man wishing to seek new lordship must notify the authorities both of the shire to which he is going and of that which he is leaving.[1] Later law prescribed a clearance from the former lord, who must vouch for his man's past conduct, and declare him free from all legal charges and claims such as might be frustrated if he left secretly.[2] The crown, moreover, was using lordship as a com-pulsory guarantee of conduct. The lawless man, or the man who had no land and goods to serve as security, must be found a lord by his kin.[3] "To go where he would", always lawful for the lawful man, and easy for the commended man of property and clean record, might be a difficult matter for the man who had no land in his own right, whose stock had been lent him by his lord, and who was of too low a station to have that weight and responsi-bility which was required of the lawful man. Nor for a man whose

1 The first administrative recognition of the private estate is, perhaps, that of Ælfred, requiring the cognizance of the ealdorman when a man leaves the *boldgetale* in which he has been serving. Ælfred, 37.

2 II Eadward, 7.

3 II Æthelstan, 2.

past and future were enclosed within the fields of a single lordship would it have seemed desirable or even possible. We may well believe successive peasant generations abode under the same mund until change became unthinkable, and yet doubt whether the law held them *adscripti glebae* or had found for the peasant a ground of dependent tenure which it had yet to arrive at for commended men of higher status. If we deny feudalism among the magnates, we should need convincing evidence to find it in the community of the village, and of such evidence there is no hint in charter, custumal, or law.

The terms upon which the Domesday *villanus*, the Saxon *tunesman*, lived with his lord hardly concern the constitution. In East Anglia the *villani* are not the principal stock of the peasantry. They are outnumbered by the *sokemen*, that is, by holders of small estates, who owe attendance to the hundred court, or to a lord who holds the immunity of sake and soke, and pay the miscellaneous customs which are due to the king from the hundred. These have an acknowledged landright, and for the most part commend themselves as they will. The North has more *villani* than sokemen, but the manorial records of the Middle Ages show us that they were *bondi* or *husbandmen*, who, in contrast to the Midlanders, enjoyed much freedom of right and lighter service. The Kentings had a free landright by custom of gavelkind: they could sue in the king's courts in the thirteenth century, and were lightly burdened, and, except for the absence of the right to sue by writ, a large proportion of the villages of Hampshire and Sussex had an almost equally free custom known as Borough English. The Midland counties and the middle South-West were the district of the most onerous villeinage, but even in the Midlands there was a proportion of comparatively free custom. This is the verdict of the charters, court-rolls, manorial surveys, final concords of the late twelfth and succeeding centuries, but it is contradicted by no evidence from the eleventh if the meaning of the Domesday *villanus* be rightly interpreted.

It has seemed best to reserve the thegns to the end of our survey *Thegnage* of the community because their status is to be explained neither by vassalage, nor birthright, nor property, nor tenure, and because attempts to treat them under one or more of those headings have led to confusion in the past, beginning from the moment when the Normans turned themselves to explain the society which they *The king's* conquered and never fully understood. The king's thegn has *thegns* already made his appearance once in Wihtraed's law, once in Ine's, and on a number of occasions in the Ecclesiastical History of Bede, where, as *minister*, he seems to be distinguished from the *comes* or gesith.[1] The mark of his status is a higher privilege than that of the latter,[2] and he is in some matters free from the common commitments of folkright. Royal patronage stands to him instead of kindred, for, like the priest, he can clear himself by his unsupported oath.[3] In origin, therefore, thegnage is an office, not a grade of the folk—the thegn may be either twelfhynd or twyhynd [4]—and it keeps this character until the rules of the folk fade out of memory. There is no indication that its holders were at first numerous. A couple of *ministri* attest Wulfred's charter of 674,[5] one thegn of Caedwalla of Wessex appears in 653,[6] and two attest a charter of Offa in 785.[7] If attestation of genuine charters is to be the test, it is not until the reign of Æthelwulf that the king's thegns begin to play an important part outside his immediate entourage,[8] and, though we must not place too much weight upon the practice of charter witness, it does indeed appear that the first great expansion of the thegnhood came with the military and political supremacy of Wessex.

The title of king's thegn may be applied to any official of high standing, but is especially used of the *ministri* below the rank of ealdorman and in constant and active service, and above all of those in immediate attendance on the king's person. We hear

---

[1] Bede, *Historia Ecclesiastica*, iii. 14. The Anglo-Saxon translator renders *miles* as *thegn* and *comes* as *gesith*. Cf. also W. de Gray Birch, *Cartularium Saxonicum*, 225, Cynewulf's grant: *Bican comiti meo et ministro*.

[2] Ine, 45: *Be burhbryce, Cyninges ðegnes lx scillinga: gesiðcundes monnes land-haebbendes xxxv scillinga*.

[3] Wihtraed, 20.

[4] III Æthelstan, Prologue: *Omnes Centescyre thaini, comites et villani*. F. E. Harmer, *Anglo-Saxon Writs*, No. 26, "all my thegns twyhynd and twelfhynd". Simeon of Durman. *De Gestis Regum*, ann. 884. The Norðleoda Laga, a Northumbrian text which betrays Celtic influence by allotting wergelds to each official rank, is the only pre-Norman code which gives the thegn a distinctive blood-price irrespective of birth (*loc. cit.* 5).

[5] W. de Gray Birch, *Cartularium Saxonicum*, 32.

[6] *Ibid.* 82.   [7] *Ibid.* 245.   [8] *Ibid.* 421 et seq.

of household officials, the *disc-thegn*,[1] perhaps the *pincerna* or butler, who might also be an ealdorman, of *hall-thegns*, of *bur-thegns*,[2] thegns of the king's bower or chamber, who survive as the servants of the Norman kings' camera, *horse-thegns*,[3] and *hrael-thegns*.[4] But, besides these holders of a working ministry about the court, there are other king's thegns of whom we can only say in general, as our texts say, that they are "very near to the king",[5] that they have "a special seat in the king's hall",[6] that they are in the king's *sundernot*, or personal service,[7] that he pays them a wage at Easter.[8] In later days the decisive act in recognizing a newly made baron was to allot him a seat at the tables of the king's hall, and authorize the livery of his own rations and those for the attendants custom allowed him in the palace. In all probability this would be the only tangible mark of the thegn's status also. As having this recognized provision about the king's person all the magnates, ealdormen, bishops, abbots, and the like were king's thegns,[9] as well as those who had no other standing but the king's ministry.

Beginning as a court officialdom—and although their title and office never became legally heritable[10]—the king's thegns were on the way to establishing themselves as a landed aristocracy by the middle of the ninth century. Principal links between the king and provincial administration, they were coming to have a foothold in the country as well as the court and to appear as county magnates. They were building estates of land upon the king's generosity, and their value in local government made the crown anxious to fortify their landed interest, limiting their court attendance to one month in three and leaving them free for the rest of the year to

The king's thegns and the land

---

1 W. de Gray Birch, *Cartularium Saxonicum*, 912.
2 J. M. Kemble, *Codex Diplomaticus*, 572.
3 Anglo-Saxon Chronicle, 897A.
4 W. de Gray Birch, *Cartularium Saxonicum*, 912.
5 II Cnut, 71. 1.   6 Geðincðo, 2.   7 *Loc. cit.*
8 J. M. Kemble, *Codex Diplomaticus*, 314.
9 Anglo-Saxon Chronicle, 897A, gives the king's thegns who died in that year as the bishops of Dorchester and Rochester; the ealdormen of Kent, Essex, and Hampshire; Eadulf, a king's thegn of Sussex; Beornwulf, the wic-reeve of Winchester; and Ecgulf, the king's horse-thegn.
10 They were renewed at the beginning of a new reign, and might be forfeited for misconduct. Cf. IV Eadgar, 2A: "All my thegns shall keep their (thegn)ship as in my father's day".

reside upon their estates.[1] Much land had been granted to individuals[2] as the reward of service and, unlike that of the gesiths of the past, it carried the free property of bookright. All these grants were, therefore, alienable at the discretion of the grantee and free of all conditions for the future.[3] There had been at least one distribution upon a national scale which can only be described as an endowment of the thegnage intended at once to secure their fidelity and to establish their material influence in the country. When Æthelwulf made his much debated decimation of his kingdom in favour of the churches he included in his benefaction his "thegns who are established throughout the said realm",[4] and,

[1] Asser, *De Rebus Gestis*, 101. *In tribus namque cohortibus praefati regis satellites prudentissime dividebantur, ita ut prima cohors uno mense in curto regio die noctuque administrans commoraretur, menseque finito, et adveniente alia cohorte, prima domum redibat.*

[2] W. de Gray Birch, *Cartularium Saxonicum*, 750 *et passim.*

[3] One royal charter only of this age, if it is correctly transcribed, represents an early attempt to fasten a condition of future service upon the recipient of book-land and his heirs—to make a holding of book-land dependent on thegn's service. W. de Gray Birch, *Cartularium Saxonicum*, 814: Edmund grants land at Weston to his thegn Æþelere, *eatenus ut vita comite tam fidus mente quam subditus operibus mihi placabile obsequium praebeat. Et post meum obitum cuicunque amicorum meorum amicorum voluero eadem fidelitate immobilis obediensque fiat. Sicque omnes posteriores praefatam terram possidentes in hoc decreto fideliter persistant sicuti decet ministro*: on condition that to the end of my life with faithful mind and bodily obedience he shall show me acceptable duty. And after my death he shall remain steadfast in the same faith and obedience to whomsoever of my friends I shall desire. And let all his successors who hold the same land hold faithfully to this provision as it behoves a thegn to do. (Notice how the king's reservation of the intention to bequeath the thegn's service after his death conforms to Saxon notions of the alienability of right, in contrast with the customary descent of the *feudum* through heirs. It is derived from the general notion of bookright.) A comparison of what is, in effect, a rough attempt to anticipate the principle of the *feudum* with a gift to a thegn in the common Saxon form will show how widely the former differs from Saxon notions. W. de Gray Birch, *Cartularium Saxonicum*, 1197: Eadgar grants to his faithful vassal Wulfoð three hides in Lesmannoc *liberaliter in æternam possessionem . . . ut illo predicto territorio voti compos vita perfruatur comite, et post obitum ejus cuicumque voluerit heredi derelinquat. Tam in minimis quam in magnis . . . immunem derelinquat. Prefatum siquidem rus omni servitio careat*: freely in eternal possession . . . so that he shall possess the said land during his life, and after his death leave it to any heir he will, free in great things and small. The aforesaid estate shall be immune from all service. The reservation of the *trinoda necessitas* which follows is, of course, that of a public obligation on all land.

[4] *Decimam partem terrarum per regnum non solum sanctis ecclesiis darem, verum eciam et ministris nostris in eodem constitutis (ibid.* 469). This is probably an original text, and is the centre of a group of charters of varying authenticity and intelligibility. By W. de Gray Birch, *Cartularium Saxonicum*, 486 (*Textus*

whatever the effect of his grants as regarded the church, the secular thegnage benefited by a series of charters conveying book-land. This endowment of 854 was typical of the second of three attempts to stabilize the king's dependants in the countrysides. The first ministry, of the gesithcund men, perhaps died away for lack of heritable right, the second, the king's thegnage, had property of which the king retained no power of regulating the descent, and so they dissipated their lands by bequest and gift, the third, the Norman enfeoffment, was to find in the *feudum* the key to the honour,[1] heritable in perpetuity, in general indivisible, and bound by perpetual service and fealty to the crown. If the thegn held other land not under bookright but under the common rules of folkright, as no doubt many did, that also was not held in any feudal tenure. It must, says a law passed within a half-century of the Conquest, be equitably distributed among his heirs.[2] Thus, while the *ministerium* of the king's thegns carried a duty of service less specific than that of feudal knight or baron, their landright was a thing apart from it, property not tenure.

There are already signs in the ninth century that with many thegns the provincial interest will outgrow that of court service, so that their attendance will come to be titular, or only exercized at the ceremonial courts of Christmas, Easter, and Michaelmas, or when the king, passing about his kingdom, resides and holds council in some provincial centre. In the attestations to charters we can trace some thegns in constant attendance in all parts of the realm, and some of these rise to be ealdormen and are clearly national figures.[3] But others seem to be provincial notables only, coming in from their country seats to Winchester or Canterbury.[4] Had Saxon government been less closely knit, the thegns might well have grown away from their ministerial origin, and survived as a landed nobility with nothing of ministry but the title. That

Functions of the king's thegns

Roffensis), the thegn Dunn receives land *pro decimatione agrorum quam Deo donante caeteris ministris meis facere decrevi.* Eadgar expresses the same motive (J. M. Kemble, *Codex Diplomaticus*, 536): *disposui ex opibus mihi a deo concessis meos fideles ministros cum consilio optimatum meorum ditare*: I have determined with the counsel of my magnates to endow my faithful thegns out of the wealth given me by God.

[1] Cf. p. 140, *infra*.   [2] II Cnut, 78.

[3] As did Eastmund under Æthelbert and Æthelred of Wessex. W. de Gray Birch, *Cartularium Saxonicum*, 506, 507, 516, 519.

[4] Like Lulla, Æthered, Wullaf, etc. *Ibid.* 449, 460, 467, 486, 501, 506, 519.

they did not do so was in part due to the fact that the king kept
in constant touch with the shires, and required of his thegns much
the same steady coöperation in the shire courts, of which they
formed the witan, as he did from the bishops, ealdormen, and
thegns about his person. The king's thegn was becoming the
knight of the shire of his day; he owed special obedience to the
king's ban,[1] and to the body of the shire-thegns the king's writs
were addressed.[2] The king maintained a tone of patronage to his
thegns, looked to them for a special standard of conduct, and
made use of their strength to afforce his reeves. In the eleventh
century he laid upon them the primary responsibility for judgment in shire and hundred,[3] Under like penalties with the king's
sheriffs and reeves, they were set to enforce the pacts of mutual
peace into which he persuaded the countrysides from time to
time,[4] to carry out the regulations against theft,[5] to force priests to
keep their rule,[6] to collect the dues of the church.[7] In such matters
the king's thegns and the king's reeves were on the same footing,
and were so treated in enactments.[8] Both came under similar
penalties for abusing their charge,[9] and where the reeve might lose
his office, the thegn might lose his thegnage.[10] These are particular
applications of the ministry which it was found necessary to
specify from time to time in royal ordinances. They were additional to duties in which the thegns were the executive hands of
the folkmoots. At least the leadership of the elaborate routine of
arrest, process serving, levying of distress, eviction for contempt
of judgment, pursuit of outlawry, and hue and cry, lay upon the
thegns who rode upon the court's errands and enforced its decrees[11]
with a growing sense of royal commission as the king's initiative
in law and order became more active. The tenth century was a
great age of the English crown, and the king's thegns were its

---

[1] *Rectitudines Singularum Personarum*, 1.
[2] F. E. Harmer, *Anglo-Saxon Writs*, No. 82. *Eadward kyng gret well . . . calle
mine ðegnas on þam scyrum þar Sancte Peter into Westmynstre hafað land inne.* Cf.
also Nos. 11, 24, 29, etc.

[3] III Æthelred, 3. 1. *Ibid.* 13. 2.   [4] VI Æthelstan, 11.
[5] *Loc. cit.*   [6] IV Eadgar, 1. 8.
[7] Northumbrian Priests' Law, 57. 2.   [8] III Eadmund, 7. 2.
[9] The king's oferhyrnes or ban of 120/-. Cf. V Æthelstan, 1. 4 and VI. 11,
and III Eadmund, 7. 2.
[10] III Eadgar, 3. The judge who gives false judgment forfeits his thegnage.
[11] III Æthelred, 3. 1, 2; J. M. Kemble, *Codex Diplomaticus*, 755.

characteristic servants, a corps of provincial *ministeriales* more obedient, more at the mercy of the king, and more readily responsive to royal mandates than the Norman kings had in their barons. They were empowered to ride in the king's stead with his writ and summons,[1] and it is in this function that we see them intervening in the shire courts or local witenagemots of the tenth century with ordinances to proclaim, and commission to advise and coöperate in their execution.[2] Some of them were very great men indeed, and, though their commissions were not regularized as routine visitations, upon occasion they fulfilled something of the function of the Carolingian *missi*. Through them, as much as through reeves and ealdormen, the crown controlled the provinces.

Thegnage means no more than service, *ministerium*. From the ninth to the eleventh century it was the normal expedient for getting done any work of exploitation or administration which could not be conveniently left to the reeves, or for discharging such public duties as could be done by deputy. So, just as the king's thegns made themselves useful about his person or seconded the reeves of the shires and boroughs, so every great royal estate and every great private franchise had its thegns also. The thegns upon the king's estates are not king's thegns—though indirectly they are thegns of the king—for they take their orders from the reeve of the estate,[3] pay their rents into his farm,[4] attend his summons to court,[5] and go upon his errands. If they are amerced their fines go to the reeve, whereas those of the king's thegns go to the crown. Probably their heriots, which are small, go through the estate farm also. "They serve the reeve of the manor."[6] While no

The lesser thegns

---

[1] Geþyncðo, 3: *He þenode cynge and on his radstæfne rad: regi servisset et vice sua equitaret in missiatico regis.*

[2] VI Æthelstan, 10: "The witan at Thundersfield ... to which Ælfheah Stybbe and Brihtnoth, son of Odda, came, bringing the king's word to the moot" (J. M. Kemble, *Codex Diplomaticus*, 755).

[3] Domesday Book, i. 269B. *Si cui jubebat in suum (prepositi) servitium ire et non ibat, iiii solidos emendebat*: if the reeve ordered any one of them to go on his errand and he did not go, he paid four shillings in amendment.

[4] As in the king's hundreds Inter Ripam et Mersam (Domesday Book, *loc. cit.*), and of Winnington in Cornwall (*ibid.* i. 120A). Cf. also *ibid.* I. 172A.

[5] *Ibid.* i. 269B: *Si ... non ibat ad placitum ubi prepositus jubebat ...*: if he did not go to the moot when the reeve ordered ...

[6] *Ibid.* i. 86B: *Tres taini tenebant T.R.E. et serviebant preposito manerii*: three thegns held it T.R.E. and served the reeve of the manor.

one may have jurisdiction over a king's thegn except the king, the lesser thegns are transferred as a matter of course with the administration to which they belong.[1] It would be hopeless to try to reduce all these small *ministeriales* to a common standard. Subjection to local custom, absence of judicial privilege, obedience to reeves' authority, seem to have been their distinctive mark, and local custom varied endlessly. The habit of each group of such thegns was that of the administration to which they were attached. Nevertheless, there seems to have been some effort to legislate for them as a class. They were spoken of as *laess-thegns, mediocres taini, meduman thegene*,[2] meaning, perhaps, medial or mesne thegns, as standing at one degree removed from the cognizance and protection of the king. They were considered to have a uniform heriot of forty shillings,[3] and a man-bote of ten,[4] and, for those derelictions of duty for which the king's thegn paid the king's oferhyrnes of a hundred and twenty shillings, the medial thegns paid forty to the reeve.

The great units of *terra regis* are especially rich in these medial thegnages, above all in the north and west, where the great extent of the economic units made a class intermediate between the reeves and the peasantry almost necessary. There, as in the king's hundreds in Lancashire, they were liable for the ordinary dues of the countryside, worked on the king's buildings *sicut villani*, made the deer-hedge for the royal hunt, guarded the fisheries, and sent reapers into the king's fields for the harvest.[5] Small thegnages of this kind may be found upon many of the great clerical estates rendering their dues into the farms of the reeves of the immunity.[6] In some, as in those of Shaftsbury,[7] they owe services of ploughing and harvesting like the king's Lancashire thegns; in others there is no specified service, and one may suspect that, beyond a money rent, their principal use to their lords

---

[1] F. E. Harmer, *Anglo-Saxon Writs*, No. 108. *Eadgar cyning . . . bead ælcon his þegna þe enig land on þan lande* (Taunton) *hafde þat hi hit ofeodon be þeo biscopes gemedon.* King Edgar bade all his thegns who had land there to hold it at the bishop's will. Cf. also, less certainly authentic, *ibid.* No. 100.

[2] II Cnut, 71. 2.

[3] Domesday Book, i. 269B, 298B, and Hen. I, 1. 14.

[4] Domesday Book, i. 179A, and Leis Willelme, 7.

[5] Domesday Book, i. 269B.

[6] As at Worcester. *Ibid.* 172A.

[7] British Museum MSS. Cotton. Tiberius, 61.

was legal, maintenance in court, pursuance of legal process,[1] and responsible errand bearing. Very commonly, such thegns had no property, and therefore no inheritance in the estate their lords allowed them. Oswald's laens at Worcester were mostly made to the thegns of his church and for three lives only. The sons of the thegns between the Ribble and the Mersey were by custom allowed to take their fathers' lands, but there was no heritable property. In some cases a measure of independence was accorded by the commutation of the thegn's works and dues for a fixed farm, while certain of the great churches produced something which bore a remote simulacrum of knight service by setting apart a number of estates as *thegnland*,[2] keeping them inalienable,[3] but writing them off temporarily from the *firma ecclesiae*. That any heritable succession was allowed to establish itself in such lands before the Conquest is unlikely,[4] though after 1066 perpetuity was achieved by the introduction of *feudofirma* (heritable farm) at the Conquest.[5]

It will be seen that these various kinds of thegnage cannot really be classified. Besides the two outstanding types which we have described, there were thegns for every conceivable ministry, among them men serving Godwin, or Witgar, or Tostig with as much honour as the king's thegns served the king, and many whose service the Normans thought to be *sicut villani*. If we take the term thegn without qualification it is a parallel to the official or ministerial element in the royal and honorial barony and the grand and petty serjeanty of the Normans, but it has no element of feudal tenure. Instead of with the *feudum*, it is associated variously

Thegnage not feudal [marginal note]

---

[1] Geþyncðo, 3. The thegn may "make the foreoath for his lord and carry his cause to the end with full right", *i.e.* can act as his proctor in folkright.

[2] Domesday Book, i. 66B: *Unam hidam quae jure pertinet abbatiae de teinlande*: one hide which of right belongs to this abbey as thegnland. The Abingdon Chronicle is particularly rich in references to the thegnlands of the abbey.

[3] *Loc. cit.*: *Haec terra teinlande non potuit ab ecclesia separari*: this land, being thegnland, could not be taken away from the church.

[4] *Cartularium Monasterii de Rameseia*, i. 233 (1087–1096): *Si vero teinland tunc fuisse invenietur . . . si voluerit, eam abbas in dominio habeat*: if it is found to have been thegnland . . . let the abbot take it into demesne if he will.

[5] The elements from which the law of the thegn and his holding were being patched into a tenure of thegnage in the twelfth century are well seen in a charter recorded by Simeon of Durham (*Scriptores Tres*, lv.) granting Ellingham *in feodofirma theineslage*. Here we have the farm (a rent of £4), the fee giving perpetuity, and the "thegn's law" carrying heriot and service. It is a kind of rustic parody of the knight's fee.

with book-land, laen, bookright for terms of lives, farm. Nor can it be brought into any formal relation to the service of Norman knighthood. Based on no fee, it carried an infinitely variable service, and the one military obligation that can be posited of it at all times and places is the normal *trinoda necessitas*—fyrd, borough bot, and bridge bot—of folkright. This even the thegn's book-land owed. It is true that every thegn was in the special service of the king, or of some reeve or lord, and that it was an age of almost constant war, but Dr. Round's enquiries[1] have shown that his character was expressed in no such uniform incidents as that of the knight. The latter's place was in the feudal host; that of the thegn in time of war was in the fyrd[2] or as the personal guard of the king, though it might entail leadership and onerous duties during a campaign.

Thegnage and the social ranks
The variable functions of thegnage give it the widest distribution in every social degree, and it becomes perhaps the most outstanding fact in the society of the late Saxon age. It is not to be supposed that every landowner was a thegn, nor that every relation of lord and man carried with it the additional obligations of the thegn's service. Nevertheless, it was prevalent enough for official documents, at least in Wessex, to assume that the shires and boroughs whom they addressed were communities of thegns. Thegn and land-holder become in loose generalization interchangeable terms, and the old grades of the folk were coming to be forgotten. *Thegen and theoden* was now as natural a classification of society as *eorl and ceorl*. It is a curious phase of social growth of which one does not easily see the future, in which—without any real promise of coming feudalism—large sections of the community have become ministerialized, in which there is little

---

[1] Round, *Feudal England*.

[2] Some countrysides were allowed to compound for the levy *en masse* of the fyrd with one man from every five hides, the generality paying their expenses. It cannot be said categorically that no religious houses looked to their thegnlands to discharge this service, but there is no evidence that they did so. The Abingdon Charter, which purports to free all St. Mary's lands of service of war for a quota of twelve "vassals" (J. M. Kemble, *Codex Diplomaticus*, 214), is a most suspect document. The operative phrase *cum xij vassallis et cum tantis scutis exerceant* is of the twelfth century rather than the ninth. In general the five-hide quota system applies to the community at large and has nothing to do with the practice of Norman knight service by which a certain number of fees defended the whole honour and left the non-feudal lands immune.

tendency towards the growth of hereditary entail in landright. But thegnage, though it lacks the perpetuity of the feudal tie, is yet working powerfully to undermine those racial loyalties which were still the most serious rivals to English unity. In 1066 the Confessor's thegns were spread throughout Mercia and East Anglia as well as Wessex. If the laws of the Saxons, Danes, and Mercians were still distinct, a common law of thegnage and royal obedience already overspread them.

The tribal quality in institutions has been largely outgrown. *Growth* There is a common *Regnum Anglorum* as the basis of English *of a* supremacy over Celt and Dane,[1] and the king bears a kind of dual *territorial society* title as King of the English and King of Britain. The kingdom as a territorial power is vaguely foreshadowed in such recurrent phrases as *Rex regionis Angligenarum*,[2] *telluris Brittanicae*,[3] *Albionis*.[4] The old racial divisions are now thought of less as maegths than as provinces of law; a Danelaw, a West Seaxna Law, a Mircna Law, are recognized as principal components of the state, and, where the administrative ordinances once legislated for the *methel* or the *thing*, they now speak of the hundred and the shire. Clearly, the land has come to hold an equal place in imagination with the race. Ælfred's code is the last to use the old kindred grades as general categories of the folk, and to apply them to the common purposes of the law as a matter of course, and a treatise *Of Ranks and Laws*, of the middle eleventh century, writes their epitaph: "Time was in English law when status and privilege went by rank. Then were the wise given their due worship, each according to his degree, eorl and ceorl. . . ." In this text we may read what has been the common trend of English law since, perhaps, the reign of Æthelstan—the virtual abandonment of the old folk grades or their formal, hesitant, and often mistaken, use, and their super-session by newer classifications which have become more real in an age of wealth and lordship. "Rich and poor",[5] *landagenda and ceorl*,[6] *landrica and tunesman*,[7] *thegn and bonda*,[8] *thegn and theoden*,[9]

[1] J. M. Kemble, *Codex Diplomaticus*, 727. Cnut calls himself *Imperator regiminis Anglici in Insula*.   [2] *Ibid*. 641.   [3] *Ibid*. 534.
[4] *Ibid*. 537.   [5] IV Edgar, 2. 2.
[6] Northumbrian Priests' Law.   [7] North People's Law, 59.
[8] VII Æthelred, 3.   [9] Geþyncðo, 1.

replace the traditional twelfhynd and twyhynd, which linger only in the archaic formulae of writs. The spread of thegnage elevates the thegn as the principal element among the magnates almost to the position of the twelfhynd man. To the Norman latinizers of English texts the thegn is *plene nobilis.*[1] Where Celtic influence is strong, the Celtic usage of accommodating the wergeld to official and not to blood rank[2] has established itself. In Northumbria, the bishop, ealdorman, king's high reeve, priest, and thegn has each his appropriate wer.[3] There is also a tendency to grade the blood-price according to the amount of land.[4] It is not clear from the text whether this is held to be true of Englishman and Weahlishman alike, but, in any case, the custom seems to be characteristic of the Celtic fringes of the North and West, and is found as early as Ine's code in respect of the *Weahlcynn* of Wessex.[5] It is probable, indeed, that the whole system of wergelds displayed in the North People's Law is part of the Celtic legacy to that Anglo-Celtic people, the Northumbrians. No purely English text explicitly deserts the theory that the wer comes by blood, until commentaries upon English law begin to come from Norman scribes.[6] The tendency is rather for twelfhynd and twyhynd to be eliminated as classifications of society, and for more precise terms of social and economic meaning to take their place. The landhlaford, even if not a thegn, is coming to the fore in legal record, and for the first time the custom of private estates is being recognized—hlaford's law,[7] which the Normans will call the custom of the manor. In all this the eleventh century is seen as an age which has lost its hold upon its primitive social rules, and is seeking new ones, though as yet unsystematically, in a world where service and landed property are coming to a new importance in social relations which is as yet undefined.

Conclusion   This is a distinctive phase of society that has no close parallel, and one of which it is not easy to see the outcome. The common impression, that it lacked stability and the essentials for growth

---

[1] Quadripartitus; II Cnut, 31. 1A. [2] Cf. the Laws of Howel Dda.
[3] North People's Law, 3-5. [4] *Ibid.* 7-12.
[5] Ine, 24. 2. Cf. also Dunsaete, 5. [6] Leis Willelme, 8.
[7] Gerefa, 1. A competent reeve should know *hlafordes landriht* as well as *folces gerihtu.*

towards unity, probably does it less than justice. It is true that it had not that uniquely strong quality of feudalism which associated every relation, power, and duty with the material interest of tenure, but its lower ranks were held together by a common respect for law and legal process which was sanctified by religion. At no period, perhaps, was it more difficult to flout the conventions of lawful behaviour and to retain a standing in the community. The Norman régime inherited this strongly legalistic basis, and owed much of its strength to it, as did every reign until late in the fourteenth century. In the very general ministerializing of society—so general that it was a common assumption that the man of landed substance would be a king's thegn—the nation had a bond of discipline and stability which was comparatively new, but it also had the older lordship which was capable of building wide-spreading connections by fealty both for the king and the magnates, and which—perhaps because it was not materialized by association with land, and could be revoked without loss of estate—seems to have been free from the grosser abuses of feudalism. We know of no episode in Saxon history so dangerous to the state as some of feudal leagues of Norman and Angevin England, and the fate of Tostig and some episodes in the life of Godwin show that the tie of commendation could on occasion break when it was turned against the king. It is true that commendation and bookright built up no continuity of property and lordship, and that these were likely to be dispersed with every generation. At the moment of the Norman Conquest the shape of English life was governed no longer by the blood-relationship which had created it, and not yet by the nexus of tenure in which the Normans were to confine it, but in the main by personal and revocable agreements between lord and man. Yet the more mobile life of the eleventh century had inherited strength from the régime of the folk and was already deriving more from the growth of monarchy.

We cannot guess the future of this society had it been left to work out its own fate. On the eve of the Conquest its bent was not fully decided. It was territorialized, but not feudalized. It had lordship but not tenure; its nobles by blood had died out and its official notables had yet to be recognized as a nobility. If ever it had reached the phase of feudalism it would have done so but slowly in the absence of foreign intervention. It is possible that, since it had already made the transition from the tribal to the territorial state and developed a stable local administration, a strong succession of native kings might have guided it to become a kingdom of the Scandinavian type, but with greater stability, a more closely knit community, and a more complex government. If the successors of Harold had failed in leadership the kingdom of England could hardly have survived, and the Humber and the Thames might again have become national boundaries; normal ability in its kings would probably have kept the united kingdom one. Thus the groundwork of a nation state had been laid, perhaps more truly than in any Continental kingdom. It remained for the Normans to engraft into the community the endurance of the fees and honours, ultimately strengthening the fabric of society, though perhaps at some sacrifices of variety and energy, and to elaborate the court and household of the king into a judicial and fiscal machine which made a new epoch in the history of government. With that metamorphosis we enter upon a third and well-defined phase of English history.

ii

THE KINGDOM OF BRITAIN

*Intro-
ductory*

During its first four centuries English history is mainly determined from below. Economic forces and the initiative of the crown make head only very slowly against the innate conservatism of the community. In the century and a half between Ælfred and the Norman Conquest this is reversed. The crown comes to the fore and transforms its own status and powers, and the country begins to respond to its leadership. In this period are created a territorial community, the unified realm, a crown pre-eminent in the most important section of the law, a national peace, and the administrative frame of shires and hundreds as we know them in the Middle Ages. Not all these prerequisites of medieval government are achieved consciously, or recognized at once for what they are, but the revolution is there in fact, and, after due credit is given to the nation for its power of adaptability, it is mainly the work of a great succession of kings. The radical change which took place in the community is in the main a reorientation imposed from above. The chaos caused by the Danish wars gave the crown its opportunity, for the nation could only survive at the cost of *Political* *unification* reconstruction. By the time of Ælfred's death Mercia, East Anglia, and Northumbria were extinct as native kingdoms, and there were no rivals to the house of Wessex except the various governments of the Danes. An English victory must, therefore, mean a single crown for all the Angles and Saxons, and, in all probability, for the island of Britain. For that reason, together with the military work of conquest, the first task of the dynasty was to find an acceptable claim and title to the united realm. No tribal kingdom of the Gewissae could long contain its diverse elements. At the death of Ælfred only Wessex was directly in the hands of his son Eadward. Mercia, under Æthelred and Æthelflaeda, preserved its identity, and the Danish powers were bound to him only by treaties of peace. In 912 Æthelred died, but the king contented himself with adding to his kingdom only London and Oxford, and "the land that belonged to them",[1] and thenceforward he extended his power piecemeal by conquest in the border districts of Essex (913), Bedford (918), and Northamptonshire (921).[2] In the last years of his reign the cumulative effect of his victories became apparent, and whole peoples began to "seek him to lord", the Danes of Cambridge and East Anglia in 921, the North Welsh in 922, while in the latter year the Lady of the Mercians died, and, against some grudging by Mercian patriots, the lordship was absorbed into the kingdom. In 924 Eadward reached his furthest North, and, at Bakewell in Peakland, there "took him to father and to lord" the Scottish king and all the Scots, Raegnald, who may have been the head of the Danish power in York, Ealdred, leader of the Northumbrian English, and the Welsh king of Strathclyde. From this moment the British empire of the English kings was in the letter complete.

We have no charters[3] from these years of Eadward's greatness— *Growth* *of the* during his early years he attested himself *Rex Angol-Saxonum*[4] and *royal* *Rex Anglorum*,[5] as did his father—but Æthelstan at once assumes *title* a status which is not in substance abandoned until the Norman Conquest. In its fullest extension the title of Æthelstan and his

[1] Anglo-Saxon Chronicle, 912A. [2] Ibid. *sub annis.*
[3] What follows does not rest on the genuineness of any given charter. These royal styles and pretensions characterize a whole phase of English diplomatic.
[4] J. M. Kemble, *Codex Diplomaticus*, 333. [5] *Ibid.* 337.

successors is Emperor of Albion or Britain, *Basileus Albionis monarchus*,[1] *totius Brittaniae Basileus*,[2] "King and Caesar of all Britain".[3] It is likely that these enhanced titles were put forward in part to discourage such imperial intervention as Charlemagne had been inclined to venture, but still more to cover the varying shades of authority and patronage which bound the English peoples to one king together with "all those races who dwell about them".[4] Though imperial in its independence and its power over conquered and allied nations, the realm of the English was still a racial one; a theory which should confine the royal right within the circle of the crown and make it a quality of the reigning monarch would have been unintelligible to the successors of Ælfred. The English peoples had come to realize their affinity, the West Saxon king now stood for all their various branches, and was *Basileus Anglicae Nationis*,[5] or *Rex Regionis Angligenarum*;[6] but

Imperium Britanniae the title was dual, as was the political fact it stood for. Over the Angles the kingdom was still a racial right, but over the Britons and the "Pagans" it was the right of the Angles as a conquering and royal race—*Imperator regiminis Anglici in Insula*.[7] Thus, alternating with the sharp definition of the *regnum* or *imperium Britanniae*, are formulae which reveal its composite origin. *Rex*, or *Basileus Anglorum*, the king is *rector*,[8] *primicerius*,[9] *propugnator*[10] of the alien races. "King of the English and mundbora over many nations".[11] The crown of the tenth century is, perhaps, best described in King Eadred's own words upon his accession: "it came to pass on the death of King Eadmund, who most royally governed the realms of the Anglo-Saxons, the Northumbrians, the Heathen, and the Britons, that in the same year I, Eadred, his uterine brother was called by the choice of the witan, and by apostolic authority received catholic consecration as king and ruler of the fourfold realm".[12] Over the diversity of peoples is set the imperial crown

---

[1] J. M. Kemble, *Codex Diplomaticus*, 461. [2] *Ibid.* 357.

[3] *Cyning and casere totius Britanniae. Ibid.* 433.

[4] *Ibid.* 372: *Basileus . . . Anglorum cunctarumque gentium in circuitu persistentium.*

[5] *Ibid.* 622, 636, 638, 640. [6] *Ibid.* 641, 743.

[7] *Ibid.* 435: *Basileos Anglorum, huiusque insulae barbarorum. Ibid.* 424.

[8] *Ibid.* 426. [9] *Ibid.* 434, 441, 442. [10] *Ibid.* 426.

[11] *Ibid.* 378, 385, 377: *Rex Anglorum et curagulus multarum gentium.*

[12] *Ibid.* 411: *Regna quadripertiti regiminis.*

with its trebly reiterated sanction of birth, election, and apostolic consecration.

The *populus Anglorum* is still the first constituent of the king- *Imperial* ship, but as time goes on the crown seeks to incorporate all its *Councils* provinces in its constitution. As in the past, the king's authority and the witan's, like the obverse and reverse faces of a coin, together give currency to national acts, and the king's power is personified in the composition of his assemblies. The normal governing force of the tenth century is the witenagemot of the real English of the South and Midlands, the bishops of the southern province, the five or six ealdormen who survive south of Trent, and lesser thegns and churchmen whom we may guess to have been southerners also. Such councils reflect the older, more common, and more real title of the king as *Rex Anglorum*. Beginning, however, with Eadward's Bakewell council of 924, the full extension of the empire is at times exemplified in a witenagemot which can fairly be called imperial. One such Æthelstan held in the autumn of 931 at Luton,[1] and another at Pentecost, 934, at Winchester.[2] To them, in addition to the English witan of the South, came Welsh kings—among them the great law-giver Howel Dda—the archbishop of York and the Northumbrian bishops, the northerners Ealdred and Uhtred, with Osuulf, later high-reeve of Bamborough, and many *duces* who by their names must have been the Danish eorls of Yorkshire and the Five Boroughs, Guthrum, and Haward, Gunner, Hadd, Scule, Inhwaer, and Halfdene. Eadmund held an assembly of this kind in 942.[3] Eadred's accession council of 946 was an especially magnificent example.[4] Six kings were with Eadgar at Chester in 973, and legend has chosen this occasion as the culminating glory of the Saxon monarchy.[5]

These great witenagemots are special and occasional demonstrations of the *Imperium Britanniae*. The attendance of the northern archbishop at more ordinary meetings, which becomes common from the last years of Eadmund,[6] is, perhaps, a better test of its reality, but in any case we could hardly expect a rapid absorption

[1] J. M. Kemble, *Codex Diplomaticus*, 353.   [2] *Ibid.* 364.
[3] *Ibid.* 392.   [4] *Ibid.* 411.   [5] Anglo-Saxon Chronicle, 972B.
[6] Eadmund is the first king to legislate with the counsel of both archbishops. I Eadmund, Prologue.

of the other kingdoms into Wessex. It is, on the contrary, a very gradual process. The basic folkright of each of the nations was still *The union* indefeasible. Æthelstan seems at times to be unconscious that his *of the* law-making can extend beyond Wessex.[1] Eadgar recognizes the *laws* variant laws: "I will that secular law shall stand in each folk as can best be established".[2] The autonomy of the Danes is especially affirmed: "I will that secular law shall stand with the Danes by as good custom as they may be able to choose",[3] and Eadgar expressly limits most of the new laws of his witan's making to the English. The imperial witenagemots of the early tenth century were, therefore, clearly ceremonial and not legislative, and not till Eadgar's reign do we find the first edicts common to all the nations. His elaborate scheme of precautions against theft and the disposal of stolen goods is imposed upon the whole Island: "the following edict shall be common to every folk, Angles, Danes, and Britons in every quarter of my realm".[4] By this enactment the Danish administrative units make their first appearance in English law, and the wapentake is appropriated to the carrying out of an English king's orders, as in Wessex and Mercia the hundred. As yet this is an exception, and Eadgar expressly promises that it shall be so: "my witan and I have chosen what the penalty shall be, let the Danes choose according to their law".[5] But the slow fusion has begun. It is possible that, at least as far as new enactments were concerned, Mercia and Wessex were now treated as a common English law.[6] Æthelred, though recognizing the Danelah as distinct, legislates for it with far more confidence than Eadgar. The ordinances of Wantage constitute a complete enactment of procedure and police regulations for the Five Boroughs, their courts, and officials. They are not all new, but by naming the reeves of the Danelah as king's reeves,[7] and by ordering that the right of Christ and the special right of the king should be protected under Danish procedure as under English,[8] Æthelred was establishing the status of an English crown in an alien folk. If Eadward and his successors were lords and mundboras of the Danes, Æthelred was their king.

---

[1] II Æthelstan, 14. 2.   [2] IV Eadgar, 2
[3] *Ibid.* 2. 1.   [4] *Ibid.* 2. 2.   [5] *Ibid.* 14, 13. 1.
[6] Mercian law was theoretically distinct in the early twelfth century.
[7] III Æthelred, 1. 1.   [8] V Æthelred, 31.

The final absorption of the Danelah into the English monarchy, *The King* inevitable though it was, came almost suddenly with the accession *of Eng-land* of a Danish king. Cnut bound both Dane and Saxon by the law of Eadgar.[1] Natural king of the Danes and king by election and conquest of the English, he spoke to his realm as one nation,[2] which, for him, a foreigner, with no native right, appeared as a territorial rather than a racial power. Alone among his contemporaries, he took his title from the English land,[3] ordered his edicts to be observed "over all England",[4] and, in the spirit of Æthelred, but more explicitly, warned every man, Dane or Englishman, that, if he defied the law of God or the king's royal right, he would be driven from the realm.[5] One, and not the least important element in this royal right of which he speaks, we may see in the full enumeration of all the special powers of the king, the *cynescipe*, in the form which custom gave them in the Danelah, the king's pleas, the *trinoda necessitas*, the special wites of the king, and the heriots of the thegns. This, at least, was a law binding "over all England". The foundation was Æthelred's work, but the strong reign of Cnut established that balance of royal preëminence and local folkright by which, in the words of the Norman legist, "the law of England is threefold, of Wessex, Mercia, and the Danelah . . . and above it we acknowledge the royal right of the king's majesty as most fearfully to be obeyed".[6] It was no empty phrase that Cnut used when he abandoned the vaguer claim to a British *Imperium*, and called his kingdom England.[7]

There remained, of course, an ingrained provincialism which *Lordship* even Glanvill recognized. The exalted titles which came into *and the* fashion in the tenth century were, in fact, deceptive. They reflected *king*.

[1] Anglo-Saxon Chronicle, 1018D. *Dene and Engle wurdon sammæle æt Oxana-forda to Eadgares Lage.*

[2] *Rationabili consideratione decrevit, quatinus sicut uno rege, ita et una lege universum Angliae regnum regeretur* (Consiliatio Cnuti (1110–1130), Proem, 2).

[3] Cnut, 1027, Proem: *Canutus, rex totius Angliae*; I Cnut, Proem: *Cnut cyning, ealles Englalandes cyningc.*

[4] II Cnut, Prologue.   [5] Cnut, 1020. 9-10.

[6] Leges Henrici Primi, 6. 2: *Preter hoc tremendum regie maiestatis imperium titulamus.*

[7] In his few charters Cnut used the title *Rex Anglorum*, but charter formulae were traditional.

the geographical extension of the monarchy rather than its effective core. That was still the *Regnum Anglorum*, and the English kings' power could grow only with the advance of purely English notions. The general hardening of the sense of political obligation is, of course, the product of many factors and is hardly susceptible of analysis. That the kingship of the Confessor was more full and more deeply felt than that of Ælfred, is true, but it is not the subject of contemporary record. Again, it will not be supposed that lordship will have the same formative effect in Saxon England as in a feudal kingdom. Since its emotional force was a loan from that of the kindred, and since it had not succeeded in associating itself with the tenure of land, it is unlikely that lordship was a stronger bond in the eleventh century than it had been in the seventh, and, indeed, the period before the Conquest is one in which authority is watching its effects closely, and passing laws to control its abuse. Nevertheless, the tie of lord and man was felt to be one of the natural relations and therefore beneficial to the state. Ælfred's condemnation of treachery was reiterated,[1] and it was one of the ties which the crown sought to turn to its own advantage in an age of conquest. As in the common social life, so in politics, the chief value of lordship is to establish a tie of sentiment and obedience where there is no tie of blood. Kings who were not native, *gecyndne*, might be received as hlaford and mundbora. A taking of Eadward to lord was, as we have seen, the form in which eorl Thurkill accepted English rule in 918, and in 921 Thurferth and the men of Northampton "sought him to lord and to mundbora", while in the lyrical passages of the Chronicle, which preserve traditional epithets and old ways of thought, the distinction between the right of Ælfred's house in Mercia and in their native Wessex is still maintained: "Eadgar, ruler of all the Angles, darling of the West Saxons, mundbora of the Mercians".[2]

The oath of loyalty   From the period of Eadward the Elder the swearing of fealty to the king became part of English political practice, and was handed on to the Norman kings as their most effective counter to the act of homage between vassals and sub-vassals. There is no proof that the oath was put to the generality in their local moots, but—of instances which have come down to us—it was taken from the witan by Eadward, Eadmund, and Æthelred, and such an oath

---

[1] II Æthelstan, 4.   [2] Anglo-Saxon Chronicle, 975E.

by the witan was representative of the nation. The oath sworn was the common hold-oath. Eadward's witan at Exeter followed its terms with the conventional formula "to love all that the king loves and to shun all that he shuns",[1] the witan at Colyton swore "faith to King Eadmund as a man ought to bear faith to his lord",[2] and, on Æthelred's restoration, that of 1014 enacted that all should "be hold to one royal lord".[3] Cnut, with that note of authority that is in all his utterances, promised at the beginning of his settled reign, to "be good lord to all his people". Until the feudalization of lordship, however, it remained a revocable and dubious tie, countered by innumerable private, and, no doubt, more effective agreements of fealty between subjects. The king himself constantly accepted the special commendation of individuals, and thereby proved that effective kingship needed specific agreements to bring it into being. In 1051 the Confessor did not dare to allow Godwin into his presence until he had induced the former's thegns to transfer their fealty to himself,[4] and it is this immediate, commended vassalage that we find in the submission of the Cambridge Danes in 921, when they took the king one by one—*synderlice*—to lord, and strengthened their act with oaths.[5] If such a fealty as that of 921 had become the rule, the crown might have acquired from it some of the security which it afterwards sought from liege vassalage, but we do not know that the experiment was repeated on a national scale, and the king continued to form his own personal connection of commended men like any other magnate. Kingship was not to be radically strengthened by such devices, although the general allegiance of the magnates was, at any given time, an enhancement of royal power.

And yet the strength of the crown was advancing rapidly between 900 and 1066. The king, once no more than the avenger of the law in the last recourse, was becoming its arbiter, partly by placing one legal safeguard after another under his special protection, partly by turning his personally given peace to legal and political ends, partly by taking over from the moots the coercive force of outlawry. In the past, outlawry had been reserved for exceptional *Outlawry* *The King and the Law*

---

[1] II Eadward, 1. 1.   [2] III Eadmund, 1.   [3] VIII Æthelred, 44. 1.
     [5] Anglo-Saxon Chronicle, 1051E.   [6] *Ibid.* 921A.

offences which were regarded as heinous—killing within the kin, or the betrayal of a lord by his man. By the tenth century it had come to be a common process of coercive procedure, and a penalty for many offences of violence. The thief,[1] the lord who connived at his vassal's theft,[2] the man of such bad repute that he could get no lord,[3] were all outlaw. Even civil offences, such as refusal to attend the hue and cry, were outlaw's work if habitual.[4] The pressure upon the outlaw became irresistible when the sentence came to hold good everywhere. At Wantage the witan of Æthelred ordained that outlawry in one district should hold good in all,[5] and the condemned man was to be outlaw wið eal folc.[6] Outlawry had been the ultima ratio of the folkmoots; given into the hands of the king it invested him with the final sanction of the law, and under Cnut the sole right of extending the peace to outlaws and bringing them back into the peace was secured to the king,[7] and the process put under his mund and the defence of his mundbryce. Æthelred, twenty years before this, had been compelled to go through the clumsy form of binding the magnates severally by oath not to harbour Leofsige of Essex after he had killed one of the king's officers,[8] but, twenty years later again, the Confessor was able to use outlawry with effect against Swegen and Godwin.[9] Not only legally, in imposing the peace, but politically, against great offenders, the crown had gained a decisive weapon. This change in procedure is characteristic of the advance of the crown and of the methods by which it was being brought about. In Cnut's appropriation of the process of outlawing and inlawing we see the private privilege of the king, his grith and mund, becoming the normal mode of restoring the lawless man into peace and folkright. A like use of the king's mund to safeguard the passage from un-law to law is found in an addition to the law of homicide under Eadmund, whereby, the promise to forgo the feud having been made, and surety to pay the wergeld given, the "king's mund is raised", and if either party breaks the peace he incurs the king's mundbryce.

Less effective in government, but of increasing importance in

The king's mund

---

[1] I Æthelred, 1. 9A.   [2] *Ibid*. I. 13.   [3] II Æthelstan, 2. 1.
[4] I Eadgar, 3.   [5] III Æthelred, 10.   [6] I Æthelred, 1. 9A.
[7] II Cnut, 13.   [8] J. M. Kemble, *Codex Diplomaticus*, 1289.
[9] Anglo-Saxon Chronicle, 1048E.

law, is the converse side of the king's authority, the right to ban. The king's wite of a hundred and twenty shillings has been exacted for attacks upon his own dignity and privilege from the time of Ine. A specialized use of it comes into being in the tenth century, and is swiftly extended. Wherever the king has enjoined or prohibited a certain course by his express orders, failure to obey makes the offender liable to pay the king's wite on the ground of oferhyrnes, or disobedience. This use begins in the reign of Eadward *The king's* the Elder—since the seventh century the Frankish kings have *oferhyrnes* enjoyed the ban—and is responsible for an unparalleled growth of the king's official responsibility for the enforcement of law and order. No very clear system guided the stigmatizing of certain offences as oferhyrnes. Rather, the authorities seem to have imposed the wite arbitrarily, wherever they felt the need of an exceptional safeguard, and principally as an incentive to the king's reeves and thegns to carry out the new peace edicts. Reeves who take bribes to pervert justice,[1] or who fail to enforce the rights of the church,[2] are liable to it. The whole machinery of the edict of Grateley, and so the newest and most effective regulations against theft and disorder, is put under its sanction.[3] It is in general used to secure enforced obedience not only from the officials but also from the justiciables of the courts. By Eadward's first ordinance, buying and selling outside a licensed borough,[4] and repeated refusals to comply with an adverse judgment in land-suits[5] are marked as oferhyrnes. Æthelstan adds the withholding of suit from the public moots,[6] and failure to ride upon the orders of the court to put defaulters under distraint,[7] and Cnut extends the oferhyrnes to the neglect of hue and cry.[8] This use of the king's ban reflects a new phase in the crown's relation to justice in which the balance of moots begins to swing from popular to royal authority. The crown is no longer only mundbora—a remote providence under which the moots work in independence—it has come to intervene, to improve procedure by edict, to watch over its working, and to punish those who hinder or rebel against it. Where once the moots, and sometimes the parties themselves, were left to execute the judgments they secured, these were now enforced by the

[1] V Æthelstan, 1. 3. [2] I Æthelstan, 5. [3] II Æthelstan.
[4] I Eadward, 1. 1. [5] Ibid. 2. 1. [6] II Æthelstan, 20.
[7] Ibid. 20. 2. [8] II Cnut, 29. 1.

king's ban.[1] Æthelstan's imposition of the oferhyrnes fine for corrupt judgment is a final and striking proof of the distance the crown has travelled towards a sense of responsibility for justice.

The king's pleas

From this enhanced sense of responsibility it is but a step to the conclusion that the offences covered by the king's mund, the king's oferhyrnes, and the king's wite, form a homogeneous body of law, and one which, in some special sense, is the business of the king. The Leges Henrici Primi[2] bring together all such pleas under the rubric *jura quae rex super omnes homines habet*, and refer to them in a later section[3] as *propria placita regis*. They are some forty in number, and, in addition to six which are said to be the *placita gladii*, pleas of the sword of the Norman Duke,[4] they include such ancient occasions of the oferhyrnes as refusing to coöperate in the *frith*,[5] failing to perform the *trinoda necessitas*, and unrighteous judgment,[6] the breaches of the king's mund under the headings of *hamsocn* or violent entry into dwellings,[7] harbouring of outlaws,[8] and bohrbryce,[9] together with those offences which could only be expiated by death unless the king extended to them his mercy, violation of the king's handgrith or peace personally given,[10] fighting in the king's hall,[11] treason,[12] incendiarism.[13] A phrase of Cnut's law[14] records as the "rights which the king has over all men in Wessex", mundbryce, hamsocn, *forsteall*, and *fyrdwite* (these he will grant only to such subjects as he wishes specially to honour), but they are, as we have seen, only a few of the more important of those royal pleas that have been coming into the king's hand, beginning with Ine and accumulating rapidly under the successors of Ælfred, and which are, perhaps, first specified as a coherent body of law in those "kingship rights in every shire and borough" claimed by Eadgar.[15]

Procedure of the king's pleas

Besides the fact that initiative in these causes lay specially with the king, and that his officers were specially bound to pursue

[1] II Eadward, 1. 3. No man shall withhold from another his right. For the third offence he shall pay 120/- to the king.

[2] Leges Henrici Primi, 10.   [3] *Ibid.* 52.

[4] But all these, except *murdrum*, seem to be synonyms of Saxon pleas.

[5] *Commoda pacis ac securitatis institucione retenta*: apparently a Latin paraphrase of II Æthelstan, 25.

[6] From III Eadgar, 3.

[8] II Cnut, 13.   [9] Ælfred, 3.   [7] II Eadmund, 6.

[11] Ine, 6.   [12] Ælfred, 4.   [10] III Æthelred, 1.

[14] II Cnut, 12.   [15] IV Eadgar, 2A.   [13] II Æthelstan, 6. 2.

them, they were pleas of the crown in the sense that the wites due from them went not into the reeves' farms, but direct to the king,[1] and—a decisive criterion for the eleventh century—in being sued under a special royal procedure, which denied the accused those safeguards and delays in which Saxon folkright abounded. He could attend no other summons until the king was satisfied,[2] on the first summons he must give pledge to the king's officer to stand to right, he must attend on the day of summons to plead without respite or essoin,[3] or, in default, be condemned in absence; he might not claim remand until his lord could come to assist him; if he refused pledge he incurred the oferhyrnes, and might be imprisoned until he found it.[4] The sum of these truncations of common folkright make up a royal procedure distinct in kind, uniform in contrast to the various provincial laws, and of a severity which reflects the weakness of popular law in a lawless age, and the readiness of contemporaries to accept a new interpretation of the status of the crown in order to counteract it. To say that this field of law, perhaps the most important of all, had come under the king's prerogative would be to speak intelligibly, but at the cost of anachronism. The Norman lawyers, who spoke of the king's rents as *dominica firma*, and of the king's thegns as *taini dominici*, called the growing body of the king's causes *dominica placita regis*[5]—they were personally his as were his demesne lands and the thegns of his household; they were *les plais ki afierent a la curune la rei*.[6] But they were merely glossing a Saxon crown-right in Norman terms. The Saxon kings, with no reasoned doctrine of *dominium* to guide them, yet saw these pleas as a coherent juris- diction appertinent to the crown and separate from folkright— part of the *cynescipe*. Before the Conquest, in the Confessor's charter to Ramsey, the concept is as fully realized as it was to be for a generation after it: "all the pleas that belong to my crown", *ealle tha gyltas tha belimpeth to mine kinehelme, omnes forisfacturae quae pertinent ad regiam coronam meam*.[7] The pleas of the crown, in substance, were already in being.

---

[1] Leges Henrici Primi, 10. 4; Domesday Book, i. 252A: *Has iii forisfacturas habebat in dominio rex Edwardus . . . extra firmas.*

[2] *Ibid.* 43. I am assuming that the legist is here reflecting Saxon usage.

[3] Essoin = the acceptance of surety for attendance at court on some future date.   [4] Leges Henrici Primi, 52.   [5] *Ibid.* 10. 4.

[6] Leis Willelme, 2.   [7] J. Earle, *Land Charters*, p. 344.

The king's reeves and the moots All this growth of royal process gave the king a new relation to the law, and the king's reeves a new standing in the moots. Asser shows Ælfred taking the lead in a renaissance of law,[1] judging ealdormen and reeves by their honesty and knowledge of custom, and revealing a clear sense of authority over their office. They hold, the king tells them, a *ministerium* from God and himself. The illiterate and dishonest the king can and will degrade. Ælfred, then, appears as the active head of the executive not only in general but in legal administration; provincial moots no longer function in isolation, for a national discipline unites them under the crown. Moreover, the reeves and ealdormen, who are so clearly recognized as the king's officers, are themselves widening the scope of their position in the courts. A commonplace of English legal history[2] is the gulf that separates the suitors as doomsmen from the presiding officer, sheriff, reeve, in Norman times justiciar. The doomsmen give judgment, the reeve demands it from them, and executes the judgment made. Thus the archaic principle that law is folkright is underlined and the way barred to a king's judiciary. But, in the crucial century and a half from Ælfred's reign, that bar was in some measure weakened. Possibly Frankish influence, certainly the authority of Isidore of Seville,[3] was accustoming English legists to apply the term *judex* not only to the witan of the moots but also to their presiding officer, and the natural evolution of the *gerefa's* function was in practice associating him more closely with the moot. Ælfred placed upon his reeves and ealdormen the duty of knowing the written law and imposing it upon the courts,[4] and regarded an illiterate reeve as an anachronism. In the new, written dooms the reeve was "wise" in a way in which the provincial suitors were not, and, since it was he who called for the judgment of the doomsmen at each point of the trial, he must have had the qualities if not the function of a doomsman himself.[5] Understandably enough, therefore, Ælfred called

The reeve as judex

---

[1] *De Rebus Gestis,* cap. 106.

[2] F. Pollock and F. W. Maitland, *History of English Law,* i. 548.

[3] Cf. especially the text *Judex,* which is largely a borrowing from Isidore. The first use of *judex* for reeve seems to be Mercian of the year 844. W. de Gray Birch, *Cartularium Saxonicum,* 443.

[4] Asser, *De Rebus Gestis,* 106.

[5] I Eadward, Prologue: "King Eadward bids all reeves that they deem right dooms according to their knowledge as it stands in the doombook"; Cnut, 1020. 11.

the reeve's office a *ministerium sapientum*, "an office of the moot", and throughout the tenth and eleventh centuries the king's officers were commonly given the name of *judex*. There is a remote Saxon anticipation in these *judices* of the Norman sheriff as justiciar of his county, and they mark an essential phase of transition in the judicial development of the country. The royal delegate was now established beside the popular element even in the provincial courts of law. Thus the old popular judgment is associated with a controlling and directing executive. If the folkmoots stand for the rule of law and for individual right, the kings of the tenth century display a new care for the general peace, and a sense that rights, and the just assessment of right between parties, are not the only concern of law, and need stronger safeguards than the old folk-right provided. With Eadward begins a series of enactments, proceeding from king and witan, and comparable with the Frankish capitularies, having for their aim the suppression of disorder, the building up of a peace of the realm, the refinement of legal procedure and its enforcement by penalty. The archaic reliance upon self-help as the sanction of individual and public right is partially eliminated, and if this is done by national edicts, it can be put into effect only because a completed system of administration gives the king access to every court, and enables him partially to command their obedience. Through the confusion of provincial forms, much of the outlines of which we have lost, this great principle has been working towards its completion, that the order, and the executive power of the assemblies rest with royal officials and are a national whole, and that a great part of the national law is the province of the king.

Linking the growth of the supremacy of the crown in law and *The king* the reforms in political administration, of which we still have to *and the* speak, is the evolution of the legal doctrine of the peace. From *peace* Ælfred to Æthelred English statesmen were obsessed by this problem, internal peace against theft and disorder and external peace against the Danes, and the legal history of the period is largely that of an intense effort to bring about a common peace in a nation where every minister and church, every local assembly, every great landowner and official, had his several peace, but where there was no peace of the realm. In this effort every witenagemote becomes a peace conference and every edict an edict of peace, and in the end they achieved a peace which, if it was not universal and perpetual, sufficed for crucial needs and occasions. The Leges Edwardi Confessoris record that the king's peace lies upon the seasons of Christmas, Easter, and Pentecost, over the four main highways, and over the navigable rivers,[1] but in practice the king's grith is applied variously, as occasion demands, to great matters and small. It may cover the individual with the king's special protection, as Eadward gave Swegen grith for safe-conduct in 1046, in spite of his outlawry,[2] or it may be used more widely to check disorder, as when in 1051 the same king, caught between the factions of Godwin and Leofric, stopped an appeal to arms by placing them both and their supporters "under God's grith and his own friendship".[3] It is not surprising that first among the commands of the Wantage edict "for bettering the peace" it stands that "the king's grith shall be established as firmly as ever it was in his father's day", and that breach of that given by his own hand shall be inexpiable.

Frith *and* grith The distinction drawn between the *grith*, or personal peace of individuals, and the *frith*, or peace set between nations—or, as in the Empire, the land-friede, or peace of a whole community—is no doubt a sound one, but in the tenth century, much to the benefit of the realm, the distinction was becoming obscured.[4] The friths between the English and the successive Danish and Norwegian armadas are the sum of individual gages of peace, the leading men of either race speaking for themselves by oath and pledge, and thereby binding those under them.[5] The grith of Ælfred, Eadward, or Æthelred is the core of the English frith, as that of Guthrum, Olaf, or Justin is of that of the Northmen, but the peaces of the great East Anglian and Mercian ealdormen are

[1] Leges Edwardi Confessoris, 12.
[2] Anglo-Saxon Chronicle, 1046E.
[3] *Ibid.* 1051E.
[4] Cf. the use of frith and grith in Anglo-Saxon Chronicle, 1002E, 1004E, and in VI Æthelred, 42.
[5] Ælfred and Guthrum's Frith, Proem. This is the frith that King Ælfred and King Guthrum and all the witan of the English race, and all the folk among the East Angles, have agreed upon, strengthening it with oaths for themselves and their subordinates.

constituents of it also, with those of many lesser men, which on occasion may be used to set up local friths while the main bodies of the nations are still at war. So the Western magnates, Ælfric for Hampshire, Æthelweard for the South-western counties, and Archbishop Sigeric, made frith with Olaf Tryggvason;[1] so also Ulfkytel and the East Anglian witan used their own griths to come to terms with Swegen in 1004.[2] Thus afforced by the griths of his magnates, who, in their turn, speak for their countrysides, the king's grith is not far from being the pledged frith of a nation. In this sense, all those, both Norse and English, who are within the frith set between Æthelred and Olaf are "King Æthelred's *frith-men*".[3] All others are outlaw, and, for the term of the treaty, to be law-worthy in the king's realm is to be in the king's frith.

The characteristics which distinguish these early experiments in the peace from its later and perfected form in English law are its partial and occasional application, and the underlying theory that the king's is only one, though the greatest, of a number of griths placed for the occasion at the disposal of the state. Much of the enforcement of law even in the tenth century was still left to self-help, licensed violence, while the Danish wars had so thrown the country into disorder that whole provinces lightly changed their allegiance. Royal efforts to beat down disorder thus reflect something of the tradition of civil warfare, and their aim was steadily directed towards the establishment of a frith. Eadward, at Exeter, with his counsellors, "seeks how our frith may be made better", and "receives oath and pledge from all the nation" that they will hold to it.[4] Æthelstan, again, at Grateley, complains "that our frith is ill kept," and "takes oaths, pledges, and sureties" from the witan there.[5] Thus the internal order of the realm rests upon much the same sworn and pledged frith, centring upon the king's personal peace or grith, but strengthened by those of the magnates, as was set up during brief intervals of peace between the Danish fleets and the English. It is now applied as the domestic frith of the nation, and comes to be the principal object of the great reforming councils of the tenth century and is embodied in their edicts.

The national frith

---

[1] II Æthelred, 1.   [2] Anglo-Saxon Chronicle, 1004E.
[3] II Æthelred, 3. 1. So, in 921, the men of Huntingdon "sought King Eadward's frith". Anglo-Saxon Chronicle, 921A.
[4] II Eadward, Proem.   [5] V Æthelstan, Prologue.

Grateley, indeed, and its sequels at Exeter, Faversham, and Thundersfield, is the inspiration of a great combined effort of king and people to put the realm under a standing frith, every magnate and reeve at those councils taking oath that "he will hold all that frith that King Æthelstan and his witan set at Grateley",[1] and the reeves exacting pledges from the communities they govern that they too will hold it. In London the response to this was the founding of a formal frith-guild, in which eorl and ceorl were bound into a common obedience to the decrees against robbery and violence, and to joint action to pursue them to justice.[2] In all this we are very near to an effective peace of the realm. It is true that its basis is as yet uncertain. The frith founded at Grateley is the sum of multitudinous griths sworn and pledged in provincial moots and royal councils, and it might well have hardened into a peace of the folk such as the German *landfriede*. On the other hand, the king's share is already predominant, his own grith the greatest peace involved, and its enforcement by the reeves ordered under penalty of the special wite for contempt of the king's authority, the king's wite.[3] By the reign of Æthelstan the king is claiming to impose his will upon the communities as to what actions or persons shall be recognised as within the peace. Upon the whole is set, as the most impressive authority, the sanction or the king's mund.[4] The king demands, and, on the whole, secures, that his people shall "frith all that he will frith",[5] and, as the administration grows ever stronger and more specialized, it becomes increasingly probable that it will be upon the king's peace that the order of the realm will in the end come to rest. Cnut promises that he "will make full frith through the power that God has given me".[6]

The hundred An entirely new set of institutions arose to make this concern for the frith effective and to give it permanency, those that centred upon the hundred. There can be little doubt that the hundreds were first formed as private associations or frith-guilds and were

---

[1] VI Æthelstan, 10. [2] *Ibid. passim.* [3] II Æthelstan, 25.
[4] *Ibid.* 25. 2.
[5] *Ibid.* 20. 3: "It shall be proclaimed in the moots that men shall frith all that the king wills to be frithed". [6] Cnut, 1020. 3.

part of the response of the countrysides to the edict of Grateley, with those of Exeter, Faversham, and Thundersfield. The *societas hundredi* is a common phrase of Anglo-Norman law, and the voluntary origin of the hundred is marked by the fact that it is protected against disobedience to its authority, judgments, and rules, not by a crown wite, but by the oferhyrnes of its principal members, the thegn's oferhyrnes of five mancuses, or thirty shillings.[1] Unlike the usage of all other courts, conviction in the hundred carries with it the normal wite and bote, and "thirty shillings to the hundred" in addition,[2] and, finally, the hundred shares in the chattels of condemned thieves,[3] a right never in Saxon law accorded to doomsmen proper, and, it might be thought, *pessimi exempli* had the men of the hundred been in origin judges of a court. In fact the function of the hundred is not at first one of judgment, rather a special application of the universal privilege of self-help against theft, by which, as the Grateley frith decreed, thieves must be hunted down by the hue and cry and slain.[4] This organized self-help under royal patronage, so characteristic of the age, we may see in the frith-guild of the *Judicia Civitatis Lundoniae*, explicitly formed to put in action the Grateley decrees,[5] charged with the duty of suppressing theft, defended by the oferhyrnes of its members,[6] enjoying a share of the chattels of felons,[7] and placed on a semi-public footing, in that it could command the service of the king's reeves.[8] Though the guild of the *Judicia* has not yet the right of oath and ordeal and cannot, therefore, technically embody a court, Æthelstan has already given it the substance of judgment. Its extra-judicial enquiries into the guilt of thieves are to have the authority of the ordeal.[9]

The voluntary hundred

[1] Leges Henrici Primi, 35; Liebermann, *Sachglossar*, p. 461.

[2] III Eamund, 2; II Cnut, 15. 2; Leis Willeme, 42. 1.

[3] I Eadgar, 2. 1. VI Æthelstan, 1. 1.

[4] II Æthelstan, 1. As late as the reign of Eadward the Elder the responsibility of following up stolen cattle lay with the loser.

[5] VI Æthelstan, Proem: "To make more effective the dooms which were set at Grateley, Exeter, and Thundersfield".

[6] *Ibid.* 7: "Let him not abandon the enquiry on pain of our oferhyrnes".

[7] *Ibid.* 1. 1.

[8] *Ibid.* 8. 4.

[9] *Ibid.* 9: "Thieves who are not manifestly guilty on the spot, but found so by subsequent enquiry (by the guild), may be redeemed by their lords or kinsmen as though they had been condemned by ordeal". The process of "enquiry"

Here we have a frith-guild anticipating the hundred in many essentials, as the hundred, when established, retains many of the significant characters of the frith-guild. The name of the hundred is there, for the guildsmen are bound by groups, or titheings, of ten, into a combined *hynden*, or hundred under a *hyndenman*,[1] and, though the intention is to form a personal association, it is quasi-territorial from the first, for allowance has to be made for tithe-ings of greater or less population.[2] It has an inchoate right of judgment, since its inquests have the effect of trial, though con-ducted without the traditional forms. The hundred is adopted and made obligatory on the whole country by Eadmund as an associa-tion of eorl and ceorl in thief-taking, and retains its oferhyrnes,[3] but it is Eadgar's fuller code that confers the formal status of a court of judgment in folkright with oath and ordeal, and which, for the first time, shows the adoption of the private organization into the machine of government. In words which would have been in-applicable if the hundred had been a pre-existing jurisdiction already exercising the ancient law and procedure, he provides that "in the hundred, as in other moots, we will that every case be conducted by the rules of folkright",[4] fixes the meeting of the court every four weeks[5]—this was the interval at which the hyndens of the London frith-guild held their meetings[6]—orders that judg-ment shall be given within a fixed term, and the parties mulcted with the thirty shilling *bot* to the hundred if they do not appear,[7]

The hun-dred as a national obligation

---

is here *geaxian*, not by formal judicial procedure and doom, but in a quite general sense. Cf. Ælfred, Introduction, 49. 3: *We geascodon = audivimus*, "we have learned". Ine, 39. If a man flee from his lord and is discovered (*hine mon geaxie*). In the tenth century *geaxian* is used of the official but non-judicial investigations of the reeve. IV Edgar, 10 (enquiry into the truth of warranty of sale).

1 VI Æthelstan, 3.

2 Liebermann considered that these titheings were preëxisting territorial units, but if such had existed Grateley would have mentioned them. The mem-bers of the *hyndens* were neighbours of standing, with slaves and commended men, a fact which at once gave the titheing the quality of a territorial neigh-bourhood. The phase during which the original grouping by ten men was being abandoned is recalled in Consiliatio Cnuti, ii. 19. 2D: *Alicubi (dicitur) vero decimatio (titheing), quia ad minus debent inesse.*

3 III Eadmund, 2.

4 I Eadgar, 7. This clause proves conclusively that hundredal *process of judgment* was new in Eadgar's reign.

5 *Ibid.* 1.   6 VI Æthelstan, 8. 1.

7 According to Liebermann the oferhyrnes was not the thirty-shilling bot, but the fine of thirty pence found in VI Æthelstan, 3, and also in I Eadgar, 3. This

and, finally, defines the duty of the hundred, like other courts, to proceed by oath and ordeal.[1] Besides these clauses, which convert the powers of informal inquest—*geaxian*—conferred by Æthelstan into a true power of judgment—*deman*—recognize the guild meetings as courts, and confine them to the strict rule of oath and ordeal, Eadgar's Ordinance of the Hundred is largely a fortification of the objects and functions of the voluntary hundred of the *Judicia*,[2] which, in turn, has been inspired by the national decrees of Grateley. Thus, the series of peace enactments from Æthelstan to Eadgar should be regarded as a whole, theft and its suppression, both equally violent, being the most notorious of contemporary threats to the frith. Reign by reign the edicts grow stricter, more elaborate, and of more general application, till they gain their full embodiment in the hundred. It is Æthelstan who licenses the hundred guild as an allowable interpretation of the intentions of the witan at Grateley. It is Eadmund who adopts the guild and makes it of universal obligation. It is Eadgar who recognizes that the inquests of the guildsmen are in substance trials, and forces upon them regular periods of meeting and the oath and ordeal of folkright. In so doing he[3] takes the final step and adds a new circle of judicature and administration to English government. It need not be suggested that the London frith-guild is the sole root of all this. It may have drawn upon similar associations in other districts whose provisions we have lost, though it is true that a report of the measures taken by the county of Kent on the same occasion that produced the *Judicia* of London[4] takes much more conservative measures to meet the king's demands. But guild

is impossible, since the latter is a variable fine, and divided between the hundred and the criminal's lord. Moreover, the thegn's oferhyrnes was thirty shillings, not pence.   [1] I Eadgar, 9.

[2] In substance, I Eadgar, 2, 3, 4, and 5, are taken from the *Judicia*.

[3] I suggested in *Essays in Honour of James Tait* (p. 164) that a lost edict of Eadmund, in which, according to Eadgar, he ordered "the doing to the thief his right", might be the origin of the hundredal jurisdiction as it is found in Kent. I now believe that this refers to the sanction of the right of extra-legal enquiry (*geaxian*) conferred by VI Æthelstan, 9, and the making of it generally applicable by Eadmund. The substitution of a folkright trial for this informal process seems to be the main purpose of I Eadgar, the "Ordinance of the Hundred".

[4] III Æthelstan: "The decree of the bishops and other witan of Kent ... (2) as to our peace, which all the people wish to be observed as your witan at Grateley decreed".

influence, almost certainly guild origin, left its mark on the hundred in name, in the element of guild profit from money penalties, and, possibly, in some parts of England, in the elective nature of the bailiffry.[1] The primary purpose of both the frith-guild and the hundred is to organize the primitive and undisciplined "riding after thieves" which is an original right and duty of the Saxon countryside. The duty and power of trial is historically an after-thought. Some such disciplining of the practice of extra-judicial remedy was essential to the effectuation of the Grateley frith, for, not only did it provide that the community as a whole should take up the defence of individuals, but it secured the country from the dangers of a lynch law which was lawful yet unregulated, and as great a source of feuds, disorders, and injustice as theft itself. The principles common to the London frith-guild and the hundred substituted community action for individual self-help, and enabled the crown to deal with an organized territorial unit instead of a formless crowd of individuals. In assuming a joint responsibility for order and for the suppression of the most prevalent form of crime, the hundred was offering itself to the crown as, for many important matters, a juridical whole in a new sense. It was this legal unity, the guild quality, almost a legal personality, of the hundred, voluntarily assumed at first and subsequently enforced, that made the hundreds susceptible to the constant imposition of new obligations and to that system of amercements upon which much of the authority of the Norman kings ultimately rested.

Spread of the hundred beyond Wessex

While its initial function in the tenth century reform is the repression of the typical disorder of the epoch and the administrative embodiment of the peace, the hundred came to play its part in a general reconstruction of government. The reconquest under Ælfred and his sons placed the crown in possession not of a government of England but of the ruins of at least eight national constitutions. Besides reconstituting her own shire system, whatever it was, Wessex was faced with the task of bringing into a common administrative scheme the trithings and wapentakes which the Danes had set up or taken over in the North, the Celtic scirs, the lathes, the rapes, and whatever local units of Essex, East Anglia, and Mercia have passed out of history. In the hundred she possessed

[1] As in the Eastrey and Wingham hundreds of Kent, and the Rotherbridge hundred of Sussex. *Victoria County History of Sussex*, ii. 172.

an institution which was readily exportable. It conformed to the contemporary fear of theft and violence, and it was voluntary in origin—lynch law legalized. As a popular special judicature it could be added to the existing moots, or set up beside them, without fear of a conflict of laws and loyalties. The *hundraed saetene*, right to initiate the hundred, *constitutio hundredi*,[1] was therefore freely conferred or imposed upon communities and influential subjects, and during the second and third quarters of the tenth century must have been carried far and wide throughout the country. It became, indeed, the one administration common to all the peoples confederate under the *Regnum Anglorum*. Not only Wessex but all the countries sometime of the Heptarchy save Bernicia have been invaded by the hundredal system by the time of Domesday. Thus, in Kent the surface of the lathes is overwritten with some sixty hundreds, some of them reckonable in acres, one conterminous with the lathe of Milton. It is the lathe courts, as at Milton and Wye, that entertain the old justice and the pleas of the crown, and, when they have decayed, the latter go to the county. The hundreds, not only in Kent, but in many parts of south England, tend to be *ad latronem judicandum*, that is,[2] they have only that specifically hundredal function which runs back in the cognizance of theft, through the edicts of Cnut, Eadmund, and Aethelstan, to the edict of Grateley and its London offshoot. Yet, as a special *The hundred* jurisdiction supplementary to older jurisdictions the hundred has *and older* often come to be blended and confused with them, and so its *jurisdic-* spread has produced that bewildering appearance of diversity of *tions* size and jurisdiction which has baffled historians. Added to the lathe court of Milton, the hundred conformed to the boundaries of the lathe, which was, therefore, called both lathe and hundred in Domesday. Milton *curia* continued to exercise both its old criminal jurisdiction and that of the hundred, and finally in the thirteenth century came to be classed as a hundred court. In East

---

[1] III Cnut, 58.

[2] E.g. Kingston Hundred (Surrey), *pro latronibus judicandis et praeceptis Regis exequendis* (*Placita de Quo Warranto*, p. 741). The private hundreds of Hampshire claim only gallows, which is a synonym for infangentheof. *Ibid.* 764, 767, 769. Cf. also Berkshire, *ibid.* 81, 152; Gloucestershire, *ibid.* 256, and Devon, *ibid.* 167, 171. In general, compare *Essays in Honour of James Tait*, pp. 155 *et seq.* Certain other pleas, usually that of *sanguinis effusio*, were attracted here and there into the cognizance of the hundred, but it is not common. Cf. Elham Hundred and Axtan Hundred (Kent), *Placita de Quo Warranto*, pp. 324 and 345.

Sussex, on the contrary, the same amalgamation produced the opposite effect; the rape absorbed the hundreds, and did their work in its three-weekly lathe court.[1] In Lancashire the administrative divisions preserved the names of both hundred and scir, and we find hundreds of Blackburnshire or West Derbyshire, which were also called wapentakes; three administrative epochs were compounded in these names. In the middle north, on the contrary, the wapentakes—whether Danish or Anglian [2]—tended to survive, and, with the hundreds as their administrative subordinates, remained courts of criminal pleas into the Middle Ages. Thus the hundred, even when remaining in the hand of the crown, was patient of almost every conceivable combination with the older circles, and the position is complicated even further by the number of private immunities. Theft and the peace went together, and suretyship for their men was freely laid upon the shoulders of lords. It was, perhaps, as much this as any sense of due privilege, which led to the widespread attribution of hundredal power to private immunists during the eleventh and twelfth centuries, whether in fee or farm.[3] We have no valid reason for carrying hundredal immunity behind the eleventh century, nor for believing that it had gained its full momentum before the Conquest, but the *hundraed saetene* of both crown and immunist acted everywhere as a corrosive against the ancient provincial scheme of the Heptarchy, and had much to do with its replacement by an English system of courts and administrative districts. We cannot, therefore, claim that this change of the hundred from the thief-taking of the Judicia to the court of all purposes of the first Norman reigns can be clearly understood. The final picture is of a judicial system upon

[1] Cf. H. M. Cam, *Essays in Honour of James Tait*, p. 24.

[2] The wapentake is usually said to be Danish in origin. There is no evidence that any Scandinavian unit of government bore that name, but *vapnatak*, "the resumption of arms", is the term for the closing of the session of the Icelandic Althing. The distribution of the wapentakes in England has not been scientifically studied. In medieval records it is used in the country between the Trent and the Tees; but learned clerks were apt to apply it arbitrarily elsewhere.

[3] The lapse of the hundredal administration into private hands probably began with the greater ecclesiastics. III Cnut, 58 (Instituta, 1103–1120): *Episcopi . . . in multis tamen locis secundum iusticiam in sua propria terra et in suis villis debent habere constitutionem hundredi, quod Angli dicunt hundraedsetene*: bishops ought in many districts rightfully to have the setting up of the hundred in their own lands and townships.

two levels, the hundred accroaching to itself all pleas in first instance, except those of bookland, and the shire holding pleas in default of judgment in the hundred and coercing those who were too strong to obey it. But the process by which this alignment was brought into being is, and will in all probability always remain, obscure.

The Danish invasions had wiped out the structure of Mercia: its *The* many ealdormanries vanished, and were replaced by the single *ealdor-* great ealdormanry, lordship, or sub-kingdom, of Æthelred and the *manries* Lady Æthelflaeda, and a great change came upon England south of the Thames also. Ælfred's ealdormen of the several Wessex shires seem to have held their charges to the end of their lives, but, as they died, their ealdormanries were not renewed. Instead, a division was made which conformed in general with the old national frontiers. Mercia remained a whole, though a second ealdormanry, centred upon Hereford, appears for a time. East Anglia and Essex—probably including Hertfordshire and Middlesex—were each left as separate provinces, and Wessex was divided under two ealdormen, sometimes called of Devon and Hampshire, and in one charter, those of the Western Provinces and of Winchester.[1] Whether Kent and Sussex lay in the Winchester province, and where the line was drawn between that province and the Western ealdormanry is not known.[2] This redistribution must have transformed the problem of English government in its lowest stratum, and, with it, the nature of ealdormanry. An ealdorman who governed all Mercia was in an entirely different position from those who once governed a single county, and, for this reason, if for no other, the tenth-century crown was faced with the need to find a new method of direct administration for the vastly enlarged area of the West Saxon supremacy. This method they had developed securely before the end of the Saxon *The* era, its components being the modern county with its sheriff, and *sheriff* the hundred; but the process of the reconstitution of the shire was too gradual to be allotted to any one reign, nor, at present, can we

---

[1] J. M. Kemble, *Codex Diplomaticus*, 698. *Æthelweard Occidentalium Provinciarum Dux*: *Ælfric Wentanensium Provinciarum Dux*.

[2] An ealdorman of Sussex appears once in Æthelred's reign.

do more than conjecture the main outline of its growth. The sheriff, *eo nomine*, does not make his appearance until the reign of Cnut, but from that of Æthelred we hear of a *scirman*, one Wulfsige the Priest, holding that position in Kent, and apparently discharging the sheriff's office,[1] and under Eadgar[2] a regulation ordering its court to meet twice yearly gives us our first mention of the modern county. In this edict, indeed, the units of shire, hundred, and borough appear for the first time together, and Eadgar's reign must, therefore, be taken as the time at which English administration reached its formal completion.

The boroughs
From the time when the Danish invasions wrecked the ancient provinces of middle and eastern England to that when the modern system emerged under Eadgar, there was, however, an interlude in civil government, during which courts and reeves retired into the fortified centres. From Ælfred's day to Eadgar's the king's reeve rules not the shire but the borough, and the borough itself is the primary unit of government.[3] A few English towns, notably Canterbury, were known as boroughs before the reign of Ælfred, but their multiplication seems to have been caused by the great Danish war of 870–920. They were the burhs, or towns "timbered" or fortified by a containing wall in the process of defending Wessex and reconquering Mercia. The first hint that they have become the primary units of organization for defence is the annal of 894[4] in the Anglo-Saxon Chronicle. Here, for the time being at least, we see the king's officers in garrison throughout a range of burhs covering most of England that was in English hands, and, as the English passed to the offensive, the building of boroughs became the routine method of securing recovered territory: "in this year Æthelflaed timbered Tamworth and Stafford burh, and in the same year, at Martinmas, King Eadward had the north burh at Hertford timbered between Maran, Beane, and Lea".[5] Taken by themselves, these facts stand for no more than a revolution in the art of war, but, as later in Saxony, strategical considerations came to bear upon the administrative system, and changed it

---

[1] J. M. Kemble, *Codex Diplomaticus*, 1288 and 929.
[2] III Eadgar, 5. 1. In succeeding charters of Cnut's reign (J. M. Kemble, *Codex Diplomaticus*, 731, 732), Æthelwine appears as shireman and later as sheriff.
[3] II Æthelstan, 20. 1.
[4] Anglo-Saxon Chronicle, 894A.
[5] *Ibid.* 913D.

vitally. Wessex before the reign of Ælfred was governed certainly by the ealdormen and moots of the provincial units south of the Thames, and possibly also by subordinate units of which the various king's towns were the capitals. For a period after Ælfred the traditional circles of government seem to have been in abeyance, and Mercia and Wessex alike were controlled from boroughs, the only courts below the witenagemots of the ealdormanries being borough courts, and the only officials under the ealdormen borough reeves. This phase may not have lasted long. The shire moot was meeting again by the time of Eadgar, and it was, perhaps, a war measure by which the civil power took refuge within the borough walls. But Æthelstan's laws assume that all courts will be borough courts,[1] and that borough reeves are in control of the royal estates,[2] while the author of the *Judex*, speaking in general of the justiciables of any moot, takes it that they will be those of a borough.[3]

A document known as the Burghal Hidage, and assigned with some probability to the years 911–919,[4] gives, evidently with some corruption, a record of the districts subject to the various boroughs of Wessex, and of several districts of Mercia.[5] For Wessex these areas are irregular, and break up the ninth-century shires, but some of the boroughs are known to have been *villae regales*,[6] royal townships, and in Sussex the burghal area seems to have had some relation to the rape.[7] It is not improbable, therefore, that the period of burghal government may have marked a time when many of the royal towns became indefensible and when the moots were withdrawn into such of them as had been timbered, and whose position was particularly strong,[8] the reeves following them, but retaining the stewardship of the royal estates whose *curiae* were abandoned. If so, burghal administration, drawing upon past institutions, preserved something, though not all, of their outlines.

---

[1] II Æthelstan, 20. 1. [2] I Æthelstan, Prologue.

[3] *Ibid.* 9. 1. As the text dates from after 980, this may already have been an archaism.

[4] H. M. Chadwick, *Anglo-Saxon Institutions*, p. 207.

[5] W. de Gray Birch, *Cartularium Saxonicum*, 1335.

[6] Southampton, Wilton, Winchester, Exeter, Bath.

[7] The burghal areas of Sussex are Heorepebura (Hooe Rape Burh?), Hastings, Lewes, Burpham, Chichester.

[8] Thus, in Dorset, Dorchester was ignored, and Wareham taken as a burghal site.

The high-reeves

The number of centres of government being thus reduced—there were four survivals in Hampshire, Porchester, Southampton, Winchester, and Twynham—and the supervision of the ealdormen being relaxed by the reduction in their number, the borough reeves must have risen in importance. In Oxford, Worcester, and Warwick, the only boroughs in their shires, they must have been sheriffs in all but name, and it is, perhaps, in these circumstances that a new title, that of high-reeve, comes into the official language of southern England. Eadmund, in his edict of Colyton,[1] speaks, apparently of the borough reeves, as *summi prepositi*, while the Chronicle reports two *heah-gerefan* as being killed in the Danish raid on Hampshire in 1001,[2] and of another, Æfic, as being murdered by the ealdorman of Essex in the following year.[3]

The shire

Against this predominance of the borough and the high-reeve, we have to place the fact that the shire had already revived by Eadgar's reign, and was holding a court twice yearly in addition to that held three times a year for the borough, and that the importance of the shire was marked by the attendance of the ealdorman and bishop at its court.[4] The phase during which the shire reasserted its supremacy cannot, therefore, be described with any certainty. It is only clear that it did in fact succeed in shaking itself clear from the rivalry of the borough, and that, as a result, the sheriff was established as the principal local officer of the crown. The appearance of Wulfsige the shireman in the reign of Æthelred gives us, perhaps, the latest date for the completion of the process. Thus, the burghal phase of administration is no more than an interlude, but one which helped to break up the circumscriptions of the Heptarchy, and to clear the ground for the English shire and hundred. In the counties of the South the larger divisions of Wessex, Hampshire, Dorset, and the other small ealdormanries of the ninth century reasserted themselves to determine the shire boundaries of the tenth. Essex, Kent, Sussex, Surrey, and the two East Anglian folks are primitive divisions of even greater age. But in Mercia the borough had the last word. The counties of the east Midlands may have begun in the burghal areas of the Five Boroughs of the Danes. Those in the west take their names from the Eadwardian boroughs built in the re-conquest, and the central

---

1 III Eadmund, 5.   2 Anglo-Saxon Chronicle, 1001A.
3 *Ibid.* 1002E.   4 III Eadgar, 5. 1.

location of their capitals and the rounded assessments in hides, 1200, 2400, and the like, which "lie into" them, are strong arguments for their creation as an act of deliberate statesmanship.[1] Indeed, though older units had not all been obliterated, by the time of Eadgar all England south of the Humber was set out to plan, the variety of the minor kingdoms, West Saxon scir, Mercian ealdormanry, and petty kingdom, drawn into one common structure of government, the moots losing their sense of provincial identity in a new common status as shire-thegns of an English king.

Returning to the main theme of kingship, and to its new status *The king's* as a political monarchy of Britain, it is difficult to determine how *fisc* far this revolution in the crown had called into being a specialized central ministry, or was supported by any organized system of finance. The tenth and eleventh centuries were not an age of record. The sole source of revenue for Wessex, until the introduction of the feudal aids after the Conquest, was the produce of the royal lands and the wites of the courts. Danegeld, which was paid seven times between 996 and 1118, was the only direct tax upon the land of the whole country, and can hardly be counted as revenue. According to Asser,[2] a distinction between the lands of the crown and the personal lands of the king had already been *Royal* established by the reign of Æthelwulf, who, in his testament, *land* commended the *pecunia regni* to his two elder sons, who were to reign simultaneously over Wessex and the Eastrey, and bequeathed his *propria haereditas* to his younger children and to remoter connections. Æthelred II, in one of his charters,[3] amply confirms this. On the death of his father Eadgar, he tells us, the witan chose his elder brother Eadward as king, and conferred upon himself the lands of the ethelings, the *terrae ad regios pertinentes filios*. On the death of Eadward, Æthelred received both the lands of the ethelings and also the *regales terrae*. These he distinguishes from his *propria haereditas* which he can alienate at will. Substantial crown lands, for whose conservation the witan felt themselves respon-

---

1 F. W. Maitland, *Domesday Book and Beyond*, pp. 502 *et seq.*
2 *De Rebus Gestis*, 16.
3 J. M. Kemble, *Codex Diplomaticus*, 1312.

sible, seem, therefore, to have been established as early as the ninth century, and it is, no doubt, the remnant of the crown demesnes which appears in the Domesday of East Anglia as *terra de regno*,[1] and in Devonshire as *dominicatus regis ad regnum pertinens*. The distinction was one which could not survive under a doctrine of feudal tenure, and lapsed with the Conquest, but, since all grants by charter were unconditional as far as the giver was concerned, it must have been a necessary restriction if the Saxon crown were not to be stripped of all its resources.

The king's farm   As seen in Domesday, the profits of these lands are consolidated into farms, or fixed renders from the shires, which the sheriff must produce annually, irrespective of the actual yield of the year, making profit or loss according to fortune. This practice of fixing a yearly quota was of such old standing in exploiting the property of individuals and religious communities, that there can be little doubt that the general principle had long governed royal as well as private finance. From as early as 836 we have the record of a fixed farm from the land of Challock in Kent,[2] and a schedule of provender "from ten hides to foster" is usually taken to be Ine's regulation of the farm to be paid to him from his land. The *regiae census*, of Ælfred may, perhaps, be taken to be the king's farm, *cyniges feorm*, that he sometimes granted to monasteries,[3] and with Æthelstan, who orders the maintenance of one poor person from every two of his farms,[4] the system is clearly established. The normal method of organizing individual estates under this system seems to have been to lay upon them the farm of one or more days,[5] presumably a sufficiency of provender to maintain their owners' household during that time. Domesday shows the principal royal manors of Wessex thus burdened by a farm or provision for one night—*firma unius noctis*—and, since the same practice was in use in the monastic estates of Winchester as early as A.D. 931,[6] it must have been one of old standing. The Chronicle calls such estates *feorm hams*.[7]

---

[1] Domesday Book, I. 183: *Istud castellum est de regno Angliae. Non subjacet alicui hundret.* "Kingship lands" would probably be the old English equivalent.
[2] J. M. Kemble, *Codex Diplomaticus*, 235.
[3] Ælfred, 2.   [4] Æthelstan, Alms. 1.
[5] The abbey of Ramsey arranged its manors in groups to render the farm of two weeks.   [6] J. M. Kemble, *Codex Diplomaticus*, 353.
[7] Anglo-Saxon Chronicle, 1087E.

How far the *feorm* was available in money is another matter. Perhaps in very early times the king circled the country, living upon his own estates, and even as late as 1006 Æthelred wintered in Shropshire upon the local king's farm.[1] It used to be held, on the authority of the *Dialogus de Scaccario*, that the *firma comitatus* continued to be paid in kind until the reign of Henry I, but this can no longer be believed.[2] Even Ælfred could clearly turn his *regiae census* into coin if he did not receive them as such; his household received wages at Easter, and he could send money to distant monasteries. Asser's account, indeed, takes a budgetary form as for a money revenue, and the provision that, where offences involve disobedience to two ealdormen, the wite shall be paid to the king half in one scir and half in the other,[3] strongly suggests a scir-farm whose reeve could not afford to allow its profits to reach the king through other channels. With Æthelstan the presumption of an organized farm becomes certainty. When, after a period of ignorance, we see the farm in the Confessor's reign, it is already the *firma comitatus* in its Domesday form, accounted for—and, presumably, for the most part, rendered—in coin by the sheriff to a treasury.

The king's *gold-horde* is spoken of in the earliest days of kingship. It is said that Eadred lodged records and his inherited wealth in Dunstan's abbey,[4] and this is the first hint of the treasure as an institution of state. A charter of Cnut's reign is recorded as being deposited "in the king's *haligdom*",[5] and a similar reference under the Confessor is Latinized *in thesaurum regis*.[6] Florence of Worcester, writing, of course, a century later, records that Harold Harefoot seized the treasure which Cnut had left to his queen Emma, and that it was at Winchester.[7] Two of the Confessor's chamberlains, Aluric and Henry,[8] called in Norman times *thesau-*

The king's treasure

---

[1] Anglo-Saxon Chronicle, 1006E.
[2] Round, *Commune of London*.   [3] Ælfred, 37. 1.
[4] *Memorials of St. Dunstan* (Rolls Series), 29.
[5] J. M. Kemble, *Codex Diplomaticus*, 1327.
[6] *Ibid.* 932.
[7] *Gazarum opumque, quas rex Cnutus Alfgivae reliquerat reginae.* This is to some extent confirmed by Anglo-Saxon Chronicle, 1035C and D. The previous citations are taken from L. M. Larson's *King's Household*.
[8] Domesday Book, i. 49A, 49B, and 151A. Aluric's lands were given to William's chamberlains, Humfrid and Alberic. It is possible that the tenure of Wenesi Camerarius Regis Eadwardi near Neatham in Hants should be added. *Ibid.* i. 47A.

rarius, already held land near Winchester before the Conquest. It is possible to suppose from this that the treasure was now a permanent institution and usually lodged at the capital of Wessex. A solid establishment of the treasure from at least the reign of Cnut is, indeed, necessary to explain the degree to which its financial methods were advanced by that of the Confessor. From before the Conquest we have clear proof of a consolidated sheriff's farm, for the Domesday entries for the Confessor's day proceed on that assumption. This the treasury was expert enough to supervise, making deductions on account of lands withdrawn from the sheriff's charge, and possessing the essentials of later treasury technique in accounting—almost certainly by tallies—and in securing a standard purity in coin of the sheriff's render. The assaying of coins for their content of silver by weighing them against a standard measure (*ad pensum*), and for its purity by melting and removing the dross from a sample of the metal (*moneta alba* or *blanca*), were in practice in the late Saxon period.[1]

Financial officials The administration of this routine seems to have lain until well into the Norman period in the hands of the king's domestic attendants. Of such officials we know very little. It is possible that there was no title of chief horderer, or treasurer, even under the Confessor,[2] but officers of the treasury there must have been. A late authority[3] asserts that the keeping of Eadward's records in his treasury was entrusted to Hugelinus, who appears in charters as *cubicularius* and *burthegn*,[4] and in Domesday as Hugo Camerarius.[5] The continuity of the office in the days of the Norman kings makes it certain that Hugo, or Hugelin, and the two other known *camerarii*[6] of Eadward were the principal financial ministers of the crown. The title is of purely domestic origin. Burthegn, officer of the king's bower or chamber, is its English form, but it was one of importance from at least the reign of Eadgar. Both he[7] and the

---

[1] Domesday Book, i. 2B, 132B, 143A, 163A, 190A.
[2] "Henry the Treasurer" was in possession of his tenement both before and after the Conquest but it is not clear that he was a treasurer in both reigns.
[3] *Cartularium Monasterii de Rameseia*, p. 170 (Larson, *op. cit.*).
[4] J. M. Kemble, *Codex Diplomaticus*, 904.
[5] Domesday Book, i. 208A.
[6] *Ibid.* i. 151A, Aluric; *ibid.* i. 47A, 151A, Wenesi.
[7] Titstan, Winstan, and Æthelsie. J. M. Kemble, *Codex Diplomaticus*, 489, 503, 572, 1247 (Larson, *op. cit.*).

Confessor seem to have had three such ministers in office simultaneously, and, except for the reference in the Ramsey Chronicle,
we have no reason to believe that any one of these was more
prominent than the others, or that the office of treasurer was led
up to by one of chief chamberlain. The keeping, accounting,
and expense of the treasure must, in short, have been part of the
routine of the king's chamber, or bower. It is, however, unnecessary to put too much weight upon the questions of origin and title
alone. The office was, no doubt, a growing one, and, while that
of Eadgar's chamberlains cannot have been purely fiscal, the
absence of a principal chamberlain or treasurer under the Confessor must not obscure our sense of the skill and experience
needed for a conduct of the treasure largely identical in practice
with that of the first generation after the Conquest.[1] Saxon
custom, as opposed to that of the Franks, was against the growth
of single officers for each office of state. Ælfred had divided each
ministry among three ministers, charging them with a monthly
term of office, and even in the Confessor's reign such ministries
as those of the *stallers* and burthegns were held by several persons
simultaneously. The absence of a single treasurer is not, therefore,
a sign of imperfectly specialized routine. It is true, on the other
hand, that the fissure between the *thesaurus* and *camera* is only
beginning in the reign of Henry I. The evolution of fiscal
administration seems to be steady and broken by no sudden
change of principle, but its specialized growth is of the twelfth
century.

A similar problem is that of the secretarial work of government. *The king's*
Primitive kings and ealdormen were not, as a rule, literate,[2] but *writers*
from the days of Theodore the charters were composed and put
into writing, and the difficult distinctions of Saxon law were
Latinized. There is some indication of a royal or conciliar secretary
at the height of the Mercian supremacy in the early ninth century.
Under Coenwulf one or more simple priests are found attesting *The pedis-*
secus

[1] "The existence of such a system indicates a relatively advanced machinery at
the Treasury" (R. L. Poole, *Exchequer in the Twelfth Century*, p. 31).

[2] Cf. V. H. Galbraith, Raleigh Lecture on History, 1935: "The Literacy of
the Medieval English Kings", *Proceedings of the British Academy*, vol. xxi.

charters over a period of years, making their cross at the foot of those of the magnates ecclesiastical and lay,[1] or as the last of the spiritual order, and before the laymen.[2] It is these men who are given the much debated title of *pedissecus* or *pedesessor*[3]—follower of the footsteps, or sitter at the feet, presumably of the king. The presence of a single priest in a subordinate position in the council, but attendant upon the king, and probably literate, can hardly be explained by any other position than that of secretary, and the forgotten names of Cuthred, Bola, Æthelheah, and their colleagues may deserve a niche in history, the first as the scribe of the great London council of 811,[4] the second as that of Clovesho in 824,[5] and the remote forerunners of the English chancellors.[6] The practice of adding the test of the *pedissecus*, with his title, to the charter, seems to have been peculiar to Mercia of the early ninth century, but Eadred at his accession council at Kingston gave land to Wulfric *pedisequus*,[7] and in 955 to the *pedisequs* Uhtred Child,[8] while a charter of 968 purports to be witnessed by *duces, disciferi, pedissequi, et ministri*;[9] but two of these charters come from a single codex, and no more can be said than that they give some support to the belief that the *pedisseci* persisted under the Ælfredian dynasty. We need not, of course, believe that their office was purely secretarial. The burthegns, from whose ranks the chamberlains of the treasury arose, began, no doubt, as general keepers of the king's chamber, and the *pedisseci*, if they were indeed the forerunners of the later secretariate, may well have come from the body of the king's priests and attendants upon the royal chapel. The latter are an important element in Ælfred's court, and, though they appear less frequently as charter witnesses in the next century, Eadred in his testament left a substantial bequest

---

1 W. de Gray Birch, *Cartularium Saxonicum*, 322, 335, 341, 373, 378.
2 *Ibid.* 357.
3 *Ibid.* 341, *Æthelheah ped. seq.*; 364, *Cudred pedisequus*; 378, 384, *Bola Pedissecus.* Preserving what tradition we do not know, the Crowland archivist seized upon these attendant priests as the composers of their versions of charters: *ego Turstanus presbyter domini mei regis Withlaphii, hoc cirographum manu mea scripsi, Ibid.* 325.
4 *Ibid.* 335.   5 *Ibid.* 378.
6 The Merovingian kings had their *referendarii* or *cancellarii* by the eighth century, so an English parallel is more than probable.
7 *Ibid.* 815.   8 *Ibid.* 911.
9 *Ibid.* 1211.

to his mass-priests, mentioning them next after the officers of the household.

That the ecclesiastics of the court were charged with the writing *The chan-* of its letters and charters we can hardly doubt, but of a chancellor *cellors* *eo nomine* there is no evidence until the reign of the Confessor, when Regenbald appears in a reputable English charter as Regenbold *cancheler*,[1] and in several Domesday entries as chancellor of William. That his qualification was that of king's priest we see from the Conqueror's mode of address to him, and his importance may be gauged from his wealth in lands and from the sixteen churches which he was able to bequeath at his death.[2] From the fact that the Confessor had a seal,[3] and from the later history of the chancery, it is fair to assume that Regenbald kept the king's seal, and saw to the drawing up of charters,[4] and of the writs which ordered the local authorities to give effect to them, and which, perhaps, were beginning to take their place. The title, and with it the enjoyment by one of the clerical ministers of a permanent charge, cannot be carried behind the reign of the Confessor, and, though Florence of Worcester gives Regenbald a forerunner in Leofric, bishop of Exeter, his authority is not decisive on such a point. The function cannot, however, but have some earlier history. Ælfric speaks familiarly in the Homilies of the king's writ and seal, and its use seems to be a certainty under Æthelred II,[5] from whose time may come the first writ which approaches the common form later used by Eadward's chancellor. Domesday suggests that such writs, under the king's seal and presented to the hundred court, had become a common reinforcement to the witness of the hundred in the establishment of a title to land before the Conquest,[6] and, if that is so, not only the chancellor of the

---

[1] J. M. Kemble, *Codex Diplomaticus*, 891.

[2] Round, *Feudal England*, p. 421.

[3] The latest discussion as to sealing in the courts of the late Saxon kings is to be found in F. E. Harmer's *Anglo-Saxon Writs*.

[4] Professor Tout (*Chapters in Administrative History*, i. 130) was of the opinion that the fact that the Norman chancellors witnessed charters proved them to have been "somewhat aloof from the clerical work of drafting".

[5] F. E. Harmer, *Anglo-Saxon Writs*, pp. 235 *et seq.*

[6] Domesday Book, i. 50A: *De ista hida . . . dicit hundredum quod T.R.E. quieta et soluta fuit, et inde habet Aluui sigillum regis Edwardi. Ibid.* i. 50A, i. 197A, i. 208A.

Confessor, but the untitled clerks who preceded him, must have needed the method and consistency in practice which only the traditions of an established writing office could give.

The king's household   Perhaps because of Ælfred's triple division of the ministries,[1] the secular household of the king developed upon lines very different from those followed by the great palatine offices of the Franks. There was no mayoralty of the palace, no one chief butler, steward, marshal, or constable, in fact no great officers who exceeded the scope of their palace ministry or appeared as officers of state. We have occasional references to the butlers (*pincernae, byrele*) and to the *disc-thegns*, or *dapiferi*, attendants upon the king's table, but there are always several of equal status, and they have no more than domestic importance and do not equal the ealdormen in rank. Eadred's will,[2] the best source in this matter, leaves eighty *mancuses* to each "disc-thegn, hraelthegn, and biriele" actually in service at his death, which is a little more than he left to each of his mass-priests. Eadgar had, apparently, three burthegns, the Confessor three stallers,[3] so that the triplication of officers begun by Ælfred seems to have persisted. One office seems to have been added under Scandinavian influence, that of the stallers, who first appear in a charter of the year 1032.[4] In later Norse history the staller was the king's spokesman on official occasions, and might represent him as justiciar, but in England, where, as with the other offices, there were always several stallers functioning together, they must have had less influence individually. Possibly misunderstanding the title, which seems to come from the high-seat or stall in the king's house, the Normans were inclined to treat the stallers as marshals or constables—Bondig the Staller appears once in Domesday as *constabularius*[5]—but the Saxon court already had its marshals, the horse-thegns,[6] and they were of little account in a state where cavalry was of no repute. We shall probably be right, therefore, in assuming that the staller was a steward of the king's hall with domestic rather than military or political significance.

It is difficult to say whether the crown gained or lost by the

---

1 Cf. p. 131, *supra*.
2 W. de Gray Birch, *Cartularium Saxonicum*, 912.
3 Larson, *op. cit.* p. 151.
4 J. M. Kemble, *Codex Diplomaticus*, 1327.
5 Domesday Book, i. 151A.
6 Wulfric and Ecgulf under Ælfred. Anglo-Saxon Chronicle, 897A.

purely domestic nature of its court. Any weakness from this cause *Resources*
was in part obscured by the greatness of the successors of Ælfred, *of the*
but the violence of the reaction against such royal favourites as *crown for govern-*
Æthelsige[1] shows that it left the throne dangerously isolated during *ment*
a minority. A mayoralty of the palace might have regularized the
position of Godwin, and, by satisfying the ambition of Harold,
have averted the dynastic quarrel of which the Conqueror took
advantage. In general, however, there is little reason to think that
the crown lacked hands to do its work. If there was as yet no
bureaucracy, the whole order of the secular thegns and ecclesiastics
was at its disposal. The minute subdivision of the country into
hundreds for the peace multiplied the reeves and brought the
king's discipline to every village. To keep in touch with the provinces, the king had legation and writ. The magnate bearing the
king's *writ and insegl*[2] was a familiar figure in the courts and to
the provincial witan,[3] initiating process, promulgating national
edicts, and advising as to their putting into action. The judicial
function of the eyre was lacking, with all its schedule of agenda
and its periodicity, but the crown itself, and with it the witan, was
itinerant. Eadgar toured his whole kingdom in winter and spring
to oversee justice,[4] and we find the Confessor hearing cases in the
west country and proroguing them to the great Christmas court.[5]
The holding of witenagemots in the principal provincial centres
was a recognized means of securing the coöperation of the countrysides in new schemes for order. Such a series of *gemots* were
those at Grateley, Exeter, Faversham, and Thundersfield which
enacted and enforced the peace edicts. To fill the intervals between
these royal iters there were the five or six great ealdormen, who,
with certain disloyal exceptions, multiplied the power of the king
and carried out his orders without standing between him and the
shires. Except perhaps for the North, the king's writs went out to

---

[1] J. M. Kemble, *Codex Diplomaticus*, 700.

[2] Domesday Book, i. 50A, 197A, 208B, etc., J. M. Kemble, *Codex Diplomaticus*, 693.

[3] VI Æthelstan, 10: "The witan at Thundersfield gave their pledges (to the peace) . . . when Ælfheah Stybb and Brihtnoth, son of Odda came to them at the word of the king"; III Æthelstan, 1: The Kentish witan have taken counsel as to the peace *auxilio sapientum eorum quos ad nos misisti*: by the advice of those witan whom you sent to us.

[4] Florence of Worcester, *sub anno* 975.

[5] Domesday Book, i. 252B: *inducias donec ad curiam instantis natalis domini*.

eorl and bishop but also to the sheriff and the king's shire-thegns. The king and the witan could appoint and depose ealdormen, and their official status seems to have been emphasized by the enjoyment of state lands *de comitatu*. Cnut turned the great ealdormanries to the account of his government in his four eorldoms, and it is probably from his reign the eorl's share of a third of the borough and county wites must be dated. If we except the treason of Ælfric and Eadric in Æthelred's reign, and the misgovernment of Tostig and his deposition by the Northumbrians, there is not much evidence that the eorldoms were failing to fulfil their purpose. If they were dangerous to unity it was certainly not from any feudal quality, which they altogether lacked, but from the possibility that racial feeling might revive and gather round any long succession of ealdormen of the same stock. This seems to have happened in Northumbria, but not elsewhere.

Summary   In contrast with the earliest phase of English kingship, that of the tenth and eleventh centuries appears as a time of rapid growth of royal power, of the invention of new ties between king and people, of the merging of the ancient racial monarchies in a new kingdom of Britain. It is the time of the reconciliation of laws under a common kingly right, of the appearance of the frame of provincial government in outlines which were to be final, in short, of the rudiments of a territorial and political kingdom. Taking our standpoint in the twelfth century, we should be conscious of a strong contrast with the feudal and bureaucratic stability of the Angevin crown. There is the cardinal difference that the rule of the house of Ælfred was based less upon the land than upon the folk. The obligatory, lasting bond of homage, riveted into the land by the material interest of tenure, was absent. The hold of the Saxon king upon his subjects was still compounded of strands of feeling and habit, the sense of racial unity finding its focus in the cyne-cynn, the personal, contracted loyalty of his commended men and of their men under them, the claim of Christian kingship. Crown and people were beginning to be interlocked in the hard structure of a royal pre-eminence in law and in a royal administration. The Saxon king was still weak where, in comparison, his Angevin successor was to be strong, but found reserves of impalpable strength where no foreign dynasty could. In many of its essentials the old English throne was like the constitutional monarchy of to-day. It had few positive powers, but it had access to reserves of loyalty and affection not to be explained by the legal rights of the crown, or even by an unbiassed estimate of the individual who bore it. Rightly carried, the crown could gather the nation to great exertions and sustain them over long periods of years. The conquest of the Danelah—ably conducted or not, we can hardly judge—was an extraordinary feat of endurance, in which Wessex was kept to a continued strain of war throughout a generation. The rallying of a disordered and demoralized nation to peace in the half-century succeeding the reconquest was an even more remarkable effort, in which Æthelstan, Eadmund, Eadred, and Eadgar point by point relied upon the response of their people to insistent leadership. Without the inspiration of the king, and, equally, without the loyal following of the subjects, nothing could have been accomplished, for all the reforming councils from Grateley onwards drew their authority from voluntary agreement. What coercive rights the crown finally acquired, it came by during the struggle to construct peace and order, and as an outcome of it.

The very effort to throw off the virus of the Viking attacks had brought the elements of stable life into being. Possessed of a uniform and intensive legal and administrative system in the shire and the hundred, of a monopoly of the higher criminal pleas and an agreed national peace, the late Saxon kings were vastly stronger than any dynasty which had gone before them. It might be just to recast the established judgment upon the England of 1066, and to say that the strength of its crown lay in an effective administration, a secure if partial control of the law, and a powerful ministerialized nobility in which it was not markedly weaker than the Norman monarchy, while its weakness lay in the fact that unity between the divergent elements of which the new realm of England was composed was only partially achieved. Here much turned upon the personality of the monarch. Only a strong king could keep the provincial nationalism of Northumbria, and the less intense nationalism of Mercia, in abeyance, and the dangers which were obscured by the exceptional abilities of the kings who ruled the country from 870 to 975 asserted themselves under Æthelred

II, and again to some extent under the Confessor. For this racial disunity the most certain and rapid remedy of that age was feudalism, and the spread of the Norman feudal lordships across the country, binding the looser constituents of English life into a new unity of material interest, marks a radical break in history.

III

FROM THE NORMAN CONQUEST TO THE REIGN
OF HENRY III

i

THE FEUDAL RÉGIME

"FEUDALISM in both tenure and government was, so far as it
existed in England, brought full-grown from France."[1] The introduction of the *feudum*, bringing with it the recognition of a perpetual right of one party in the lands of another, created a revolution
in the upper layers of social life in England, and set new principles
at work in its constitutional and political history. Two things
made this wholesale change practicable, the conversion of English
legal and administrative procedure from kindred to territorial
organization in the preceding hundred and fifty years, and the old-
established use of lordship and vassalage, which, though not
territorial, made a workable bridge to feudalism. It is difficult to
say precisely how the destruction of the ancient alodial right of
Englishmen and its replacement by feudal tenure was justified.
Heir though he was of the Confessor, the Conqueror is said to have *The theory*
asserted the king's lordship over every acre of land in England, by *of the*
however many degrees of tenure it was separated from the throne.[2] *Conquest*
But besides this, which is difficult of proof, there was the sentence
vouched for by the *Dialogus de Scaccario* that all who resisted the

---

[1] Stubbs, *Constitutional History of England*, i. 273 n.
[2] F. Pollock and F. W. Maitland, *History of English Law*, i. 69. "The great
generalization which governs the whole scheme of Domesday Book." Anglo-
Saxon Chronicle, 1066E. Archbishop Ældred and the Ætheling's party "bought
their lands" of the king. A century later Richard de Luci claimed, "*de conquisitione
apud Bellum facta feodati sumus*": we were enfeoffed as of the conquest made at
Battle. M. M. Bigelow, *Placita Anglo-Normannica*, p. 221. *Placita de Quo Warranto*,
4. *Manifestum est quod in conquestu Anglie quelibet jurisdictio ad Coronam Regiam fuit
annexa*: it is patent that by the conquest of England every jurisdiction was
annexed to the royal crown.

Conquest thereby forfeited their landright, though such forfeiture was harder measure than was usually meted out to rebels under Norman feudal law. Upon the theory of forfeiture the battle of Hastings and the succeeding risings in the North, West, and East were almost, though not entirely, sufficient to absolve William from putting forward any other principle.[1] In practice each considerable estate seems to have been allotted to a Norman as its Saxon owner incurred confiscation, the former entering into the latter's general right; those who were allotted no such "antecessor" would be expected to justify their possession of any manor by royal writ and seal.[2]

Introduction of the feudum

On the whole, the evidence is not sufficient to prove that, even in 1086, the surveyors saw absolutely clearly the nature of the contrast between the landrights of the Saxon and the Norman (any attempt to prove that they used *tenuit sub* to denote commendation, and *tenet de* of tenure in Norman fee, breaks down at once),[3] but the whole tenor of Domesday is best explained by the assumption of the universal overlordship of the king and of the rules of the fee. Not only is the term *feudum* frequently used in Domesday for the grouped manors which have come into the hands of the principal Normans,[4] while it is so rarely applied to Saxon landholding as to seem to be used in error,[5] but the earliest-known Norman writ professes to grant *in feudo*, and in this presents an

---

[1] Anglo-Saxon Chronicle, 1067E. On his return from Normandy William "gave away the lands of all whom he came against".

[2] A test case seems to be that of Tederley (Domesday Book, i. 50A). Three freemen held it before Hastings. Two of them were killed there and Alwin Ret got possession. The men of the hundred say "*quod nunquam viderunt sigillum vel legatum regis qui saississet Aluuinum Ret . . . de isto manerio et nisi rex testificetur nichil habet ibi*": they have never seen the seal or any messenger of the king to seize Alwin of this manor, and, unless the king will warrant him, he can have nothing there. The Confessor's writ is commonly pleaded when the right or the crown is affected, as when grants are made from the royal demesne (*ibid.* ii. 409B), king's farm (*ibid.* i. 60B and i. 197A), royal soke (*ibid.* i. 208B), king's forfeitures (*ibid.* ii. 195A), quittance from geld (*ibid.* i. 154B), rights in boroughs (*ibid.* i. 208A). There are a few exceptions.

[3] Cf. p. 81, *supra*.

[4] *Feudum Lisois* (Domesday Book, i. 212B); *feudum quem emit Willelmus episcopus* (*ibid.* i. 134A); *Rogeri Comitis* (*ibid.* i. 62B).

[5] *Ibid.* i. 19A and i. 23A. Certain other cases such as the *feuda* or *honores* of Eadnoth, Brictric, Asgar, Phin Dacus, and Wisgar, are those of Englishmen who survived the Conquest a while and so may have held in fee from William.

abrupt contrast with any writ of the Confessor.[1] The handling of
lordship and landright within each of the Norman honours testifies *The fee or*
to the change which has taken place. A simple and quite normal *honour of*
instance of this is the Domesday fee of Geoffrey de Mandeville, *Mande-*
which reveals the structure of an honour over a range of differing *ville*
custom from Surrey to East Anglia. Primarily, Geoffrey was the
successor of Asgar the Staller, and the jurors challenged the right
to his four Surrey manors *quia ad terram Asgari non pertinent.* They
had never seen the king's writ for them, and he held them *injuste,*
sine dono regis et sine waranto.[2] He should, another entry implies,
enjoy only *quod posset deratiocinari ad feudum suum,*[3] principally the
feudum or *honor*[4] of Asgar, who was his chief antecessor. That was
the English view. What was finally reckoned in this *feudum* is,
however, a striking proof of the change that feudalism had wrought
in a generation. The chief weight of Geoffrey's inheritance from
Asgar lay, indeed, in the latter's own property, something round
two hundred and fifty hides in the Midlands,[5] but, though one
entry expresses the opinion that the fee of Asgar should be interpreted as including no more than his personal estate of land, at
most the lands of those men who could not leave his lordship,[6] the
whole of the Mandeville fee in Cambridgeshire, most of it in
Hertfordshire, and part of the lands in Buckinghamshire and
Middlesex, is made up of lands held under the Confessor by freemen who had property in their land, and the right to sell,[7] or
otherwise dispose of it, and who had entered only into the voluntary and revocable tie of commendation with Asgar. In all, about
seventy hides were added in this way, and some forty freemen
and sokemen, in purely personal vassalage to Asgar, found themselves involved, on his fall and the transference of his succession to

---

1 Cf. the writ printed by Professor D. C. Douglas, *English Historical Review,*
xlii. p. 247, conferring lands to Peter the king's knight, *"feodo libere". In*
dominio is, however, more common under the Conqueror and Rufus than *in*
feudo; cf. *Chronicon Monasterii de Abingdon,* ii. 8.

2 Domesday Book, i. 36A.   3 *Ibid.* ii. 61A.   4 *Ibid.* ii. 412B.

5 In Berks, Oxford, Cambridge, Herts, Northants, Warwick, Essex, Suffolk,
and Middlesex.

6 Domesday Book, ii. 57B: *Non fuit de feudo Ansgari sed tantum fuit homo suus.*
This distinction is much more accurately maintained in the Domesday record
of the *honor Ordulfi* in Devonshire. *Ibid.* i. 105, iv. 190, 201, 468.

7 One had exercised this right and sold to the bishop of London, but the
latter had not succeeded in getting the land from Geoffrey.

Geoffrey, in the feudal structure of the Honour of Mandeville, to which their lands—held by themselves henceforth as dependent tenants, or taken from them by forfeiture or violence—were now annexed in perpetuity.

Eadric of Laxfield's mund-byrdnes

Beside this very moderate instance of what the doctrine of the fee could do to alter the map of land-holding, we may set the extreme case of an east-country honour in a district where the free landright of small men was the rule. The power—the mundbyrdnis, contemporaries would have called it—of Eadric of Laxfield in Suffolk, with some minor additions from those of Halden and others, passed to William Malet at the Conquest and in 1076 to his heir Robert.[1] There was, of course, a proportion of demesne land which had been the personal property of Eadric, but, besides this, fourteen hundred *liberi homines*, commended for the most part to the latter, were caught into this new complex of Norman right, and confined permanently within Robert's fee. This is the application of feudal tenure to a whole countryside which had formerly lived under the loose bond of commendation, and it is worth reflecting on the history of Eadric's men during the years about 1066 and on the effect of the Conquest enfeoffment upon such complexes of right and indirectly upon the history of the nation. Eadric's power was an extreme instance of the brittleness of Saxon lordship. Its base in landed property was very narrow, for it rested mainly upon a wide connection of commended men. At some period before the Conquest Eadric was outlawed,[2] and the impermanence of his estate was at once revealed. The commended men scattered; some took lordship with the king, some with Harold, or Godric,[3] and nothing was left but the comparatively insignificant core of Eadric's real property, then in the king's hand. Again before the Conquest, he was inlawed, and presumably restored to favour, and Eadward granted his men leave to seek him again as lord,[4] and the majority, though not all, seem to have done so. In this phase of its history the connection passed to William Malet, who, at the Conquest, was seized[5] of Eadric's lands and men alike. William's seizin did not in most cases

[1] Domesday Book, ii. 304A *et seq.*
[2] *Ibid.* 310B.   [3] *Ibid.* 310B, 313A, 317B.
[4] *Ibid.* 310B: *Dedit etiam brevem et sigillum ut quicunque de suis liberis commendatis hominibus ad eum vellent redire suo concessu rediret.*
[5] *Ibid.* 317 *et alibi.*

drive the commended men from their lands, for they were mostly men of no importance, but it involved them in a new *dominium* of a tenant-*in-capite*, which pervaded the whole, made it henceforth indivisible,[1] a fee and an honour,[2] and introduced between the *dominus superior* and the immediate tenants of the soil a group of Normans whose names, Glanville, Gulaffre, and so on, proclaim them the ancestors of the tenants in knight service of Henry II's day.[3] The connection in the Confessor's reign was personal, revocable, dependent upon the mere right of patronage in Eadric, and by the one fact of his fall scattered into its elements, and, had it not been for the change from Saxon to Norman law, the same scattering would have been repeated within a few years, on the death of William Malet. But the one act of William's seizen made it a whole and heritable, and did what six hundred years of Saxon custom had failed to do, stamping an indelible unity upon Eadric's countryside. Robert Malet after him succeeded to a legal unit, the honour of Eye, which, surviving forfeiture to Henry I, transferred unbroken to Stephen of Blois, returning to the crown at his death, used as a bait to draw Boulogne into war on the side of the young Henry in 1173, granted to the Duke of Louvain by Richard I, passing then to Richard of Almain and the house of Lancaster, became a permanent factor in English history.

The honour of Eye

Beyond setting up the perpetual complementary rights of lord and man,[4] the doctrine of the fee made no general change in the custom of the land. Any description of durable profit could be held in fee, an office, as of bailiff or forester, a rent,[5] land, and, consequently, we find the principles of feudal custom applied to the full gamut of Saxon rights, which are taken over wholesale into Norman tenure. Domesday records meticulously every item of custom from the Confessor's reign that can be profitable as valid in William's, but it shows that almost nothing has been added— apart from illicit encroachments—upon any new principle, for to

---

[1] Since baronies were indivisible except between coheiresses.

[2] *Dominus meus Willelmus rex Angliae . . . honorem mihi dedit* (charter of Robert Malet to Eye Priory, F. M. Stenton, *English Feudalism*, p. 56, and *Monasticon Anglicanum*, iii. 405).

[3] *Red Book of Exchequer*, p. 411.

[4] *Eadem terra est de feudo abbatis . . . et Stephani qui de abbate eam tenet: Cartularium Monasterii de Rameseia*, i. 141.

[5] *Ibid.* i. 153: *Concessimus . . . ut duo miliaria anguillarum habeat in feuodum et hereditatem:* two thousand eels in fee and inheritance.

hold in fee does not in itself give the right to any category of public jurisdiction with which the Saxons were familiar, nor to those rents in money, kind, or labour which were known as *consuetudines*. This is especially marked in the Malet fee in Suffolk,[1] and others like it. The commended men, of whom it is largely made up, had come in to Eadric of Laxfield still bound by and bringing with them their ancient public obligations. Almost all of them were under the soke, not of Eadric, but of their hundreds, or of the ecclesiastical lords of East Anglia. Accordingly, Malet seldom had the sake and soke, except in his demesne manors,[2] and often had not the customs. The fine confusion of a predominantly free Saxon countryside was carried into the Norman honour. In most of the demesne manors Malet probably had the customs and the soke, a few of the men outside the demesne are said to be his sokemen, the vast majority of Eadric's commended men were of the soke of the abbots of Ely or Bury St. Edmunds, the rest mostly in that of the king or of the king and earl jointly, and as it was in Eadric's day, so it remained in William's. The new honour of Eye had not the soke over a great proportion of its lordship.

The small-holders   Just as the creation of a fee did not destroy the external commitments of its members, so, equally, it left their internal rights intact in substance. An honour and its component manors might contain freemen, sokemen, and villeins. Of these the freemen who passed from the lordship of Asgar or Eadric into the feudal lordship of Mandeville or Malet, did not cease to be *liberi homines*. They retained their right to sell their land, and their right of inheritance. They had lost only their right to seek a new lord with their land, for, if they sold their holdings, their successors must enter into the lordship and hold of the manor and the fee in which the land lay. In law—in fact, no doubt, there was often irregularity and oppression—no iota of their custom could be changed, no rent added and no new custom imposed.[3] The sokemen, those freemen the suit of many of whom had been cut away from the

[1] Domesday Book, ii. 304 *et seq.*

[2] His grant to his foundation of Eye of sake and soke in certain lands, and all rights and liberties which the Conqueror gave him, can mean no more than granting soke where he had it. *Monasticon Anglicanum*, iii. 405; and F. M. Stenton, *English Feudalism*, p. 56.

[3] Leis Willelme, 29. No exaction beyond their due rent shall be made from the cultivators.

hundred court and thrown under a lord by a royal grant of sake and soke, retained their right in the soil as it had stood under the Confessor, though henceforth it was blended with the feudal right of a lord. The villeins, if their right was descended from that of the geburs who took land by contract, could hardly be touched by the change to feudal lordship, since the landright already lay with their lords. If Norman theory touched them at all, it would be to sanction and stabilize an existing propertyless and dependent security. "No lord may eject his cultivators from their land as long as they can do their due service."[1] "*Nativi* who leave the estate where they were born" are to be arrested and sent back.[2] In law, even in fact, Norman lordship made little difference to the economic and social structure of England in its lower ranks.

With the exception of that feudal justice of which we shall speak later, the same conservatism prevailed in jurisdiction. It has been held[3] that the baron was essentially the same as the king's thegn, and that both had a distinctive and identical right of justice, in Normandy justice over thieves taken within the honour and *causes citeines*, and in England sake and soke and infangentheof. If we are to accept this theory we must be careful upon what grounds we do so. The qualification of baronial status becomes of the greatest importance in the later history of parliament. The baron's right was in part derived from and associated with a territorial barony, indivisible and heritable. In this territorial sense king's thegnage did not exist, but was an immaterial thing, a *ministerium*. Again, though a parallel development of the law of theft in both countries had given the barons a *justice de leur larruns*[4] in Normandy which is hardly to be distinguished from infangentheof, the *causes citeines*, if they are rightly explained as "civil causes", are not the English sake and soke. Such niceties of distinction might well be obscured in the disorder of the Conquest, but, setting them aside, it is clear that there was no common right of jurisdiction in the thegnage. Some king's thegns had their soke and some had not. Jurisdiction was, in fact, granted freely to men of importance both

Marginal note: Jurisdiction: king's thegnage and barony

---

[1] Leis Willelme, 29. 1. According to Liebermann the Leis Willelme dates from between A.D. 1090 and 1135.

[2] *Ibid.* 30. 1.

[3] R. R. Reid, "Barony and Thanage", *English Historical Review*, xxxv. p. 161.

[4] Tres Ancien Coutumier, 41.

before and after the Conquest,[1] but in Domesday it is determined by no criterion of rank, and in the *Quo Warranto* it is claimed not by right of barony but by special grant or by prescription proved from manor to manor.[2] Indeed, it is in the manor, and not in the honour or the barony, that the right of sake and soke and infangentheof inheres. It is a franchise of certain individuals, part of the special right of a Saxon antecessor, or created by special grant after the Conquest,[3] and in the main its distribution is perpetuated, not obliterated, by the coming of feudalism. Private hundredal justice is comparatively rare, and there is never any doubt that it lies at the king's discretion.[4] But, though it does not seem possible to establish an identity of king's thegn and baron on the ground of jurisdiction, or indeed to determine any fixed jurisdiction or administrative immunity for either, the two titles are persistently associated in early Norman texts. The baron of the Leis Willelme is clearly intended to parallel the "king's thegn who is nighest to him" of Cnut's Law[5] in the clause fixing reliefs, and, like that of the king's thegn, the baron's person is justiciable only by the king. There seems to be between the two ranks a rough identity of personal quality, and this is derived from their "immediacy" to the crown; "the king's thegn who is nighest to him", *barones dominici mei.*[6] Moreover, there is at least something of the ministerial function of thegnage in the king's barons. They are the king's leading judges in the counties[7] and we find them used freely as justiciars when the royal justice becomes itinerant. If the identity were not

---

[1] Domesday Book, i. 1B. The Kentish Domesday gives us our one exhaustive list of the holders of sake and soke in any administration, and though many of the king's thegns of West Kent have justice over their men and lands, others (Alnod Cild, who was certainly, and Godric Carlesone, Turgis, and Norman who were almost certainly king's thegns) have none.

[2] The Leges Henrici Primi (20) attributes sake and soke to bishops and earls, but in the next clause speaks indirectly of baronial lands in which the king has soke. In the pleadings in *Quo Warranto* William de Say explicitly disclaims rights of jurisdiction throughout his barony in Kent. *Loc. cit.*, 315.

[3] *Placita de Quo Warranto*, 123: *quo ad . . . infangenethef . . . illa libertas est mere regalia quod nulli licet in regno hujusmodi libertatem habere sine speciali facto domini Regis:* as for infangentheof, that liberty is fully royal, so that no one in the realm can have such franchise without the special act of the lord king.

[4] *Ibid.* p. 179. *Nullo liceat hundredum habere nisi specialiter de dono domini Regis:* no one may have the hundred except exceptionally by the gift of the lord king.   [5] Leis Willelme, 20. 1: II Cnut, 71. 1.

[6] Hen. I. Ordinance of Shires and Hundreds.

[7] Leges Hen. I. 29. : *Regis judices sint barones comitatus.*

expressly made by contemporaries we should still conclude that
the general place of the king's thegn in the royal system of Confessor was taken by the baron of the Conqueror. Baron, like thegn,
is an ambiguous term. There is an honorial baronage, barons of
the king's tenants-in-chief, and in a general sense, as thegn need
mean no more than minister, so *baro* may mean no more than
homo. All the king's tenants-in-chief are in that sense his barons.
Yet, just as truly as king's thegnage existed, there are barons
par excellence—in later days they will be called *majores barones*—
and in the absence of any more definite criterion, since some
criterion we must believe existed, we may take it that they were
those who, like the king's thegns, had constant access to his person
and court, a place in his hall and at his table, at least at the three
great feasts of the year, and during that period livery along with
the household for such attendants as custom allowed, in short, that
they were there with an established place in the great hyred or
curia.[1] The creation of the abbey of Battle brought a new spiritual
barony into being, and the sole clause of the charter[2] bearing upon
the secular status of the abbot allots his place and living in the
curia. It may be that we see in this curial, dominical status the vital
fact in the creation of a baron. In a feudal state which associated
tenure closely with office the heritable honour *per baroniam*, which
chiefly distinguishes barony from thegnage, is a necessary outcome of the changed state of land-law. Barony, we might say, is
king's thegnage feudalized, and for that reason destined to play a
very different part in the life of the nation.

Apart from the greater justice, there is the justice of the manor *Manorial*
court, and we may legitimately doubt whence this has come. It is *justice*

[1] There is some evidence that certain of the king's ministries carried barony
with them, for in the reign of Henry III Hugh de Ver held much of his land
"*per baroniam essendi camerarius regis*", and this is in itself indicative of the
personal and ministerial quality of baronage. Public Record Office. *Inquisitions
Post Mortem*, Henry III, 31 (1). The Chamberlain's barony is a composite one,
including some of the manors which Aubrey de Ver held in 1086. Since
Geoffrey de Coutances' manor of Kensington is incorporated in it, his barony
can hardly be of the Conqueror's reign. The de Ver chamberlainship was
created by charter of 1133. J. H. Round, *Geoffrey de Mandeville*, p. 390.

[2] H. W. C. Davis, *Regesta Regum*, no. 60 (1070–1071). The abbot is authorized
to come to court at Easter, Whitsuntide, and Christmas, and to have the court-
livery of victuals and lights for himself and two attendants. This is the "seat
in the king's hall" of Cnut's thegns. The Abbot of Battle owed no knight
service but was summoned personally to the host and to Parliament.

certain that the Norman lord could hold a court for his men from the mere fact of being a lord,[1] and, indeed, every lord of a manor seems to have done so, and to have claimed that it was of common right,[2] and needed no royal grant such as was necessary for the enjoyment of sake and soke. A memorandum, apparently of the early fourteenth century,[3] tells us what that jurisdiction was—debt under forty shillings, contracts and conventions made within the power of the lord, cattle wounding *et hujusmodi*, damage to crops by animals, assault not leading to bloodshed, trespass or damaging of timber where the king's peace was not involved, and actions about land by writ of right up to the stage of their removal to the king's court for the grand assize. Action upon the writ of right is held because all causes arising out of the land-tenure of freeholders were in principle tried in such courts, while their removal to the king's court was mainly subsequent to the reforms of Henry II. *A fortiori*, the customary tenures must have been justiciable there also. Both might follow from the feudal doctrine that lordship of itself carries jurisdiction, and, as there is no evidence to carry it behind the Conquest, we may well believe it to have been Norman. As to the trespasses and petty assaults, it is to be noted that they are such as Saxon folkright seems to have left out of account. In the codes they are either ignored, or else explicitly left to the individual to find his own redress.[4] It is possible, therefore, that, while the hundred was set up to put the outstanding and more dangerous field of self-help against theft under the check of a jurisdiction, the townships may have acted informally for less important disputes between neighbours, and this is the opinion which was held in the first half of the twelfth century. The Leges Edwardi Confessoris describe such matters[5] as township or titheing causes, despatched *inter villas et inter vicinos* by the titheing men, who refer more important causes to the hundred. They were, it is

---

[1] Leges Henrici Primi, 55. 1.

[2] *Placita de Quo Warranto*, p. 313. *Habere liberam curiam de tenentibus . . . non est libertas nec regale*: to have free court of tenants is neither a franchise nor a royal right.

[3] British Museum MSS. Arundel, 310, f. 86A.

[4] There is no penalty in folkright for assault *sine effusione sanguinis*. Trespassing cattle might be killed on the spot if they did damage. Ine, 42. 1. There is a composition for felling timber in Ine 44, but in no later law.

[5] *Videlicet de pascuis, de pratis, de messibus, de decertationibus inter vicinos et de multis hujusmodi*. Leges Edwardi Confessoris, 28. 1.

implied, a petty arbitration of Saxon date, but post-dating the creation of the hundred, licensed by the witan when it was found that the hundred and frankpledge did not suffice to prevent all cause of dissension. There is reason, then, to think that the jurisdiction of the manor is adequately accounted for by a combination of Norman custom together with such small matters of dispute as had come under the law's notice only at the end of the Saxon epoch, and had been allowed to fall to the comparatively new units of the townships. Thus feudal justice as such was confined within very narrow limits, and where the higher justice came into the hands of subjects it was by grant of the king. Short of unpardonable laxness by the crown, there was no danger of a general liquidation of the judicial system among the feudatories.

The administrative framework of Eadward's day was equally *Adminis-* resistant and continued to serve the Conqueror. Feudal tenure *tration* gave of itself no freedom from hundred or titheing, no exemption from suit of hundred and shire. Unless by royal grant, no fee was immune from the entry of the crown's bailiffs to serve the king's writs, or make arrest, or take pledge, or follow up stray cattle. Feudal land as such was not privileged. Its tenants performed suit, followed the hue and cry, made presentment of Englishry, were viewed in their frankpledges, kept watch and ward upon the roads or the sea-coast. Conversely, if individually or by communities they made default, their duty was brought home to them by personal or common amercement with the rest of their shire or hundred. In respect of all this the land and tenantry were said to be "geldable",[1] or to be "in scot[2] and lot" with the shire, and, though there were countless exemptions, the greatest barons were forced to admit that part of their lands were geldable, and the

[1] The geldable is that portion of the shire not in any immunity, but fully under the king's administration. Cf. *Placita de Quo Warranto*, p. 224. Custom varies, but the obligations of the geldable in Lincolnshire are a fair example: *solebant esse geldabiles, dare auxilium vicecomitis, murdrum, commune amerciamentum, et facere unicum adventum ad wappentachum . . . et dare visum franci plegii*: they used to be geldable, giving sheriff's aid, murdrum, common amercement, making one suit to the wapentake with view to frankpledge. *Ibid.* p. 408. So at Winchcombe in Gloucestershire: *esse geldabiles et facere sectam ad hundredum domini Regis et facere vigilias et dare theloneum et amerciari inter alios de villa*: geldable, and making suit to the hundred of the lord king with watch and ward, paying toll, and being liable to amercement with the rest of the township. *Ibid.* 250.

[2] The Confessor's phrase *scotfreo fram heregelde aud fram eghwilc oðer gafol* (F. E. Harmer, *Anglo-Saxon Writs*, No. 15) is as near as a Saxon king gets to this.

crown continued to assert that immunity from the administrative duties of the geldable was not of the common right of feudalism,[1] and that the right to them constituted *regalia, mere domini Regi spectantes.* Within the franchises the provincial routine of law and administration was perpetuated by franchisal bailiffs,[2] and from the reign of Henry II these officials became subject to recurrent enquiries as to their conduct. Thus the English countryside absorbed feudalism into its communities. Royal power reached downward to involve the common men of the titheings, shires, hundreds, and boroughs through threads of authority which were purely Saxon, and in this the Conqueror is most clearly seen to be the heir of the Confessor. These, as much as the high matters of justice for which the name *cynerihta* was reserved, convey the real continuity of the English and Norman crowns.

Continuity of Norman with Saxon England   In the light of this summary we may hazard some very general conclusions as to what the introduction of feudalism did and did not do in England. Feudal tenure had no immediate revolutionary effect upon the mass of the people, in so far as the essentials of their material life, their security of holding, and their personal status were concerned. Outside the honours, the landed rights of all free men had their defence in shire and hundred as before. Not even an earl's right carried the jurisdiction of shire or hundred without special grant. Earls and barons had an immunity as such, but it was of their own persons only. They claimed to be tried by their peers, and though much of their land might be subject to common amercement, they themselves were not.[3] For at least a further generation hundred and shire functioned as before. There was no sudden radical change of system, nor, as has sometimes been suggested, revival, for since the reign of Æthelred no decline in

1 *Placita de Quo Warranto*, p. 245: *Private persone . . . non habuerunt potestatem aliquem feoffare de hujusmodi (sci. libertatibus de visu franciplegii et weif) cum sint mere ad Coronam domini Regis spectantes:* private persons could not enfeoff others of this kind of franchise, etc.

2 *Ibid.* 677: *Tenere duas magnas curias in eodem manerio et in curia illa placitare omnia placita que vicecomes placitat in turno suo:* to hold two great courts in the said manor, and in them to implead all pleas that the sheriff impleads in his tourn.

3 Barons ought to be amerced before the king's council. Letters Close, 3 Hen. III, p. 383.

4 William I, Latin Articles, 8. 1: *Requiratur hundred et comitatus sicut antecessores nos tri statuerunt.*

the English system had taken place. The essentially popular basis of justice was untouched. As in the sheriff's courts, so in the courts of those magnates who held private jurisdiction of the hundred, or sake and soke, the custom of the countryside prevailed, and even down to the manorial courts, the lord's reeve was no more than incorporating officer of the court, and villeins, as judges of the manor custom, determined each other's right. Judgment by suitors was as proper to feudalism as to the system which it superseded, and the two systems were not far apart. Almost all the kindred procedure had been eliminated from the old English local moots before the Conquest, and for it had been substituted judgment and oath-helping by neighbours, preferably neighbours of the same order and standing as the litigants; this preference for an equivalence of the standing of judges and parties conformed strictly to Norman prejudice and lent itself readily to feudal expression. Judgment by neighbours, for choice of equal rank, developed into judgment by tenants of the same administration or liberty, preferably equals in tenure. The *judicium vicinorum*, almost imperceptibly modified, passed into the *judicium parium* which was the ideal, if not the rule, of Norman justice.[1] We shall, in fact, misunderstand the course of history if we fail to realize the flow of the broad stream of English custom across the line of the Norman Conquest and into the Middle Ages. That custom, and the community it has formed, remain the basis of the English state, and, as time goes on, the crown is content more and more to go down into the county courts and hundreds to find lawful men to activate its procedure in common law and administration. The drawing together in a common task of government of a crown which claims an English descent and a nation which has not abandoned its immemorial custom is one of the two outstanding facts of the Middle Ages. In this we see the English nation coming to the lordship of feudalism and yet preserving the essentials of community. But this is only one, though, perhaps, the more powerful of the two impulses which determined the rise of the English polity. The Norman Conquest brought into England a crown which was in two minds between its royal Saxon and its Norman

[1] Leges Henrici Primi, 31. 7: *Unusquisque per pares suos iudicandus est et eiusdem provincie*: every man is to be judged by his peers and those of the same administration.

ducal right, but which in the end did its work through its feudal power of jurisdiction. Royal lordship proved to be more effective than the Saxon cyneryhta. Still, for two centuries and more, England had rulers who, according to their individual temperaments, behaved now as king and now as lord. The cleavage between the two societies and the two races was not, of course, absolute. The gradation from the highest feudal tenure to the lowest servitude was by imperceptible stages. But in broad outline it is the fissure within the nation set up in 1066 which gives to the central institutions of medieval English government their characteristic trend, for from feudal discontents, arising from specifically feudal burdens, and from the ambitions of a few feudatories, came first rebellion, and as rebellion failed, a more considered resistance to the crown which broadened into a common interest with the nation.

Feudal theory   The material detail of feudalism, its incidents, and the struggle between the crown seeking to turn them into an elastic source of revenue and of the feudatories refusing to exceed their customary liabilities may, for the moment, be deferred. They are the absorbing consideration of a later age. But some description of the ideas which inspired the feudal order and led to the more notable actions of its leaders is necessary, for it is against a background of feudalism that the kings fought their way to an overmastering crown, and not the least part of their struggle was to resolve within their own minds the implications of their dual status as lord and king. The units of feudal society are fees, baronies, and earldoms, the two last impartible in law. The term honour was applied in general to any of them which achieved a degree of structural unity, and, though the doctrines of tenure came to pervade all relations of life, it was in the honour that feudal values *The honour* were brought to a focus and most clearly expressed. The Mandeville barony, of which something has been said already, shows the honour well enough in its average form. Except in the North and upon the Welsh Marches, it is rare for the lands of any one lordship to lie contiguous to each other. The scattering of manors in several counties, each with its own customary court and officials, is the common rule, and the honour appears, therefore, rather as a confederation of social-economic units than as a compact whole, the superstructure of central obedience and common administration and jurisdiction which reconciles this disunity being an outcome of Norman lordship and concerned solely with the strictly feudal elements, tenures in free fee, tenures in knight-service.

The binding tie of this knightly and baronial feudalism is the *Homage* swearing of homage.[1] It is distinguished from the oath of fealty and the English hold-oath by its greater precision, by identifying the tie of lord and man with that of tenure. Being made for a certain tenement, and constituting a contract by which that tenement is held, it has a material guarantee in law. The hold-oath was a solemn promise, the breach of which incurred moral reprobation; the breaking of homage gave rise to an action at law, and made the tenant liable to lose his tenement. It was a most solemn act, bringing into being the most deeply felt relation of the feudal world, and it bound the heirs of both lord and tenant in perpetuity.[2] Its action was symbolical of fidelity and reverence on the part of the man, who knelt bare-headed, and of dominance and protection on the lord's part, as he received his vassal's hands between his own.[3] The material purport of the ritual was a contract; upon the vassal's side to "become your man for the tenement I hold of you, and bear faith to you of life and members and earthly honour against all other men, saving the faith I hold to our Lord King"; upon that of the lord to maintain his tenant in his tenement, rights, and custom, to warrant his tenure in law, and to defend him against all other men. "Homage is a bond of law by which one is holden and bound to warrant, defend, and acquit the tenant in his seisin against all men, in return for a fixed service named and expressed in the gift, and whereby the tenant is bound to keep faith with his lord and to perform the due service: and such is the relation of homage that the lord owes as much to the tenant as the tenant to the lord, save only reverence."

It is necessary to dwell upon this act and its implications because *Homage a* *contract*

---

[1] F. Pollock and F. W. Maitland, *History of English Law*, i. 296-307.

[2] The lord can be compelled to take the homage of his dead tenant's heir or show cause *quare non fecerit*. Glanvill, *Tractatus de Legibus*, ix. 4.

[3] *English Historical Review*, xlii. 247. A writ of William I records, *Petrum . . . militem Sancti Aedmundi et Baldewini abbatis manibus iunctis fore feodalem hominem.* Black Book of St. Augustine's (British Academy), ii. 462: *Domini sui quorum homo manibus suis fuerit.*

it is the strongest sanction of the unity of the honour,[1] and because in it feudal England, in common with the feudal world, brings to the surface much which underlies its theory of society, but in England, at least, seldom gets explicit acknowledgment. It is, in fact, the clearest formularization of the feudal contract—a concept, which, though it is never openly embodied in a general feudal code, yet haunts the background of English politics for at least two centuries, and from time to time finds outlet in action. In virtue of the contract of homage and of the tenure which it set up, the lord could exact from his tenants in fee and inheritance service which was fixed by agreement at the creation of the tenure [2] or had become customary. A substantial proportion of the tenements granted by lay and spiritual lords would be given to be held *per servitium militare* with the original intention of meeting the *servitium debitum* or service of knights demanded by the Conqueror from the tenant-in-chief, and, at least by the reign of Henry II, these would have come to owe a number of incidents which are substantially the same throughout England; relief, or fine for entering upon the tenure; wardship and marriage, by which the tutelage of heirs under age and of their estates lay with the lord together with a veto upon marriage to anyone in the lord's disfavour; aid, or an agreed subsidy usually demanded when the lord's eldest son was knighted, or his eldest daughter was married, or to ransom his body from captivity; and scutage, recoverable from the sub-tenants when the king had levied it upon the tenant-in-capite. In a more general way, feudal lordship reproduced or perpetuated many of the privileges and restraints of Saxon lordship, the power of advocacy by the lord,[3] and the right of the man to plead the lord's cause for him at law, the prohibition of joining in judgment upon one's lord, even in a plea of the crown,[4] and the general obligation of lord and man to maintain each other against all others in litigation and to provide good counsel for the furtherance of any purpose either may have at heart. Such coöperation, recalling the legal value of the Saxon mund, was still a principal motive

Feudal service

---

1 So much so that "the homage" can be used as a synonym for "the honour", *Cartularium Monasterii de Rameseia*, i. 155.

2 Glanvill, *Tractatus de Legibus*, ix. 2: *Fiunt autem homagia . . . de servitiis de redditibus certis assignatis in denariis vel in aliis rebus.*

3 Only a lord could replace the kin in bringing accusation of homicide. Glanvill, *Tractatus de Legibus*, xiv. 3.   4 *Leges Henrici Primi*, 30 and 32. 2.

in the relation of lord and vassal, and explicitly specified in some charters as a condition of tenure.[1]

The law which provides the ceremony of homage for the form- *Diffidation* ing of the contract between lord and man has an equivalent form for its ending, the *diffidatio*. The condition of vassalage is fidelity and service upon the one hand and warranty and protection upon the other. The tie cannot lightly be broken, but either lord or man, by failing to perform his share of the contract and refusing redress after legal complaint, gives to the other the right to defy him in ritual form, to put him out of his faith, and to coerce him with all the means in his power. The conditions under which a vassal may consider himself free of his homage are carefully de-limited. They are the taking away of the fee or right for which homage is due, or the deserting of the vassal in mortal necessity.[2] The diffidation must be made in due form and after a year's delay, during which the tenant must require redress from his lord, inform-ally by the intercession of his peers, of his neighbours, and familiars, and legally of any independent jurisdiction to which he may have access.[3]

[1] *Black Book of St. Augustine's* (British Academy), ii. 462: *Eo tenore quod Hamo Dapifer, si opus fuerit, ecclesiae et michi vel successoribus meis de placitis in comitatu sive in curia regis contra aliquem baronem consulat, adiuvet et succurat, exceptis dominis suis quorum homo manibus suis fuerit*: on the condition that Hamo Dapifer shall give counsel and maintenance to this church, to me and my successors, in pleas in the shire-moot or in the king's court if need arise, except against those lords of whom he shall have become the man. *Chronicon Monasterii de Abingdona*, ii. 133. *In curia etiam regis si abbate placitum aliquod forte habendum contigerit, ipsius abbatis parti idem aderit, nisi contra regem*: and if the abbot shall have any plea in the king's court he shall adhere to the part of the said abbot, save only against the king. *Cartularium Monasterii de Rameseia*, i. 153: *Quia vero predictus Robertus vir nobilis erat et sapiens . . . retinuimus hominium suum ad servitium ecclesiae*: and because the said Robert was a man of worth and wisdom we retained his homage for the service of the church.

[2] Bracton, *Note Book*, i. 78. Leges Henrici, 43. 8.

[3] *Ibid.* 43. 9. The ground of the loosing of homage is well put for Richard Marshal by Matthew Paris (*sub anno* 1233): *Proditio non egi contra Regem, quia sine judicio parium meorum et injuste ab officio Mariscalciae me spoliavit . . . cum semper paratus essem in curia sua juri parere, et stare judicio parium meorum. Unde homo suus non fui, sed ab ipsius homagio non per me, sed per ipsum licenter absolvebar*: I have done no treason against the king, for he has disseized me of my office of the Marshalsea unlawfully and without judgment of peers . . . whereas I have ever been ready to appear in his court to fulfil the law and to stand to the judgment of my peers. So I was not his man (when I took arms against him), but stood absolved from his homage rightfully, and not by my own doing but by his. Cf. Wendover, iii. 65.

Limita-
tions on
feudal
right

Feudalism is, therefore, contractual, but there are effectual limitations upon its tendency to disintegrate, especially so in England, where feudal custom is a newcomer and has to adjust itself within a law of violence which is still in full force. In contrast with Normandy, war between subjects has been illegal for centuries, and the right of lord and man to fight each other's battles is narrowly confined by old-standing restrictions upon violence.[1] Again, feudal justice has safeguards for both lord and man arising out of its own constitution, which guarantee the right of judgment in open court. No man can forfeit his heirs' right except for felony,[2] or betrayal of his lord,[3] or persistent default of service, and in the event of denial of justice by the lord, such as the rules of diffidation have in mind, the vassal has a right of action in the king's court,[4] to which he would be required to have resort rather than to self-help. He must, in short, appeal to the king,[5] and is, indeed, required to do so. Conversely, the king accepts the honour jurisdiction as part of the public order, will afforce his baron's courts for them if they are too feeble to act alone,[6] and will compel the tenants to take their legal action therein.[7] By such

---

[1] Leges Henrici Primi, 82. 3. [2] *Ibid.* 88. 14.

[3] This is broadly interpreted, and may include advocacy of another's legal plea against one's own lord. *Ibid.* 43. 3. A good instance of the grounds upon which the king may exact forfeiture of lands is that of Grimbald of Bayeux (H. W. C. Davis, *Regesta Regum*, 76): *Pro reatu infidelitatis suae et crimine insidiarum suarum quibus adversus me perjuraverat*: for his infidelity and for the crime of conspiracy with which he forswore himself towards me. So, in 1172, *Adam de Port calumniatus est de morte et proditione regis*, and was outlawed and his fee declared forfeit: Adam de Port was accused of conspiring the death and betrayal of the king. Benedict, i. 35.

[4] The lord is said to lose his court if he denies justice to a litigant, that is to say, the plea is removed to the court of the king. Leges Henrici Primi, 57. 5.

[5] *Ibid.* 59. 19. The transference of the plea must be effected by a formal denunciation of the lord's default, *curiam domini sacramento falsificare*, an oath being taken upon the Gospel. M. M. Bigelow, *Placita Anglo-Normannica*, 212. Glanvill, *Tractatus de Legibus*, xii.

[6] Letters Patent, 6 John, p. 51: *Nolumus quod judicia curie Pagani de Rupeforti de Hathfeld remaneant per defectum hominum . . . immo precipimus quod judicia curie illius procedant et fiant per milites de comitatu de quibus Vicecomiti Essexie precepimus quod illos illuc venire faciat*: we are unwilling that judgments shall go unmade in Pain de Rochford's court of Hatfield for default of suitors and therefore we command that the judgments of his said court shall proceed and be made by those knights of the county whom we have ordered the sheriff of Essex to make to attend there.

[7] So Henry I orders that if Goscelin has any claim in the lands of St. Mary of Abingdon *eat in curiam Abbatis, et ipse Abbas sit ei ad rectum: et defendo ipsi*

safeguards every door to violence is closed, while the doctrine of mutual responsibility of lord to man is approved and reinforced. There is, therefore, no inevitable antagonism between the crown *Rule of* and the legalized feudalism of the twelfth century, and such ex- *Law* pressions as "feudal anarchy" are peculiarly inapt to describe the normal mind of feudalism, which maintained, on the contrary, an all-pervading respect for law, a respect so strong that it asserted its sanctity above that of any of the authorities which were empowered to carry it out. The rule of law was the most clearly realized political principle of the feudal age, governing the conduct of lord and vassal alike,[1] and the right of diffidation, the right to denounce the contract of homage, was valid precisely and only when the supreme judicial authority failed in its trust of affording fair trial of right; for equally fundamental was the principle that, as the lord was bound to offer fair judgment, so the vassal was bound to place himself upon it. The feudal subject might rebel not when he felt himself to be wronged, nor when he had suffered material loss from the action of the state or of individuals, but when in pursuing the proper channels of law he was refused judgment, a judgment which when lawfully pronounced, whatever its verdict, he must accept.[2] It will be seen by this that the English feudatory was under two degrees of obligation, derived from successive layers of history. As a member of the English community, either by birth or in right of his Saxon antecessor, he was born into a birthright of English law, which he could neither evade nor annul. This was subject to no contract, and constituted an unbreakable tie, one the breaking of which was inconceivable. No English magnate of the feudal age ever formed the ambition of breaking loose from the community of English law, and turning his fee into an independent state. But, with the authority to which the protection and

Abbati quod non respondeat inde Goscelino in alio loco: let him enter the abbot's court, and let the abbot there do him right; and I forbid the abbot to answer Goscelin in any other place in this plea. *Chronicon Monasterii de Abingdon*, ii. 93.

[1] The dealings of the lord with his vassal must be *justa secundum considerationem curiae suae et consuetudinem rationabilem*. Glanvill, *Tractatus de Legibus*, ix. 8.

[2] Both aspects of this principle are shown in Langton's justification of a subject's refusal to support his prince in a disseisin not preceded by legal judgment. "If the king attacks a castle unjustly are his people bound to support him? If without judgment, no. If after judgment, yes: *cum populus non habet discutere de sententia*." F. M. Powicke, "Stephen Langton", p. 95. Note I.

enforcement of the law was entrusted his relation was conditional, or so it seemed to an aristocracy which had become steeped in Frankish feudalism. Because the *feudum*, bestowed by a lord and earned by the service of a vassal, had come to be the universal land-right of Normandy and therefore predominant in England, the holders of English fees thought of themselves as first and foremost vassals, whose duty towards the king was created by enfeoffment and was therefore subject to the conditions and limitations of feudal tenure and by the terms of homage revocable. In so far as they could see beyond the individual relation, the king appeared to them as the guardian of the national custom, whose claim to obedience, either by divine or secular right, was nullified if he failed to fulfil his trust. The maxim that the power of a king who acts as a tyrant is illegitimate, which almost exhausts contemporary theorizing about monarchy, and to us seems to be an ineffectual truism, was thus in the twelfth and thirteenth centuries the corner-stone of legal security.

*Feudal
revolt*

Feudal action, therefore, as long as it is guided by principle—and it is rarely that the individual can divest himself of the preconceptions of his age—is primarily legal: but, when refused legal redress, the aggrieved party is entirely within his rights in declaring his obligation of vassalage at an end, making war upon his king, and coercing him by every means in his power to do him right. From its very nature, we cannot go to crown records for this strand of theory, but it governs the treatment of historical events in chronicles and popular literature. One of the few surviving romances of English chivalry, the legend of Fulk fitz Warin,[1] gives an excellent example of the behaviour that was thought proper from an injured vassal to his king. Maurice fitz Roger of Powys had ejected Fulk's father, Warin, from his fief of Blancheville, and Fulk, as his heir, had claimed justice and been denied it by King John. Fulk defies him in these terms: "Lord King, you are my liege lord, and I was bound to you by fealty as long as I was in your service and held lands of you: and it was for you to maintain me in right, and you failed me in right and common law. Never was there good king who denied his free tenants right in his court.

[1] The historical Fulk fitz Warin was lord of Whittington, and was one of barons excommunicated by Innocent in January, 1216 for his opposition to John (Rymer, *Foedera*, i. 139). The romance is of the early fourteenth century.

For this I render you back your homage." This is not history but romance, popular sentiment, and it shows what was acceptable among the French-speaking gentry for whom the tale was written, for Fulk was the idealized hero of the revolt against John. Coming nearer to history, for he was a clerk in Henry's employ, we have Jordan Fantosme's account of the reasoning of William the Lion before he entered the war of 1173 against the elder Henry.[1] He is represented as regretting, on the ground of right, his promise to join the son in rebellion: "to the old king, equally, he owes homage and service, true allegiance. It is not right that he should make war on his lands without first demanding his inheritance" (Northumbria, to which Henry II denied his claim). "If he refuse, then he may, at his will, renounce his homage without blame." In the same category of war made by individuals in legal form and without sense of illegality, to secure their right, we may place the action of the sons of Robert de Beauchamp in 1138 when they fortified Bedford against Stephen: "not that they meant to deny their due obedience or service to their lord, but because they had heard that the king had given the daughter of Simon de Beauchamp to Hugh le Poer with her father's honour, and they feared to lose their whole inheritance".[2]

We should probably find this grievance of default of justice, with its consequence of legal diffidation, at the back of most feudal "revolts". They are hardly rebellions as we understand it, and certainly not treason. The term *gwerra* used for them could bear the sense of right sought by legitimate force, almost of wager of battle. That of 1173 was led by men whom Henry II had "disinherited",[3] that of 1191 was mainly caused by the Chancellor's resumption of Richard's sales of honours to finance the Crusade,[4] *The barons and the crown* and the terms of peace required that the former should "disseize no one without judgment of the king's court". In the long discontents against John, the charge of selling and withholding justice was fundamental to the opposition case. Indeed, with so many warnings that the sanctity of law did not in itself guarantee the rights of individuals, the voluntary nature of vassalage was from

---

[1] Fantosme, p. 227.   [2] Orderic, III. xiii. 17.
[3] Ralf de Diceto, 371. The disinheritance was, no doubt, in part of royal castles which had been held long enough to breed a sense of prescription.
[4] Richard of Devizes, §§11-32.

time to time made an excuse for exacting a specific contract at the moment of homage, and even for anticipating its withdrawal in given circumstances. Robert of Gloucester did homage to Stephen in 1136 *sub conditione quadam*,[1] as did the bishops,[2] and withdrew it in 1138 "according to the customary form", and in 1199 the earls of Derby, Chester, Warwick, and others sold their fealty to John on the condition *ut redderet unicuique jus suum*, which *jus* we may take to be such definite objects as the share of the Peverel lands which had been pursued by the earls of Derby since 1153, and the Chester claims in South Lancashire.[3] The safeguard of the Great Charter of 1215 rested, indeed, upon a wholesale application of this principle, for the homage of twenty-five of the greatest barons was sworn on condition of the charter's observance and revocable on its breach. Thus, on the part of those barons who stand as types of the feudal order, there is a deep sense of their feudal status. Let the king touch their individual *jus*—and the ramification of claims and counterclaims was too intricate to admit of legal settlement without cavil—and they are ready with the cry of default of right and the weapon of withdrawal of homage. Almost always, it would seem, the quasi-legal conventions are preserved, and the form of diffidation gone through. Robert of Gloucester, as against Stephen in 1138,[4] on a personal issue, and the barons of the Charter before Runneymede,[5] in a general cause, equally present their defiance and so hold to convention in making war on their king, and Henry III himself against Richard Marshall in 1233 and before Lewes in 1264, feels bound to use the ceremony of diffidation against the rebels before he takes the field:[6] *vos tamquam nostrorum . . . inimicos diffidamus*. The feudal standing of monarch and subject as parties to a revocable compact appears in this defiance of his subjects by a king, as it does in the letter of the charter barons to John denouncing him as perjured *et baronibus rebellis*.[7]

Divided loyalties

It is hard to determine how far this feudal diplomacy was backed

[1] Malmsbury, 707: *Scilicet quamdiu ille dignitatem integre custodiret et sibi pacta servaret.*

[2] *Quamdiu ille libertatem ecclesiae et vigorem disciplinae conservaret.*

[3] Derby actually got his demands in 1199 (*Rotuli de Oblatis*, 3). Chester had to wait for his until a later crisis at the end of the reign. *Placita de Quo Warranto*, 387.

[4] *Historia Novella*, i. §18.   [5] Coventry, 219.

[6] Rishanger, p. 28.   [7] Wendover, ii. 117.

by feudal power. The most considerable warlike efforts of individual barons seem to have been made with foreign mercenaries.
Ralf Guader intended to hire a Danish force, Robert of Gloucester
won the battle of Lincoln with Welsh mercenaries, and in 1173
Leicester, Mowbray, and Norfolk fought with armies of hired
Flemings. The amercements in the Pipe Roll of 1175 and 1176
reveal almost no trace of any English following.[1] Indeed, the cross-
currents of obligation in which the English vassals were involved
made it hard for king or baron's strength to gather head. Homage
might be done to several lords for different tenements, and those
lords might be at variance. If the tenant were drawn into advocacy
of one lord against the other at law, or had to take up arms, he
should by feudal custom forfeit the tenement held of the lord he
had deserted. The lord, also, though he exacted the strict letter of
service from the man whose homage he shared with his enemy,
might still lose the full and willing support of his vassal. Many
devices were put forward to solve this kind of dilemma. The lord
could at least insist that the resources of the fees held of himself
should not be used against him.[2] Many vassals, however, felt that
they had discharged their obligation if they rendered their strict
servitium debitum to their lord, and might use the rest of their
resources as they liked, even to the point of throwing them on the
side of his enemies. The count of Flanders had a standing agreement with England to limit his service to the king of France in
this way, and the same evasion was apt to be made in England.[3] In
1141 many barons came in person to Stephen's host at Lincoln
with their customary quota, but sent the rest of their men to join
the Angevins against him,[4] while in 1215, after their knights had
gone over to the opposition, certain of the magnates felt bound to
continue with the king *tanquam domino adhaerentes*.[5] Some attempt
was made to clear up this ambiguity by introducing the conception
of ligeance,[6] liege homage, and liege fealty, which set up a prior *Liege*
claim upon the service and fidelity of the liege vassal, and it was *homage*
further accepted that a man's liege lord should be he of whom he

[1] There was some disturbance in York, and round the Mowbray's stronghold
of Thirsk.   [2] Leges Henrici Primi, 59. 12A.
[3] Cf. the treaty between the earls of Chester and Leicester (1147-1151).
Stubbs, *Select Charters*, p. 140.
[4] Orderic, III. xiii. 21.   [5] Coventry, 220.
[6] From *ledic*, "direct or unrestricted", as opposed to *simplex homagium*.

held his principal fee, *cujus residens est*.[1] The effect of this, of course, would be to strengthen the hold of the king upon the barons, who held their *capita honorum* from him, but also that of the barons over the tenants of the fees held in mesne tenure from them. On the whole, it would tend to arrest the dissipation of feudal loyalty and so solidify the sense of unity in the honours, and it had little bearing upon the main problem of the eleventh and twelfth centuries, the reconciling of the king's claim to general obedience with the special obligations of tenure. Besides the ambiguities inherent in the feudal system itself, there is the fact that by Norman, but still more by English tradition, the royal person was something more than lordship.

Fealty to the king Whatever had been his rights in Normandy, the Conqueror inherited a claim to, or at least an expectation of general fealty, which the English kings since Eadward the Elder had received from the nation through the mouths of the witan. This had been thought of as a taking of the king to *cynehlaford*, and it had apparently been sworn in the form of the ordinary hold-oath of man to lord. Under the Norman kings this fealty to the king was renewed in every reign, at the celebrated meeting at Salisbury in 1086,[2] to

[1] Leges Henrici Primi, 55. 2. Some charters require that the homager shall remain resident, and thus not impair his ligeance. *Cartularium Monasterii de Rameseia*, i. 144.

[2] The oath of 1086 has been a source of debate, and historians have given it a kind of fundamental importance as "The Oath of Salisbury". It does not seem, in fact, to differ essentially from the swearing of fealty in the next year to Rufus, in 1100 to Henry, or from the hold-oaths sworn to Eadward the Elder, Eadmund, or Æthelred. The combination of respect and hesitation with which it has been approached arises from the fact that, though explicitly stated to have been exacted from sub-tenants as well as from tenants-*in-capite*, it has been taken for an act of homage. The English term used when homage is intended is usually *manraed*, though this is a distortion of its original meaning, and in 1086 the Anglo-Saxon Chronicle—of which Florence of Worcester's account can hardly be more than a paraphrase—is clear that the oath sworn was the hold-oath: "they all bowed to him, and became his men, and swore hold-oaths to him". But behind any question of contemporary terms lies the simple fact that an oath of homage from mesne-tenants to the king was at that time impossible in law. The same tenement could not bear a double or multiple homage to a series of superior lords, since homage carried liabilities of relief, wardship, marriage, escheat, and other personal services which could not be shared. By the time of Glanvill's tractate (*Tractatus de Legibus*, ix. 2), a restricted form of homage had been devised, which excluded liability for the feudal incidents while carrying an equal sense of general submission, and this was taken to the king and to the king only, and created no conflict of services when he exacted it from the vassals of his barons. *Fiunt*

Rufus in 1087, when "all the men of England bowed to him and swore oaths",[1] to Henry in 1100, when "all the men of this nation bowed to him and swore him oaths and became his men".[1] Stephen, more Norman and less statesmanlike than his predecessors, seems to have pretermitted the rite, but it was renewed by Henry II, and more effectively, since it was sworn to by all classes in their hundred moots, and thenceforth it became a part of the normal routine of government.

The Saxon hold-oath and Anglo-Norman fealty were, however, in practice less effective than the full tenurial bond, and may be said to have maintained a conflict of principles within the state rather than to have nullified the effects of homage. Feudal sentiment enforced duty to an immediate lord: monarchical and national tradition placed the peace of the realm and sworn fealty to the crown above it. It cannot be said that the conflict was effectively laid to rest in any reign until that of Edward I. It is true that common law closely restricted the limits within which a man *Conflict of royal and feudal principles*

autem homagia de terris et tenementis liberis tantummodo de servitiis de redditibus certis assignatis in denariis vel in aliis rebus. Pro solo vero dominio fieri non debent homagia alicui excepto principe. This may well have been the *ligeantia* exacted from his barons' knights by Henry II in 1166, the homage twice sworn to the young king and to Henry of Anjou himself in 1153,—it would serve its purpose of constituting an immediate or prospective recognition of right in him who received it, without setting up a conflict of immediate obligations *de servitiis,* which was precisely what Henry fitz Roy made the pretext of his revolt—but there is no mention of it in the Leges Henrici Primi, and certainly no reason to suppose it had been invented by the reign of the Conqueror. Fealty was a much less tangible tie than homage, if only from the fact that, while homage was protected by an action at law, and its breach would lead to the loss of the tenement from which it was due, a breach of fealty, unless aggravated by criminal acts, was no more than a moral offence. It was proper for the king to take fealty of the whole nation as far as they could be approached effectively, and by the time of the Conquest it was usual for the king so to do. It was an oath which might be sworn to without difficulty by all subjects "whosesoever men they were": but it could not have the rigid legal effect of homage, and was, no doubt, apt to cover many degrees of feeling towards the king, and to admit of all sorts of subordinate commitments which were not felt necessarily to conflict with the general allegiance of the subject. Probably, the difficulties of the Conquest made it advisable to postpone the ceremony until the end of the reign, while Rufus and Henry carried it through on their accessions. The knowledge of the English tenantry gained from the Domesday survey may also have helped to make it possible. A sense of its having marked the culmination of the reign may have led the Chronicler to give it a somewhat misleading emphasis compared with that allowed to earlier and later instances of equal constitutional importance.

[1] Anglo-Saxon Chronicle, *sub annis.*

could support his lord without committing felony, and that the oath of homage and charters of enfeoffment included the phrase *salva debita fide Domini Regis*, or the like, but in practice, as we have seen, feudal motives prevailed in many crises of history, and feudal convention was followed. It is, indeed, far from clear that the strongest kings were consistent in holding aloof from feudal motives. Rebellions were made as legally justified war against the king, and were so accepted by him. That of 1215, the rising of the Marshal in 1233, end, not with punishment, but with a peace; *hominium et fidelitatem de novo facientes*. The treaty ending the war of 1173–4, when the barons were at Henry's mercy, shows a nice discrimination, by which what we should hold to be the crime of rebellion and treason is condoned, and the common law offences committed in the course of it are left open to prosecution.[1] Here the exact letter of English feudalism as set out in the Leges Henrici Primi seems to have been observed—the right to urge the cause of a lord, in this case the young king, to whom homage had been done, but with no privilege to commit felony. No forfeitures follow this revolt, and, indeed, that rebellion as such is treason is not a doctrine of public law until the fourteenth century.[2] The great forfeitures of the twelfth century, those of Robert of Bellême,[3] William Peverel, and Henry de Essex, were for felonies in the strict feudal sense, betrayal of a lord, poisoning, desertion of a lord on the field of battle. If the chroniclers are to be believed, the strongest of kings were capable of strange lapses into feudal sentiment. The civil war may explain such concessions of hereditary jurisdiction as the Empress Matilda made to Aubrey de Vere or Geoffrey de Mandeville, *convenciones* in treaty form guaranteed by the count of Anjou and the king of France,[4] but Henry I needed to be convinced of his right to disinherit Robert

---

[1] Foedera, i. 30: *Omnes illi qui recesserant ab eo post filium . . . ad pacem ejus (Regis patris) revertantur; . . . ita quod de . . . morte vel perditione alicujus membri respondeant secundum judicium et consuetudinem terrae*: all those who seceded from him with his son may return to his peace, answering for death or maiming by judgment and the custom of the land. Even after Evesham the Dictum de Kenilworth admitted the rebels to peace—*non fiat exhæredatio sed redemptio*. Stubbs, *Select Charters*, p. 407 (citations throughout are from the Ninth Edition).

[2] In 1386 Gloucester took legal advice as to whether a right of diffidation still existed. *Rotuli Parliamentorum*, iii. 379.

[3] Orderic, III. xi. 3. *Crimen proditoris confessus.*

[4] J. H. Round, *Geoffrey de Mandeville*, p. 176.

de Bellême,[1] and accorded the earl's captured garrison of Bridg-north freedom and the honours of war *quia fidem principi suo servabant ut decuit.*[2]

Feudal aims, therefore, seem to have been limited by the very doubtful hold which any feudatory outside the Welsh March had upon his lesser tenantry, by the restrictions of common law and the law of felony, and by the essentially legalistic outlook en-gendered by feudalism itself. But the Norman barons and their *The com-* knight tenants and greater freeholders formed to a limited degree *munity* a community within the community, governed as to part of *of the honour* their actions by ideals of tenure and chivalry, and often taking action against the king on purely feudal grounds. The executive machinery of a great lordship was not unlike that of the king-dom,[3] which was itself still rudimentary and domestic. No lay honour seems to have developed a regular chancery, but at least one private exchequer, that of the earl of Gloucester at Bristol, is known, and the greatest men, like Stephen when still count of Mortain and lord of Furness, Eye, and much else in England, address their writs to their justiciars, though it may be suspected *Organiza-* that the title often stood for no specialized office.[4] The *dapifer* or *tion of the honour* seneschal occurs frequently, holding courts in his lord's absence, receiving fealty and giving seizin,[5] and, in the greater immunities, occupying the bench together with the visiting justices of the crown. The dispenser appears as directing issues for expenses and alms. Constables, originally commanders of the knights of the household, act in the twelfth century more commonly as castellans of individual castles, and rarely, as at Richmond and Chester— where the lords of Mold, themselves powerful barons at Widnes and elsewhere, held the hereditary constableship of the earldom—

[1] Orderic, III. x. 16.

[2] *Ibid.* III. xi. 3. Cf. with this the lenient treatment accorded to the vassals of Simon de Montfort after Evesham. They were fined only a tenth of the pro-portion of their revenue that the principals had to pay to make their peace. Dictum de Kenilworth, 29; Stubbs, *Select Charters*, p. 407.

[3] F. M. Stenton, *English Feudalism*, pp. 65-82.

[4] Cf. Waleran of Meulan's writ to his justices of Sturminster, who can hardly have been more than manorial reeves. *Ibid.* p. 67.

[5] *Chronicon Monasterii de Abingdon*, ii. 59: *Investituram, id est saisitionem, accepit per manum Picoti, dapiferi Albrici* (de Ver).

do they remain, even in title, military chiefs of the whole honour. In general, there is less rigidity, and probably less effective special. ization of function in baronial than in royal administration, but the impression given is still of a system amply sufficient to the full exploitation of the estates, and to their coördination as military, and, to a lesser degree, social units.

Social unity is, indeed, for the most part confined to the feudal gentry whose mesne tenure is the binding force of the honour. The free tenants of the fees of a great lordship were involved in a common obligation to the *dominus superior*, and as time went on *Honorial* their tenure and service tended to take some measure of local *courts* uniformity, and to be thought of as the custom of the honour.[1] The knights could be spoken of as *pares* of the honour,[2] as mutually associated in one law, and so a new institution came into being, the latest juridical institution to be created by the spontaneous vigour of private right, and the last to emerge before the crown assumed and retained the initiative in all judicial and administrative change. As with the hundred, so with the honour, the test of its vitality is that it had the strength to embody its community in a court. Above the manor courts or soke courts, which any considerable barony would, as a rule, include, with no point of contact with them, confined to the suit of tenants in fee and interpreting feudal custom throughout the honour, rose a *curia domini, curia baronum, curia militum, magna curia*. It can hardly be doubted that the power to hold such courts is a product of the rules of the *feudum*. The estates of the Saxon thegns, quickly acquired and lightly dispersed, gave neither time nor motive for them to arise. The Norman magnates and their tenants in fee must look forward to a permanent association between their heirs. There must be a *modus vivendi* for all time. Such courts are clearly defined by the reign of Henry I. They excite no criticism and are of accepted standing. They owe their validity purely to the honorial

---

1 Chester, an exceptional case, of course, produced a comprehensive code of feudal custom in the Magna Carta of the earldom. Cf. J. Tait, *Chartulary of Chester Abbey.*

2 *Cartularium Monasterii de Rameseia*, i. 154: *Per servitium duorum militum in omnibus servitiis quae facient compares sui de eodem feuodo*: by service of two knights in all services which are done by their peers of the same fee.

right of their lords. They are not confused with the *halimotes* of the manors, nor with the jurisdiction of soke which came from the English,[1] but are privileges in the common right of Norman feudalism, lord's right from the very fact of lordship. This right is so explicitly set forth by the Henrician jurisconsult who sought to coördinate feudal custom with Saxon law, that we may be sure that he saw it to be part of a new, though settled, order. The right to exact suit as from man to lord is explained, and with it the basic right to endow the suitors with the quality of doomsmen,[2] and so to bring a court into being, and they are of common right for all who hold in fee. It is, however, to be noted that they are already forced to conform to an established territorial scheme, they are already honorial. A lord may summon men to his court from the furthest manors of the honour, but not from beyond it,[3] however far his lordship may extend, and in time it will come to be contended that even that right is not valid unless suit is specified in the charter of enfeoffment. The judicial fact of the honour determines the suit, not the personal fact of lordship and tenure, and this, no doubt, is the prime factor making against the absorption of one honour by another and the growth of feudal sub-states within the nation. Within fifty years of the Conquest, therefore, the honours had become substantive parts of the English legal and social system, had defined their legal boundaries, determined the obligations of their members, and embodied their jurisdiction in permanent courts, but, at the same time, had reached their furthest extension.

Except when the honour included some pre-existing public administration—as in Holderness, where the lord appointed a sheriff, and the honorial suit was done to the wapentake—the honorial court could have had very little relation to the customary tenants, sokemen, and small freeholders, that is, to the bulk of the population. We can see this in such an honour as that of Boulogne, which had manors in Essex, Kent, Surrey, and Suffolk, whose knightly tenants did suit every month to the honour court of Witham in Essex, and to a six-monthly court at St. Martin-le-Grand, while the manorial tenants were confined to their manor

[1] Leges Henrici Primi, 9. 4; 56. 4; 57. 8.
[2] *Ibid.* 32. 3: *Si dominus placitet contra hominem suum, potest in consilio suo habitos judices informare, si opus sit*: if a lord brings a plea against one of his men, he may constitute judges in his own council if need be.
[3] *Ibid.* 55. 1A.

courts, and were in some cases involved in forinsec[1] jurisdictions.[2] An attempt to extend the honorial suit beyond the free tenants might be resisted, as when the men of Thanet asserted that their duty was only to their halimotes, and refused to attend St. Augustine's court at Canterbury even upon personal summons. Remarkably enough, the Kentish peasantry and the king's chancery were at one in asserting the reality of the older outlines of land-right and jurisdiction as against the feudal honour. For many common purposes of administration and judicature the crown would not recognize honour or barony. The right to neither could be sued for *eo nomine* by writ. Thus, when in 12 Edward I[3] the crown "challenged the barony of Dalston with its appertinences as his right against the bishop of Carlisle," the bishop was able to reply that the writ was not good in form, *debet enim dominus Rex petere per maneria, vel per messuagia, vel in aliquo certo loco*,[4] and his objection was acknowledged and the object of the writ amended to *manerium de Dalston . . . cum omnibus membris suis, tam in dominicis quam serviciis, redditibus et villenagiis, et cum advocacione ecclesie et tota soka et omnibus pertinenciis suis*, the specification of the barony as the object of the suit dropping out. Throughout the Edwardian enquiry *de quo warranto* the crown refuses to recognize any general honorial or baronial immunity[5] from royal courts or administration as apart from what is proved as the privilege of the component manors or justified by a general royal charter.

The court and the honorial community   The interest of honorial justice, therefore, lies in the history of the feudal aristocracy, the barons, and their free tenants, and has only an indirect reaction upon the nation. Responding to the Norman instinct for judgment of like by like, the honour court provided a forum where the knights sued for their tenures, where

[1] *I.e.* foreign to the honour, belonging to some exterior court public or private.

[2] As with Boughton Alulf in Kent, whose holder in knight service did suit to Witham, while his tenants in gavelkind attended the abbot of Battle's court of Wye. So also, the Lincolnshire townships of the honour of Eye do their suit to the wapentake of Sedgebrook in that county. Public Record Office. *Calendar of Inquisitions Post Mortem*, iii. 604.

[3] *Placita de Quo Warranto*, p. 112.

[4] "Manor by manor and messuage by messuage, or as incident to some place named."

[5] So Ralf de Beauchamp's claim of view in Eton on the ground *quod capud baronie sue est* is rejected by the king's proctor. *Placita de Quo Warranto*, p. 3.

feudal custom could develop and clarify its rules, and where feudal policy and interests were furthered. Like the *curia Regis*, it was at once a court of justice and a council in which the lord sought the advice of his men.[1] "The baronial courts of the Norman age did justice between their peers, advised their lords in the crises which continually arose in the history of every great fee, and thereby evolved in course of time a coherent scheme of rights and duties out of the tangle of personal relationships produced by the sudden introduction of feudal tenure into England".[2] The period during which this influence was at its height was hardly more than a century. With the creation of the assizes under Henry II a form of trial better than ordeal by battle was offered by the royal courts, the barons were rarely empowered to administer it, and their courts quickly fell out of favour. They remained, however, the pivots upon which social and political feudalism turned. Much of the domestic history of feudalism was enacted in the lords' courts, and with their witness and warranty. Robert de Bagpuize wishes to add to the lands of his younger brother, John. He grants him a knight's fee in Bentley and Barton with the witness of William Ferrers of Derby, of the earl's brother and uncles, of his steward, and of certain knight tenants of the honour. John then becomes his brother's man *in curia domini mei Comitis Willelmi de Ferrers*.[3] William fitz Richard makes a clean partition of inheritance with his brother Gervase. It is done by resigning the estate, a knight's fee, into the hand of Geoffrey Ridel, the lord, whose court then makes recognition of the surrender, upon which Geoffrey gives seizin to Gervase and receives his homage.[4] The security of family settlements might often rest upon this recognition by the lord's court.[5] Again, the incidents of knight service call at times for

---

[1] The honorial court as council is well illustrated in the case of Abingdon (M. M. Bigelow, *Placita Anglo-Normannica*, p. 168). The abbot receiving what he believes to be an unjust order from King Stephen to return certain lands to Turstin Basset, *adunata . . . curia sua, diem statuit quo, habita deliberatione, excogitaret quid super hoc responderet*: summoned his court and appointed a day when he might take counsel what answer he should make in this affair. For another instance in the honour of Battle, *ibid.* pp. 115 and 178.

[2] F. M. Stenton, *English Feudalism*, p. 44.

[3] I. H. Jeayes, *Derbyshire Charters*, 239.   [4] *Ibid.* 1078.

[5] Thus the abbot and chamberlain of Ramsey bring "before the barons of the church of Ramsey" an agreement they have come to in the chapter, and the barons *recordati sunt et concesserunt. Cartularium Monasterii de Rameseia*, i. 142.

adjustments and concessions, and these also may be made before the lord or his seneschal. So Richard de Curzon, who has had to pay the customary aids to the earl Ferrers, and has been helped to do so by Thomas Curzon of Kedleston, in return excuses Thomas the same aids to himself, and does so with the witness of Ralf fitz Nicholas, the earl's seneschal.[1]

Wardship and marriage

Another side of feudal obligation, which worked to give the honour a common interest, and to produce a uniform honorial type, was the lord's right of wardship and marriage. The tutelage of heirs under age and of their lands brought every family into intimate personal relationship from time to time with its overlord, in whose household the heir would be bred up, and with whose patronage and good-will marriages were made. At its best, this could inject a kind of paternalism into the feudal bond,[2] and the interweaving of lordship and family ties within the honour could make it a very close community. The knight tenants, in the larger honours barons of their lords, formed his council (judgment and counsel being, indeed, inseparable functions), and, as the domestic fortunes of the tenants were again and again conducted under his guidance, so they lent their counsel and consent to the lord's actions,[3] which thus became, as it were, public acts of the honour, as those of the king and his *curia* were public acts of the realm.[4]

The year 1066 was the beginning of innumerable adjustments due to the passage of the community from organization first by kindreds and then by neighbourhood to a feudal grouping, but they are too intricate to be presented as an intelligible whole. The reception of Norman feudalism, with the rise of the honours, and their impact upon politics and the constitution, has, on the contrary, effects which are plain to see. *Ex conquestu* there sprang into

---

[1] I. H. Jeayes, *Derbyshire Charters*, 1500.

[2] So Henry I gives the daughter of Geoffrey Ridel in marriage *requisicione et consilio . . . parentum suorum*: by the request and counsel of her relatives. Here we have the two interests blended in the petitioners, that of the family implied in the request, and that of the lord who is counselled that he may justly and in his own interest make the marriage. Stenton, *English Feudalism*, p. 259.

[3] *Chronicon Monasterii de Abingdon*, ii. 20. Hugh of Chester says: *locutus sum . . . cum meis baronibus, et inveni in meo consilio quod concedam eam* (*terram*) *Deo*: I have taken counsel with my barons, and have been convinced in my council that I ought to give the land to God.

[4] *Ibid.* ii. 136. The abbot grants *consensu omnium monachorum et auctoritate militum*: by the consent of all the monks, and by the authority of the knights.

being a hundred or more feudal dynasties, of which at least the greater were responsible for a dual effect upon the life of the nation. The reigning tenant by barony had his place in the *consilium regis*, which was the highest court of the realm, while for the same lord the *caput honoris* was the centre of a provincial policy which aimed at the extension of family lands by marriage, by legal finesse, and, in some extreme instances, by selling the support of a great landed interest to the crown. The first, the influence of the barons, individually or together, in the king's council, was a constant factor, effective even under the strongest Norman kings: but until the last decade of the twelfth century, when custom and common law began to be threatened, it was applied equably and produced its effects without challenge. The duty of the vassal in the lord's *curia* was to give him favourable counsel. A basic identity of interest was assumed, and the right or duty to oppose the lord's will arose only in extremity to save him from his own folly.[1] From its very nature the great council of the Norman kings was unfitted for the functions of a parliament, and the nature or authority of counsel, the place in government of the king's personal will, the relation of both to the supremacy of the law, were matters which were beginning to exercise a handful of lawyers and churchmen only. It would take a hundred years from the Conquest to digest them into political creeds.

Thus the strength and ambition of the Norman feudatories at first found an outlet in domestic diplomacy. The interests of the greater honours were pressed individually, and from generation to generation determined the attitude of their lords to their neighbours and to the crown. The great lords of the Welsh March were possessed of regal powers[2] within their lordships, and had their enmities and alliances with English barons and foreign powers, and, until the crushing defeat of eight of the leading families in 1174, or, perhaps, even until Evesham, there seemed to be no necessary limit to the ambitions even of the purely English magnates. Between 1073 and 1098 the Montgomerys, already possessed

External diplomacy of the honours

---

[1] Becket's words to Henry II—*eo quod dominus, debeo et offero vobis consilium*—might have been taken for, and probably was, a calculated impertinence but it was good custom. Letters of St. Thomas (ed. Giles), no. 179.

[2] Cf. Hugh de Louther's comment upon the Mortimers' powers at Cleobury: *predicte libertates faciunt quandam coronam integram per quam quis est rex. Placita de Quo Warranto*, p. 675.

of Shrewsbury and South Lancashire, conquered all middle Wales, imposed their overlordship on Cardigan, and founded a third Montgomery lordship in Pembroke. When Robert of Bellême rose in 1102 it was in alliance with the princes of Powys, the king of Dublin, and the Norse king of Man. If the earls of Chester had realized at any one time all their claims by inheritance, conquest, and royal grant, they would have held, besides Chester, North Wales to Anglesey, Cumberland, South Lancashire, Staffordshire, the honours of Bligh, Peverel, and Eye, the sokes of Torksey, Oswardbeck, Mansfield, Rutland, and Stanley, the towns and castles of Stafford, Derby, and Nottingham.[1] These are extreme instances, but within such great fields of forfeited or unrealized ambitions, which were never really abandoned, there was motive for generations of intrigue, of which the crown was inevitably the focus. Confused with these *jura* of inherited and acquired lands, indeed, in this age of feudalized administration, never distinguished from them, were devolved rights of government, justiciarships, shrievalties, custodies of castles, granted in any moment of the crown's weakness, and in every degree of fee and inheritance, farm, grant for terms of years, or during pleasure. These, in earlier times a pretext for rebellion,[2] became in the thirteenth century the least reputable part of the political pretension of the magnates, so that the need for good government was identical in their minds with the government of the provinces by baronial sheriffs and the lodging of the principal castles in the hands of English nobles. Between 1135 and 1232 such claims were pressed against the crown not only by the earls of Chester, but by the great line of feudatories, Leicester, Derby, Aumâle, and Norfolk, which lay across the north Midlands, and whose lands, almost marching with each other, became the fixed centre of baronial opposition in the Middle Ages. The Marchers, on the contrary, possessed by custom of almost royal rights in their honours, and threatened by the rise of Gwynedd, remained, upon the whole, loyal. They saved the crown in 1174, in 1216, and in 1265, though, no less than the disloyalty of those who were beyond the danger of the border,

---

[1] Rymer's *Foedera*, i. 16.

[2] For example, the young Henry bribed the earl of Norfolk in 1173 with the promise of the constableship of Norwich castle in fee and inheritance. Benedict, i. 45.

their loyalty was determined by honorial interests.

There were few of the great families that did not at one time or another seek to get from the crown by force, individually or by sectional leagues, what they could not get by law, but feudal grievances and the wars they occasioned widened as time went on, fastened upon causes which were common to the whole order, and were urged more peacefully. There is no one time at which we can say that the old local ambitions are extinguished, or that the barons have taken to legitimate courses as an opposition in council, but, as the crown grows stronger, single adventures have less and less prospect of succeeding, and the spirit of opposition becomes a struggle to limit feudal obligations, against the rise of too powerful ministries, and even, under John, to defend the basic rights of person and property. The families who made the last league for purely selfish aims in 1173 are foremost in what was in some measure a war for common right in 1215.

In a very real sense, then, the conciliar elements of our constitution, and the temper in which it worked to keep the crown responsible to the law and to perpetuate the elementary rights of the subject, owed much to feudalism. The king's *curia* of feudatories acquired in the thirteenth century the methods and outlook of a political assembly, though it was that of a very narrow-minded one, and though the specialized quality of feudal counsel was only changed to the free spirit of parliamentary counsel by a painful process of evolution. The material strength which made sustained opposition possible was the indefeasible feudal right in the soil of the honours. The habit of opposition grew imperceptibly out of feudal ambitions and broadened until it was a general cause, and the right, in the last recourse, to oppose the crown with war was no more than the right of diffidation derived from the contractual element in homage. No doubt other systems of right and other ways of thinking might have thrown up habits and conventions of constitutional action not unlike those of the thirteenth-century baronage, but as a matter of history it is from the act of homage that these are in practice deduced. *Constitutional element in feudalism*

History, therefore, cannot afford to ignore the habit of thought bred in the private life of the honours, and, far more than the tenets of the schoolmen, with which it often conflicts, it is the governing thought behind political action. It will be centuries

The Honour of England from the introduction of tenure and homage before the leaders of English politics will entirely rid themselves of the notion that the *regnum Angliae* is no more than the greatest of the honours, and from this half-conscious prejudice come most of the extreme actions in the cause either of king or barons. The limits of the range of English medieval politics are the belief of the king and his servants that the crown is a tenure of the honour of England,[1] and its lands and profits his demesne, and, against this, the belief of the feudatories that, as barons of that same honour of the realm, they are the *communitas regni*, the repositories of its law, its natural judges, and coadjutors with the king in his task of government— counsellors in the *commune consilium regni*, and at need masters of the king. However unwilling the magnates may be to do the practical work of governing, they recur again and again in opposition to the simple type of the honour as their ideal of the state. Against the *curiales* of Henry I, against Longchamps, Henry III, and Edward II, the basis of baronial politics, even under the sophistication of the fourteenth century, is the return in one recasting or another to the unity of the feudal *curia*, to government by the king with and through his peers. The justiciars of the king should be his barons, his great officers, if not barons, at least such as they can trust and appointed in concert with them, his primary council the *curia* of his tenants in chief, the whole held steady, as in the Charters, by the recognition of a fundamental law, of which their tenure and franchise is a part. This was an ineffectual barrier to oppose to the inevitable pressure of the state towards subdivision of ministry, skilled officialdom, and impersonality of government—upon every occasion when a feudal party secured control it came to disaster—but, variously embodied according to the circumstances of the time, it was the governing concept of medieval opposition and the forerunner of constitutionalism in parliament.

ii

FEUDAL MONARCHY AND BUREAUCRACY, 1066–1189

One essential of the strength of William's kingdom, as of that of all the kings who came after him, was that it was territorial. That

[1] *Barones mei honoris*, Henry I. Ordinance of Shire and Hundred.

is to say, that he could address his writ to the presiding official of *The* any administration with the effect of binding the court and all the *Norman* persons who lived within that administration; that he could place *crown* all such persons under common amercement for default of administrative duty or false judgment. These rights of territorial kingship he owed partly to his predecessors from the year 900. One bond which held the realm together was still the English expedient of the peace[1] and the English oath of fidelity.[2] To this, feudalism added something which English kingship had not known, the jurisdiction inherent in feudal lordship, by which it was within the lord's right to hold court for all the pleas of land of his men—the men *i.e.* who held of him direct, his tenants in capite—and the complementary right to make justiciars to hold pleas, to maintain the authority of his courts, to compel attendance at them and to enforce their decrees. In this right the folkmoots of the shire and hundred became with a new meaning courts of his lordship;[3] sheriff and bailiff merged into his general justicial power as minores justiciarii regis. There was, perhaps, no conscious innovation. Cnut legislated mainly to confirm what his predecessors had devised. Most of the enactments bearing the Conqueror's name are conservative in intention.[4] His recorded "institutes"[5] secure that Normans shall enjoy their own custom of pleading when challenged by the English, and shall not be called upon to offer the difficult formulaic Saxon oaths.[6] The Ten Articles, which were compiled after 1100, and the Leis Willelme, which may be as early as 1090, are mostly excerpted from the law of Ælfred and from Cnut's second code, and what is new to us is yet small matter of English custom. In substance, William's intention was to grant the law of the Confessor to the English and to make the

[1] The Charter of Henry I makes the first explicit claim that the king sets the peace of the realm—*pacem firmam in toto regno meo pono*—but it is only a shade more categorical than Cnut's promise that he will "make full frith everywhere". Cnut, 1020. 3.

[2] William's Ten Articles, 1 and 2. Anglo-Saxon Chronicle, 1085E. "There came to him . . . all the landholding men of any worth over all England, whosesoever men they were . . . and swore him hold-oaths".

[3] *Concedo et precipio ut amodo comitatus mei et hundreta . . . sedeant sicut sederunt in tempore regis Eadwardi.* Henry I, Ordinance for his Shires and Hundreds.

[4] *Ut omnes habeant et teneant legem Eadwardi Regis in terris et in omnibus rebus*: William I, Latin Articles, 7. All men shall have and maintain the law of King Edward in lands and in all things.   [5] William. Lad.   [6] *Loc. cit.*

Normans immune from it only where it might bear upon them unfairly. Contemporaries were, indeed, hardly conscious that the régime had changed with the ruler,[1] and habitually confused the incidents of Norman custom with their nearest English analogies.[2] Yet the change was from a king holding a few pleas and folk-moots largely self-determining to a king holding a universal jurisdiction throughout his lordship, and, in the end, that would move many landmarks and open the way to a king's law.

The Norman curia

The Conqueror was elected by customary acclamation, and swore the traditional oath to the Church and the Law.[3] The crown-wearings continued at the three annual feasts,[4] and were held at Gloucester, Winchester, and Westminster. The Chronicler of Peterborough, writing in English, calls them *hyreds*,[5] households, and says that some of them at least were accompanied by a witena-gemot. Later chroniclers speak of them as *curiae* or *concilia*. They were, unlike their Saxon predecessors, meetings of tenants who had done homage to the king, but we cannot believe that this restricted William's practical right to summon whom he would, or gave any prerogative of attendance against his will. He could call the men who held immediately of him within his honour to counsel with him. The duty to attend was at times enforced by penalties.[6] The chronicler tells us that "all the great men of England, archbishops, bishops, abbots, earls, thegns, and knights", were with the king at his crown-wearings, so that, though it is probable that the baron, like the king's thegn before him, had a ministerial quality which gave him a place in the king's hall by custom,[7] and placed him under a special obligation in council and in war, at court, and in the provinces, the *curiae* were by no means confined to prelates, earls, and tenants *per baroniam*. Pleas were judged at these assemblies, as in the Confessor's reign, and deci-

---

[1] This is very noticeable in the references to the Norman *curiae* in the Anglo-Saxon Chronicle. So, Geoffrey Baynard's appeal of William of Eu for treason was tried in the witenagemot held at Salisbury immediately after Epiphany 1096. Odo of Champagne was also convicted there on the king's oath and suffered forfeiture. Anglo-Saxon Chronicle, 1096E.

[2] Cf. Leis Willelme, 20.   [3] Florence of Worcester, 1066.

[4] Anglo-Saxon Chronicle, 1086E.

[5] While Domesday calls Eadward's hyreds *curiae*.

[6] Anglo-Saxon Chronicle, 1095E. Robert Mowbray was put out of the king's peace for refusing to attend the Easter court.

[7] H. W. C. Davis, *Regesta Regum*, no. 60.

sions made on all questions too serious to pass as executive routine, but a comparison between the authority of the king and the magnates within the council would have little more meaning in Norman than in Saxon times, though the temper of the Conqueror and his sons was such as to dominate any constitution. If we believe—it is, of course, possible to do so—that the Anglo-Norman *curia*, almost exclusively Norman in blood, and bound to the king by feudal tenure, had little sense of English tradition, still the feudal *consilium* is the Teutonic moot passed through the tincture of feudalism. It retained the basic assumptions of the latter as to the nature of law and judgment.

It is still true of the *curia* as it was of the witenagemot, that the king cannot give a valid sentence without the *judicium sapientum*;[1] he calls for their judgment.[2] It is also true that their joint authority inspires every act of state. The term 'folkright' dies at the Conquest, but the *consuetudo Angliae* which takes its place is equally authoritative and all-sufficient as a body of principles for public and private action.[3] Reforms through administrative edicts—true legislation is in the future—are still thought of as the fuller expression of a law which is essentially immutable, and so, by extension, judgments, and as such are made by the king in and with the highest court of the realm: *communi concilio et consilio . . . omnium principum regni mei emendendas iudicavi.*[4] The revenues of the crown as well as of subjects, except in so far as they are gifts *ex mera gratia* from man to lord, are so stabilized by custom that they cannot well be modified without a judgment. The Treasury and the Exchequer are courts of fiscal causes from the beginning. Even war, as between the king and his overlord of France, is so conditioned by the overruling conventions of European feudal law as to seem a judgment of the

(marginal note: Law and judgment)

---

1 H. W. C. Davis, *Regesta Regum*, 118. An instance of 1175 shows how rigidly Henry II interpreted this limitation. The abbot of Battle brought to him a charter which had perished with time and asked for its renewal: *non hoc, inquit rex, nisi ex judicio curiae meae facturus sum*: I must not do this, said the king, without judgment of my court. M. M. Bigelow, *Placita Anglo-Normannica*, p. 221.

2 Loc. cit. *Inquit Ricardus de Luci . . . 'quoniam judicium nostrum . . . exigitis . . . [sic] adjudicamus':* since you have demanded judgment from us we pronounce judgment.

3 Cf. the suit for the Bigod inheritance. *Ibid.* 230 (1177). *Dominus rex . . . praecepit eis Lundonias venire, ut ibidem consilio comitum et baronum suorum eis secundum rectum et patriae consuetudinem satisfaceret.*

4 William I, Episcopal Laws, I.

curia of the English vassals—*judicium super eum ire*—and coercive action against a subject by the mere authority of the king—*ire super eum sine judicio*—is the act of a tyrant. It is true that the Norman reigns see a partial withdrawal of the magnates from the routine of justice, and the beginning of the transference of their function to professional judges of no tenurial standing, but there is no sign of this in the first generation of the Conquest, and—long after they have ceased to try the demesne pleas of the crown, and the pleas of parties other than those of their own order—the magnates habitually join in those acts of state, which it would be truer to the mind of the age to call judgments of state, but which are the rudiments of legislation. The king, then, must in theory act with his council, and, indeed, in so far as his outlook is that of feudalism at its best, he will wish to do so, and will think that his power is best served, and his dignity highest, when his whole honour is gathered about him in his great court of magnates.[1] There is, thus, much in the underlying truth of the Conquest régime to explain the English belief in the continuity of government and the legists' appraisement of Norman institutions in English terms.[2] Whether that sense of standing for the nation that the witan had held in the tenth century and the magnates were to regain in the thirteenth, was entirely replaced by the sense of individual standing and vassalage, no evidence remains fine enough to determine.

The Norman curia

We must not, then, look for rapid change in the administrative framework of the community. But the spirit in which institutions were worked was feudal, and, inspired by the Norman tenurial relation of lord and man, conformed to the Norman feudatories' conception of the kingdom as the greatest of feudal honours. In the course of a generation that will give the sheriffs a new jurisdiction. At first government was aristocratic rather than specialized or

---

[1] Counsel is an obligation upon the baron: *Letters of St. Thomas* (ed. Giles), no. 179. Becket to Henry: *eo quod dominus, debeo et offero vobis consilium meum.*

[2] It is curious to notice the strength of the English contingent at the Whitsun *hyred* of 1068. Of the witnesses of a grant to Wells (H. W. C. Davis, *Regesta Regum*, 23), six out of nine bishops, all four abbots, two out of five earls are English, and, among about twenty other notables, are some of the Confessor's greatest thegns, Ælfgeard Thorne, Bundi the Staller, Robert fitz Wimarc, Azor, Brixi, and Brihtric, with other lesser Englishmen.

official. There were baronial sheriffs and the barons were the mainstay of the king's capital *curia*. A professional council of justice was not of the Conqueror's reign. Only the king's *hyred* was permanent, for it was his household. The crown-wearings, though they were households, *curiae*, were baronial also, for under the paternalism of feudal crowns the magnates were *dominici barones regis*.[1] Already the whole *curia* did not withdraw when the councils dispersed, nor was William without baronial attendance in the intervals between the great festivals. There are few writs which are not witnessed by at least some of those who were nearest to him, Montgomery, Warenne, Clare, his brothers, or some of the bishops. There were curial officers who were barons, and so in constant attendance, the *dapifers*, William fitz Osbern, and later Eudes and Hamo, the constables who were heads of the knights, riding servants, huntsmen, and foresters, and their deputy, the marshal. But, beside them, were literate ministers, the chancellor, *cubicularii* or chamberlains, and the chaplains. There were thus already the elements of a curial government which were always about the king.

Within the household there were already signs of departmentalism. The chamber, as under the Confessor, ministered to the king's person, the chancellor, perhaps, already had his clerks and supervised the writs, the chapel had its staff of king's priests and chaplains. It is probable that any act of moment received the consideration of the familiar barons and the more dignified officials, the stewards or *dapifers* certainly, and perhaps the *pincernae*—butlers. The constables and the chancellor stood upon a lower plane, but their prestige was rising. The directive force of government was, however, still baronial rather than official. It was through such barons as were resident in the household, a small body of great men, with such ministers as could not be dispensed with, that the king habitually acted between the great councils. In this sense, though in this only, there was a "lesser *curia*". It was no defined body, its only essential member was the king, and it might vary from day to day. If in the Conqueror's day any one officer was required regularly to witness the king's precepts, it was the *dapifer*, as in the honours, and even his witness was not essential.

The lesser curia

[1] Hen. I, *Comitatus et Hundreda*, 3.

When William was in Normandy a similar group remained in control in England, and its principal members, often Lanfranc, Odo, or Geoffrey, acting alone, signified to the other barons the commands received from the king. No one claimed a sole title as Justiciar. They informed their peers what William required "of us his barons".[1] If the ideal of *curia* in its fullness was the great assembly of the vassals at the crown-wearing and its common expression in practice the counsel of a few of the greatest of them, there was no sense of contrast between the two. Both were thought of as *curia regis*, both were *rex cum consilio baronum*. In this the history of the *curia* is that of the witenagemot reset in terms of baronial tenure. Justice seems to have been little more centralized under the Conqueror than under the Confessor. It was the exception for it to be summoned out of the counties. If it was, it was to a court of barons. The title *justitiarius*, later confined to judges with special royal commissions, stood for the king's deputed jurisdiction over his feudatories as lord, but it was still unspecialized in application, and continued to be so until the reign of Stephen. The *justitiarii regis* were not yet a defined ministry, still less a special judicature. There was no chief justiciar. Pleas of the crown continued to come before the sheriffs, and, though occasional courts were held in the provinces by magnates under special commission, these also were not yet a settled institution.

The enfe-offment This is a confused and little-known reign. There is the skill to exploit the advantages of both the kingdom and the duchy, with the notion of the king's lordship running through all. The Conquest was carried through with confident empiricism. In the South and Midlands, where the Normans were secure, the grouping of the lordships upon the day that Eadward was quick and dead was allowed to determine the permanent lines of English landlordship. Upon the frontiers, where the Conquest still had enemies, the Norman palatine system was applied in its pure form. The lords of the five baronies which defend the Channel in Sussex are the palatines of the southern border of Normandy, Eu, Mor-

---

[1] Lanfranc to Earl Roger: *Dominus noster . . . salutat vos et nos omnes sicut fideles suos . . . et mandat ut quantum possumus curam habeamus de castellis suis*: our lord greets you and us his faithful men . . . and bids us take as good care of his castles as we may.

tain, Warenne, Braiose, and Montgomery. The great earldoms were not done away with, but left to stand the test of time, though one may doubt whether Eadwine and Morcar, half guests, half hostages, would have been allowed to resume their full power. The earldom of the East Angles was retained for Ralf Guader, and William persisted in keeping that of Northumbria intact until two English earls had failed him and Commines had been murdered with all his knights. The enfeoffment was like the settlement of an army upon the land. Whatever the relation of the Norman successor to the land and its folk, to the king he remained a unit of the feudal host, and his tenure in peace was allotted him as an earnest of future service in war. The units of the host lay upon the land in the tens and multiples and fractions of tens with which it was organized for the field, a full constabulary of ten knights from the barony of moderate size, from many fewer, from a handful of great men, more. The extent of land held had only the very roughest relation to the *servitium debitum*,[1] for it was the result of no assessment, and was to all appearances made in the first years of the Conquest before the land was fully conquered or the Domesday survey thought of.[2] Some estimate of the standing of the recipient in the host was, perhaps, the determining factor of his obligation, and some rough approximation in office or rank to that of a Saxon antecessor the sole considerations in the choice made of his fees.

The county and hundredal systems were treated in the same *Administration* spirit. Inevitably, they remained the mainstay of law and order, but, since a completely English officialdom was impossible,[3] and the Conquest could provide no sufficient body of *ministeriales*, the barons were sheriffs in the counties of their chief power, and some retained the shrievalty in their own hands throughout their lives, and even handed it to the second generation, or nominated dependants. Both these expedients, the palatinate and the baronial shrievalty, were dangerous. During William's reign or soon after it, much of his work had to be undone: the palatines rebelled one by one and their honours were destroyed, and under Henry I a

---

[1] Thus, the abbot of Abingdon owed sixty knights, the abbot of Ramsey four.

[2] Cf. J. H. Round, *Feudal England*.

[3] Many Englishmen were retained as sheriffs.

shrievalty of royal ministers replaced the barons. They were, no doubt, necessary during the phase of consolidation, and in that phase least dangerous. As long as Gospatric and the Confessor's kindred troubled Northumbrian loyalty from their lodgment among the Scots, an English rising might be feared, and the Normans served themselves best by obedience to the king. Nevertheless, the greatness of the Conqueror was not that of the legislator or of the founder of new systems of state, but a greatness of character so strong and equable as to approach genius. So formidable was his will that he could afford to rule by deputy, to declare his English kingship and assume that he would be obeyed as English kings had been, granting great latitude of tenurial and administrative power to a handful of feudatories, requiring that they should exercise it in his interest and not their own. "Among the rest there must not be forgotten the good peace he made in this land. He was a stern man and terrible, so that none dared to thwart his will. Earls who went against him he put in fetters, and bishops he deposed from their bishoprics, and abbots from their abbacies, and at the last he spared not his own brother." [1]

The Norman crown   Yet, though its founder was no innovator, the future of the Norman crown was to lie along new lines. The native English kings had summoned the goodwill of the nation to make peace and order an institution. This was no longer enough, for the coming of feudalism set loose forces which would gather will and direction of their own if they were confronted by nothing more lasting than the common will to peace. That had been born of the reaction from the miseries of the Danish wars, and rested on sworn coöperation and the leadership of a succession of great kings, whose personal landed estate would hardly have sufficed to maintain the throne in a feudal age. Such landed power the new royal house was better suited to supply. It is not fanciful to see in the half-feudal dynasty of the Norman kings an intensified interest in what may be called the demesne concerns of the crown. The *cyneryhta*, the *jura regalia*, had been developed by the Saxon kings to place part of the law under the direct protection of the monarch

[1] Anglo-Saxon Chronicle, 1086E.

in a special way, as part of his equipment for the maintenance of law and order. Feudalism associated power, office, and material wealth from the crown downwards, in the comprehensive notion of *dominium*. And the outcome of that was jurisdiction. Both as wealth and power, the crown of England was honorial and its lands and rights were demesne of the king. As late as 1264 the gravamen against Henry III was that he treated the realm as the same unfettered demesne as an earl's honour. Thus, while the Ælfredian kings expended their energy upon the strengthening of provincial life, the hundred, the peace, and the new punitive element in the law, and achieved substantial success, the Norman kings, enjoying *dominium*, turned inwards to the resources of the crown itself. The springs of Norman monarchy are jurisdiction and the *terra regis*. Its genius goes to the fostering of this permanent fund of wealth, and of the trade in justice which had no visible limits if it were pressed actively and efficiently. To further this there came into being a domestic bureaucracy which, without at once departing radically from the traditional routine of government, so minuted, exacted, and augmented the *jura regalia* that they became the object of a new art of government and of a yet closer relation of the crown to the community.

The Conqueror set himself from the beginning to increase the *The fisc* revenue and estates of the crown. After the Conquest he kept as *terra regis* lands which brought in roughly double the revenue of the Confessor, some £11,000 yearly, as against the £30,000 of rents which were allotted to the hundred and seventy baronies.[1] He used the old machinery of exaction and account. Beyond a possible increase in their number, the record of the chamberlains' holdings in Domesday[2] suggests no difference in the composition of the chamber and treasure; the Chronicle for 1087 gives us our first clear mention of a treasure-house at Winchester, but it is doubtful evidence for the date; the Survey reflects no radical change in the fiscal system such as any break in the routine of the chamber might cause. The only visible alteration in policy, made

[1] W. J. Corbett, *Cambridge Medieval History*, v. 507.
[2] Humfrid and Alberic, chamberlains of William, succeeded Aluric, a chamberlain of Eadward in his lands. Domesday Book, i. 49A, 49B, 151A. The mention of Henry the Treasurer may stand for the regular association of one of the chamberlains with the treasure. Whether this dates from Eadward's reign we do not know.

in a number of districts, but quite without system,[1] is the insistence on blanched money—coin assayed by melting and refining—or payment *ad pondus*, by weighing a sample of coin against a fixed standard, as against the cruder payment *ad numerum*, which was the commoner practice under the Confessor, though the more accurate processes were known and practised, especially upon Eadward's demesne. This may reflect a more businesslike policy in the chamber—payment *ad pondus* might add 30 per cent to the value of the farm[2]—but it is so local and unsystematic[3] that it is more likely to be the result of intelligent exploitation by the sheriffs. The heavy increases in the nominal rates of the farms, equally unsystematic,[4] are also, in all likelihood, due to shrieval initiative. The Chronicle puts the blame for the racking of the royal estates upon the king,[5] but there is little sign of any attempt to devise a common policy for the realm, or to attack the inconsistencies in the management of the king's estates. Conservatism, a very free hand for local authorities, and sporadic severity of exactions, seem to have taken the place of policy in William's exploitation of his demesne.

The Chamber and the treasure

The Chamber must have continued, as under the Confessor, to be the authority by which the king's cash was carried with him and spent. It remained intimately domestic, but, though there is only a single indication of this in the Pipe Roll of Henry I, it retained

[1] This occurs in Surrey, Wiltshire, probably Hampshire, Buckinghamshire, Cambridgeshire, Northamptonshire, and Sussex. In Oxfordshire and Huntingdonshire payment was still *ad numerum* in 1086. Parts of the west, especially Herefordshire and Devon, already payed in blanched money T.R.E.

[2] Domesday Book, i. 16A. For the technical reasons leading to this change see *Dialogus de Scaccario*, i. 7, though the change is wrongly attributed to Henry I.

[3] The chaos which existed in the fiscal scheme of a great royal manor may be seen at Dartford. T.R.E. its farm value was £60. The French reeve who farmed it in 1086 said that it was really worth £90. The English jurors said that it ought still to be at £60. The actual farmer in fact paid £82 : 13 : 2 in coin assayed by three different methods. Domesday Book, i. 12B.

[4] The royal manors of Leicestershire had their farms roughly doubled between 1066 and 1086, while those of Cambridgeshire were left at the old amounts but were put under the stricter form of assay. At Havering in Essex the value T.R.E. was £40, but the sheriff was taking £90 in 1086. *Ibid.* ii. 3A.

[5] "The king farmed his land as dearly as he might. If a second came and bid more, and a third, he let him who bid most have it, and cared nothing with what sin the reeves must exact it of poor men." (Anglo-Saxon Chronicle, 1086E.) The large sums paid by farmers *de gersuma*, *i.e.* as premiums, were, no doubt, an additional burden on the land.

enough of its fiscal habit to be expanded into a household exchequer by Henry II, receiving many payments directly, and
making payments for wages and expenses. The treasure, which at
some period of the eleventh century had come to lie at Winchester,
began to attract the regular attendance of one or more of the
officers of the Chamber, and slowly to gain an identity of its own.
In Rufus' reign, and again in that of Henry I, an occasional turn of
phrase speaks of one or other of the chamberlains as *cubicularius et
thesaurarius*. One Herbert is the bearer of this double charge under
Rufus and Henry I, and under Henry Geoffrey de Clinton gives
himself the same ambiguous title, now *camerarius* and now *thesaurarius*. In 1129-30 he accounts *pro ministerio thesauri Wintonie*.[1]
Still, however, the fiscal arrangements seem to be completely
fluid. For a term previous to Clinton's, William Pont de l'Arche
accounts to the commission of audit of the treasure,[2] his office
being a *ministerium camere curie*.[3] The treasure is a material fact. It
has a normal location at Winchester, some form of account has to
be made there, and it comes to require the constant service of
a minister, and his ministry may lead to his being spoken of
currently as *thesaurarius*. Courts may be held there for the settlement of fiscal causes. But seventy years after the Conquest there is
no exclusive or permanent office of treasurer, and the qualification
for custody of the treasure is still office in the king's Chamber.[4]
Nor can we feel certain that the custodian at any given time was
immune from intervention, coöperation, or supersession by one
or other of his fellow chamberlains of the *camera*. For the first
recognition of a treasurer as equal with and distinct from the
Magister Camerarius we must wait until after the reign of Henry I,[5]
and, in its purely domestic nature as a phase of the ministry of the
king's private chamber, held by lay, and therefore illiterate, servants, the Treasury of the Norman kings has its affinities with the
past rather than with the future.

[1] Pipe Roll, 31 Henry I, p. 105: *Idem Gaufridus reddit compotum de ccc et x marcis
argenti pro ministerio thesauri Wintonie*: the same Geoffrey renders account for
three hundred and ten marks of silver for the ministry of the Winchester
treasure. It is possible that he was acting as subordinate to Robert Mauduit.
Ibid. p. 37.   [2] *Ibid.* p. 130.
[3] He had apparently bought it with the heiress of Robert Mauduit. *Ibid.* p. 37.
[4] *Chronicon Monasterii de Abingdon*, ii. 116. Herbert, sitting *in curia apud
Wintoniam in thesauro*, is entitled *Herbertus Camerarius*.
[5] *Red Book of the Exchequer*, pp. 807 *et seq.*

The
Exchequer

Upon this small and comparatively unspecialized staff of clerks was imposed a task which increased in elaboration as time went on. But, though the rule of progress was uncalculated, almost automatic, evolution, the twelfth century was already making a beginning of science in law and government. At some time near its outset conscious planning of a new kind seems to have been brought to bear upon the working of the king's fisc, and to have added to the Treasury an entirely new office of receipt and account, the Exchequer. For the period of its institution we are dependent upon charters to which dates can only be affixed within wide terms of years. In these the term *scaccarium* itself [1] appears in some year not later than 1118, the *curia* is found in the Exchequer in a charter from between 1108 and 1127, and in others from between 1110 and 1127 Henry speaks of record *in rotulis meis,* and in all probability refers by this to the Great Roll of the Pipe, or central record of the Exchequer.[2] From the fiscal year 1129–30 a complete roll of the Exchequer survives. The general character of the Exchequer is that of a commission of receipt of revenue, and of audit of accounts, which is also a court in which disputes arising during the audit may be settled. In the reign of Henry II it meets at Westminster, and summonses the sheriffs of every shire, together with many others who have separate charges, to present their revenue account for the year, together with that of all arrears and of any deductions to which they may be entitled on the ground of expenses, previous payments, or diminution of profits due to exemptions granted by the king. That such an account had been made for some generations, more lately in the Treasury, before whatever session of chamberlains or *cubicularii* and magnates were deputed to receive it, is a conclusion we can hardly avoid. What is new in the Exchequer, and stamps it as one of the achievements of an inventive age, is its centralizing of various branches of fiscal administration, the completeness of its arrangements to secure adequate knowledge and authority for its action, and its new method of calculating its accounts.

The staffing of the Exchequer points to its being a composite

[1] T. F. Tout, *Chapters in Administrative History,* i. 93.
[2] A custumal of Ringwood of 39 Edw. III (Public Record Office. Rentals and Surveys. General Series. Portfolio 14, 54) professes to quote from *pipa Domini Regis apud Westmonasterium . . . in anno viij⁰ regis Henrici Primi,* i.e. 1107–8. A charter printed in D. C. Douglas, *Feudal Documents from the Abbey of Bury St. Edmunds,* p. 67, suggests that there was no exchequer in 1104–6.

body put together *ad hoc* from the personnel of the Treasury, the *The Exchequer centralizes the accounts of all branches of the curia* Chamber, and the wider circle of the *curia*. Each of these sets of officers brought its particular aptitude and authority to the audit. The treasurer, as soon as one existed, with two chamberlains who shared his acts and responsibility, received only the sheriff's *compotus* of the *firma comitatus*, that is, the revenue which we must believe to have been accounted for in earlier times to the Treasury. He, or rather his scribe, wrote this, with all other items, upon the principal roll of the Exchequer, which, from its shape, was called the Roll of the Pipe. For all items, except the record of the sums actually paid *in thesauro*,[1] his roll was subject to the correction of the chancellor. For payments *in thesauro*, that is, for the coin of which his office of the treasury was the storehouse, his authority was absolute. This division in the authority of the roll points again to the composite origin of the Exchequer, and to the historical evolution of the work of the Treasury officials *ad scaccarium* from their function in the Winchester Treasury. The officialdom of the *curia*, with the chancellor and his clerk, seems to have been superimposed upon this Treasury machinery in part as a check—the chancellor's clerk checks and copies the roll of the treasurer—in part for its special function of drafting, for the chancellor has charge of all writs issued from the Exchequer. But it also has its separate field of knowledge arising from the chancellor's custody of escheats.[2] All outstanding revenue owed by the sheriff in arrears of his farm is noted and exacted from him by the chancellor's clerk.[3] The chancellor, in fact, is the accounting officer for all the king's casual revenue, as being in a general sense his secretary, while the treasurer accounts for the ancient crown revenue of the *firma comitatus*. Similarly, the constable, who in the household was charged with the supervision of the king's domestic ministers, especially those of the military household and the officials of the hunt and the forests, attends, or sends his deputy to the Exchequer,

---

1 *Dialogus de Scaccario*, I. v. E: *De omni scriptura rotuli cancellarius eque tenetur ut thesaurarius, excepto dumtaxat de hoc quod scribitur "in thesauro receptum"*: the chancellor is equally accountable with the treasurer for the writing of the whole roll, except for what is entered as "received into the Treasury". It was thought by some that the treasurer was only responsible for that part of the roll which recorded payments *in thesauro*. *Ibid.* I. iii. B.

2 That is, estates falling in to the crown by failure of heirs, etc.

3 *Dialogus de Scaccario*, I. vi. C.

in general to confirm the witness of the chancellor to all transactions, but in particular to compute and pay the liveries of officials
of his own ministry.[1] His representation of the *curia* is further
emphasized by the fact that his clerk brings with him the record
of all writs issued in the course of his function and presents them
in the Exchequer.[2] Having regard, therefore, to the diverse
elements of administration which compose the Exchequer, it
would be fair to assume that one of the chief motives for its creation was the desire to centralize and bring under a common
authority the various offices which had been growing haphazard
and without decisive common control.[3] Such a scheme would
have suggested itself above all to that masterful and ubiquitous
man of King Henry's affairs, Roger of Salisbury, who impressed
the next generation as having been, what in fact he was not,
justiciar, chancellor, and treasurer at once. The constable with his
domestic pay-roll, the chancellor with his irregular revenue from
amercements, escheats, and so forth, the Treasury with its old-
established hold upon the *firma comitatus*, are brought to a common
place and system of audit, and their accounts digested upon a
common roll. The foundation of the Exchequer was, in fact, the
essential preliminary to a consolidated royal revenue, and to a
national control of expense.

Exchequer court   No Norman system of audit is possible without a court, still
less the vast audit of England. In every rent and due, in every
individual's obligations, in every reeve's powers, there lurks the
potentiality of dispute. Where no two manors' customs are
identical, where shires are fields of divergent law, there must be
an arbitrating authority between the subject who pays and the
official who exacts.[4] The Exchequer, therefore, is a court, and
perhaps it is in this form that it would must readily present itself
to contemporaries—*Curia Regis ad scaccarium*.[5] Of that court all

---

[1] *Dialogus de Scaccario*, I. v. F.: *Stipendarii regis . . . sive sint residentes in castris regis sive non.*   [2] *Ibid.* I. vi. D.

[3] To secure such control magnates were detached from the *curia* to the Exchequer, and the *Dialogus* dwells upon the inferior status of the Treasury officials to that of the non-official element.

[4] *Ibid.* I. iv. C.

[5] M. M. Bigelow, *Placita Anglo-Normannica*, p. 174. At the beginning of Henry II's reign the abbot of Battle had to complain that the sheriff had received certain dues from his land unjustly, *quo cognito, abbas unum ex monachis suis cum cartis . . . libertatum suarum ad scaccarium transmisit . . . Monachus vero eo perveniens coram*

the primary officers were deemed members, and, presumably, could act through their deputies. But the crown explicitly recognized the judicial nature of the audit by adding from time to time magnates who had no *ex officio* standing in the Exchequer, but who had knowledge of special value, or prestige.[1] The treasurer and chamberlains, at least, were too near their petty ministerial origin to be freed from curial supervision.[2] The king himself sat there at times, either to intervene in a plea of special moment, or to dispatch some cause in the convenient surroundings of the fisc with its records and special experience. Well into the thirteenth century he might entertain a cause in his council and upon its revealing financial implications remove himself, the cause and the counsellors into the Exchequer, and there conclude it. More normally he will detach barons to act for him, but king or baron there must be if the authority of *curia regis* is to inhere in any commission of the early feudal age. Magnates who are commissioned to the Exchequer are the future Barons of the Exchequer, for that function hardens into a defined legal office of the crown.[3] At the time of which we are writing, they must have been a variable body, barons in the Exchequer, but in no permanent sense of it.[4] By the reign of Henry II the justiciar comes to sit there, and certain persons other than the Exchequer's permanent officers are present at every session, the bishop of Winchester, and Master Thomas Brown, lately head of the Sicilian *dogana*, but now in

Roberto comite Legacestriae et Ricardo de Luci . . . et coram aliis baronibus scaccarii . . . restitutionem ablatorum expetit: when this was found out the abbot sent one of his monks to the Exchequer with the charters of his liberties. The monk presented himself before Robert, earl of Leicester and Richard de Luci and the other barons of the Exchequer, and demanded restitution. The court had the money restored, the tallies broken, and the record expunged from the roll *"unanimi judicio"*. *Ibid.* p. 235. The Justiciar pronounces the judgment of the Exchequer on the liberties of Abingdon.

1 *Dialogus de Scaccario*, I. iv. B: *Quidam ex officio, quidam ex sola iussione principis resident.*

2 The Discipulus asks, *numquid a thesauraris compotus suscipitur cum illic multo sint qui ratione potestatis maioris videantur?*: why should the Treasurer receive the account when there are many others of higher station there?

3 The earliest official use of the title seems to occur in a writ of *Nigellus Eliensis episcopus et baro de Scaccario* (*circa* 1156). M. M. Bigelow, *Placita Anglo-Normannica*, p. 188. The distinction between the executive origin of the treasurer and chamberlains and that of the barons of the Exchequer in audit and judgment, is presented in the practice of directing writs of *liberate* to the former, writs of *computate* and *perdono* to the latter. *Dialogus de Scaccario*, I. vi. A.

4 *Barones esse dicimus eo quod suis locis barones sedere solebant. Fleta*, ii. 26.

exile and in English service. He keeps a roll "of the king's secrets", which may have been the origin of the roll of the King's Remembrancer.

System of account In this accumulation of authority, and even more in the expert system of account, the Norman age has found something new in government. The processes in the Lower Exchequer of receipt, of which we have said nothing, weighing, counting, blanching, storing, and issue on *liberate*, may not have been greatly in advance of Old English usage. The Upper Exchequer, that Exchequer of account which we have been describing, has at the centre of its practice a method of computation and of displaying its results vividly, which is so new and so characteristic of the early twelfth century that it has been thought to be the discovery which itself inspired the creation of the Exchequer. It is, in fact, that from which the Exchequer takes its name. The *scaccarium* is the squared cloth, divided into columns for tens of thousands, thousands, hundreds of pounds, pounds, shillings, and pence, upon which counters were placed to demonstrate to the illiterate sheriff the sum of his account, and to compute it after the manner of the abacus. By this "game of the abacus" a more ready reckoning than in the past was possible, and the Pipe Roll upon which it was entered opened a new conspectus of provincial life to the crown, which was for the first time provided with the guidance of statistics. Authority, knowledge, the growth of ordered routine, all in some measure achieved within the Norman reigns by the concentration of the divergent ministerial functions within it, combine to make the Exchequer the pivot of the Norman and still more of the Angevin state. It marks, indeed, an epoch in the art of government.

The king and justice The function of the Saxon king was not a jurisdiction; rather, he ordered the defaulting moot to act. He had no inherent right, in the feudal term, justiciare, and the moots, as a whole, enforced their own authority, kept their own order, carried out their own distraints and arrests,[1] had their own oferhiernes.[2] None of the Saxon cyneryhta were abandoned by the Conqueror, but with time they gradually lost their force; the power of the Norman

[1] II Æthelstan, 20, 1 and 4. II Cnut, 10, 25, and 25a.
[2] II Cnut, 15, 2.

kings in law flowed mainly from a concept of jurisdiction as inherent in all lordship which they inherited from the Frankish West. This jurisdiction was an outcome of dominium. In Maitland's words,[1] "jurisdiction is a proprietary right, intertwined with the laws of property and of personal status, implicated with the land law", and such a function the Saxon kings, in their world of folkright and alod, could scarcely achieve. The right of jurisdiction implies the right to appoint justiciars, and we are soon aware of the spread of the king's justiciarate across the legal maze of Anglo-Norman England. The network of authority, *justiciandi, jus faciendi* comes to be unbroken, from the justiciarships of the king's great *familiares* to the sheriffs,[2] the bailiffs of the hundreds.[3] Jurisdiction, jurisdiction of lordship, jurisdiction of kingship, is a part of Norman landright, running *ex conquesta Angliae*. It makes valid all the bailiffrics of England.[4] Through it the Norman and Angevin sheriffs exercise their dual function of holding pleas and making distraints.[5] The Anglo-Norman law-books are slow to find terms for this. Even Glanvill has not the word "jurisdictio", and the early legists exhaust themselves in such synonyms as "jus", "censura", "districtio", "observancia", to supply its place. Most of all they use that overworked word "justitia", with a dozen slants and nuances, to mean the moral quality of justice, the power of justice, an occasion of judgment, an act of judgment, and the persons who apply it.

A wrong turn may therefore be given to the legal history of this period by a false kind of emphasis upon such trials as that at Penenden and its like. The Conqueror has justitia, jurisdiction, but it is his successors who find a permanent embodiment for it in persons and offices. Geoffrey of Coutances, and those who acted upon similar occasions, had no permanent title and office of justiciar. Those who are known to have been left in charge of the realm when William was in Normandy, had no title of chief

---

[1] Pollock and Maitland, *History of English Law*, i. 527.

[2] Leges Henrici Primi, 29. 1b.

[3] *Loc. cit.*

[4] *Justiciarius dicitur ballivus patrie qui, institutus a principe vel duce, justiciandi et jus faciendi subjecto sibi populo obtinet potestatem. Summa di Legibus Normannie*, iv.

[5] Glanvill, *De Legibus*, xii. 9.

justiciar.[1] The notion of a developed justiciarship introduced by the Conqueror has also led to the belief that the eyres were borrowed directly from the *missi* of the Emperor. No such anticipation of the Angevin justiciarship seems to be warranted by the evidence, and, indeed, the *Constitutio Domus Regis* of Stephen's reign has still no place for Magnus Justiciarius. In the Conqueror's reign, and for long after it, *justicia, justiciarius*, was a universal term for those who presided at any court, if only for a single great plea—*quibus mei imposuit hanc justitiam*. The sheriff,[2] the bailiff or doomsmen of a hundred,[3] honour,[4] borough,[5] or manor,[6] all, as summoning and directing the courts in which they sat, were *justiciarii*. The writ which initiated the trial at Penenden[7] went out, naturally, to Lanfranc, Geoffrey, Roger, count of Eu, Richard fitz Gilbert, Hugh de Montfort, and all the *proceres regni Angliae*—*quibus hanc justitiam imposui*—and, though when the day came it was Geoffrey who was *in loco regis*, he was doing no more than his fellow barons had it in their quality to do by royal precept. All, if not *justiciarii*, were judges, since *regis judices sint barones comitatus*,[8] and between the *multi barones coram quibus* Odo and the abbot of Evesham sued each other in 1077,[9] between Lanfranc, Geoffrey, and Count Robert trying the liberties of Ely *ex precepto regis*, and Lanfranc, Eudo Dapifer, William des Arches, and Ralf de Curbespine trying the right of Saint Augustine in Newington as part of their routine as *barones comitatus*, there can have been little difference—to be

[1] H. W. C. Davis, *Regesta Regum*, 78-83. The editor describes certain of these as being by "Lanfranc (as Justiciar of England)", but no reason can be assigned for his doing so.

[2] *Cartularium Monasterii de Rameseia*, i. 149; *Chronicon Monasterii de Abingdon*, ii. 43; H. W. C. Davis, *Regesta Regum*, 59; M. M. Bigelow, *Placita Anglo-Normannica*, p. 165.

[3] *Chronicon Monasterii de Abingdon*, ii. 118. *Justiciarii hundredi*.

[4] Howden, i. 225. Becket is made to speak of *justitiarii curiae meae*.

[5] M. M. Bigelow, *Placita Anglo-Normannica*, p. 165. *Justiciariis et ministris de Rouecestra*.

[6] F. W. Stenton, *English Feudalism*, p. 67. Waleran de Meulan addresses his "justices of Sturminster".

[7] M. M. Bigelow, *Placita Anglo-Normannica*, p. 4.

[8] *Leges Henrici Primi*, 29.

[9] M. M. Bigelow, p. 20. William's letters seem to assume that Lanfranc, Robert of Eu, Haimo the sheriff, Haimo Dapifer or Richard fitz Gilbert will normally be directing justice in the county of Kent—at least such cases as affect

precise, the difference of the reception or not of a writ *ad hoc*. Normally, the king moves the *proceres* to hold his pleas by writ. He does not yet create fixed jurisdictions or judicial offices.

It is true that the practice of commissioning one or more barons to try a single plea *ex precepto regis, loco regis*, was, as far as records go, common in the first two Norman reigns and also that the commission was likeliest to fall upon one of a few men, Lanfranc, Odo, Geoffrey, Robert of Mortain, Hugh de Montfort, Richard fitz Gilbert, being those most commonly chosen. But this seems not to have conferred upon them in their day that permanent title of justiciar which was attached to these magnates by Heming, Orderic, Malmsbury, and other later writers. The first officials whose title to be justiciar and little else the eleventh century would have recognized are found not in the circle of the baronage but in the shire and in the king's *curia*, for, from Rufus' reign, the sheriff had usually[1] been stripped of all but the pettiest pleas of the crown, and had beside him a *justicia comitatus*,[2] whose office was a normal part of shire administration until the accession of Henry II. Passelewe was one of these justices—for Norfolk—about the year 1100, Henry I granted the Londoners the right to choose their own resident justice and keeper of king's pleas, while Stephen and the Empress competed to buy the loyalty of Mandeville or Miles of Gloucester with the justiciarships of their counties in fee.

At the same time as these professional but stationary justices of the county came into being, the earliest itinerant commissions were going out. If we can believe our authority,[3] Devon and Cornwall were thus visited in 1096 by the bishop of Winchester, the king's chaplain, William Capra, and Hardin fitz Belnold *ad investiganda regalia placita*. It will be noticed that the types of royal justice by commission were multiplying, the precept to one or more barons to try a single plea or group of pleas urged by one

Meaning of justiciar

the royal demesne—even while the king is in England. This is much like the function of the Saxon shire-thegn.

[1] Not always, for the reversal to trial of pleas of the crown by the sheriff was still a recognized abuse in 1215.

[2] The two offices were at times reunited in one man, *e.g.* Hugh de Buckland *Berchescire vicecomes, et publicarum justiciarius compellationum*: *Chronicon Monasterii de Abingdon*, ii. 43 (1087-1100).

[3] M. M. Bigelow, *Placita Anglo-Normannica*, 69.

plaintiff, the itinerant commission to investigate all outstanding pleas of one type—as, for instance, pleas of the crown—or the resident justiciar. With this went an equal variety of venue, though the court summoned is usually one of the customary jurisdictions of the past, the shire-court, the moot of several shires, or, on occasion, the entry of a king's delegate into the court of an honour at the request of the immunist.[1] Slight as the evidence is, it seems that the reign of Rufus began a definite change in the king's exercise of these various forms of judicial initiative, which was being gradually withdrawn from the baronage into the household of the king. The commission of 1096 was made by a bishop and a king's chaplain, and the only recorded commission on a private plea, that between Pagan Peverel and the abbot of Ramsey,[2] was held by "H. Camerarius", almost certainly Herbert the Chamberlain. It is therefore possible to accept the somewhat late authority of the Peterborough Chronicle that Ralf Flambard "was the driving force of all the king's moots throughout England",[3] and to divine a little of what nature these moots were.

Both the developments which we have been considering, the shire justiciars and the occasional commissions, have elements of the later itinerant justice, though neither possesses them all. The shire justices are professional in habit—some are drawn from the shrievalty and the exchequer[4]—they try the whole range of the royal pleas, but they are resident, not itinerant. In the reign of Henry I an occasional commission seems to have been issued which combined the qualities of the two types of justice, and which was near to, though not identical with, the itinerant justice of his grandson. Their nature is revealed only by the single instance in the Pipe Roll of 31 Henry I, the session of Geoffrey de Clinton and his colleagues which was known as the Pleas of Blythe. This superseded the justiciars of the counties for the nonce, for it dealt with at least three shires, Derby and Nottingham, and Yorkshire, possibly including Westmorland and the extreme North as outliers of the Yorkshire sheriffdom;[5] it evidently dealt with the

1 Cartularium Monasterii de Rameseia, i. 239.   2 Ibid. loc. cit.
3 Ealle his gemot ofer eall Engleland draf: Anglo-Saxon Chronicle, 1099E.
4 Chronicon Monasterii de Abingdon, ii. 43.
5 E.g. from Notts-Derby, placitum de quo implacitatus fuit apud Blidam. Pipe Roll, 31 Hen. I, p. 10. Yorkshire-Northumberland, de xxxv marcis argenti de placitis de Blida. Ibid., p. 25.

general pleas of the country, for the profits were substantial, but it was not itinerant through the counties like the later eyres. Geoffrey settled himself at the royal manor of Blythe and there summoned the North to him, nor did he summon the counties by hundreds and vills as did Henry II's justices, but had before him the shire courts in their ancient constitutions.[1] The session was therefore judicial and not, as it came to be later, largely inquisitional. Of such a kind, transitional from the new to the old, may have been that "strong moot" which Ralf Basset held at Hundehoge in 1124 and "hanged there in a little while four and forty men",[2] and Clinton himself had been trying pleas in the South-Eastern counties, and, apparently upon two occasions in the Middle West.

It is noteworthy that the chronicler, now almost contemporary, calls the Hundehoge pleas a witenagemot.[3] In this, an English writer sees the present in the light of the past. For him, the ancient English judgment, the witenagemot, even one summoned by the king's writ, obscures the royal jurisdiction by which it is called. Thus seen, such courts descend from the witan who decided the rights of Rochester under Æthelred and William. More truly, in trying, as they apparently do, not a single plea or a group of pleas, but all the royal pleas of the shires summoned, they are in the line of the *justiciarii comitatus*. At much the same time as the pleas of Clinton, Walter l'Espec and Eustace fitz John, both Northumbrian barons, were moving about Yorkshire, Northumberland, and Westmorland, and the vacant bishopric of Durham, apparently conducting an enquiry into the state of the king's lands, seeing to the refortification of castles, and the restocking of the king's manors,[4] but also holding pleas. No more than the pleas of Blyth can these be taken as identical with the later eyre justice, but they have with it the similarity that they combine the care of the *terra regis* with justice, and so have something of the eyre's omnicompetence. To become the itinerant commissions of Henry II they need to combine these jurisdictions and to take the further step of carrying their court through the several counties of their

[1] The *judicatores comitatus*, Pipe Roll, 29-30 Hen. I, p. 27.

[2] Anglo-Saxon Chronicle, 1124E.

[3] *Ibid. Thaes ilces geares . . . held Raulf Basset and thes kinges thaeines gewitenamot.*

[4] *In restauratione maneriorum Regis per Walterum Espec et Eustacium filium Johannis:* Pipe Roll, 31 Hen. I, pp. 24, 33.

commission, instead of summoning the shires to them as did the pleas of Blyth.

The chief justiciar No chief justiciar, *secundus a rege* and head of the judicial body *ex officio*, had arisen in Henry I's reign out of this variety of commissions. It is, however, likely that a specialized group was beginning to detach itself from the multitude of officials who did justice, resident or itinerant, up and down England, and that, in distinction from those who did justice in a shire or a hundred, they were coming to be called *justitiarii regis totius Angliae, capitales justitiarii*, justices of the king's capital *curia*, whose commission is valid throughout the realm.[1] No more than this is, perhaps, meant in a writ of Henry I promising Holy Trinity, Aldgate, that its men shall not plead *nisi coram me vel capitali justitiarii meo*.[2] The justice the canons were most likely to fear was that of the sheriff or justiciar of London; Henry puts them under his capital judiciary. It is, again, likely that within the group of the *capitales justiciarii* the preëminence of one or more outstanding personalities was recognized, together with the king's especial reliance upon his initiative. Ranulf Flambard, the Chronicler says, was the driving force of Rufus' "moots throughout England".[3] Only such a gradual narrowing of the authority and title of *capitalis justitiarius* upon first a few and then a single justiciar will explain the confidence with which the historians of the middle twelfth century attribute preëminence to Roger of Salisbury[4] at a time when at least Richard[5] and Ralf[6] Basset were also *capitales justiciarii*, and when Henry while in Normandy was ordering "his justiciars" to defer to Anselm.[7] All agree that Roger was the virtual head of the kingdom, yet neither chronicler nor record can give us the technical formula of writ or commission which would convince us that his authority was one of recognized sole Justiciar of England. In the one writ preserved

---

[1] So of Ralf Basset, *Chronicon Monasterii de Abingdon*, ii. 170, *in omni Angliae regno justitiae habens dignitatem*. Thus in Glanvill we have *capitales barones regis* for barons holding immediately of the king (*Tractatus de Legibus*, ix. 6), and *capitalis curia regis* for the court *de banco* or *coram rege* as opposed to the eyre (*ibid.* ix. 11).

[2] Rymer, *Foedera*, i. 12.   [3] Anglo-Saxon Chronicle, 1099E.

[4] William of Malmsbury, *Historia Novella* II. Epistolae Herberti Losingae, p. 51.

[5] Henry of Huntingdon, *De Contemptu Mundi* (*Anglia Sacra*, ii. 701); Orderic, xiii. 26.   [6] *Chronicon Monasterii de Abingdon*, ii. 170.

[7] Stubbs, *Constitutional History*, i. 378.

from his government during Henry's absence he styles himself, by a title often use of the seneschal, *procurator regni Angliae*.[1]

The same process of specialization was carried through in local *The curial* administration. Henry I's edict ordering the trial in the county of *sheriffs* pleas between tenants of different honours[2] made it no longer a court only in default of justice in the hundred but a jurisdiction in first instance. Now, if ever, it called for the direct grasp of the king's hand. The heirs of Baldwin of Exeter, Hamo Dapifer, Robert of Stafford, Hugh de Port, and Hugh de Grantmesnil, were all holding in the second generation sheriffdoms granted by the Conqueror. The move to extricate local administration from the feudal monopoly had been begun on a small scale under Rufus. The county justiciars were beginning to relieve the sheriffs from the greater pleas, and at least two sheriffs were in office before 1100 who were landless and owed their position solely to the crown. These were Osbert the Priest in Lincolnshire, and Hugh of Buckland, who held several midland shires together. The position was not greatly altered by Henry's accession, though Leicestershire and Shropshire were forfeited by the risings of 1102, but after Tinchebrai in 1106 the pace of reform quickened. By 1110 Surrey, Cambridge, Huntingdon, Leicester, Warwick, and Northants were held by men of no more than knightly rank, while the future chamberlain of the treasury, William Pont de l'Arche, held Wiltshire and Hampshire. Hugh of Buckland held at that time eight shires together. The distribution of the counties already shows a clear correspondence with the process of elaboration and definition which was being pursued in Henry's *curia*. The new sheriffs appeared to the clerics and nobles who suffered under them as men of no standing, unscrupulously subservient to the king's greed for money. Actually, many of them were drawn from that small body of the king's ministers who had served a clerical or financial apprenticeship and were imbued with the skill and zeal of office which were bringing the Exchequer into being. Such certainly were William Pont de l'Arche and Aubrey the Chamberlain in the first half of the reign, and Ralf Basset and Geoffrey de Clinton in the second, all men with experience in the *camera*, while to them we must add those who rose through the

---

[1] D. M. Stenton, *English Historical Review*, xxxix.
[2] Edict for the Shire and Hundred (1109-1111), 3.

minor reeveships of the crown, men such as Serlo de Burg, whose first substantial charge was the custody of the see of York from 1114 to 1119 *sede vacante*. Better accounting at the Exchequer audit, the authority of the Exchequer court and its accumulation of precedent, were carrying the influence of the *curia* into the counties. Sheriffs were being appointed no longer to appease local interests but to reflect Exchequer policy. On occasion they were being fined for corruption or incapacity, and one, Restold of Oxfordshire, was dismissed. It is possible, of course, to exaggerate both the independence of the baronial sheriff and the degree of control that the crown could exercise even over its own nominees. Local government was never free of abuses in the Middle Ages. But, as long as the custody of the royal castles, the initiation of the pleas of the crown, the order of the county through the frank-pledge and the pursuit of felons, and even the incorporation of its courts and the execution of writs, lay with a hierarchy of bailiffs of which the sheriff was the head, the king's power could only reach the provinces through an obedient shrievalty, and a great feudatory who was also sheriff over a long term of years might enjoy something approaching palatine status.

The inquest
In procedure, as in most other matters, the Normans were alternately conservative and experimental. From their Frankish contacts they brought, as an incident of jurisdiction, what is perhaps the most vital weapon of medieval administration, the sworn inquest, but they used it occasionally and without much system. The Saxons had rid their form of trial of that element of unreason and bias which was inherent in the solidarity of the kin for oath-helping. They used witness and compurgation by independent voices of the neighbourhood. But they could not arrive at a sworn verdict without going through a complete form of trial between parties, and the oath-helper, swearing to the general credibility of his principal's oath, could not be interrogated as to questions of fact. Nor, apparently, could the king or his ministers put the subject upon oath *ex officio* in order to obtain such facts as were necessary in the course of administration or to establish his customary rights. The member of the community was, in short, still irresponsible to anything but the routine of folkright, and in this, as in so many other matters, is not to be called a subject. The Frankish kings, on the other hand, perhaps drawing upon Roman

procedure, had succeeded in extracting the oath from its place in the form of trial, and had converted it from a privilege to an obligation, and the Conqueror was able to put specific questions as to fact and law, and to demand a sworn answer from the men of the county and hundred, or to nominate groups of individuals who were likely to have special knowledge to declare it upon oath. Possibly the Norman kings made more use of "recognition", as this method of ascertainment was called, than records survive to prove—the outstanding example is the Domesday inquest, when the whole nation answered by sworn inquests of hundreds and vills to innumerable questions of ownership, possession, extent, value, and custom which were the aftermath of the Conquest— but examples of its application to ordinary justice are not common, and for the most part proof of right was still committed to the old practice of challenge between parties, trial, oath, and witness. Mainly from the somewhat doubtful source of the Liber Eliensis, we have instances of recognition even in William's reign. To establish what lands the church of Ely held at the Conquest "Englishmen who know how the lands of the said church lay on the day that King Eadward died" were elected *et ibidem jurando testentur*,[1] or later the bounds between the king's manor of Torksey and the neighbouring manor of Stow were sworn to by the "lawful men of Lincolnshire"—*facite recognoscere per probos homines de comitatu*.[2] Yet, were it not for the one wholesale instance of Domesday, the number of cases and the authority on which they rest would hardly be sufficient to persuade us that inquest was more than a power unrealized or held in reserve in William's day, or even Henry's. The Leges Henrici Primi, so generous in detail of the older forms of trial, omit inquest altogether from their survey of Norman justice.

Important as Henry I's revolution is in the history of administration, it is almost more so in revealing the mind of the Norman monarchy as to its own function in the state. The demesne interest of the crown, its interest as the greatest of all lords of estate, had come progressively to the fore as its avowed preoccupation during

Centralizing trend of royal policy

[1] Such questions were later the matter of the possessory assizes. M. M. Bigelow, *Placita Anglo-Normannica*, p. 25.

[2] *Ibid.* 139. So, in Rufus' reign, the shire of Northampton is convened to "recognize" whether land at Isham is thegnland or farm. *Cartularium Monasterii de Rameseia*, i. 233.

three successive reigns. Rufus allowed Flambard to do his exaction for him; Henry I openly devoted himself to enriching the crown by shrewd and businesslike government, working through men who were too insignificant to share the king's responsibility, and who at times were revolted by the work they had to do.[1] This was not the rôle either of an English king or of a feudal overlord as they had been understood in the past. It carried Henry away from that close coöperation with the feudatories which the Conqueror and probably Rufus had maintained, and which was the traditional basis of the régime. It is true that a section of the baronage put itself out of court by rebellion, and that a few, notably Robert of Mellent, worked amicably with Henry to the end, and it is probable that he would have ventured no major act of state without the form of baronial counsel. But, for all that, a gap had opened between the crown and its vassals, and it is most unlikely that feudal England could have been driven much further along the course that Henry had set. It was one which Henry II followed with far greater caution, and which caused civil war under John and Henry III. Though the king exacted his farms, and fines, and amercements remorselessly, sold his justice and withdrew his ministries from the hands of the magnates, so that the crown of England was contracted to the scope of a particular interest, its feudal quality was not and could not be shaken. Indeed, it might be said that in displaying the *terra regis* and the *jura regalia* as the greatest and most jealously cultivated *dominium*, Henry was stimulating the least desirable elements in feudalism. At its best a feudal realm achieved stability by the collaboration of the king and the feudatories, and government was the expression of a common mind. Neither the governing theory of feudal relations nor any feudal state which then existed could have borne the strain of a crown which abandoned the pretence of good lordship and governed to the last iota of its right. Upon this rock successive English reigns foundered. The king who so governed realized the type of the tyrant as tyrants were estimated in the twelfth century, and could not take the further, as yet inconceivable, step of legiti-

---

[1] Cf. the admission of one of Henry's justices: *Induimus animos tyrannorum: et hanc rabiem nobis induxere divitiae:* lured by the madness of riches we have become tyrants. Leges Henrici Primi, 6. 5B. Cf. F. M. Stenton, *English Feudalism* p. 218.

mizing a despotism. Far from destroying feudal right, Henry's reign is that in which the law of English tenure is formulated. The so-called Leges Henrici Primi, our most purely feudal code, were compiled by a justice of the king's *curia* in Henry's reign, and they mark the high-water mark of feudal right in England. In organizing its *curia*, crystallizing its rights at their highest value and developing new ministries, the crown was followed, though at a distance, by the magnates. In Henry's reign and in Stephen's the great honours achieved their maximum unity, and their lords began to exploit their economic resources. An extreme consequence of this feudal growth might be the adoption of an interpretation of feudal monarchy which made it nothing but lordship. Such a theory was latent in England until Henry's ruthlessness brought it to the surface, and then, when the conflicting claims of Stephen and Matilda gave it its opportunity, it asserted and forced Stephen to accept the crown on an avowedly contractual basis.

If the history of the twelfth century is to be that of one process only—the growth of monarchy and centralized administration—the reign of Stephen is empty of interest. Stephen succeeded as the choice of the great Conquest baronage, who had realized to what end Henry I's reign was leading them, who resented the loss of shrievalties and castellanships, and feared a continuance of the rule of the *novi homines* under a crown weakened by a female succession. It is said that the barons' first choice was Stephen's elder brother Theobald, but they rallied immediately to the king, and his first court at Reading was attended by such of the really great men as could reach it—Bigod, Say, three of the Clares, and Robert de Ferrars—and his Lenten court at London was "among the most splendid ever held in England for the numbers and the rank of those who attended".[1] On the other hand, with certain exceptions, Henry's servants, some of whom were already established as barons of secondary rank, held aloof,[2] or received Stephen with reservations. Thus from the beginning the future civil war was foreshadowed by a cleavage of loyalties, in which Henry's sons

Reaction under Stephen

[1] Henry of Huntingdon, *Historiae*, Lib. viii.
[2] Keeping to their castles and refusing homage because of their oath to Matilda, and because they feared the barons. *Gesta Stephani*, 15.

and servants temporized with the barons' king, and waited for the moment when they should be able to bring back the throne to the direct line and restore their own supremacy. The war which broke out in 1138, and continued intermittently for fifteen years, roughly conformed to this cleavage between the old and new nobilities—it was a division of society which was to persist for another half-century. Robert of Gloucester could count upon the steady loyalty of men like Payn fitz John, Eustace fitz John, Miles of Hereford, Geoffrey Talbot, and William fitz Alan, while, though there were men of violence like Mandeville who kept no loyalty, and though exceptional quarrels, such as made Stephen break with the earl of Chester in 1141, might shake their allegiance, the king was followed by the great feudatories with as much consistency as any claim was likely to evoke in the early twelfth century. The social division carried with it a territorial one also, since Henry had enfeoffed his son Robert in Gloucester and entrenched his *curiales* strongly in the March of Wales, and the war soon settled into a deadlock based upon rival governments of the east and west.[1]

Assertion of feudal theory

With power thus balanced, the North exposed to the invasion of David the Scotch king, and Stephen and the Empress outbidding each other as embodiments of feudal lordship, the reign yields no precedents for strong kingship. It has, indeed, been doubted whether the administrative machine continued to work beyond the immediate range of London, whether the Exchequer continued to sit, or the courts to meet with any regularity. On the whole, the scanty evidence points to a weakened action of government within the spheres of the two parties, and to its partial cessation in areas where neither could maintain a stable power.[2] The interest of the reign, however, lies not there, but in the assertion of what may be called the alternative political theory of the day, that which had played a great part under the Conqueror, had been forced into the background by Henry I, and which now imposed itself more freely than at any time in English history. Stephen's accession charter strikes a far lower note than had that of Henry. Where

[1] In 1138 Robert of Gloucester had a strong hold upon Kent, where he held Dover and Canterbury and was supported by Walkelin Maminot, but this was soon lost. Orderic, III. xiii. 17. The garrison of Wallingford came to be the easternmost point of the Angevin power.

[2] J. H. Round, *Geoffrey de Mandeville*; G. L. Turner, *Transactions of the Royal Historical Society*, New Series, xii.

the latter speaks only of hereditary right—*post obitum patris sui Dei gratia rex Anglorum*, Stephen's appeals to election—*Dei gratia assensu cleri et populi electus*. Since the direct line was broken and Stephen's right plainly elective, not too much need be made of this, but the principal friends of Matilda enforced its meaning by a pretension which is drastic as from English vassals to their king. Robert of Gloucester appealed to the contractual clauses in the formula of homage, making his submission to Stephen "on conditions, that is to say for as long as the king should maintain him in his honour, and keep his pledges entered into",[1] and in this he was followed by the prelates, who thus exploited the feudal relation to bind the new king to the "liberties of the church".[2] It is this element of contract and convention as between king and vassal which gives the reign its special interest, and saves it from the character of anarchy. In 1138 Gloucester's conditional allegiance had its sequel in a formal diffidation, "revoking his homage and withdrawing his friendship and fealty in the ancient customary forms";[3] in this Gloucester was followed by the barons of Matilda's party, and as the kingly power is relaxed the relations of both Stephen and Matilda with their supporters seem more and more to be determined by the tacit recognition of a contract. The charters by which both sovereigns bid for support take on many of the forms of private agreements between equal parties,[4] and they are required to grant away all and more than William I had allowed to the magnates or Henry I had reclaimed from them. The sheriffdoms revert to the great barons, those who are best worth placating, and now they are granted not during pleasure but in fee and inheritance. With the sheriff's administering powers go the judicial authority which has lately been created in the *justicia comitatus*. Between such hereditary viscounties and the palatine earldoms there is, indeed, hardly more than a difference of name. The most striking of these immunities was that of Geoffrey de Mandeville who received the shrievalties of London, Essex, Middlesex, and

1 William of Malmsbury, *Gesta Regum*, 707: *Homagium regi fecit sub conditione quadam, scilicet quamdiu ille dignitatem suam integre custodiret et sibi pacta servaret.*
2 *Loc. cit. quamdiu ille libertatem ecclesiae et vigorem disciplinae conservaret.*
3 William of Malmsbury, *Historia Novella*, i. 18: *Regi more majorum amicitiam et fidem interdixit, homagio etiam abdicato.*
4 J. H. Round, *Geoffrey de Mandeville*, p. 11: *Ego ut dominus et Rex convencionavi ei sicut Baroni et Justiciario meo.*

Hertfordshire in fee and inheritance, but this is only the most extreme of several instances, of which Miles of Gloucester's shrievalty of Hereford, and the creation of fifteen earls, not endowed with territorial earldoms but still enriched by grants of revenue and lands from the fisc, which seriously weakened the crown, are others.[1] This was the position which faced Henry II when he succeeded to the throne. Not only was the local government largely feudalized, but the king's castles had been allowed to lapse into the hands of the King of Scotland, William de Warenne, the earl of Chester, the earl of Norfolk, and others, the royal demesne had been freely alienated, and both Stephen and Henry had been forced to recognize an immense power in the earl of Chester, which stretched from one side of the north Midlands to the other. It was fortunate for Henry that the two Midland powers of Chester and Peverel destroyed each other by William Peverel's murder of earl Ralf in 1153 and that these two great honours fell into the hands of the crown. The work of Henry I was in fact to be done again, and with far greater thoroughness and with a new wisdom in political practice which would enlist instead of alienating the mass of the nation.

Angevin   In the obscurity of the reign of Stephen England shared only
kingship   partially in the swift intellectual movement of the times, and the men who took control after the peace seem by contrast in advance of their predecessors by more than a normal generation. Henry, Becket, Richard de Lucy, Glanvill, Richard fitz Neal, each in his own way, was more than a man of affairs, and was prepared to develop the routine of administration in the light of principles which he desired to see realized in law and government. This power of systematic design, at least in degree, new, reached far into the background of thought.[2] It was the time of the first treatises upon the state, and in the light of the new science of politics the twelfth-century crown first realized how far it had come from the restricted kingship of the eleventh, and found justification for a new scope and meaning in monarchy. Past

---

[1] *Omnia pene ad fiscum pertinentia minus caute distribuerat.* Robert de Monte, *sub anno* 1155.
[2] Cf. F. M. Powicke, *Stephen Langton*, p. 91.

theorizing about the crown had assumed that the king's function was limited to a narrow range, and his right scarcely more than *primus inter pares*. The compiler of the Leges Henrici Primi ranked the king's law as the most exalted, but recognized the popular laws of Wessex, Mercia, and the Danelah as of equal and independent validity.[1] Hugh of Fleury[2] made the crown his subject, but was concerned primarily with defining the boundary between the *regnum* and the *sacerdotium*. To neither of these writers was sovereignty itself a conscious problem, nor had they any inkling that it might come to be the impulse of every act of state, and the prime question of politics. But the men of Henry II's generation knew that there was coming to be a new power for which there was as yet no name, unrealized, and therefore bound by no limits, and this they sought to understand and to justify. There must be a divine virtue in princes, says John of Salisbury, since all men submit to them, and offer their necks to the axe.[3] The mystery of tyrannous kings must be accepted as a judgment upon their peoples. Like Attila, they are the scourge of God. He who resists power resists God. It is not to be wrongly used, being a trust for the execution of justice, and the evil king is responsible to Heaven. Nevertheless, acting in the spirit of their office, kings are not to be questioned; their will has the force of law, and is, in fact, the sole guarantee of justice and public good. All this will come to be the commonplace of medieval thought about kingship, and treads so nicely the line between responsibility and irresponsibility that it can be used to justify almost any political creed. But such writing is an historical event because it abandons the old unspeculative acceptance of official acts as conforming to or offending custom, and therefore good or bad *per se*. It is the first recognition of power and will in the state, forces not to be confined within the customary right of the king, already outgrowing his traditional functions, and to be estimated only in terms of a more sophisticated political experience than that of Norman England. When English kingship comes to be thought of in terms of the Digest, Cicero, and Vegetius Renatus, the subject matter is the crown rather than

---

[1] Leges Henrici Primi, 6. 2: *Legis etiam Anglice trina est particio . . . preter tremendum regie maiestatis . . . imperium.*

[2] Baluze, *Miscellanea*, ii. 184. The exordium to the *Dialogus de Scaccario* follows Hugh very closely.

[3] John of Salisbury, *Policraticus*, iv. 1.

the king, and the concept of a crown which is the embodiment of the community is not far from explicit utterance in John of Salisbury's *princeps est potestas publica*[1]: *publicae ergo utilitatis minister et aequitatis servus est princeps: princeps personam publicam gerit.*[2]

Growth of definition in feudal obligations It is true that Roman formulae fit the English twelfth century badly, but there was beginning in every sphere a process of analysis and consequent definition of what before was ill-defined. The king's government began to move according to general rules, its offices and routine were stereotyped, law was coming to be treated as a science—and there the result was something of a revolution—and the custom of feudalism, which had had only a general uniformity, came, though less effectively, under review. In this last sphere the realization of the crown that vagueness might be manipulated to its own profit, and the slower realization of the feudal order that its obligations were being increased and its right delimited thereby, led up to the tension and conflict of the Charter. In the course of this clarification and intensifying of its practice the crown made contact with the community at the expense of localism, conservatism, and the immunity of the honours. Henry II himself was a feudalist in politics, but his was a feudalism rigidly confined by rule, in which obligations to the supreme lord were multiplied and strictly enforced. In this spirit, he saw that the oaths of homage and ligeance were exacted and repeated[3] from the feudal order. No longer was the taking of liege homage from the knights of the king's barons an exception[4]—it was taken in a new form *de dominio solo* and generally imposed upon the honours in 1166—and fealty taken in the hundred courts was made the common link between the king and the countrysides.[5] Fealty and homage so reiterated, and becoming matters of routine, were, perhaps, intended to extract more from the feudal oaths than they traditionally carried, and they were in fact being brought home to those who took them with a new literalness. An administrative order to a great man was apt in Henry's reign to be enforced by

[1] John of Salisbury, *Policraticus*, iv. 1.   [2] *Ibid*. iv. 2.
[3] The duty of exacting homages which had not been performed was enjoined on the justices in 1170 and 1176.
[4] *Red Book of the Exchequer*, vol. i., and J. H. Round, *Feudal England*, p. 236.
[5] Assize of Northampton, 6: *Justitiae capiant domini regis fidelitates . . . ab omnibus, scilicet comitibus, baronibus, militibus, et libere tenentibus, et etiam rusticis, qui in regno manere voluerint.*

a reminder that the recipient had sworn oaths to the king, and that he expected not only a vassal's service in extremities, but specific obedience to his writs.[1] *Ligeantia* is hardening towards allegiance—obedience of the subject—though without offence to the letter of feudalism, and John, with his habitual distrust of the feudal tie, will propound this altered fealty as the basis of a commune of England, binding all men against the foreign and domestic enemies of the crown.[2] By that time he was not alone in seeing it as the political form of the future.[3]

The drawing of the community into responsibility to the crown is seen in Henry II's new process of law. It is an exercise of the Norman king's practice of redressing disseizin, but now done after inquest and not by a mere equitable re-seizin without trial.[4] Since the Conquest the crown had, and from time to time used, a means of arriving at facts more precise and quicker than trial and judgment, the inquest of sworn recognition. The simplest and most far-reaching of legal revolutions was achieved by eliciting the crucial point of fact in a series of different types of action, making the issue of the trial turn upon that one point, and submitting it to a sworn inquest of neighbours. Of the possible actions concerning land some were seen to turn upon a claim that the defendant had obtained possession wrongfully from the plaintiff —*novel disseizin* [5]—others on whether the plaintiff's ancestor had died in possession—*mort d'ancestre*[6]—while, if the right of property which underlay the fact of possession were challenged, that too could be tried by inquest—*magna assisa*.[7] In ecclesiastical matters, the possession of patronage might be determined by enquiring

The inquest

---

[1] M. M. Bigelow, *Placita Anglo-Normannica*, p. 241. The justiciar enjoins Archbishop Baldwin to withhold legal action against Christ Church *per fidem quam ei (regi) debes et per sacramentum quod ei fecisti.* In 1166 the return of the *servitia debita* of the knights was enjoined on the barons *per fidem et ligantiam quam (mihi debetis)*: Stubbs, *Select Charters*, p. 173. The commonalty are required to equip themselves and hold their arms *ad fidem domini regis et regni*: Assize of Arms. Letters Patent, 4 John, p. 72, prohibits the clergy from demanding new taxes from the laity *in fide qua nobis tenemini* (*ibid.* 76), prohibits the Irish lieges *in fide qua nobis tenemini* from answering any but the king or the justiciar's writ.

[2] Gervase of Canterbury, ii. 96.

[3] Cf. the London *pseudo-leges* of William I (c. 1210), *Statuimus ut omnes liberi homines regni nostri sint fratres conjurati ad monarchiam nostram et ad regnum nostrum.*

[4] *Chronicon Monasterii de Abingdon*, ii. p. 166; *Chronicon Monasterii Gloucestria*, i. p. 242; *Cartularium Monasterii de Rameseia*, i. p. 234.

[5] Assize of Northampton. Stubbs, *Select Charters*, p. 152.   [6] *Ibid.* p. 151.

[7] Glanvill, *Tractatus de Legibus*, ii. x.

*The
Assizes*

who made the presentment upon the last vacancy—*darrein presentment*[1]—and a whole class of litigation could be avoided by enquiry
whether disputed land were held in frankalmoign or lay fee—
assize *utrum*—and should be justiciable in the spiritual or secular
court. Where Henry I would eject a disseizor by his mere will,
Henry II would do so by form of assize.[2] For each of such actions
a single writ would suffice, and might be issued in common form
as sued for. In addition, Henry enacted that no action for free
tenement should be entertained without king's writ. The effect
of this procedure was to deprive the defendant of the delays of
the old process of judgment and also to prevent his possession
being troubled by the threat of force inherent in challenge to
ordeal by battle, and, although assize was not made obligatory

*Growth of
king's law*

but was at the discretion of the defendant, its advantages were
sufficient to bring about its general adoption within perhaps a
generation. So the king's law grew at the expense of the law of
the honours and of trial before the sheriffs, for the assize could be
taken only before a king's justiciar, and every defendant who put
himself upon it came out of the court of his lord and took his
trial before that of the king. The courts of the itinerant justices
who took the assizes began to be called *curia regis* equally with
those held *coram rege*, and the king's processes administered under
the assizes came to make up the great body of the law. Initiated by
uniform writs which ran through every county and franchise,
it had issue in uniform procedure, and was everywhere matter
of common jurisdiction. Superseding the variant customs of the
Danelah, Mercia, and Wessex, and the customs of the honours, this
king's law became recognized as the Common Law of England.

*The
inquest in
adminis-
tration*

In extending the *recognitio*, even permissively, to every disputed
case of property and possession, Henry was revolutionizing the
procedure of civil law, but he was not acting without precedent.
His predecessors had used the inquest to ascertain facts which were
essential to determining landed right, though they had used
it only occasionally—in the Conqueror's reign almost solely in
order to get an English verdict on the position in the Confessor's
day, in later reigns more generally, but still not often. In the

[1] Glanvill, *Tractatus de Legibus*, xiii. 21.
[2] Up to 1166 he was still using forceable re-seizin. Cf. *Chronicon Monasterii de
Abingdon*, ii. p. 223; *Historia Monasterii Sancti Augustini*, p. 409; Douglas,
Feudal Documents of the Abbey of Bury St. Edmunds, p. 94.

administrative use of the inquest, however, Henry seems to have been entirely an innovator, and in making it the almost invariable means of securing the knowledge necessary to action he was creating something new in the practice of the state—government which could establish its rights and assess its revenues by information which was authentic because local and sworn to by oath. It was an essential, perhaps the one essential equipment of bureaucratic monarchy.

As recognition became part of the routine of the counties it established the habit of response and obedience to the crown. The earliest enactment of inquest as the basis of administrative action is that of criminal presentment by the Assize of Clarendon[1] in 1166. The hundreds by the oath of twelve men, and the townships by four, are required to make presentment of all felons.[2] This is an administrative expedient, but it also has judicial effect—it is the forerunner of our grand jury—since the sworn accusation by neighbours deprives the accused of the right to make a rebutting oath, and drives him without preliminary to the test of ordeal.[3] Even if cleared by the ordeal, the accused must abjure the realm or be outlaw, unless he is of hitherto unblemished repute.[4] The verdict of the *jurati* is, therefore, for practical purposes equivalent to a judgment, and, though the principle that notorious ill-fame deprives the accused of the right of defence by oath is of Saxon origin,[5] this is the first wholesale attack upon the cumbrous machinery of the old English trial as the Normans perpetuated it, and, except for its stronghold in the larger boroughs, the older criminal justice was soon swept away.[6] Upon the administrative side presentment reinforces the responsibility of the countrysides for their own immunity from disorder and theft, and its perfected form in the *Edictum Regium* of 1195 provides for a regular delation of felons to knights assigned *ad hoc*, who have been taken to be the first forerunners of the justices of the peace.[7]

It is possible that the settled years of government were begun by

Criminal present-ment

---

[1] Stubbs, *Select Charters*, p. 170.

[2] Assize of Clarendon, 1.　　　　[3] *Ibid.* 2.　　　　[4] *Ibid.* 14.

[5] There is here an interesting dovetailing of Saxon and Frankish procedure.

[6] Some resistance from those who stood by the old safeguards of Saxon or Norman trial is shown by the many fines for refusing to swear to the king's assize which were exacted by the eyre of 1166.

[7] Howden, iii. 300.

Inquest of sheriffs a general inquest as to secular services in 1163.[1] A few years later we find recognition applied to almost the whole field of administration.[2] The inquest of 1170 is known as the Inquest of Sheriffs, but its verdict was to be given equally upon the administration of bishops and barons in their own estates, upon that of the bailiffs holding royal custodies, of the foresters, and of the holders of any itinerant office. It was, in fact, a general inquest upon grievances throughout the country both under royal and baronial officials, and into any leakage of revenue, as from the *aide pur fille marier*, the chattels of felons, or amercements, and finally as to the state of the royal manors, and is as remarkable in its scope as the Domesday survey itself. The immediate occasion of this inquest may have been dissatisfaction with the officialdom of the day—many of the sheriffs were displaced after it—but its historical importance is as

Royal commission and local verdict the beginning of a new practice of administration, the regular association of a commission from the *curia* with the independent verdict of the hundreds and vills upon the conduct of provincial officials and their handling of the sources of revenue. In 1170 the inquest was taken before a commission of barons itinerant. Later their place was taken by a routine of *justitiarii itinerantes*, and the

The eyre first list of the articles of enquiry of the general eyre which has survived, that of 1194,[3] has much in common with those of 1170. The Inquest of Sheriffs, in fact, set the precedent for a recurrent inquest by the shires and hundreds upon the king's affairs, and in some measure upon their own.[4] Inquest was also applied to a widening range of subjects for which special juries were empanelled. Glanvill tells us of juries to delate encroachments—purprestures—upon the king's rights,[5] to decide the degree to which criminals might be amerced without ruin—*salvo contenemento*[6]— and to decide disputed bounds,[7] while in 1185 verdicts upon heirs under age within the king's lordship were entered upon the *Rotuli de Dominabus*. Towards the end of the reign two great constructive

---

[1] Ralf de Diceto, 311.
[2] Inquest of Sheriffs. Stubbs, *Select Charters*, p. 175.
[3] *Ibid.* p. 252. A link between the enquiry into the king's demesne in 1170 and the regular practice of such enquiry in the eyres is afforded by the undated articles which Benedict and Howden associated with the Assize of Northampton. Howden, ii. 89.
[4] Cf. clause 25 of the Articles of 1194.
[5] Glanvill, *Tractatus de Legibus*, ix. 11.   [6] *Loc. cit.*   [7] *Ibid.* ix. 13.

innovations, the Assize of Arms and the assessment of the Saladin Tithe, were both prepared by inquest, and in Richard's reign the precedent of the latter is consolidated by the assessment by inquest of the carucage tax of 1198. The crown will in future rely upon countryside verdicts for the statistics upon which its increasingly ambitious and complex finance and administration is to rest. After 1194, at least, the juries will commonly be elected,[1] and not least important for the future is the fact that in the revived contact of the monarchy with the community the villein's oath will be accepted equally with that of the free.[2] Thus, the division between free and unfree tenure, which had gained recognition in law, failed to effect a lodgment in the constitution. Much of the development of the English state turns upon this point of administrative practice.

As the monarchy increased its demands upon the counties, it became necessary to strengthen and regularize their supervision from Westminster, which was now to some extent a capital of government.[3] The unspecialized shrievalty and the compromise *The* of the shire justiciary were outgrown.[4] With the experience *judiciary* gathered in Henry I's reign to draw upon, an itinerant judiciary was certain to be adopted, and Henry gave his whole genius to devising a system and to experimenting with men of various temper and qualifications to exercise it.[5] As with procedure, so with the machine which directed it, the king's work was done by trial and experience, and revealed its final form only towards the

---

[1] The Articles of the eyre of 1194 (Stubbs, *Select Charters*, p. 252) order the election in each county of four knights, who are to elect two knights from each hundred, who in their turn are to choose ten knights or freemen to form with them the grand jury of the hundred. The procedure may, of course, be older than 1194.

[2] By the Assize of Northampton the presenting jury must be knights or freemen, as again in 1194. The four men of the vill would, of course, sometimes be villeins, as might the *quatuor vel sex viri legitimi*, who were to swear to assessments under the Saladin Tithe. The jurors of the assizes, as dealing with free tenements, were naturally freemen. Villeins swore to the Inquest of Sheriffs—though Benedict (p. 5) considered the result unsatisfactory—and to the carucage assessment of 1198.

[3] The Exchequer began to sit there regularly from 1156. T. F. Tout, *Chapters in Administrative History*, i. 102.

[4] Sheriffs were prohibited from holding pleas of the crown in their own shires in 1194, and by Magna Carta from hearing them at all.

[5] Ralf de Diceto, 434: *Abbates modo, comites modo, capitaneos modo, domesticos modo, familiarissimos modo, causis audiendis et examinandis praeposuit.*

close of his reign. The Assize of Clarendon of 1166 is in the form of instructions to justiciars who are to combine a fiscal review of the counties with a drastic purge of their crimes by presentment. The eyre which it instructed was carried through in the same year by Richard de Lucy and Geoffrey de Mandeville, and may be distinguished from the later itinerant judiciary, which made use of more justices, and included men of lesser rank. The eyres, indeed, take during the first half of the reign the form of special commissions to which the hearing of general pleas is secondary, and, while the eyre of 1166 inaugurated the presentment of criminals under the new Assize of Clarendon, that of 1167 was concerned with forests, that of 1168 was sent out to collect the *aide pur fille marier*, while the commissions of 1170 were to take recognition of the sheriff's delicts, and that of 1173 was for the collection of a tallage. Most of these commissions also held pleas, but they are clearly characteristic of the formative period in the greater emphasis on their fiscal than on their judicial function and in the variety of experiments which lead up to the perfected system. The eyre of 1166 was made by two justiciars who reviewed eighteen counties unsupported, those of 1168 and 1173, as befitted their primary purpose, were made by barons of the Exchequer, the Inquest of Sheriffs was carried through by large groups of commissioners, acting each over perhaps half a dozen counties, and, for obvious reasons, contained an element of the non-official baronage.

Itinerant commissions

It is in 1176 that we are first conscious that experiment is over and the time come for the parcelling of the kingdom into areas for regular judicial visitation. Six groups, of three justices each, perambulated the country, and dealt with almost all the business which came to be that of the eyre, criminal pleas, the assizes, and every kind of plea initiated under the king's writ, provided that it did not concern a tenement of more than a half knight's fee, together with the normal enquiry into the royal demesne, escheats, and other profitable rights of the crown. Three years later experience dictated a recasting, though not a revocation of the scheme of 1176. The eyres were reduced from six to four, each with five justices, and, because the justices of 1176 were found to be oppressive, a bishop was associated with each of the three southern commissions, and Ranulf Glanvill, about to succeed de Lucy as

chief justiciar, with that of the North. The two experiments of
1176 and 1179 mark the final achievement of Henry's work in
this sphere, and the beginning of an annual eyre as the principal
weapon of provincial administration and justice. In 1194 the
further precaution was taken of removing from the sheriffs even
the keeping of the pleas of the crown, their reception, record, and
the production of parties before the justices, and of entrusting
them to three knights and a clerk elected in every county. The
instructions of that year exemplify eyre jurisdiction in its completed form. Inspired by Hubert Walter, they set out the pleas
of the crown by name as the principal business of the session, the
grand assize for property of an annual value of less than five pounds,
the affairs of the Jews, the state of the king's wardships, escheats,
farms, and churches, while with this judicial and inquisitorial
work goes the collection of tallage of boroughs and demesne
townships of the crown. In this form the eyre typifies the final
coördination of central bureaucracy with the communities of the
counties as the administrative system of Henry's choice, and the
permanent system of the Angevin state.

As in the provincial judiciary, so in the central *curia* and its staff, *The*
an ordered scheme emerges from Henry II's reign and fulfils the *central*
undeveloped precedents of his grandfather. Henry never allowed *curia*
the routine action of any office to establish a bar between himself
and the free exercise of his own judicial function. Difficult or
momentous cases were regularly reserved for the king's consideration, and even when he was abroad he allowed his subjects free
access to himself, and from time to time issued writs to the appropriate officials over the justiciar's head.[1] The latter deferred matters
beyond his own judgment to the king over seas.[2] Nor, it would
seem, did Henry abandon the principle that the commission of his
justices was a special form of the authority of the king *in consilio
sapientum*. Much judgment was done with the counsel of his
barons, and the principal assizes of the reign were evolved in such
baronial *curiae*. And yet it is during Henry's reign that the great *The chief*
offices of state assume unmistakable identity and establish their *justiciar*
full dignity. If the preëminence of Roger of Salisbury was rather
personal than of office, and was felt equally in the justiciary, the
Chancery, and the Treasury, the beginning of Henry's reign pro-

[1] M. M. Bigelow, *Placita Anglo-Normannica*, 233. [2] *Ibid.* 242.

duces a Chancery with an increasing clerical staff, a Chief Justiciarship of the title of which there can be no doubt, and a Treasurer
with settled and defined duties. The essential function of the chief
justiciar's office is identical with that of his subordinate colleagues
—the function of judgment—and it is a reminder of his emergence
from the rank and file of the judiciary that there are two chief
justiciars holding office together during Henry's early years.[1] But it
has become a permanent distinction,[2] and we can see that the chief
justiciar habitually acts as the leader in every court, and is often
entrusted with any routine powers that the king is disposed to
delegate when he is not in England, though he may find himself
disavowed in the most serious matters, as did Richard de Lucy
when he suspended the forest regulations during the revolt of
1173.[3] When the king refers a petitioner to his *curia* it is
the justiciar whom the suitor approaches.[4] Richard de Lucy is
constantly found taking a decisive lead in discussions between the
judges,[5] and, when they have agreed, the justiciar announces their
judgment,[6] as Robert of Leicester pronounced judgment upon
Becket. A plea for justice from a great vassal will now as a rule
receive from him its immediate answer.[7] At times the king, though
present, will retire from the court and leave the justiciar to preside.[8]
When he is abroad he will sometimes address the earl of Leicester
or Richard de Lucy by name, ordering them to set the county
court or some appropriate official to action.[9] Intermittently during
the king's absence the chief justiciar will issue writs under his own
name, which are qualified as *brevia de ultra mare*.[10] The fact that he
is the chief justiciar in every court gives him the presidency of the
Exchequer, and there Glanvill pronounces the judgment of the
curia in scaccario after consultation with the bishops and justices
who sit with him.[11] Besides leading in the courts, the chief justiciar
will have occasional duties of legal administration of a dignified
kind to perform, as when the earl of Leicester accompanies

---

[1] Richard de Lucy and the earl of Leicester.
[2] Richard de Lucy held from 1154 to 1179, Ralf Glanvill finished out the
reign.   [3] Howden, ii. 79.
[4] M. M. Bigelow, *Placita Anglo-Normannica*, 221.
[5] *Loc. cit.*   [6] *Ibid.* 214.   [7] *Ibid.* 239.
[8] *Ibid.* 199.   [9] *Ibid.* 204.   [10] *Ibid.* 210, 241.
[11] *Ibid.* 235. It is perhaps as from the Exchequer that the justiciar sanctions
expenditure on castellation and other royal works. Pipe Roll, Hen. II, ann. 13.
(Lancs). *Ibid.* ann. 14. (Lancs).

Reginald of Cornwall to verify Becket's plea of illness as a reason for disobeying the king's summons to trial.[1] In short his office is to do *vice rege* all that the king does in his *curia* in demanding, advising, and pronouncing judgment, and to give the necessary effect to the court's verdict, either by himself approaching great persons who cannot be handled by subalterns, by issuing writs to executive officials, or by ordering their preparation by the chancellor. In the king's absence this may become, in fact at least, a vicegerency.

The process of specialization which produced the chief justiciarship and the eyre also brought the jurisdiction of the central *curia* to definition. This had remained, at least in theory, as a function of the council of magnates, stiffened by curialists learned in law, and under the personal presidency of the king, and in theory, indeed, this remained its ultimate authority whatever adjustments of routine and personnel were adopted;[2] but it is clear that, at least by 1154, the king had been delegating his powers on occasion.[3] A precedent had, of course, existed from at least the Conquest in the commissions detached to try some one important plea, and latterly the itinerant judiciary had familiarized the country with the idea that king's justice could be done other than *coram rege*. With this went the assumption that the king's commission to a justiciar gave him the judicial power of the king *in consilio magnatum*, and made him the peer in judgment of the king's barons, and without this assumption the benches of the law could never have come into being. In virtue of this fiction delegation was regularized in 1178, and a commission of five justices was appointed to try the pleas of the kingdom, such as involved difficulties being reserved for the king and his council. Henceforth, as the charter tests show, Henry travelled with the Justiciar and two other lay justices,[4] and from this court, which tried a mixed justice of common and crown pleas, the later benches were derived.

The court of 1178

[1] M. M. Bigelow, *Placita Anglo-Normannica*, 215.

[2] Causes beyond the competence of the five justices of 1178 were to be presented *auditui regis, et sicut ei, et sapientioribus regni placeret, terminaretur*: to the audience of the king, to be determined by his pleasure and that of the wise men of the realm. Benedict, i. 208.

[3] Thus, in 1175 the abbot of Battle is referred by Henry to the *curia* under Richard de Lucy. M. M. Bigelow, 221.

[4] Usually, Robert de Witefeld, William de Bendings, or Michael Belet. Delisle, *Recueil des Actes de Henri II*, ii. pp. 122, 141, 210, 248, 307, etc.

At some period after 1178 a division took place between king's bench pleas and the *placita communia*, and the Great Charter accepted a court of Common Pleas as an established fact and fixed its session at Westminster, where all subjects might have fixed and easy access to justice.

Thus, during Henry's reign, the law, the courts, and the officials reach a condition which at least foreshadows their final state. There is as yet little feeling that the crown is bound by its own routine,[1] and, though the Exchequer's jurisdiction is made necessary by financial disputes, while that of the King's Bench—though not yet clearly defined—safeguards the rights of the crown, and Common Bench those of private parties, it will be long before the king or the justiciar will feel bound to refer every plea to its appropriate court. Much justice, also, is still done, and will continue to be done, in unspecialized great councils. But, in spite of this, law is diverging into separate streams, which find their channels in the several courts, and the general shape of the system will not be altered. That it was recognized and accepted as a system, and one directed to the public good, we may be sure from the general approval given it by the rebellious baronage in the Charter.

It is common to speak of household government or personal government in this period. I doubt if either term is apt. The king's will pervaded every part of the state, so that "personal government" tells us nothing new, and most of the household offices hardly rose above the hall, the kitchen, and the dispense. A much truer picture is given if we think of the executive as a growing corps of skilful clerks and forceful laymen distributed over the shrievalties, the castles, the custodies of escheats, the various commissions such as the keeperships of the wines, the ships and the ports, the mint, the exchange, the stanneries, and so forth, all of them constantly responsive to the royal precept, known to the king, responsible to the king alone. If we need a general name, we might call this familiar government, for again and again the de-

---

[1] John will plead the *lex scaccarii* as a justification of his action against Braiose. *Liber Niger Scaccarii*, i. 378.

scription of *familiares*, familiar clerk, *dilectus et familiaris*, is given to these royal agents. They are the *iniquissimi consiliarii* of the hostile chronicles, the king's *familearis* of all ranks, and through them the reign is governed. It is not yet a metropolitan government and the counties, the castleries, and the custodies are kept in tune and obedience by the constant itineration of the king.

As coördinating authorities under which these men mostly act, we should probably single out the Seneschalcy and the Chamber. The Seneschal's was the office for the provisioning of the king's hall and household and his eyres, and seems, under the Angevins, to have replaced the Constableship as the head of the *Familia Militaris*. Castellanships, in many cases shrievalties, commands in war and diplomatic missions fell regularly to the senior Knights of the Household. They were the backbone of the secular, unlettered half of government. Upon the clerical, financial side the one office of weight was the Chamber, but the importance of that was such as to make it a major factor in administration.

Absence of record may cover some development already made *The* in the Chamber of Henry I. The Pipe Rolls of Henry II and the *executive* Chancery Rolls of John bear witness to it on every page. A separation between the Chamberlains of the Exchequer and the Chamber was made in 1158, in which year Waren fitz Gerald ceased to function there, and the Chamber was thenceforth left free to develop as an office in its own right. Successively, the characteristic officials of an Angevin *officium* made their appearance, a household chamberlain, Richard Ruffus in 1166, a Clerk of the Chamber in the early 'seventies. The Ushership of the Chamber must have been a much older office, but the first usher to appear in record is Walter de Camera who attests charters from about 1182. It is already a lesser treasury, following the king, and receiving and spending for his daily work of government. Under Henry and John it was vital as the personal treasure, receiving money from the Treasury,[1] from escheated honours such as Rayleigh and Boulogne, from various offices,[2] from sheriffs,[3] custodians,[4] or the

---

[1] Letters Close, John, pp. 28, 74, 75.

[2] *Ibid.* 22, 39, 74.   [3] *Ibid.* 19, 25, 34.

[4] *Ibid.* 34, 72, 108. During the vacancy of the bishopric of Exeter in 1207 it was in the custody of king's clerks and its revenues were paid into the Chamber. *Ibid.* 76. Formerly it would have been in custody of the chancellor *sede vacante*.

The Chamber

king's debtors,[1] who were ordered to pay direct into the Chamber, the Exchequer writing them quit on the king's writ of *computate*. In turn, it might, if convenient, make livery of cash for every exceptional or urgent service, for the king's personal needs, the wages of mercenaries,[2] pensions,[3] garrison or repair of castles, equipping of vessels, or for innumerable other needs.[4] As the immediate source of finance for the executive, it was itinerant with the king, and it followed him abroad in 1206 and 1214, drawing as much as twelve thousand marks at a time[5] to constitute his war-chest.[6] Often using the small seal,[7] and staffed by his confidential clerks, it was the organ of his personal diplomacy—the charters by which he bound reluctant barons to special subservience were stored in the Chamber[8] and Chamber clerks were often charged with the invidious business of the baronial hostages[9]—and by providing messengers between the various offices and officials it was the motive force of government. Constantly these move about the country, bearing letters to sheriffs, justiciars, and custodians of every kind, and moneys by which the king's orders may be carried out. Reflecting the government of the realm in miniature, and forming the web of com-

[1] Letters Close, John, pp. 29, 36, 66.
[2] *Ibid.* 21.
[3] Letters Patent, 8 John, p. 5.
[4] J. E. A. Jolliffe, "The Camera Regis under Henry II", *English Historical Review*, Vol. LXVIII.
[5] Letters Close, 8 John, p. 75.
[6] At Porchester in 1205, when the king believed himself to be on the point of sailing for France, it became the immediate treasury of receipt, receiving 900 marks by the hands of London citizens, 350 marks from Hugh Nevill from the forests, and 300 marks from the Treasury of Ireland. *Ibid.* 7 John, pp. 35, 36. At the end of the reign payments are beginning to be made into the inner chamber of the Wardrobe, which was soon to supersede the Chamber. Letters Close, 15 John, p. 145.
[7] This practice began, according to Professor Tout (*Chapters in Administrative History*, i. 158), "at least from 1208". The letters issued from Poitou in 1206 *per parvum sigillum quia magnum non erat praesens* (Letters Patent, 8 John, p. 66), must have formed a precedent. It is in 1208 that we first find an admission that the small seal is coming to be appropriate to the Chamber: *has litteras fecimus signari parvo sigillo nostro, quia hec debita volumus reddi in cameram nostram, quas fecissemus signari majori sigillo nostro si ea ad scaccarium nostrum reddi vellemus*: we have had these writs sealed with our small seal because the debts they refer to are to be rendered into our chamber, etc., etc. (Letters Close, 9 John, p. 115).
[8] Letters Patent, 8 John, p. 66.
[9] *Loc. cit.*

munication on which it is borne, the Chamber causes the whole system to feel and respond to the king's will.

As an outward manifestation of the growing expertness of the *Growth of* age, rolls come into being for one branch of the administration *record* after another. The Exchequer had recorded its business from the beginning. To that, perhaps, it owed that continuity of tradition in which it spoke of the *lex scaccarii*. From 1195 it, or rather the Treasury, was preserving record of the fines or agreed settlements made between party and party, and it came to be a repository of much court record. Chancery rolls in general date from the reign of John, and it has been conjectured that the need for more consistent record may have arisen when Longchamps, driven from the judiciary and the Exchequer by the revolution of November 1191, retained the chancellorship, and carried out what duties he was allowed to perform without access to the Treasury. The roll of the king's letters patent [1]—open in charter form with pendant seal—or close [2]—folded and sealed—the *Rotuli de Oblatis* of fines offered to the king for privileges or favour, [3] and the Charter Roll, [4] all mark at once the increasing subdivision of business, and the mounting volume of information by which the Angevin offices governed reign by reign more intensely and surely.

The task of the Angevin monarchy was not alone to rule by *Crown* ever-improving devices of government, but to remain in harmony *and* with the prevailing social forms and to turn them to its service. *community* It has already been said that Henry accepted the implications of feudalism to the full. And yet, paradoxically, his reign saw such a narrowing of the scope of feudalism and its liberties that the whole outlook of the landed aristocracy was permanently modified, and their ambitions diverted into quasi-constitutional channels. At the beginning, the flow of military power, which had swelled unchecked under Stephen, was arrested. The destruction of the adulterine castles and the withdrawal of the royal castles from baronial custody was apparently completed by about 1160. In 1166 the baronial knighthood was bound by oath to the king. Not only the *servitium debitum* or customary obligation, but any additional knights whom policy had led the lord to enfeoff—the

[1] From September 1201.   [2] From June 1204.
[3] From 1199.   [4] From 1199.

novum feoffamentum—and those kept at salary in his household were forced to do liege homage. Thus, faith to the king was made the primary sacramental duty of all the military tenants of every baron. The rebels who rose in 1173 had no sufficient following of familiar knights, and fought their campaign with hired Flemings.

Clarification of the law of tenure   It is easy to exaggerate the degree to which the rules and incidents of feudalism were already determined in the Norman reigns. The reign of Henry II saw a clarification of feudal custom such as was characteristic of him. Twice general inquests were made into the conduct of feudal liberties, and, on the whole, the power and profits of the king as supreme lord were markedly increased. A preliminary question might have been whether the obligations of knight service lay upon all the fees held under the barons, or only upon those of the *servitium debitum* of the Conquest enfeoffment.[1] By 1166 Henry had decided this crux in favour of the crown. All fees, *de antiquo feoffamento* and *de novo*, came under contribution to the aide *pur fille marier* and the scutage of 1168,[2] and all were subject to a new homage *de solo dominio*. Thus, at the outset, Henry destroyed the threat of a new, uncovenanted feudalism, such as arose in the fifteenth century, and which might have grown in the twelfth from the swelling of the military households of the barons by enfeoffments free from royal oath and service, or by the retaining of landless knights.

The assessment to knight service

The incidents of knight service: aid   So far Henry went in bringing obligation to rule. But, while the assessment could be settled at a stroke, the number and nature of the incidents of service could not, nor was a degree of uncertainty unfavourable to the crown. Definition, when it came, was at the demand of the feudatories. Glanvill doubted whether a lord might not exact an aid for the general purposes of war,[3] and if this had become an established right, the coming struggle over scutage might have been avoided, and the quarter of century of war from 1192 to 1217, which wrecked the Angevin system of finance, might have been paid for without a clash with the baronage. But Glanvill

---

[1] J. H. Round, *Feudal England*, p. 285. The clerical tenants preserved the distinction between the old and new assessments and continued to protest against the latter.

[2] Before 1166 scutage was taken from the fees of the *servitium debitum* only. *Ibid.* p. 273.

[3] Private charters exist in which the lord claims aid for the redeeming of his honour, which is almost the general aid of Glanvill. Glanvill admits, however, that current usage is against such aids: *obtinet autem quod non.* Glanvill, *Tractatus de Legibus*, ix. 8.

did not venture to put forward such aids as the clear right of the crown or of any lord, and, by a definition which did at least full justice to the feudatories, the occasions of aid came in this reign to be accepted as those four—upon the lord's accession, for the knighting of his eldest son, the marriage of his eldest daughter, and for the ransom of his body[1]—which were to be sanctioned by the Great Charter; Henry II, in fact, took only one aid during his reign, that for the Saxon marriage of Matilda. Nevertheless, *auxilium* was a term of dubious application. It was extended to aids from freemen, towns, and royal demesnes, and others not of the feudal order, and its sanction, whether by the authority of the lord or by the mere grace of the tenant, was then not fully determined.

Equally doubtful were the rules of service in the host. It does not seem that they were questioned in Henry's reign, and he was able on occasion to extend the traditional forty days to service of a full year,[2] or to add an additional levy of serjeants for an extended period, as he did for the Welsh war,[3] but subsequent reigns saw the duty of serving beyond the seas, the nature of the contingents, and their time of service, all become political issues. Where there was such doubt as to the service itself it was certain that its commutation into scutage would be open to manipulation by the king. The solid basis of the composition known as scutage seems to have been the buying-off of a traditional forty days of *servitium debitum* at the accepted rate of eightpence a day, the pay and maintenance of a single knight. The standard rate of scutage was thus two marks, and at that rate it was exacted in 1159. It is therefore unlikely that any formal institution of scutage as a new tax is to be looked for. Domesday shows us that even the fyrd service of the Confessor was susceptible of a similar composition, and scutage from individuals, especially from the ecclesiastical honours, is recorded in the reign of Henry I,[4] though we know of no occasion when even a great part of the baronage bought off their service. But the imposition was seldom allowed to rest at

Service in the host

Scutage

---

[1] Glanvill, *Tractatus de Legibus*, ix. 8.
[2] Benedict, i. 138. This was in 1177, when the rebels of 1174 were still in need of conciliating the king.
[3] J. H. Round, *Feudal England*, p. 282.   [4] *Ibid.* p. 268.

that. From 1166 it was exacted not only from the *servitium debitum*, but from all fees, and it was apt to be supplemented by levies from lands not held in barony or knight service, or to be coupled with additional military exactions from the barons. Thus, in 1159, a far larger sum was raised in the form of gifts—*dona*—from the ecclesiastical tenants than was derived from the scutage of their *servitium debitum*,[1] while in 1165 many of the greater tenants, both spiritual and lay, paid several times their scutage liability in contributions to the special levy of serjeants.[2] The impression left by Henry's treatment of scutage is one of adroit manipulation, by which the basis of the contributions to his wars was kept an open question, and considerable sums raised without any manifest breach of principle. Scutages were taken seven times during the reign, never at more than the two marks which were a fair composition for the forty days' service, often at a pound or a single mark. There is better evidence to show their exaction from the lands in the king's hand than from those of the feudatories, and little to show that the alternative of payment was forced upon barons who preferred to serve. The question of consent, soon to become a burning one, was thus never forced to an issue, and was, perhaps, hardly within the competence of the twelfth century, with its automatic response to custom, to raise.

Personal relations of feudalism

But the uncertainties of feudalism went deeper than this. Besides his essentially public obligations, the tenant was involved in a dependence which survived from his tenure's origin in a voluntary seeking of lordship, and which had been devised for a lord and not a sovereign. Into this relation remote forerunners had entered in the confidence of good lordship, but in the twelfth century it already put the goodwill of king and subject to an impossibly high test. In every fee there were recurrent crises which placed the holders at the king's mercy. Every tenant-in-chief under age was in the king's wardship. If he were of sufficient importance, he might be required to live at court and receive his upbringing there, or the king might place him under the tutelage of a sheriff, or sell his wardship to the highest bidder. Until he came of age the profits of his estates went to his guardian, upon whom he depended for a maintenance suitable to his rank. The fate of the women of the feudal families was even more completely in the king's hands.

[1] J. H. Round, *Feudal England*, p. 279.   [2] *Ibid.* p. 282.

As the guardian of the heiress or widow of a dead vassal their marriage was at his discretion, nor could a feudatory marry his daughters during his own lifetime without the king's leave. Such invidious rights placed immense influence in any lord's hands, and especially were they a most dangerous privilege for monarchy. Its control of wardship and marriage might be a powerful weapon of feudal diplomacy by bringing the great honours within the circle of the royal family or marrying their heirs to the king's *Wardship and marriage* friends, and, though his grandson was a greater exponent of this policy, Henry II used it to secure the earldom of Gloucester and the marriage of its heiress for John. But there was a corresponding danger in the intimacy of the relation of wardship. The king, as overlord, was the virtual head of every magnate's family, and the position was one which could not be filled acceptably unless he in some degree realized the conventional ideal of lordship. Both William des Longchamps and John owed some of their personal unpopularity to their indifference to decency in this relation.

The gap between the death of a tenant and the seizin of his heir *Relief* was an especially dangerous time, for the inheritance was in the king's hand. The new tenure should in theory be established by the payment of a relief. The knight's relief, according to the Leis Willelme and to Glanvill, was a hundred shillings, but Henry I's charter promised only that it should be reasonable and just, and the baron's relief was at the king's mercy. In fact the king took what he would or could. Henry I's single Pipe Roll is full of entries of payments *pro concessu terrae patris sui* and the like, and many of them were high.[1] There are few such reliefs in Henry II's rolls, presumably because they were not accounted for at the Exchequer audit, but, in the separate roll *De Oblatis*, which appears in John's reign, they rise to far higher amounts.

In spite of much individual hardship, there seems to have been little tendency for private grievances to gather head in concerted unrest under the old king after 1174. Still less is there any sign of constitutional resistance. In this again, however, as in some other matters, the reign of Henry II is one of those profoundly formative periods the effects of which are not seen till after a lapse

---

[1] Pipe Roll 31, Hen. I (Oxford), John de St. John, 160 marks. *Ibid.* (Notts), Ralf Halselin, 200 marks. *Ibid.* (Hants), Herbert, son of Herbert the Chamberlain, 353 marks.

of time. In retrospect, one may fairly attribute to it the creation of the Common Law and its courts, of a sense in the provincial communities, willing or unwilling, of solidarity with the government, and, both in response and reaction to these, the preparing *Baronial* of a reasoned temper of opposition among the barons, who had *attitude to* reacted to earlier and more brutal assertions of royal power blindly *reforms* and by rebellion. No one of these developments reached finality in the king's lifetime, but the changed mood of the baronage grew so quickly to a crisis under his sons that its origin within his reign should be explained in so far as it can be. To the feudatories the government of Henry brought at one and the same time a new and welcome security of right in their tenures, and an increasing knowledge that they were at the mercy of the crown's interpretation of the obligations that arose from them. That land actions should need the sanction of a royal writ, that no seizin should be disturbed without reasonable process, nor withheld without cause shown— both before the neutral court of the king—gave to landright a solidity which it had not had before.[1] Harshly as he could act, we know of occasions [2] when Henry might have procured judgments which would have brought him considerable accessions of power, and when, by his own voice, he decided against his own interest. The barons rightly felt that such security was cheap at some loss of jurisdiction, and no challenge to the constructive side of Henry's revolution in justice ever found a place among their grievances. Nor was it easy to accept the king's law, and at the same time to reject the courts and officials that directed it, though from time to time the barons were inclined to question whether the justices could be regarded as their natural judges and to claim that judgment should be resumed by the full *curia* of the magnates when one of their own order was arraigned.

The But, in spite of much that was agreeable to the barons, the *danger* reforms of Henry II created constitutional opposition in its *of the* medieval form. By crushing the revolt of 1173-4 he had shown *reforms* the feudatories that they could gain nothing by extreme indi-

[1] In 1208 the Irish feudatories were assured, as of a valuable safeguard, *nec aliquis vobis aliquid auferat nec vos possit dissaisire de liberis tenementis vestris per alicujus breve nisi per nostrum vel Justiciarii nostri*. Letters Patent, 9 John, p. 76.

[2] Benedict, i. p. 133. In one of these the beneficiary was the earl of Leicester, who two years before had been in rebellion, and who put himself in the king's mercy, fearing to plead against him.

vidualism, and, by bringing every legal action under writ, and permissively under assize, he had diverted their interest from sheriffs' courts and honorial courts to his own, whether itinerant or *de banco*. Criticism would henceforth be directed upon a central judicature, and legal process now drew its chief authority from the crown. Henry's legal revolution had made good justice available, but he sold it for what it would fetch; since pleas of land could not now begin without a writ, he could set his own price. Richard de Morvill paid two hundred marks for a writ of right to bring action for his wife's land in the sixteenth year,[1] and it is not surprising to find him in revolt in the twentieth. The instance, indeed, is an extreme one, and, on the whole, Henry's prices were lower than John's, and, perhaps, than those of his grandfather, but his enemies were able to call him *dilator et venditor justitiae*. Indeed, the *Selling of* demands of all feudal kings kept no proportion that we should *justice* recognize. The sums paid for the king's peace in 1175 after rebellion were comparatively low beside the price of offences which we should think far less. Hamo de Masci bought his peace for three hundred marks.[2] Richard fitz Roger, for marrying his daughter without the king's leave, had all his land sequestrated, and redeemed it for a hundred pounds, though it was only seven-tenths of a knight's fee and some carucates of thegnage.[3]

Upon the criminal side of law, moreover, there remained an *Arbitrary* element of uncertainty as to penalty. The fixed compositions, wer *element in* and wite, of Saxon law had come to be succeeded by a system, or *procedure* lack of system, by which the convicted party was "in the king's mercy", as might happen to communities as well as individuals, and, though it was becoming usual to decide the fine which the king might impose *in misericordia* by an oath of neighbours and to restrict it to a sum which did not cripple the culprit, arbitrary and excessive amercement was not unknown. It seems, moreover, established that Henry II was not above setting aside the due course of law, and resorting on occasion to arbitrary imprisonment, to which the penalty *pro despectu brevi regis* easily lent itself. As against this ill-defined prerogative in criminal law, there was already established the notion that the crown was bound by its own procedure. It is probable that Henry's thirty-five years were sufficient

---

[1] Pipe Roll, 16 Hen. II (Lancs).
[2] *Ibid.* 22 Hen. II (Staffs).   [3] *Ibid.* 26 Hen. II (Lancs).

to accustom the barons to a common law which was conterminous with the nation and brought it under a common guarantee
of right, and in this they were no more than abreast of an age
which was turning to legal antiquarianism to satisfy a new sense
Common of the value and unity of the English legal heritage.[1] Richard on
right his accession felt it right to release all those who had been imprisoned in his father's reign without legal process, and, in so
doing, admitted that no subject ought to suffer in his civil rights
except *per commune rectum*.[2] The succeeding reigns were to show
that the barons accepted "common right" without reserve, and
were ready to pose as its legitimate defenders if the king, as
principal trustee, made default. It is true, as has already been said,
that the great councils were inadequate as a means of bringing
pressure upon the crown, and that opposition was fitful and took
in extremity the feudal form of diffidation and war, but the
lawyer's aphorism, *quod aequitatis servus est princeps*, was dangerously near to being given a political interpretation[3] and becoming
a principle of political opposition. There is much in the risings
of 1191 and 1215 which foreshadows the more purely political
activity of the later thirteenth century.

Prospect of By the end of the twelfth century, therefore, it can no longer
later be taken for granted that the feudal order will be indifferent
opposition to law and order. This change in outlook was in itself a major
revolution in the constitutional situation, but its effects were
hastened and made inevitable by the ambiguous standing of the
magnates' special custom, that of knight service and baronage.
Henry's government had been conservative in taxation with the
one exception of the Saladin Tithe, and had supported itself by
feudal services which were not intolerably burdensome. There was
almost no incident of military tenure, relief, wardship, marriage,
scutage, aid, or bodily service which was free from ambiguities.
Yet the belief of the barons, as of all other free men, was that their
obligations were fixed by custom, and beyond the power of their
lord to vary. On the whole, Henry II, though he introduced variations into its incidents which had no warrant in the past, seems to

---

[1] As in the London texts of the Laws of Cnut, the Confessor, and the
Conqueror.

[2] Howden, iii. 4.

[3] Giraldus, *De Principis Instructione*, viii. 33: *Terrena justitia . . . per quam
humana societas et cohabitatio confoederantur.*

have satisfied his tenants that he was remaining within the general scope of custom, that he was not making the vagueness of their services an excuse for increasing them beyond measure, nor turning customary dues into an elastic source of revenue. Here, again, the Angevin dynasty might be on the edge of a drastic clarification. It only needed a period of unbroken war, a burden for which the customary services of feudalism were never devised, to make the need for a steady and greatly increased revenue imperative. When that happened there would be a strong temptation for the crown to find its money in the only quarter where it had a traditional right to ask for it, from its vassals, by exploiting the element of indefiniteness in feudal service. The reign of Henry had prepared the way for opposition as much by its reforms in the field of law as by its conservatism in finance. Careless or unjust administration, coupled with an attempt to turn customs into unlimited, arbitrary taxation, would almost certainly precipitate a reaction.

iii

ANGEVIN MONARCHY IN CRISIS. 1189-1216

From 1066 to 1189 there had been a steady growth in the power of the crown and in its resources of administration. But that power in the English polity which resided in the council of the notables, or in its local assemblies, had, no doubt, survived without much real diminution. With the accession of Richard we come to a new phase of its evolution, in which the community begins to realize the potentialities of bureaucracy for oppression, while the baronage remembers that it is an integral part of the government, and begins to reclaim in action what it has never lost in principle. In part this is due to the fact that officials are multiplying and government is becoming more intense, in part to the fact that the loss of Normandy freed a proportion of the barons from continental interests, but most of all to a change in the tenure of the crown. Only one king between 1066 and 1189 was weak, and none was wholly tyrannous, while from 1189 to 1272 the throne was occupied first by a Crusader, then by an incalculable egotist, then by a minor and a monarch of obstinate but weak will dominated by foreign politicians. Under such kings the baronage, which had partly shed its particularist ambitions, and was coming to think of itself as leader of the community, entered increasingly into the foreground of history. The reign of Richard continued the routine of his father, and, though it produced certain elaborations of Henry's methods of local government which have rightly aroused the attention of historians, its essential interest is in the abandonment of the Henrician bureaucracy to justify itself to the country under vicegerents in the absence of the crusading king. From December 1189 to October 1191 England was in the hands of the Norman William des Longchamps—a man of no standing save such as his abilities had gained him in the service of Geoffrey of York and as chancellor to Duke Richard—who combined the offices of justiciar, chancellor, and legate, and thus concentrated in himself the responsibility of both church and state. Than this no better test of the solidity of Henry's governmental system could have been devised.

Accession of Richard I

The strength of the feudal relation as it had been left by Henry enabled Richard's lordship to be assumed from the moment of his father's death. Queen Eleanor went at once upon a provincial progress, receiving the homages of all freemen to Richard as *Dominus Angliae*. The coronation itself, which followed two months after Henry's death, confirmed the dignity of the crown by its unusual pomp and by its conformity with English precedent. Ceremony apart, the situation was overshadowed by the need to devise what must in effect be a continuance of the régime without the ruler. The past seventy years had seen the daily government of the country withdrawn from the baronial counsellors by imperceptible stages, and entrusted to *familiares*, of whom only a minority were barons, but whose actions might still, upon a favourable interpretation, be thought of as those of ministers of the king in an honorial state. Richard's original scheme for government during his absence continued this tradition. A committee of the judiciary was appointed with the bishop of Durham and William de Mandeville, earl of Essex and Aumale, as principal justiciars. The former, being newly earl of Northumberland, was probably chosen for his power over the North, while Mandeville was one of the greatest earls and a trusted statesman of Henry II. With them were associated *ad regimen regni* four of the justices of the late reign. Geoffrey fitz Peter, William Briwere, Robert de Wihtefeld.

Government in Richard's absence

and Roger fitz Rainfrai. William des Longchamps was made chancellor of England. The commission of government thus represented both the professionals and magnates of the *curia*, and perpetuated their close relation with each other, and Richard sought to make its task easier by placating the most influential of the magnates by wholesale grants of local authority. Of Henry's ministers, Hubert Walter was made bishop of Salisbury, Richard fitz Neal, the treasurer, bishop of London, Godfrey fitz Lucy, bishop of Winchester. William Marshal was given the honour of Pembroke. Hugh, bishop of Coventry, was allowed to buy three sheriffdoms, the bishop of Winchester that of Hampshire.[1] Of Henry's sons, Geoffrey was assured of the archbishopric of York and forced to take orders and to swear to absent himself until Richard returned, while to John, the most dangerous factor of all, were given the earldom of Gloucester, the counties of Cornwall, Devon, Somerset, Dorset, and Derby, and the castles of Marlborough, Lancaster, Ludgershall, the Peak, and Bolsover. On the whole, this commission of government retained its hold upon the country to an extraordinary degree during the four and a half years of the king's absence, and might have been entirely successful had it not been for the death of William de Mandeville and the supersession of the bishop of Durham by the chancellor, William des Longchamps, who from December 1189 combined the offices of justiciar,[2] chancellor, and legate.[3] The consequence of his rise to power was to destroy the balance of forces which Richard had planned, and to throw into the background the judiciary and with it the baronage, since Longchamps habitually used his title of chancellor[4] and governed mainly through his influence in the Exchequer.

Longchamps' career is an illuminating example of the power which had come to be latent in the offices, and which the par- *Longchamps' predominance*

[1] An equal motive for these grants was, of course, the great sums for which they were bought. They were made to ecclesiastics and courtiers and, if the cession to John be regarded as upon a different footing, their extent and unwisdom has been exaggerated.

[2] Whether he should be given the title of chief justiciar is doubtful. Richard's commission from Bayonne (June 6, 1190) does not give it. Diceto, ii. 83.

[3] The combination of supreme spiritual and temporal power came to be feared, and was afterwards objected against the appointment of Hubert Walter. Diceto, ii. 128.

[4] *Epistolae Cantuariensis*, 367-370.

ticular distribution of office in 1189 brought to the surface. Under Henry II the routine of administration had been stereotyped, and the officials responsible would no longer act unless they had the authority of writ from the appropriate minister authenticated by the king's seal.[1] In Henry's reign the seals were already two, duplicate seals of majesty, one resident in the Treasury, and the other, *sigillum deambulatorium*, itinerant with the king. It is possible that there was also a third, small seal for less formal business.[2] Most of the routine of government turned upon the two greater seals, and both were in the custody of the chancellor,[3] who supervised the form of all writs personally or through his deputies, and by sealing them gave them currency and effect. When the king was in England, or was represented by a strong justiciar, the sealing function of the chancellor was, no doubt, automatic, though it has been suggested that Henry II's preference for employing a vice-chancellor or *custos* was based on experience of the obstinacy of chancellors. Then the writs of the Exchequer—*liberate, computate*, and *perdono*—would nominally be ordered by the chief justiciar, the legal writs would be matters of routine, and letters ordering less specialized action would proceed from the initiative of the king and *curia* in the form of letters close and patent. But immediately on the departure of Richard and the death of William de Mandeville, Hugh of Durham being left sole justiciar, the strength of a recalcitrant chancellor became apparent. Hugh's authority was rejected by the barons of the Exchequer.[4] Whether this was brought about by the chancellor refusing to seal writs at his order, or by the treasurer refusing to initiate them, we do not know, but it must have been due to Longchamps' influence in the Exchequer, and its effect was to deprive Hugh of all financial resources. For this reason, if for no other, his justiciarship was inoperative from the outset, and Longchamps secured his supersession from Richard without difficulty.

It is significant that when installed in power Longchamps habitually emphasized his title as chancellor—the more so if he

[1] *Dialogus de Scaccario*, i. 15.

[2] For much of what follows see T. F. Tout, *Chapters in Administrative History*, vol. i.

[3] The seal of the Exchequer, that in *thesauro*, was in the treasurer's charge, but was kept in a bag sealed by the chancellor.

[4] Devizes, §15: *A baronibus scaccarii non receptus.*

had the status of Chief Justiciar—governing *per breve cancellarii*.
The reason for this must be that he had merely replaced Hugh of
Durham, and had not rid himself of the four justiciars associated
ad regimen regni, for whose authority in the general business of the
kingdom Richard had left a small seal, *regia maiestate signatum*,
taking the deambulatory seal with him.[1] In the autumn of 1191,
when it was safe to do so, these justiciars testified that Longchamps
had habitually ignored them in all matters of importance, and it
is to be supposed that it was to make this independence effective
that he refused to use the king's seal, and as a rule authenticated
his acts of government with his own private seal. The chancellor's
writ, therefore, appears during this interlude of masterless government, as expressing the personal will of the chancellor, who, controlling the Exchequer through the great seal *in thesauro*, and the
rest of the administration with his signet, evades every constitutional check upon his power, and is truly, as William of Newburgh
says, *Caesar et plus quam Caesare*.[2] Thus, the effect of check and
balance, which highly developed administrative offices are bound
to exercise upon each other, was nullified, and the united power
of the Angevin bureaucracy flowed through the chancellor's single
will. Supreme in the Exchequer, he was able to maintain a mercenary army of knights and sergeants by drafts upon the farms of
the counties[3] and upon the Treasury,[4] to garrison the castles in his
own, and, as he maintained, in the king's interest, and to move
about the country in safety. His personal retinue was of a thousand
men-at-arms, and the sheriffs were empowered to establish their
own mercenary guards *pro pace servanda*.[5] More limited, but
formidable when freed from royal supervision, was his power in
Chancery. The see of Canterbury was in the chancellor's custody
sede vacante. He used his authority to inhibit Walter of Coutances'
intervention in the imminent election,[6] and to scheme for his own
succession, which would have made him impregnable. As chancellor, the escheats were in his special charge,[7] and the crown ward-

---

[1] T. F. Tout, *Chapters in Administrative History*, i. 148 and note.
[2] William of Newburgh, p. 331.
[3] Pipe Roll, 3 Rich. I (Kent).
[4] *Ibid.* (Tower of London). Henry de Cornhill accounts for £1200 *de thesauro
per breve cancellarii . . . ad faciendum liberationes militum.*
[5] *Ibid.* (Staffs). W. Newburgh, 334, calls them *armatae inmanum barbarorum
catervae.*   [6] Diceto, ii. 93.   [7] *Ibid.* ii. 91.

ships placed in his hands the heirs of a number of the great honours. Beyond all this was that general power over the *negotia regni* which he should have exercised in concert with the justices his subordinate colleagues, but which he in fact exercised by his sole discretion and by his personal writ.

Baronial opposition The form taken by reaction against such an exaggeration of the bureaucracy cannot but be of historical importance. How far the country had travelled from the mood of 1173 is proved by the closeness with which all parties to that reaction adhered to the spirit of Henry's government. The first occasion of opposition was, it is true, such a grievance as might have been urged twenty years earlier. Gerard de Camville's castellanry of Lincoln was reclaimed by the chancellor for the king. He did homage to John to gain his protection, and the two raised the cry that it was against custom that such custodies should be taken from men of standing in the realm and given to obscure foreigners.[1] But, though John's opposition began with an echo of feudal ambitions and concealed a plot to oust Arthur from his claim to the succession, and though it came near to an armed clash with the king's officers at Lincoln, Tickhill, and Nottingham, it gathered no feudal support, and was almost immediately brought under the control of more responsible forces. Assessors, among whom the earls Warenne, Albini, and Clare represented the chancellor, met at Winchester on April 25, 1191, and imposed a settlement, favourable to John, but preserving the form of royal supremacy, since his castles were to be surrendered, though only as a prelude to their return to his castellans. Soon after this Walter de Coutances, archbishop of Rouen, reached England with letters from the king, though he did not for some time produce them. They were designed to adjust the balance of the government, if necessary; one was addressed to Longchamps and the other justices of the commission, authorized Walter to associate himself with them, and ordered them to do nothing without his advice, while an alternative commission to William Marshal and his colleagues authorized them to act without the chancellor if he should appear unfaithful.[2] By the middle of May, therefore, there was in England, though as yet unknown to any but its bearer, a commission alternative to that of Longchamps, which might become available

[1] Devizes, §38.   [2] Diceto, ii. 90, 91.

to legitimate any opposition which should justify itself in Walter's judgment. It was in these circumstances that, taking advantage of the truce and of the failure of the archbishop to produce Richard's letters, the chancellor again moved against Camville in the summer. It is noteworthy that he thought it possible to call out a third of the feudal levy to support him, and that an arbitration similar to the last, with the justiciars and the earls still upon his side, produced for him a better settlement than the last. The final crisis came when the justices were dispersed about the country upon eyre, and it was, perhaps, the first in which moderate men could have felt Longchamps to be entirely in the wrong. Archbishop Geoffrey, still bound, according to Longchamps, by his oath not to enter England, freed from it, according to his own account, by the king, landed at Dover, and, on the chancellor's instructions, was arrested. Probably without the latter's connivance, he was somewhat roughly handled, and kept for eight days a prisoner in Dover Castle. Parallels, not entirely justified, with the martyrdom of Becket were imagined,[1] and during those eight days the whole country united against Longchamps, making, as Giraldus says, the archbishop's cause their own.[2]

The most striking feature of this movement is that it was, within the range of ideas of the day, constitutional, that is to say that it produced no free-lance outbreaks for sectional ends, that its first appeal was to the justiciars,[3] that it drew together the spiritual and temporal baronage to a common cause, and brought them to a succession of meetings at Marlborough, Reading, and London whose claim was that, although ready to use force, they were the feudatories in legitimate council. From the moment of John's general summons issued from Marlborough[4] the crisis was, indeed, a rivalry between the chancellor and his opponents to set the stamp of constitutional legality upon their own standing, and to brand that of the other party with rebellion. The justiciars and

[1] *Epistolae Cantuarienses*, 370.
[2] Giraldus, *Vita Galfridi*, 397.
[3] *Ibid.* 396: *Primo . . . Willelmum Marescallum . . . deinde Willelmum Briware . . . et Galfridum filium Petri . . . Rothomagensem quoque Archiepiscopum Walterum . . . et Episcopum Wintoniensem.*
[4] This convoked the notables *sicut diligitis honorem Dei, et ecclesiae, et domini regis, et regni, et meum . . . tractaturi de quibus magnis et arduis negotiis domini regis et regni*: the question of authority is evaded, but the summons is upon the king's business. Diceto, ii. 98.

the barons summoned Longchamps to appear before them to receive the *judicium regni*.[1] He, in his turn, cited the magnates for treason, the bishops by their regalia and the barons by their baronies, and ordered them to desert John as conspiring to the crown.[2] Upon this the magnates advanced through Oxford to Reading, and there, hearing for the first time the text of the king's letters associating the archbishop of Rouen with the government [3] and the statement of the justiciars that they had been deprived of their due authority, prepared to meet Longchamps as a constituted government under the royal authority of Walter de Coutances and those who were now his colleagues.

Constitu-tional basis of the opposition
All this, inevitable in view of Richard's absence and John's ambitions, is interesting mainly as anticipating the later movement of the Charter, with which it has in common the nature of the provocation which caused it, its considered and moderate aims, and its regular course of action. Above all, it is clear that, in spite of the rapid growth of officialdom and *ex officio* action, the baron-age, lay and spiritual, have maintained their sense of being an integral part of the régime—*judices* if not—without special com-mission—*justiciarii regis*, and counsellors. It is this that they assert against a chancellor who is only one of five justiciars, whose authority is the king's letter ordering the obedience and counsel of his lieges, but who has consistently avoided that counsel and governed alone.[4] Not only the special grievance of Gerard de Camvill and his patron John, but the general grievances, true or false, of unjust levies and abusive treatment of the royal wards in his care as chancellor, aroused individual resentment and might have been pressed with individual violence. Instead, John's treason-ous aims were subdued to the common purpose, and the opposition moved through increasingly constitutional stages till it embodied the new government under the king's commission. To the baron-age archbishop Walter appealed as to the legitimate force by which the king's letters might be put into effect when the executive had got out of control, *ut in cancellarium unanimimiter insurgerent*,

[1] Giraldus, *De Vita Galfridi*, 397.   [2] *Loc. cit.*
[3] *Diceto*, 400. Benedict (ii. 213) says the commission was not produced till the last moment in London, but this hardly seems possible.
[4] Howden, iii. 143. Giraldus, *Vita Galfridi*, 400. *Alii justiciarii, quos ei socios et coadjutores a principio rex adjunxerat, publice proclamarunt, quia nihil omnino eorum consiliis actum est.*

et eum tanquam inutilem regi et regno a potestate dejicerent, aliumque magis accomodum communi consilio instituerent.[1]

The chancellor was, indeed, deposed from the supreme power *sententia diffinitiva, communi censura omnium,* and, from the moment of his elimination, abruptly the government reverted to its due monarchical style. The arrogant authority of the chancellor's writs, *Willelmus Dei gratia Eliensis episcopus, apostolicæ sedis legatus, et domini regis cancellarius,* with the convenient *teste meipso* avoiding the conciliation of witnesses, gave place again to the fiction of the king's presence, *Ricardus Dei gratia rex,* and the test of the new justiciar.[2] The wheels of the constitution settled back into their wonted coördination. Archbishop Walter is put in Longchamps' place; not absolutely—he is to act by the will and assent of his associate justiciars, and by the counsel of the barons of the Exchequer,[3] who are changed for supporters of the *coup d'état.*[4] The seal, to Longchamps' exasperation, is borne for the new ministry by his old subordinate, Benedict of Sansetun.[5] Government is of set intent brought again under the king's seal,[6] and in this we may see how clearly the opposition had analysed the disruption of Henry's machine, and the evils of an irresponsible executive. The St. Paul's council of October 8[7] takes on something of the pretensions of a constituent assembly, and, having recreated a régime,[8] invests John with the empty title of *summus rector totius regni,* and grants the Londoners their commune. Until Richard's return

Reconstruction of the Government

---

1 Giraldus, *Vita Galfridi,* 400. To rise against the chancellor with one accord and depose him as useless to the king and kingdom, and to appoint a more suitable person by common consent.

2 *Epistolae Cantuarienses,* 377, Oct. 10, 1191.

3 Howden, iii. 141.

4 Devizes, §50.

5 Howden, iii. 154.

6 *Epistolae Cantuarienses,* 378 (John and Walter to Christ Church): *Propter praeteritas quas audisti contentiones communi deliberatione fidelium domini regis statutum est, ut sub sigillo domini regis de negotio regis mandata regia fiant communiter et discurrant:* because of the late dissensions of which you have heard, it is decreed by common deliberation of the king's lieges, that the king's writs upon his affairs shall run under the seal of the lord king.

7 Howden, iii. 141.

8 *Justiciarius supremus post comitem, justiciarii errantes, custodes scaccarii, castrorum constabularii, omnes novi de novo instituuntur:* a justiciar ranking first after earl John, justices in eyre, Exchequer officials, castellans, all new men with fresh commissions. Devizes, 50.

frequent councils[1] secure that the regent judiciary, already brought into harmony with the Chancery and Exchequer, shall not again lose touch with the magnates, and in executive routine and in every crisis of those troubled years we find the justiciars acting in common[2] in the interest of the crown.

Nature of the crisis of 1191   Taken in its essentials, apart from the personal factors of John's treason and Richard's ambiguous policy, the episode of 1189-91 reveals the dangers of Angevin administration when the departments were not kept under rigid control, and the attitude of the barons towards it. To put that attitude into words is, no doubt, to give it a precision which it did not yet possess. The conventions of feudalism in private relations were already defined; the action of a council of tenants-in-chief in a constitutional crisis was not. In 1191, therefore, step by step, the profounder issues of constitutional right were evaded because not clearly seen. There is confusion, which, indeed, corresponds to reality, between the rights and functions of the king's born counsellors, the barons, and those of his commissioned officers, the justiciars; the lines between counsel, judgment, and constitutional action are altogether blurred. The baronial attitude is one of acceptance of the principles of Angevin government, but of acceptance upon the implied understanding that the executive of judiciary and finance is in essence a contracted expression of government by *rex in consilio sapientum*, that its action must follow accepted channels, secure that warrant of the seals which guarantees its coördination under the crown, and be kept in general conformity with the views of the wider and vaguer *curia* of the magnates. These are indefinite principles drawn from the accepted relation of lord and vassal rather than from experience of politics, but, in the light of them, the barons retained their sense of being the natural counsellors of the king, and were capable in emergency of laying hands upon the parts of the executive and moulding it to their convictions. 1191 was in the nature of a *coup d'essai*. Within a generation they were to find a greater cause and a more formidable antagonist, but this

---

[1] As in 1192 at Windsor, Oxford, London, and Winchester to counter John's disposition to visit France. Devizes, §75.

[2] Howden, iii. 187, 204, 205, 207, 210, 212, 225. So, in November 1191, John, Walter, *et alii justitiarii nostri* intervene in the Canterbury election *communi familiarum et fidelium nostrorum consilio*. *Epistolae Cantuarienses*, 371.

view of the constitution was to guide them for the next century.

The crisis of 1191 marks the entry of the baronage into the political field, not as individual parties to tenurial contracts but as critics of and participators in government, and is, in a sense, a prelude to the greater effort of 1215, but it has the exceptional qualities of a crisis and of an absent crown. With that revolution before us it becomes profitable to enquire how far the magnates claimed, or were accorded, a share in government not in crises but in the common course of affairs, for what acts of state the *consilium et consensus baronum* was required.

The old tradition was government with counsel, as that of the Saxons had been government by *sapientes*. There is as yet no notion of treating the *consilium* as a body whose function it is to oppose, nor any demand for a defined council of fixed membership. If anything, the barons are losing influence between 1154 and 1189. The great feasts which they attend have lost their business function. The king conforms with ceremony and then passes on to work through the year in a series of councils whose composition is determined by the place where they are held and the business to be done.[1] Henry kept the *Baronial counsel* Christmas court of 1176 at Nottingham, and then moved at once to Northampton—the road centre of the north Midlands—and held a great council with the bishops, earls, and barons of the kingdom. Flemish ambassadors were received and dismissed with proposals for an alliance. William of Albini was made earl of Sussex and given his father's lands. The honours of the earls of Chester and Leicester were restored to them, their rebellion being now purged. One great judgment was delivered, that between the earl of Leicester and William de Cahaignes, and the canons of Waltham resigned their house into the king's hand. This was clearly government *cum consilio magnatum* at its fullest. But in February the king was at Winchester, with what attendance we are not told, though evidently with no great assembly, and there ordered a levy of the feudal host, not for the customary forty days, but for a full year at the barons' charges, and this we are told he did at the prompting of his household, *per consilia familiarum*

[1] The following is the account of Benedict of Peterborough.

suorum.[1] On May 2, at Geddington, a king's house on the North Road, Henry summoned the archbishop of York and three bishops and many earls and barons to meet him *ad tractandum de pace et stabilitate regni*. On the 8th he was at Windsor, and met a much fuller council, "almost all" the bishops, earls, barons, and knights: in fact, the feudal levy that he had ordered in February. Again there was much debate as to the peace and security of the realm, and by the counsel of the bishops, earls, and barons, the castellans were removed throughout England and knights of the king's household placed in their stead, the earl of Chester's castles were given back to him, and he was commissioned to reduce Ireland to order in anticipation of Prince John's visit. Later in May a conference with the Welsh was held at Oxford, their princes did homage, and John was made king of Ireland in the presence of the magnates of the new realm, and certain honours were allotted to the service of Waterford, Wexford, and Dublin.

In all this there is clearly no rule, save that the king acts with counsel, and probably with as much compliant counsel as he can get. The principle is nothing more defined than common sense making the best of time, place, and persons in using the baron's duty of counsel. There is no jealousy as to attendance or exclusion,[2] and, unless we may find it in the making of an exceptional feudal levy "by the advice of the king's familiars", no attempt to evade discussion. Equally there is no attempt to prescribe a quorum without which initiative is invalid. Indeed, the line between the *familiares* and the wider circle of magnates is not yet one of class or office if we exclude the now established practice of judgment through a high court of justiciars not all of baronial rank. The group of barons who act with Henry throughout their lives— William de Mandeville, the earl of Arundel, Richard de Humez, and a few more—are *familiares*, but emphatically of the great baronage. Officials like Richard fitz Neal, or Richard de Lucy, are men of hardly lesser rank, and after 1177 the chancellor was the king's son. The king, indeed, has come to be the one fixed centre of government, and *consilium*—*magnum* or otherwise—does not call

---

[1] The collection of the Saladin Tithe in 1188 was determined *consilio fidelium* (*regis*), which seems to point to a similar group of *familiares*.
[2] The king forbade access to the court to the rebels of 1177 until they had purged their offence, but this is an evident exception.

for the definite article. Counsel seeks no stable embodiment, but is spoken through the mouths of *sapientes, familiares, magnates regni*, who come and go as the king's affairs or their own move them. Such varied counsel is accepted as a fulfilment of the principle that the king's councillors are his barons, for, on the whole, the magnates trust and accept the régime.[1]

It is certain that however far back in English or Norman history we go we shall find that the function of judgment was inherent in assemblies of notables. So much is basic in the public life of the northern world, and, while the reign of law was supreme and legislation as such unknown, this one function embodied public life at its fullest in the *curia*. This was true of honour and kingdom alike. But by the twelfth century it was no longer enough. Innovations in custom were becoming too numerous to pass uncriticized, and refinements in the procedure of courts were in sum altering their whole basis. Acts of state could no longer be explained solely *Assize* as judgments or recognitions of custom. With the reign of Henry II a new device, the assize, comes into politics. It is something set by agreement—*assisa statuta, assisam statuere* are common amplifications—and it marks the first realization that custom can be changed by the will of those who live under it or govern by it. With the assize we are at the headspring of English legislation, which, strangely, descends not from the national code-making of the eleventh century, but from the agreements of feudal tenants and their lords. The assize may be used for a number of cognate purposes, but it keeps within a narrow range. It may settle and declare points of custom which are open, it may bring inequalities of custom to a common rule among peers of any honour or administration, or, more fruitfully, it may make innovations in procedure or service such as are felt to lie within the spirit, but not the letter, of existing custom. The same principle of agreed and established, assized clarification or innovation may be found in the *redditus assisae, opera assisa*, of most manors, in the standards set for the staple trades, such as the assizes of Cloth, Bread, and Ale, or in the assizes of the Forest or of Arms, which bind all freemen of

---

1 The undifferentiated standing of officials and magnates in counsel is expressed in a favourite phrase of Richard's *communi familiarum et fidelium nostrorum consilio* (*Epistolae Cantuarienses*, 379 [1191]), *a plerisque magnatibus et familiaribus nostris suaderetur* (Diceto, ii. 128 [1195]).

the realm. The distinguishing marks of the assize, by which in combination it is distinguished from the *judicia* or recognitions of the past, are that it is admittedly new enactment, that it requires the consent of the lord or prince,[1] and that it must apply throughout the area of administration for which it is promulgated.[2] In this it is *communis assisa*, and is not the effect of individual submission but of common assent,[3] though such assent may be expressed without the formality and conclusiveness of the decisions of assemblies in later days. Such assizes, essentially legislative, will, if they are applied often enough and to matters of sufficient importance, bring the problems of will and authority, counsel and the initiative of the prince into an entirely new light.[4]

We must not exaggerate the importance of assizes at the beginning of the thirteenth century. They were the first link in the chain of legislation, and this link was from the beginning partly held by subjects, so that legislation began with the principle of assent; but they were the first link only. The legal assizes of Henry II were, of course, of the greatest value for the future, and to some extent their importance was realized at the time. During an episode of legal revolution the acquiescence of the magnates was vital. Henry had promised "that all my men shall enjoy their liberties and free customs" undisturbed,[5] and not without "long and deep counsel" could he have disquieted, as the proprietary and possessory assizes did, that ancient custom which accorded to all freemen

Limited scope of assize

---

[1] Letters Patent, 8 John, p. 72: *Est inauditum tempore antecessorum nostrorum et nostris quod assisa nova statuatur in terra alicuius sine assensu principis terre illius*: it has been unknown in our time or our ancestors' that a new assize should be set up in any land without the prince's assent.

[2] Glanvill, *Tractatus de Legibus*, ix. 10, distinguishes between what is *per assisam generalem determinatum* and *consuetudo singulorum comitatuum*.

[3] Assize of Clarendon, 1: *Facta a rege Henrico . . . de assensu Archiepiscoporum, episcoporum, abbatum, comitum, baronum, totius Angliae.* The Grand Assize was made *de consilio procerum*: Glanvill, *Tractatus de Legibus*, ii. 7. The assize of the Forest, *per consilium et assensum (magnatum) totius Angliae*: Stubbs, *Select Charters*, p. 186.

[4] It is possible that Glanvill saw some relevance to this in his paraphrase of the Institutes: *Leges Anglicanas licet non scriptas, leges appellari non videtur absurdum . . . eas scilicet quas super dubiis in concilio definiendis, procerum quidem consilio et principis accedente auctoritate constat esse promulgatas*: English laws may be called laws without absurdity, although they are unwritten ones, since they are promulgated . . . by the authority of the prince and the counsel of the notables. Prologue, Glanvill, *Tractatus de Legibus*.

[5] Coronation Charter; Stubbs, *Select Charters*, p. 158.

a defence of their life and lands by oath and ordeal. As it was, many feared and resisted the change.[1] But normally assize was rare, and consisted of minor standardizations of the material incidents of custom. There seem to have been four recorded assizes during John's early years, all *communi consilio baronum, per commune consilium regni,* and the like. The most important, perhaps, was the assize of money in 1205,[2] the least so the fixing of the price of lampreys *per consilium baronum nostrorum.*[3] The importance here is one of theory, and for the future. It is hardly likely to precipitate a constitutional struggle or to count among the major pretensions of the charter. Yet it is all that stands for legislation in this age and its nature is apparently already realized.

Royal finance is equally limited by its feudal preconceptions. *Authority* Only upon rare occasions did the aids conflict with custom. *of the* When, therefore, Howden and Coggeshall tell us that the aid for *aids and* the acknowledged occasion of Richard's ransom was authorized *services* at once by request of the king and by statute or edict of the justiciars,[4] contemporaries must have been much less conscious of the contradiction than are we ourselves. A king's ransom was a recognized occasion of aid; for the amount he must observe custom, and since custom will ultimately be determined by his court,[5] he is to some degree at the mercy of his vassals. Thus it is that the fact or fiction—it could be either in any given instance— that the aid is an act of grace, recurs uncriticized in royal and baronial correspondence,[6] while, at the same time, the earlier instances of resistance are individual and based upon some peculiarity in the tenure of the objector. It is the same with the duty of corporal service. When it is resisted it is usually by individuals who plead some special right—the refusal of 1205 to serve beyond

---

[1] Pipe Rolls, 13 Henry II, *passim.* Fines of those who refused to swear to the king's assize. Cf. also *Dialogus de Scaccario,* II. x. F.

[2] Letters Patent, 6 John, p. 54.

[3] *Ibid.* 8 John, p. 68.

[4] Howden, iii. 210; Coggeshall, 101.

[5] Glanvill, *Tractatus de Legibus,* ix. 8: *Iuste secundum considerationem curiae suae et consuetudinem rationabilem.*

[6] *Humiliter postulavit ut universi . . . tale auxilium facerent ei ad redimendum eum, unde ipse sciret eis grates.* Howden, iii. 208.

the sea was professedly in the king's own interest—or by groups
who claim some difference of tenure in common. St. Hugh in 1198
pleaded that the see of Lincoln was exempt from service abroad,
and in 1213 the *Northanhimbrenses* claimed the same, though they
held by lay barony—"their charters" confined their service to
England[1]—no doubt recalling that, in the case of some at least,
their Saxon antecessors' service was that of *endemot* or defence
between the Rere Cross of Stainmore and the Scotch border.[2]
Such resistance was hardly a "landmark in constitutional history".[3]
Rather, it revealed the absence of any sense of the nation or of any
beyond a feudal responsibility, and it was probably coming to be
realized as hopeless even in the reign of John. In 1205 the *assensus*
of magnates was held sufficient to bind the knights of England to
combine to produce a tenth of their number for an indefinite
term of service and to impose forfeiture on those who defaulted.[4]
The king himself determined the period of service[5] and soon was
visiting individual defaults by disseizin without trial.[6]

Consent to
exceptional
aids

On the other hand, it would seem that already in John's reign
the feudal conscience was awake to the distinction between customary aids on the lord's accession and on the three non-recurrent
occasions, and exceptional aids for other purposes, such as Glanvill
thought to be doubtfully due, and that for such it was beginning
to apply principles which were later of vital importance to the
constitution. The latter were held to be of mere grace,[7] and
latitude was allowed to the king as to their nature and incidence,

1 Coggeshall, p. 167: *Asserentes non in hoc ei obnoxios esse secundum munia*
terrarum suarum.

2 Thus Patrick of Dunbar owed service of defence (*inborh* and *outborh*) in
the march between England and Scotland for the barony of Beanly. Public
Record Office. *Inquisitions Post-Mortem.* Edward I. ii. 741. The cornage tenures
of Cumberland serve "in exercitu Scocie", *Testa de Nevill*, i. 350, and do not
pay scutage under Henry II. Others pay. Pipe Roll, 18 Henry II.

3 Stubbs, *Constitutional History*, i. 548 (of St. Hugh in 1198).

4 Letters Patent, 6 John, p. 55.

5 Letters Close, 6 John, p. 54: *standum nobiscum ad minus per duas quadrage-*
simas: to remain with us for at least two periods of forty days.

6 *Ibid.* 14 John, p. 117.

7 Glanvill, *Tractatus de Legibus*, ix. 8. Cf. John's appeal to the barons of Meath
and Leinster for an aid: *precamur eciam quatinus pro amore nostro auxilium . . .*
faciatis ad civitatem nostram Dublin firmandam, tantum inde facientes quod justis
petitionibus vestris nos libentius exaudire debeamus: we pray you, as you love us
. . . accord us an aid. Letters Patent, 8 John, p. 69.

so that a very fruitful license to experiment and innovate was permitted. Both king and subject might find it convenient to go beyond the traditional fixed levy upon the knight's fee. We may see these principles at work in the treatment of the aid of February 1207. No expedition to France could be pleaded as an excuse for a scutage, and seven scutages had already been taken since John's accession. He now asked for a proportion of revenue from the churches, which was refused, and the burden fell upon secular lands. At Oxford an aid of twelve pence in the mark of revenue, commonly referred to as a thirteenth, was granted *per commune consilium et assensum concilii*.[1] In addition, the king appealed to the clergy of Canterbury, citing the generosity of the council; but, being put off by promises of consideration which were not fulfilled, wrote a second letter asking that each individual should state upon a roll the amount that he personally was prepared to give. The difference in basis between these two levies is clear. The clergy could not be brought to the point of grant. The king, therefore, was at their mercy—since the aid was secular and for the general purpose of defence—and he bargained with them as individuals, though the interdict and the outlawry of the clergy were scarcely two months old. Of the obligatory nature of the secular aid, however, though it was for general defence, fell upon all who held lay fees, and was in an unaccustomed form, and so failed in every test of custom, there was never any doubt since it had received "common assent". Those who evaded it were to lose their lands or be reduced to slavery, the Northern religious houses, which had allowed their neighbours to hide their chattels with them to avoid assessment, were brusquely ordered to return them to their owners,[2] and the constable of Richmond,[3] who had made default, found his castle of Richmond sequestrated, and in eight days made his submission.[4] Aid granted by the order concerned, although not one of the three sanctioned by custom, is already valid and binding. Aid not so granted is dependent upon the mere grace of individuals.[5] How long this has been true we

---

[1] Letters Patent, 8 John, p. 72   [2] *Ibid.* p. 71.
[3] *Ibid.* p. 73.   [4] *Ibid.* p. 73.
[5] As, presumably, with the Londoners' aid of 1205, of which John received into the Camera 900 marks *de promisso quod nobis fecerunt ad auxilium nostre transfretacionis.* Letters Close, 7 John, p. 35. Mesne tenants were less fortunate and the king constantly granted his tenants-in-chief writs for aids for such various

cannot say, but it is possible that we may see the power of the *consilium* to bind the generality hardening during the first decade of John's reign. In 1199 the Cistercian abbots objected that they were bound not to make aid to secular powers *nisi communi consilio et assensu generalis capituli*,[1] while the canons of York pleaded the "liberties of their church". John did not feel able to put any of the penalties of 1207 in force against the abbots in 1199, and contented himself with putting them out of his protection, and turning their beasts out of his forest pastures. In 1207, on the other hand, Geoffrey of York resisted the aid, apparently as affecting the secular tenants of his church, and, with no more mercy than was shown to the constable of Richmond, his see was sequestrated, and he went into exile. In eight years practice, or theory, or both, have hardened, and the right of both king and magnates has moved towards definition.

Scutage Scutage, unlike aid, seems to have been upon a prerogative basis, and there is no evidence of baronial consent. At least in his later years, John's practice was to proclaim a campaign, designate certain barons to follow him *per preceptum regis*,[2] perhaps even to allot others to garrison and council at home,[3] to issue writs granting their scutage to those who were crossing with him, and then to order the Exchequer to collect from the remaining fees at the prescribed rate and without further parley. *Scutagium statuimus*[4] is the phrase which governs the enactment, and, short of insisting on serving personally at many times the cost of the scutage, forcibly preventing the king from leaving England, or proving that he had never intended to do so, there was little customary ground for resistance. Indeed, this was not the end of the king's exactions on

purposes as the payment of their reliefs, or their debts, to equip them for his own service, and the like. The Charter reduced the aids of mesne tenants to the three customary aids of the realm, though this was not strictly observed.

1 Coggeshall, p. 102.

2 Hugh Peverel was excused scutage in 1214 as he was in Poitou *per preceptum regis*. Letters Close, 16 John, p. 167.

3 Letters Patent, 16 John, p. 118. Barons urged to come to France *exceptis illis qui de consilio venerabilium patrum nostrorum domini Petri Wintoniensis Episcopi Justiciarii*, etc. . . . *in Anglia moram sunt facturi.*

4 Letters Close, 16 John, p. 166: *Statuimus tres marcas capi de scutagio ad opus nostrum de singulis feodis. Ideo vobis mandamus quod scutagia illa . . . capi faciatis . . . preterquam de feodis militum . . . pro quibus litteras nostras de scutagio suo habendo warantum suscepitis.*

the score of scutage. John used even more summary methods at times, ordering his sheriffs to collect the levy direct from the sub-tenants over the heads of their lords,[1] and even permitting a magnate in favour to impose a scutage upon his tenants when there was none ordered from the realm.[2] Thus, the normal limitation of the sub-tenants' liability to the occasion *quando scutagium regis currit per patriam* was nullified, and a dangerous door was opened to indirect taxation of the lower grades of feudal tenure.

The executive, the most powerful force in the state, was *The* growing beyond the range of criticism and control. It had arisen *executive* within the sphere of the king's household, and was as personal to him as the household of any lord. Only in war, when the king's officers were in part his barons, could the voice of the council be effective, as when the king's galleys were allotted their stations *communi consilio baronum* in 1205,[3] or when the barons destroyed the king's hopes of an invasion of France in that year. Even here the constraint was military rather than constitutional, for the king was ready to turn from the barons to his bachelors, the squires and knights of his military household, and to lead a mercenary host out of England. Indeed, as John drew away from feudal towards mercenary war, the influence of English chivalry declined. The two most impressive and typical military achievements of the reign, the organization of sea-borne transport and supply under William de Wrotham, master of the king's ships and archdeacon of Taunton, and the defence of the West Country castles in 1216, turn entirely upon the trained capacity of officials and the loyalty of portsmen and mercenaries and are royal enterprises far beyond the scope and control of feudal magnates The administration as a whole could be and was given a quasi-military character which favoured John's tendency to treat it as an extension of his military household. Longchamps had shown how the shrievalty could be militarized, and in the second half of his reign John made free

---

[1] Letters Close, 8 John, p. 46: *Mandatum est Vicecomiti Kancie quod non distringet Johannem de Augi ad reddendum scutagium de tenemento quod tenet de feodo comitis Arundel . . . quia idem comes inde domino Regi respondebit.*

[2] *Ibid.* 14 John, p. 127. In 1212 he authorized William of Salisbury to take a scutage of three marks from his lands in seventeen counties. There was no national scutage in that year. Entries in the Fine Rolls suggest that John was allowing scutages to be taken in order to enable magnates to pay their fines to him. *Rotuli de Oblatis*, 16 John, 531.

[3] Letters Patent, 6 John, p. 52.

use of his foreign captains as sheriffs,[1] and, while the order of the realm rested ultimately upon the strength of the castles, their personal control by the king was so jealously guarded that at crucial moments, as in 1212, the custodians would not accept the authority of letters patent for their surrender, but demanded their delivery by a known intimate of the king.[2]

It is evident, therefore, that the reigns of Henry II, Richard I, and John are a period when many aspects of society, the state, and government are undergoing a process of analysis and clarification, with the result that the underlying principles of medieval politics are emerging into conscious appraisal. It is becoming probable indeed that certain of them will conflict with others. The feudatory sees the state as an honour upon a large scale. He knows that if its law is to be changed it must be by common assent of the tenants-in-chief, and that equally its contributions to the king are fixed by custom and cannot be increased arbitrarily or changed as to their nature. He knows that every judgment should be by the court of vassals, and he is only slowly realizing that the executive cannot be adequately discharged by a few great officials of baronial rank—stewards, constables, and the like. Even the sheriffs have at times been barons. But against all this the king has been governing through familiars and ministeriales. The Chamber, the Seneschalcy, the Chancery, and the Exchequer are its characteristic servants. Even judgment is being done on a large scale by justiciars, fewer and fewer of whom are of clear baronial standing. The principle of consent to non-customary taxation is not to be denied—but what is custom? The quarrels of the future, the very real constitutional differences of the thirteenth century come into view as soon as the skill of an analytical age has had time to exercise itself upon the raw mass of custom. The coming age, because it is one of perfected and rationalized law and administration will, for that very reason, be one of constitutional strife.

[1] 1208; Gerard d'Athies, Gloucester and Hereford: Philip Marc, Notts and Derby.

[2] Letters Patent, 14 John, p. 94: *Quia credimus vos nolle castrum illud* (*Tickhill*) *liberare sola litterarum nostrarum auctoritate, mittimus ad vos dilectum et fidelem nostrum Magistrum Ricardum de Marisco. Ibid.* 16 John, p. 116. This came to be a normal safeguard under Henry III.

Nevertheless we must expect the constitutional principles of the opposition to John still to be, for the most part, those deducible from the rules of tenure and to reflect a very rudimentary political experience. The Articles of the barons and the Great Charter stood mainly for two things, the reassertion of the Henrician common right, generally, but especially as it affected the great feudatories, and the clarification of the uncertainties of feudal custom, with some attempt to reintroduce the conventional standards of lordship into the relation of the king to those who were his subjects but also his vassals. Both of these ends would have been secured in a more experienced age by setting a permanent control upon the actions of the crown and its officials. The barons of 1215 sought the same end by the only means they knew and attempted a recognition of certain essential points of the law; we know now that no code of custom, however full, can of itself provide against every possibility of misinterpretation and abuse. The real problem was one of administration and of the character of the king, for no king could govern the Anglo-Norman baronage who did not himself exemplify the virtues of good lordship. Alone of his brothers, John was temperamentally *mauvais sire*, for chivalry and feudal convention, both in their strength and weakness, were antipathetic to him. He despised the military and administrative incompetence of the knightly order and its lack of conclusive purpose. He knew his barons to be treacherous subjects and contemptible enemies, and found loyalty, courage, and the skill of the new age in mercenaries and civilian clerks. But he underrated the cumulative force of a moral code which was higher than his own, and decisively nearer to that ideal of right Christian government which was held by all thinking men of his day. How *John and* far he was a tyrant to common men is doubtful. At least he knew *the people* where Angevin government pressed them, and in 1212, when he had discovered the treachery of his barons, and was confiscating their castles, he bid high for the support of the counties and boroughs, restoring the forest custom of his father,[1] and limiting the prises of his galley captains upon the ports.[2] In 1213,[3] and again

---

[1] Coventry, 214. Annals of Dunstable, *ann.* 1211. A writ of May 1212 ordering knights who are not verderers to meet Brian de Insula in every county north of Trent suggests that this concession was planned before the baronial treason. Letters Close, 14 John, p. 129.   [2] Coventry, 207.

[3] Letters Patent, 14 John, p. 97. Inquisitions on oppressions by the sheriffs of

in 1215, under the prompting of Nicholas of Tusculum, he entered upon an enquiry as to the sheriff's exactions, though the second inquest was interrupted by the barons' rising. The best known of his local officials were men who had served the nation well under Richard.[1] With his subjects, other than of the knightly order, he was accounted peace-loving and charitable.[2] London owed him gratitude for his share in creating her commune, and throughout his reign he sold municipal liberties freely. In return, reading the king's heart rightly or wrongly, the country did not follow the barons against him. London was surprised into admitting the barons' army and could not shake it off,[3] but the ports stood by him with persistent loyalty,[4] York stood a siege for him in 1216,[5] and beyond the range of the rebels' arms the land lay quiet.[6]

Yet we cannot doubt that John was a bad king for his age. Nature and experience turned his familiarity with the great feudatories into dislike and suspicion. When it was inexpedient to retaliate, as with William Marshal in 1205, he left the offender in no doubt as to the bitterness of his resentment. When, as against the Braioses, he was free to act, his revenge went beyond all reason. As the reign went on his temper hardened into contemptuous rejection of all the normal sanctions of vassalage, and to a suspension of many of the safeguards of common right.

Lincolnshire and Yorkshire. In 1212 he had allowed the knights of at least one shrievalty (Somerset-Dorset) *habere vicecomites ex seipsis*. Letters Close, 14 John, p. 131. Cornwall was entirely disafforested. *Ibid.* 16 John, p. 197.

[1] W. A. Morris, *Medieval Sheriff*, p. 163.

[2] Coventry, 207: *Viduis dicitur propitius extitisse, et pacis provisioni, quantum ad temporalia attinet, satis sedulus extitisse*: he is said to have been merciful to widows, and to have exerted himself constantly to maintain the peace in secular matters.

[3] Coventry, 220. Wendover, 116.

[4] Coggeshall, 181. The Cinque Ports submitted to Louis in collusion with John. Annals of Dunstable, 46. Seaford provides an interesting example of a borough which adhered to John against the orders of its rebel lord Gilbert de l'Aigle: *eidem Gileberto nec alicui alii inimico nostro aliquid unquam facere voluisti quod ad dispendium corone nostre redundaret*: you have never willingly helped the said Gilbert or any other enemy of ours against the interests of our crown. Letters Patent, 18 John, p. 196 (John's letter of thanks to the town).

[5] The mayor was rewarded with a grant of rebels' lands in 1215. Letters Close, 17 John, p. 260.

[6] There were riots in Northampton, and a baronial force at Exeter was dispersed. Coventry, p. 220; Annals of Dunstable, 48.

Judging from the Close, Patent, and Fine Rolls, John preserved the system of his father and brother without any glaring abuses during the first half of his reign, and remained upon terms with his barons which allowed of their meeting in council.[1] In 1205 came *John and the feudatories* the refusal of service beyond the sea by the magnates of the host, and in July Hubert Walter's restraint was removed by death. The year 1207 saw the quarrel with Rome, and 1208 the interdict and the sequestration of the church lands. For four years from 1208 the Chancery Rolls are lacking, but the sparse records of the chronicles suggest a growth of tension. The Christmas reunion of chivalry had been held by John for one day only in 1204.[2] By 1209 the barons attended reluctantly from fear of the king.[3] When we have the light of the Rolls again we find John upon the point of discovering the treason of 1212, and it is not too much to say that in this second phase of his reign he has changed from a king in the hard Angevin tradition to one who, at least to his nobles, is a tyrant.

No doubt the change was gradual. Already before 1208 the bad *Baronial* precedent had been set of taking the heirs and friends of the barons *hostages* as hostages, and so betraying the king's mistrust for the loyalty sworn in homage. It would seem to have begun, perhaps pardonably, with the taking of hostages from the Irish barons. In 1212, at least for the northerners, it had become almost a normal incident of tenure.[4] They were not always badly treated. The sons of Richard de Umfraville came in charge of their tutor, and were set to serve the queen's table,[5] but the pressure which could be brought to bear through them is shown by John's words to earl David in August 1212: "you have given us your son as hostage . . . therefore we order you to yield us your castle at Fotheringhay".[6] As John cut away his vassals' duty from its legiti- *Disseizin* mate basis and put it upon one of fear, he was also undermining their common law right. It is impossible to tell how many of John's

---

[1] Thus, in the spring of 1207 there were councils at London and Oxford, and an aid was granted.

[2] Wendover, ii. 9.   [3] *Ibid*. iii. 231.

[4] In 1212-13 we know of hostages held from Vaux, Lucy of Egremont, earl David, Muschamp, Umfraville, Merlay, Mowbray, Bruce, Clifford, Lindsay, Avenel, Comyn, Patrick of Dunbar. It is fair to say that he was only using a primitive right of the Norman dukes.

[5] Letters Close, 14 John, p. 122.   [6] Letters Patent, 14 John, p. 94.

orders to take lands into his hand were disseizins without judgment—possibly all that are minuted *per preceptum Regis*, and they
are many—but of some instances we can be certain. In May 1212
the king ordered Ralf Berners to be disseized of his lands and his
nephew given seizen if he did not cross to Poitou,[1] and in the same
year the custos of Warkworth is warned that if he does not at once
produce the pledge which his lord, earl Ferrars, has promised the
king, the earl will be disseized of certain lands he holds in fee-
farm.[2] Here John is using disseizin as an act of administrative
routine, a kind of stronger distraint, and that he had come to
adopt it as a principle we can infer from his admission in June 1215,
"we are to restore to our barons all those lands, castles, and rights
of which we have disseized any of them unjustly and without
judgment".[3]

*Charters
of fealty*

From 1212 an increasing number of the barons passed under a
system which joined both these devices of terrorism, the exaction
of hostages and the denial of legal defence, into a yoke which was
inescapable. The pledge of hostages began to be supplemented or
exchanged for a special charter from vassal to king, which renewed
the obligation of fidelity, renounced all treasonous correspondence, and agreed that by the mere fact of such treason the lands,
and in some the life, of the tenant should be *ipso facto* at the mercy
of the crown. Apparently such charters developed out of John's
agreements with foreign auxiliaries who were not bound to him
as "natural lord"—the first of the kind seems to be that which
gave a lodgment in English feudalism to Savary de Mauleon in
1206[4]—but after 1212 they become increasingly common as between the king and his native vassals. On August 24 of that year,
within a week of John's discovery of the plot to seize him in the
host, Richard de Umfraville yielded him a charter[5] promising his

---

[1] Letters Close, 14 John, p. 117. So Richard fitz Henry was disseized for not
joining the army in 1213, and was only to be restored on compliance. *Ibid.* 15
John, p. 148.   [2] *Ibid.* 14 John, p. 119.
[3] The bulk of the lands referred to were probably seized after the barons had
made their diffidation (*ibid.* 16 John, p. 200), but as early as 1213 the king found
it necessary to command an inquisition whether Geoffrey de Lucy has been disseized of Newington *per voluntatem nostram vel per judicium curie nostre* (*ibid.* 15
John, p. 136). Other instances are Fine Rolls, 15 John, p. 471. Another not uncommon device of John's was to sell a writ for an inquisition to one party, and
a second quashing the effect of the inquest to the other. Fine Rolls, p. 23.
[4] Letters Patent, 8 John, p. 66.   [5] Letters Close, 14 John, p. 122.

four sons as hostages with the cession of Prudhoe castle, and agreeing that if he should be discovered to have had part in the recent
treason, his sons, his lands, and his castle should be at the crown's
mercy, and that "we may do with his body as with that of a
traitor". The substance of this charter was suggested by suspicion
of treason, but John was quick to see its possibilities in the general
field of vassalage. In September 1213, John, constable of Chester,
could only secure his inheritance by binding himself by a similar
charter by which, though it acknowledged the special loyalty of
his father and himself,[1] he agreed *quod si unquam a servicio domini
regis recesserit et ad inimicos domini Regis divertit omnes terre sue et
tenementa sua domino Regi incurrantur.*[2] When, in the spring of 1216
many barons came to make submission, they found that they
could only do so by placing their lands and liberties outside the
law by such a *carta de fidelitate Regi.*[3] The king's plans for the
future state of his barons may be seen by the terms upon which
Gilbert fitz Reinfred,[4] one of the oldest servants of his own and his
brother's reign, but taken in arms in Rochester castle, purchased
his peace. He paid 12,000 marks, gave up Kendal and Merhull
castles with twelve hostages from the principal families of north
Lancashire, recanted his oath to the charter and to all the king's
enemies, swore to serve John faithfully all his life, and to submit
to perpetual disherison if he broke any part of his agreement. It is
fair to say that the charters of fealty were first prompted by a
legitimate fear of treason, and that record of them is most common
in the last year of the reign, when they became general. But a
clause of the charter[5] demands the giving back of all such charters
delivered to the king, and they must have been numerous by
1215. Had John reëstablished his power, there can be little doubt
that they would have superseded the legitimate feudal tie with its
patiently evolved safeguards of law. Their essence was that they
disclaimed the right of legal defence in advance, and made the

[1] *Pro bono et fideli servicio predicti patris ipsius . . . et servicio ejusdem Johannis
quod bonum et fidele dominus Rex spectat habere.* Fine Rolls, 15 John, p. 494.

[2] *Ibid.* p. 495: that if he ever went back from the service of the lord king, and
joined his enemies all his lands and tenements should be forfeit to the lord king.

[3] *Secundum tenorem aliarum cartarum quas alii qui ad pacem domini Regis venerunt
fecerunt.* Fine Rolls, 17 John, p. 575.

[4] W. Farrer, *Lancashire Pipe Rolls,* p. 257.

[5] Magna Carta, 49: *Omnes . . . cartas statim reddemus que liberate fuerunt nobis
ab Anglicis in securitatem pacis vel fidelis servicii.*

king's mercy the normal state of vassalage. They made homage meaningless, put tenure upon the ground of private agreement, and were, in effect, the forced acceptance by great individuals of that disherison without trial as the sanction of the king's precepts that John was making the rule in dealings with his feudal subjects as a whole.

The approach to the Charter   It was with this overwhelming threat to common right, and especially with certain great instances of its operation in their minds, that the barons approached the crisis of the charter. The natural point of departure for opposition in 1215 was, indeed, a legal one. In 1191 it could be maintained that the status of the chancellor was irregular, and there was a premature concentration upon the powers of the justiciary and the use of the seals, which was really beyond the natural capacity of the age. Not for sixty years would these issues be incorporated into an attack upon the crown as such. In 1215 the executive was that of the king without doubt, and its legitimacy was therefore beyond challenge. Only his use of it could be attacked, and that, with the ideas of that generation, could only be approached by the one channel in which he was responsible for his actions. The king was custodian of the law. Law must be restated and reaffirmed. There could be no disposition to criticize the basis or authority of administration; only to bring it back to its subservience to custom. It is said that at St. Paul's in the summer of 1213 Langton encouraged the barons to believe that they might recover their lost rights—*jura*—and that this was the mainspring of the revolt. The primary meaning of such terms would be concrete, relating to individual claims by inheritance or to defined points of customary right. The magnates had bargained with John upon his succession, exacting a promise *quod redderet unicuique illorum jus suum*,[1] such *jura*, no doubt, as the Ferrars claim to a share in the Peverel lands, which the earl did indeed receive in 1199.[2] The course of the charter negotiations shows that such rights were in the forefront of the barons' minds, and the first of all their demands, propounded five weeks before the general programme of the barons' Articles, and a

[1] Howden, *sub anno* 1199.
[2] The hundreds of Hecham, Blisworth, and Newbottle. Fine Rolls, 1 John, p. 3. The *comites Angliae* made the same claim before they would cross the sea in 1201.

condition to entering into treaty at all, was for the restoration of the course of law. "We have conceded to the barons who are against us that we will not take nor disseize them nor their men": *nisi per legem regni nostri vel per judicium parium suorum in curia* Restora-*nostra*.[1] Upon that same day, May 10, the parties to two of the *tion of* great causes of the day, the Braiose bishop of Hereford and *judgment of court* Geoffrey de Mandeville, ventured to test the king's sincerity in the restoration of legal process, and brought their causes into court. Geoffrey's case shows how plainly the special charters of the king stood for the opposition in the forefront of his denial of the common course of justice. A year earlier he had been granted the marriage of the heiress of Gloucester with her honour, for which a fine of 20,000 marks was imposed by way both of marriage purchase and relief. By charter he had agreed to complete his payment in sums of five thousand marks at successive terms within the year, and to surrender all his lands to the king if he failed at any one term.[2] In brief, much like his peers, who were forced to warrant their loyalty by putting themselves in the king's mercy, he had risked the tenurial right of all his lands, and debarred himself from legal action upon his bargain. Assured now of the judgment of his peers, he wished "to have the judgment of our court as to the debt which is being exacted from him for having the Countess Isabella to wife".[3] With him all those who had been deprived of their lands by the king's mere precept, and those who had offered up their right by charter, would, by John's surrender of May 10, be restored to the primary right of their tenure—judgment.

In May the magnates were still concerned to restore a safe legal *The* basis for themselves, for without it they could not have remained *barons'* within range of the king's power. The privilege of May 10 is *right in judgment* therefore for the king's barons in the king's court. The legal programme of the Articles of the barons and the Great Charter[4] broadens to the full scope of the law, covers the right of all those who have a tenure in fee or socage, and makes provision for improvements in Henry II's procedural changes in the light of a

---

[1] Letters Patent, 16 John, p. 141: except by the law of our realm or by judgment of their peers in our court.

[2] Fine Rolls, 15 John, p. 521.   [3] Patent Rolls, 16 John, p. 141.

[4] The authenticity of the so-called Unknown Charter and its origin remain matters of pure speculation, and it seems unsafe to use it in argument. Cf. W. S. McKechnie, *Magna Carta*, pp. 171-5, and Appendix.

generation of experience. It is, in fact, a restoration of Henry's law with such adjustment as time has suggested. The primary legal clause, from which all the others take their tone, reflects the fact that a process older than the assizes of Henry still holds part of the field, and that—perhaps especially for their own order—the magnates wish it retained. The king promises that no free man shall be imprisoned, disseized, or outlawed *nisi per legale judicium parium suorum vel per legem terrae*.[1] By one of the two forms, either assize or *judicium*, every man must be accorded fair trial of right. By 1215 most causes will, indeed, be decided *per legem terrae* but without judgment in the archaic sense of the term which still prevailed.[2] For every freeman there remained, however, the choice of the older English medial doom in civil causes and the Norman judgment after suit and witness, and the barons believe, and in part establish, that as barons they are immune from presentment for crime, and may seek judgment of court for that also. In May they had expressed this immunity as a right to judgment *in curia regis*: in June they found a more accurate and comprehensive term, the *judicium parium*, which, though it failed to become a decisive factor in English common law, was part of the feudal theory of justice. For the freeman not of baronial rank the judgment of peers would be fulfilled by judgment in his county, for the baron it meant trial by his own order in the king's presence, or at least in that of his chief justiciar, and they must have had in mind that virtuose stroke of law by which John had evaded trial of Eustace de Vesci and Robert fitz Walter before their peers in 1212.[3]

Safeguards of common law

Except for this touch of conservatism, the demand of the Charter is for the regular application of the common law as it then

---

[1] Magna Carta, 39.

[2] If the subject has been presented by his neighbours on a criminal charge under the Assize of Clarendon, or has applied for a writ of assize, there will, of course, be no *judicium parium*, for he will go at once to the ordeal, or stand or fall by the inquest. *Judicium parium* and *lex terrae* are therefore contrasted with each other. These processes, though not yet old, are assizes, and therefore part of the *consuetudo patriae, lex terrae*.

[3] Robert fitz Walter was cited for treason in four successive courts of his county of Essex, and outlawed by a Saxon enactment whose antiquity must have commended itself to the most austere defender of custom among the barons. But it was custom applied by the commonalty of a county under the eye of Geoffrey fitz Peter. Letters Close, 15 John, p. 165. Howden says that the same procedure was adopted in the case of Eustace de Vesci. The Devil was quoting scripture, as John often liked to do.

stood, and the Charter's legal clauses stand in natural succession to the great assizes of Henry. Experience must have taught the need of dividing the pleas of the crown, with their restricted right of delay and essoin, from the common pleas between subject and subject, and the Charter demands that *communia placita* shall no longer follow the king, but shall be tried in some fixed place.[1] It is the first clear recognition of a Common Bench. The assizes are to be taken four times a year by justiciars in every county,[2] and in this the whole Henrician system of writs and processes as Glanvill described them is seen to be accepted. Of all Henry's work, only the writ called *Praecipe*, which placed the justiciars in immediate jurisdiction of any cause to which it was applied, was singled out for condemnation: it deprived the plaintiff equally with the defendant of his choice of jurisdiction, and was a direct invasion of the judicial immunity of his lord. Thereby, "a free man might lose his court",[3] and the defendant his choice between judgment and assize.

The clauses dealing with the administrative safeguards of justice *Administrative* are in advance of anything which has gone before them. They *safeguards* include a curious attempt to reconcile the old judicial quality of *of justice* the *seniores* of the shire communities with the new commissioned justice; the itinerant justiciars are to have four knights elected by the county courts as associates in taking the assizes.[4] Here, too, we may detect the contemporary reverence for peerage. Glanvill's rule that amercements should be assized by the oath of neighbours and should not exceed the capacity of the payer is reiterated,[5] no king's officer is to have the right of putting men to the ordeal without adequate witness,[6] the writ *de odio et atia*, protecting the subject from malicious prosecution, is to be free to all,[7] and to no man "will the king sell,[8] or deny, or delay justice."[9] The process

---

[1] Magna Carta, 17.   [2] *Ibid.* 19.   [3] *Ibid.* 34.
[4] *Ibid.* 18.   [5] *Ibid.* 20.   [6] *Ibid.* 38.   [7] *Ibid.* 36.
[8] A reasonable and uniform charge for writs was never abandoned, but the monarchy had been used to selling inquests at prices which corresponded, if with anything, with the wealth of the suitor and the value of the land sued for. Thus in 1213 Alan of Galloway fined 340 marks for an inquest as to his mother's lands. Fine Rolls, 15 John, p. 467. A simple instance of the sale of justice is that of William de Braiose who buys a trial *coram rege* and will pay 700 marks if he wins and £100 if he loses (*ibid.* 1 John, p. 46). In the year 1200 William de Mowbray fined 2000 marks *ut dominus rex faciat eum deduci juste et secundum consuetudinem Anglie in loquela quae est inter ipsum et Willelmum de Stutevilla* (*ibid.* p. 102).   [9] Magna Carta, 40.

of stripping the sheriffs of their power of justice is completed, and none of the resident provincial officials are henceforth to hold the pleas of the crown. Taken together, these provisions well represent that phase of English jurisprudence when the practice of popular justice was giving place to judgment by special commission, and go as far towards securing that the new judiciary shall be an independent one as was then possible.

Feudal obligations defined Most of this legal matter may be regarded as the vindication of preëxisting common right. The second great work of the charter is to bring to an end the indefiniteness of feudalism. For the first time the custom of English feudal tenure ceases to be a fluctuating, variously interpreted convention between lord and man, and takes its place as a defined component of English common law. We have seen how the feudalism of Henry lacked that fixity which might have safeguarded it from exploitation by John. The latter was no innovator in this, but his exactions were ceaseless and heavy, falling especially upon the open points of relief, wardship, marriage, aid, and scutage, and to prove them it should be sufficient to point to the rolls. They contain such outstanding cases as John of Chester's seven thousand mark fine for taking up his barony,[1] or William de Braiose's five thousand marks for his Irish lands— which ended by ruining him [2]—and they bear constant witness to the sale of wardships at prices which could hardly be recovered by fair means during a minority,[3] to fines exacted before their dower was accorded to widows,[4] for leave to remain unmarried [5] or marry where they will,[6] for the marriage of heirs and heiresses.[7] The charter seeks to fix what can be fixed at a reasonable level, enormously lower than the average exaction of the crown, and to protect women and minors in those relations with the king which were unavoidable in feudalism and capable of abuse, but which could not be reduced to figures. Relief is to be divorced

---

[1] *Fine Rolls*, 15 John, p. 483. Thurstan Banaster fined 500 marks for Makerfield (*ibid.* 15 John, p. 488). Its farm stood at about £23 when it was in the king's hand (W. Farrer, *Lancashire Pipe Rolls*, p. 246). This would be about fifteen years' purchase, and the last holder, Warin Banaster, had already been fined 400 marks in 1204 (Fine Rolls, 6 John, p. 207).

[2] *Ibid.* 6 John, p. 232.
[4] *Ibid.* 6 John, p. 232.
[6] *Ibid.* 2 John, pp. 91, 96.

[3] *Ibid.* 7 John, p. 316.
[5] *Ibid.* 2 John, p. 82.
[7] *Ibid.* 1 John, pp. 8, 24, 45, 57.

from the value of the inheritance and fixed at what the barons believed to have been its "ancient" rate, an earl for his barony, and a baron for his, a hundred pounds, a knight for a full knight's fee a hundred shillings, and from fractions of fees less.[1] No more than reasonable profit, without waste of men and chattels, is to be taken from estates under wardship,[2] and the estate is to be returned to the heir in full order when he comes of age.[3] Heirs are to be married within their own rank—*absque disparagatione*[4]—and after due notice to the kin. Widows shall not be compelled to remarry against their will[5] and shall receive their inheritance, marriage portion, and dower without fine.[6]

The greater levies, being general to the whole feudal order, could be determined by assize, and were capable of more precise definition. No scutage or aid, except the three customary aids, and those at a reasonable rate, were to be taken *nisi per commune concilium regni*,[7] the authority of such councils being the inherent function of tenants-in-chief of making provision or assize in the court of their lord. Such assizes were of original feudal right, and, according to the assumptions of feudal statesmen, were treated as equivalent to those of the community at large. The amount of the aid or scutage was to be decided by assize *secundum consilium illorum qui presentes fuerint*,[8] and in order to obtain this common voice the king would summon his tenants in chief, the greater barons directly by writ, and the lesser barons through the sheriff. The assembly would thus be the *curia* of the king's immediate tenants and nothing more. The *regnum* is regarded as the circle of the immediate vassals: indeed, though the charter recurs several times to the term "community", that community's contact with the crown is always thought of as being maintained indirectly through the medium of tenure. That such a council could hardly meet is, perhaps, of little importance, and was, indeed, recognized at the time, but, in addition, its sessions were limited to those occasions, which it was hoped would be rare, when an exceptional levy was demanded, and its function was purely that of assizing the aid.[9] *Commune consilium regni*, thus defined and applied, meant,

Aids and scutages

Commune consilium

---

[1] Magna Carta, 2.   [2] Ibid. 4.   [3] Ibid. 5.
[4] Ibid. 6.   [5] Ibid. 8.   [6] Ibid. 7.
[7] Ibid. 12.   [8] Ibid. 14.
[9] Ibid. 14: *de auxilio assidendo.*

therefore, far less than the terms suggest, and, since such counsel lay in the full tradition of feudal assemblies, the Charter's greatest innovation may be thought to lie in the insistence on formal summons and the right of attendance. In the light of the barons' tendency themselves to assume the status of a national representative it is not surprising that in 1216 the whole clause was dropped, for, while it called for attendance far beyond the circle of the barons, it held nothing of direct value for the shires and boroughs. The financial check had a more important future. It was, no doubt, implicit in the feudal relation, but here it was set out for the first time explicitly, and, because of the wide interpretation which the word "aid" had been given during the past twenty years, it was one capable of covering other forms of taxation than those based on the fees. The subsidies upon revenue and other chattels which were to finance the crown during the following period were in origin varieties of the aid. The tallages of London were reckoned as *auxilia*, and safeguarded by the same clause as the aids of the barons, though the privilege was soon let slip.

The defensores   Of constitutional plan the Charter contained little. Its final clause is a provision which has been thought to aim at a kind of executive council, and which seems to have had something of the effect of such a council in the August of 1215, but the intention of which was in fact very different. The barons are to elect twenty-five of their number "to observe, hold, and make to be observed the peace and liberties which we have conceded to them". If those liberties are broken and the king refuses amends, the Twenty-Five are to rouse the *communa regni* against him, and make war against his lands, castles, and possessions, saving his person and those of the queen and the princes. Of this body it may be said outright that they in no way anticipate the conciliar committees of the succeeding reigns. Their function is the diffidation followed by the lawful rebellion of feudalism, their status is that of *fidejussores* such as swore to most treaties in the twelfth century, twelve or more barons of the kings of France or England, or the count of Flanders, pledging themselves to renounce their liegeance and make war upon their natural lord if he breaks the treaty to which he and they have set their hands.[1] A device essentially the same had been used

[1] Cf. the Treaty of 1201 between John and Philip. Howden, iv. 175. So also the Treaty of Falaise.

by John in the charters which he exacted from the barons *de fidelitate*,[1] and it had been the normal guarantee of conventions between English parties for three generations.[2] There was thus no conciliar scheme of control, it was some years too early for that; but there was this advance, that, for the first time, the crown was forced to sacrifice its servants to administrative expediency. John is to remove from office all the adherents of Gerard d'Athies and certain other foreigners[3] and to confine his choice of justiciars, constables, sheriffs, and bailiffs to such as know the law and are willing to observe it.[4] There had never before been any tendency to turn the tables on the king and claim to determine the custody of his castles,[5] but from this time onwards the control of castles and counties becomes a recurrent issue of politics, and in the reign of Henry III every change in the political balance will be reflected in a change of constables and sheriffs.

The Great Charter offers little to reward the historian in search *General* of "constitutional precedents"; perhaps the assizing of the aids *effect* and the design for *commune consilium* might be accepted as such. It *of the charter* was, indeed, essentially what the king called it, "a peace between us and our barons"; we cannot detect any very deep stirring of the nation, and if John had lived another twenty years it might almost have come to be forgotten. The political events which surrounded it and every clause of its articles bear a feudal colour, though it is that of Henry's tamed and legalized feudalism.[6] The rising was not treason—indeed the barons asserted that the king had rebelled against them[7]—it was preceded by diffidation,[8] carried through in legitimate warfare,[9] closed with a peace, "so

---

[1] *Rotuli de oblatis*, 15 John, p. 494. Twenty knights of the constable of Chester swear *si predictus Johannes a servicio Domini Regis recesserit . . . ipsi cum omnibus tenementis suis ad Dominum Regem se divertent.*
[2] Cf. the charter of Treaty between Stephen and Henry of Anjou. Rymer, *Foedera*, i. 3.   [3] Magna Carta, 50.   [4] *Ibid.* 45.
[5] In August 1215 castellans were being appointed *de communi consilio* (Letters Patent, 17 John, p. 181). The barons were also seizing the shrievalties (Coventry, 224).
[6] Those clauses touching the villein and the merchant may be explained by the profit these classes brought to the land-owner. The king and other great persons had their own merchants, *mercator meus*, under their personal protection.   [7] *Perjurus et baronibus rebellis.* Wendover, ii. 117.
[8] *Regem diffiduciantes . . . et hominia sua reddentes.* Coventry, p. 219.
[9] *Guerra mota inter Dominum Regem Johannem . . . et barones Anglie* is the normal formula of the rolls.

that we have taken again our barons' homages".[1] The text itself is a medley of recognition, assize, and feudal *conventio*. Its ultimate sanction is the implied feudal contract and its immediate safeguards the *fidejussores* of feudal treaties and the *diffidatio*. Yet, taken together, the events of 1215-16, the Great Charter, and the death of John, constitute one of the crucial episodes of English history.

The legal changes of Henry II have come to stand to us for a great reform, a common law, and a general safeguard of right. So the great lawyer intended each assize individually to be. But collectively they might have turned into something different. When it became true that no claim for free tenement could be initiated without the king's writ—and this was established when Glanvill's book was written—a profound revolution had been completed. Since the beginning of her history—though decreasingly so during the Norman reigns—the law of England had been put into motion by the self-directed machinery of moot jurisdictions which were in effect autonomous legal republics. The oath of a plaintiff of sound lawful standing was of itself sufficient to throw open to him the court of shire or hundred, to bring his antagonist into court, and to command judgment of his cause. No change could affect the fibre of life more deeply than one which destroyed this open access to law and denied the courts to those from whom the king's writ was withheld. Henceforth the civil rights of any Englishman were at the discretion of a power other than that of himself and his neighbours. Henry II was, in fact, probably the first king of whom even an unjustified accusation of denying or delaying justice could have had any real meaning.

The sanctity of law

Between 1154 and 1216 the system by which the king accorded judgment as a royal boon and not a right was itself upon trial. This was the first great test of the responsibility of the crown, for such a power could be exercised with various effect. If the belief that almost all men of learning held—that the king was trustee for the law which must itself determine his actions—were to become fact, then the king's will must be an impersonal force, activating procedure automatically, having issue, often by deputy, in impartial judgment. The personal will of the king must become a fiction, while the authority of the crown through its writs remained the

[1] Letters Patent, 17 John, p. 143: *Firma pax facta est per Dei gratiam inter nos et barones nostros . . . ita quod eorum homagia eodem die ibidem cepimus.*

most formidable guarantee of legality. The rising tide of early thirteenth-century thought, with its desire to bring political expediency to the test of moral law,[1] was against *vis et voluntas* and in
favour of the triumph of reasoned order in jurisprudence, but it
was exposed to an assault by men of action who put reason of
state before individual right, and would make the king the master
and not the servant of law. This was the threat to which English
law was at least occasionally exposed under Henry II, and which
materialized as a sporadic attack upon the great units of property
under John. In his last year many of the strongest feudatories
were at his mercy, and, had his reign continued, the whole basis
of common law might have been subverted. Exacted by magnates,
the liberties of 1215 were appropriated by a commonalty of free
men. In 1219, when the judgment and assize of the county of
Lincoln in favour of Gilbert de Gant had been traversed by the
Marshal's writ, the full county court appealed to the *libertas concessa
et jurata*, and made a great baron's cause that of the community
of the realm—*cum eo et pro eo acclamante, immo pro se ipsis, et pro
communi totius regni.*[2]

To the enlightened, therefore, the "liberties of free men" were *The
freeman
of the
Charter*
those of the community at large. To say in retrospect that they
and the community they protected were alike of the feudal order
is almost meaningless. If by the accusation of feudal interest
the individualist spirit of 1173 is meant, that had been dead for
forty years as an effective force, though echoes of it recur for a
couple of centuries; if the ordered, writ-controlled feudalism of
Henry II, it was precisely a reassertion of feudalism that was
needed, for his reign had made tenurial right part of a common law
of the realm. The two seem in that day identical. There is and
can be no claim to speak for the magnates alone. Relations are too
closely interwoven, the man of great tenure in one county is too
often the small tenant of another, to make anything short of a
general defence of the law of free tenures possible. In a society in
which the greatest earl was at once lord of hundreds, subject in
royal and private hundreds, tenant by barony, knight service,
serjeanty, socage, fee-farm, and term of years, the concept of the
liber homo, standing for all tenures—other than the precarious right

---

[1] F. M. Powicke, *Stephen Langton*, p. 90.
[2] *Royal Letters of Henry III* (ed. Shirley), i. 20.

of villeinage—can be nothing short of the type of the community.
The Without any sense of incongruity, therefore, the magnates use the
communa terms of political community which are at this very time making
of the their way into common speech. They speak of *communa totius*
Charter *Angliae, commune consilium regni.* But their understanding of
politics is still not that of the state but of the fee. For them the
regnum is primarily the *dominium* of the king over his immediate
tenants. The mesne tenures remain in the background, taking their
place through the derived right of the tenures *in capite.* Upon the
fringes of the feudal order are persons and tenures—burgesses and
sokemen of varying degrees of independence—whose place in the
communa they would find it difficult either to define or deny.
Villeins, who have no land in fee, or landless freemen, are beyond
their view, which is essentially one of a community of tenures. It
is a political idea which needs to be clarified and translated into
the terms of the state; yet, imperfectly detached from notions of
tenure as it is, this baronial conception of *communitas,* and the sense
of their own quality as its natural representatives, inspires the
baronage to act as a national opposition in the thirteenth century,
and is an important phase in the growth of constitutional theory.
For the first time, though imperfectly, it is asserted in the Great
Charter.

To the edge of such community the country had been brought by
sixty years of Angevin rule. The federalism of the past, federalism
of races and laws under the Saxons, of feudal honours under the
Normans, was now reconciled under the growing predominance
of the crown. Law was one in essentials throughout the kingdom,
and the dependence of judgment upon the king's writ had turned
folkright into king's law. A legal community of the realm was
now a realized fact, and a political community could not be far in
the future. The national fibre had, moreover, been strong enough
to impose its virtue upon the government. Thirteenth-century
administration derived most of its efficacy from inquest, and therefore rested upon the integrity and independence of the legal
communities of the shires. In this it inherited the spirit of the
English past. Under John, working through the magnates, this
spirit had set final limits beyond which the crown might not
depart from tradition, and it may be thought that what was best
in both régimes had survived—the strength of Saxon provincial

communities and the administrative efficiency of the foreign crown. Because this balance of the two traditions had been achieved, and would not be substantially changed in the future, the death of John closed a stage in English history. For the future, the struggle for civil right being won, the concern of the nation is to be the imposition of political control upon the crown, and the battle shifts from the ground of law to that of the constitution.

iv

CROWN AND UNIVERSITAS. 1216–1272

The death of John on October 19, 1216, destroyed his tyranny *The new* at the moment when it seemed to be becoming secure, and the *reign* balance reverted to that baronial ·interpretation of the régime which had prevailed in the movement against Longchamps and, more crudely, in that of the Charter. As was usual in these recurrent reversals, the form of the executive was not challenged, and the majority of John's officials were retained. William Marshal replaced or afforced Hubert de Burgh as justiciar in the crisis of the king's death,[1] but resigned almost immediately. Hubert, Richard Marsh the chancellor, the chamberlain Geoffrey Nevill, continued in office, as did the justiciar of Ireland, and many of the sheriffs. The government was, in fact, John's, but with a policy which differed from that of the opposition only in being more deliberate. The minority of the king drove the magnates to the partial precedent of 1191, and on or before November 20[2] the marshal was bearing the title *Rector Regis et Regni*. Unlike the Supreme Rectorship of John, his office was a real one. There was no regent judiciary to dispute his power, and until his death in 1219 writs ran under his private seal and over the witness *Teste Comite.*[3]

A great council at Bristol from November 13 to 20 founded the new reign. There homage was sworn, the king was crowned, the Charters reiterated, and the Marshal assumed the rectorship. The caution of the guiding magnates, and perhaps the policy of

---

[1] Letters Close, 1 Henry III, p. 293 (Nov. 13): *Teste Comite Willelmo Marescallo Justiciario Anglie apud Bristollium.*   [2] *Loc. cit.*

[3] *Quia nondum habuimus sigillum has litteras sigillo dilecti et fidelis Comitis Willelmi Marescalli rectoris nostri et regni nostri fecimus sigillari. Ibid.* p. 293. The influence of the legates was constant and at certain times crucial, but since they acted by Apostolic authority their action was not directly constitutional.

the legate, took care that the right of Henry should in no way be tarnished by the recent challenge to his father's. An affirmation of the Charter was essential from every point of view, but it was to be detached from the events of 1215, and to appear as a spontaneous act of the new reign and its counsellors. "Our late Lord and Father being happily passed from the light of our day, and his soul gathered to the elect . . . we have heard how indignation arose between the said lord our Father and certain of the nobles of our realm, whether with good cause or none we know not . . . wherefore, according to every man his right . . . and abating in our realm all evil customs . . . we will to restore the good days of our forefathers."[1] The new charter of liberties issued from Bristol three weeks after the king's death, immediately after the coronation, and as a response to the homage of the lieges. It was substantially the same as that of 1215. Clauses Twelve and Fourteen of the former, calling for the assent of *commune consilium* to aids and scutages, and defining common counsel as the assembly of all tenants-in-chief, were omitted as *gravia et dubitabilia*, and with them the clause which limited the aids of mesne tenants to the three customary occasions.[2] Half the baronage was in homage to Louis of France, and likely to remain so, and the counsellors of the minority could not make supply contingent upon the remote possibility of a *commune consilium regni* as defined in 1215. Perhaps the provision of the reissue of 1217, that scutage should be taken as it was in the time of King Henry II, expressed the general intention to get the consent of the *curia* without attempting to define its composition.

The Charter reissued

A minority was, indeed, calculated to prolong the Henrician transition phase of government by a developed executive in ill-determined relation to an acknowledged tenurial right of counsel, and in November 1216 the barons were well placed to hold their own. Lands and custodies were left as they were held before the war, and, though it was agreed that no binding alienations of royal lands should be made until Henry's majority,[3] many great men were

Nature of the régime

---

[1] Stubbs, *Select Charters*, p. 333.

[2] The magnates were, in fact, authorized to take aids from their tenants for very varied purposes. Letters Close, 1 Hen. III, pp. 319, 330.

[3] *Ibid.* 4 Hen. III, p. 437: *communi omnium magnatum nostrorum consilio provisum esset ne quid sigillo nostro firmum fieret usque ad etatem nostram.*

bought with grants of castles or counties in ward.[1] Territorially
the magnates were stronger than at any time since 1154,[2] and the
government dealt more loosely with nobles and officials than was
the habit of the Angevin kings.[3] William Marshall, and, in the early
years of his predominance, Hubert de Burgh, ruled with a
varying group of officials and barons, sometimes small, sometimes
large, occasionally swelling to *commune consilium*, and apparently
determined only by the nature of the business in hand. There was
no defined *consilium regis*, but the function of counsel inherent in
baronage was called upon as it was needed.[4] The witness to letters
and writs gives us our only hint of the composition of the council,
and they record only such names as were needed to warrant the
chancellor in affixing the great seal. But over long periods we find
letters close and patent going out *teste Comite coram Episcopis
Londoniense et Wintoniense*, or *teste Huberto coram Episcopis Bath-
oniense et Sarisberiense*,[5] and we may infer that small groups of
magnates, working with the necessary clerical and official advice,
were the *consilium regis* by which daily administration was being
done. A summons to the prince of Connaught in 1226 was
witnessed by two bishops, the justiciar, the earl of Gloucester,
Richard of Argentien, Hugh Mortimer, the steward Geoffrey de
Crowcombe, five *curiales* of no special note, the archbishop of
Dublin, Roger Waspail the seneschal of Ulster, and three Irish
tenants, Geoffrey de Costentin, Nicholas of Verdun, and Walter
de Riddleford.[6] By this test Henry's minority councils were in
the common course much like those of John; but aids, scutages,

---

[1] Aumâle received Rockingham and Sauvey in December 1216 (Letters
Patent, 1 Hen. III, p. 13), and Salisbury Sherborne castle and the county of
Somerset in March 1217 (*ibid.* p. 38). In certain cases, as with Ferrars, Walter
de Lacy, Brian de Insula, and Reginald de Braiose, the castles were to be retained
until the end of the king's fourteenth year.

[2] The fact that William Marshall the younger held Marlborough and
Ludgershall was a strong motive for giving him the king's sister as wife.
Royal Letters of Henry III (ed. Shirley), i. 244. Fawkes was accused of making
a large fortune from his counties. *Ibid.* i. 313.

[3] *Ibid.* vol. i. pp. 19, 47, 71, 73.

[4] So Lechlade was granted to Fawkes de Breauté *per ipsum Marescallum et
consilium domini Eboraci Archiepiscopi et Episcoporum Wintonensis, Dunholmensis,
Willemi Briwere*. Letters Close, 2 Hen. III, p. 371. Llewellyn was accorded a
day of trial *de consilio venerabilium patrum Cantuariensis Archiepiscopi, Episcopi
Herefordensis, Huberti de Burgo Justicarii nostri et baronum nostrorum Marchie.*
Ibid. 4 Hen. III, p. 434.

[5] During the years 1224–5–6.

[6] Letters Patent, 10 Hen. III, p. 48.

hidages, carucages—imperfectly distinguished from aids—were faithfully demanded from the *commune concilium*, in spite of the dropping from the Charter of the obligation to do so.[1] In 1230, when both the king and the justiciar left the country, the regency of the chancellor and Segrave, the sealing of the various classes of writs, and the custody of the seals, were determined *de communi consilio*.[2] Here, as at Bristol in 1216, the refounding or recasting of the government was matter for the whole body of the feudatories.

Coöpera-tion of crown and baronage   The minority is the last series of years during which the crown and the baronage act together uncritically upon the old feudal assumptions, largely unconscious of divergent interests. Many factors made it possible for them to do so, the prestige of the Marshal, the Apostolic overlordship transcending local rights and ambitions, the childhood of the king. On the whole, the clauses of the Charter in which the magnates had thought specially for themselves were adhered to. The custody of many of the royal castles was in their hands and gave them a kind of inviolability,[3] reliefs were kept rigidly to the low sums determined in 1215,[4] there was no conspicuous abuse of wardship and marriage, and, though the barons were usually content to submit their causes to assize, they would on occasion demand judgment of their peers.[5] But, as Henry grows towards manhood, signs of strain begin to appear, and it is seen that the thirteenth century will have to deal with con-

[1] Letters Close, 4 Hen. III, p. 437: *concesserunt nobis sui gratia communiter omnes magnates et fideles totius regni nostri donum.*

[2] Letters Patent, 14 Hen. III, p. 339: *de communi consilio comitum et baronum et omnium fidelium nostrorum qui nobiscum aderant apud Portesmue ante transfretationem nostram.*

[3] Fawkes de Breauté, who held six of them, said that if the English barons wanted to try his strength, "he would give them such a war as all England could not hold".

[4] Letters Close, 4 Hen. III, p. 438. The earl of Warwick, £100. For a list of knight's reliefs at 100s. the fee cf. Letters Patent, 2 Hen. III, p. 173.

[5] Letters Patent, 10 Hen. III, p. 82. The young king is made to grant that *dominus rex . . . faciet habere dicto Comiti Marescallo judicium parium suorum de . . . jure et saisina* as to his right in Caerleon. The right of amercement by peers is preserved in the instructions to justices. Letters Close, 3 Hen. III, p. 383. Barons to be amerced *coram consilio nostro*. Refusal of judgment by his peers was one pretext for Richard Marshal's revolt in 1233. Cf. Matthew Paris, *Chronica Majora, sub anno*.

stitutional problems altogether different from those of the past. *Narrowing* Like other "national" governments, that of Henry's minority *of the basis* owed much of its strength to a few individuals who were thought *of the* to be strong and of wide sympathies, and to its adoption of a *govern-* middle course in politics. As time went on, it began to lose its *ment* inclusive character. In the summer of 1217 it had rejected the demand that the earl of Chester should be associated with the marshal as rector [1]; in May 1219 the marshal died, and Pierre des Roches, linked in the unofficial mind with John's rule, was given the guardianship of the king; in 1221 Langton induced Honorius to recall Pandulf from his legation. So it happened that at the very time when the government was announcing the end of the troubled years and celebrating it by the second coronation of the king in May 1220, the circle of its supporters was becoming dangerously narrowed and division was beginning among its leaders.

Nevertheless, this was the moment chosen to initiate a new *Hubert de* policy which came to appear more and more that of the justiciar, *Burgh gains in* and which ended in opening again that gulf between the more *power* independent of the baronage and the crown which the com- promise of 1216 had closed. The minority satisfied the extremists because their hold upon the custodies made them secure in the provinces. In the autumn of 1219 William of Aumâle incurred excommunication for defying the edict against the holding of tournaments, and subsequently refused to surrender the castles of Rockingham and Sauvey. [2] Perhaps as a consequence of this, the coronation was made the justification for an attempted resumption. The Pope wrote ordering ecclesiastical and other magnates to return the royal castles to the king, [3] and on August 9, 1220, there appeared the writ for the first general enquiry *quo warranto* in English history. All those who held royal demesne were ordered to prove their warrant for doing so at the Michaelmas Exchequer. [4] The adventure was not carried through. The reduction of Aumâle cost the country a scutage and a campaign, and there is no sign

---

[1] *Royal Letters of Henry III* (ed. Shirley), i. 532. Later the Pope considered the failure to secure the full coöperation of Ranulf Blundevill as a danger to the régime. Cf. *Ibid.* i. 225.

[2] Letters Close, 4 Hen. III, p. 434.

[3] *Royal Letters of Henry III* (ed. Shirley), i. 535.

[4] Letters Close, 4 Hen. III, p. 437.

that the *quo warranto* returns were acted upon, or, in fact, made. But the episode was significant. Hubert was turning against the less responsible feudatories, and henceforth his government could no longer claim to be that to which they had acceded in 1216. The policy of resumption was pursued, but cautiously. In November 1221 Corfe was recovered from Peter de Mauley,[1] and Bolsover and the Peak from earl Ferrars[2] in the summer of 1222. The earl left the council in anger, and the earl of Chester, hitherto one of the crown's principal supporters, protested to the verge of rebellion, but once more unity was outwardly maintained. It was broken finally when in 1223 the Pope declared Henry of age and Hubert carried through a wholesale resumption at the expense of Fawkes de Breauté and the earl of Chester.[3]

Move against the feudatories

It is evident that Hubert's action was made possible by divisions which had been growing for some time within the ranks of the magnates. Fawkes attributed his disgrace to the treachery of the English barons[4] and as early as 1221 he had attracted the enmity of the Courtneys and the younger William Briwere in the West, and knew that the king's uncle Salisbury was behind their hostility.[5] At that time he was so sure of Hubert's friendship that he begged him not to judge them too hastily out of favour to himself. But a year later he had quarrelled with the young earl Marshal,[6] and the earl was already betrothed to the king's sister. In 1224 Shrewsbury[7] and Pembroke[8] urged the case against him in concert.[9] Thus, the crisis of 1223 presented itself to contemporaries not as a turn away

[1] Letters Patent, 6 Hen. III, p. 321.

[2] *Ibid.* 6 Hen. III, p. 335. Ferrar's custodies of Bolsover and the Peak terminated with the completion of the king's fourteenth year according to an agreement of 1216. *Ibid.* 1 Hen. III, p. 1.

[3] As to Chester, the motive for depriving him of his hold on the north-west Midlands was probably his intervention to defend Llewellyn from the royal expedition of 1223.

[4] *Royal Letters of Henry III* (ed. Shirley), vol. i. pp. 221-222.

[5] *Ibid.* vol. i. p. 172.   [6] *Ibid.* vol. i. p. 175.

[7] *Ibid.* vol. i. p. 221.   [8] *Ibid.* vol. i p. 222.

[9] Fawkes submitted, as did Chester and others, to the deprivation of his castles and sheriffdoms in January 1224, but was involved in a number of private actions for redress, some of them fomented by Salisbury and Pembroke, and was finally ruined by his brother's violence against Henry of Braybrook, one of the justices who had presided in his cause. He was proclaimed *inimicus manifestus regis* on July 11, and soon after left the kingdom.

from the baronage, but as the ruin of a faction.[1] Though Chester
and Llewellyn[2] favoured Fawkes and resisted the redistribution of
power—civil war was only narrowly avoided at the Christmas
council of Northampton[3]—a substantial body of nobles stood by
Hubert and made his action possible. Nevertheless, in historical
perspective, the proclamation of Henry's majority, accompanied
by acts which bear every mark of a conscious shifting of the
centre of power,[4] may be taken as the beginning of a new phase
of monarchical government. The redistribution of the custodies
was so managed as to restore the provincial authority which had
passed from the bureaucracy in 1216. The earl of Chester lost
the castles of Shrewsbury, Bridgnorth, and Lancaster, with the
custody of the counties of Stafford, Shropshire, and Lancaster;
Fawkes surrendered eight castles and the county of Oxford;
Engelard de Cigogné, Windsor and Odiham; Pierre des Roches,
Winchester, Porchester, and the county of Hampshire. In all, about
thirty castles changed hands,[5] and were entrusted for the most
part to the king's servants and knights, men who drew their *Resump-*
liveries from the Chamber, and most of whom had seen service *tion of*
under John and been moderately endowed from the forfeitures *castles*
of 1215.[6] John's experiment of entrusting the counties as custodies
at will, and not at farm, was also revived, so that the sheriffs

1 It is noteworthy that the earl of Salisbury had confirmed to him the
custodies granted him by John, and was allowed to dispose of them in his will
(Letters Patent, 10 Hen. III, p. 12), and that William Marshal was made justiciar
of Ireland (*ibid.* 8 Hen. III, p. 437). In Rome it was feared that the barons as a
whole would be moved to rebellion. *Royal Letters of Henry III* (ed. Shirley),
i. 240.

2 Cf. Llewellyn's bold and dignified explanation of his defence of Fawkes
(*ibid.* i. 229), and the Earl of Chester's (*ibid.* i. 233).

3 *Ibid.* vol. i. p. 225. A fragmentary safe-conduct suggests that Gloucester,
Aumâle, the constable of Chester, Brian de Insula, Robert de Vipont, and
Engelard de Cigogné were involved (Letters Patent, 8 Hen. III, p. 481),
and this is roughly the list given by Matthew Paris (*Chronica Majora, sub
anno* 1224).

4 Matthew Paris (Stubbs, *Select Charters*, 322), says that the Pope's letter
empowered Henry to govern thenceforth *cum suorum domesticorum consilio* and
that the barons protested.

5 Letters Patent, 8 Hen. III, pp. 417-420, 427, 429.

6 Hugh Despenser (Letters Close, 2 Hen. III, p. 345; *ibid.* 6 Hen. III, p. 494);
John Russell (*ibid.* 17 John, p. 232; *ibid.* 2 Hen. III, p. 345); William de Einesford,
Senescallus Regis (*ibid.* 7 John, p. 43); Stephen Segrave (*ibid.* 2 Hen. III, p. 365);
Robert Lupus (*ibid.* 9 John, p. 108; *ibid.* 9 Hen. III, p. 500); William de Rughe-
don (*ibid.* 9 Hen. III, p. 508); Waleran Teutonicus (*ibid.* 16 John p. 218; *ibid.*

henceforth returned every detail of their revenue, and the Exchequer might hold them to an itemized account.

Clerical element in Hubert's government

There was a strong clerical element in this government of Hubert. The bishops took a leading part in the recovery of the custodies,[1] and the suffragans of Canterbury came of their own free will to the siege of Bedford, and granted a special carucage from their demesne lands.[2] From its inception, that is from the winter of 1223, to the beginning of 1226, the bishops of Bath and Salisbury—sometimes joined by the bishop of London and the inescapable William Briwere—are the usual witnesses to the justiciar's executive acts. The basis of the government is also narrower. The phrase *per consilium regis, coram consilio regis* is markedly rarer than in the early years of the reign. In consequence the household executive, which had been so powerful under John, and of which we hear little at the beginning of the minority,

The Wardrobe

wakes to a new activity. The Wardrobe had begun to replace the Chamber in the last years of John; in the first years of Henry the Seneschal replaced both Chamber and Wardrobe as receiver for the Household;[3] but a Roll of the Wardrobe is again mentioned in 1217, and after about 1219 the Chancery Rolls show it drawing upon the Exchequer for the king's personal expenses. The crisis of 1223–4 is reflected by the dismissal of its principal clerk, Peter des Rievaulx, son of the discredited bishop of Winchester, and almost immediately the office is thrust into the foreground as a principal department of state. Much more markedly than under John, the Wardrobe of the years 1224–7 becomes the receiving and spending department for a considerable proportion of the revenue. Under the new clerks, Walter de Brackley and Walter de Kirkham, the Wardrobe receipts spring from the £2000 of 1223 to £9000, £8800, and £6700 in the eighth, ninth, and tenth years, so that they almost equal those of the Chamber of John.

---

9 Hen. III, p. 511); Walter de Fauconberg (*ibid.* 7 Hen. III, p. 561). T. F. Tout, *Chapters in Administrative History*, i. 203 *n.* Richard of Argentien, *Senescallus Regis*; Tout, *op. cit.* i. 203 *n.*; Ralf fitz Nicholas, *Senescallus Regis*. Letters Patent, 11 Hen. III, p. 162.

1 About half were resigned into the hands of one or other of the bishops.

2 Letters Patent, 8 Hen. III, p. 464.

3 Or his deputy Robert de Bareville. Letters Close, 3 Henry III, pp. 384, 386, 401 ; 5 Henry III, pp. 444, 457, 458.

It is not difficult to see that this rise was due to a revival of John's *The Wardrobe and finance* fiscal policy at the expense of the Exchequer. Under Peter, the Wardrobe had drawn upon the Treasury, which retained a virtual monopoly of receipts, or had received minor sums directly from sheriffs and debtors. Under Kirkham and Brackley the whole render of certain taxes was diverted. The bishops paid the clerical carucage of August 1224 into the Wardrobe,[1] Fawkes' great fine of seven hundred marks was taken over by its clerks from the Temple,[2] and the chattels forfeited by his fellow-sufferers were received there without passing through the treasurer's hands. During the same period items of revenue which had been received in the Exchequer were transferred immediately en bloc to the Wardrobe, as was the tallage of the Jews of 1225.[3] In addition, the principal tax of that year, the Fifteenth granted in February, was cut out entirely from the purview of the Exchequer, received by a special commissioner at Winchester,[4] and committed to the bishops of Bath and Salisbury, Hubert's confidants, by whom it was delivered to the Temple, the Wardrobe, or the Treasury, or transmitted direct to the army in Gascony through the hands of Walter de Kirkham or others as occasion demanded.[5] Until the beginning of 1227, when it seems to have been exhausted, the crown was assured of a revenue[6] independent of the Treasury. A Treasurer of the Chamber or Wardrobe appears,[7] with functions like those of the Clerk of the Chamber of John.

The effect of all this may not have struck contemporaries. It was what, in one degree or another, had been the Angevin monarchy's financial practice almost from the year of Henry II's accession. Hubert continued to conform to the general lines of the settlement of 1216, and bought the aids of 1225 by a final recasting and reissue of the Charter, though it may be significant that it was issued *spontanea et bona voluntate regis*. Nevertheless, by eliminating Fawkes and restricting earl Ranulf's hostile influence to his

---

[1] Letters Patent, 8 Hen. III, p. 473 *et seq.*

[2] *Ibid.* p. 467.   [3] *Ibid.* 9 Hen. III, p. 513.

[4] William de Castellis, who sat from June 17 to July 20 and from September 29 to November 21, 1225. *Ibid.* p. 541, and 10 Hen. III, p. 6.

[5] Letters Patent, 9 and 10 Hen. III, *passim.*

[6] The fifteenth is said to have raised a sum of 87,000 marks: Stubbs, *Constitutional History*, ii. 38.

[7] T. F. Tout, *Chapters in Administrative History*, i. 196.

own earldoms, the justiciar had enabled bureaucracy to resume that course of development which had been interrupted by John's *débâcle*, and this time it was no longer crippled by being linked with an attack upon civil liberties. What Hubert restored Henry inherited, and his personal rule is an exaggerated outcome of the justiciar's last eight years of government.

Unpopularity of Hubert

Hubert's fall in July 1232 may be ascribed to many reasons. The Angevin system was essentially monarchical, and intolerable when it lacked the grace of divine and seigneurial right. William des Longchamps, Hubert de Burgh, and Simon de Montfort were all hated because they carried an authority which was essential to them, but which the nobles would bear, if at all, only from a king; and of necessity they strengthened their material power in a way which made the older feudatories more jealous still. As earl of Kent, lord of much of South Wales, holding profitable wardships and custodies, brother by marriage of the Scotch king, Hubert was growing as far beyond the ancient nobility in territorial power as he was below them in birth. Since the Angevin régime lacked the theory of a conventional crown,[1] these grand vizierates were bound to appear intermittently, and were always disastrous to their holders. Inevitably, Hubert had made many enemies, among them the greatest of all, Ranulf Blundevill, *semper mihi molestus*, and, towards the end, the young king, whose initiation into knighthood he turned to lasting discredit. Indeed, the bungling of the French war of 1230, the defeats in Wales, and the confusion in the finances, go far to justify Henry's desire for emancipation when at the age of twenty-five he had been twice crowned and twice proclaimed of age.

Rise of Pierre des Roches

The seizure of power by Pierre des Roches in the spring of 1232 had, therefore, some practical excuse. It produced a measure of financial reform[2] and satisfied the desire of all parties for the humiliation of the great justiciar. Peter, however, though he was perhaps the one man who had the standing and adroitness to unseat the government, fell short of some quality which was

---

[1] The notion of an impersonal crown as a legal entity distinct from its wearer does not appear until the fourteenth century.

[2] M. H. Mills, *Transactions of the Royal Historical Society*, 4th series, x.

needed to govern the England of 1232. Deliberately, he displayed his belief that the baronage had not changed,[1] denounced compromise, turned the *coup d'état* against the magnates who had favoured it, and reverted to the methods of John to cow them into submission. The first sign of unrest called forth government reaction in the full spirit of the almost forgotten tyranny, and, after sixteen years of security of law, pledge by hostages[2] and the hated charters of special fealty[3] were revived, and mercenaries were brought in from Poitou and Brittany. Peter had clearly learned nothing of English politics since 1216. The barons of 1232 were, however, no longer weak nor divided. Refusing to obey successive summonses to council, they demanded the dismissal of the Poitevins, and were joined by the clergy under Edmund Rich. The marshal, earl Richard of Pembroke, who had retired from the court and been proclaimed traitor, found general support, and the magnates raised the old cry of right of trial by peers. By April 1234 his success against Henry in the field brought the king to admit that he had been wrongly counselled and to dismiss the Poitevin ministers. The episode of the return of Pierre des Roches to power and his defeat brings together elements both of the past and of the future. The bishop, himself one of the most notable financiers and soldiers of the last generation, had played his part in a violent and unscrupulous age, and the appearance of better times did not convince him. He assumed that sixteen years had *His re-* made no essential change, and that the barons would take advan- *actionary policy* tage of any show of weakness, and could best be kept in hand by suspending their civil rights at the first sign of disobedience. He began, in short, at the point at which he had last laid down power. Outwardly, therefore, his short ministry is of the past, and is the last echo of John's tyranny and the last threat to common right. It was met by a violent burst of opposition, in which church and

---

1 Matthew Paris, *Historia Minor,* ii. 354: *Quod adhuc reliquias odii et guerrae, quas olim Angli contra regem Johannem . . . suscitabant, merito debet habere suspectas:* the remnant of the former war and hatred which they had stirred up against King John in the past ought still to be guarded against.

2 The barons of the March gave hostages at the Worcester council of 1233. *Letters Close,* 17 Hen. III, p. 312.

3 From William Mauduit, John of Evreux, Matthew de Meung, Richard Marshal. Earl Bigod, Thomas Grelley, Walter Clifford, Robert Musard, Henry of Erleigh, and Morgan of Caerleon: *ibid.* 320. These are enrolled between August 16 and 25, after the opposition of Richard Marshal and the Bassets.

baronage united, and the threat of another suspension of the law after John's model was laid for ever.

But, reactionary in the weapons they chose to deal with the baronage, Pierre des Roches and his followers conducted their campaign within the court with a very different order of ability, and with results which were to be the model for Henry's personal government in later days. There the problem was to rehabilitate the authority of the king, and through him to gain power over the administration. Symptoms of Henry's emergence from tute-

Pierre des Roches and the household

lage may be seen some years before the justiciar's fall. When the Breton campaign of 1230 declined towards failure he had wished to throw the government into the hands of a legate, and Hubert barely succeeded in dissuading him.[1] On his return to England he broke with the custom of the minority, which for fourteen years had conducted all business of state under the personal seals of the Marshal and Hubert, and in November 1230 began to issue letters close under the seal of Geoffrey de Crowcombe, his household steward.[2] In December he first used a private seal of his own. In 1231, when Pierre des Roches, the victim of 1224, was allowed to return, Hubert's late clerk Ralf Brito was displaced from the Wardrobe, and the bishop's son Pierre des Rievaulx became

The household against the great offices

treasurer of the Chamber. By June 1232 the power of the executive was sharply divided, the household being controlled by Hubert's enemies, Geoffrey de Crowcombe as steward, and Peter des Rievaulx as treasurer, while the justiciarship, the Chancery, and the treasurership of the Exchequer remained to Hubert and his associates of the minority.[3] It now became evident that, in spite of its long abeyance, the king's will was still formidable if he could be brought to assert it, and that the household had been so far developed as to make it a rival to the great offices, in that, even without displacing their holders, it could be used by adroit management to neutralize their functions. In Pierre des Roches,

[1] *Royal Letters of Henry III* (ed. Shirley), i. 379.

[2] T. F. Tout, *Chapters in Administrative History*, i. 210 *et seq.*

[3] The principal magnates who were favourable to Pierre des Roches' coup were probably those of whom a Letter Patent of 3rd September 1232 says that they were retained on urgent business about the king, *i.e.* the earls of Chester, Cornwall, Pembroke, Warenne, and Derby, and the constable of Chester. The marshal soon changed his views, but, according to Matthew Paris, the predominance of the foreigners was not recognized as a grievance until Christmas 1233. Letters Patent, 16 Hen. III, p. 498.

who knew the courts of the Pope and the Emperor, the justiciar of England had an enemy who had little sense of the compromise upon which the minority rested, but who could meet him with a more subtle understanding of the intricacies of power than even his own thirty years of administration had given him. Instead of attacking the apparent sources of his strength, his own justiciarship and the episcopal tenure of the Chancery and Treasury, the Poitevins seemed at first to strengthen them. As late as June 15, 1232, Hubert was made justiciar of Ireland, and at almost the same time the bishop of Chichester was confirmed in the Chancery and the bishop of Carlisle in the Treasury, and all three grants were made by charter and for life. Such charters could be issued upon the eve of revolution only because the charges which they confirmed were already discounted in the plans of the opposition, and they were soon seen to be preliminary to the reduction of the great offices of state under the dictation of the newer offices of the household.

There Pierre des Rievaulx was already supreme. On June 11 he had been made keeper of the king's Wardrobe and Chamber, and treasurer of the household for life, with power to remove any of its officials at will. On June 15 he became keeper of the king's small seal, also for life. Thus, for the first time the various branches of the household were coördinated into a whole under a single minister, while the consolidated ministry was removed from the check of the Chancery by obtaining the freedom of its own seal. Captured and reconstituted by the opposition, the domestic ministry was now to establish points of contact in the offices of state from which to destroy their initiative and secure their conformity with household policy. The creation of a keepership of the small seal had already to a large degree neutralized the influence of the Chancery. The next to be dealt with was the justiciarship of Ireland. On July 28 Pierre des Rievaulx—now Treasurer and Chamberlain of Ireland—was empowered to associate a deputy with the justiciar in the receipt of the Irish Exchequer in the justiciar's special prerogative of exacting the fines of the Irish tenants without royal precept, and in the taking of all assizes. For all these functions Peter's deputy was to keep *contra alios rotulos* a separate roll.[1] Three months later a somewhat similar check was

---

[1] Letters Patent, 16 Hen. III, p. 493. As was said in another connection, "to keep his roll in witness against" them. Cf. Tout, *op. cit.* i. 248.

placed upon the Treasury of England, still in the hands of Walter of Carlisle, by the intrusion of a clerk of Peter des Rievaulx *residens ad Scaccarium regis loco suo*, who shared with the treasurer and chamberlains a key to, and, presumably, the custody of the main treasure.[1] With the substitution of Stephen Segrave for Hubert de Burgh, the justiciarship was reduced to its function as head of the judiciary, and ceased to be a serious political factor. The design of subordinating the ministries of state to the household is unmistakable. How far the spread of Peter's authority over the provincial administration was part of the same policy of extending domestic government is doubtful. Though it had that effect for the moment, it was not maintained after the Poitevins' position was established, but during the rest of 1232 Peter received almost every provincial custody, all the counties[2]—except the few already granted for life and those held by Stephen Segrave—a number of the castles,[3] the forests throughout England,[4] the custody of all wardships and escheats,[5] of all sees to fall vacant in Ireland,[6] of the vacant see of Canterbury.[7] In January 1233 the Treasury of the English Exchequer was added,[8] and all these were to be held for life. The ministry lasted barely two years, but its effect upon the structure of government was decisive, for on the fall of Pierre des Roches and Pierre des Rievaulx in April 1234, there was no going back upon the advance which their period of power had achieved. Henry's personal rule was to be based upon the household.

Pierre's ministry a turning-point   Thus there ended that transition phase of constitutional growth, during which the powerful, intricate, and potentially tyrannous bureaucracy had sought to tread a middle course between the crown and the baronage, embodying itself in a group of magnate officers devoted to the system rather than to the king, and themselves tenants by barony in lay and ecclesiastical right. Inevitably, it had left unsatisfied every party to the compromise, and it had failed in every major enterprise, but it had gained time for the nation to reflect. The issue between crown and baronage had been confused and delayed for eighteen years, and the new generation

---

[1] Letters Close, 16 Hen. III, p. 118.
[2] Letters Patent, 16 Hen. III, pp. 486-489.
[3] *Ibid.* pp. 487-502.　　[4] *Ibid.* p. 489.　　[5] *Ibid.* p. 491.
[6] *Ibid.* p. 495.　　[7] *Ibid.* p. 486.　　[8] *Ibid.* 17 Hen. III, p. 7.

reopened it with more moderation and with a better knowledge of government. The year 1234 marked the reëmergence of the king as head of the executive. We have seen the three great offices of the justiciar, the chancellor, and the treasurer in the main as defences of the minority against disruptive forces, and exposed at times to feudal opposition. Nevertheless, it was evident that Hubert's government never departed from reasonable conformity with its foundation principles, and could always rely upon a sufficient though varying party among the barons. Indeed, as the minority was again and again prolonged, the great offices were beginning to be tinged with that feudal quality which overcame all ministries which were held for a long term of years. The strength of Hubert's position lay partly in his earldom of Kent, his custodies of Gloucester and Gower, and the rest, and Nevill and Mauclerc had been bishops before they received the Chancery and Treasury. The Chancery was a charge from which the routine profits went to the chancellor, and from February 1227 Ralf Nevill had held by charter and for life. In 1232 Hubert received the justiciarship of Ireland, Nevill, by a second grant, the Chancery, and Mauclerc the Treasury for life. Besides their natural resistance to the spirit of change inherent in personal government, it could not but be that such offices, held indefinitely, should form associations and habits of coöperation among the moderate baronage. Their procedure and traditions reflected their fixity of tenure, and responded slowly to innova- *The king* tion. Already John could speak of the "law of the Exchequer". *carries on* Henry III therefore saw in these offices a perpetuation of his *Pierre's* *tradition* tutelage and an opportunity for undue influence by the magnates. It was not in the manner of the thirteenth century to diminish the state of the crown by the suppression of such ministries, but abundant precedent existed for their reduction to a ceremonial function. The hereditary stewardship of England had long become an anachronism, and from 1233 to 1241 the king kept the marshal-ship in his hand at the cost of a rebellion.[1] In 1238 the Chancery was similarly attacked. Ralf Nevill could claim that he had been granted his office by the council of the realm,[2] and was too strong

---

[1] Letters Patent, 26 Hen. III, p. 266.

[2] Matthew Paris, *Chronica Major, sub anno* 1223. *Assensu totius regni, itaque non deponeretur ab ejus sigilli custodia nisi totius regni ordinante consensu et consilio.* There may be some exaggeration in this.

to be removed, but the seal was taken from him, lodged in the Wardrobe, and entrusted to keepers from among the Wardrobe clerks. From that year until Nevill's death in 1244 the chancellorship was a profitable title divorced from the power of office, and from 1244 the character of its holders changes in accordance with the policy of governing through the personal servants of the king.

Reduction in rank of the great offices There are no more magnate chancellors for life, but Wardrobe clerks, or knights of legal training, to whom the title of chancellor is at times accorded, but who are often, and perhaps better, characterized as *portitores, custodes sigilli regis*. At least intermittently, the great seal,[1] whose acts had become bound by precedent, was held out of Chancery by its keepers, removed from the knowledge of the Chancery clerks, and its acts recorded in the Wardrobe. At such times the king was relieved of all constraint save such as the more elastic methods of his domestic clerks might impose. As a result, the privy seal[2] almost passes out of record. The king had resumed what he, no doubt, regarded as his natural prerogative of authenticating with the seal of majesty.[3] On going abroad in 1242 he took the great seal with him, and would only accord the

Henry resumes custody of the great seal Exchequer a specialized form of his small seal to use in his absence, and in 1253 the great seal was laid up in custody under the seals of the regency. No action could more clearly symbolize Henry's refusal to accord any measure of initiative to the great departments, and his intention himself to embody the reign.[4]

The two other offices of state did not present the same resistance as the Chancery. Both had yielded to the attack of the Poitevins, and with their fall were in the king's hand. Hugh de Pateshull, one of the most active justices of the minority, was given the custody of the Treasury *quamdiu regi placuerit*, and in 1240 was succeeded from the treasury of the Wardrobe by William de Haverhill. Payments in which the king had a personal interest were transferred from the Exchequer to the Wardrobe according as he was

---

[1] As to the seals and their importance cf. T. F. Tout, *Chapters in Administrative History*, vol. i.   [2] Cf. p. 217 *supra*.

[3] Of writs so authenticated the Chancery clerks knew nothing unless they subsequently received them to enrol. T. F. Tout, *Chapters in Administrative History*, i. 287.

[4] The standing of the untitled custodians who held the great offices must not be underestimated. In 1244 William de Haverhill is described as *non solum de magnatibus sed de majoribus regni*. Letters Patent, 28 Hen. III, 426.

in England or abroad,[1] and in his absence the small seal was used to authenticate the writs of the Exchequer. Against such rivalry in the Exchequer and as the judicial benches took shape the justiciarship was becoming no more than a presidency of the judicature. The appointment of Segrave had in itself been a sign that the office was to be emptied of political importance,[2] as indeed it must be if the king's majority were to be more than a fiction, and with his dismissal it was not revived. In fact, only a strong king, or one so weak as to submit to domination, could afford a strong justiciarship, and of these Henry III was neither.

Although it was much drawn on to staff other offices, Henry's Wardrobe remained a household treasury, except in war-time, when it became more important than the Exchequer of London. On the fall of Pierre des Rievaulx, Walter Kirkham occupied the treasury of the Chamber, no doubt somewhat in the spirit of his patron Hubert de Burgh, and was associated with William de Haverhill, whom Professor Tout has called "the first holder of the office afterwards described as the controllership of the Wardrobe".[3] From 1236 to 1240 he was succeeded by an English Templar, Geoffrey, who had served his apprenticeship as almoner to the king, and who brought the financial ability of his order to the service of the state. In these circumstances, like the Chamber before it, the Wardrobe achieved an essential and unobjectionable place in the constitution, in so far as it served a legitimate need as a private exchequer—its receipts and expenses remained level at about £9000 a year—smaller than those of the Chamber of John—and could develop uncriticized. In the process of this growth it became the centre of secondary offices like itself, the queen's Wardrobe, established on the king's marriage in 1236, and the Wardrobe of the prince,[4] which from time to time rendered their accounts either to the king's Wardrobe or the Exchequer, and towards the middle of Henry's reign it became evident that the endless process of subdivision was to be repeated within the king's Wardrobe itself. The purchase of stores for the household, in-

Henry III's Wardrobe

---

[1] As were the pensions of his brothers of Lusignan. Letters Patent, 26 Hen. III, p. 309.

[2] After his fall Segrave maintained that he had never been in the inner circle of the counsellors as justiciar. Matthew Paris, *Chronica Majora, sub anno* 1234.

[3] T. F. Tout, *Chapters in Administrative History*, i. 244 *et seq.*

[4] Letters Patent, 43 Hen. III, p. 6.

volving knowledge of prices and qualities, storage, and transport which were alien to the accountants' training of the Wardrobe clerks, was beginning to find its appropriate organization and its separate officials. From these outside activities of the Wardrobe, which first became systematized in the late 'thirties, the Great Wardrobe of the fourteenth century arose.

Henry's personal policy

Such, in roughest outline, was Henry's curial machine. It was a product of the time rather than the man, for he had no very strong will, and for long periods undertook no great enterprises of state. The instinct to withdraw the crown within an inner structure of domestic offices was, in him, that of a weak nature which feared the concurrence of the feudatories in open council. Henry's very weakness left the way open to change. Far from sharing the illegalism of his father's reign, his was a time of security of right and of rapid development of process, during which, in the abeyance of the chancellorship, the number of available writs was multiplied many times and the courts took the final shape of their jurisdiction. The writing of Bracton's treatise falls in the years immediately before the upheaval of 1258. The reign was wrecked on personalities. Some recognition of the baronage as the ultimate sanction of government, and a more moderate exercise of the feudal prerogatives of the crown, would have freed Henry to exploit the administrative ability of his Chamber and Wardrobe uncriticized.[1] But, though his positive contempt for his native vassals was less marked, Henry shared his father's respect for foreign capacity. His papal overlord condemned English jealousy of foreigners,[2] and as a catholic and the head of a royal clan which stretched from Poitou to north Italy, he himself never learned to reckon with insular feeling. Disinclined to make his own will decisive, he turned in times of difficulty to a papal legation, which was, perhaps, his ideal of security, to his mother's sons and brothers-in-law of La Marche, and to his wife's Provençal and Savoyard relatives. With this foreign leaning it was easy to make his retreat from the feudal *curia* appear as a dereliction of English

The foreign favourites

[1] With the exception of Pierre des Rievaulx, who was dismissed from the Wardrobe, the barons accepted Henry's existing ministers almost without exception in 1258. T. F. Tout, *Chapters in Administrative History*, i. 296.

[2] *Royal Letters of Henry III* (ed. Shirley), i. 540.

kingship, and to give special bitterness to the hatred which was incurred by any medieval government which taxed and administered great estates of royal demesne. The anti-foreign cry had been raised against William des Longchamps, against John's mercenaries and Pierre des Roches. It was raised again when William, elect of Valence, came to England with the queen, and was found to have mastered the king's confidence at the Northampton council of 1236. Suspicion was maintained by Otto's legation in 1237, though William of Valence withdrew in 1238 in order not to compromise Henry with his subjects. In 1240 the king's Wardrobe fell into the hands of Pierre d'Aigueblanche, William of Valence's treasurer. The period of foreign control of the Wardrobe lasted until 1258,[1] but those who exercised it were able and apparently not unpopular, and the Chancery, Treasury, and Judiciary remained the preserve of Englishmen. The real target of anti-foreign feeling was not the working clerk, but the nobles of Henry's family who came to fill the court and set the tone in counsel, who took their share of the wardships and custodies with the English, and whom the feudal confusion of lordship and wardship set to interfere in the fortunes of the greatest English families. The migration of brothers and uncles began in 1241 with Peter of Savoy, the uncle of the queen, Bernard of Savoy, and, a little later, Peter, son of the count of Geneva. Of the king's half-brothers, sons of Isabella by Hugh of La Marche, Guy de Lusignan was in the king's service in Gascony in 1242, and all four, William, Guy, Geoffrey, and Aymer, settled in England in 1247. The charge of pillaging the wealth of England which was commonly made against the princes of Savoy and Lusignan is hardly confirmed by the records. They were active statesmen, who served the king at court and upon foreign missions, and Thomas of Savoy came to be essential to Henry's continental system. Henry treated them as it was usual to treat important foreigners, and even Englishmen, whose fidelity was desired, and settled yearly sums upon them, nominally secured by promised grants of land, but actually issuing as pensions from the Wardrobe or the Exchequer.[2] Where lands were given

---

[1] Peter Chaceporc, 1241-54; Artaud de Saint Romain, 1255-7; Pierre des Rievaulx, 1257-8.

[2] Thomas of Savoy received 500 marks yearly (Letters Patent, 30 Hen. III, p. 489), William of Valence £500 (*ibid.* 31 Hen. III, p. 509), Guy de Lusignan

they were usually an endowment from the escheats upon the foreigners' first coming to court, and were not greatly increased in later years. Peter of Savoy, who was given custody of the earldom of Richmond, and William of Valence, whose wardship of the heiress Joan de Monchesni[1] led to his marriage and to the revival of the earldom of Pembroke in his favour, were the principal beneficiaries, and such grants hardly formed more than a suitable lodgment in the feudal hierarchy if Henry's policy of grafting his French relations into the English feudal stock were to be carried through. Whether the anglicized aristocracy of the Normans would submit to a further indraft from the Continent, and that from the doubly alien families of the Languedoc, was another matter.

Feudal diplomacy   It would, however, be unfair to ignore the element of policy in Henry's dealings with his relations; his son did the same with no sense of wrong. Amid the growth of new institutions it is easy to forget that the king had lost none of the rights of a feudal lord. How careful of feudal convention Henry could be we may see in his formal diffidation of Richard Marshal in 1233[2] and of the Montfortians before Lewes,[3] and in this relation, where his action was most personal, he appears, especially in his later years, as a persistent, though, perhaps, too ambitious manipulator of the domestic diplomacy of feudalism. From time to time in his long reign many of the great honours passed into his hands in wardship or escheat. Henry had been taught to study the example of the French crown[4] in the use of the lord's right of marriage to draw the counties of Namur and Ponthieu into dependence. Hubert de Burgh applied the same policy in marrying the earl Marshal to the king's sister, and when Henry grew older he used the marriage of his own children and of the princesses of Poitou and Savoy to extend the family tie over the principal English feudal

---

300 marks (*ibid.* p. 502), Geoffrey de Lusignan £500 (*ibid.* 41 Hen. III, p. 406). When we consider that the practice of pensioning the Poitevin nobility reaches well back into the period of Hubert de Burgh (William l'Archeveque was given a pension of 100 marks in 1226: *ibid.* 11 Hen. III, p. 102), that a good pension for a king's clerk was 60 marks, and that Simon de Montfort allowed himself to receive a pension of 600 marks, these amounts do not seem excessive for the king's brothers.   [1] Letters Patent, 39 Hen. III, p. 419.

[2] Wendover, ii. 55.   [3] Rishanger, *De Bellis*, p. 28.

[4] *Royal Letters of Henry III* (ed. Shirley), i. 246: *considerante etiam exemplum quondam regis Franciae Philippi.*

houses.[1] In individual cases these marriages were not always suc- *Extinction* cessful. Gloucester had his Poitevin marriage annulled, and the *of the feudal* whole policy was arraigned in 1258.[1] Nevertheless effective opposi- *dynasties* tion seems to have been delayed for many years by the friendship which Henry established with Richard de Clare during the latter's minority, and by the accumulation of the earldoms of Leicester, Pembroke, and Richmond in the hands of his relations. These earls formed a firm royalist group in the 'fifties, and it was only the quarrel within that group which gave back to the baronage its natural leaders and made the crisis of 1258 possible. Moreover, Henry pursued a steady policy of keeping the great escheated honours in his own hands, which, together with the disaster of Evesham and the extinction of a number of honours by intermarriage or the failure of heirs, helped to bring about a social revolution. The baronage with which Edward had to deal was far less formidable in power and ambition than that of Henry's early days. In 1216 the number of earldoms held by Englishmen not of the court circle was twenty-three. In 1272 only Warwick, Hereford-Essex, Gloucester-Hertford, Norfolk, Lincoln, Surrey, and Huntingdon survived. Edward held Chester; Edmund Leicester, Derby, Lancaster, Aumale; Henry's son-in-law, Count of Brittany, held Richmond; and Valence held Pembroke. The great line of feudal dynasties, Chester, Derby, Leicester, which had repeated its traditional opposition in 1173, 1215, and 1264, had vanished, and how little weight remained in the surviving earldoms Edward's treatment of the tenure of Bohun, Clare, and Bigod was to prove. Partly by good fortune, partly by the policy of a weak but consistent ruler persisting through two generations, the thirteenth century saw the end of the great

---

1 *Volens omnes Regni sui nobiles degenerare.* Matthew Paris, *Chronica Majora,* sub anno 1252. John, earl of Surrey, *m.* Alais de Lusignan; Robert, earl of Derby, *m.* Mary de Lusignan; Baldwin, earl of Devon, *m.* Margaret of Savoy; Edmund, earl of Lincoln, *m.* a daughter of the marquis of Saluzzo; John de Vesci, *m.* Mary de Lusignan; Gilbert, earl of Gloucester, *m.* Alais de Lusignan; Joan de Monchesni, *m.* William de Valence; Matilda de Lacy, *m.* Peter of Geneva. *Murmur et indignatio per Regnum, ibid. sub anno* 1247. The barons claimed that marriages of great feudatories in ward should be arranged in consultation with them. *Ibid. sub anno* 1238.

2 A later John de Warenne complained that he had been forced to marry Joan de Bar when in ward to Edward *vi et metu qui cadere poterant in constantem virum.* Northern Registers (Rolls Series), p. 229.

territorial units of the Conquest. The fourteenth century nobility was to rise upon the impulse of the Hundred Years War, and was royalist and inspired by the nationalistic ideals of the Round Table and the Garter.

With the exception of the Gascon war of 1253-4, Henry carried through no single enterprise of moment. Upon the surface of events his will played feebly, straying from object to object, and withdrawing nervously before an opposition which became automatic as the belief in his unkingliness hardened. But, though he could never master any crisis or outface any opponent, he had an inner fixity of purpose which conformed to those currents of the time which were setting away from feudalism. To this half-realized drift of events the recurrent opposition of Henry's reign *Baronial* was a reaction, and, as its direction revealed itself, so the policy *opposition* of the barons, at first opportunist and individual, began to draw together and to clothe itself in constitutional form. In the beginning it was an opposition of distrust rather than of grievance, and for many years it exhausted itself in complaints of ill-advised and foreign guidance, and restless schemes for baronial counsel, which, lacking the coöperation of the crown, it had not the vitality to carry through. It was, indeed, the malaise of feudalism under the first king who placed no value upon the tenurial incident of counsel, and who yet offered no positive target of misgovernment. Baronage was being deprived of significance both as a territorial power and in the *curia*, for, as the writer of the Song of Lewes complained, *rex vult sibi vivere*.

In weighing the motives of the baronial opposition we must remember to what forces the baron was exposed; the justices, the chancellor and his writs, the king and his rights of wardship and his demands for aid, the incidence of government upon their great franchises, rather than the general plight of the country. A baron of the king is a dangerous man for a sheriff to handle.[1] Provincial maladministration may to some degree pass him by. The common law, the judiciary, the great offices, and the council will be the

---

[1] So the county of Lancaster, having tried to levy a distress upon Montbegon of Hornby, refers the whole matter to the council *cum ipse magnus homo erat et baro domini regis.*

first consideration of the feudatories, for, much more than the shrievalty, each of these has maintained its hold upon that peerage of baronial immunities which is, in the eyes of the magnates, the *communitas Angliae*. But this central mass of the baronage fades into the classes above and below it. The substantial knight tenant, the baron with few fees, may feel his interest to be with the mass of county freeholders. At the other end of the scale there is a tendency for a separate order of the earls to come into being. There is at times a desire to distinguish between the *magnates, proceres*, and the *universitas baronum*. De Montfort, with his stewardship, the residual claim of his sons to the throne, and his Welsh alliances, never worked easily with the *universitas baronum*, and Gloucester and Warenne also were involved from time to time in more exalted ties of policy. Thus there were always rifts in the opposition, which tended to widen as soon as it had achieved success.

Again, we must remember that opposition to personal monarchy *Political* was no longer entirely governed by the near view of practical *theory of* politics. Throughout western Europe these two generations were *opposition* concerning themselves with the problems of law, authority, and counsel, setting the *regale dominium* against the *regimen politicum*. England was poor soil for political definitions, but that sense of the responsibility of kingship which was diffused throughout Christian thought was here and there being intellectualized and brought to a more definite application. Difficult to localize or define, the same thought inspires the most diverse quarters. Alike for Bracton and the anonymous cleric of the Song of Lewes the king has his associates, almost his masters, in his council, and his native counsellors are the barons of his realm.[1] Less specifically, this was the doctrine of the Franciscans and of Grosseteste, and the leaders of revolt in two generations, Richard Marshal and Richard Seward, and again Simon de Montfort may have found inspiration in Grosseteste's friendship and writings.[2] More practically, the

[1] Bracton, *De Legibus Angliae*, II. xvj. 3: *Rex autem habet superiorem . . . item curiam suam, videlicet comites, barones, quia comites dicuntur quasi socii regis, et qui habet socium habet magistrum*: Moreover the king has a superior in his court, *i.e.* his earls and barons, for by earls (*comites*) is meant companions of the king and he who has a colleague has a master (probably an interpolation, but an early one).

[2] Simon had read Grosseteste's treatise *De Principatu Regni et Tyrannidis* in common with the third of this group of friends, Adam Marsh. C. L. Kingsford, *The Song of Lewes*, Introduction and Appendix.

king's minority focussed attention upon the ministers and counsellors and upon the crown. The problem of the central will, its
relation to the kingdom, its control by external forces, and the
channels through which it made itself felt, in short the problem of
sovereignty, must inevitably have forced itself upon the political
leaders of England within measurable time, but the reign of a king
whose acts were the reflection of a succession of advisers stronger
than himself shortened the period of consideration and compelled
an unnaturally quick solution, all the more so because from 1240
onwards the counsel which influenced the king was principally
that of foreigners. For this reason the conciliar schemes of 1244
and 1258 have the violence of immaturity and revolution, though
they are inspired by the oldest elements in English political
thought.

The baron's view as to their own constitutional status is a confusion of the ideas of two epochs slowly clearing as the reign goes
on. First is a survival of the older conception of the feudal *curia*,
that the king's natural counsellors are his barons, that his principal
officials should be barons, or at least such as the barons can
associate with their order, and that what affects the generality or is of
great moment—*magna negotia regni*—should be decided in full
curia of the magnates. According to this curial view of the realm
—curial or honorial because all institutions should draw their
strength from the *curia* of the vassals and take their tone from the
chivalrous and domestic ideals of the honour—the political
function of the barons is exhausted in the service and counsel of
the king, and the furthering of his ends, and the *commune consilium*
is the king's *curia* swollen to its full membership. Governed by
this survival of an ideal feudalism[1] which has been unrealizable
for half a century, and inclined to revert to the simplified structure
of the private honour as the norm of the state, the barons reject
Longchamps as of base birth and substitute for him baronial
justiciars in the king's name, grudgingly accept de Burgh as a
magnate of new standing, and find it their first gravamen against
Henry III that he rules without a justiciar, chancellor, and treasurer

---

[1] Henry himself at times appealed to this kind of loyalty: *Ecce Rex . . . ex
abrupto advenit . . . protestans quod eorum honor suus foret et e converso*: he came in
suddenly and protested that their honour and his were inseparable. Matthew
Paris, *Chronica Majora, sub anno* 1244.

of baronial or prelatical rank, and takes counsel with foreigners. Secondly, supervening upon this older notion, and never perfectly extricated from it in Henry's reign, is the more modern notion of the assembly of the barons as an institution of the community rather than of the crown, whose affinities are with the *universitas regni* or body of tenants in chief, for which it acts as representative, approaching the government from without, and "parleying" with the king and his council in meetings which are coming to be called *colloquia* or *parliamenta*. In this phase—the two phases overrun each other—the breach in the *curia* is accepted. It is taken for granted that the baronage can associate themselves with the crown only by mastering it. They begin to claim a constitutional control in order to recall the king to his trust; the more enlightened will say to his trust for the *communitas Angliae*, those less so will think of it as a trust for the *universitas* of tenants in chief. We cannot, of course, interpret the *parlemenz* of the Provisions of Oxford as incorporating a developed estate of the realm. Nevertheless, the assembly of magnates, representative of a nation-wide if not a national constituency, summoned to meet the king and council *pur treter des besoingnes le rei et del reaume*, is a necessary passage in the evolution of parliament, and a profound break with the curial and tenurial outlook of the past.

The barrier to progress along this line was the belief of the feudal order that counsel was an incident of tenure and that the assembly of the magnates was the king's council par excellence, as, exceptionally, it still was for John.[1] This view was flattered by the fact that Henry never really abandoned the practice of summoning the council of the whole baronage at intervals, nor tried to take aids without its consent. The notion of the *commune consilium* as a body of opposition was thus slow in forming. Conversely the magnates won with difficulty to the conception of a king's council distinct from the *commune consilium* of the feudatories, and which should attend unremittingly to the king's business, and put itself under special vows of secrecy and integrity. Such an idea was

The problem of counsel

---

1 Cf. John's use of *magnates regni nostri* and *concilium nostrum* as equivalent phrases. Letters Patent, 8 John, p. 72. A late instance before 1258 when the term *curia regis* was used of the assembly of magnates acting legislatively with the king is at the council of Merton in 1236, *provisum est in curia domini regis . . . coram majore parti comitum et baronum angliae. Statutes of the Realm*, i. 1.

essentially opposed to the feudal strand of thought in the minds of both king and magnates, for feudatories who were admitted to a special council submitted themselves to a new kind of obligation and were required to bind their consciences to unfamiliar standards,[1] and to show a new kind of discretion. Homage and fealty bred feelings and loyalties of quite a different order. Thus, the barons were reluctant to detach themselves from their equals,[2] and for the same reason the king rarely found suitable counsellors among his magnates, unless, like William Marshal, Montfort, Warenne, or Salisbury, they owed him a family loyalty also. According to the papal view he was free to ignore tenurial qualification as soon as he came of age, and to govern *cum consilio domesticorum*,[3] but Henry was hesitant as a doctrinaire and satisfied to evade the issue by giving his foreign relations a titular footing in English feudalism and using them together with his clerks and sufficient of the more compliant of the English barons to placate moderate opinion. Both sides, therefore, were slow to clear their minds as to what was the actual issue. It took many years for the baronial assembly to exchange the habits of a feudal *curia* for the persistent independence and mutual loyalty of political opposition.

In so far as the barons had a consistent view, they continued to maintain that the *commune concilium* was the primary council of the realm, and to complain if great affairs of state were done without it. The king and his barons should be at one. They were aggrieved that the imperial marriage of 1236 and the Poitevin alliance of 1242 were carried through without their advice, and in 1237, when summoned only to grant an aid, they expressed their surprise that no *magna negotia regni* were put before them.[4] They could not help realizing that the *domestici* and *familiares*, who were always with the king, had to be reckoned with as a secondary council. They knew it bridged the intervals between the meetings

[1] The conflict between the two kinds of counsellor, and the failure of contemporaries to understand it is well illustrated by the quarrel between Richard Percy and Gilbert Basset recorded by Matthew Paris, *Chronica Majora*, *sub anno* 1237.

[2] *Sine paribus suis tunc absentibus nullum voluerunt responsum dare*: they would make no answer without those of their peers who were absent. *Ibid. sub anno* 1255.

[3] *Ibid. sub anno* 1223.

[4] *Ibid. sub anno* 1237. *Imperialia et alia ardua negotia.*

of general councils, but they were jealous and affronted if it showed signs of becoming the primary council. The mind of the king must be fully open to his magnates;[1] there was no more certain occasion of offence than for one of the permanent council to affect secrecy with the king in the presence of the barons; he might be reminded that they were the king's intimates also and were not to be treated as outsiders.[2] Henry, for his part, gave intermittent justification for the belief that he was withdrawing himself from baronial counsel. Coming to London, the magnates often found themselves still without access to the king's person and that familiarity of his court which vassals ought to enjoy. At times when the *colloquium* of barons assembled at Westminster he removed from the Palace to the Tower, and would only address them through one of his clerks[3] as speaker.[4] Frequently they found the real identity of the court was not the king's. They had been brought not to hear their natural lord but the elect of Valence as in 1236, or a Roman legate as in 1237. In reaction, they began to accept the breach in the traditional unity of the *curia*. Since he is not with them as in his council, they counsel with each other rather than with the king, withdraw and debate secretly,[5] and return with a common answer.[6] Their solidarity becomes proof against bargaining. Individuals and groups learn to refuse to answer *sine communi universitate*.[7] In 1244 a committee of twelve drawn from prelates, earls, and barons is empowered to answer for the whole. The constitutional problem is a difficult one. General assemblies cannot be multiplied indefinitely, and individual barons will not easily adapt themselves to the functions of *familiares*. If they do they become suspect themselves.[8] Nevertheless, it is this expedient which is tentatively adopted, and in 1237 a baronial wing is added

[1] *Vestrum omnium, quasi fidelium et naturalium hominum, consiliis se subdere*: to be guided by the counsel of you all as of his natural lieges. Matthew Paris, *Chronica Majora, sub anno* 1237.

[2] *Ibid. sub anno* 1237.

[3] As through William of Cailli in 1237.

[4] *Quasi mediator inter Regem et regni magnates. Ibid. sub anno* 1237.

[5] *Secesserunt in locum seorsum secretiorem . . . inierent consilium*: they went aside by themselves and held counsel. *Loc. cit.*

[6] *Ibid. sub anno* 1242: *Magno inter eos tractatu praehabito . . . dederunt consilium*: they offered counsel after preliminary discussion among themselves.

[7] *Loc. cit.*

[8] As did the earls of Lincoln and Leicester in 1237. *Ibid. sub anno.*

to the council. This was perhaps the first explicit recognition of a permanent council as a separate entity, and Henry underlined its distinctive standing by exacting from Warenne, Ferrars, and John fitz Geoffrey, the baronial nominees, an oath that they would refuse bribes and give impartial counsel. It was a declaration of policy. The oath of homage no longer qualified the greatest vassal to share the inner confidence of the king.[1] Henceforth there were two councils recognized as there had long been two in function; the one permanent, advisory, and executive; the other occasional, critical or revisory, increasingly obsessed by political grievance.[2]

On the whole, this dualism in the *curia* seems to have conformed to Henry III's views, and he emphasized it from the 'forties onwards in a way which became increasingly distasteful to the barons. The king continued to summon the magnates, but not at regular intervals, and with the limited purpose of granting aids or debating war-like enterprises for which the military action of the barons would be necessary. Writs have survived summoning the magnates to advise on, or mentioning their agreement to, the Scotch expedition of 1244,[3] the subsequent Welsh campaign,[4] and that of 1258,[5] and to solicit aid, as for Gascony in 1254,[6] when a campaign had already been begun, and there are, of course, other notices of such councils in the chronicles. Henry's rule, indeed, was roughly according to the letter as opposed to the spirit of the Great Charter. He had no chance of getting an aid without the *commune consilium*, and, except for bargaining with individuals, did not try to evade it; and sometimes, though not always, he went further than the Charter demanded and asked the opinion of his magnates on the policy for which the aid was required. But further than this he would not go. Just as he withdrew the administration within the circle of the domestic ministers, so he

---

1 Apparently the first instance of a sworn council was in 1233.

2 Cf. the writ of 38 Hen. III when the king was in Gascony: *vobis mandamus quatenus sitis apud Westomonasterium coram regina nostra et Ricardo comiti Cornubiae fratre nostro et aliis de consilio nostro . . . audituri beneplacitum nostrum et voluntatem et cum praefato consilio nostro super predictis negociis tractaturi. Report on the Dignity of a Peer*, iii, p. 12.　　　　　　　　　　　　　　　3 *Ibid.* p. 9.

4 *Ibid.* p. 11.　　　　　5 *Ibid.* p. 17.　　　　　6 *Ibid.* p. 12.

7 *E.g.* to hear the claims of the Scotch king in 1237, to consider the war in Poitou in 1242, and in 1246–7 to find means of meeting the papal demands.

retained the general conduct of government, the allocation of the castles, counties, escheats, and wardships, the judiciary, the itinerant commissions, the sanctioning of writs, as the prerogative of himself and his familiar council.[1] In taking upon itself the discontents of its order, the general *colloquium* had, in Henry's view, disqualified itself for that favourable counsel which a lord might demand from his vassals.[2] Upon the one side and the other, the breach in the feudal *curia*, long a fact, was becoming avowed.

When once the end of the traditional union of crown and baronage in a joint feudal régime was realized a struggle to control the king was inevitable. During the minority the magnates could still regard themselves as constituents of the government in right of their tenure in chief of the honour of England. They felt secure in the new safeguard of a reaffirmation of the Charters. Progressively, as they were forced into the position of spectators and saw clerks and foreigners in the great charges of state, there grew in their minds the possibility of seizing upon the government and dominating it from without. A precedent for baronial control of the executive had already been set. Bishop Nevill could claim to have been given the chancellorship *in communi consilio regni*. By the 'forties the barons were becoming critical of the detail of government. In 1241 they secured the relegation of the customary revenue to trustees from the Temple and the Hospital.[3] In 1242 they refused an aid on the ground of previous grant, and questioned the method by which escheats were kept, emphasized the great exactions of the recent eyres and pleas of the Forest, and doubted

---

1 The king's claim to supremacy over the executive is very clearly put in *The Song of Lewes*, 11, 492 *et seq.*: "it is no affair of the magnates to whom the king entrusts his counties and castles, or employs as his justiciars. He is determined to have whom he will as chancellor and treasurer, to choose his ministers from any nationality, and to appoint and dismiss his ministers at his discretion. Every earl has this degree of control within his own honour, as, indeed, the king desires him to have it." Cf. also Matthew Paris, *Abbreviatio*, 291.

2 As late as the Lincoln parliament of 1301 Edward I insisted that the magnates were bound by their oath (of homage) to offer no counsel and put forward no claim which might trench upon the *jura corone*: *prelati, comites, barones, et ceteri magnates . . . ad observandum et manutenendum jura regni et corone una nobiscum juramenti vinculo sint astricti*: prelates, earls, barons, and other magnates are equally bound by oath with ourselves to observe and maintain the rights of realm and the crown. *Report on the Dignity of a Peer*, iii. p. 121.

3 Letters Patent, 25, Henry III, p. 249.

Opposition aims whether they had been properly collected and kept. They are sceptical of the king's guarantee of the Charter, and they will not be placated by his offer to redress any grievance that individuals put forward. In short, they are at last disillusioned with the old safeguards. Reaffirmation of the Charters has come to be a form. The *commune concilium* is summoned to reflect the king's intentions. At first they are inclined to resort to old methods. Only obstinate insistence can restore reality to the feudal constitution. In 1244 —again the authority is that of Matthew Paris[1]—they fulfilled the implied threat of 1242, and approached the king, not with individual complaints, but with a programme which was a practical challenge to Henry's whole view of the state. They would go back to the old ways. Four nominees of the barons were to follow the king, of whom two at least were to be in constant attendance.

Scheme of 1244 As with the barons who coöperated with Henry II in the work of government, it is hard to say whether they were regarded as justiciars or counsellors. They were to combine executive and advisory functions, their title, if any, was that of conservators of the Charters, they were to sit with the king to give immediate remedy for legal wrongs, to deal with the king's treasure according to their view and provision, and the chief justiciar and the chancellor were expected to be chosen from among them.

The remedy for the assumed defects of the council, the elected *conservatores*, is, in fact, an idealization of some less specialized constitution of the twelfth century. The rest of the scheme, because it deals with concrete abuses, is of its own day, and shows that the opposition have come to some understanding of Henry's system and of their own disabilities under it, by which the reality of power is escaping them. The target is now the personal government and specifically the lapse of the great offices, particularly that of the chancellor, which is responsible for the impoverishment of the crown by the wasting of escheats and for a threat to the security of landright by the issue of writs against precedent and custom.[2]

---

[1] Historians have neither accepted nor rejected Matthew's account very confidently, but it bears some marks of being a contemporary draft or memorandum, and the confusion of functions suggests inexperience. Strong reasons have been advanced for associating it with the crisis of 1237–38. N. Denholm-Young, *English Historical Review*, vol. lviii. pp. 401 *et seq.*

[2] *Per defectum cancellarii brevia contra justitiam pluries fuerant concessa.* Matthew Paris, *Chronica Majora*, *sub anno* 1244. Writs with the *non obstante* clause, noticed

With the Great Seal at Henry's discretion, a wide door was open for that legal experiment altering right which the barons most of all feared. Henceforth, therefore, there was to be a justiciar and a chancellor elected by the magnates, not to be changed without *commune consilium*, and to prevent such evasions as the merely titular chancellorship of Nevill, all writs were to be invalid if the king deprived the chancellor of the seal. As a further safeguard, two of the justices of Common Pleas, and the justice of the Jews were to be elected, and some action unspecified was to be taken as to the eyre jurisdiction. Aid will be unnecessary if the chancellor conserves the escheats instead of giving them to foreigners and the conservators handle the royal treasure wisely. To that end two elected barons are for the future to serve at the Exchequer.

The interest of this programme is not as a constitutional actuality, which it never was, but as a scheme which, even if it came from the brain of Matthew Paris only, would still reflect the uncertainties of a transitional phase of thought. In it we see the barons in mid-course of their evolution from a curial to a parliamentary status. They are already sound critics of the executive, but they have lost their old standing and their future function in the state is yet to find. The parts of the Angevin machine are already so familiar that each can be effectively padlocked by the check of baronial deputies, but, as reconstituted, that machine is expected to run of its own motion under the conservators. The feudal creed that the first duty of a vassal is to serve his lord in council is set aside as an anachronism; in fact the scheme will release the feudatories from a curial duty which has no longer any meaning. The *universitas* is not to be again summoned until the conservators find good cause; the *conservatores* will be the king's chief councillors. The offices which on the first occasion are filled by election may in future be left to the nomination of the conservators, who, like the Twenty-Five of the Great Charter, are in name and function conservators of feudal liberties. Upon the positive side there is nothing, no sense that the *commune consilium*, having lost its function of afforcing the crown, may find a new one as the voice of the *universitas*, criticizing and opposing where the interests of the crown and the community are at variance, conveying

as a new abuse in 1250 and frowned on by conservative justices, were particularly unpopular, as was the *quo warranto* writ when used of land.

advice and support where they are identical, that it may need to meet regularly, and even to compel the king to meet it, to "hold parliament" with it. If this reflects reality, to be a baron of the king meant in politics less than for some time before or after, for the *commune concilium* has become meaningless or burdensome and the parliament is as yet some years in the future.

This constitution was never put into force. If it had even that degree of authority, it was a party document such as those provisions which the prelates drew up in 1257 "to be given effect at some more favourable conjuncture".[1] At any time during the next fourteen years the occurrence of such an opportunity seems to have waited only for some coincidence of persons and events which should carry the gathering impatience with Henry across the line of action. He himself displayed a genius for bringing the magnates to the verge of an explosion and then dissipating the tension by ingenuously displaying his alarm and his haste to placate them. In a succession of general councils, whenever an aid was asked for, in 1248, 1249, 1255, the same comedy was played, the confirmation of the Charters, which no longer convinced anyone, was demanded and granted—Henry himself liked to take a leading part in the ceremony of pronouncing excommunication against those who should break them—and the more solid sceheme for the restoration of the great offices was as regularly presented and refused. Aid was denied the king, and he proceeded to pay his way by papal taxes on the clergy, by begging from individuals, pressing the pleas of the forest, selling his woods, and cutting down his household expenses to a degree which his subjects thought disgraced the nation.[2]

Preliminaries to revolt There was no apparent reason why this cat-and-dog relation should not have been continued indefinitely. The rank and file of the barons were under a growing sense of responsibility to the feudal classes, but with the magnates the king's position even improved. In 1255 Gloucester, Leicester, Warenne, Lincoln, and Devon were all upon his side. Richard of Cornwall, whose prestige and wealth were enormous at that time, was neutral, and blocked all action. The archbishop of Canterbury was abroad,, and was no party man when at home, and the see of York was

[1] Matthew Paris, *Chronica Majora, sub anno* 1257.
[2] Letters Patent, 39 Hen. III, p. 433.

vacant. The Poitevin lords had grown rich, confident, and secure. The *universitas* felt itself leaderless and became resigned to inaction. Henry could not rally the baronage to himself, and when Rostand brought the royal ring of Apulia to Prince Edmund in 1255 even Richard would take no share in its acceptance, but still the group of English and Poitevin magnates who dominated the council[1] were strong enough to discourage opposition, and were working with the king to carry the Sicilian scheme forward,[2] although Norfolk, Hereford, and Oxford held aloof. There still need, perhaps, have been no constitutional crisis, or at least none that could not have been overridden, had not the always precarious peace of the royal family been shattered in the autumn of 1257 and the spring of 1258 with an effect not greatly less than that of the breach which preceded the Wars of the Roses. Henry himself had quarrelled with the earl of Norfolk two years earlier, and had been upon the verge of a quarrel with his son Edward, now lord of Chester, Gascony, and Ireland, which had caused him to reflect upon the family wars of his grandfather. In May the influence of Richard was removed when he sailed for Germany and the lesser members of the family were left to face each other uncontrolled. The Welsh war, falling upon the perennial jealousies of the Welsh March, broke the vital alliance of Leicester and Gloucester with the Poitevins. The former were accused of inspiring Llewellyn's ravaging of William of Valence's earldom of Pembroke.[3] In this confusion of hatred and suspicion the *universitas* at last found its leaders. Leicester denounced the immunity of the king's brothers from legal accountability and made it the pretext for some show of turning for justice from the king to the barons.[4]

This time, also, the crisis might have faded into the usual stale-mate had not Henry been compelled to persist in demanding an

1 Letters Patent, 40 Hen. III, p. 451. Henry announces that privileges concerning the affair of Apulia are being sealed with the counsel of the bishops of Hereford and Winchester, William de Valence, Geoffrey de Lusignan, the earls of Gloucester and Warwick, John Mansel, and others.

2 Gloucester and Leicester were committed to the manœuvres by which the money for Apulia was borrowed and secured. *Ibid.* pp. 498, 563, Leicester and Richmond were commissioned to Rome in the affair as late as June 1257. *Ibid.* p. 567.   3 Matthew Paris, *Chronica Majora*, *sub anno* 1257.

4 Matthew Paris, *Chronica Majora*, *sub anno* 1258: *Non tamen regi sed universitati praecordialiter est conquestus*: he complained warmly not to the king but to the baronage.

aid, since he had gone too far in Apulia to retreat. Thus he kept the barons meeting at intervals during the first half of 1258, and, in the course of what was almost a single prorogued council, they worked themselves into a mixture of fear, mutual loyalty, and anger, which produced a revolutionary impulse such as had not been seen for forty years. It was the mood in which the Londoners locked their doors against the Cahorsins and Jewish assassins, in which sober clerks estimated the crown's current expenditure at 850,000 marks,[1] and country gentlemen dismissed their cooks for fear of Poitevin poison.[2] But it also had the genuine political grievances of two generations to work upon. Not only the magnates, but the church,[3] and, as it proved later, the lesser feudatories, had had time to clarify their discontents and to prepare themselves to seize upon any real break in the stability of the realm.

Outbreak of the revolt of 1258   The beginning of the crisis was the work of a group of the greater magnates. They had made it inevitable by breaking the king's circle, and the ultimatum was presented to him by his personal enemy Roger Bigod. It demanded the expulsion of the foreigners[4] and a reform of the realm impoverished through them by the counsel of English nobles. In return, they would persuade the *communitas regni* to grant an aid for Sicily. This was on April 30, 1258. On May 2 Henry promised to submit to a purge of his government by the provision of a committee of twenty-four, twelve of his own party and twelve chosen from that of the barons. He and the Prince bound themselves to accept its decisions and to meet parliament on June 9 at Oxford to give them effect. Of the grievances which precipitated the crisis, other than the sense of their loss of constitutional function and the hatred of the king's family, we may judge by the so-called Petition of the Barons, which is thought to have been drawn up by the twelve baronial *Demands of 1258: petition of the barons* commissioners in the interval before the Oxford parliament.[5] They are of the familiar type, supplementary to and corrective of the

1 Matthew Paris, *Chronica Majora*, sub anno 1257: *Quod est horribile cogitatu*, and also, it must be said, entirely untrue.   2 *Loc. cit.*
3 Cf. the bishop's Articles of grievance compiled in 1257 but withheld "for a more favourable occasion". Matthew Paris, *Chronica Majora*, sub anno; *Additamenta.*
4 Safe-conduct for the king's brothers to leave England under conduct of the earls of Hereford, Warenne, and Aumâle was issued on July 5, 1258. Letters Patent, 42 Hen. III, p. 640.
5 R. F. Treharne, *The Baronial Plan of Reform, 1258–1263.*

standing articles of the Charters, and there is a visible reaction against Henry's exploitation of feudal right for the advantage of foreigners.[1] Castles are to be entrusted to native Englishmen, and heiresses are not to be disparaged by marriage to men not of English birth. The reference is evident, and beyond this there is little that is new—minor inconveniences of the use of wardship, abuses of the king's right in the forests, of his use of escheat, of sheriffs' claims to more suit than is their right, of their misuse of the *murdrum* fine and so forth, and of the Wardrobe's buyers' purchases by way of prise.

The crisis was, it seems, no revolt against intolerable wrongs. *Provisions* There was no general threat to the common law as under John, *of Oxford* and there had been no forced levies. Rather, at the end of a long period of maturing political experience, the time was ripe for a readjustment of the status of king, council, and *communitas regni*, which could no longer be expressed in the old formulae of the *curia regis*. It was likely that the occasion would release almost more than was required of the political inventiveness of the barons, which had been stored up during thirty years of enforced inactivity, and though there was, perhaps, no single article of the reforms for which precedent could not be found, the Provisions of Oxford sum up the end of an epoch because they recognize the changes which Henry III's reign have brought about and stereotype them in a constitution. The scheme of 1258 was realistic where that of 1244 was reactionary. It abandoned the past frankly. The confusion of executive and judicature in a committee of baronial justiciars was dropped, and the contemporary division of powers and functions accepted. Specifically, the permanent advisory council was recognized and made the centre of the system, to which end four electors were taken from the two parties and empowered to choose fifteen magnates as king's councillors. The *commune consilium*, on the other hand, was relegated to what had *Parliament* come to be its true function as an assembly roughly representative of the *universitas* and watching conciliar government from a distance, informing the permanent council as to the state of the community, and treating with it *des communs besoignes del reaume et del rei*. It is not a serious anachronism to say that the intermittent assemblies of the barons had been becoming decreasingly obedient

[1] Petition of the Barons, 4 and 6.

to the canons of the feudal *curia* and increasingly independent, or, as we may almost say, parliamentary, for the sense of parliament is a parley of antagonists. From 1246 Paris called such assemblies parliaments; the term is used officially of the Easter parliament of 1255,[1] and the Twenty-Four ordain in the Provisions that there shall be three *parlemenz* every year at Michaelmas, Candlemas, and three weeks before the feast of St. John. This is the end of a prolonged and gradual evolution in public life, which now receives statutory recognition. The problem of the organization, and, indeed, that of the composition of the *universitas* for parliamentary purposes, remains to be solved. For the time being it is content to elect twelve of its body as a convenient channel through which to treat with the council at every parliament, and itself to remain in some obscurity.

The great offices   The provisions dealing with the executive mark the triumph of the long-standing demand for the restoration of the great offices to their former substance and rank—at least to their independence from the king and the household. The justiciar is to be more than a mouthpiece for the issue of judicial commissions. He is to "amend according to the law the wrongs done by all other justices and bailiffs and earls and barons", in short, to be the guardian of common right. This he is to do by the counsel of the king and of the great men of the realm and according to the provision of the Twenty-Four. He is not to take bribes or fees, and therefore he is allotted the great salary of a thousand marks a year. His office is for a year only, and then he must answer for his term before the king's council and his successor. In fact Hugh Bigod's justiciarship produced the great part of what redress the commonalty received from the baronial government. The chancellor equally is responsible to the council for everything but the routine of his office. He may seal writs of course without reference, but the great wardships and escheats, which have played so large a part in the king's personal rule, must be granted only with the consent of council.[2] The general restriction on the seal's use is a clumsy one; nothing is to be sealed which is against the ordinances made by the Twenty-Four, but, no doubt, the assumption is that the chancellor

[1] Letters Patent, 39 Hen. III, p. 399.
[2] A revival of the practice of the minority when escheats were disposed of *per commune consilium*. Letters Close, 3 Hen. III, p. 384.

will obey only the precepts of the council. The Treasurer's office is to be annual; "good men" are to be put into the Exchequer by the ordinance of the Twenty-Four. All the issues of the realm are to be paid there, and further order is to be taken as it seems necessary. As in all changes of government in this age, the provincial charges were taken into account. No baronial government felt itself safe unless the principal royal castles were lodged in the hands of its leading members. As in 1216 so in 1258, the leading *Provincial* magnates of the opposition took security in fifteen of the chief *government* castles[1] before the work of reform was begun. For twelve years the king's precept would be insufficient to compel their surrender without warrant of a majority of the council. The sheriffs were to be vavasours of the counties in which they served, salaried, and appointed for a year only.

The fact that the Provisions of Oxford could be pressed through during the few weeks of the Oxford parliament suggests that they embodied changes which had become a familiar prospect to most public men. Indeed they were approved by such royalists as Walter de Kirkham and Peter de Savoy. They were brought in almost without change of ministers, Lovel retaining the Treasury[2] and Wingham the Chancery. Only Pierre des Rievaulx was removed from the Wardrobe. But in the hands of the reformers the constitution of the Provisions of Oxford was unworkable for *Defects* any length of time. It lodged all authority in the council, and pre- *in the* supposed the elimination of the king's will, while requiring the *Provision* form of his consent to every act of government.[3] Yet without a single dominant will the council was itself ungovernable. The nervous ingenuity with which its original membership was contrived betrays its instability. It represented, or was under pressure from, a dozen interests which were only united by hatred of the Poitevins—the magnates of the king's party, the group of Norfolk and Hereford, the persons and interests of Gloucester and Leicester, the habitual conservatism of the *universitas* of the barons, the more radical bachelors, and the unrepresented mass of freeholders, who

1 Letters Patent, 42 Hen. III, p. 637. June 22, 1258.
2 Until November 1258. *Ibid.* 43 Hen. III, p. 1.
3 *Et nus averun ferm e estable quanque lavant dit conseil ou la greinure partie fera*: and we will hold established whatsoever the said council or the greater part of it shall do. *Ibid.* 42 Hen. III, p. 645.

had the best reasons to press consistently for reform.[1] Only at its peril could the council of the Fifteen put its quality of a reformed government to the test, and commit itself to action. The balance achieved in the summer of 1258 was, indeed, at the mercy of every change of favour or circumstance. The momentary absence of the chancellor in July 1259[2] let slip a writ from Chancery which might have embroiled the council with the pope.[3] The Peace of Paris took the king to France and made necessary a duplicate government, whereof the king's half was rapidly converted to be a replica of his personal rule, and a royal party was re-knit. Simon played his own hand in the negotiations for peace, and quarrelled violently with Gloucester. By the time of his return in April 1260 Henry was able blandly to address the justiciar and the rump of the council with an assumption of common anxiety for the peace of the realm now threatened by the alliance of Montfort and Prince Edward, while at the same time he withheld the writs for a parliament which might have rallied the supporters of the Provisions. The crown was showing itself indispensable, and that

Decline of baronial unity Henry was able to dismiss the justiciar and chancellor in April 1261, and to absolve himself from his oath to the Provisions, was due less to his personal skill, though he made no mistakes, than to the fallacy essential to a scheme of government which affected to rule a monarchical system without a king. The victory of Simon's party in 1263 was no more than a check to the coming victory of the crown, and the *Forma Regiminis*, which confirmed it by contracting effective power to the voice of three electors or nominators of the council, acknowledged those vices of division of authority and faction which no baronial government could shake off. As with Cromwell after him, only the assumption of the crown could have perpetuated Simon's rule, and the Edict of Kenilworth, which pronounced the sentence upon the baronial régime in 1266, opened with the reassertion of the personal

---

1 The efforts made to accord such reform are described in a proclamation of October 20, 1258, and their official embodiment is in the Provisions of Westminster. The eyres of the justiciar and the other commissions which sought to redress local wrongs are described by Professor E. F. Jacob in his *Studies in the Period of Baronial Reform*.

2 Letters Patent, 43 Hen. III, p. 29.

3 *Ibid*. p. 35: the safe conduct for Valascus, the papal nuncio for the affair of the diocese of Winchester.

authority of the monarch—"that the most serene prince lord Henry shall have and fully hold his lordship, authority, and kingly power".[1]

Between 1258 and 1265 the forces of feudalism and monarchy, which had been fencing with each other for a generation, were brought to measure their strength and to declare their principles. Politically, the victory of the future king at Evesham was decisive. The original nobility of the Conquest, which had been the mainstay of the rebellions of two centuries, was destroyed as a distinctive force, and left the field to the newer, and for the time being weaker, nobilities of the North and the Welsh Border. As clearly as does their fall, the barons' moment of success reveals to what a point the nation had advanced beyond even the more moderate conceptions of feudalism. The Provisions of Oxford, designed *Triumph* to constrain the king, go almost the whole way to accept the *of the* monarchical state. Government of the realm by a feudal king in *cal system* and through the *curia* of his vassals is abandoned even in the modified form in which it had been entertained fourteen years earlier. The government of the Provisions takes over the division of executive functions, the specialized and powerful bureaucracy, even the members of the king's government. It recognizes the permanent sworn council as the motive force of the state, and relegates the *universitas* of the tenants in chief to a parliamentary status. Faced with the necessity of justifying twenty-five years of opposition, the barons establish control of the king's will, but capitulate to the monarchical régime. It was, perhaps, a natural reaction to a period during which the art of monarchy had been advanced while the king had lost the respect of his nobles, but it was an abandonment of the basic thesis of feudalism. No longer was it even conventionally maintained *quod debet rex omnia . . . facere in regno . . . per judicium procerum regni*.[2]

Yet the effects of Henry's misfortunes and of the baronial movement were very far from being extinguished at Evesham. The story of the first three-quarters of the thirteenth century is superficially one of discord, triviality, and failure. Without great causes and therefore without great men, it is a time of disillusionment with the older ways, while the new growth of the Edwardian

---

1 Dictum de Kenilworth, 1. Stubbs, *Select Charters*, p. 407.
2 Leges Eadwardi Confessoris, xi. 1. A6 (early thirteenth century).

Summary reigns is as yet unattainable. But for that very reason it is one of the great formative periods of English constitutional life. If one formula should be chosen above all others to explain it, it must be that the old coöperation between the crown and the vassals in the feudal state is dissolved. The nature of the vassal's counsel changes, ceases to be a fortification and a willing servant of the will of the supreme lord, and is diverted into independence, criticism, and distrust. *Commune consilium* comes to be something that the king has reason to fear, because it embodies a will which is self-determined and for the most part antagonistic to his own. It becomes parliamentary instead of curial. For its part, the crown goes its own way also, carried by the growing complexity of government to associate itself with advisers and ministers whose standing has been won by efficient service. A new council grows up about the king, skilled in the writs and rolls of Chancery, Treasury, Chamber, and Wardrobe, and engaged by every interest to forward the crown's official policy. In so far as the genius of English political institutions is determined by a permanent principle of opposition between the executive on the one side and the community and those who speak for it on the other, an opposition of court and country, the reigns of John and Henry III were decisive of the temper in which our parliamentary government should be carried on. Without this dualism it would have been impossible. Upon neither part is the process of evolution yet complete. The institutions which will one day arise to embody the national will to opposition are yet undreamed of. That will itself is still hardly more than a persistent instinct to distrust and hamper government in an aristocracy which has lost its traditional part in the régime. Those who have the opportunity to express what is under Henry still a grievance rather than a policy have but a doubtful qualification to do so, for the rule that defined *commune consilium* in the Great Charter was never practicable and has become increasingly untrue to legal and social reality. As a political order their day is over. Of the multitude of tenants who could have claimed to come to the *commune concilium* of 1215, less than a hundred will find a place in the *magnum concilium* of parliament, and the commons representation will depend upon a theory of politics of which feudalism knows nothing. Parliament, with a handful of royal nominees standing for the feudal magnates, and its elected deputies of the *Communitas Angliae* of all free men, is a creation of another world from that of Henry's middle years. But, in spite of this, every move in the slow integration of parliament is an answer to the problems set in these two generations. The crown, which under Henry has narrowed its confidence to a domestic officialdom and turned inward to exploit its demesne right, sets itself under his successor to exploit the realm of England with greater courage, and can afford to rebuild the *commune concilium regni* upon a new basis of parliament, choosing what can best serve it from the remnants of feudal counsel and from the rising political capacity of the communes. But it takes, and cannot but take, into the new régime of the community those forms of political consciousness which have been bred under John and Henry. Parliament will be neither the undifferentiated council, judicature, and executive which was the primitive feudal *curia*, nor the useful servant of prerogative which Edward I perhaps thought to make it. The magnates, even the commons whom he summons before him, will bring with them something of the old judicial function of the *curia* and the form of humble petition which was appropriate to the rule of a king governing by prerogative in council; but in the long run more of the spirit of opposition. From the fissure in the unity of the feudal *curia*, first apparent under John, and hardened into persistent antagonism under Henry, comes that principle of division and balance, statute in the form of redress of grievance, revenue bought by concession, the alternate domination of parliament by court and country, which became the established rhythm of parliamentary government.

IV

1272-1377

i

THE NATIONAL AND LOCAL COMMUNITIES

Franchise brought to rule IT is in the third quarter of the thirteenth century that we first become certain that feudal principles are losing hold. It is not that positive feudal rights are lost; on the contrary, the crown analyses and recognizes them; but by the act of recognition their further growth is stopped. The vagueness in which feudalism flourished begins to clear at the end of the twelfth century. Charters affect a new precision as to what they give, and purport to convey every known incident of privilege, current or obsolete, appropriate or not to the locality of the grant. Neither chancellor nor grantee could say what may or may not be the admissible limits of franchise, and, for that reason, they are determined that no liberty of which they have ever heard shall be omitted. Conversely, the regular entry of the king's justices into the county courts is causing immunities to be examined and referred to the *curia* when doubtful,[1] and what is not in writing is becoming hard to establish on the ground of mere prescription or as inference from general phrases. By the middle of the thirteenth century the *quo warranto* enquiry and the "subtlety" of royal lawyers are established feudal grievances, and if the immunist "exhibits his charter and claims some certain franchise as being implicit in a general clause, it profits him nothing unless the said franchise is mentioned in express terms".[2] The clergy considered that such judgments were

[1] Cf. the instructions to an eyre of 1218 (Letters Close, 3 Hen. III, p. 383): *Omnes autem demandas que coram vobis fuerint quas homines exigunt de libertatibus, videlicet quas dominus Archiepiscopus Cantuariensis, Gilbertus Comes de Clara, vel alii exigunt in respectum ponatis . . . coram consilio nostro apud Westmonasterium.* Where liberties had been exceeded the eyres were already seizing land and franchise into the king's hand. *Ibid.* p. 400.

[2] *Rotuli Parliamentorum*, i. 57. The abbot of St. Mary's, York, complains of the *subtilitas modernorum* in explaining away the *verba generalia* of charters.

violations of the Great Charter: *mirabile est dictu quod longissima* Denial of
possessio non prodesse contra regem.[1] Indeed, the denial of the inde- *right by*
feasible right of time marks the end of unchallenged feudal *prescrip-*
tion
privilege, for it is as much as to say that all right comes from the
king. King's proctors claimed that a rule had been made by common council of the realm[2] that any claim to franchise by charter
must be established by definite and unambiguous words in the
grant, and for his great enquiry *quo warranto* Edward I could claim
and in part make good that time establishes no prescription
against the crown—*quod nullum tempus occurit regi.*[3] Finally,
Edward will go beyond even this and assert that when franchise
clashes with the welfare of the community the king may by
prerogative declare it void.[4]

But no reign is less open to the charge of being an age only of *The idea*
decline than that of Henry III. The great feudatories are losing *of com-*
munity in
their old constitutional place, but new orders are rising to take *the shire*
their share; it is the age of the coming to maturity of provincial
government. The presage of this is a gradual change of life in the
shires and boroughs, which will have to develop many of the
characteristics of true communities before they are qualified to
play a constitutional rôle. The shires never in this age became truly
counties corporate; indeed, their community, even for administrative purposes, was only slowly attained. The shire had been a
unity of law since its creation, and from the time of Cnut was
entrusted with administrative action such as the pursuit of
criminals, but the Norman kings did not summon it as a whole
for other than legal business, or make it corporately responsible for
more than judgment [5] and a very few acts of local government.
For failure in these it could be amerced as a unit; but more than
this it had not entered into the mind of government to do, and
small experience of constitutional unity could come of it. Henry I

[1] Articles of the bishops: it is much to be wondered at that however long
possession (of franchise) is proved it should not be accepted as valid against the
king. Matthew Paris, *Chronica Majora, Additamenta, sub anno* 1257.
[2] *Placita de Quo Warranto*, p. 210: *de communi consilio regni Regis nuper
provisum.* [3] *Ibid.* p. 4.
[4] *Rotuli Parliamentorum*, i. 71. *Dominus Rex, pro communi utilitate, per prerogativam suam in multis casibus est supra leges et consuetudines in regno suo usitatas:*
by prerogative and for the good of all the lord king is above the laws and
customs of his realm in certain cases.
[5] *Leges Hen.* I, 48, 2.

could conceive of no use for the shire except its judgment between honours, or some exceptional call for judgment or inquest upon the demesne rights of the crown,[1] nor, as we have seen, did he base upon it his occasional experiments in itinerant justice. Moreover, such rudimentary public functions as the shire possessed were gravely trenched upon by feudal immunity, since the view of frankpledge and freedom from amercement and common fine, and even from the sheriff's tourn, were common forms of franchise. Many barons and ecclesiastics could withhold their tenants' suit from shire and hundred and exclude the king's officers from entering their land after strayed cattle or to enforce pledge, while some received and served the king's writs, so that no sheriff or royal bailiff had any power within their franchise.[2] Far from being a single community at the disposal of the king's agents, the county was a patchwork of administrations, some where the king had all, some where a greater or less degree of privileged right prevailed, and much of which it could be said, *ibi domino Regi nihil accrescit*—"here the lord king has nothing". Alike in borough and county, franchise and community were opposing forces.

Royal action in the shire

Until the middle of the twelfth century the tide was with such feudal enclaves, but with Henry II a process of attrition began. At a stroke, the Assize of Clarendon re-created for the justices a community which had been partially lost to the sheriffs, placing the oath of every man of whatever fee at the disposal of the justices' inquest, and giving entry to the royal sheriffs into every bailiffry —"even the Honour of Wallingford"—to arrest under the Assize.[3] This was no isolated measure, for not only were the franchises brought into the machinery of the Inquest of Sheriffs, but the king tried to cancel the commonest of all immunities, that of view of frankpledge.[4] The shires were to experience a first lesson in administrative unity under the session of the justices, for it was the channel through which Angevin government was directed as

---

[1] Hen. I, Ordinance of the Shires and Hundreds, 1: *Precipio ut amodo comitatus mei et hundreta in illis locis et eisdem terminis sedeant, sicut sederunt in tempore regis Edwardi, et non aliter.* 2: *Ego enim, quando voluero, faciam ea satis summonere propter mea dominica necessaria ad voluntatem meam.*

[2] *Placita de Quo Warranto*, p. 675: *ita quod nullus vicecomes, ballivus, aut minister Regis manerium aut membra predicta ingrediantur ad districciones aliquas facere pro tallagiis sectis aut aliis consuetudinibus.*   [3] Assize of Clarendon, 11.

[4] *Ibid.* 9. Unlike Henry's other assizes, this rule had no visible effect.

it grew. The swearing of allegiance, the presentment of crime, the assizes, the affairs of the king's demesnes, escheats, custodies, the conservation of the peace, the assize of arms, all were under the survey of the justices or passed under the verdict of the hundreds, vills, and boroughs which made up the shire and which collectively soon came to be spoken of as *commune comitatus*.[1] Duties imposed one by one bred a habit of obedience until, within fifty years of the Assize of Clarendon, the shire was summoned to the justiciars' sessions to hear and obey the king's commands at large—*ad audiendum et faciendum*,[2] as in the later writs of parliament.

In community the shire could do much that it could not do in its first judicial function, or could do it more easily. Common obligation created a common outlook, and the counties began to take an effective part in their own government. To some extent the crown encouraged this as an offset against its own bailiffs. Petitions were admitted to claim local liberties,[3] and John, especially, consulted the shire on such matters as forest administration,[4] and the rights of the debtors of the Jews.[5] Almost certainly, by summoning four knights from every shire *de negotiis regni*,[6] he set the precedent that de Montfort and Henry III were to follow forty years afterwards, though it was as yet no more than a measure taken in a crisis, and had no immediate sequel. Beginning with John's reign the shires were to act upon their own initiative and in their own interest, combining to buy privileges and to secure the appointment of officials whom they could trust.[7] As the magnates withdrew into opposition and were confined more and more to their rare appearances in parliamentary meetings with the king and council, the counties fell into the hands of knights or freeholders and the stewards of the magnates, who declined to attend in person and were exempt by privilege from doing so.

Common action in the shire

---

[1] Assize of Northampton, 1.

[2] Letters Close, 3 Hen. III, p. 380: *audituri et facturi preceptum nostrum*.

[3] Letters Patent, 16 Hen. III, p. 456. Cumberland secures the reduction of the king's sergeants of the county to four.

[4] *Ibid.* 14 John, p. 129.   [5] *Ibid.* p. 132.

[6] Stubbs, *Select Charters*, p. 282.

[7] Pipe Roll, 8 John (Lancs.). Lancashire fines 100 marks to have Richard Vernon as sheriff. Letters Patent, 10 Hen. III, p. 45: Somerset and Dorset receive leave to elect a sheriff. *Ibid.* But when John sells the forest rights of Devon it is not as yet to the county but only to certain persons who subscribe to the fine. *Ibid.* 8 John, p. 70.

*The
change
from
feudal to
national
aids*   The shire must become a taxable community before it can
qualify to take its place beside the magnates as a community in
parliament with a voice in taxation. In the twelfth century the
great tenants-in-chief were intermediaries between the crown and
large sections of land and people, but during the thirteenth group
after group of tax-payers were extricated from their control and
brought into immediate responsibility to the Exchequer. The responsibility of the magnates came to be confined to their own land
in demesne and villeinage, and was finally abolished altogether,
and their knights and free tenants fell away into the body of the
county, which thus became a fiscal unity immediately accountable
to the crown. Setting aside the Danegeld and the Saladin Tithe,
the first of which was obsolete and the second, being upon the
ground of religious obligation, no analogy for secular action,
the taxation of Henry II's reign had been feudal. He tallaged his
demesne—in which royal boroughs, farms, and ministerial tenures
were included—and received aids and scutages from his tenants-in-
chief by military service. Both forms of revenue seem to have
passed through the sheriffs' hands, but the county as such was not
the basis of the tax. The honours bore it, and the non-military freeholders, free socagers, and the like, must have gone untaxed. The
military sub-tenants of the honours seem not to have been bound
by a scutage or aid imposed upon their lords unless the latter were
empowered to recover it by writ.[1] The taxing power of the crown
—it was upon customary occasions and not a true taxing right—
thus originally treated the lordship as a whole under the tenant-in-
chief, and was feudal, in right of tenure; but the earliest Chancery
enrolments show John carrying the crown's action into the stratum
of the mesne tenures. It seems clear that he empowered the sheriffs
to collect scutage directly from the knights of the honours.[2] At
the same time as this departure from feudal correctitude was
hazarded, there came a shifting of the basis of taxation which

---

[1] Pipe Roll, 15 Hen. II (Yorks.). The abbot of Ramsey made special agreements
with his tenants to recoup him for the *auxilium expedicionis*. The bishop of
Norwich makes an aid to the king, who orders the burgesses of Lynn to recoup
him by an aid from themselves. Letters Patent, 11 Hen. III, p. 114.

[2] Letters Close, 7 John, pp. 43 and 46. The marshal's government returned to
precedent in this matter (*ibid.* 2 Hen. III, p. 371), but the sheriff would distrain
in case of recalcitrancy (*loc. cit.*). The same precedent was followed in 1235
(*ibid.* 19 Hen. III, p. 188).

made established rules difficult of application, and indeed for a time left the crown without any settled principle. In 1198 Richard went beyond the feudal aid on the demesne and the knight's fee, and laid a five-shilling *auxilium* upon the plough; in 1204 John took a seventh of their moveable property from the earls and barons and from the parochial and conventual churches; while in 1207 was set the vital precedent of taxing the whole nation, not upon the fee or the plough, but upon the sum of the year's rent and the chattels of every subject. The levy of 1207[1] was, in fact, the beginning of national taxation, and the change from a feudal to a national basis was expressly realized. The tax, a shilling in the mark, loosely referred to as a Thirteenth, was to be upon every layman who had chattels to the value of a mark throughout England *de cujuscunque feodo*. The tax upon moveables was to assert itself as the chief source of revenue in the thirteenth century though not entirely without opposition; as late as 1232 the bishop of Durham, Gilbert de Umfraville,[2] and other northern immunists, claimed that the Fortieth could not be levied within their liberties, and resisted payment for three years. Liability and consent were not, however, all. New tax-forms raised new questions of authority and machinery of collection which must affect the whole structure of the county. The matter of assessment alone was of the first importance, for assessment was at this time akin to assent,[3] since in every appeal for aid the assumption was that the vassal desired to aid his lord and that his gift was only limited by his capacity.[4] *Providere quale auxilium nobis impendere voluerint*—"to ordain how much aid and of what nature they will give us"—is the phrase used in summoning the vassals to debate supply, and the practice of allowing the individual to determine his own capacity was not unknown.[5] Thus assessment and collection were a practical problem hardly different in kind from that of grant. Every levy

[1] Letters Patent, 8 John, p. 72.

[2] On the ground of the regalian status of Redesdale. The bishop, no doubt, stood on his palatine immunity. Letters Close, 19 Hen. III, p. 184. The earl of Chester had even been able to refuse a papal Tenth in 1229. Stubbs, *Select Charters*, p. 323.

[3] Indeed the phrase *assisare auxilium* originally conveyed the idea of assent.

[4] This is particularly clear in the *auxilia* of the boroughs of 1227, assessed by the communities themselves *per se secundum facultates suas*. Letters Close, 11 Hen. III, p. 114. Thus the question of consent arises, but only at the stage of assessment.

[5] Letters Patent, 8 John, p. 72.

brought it to an issue and the expedients adopted were inevitably tests of the unity or disunity of the county. The task was entrusted to commissions under the title of collectors or justiciars, assigned to each county, sometimes from among its own knights and free-holders but with the addition of a king's clerk. These, in coöpera-tion with the sheriff, put in action the current scheme of assessment, received the tax, and conveyed it to the Exchequer or elsewhere as directed.

Growth of fiscal unity in the shire

With each new method of assessment, the crown gradually ad-vanced the disintegration of the fiscal unity of the honours and brought all but their lords' demesne into the body of the shires, which thus became consolidated communities for the levy of aid. So was created that division between baronial and county assess-ment which later extended to the right or duty of the two groups, nobility and communes of the counties, each to tax its own order. The consolidation of the county was, it is true, only arrived at slowly. In 1225 [1] the assessment for the Fifteenth was made under two separate schemes—on the one hand the *feuda*, the demesnes and villeinage of earls, barons, and knights, *i.e.* all the land held in knight service, and, on the other hand, socage, burgage, and other rentals and freeholds—the feudal land being assessed by oath of the reeves of liberties. But a number of spiritual magnates were allowed to extend their immunity of assessment to cover the lands of their burgesses and free tenants, and some to join their bailiffs with one of the justiciars for the assessment of their knights. [2] In 1232 the Fortieth was assessed by the oath of elected men in every vill, but the stewards of baronies and liberties were accorded a roll, and permitted to collect and distrain for the tax throughout their lord's lands, [3] while the earls of Cornwall [4] and Pembroke, [5] the masters of the Temple and the Hospital, and most of the spiritual magnates, were allowed to stand aloof and find their own machinery of assessment and collection. In 1237, however, most of these exemptions had vanished. Gilbert de Umfraville was allowed

[1] Letters Patent, 9 Hen. III, p. 560. The clerical carucage for the siege cf Bedford was assessed and collected by the clerical magnates from the lands of their knights, free tenants, and villeins as well as from their demesnes. *Ibid.* 8 Hen. III, p. 465.　　　　　　　　　　　　[2] *Ibid.* pp. 571-575.

[3] The clergy were apparently allowed special commissioners for their estates, though they were assigned by the king. Letters Close, 16 Hen. III, p. 160. *Ibid.* 17 Hen. III, p. 283. The northern immunists refused this aid outright.

[4] *Ibid.* p. 291.　　　　　　　　　　　　[5] *Ibid.* p. 295.

to make his own levy in Redesdale,[1] and the clergy were given liberty to collect the aid within their fees when assessed, though few seem to have availed themselves of the privilege;[2] but, apart from these minor exceptions, the collectors of the Thirtieth were able to summon the men of the vills throughout the counties without the intervention of their lords, to whom no more was allowed than to send their stewards to attend the assessment if they saw fit to do so.[3] Thus, though it had been clung to as a valuable safeguard of feudal liberty,[4] the magnates' right of separate assessment had by 1237 been restricted to their personal goods and revenues. Those in mesne tenure, knights, freemen, and villeins, had been progressively detached from their lordships and absorbed into the body of the shire. The sole fiscal immunity in the counties was now that of the crown itself, whose demesnes were to be subject to tallage and exempt from the general tax upon moveables until the sixteenth year of Edward II, when they also were for the first time included in the vote of the counties.[5] For taxation, therefore, the *communitas comitatus* was already a fact in the last two decades of Henry III, and it seems right to associate with this recognition of a consolidated shire unit the innovation *Fiscal* that on the next occasion of a general aid, in 1254, knights were *constituency a* summoned to the king *vice omnium et singulorum* in their counties. *prelude to* With the precedent of 1237 as a guide, a single constituency *parlia-* of each and all in the shire was at last available as a basis of *mentary* representation. *constituency of*

The question of whose consent was necessary was hardly *the shire* capable of solution until the process which has just been outlined had brought into being a unified constituency for taxation. It had remained open for half a century, the Crown using one method and one formula after another to secure aids. John had overridden the tenants-in-chief and collected the scutage from their knights,[6]

---

[1] Letters Close, 22 Hen. III, p. 45.

[2] The archbishop of Canterbury, the bishop of Winchester, the abbot of Cluny, and a few others. *Ibid.* pp. 8, 9, 15, and 18. In the reign of Edward I the Knights Taxers were ordered *taxer en ceste taxacione les biens as vileins des Ercesvesqes, Evesqes, Religieux, e de toutz autres Clerks, qui quil seint. Rotuli Parliamentorum,* i. App. p. 239.   [3] Stubbs, *Select Charters,* p. 358.

[4] *Ad conservationem libertatum vestrarum concessimus* . . . Letters Close, 17 Hen. III, p. 285.   [5] *Report on the Dignity of a Peer,* i. p. 283.

[6] For the *auxilium* of two marks on the fee in 1235 the sheriffs distrained for default, but *ad mandatum domini.* Letters Close, 19 Hen. III, pp. 186, 188.

and, since the tax on moveables was invariably granted by *commune consilium*, must have been considered as being taxed in the right of their lords. Nevertheless, the crown began to betray uneasiness as to the authority of its taxes, and to lay claim to a width of consent which it certainly never received. John was content to rest upon the *commune consilium et assensus concilii nostri*, but Henry III claimed the consent of *omnes magnates et fideles totius regni* for the carucage of 1220,[1] and for the Fortieth of 1232 that of the "clergy, earls, barons, knights, freemen, and villeins of the whole realm".[2] It is almost certain that no representatives from the lower tenures were called to London, and unlikely that they were consulted in their counties and hundreds,[3] yet for the Thirtieth of 1237 the same protestation was virtually repeated: the earls, barons, knights, and freemen have granted the aid "for themselves and for their villeins". Thus, Henry III never ventured to assert bluntly that the assent of the magnates to taxation carried with it that of the counties, and, consent and assessment being closely identified, their right to bind anyone but the tenants of their own demesnes became ever more doubtful, especially when the whole business of assessment and collection was taken out of their hands and given to knights elected by the county. The magnates were, indeed, the first to admit this, and it was at their instance that knights were first summoned to consent to an aid in 1254. A generation after this it had become an established principle that the community of each county was the author of the aid, giving its individual consent through its elected attorneys, the knights.[4]

The knights of the shire   In less than a century, therefore, the shire had achieved much of the quality of a fiscal and administrative community. In practice, its voice was that of the knights of the shire. The term *miles comitatus* denoted property, prestige, and tenure within the shire, rather than tenure *per loricam*,[5] and distinguished the independent

---

[1] Stubbs, *Select Charters*, p. 349.   [2] *Ibid.* p. 356.

[3] A dispute in the county court of Yorkshire as to the authority of the carucage of 1220 seems to have been a protest by the bailiffs of the local magnates that their lords had not been consulted in *commune consilium*. It may have represented an appeal by the lesser landholders to clause 14 of the Great Charter.

[4] *Rotuli Parliamentorum*, i. App. p. 226: *Decima, quam tota communitas comitatus Warwick Regi in subsidium guerre Regis concessit* (22 Edw. I).

[5] Perhaps over £20 yearly rental.

landowner from the bachelor or stipendiary knight of the king's household, such as usually rose to castellanships and custodies of escheats and bailiffries and sheriffdoms. Their activity in the thirteenth century is associated with the withdrawal or ousting of the greater barons from the routine of government. Since the reign of Richard I the recurrent special commissions which supplemented the eyres were no longer drawn from the barons, and, in the latters' stead, the knights were making their appearance upon the fringes of government. The knight of Henry III's reign might at intervals find himself a justiciar, though for a few days only, for much of the justice upon assize was done by inquest upon individual cases. For such causes a day and place were appointed within the county, and three or four local freeholders were assigned as justiciars,[1] with a king's clerk joined with them *ad hanc justiciam*. Similar commissions as justiciars[2] were issued to the knights who assessed the taxes upon moveables, and these again were drawn from the counties within their circuit, except for one or more official members. These knight-justiciars were, of course, in addition to the elected knights who on some occasions did the actual work of assessing the hundreds, and they may be supposed to have learned their work in the subordinate capacity. Other commissions, for the tallaging of the king's demesnes, for inquisitions into assarts or purprestures, breaches of the peace, or for such exceptional enquiries as that which followed the fall of Pierre des Roches in 1234, administrative duties, the assigning of knights to receive the oath to the peace in the Edictum Regium of 1195, with the custody of felons,[3] the enforcement of the Assize of Arms,[4] called for constant service by the knights of the counties, and occasionally they rose into official prominence as sheriffs or escheators, or, *The* as in 1226,[5] came to the council with presentments of county griev- *busones* ances. In the early 'thirties there were in Hampshire about a score of knights who had had experience under one sort of commission

1 Letters Patent, 7 Hen. III, p. 409: *X. Y. et Z. constituti sunt justiciarii ad assisam capiendam quam A. aramiavit . . . versus B. de recognitione utrum.*

2 *Ibid.* 9 Hen. III, p. 560 (For the Fifteenth of 1225): *Rex X. Y. et Z. salutem. Assignavimus vos justiciarios nostros ad quintamdecimam omnium mobilium assidendam et colligendam in comitatibus A. B. et C.*

3 Stubbs, *Select Charters*, p. 258.

4 *Ibid.* p. 362.   5 *Ibid.* p. 353.

or another as justiciars, who had no official connection with the central administration, but were county landholders of moderate means.[1] Such county notables, knights who were foremost in the judgment of the local courts and in provincial administration, were distinguished by Bracton and others as *busones*, and were a recognized class in the community, the product of a new age. They emerge as a quasi-official administrative class as the shire outgrows its feudal disunity, becomes a fiscal whole, realizes a new kind of identity: they are the fore-runners of those who will take the newly integrated shires as their constituencies and represent them to Parliament.

Early history of the borough

Self-government and the sense of communal unity were even stronger in the boroughs. They possessed a kind of immunity from the beginning; indeed they were older than the shires by half a century. The earliest towns seem to have been centres of provincial government, like Wye, or Bamborough, or Winchcombe: some of them were, of course, national capitals, and others, like the Cinque Ports, began as trading stations, perhaps even for the petty trade of monasteries or lord's halls. During the Danish wars the fortified town or burh became the sole centre of government, and for a period of years at the beginning of the tenth century England was governed by borough reeves, while as yet there were neither shires nor hundreds. The boroughs emerged into the settled régime of the eleventh century with courts and administrations covering the urban area and a greater or smaller portion of the surrounding fields, but they had become subordinate to the shires in which they lay. Even London was not a county, though its sheriffs farmed the county of Middlesex from the reign of Henry I, and the rule that the pleas of the borough courts were those of the hundred probably had no exception before the Conquest. The burgess of the eleventh century was an agriculturist rather than a craftsman if London and some of the larger seaports

[1] A typical instance was Walter de Rumsey, in private life steward of Rumsey Abbey. He was justice to enquire into breaches of the peace in Hampshire in 1218, into assarts of the forest in 1219, upon a case of homicide in 1221, for the assessment of the Fifteenth in 1225, for an assize of darrein presentment and one of novel disseisin in 1226, and for another in 1228, all three at Winchester. He was added to the eyre for his own county in 1227, made escheator of Hampshire in 1232, and was collector for the county for the feudal aid of 1235. Letters Close and Patent, *passim*.

be excepted, and the towns were dominated by privilege and rank. Beginning as places of justice and defence, they were under the control of the ministerial nobility. For the discharge of his service of judgment and administration every king's thegn had his borough residence, and the borough thegns were a synonym for the borough community,[1] as were the shire thegns for that of the shire. They brought their privilege with them, and even London was riddled with the sokes and immunities of the king and queen and the great ecclesiastics, while one of its wards, the Knightengild, perhaps took its name from the franchise of a gild of London thegns. As late as the reign of John the soke and the soke reeve were important factors in London government and found their place in the London Custumal.

Thus, the borough inherited the elements which were universal *Borough* in Saxon politics. As a community it was a folk of freemen em- *constitu-* bodied in its court—in London the "folkmoot"—its custom, vary- *tion* ing from district to district, but conforming to the broad lines of old English court procedure by oath and ordeal. As an administrative area it was under the government of a royal reeve, port-reeve, or borough reeve, who presided over the court, took its wites for the king, enforced its judgments, and directed its frankpledge. There was, therefore, much in the boroughs which derived from and was governed by inflexible and conservative institutions. All Saxon courts proceeded by rules coming out of a remote past and preserved a nucleus of custom of fabulous antiquity. The burgesses clung to these forms through the Conquest,[2] bargained with the Norman and Angevin crown for exemption from the new law, and became the last stronghold of ancient Teutonic process in an age of legal revolution. In the London of Henry III's reign the old procedure of defence by compurgation[3] remained the palladium of the burgess oligarchy, by which the aldermen and the conservative burgess families defended themselves against the unholy

1 J. M. Kemble, *Codex Diplomaticus*, 857: *Eadward king gret Willem bisceop, and Leofstan and Ælfsi porterefan, and alle mine burhthegnes on Lundene.*

2 The Conqueror grants that the Londoners shall "be worthy of all their law as they were in the reign of King Edward". Stubbs, *Select Charters*, p. 97.

3 Charter of Henry I to London: *per sacramentum quod judicatum fuerit in civitate se disrationet homo Londoniarum. Ibid.* p. 129. *Placita de Quo Warranto* (Edw. II), p. 449: *et quod nullus de misericordia pecunie judicetur nisi secundum legem civitatis quam habuerunt tempore Regis Henrici avi Regis Henrici avi Regis Henrici avi Regis nunc.*

alliance of the crown, a democratic mayor, and the commune. Here and elsewhere the defence of borough liberties took the form of a fanatical clinging to archaic rules of court. Moreover the administrative machinery, similar to that of shire and hundred, shared its inelasticity; the future self-governing corporations of the towns and cities set out equipped with nothing more than courts confined to judgment between parties and even more conservative than the courts of the counties, and governing officials who were stewards of a lord's demesne. Beneath the reeves' government the burgesses were headless, without unity beyond that of their common membership of their court: even their lordship was sometimes divided among several lords, and their primary allegiance might be less to their borough than to some external manor in the shire.[1]

Burgess organization   Within this inexpensive framework there lay and worked the most mutable social material of the age. The free play of money, sale and purchase, credit, interest, and wages, were closely restricted by convention and a public opinion which condemned usury and held by the rule of the just price; much of the industry of the lesser towns was still agrarian, and tenure and lordship preserved a degree of stability even in London. But, in spite of all this, the burgesses of even the smallest boroughs were beginning to look beyond fixed rents to profit, and to see that buyers and sellers could find more useful social forms in the free association of equals and rivals in craft or commerce than in the passive and defensive devotion of man to lord. Slowly, therefore, lordship and tenure began to be undermined by newer and more real loyalties, and the mutual oath of gilds and communes became stronger than the oath of fealty. Had the burgesses found nothing to serve their turn but the public powers of the *firma burgi*—the right to compound for the king's dues by a farm—tradesmen and artisans would have remained within the shell of the Saxon borough without a law merchant, without action for debt or contract, without rules for employment, apprenticeship, or standards of craft, without power to protect their merchants in foreign parts,

[1] Thus the burgesses of New Romney were for the most part tenants of the archbishop's honour of Newington, and under that manor they are entered in Domesday, where all mention of the borough is omitted. Domesday Book, i. 4A.

or to govern themselves as the crowded populace of a city. The borough as such was powerless even to levy upon its burgesses for the care of streets and bridges or to keep a common purse.[1] It could judge, collect the king's dues, and keep the king's peace, but for the townsmen themselves it was no better than a negative safeguard, an immunity.

Some of these freedoms they arrived at indirectly by grant of *The gild* the gild merchant, which may have come into the towns by way of English *cnihtengilds*[2]—the earliest is of about A.D. 860[3]—or may have been a spontaneous growth of Norman England. By this they got franchise of tol and team—the right of warranting sale —with the assize of weights and measures which went with it. The gilds were spreading through the towns soon after the Norman Conquest, and must have given an outlet to burgess activity for a generation before the *firma burgi*[4] was commonly enjoyed. The root privilege of the gild was the right of retail trade within the franchise, but it seems also to have conferred a power of positive action. Thurstan granted a *hans hus* or gild hall to Beverley *ut ibi sua statuta pertractent ad totius villatae emendationem*,[5] and most gilds achieved a very full organization under a gild alderman, a group of governing jurats, a treasurer, and a court of morning-speech. Not every town had a gild merchant—London found a substitute in its aldermen and *probi homines*, and later in its commune—but many found in the morning-speech the authority to fix standards of work and wages, enforce contracts, to give sanction to the rules drawn up for themselves by the several crafts, and to apply those conventions of fair trading for which there was as yet no action at common law. Especially where the burgesses did not as yet farm the bailiffry, there was a natural tendency to concentrate upon the gild at the expense of the borough. The rota of those capable of responsibility was small, and the jurats or *judices* of the town

1 The lesser towns had to apply to the crown for grants of murage, pontage, and pavage for these purposes. F. Pollock and F. W. Maitland, *History of English Law*, i. 662.

2 F. W. Maitland, *Domesday Book and Beyond*, p. 191: "When, not long after the Conquest, we catch at Canterbury our first glimpse of a merchant-gild, its members are calling themselves knights: knights of the chapman-gild".

3 W. de Gray Birch, *Cartularium Saxonicum*, 515.

4 Cf. *infra*, p. 320.

5 Stubbs, *Select Charters*, p. 131. "With right to make statutes there for the good of the town."

must also be jurats of the gild, and sit both in the public court—the portmanmoot or hustings—and in the morning-speech of the gild also. Thus there was a useful confusion between the spheres of the gild and the borough; where the latter could not act the gild was to be found levying upon its members for the expenses of the town,[1] and the gild merchant might come to regard itself as the real source of borough government.[2]

The gild a solvent of feudalism   Whatever their later history, the gilds merchant of the twelfth century were powerful solvents of the feudalism of the towns. The portmanmoots had been subject to the prevailing aristocratic trend in judicature. The lawmen's office of the Danelah boroughs and the aldermanries of London and Canterbury were originally heritable and could be bought and sold. The gild, on the other hand, was a community of presumed equals; the phrases *communitas gildae*, even *communa gildae*, are not uncommon. The morning-speech, though the predominant merchant families no doubt had their way, was an open aristocracy of wealth and ability, and, while the elective principle was not native to the borough, it was everywhere recognized, at least in name, in the gild. Moreover, the rise of the gilds accompanied a progressive decline in the landed interest, and in the judicial and administrative immunities which had arisen from them to divide the borough structure. Legal change was in any case reducing the soke and manor courts to the rank of a minor justice of trespass and the peace; the suit of burgesses to external courts was cancelled by the almost universal privilege "not to plead outside the walls", and, with the bait of gild privilege,[3] the tenants of the intra-mural franchises were less and less disposed to cling to their immunity from amercement, common fine, and tallage, or to claim the protection of their lord's reeves. Bargains by which such discordant groups as the bishop of Lincoln's fee in Leicester[4] accepted the full obligation of scot and lot in return for the right of gild marked the abandonment of

---

[1] M. Bateson, *Leicester Borough Records*, II. xlvii.

[2] At Bedford the burgesses claimed to be able to extend the full borough franchise to non-burgesses by making them members of the gild. *Placita de Quo Warranto*, p. 18.

[3] Great landholders found it worth while to seek membership of town gilds as did the earl of Norfolk and the East Anglian religious houses at Norwich and Ipswich.

[4] M. Bateson, *Leicester Borough Records*, i. 192.

franchise for burgess freedom, and brought the boroughs nearer to effective community. It was a minor revolution in English social life, the difficulty of whose achievement we have lost the ability to estimate, when the men of bishops, earls, and barons surrendered their special status, and placed themselves at the king's mercy with their fellow burgesses, accepting the disabilities of tenants on ancient demesne of the crown.[1]

Without the stimulus of the gild, constitutional growth was slower but not impossible. Every English court and the population it served had the potentialities of political self-government, and we have already seen the counties make some advance towards it in the first half of the thirteenth century. Both in their popular composition as folkmoots and in the official groups of doomsmen which had formed within them—lawmen at Lincoln and Cambridge, deman at Chester, aldermen in London, jurats in the Cinque Ports—the boroughs had a root of self-government, though it was hard to bring it past the phase of judgment to counsel and law-making. The greatest borough of all contrived to govern itself until the reign of Richard I without a gild merchant or a commune, using, presumably, its port-reeve and aldermen to pass by-laws by way of assize,[2] and its folkmoot as a general assembly for frankpledge and the hearing of the king's precepts. Nevertheless, it is clear that the habit and expectation of controlling their own affairs bred in the gild merchant counted for much, and were preparing the towns to desire more explicit recognition. They were in fact managing their own affairs roughly upon the basis of equal citizenship, but they were doing so either on sufferance, as *probi homines* called in at discretion to advise the judicial oligarchs as in London, Norwich, or the Cinque Ports, or, more questionably still, by using the machinery of the gild to do that business which the town could not.

The struggle between these two principles, the rigidity of royal or seigneurial administration and the free industrial or commercial coöperation of fellow townsmen, is the main theme of borough history in the Middle Ages. It is that which we have already seen in

[1] *Placita de Quo Warranto*, p. 158 (Derby): *Quicunque in burgo manserit cujuscunque feodi sit, reddere debet cum burgensibus tallagium* (Cf. also Nottingham).
[2] Such as the Building Assize of 1189. *Munimenta Gildhallae*, i. 319; F. Pollock and F. W. Maitland, *History of English Law*, i. 660.

the counties, but fought out with clearer purpose and a more decisive result. In part the deadlock was solved by the reception of the foreign political form of the commune, but the crown would hardly have admitted the commune into its cities had it not already bartered away a great deal of its demesne right. The twelfth century saw a series of bargains to buy out the seigneurial right in the court of burgesses and the burgess tenements, to secure the election of the reeve and his subordinates, and to compound the rents and profits for a fixed *firma burgi*. The rudiments of this process appear in Domesday—Dover has already bought out its sake and soke[1]—but it is one which proceeds irregularly. The majority of the greater towns answer for their own farm by the year 1200 and a number claim to have done so since the reign of Henry II; but there are exceptions, of which Winchester is the chief. Leicester is buying itself free from the lordship of the earl item by item until well into the fourteenth century.[2] London secured its farm in the later years of Henry I. Its charter[3] gave the citizens the right to elect bailiffs, who should also be sheriffs of Middlesex, a shire justiciar, who should also hold and keep the crown pleas of the city, and to render the king's profits, both for city and county at a farm of £300 for all issues. By this charter, except for the difference between farm and fee-farm, *i.e.* farm in perpetuity, the position of the Londoners was that of the de Viponts in their hereditary shrievalty of Westmorland, or of those short-lived sheriffdoms and shire justiciarships which were granted to Geoffrey de Mandeville and Miles of Gloucester a few years later, and the parallel is worth considering. Neither the London liberties nor those of the magnates offered the basis of a new political life. The boroughs got from their farm not a general power, nor authority to advance their political form towards self-government, but immunity. They were no longer at the discretion of a stranger who could make his profit by inventing reasons for amercement or exceeding the dues of custom. But in their courts, their rents, and services, nothing was changed. Some more positive recognition was wanted if the burgesses were to govern themselves in their own right and not as farmers for the crown.

The firma burgi

---

[1] Domesday Book, i. 2.
[2] M. Bateson, *Leicester Borough Records*, passim.
[3] Stubbs, *Select Charters*, p. 129.

This they found in an idea of community, most intensely *The idea* realized in the boroughs, though even there it is rather a general *of com-* concept of the state, varying in intensity according to time and *munity* place, than a borrowing of specific foreign institutions. It was, *borough* indeed, an influence that affected all England in the thirteenth century, changing the value of political forms, modifying political action, and breaking down the restrictions and immunities of feudalism. Its governing idea is the recognition of a general political association of which the basic right, status, and duty of all the members are identical, and where obedience and loyalty are owed equally by all to the political form in which the commune is embodied. That form is immaterial to the political concept, and the fact that the term commune suggests first to our minds the self-governing town is a mere accident of modern historical study. We shall treat it in what follows as only one of many types of commune, for in the Middle Ages the word is universally applied, though with varying reality—the commune of the county, the realm, the borough, the commune of parliament, communes of merchants. The capacity to perform a joint legal act seems to be sufficient to gain for its makers the name of commune with contemporaries. Communes were apparently instituted formally only in a few of the great boroughs and over a period of about twenty years. A forgotten pioneer, Thomas de Ultra Usa, tried to set up a commune of York during the anarchy of 1174,[1] there is London's commune of 1191,[2] and of those cities which had mayors under John, Oxford, Winchester,[3] York,[4] Bristol,[5] and Lynn, three soon claimed the status of communes,[6] and were among the first to use a common seal. These city communes certainly stood for something very definite. In 1175 York was punished as for a revolutionary act, and Richard I's chronicler feared them as *tumor plebis*. Winchester thought the commune worth having without a farm of its bailiffry. Indeed, it is likely that at the beginning of its history, while its meaning was still

---

[1] Pipe Roll, 22 Hen. II (Yorkshire).
[2] J. H. Round, *Commune of London*, passim.
[3] Letters Close, 6 John, p. 2. Northampton also. *Ibid.* 16 John, p. 188.
[4] *Ibid.* 15 John, p. 150.
[5] Letters Patent, 18 John, p. 195.
[6] Letters Close, 5 Hen. III, p. 405 : *Littere majoris et commune Londonie et Majoris et commune Wintonie et proborum hominum Suthhamtonie.*

clear cut and foreign, the *communa* had much to offer to the
theory and even the practice of corporate life. The boroughs had
become partially feudalized, their only bond of unity was the
feudal oath, and the burgesses were the men of this or that soke
or manor if they were not the men of the king by a supposed right
of ancient demesne; the commune offered them an oath to their
city and to their confraternity.[1] It will not do to insist that any
single implication of this oath was realized and applied, but
London under its commune was tallaging itself for civic purposes
consensu omnium, de cujuscunque feudo, while many boroughs still
needed royal license to do so. Associated with the commune is the
mayoralty, though it cannot be said with certainty that it arose
from it. In London the first mayor was in office within two years
of 1191, and the mayoralty soon identified itself with the popular
element in the folkmoot. As an institution it answered to the
political unity promised by the commune, for, unlike any other
civic office, it conferred authority over all the discordant parts of
the borough,[2] the king's bailiffry, the aldermen, and the craft gilds.
It embodied in itself both the elective right of the community
and the royal commission, so that the king appointed a mayor to
Lincoln as *ballivus noster et major vester,*[3] and, being added to
the court of aldermen or jurats, it represented the town to the
outside world.[4] Either as an outcome of the commune, or as an
alternative way of conferring the same benefit, the mayoralty
coördinated the borough into an entirely new unity of authority.
Among the Gildhall memoranda is a draft for a communal oath
with *echevins, cent pairs,* and *prudeshommes.*[5] There was no such
formal reception of the commune as this, and no English town

*The
mayoralty*

---

[1] For the same reason the phrases *communa gildae, communitas gildae* were
applied to the gild merchant.

[2] The general power of the mayor and the delimited office of the bailiff are
distinguished in the *quo warranto* plea of Nottingham (*Placita de Quo Warranto,*
p. 618): *Major . . . presit ballivis et aliis de eadem villa in omnibus que pertinent ad
. . . ejusdem ville regimen et juvamen. Ballivi . . . ea que pertinent ad officium suum
exequantur:* the mayor is over the bailiffs and others in the town in all things
which pertain to its government and welfare. The bailiffs do that which pertains
to their office.

[3] Letters Patent, 2 Hen. III, p. 160.

[4] F. Pollock and F. W. Maitland, *History of English Law,* i. 681 n.: *Et factum
maioris in hiis que tangunt communitatem est factum ipsius communitatis.*

[5] J. H. Round, *Commune of London.*

altered its constitution to suit a foreign model. No doubt, if its full implications had been realized, the aristocracies of the towns themselves would have been the first to repel it. But the communal doctrine lifted civic patriotism on to a new basis. It was a theory of political association alternative to feudalism, it was allowed to establish itself beside the law of tenure in the towns as alternative to feudal loyalty and to make demands additional to feudal obligations. It gave a colour of constitutional right to the inevitable advance of industrial over agrarian factors in borough government, and in the end it made the civic status of the burgess more important than any status by tenure which might survive.

Communal practice was at its strongest in London, where *communa* became the cry of a violent democracy.[1] Here an almost Italian precision of civic consciousness was achieved, the folkmoot standing for the *parliamento*, while the London magnates followed the aldermanry as the *grandi* clung to the consulate of the Italian cities. Other towns passed through the same conflict, though less consciously and with less disorder, but on the whole the boroughs soon forgot the enthusiasm of the commune and passed under a government of crafts and liveries; community, therefore, did not in the long run mean popular government, but rather a transfer of power from an aristocracy of lords of sokes, manors, and burgess tenements to one of traders. But, though the struggle between the classes was short-lived, the two centuries during which urban franchise was pieced together left their mark on the nation, since they brought the boroughs into being as *Growth of* separate units of administration and converted burgess right from *borough* a variety of tenure to the status of an independent order of the *immunity* state. While the counties had been developing powers of selfgovernment and absorbing the elements of feudalism into their community, a similar but more persistent instinct had been withdrawing the threads of local government and taxation from the sheriffs, and giving the principal boroughs independence within the counties in which they lay. After a period during which the Angevin judiciary had held borough and hundred in a common responsibility to the eyre court of the county, English administration was coming to be split into two distinct elements, standing for the respective interests of the minor landed gentry and free-

[1] *Liber de Antiquis Legibus* (Camden Series), *passim*.

holders and the organized wealth of industry. The order in which the various immunities were come by varied. On the whole, the freedom from external lordship was earliest. No burgess could be involved in villein status, or put into court on any subject's plea beyond the walls of the city, and this, the right to immunity from foreign courts, destroyed equally the county's claim to burgess suit. Londoners were even allowed to set a court at the Tower for the justices of the king's pleas, and some other towns were privileged to be the place of session of the eyre,[1] and to have their special session of gaol delivery.[2] Almost all had the trial of civil right in their hustings and that minor criminal justice which was known as the *placita vicecomitis*. On the administrative side the election of bailiffs gave a certain security, but it left the borough at the obedience of the sheriff. In most large boroughs, therefore, city coroners were elected[3] and the bailiffs of the town were allowed to present the farm in person at the Exchequer,[4] and in the thirteenth century many came to have the return of writs of both Exchequer and common law courts. It could then be said that "no sheriff or bailiff of the king or any other person might enter the borough to perform his office,"[5] except in case of default by the bailiffs of the franchise. This was the liberty which in another connection was said to be "a crown in itself"; in simpler terms it was complete exemption from the government of the county, and, although the phrase belongs to a later century, it was in this right that some towns came to be called counties corporate, and to have the title of sheriff for their reeves. By the reign of Edward I an important group of boroughs stood outside the *corpus comitatus* and presented a distinct problem of government.

Fiscal unity of the borough   As in the counties so in the towns, the rise of the boroughs towards a parliamentary status is heralded by the clarification of their fiscal relation to the crown. Upon what ground the early

---

1 *Placita de Quo Warranto*, p. 158: *et habere quod comitatus de Derby imperpetuum teneatur apud Derby.* Lesser towns, such as Dunwich (Stubbs, *Select Charters*, p. 311), had liberty *quod nullam sectam faciant comitatus vel hundredorum nisi coram justitiis nostris*, and that by suit of twelve representatives.

2 *Loc. cit.*: *et quod Rex et heredes Regis mittent justiciarios nostros usque burgum predictum ad gaolam predictam . . . deliberandum.*

3 Cf. Stubbs, *Select Charters*, p. 306. John's charter to Northampton.

4 *Ibid.* p. 305. John's charter to Nottingham.

5 *Placita de Quo Warranto*, p. 158.

boroughs were treated as royal or seigneurial demesne[1] we do not know. As late as the reign of Henry II this is the basis of a curious classification in which cities, boroughs, thegns, drengs, *firmarii*, and demesne vills are grouped together as liable to tallage: lords of franchises might tallage their boroughs when the crown tallaged its demesne.[2] From this base, tenurial status the towns gradually rose during the twelfth and thirteenth centuries. Perhaps the first phase of advance can be found in the assertion by certain of the larger towns of their own fiscal unity. Early in John's reign Derby and Nottingham, and, no doubt, other towns, secured the elimination of tenurial immunities from taxation, and every burgess, of whomever he held, must join with the town in tallage.[3] But not all towns cared to deal with the king's tallagers as communities,[4] and well into the fourteenth century the tallagers were licensed to tallage the burgesses by poll or in common as they thought best.[5] Individual responsibility was the answer to persistent abuse of joint levies upon the community, but upon the whole the communal system was gaining ground, and the power of bargaining which it gave began to lift the burgess out of the demesne status. Arbitrary assessment had indeed been increasingly difficult to apply as Henry III's reign proceeded. Again and again the sums imposed had to be reduced, and for many towns an agreed amount settled into custom. London came to regard 1000 pounds as the limit of its tallage and in 1255 resisted the king's demand of 3000 marks, and offered 2000. Henry complained that the citizens' conduct was equivalent to a claim to be taxed by voluntary aid instead of by tallage,[6] but, indeed, the time was coming when it would be more profitable for the crown to transfer the towns to the voluntary system. Already the difficulty of estimate had made it necessary to allow the greater towns to tallage themselves through elected burgesses, and the narrow

Transition from tallage to aid

1 *Placita de Quo Warranto*, p. 241: *Burgus de Gloucestria qui est de antiquo dominico Corone.*

2 Letters Patent, 7 Hen. III, pp. 373, 385. Chichester, Exeter, Wilton, tallaged for the queen-mother when the king tallaged his demesne.

3 *Placita de Quo Warranto*, pp. 158, 618.

4 In 1243 London was tallaged by an individual canvass.

5 Letters Patent, 44 Hen. III, p. 76; *Rotuli Parliamentorum*, i. 449 (8 Edw. II), *separatim per capita vel in communi, prout ad commodum nostrum magis videritis expedire.*

6 Letters Close, 39 Hen. III, p. 160. *Optulerunt domino regi duo milia marcarum nomine auxilii.*

difference between an aid and a tallage imposed arbitrarily and
then reduced on the ground of poverty or custom to what the
burgesses were willing to pay was further obscured by the fact
that custom already extended the tallage to the franchises and
would make towns in seigneurial demesne equally liable with
their free neighbours. In 1297, therefore, the Eighth granted by
the citizens and burgesses, though it is still linked with tallage by
the taxing of the crown demesne with the boroughs, is levied not
only from those of the king but from the mesne boroughs also—
*totes citiez e Burghs, petitz e grantz de Reaume, qui quil seient, e de
quinque tenure ou fraunchise.*[1] Under Edward II the rare tallages are
made at the same uniform fractions of revenue as the aids,[2] tallage
and aid have become almost indistinguishable, and the boroughs
contribute regularly to the latter, and, having shaken off their
connection with the demesne,[3] stand as a distinct and independent
order of the community.

By the end of the thirteenth century the compactness of community in the towns had become such that "a new line had to be
drawn between the boroughs and other *communitates*. Bracton
saw this, though he saw it dimly."[4] Nevertheless it is true that
communa, used almost exclusively of the boroughs, and *communitas*,
with reference to the county, are latinizations of a single vernacular
term *commune* which was modifying the estimate in which
institutions were held both in country and town, and was making
The idea possible a readjustment of national institutions. At points we may
of com- believe that the fact that the commune was so clearly exemplified
munity in the boroughs may have influenced the country's rulers con-
and the sciously. The commune in the boroughs achieved its greatest
nation reality under John, and we cannot dissociate it from his innate
antipathy to feudalism and willingness to foster any rival political
theory. He gave the commune to London under Richard, and, in
his own reign, almost certainly to Winchester [5] and perhaps to
York and Bristol. He instituted a sworn commune of England
for the defence of the realm and the preservation of the peace

[1] *Rotuli Parliamentorum*, i. 239.
[2] In 1314 a Fifteenth of moveables and a Tenth of revenues. *Ibid.* i. 449.
[3] As from 1319. *Ibid.* i. App. 455.
[4] F. Pollock and F. W. Maitland, *History of English Law*, i. 687.
[5] Which acquired a commune between 1190 and 1220 (Letters Close,
5 Hen. III, p. 445).

in 1205,[1] the thought of which must have been near to that of the contemporary London compilation of the Articuli Willelmi, *ut omnes liberi homines totius regni nostri sint fratres coniurati ad monarchiam nostram.*[2] Two years after his proposed *commune* of the realm, he transferred taxation from a feudal basis to the community at large, and in so doing repeated the phrase by which the boroughs were securing the right to tax the tenants of the intra-mural immunities to their tallage: *quicunque . . . cujuscunque feodi sit reddere debet simul cum burgensibus talliagia*[3]: *quilibet de cujuscunque feudo sit . . . det nobis in auxilium.*[4] Thus the crown was not above using the practice of the *commune* to support its innovations upon feudal custom.

The theory of community, though in a less concrete form, also played its part in the rise of baronial opposition. It applied less aptly to equals in tenure than to association in urban or rural groups, nor does the honour ever seem to have been considered in terms of the *commune*, but it was, perhaps, by some extension of the earlier and more limited use that the body of the tenants-in-chief came to be spoken of as *communa, communitas,* or, quite as often, as *universitas, regni,* the *regnum* being thought of in this connection as the special lordship of the king over his immediate vassals rather than the sovereignty over all subjects.[5] The gradual expansion of loyalty from the ideal of a special fealty of *barones dominici* to the king to one of faith to some imperfectly defined national cause was, no doubt, prompted first by the partial breakdown of the exclusiveness of the baronial circle. Many baronies had fallen into fractions between coheiresses, and the number of tenants *per baroniam* was vastly greater than that of the baronies. The simple knight might often be richer than his "baronial" neighbour.[6] Yet the transition was certainly made easier by

The tenants-in-chief as communitas

---

[1] In 1202 John had already tried a temporary, regional commune in the district about Harfleur as a means of rapid and coordinated defence against Philip. Letters Patent, 4 John, p. 14.

[2] *Willelmi articuli Londoniis retractati,* 9.

[3] *Placita de quo Warranto,* p. 158.   [4] Letters Patent, 8 John, p. 72.

[5] In this sense Henry I spoke of the *regnum* as an honour of which his barons were the members, *barones mei honoris.* Hen. I, Ordinance of the Shires and Hundreds, 3.

[6] The *Modus Tenendi Parliamentum* was ready to assert that the tenant *per loricam* should be deemed a baron for parliamentary purposes if he held as much as thirteen and a third fees.

a background of theory, however, imperfectly apprehended. The authority of the *communitas regni* was constantly urged against Henry III, and, on one occasion at least, the magnates asserted their need of a common seal of the *universitas*.[1] This use had, as we shall see, a considerable future in the vocabulary of parliament, but as yet it was not the opposition that exploited the idea of community with the greatest effect, but the crown, which, by using it to effect the awkward transition from the feudal limitations upon its dealings with the counties and boroughs, made the word "commune" a vital one in the terminology of the national assembly. There was never any likelihood of the English estates establishing themselves upon the ground of tenure; the many kinds and degrees of tenure and their lack of clear differentiation made them unsuitable for representation in a national council. Indeed, the general and uniform taxation of moveables, and with it elected representation, were possible only in so far as the immunity which so many tenures carried was overridden and the innumerable interwoven interests of property, tenure, and lordship, which neighboured each other in the shire, were endowed with some fiction of joint personality. It was not tenure-in-chief, nor tenure by barony, nor knight service, nor the forty-shilling freeholder, nor freehold as such, which came to be represented in parliament, but the combination of all these—and through them even of the villeins—into the community of the shire; the constituencies of parliament were to be *les communes de la terre*, the communities of shires and boroughs, the commons. The rise of the shire to a measure of community accompanies and makes for the evolution of its fiscal and administrative unity, and both are expressed in the writ forms of the summons to elected representatives: *ex parte communitatis comitatus*,[2] *vice omnium et singulorum*,[3] *pro comunitatibus eorundem comitatuum habentes plenariam potestatem*.[4]

The implications of a claim to communal status were so im-

The parliamentary commune

---

[1] The earls and barons seem to assert their representative quality in 1244 in demurring to an aid *quod sine communi universitate nihil facerent*. Stubbs, *Select Charters*, p. 327.

[2] *Report on the Dignity of a Peer*, iii. p. 35 (49 Hen. III).

[3] *Ibid.* p. 13 (38 Hen. III).

[4] *Ibid.* p. 46 (11 Edw. I). The formula occurs as early as 49 Hen. III in the summons to the capitular clergy (*ibid.* p. 36).

perfectly understood [1] in the counties and even in the towns, that it is perhaps surprising that the *commune* should have had so large a share in the transition from feudal *curia* to parliament. This was, indeed, its most important achievement in England, where social relations and the routine of provincial life outside the towns continued to be governed by feudal motives and the custom of tenure, and, as time went on, by the free play of money. It helped, half consciously, to free the crown partially from its commitment to the magnates for aid and counsel, and—by recognizing *communes des comtés*—to weaken their claim to be the *communitas regni*. It brought the crown into direct contact with all grades and kinds of tenure with a new colour of constitutional right, and it provided a ground of principle when parliament was being brought into being empirically and almost entirely at the crown's discretion. For such reasons the period during which the threads of ancient right were summarily cut by giving the qualities of a *commune* to any group which it was inconvenient to deal with as individuals is a phase in the history of the constitution which it is impossible to ignore; a new non-feudal colour spread over the administrative organization of the provinces with an influence upon the growth of parliamentary estates which is difficult to analyse but none the less real. In Scotland the line of growth is clear. As in England, the tenants-in-chief establish themselves as the *communitas regni par excellence*. They are joined in the first half of the fourteenth century by two other *communitates*, those of the clergy and burgesses, and these, by their representatives, take their place as the three "communities", the future three estates, of the Scotch parliament. In England the process is less simple, but the principle is the same. The English baronage asserted during the thirteenth century a *communitas regni* which was understood, with more or less clarity, as an embodiment of the principal tenures-in-chief of the crown; but with the loss of the Barons' Wars there came a break in baronial tradition. Only a minority even of the magnates attended the parliaments of the fourteenth century, and their attendance was so plainly at the will of the crown that, though the *communitas procerum* holds its place in the

[1] There are, as has been said, many uses of the term in a vague and general sense. The *communitas bacheleriae Angliae*, and so on.

language of parliament for a time,[1] the fiction of a parliamentary community of nobles was hard to maintain. By the reign of Edward II the representatives of the *communes* of shires and boroughs had attracted the title of *communitas regni* to themselves,[2] and, in default of an equivalent *communitas baronum*, the "three communities of parliament" were never adopted into English constitutional phraseology. The magnates in parliament never, in fact, after Evesham recovered that clear sense of embodying an order which had inspired them as a *curia* of feudal tenants *in capite* and might have justified them in claiming the status of a parliamentary *commune*. In the Edwardian parliaments they represented nothing, the commonalty became the one community of the English parliament, and it was only when the stability and continuity of the magnate element was being established in the patented peerage of the fifteenth and subsequent centuries that they were able to assume a fixed legislative status by the vaguer title of "estate". Even so, community plays a great, perhaps a decisive part, in the first vital century of parliamentary history. The view of the counties and boroughs as *communes*, achieved so laboriously in the face of feudal privilege, and held firmly by the year 1300, not only made it possible for the crown to handle them as units and deal with them through their representatives, but it also blocked the way to direct negotiation with individuals and groups. By the ninth year of Edward II the crown had ceased to approach the royal demesnes directly for the aid on moveables, and the shire faced it as an indivisible whole. Edward I and Edward III were disinclined to complicate their task of ruling and fighting by debating political abstractions, and accepted the community notions which were making headway in provincial organization and used them without question as material for their

---

[1] So of the "Bill" of the prelates and *proceres* in the Lincoln parliament of 1301, *non placuit Regi set communitas procerum approbavit.* Parliamentary Writs, i. 105.

[2] *Ibid.* ii. 157. The grant of service for the Scotch war in 9 Edw. II was made by the *magnates et communitas regni.* This is explained in the writs as referring to the earls, barons, *liberi homines et communitates.* It is probable from the phrase *les Contes, Barons, et la communante de la tere* in the First Statute of Westminster that the transference had taken place by the beginning of the reign of Edward I. An assertion of the community of the barons is made in 1272, when certain magnates wrote in the name of the *communitas procerum* to announce the accession of Edward I. Rymer, *Foedera,* i. 888.

machine of parliament. The *communitas*—in the French vernacular, *commune*—became, indeed, the most versatile political concept of the day, and, with all the exceptions which are to be found in the practice of any inchoate theory, it played something of that directive part in the growth of public institutions that was played by notions of tenure in the preceding age. Indeed, it is mainly because of this change in terms and in the beliefs they stood for that with the accession of Edward I, most of all in his dealings with parliament, we are conscious that a new age is in being. Feudalism, if the episode of the Ordinances be excepted, has ceased to be a general standard to which the validity of institutions and acts of government is automatically referred. It is yielding to monarchical empiricism, community, and economic realism. A parliament embodying the elected representation of shires and boroughs in a Communes'—Commons'—House is as natural an outcome of the age in which community is the basis of political thought as is the witenagemot of that of the law-worthy folk, or the *commune concilium* of tenants-in-chief of that of the feudal honour.

ii

PARLIAMENTARY MONARCHY

The progress of our constitution is so slow, proceeds by such slight advances, and is subject to so many reversals, that it is impossible to divide its history into compact periods. Nevertheless, there is something to be gained by surveying that progress at long range and watching the emergence of new principles of the most general kind. Political history imposes the accession of Edward I as the beginning of an age, and it is possible to see in the reign of the three Edwards the consolidation and completion of a new phase of the constitution. Speaking with the widest latitude, the reign of Henry III had seen a weakening of feudalism as the idiom of practice and theory in political life. It was no longer so easy to believe that the *regnum* was no more than a supreme and intricately ordered example of honorial government, and one merit of the reign of Edward I is that he had the courage or the insensitiveness to break with the feudal past, and to found what, at least as a system, was a new régime, upon the basis of prerogative

Summary of the period

exercised in parliament. But Edward did no more than increase the force of the king's will as prerogative and give the future estates their earliest essays in politics. In prerogative a source of authority was put forward for legislation now that new law was coming to be made, but the state still waited for a reconciliation of its uncoördinated parts. The principle of government was still discord rather than harmony; Chamber and Wardrobe were rivals of Chancery and Treasury, the Great conflicted with the Privy Seal; the king taxed on the right hand by a consent imposed by the ancient rules of tenure, and on the left with the rising strength of prerogative; parliament, as yet no more than the servant of the king, was hardly an effective critic, still less the master of this complexity and disunity. In the reign of Edward II there opens the struggle to impose interdependence and common subordination upon the ministries, to consolidate taxation upon a single authority, and to bring the whole under the survey of the magnates in parliament; but throughout the reign the objects aimed at are never clearly seen. The problem is clarified by victories won in turn by the dying feudal cause, by parliament, and by the domestic officers of the crown, each crisis adding its legacy of experience. Some order is gained after the victory of the middle party and the Despensers, but it is precarious. At any time the king might have defeated opposition politics and established government upon the Chamber, the Wardrobe, and the Privy Seal. The striking of the final balance is, therefore, the work of the long reign of Edward III. Naturally opportunist, ready to be compliant at home in return for the nation's generosity in paying for his crown of France, he came to see that the household offices should be used, not as Henry III had used them, however feebly, as a personal administration threatening at any moment to take power openly, but either as working offices with little influence, or as responsible ministries embodying the will of the king, but of the king as head of the state, leaving the main work of administration to Chancery and Treasury, and coördinating them with each other and both with the crown. When this reconciliation between the offices of the household and the offices of the state had been accomplished, and when parliament had come to be accepted as the controlling influence within which the various powers of the executive performed their functions, the parliamentary monarchy may be said to have been firmly established. It was a new political form, replacing the régime of feudalism, though embodying much that survived from feudal theory.

In spite of Henry's six final years of uncontrolled rule, the *Position at Edward I's accession* of Edward I had something of the character of a restoration. For the first time since 1258 a clear personal will coördinated and directed the state. In Edward the country found a leader more single-minded than de Montfort, and one whose instinct in what he felt to be essential for the good of the country chimed more exactly with its own than that of any king since the Conquest. War for the king's right in Poitou, wherein Henry had vainly tried to convince the barons that "his honour was their own", gave way to the more real menace of the Welsh and Scotch borders, "to which, God willing, we mean to put an end, thinking it best and most seemly that we and our people should labour and spend for the common weal at this one time for the utter extirpation of the evil".[1] It is a change of aim which justifies a new language from the king to his people, confidence and leadership, the capacity to accept and use the real distribution of forces within the nation; only when the threat is to Gascony has Edward to descend to persuading. The conjuncture was one where a generation had reached the end of its capacity for effort and events waited for a fresh impulse. Edward was no doctrinaire, certainly no democrat; there was little that was entirely new in his scheme of government, or, if there was, it was in the clearer assertion of prerogative. He ignored theory and made his way straight to action, and his reign carried the country no further than the phase of experiment in what we call parliamentary government; what he did was not final in form and might have been undone by a strong king following him. Nevertheless, much that was settled neither by the baronial rebellion nor by the return of Henry III to power had found by the end of his reign at least a provisional answer, or, more strictly, a choice of answers. The ministries of state, the county and borough communities, the king's council and the *colloquium* of the magnates had come far since the death of John, changing their functions and shedding many of the

[1] Parliamentary Writs, i. 10.

prejudices and pretensions of feudalism. Under the feeble and de-
bilitating rule of Henry III the feudal control of the state had lost
its vigour, the experiment of replacing it by a nominated council
of magnates had failed in 1261, and the field was open to a king
who could make the crown the centre of unity. It was, in fact,
a point of history when everything turned upon the accession of
a king who could ignore the jealousies and prejudices of the last
reign and was prepared to take parties and institutions as they
stood and to reconcile them in a practical order of government.

Change in   The liberal historians of the nineteenth century accepted the
the theory entry of the commons into parliament as the outstanding con-
of law   stitutional event of this period, and saw in Edward I the creator
of English constitutionalism. The growth of representative institutions at this time and during the preceding half-century is, indeed,
one of the outstanding facts of English history. We shall, however,
miss its true significance if we forget that it was accompanied and
made possible by a change in public life which determined not
who should participate in politics but the very basis of taxation
and law-making. Until well into the thirteenth century the primitive conception of a society living within the frame of an inherited
law had deprived the king of the quality of legislator and
restricted the *commune concilium* to recognition of custom and
participation in adjustments of right and procedure by way of
assize. Vital changes were, no doubt, made, but they were made
in such a way as to obscure their real nature as legislative change.[1]
The right to legislate, therefore, never came into dispute. If a
choice of the crown, or of the *commune concilium*, or of both conjoined, as legislator had been faced, the last would have been chosen
without question, but the issue was, in fact, scarcely realized.
Thus it was that the country approached a second great period of
legislative activity, comparable to that which Henry II had carried
through under the colour of assize, unprepared with any clear
opinion as to where lay the right to make new law. With the
accession of Edward the community was upon the edge of a new
phase of making law by statute,[2] that is by enactment consciously

---

[1] Bracton considered it right *legem in melius converti* but not *legem mutari*.
F. Pollock and F. W. Maitland, *History of English Law*, i. 176 n. So the barons at
Merton in 1236, *nolumus leges Angliae mutari*.

[2] *Ibid*. i. 178 *et seq*.

changing or adding to the body of unwritten custom and done by a mere act of authority. What this meant is only in process of realization under Edward. The recording of enacted statutes, the corpus of written law as opposed to custom, later to be gathered into the Statute Roll, is an innovation of his reign, and its first-fruits is the Statute of Gloucester. The very force and nature of statute is still doubtful, and will remain so for a generation, and, since the basic conception of law as custom is shaken, it is a time of confusion as to the ultimate authority from which the new law which is not custom comes. Extreme and contradictory views are possible among men who are almost contemporaries, but the drift is towards prerogative. For Bracton and Grosseteste, enacted law is the exception, and is the province of the king in the council of his barons. For the Edwardian Britton, all law is statutory and its initiation lies with the king. Britton would find many to contest his view, but the doubt is there, and, beneath the play of political events, the age is committed to a search for something radically new in its polity, a legislator—the king if the demand at once for change and stability is to bear down the feudal right of the past and the rising activity of the *communes*; some revival of feudal councils, or some new council or councils of the nation, if the older view of the popularism of law is to prevail.

In so far as it is possible to generalize about a problem upon *The* which the Edwardian lawyers and statesmen had themselves no *magnates* steady mind, doctrines and practices drawn from two separate *and* *legislation* phases of history contributed to the theory of legislation during the fourteenth century. The older strand of thought, arising out of the feudal past, endowed any assembly of magnates summoned by the king with some of that power to declare custom and to innovate by assize which inhered in the character of the tenants-in-chief and especially in *commune consilium*. This power had been effective only rarely during the reign of Henry III—the Statute of Merton was perhaps the last occasion on which it was unequivocally admitted by the crown[1]—and the failure of the baronial reformers had gone far to discredit it. This full power to provide, to make law, is replaced, and that only intermittently, by that *assensus* of the clergy, magnates, and *communitas* by which the first

[1] The Provisions of Westminster, claiming much the same authority as those of Merton, are a document of the opposition.

Statute of Westminster and Edward's last Statute of Carlisle were issued. Theoretically, it remained as a possible ingredient of any share the barons might be asked to take in a future parliamentary model, and in successful opposition they tended to revert to it. It was recognized at Lincoln in 1301, when that strand of political theory which rested the stability of law upon the Great Charter with the *consilium regni* as its guardian experienced a revival, but taking the general trend of theory rather than any specific enunciation, it would seem that such legislative function as the barons derived from their curial past, at best never clearly defined, was losing in efficacy by the reign of Edward, and that the idea of claiming a similar function for the commons was still not yet entertained.

The reign of Edward was thus a time of slack water between the dying impulse of feudalism and that political life of parliament which was in the future; momentarily it was possible for the crown to emerge in the decline or absence of rivals as legislator
Preroga-
tive and
legislation
by prerogative. Such prerogative was a newly emergent power, but it was held firmly and just so long as to determine the form of legislation when parliament came to maturity. The king as legislator was a new factor in the thirteenth century. His was, indeed, a power arising imperceptibly, evading criticism by its intangibility, a principle built up from the gradual transformation throughout a century of the king's relation to privilege, and therefore to law. Franchise, once it was subject to inquest, had come to be no longer regarded as inherent in landright or indefeasible. Even the verdict of the countrysides was not now accepted as final as to its validity. Edward, on the contrary, claimed that custom itself was at the mercy of prerogative when
Preroga-
tive and
petition
it conflicted with the public interest,[1] and, though this might be an extreme view, as a matter of practice under Henry III, in the theory of Bracton, and by express order in council under Edward, all franchise had come to be subject to justification by the express words of royal charters. Every liberty not warranted by charter must be sued for to the king, and, in addition, all redress

---

[1] *Rotuli Parliamentorum*, i. 71: *Dominus Rex pro communi utilitate, per prerogativam suam in multis casibus est supra leges et consuetudines in regno suo usitatas.*

not obtainable in the common course of law[1] could be obtained only by his grace and favour. The result was to inject a new virtue into the crown. It became the target for innumerable petitions from individuals for warrant of privilege,[2] which it withheld or conceded at its will. Petition and grant in the king's Council became one of the busiest functions of the crown. This was in itself a making of law, albeit of private law, privilege, and the more numerous the petitioners, the greater the group of the beneficiaries, the nearer shall we be to calling it legislation. Grant of liberties to the *commune* of one county[3] in answer to the petition of that county may leave us doubtful—is it privilege-making or law-making? If the *communes* of all the counties unite to petition, the king's grant of what they ask will make law of general application, will be a change of national custom—legislation—and legislation by the king's sole prerogative moved by the petition of his subjects: *Dominus Rex ad Parliamentum suum . . . de gratia sua speciali et etiam propter affectionem quam habet erga Prelatos, Comites, Barones, et ceteros de regno suo concessit*[4]: "the Lord King at his Parliament has granted". It is not, moreover, the commonalty alone that petitions. The magnates, both prelates and others, make petition at the king's parliament,[5] and, in the guise of petitioners to the king to confirm old law or concede new, seem to occupy the common ground of subjects rather than that from which the barons of Merton declared *nolumus leges Angliae mutari*. Much will depend upon whether they are to take the first or the second, the higher or the lower status in parliament. If they assume at once the rank of a feudal *curia*, they will in some measure inherit its function and control the legislation from the beginning. If they appear as petitioners, there must be a long struggle before their petitions can acquire a coercive power over the initiative of the crown.

By the accession of Edward, however, the possible claimants to

---

[1] *Tortz et grevances faites a eux, qe ne poent estre redrescees par la commune Ley ne en autre manere santz especial garant. Rotuli Parliamentorum.* i. App. 444.

[2] *Ibid.* i. 50: *Priorissa de Amesbir' . . . petit quod Rex ei concedat fines et redemptiones hominum et tenentium.*

[3] *La commune de Cestresire prient a lour Seigneur le Roy. Ibid.* i. 6. *Communitas ville de Gloucestre conqueritur . . . et supplicat Domino Regi. Ibid.* p. 47.

[4] *Ibid.* i. 36.

[5] *Ibid.* i. 35. So also the Statute Quia Emptores: *Dominus Rex in Parliamento suo . . . ad instantiam Magnatum Regni sui, concessit, providit, et statuit. Ibid.* i. 41.

Council and legislation act as legislator were no longer two but three. Between the king and the feudal Council, and widening the gap between them, there had arisen the permanent sworn council of state, and, since it contained the principal ministers and the king's intimates, and had the almost decisive advantage of knowledge of administration, constant session, and continuity of policy, it was likely to be the strongest claimant of the three. Its claim was especially valid because the developments of the last fifty years or so had placed the council athwart the line of that main stream of future legislation, the subject's right of petition and the king's power to redress grievance. After the courts of King's Bench and Common Pleas and the court of the Exchequer established their several spheres of jurisdiction, the Council retained a function which was more restricted but no less preëminent than that of the undivided *curia*. It remained a court of reference for all causes which came before the Benches, the Exchequer, the eyre, and the courts of justices assigned, and which yet in any way exceeded their competence. It often instructed the justices to transfer cases involving important interests to its own consideration, and it admitted of direct petition from individuals or communities, which might be referred to the appropriate court or answered directly by the king in Council. It was the supreme court for the consideration of franchise. The amount of justice dispatched *coram ipso rege* diminished after the reign of Henry II, but the number of petitions for extra-legal redress and relief from the undue harshness of the law or for new privilege, the germ of prerogative law-making, increased—the emergence of a special jurisdiction of Chancery under the Edwards is proof that this was so—and the permanent Council became more and more a body for the hearing of

The Council as the germ of parliament petitions. By the middle of Henry III's reign[1] it had already adjusted itself to this influx of legal and extra-legal business by concentrating it upon certain seasons of the year, when it sat at

---

[1] Letters Close, 3 Hen. III, pp. 383, 409, 410. The Michaelmas session of the Exchequer early came to be used for this purpose, the Council conferring with the barons of the Exchequer and sitting in the Exchequer to receive reports of inquests and to hear pleas of right. *Ibid.* 4 Hen. III, p. 437. Sheriffs enquire into the present tenure of King John's lands, especially of the *terrae Normannorum—et inquisicionem illam . . . facias scire nobis et consilio nostro . . . apud Westmonasterium in Crastino Sti. Michaeli*—all those who hold such lands attending with the sheriffs to show cause.

Westminster for readiness of reference to charters and to the rolls of the Treasury, and ordered the attendance of any justices who might have been upon eyre or commission, of the barons of the Exchequer and the justices of the Jews, and also of the benches—a full quorum of legal and conciliar lore.[1] These special sessions of council became stereotyped before the end of Henry's reign, and early in that of Edward they appear as a sharply distinguished organ of the state of extreme importance under a name which they share with the *colloquia* of the magnates—Parliament, *concilium regis ad parliamenta sua* or *in parliamento*.[2] This parliament of law and council of Edward was a large body.[3] It consisted of the sworn counsellors of state, afforced, since the matter before them was principally legal, by the justices of both benches, and the barons of the Exchequer.[4] It contained, of course, the great officers of state, notably the chancellor, and, since it entertained petitions not only from individuals but from communities, and since the power of the king to create new privilege, to which it was hard to set a limit, was habitually exercised with the advice of his parliaments of council, the latter's jurisdiction constantly verged upon legislation. Edward, accordingly, associated the council with himself as the authority of statute.[5] Any lapse of the impulse of the magnates to act as mouthpiece of the *universitas regni*, and any failure of the communes to establish regular constitutional access to the crown by representatives—both possible eventualities in the generation that followed the battle of Evesham—might at any time have left the council *ad parliamenta*, since it embodied the king's prerogative,[6] not only the highest jurisdiction but the

The Parliament of Council or Council in Parliament

---

[1] These sessions, sitting most commonly a fortnight after Easter and Michaelmas, were clearing-houses for petitions for favour and examination into franchise. In the 'fifties meetings of the *colloquium* of the barons were often summoned to coincide with them, and rolls and chronicles sometimes accorded the title of *parliamentum* to the occasions of which they formed part. The material and some of the function of parliament existed in them. Cf. J. E. A. Jolliffe, *Some Factors in the Beginnings of Parliament*. Transactions of the Royal Historical Society, vol. xxii.   [2] *Rotuli Parliamentorum*, i. 15.

[3] 70 in 1305. F. W. Maitland, *Memoranda de Parliamento*, p. cvi.

[4] For the composition of the Council in Parliament in 1305 cf. *Ibid.* p. xliii.

[5] *Rotuli Parliamentorum*, i. 78: *per ipsum Dominum Regem et consilium suum provisum est. De commune consilio statuit* (*Rex*).

[6] It is curious to notice how closely king and Council are identified in their official acts. Even the routine questions to petitioners take form of a joint address from king and Council: *et super hoc, per ipsum Dominum Regem Anglie et consilium suum quesitum est. Ibid.* i. App. 226.

sole legislative authority of the realm. In this phase of its history, the embryo legislative function of the Council was indeed already detaching itself from the mass of legal business; by 1280 petitions triable by the benches, the Exchequer, or the chancellor were given only a first hearing by Council, and found a *complementum justitiae*, as it was called,[1] in the old-established courts. Reserving its full judgment for a residuum of doubtful causes, such as oftenest called for legislation, the Council might have come eventually to recognize its function as essentially that of a legislature, and the very terms of the Council's resolution of 1280 show that upon this matter it was very near to realizing its new function; "in this manner the king and his Council may be able to attend to the great affairs of his realm (the *magna negotia regni* that had been laid before the barons under Henry), and of his foreign lands without charge of other affairs".[2]

Definition of parliament   It may need an effort of imagination to detach our minds from the subsequent meaning of "parliament" as an assembly of the peerage and the representatives of the people, but the rolls of the early Parliaments leave no doubt that in this phase of their beginning their only essential elements were the king, the sworn Council, and the various justices, and that the "parleying" from which they took their name was primarily legal. *Placita et petitiones*, trial of causes and petitions for legal redress, are the only business upon some of these rolls. The hearing of such *placita* and petitions seems to be the fact which distinguishes a parliament from the various *colloquia*, *tractatus*, and so on, which the king held from time to time with his magnates, with representatives of shires and boroughs, with the clergy, with merchants; the presence of the king, the Council, and the judges, seems to be the fact which distinguishes a parliament in composition from such other assemblies. Chancery marked parliaments proper by issuing writs of summons *de veniendo ad Parliamentum*, *de Parliamento tenendo*; writs for other assemblies it endorsed *de veniendo ad tractandum*, *de subsidio petendo*, *de tractatu habendo*, and the like. An assembly embodying prelates, magnates, knights, and burgesses, without the Council, and summoned *ad colloquium habendum*, would be no parliament—in the reign of Edward III it would be called a *Magnum Concilium*. A

---

1 *Memoranda de Parliamento*, ed. F. W. Maitland, p. 131.
2 Letters Close, 8 Edw. I, p. 56.

meeting only of the king, the Council, and the justices to try *placita* and hear petitions might, on the other hand, be perfectly a parliament.

The future of legislation would turn chiefly upon how far the *Possible* Council in Parliament was left to realize its potentialities without *alternatives in* rivals. A consistent lead by Edward during his thirty-five years *develop-* reign might have encouraged it to do so. The *colloquium* of the *ment* magnates might have been summoned only to grant aid, the shires and boroughs, assize being near to assent, might have been approached through justices *ad auxilium assidendum*, or formal assent to aid might have been got in the courts of the shires,[1] and the cities and towns tallaged as ancient demesne. Alternatively, an estates system, either of the old *universitas* or with deputies of all orders, might have been created, and allowed, like the *états* of France, to vote subsidies and present grievances at a safe distance from contact with the real centre of government in the conciliar *Parlement*. As in France, this would have answered the political ambitions of the nation till the monarchy had reached its full growth, and the end would have been that of the French *états généraux*, a prerogative taxation by tallage and estates convinced of uselessness and falling into desuetude. Thus, the death of Henry left the field open to experiment. The constitutional force of feudalism was partly spent, and the king's prerogative was rising towards the ascendant, and it might be necessary to reconstitute the *commune concilium* about this centre and upon a new system. Given a king of Edward's qualities, one thing alone was certain, that the Council, especially the Council in the Parliament, would be increasingly the motive force of government. The composition of his father's councils was, indeed, retained and accentuated. Knights, justices, clerks, and officials of the household were the mainstay of Edward's Council and filled the great offices. No

---

1 As was done in 1282 when John de Kirkby went the round of the country negotiating supply—*curiale subsidium*—in the shire courts (Stubbs, *Select Charters*, p. 457), and, on a smaller scale, in 1292, when the barons owning land in Wales and the *communitas* of Chester gave a Fifteenth. Stubbs, *Constitutional History*, ii. 129. The recurrent assemblies of merchants to grant exceptional customs are a device of the same kind. The towns granted a Sixth by separate negotiation in 1294.

great ministers of the baronial type served during his reign, but men like Burnell and Hamilton as chancellor, and Kirkby as treasurer. Against such men the cry for baronial ministers could not be raised, for Edward was strong enough to value able servants and ruthless in sacrificing them when it became necessary to save his credit.[1]

The "parliaments" of that collection of *placita* and *petitiones* which we know as the *Rotuli de Parliamento* are primarily such meetings of the Council *ad Parliamenta* as we have been describing.[2] But Edward, and probably in the last decade of his reign, Henry before him, had been in the habit of afforcing them by summoning a selection of the magnates, and even representatives of the communes by a writ *De Veniendo ad Parliamentum*. The *colloquium* or *parliamentum*[3] of Henry's barons was upon occasion conjoined with the Parliament of Council. The purpose of this addition of the magnates to parliament was the holding with them of *colloquium et tractatus* upon great affairs of the kingdom, which the king and Council did not care to dispatch alone, and the nature of which is generally stated in the summons. They are such matters as the affairs of Gascony or Scotland, the demands of the Pope, or the peace of the realm, and, taking the first place upon the agenda of the later parliaments of the estates, they came to be distinguished as "the king's business", "les busoignes le Roy", as opposed to the *placita* and *petitiones* of subjects. It has been held that "this amalgamation of 'estates' and 'parliament' constitutes Edward's claim to be the creator of a model English parliament".[4] Taken together, the evidence of the writs of summons, of the petitions in parliament, of the more representative memoranda of the parliament of 1305, of the preambles to statutes, and of the chroniclers is fatal to the view that Edward was the sole pioneer in this. From the beginning of Edward I's reign the magnates were summoned by writs which the Chancery advisedly classed as brevia *De Veniendo ad Parliamentum*. The

[1] As the treasurer William Marsh was sacrificed in face of the outcry against the taxation of 1295, and Hengham, Weyland, Bray, and Stratton after the king's absence from 1286 to 1289.

[2] *Report on the Dignity of a Peer*, iii. p. 170.

[3] Chroniclers, using the older and more general meaning of the term, sometimes gave the name *parliamenta* to what were only *colloquia* of the magnates.

[4] A. F. Pollard, *Evolution of Parliament*, pp. 47 *et seq.*

assembly of 1275 included prelates, earls, and barons *et la communaute de la tere*; in the words of its Statute of Westminster, it was *le primer parlement general apres le corounement*.[1] The phrase presupposes earlier "general parliaments"[2]—the Edwardian Close Roll[3] calls the assembly at Winchester after Evesham a parliament—and it might be inferred that the clerks who drafted it were of the opinion that some at least of those sessions of Henry's reign, to which not only the unofficial historians of his day but the king's secretaries gave the name of parliament, were essentially like that of 1275.[4]

1 Stubbs, *Select Charters*, p. 442.

2 It may, however, be suggested with some hesitation that *generale* or *plenum parliamentum* was used rather of the full session of the conciliar parliament, as opposed to the various committees of triers of petitions appointed during its term or to the chancellor's court, than of a full assembly of "estates".

3 Letters Close, 4 Edw. I, p. 274.

4 Letters Patent, 39 Hen. III, p. 399. A parliament three weeks after Easter, 1255. This was Matthew Paris' parliament of *omnes nobiles Angliae tam viri ecclesiastici quam saeculares, ita quod nunquam tam populosa multitudo ibi antea visa fuerat congregata*. It met *in quindena Paschae, quae vulgariter Hokeday appellatur*. There is no doubt that the magnate assembly of Oxford in 1258 was called a parliament in letters patent and the Provisions of Oxford gave the title to their triennial sessions of the Council with the representatives of the *universitas*. Knights were summoned *ad Parliamentum* in 1264, twenty-five earls and barons were called in 1261 *ad instans parliamentum* (*Report on the Dignity of a Peer*, iii. p. 23), and clergy, barons, knights, and citizens were similarly called *ad instans parliamentum quod erit Londoniis in octavis Sti. Hilarii* in 1265. The objection that "there are between 1275 and 1298 nine assemblies summoned by 'parliamentary' writs, and fifteen sessions whose business is recorded in the rolls, and . . . not one of the nine coincide with one of the fifteen" (A. F. Pollard, *Evolution of Parliament*, pp. 47 *et seq.*) is not quite conclusive. All the rolls of Parliament, *i.e.* the collected *placita* and *petitiones*, are wanting for the years 1-6 and 6-18. Chroniclers record "parliaments" attended by magnates and representatives at intervals throughout the reign, and the nature of our record is certainly insufficient as evidence to prove that these were not parliaments in the strict sense. There seems, therefore, no reason to regard parliaments in which the Council are joined by magnates and representatives as an innovation of the last years of Edward's reign, nor, necessarily, of Edward's reign at all. Henry III almost certainly had recourse to them, though Simon de Montfort, though he might summon knights to a *colloquium*, had not the royal power which alone could summon a parliament. During the last two decades of Henry III's reign the use of the term parliament was probably in process of becoming fixed. Many assemblies which seem to merit the description are not officially so called, or at least we have no record of their being so called, and it would not be surprising if further research revealed the fact that the principal difference between the later assemblies of Henry III's reign and the earlier assemblies of Edward I's were one of name. Certainly, the parliamentary business of *placita* and *petitiones* seems to have been carried on actively in Henry's parliaments.

Fluidity of Thus, although it is true that the parliament of the future was to
parlia- consist in the interlocking of the *colloquium* or *parliamentum* of the
mentary
institution magnates with the parliament of Council, and that some precedent
in 1272 for this was certainly set in Edward's third year, and probably
under his father, the whole constitution was still fluid at the
beginning of Edward's reign, and remained so in some measure
until its end. Among the dubitabilia, as to which the policy of the
king was likely to be decisive, we may place the choice of magnates to receive the direct writ—the basis of the future House of
Lords—the calling or not of representatives from the *communes*
of the counties and boroughs, and the degree to which assemblies
other than parliament were to be used to dispatch more or less of
the *ardua negotia regni*. As to the powers of parliament and its
several members when summoned, the situation, in the ambiguous
phase of law which then prevailed, was even more obscure. Were
the magnates to be legislators in their traditional feudal character,
or counsellors whose advice might be set aside, or assessors whose
assensus was valuable but not vital to statute, or simply petitioners
awaiting the result of the king's discussion with his Council? Was
statute to be by authority of the king in the inner parliament of
Council, or in the parliament with Council and magnates together? And were the representatives of the *communes* summoned
in any legislative capacity at all? Finally, were magnates, or magnates and *communes*, to be incapable of granting aid except in
parliament, or would local or general non-parliamentary assemblies suffice, and could the magnates act in their old capacity to
grant on behalf of the *communes* as well as for themselves, or must
the latter be consulted through their representatives? None of these
questions was settled when Edward came to the throne nor were
they finally answered during his lifetime, for they only arose in the
light of later experience of the working of parliamentary institutions; but his reign established certain precedents of value.
According to the answer that might be given to them, there was
material for perhaps a dozen constitutions other than that which
ultimately grew into being.

It may be said at once that no statute ever issued except from parliament, that is from an assembly of which the parliament of Council

at least formed a part. The *colloquium* of magnates alone—the *Magnum Concilium* as it came to be called under Edward III—never legislated. In that sense the king in his Council in his parliament was the centre of the state. It is nevertheless true that other forms of assembly, without parliament, were summoned late in Edward I's reign, and long after it, and that they were concerned with deliberative business which we should call parliamentary—but which contemporaries would not [1]—though none of them was summoned by the writ *De Veniendo ad Parliamentum*.[2] Throughout his reign Edward continued indifferent to the exact composition of these occasional assemblies. At his convenience he summoned them in any part of the kingdom, from all classes that he wished to use, and laid upon them any fiscal or executive burden they could be induced to bear. If there is any principle it is that a proportion of magnates should be present in any council that is required to grant a general aid. Such assemblies were more variously constituted than was parliament, were often summoned to deal with some immediate crisis, and had at times so strong a military quality that they are hard to distinguish from simple summons to service in the host. Such is the summons to some two hundred barons and knights to come to Ross on the Nativity of the Virgin in the 25th year *de quibusdam negotiis nos et regnum nostrum specialiter tangenciis . . . locuturi et tractaturi*.[3] It was in an assembly of the host summoned by writ of bodily service for Gascony [4] that the most dangerous crisis of the reign was fought out in July 1297, the confirmation of the Charters being granted, and reconciliation

Non-parliamentary assemblies

---

[1] Professor Tout's comment upon one of these assemblies summoned to *magnum consilium* in 1338, that it "can fairly be reckoned a parliament" (*Chapters in Administrative History*, iii. 80 n.), ignores the radical character of parliament as containing the Council *ad parliamenta* and entertaining *placita* and petitions.

[2] The distinction between parliament and other assemblies is very clearly marked in the writs of 17 Edw. II, (a) for a *tractatus* at Hilarytide to which lay magnates, knights, and burgesses were summoned by writs *De tractatu habendo*, and (b) the parliament summoned for the Purification by writs *De veniendo ad Parliamentum*. The difference was, no doubt, that parliament sat to hear all petitions, while the *tractatus* was summoned to discuss some certain matters of general import. *Report on the Dignity of a Peer*, iii. p. 344.

[3] *Ibid.* iii. p. 83.

[4] It is noteworthy that the form of the writ for this meeting was actually challenged by the malcontent nobles, but on the ground that it did not specify the place to which the host was to go and gave insufficient time for preparation. That it was insufficient as a summons upon which aid was granted and great affairs discussed seems to have occurred to no one.

made between archbishop and king. Others are called with the
express intention of massing the feeling of the nation behind the
king in some dangerous or invidious business, as when the laity,
magnates, and representatives of shires and boroughs, are called
to Shrewsbury to advise on the fate of David in 1283.[1] They are
used as a means of securing sectional aid or administrative coöperation[2] from those who have not been called to parliament, as in
1283 when two provincial assemblies are called *de subsidio petendo* to
Northampton and York. Here the magnates were not summoned
—being then in personal service with the king in the field—the
king himself proposed not to be present, but the clergy and
representatives of the *communes*—who did attend—were induced
to render some personal contribution to the war of which we do
not know the nature. Wykes records assemblies of magnates in
1286 and 1288 which were not parliaments, but in one of which
aid was granted, and in the other deferred, for the whole kingdom.
In these non-parliamentary assemblies there was far more elasticity
than in parliament; Edward maintained Henry's practice of going
beyond the circle of the baronage on such occasions, and in those
which were summoned to grant an aid there seems to have been
no reason to secure a large assembly. Half the full parliamentary
list of magnates, acting if they so wished through attorneys, was
considered sufficient to commit their order to the aid of 34 Edw. I
for knighting the prince of Wales.

The
magnates
in
parliament
    Routine business of state Edward did in his Council, since this
was the highest court of justice, and because, even more than his
father, he treated every administrative order and every change in
custom as matter of prerogative, the king in Council in parliament
was the essential authority of statute. It was, perhaps, with very
little desire of giving greater validity to acts which needed no
confirmation that Edward summoned other elements to parliament, but rather to keep himself in touch with national feeling,
to maintain that sense of national leadership with which he had
begun his reign, and to get independent advice as to the effect in
practical working of statutes and judgments. Since, therefore, the

[1] *Parliamentary Writs*, i. 16.
[2] As with the knights called to York in 1300 *ad faciendum et exequendum pro
observacione cartarum. Ibid.* i. 87.

utmost variety prevailed in the composition of assemblies other than parliament, it is not surprising that the structure of the afforced parliaments also reflects the free choice of the king and his needs, rather than feudal right. Baronial franchise had, indeed, become almost useless as a qualification for political power. Tradition and existing realities both demanded some recognition of the community of the tenants-in-chief, and at least the greater of them were accustomed to individual summons. But the application of this principle was vague enough to give scope for almost any plan which might commend itself to the king. During the baronial wars there had been much talk of the *universitas regni*, and again under Edward II a distinctive political right was claimed for the *baronagium*. Under Henry III, at least when the crown was weak, it is probable that this baronage assembled much as it liked, and often in great numbers.[1] But those who put themselves forward upon such vague qualifications in time of unrest were in no position to establish a legal claim to summons to any formally constituted parliament.[2] The same forces that had been favouring the drawing together of the shire community into a suitable constituency for parliament had been working for the disintegration of the baronies: baronage had almost ceased to denote a political order and was now little more than a variant of free tenure, and tenure *per baroniam* had itself developed intricate degrees. Tenants of a whole barony were few, tenants *per baroniam*, holding a fraction in right of partition of coheiresses,[3] were very numerous, and often of little standing. Barony was coming to be blended with the unprivileged tenure of the counties, and was ceasing to be a valid determinant of parliamentary or any other public status. Apart from the decline of the tenure, the right to summons had never received more certain definition than the vague rule of Magna Carta, and recent usage had set no clear precedent.

[1] Matthew Paris, *Chronica Majora*, anno 1255: *Omnes nobiles Angliae . . . ita quod nunquam tam populosa multitudo ibi antea visa fuerat congregata*, attended the Hokeday Parliament.

[2] At an earlier period the lords of Yorkshire denied the validity of an aid because they had not been summoned to the *commune concilium* which granted it. *Royal Letters of Henry III* (ed. Shirley), i. 151.

[3] The distinction between those who held a whole barony—*integra baronia*—and those who held only a fraction of one *per baroniam* had certain legal and constitutional consequences in the reign of Edward III. It is doubtful whether they were recognized under Edward I.

Edward's
roll of
parlia-
mentary
magnates

It would have been uncharacteristic of Edward I to prejudice the immediate usefulness of his parliaments by leaving the right of attendance to be asserted as a franchise. In so far as the magnates were not indifferent,[1] the result would have been litigation for which even the principle was lacking, and an indefinite period of debate. The author of the *Modus Tenendi Parliamentum* despaired of using tenure as a qualification, and, with a kind of premature Whiggery, asserted it upon the ground of landed wealth, and claimed the direct writ for all those who held thirteen-and-a-third knight's fees or more,[2] whether by barony or not.[3] Edward, less trustful of wealth as a guarantee of loyalty and wisdom, took an even cruder test. The list from which the chancellor's clerks dispatched the writs *De Veniendo ad Parliamentum* to the secular magnates in his last eight years was the list of summons to the host to Carlisle at Pentecost 1299.[4] From this roll of eleven earls and a hundred and four other magnates—not all of them were barons[5] and some not even tenants *per baroniam*—with frequent omissions, and more rarely with the addition of a name or so, parliaments continued to be summoned until the end of the reign.[6] The heads of many baronies and honours were omitted from it, and were thus disfranchised; some who had regular summons can have been no more than knights; but it had the advantage of settling outright

[1] Cf. F. W. Maitland, *Memoranda de Parliamento*, lxxxvii.

[2] Some baronies were mere fractions of such an estate. Cf. that of William Martin, who sat in Edward I's parliaments. It was *integra baronia*, but consisted of the manor of Blagdon (Somerset), of one knight's fee. Public Record Office, *Calendar of Inquisition Post Mortem*, vi. 707.

[3] Stubbs, *Select Charters*, p. 501.

[4] Parliamentary Writs, i. 321. There is no consistent evidence as to practice earlier in the reign, but the roll for the Salisbury parliament of 25 Edw. I is identical with that for the host of Newcastle of the same year, the same order of names being followed throughout, though thirteen magnates who were called to parliament were not called to the host (*ibid*. i. 51, 302). As a result of the change from this list to the one adopted finally in 1299, some thirty magnates were cut out and others substituted. Such men as Ralf Nevill of Raby, Ingelram de Gynes, and Gilbert de Gaunt were not summoned for the rest of the reign.   [5] In the sense of not holding *baroniam integram*.

[6] The summonses for Edward's last large parliament, that for Carlisle, at Hilary 1306, are identical with the military summonses seven years earlier in the order of the names and the men summoned, with the exception that, out of the hundred and four magnates, other than earls, who were called to the host in 1299, thirteen are omitted in the parliament of 1306, and five names are added, Edmond Deyncurt, John de St. John of Lagenham, Geoffrey de Geynville, Amalric de St. Amand, and Henry Tregoz. *Ibid*. i. 181.

a problem which was insoluble by any rule then existing, and it provided Edward with magnate counsel of proved fidelity and wisdom, since it was that of men whom he had chosen to lead the Scotch war. Had Edward I lived longer or had Edward II retained his list of council unchanged, peerage of parliament might have been established in the descendants not of those called to the "model" parliament of 1295, but of those summoned to the first, abortive war of Caerlaverock. As it was, the principle of treating the prelates, the earls, and a minority of the baronage, arbitrarily chosen from time to time, as a parliamentary peerage, dates in fact from Edward I, though it was not admitted as a principle, nor stereotyped as the basis of an hereditary right, until after a long period of maturing prescription which was perhaps hardly completed in the fifteenth century.

With this extremely artificial treatment of the future second *Commons* estate in mind, we shall not look for Edward to be very strictly *in* bound by precedent in his treatment of the other parts of *parliament* his parliament, nor to be governed by popular principle for its own sake. The famous dictum *quod omnes tangit ab omnibus approbetur* seems to have been nothing more than an effort to convince the archbishop and his suffragans that further aid for the relief of Gascony, which Edward suspected would be refused on the ground that the clergy were not concerned, was really in their own interest.[1] Nevertheless, the tide already ran in that direction. Omitting royal and seigneurial demesne, the shires had long been taxable unities,[2] sometimes assessed and levied upon by resident knights. Upon these developing constituencies Edward fastened, his originality lying mainly in the fact that, with a few exceptions in the earlier part of his reign and after a certain amount of experiment, he established the practice of summoning the counties and boroughs to parliament, instead of staving them off into occasional *ad hoc* assemblies. The first step towards the association of the

[1] *Res vestra maxime sicut ceterorum regni ejusdem concivium agitur in hac parte*: your interests are equally involved with those of the rest of the realm in this affair. Stubbs, *Select Charters*, p. 480. Edward had tried to establish this sense of common interest in a writ to the archbishop of York of the previous year— *quos communiter negocium istud tangit*—but without as yet suggesting the propriety of all concerned lending their consent. Parliamentary Writs, i. 25.

[2] Cf. *ante,* pp. 310 *et seq.*

knights with the clergy and magnates in granting aid may, perhaps, be taken as that occasion in 1254 when the magnates would not pledge the counties for an aid for Gascony, and knights were summoned *vice omnium et singulorum* to make a grant.[1] The practice seems to have had many precedents by 1272. Knights were summoned in 1264 and 1265, and possibly later in Henry's reign, and with a hardening sense of their representative quality, of their speaking with the authority of the communities,[2] which were to hold *ratum et acceptum*—valid and agreed—whatever was done in their name.[3] Throughout the reign of Edward representatives were called at intervals to provide aid in special assemblies, and upon a number of occasions to parliament.

As has already been suggested, much would turn upon what the magnates and the representatives were required to do when present at parliament. Edward's parliament was not yet a body of fixed constitution. Rather, it was a *colloquium* between the Parliament of Council and certain magnates and representatives of communities, selected, and differently selected, from time to time according to the king's convenience and his judgment of what was convenient for the realm. Nevertheless, certain combinations of these elements were beginning to recur more frequently than others, and the "model" parliaments of 1295 and 1296, containing prelates and magnates, proctors of the clergy, knights and burgesses, were so nearly an epitome of the nation's life that this form came in the end, though hardly in Edward's reign, to be accepted as the proper constitution of a full parliament. Equally, certain broad principles as to the function of these various elements when attending parliament were beginning to emerge, though they were not those which were finally to prevail. Except in 1275,[4] the *communes* were never summoned to parliament with

Function of communes in parliament

[1] *Royal Letters of Henry III* (ed. Shirley), ii. 101.

[2] *Vice omnium et singulorum* (1254), *pro toto comitatu* (1264), *pro communitate comitatus* (1265).

[3] Cf. J. G. Edwards, in *Essays presented to Dr. Salter*, p. 149.

[4] An exception occurs in the October parliament of 1275, but the representatives summoned were not ordered to be elected, and were to be *de discrecioribus in lege*. Unlike the elected knights of later parliaments of the reign they were commissioned *ad tractandum cum magnatibus*, and shared in the enactment of a statute, that of Westminster I. C. H. Jenkinson, *English Historical Review*, vol. xxv. This plan was not repeated in any subsequent assembly summoned by writ *de veniendo ad Parliamentum*.

any fuller commission than to execute what others had decided.[1] The magnates came to discuss—*tractaturi vestrumque consilium impensuri*—and the representatives might be asked for advice on occasion,[2] but they were required to have full power from their shires and boroughs only to hear and do—*ad faciendum quod tunc de communi consilio ordinabitur;*[3] it was not until the Lent Parliament of 1313 that their parliamentary writs began to summon them *ad consentiendum*.[4] The commission *ad faciendum* is the same power that is required for them when they are called to non-parliamentary assemblies to hear and carry out some particular executive enactment, as at York at the Ascension of 1300, when knights attended *ad faciendum et exequendum pro observacione cartarum*, or in 1283, when called to York and Northampton to receive the king's precept, *ad audiendum et faciendum*, for some unspecified coöperation in the Welsh war, one outcome of which was the grant of the Thirtieth. Knights who were elected to the parliament of 1295 *ad audiendum et faciendum* were later nominated by the king to assess and collect the Eleventh and Seventh in nineteen out of the thirty counties[5]: and this, together with the convenience of receiving petitions during the time of parliament, and by the hands of accredited representatives, may be the king's principal motive in summoning the *communes* to parliament. For elected knights participating in counsel and sharing in decisions made, we must look for the most part outside parliament to special non-parliamentary gatherings, especially to such as are called to grant an aid. To the Shrewsbury meeting which considered David's fate, knights and burgesses were summoned because "the King wishes to speak with them upon that and other matters".[6] In 1290 they were called to Westminster after parliament had dispersed to consider certain requests for privilege put forward by the magnates, and again it was *ad consulendum et consenciendum*.[7] Four years later they were called at Martinmas, not to parliament but to

---

1 Cf. Parliamentary Writs, *passim*.

2 As for the Statute of Carlisle which drafted *post deliberationem plenariam et tractatum cum comitibus, baronibus, proceribus et aliis nobilibus ac communitatibus regni sui habitum*: after deliberation and consideration with the earls, barons, notables, other nobles, and communities of the realm. *Rotuli Parliamentorum*, i. 217.   3 Parliamentary Writs, i. 183.

4 *Report on the Dignity of a Peer*, iii. p. 223.

5 Parliamentary Writs, i. 34, 45.

6 *Ibid.* i. 16.   7 *Ibid.* i. 21.

colloquium—the object of which was, apparently, an aid for the Gascon war [1]—again to offer counsel, but also to consent to what the earls, barons, and *proceres* should have decided. In 1306 they were called *ad tractandum et ordinandum de auxilio . . . faciendo et ad consenciendum hiis que ordinabuntur in hac parte.* This last phrase defining their powers in 1306 was identical with that in the writ on the same occasion to the clergy and magnates,[2] and it is in such councils, and such only, and not in parliament, that the *communes* of the shires and boroughs are seen to share some measure of deciding power with the magnates.[3] There, as readily as they later will in parliament, they exercise the ancient right of all feudal lieges to determine the occasion and amount of aid.

Function of the magnates in parliament   The standing and function of the magnates in parliament was less clearly determined, but it was far short of that which they had occupied in former reigns. Their writs summoned them *ad colloquium et tractatum* and with the underlying assumption that their attendance was justified less by a routine membership of a supreme governing body of parliament than because some special circumstances moved the king in parliament to consult them. The summons, therefore, was to special business, and not to the whole session of parliament. At times the writ would say what that business was, as in 1299 about Gascon affairs—*super negociis nostris transmarinis* [4]—or in 1304 the better establishment of the realm of Scotland,[5] or in 1296 to fulfil the promise of an aid.[6] Or the magnates might be informed that the reason of their attendance would be told them when they reached parliament,[7] or be summoned simply to give their opinion about certain arduous matters unspecified, which the king did not wish to dispatch without their presence.[8] They were summoned, then, to consider what should be put before them by king and Council in parliament, not to the full range of the Council-in-parliament's business. Much of the work of the session might be dispatched before they came, much which was done while they were technically at parliament would never be brought to their notice, and they were

---

1 Parliamentary Writs, i. 26.   2 *Ibid.* i. 164.

3 The nearest they get to such power in Parliament is when they are admitted to "deliberate" in 1306. Cf. note 1, p. 351 *supra.*

4 *Ibid.* i. 78.   5 *Ibid.* i. 136.

6 *Ibid.* i. 47.   7 *Ibid.* i. 81.   8 *Ibid.* i. 28.

often dismissed while parliament had several weeks to run. Their attendance was to limited agenda predetermined by the king. It follows therefore that, though feudal tradition gave to every baron and indeed to every tenant-in-chief the right of counsel, the magnates in parliament did not constitute, nor were even added to, the king's sworn Council for the period of parliament.[1] Their summons invites them only to attend *cum ceteris magnatibus et proceribus regni*, while the councillors' writ summons them *cum ceteris de consilio nostro*.[2] They remain an external body called to intermittent *colloquium* and *tractatum* with the Council during the period of Council's session *ad Parliamenta*. Though it will come in Edward II's reign, there is as yet no merging of the magnates and Council into one body during the session of Parliament either for judgment or legislation.[3] Statute is, indeed, in strict form, not made by the magnates, though their assent may be recorded, and the distinction set up between magnates and councillors is maintained in the rolls of parliament. According to the letter of their preambles it is the king, *rex in consilio*, who makes statutes. Never after the First Statute of Westminster do the lords join in enacting it. They will not do so until the period of the Ordainers under Edward II.

Devised to make prerogative strong, and yet sensitive to the

[1] Cf. the proclamation during the parliament of 1305: "Archbishops, Bishops, and other Prelates, Earls, Barons . . . the King wishes to return for the time being to their countries . . . except for those Bishops, Earls, Barons, Justices, and others who are of the Council of our Lord King. Let them not go without special leave of the King". *Rotuli Parliamentorum*, i. 159.

[2] This form of writ was issued to a few magnates in the very small Parliaments of 1297 and 1305. But it is likely that they were magnates who were also members of the sworn Council.

[3] Mr. Baldwin's view that "the identity of the Council was immediately lost when any larger assembly was brought together", though true of the period of the Ordinances, does not seem to be borne out by the records of Edward I. J. F. Baldwin, *The King's Council*, p. 307. Thus in the Easter Parliament of 1285 *plures de regno tam Prelati . . . quam comites et Barones* petition the king as to the confirmation of charters and he answers them *habito super hoc cum suo consilio tractatu*. Letters Close, 13 Edw. I, p. 331. A clear sense of the distinction between provision and judgment, and of the more restricted function of assent to them or petition for them, is shown in an objection made in 1414 to the judgment upon the earl of Salisbury: *come les ditz declaration et juggement ne furent donez par le Roi, mais soulement par les Seignurs Temporels, et par assent du Roi; quelle juggement doit estre donez par notre Seignur le Roi qi est soverein Juge en toutz cas, et par les Seignurs Espirituels et Temporelx, ove le assent de les communes de la terre ou a lour petition. Rotuli Parliamentorum*, iv. 18.

needs of the nation, and set against a background of unstable and variable survival from past constitutionalism, the Edwardian parliament appears as a new institution, hardly as yet more than an experiment, but marking a radical break with that growth of the constitution which had hitherto proceeded smoothly from the root of the feudal *curia*. It contains elements which are old, but they have been so re-set that their practical effect is new, and they might well carry government away upon fresh lines at a tangent from the past. The magnates retain the function of *tractatus et colloquium* which the baronial *curia* had exercised, though decreasingly, under Henry; but it now takes the weaker form of petition and advice, and the baronage as a whole has lost its standing. The magnates of Edward's parliaments were a minority, arbitrarily chosen by the king, and given a parliamentary status artificially maintained. Much time would be needed to harden their status into parliamentary peerage, leaving many of their peers in tenure to lapse into the body of the unprivileged commons. Nor do those who were summoned seem to have been given the full standing of the Council in parliament. Their rudimentary legislative function, which had been growing in the past, was rarely appealed to by Edward after 1275, if at all.   The most they are called upon to do is to "assent to", to "approve" the action of parliament.[1] Edward's rule was to legislate by prerogative, sometimes upon petition, and though the assent of the magnates was recorded more often than that of the representatives it was clearly not essential to the validity of statute.

By the parliament of 1306 the future commons had come to the verge of securing for themselves an extension of the barons' much attenuated function of council and assent. They did, in fact, enjoy it from time to time in occasional non-parliamentary assemblies, for which their writs of summons were identical with those of the clergy and the secular magnates. They actually established their right to join the *universitas regni* upon questions of supply. But they carried no legislative right into parliament. To parliament they were summoned *ad faciendum*, and their

---

    1 This intermittently recorded *assensus* is to be contrasted with the power of the feudal *curia* to "provide", *i.e.* to decree enactments. Cf. the Statute of Merton: *ita provisum fuit et concessum, tam a predicto Archiepiscopo, Episcopis, Comitibus, Baronibus quam ab ipso Rege et aliis.*

function was that of an executive link with the counties and boroughs. Their share in future legislation will always be that of petitioners. Thus, though a planned constitution was probably no part of Edward's conscious policy, circumstances and his habitual decisiveness in dealing with involved issues conspired to make his reign a time of vital readjustment. The new parliament was not the old *curia*; rather, it was a servant and petitioner of the prerogative. In spite of the fact that he was not bound to work through them, the rapid succession of parliaments afforced by magnates, knights, and burgesses in his last decade sufficed to establish them as the norm of English government, and issues which might have been, and in the earlier years of his reign were, fought out in assemblies gathered *ad hoc negotium*,[1] were gradually drawn into the orbit of parliament, and in time, though not immediately, became matter for parliament alone. It is this, perhaps, as much as the new mechanics of parliament, which makes the reign of Edward crucial—that all the great business of state is coming to pass under prerogative, and prerogative chooses parliament as its vehicle.

The hesitation between feudalism and the political community, which distracted all forms of public life in this generation, is well shown in the confusion as to the basis of national finance, which, in spite of bold language in the *Confirmatio Cartarum*, lasted throughout the reign. There has, perhaps, never been a period of greater diversity of principle in taxation. The purely feudal taxes persisted. In 1279 the king took a scutage of forty shillings for Wales, in 1290 an *aide pur fille marier*, and in 1306 one for the knighting of Prince Edward. Only the aid of 1290 was made in parliament, and that in a parliament which seems to have been attended by a minority of magnates only, and those not summoned by parliamentary writ, and to have been vouched for only *quantum in ipsis est*.[2] The tax upon moveables was an established

Supply under Edward I

---

[1] E.g. in occasional *colloquia* with a handful of magnates, with clergy alone, and in 1303 even with an assembly of merchants *ad colloquium et tractatum*. Stubbs, *Select Charters*, p. 496. H. S. Deighton, "Clerical Taxation by Consent", *English Historical Review*, vol. lxviii.

[2] *Rotuli Parliamentorum*, i. 25.

principle, but, though he took a Fifteenth in 1275 and again in 1290, and a Thirtieth in 1283—of which only the first was strictly parliamentary[1]—it seemed for a time that Edward intended to evade the unequivocal necessity for consent which attached to the aids, and to find his revenue as far as he might by prerogative, or upon the ground of custom. The magnates of the parliament of Easter 1275 sanctioned the *magna et antiqua custuma* upon exports of wool and leather as permanent revenue, but in 1303 Edward added to it the *nova custuma* by a private bargain with the alien merchants. Between 1288 and 1294 perhaps the largest source of supply was the crusading Tenth imposed by papal authority for two successive periods of six years, and, in addition to such extraneous aids, years of crisis, such as 1294 and 1297, brought unconcealed prerogative taxation into action, in the former year in the seizure of the cathedral treasures and the wool and leather of the merchants and in the forcing of the clergy to yield a moiety of their revenues upon pain of outlawry, and in 1297 the maltolt upon wool, and what was again virtually a forced levy of a Third upon the clergy. Besides these taxes, which contemporaries contested as unconstitutional, the personal lordship of the king admitted as late as 1304 of a tallage of the royal demesne and of the boroughs, of a "gracious aid", *curiale subsidium*, from the towns in 1282, and in 1292 of a Fifteenth from the royal earldom of Chester, both of which, though aids in form, were probably polite substitutes for tallage.

Extra-parlia-mentary grants

Between 1279 and 1295, and 1297 and 1301, and again from 1301 to the end of the reign, all taxation was in the strict sense extra-parliamentary. That is to say it was either prerogative or derived from custom, or granted in special assemblies not summoned by writs *De Veniendo ad Parliamentum*. There was as yet no clear idea that aid was an inalienable function of the whole parliament; at times official language suggests that the magnates granted for their order, while each of the counties gave individual assent to its own grant;[2] but some kind of assembly of a more or

[1] The grant of 1283 was made by the provincial assemblies at York and Northampton.

[2] *Rotuli Parliamentorum*, i. App. p. 226: *Decima quam tota communitas Warr' Regi in subsidium guerre Regis concessit (ibid.* 22 Edw. I). *Ibid.* p. 242: *Quinta decima . . . Nobis nuper in Parliamento nostro Lincoln' a communitate comitatus predicti, sicut a ceteris communitatibus aliorum comitatuum (ibid.* 29 Edw. I).

less representative nature was usually called to accord it. The principle of consent was never seriously challenged, and even the *curiale subsidium* of Kirby's quest for aid in the counties must have been sued for in the county courts. The Thirtieth of 1283 was granted in provincial assemblies of knights and clergy. Knights granted a Tenth at Westminster in 1294, and knights and barons an Eighth in 1297, though the first was done in a *colloquium*, not a parliament, and the second in the host called by writ of military summons *De Veniendo cum Equis et Armis*, and without representation. The aid to knight the prince was made in an extra-parliamentary assembly of clergy, magnates, and knights at Pentecost 1306. Special meetings of the clergy out of parliament, as at Ely in 1290, were, perhaps, the commonest way of raising clerical subsidies. On the other hand, taxation could be and was made in parliament. The parliaments of Michaelmas 1275 and 1279, of November 1295, at Bury in 1296, and at Lincoln in 1301, all granted taxes on moveables, and in a Council *ad Parliamenta* in 1290 those magnates who were present granted the *aide pur fille marier quantum in ipsis est*. But it is clear that taxation in parliament was no more than the seizing of a convenient occasion. How indifferent the magnates were to the nature of the assemblies as long as they were substantially representative of the order taxed is shown by the protest against the taxation of 1297. An Eighth from barons and knights and a Fifth from the burgesses were granted in July by a section of the magnates in the host; the taxes were quashed by a parliament which met in October after Edward's sailing, but not as unparliamentary, but because they were conceded before the king had made that Confirmation of the Charters for which they were held to be the reward. The financial safeguards in the *Confirmatio Cartarum* itself are subject to the same limitation of outlook. The pressure under which the grants of 1297 had been made gave some ground to fear for the immemorial principle that aid was by the mere grace of the vassal, and Edward was recalled to the promise of the Great Charter. He will not, nor will his heirs, says the *Confirmatio*, "take such aides, mises, and prises *fors qe par commun assent de tut le roiaume*".[1] He is not bound to parliament, for that is not as yet regarded as the sole vehicle of feudal constitutional right. A meeting such as that of Pentecost

Grants in parliament

[1] Stubbs, *Select Charters*, p. 490.

1306 *ad tractandum super auxilio ad militiam Edwardi* will amply fulfil the sixth clause of the *Confirmatio Cartarum.*

But, though the principal constitutional issues were for the time being in abeyance, Edward's government was too strong and impartial not to arouse opposition. Much of his achievement had lain in the realm of common rather than of constitutional law, and it was here, rather than through parliament, that his rule pressed upon the privileged classes. The Statutes of Westminster, Winchester, and Gloucester, *Quia Emptores*, and *De Religiosis*, the great inquisitions of 1274 and 1279, show him defining, elaborating, and restricting the rules of franchise, legal administration,[1] and public order with a purpose of which the general end is unmistakable. The power of the crown and the rights and conveni-

Feudal privilege threatened by Edward's reform

ence of the generality are the supreme tests of the pretensions of groups and individuals. The subject, not the franchise, is the unit of Edward's scheme of state, and common law, partnered by a jealously guarded regalian right, outweighs the validity of all other custom in England. Such a purpose was not to be maintained without a steady assertion of will against the multitude of individual ambitions inspired by the fresh opportunities of the times or by the surviving privilege of the past.

Bureau-cratic tendencies

The long campaigns in Wales and Scotland and the problems of administering those countries as additional provinces of the realm would in themselves have forced Edward to exaggerate the bureaucratic tendencies in his father's government,[2] and from the 'nineties onwards a certain revival of baronial opposition forced him at once to narrow the circle of the ministers and to throw some of the executive routine upon the knights and burgesses of parliament. The domestic ministries, and especially the Wardrobe, became more and more important in government, and the bureaucratic element in the sworn Council increased at the expense of the magnates, some of whom Edward was pur-

---

1 Among the reforms of legal administration at this time may be placed the *Nisi Prius* circuits of Statute of Westminster, II. 30, the fixing of four circuits of assize for biennial visitation in 1293, the addition of commissions of Gaol Delivery to those of assize in 1299. Stubbs, *Constitutional History*, ii. 284.

2 T. F. Tout, *Chapters in Administrative History*, ii. 60 *et seq.*

suing in a spirit of personal revenge. As under Henry III, the Wardrobe was the travelling treasury; it received revenue direct from the collectors of taxes, issuing tallies by which they could acquit themselves at the Exchequer, and from 1296 the normal relation of the two offices was reversed and the Exchequer became in practice dependent upon the Wardrobe. The pliability of Wardrobe traditions favoured the more liberal principles of finance to which the king was forced by the clamour of all classes against taxation. Through the Wardrobe he could borrow without check or criticism, and revenue prospects for years ahead were anticipated by loans from foreign bankers secured upon the Exchange and the Customs. By 1289 the king owed £107,000 to the Riccardi, and in his later years borrowed almost as freely from the Frescobaldi. John had been £200,000 in hand in 1213.

Irregular as it was, according to more modern principles of finance, this use of the Wardrobe was nothing new. It was unavoidable with armies out on the remote campaigns in Wales, Gascony, and Scotland. But, governed by no general financial policy, it involved the Crown in serious difficulties by the end of the reign, though they were difficulties which a generous agreement by the subjects to pay for Wales and Scotland by a short period of stiff taxation might easily have met. It would be unfair to justify baronial opposition upon the ground of these financial irregularities, of which the magnates were largely unconscious. Some attempt was made to clear up the arrears of the Wardrobe under the Ordainers, and the attempt was repeated in 1322, but on the whole the nation realized only a few of the symptoms of which the financial problem was the cause. Opposition under Edward I found little new to say and drew its programme from the past. The feudal order had modified its claims and held them for the most part in abeyance, but it had not renounced them, and, beneath the salutary innovations which we are bound to regard as the primary interest of the reign, the grievances and desires of the medieval subject worked as they had in every generation and were not greatly changed. Edward's taxes, his purveyors, customs gatherers, and tallagers, were as much hated as those of John, for government was unpopular in proportion as it was strong, and the system rather than the immediate policy of the reign made for harshness and extortion.

Ineffective nature of the opposition

Thus, there was opposition in Edward's reign, though of the traditional ineffective kind, attacking every incident of taxation or administration separately when grievance was felt, justifying the sense of wrong by the abuse of custom, seeking remedy in the many times discredited device of a reissue of the Charters. In the absence of any new constitutional theory the various interests defended themselves individually, the clergy—the butt of the crown in the taxation of the years 1294–8—fighting on the special ground of the traditional exemption of their spiritualities and of the bull *Clericis Laicos*, and a section of the magnates in 1297 taking some obscure and unverifiable ground of privilege, the drift of which has never been clear.[1] In that year the Constable and the Marshal stumbled into a constitutional quarrel in the course of urging an individual grievance, and, drawing a certain number of the magnates after them, broadened their demands to question, as

The year 1297

they had some reason for doing, the future of taxation, and especially the increased customs duties imposed three years earlier by prerogative decree. In form, at least, the crown suffered a defeat, and, though Edward's surrender was caused only by the coincidence of three essentially separate problems, the French war, the quarrel with the magnates, and that with the clergy, he promised to respect the principle of consent for "all such aids, tasks, and prises" as his recent levies upon the wool, and submitted to a covering grant from the Pope when he taxed the clergy's spiritualities, as he continued for the rest of his reign to do. Moreover, once set in motion, the demand for redress was not satisfied by the general terms of the Confirmation of 1297, and the grievance was renewed from time to time when the king was least able to resist it.

The support of the magnates for the Scotch war of 1298 had to be bought by a further confirmation of the charters and the promise of a perambulation of the forests, by which the foresters' encroachments of recent years might be detected. The problem of the forests, once raised, involved the king in long and intricate negotiations. He anticipated that the perambulation with its

---

[1] As to the constable and marshal that they were bound only to personal attendance upon the king in transmarine wars, and for the rest, with a new straining of the letter, that the clause *affectuose rogamus* in the writ of summons might be taken as license to abstain from attendance if they so desired.

inquests would invite pleas for redress, warned the country that the Council could not postpone the urgent concern of papal affairs to a flood of forest litigation, and stipulated that the returns should lie with him until they could be released for action with safety. He would take no steps which might prejudice the *jura regni et corone*. Even under these restrictions the complaints widened to include the usual range of grievances. In a parliament in March 1300, with clergy, magnates, and commons, the Great Charter and the Charter of the Forest were reënacted, and the public appetite for their reiteration was gratified by a decree that they should in future be published four times in every year. Twenty new articles, *articuli super cartas*, were added, much in the spirit of those of 1297, but with certain reversions to the stock-in-trade of past opposition, which show that the spirit of 1258 was not entirely dead.[1] In the forefront remained the demand for an enquiry into abuses of the Charters and especially of the Forest Charter. It was now satisfied by the grant of an elected commission, a concession destined to force Edward into his most serious quarrel with his secular lieges. The knights elected in every county carried through their enquiry in the summer of 1300, and by September their report was in the king's hands.[2] Edward summoned parliament for Hilary 1301 to Lincoln to consider it, warning the magnates that they were equally bound with himself to maintain the *jura corone*. The commissioners attended as knights of the shire,[3] and all the foresters of every county came with them to give expert counsel. A rather obscure wrangle between the king and the magnates ensued at Lincoln, in which either party sought to throw upon the other the responsibility for any encroachment upon the rights of the crown that possible concessions might cause. An outlet to the deadlock was found in the presentation of a series of articles, introduced by Henry de Keighly, one of the commissioners for Lincolnshire,[4] but backed by the mag-

Articuli super cartas

Parliament of Lincoln

---

1 Of these the licensing of the election of sheriffs where the counties desired it is the most striking.   2 *Report on the Dignity of a Peer*, iii. p. 121.

3 From the writs (*ibid.*) it is evident that the knights who attended at York in March 1300 were appointed commissioners to enquire into abuses of the Charters, and were again summoned to Lincoln at Hilary 1301, to parliament, as knights of the shires.

4 He was, of course, a parliamentary representative of the county, but presumably offered his bill of grievances in virtue of his membership of the forest commission.

nates and formally accepted by the king. The parliament of
Lincoln is interesting as much for Edward's attempt to rally the
magnates to the interest of the crown and its rights as against a
too generous interpretation of the Charters as for its hint of a
coming renewal of opposition, but the dismissal of the treasurer
was demanded—an avowal of dislike for Edward's government
which could hardly have been made at any earlier period of the
reign.

Dislike did not, however, gather head to extreme action during
the king's lifetime. Edward's reign was for contemporaries, and
still remains, one whose balance of good and bad it is difficult to
assess. It is a period in which the greatest variety of constitutional
form prevails. Survivals and new experiments are so evenly
balanced that it is only in the light of later history that we can
determine the real direction of the reign. At Edward's death two
constitutional principles seem likely to prevail, the primitive
principle of consent to taxation, and the new principle of the
change or adjustment of law by prerogative. The latter will certainly be exercised in parliament, but there is as yet only a probability that the enacting body in parliament will be wider than
the permanent Council. Taxation will continue to be by consent
unless the customs and some extension of tallage come to outweigh the taxes on moveables in importance, but on the whole it
seems improbable that consent will be given in parliament. Non-
parliamentary assemblies, perhaps provincial negotiation, seem
more likely here, and if they prevail there will be no true parliament but an estates system upon the model of France. The reign of
Edward I, though it propounds a number of alternative answers to
the problems raised by the break-up of the feudal régime, and
offers at least some experience of the Parliament of Estates as a
possible substitute for the *commune concilium* of feudalism, leaves
the nation upon a point of doubt. A strong volition, royal,
oligarchic, or popular, might deflect the constitution into any one
of several paths, and the final choice is yet to be made.

The natural corrective to monarchy had been in abeyance since
Evesham. Although the growth of opposition cannot be ignored
in any account of Edward I's reign, its real interest lies in its

history during that of his son, and then less in its conscious principles than in the effect upon parliament of the mere fact of opposition.

The crown which Edward II inherited was not a popular one. *Accession of Edward II* His twenty years of incompetent rule gave such a check to the smooth increase of kingly power as to alter the whole history of monarchy and of that parliamentary system which it had built to serve it. Edward I had left the Council supreme in parliament. Under him the magnates were spectators and auditors whose agreement might be sought at the king's discretion, and the commoners petitioners and executants of parliamentary decrees in their constituencies. By the end of his son's reign the magnates had established themselves as the king's primary Council in parliament, absorbing the sworn Council into their larger body, and resuming their primitive function as the enacting authority of legislation. The *communes*, in their turn, had also drawn nearer to the centre of parliament, and now occupied a status distinctly more influential than that held by the barons in 1307. Their advice and assent to policy was called for as that of the barons was by Edward I, but with the added advantage that it had at least once been by statute declared essential.

We cannot attribute this profound change to the intention of the Ordainers. They were moved by the perennial causes of medieval opposition. They disliked paying aids, thought that the king should live of his own and avoid the expenses of war, at least of war in Gascony, and found Gaveston as dangerous as the foreign advisers of Henry III and more offensive. They were less capable of devising a constitutional revolution than the barons of 1258, and, except for a demand that the Wardrobe should cease to anticipate payments to the Exchequer, they put forward no scheme of reconstruction. They accepted the very restricted parliamentary assembly of magnates convoked by Edward I and they gave no fresh encouragement to the *communes*. If anything, they would have narrowed the governing clique still further and proceeded by ordinance *du commun assent del roy e de ses countes*.[1] The movement of the Ordinances was, therefore, no overt attack upon the Edwardian constitution as embodied in parliament, or

[1] T. F. Tout, *Chapters in Administrative History*, ii. 193 n., citing the *Mirror of Justices*.

Edward II's early parlia- ments

at least it was not attacked upon what at the present day seems the obvious ground of the monopoly of the parliamentary writ by a handful of magnates and the exclusion of the *communes* from a full share of legislation. The slightness of the change produced in the summonses to the baronage caused by the accession of Edward II is, indeed, remarkable. The first two parliaments of the reign were made up of a selection from those who attended Edward I's last parliament at Carlisle.[1] That of Easter 1309 admitted Cromwell, Tiptoft, Butler of Wem, and Grelley of Manchester[2]; but the success of the opposition caused no influx of barons discontented at past exclusion,[3] and the parliament of March 1310, when the magnates carried their demand for a committee of Ordainers, contained only thirteen names which were strange to the later parliaments of Edward I.[4] Of the six first parliaments of Edward II's reign, only the first and last contained representatives of the *communes*. The attack was not, therefore, upon any lack of popularism in Edward I's parliamentary legacy.

Constitu- tional change under Edward II

Probably not a tenth of the record which was actually made of the work of parliament during the reign of Edward II has survived, and whole periods of years have left us nothing. In addition, the records were, of course, not intended to assert principles, of which, indeed, contemporaries were largely unconscious. The ambiguous term *consilium* is still used when we should be glad of a precise statement as to the particular manifestation of counsel intended. Nevertheless, it is clear that the beginning of the reign saw not the least decisive of the reversals which have from time to time overtaken English political forms, and the clerks of parliament were compelled in some measure to change their terminology to reflect it. In brief, the change is that the sustained mood of opposition, of which the appointment of the Ordainers in 1310

1 *Report on the Dignity of a Peer*, iii. pp. 174, 178.
2 *Ibid.* 189.
3 It is true that of the thirty-two men who launched the ordinances, five had been neglected in the parliaments of Edward I, William Marshal, Tiptoft, Botetourt, Baddlesmere, and Cromwell.
4 *Ibid.* 197. The king himself complained that the ordinances were the work of a small caucus. Eleven bishops, eight earls, and thirteen barons took the responsibility for them. *Rotuli Parliamentorum*, i. 443.

and the publication of the ordinances in 1311 are typical, revived the ambition of the baronage to dominate the crown and the government, that it was at least temporarily successful, that it brought about a profound change in the status and functions of the magnates in parliament, and in the end profoundly modified those of the *communes* also. That the baronage fastened upon parliament at this time—and not upon some convocation independent of parliament, like the convocations of the clergy—is, perhaps, the most important single fact in the course of parliament's evolution.

The Council in Parliament of Edward I, that enacting group *Magnates* which was the real core of the constitution, was not the baronage *become* but the sworn permanent Council of the king. It was this which *Council in* received, considered, and answered petitions, at times seeking the *Parliament* *consilium* and even the *assensus* of those who were summoned by the magnates' writ *ad colloquium et tractatum*. The Council in Parliament of Edward II, at least over that portion of his reign after he came under baronial influence—from which most of our rolls of parliament are derived—was the *commune concilium* of the magnates or an active group of them who were regarded as representative of their order, and who were not sworn of the permanent Council. Departing from the opposition programme of the thirteenth century, the Ordainers rejected the permanent Council[1] as the centre of parliament. Redress of wrongs, they said, should be by the king and his prelates, earls and barons *ad querimoniam vulgi*,[2] and upon this principle, a reversal of the practice of Edward I, but having good medieval theory behind it, they tended to treat the whole body of the magnates in parliament as the primary Council. By them auditors were appointed to try petitions[3]—less than this had been refused them by Edward I[4]—

[1] One good reason for this may have been a failure of Edward II's Council to carry on the steady application of remedies offered by that of Edward I. In 1310 the knights and burgesses complained that "they found no one to receive their petitions, as was done in parliament in the days of the lord king his father." *Rotuli Parliamentorum*, i. 444.

[2] *Annales Londonienses*, i. 211. Stubbs, *Constitutional History*, ii. 353.

[3] Cf. the account of the Lincoln parliament of 1315. *Ibid.* ii. 350.

[4] At Lincoln in 1301 the magnates begged that complaints against breaches of the charters should be tried by *auditours a ces assignez qe ne soient pas suspecionus des Prelatz Contes e Barons.* Edward replied "*non per tales auditores.*" *Parliamentary Writs*, i. 104.

and many petitions seem to have been heard by the whole or
a preponderance of the magnates under the title of *Magnum
Concilium*.

Magnum   This *Magnum Concilium* as the centre of parliament[1] appears first
Con-   in 1312, though, since the rolls of the previous years are wanting,
cilium   it may have come into being earlier. It acted principally when
the regalian right or the conduct of royal officials or the requests
of great persons were concerned,[2] and, although a *concilium*—presumably the sworn Council—was sitting at the same time, it was
as an independent body, and from time to time referred cases to the
Magnum Concilium as to an overriding authority[3]; on occasion its
decision was reversed.[4] During 1315 the heading *Coram Magno
Consilio* covers the whole recorded business of parliament.[5] In
later years only occasional entries show that the great as well as
the ordinary Council has been in action. From the material at hand
it is hardly possible to be positive as to its precise constitutional
affinities, but it was in all likelihood the general body of the peers.
The name was used in later days of meetings of magnates without
parliament[6] and usually without the lower grades, and also for the
small continual councils of the Lancastrians, but the rolls suggest
that in Edward II's reign it was identical with the parliamentary
magnates, or at least composed of such a proportion of them as was
deemed to stand for all. It may well be that, while the appearance
of the *Magnum Concilium* stands for the assumption of control by
the lords of parliament, its exact relation to *commune concilium* on
one side and the sworn Council on the other remained undefined;
upon one occasion the *Magnum Concilium* postpones a decision
to the next parliament because "certain great lords, prelates and

1 *Rotuli Parliamentorum*, i. 288: *Placita coram Magno Consilio in Parliamento.* . . .

2 As with the petition of the Countess of Ulster *coram Rege et Magno
Consilio suo* in 1334. *Ibid.* ii. 73.

3 *Ibid.* i. 419: *remittatur peticio cum transcriptis coram Rege et Magno Consilio.
Ibid.* i. 306. *Responsum est per consilium quod* . . . *Postea recitata fuit ista petitio
cum responsione coram Magno Consilio.* Thus John Mowbray petitions the king
and Council in 1334, and because he is asking for a revocation of outlawry
"nothing can be done *sine Magno Consilio*". *Ibid.* ii. 74.

4 *Ibid.* i. 296.

5 *Ibid.* i. 288.

6 The first instance of this use in the rolls seems to be in 1371. *Ibid.*
i. 304.

others, are not at this Parliament, and those that are will not undertake to give judgment without them",[1] and on another Mortimer of Chirk's claim to lands resumed under the Ordinances is postponed "because such lands are not to be restored without the common assent of the magnates, and the number now in Parliament is insufficient for the purpose".[2] The *Magnum Concilium* may be referred to simply as the *majores*.[3] Such phrases would be consonant with a Council which regarded itself as a quorum of the whole of the lords in parliament, sitting in the place of the sworn Council in Parliament of Edward I.[4] As a rule the petitions which come before it seem to involve royal right or the action of officials, and in such causes the form of the petitioners' address occasionally varies from the usual *a nostre seigneur le Roi et a son conseil*, and is made *a nostre Seigneur le Roi et son Conseil, Prelatz, Countes, et Barons de sa terre*.[5]

The character of the Great Council of the rolls of parliament of Edward II as a subsuming of the king's Council *ad Parliamenta*—and so of the parliament in the sense in which it was hitherto understood—into the whole body of magnates summoned, is probably identical with the usage of the early fifteenth century. From the ninth year of Henry V we have the so-called "Book of the Council", considered by Sir Harris Nicolas[6] to have been compiled by the Council's clerk, and therefore authoritative as to its view of its own procedure and composition in that and succeeding reigns. It seems from this book that the sittings of the ordinary or continual Council were afforced during times of parliament or after special summons by the lords spiritual and temporal and the judges. The minutes of such sessions during parliament continue to be embodied in the book of the permanent Council's proceedings, the same business is done—though many of the

---

[1] *Rotuli Parliamentorum*, i. 306.

[2] *Ibid.* i. 305.

[3] *Ibid.* i. 336.

[4] By the middle of Richard II's reign the term Grand Conseil is clearly being used for the permanent council which was set by parliament to control the king. *Ibid.* iii. 258.

[5] As in Hugh of Audley's claim to the earldom of Cornwall, lapsed after Gaveston's forfeiture into the king's hand. *Ibid.* i. app. 453.

[6] H. Nicolas, *Proceedings and Ordinances of the Privy Council*, v. 1 *et seq.*

petitions at that time being promoted in parliament come up
for disposal—but the Council is joined by the peers and the
justices, who apparently participate upon equal terms, and lend
an equal authority to judgment and decision. Thus throughout
July 1423 the continual Council of the minority is in session
attended by all or the majority of the following sworn councillors
—the duke of Gloucester, the archbishop of Canterbury, the
bishops of Winchester and Worcester, the duke of Exeter, the
earl of Warwick, the lords Fitz Hugh, Cromwell, and Tiptoft,
the chancellor, treasurer, and keeper of the Privy Seal. There is
then a gap in the proceedings, parliament meets upon the 21st
October, and they are resumed on the 23rd October, "present the
Duke of Gloucester, the Archbishop of Canterbury, the Bishops
of Winchester, Norwich and Worcester, the Earl of March with
divers other lords *of the Parliament*,[1] the Lords Cromwell and
Tiptoft, the Chancellor, Treasurer, and Keeper of the Privy Seal
and all the Justices, serjeants, and attorneys at Law of the King".[2]
During the session, meetings of the ordinary Council are taking
place, and it would be easy and natural for any particular cause to
be referred from the smaller to the more general meeting as they
were under Edward II. On the available evidence it can hardly be
said that the name *Magnum Concilium* was given consistently to
these councils of the lords in parliament,[3] but that it was occasionally so used until well into the fifteenth century is certain.[4] In
general, Great Council seems to be a common description of any
body considered to be representative of the magnates, whether
nominated in parliament as a continual council, or summoned by
writ of Privy Seal to a special Council, or summoned under writ

[1] So again in 1425, *et aliis dominis de parliamento*. H. Nicolas, *Proceedings and
Ordinances of the Privy Council*, iii. 169.   [2] *Ibid*. iii. 117.

[3] The term *Magnum Concilium* seems at times to be a mere honorific description of the continual council as well as a name for the occasional meetings of
magnates which were still summoned. *Ibid*. iii. 95, 113, 222, 271. A specially
summoned council of magnates contrasted with the *consilium privatum*—no
doubt the permanent council. *Ibid*. iii. 322.

[4] Thus, during the July parliament of 1432, there are meetings described
alternatively as being of the *domini magni consilii Regis in camera consilii parliamenti* and of the *domini consilii Parliamenti. Ibid*. iv. 120. So (*ibid*. iv. 287) the
king . . . "hath by his greet consail in parlement be advised". On the other
hand, in April 1434 a great council was summoned, clearly as a substitute for
parliament, and under writ of Privy Seal, and also sat *in camera parliamenti.
Ibid*. iv. 210.

of the Great Seal to parliament, as was the case with these *Magna Concilia* of Edward II's parliament.

The essential fact of Edward II's reign is, no doubt, this capture of the Council in Parliament by the magnates, since it gave back, at least to an important section of the feudal order, that power of judgment which the whole *commune consilium* had possessed a century ago, and which it had been steadily losing. When normal times return the peers survive as the authority to which, with the king, the commons make their petitions, and, by bringing parliament under the control of the one order of the realm which was capable at that time of claiming it, the episode of the Ordinances was decisive of much of later parliamentary history, perhaps of the survival of that institution at all. The *communes* were, moreover, soon to find a more defined place in parliament, for the magnates, having established the supremacy of parliament and their own control of it, made less than they might have done of their opportunity. Lancaster, at least, though his party was that of the Ordainers, showed no disposition to carry out their constitutional policy. According to the Ordinances, parliament was to have had an overriding voice in peace and war, power to prevent the king from leaving the kingdom, and to appoint a regent when he did so. All the great officers, from the chancellor to the controller of the Wardrobe, were to be named by counsel of the barons in parliament. Government of this kind, which dispensed with the sworn magnate council of the Provisions of Oxford, would have required frequent parliaments, and the Ordainers determined that they should meet once or twice a year; but, no sooner had Lancaster come into power, than they ceased altogether. During the two years and a half from January 1316 to August 1318, when Lancaster lost his influence, only one parliament was summoned, and that was twice prorogued and then dismissed. By this indifference to what was coming to be recognized as the legal course of government, the baronage put an invaluable weapon into the hands of their enemies, and, by a curious reversal, first the middle party of Pembroke[1] and later the king and the Despensers became for the time being the champions of parliament in all its branches and especially of the commons. Indeed, like several of our more

The Ordainers and parliament

---

[1] The York parliament of October 1318 took up the Ordainers' abandoned policy of enforcing the Ordinances in parliament.

incompetent kings, Edward II was inclined to advance popular principles. It can hardly be a coincidence that the change in the parliamentary writ of the *communes* to a form summoning them to consent as well as to obey dates from the Lent parliament of 1313, when the earls, still in disgrace for Gaveston's death, were ignoring the king's writs and avoiding parliament. The moment was opportune, for the *communes* themselves were beginning to recognize the value of parliament. A petition in 1310 urges that properly constituted authority shall be present to receive petitions needing redress other than that by common law,[1] and in 1315 this petitioning power was for the first time turned against the magnates, and the king promised to withhold the exceptional legal commissions which they were beginning to use against their poorer neighbours.[2] In 1316 the *Communitas Angliae* asked that those who sought the office of sheriff should be obliged to forgo all private agreements with great neighbours and *faire office de vicomte pur le Roi et pur le Poeple*.[3] Thus, the interest of both crown and people combined with the incapacity of baronial leadership and the first warnings of the over-mighty subject to thrust the commons forward. The knights were beginning to see their function in a clearer light, they attend *pur eux et pur le poeple*,[4] and, if the *Modus Tenendi Parliamentum* is really a product of this reign, we must recognize that some surprisingly ambitious claims as to the status of the commons were current. To the author of the *Modus* they were the one essential element of parliament, without which no parliament was valid, "because they stand for the community"— *quia representant totam communitatem Angliae*—while of the magnates the best that can be said is that each stands for himself.[5] That such theories were in the air we may well believe, since the parliament after Boroughbridge declared that all matters concerning the king and the realm were in future to be accorded and established by the commons as well as by the prelates and magnates. This is less likely to refer to legislation by statute, in which the commons' place was to be that of petitioners, than to that congeries of questions of policy, *les busoignes le Roi*—Scotland, Gascony, or the peace of the realm—which confronted most parliaments before they

Increased influence of the commons

Commons' petitions

---

[1] *Rotuli Parliamentorum*, i. 444. [2] *Ibid*. i. 290.
[3] *Ibid*. i. 343. [4] *Ibid*. i. 444.
[5] *Est pro sua propria persona ad Parliamentum et nulla alia.*

could come to their own concerns[1] of grievance and petition, but even petitions by the commons are beginning to have a new authority. Petitions of the *Communitas Angliae*, petitions *pur tote la commune*, have become more frequent, though they are not always formally urged by the knights[2] nor will it be for many years that the common petition will emanate only from the commons and become the initiating force of parliamentary legislation.

The accession of Edward III thus followed upon a period of *Revolution* rapid parliamentary growth. It would be natural to expect that it *of 1327* would be still further advanced by the overthrow of the throne and the forced abdication of the king. It is true that the revolution of 1327 was carried through in as strict a parliamentary form as Edward himself had observed after Boroughbridge, but, like revolutions of later days, it could not solve the contradiction that the prerogative was itself the maker of parliaments. Though the prince sent out the writs they went out in the king's name. So, when parliament met, though it came near to the point of deposition, setting its charges against Edward in six articles of incompetence, evil counsel, loss of provinces, oppression of the church, default of justice, and incorrigible misrule, and adopting them by almost general acclamation, though an oath to maintain the cause of the queen and the prince was taken by the prelates and magnates, and the prince was brought to Westminster to be acclaimed by the people as the future king, the vacancy of the throne was the act of Edward II himself. Deputies of the prelates, earls, barons, and judges went to Kenilworth, the king yielded the throne freely to his son, and only then, not in the act of a sovereign assembly, but by the withdrawal by procuration of all the several

---

1 The assent of the commons to statute was not assumed to be necessary until the reign of Henry V. The substance of the declaration of 1322 was in fact observed for the future, and in 1369 Edward III was able to tell parliament with justice that "he had at all times during his reign acted with the advice by the counsel of the magnates and commons *en touz les grosses busoignes qe toucherent lui ou son Roiaume* and that he had at all times found them faithful and loyal". *Rotuli Parliamentorum*, ii. 299.

2 In 1325 certain persons who hold the forfeited lands of rebels proffer a petition *pur tote la commune*. *Ibid*. i. 430. In 1315 there is a petition *quorundam de Regno, petentium pro se et communitate*. *Ibid*. i. 295. A transition form which is almost that of the common petition occurs in 1314: *Prie la Comunalte de la terre, nomement ceux de l'eist de Londres. Ibid*. i. 308. Cf. G. L. Haskins, *Speculum*, xii. 315.

fealties of the lieges,[1] was the allegiance to the king broken. In so far as precedent was followed, it was that of the diffidation of John, in so far as parliament set the course of events, the prelates, magnates, and high officials assumed that they themselves were parliament, and no intelligible precedent was set for the future. The facts were, indeed, unprecedented; an abdication, and a diffidation which had lost its authentic feudal quality yet was not claimed as the act of a community embodied in parliament;[2] and they were so little reconcilable with contemporary or former experience that the theory of parliament could gain little from them.

State of parliament at Edward III's accession But, setting aside the palace revolution of 1327 and the national discontent which it brought to a focus, it is a very much changed parliament which emerges from Edward II's reign. In form at least, the magnates are now its centre and the *communes* are being admitted to a greater share of business. Parliament, it may be said, has come in a rough and unsystematic way to be shared between the king and the nation. The future, however, is even yet unsure. The particular adjustment of forces to which Edward III succeeded might have proved to be nothing more than a momentary balance struck by the weight of political parties as the last twenty years had left them. The grip of the nobles on the *Magnum Concilium* might have been relaxed again, the *communes* might have fallen back into their original impotence. As it happened, the general balance of 1327 was preserved without essential modification for the next two centuries; but, even so, almost the whole of the constitutional history of parliament remained to be written.

In fact, it was the outward form of parliament which, in broad outline, had been settled by 1327. Though it was still to meet without one or other of its components upon occasion, and though the non-parliamentary assembly of magnates[3] persisted at increasingly

---

[1] Stubbs, *Constitutional History*, ii. 380 n.: *les homages et fealtez a vous Edward roy d'Engleterre . . . rend et rebaylle sus.*

[2] *Ibid.* The renunciation, made by William Trussell, was that of *prelatz, contez et barons et altrez gentz en ma procurage nomes*, and thus preserved a convenient vagueness as between a possible authority of parliament and that of the individuals named. Legally the act is not better defined than that of the twenty-five barons whom the Great Charter empowered to make diffidation for the "whole commune of the realm".

[3] The meeting of estates out of parliament, sometimes including prelates, clerical proctors, magnates, knights, and burgesses (*e.g.* in July 1338 at Northampton), was an occasional feature of Edward III's reign.

rare intervals until the age of the Stuarts, it had become essential
to great affairs of state.[1] For the time being, the weightiest business
of all was likely to engage those magnates who were coming to
call themselves the Peers of the Realm, though they were as yet
no more than counsellors summoned at the king's discretion.
They undertook the great treason trials with which Edward III's
reign began, the quashing of Lancaster's process, the condemnation of Mortimer and his accomplices, the retrial of the case
against Edmund, earl of Kent. It is clear that they were acting
again, as their feudal ancestors had acted, as the highest court of
the realm, the greatest council of the king—*come juges de Parlement.*[2] Though they would not admit that their jurisdiction
extended to each and every trial in first instance, they habitually
heard petitions from all conditions of men, which were "read and
heard" "before our Lord the King, Prelates, Earls, Barons, and
other magnates of the said Parliament",[3] and answered "by their
request and assent". As common petition by the knights and
burgesses became the rule, their assent began to have the force of
legislation. The term *Magnum Consilium* was still used,[4] and it was
an apt description of the number, dignity, and high function of the
peers acting as the king's primary council in parliament. The *Growth*
opening of the Hundred Years War gave a strong stimulus to the *in the*
growth of the internal order of parliament and especially to the *structure of*
rise of the commons. The political matters put before it became *parliament*
more and more absorbing. From point to point Edward consulted
it upon the critical phases of war and truce, and left the organization of support from England in the hands of Council and parliament working together. Successive sessions record little but
national business, in which the commons are treated almost upon
an equal footing with the magnates, while their separate identity
is preserved and accentuated. The parliament which emerges from
this process of internal evolution is seen to preserve the dualism of

---

[1] *Rotuli Parliamentorum,* ii. 69: *le Roi . . . fist assembler un Conseil a Everwitz
des Grantz et autres tielx come poet illocques avoir. A quel conseil feu avis, que
les busoignes estoient si chargeantes q'il busoigneroit a somondre Parlement.* The
statute of 1340, decreeing that all aids shall be granted in parliament, is a landmark in this matter. *Statutes of the Realm,* i. 289.

[2] *Rotuli Parliamentorum,* ii. 54.

[3] *Ibid.* ii. 123: *par les Prelatz, Countes, Barons, et autres du Parlement.*

[4] *E.g.* in 1334. *Ibid.* ii. 73.

its origin in the bringing together of the *colloquium* of magnates
and the parliament of the Council. Sprung from these two roots
of *colloquium* and supreme court for redress, the session proceeded
Order
of the
session
by two stages.[1] In the first, *colloquium*, the business of the
king, aid, and counsel of state, which formed the matter of the
chancellor's charge to the lieges, and for which the writs were
avowedly issued, divided parliament according to its grades, and
a series of sectional meetings in the White or Painted Chambers,
or in the Chapter House of the Abbey, broken by occasional visits
from grade to grade for consultation, prepared the magnates and
the representatives to face the king with a considered view of his
difficulties and of the means to be taken to meet them. With this
they returned, reconstituted the full parliament, and made their
answers. In the second, we are back in the ancient judicial parliament of Edward I, the magnates sitting with the king in their
capacity of Great Council, or acting under individual commissions
as triers of petitions.[2] Before this session the commons appear in
their original status as petitioners: "if they have any petitions of
grievances done to the common people or for amendment in the
law, let them put them in to the parliament".[3] The king, together
with the Council of magnates,[4] accedes to or refuses their petitions,[5]
refers them to some other form of redress, or promises to consider
the matter further.

Relation
of the
order
of the
session
to the
structure of
parliament
These two phases of the parliamentary session, and the procedure made necessary by them, determined the later division of
parliament into two houses and three estates. The upper and lower
houses come, of course, from the primitive division between the
king's Council and its petitioners. In presenting themselves before
the official Council of Edward I, or before the *Magnum Concilium*
of Edward II and Edward III, the commons appear as an external

---

[1] The first record of some such division appears in 1315. It may well have
been derived from the primitive dualism of *colloquium et tractatus magnatum* and
council *ad parliamenta. Rotuli Parliamentorum*, i. 350.

[2] In such apartments of the Palace as the Chamberlain's Room and the
chamber of Marcolf. *Ibid.* ii. 309.   [3] *Ibid.* ii. 237.

[4] *Ibid.* ii. 237: *si vindrent les dites Communes devant nostre Seigneur le Roi et touz
les Grantz en Parlement et monstrent.... Ibid.* ii. 238: *il plest a nostre Seigneur le
Roi et a les grantz de la terre.* Upon occasion petitions are endorsed *les Seigneurs
se aviserout. Ibid.* ii. 318.

[5] *Ibid.* ii. 319: *le Roi et lez Seigneurs ne sont pas en volunte a ceste foitz de change
la commune ley.* The magnates have recovered the status of the barons of Merton.

subordinate body, and, though they find unity for themselves in joining to present common petitions, there is never any tendency for them to become merged in the magnate Council. The idea that the knights could ever have joined the lords of the Council in a joint house rests upon nothing tangible and ignores a fundamental division in the structure of parliament. On the other hand, if the two houses arise from the second, petitioning, phase of the session, the three estates are formed in the sectional consults of the first phase, the debate and advice upon "the king's business", the consideration of aid and the *magna negotia regni*. The division into two houses is foreshadowed in Edward I's writs, which calling magnates *ad colloquium et tractatum de quibusdam arduis negotiis que regnum Anglie tangunt*", and knights and burgesses *ad audiendum et faciendum quod tunc de communi consilio ordinabitur*, though, since the change made in the commons writ in 1313 and the declaration of 1322, the commons have entered into a share of deliberation upon the king's business.

In proportion as the full parliament came to be the principal forum in which policy was debated, the three estates began to take their form. It was during the reign of Edward II that the proctors of the parochial and capitular clergy began to hold back from parliament. They felt safer in their convocations[1] in a reign when any parliament might be required to condone a *coup d'état* or to proclaim judgment of death upon a defeated party. The prelates and magnates, on the other hand, began to claim the right to private consultation within parliament, and so confirmed the principle of separate orders. Behind this grouping we can see vaguely defined a conception of estates of the realm, since the earls and barons in parliament claim to stand for "their peers of the land", *Beginning* those who hold *par baronie*, and to grant aid for their demesnes *of division* as well as for their own.[2] Much of the business of the early years *houses* of Edward III's reign could only be done by the secular peers— the removal of Edward of Carnarvon to Kenilworth, the trial of the Mortimers—and even upon general matters they and the prelates were inclined to debate separately.[3] At the Salisbury

[1] It was even difficult to enforce their attendance at Convocation when the king's business required it. *Rotuli Parliamentorum*, ii. 146. [2] *Ibid*. ii. 107.
[3] *Ibid*. ii. 52. In 1315 the prelates and magnates still debated together in the chapter-house of Lincoln. *Ibid*. i. 351.

parliament of 1330 the prelates *estoient assemblez au dit Parlement en une meson pur conseiller sur les busoignes nostre Seigneur le Roi*, and in this they were copied, in the parliament of the Nativity of the Virgin in 1332, by the other two orders.[1] At the ensuing parliament all three grades made their replies separately to the crown. During the king's absence in 1339 and 1340 parliament undertook the burden of supply and internal peace, and the commons took an active part.[2] At Easter 1343 the identity and independence of the future two houses was further emphasized by the dispatch of the prelates and magnates to the White Chamber, and the knights and burgesses to the Painted Chamber to discuss the king's business separately,[3] and their replies, together with the bills of grievance which the knights and burgesses attached to them, mark an advance in parliamentary procedure. In this parliament we hear for the first time the name of the reporter of the commons' advice, Sir William Trussell, who has been taken as the first in the line of the commons' speakers.[4]

Commons'   In time, also, the habit of separate debate began to reflect back
petitions   upon the form of petitioning and to bring the petition of the commons into being as an unique parliamentary function, exercised without the magnates, though sometimes after consultation with them. Independent discussion made the older joint petitions "by Prelates, Earls, Barons, and the commonalty of the realm" an anachronism, and in 1343, although there was still only one clerk of parliament,[5] the commons' deliberations found record

---

1 *Rotuli Parliamentorum*, ii. 66: *euent trete e deliberation, c'est assaver les ditz Prelatz par eux mesmes, et autres Grantz par eux mesmes, et auxint les chivalers des countees par eux mesmes.*

2 At Hilary 1332 the twelve magnates of the duke of Cornwall's council, the other prelates and magnates, and the knights and burgesses treated of the king's business as three orders. Their conclusions were reported to the king by the chancellor. *Ibid.* ii. 69. The presentation of a formally digested common opinion will certainly be made by a single person in the name of the rest. In 1343 the knights and burgesses "replied by Master William Trussel". *Ibid.* ii. 136. *Ibid.* ii. 117: *apres grant trete et parlance entre les Grantz et les dites Chivalers et autres des Communes.*

3 *Ibid.* ii. 136. By 1376 the chapter-house was "the ancient place" of the commons. *Ibid.* ii. 322. The allocation of the chapter-house of Westminster to the commons dates from Hilary 1352. *Ibid.* ii. 237.

4 *Ibid.* ii. 136: *Vindrent les Chivalers des counteez et les Communes et responderent par Monsieur William Trussell.* In 1377 *Monsieur Thomas de Hungerford, Chivaler . . . avoit les paroles pur les communes d'Engleterre. Ibid.* ii. 374.

5 *Ibid.* ii. 147.

in a special section of the roll under the heading "Petitions of the Commons and the Responses to them".[1] In 1348 the commons' petitions were still more clearly marked by being delivered to the clerk of parliament, while the petitions of individuals continued to be handed to the chancellor. The former were answered seriatim *par nostre Seigneur le Roi, et par les Grantz en dit Parlement*, and in 1344[2] the commons asked that the answers should be circulated to the shires and boroughs in the form of letters patent "for the comfort of the people". At this time the "grievances of the Commons" become an accepted feature of parliamentary procedure; they are invited in the opening address of the chancellor or chief justice; the commons themselves become jealous that their bills shall contain nothing that is not genuinely national in scope,[3] and thus the rule of legislation by petition of the commons and assent of the king and peers is roughly foreshadowed. In 1376 a petition was rejected on the ground that it had not been sponsored by the commons.[4]

It will be seen, also, that a radical change has overtaken the normal course of legislation. It has been by provision of the *commune consilium* of tenants-in-chief, then by the more or less absolute prerogative of king in Council in parliament, and lately, under Edward II, by the king and magnates in parliament, and the last form of authority has never been in form dispensed with. But in the past its inception has lain with the king and his men learned in the law, more rarely with the *proceres*. Now it is coming to lie with the commons. From 1327[5] the petition of the commons is mentioned as the initiating force in the preamble of statutes, while the authority of enactment remains that of the king and magnates. Common petitions, which, since they have adopted them and sponsored them to parliament, have come to be the commons' petitions, are a normal, though not the only,[6] prelude to statute, *(margin: Commons initiative in legislation)*

---

[1] *Rotuli Parliamentorum*, ii. 139. In 1344 there was similar schedule for petitions sent to the king by the prelates and other clergy.   [2] *Ibid.* ii. 150.

[3] In 1372 they complained that personal grievances were being clothed in the form of common petitions. *Ibid.* ii. 310.

[4] *Ibid.* ii. 333: *Pur ce qe ceste Bille ne fust mye advouez en Parlement.*

[5] *Statutes of the Realm*, i. 255.

[6] In the last parliament of the reign the commons declared that "we will not be bound by any Statute or Ordinance of yours made without our assent , but the dying king put the demand aside; "let this matter be more explicitly declared". *Ibid.* ii. 368.

and prompt the majority of ordinances. To say this is, of course, not to say that the commons' petitions always, or even frequently, issued in statute. They were often not intended to do so, for the greater number demanded only the putting into effect of existing law, the redress of partial grievances, or some change in administrative routine, which could best be effected by ordinance in council[1] or letters patent. In 1351 the commons sponsored thirty-nine petitions. To three of these the king, in giving favourable answers, added in

Statute effect *accorde est qe le respons de ceste petition soit mis en Estatut*, and they were adopted in parliament as the Statutes of Labourers, Provisors, and Servants. To others the answer was that "it pleases the King well that the said law should be enforced as heretofore", "that the said statute should be held and kept". Of some the petitioners were invited to appeal for redress to the Council. Others the king considered unreasonable and refused. Of a few, *le Roi s'avisera*. Statute, therefore, is a comparatively rare necessity, adding to the corpus of standing law of which the Charters are the heart,[2] and seems to be prompted less by the comparative importance of the object aimed at[3] than by the desire to give the king's concession that permanence which was attributed to the Great Charter and to place it beyond alteration or revocation; for it is already an old belief that statute is the province of parliament and can be annulled by parliament alone.[4] The latter years of the reign

---

[1] Thus in 1362 the commons ask that the king in Council shall make an ordinance increasing the currency, *ordeiner plente d'or et d'argent*, Rotuli Parlia-mentorum, ii. 271. In 1363 the commons were asked "whether they wished to have the matters accorded embodied in statute or ordinance". They chose the latter so that any necessary amendments might be made in the next parliament. As between ordinance in parliament and ordinance in council the commons seem to have been influenced chiefly by the fact that the council was not a court of record and they preferred certain matters to be entered on the parliament roll. *Ibid.* ii. 253. There is little appearance of jealousy as to authority. Mr. H. L. Gray observes that the legislation of only six of the ten parliaments following on 1343 directly answered commons' petitions (*Commons' Influence on Early Legislation*, p. 225), but, as is pointed out above, statute is not the only acceptable answer to petition.

[2] Cf. the archbishop's charge to parliament in 1422: "their liberties and franchises by them rightfully enjoyed and never repealed, nor by the common law repealable." *Ibid.* iv. 423.

[3] In 1363 a special statute was devoted to the return of strayed falcons to their owners. *Ibid.* ii. 282.

[4] In his last parliament Edward III acknowledged *qe les Estatutz faitz e a fairs en Parlement . . . ne purroient estre repellez sanz assent du Parlement.* *Ibid.* ii.

showed a certain hardening and definition of the nature of statute.[1] Judges were refusing to exercise their past laxity of interpretation and protesting the sacredness of its letter, to the profit of Chancery, whose market for equitable redress was strengthened by the timidity of the common lawyers, but also to the advantage of the authority and fixity of statute. Ordinance of king and Council began to be subordinate to statute. The Ordinance of the Staple of 1353 was not thought to have sufficient force till the ensuing parliament adopted and reënacted it.[2] From this period dates the first statute roll, into which the Chancery clerks incorporated the legislation of previous years from the accession of Edward I.

Parliament is, nevertheless, to some degree at the mercy of the king, the chancellor, and the triers of petitions, for the form that statute or any other answer to their petition may take. Commons do not yet put their grievance in a draft which itself contains the literal form of the required redress.[3] Statutes and ordinances are cast in such form as the Council considers will secure the substance of the commons' demands in so far as the king is advised to grant them,[4] and they may not be seen by the actual parliament which has moved them. Some bills may be suppressed by the triers, and it is suspected that the king has this done to petitions he does not like.[5] The aggressive parliament of 1340 was allowed to assent to the king's assignment of triers for their petitions and to associate certain commoners with them, but this was an exceptional concession.[6] In the last years of Edward III's reign the commons are, it is true, beginning to assert that the main purpose of parliament is

Treatment of commons' petitions

368. In 1351 the commons had asked that no statute should be altered on the petition of individuals nor its application modified. The king, however, asked for more explicit petition before he gave an answer, and this the commons do not seem to have been able to provide. *Ibid.* ii. 230.

1 Plucknett, *Statutes and their Interpretation*, pp. 121-122.

2 Professor Tout thinks that the petition of the commons in April 1354, that all the ordinances made in the late council should be "affirmed in this parliament and held for statute for ever", "suggests the exact date of the final differentiation of statute and ordinance". (*Chapters in Administrative History*, iii. 182 n.) This is, perhaps, too rigid a judgment.

3 On the part taken by the commons in composing the form of statute cf. H. L. Gray, *Commons' Influence on Early Legislation*, pp. 201 *et seq.*

4 "The king will ordain what it seems to him should be done with the advice of his Great Council." *Rotuli Parliamentorum*, ii. 320.

5 *Ibid.* ii. 272: *Lesquex Seigneurs et autres assignez, si rien touche le Roi, font endocer (endorse) les billes Coram Rege: et issins riens est fait.*

6 *Ibid.* ii. 113.

to redress their grievances,[1] and to insist that their petitions shall be fairly dealt with within the period of the session.[2] Common petitions are coming to be dealt with as a whole before parliament passes to those of individuals.[3] In 1363 the petitions with their answers were read by the chancellor in the White Chamber before the king, prelates, magnates, and commons. There were, moreover, intermittent efforts to associate redress with supply, either, as in 1352, by inscribing the promise of the aid upon the same roll with the petitions,[4] or, as was done for a while in the sixties, by postponing the grant until the petitions had been heard and answered.[5] On the whole, however, the form of legislation grew throughout Edward III's reign without serious conflict, and, therefore, without adding much to the theory of its nature. Edward's subjects would have been satisfied with some such generalization as that statute was law promulgated in parliament by the king's grace at the petition of the commons, and with the counsel and consent of the lords. Of these elements, the king's grant was still the chief essential, at least its supremacy was not overtly challenged, and he had not yet promised that he would make statute on none but common petition.

Indeed, there were few signs of conscious innovation. Exceptionally in 1340 parliament granted a Ninth "on the condition that the king would grant their petitions",[6] but such methods were not consistently applied, and were rather devices to make effective the petitions of the current parliament than considered contributions to parliamentary practice. They were used and dropped according to circumstances.[7] The Peers had lost the mood of consistent opposition and had been caught up into the king's cause and the ideals of the Round Table. They were a nominated group

---

[1] H. L. Gray, *Commons' Influence on Early Legislation*, 113. "Since this Parliament was summoned to redress the divers grievances and mischiefs done to the Commons."

[2] "Please the king of his good grace to ordain that the said bills should be seen, answered, and endorsed before the departure of the said Parliament." *Rotuli Parliamentorum*, ii. 272.

[3] *Ibid.* ii. 243. "After the petitions of the commons were answered, a petition was entered by Sir John Maltravers, etc., etc." (1352).

[4] *Ibid.* ii. 237.   [5] *Ibid.* ii. 273.

[6] *Rotuli Parliamentorum*, ii. 113.

[7] From 1365 to 1376 the grant of aid was again allowed to come before the consideration of petitions.

of about fifty earls, barons, and even bannerets, most of whom had made their names in France. Nor, till the very end of the reign, had the commons that sense of rising power that we are apt to attribute to them. The burgesses made little showing, except, perhaps, the Londoners, and they preferred to urge their petitions as an independent force in parliament. The knights showed nothing of the conscious authority which inspired the feudal barons of the early thirteenth century. We should be wrong to discount altogether the forms of ceremony and address which accompanied the growth of respect for the king's person and formal deference to the crown. It was fact as well as form that redress was now obtained by petitions to the king's grace. The victory of Edward I's prerogative had not yet lost its substance, nor was the modest address of the commons, "*a lour tres-doute et graciouse Seigneur le Roi supplient ses povres liges Communes*", entirely without meaning. It is the unnoticed pressure of reality, rather than any conscious assertion of principle, that is bringing parliament to express a national will and make it respected.

Any account of the fourteenth century would be incomplete it *The* it were treated as a story of new growth only. Before parliament *opposition* could find its full strength it was forced to destroy much which *to the* *crown* had had its value in the past. There is a story of opposition— principally that of feudalism against the rapid retrenchment of its influence by the crown—which recurs intermittently through the reigns of the three Edwards, and under Edward II has a success of far-reaching consequence.

The evolution of parliament is that side of the reigns of the three Edwards which has most apparent relevance to later history. There is, however, another side to the constitution which seemed more important to contemporaries—perhaps, indeed, at that time was more important. Parliament met to secure redress of grievances which common law could not deal with. It was still a meeting of petitioners at law, and it was occasional only. Largely beyond its understanding, and almost wholly beyond its control, lay all those factors of government which we call executive, and they constituted perhaps the most pressing problem of the fourteenth century, for they had become numerous, powerful, jealous of their tradition and of each other, Chancery, Treasury, Chamber, Wardrobe, and their several officers pursuing a constant struggle to consolidate and extend each its particular sphere of power, and to fend off external criticism. Of this rivalry the most aggravated and dangerous form was the cleavage between the two offices—the Chamber and the Wardrobe—which had had their origin in the Household, and the Chancery and the Treasury, which they had from time to time almost superseded, the former working through the warrant of the Privy Seal, and affording the readiest weapons for a king who wished to develop his own personal policy. These executive offices were the target of most of the opposition of the early fourteenth century, the baronage seeking to depress the Wardrobe and the Chamber, to strengthen the Chancery and Treasury, and to keep the latter under baronial control, while the king preferred to withdraw his initiative within the offices of the Household.

Had the barons succeeded in their policy, the result might well have been disastrous. It would have meant the guidance of the executive routine not by the single will of the king, but by that of an external body of magnates. Its best chance of success—indeed, its only one—would have been the maintenance of a strong permanent Council of magnates, such as was called a continual Council in the fifteenth century, and it is to be doubted whether the barons of the fourteenth century had the application or level-headedness to keep such a Council in effective action. If, on the other hand, the king had succeeded in directing the main functions of government away from the Chancery and the Treasury, that might well have been the prelude to despotism. There would have been little check upon the expenditure of revenue, and provincial and central government would have been freed from the rules imposed by the need to secure the Great Seal for the king's precepts. We have become familiar with this conflict under Henry III. It is largely in abeyance during the reign of Edward I, breaks out violently in that of Edward II, and receives its final quietus under Edward III by the recognition of the king and his ministers that the king's government must be carried on, not by encouraging and exploiting the differences between the various offices, but by finding the most useful function of each in the state, and establishing a recognized subordination of parts to the whole.

To this Edward III contributed by his willingness to abstain from undue interference with the minutiae of government, and, as long as support for his French enterprise was forthcoming, to allow the various ministries to find their own levels within a balanced constitution. Turning from parliament, therefore, we must give some attention to this gradual process of adjustment within the executive and to the various phases of opposition which arose during its accomplishment.

At the accession of Edward II it seemed possible that the strong, *Adminis-* but latterly inefficient, administration of Edward I would be carried *tration* on with better acceptance. The household of the Prince of Wales *policy of* *Edward II* was drawn upon to dilute the officialdom of the last reign, but only Walter Langton, the treasurer, and the old king's weapon against the earls, was sacrificed. The barons who had been in opposition under his father rallied to Edward, and the abandonment of the Scotch war may, perhaps, be taken as the first-fruits of an alliance of king and magnates in a policy of peace. The break up of this first season of fair weather is to be attributed in part to the despair of the more zealous of the ministers of bringing order into the financial chaos bequeathed from the past—Benstead, and then Droxford, succeeded to the Wardrobe, and, failing to achieve reform, drifted into opposition—but still more to the folly of Gaveston and the irascibility of the earls. Gaveston was exiled—for a second time— in 1308, and in 1309 the Stamford Articles revealed what political *Opposition* programme, other than hatred of the favourite, the magnates had *of 1309* to offer. It was of the most conservative character, and, except for the cardinal fact that it was chosen as the governing body of the state, little use was, in fact, made of parliament. There was hardly a phrase in the Ordinances which might not have been taken from the Articles of 1300, or, indeed, from the earlier programmes of opposition under Henry III. The subordination of the Wardrobe to the Exchequer in finance, of the Exchequer to the Chancery in the framing of writs, the appointment in parliament of the great officers—to whom were added the keeper and controller of the Wardrobe—together with the principal members of the king's Household, exhausted the political inventiveness of the Ordainers, and established a baronial control of the government without effective reform in administration. To this conservative revolution the king reacted as his predecessors had done to earlier challenges of the same kind, suppressing the chancellorship and treasurership, since he might no longer make his own appointments, and ignoring the promise of that purge of the Household which was the real desire of the baronage. Then followed a struggle between the barons and the king for the control of the Chancery and the Treasury, in which the former drove the king's representative from his presidency of the Easter exchequer, and the latter frightened the Chancery clerks into sealing proclamations of Gaveston's loyalty which had been drafted in the Wardrobe. In 1312 constitutional manœuvres were driven out of the minds of both parties by the tragedy of Gaveston, and by Edward's attempt to cover up his shortcomings by a renewal of the war with Scotland, but Bannockburn, throwing him upon the mercy of the country, and shutting up the nation with its own domestic rancours, brought him to humble himself to the Ordainers. For the first time, the Ordinances would be executed without fear of defiance or evasion by the king. At the York parliament of 1314 the

Triumph great offices and the ministries of the Household were filled with
of the baronial nominees. "The opposition had become the govern-
opposition ment." [1] It was not, however, until 1316, that that "government" passed the phase of administrative interference, and attempted to establish an adequate conciliar control. Lancaster was set at the head of the Council established at Lincoln in that year, *de consilio Regis capitalis*, but his idle interventions and his still more troublesome lapses into indifference had already discredited him with his own party, and, at the outset of their enterprise of governing England, the cause of the barons went to pieces. Warenne took the field against Lancaster, Lancaster's supporters fell into disorder for lack of leadership, and those who were of neither faction, Roger d'Amory and Bartholomew de Badelesmere, under the guidance of Edward's cousin Pembroke, came to the fore as a middle party, not hating or favouring either extreme, but looking to the rehabilitation of the king and the reconstruction of a government which, in its three elements of crown, council, and ministries, was losing all cohesion and exhausting itself in a crossfire of mutually conflicting writs and precepts. In April 1318 the

[1] T. F. Tout, *Chapters in Administrative History*, ii. 202.

process of reconciliation was complete. The king and the earl gave *The* sureties for their future conduct to each other in the Treaty of *middle* Leake, and Lancaster, by forfeiting all hold upon the Council except *party* a single representative, passed out of effective influence. The power that he had lost, or failed to make good, went to a Council like that of 1258, and from this Council, in which Pembroke predominated, and by which Badelesmere was made steward of the Household and Hugh Despenser chamberlain, the first great administrative reforms proceeded in the Household Ordinance of York.

The way to reform had been to some degree prepared by the *Household* work of the Ordainers. The trend was, of course, towards im- *Ordinance* personal government and the exaltation of the office above the *of York* caprice of the king, and it was undertaken with some measure of skill. Like his predecessors, Edward had made his personal policy effective by writs under a Privy Seal kept in the Wardrobe and unchecked by external authority. It was the special weapon of prerogative. The baronial answer to its arbitrary use was twofold, to restrict the occasions on which it could be used to the detriment of the Great Seal, and to bring the Privy Seal under the guardianship of a nominee of their own.[1] In the first year of Edward II, as under his father, the controller of the Wardrobe united with that office the personal secretariate of the king and the custody of the Privy Seal. Its use to withhold redress at common law was *The* petitioned against in 1309, and prohibited in the Ordinances of *Privy* 1311,[2] by which the commissioning of sheriffs by writ of Privy *Seal* Seal was also forbidden. But these were mere elaborations of Edward I's concessions of 1300—perennially ineffective—and the vital contribution made to the future of the seal in 1311 was the ordinance that in future "a suitable clerk be appointed to keep the Privy Seal". This was the beginning of the keepership as a distinctive charge, intended to acquire those standards of office which put the established ministries beyond the personal caprice of the king, and guaranteed of independence by its inclusion among those offices the holders of which should be elected in parliament.

Under the guidance of Roger Northburgh and his successors the Privy Seal developed along the lines of a separate office, accumu-

[1] T. F. Tout, *Chapters in Administrative History*, ii. 282.
[2] Clause 32.

lated a staff of subordinate clerks, and, as might have been expected
from the auspices under which it was created, began to pass out
of the circle of the Wardrobe and to be drawn into the Council
where the baronial reformers predominated. Writs *per assensum
concilii* testify that the seal is being affixed in council and has
ceased to be private to the king. Indeed the keeper remained in
London, employed by the Council, while Edward was residing
in the North and conducting his correspondence with the still
more personal warrant of the Secret Seal. Thus the Privy Seal
was following the course of the Great Seal at the end of the
twelfth century, and the Ordainers, like the barons of 1258, were
seeking to bring its use under constitutional control. It is a feature
of the revolutions of this time that most of the constitutional
changes enforced by successful opposition are adopted by the
crown when its power is restored, and the enhanced status of the
keepership under the Ordainers survived the victory of the middle
party and the king's victory of Boroughbridge without much
diminution. It has been said that "if the Keepership of Northburgh
represented the triumph of the Ordainers and that of Charlton
became an emblem of the Pembrokian compromise, the next
keeper"—Baldock, who held the seal from 1320 to 1323—"stood
once more for curialistic policy",[1] but, although the controllership
of the Wardrobe came again for a time to be held by the keeper,
the functions of the two offices were not confused, and the office
of the Seal remained distinct and important. We shall see that it
had a part of real value to play in the reign of Edward III. Baldock
was, in fact, the most important official of his day. After he had
been raised to the Chancery his intelligence inspired the government of Edward and the Despensers, and Baldock's successors,
justices and clerks of Chancery, with no experience of the Wardrobe, carried the Privy Seal yet further from dependence upon the
Household and developed its identity as a second Chancery.

*The
Wardrobe*   The history of the domestic offices under Edward II follows
closely the course of development of the Privy Seal, their special
warrant. Upon the whole, the characteristic of the period is the
reduction of the disorderly independence of the Household offices
and the reconstitution of the authority of the older and greater
offices of state. The Wardrobe, being the principal source of the

[1] T. F. Tout, *Chapters in Administrative History*, ii. 299.

private finance of the king, and the open sluice through which the revenues of the crown had been poured out for his uncontrolled expenditure, presented itself to the Ordainers as an office whose activities must be curtailed, and figures only negatively in the Ordinances. Its keeper and controller are to be appointed in parliament, and all the issues of the kingdom are to be paid directly into the treasury of the Exchequer. In so far as this rule was made effective, the Wardrobe would be deprived of its power to order the payment of revenue to itself upon writs of Privy Seal, and would become dependent upon the Exchequer, where the king's private expenditure could be controlled and limited. The abolition of the financial independence of the Wardrobe was, in fact, the sole means by which the king could be made to live of his own, and it is conjectured that the cutting off of the Wardrobe's separate access to revenue at a time when the Exchequer was at the mercy of the earls had much to do with the fall of Gaveston and the king's submission to the Ordainers.[1]

Equally restrictive are the ordinances made by the middle party at York in 1318 and at Cowick in 1323, for, while accepting the organization of the Wardrobe as it then stands, the first deals with it—together with the rest of the Household—as a staff of officials whose status and duties are to be defined and thus deprived of the indefiniteness of function upon which their importance thrives, while the second puts into effective working that Exchequer control which had been broadly asserted by the original Ordinances. In this, as in so much else, the reign of Edward II was a decisive one, for the Wardrobe, perhaps that one of the domestic offices which was most dangerous to the proper authority of Chancery and Treasury, then reached and passed its maximum of importance. The policy of the Ordainers was in part ineffective, but it was inherited by Pembroke in 1318, and, in a less aggressive but no less salutary form, by the royalist government of the Despensers. Under such governments many factors conspired to constrain and reduce the old undirected growth of Wardrobe influence. The detachment of the Privy Seal deprived it of its character as a domestic chancery, the York ordinance confined its several

---

[1] *Chapters in Administrative History*, ii. 235 n. The Wardrobe receipts of 1307-8 were some £78,000, and, in addition, it received five-sevenths of the income of the Exchequer. In 1312-13 they had fallen to £8400.

officials within the restrictions of recognized function, and the ordinance of 1323 systematized the restored primacy of the Exchequer and reduced it to routine and rule. Regular Wardrobe accounts were to be made the personal business of every executive officer through whose hands its moneys passed, the keeper of the Wardrobe was allotted a personal responsibility for the whole, the general account of the Wardrobe was to be rendered to the Exchequer, and the treasurer was given power to punish all defaults in account by the arrest of the offender and the seizure of his lands and goods. A third ordinance of 1324 prohibited the keeper from receiving any moneys except from the Exchequer, and the Great Wardrobe, the external purchasing staff of the Wardrobe, was now detached from its parent office, and its clerk directed to make his account to the Exchequer alone. There was some return by Edward III to the older independence of the Wardrobe when war conditions made a revival convenient, but upon the whole its great days were over. An office among others, and with its subordinate nature now recognized and confirmed by a succession of ordinances, the Wardrobe of Edward II's later years is well characterized by the phrase which then came into use, "the Wardrobe of the Household". Its place in history would henceforth be a minor one as a domestic office of the king.

The Chamber   In contrast with the slow decline of the Wardrobe under Edward II is the meteoric revival of the still older office of the Chamber, which flourished for a few years, carried the weight of the king's personal policy when the Wardrobe and the Privy Seal were under the jealous eyes of the baronage, and bid fair to establish itself as a permanent bulwark of prerogative in the heart of a constitutionalized state. Its progress was that of all its forerunners in the monarch's private service. As the Wardrobe once diverted money from the Chamber in the early days of its own growth, so the Chamber began to avenge the past by receiving the direct payment of Edward's foreign borrowings *pro quibusdam secretis faciendis,*[1] as to the nature of which the king "refused to inform his Wardrobe". In 1309 the Chamber came by a capital of land from which a permanent revenue might be expected. The custodians of the estates of the disgraced treasurer, Walter de Langton, and of

[1] T. F. Tout, *Chapters in Administrative History,* ii. 315 n.

part of the vastly greater lands of the Templars, were ordered to *The* make their account to the Chamber. In 1310 all the Templars' *Chamber* lands were under the single custody of Wingfield, "clerk of the *lands* King's Chamber". In 1311 the partial execution of the Ordinances diverted revenues of the Chamber lands to their proper account at the Exchequer, but a few weeks later the king succeeded in imposing a compromise by which the Wardrobe was made responsible. In 1312 much of the estate of Edmund of Cornwall's widow was added to the same fund of estate, and before the end of the year the Chamber had again replaced the Wardrobe as the office of receipt for its revenues.

The Chamber seems to have come under little criticism from the Ordainers. In 1313 it is found in possession of its own, the Secret Seal, and by 1318 the office of chamberlain is of sufficient importance to be added to those whose holders need the confirmation of parliament and to be taken by the younger Hugh Despenser. From 1322 to 1326 it was the chief weapon of that régime which passed for personal government and was in fact the rule of the Despensers. Great estates, the forfeit of successive treasons, were added to the Chamber's account, the lands of Badelesmere in 1321, in 1322 those of Mowbray together with the castles, lands, and moveables of ninety-three principal rebels, and, again, the forfeitures after Boroughbridge. It would seem that Edward had in the immense resources accumulated under the Chamber a promising source of revenue by which the crown might maintain itself without parliamentary grant, and it is characteristic of his lack of persistence that it was never reasonably exploited,[1] and that the temporary emergency of the Scotch campaign of 1322 induced him to abandon it. In July the issues of the Chamber lands were diverted to the Exchequer, then at York for the conclusion of the war, and when the truce was resumed the Exchequer continued to receive them. While they were the property of the Chamber these revenues were expended on the furthering of Edward's personal aims, upon the expenses of the messengers of

---

[1] The sum that reached the crown was about £2000 a year. The real revenue must have been vastly greater. T. F. Tout, *Chapters in Administrative History*, ii. 355. It is too much to say that the curial officers and the private seal were equal rivals to parliament and the great offices under so negligent a king as Edward II, but their failure under him closed an obvious line of alternative growth.

his secret seal, the maintenance of his ships, and upon the wages and equipment of men-at-arms in his special service. Intelligently used they might have saved the king in 1326. It has been well said that the Chamber lands might have been made into a state within the state, and the reversal of the policy which brought them together is a rare instance of the crown voluntarily foregoing one of the most promising aids to its own absolutism. Without the resources which its lands had given it, the office lost its influence at Edward's fall, and under his successor it returned to the comparative obscurity whence his personal needs had drawn it.

The Household under Edward III   Under Edward II the development of the domestic seals and offices is either curialistic in an unfavourable sense, that is to say, it is designed to obscure the responsibility of officials and to free the king to follow his own course, or dictated by the malcontents. Under Edward III the situation is changed; the king, the nobility, and the commons are substantially at one to support the war, and the king is trusted, and in the main rightly trusted, to exploit what adaptability and specialized capacity in the national business exists in his household, even though it should trench upon the independence of the older ministries. The day is gone when the Chancery and Treasury are supported against the crown by a jealous nobility. The king, as we have seen, works in harmony with the orders in parliament, and in administration he is given and deserves a freer initiative than ever before. The first manifestation of this new spirit is in the Walton ordinances issued in July 1338, when Edward was upon the point of sailing for

Walton ordinances   Flanders.[1] The principal effect of these is the bringing of Treasury and Chancery for certain purposes under the control of the Privy Seal; their most striking feature—in the light of the struggle for the seal in the last generation—is the unconscious confidence with which Edward applies what has once been the weapon of an unprincipled prerogative, and is still largely under the king's own hand, to discipline the great offices which till now have been regarded as the strongholds of administrative independence and probity. By the Walton ordinances every payment made by Treasury—except routine and fixed fees—was henceforth to be

[1] T. F. Tout, *Chapters in Administrative History*, iii. 69 *et seq.*

warranted by a writ of Privy Seal. Chancery writs of *liberate* where they were still employed were to be accompanied by such writs; in time, indeed, they came to be largely supplanted by them. That such a use of the Privy Seal could be accepted as a reform is *Supremacy* explained by the regularizing of the keepership which the opposi- *of the* tion of the last reign had effected, and its use for warrant of *Privy* *liberate* is proof that the traditions of the office had already formed *Seal* along sound lines. Warrants were to be issued "with the assent of the king and of a sufficient person appointed for the purpose", they were to be enrolled by a permanent clerk, with a counter-roll kept by a clerk of the Chamber, and all Exchequer issues upon order of the Privy Seal were to be audited annually by a clerk using the counter-roll, together with an independent commission of a bishop and a banneret. As a final and vital safeguard, the writ was to avoid vagueness of statement as to the ground upon which the issue was warranted—such as "for the King's secret needs"—and to embody its precise purpose. Such a use of the Privy Seal, in the best traditions of public service, constitutes a revolution in its conduct, and no less a revolution is marked by the curbing of Chancery and Treasury initiative. Most significant of all, the crown, using the most characteristic weapon of its prerogative, has replaced the magnates as the motive power of reform and control. "Chancery and Treasury were henceforth in leading strings",[1] the hand which held them was that of the king, and the change was very far from being the former indiscriminate extension of royal influence, for the Wardrobe was included under the extended authority of the Privy Seal. How far it corresponded to a new and more popular orientation of the crown may be seen by the association of the clauses bringing the great offices under the seal with a further curtailment of their power in the interests of the provincial communities. The sheriffs and all other "great officers of the shires", and the customers of the ports, were in future to be elected annually "by the good men of the shire", and to be such as they could answer for at their peril. It was a reform long petitioned for in previous crises, and now made doubly necessary by that decline in the integrity of the provincial officialdom which had followed upon the death of Edward I, and it was made, not under pressure, but as a spon-

[1] T. F. Tout, *Chapters in Administrative History*, iii. 71.

taneous act of crown.[1] The great offices were coming to be ground between the upper and nether millstones of popular initiative and a crown which trusted and was accepted by it. The Walton ordinance deserves to be understood for the light which it throws upon the changed and happier adjustment of the constitution which prevailed under Edward III. Professor Tout, perhaps with some exaggeration, has said that the committee of audit of the ordinance "was clearly intended to be the keystone of the monarchical arch, with the office of the privy seal, the chamber, the king's council, and the local courts on the one side, and the chancery, exchequer, and wardrobe on the other".[2] Whatever the ordinance's original intention, the need to give freedom of action to the Exchequer during the Flemish campaign made it impossible to maintain the more stringent restrictions upon it, but the former jealousy no longer attached to the domestic offices, and the Privy Seal and the Wardrobe provided a secondary government for the king in Flanders and were accepted and supported by parliament as such.

The year 1341   With the force of this unanimity behind it, the general settlement of the government under Edward III was strong enough to survive the storm of the king's quarrel with Archbishop Stratford and the malcontent parliament of 1341. Arising from the inadequacy of medieval administration to maintain adequate supply for an expedition and a mercenary alliance on the scale of that of the Low Countries, the dispute developed into a wholesale attack by the king and his curialist barons and officials upon the Chancery and the Exchequer, for which the archbishop and the clerical ministers stood. Behind the latter the secular magnates of the Lancastrian tradition ranged themselves, and the stage was set for a repetition of the events of 1311, with Stratford playing the rôle of Winchelsea and appealing to memories of Becket. The demands of the parliament of 1341 brought out again the time-worn counters of opposition, election of the great officers, oath to the Charters, judgment of lords by their peers in parliament. But in all this fury—the controversy was waged in speech and

---

[1] It was somewhat sparely acted upon.
[2] T. F. Tout, *Chapters in Administrative History*, iii. 76: "The specific task of the committee was to secure the harmonious working together of the various elements of the administration in the execution of the royal will".

writing more violent and more explicit than upon any previous occasion—the significant fact is that there was no real victory for either party. The very fact that the issues were now realized with a new and complete clarity guaranteed that the struggle should not be urged to a conclusive issue. Forcibly as king or prelate might urge the claims of their contrasting views of the state, the experience of fifteen years had told them that it was upon the Edwardian compromise between prerogative and parliament that the government must finally be rested. There were formal, indeed, in some matters, admittedly feigned, concessions by the king, and an equally formal submission to the king by the primate. When all was over the anger died away, and for a quarter of a century king and parliament worked in general harmony.

But, more striking than this temporary tolerance of household *Reduction* activity, more lasting than the quarrel of the king and the ministries *of the* in 1341, and more typical of the growing consolidation of the whole *influence* *of the* state as a uniform machine of public government, is the gradual *Household* reduction of the scope of the domestic offices. This was brought *offices* about voluntarily, though the increasing influence of parliament may have been its ultimate cause. The king, or the ministries acting for him, gradually extinguish the independence of those departments which were outlets for the king's personal will, and return the full control of business to the great impersonal offices of the crown. We have seen how the Privy Seal was officialized and claimed for the public service. During the same period the private seal or Griffin ceased to be applied to precepts of importance. The king's seals were thus all in the hands of public servants, who were bound to consider the rules of their office as well as the king's wishes.[1] The campaign of 1338–40 was the last upon which the Great Wardrobe followed the king abroad as a travelling treasury, and the year 1359–60 the last in which, from its now stationary office at Westminster, the main Wardrobe handled the bulk of the finances of a campaign. It was returning to its primitive function of disbursing and accounting for the king's Household. The same declension came upon the subordinate offices of the Great and Privy Wardrobes, though the latter's importance had never been great. In 1356 the practice of entrusting the Chamber with the custody of part of the royal estates was discontinued, and

[1] T. F. Tout, *Chapters in Administrative History*, iii. ch. 9, and v. ch. 17.

the voluntary action of the crown put an end to what might have
been an important source of personal revenue. In 1360 the
accountability of the Great Wardrobe was incorporated in that of
the Exchequer. A feature of the time which is a practical expression
of the increasing unity of government is the massing of the lesser
offices under the shadow of the old great offices at or near Westminster. In 1361 the Great Wardrobe settled at St. Andrews in
the south-west of the city. In 1365 the commons petitioned that
the king's bench should be settled at Westminster, or, when
necessary, at York. Such quiet adjustments of ministerial relations
were among the best fruits of a reign whose share in the settlement
of constitutional form has received scant justice. If Edward III
makes a greater showing in the now unpopular rôle of the conqueror of France, much credit is also due to the spirit of compromise and accommodation which made him accept administrative change without resistance and almost without comment. The
unification of the administration under the crown, the rough
conformity of the king's will to parliament, and a willing response
by lords and commons to the unending demands of the French
war, were the outcome of the administrative planning of his
earlier years, and of the new understanding that had been won
from the very violence of the brief storm of 1341. Until the king's
physical decline and the Good Parliament, England enjoyed more
ordered government than it had known since the days of Edward I,
and our constitution made a full generation of progress towards
maturity.

Revenue   The problem of revenue followed much the same course of
alternate clash and compromise as did that of administration.
The attempt to build up a new and personal revenue for the crown,
to give the king a landed estate which should be beyond the reach
of treasurer and chancellor and therefore immune from parliament, was in part a reaction to the decline of the prerogative power
of taxing by the crown. The issue was still seen only obscurely.
No parliament of Edward II's reign would claim that all supply
must be parliamentary. Such new fiscal principles as gained
acceptance in the fourteenth century did so because the facts that
underlay them were changing, not because the age had a new

theory to propound. The governing rule is that of the past: aid is by the free will of the subject; the king should live of his own. If the scope of the king's right to tax is narrower than it has been in the past, it is in part because scutage and the obligatory aids bear a small proportion to the vastly swollen mass of revenue, and in part because "the king's own" has come to mean less as his feudal status loses reality and his sovereign hold upon the nation hardens. On the other hand, the limitation of prerogative taxation was not achieved without a struggle. Neither parliament nor any-one else had any power over the king's demesne right. Edward I had defended the sanctity of the *jura regalia* wherever they seemed to be threatened, and, in the absence of any clear distinction between the sovereign and feudal qualities of the king,[1] his right to exploit the latter was limited by no existing principles as long as he kept within the rules of common law.

The fiscal history of the fourteenth century is that of a desultory *Pre-* duel between the king and the commons, in which the former *rogative* sought to supplement the aids by exploiting the profits, allowable *revenue* according to feudal theory, of his demesne lordship of the *Regnum Angliae*. Of these profits the oldest and the most easily come by was the tallage. The common right of feudalism left not only the royal lands but the royal cities and boroughs at the king's discretion as demesne,[2] for in their beginnings the townsmen were tallageable with tenants on ancient demesne. But by the fourteenth century the burgesses had risen in public estimation; "our cities and boroughs are nobly enfranchised, such franchises being heritable and approved, as of lordship, for the maintenance of lawful merchan-dise, wherein the greater part of the riches and common profit of all realms consists".[3] Tallage, therefore, was becoming an anomaly, *Tallage* the more so when the burgesses, taken into parliament with their

---

[1] The Ordainers maintained some such distinction in their doctrine of an impersonal crown, but it was not expressed with any clarity.

[2] As late as 1315, when trying to enlist the special favour of the king, the burgesses of Lostwithiel address him as from *ses demeigne gentz de sa Ville de Lostwithiel. Rotuli Parliamentorum,* i. 296.

[3] *Ibid.* ii. 332. The schedule for the Poll Tax of 1379 contains an interesting comparison of various civic classes with other ranks to whom they were to be reckoned as equivalent in wealth: "the Mayor of London pays like an Earl, £4; the Aldermen of London, each like a Baron, £2; the Mayors of the great towns of England, each like a Baron, £2; all the Jurats of the good towns and the great Merchants of the Realm pay as Bachelors, £1." *Ibid.* iii. 58.

fellow *communes* of the shires, shared with them the common aid upon moveables and even paid it at a higher rate. As early as the reign of Henry III there were signs that arbitrary tallage as demesne no longer accorded with burgess ambitions, at least in the greater towns, and the estimates of the tallagers were constantly subject to revision in favour of communities who claimed to have established a customary limit to their liability. Towards the end of the reign, London asserted that its tallage must not exceed two thousand marks, and its pleading was so directed that the king accused the citizens of claiming the right to contribute by way of gracious aid rather than by tallage, or, in other words, of denying their demesne status. In so far as the citizens were seeking to shake off the king's demesne right, their case was strengthened by the financial policy of Edward I, though it was not such as to put an end to doubt. Under Henry the royal demesnes and the boroughs had been granted exemption from the general aids in acknowledgment of their tallage,[1] but in 1283 Edward prejudiced his right in some measure by begging a "courteous aid" from towns and counties alike, and by including the burgesses in the aid of a Thirtieth which was granted in the same year. In 1294, while the special position of the boroughs was recognized by their exclusion from the Fifteenth, and by the fact that they were not summoned to the parliament which granted it, they were allowed to negotiate separately with the king's commissioners, and their grant of a Sixth must have been capable of explanation either as a tallage or an aid. Their final inclusion within the aid-paying community may, perhaps, be dated from the burgess grants of a Seventh in 1295 and an Eighth in 1296, but to be invited to join in the gracious aid of the community was not necessarily to be freed from the bondage of the demesne, and for many years the towns continued to suffer the rigour of both conditions. In spite of appearing regularly in parliament, and contributing a larger aid than the counties, they were tallaged in 1304, in 1312, and again in 1332, though on the last occasion the levy was not collected. On none of these occasions was there any

---

[1] The statement (Parliamentary Writs, i. 12) in the schedule for the assessment of the Thirtieth of 1283 that the burgesses had been taxed to the aid in the "days of the King's ancestors" is contradicted by the records of Henry III's reign.

general criticism of the crown's claim, nor does that claim ever seem to have been explicitly abandoned.[1] Rather, it fell naturally into desuetude with the changed status of the burgesses, the absorption of the demesne into the fiscal community of the shire, and the rise of other ways of taxing the towns, but its history is, for that reason, the more significant as showing the slow change of constitutional practice without crisis and even without conscious innovation. The most purely arbitrary of our taxes dies slowly with the decline of feudalism and not by any conscious effort towards the freedom of the subject.

The customs arose from the demesne right of the king, as did *The* the tallage, but from a different aspect of it and upon a different *customs* principle. They were increasingly important in the fourteenth century, and, from the ease and rapidity with which the wool subsidy could be collected, it became the mainstay of supply during the Hundred Years War. If prerogative taxation was not to become the rule, the control of the customs was therefore of the utmost importance to parliament, and it presented a problem of the greatest complexity, since it was one for which the traditional rules of gracious aid had no formula. Custom, the levy of dues upon the movement or sale of merchandise, is a right of feudal lordship which we may, perhaps, derive remotely from the franchise of toll and team, and as such, of course, as much part of the right of the crown as of that of many of the magnates; in its lowest form it was made up of various minor tolls and dues, varying with the custom of each district, and in its highest it extended

[1] The term tallage is a general one, the tallage of the demesne, and of the towns in right of demesne, being no more than a particular application of it. It is commonly used, especially by chroniclers, as a synonym for *auxilium*, *carucagium*, and the like, and for that reason it is unsafe to give it a special meaning when it is not applied explicitly to the prerogative taxation of boroughs. Hemingburgh's Latin version of the *Confirmatio Cartarum* purports to place tallage with aid upon a voluntary basis, and it was taken into the body of the Statutes of the Realm and appealed to in the Petition of Right. But the authentic French text has no mention of tallage, and Hemingburgh probably used the term in the general sense of "levy", with no special reference to the towns. The concessions made in 1348, 1352, and 1377 seem far too vague to be attached to the tallage of boroughs in virtue of demesne. *Rotuli Parliamentorum*, ii. 201, 238, and 365. But cf. Stubbs, *Constitutional History*, ii. 402. Cf. the use of "subsidy or tallage" as a general phrase for all kinds of taxation in 1376: *Rotuli Parliamentorum*, ii. 323. As late as 1450, Cade's followers complained of the excessive "taxes and tallages" which were inflicted on the country.

to the right of the king to license, direct, or arrest traffic through-out the honour of England, and of other lords to do the same in the palatinate of Durham, the lordships of the Welsh March, the lordships of the Irish Pale, and so forth.[1] By the crown it had already been used under Henry III to regulate shipping during the recurrent war with France, and, by a very ruthless interpretation of the right of arrest, to seize the goods of the merchant and to hold them until he had made his peace with authority by fine.[2]

Magna et Antiqua Custuma   One of the first acts of Edward I was to put the customs upon a regular instead of a variable basis and to treat with the mer-chants of England as a whole in order to secure their acceptance of a national tax. This was in 1275, when, "at the instance and request of the merchants" in parliament, he accepted from them a grant of half a mark from every woolsack exported, and a mark from every last of hides to him and his heirs, which became established as the *Magna et Antiqua Custuma*. The concession was said to have been made in parliament and by consent, but it was not only or principally the consent of the magnates acting in parliament as *commune consilium*, as would have been the case with an aid. The act of assent was composed of two elements, the "request" of the *communes de Marchaunz de tot Engleterre*[3]—which was given, in all probability, in consideration of some remissions of custom which are not recorded[4]—and of the individual con-sents of a number of great men confirmed by their letters patent severally issued, *unusquisque pro se*.[5] The reason for this procedure is clear, and explains much of the subsequent constitutional history of the customs. The *Magna Custuma*, being in its nature a com-mutation of certain customary rights enjoyed by the king in the royal ports and demesnes but also by the majority of the magnates within their franchises, was not an aid, did not affect the *com-*

---

[1] Thus Abbot Sampson claimed that Richard I had no right to regulate the tolls in the town of Bury, where he had no demesne right, and where that right belonged wholly to the Saint.

[2] In 1218 the marshal arrested the wool of the merchants at Bristol, and exacted six marks upon the sack for its release. Stubbs, *Constitutional History*, ii. 200.   [3] Parliamentary Writs, i. 1.

[4] Possibly, also, in recognition of the fact that a three years' embargo on the export of goods to Flanders had recently been lifted.

[5] *Ibid.* i. 2.

munitas regni directly, and so was not strictly subject to the consent of *commune consilium*. The consents legally necessary were first that of the "community of merchants", since they were submitting to a new composition for a variety of dues, and, second, that of those magnates—the letters patent of twelve secular lords are recorded —who gave their consent as individuals because they were foregoing their tenurial right, and allowing the new customs to be collected by the king's officers within their franchises.[1]

How far the bargain between king, magnates, and merchants could be construed to involve the *communitas regni* and to need the added sanction of its consent, came in the future to be a constitutional issue. In 1275 it existed only as a possible complication of the position created by the *instancia et rogatus mercatorum* and the consequent letters patent of the magnates, but it cast a doubt over the transaction and confused the formulae in which the king announced the grant to the appropriate officials. The authority of the individual letters patent, rightly described in one writ as that of *quidam magnates terre nostre*,[2] is in others given more loosely as that of *touz les granz de Realme*,[3] and in one as that of *Archiepiscopi, Episcopi, Abbates, Priores, Comites, Barones, Majores, et tota communitas regni nostri*.[4] On this, the first occasion when the customs appeared as an issue of importance, they were treated principally as the demesne concern of the king and a number of holders of franchise. The national interest in them was not consistently affirmed, and was certainly not fully realized, and a precedent was unconsciously set for the king to bargain in the future with the merchants and with any other parties who might be thought to be concerned. But still the shadow of future parliamentary claims to assent already lay over the king's right. The customs were to share neither the clear prerogative justification of the tallage nor

1 So William de Valence: *nos (Willelmus) ad instantiam predictorum mercatorum concedimus pro nobis et heredibus nostris quod idem Dominus Rex et heredes sui in singulis portubus nostris in Hibernia tam infra libertates quam extra habeant dimidiam marcam de quolibet sacco lane etc. etc. . . . percipiendam per manus custodum et ballivorum ipsius Regis*. Parliamentary Writs, i. 2.

2 *Ibid.* i. 1, no. 4.   3 *Ibid.* i. 1, no. 2.

4 *Ibid.* i. 1, no. 3. This is, perhaps, an inaccurate expansion of the formula used in the king's letters patent ordering the arrest of wool until Holy Trinity 1275: *prelati et Magnates ac tota Communitas Mercatorum Regni . . . concesserint* (*ibid.* i. 3, no. 11), but it shows that the constitutional nature of a consent given by private parties but within parliament was not clear to Chancery.

the equally clear parliamentary authority of the aids, but would occupy a debatable ground between the two, the centre of converging rights and interests which had yet to be clarified and reconciled with each other.

The taxation of 1294 and 1297 was governed by national crises and hardly represented Edward's considered policy. In both years he ignored any possible right of common consent and proceeded upon the assumption that the customs were at the discretion of the king and the merchants, and in 1294 the tolts upon wool and leather were raised to the enormous sums of three and five marks respectively.[1] In 1297, by a procedure which could have no constitutional justification, except the theory that the foreign merchants, like the Jews, were collectively within the king's demesne right, the wool of the greater traders was seized, the king giving security for future payment, while the lesser merchants were allowed to purchase exemption for a maletolt of forty shillings and to proceed with their trade. The violence of this action brought a protest from those who claimed to represent the nation, and in August 1297 the marshal and the constable included the prise, or seizure, of wool in their grievances. Edward abandoned a policy which in any case could hardly be repeated, and the Confirmation of the Charters granted that the recent prises should not create a precedent, revoked the maletolt of forty shillings, and promised that in future no such tax should be taken without consent of the commonalty of the realm. Three years later the constitutional position was set in a much clearer light by the admissions made in the *Articuli super Cartas*. For the first time the crown recognized a national concern in its handling of the merchants— "the most part of the community of the realm feels itself heavily burdened by the maletolt upon wool"[2]—and a line was drawn between the great and ancient custom of 1275, recognized as a fixed due, and any new levies to which, if they should become necessary, the common consent and goodwill of the community of the realm would have to be obtained. In addition to this, the events of 1275 were referred to in terms which threw upon them a retrospective recognition of parliamentary authority: even the *Magna et Antiqua Custuma* appears as "the custom upon wool,

---

[1] Stubbs, *Constitutional History*, ii. 551.
[2] *Confirmatio Cartarum*, cap. 6.

wood-fells, and leather granted to us aforetime by the said community of the realm ".

An acknowledgment extorted from the king in August 1297 could hardly be maintained when his authority was restored. It is, rather, remarkable that the assertion of the community's control of the customs should have been made at so early a date, for it went beyond the strict letter of constitutional right and prejudiced the *jura regalia* to a degree which Edward could certainly never have admitted. In consequence, we find him six years later turning again to the customs for revenue, and, though restricting his demands to very moderate proportions, acting with complete indifference to the constitutional principles he had been forced to admit in 1297. In 1303, his mind having been, perhaps, clarified by opposition, he proceeded towards both English and foreign merchants upon the ground of demesne right only, summoned first the Italian companies and then the English burgesses to York,[1] and, dealing with them not in parliament but in the Exchequer, offered them a bargain to which there should be no other parties, and in which no national interest was recognized. He promised a "quittance of our prises together with divers liberties".[2] The Italians agreed to add 50 per cent to the *Antiqua Custuma* in return for these concessions: the representatives of the English cities and boroughs, being offered the same bargain, refused to increase "the customs anciently due and accustomed". Edward did not press the matter—the profits of the duty would come mainly from the foreigners, in whose hands the export trade mainly lay[3]—and the *Parva et Nova Custuma* remained as an acknowledgment of the right of the crown to burden the foreign merchant by agreement, and without recognition of any parliamentary interest in the transaction. In spite of one striking victory for the principle of common consent in 1297, Edward I's dealings with the customs left him in possession of the main point of prerogative right, but with the warning that it could not be pressed too far without rousing the general resistance of the nation.

Under Edward II the customs were only occasionally a con-

Parva et Nova Custuma

[1] Parliamentary Writs, i. 134.
[2] *Ibid.* i. 406.
[3] In 1273 English merchants conducted 35 per cent of the export of wool.

stitutional issue. In 1309 [1] the Community of the Realm petitioned upon the ground of hardship against the "little customs on wine, cloth, and goods sold by weight", which formed part of the *Nova Custuma*—they were said to raise prices 50 per cent against the consumer—and the king, taking the same ground of expediency, promised to suspend the custom for a year to see where the burden really fell. In 1311 the Ordinances abolished all customs and maletolts which had been imposed since the accession of Edward I and denounced the treaty of 1303 which had brought into being the *Nova Custuma*. The prerogative use of the customs was thus definitely ranged amongst those practices which were against the Great Charter. New customs, it was said, must be by consent of the magnates. The *Magna et Antiqua Custuma* upon wool and leather was expressly saved to the crown, and, though the economic effect of uncertain and arbitrary charges seems to have been more fully understood than it had been in the past, the basing of the restriction of the king's action upon the text of the Great Charter and his promise to secure the consent of the "baronage",[2] carried the case of the opposition little further. In this it shared the vice of almost all the work of the Ordainers and would hardly be a sufficient safeguard in the future. Accordingly, in 1317 we find Edward borrowing from the merchants by way of a duty of ten shillings on the woolsack, five shillings on the tun of wine, and so forth, and turning his victory of 1322 to account by reviving the *Nova Custuma*, and placing a heavy subsidy upon the wool of both native and foreign merchants. Under Edward III the farming of the subsidy and the customs in anticipation, with a formal act of grant by parliament *ex post facto*, avoided a constitutional deadlock and assured the king of an easily accessible revenue.

Crown and opposition thus avoided serious disputes over the customs as such. As soon as they secured parliamentary tolerance, if not recognition, the main question of authority was at an end, and much the same compromise between the ancient rights of the crown and the claims of parliament was followed in the treatment of the wool subsidy. This had been resisted under Edward I and Edward II, but the initial popularity of the French war, and the idea that trade would benefit from the conquest of France, re-

[1] *Rotuli Parliamentorum*, i. 444. Cf. Stubbs, *Constitutional History*, ii. 553, for what follows.   [2] *Rotuli Parliamentorum*, i. 282.

moved some of the objections to a commercial tax. When the
king was in Flanders the merchants could be required to pay at
least a proportion of the levy in cash to the Wardrobe in Bruges.[1]
King and parliament, therefore, collaborated to make it profitable.
In 1332 the magnates advised Edward to have recourse to the
merchants, and he imposed a half-mark on the woolsack and a
pound upon the last of hides, and followed this impost by a slightly
larger one in 1333. Between 1336 and 1340 the parallel authorities
of king and parliament were curiously illustrated. In the former
year the king arrested the wool at the ports and parliament imposed the heavy tax of two pounds on the sack from natives and
three pounds from aliens. In 1337 the arrest on the wool was, on
the contrary, made by statute, and the king in Council set the
subsidy at two and four pounds upon natives and aliens. In 1339
the magnates attached to their grant the request that the maletolt
should be abandoned, and themselves substituted for it a tax of
forty shillings.[2] In 1340 parliament in a changed mood, resolved
itself into a series of committees to negotiate with the several
groups and individuals of the English, Italian, and Flemish merchants[3] to secure the arrested wool and the payment of maletolt
of forty shillings. Throughout the period parliament showed no
reluctance to recognize the need to finance the war, though it would
not assent to the king's view that the burden of indirect taxation
falls solely upon the exporter. By 1343 it had brought itself to
insist that it ought in reason—perhaps it was not sure of the point
of law—to have the assent of the commons.[4] The king in reply
evaded the constitutional issue and pointed out that, since the
price of wool was fixed by statute, it could no longer be lowered
to the disadvantage of the English producer. From this time onward, however, Edward took the precaution of anticipating any
question in parliament by pledging the whole of the customs to
a group of English merchants, the magnates rejected the commons'
protest in 1346 because of the emergency of the war,[5] and in spite
of resistance, which was based upon the statute of 1340, the practice

---

1 Rotuli Parliamentorum, ii. 120.   2 Ibid. ii. 104.
3 Ibid. ii. 122: dont, Seigneur . . . nous ferroms de jour en autre a traiter ove
Marchandz et totes maneres de Gentz ove queux nous purroms.
4 Ibid. ii. 140: qar ce est encontre reson, qe la Commune de lour biens soient par
Marchandz chargez.   5 Ibid. ii. 161.

Parlia-
mentary
control of
subsidy

was continued until 1362,[1] when the king promised that no subsidy or other charge should be placed on wool or leather without assent of parliament. In 1371 he repeated the assurance and apparently recognized his previous promise as constituting a statute.[2]

The technicalities of revenue, though the indirect taxes might rise to fifty thousand pounds in a single year, would not be of great interest were they not part of the process by which the various elements, public, private, feudal, and sovereign, of the king's power were being brought into a single concept of royal authority exercised under the eye of parliament. Under Edward III prerogative revenue might well have become a fatal issue between king and people. By 1377 that risk had been averted by good sense on either side, while at no single moment was the conflict of prerogative and parliamentary taxation such as to cause real anxiety to the crown. It is an immense result to have been achieved without serious constitutional discord, and it is typical of the process by which the country was moving from a feudal to a parliamentary régime. Feudalism looked in general to a fundamental custom as the security for its right, and to feudal war, more or less violent, as the law's safeguard. The Great and the Forest Charter and the host of armed vassals in *commune consilium*, or, in the last recourse, in rebellion, were the two bases upon which the thirteenth century rested. We may see the progress towards a less archaic view of the state in the appearance of the first additions to the body of fundamental law, the *Confirmatio*

Summary
of the
progress
under the
Edwards

Cartarum, the *Articuli super Cartas*;[3] perhaps, also in the ordinances of 1311. By the broad fact that they took parliament as the executant of their policy, the Ordainers were leading the country away from the feudal habit of amendment or redress by royal prerogative under threat of diffidation. But the victory of parliament, a real one over the ensuing period of fifty years, was not won in any spectacular defence of liberties, was made possible, indeed, by a

---

[1] *Rotuli Parliamentorum*, ii. 271.   [2] *Ibid.* ii. 308.

[3] In the first century of its history statute in parliament gained its peculiar authority as much from its association with the Charters as from any notion of the preëminent right of parliament. *Qe la Grande Chartre, la Chartre de la Foreste, et les Estatutz faitz avant ces heures . . . soient fermement tenuz et gardez*, is the first petition of parliament.

process of slow and piecemeal reform which destroyed the usefulness of the great feudal leagues of the past. Common and frequent
petition, without the threat of force, took the place of prolonged
discontent and the abrupt presentation of a confused cahier or
grievances at the point of the sword. Changes no longer came by
violent crises divided by long periods of sulking, but by the
milder pressure of successive parliaments. There was much that
was imperfect and inconclusive in the petitions and statutes of the
fourteenth century. The commons' requests were often ill-con-
ceived and badly presented, so that the power of the king and
Council to reject, to distinguish, and to recast petitions was as vital
to the country as the right of petition itself. But the great fact that
the crown and nation were kept steadily informed of each other's
needs, and that what was common ground between them could
be embodied in the new expedient of statute and so be added to
the permanent body of law, was a revolutionary change from the
rigidity of feudalism. In so far as it had the imagination to do so,
the nation obtained the power to determine its own future and to
shake off the dead hand of the past. In statute, indeed, and in the
less permanent ordinances in parliament and letters patent, was
found a new power to change not by rebellion nor by the unchecked initiative of officials. It hardly detracts from the greatness
of the change that few of the constitutional principles of parliament were yet established, or even recognized for what they
would come to be. That maladministration, or law which had
outgrown its usefulness, or innovation that created hardship, were
already habitually petitioned upon by the representatives of all
the shires in common, that the king habitually accepted such parts
of common petitions as were unobjectionable, and gave them
permanence as statutes, that statute in parliament had come to be
established as the highest kind of law, overriding all prescription,
all these things as the settled practice of parliament make up a far
more significant phase of the constitution than the period of
crystallization which succeeds it. It is to the reigns of the three
Edwards that we owe the creation of parliament, and the peaceful
and almost unnoticed growth of its most essential principles.

Nevertheless, Edward's reign was not to be lived out in complete unanimity. The peace of 1360 created a financial crisis, since the motive for the granting of extraordinary aids vanished. The Exchequer tried to bring revenue and expenditure together by systematic finance, and even produced between 1359 and 1364 the first national budgets, though they were inaccurate and incomplete; but the attempt to carry on a peace government without the revenue which a fourteenth-century parliament would only grant for war had little prospect of success. When the sums allocated for various unavoidable charges were written off, the king had barely £3000 a year to spend, and the deficit for 1362–3 was £55,000, and that for 1364–5 £65,000. As against this, the French ransoms had brought in some £200,000 by 1364. In the face of this it is remarkable that a parliament was found in 1369 to advise Edward to resume the crown of France, and to grant a three years' subsidy upon wool and a clerical tenth to promote his claim. Indeed, the opposition which clouded the last years of the reign first showed itself in excessive loyalty to the crown, when, after the unhappy experience of the campaign of 1370, the court party in the parliament of 1371 attacked the ministry of William of Wykeham and Bishop Brantingham, and in general the prelate in office, much as Edward had attacked Stratford thirty years earlier. Disillusion was coming upon the country, but it did not yet involve the king or the princes. Nevertheless, from this time onwards opposition grew. The lay ministry—Scrope of Bolton and Thorpe as treasurer and chancellor—blundered in finance, the prince returned ill from Gascony, and the king was compelled to emerge from retirement and take the relief of La Rochelle upon himself. One by one the great figures of the court were discredited: Pembroke was captured in 1372, Edward's expedition failed, John of Gaunt ruined his reputation by the *chevauchée* of 1373. After 1373 the king's age kept him inactive and, though he came to parliaments, most of his time was spent at Windsor, Sheen, or Eltham. Councils were held at Westminster without him, and his influence upon the detail of government declined. The prince, also, was ill, and John of Gaunt was absorbed in foreign schemes, and often abroad. The influence of Alice Perrers began to dissolve the court party, which had already suffered from the loss of its leader Pembroke. In April 1376 the first parliament for three years, which was to gain the name of the Good Parliament,[1] met under the influence of the Prince of Wales and William of Wykeham, convinced that the virtue had gone out of the old king's reign, and prepared to attack the whole conduct of its recent years.

As the exponent of the accumulated discontent of the years since 1373, the Good Parliament is proof of the extent to which the general frame of government, and the relation of its parts to each other and to the whole, had found stability and acceptance. The leaders of the opposition, and its temper, were utterly different from those of the reformers under Edward II. The demand was now not for revolution, but for the right use of the constitution as it then stood, for the punishment of those who had worked the system corruptly and for an enquiry into the misdirection of the king's finances. The impulse of what had been the Lancastrian party of feudal constitutionalists was now almost entirely spent. The attack was a parliamentary one, directed, more than by any other influence, by the commons, and, in so far as they were strengthened by support from outside their order, it was by the encouragement of the prince, and of William of Wykeham, who had lost his chancellorship in 1371 to the party whose successors were now themselves under impeachment. The commons called, as they had sometimes done in the past, for the advice of twelve of the lords, but those whom they helped to choose for the task were not of the temper of the Ordainers, and stood rather for the sound military and administrative loyalty of the middle years of the reign. The gravamina of the opposition were presented as commons' petitions through a prolocutor, Peter de la Mare, and their first requirement was for an audit of accounts. The Staple had been manipulated to enable individuals to rob the crown, the king had incurred debts to his favourites at exorbitant interest, and they had been allowed to buy up his bad debts from his creditors and secure their payment by court pressure. The courtiers and merchants specially indicted were the chamberlain, Lord Latimer; Richard Lyons, who had acted as broker for the wool subsidy; William Ellis of Yarmouth, his deputy; and John Peach, who had

The
Good
Parliament

---

[1] The best contemporary account of the Good Parliament is found in the *Anonimalle Chronicle* (ed. V. H. Galbraith), and in the *Chronicon Angliae, 1327–1383* (Rolls Series). The former is of exceptional value as a record of the detail of procedure.

bought the monopoly of sweet wines for London. At a later phase
in the crisis Alice Perrers was accused of securing unjust sentences
by maintenance, and banished upon the curious ground of the
statute prohibiting women from practising in the courts of law.

All this is significant of a new though, perhaps, transitory
strength in the commons, and of the decline of the leading power
of the magnates, and it has the constitutional interest of being the
first great occasion when impeachment by the commons was
directed against ministers who were not also in the enmity of the
king. Still greater interest is to be found in the fact that no
minister, except the chamberlain, nor any part of the constitution
was attacked, that all the commons' indignation was reserved for
les privez le Roi, and that their demands for change sought for the
strengthening of the constitution in the form into which it had
already settled. To almost all the commons' petitions Edward
could answer that they were already provided for by statute, and,
in granting the afforcement of the Council by certain lords named
in parliament,[1] he was able to insist that the chancellor, treasurer,
keeper of the Privy Seal, and other officers should not be subject to their censure. "The king and his sons" were actually made
the judges of any councillor who might be accused of taking
bribes. So far had matters come from the days when the main
purpose of every opposition was to secure control of the great
ministries,[2] and to fetter the king with baronial councils. Edward
III's reign at its weakest produces not a constitutional crisis but an
attack upon ministers and financial incompetence. It is clear, also,
that the knights are confident of their power to serve the country
and express its grievances adequately, for annual parliaments and
the election of representatives [3] "by the best men of the counties"
are the only constitutional demands of permanent importance made
in 1376. The Parliamentary Crown may be said to have achieved
its settled embodiment and to have been accepted by the nation.

[1] Apparently not as a measure of distrust, because the number of "officers
the king has had about him are insufficient for such great government as the
wars at the same time in France, Spain, Ireland, Guienne, and Brittany call for".
Rotuli Parliamentorum, ii. 322.

[2] Richard Lyons' handling of the impositions on wool "without any controller, record, or responsibility to the Treasurer", is reminiscent of the former
tendency of the household offices to become irresponsible, but the attitude of
the commons is entirely different from that of their predecessors. *Ibid.* ii. 323.

[3] *Ibid.* ii. 355.

V

1377-1485

i

THE DECLINE OF THE MEDIEVAL COMMUNITY

"BEHOLD, Lords, whether there was ever Christian King or Lord *Intro-* that had so noble and gracious a lady to wife and such sons as our *duction* Lord the King has had, both Princes, Dukes, and others. For of the King and his sons all Christian peoples have had fear, and by them the Realm of England has been most nobly amended, honoured, and enriched, more than in the time of any other King. And our Lord the King may here, by the grace of God, see the son of his son, and has sent him as his Lieutenant to this Parliament to give you comfort and joy of him, as it is said in the Scriptures, 'This is my beloved son, this is the desired of all nations'. But if we his subjects desire and will to prosper in his grace in this year of Jubilee, and to take comfort from him who is the Vessel of Grace or chosen Vassal of God, needs must that we set ourselves in all virtue to receive that grace and to flee all wrongdoing."[1] These were the words of Adam Houghton, the chancellor, in his charge to parliament in the Jubilee year of Edward III, in what was to be the last parliament of his reign. As a forecast of the immediate future it went beyond any natural good fortune that a realm under a minority could expect, but not beyond the reasonable hope of one who looked back upon the long stability of England under the Plantagenet kings. In spite of intervals of factious rebellion, the English state had grown steadily in strength and unity in the past two hundred years, till it was to all appearances the most firmly based in Europe, and the commons acknowledged that Edward had "set them beyond the servitude of other lands".[2] The chancellor's words, however, contained a warning. If the crown was at once stronger, more national, and set more equably

[1] *Rotuli Parliamentorum*, ii. 361.   [2] *Ibid.* ii. 276.

towards every member of the state, than it had ever been, that virtue which he posited as the condition of future prosperity was a fact no longer to be assumed without question. If we may take it to be that peculiar virtue upon which Angevin, Norman, and Saxon government had in fact rested, the virtue of the lawful man, whose oath was unquestioned, and whose integrity was the safeguard in turn of Saxon judgment and Norman inquest, the fourteenth century had degenerated from the past. Part of the appearance of decline in public virtue is due, no doubt, to changes in the nature of records, and to the new power of the commons to present fraud and violence before the parliament in general terms. Common petitions tell us more and more explicitly what are the prevailing social vices. But even so, the parliament rolls show that the honesty of provincial courts was declining, that the law itself was coming to be a weapon in the hands of the unscrupulous, and that open violence was on the increase.

The beginning of decline in justice   The period of the Ordinances either gave the opportunity for misconduct or encouraged the counties to appeal against it. In the Hilary parliament of 1315 the commons turned the weapon of petition for the first time against the lords, and showed how county influence could be used to pervert the forms of justice into oppression. The matter of the petitions[1] is to be familiar in time to come, but in that year it was new. Lords invent trespasses on the part of their enemies and secure commissions of oyer and terminer for justices who are favourable to them. They influence the sheriffs to appoint days of trial without warning the defendants, and so they lose their case by non-appearance. They appoint places for trial in *Period of the Ordinances* remote districts where their victims dare not come, and have juries empanelled who know nothing of the cause. In suits of land great lords maintain each other, so that the opposing parties dare not proceed. Much of the technique of the legal tyranny of the fifteenth century seems already to be familiar. It can hardly have been entirely new in 1315, but at least it has never been so clearly and so generally exposed. Already the principal vices which were to bring the medieval order to ruin are present, lordship unlawfully exercised,[2] the corruption of juries, sheriffs who use the letter

[1] *Rotuli Parliamentorum*, i. 290.

[2] Matthew Furness could not be sued in the county court of Somerset *pur sa seignurie*. *Ibid.* i. 289.

of the law to deny fair trial, justices whose decision is prearranged. Innocent men, it is said, may be put falsely upon their defence for charges involving a few shillings, and led from process to process till their amercements amount to hundreds of pounds and their estates are sold to pay them. Two stock figures of the coming anarchy, the lord who "maintains" his friends at law by the un-avowed threat of his wealth and influence, and the conspirator, are already a threat to the commons at large. Conspiracy, indeed, has come to be a profession, and holds whole counties in its power. "They boast that the King and his Council can never touch them".[1] It is noteworthy that the very explicit complaints of the commons got little sympathy in this time of baronial government. The Council refused to be alarmed: "Let those who so suffer seek their remedy at Common Law".[2] Nor were they more than occasionally referred to in the next generation.

The reign of Edward III seems to have taken means to restore *Recovery* order to a fairer level. Besides such devices as the annual nomina- *under* tion of sheriffs, which was imperfectly observed, the Conservators *Edward III* of the Peace were, by statutes of 18 and 34 Edward III, empowered to hear and determine charges of felony, and now, as Justices of the Peace, acted in the intervals between the itinerant commissions. Nevertheless, the declining strength of the reign weakened the local peace also, and the petitions of the Good Parliament de-nounce much the same state of affairs as did those of 1314 and 1315. It is to be noticed, however, that the intervening half century has brought about a change. In 1315 much of the blame was laid upon the sheriffs. Not only the community, but several counties individually, then complained that their people were being undone by "false juries" chosen by the sheriffs.[3] In 1376, though the *Com-* commons do not trust the shrievalty entirely—they repeat the *plaints at the end of* demand for annual appointment—they attribute the dishonesty *Edward* of juries rather to the "little ministers", bailiffs, sergeants, and *III's* others, and seek a remedy in laying a responsibility for checking *reign*

---

1 *Rotuli Parliamentorum,* i. 299. "The community of England complains of conspirators who are in every City, Borough, Hundred, and Wapentake in England bound by oath to maintain and procure false parties against law and right, and have allied to themselves many of the jurors of assizes and inquests".

2 *Ibid.* i. 290.

3 *Ibid.* i. 291. Lincoln.

all juries upon the sheriffs themselves.¹ A period of steady administration had clearly led to a better control of the shrievalty, and the Good Parliament no longer wished it or the Justiceship to be elective offices. On the other hand—and the symptom was a dangerous one for the future peace of the realm—the illness of Edward, which had made possible the financial scandal of Latimer and Lyons, was also encouraging the court to extend its influence into the counties, and to use the power of the crown to pervert local government; sheriffs were being nominated *par brocage en la Courte du Roi*,² justices of Assize and Gaol Delivery were being sent out into counties where they had their lords and friends,³ justices of the Peace were being appointed by maintainers, and commonly practised maintenance themselves,⁴ and even the officers of the Exchequer were using their hold over the sheriffs to coerce them into dishonesty.⁵ The remedies suggested show an equal disillusionment with provincial election and with the crown in its weakness as the source of commissions. The commons asked that the justices of the Peace should be nominated in parliament.

But, although the corruption of the court in Edward's last years gave a foretaste of the future disintegration of society from above, the full danger was not yet evident. At the beginning of Richard's reign, though the Chancellor warned parliament that "the rule of force was coming to be divorced from the rule of law",⁶ the problem was still seen as a local one. The lords were confining themselves to the less blatant form of indirect pressure known as maintenance, livery was only realised as a danger when it was adopted by associations for conspiracy, violence seems to have been confined to bands of robbers and to the disorderliness of vagrants and unemployed labourers, and parliament still hoped to deal with it by the local machinery of the peace. In general, the middle rank of country gentry, in alliance with the sheriffs, were

¹ *Rotuli Parliamentorum*, ii. 331.
² *Ibid.* ii. 331. In the middle years of Edward III's reign there had been a marked tendency to return to the feudal practice of appointing earls to life shrievalty of counties. T. F. Tout, *Chapters in Administrative History*, iii. 188.
³ *Rotuli Parliamentorum*, ii. 334.   ⁴ *Ibid.* ii. 333.
⁵ In the next parliament the officers of the Exchequer were accused of intimidating the sheriffs to procure maintenance, *Ibid.* ii. 368.
⁶ *Ibid.* iii. 33.

looked to as sufficient to restrain the active crime of the provinces. The commission of the justices of the Peace had, indeed, wholly exceptional powers at this time, and was even coming under suspicion as a danger to feudal privilege.[1] Subordinate to the sheriffs, *The justices of the Peace* in the sense that they rendered the records of their sessions to them, they yet had a far higher justice than the old *placita vicecomitis pro pace servanda*. The ordinance of 1380[2] gave them the jurisdiction of the Statutes of Winchester, Northampton, and Westminster for the conservation of the peace, power to bind any person to keep the peace, power to search out by inquest, hear, and determine a list of offences typical of the day, robbery, maiming, homicide, the bearing of livery for purposes of maintenance or conspiracy, breaches of the Statutes of Labourers; in short, to exercise in their quarterly session far greater power than the sheriffs had held within the last century and a half, and virtually to replace the criminal jurisdiction of the eyre and gaol delivery. After the Peasants' Revolt the commons asked and obtained that the justices might hold session upon emergency when and where they thought fit,[3] and in 1392 they were given the extraordinary power of raising the counties against those who invaded their neighbours with bands of men-at-arms and archers, and the sheriffs were to place themselves under their orders.[4] Unlike that of the sheriffs, but like that of the eyre, their commission ran through every franchise. The whole jurisdiction was an extraordinary experiment in justice which was at once anti-feudal and a reversal of the hitherto universal trend towards centralization. It was typical of the day, in that it conformed to the rise of the county community and to the growth of a county interest neither feudal nor royal. Whether that interest would prove strong enough to master the problem of order within its own communities would depend at least upon the tolerance of the magnates. Significantly, the commons wished the commission of the Peace withheld from the lords,[5] and preferred provincial landowners, not necessarily

---

1 In 1380 the prelates protested against the justices' commission to try charges of extorsion as likely to impinge upon the rights of the Ordinaries. *Rotuli Parliamentorum*, iii. 83.

2 *Ibid.* iii. 84.

3 *Ibid.* iii. 118.

4 *Ibid.* iii. 290.

5 *Ibid.* iii. 44.

learned in the law,[1] but independent,[2] to visitations from Westminster.[3]

Deteriora- It is apparent that the position deteriorated fast under Richard II.
tion under The nation was coming to be sick both in head and members.
Richard II Most fatally, the central judicature was losing its independence,
and the judges of every class, forgetting that they should be as lions
beneath the throne, were seeking lordship. By 1384 "the justices
of both Benches and the Barons of the Exchequer were retained
and salaried by lords and others",[4] and habitually took great
bribes. Justices of Assize were commonly sent into their own
countrysides, where they had formed ties of lordship "and had
great alliances and affinities".[5] Judgments, when rightly rendered,
were made valueless by falsification, perversions of the verdicts
really returned, or erasure from the rolls,[6] and in the provincial
courts it was often impossible to obtain any sort of record by
which a case might be carried in appeal. Ordinances were made to
stop these abuses, but, whatever betterment may have resulted in
the central courts, the commons came to lose all faith in the
itinerant commissions, and to regard the eyre, trailbaston, and oyer
and terminer as disastrous to the counties they visited and devoid
of all judicial value. They would welcome commissions of oyer
and terminer if assigned to men of standing in the district to be
visited and chosen in parliament,[7] though the hold of Chancery
had been so far loosened that numbers of such commissions never
reached the persons to whom they were assigned,[8] but almost
yearly after 1382 they petitioned against the itinerant judge from
Westminster under whatever commission he came.

Clearly, the decay of the integrity of royal justice brought the

---

[1] They held that two justices with legal knowledge among the six or seven
in the county would be sufficient. *Rotuli Parliamentorum*, iii. 65.

[2] In 1439 the commission had to be withheld from all who had less than £20
in yearly rent, since the poorer justices had proved open to bribery and intimidation. *Ibid.* v. 28.

[3] *Ibid.* iii. 90. The commons pray that during the war justice of eyre and
trailbaston may not run among the poor commons, but that the justices of the
Peace shall hold their courts according to the tenor of their commission. Commissions of oyer and terminer were especially hated, and commons petitioned that
they should only be issued if the plaintiff could get three substantial men to
back his application. *Ibid.* iii. 94.

[4] *Ibid.* iii. 200: *sont de retenue et as fees des Seignurs et autres.*

[5] *Ibid.* iii. 139 and 200.   [6] *Ibid.* iii. 201.
[7] *Ibid.* iii. 140.   [8] *Ibid.* iii. 498.

nation to the edge of incalculable possibilities. The high royalist principles of Richard II, the foreign and English titles of the princes, his French alliance, and the luxury of his court, were worthless substitutes for the primitive legal virtue of past generations[1] and the iron administration by which the stronger of his predecessors had kept the realm in check. Social and political life was passing into a dissolution, and the forms in which it would reconstitute itself were still not to be conjectured. Richard II's commons seem to have diagnosed the danger rightly, and to have seen it as one in which the provinces must find their own salvation with little help from a corrupt or powerless judiciary. To raise the justice of the Peace to a judicial monopoly in his county, to make his authority as far as possible ubiquitous and immediately applicable when disorder broke out, and to give him the military support of the shire, was the general purpose of their petitions. The policy, sound enough in the circumstances, though it involved the admission that the Angevin judicial bureaucracy was no longer trustworthy, was vitiated by one unavoidable weakness—the commons had not the support of any sufficient body of the magnates, who, indeed, were themselves learning to profit by anarchy, and they neither dared to employ them as justices nor to attack them in their petitions. They could not venture to go above the substantial shire-knight for their justices, and, beyond a general accusation of maintenance, they never dared to force their charges against the nobles home; the small man who took a lord's livery or sought his favour against the king's law was petitioned against; the great man who shared his guilt equally went unquestioned, or it was left to the crown to draw the inference of his implication and to turn the edge of the statute against him.[2]

It is not entirely safe to assume that disorder and conspiracy is *Recovery* accurately reflected by commons' petitions, but if we take them *under the* as a rough guide we shall be inclined to conclude that the reign *first Lancastrians*

---

[1] Though the complaint that the justices of the Benches were in the fee of the nobility may partly explain that habit of putting aside their opinion in favour of his own when causes were on trial before Council which was the practical expression of Richard's principle that the "law is in the king's mouth".

[2] Thus in 1393 the commons' petition for a penalty of £20 for those who obtain writs from nobles to hinder their adversaries from proceeding against them at Common Law. The crown includes in the penalty the lords who issue such writs. *Rotuli Parliamentorum*, iii. 305.

of Richard II saw the first serious deterioration of public order, that the accession of Henry IV was marked by some attempt to grapple with the problem, that this was not entirely unsuccessful, that the reign of Henry V was one of good peace,[1] and that a really acute phase of the disease set in again in the thirties after a generation of comparative improvement. The accession of Henry Bolingbroke was at least marked by the first attack upon livery as a crime of lords rather than of their retainers and by the restriction of it to its legitimate use as part of the decencies of a great *Statutes* man's household. By a statute of 1399 livery of company, *i.e.* the *against* military livery of the squires, men-at-arms, and valets, was done *livery* away with in England in time of peace, except for the servants of the king, and even the king's men were to wear it in the presence only.[2] In 1401 the livery of peace, the badge and livery of cloth, was restricted to the counsellors, ministers, and menials of the magnates, though the king's livery and the prince's livery of the Swan might be worn throughout the realm by the noble families and by gentlemen of lesser rank about the court.[3] The penalty for disobedience to this new sumptuary law was fine at the king's mercy, and it was not till twenty years later that its abuse became again a subject of complaint in parliament.[4]

Disorder, conspiracy, and forcible disseizin did not cease during the reigns of Henry IV and Henry V, but they would seem to have been in part warded off to the frontiers[5] and to have been less a chronic condition than an outcome of the periodic rebellions. The violence of the nobles is specially mentioned in the autumn parliament of 1402,[6] and in 1417 the general unrest, which the authorities associated with the Lollard movement, showed itself

---

[1] An assize which the parties proposed to attend "with strong party on bothe sides" was in 1420 sufficient to provoke a letter to the Council from Sir Thomas Erpingham then an "agid man evermore willyng and desiryng good pees". The Council admonished the parties to present themselves attended by none but men of law. H. Nicolas, *Proceedings and Ordinances of the Privy Council*, ii. 272.   [2] *Rotuli Parliamentorum*, iii. 428.
[3] *Ibid.* iii. 477.   [4] *Ibid.* iv. 329 (1427).
[5] Henry V's first parliament presented a series of articles for the restoration of the Peace which they considered to have been indifferently guarded in the last reign. "Due obedience to the laws within the realm" came last in a list calling for good governance in Ireland, the Marches of Wales, Scotland, and Calais, the Duchy of Guienne, and the safety of the sea. *Ibid.* iv. 4.
[6] *Ibid.* iii. 497.

in "assemblies in manner of insurrection armed and arrayed to make war".[1] But, as in the matter of livery, the handling of the danger was more decisive than it had been under Richard, or than it came to be under Henry VI. The powers of the justices of the Peace were extended; after the rising of Kent and Salisbury Council decided to allot them armed retinues salaried by the crown [2] and the commission was sometimes used as a summary, quasi-military jurisdiction over wide areas of country, as when in 1406 Prince John and Ralf Nevill held it jointly "for the parts of the North";[3] but there is also renewed confidence in the central judicature. The chancellor was enjoined to accord special assizes without suit at common law in the case of violent disseizin, to punish the aggressors with imprisonment,[4] and to associate with each such commission a justice from one or other of the Benches. The justices of the Benches had, moreover, regained the country's confidence as justices in oyer and terminer, and in the dangerous year 1417 it was to such commissions, nominated by the chancellor, that the government of Bedford had recourse.[5]

If the first two Lancastrian reigns gave the country some small *Decline of* measure of that "abundant governance" that the commons *justice* demanded of Henry IV, five years of minority would seem to *Henry VI* have brought all the old evils to the surface. Council was making a creditable fight against the growth of faction upon a national scale, but corruption and conspiracy were regaining their hold on the provinces. 1427 was a great year of grievance. The justices of the Benches were retained in private interests,[6] the justices of the Peace were being made helpless by maintenance, the livery statutes were not kept, the election of the shire knights was corruptly managed, assize jurors were bought, the sheriffs were the tools of greater men, and, through their power over juries, the law of the country was at their mercy.[7] In 1430 the dangers of maintenance

---

[1] *Rotuli Parliamentorum*, iv. 117.
[2] H. Nicolas, *Proceedings and Ordinances of the Privy Council*, i. 109.
[3] *Rotuli Parliamentorum*, iii. 604.
[4] *Ibid.* iii. 497.   [5] *Ibid.* iv. 114.
[6] William Paston of the Common Bench was said to have had retainers of fifty shillings yearly from the town of Yarmouth, of the abbot of Ramsey two marks, of the town of Lynn forty shillings, and so on, "against the king for to be of their council for to destroy the right of the king". *Paston Letters* (ed. Gairdner), no. 19.
[7] *Rotuli Parliamentorum*, iv. 329-331.

figure in the chancellor's charge as one of the principal reasons
for the summoning of parliament.[1] Council also was induced in
this year to pass a self-denying ordinance renouncing livery
and maintenance for its own members.[2] The virtue of the
lawful man and the sanctity of oath, upon which the English
Attempt to system had rested for a thousand years, had been replaced by
reform the their characteristic perversions, maintenance, false verdict, and
jury system fraud. The parliament of 1432, believing that integrity might still
be found in the substantial landholders, wished drastically to
narrow the field from which the most vital juries—those of attaint,
which pronounced upon verdicts challenged as false—were chosen,
and would have excluded all who had less than five pounds of
annual rent of freehold from such panels.[3] To this the Council
refused its consent, though it had accepted a parallel petition for
the limitation of parliamentary franchise to the forty-shilling freeholder, and it is, indeed, likely that the decay of political morality
had spread to all classes. Without the restoration of a strong crown
and some sharp restriction of liberty there could be no reform.
Neither Henry IV nor Henry V had had the qualities needed for
such a lead from the crown, the lords were indifferent or guilty;
the knights of the commons, still holding to the tradition that shire
government was the prerogative of their class, could see no solution but the fortification of the commissions of the Peace and an
occasional resort to oyer and terminer in times of crisis. By the
thirties things had gone so far that neither of these jurisdictions
could surmount the strength of local interest and the prevalence
of conspiracy, and both were sharers in the very abuses they were
set to repress.[4] Fifty years earlier the chancellor had warned parliament that "law and might were divorced in England"; the

---

1 *Rotuli Parliamentorum*, iv. 367.
2 H. Nicolas, *Proceedings and Ordinances of the Privy Council*, iv. 64.
3 *Rotuli Parliamentorum*, iv. 408. Raised to £20 a year in 1436. *Ibid.* iv. 502.
4 H. Nicolas, *Proceedings and Ordinances of the Privy Council*, v. 39. A curious
instance of the clash of these two jurisdictions occupied the Council in 1437.
Two commissioners, Peke and Ludshope, had been sent to enquire into felonies
and insurrections in the Midlands. They set up their sessions at Silshoe, whereupon Lord Grey, a justice and of the quorum of Bedfordshire, came with sixty
armed men, complained that it was his town, that the intention was to "vex his
tenants", and threatened that if the court was continued he would set up his
own sessions and take the enquiry into his own hand. The king's commissioners
were forced to withdraw.

commons of 1436[1] confessed the truth of his warning in the bitter experience of its fulfilment: "Please oure said Soveraigne Lord to consider, that the Triall of the Life and Deth, Landes and Tenementz, Goodes and Catalles, of every Persone of his Lieges remayneth and stondeth, and dailly is like to be hade and made, by the othes of enquestes of xii men, and to considre also ye grete dredeles and unshamefast Perjurie that orriblely contynueth and dailly encresseth in the commune Jurrours of ye said Roialme".[2] In 1442 the chancellor's charge to parliament turned mainly upon the "horrible crime of perjury more prevalent in these days than ever before",[3] and a few years later a justice of Common Pleas, whose honesty had won him the name of the "Good Judge", felt it necessary to urge a friend, who had been wrongfully ejected from his tenement, not to have recourse to law, "for, if you do, you will have the worse, be your case never so true. For he is feed with my Lord of Norfolk, and is much of his counsel, and also you will get no man of law in Norfolk nor in Suffolk to be against him, and, forsooth, no more might I, when I had a plea against him. Therefore my counsel is that you make an end, whatsoever the pay, for he will else undo you and bring you to nought."[4] England had fallen into that most irreparable form of tyranny in which centuries of effort have built up the safeguards of individual right upon the guarantee of popular verdict, and fear and favour have made honest verdict unobtainable.

Generations probably do not vary greatly in their inherent *Underly-* capacity for virtue. A decadent age is one in which energy, *ing causes* devotion, and altruism have been diverted from their conventional *of the* channels into others which are either indifferent or inimical to *of order* established institutions. At such times traditional social and political practice is upon the defensive, and, finding it without a creed, the idealist is apt to be driven to extremes of impracticable theory, and the unimaginative mass finds secondary and often unworthy objects for its loyalty and ambitions. It would be difficult, though

1 *Rotuli Parliamentorum*, iv. 501. So again in 1439, false indictments, perjury, conspiracy by sheriffs, etc. *Ibid.* v. 28, 29.
2 *Paston Letters* (ed. Gairdner), no. 42.   3 *Rotuli Parliamentorum*, v. 35.
4 *Paston Letters*, no. 28. *Rotuli Parliamentorum*, v. 181.

of extreme interest, to determine the underlying causes of the disillusionment which came upon the end of the fourteenth and the first half of the fifteenth centuries. There had been a succession of party revolutions, beginning with the reign of Edward II, in which one group of the ruling caste after another had convicted its rivals of treason, and from the Good Parliament onward the royal house allowed itself to be involved. There was, no doubt, weariness and some despair with the war, and the insecurity of the sea was bringing ruin to the ports of the Channel. But the causes of disillusionment went deeper and had troubled men of thought and religion while the reign of Edward III retained something of its glory and while social disorder was still kept within bounds. A significant change had long been growing upon the temper of scholastic thought. In the thirteenth century, in so far as the theory of the state went beyond legal and moral generalizations as to the duty of the ruler, it was catholic in the sense that it sought to reconcile the existing orders of men and institutions within a universal whole, and so leaned towards a constitutionalism which found a political function for every estate. As the work of men of learning and religion, it lacked urgency of feeling and was neither very deeply reasoned nor the fruit of much experience. In England this mild constitutionalism had shown itself in the clerical support which the barons had enjoyed in 1258, but it did not survive the test of political strife, and already in the papal and imperial quarrel of the early fourteenth century controversy was stirring deeper levels of thought; the left wing of the Franciscans was attacking the material

Break-up of the catholic unity basis of the church, and Marsiglio and John of Jandun were fore-shadowing a secular justification of the empire. Such radical questionings were unlikely to form a unified system, nor did the various critics of the catholic world-order necessarily draw upon each other, although authority, challenged for the first time, tended to confuse them in a general condemnation. Wycliff's doctrine of dominion by grace, in fact a very specialized application of the accepted doctrine of the divine trust of all rule, was consistently denounced by Rome as "the heresy of John of Jandun of cursed memory", and in this there was at least the truth that it was a rationalizing of political pessimism, reflecting no reality

Political infidelity save that inner unrest which its creator shared with his generation throughout Europe. Such theory had indeed no value for the

times, as Wycliff himself confessed, and, though the two movements can hardly have had any close relation to each other, the
vague and exalted Christian democracy of the Peasants' Revolt
more nearly expressed the political creed of Lollardry than did
the principles of any movement or party of the day.

Wycliff himself feared so modest a threat to the stability of
property as the confiscation of the lands of the alien priories, withdrew before the consequences of his own doctrines, and left them
to trouble the country for fifty years, during which Lollardry and
social rebellion became firmly identified in the mind of the
orthodox.[1] The wide spread of Lollardry among the poor was a
symptom of a general refusal to accept the old fixities of social
order, and especially those burdens and duties which had no warrant
but custom or ancient agreement. The rising of 1381 was in the
main one of free peasants, copyholders, gavelkinders, sokemen,
small burgesses, who, if they were under any shadow of villeinage
at all, had ceased to regard it as anything but an invidious and
unreal survival. Asserting the human dignity of the individual, the
natural man in his right in the Christian community, they saw its
chief enemy in a conventional rule of law, and vented their anger
upon monastic and borough archives and upon the lawyers. The
suppression of the rising and the hanging of its leaders could not
restore that essential of civil life, belief in the validity of the law's
right over the subject. Scepticism of its claim, and readiness to
deny legal rights upon general grounds of humanity and public
interest, often associated with religious libertinism, continued to
show themselves, occasionally in the form of serious risings as in
1417 and 1431, more constantly in resistance to particular obligations by individuals which yet reveals the rebellious mind of the
objectors.[2] By the second quarter of the century any heat of

1 Cf. the commons' petition of 1414 against Lollardry: "forasmuch as great
insurrections have been lately made in England . . . by those who are of the
sect of heresy called Lollardry with the intent to annul and subvert the Christian
faith and the law of God within the said Realm, and also to destroy our right
sovereign Lord the King and all manner of estates of the said Realm, as well
spiritual as temporal, and all political order (*toute manere pollicie*), and the very
laws of the land". *Rotuli Parliamentorum*, iv. 24.

2 Like that friar John Bredon, who, in supporting certain recalcitrant
parishioners of Coventry against the priory of St. Mary there, called the Prior's
rule the "Thralldom of Pharaoh", and committed himself to the dictum that
"eny custom howe long so ever hit be, thowe hit be of a hundred yeres, if hit

feeling and thought in such matters seems to have come to be confined to the masses, or to an occasional eccentric among the clergy or the learned; after the one effort of 1381 the social discontents did not gather head in rebellion. But the dead-weight of indifference and disillusionment paralysed those who had the task of maintaining law and order upon the established principles. Men continued to act wrongly in practice because they had no guiding principles of thinking.

If the strength of the age was renouncing the old habits of loyalty, belief, and obedience, it must needs find others by which to live. While the schoolmen had nothing or, rather, worse than nothing to offer for their guidance, the times were alive with new sources of power and the community set itself instinctively to exploit them unguided by the traditional sanctions of authority and with leaders who had no altruism and little political sense. It would be wrong entirely to eliminate the original structure of feudalism from the living forces of the fifteenth century. Some of the Conquest honours survived more or less intact, though the first Norman nobility had passed away. But that feudalism which had been so mastered and confined by the Plantagenets as to be a safeguard of provincial stability rather than an excuse for disorder had lost much of its force. That trend in legislation of which *Decline of* Edward I's statute *Quia Emptores* was the type, whatever its in-*feudal* tention, had made for the dissolution of great honorial estates, *authority* and the number of small tenures which were immediate to the crown had increased largely, while at the same time the decline of feudal values had been emptying the tenurial tie of its implications of loyalty and strengthening its meaning as a business contract. Commutation of services had begun to undermine the solid villeinage of the midlands—though the midland peasantry were still politically inert beside the turbulent gavelkinders and free

be in prejudice of commone wele it is unlawfull". The Council scented civil as well as ecclesiastical sedition—"against God's law and oures"—and the friar had to recant in the parish church. H. Nicolas, *Proceedings and Ordinances of the Privy Council*, vi. 43 (1446). So in 1440 the abbot of St. Edmunds complains that "daring misdoers daily make resistance and interrupt the franchise against all good rule of the law of your realm, and will suffer no law to be executed therein". *Ibid.* v. 125.

sokemen of the east—and tenure by copy of court roll was giving a new stability even to villein right. The peasantry were not alone in their impatience with the older, tenurial lordship. A commons' petition of 1379,[1] though it is true that it was directed to the one point of contribution to the payment of members of parliament, objected to lords taking the phrase *lour Hommes* so widely as to include those who hold freely or by court roll. It might indeed have been well for the peace of the country if the oaths of homage and fealty had retained more of their force, for the common law had made its terms with them and brought them within sufficient safeguards. The feudal oaths required man and lord to maintain each other at law, but not to the point of perjury or intimidation, and their right to use force in each other's defence had since the twelfth century meant almost nothing. But, as the exploitation of land for living had given rise to feudalism in the past, so now the coming of capitalism and wealth for profit was working towards a new integration of society, which was to reproduce the worst features of feudalism without its stability and almost without restraining rules. Edward III's battles were fought chiefly with *Rise of* English mercenaries, and, as the war dragged on into the second *extra-legal* generation, the fortunes and reputations made in France brought *lordship* to the fore men who had neither tradition nor property in land. Of these military notables the bannerets were the type. They were men who had served the king with at least ten lances, and who had been ennobled for their service upon the field of battle, and among them were such men as Sir John Chandos, the Fleming Walter Manny, Cobham, Dagworth, and Calverley. Many of them sat among the magnates in parliament, where the bannerets are recorded as the lowest estate of secular nobles, and, of course, in the Council, and his Gascon birth did not prevent Guichard d'Angle from being made an English earl of Huntingdon. The *The new* influence and popularity of the bannerets was not without its *chivalry* effect upon the prestige of the titular nobility, as an incident recorded by Froissart shows. The earl of Oxford, sitting at the prince's table, protested at the cup being presented to Chandos before himself. Chandos told him, "for all who liked to hear", that he himself served the king with sixty lances, Oxford with only four, and that he had waited to be ordered by the king before he

[1] *Rotuli Parliamentorum*, iii. 64.

came abroad: "So I may of right be served and walk before you, since my dread Lord the King of England and my Lord the Prince will have it so". In fact thirty years of war were bringing into being a new chivalry, more exacting than the old and calling forth loyalties which cut across the remaining feudal ties, and the Order of the Garter, which was its focus, has been called "a new nobility by livery". Like feudalism before it, this new social relation had its material nexus, not usually of land, as was that of the former, but of pensions and wages. From the king, who made his newly created dukes and earls pensionable upon the Exchequer, downwards, the propertied classes were reviving the old voluntary associations of lord and man which had prevailed in the tenth century, divorced, as those still were from land, and contracted by indentures for a term of years or for life, but, unlike them, unfettered by legal restrictions, and as time went on increasingly indifferent to right and wrong. The origin of the revival was

The new lordship military, and it never wholly lost its military character. Edward I had gradually replaced the *servitium debitum* of feudalism by the more adaptable and efficient system of salarying barons, bannerets, and knights to raise their own contingents for his wars, and they in their turn began to retain knights and troopers in permanency. A transitional form between the old enfeoffment and the new salaried indenture may be seen in those grants of lands by great nobles in Edward I's reign, of which the earl of Norfolk's cession of the manor of Lidden in Norfolk to John, Lord Segrave, is typical. Segrave was to bear the earl's livery "in as rich a guise as any banneret may", to serve him for life within England, Wales, and Scotland against any man but the king with six knights and ten men-at-arms, and beyond the sea with twenty knights at hire. Such treaties, accompanied sometimes by leases of land, but more often at wages, soon spread beyond the circle of the mag-

Indenture and livery nates and formed associations of liveried and salaried retainers under men of standing which were invaluable to the campaigns in France but which gradually crept into civil life and began to constitute a new and dangerous kind of seigneurial influence. For a long time these "affinities", as they were sometimes called, escaped the criticism of parliament, to which only covins and conspiracies which used livery for confessed robbery were suspect. As late as 1389 livery was permitted by statute for those who had bound themselves as retainers by sealed indenture for life.[1] Until the middle of the fifteenth century it is, perhaps, true that the life indenture was the least dangerous form of the new salaried association, but with the reign of Richard II indenture for the period of a specific undertaking was being encouraged upon such a scale as to offer the opportunity of rebellion to any noble who could put his hand upon a supply of ready money. Neither king nor parliament saw the danger but rather encouraged it. In 1382 six hundred men-at-arms and nine thousand archers went to the Scotch war under the banner of John of Gaunt. Lancaster himself, Buckingham, and Bishop Despenser, were encouraged to lead armies out of England upon their own concerns but with public sanction and support, and, by these licensed arrays of thousands of the king's lieges in the pay and livery of a subject, the growth of the abuse proceeded logically until in 1403 the Welsh Border and the North could be raised "by gathering of power and giving of liveries",[2] and brought to battle with the king at Shrewsbury. Nor was it possible to go to extremes with the rebels even when Hotspur was dead and Northumberland a prisoner. The lords, "having heard and understood as well the Statute of Treasons of 25 Edward III as the Statutes made against Livery", adjudged the earl, who, though he had marched towards Shrewsbury, had not reached it, not guilty of treason "but guilty of trespass only",[3] and he "humbly thanked them for their righteous judgment".[4]

The reign of Henry VI saw an intensification of all those relations *Revival of* which honest men feared under such names as covins, affinities, *seigneural* indentures, and the like, and which now flourished so in peace as *justice* to place standing armies at the disposal of the more powerful lords, and so to fill the courts of the shires and the hundreds, the shrievalties, the benches of the justices, and the jury lists with men sworn "of their affinity", that the king's writ was of no

[1] *Rotuli Parliamentorum*, iii. 265.

[2] *Ibid.* iii. 524. "Secretly assembled and marching to join him (the earl) with the crescent badge on their arms". H. Nicolas, *Proceedings and Ordinances of the Privy Council*, i. 210.

[3] *Rotuli Parliamentorum*, iii. 524. Hotspur and Worcester were taken as the principals and condemned of treason, but their lands in fee tail were allowed to descend to their heirs. *Ibid.* v. 12.

[4] The commons had maintained that the lords must of necessity know much of the rebellion which the king could not know, and demanded that they should conduct the trial *sanz curtoisie faire entre eux en ascun manere.* Ibid. iii. 524.

effect except for the men of the predominant party. One curious
result of this hardening of local power in the hands of provincial
partisans was a sinister parody of those franchise jurisdictions
which had long ago lost their vigour to the Benches, the Eyre, and
the itinerant commissions. Some lords were great enough to set
up conciliar tribunals of their own, trying causes[1] and issuing
writs of summons counter to those of the king, and forcing
plaintiffs to show cause why they had had recourse to the royal
courts against the lord's retainers.[2] Others, less sure of their
immunity, used the hundred and wapentake courts, where "the
little ministers" were most easily intimidated, and brought actions
there for trespass against those who defied them. For their own
persons, the lords resisted or evaded the king's jurisdiction and
ignored writs of the Great and Privy Seal summoning them to
Chancery or Council.[3] In these ways, and by every device by
which an intricate and supposedly popular court procedure could
be turned to the advantage of a predominant clique, the centralization of three centuries was undone, and the country came to be
parcelled out into spheres of influence, where no will prevailed
but that of the great man and his affinity. The commons could
say against one who is generally held to have had the county's
welfare at heart, Henry VI's earl and duke of Suffolk, that he "had
made Shirreves to be appliable to his entent and commandement
. . . whereof ensued that they that would not be of his affinitie in
their Countreys were oversette, and every mater true or fals that
he favoured was furthered and spedde".[4] So, the lord Percy of

---

[1] *Rotuli Parliamentorum*, iii. 285: "The king's lieges are made to come before
the Councils of divers lords and answer there for their free tenements which
ought to be proceeded on according to common law".

[2] *Ibid.* iii. 305: "So that the said plaintiffs dared not proceed".

[3] One Northerner, Percy of Egremont, "withdrew him from his dwelling
place accustomed, and kept him apart in secret places" when summoned to
answer to Council and parliament for his disorders in the North. *Ibid.* v. 395.

[4] *Ibid.* v. 181. It is worth recalling that five years before parliament had
represented to the king that Suffolk "hath been to labour all his days for
conservation of the peace in the King's laws within this Realm in repressing
and expelling all manner riots and extortions within the same". *Ibid.* v. 73.
But the *Paston Letters* amply illustrate the prevalence of his influence in East
Anglia, cf. *Paston Letters* (ed. J. Gairdner), nos. 53, 56. "There xal no man
ben so hardy to don nether seyn azens my lord of Southfolk, nere non that
longeth to hym; and all that have don and seyd azens hym, they xal sore repent
hem", no. 66.

Egremont from his Cumbrian stronghold terrorized the neighbouring parts of Yorkshire, Cumberland, Westmorland, and
Northumberland: "whereof your people of the same shires have
been and yet be, sore hurt, vexed, and troubled, and dare make no
entry, nor action attempt upon nor against them at the law, for
fear of death, to their likely destruction".[1]

The power which was displayed in successful opposition to the
normal course of the law was a tremendous incentive to lesser
persons to seek lordship, and the strength of the greater families
grew by its own momentum. The crown itself, forgetful of the
carefully sustained policy of attrition, by which the older feudalism
had been reduced to manageable scope in the twelfth and thirteenth
centuries, lent itself to the building up of local supremacies for the
great families of the Welsh Border and the North. It was held that
"March should suffice against March", and to realise this economy
of force Edward III and his successors deliberately put lands,
custodies, and offices into the hands of the Nevills and Percies,
until only the accident of their mutual hatred saved the north of
England from being at their mercy. The Percies' achievement of an *The
Nevills
and
Percies*
exceptional standing was in part the work of Edward III, by whom
Henry Percy IV was made earl of Northumberland and earl marshal.
By this earl's marriage with Maude de Lucy, widow of Gilbert de
Umfraville, the de Luci honours of Cockermouth, Copeland, and
Wigton were gained in 1385, together with the Umfraville's castle
of Prudhoe. Richard II made him warden of the Northern
Marches, and, for his support of Henry IV, he received the Isle of
Man in inheritance, the custody of the lands of Mortimer, and the
constableship of England. In 1403 the district of southern Scotland
—Roxburgh, Selkirk, with much of Berwick, Peebles, Dumfries,
and Lanark—were made over to him, though his power there was
not made good before his rebellion and fall. The Nevills had always
been barons of importance in the North. They rose to an equality
with the Percies under the first earl of Westmorland, Ralf Nevill
of Raby, who made his career under Edward III and Henry IV,
the latter giving him the castle and honour of Richmond, the
custody of the Dacre heir and lands, and part of those of the earl of
Wiltshire in minority. Lord Furnevall, Ralf's brother, was given
Annandale and Lochmaben Castle. In the fifteenth century a

1 *Rotuli Parliamentorum*, v. 395.

persistent marriage policy made the Nevills more powerful than their rivals. Ralf's second son acquired the earldom of Salisbury by marriage with the heiress of the Montacutes, his fourth son became Lord Latimer, and the fifth married Elizabeth Beauchamp and became Lord Abergavenny. His sons-in-law were Lord Dacre of Gilsland, Lord Scrope of Bolton, Richard, duke of York, Henry Percy, earl of Northumberland, and Humphrey Stafford, duke of Buckingham. In 1459 parliament reminded the king of the earl of Salisbury that "he and his had in rule all your castelles and honourable offices fro Trent northward".[1] It was the North that first became entirely unmanageable by the crown at the approach of the Wars of the Roses in 1453 and 1454, when the feud of the younger Nevills with the Percies called out large armies and caused the pitched battle of Stamford. For this the crown was in some measure to blame, for since the beginning of the fourteenth century it had neglected that careful diplomacy of marriage by which Henry III and Edward I undid the domestic league of their nobles, and drew them generation after generation into the royal circle. A far-reaching marriage policy such as Ralf of Raby's would have met with decisive opposition from either of these kings.

Affinities   Besides the titles and the lands properly annexed to them that these great lords held, and which the crown could in some measure have controlled, there was the ever growing accretion of influence which flowed in to such centres of "good lordship" during the fifteenth century, and which neither Council, parliament, nor king seemed able to check. The crown was content to bribe the principal magnates into loyalty by grants of land and custodies, and there were a countless number of subjects who were willing to buy protection on the same terms. When Henry IV's earl of Northumberland fell, a special section in the act of forfeiture was needed to deal with "the lands with which persons have enfeoffed the Lords Northumberland and Bardolf for the great confidence they had in them for the furthering of their desires".[2] Thus landed wealth accumulated more by the mere attraction of its influence. There was, moreover, a vast system of affiance with-

[1] *Rotuli Parliamentorum*, v. 347.
[2] *Ibid.* v. 11: *pur la graunde affiance que gentz que eux enfefferont avoient a eux, de fair ou perfournere lour voluntee.*

out land, in which an exchange of pledges by way of indenture—
"saving the faith due to the King"—bound lord and client to
support each other, so that by 1450 whole countrysides stood in
the same patron's obedience, as did northern Yorkshire to the
Nevills, Cumberland to Henry Percy, Lord Egremont, and
Suffolk to the duke of Suffolk. There the duke in the days of his
ascendancy was a better patron than the crown and the king admitted that it was so.[1] All this had its effect in the sphere of law
before it came to be openly decisive in politics. From soon after
the accession of Henry VI the local courts became inaccessible to
any but the predominant party, traps for the man who had not
lordship, where he might be ruined by false indictments, bought
juries, and partial judges. Even the great ecclesiastics were at the
mercy of oppressors "coveryng theym under lordship".[2] In the
middle of Henry's reign "affinities" and livery began to tell in
politics also. Parliament could be overawed by them, men came
"armed and arrayed in manner of war" to the elections,[3] and, if
held in one of the great spheres of lordship, they were helpless like
the parliament of Bury St. Edmunds in 1447, or the Lancastrian
parliament of Reading in 1453.[4] At last the Yorkist influence in
London became so strong that the king could not with safety hold
parliament there. The government itself was in part to blame for
bringing force into parliament. In 1449 Suffolk urged the lords
"to come in their best array and with strength";[5] for the parliament of February 1454 the great lords engaged whole quarters
of the city—Somerset bought up the lodgings about the Tower,
St. Katherine's, Mark Lane, and Thames Street—and sent the
weapons and harness of their retinues before them, riding up
themselves with armies of "every man that is likely and will go
with them" raised by public proclamation in the shire towns.[6] In

---

[1] H. Nicolas, *Proceedings and Ordinances of the Privy Council*, v. 125. The
abbot of St. Edmund's to the king, 1440: "the earl of Suffolk is a grete lord
in the cuntre and goodly to your said monastery. Like it unto your hieghnesse
and good grace to geve him in comaundement undir your grete seal to support
and maynteyne and defende youre seide monasterye and correct suyche personys
as be there mysdoerys and opresseres." (The king issued letters patent to that
effect.)

[2] *Loc. cit.*   [3] *Rotuli Parliamentorum*, v. 8.

[4] Stubbs, *Constitutional History*, iii. 167.

[5] *English Chronicle* (Camden Society), p. 62.

[6] *Paston Letters* (ed. Gairdner), no. 195.

February 1458 the Lancastrian lords came "with great power", and it was left to the Londoners to proclaim that they came against the peace and to refuse them lodging.[1] The royal family itself is carried away inevitably in the current towards militarism and begins to build up vast liveried associations throughout the country.[2] Such was the end of the long chain of decline through the petty dishonesties of juries, the weakness of bailiffs and justices, and all that decay of strength and integrity in local government which at last brought it about that dependence and lordship were necessary for survival both for the great man and the small. It is the end of an age if, as we well may do, we take the supremacy of the law as the cardinal principle of the medieval world; and the attempt of the weakened monarchy to master disorder and con-spiracy by the traditional expedients of continual council and parliament, and its substantial failure, is the main theme of the constitutional history of the fifteenth century.

ii

PARLIAMENT, COUNCIL, AND THE NEW FEUDALISM

Intro-
duction   The history of the constitution in the fifteenth century sees much advance in practice without the formation of adequate constitu-tional theory to direct and maintain it. There is no doubt that parliament is already esteemed the highest embodiment of the government of the realm. But historically this is so because in the past parliament was the highest court of the king, that in which he himself sat and with the fullest pomp and power of his regality. The estates have come to be conjoined with the parliament, the Great Council sits in parliament, and brings with it what survives of the virtue of the ancient *commune consilium* of magnates, and the commons have risen to a new status, in which their assent is necessary to the full and common consent of the realm. But when we come to examine this in practice, its effect is seen to be partial, imperfectly applied, and intermittent. The feudal authority of the

---

[1] *English Chronicle* (Camden Society), p. 77.

[2] In 1459 Queen Margaret "made her son called the Prince give a livery of swans to all the gentlemen of the county (Chester) and to many others through-out the land". *Ibid.* p. 80.

commune consilium is in process of being forgotten, that of the commons is new and unconsolidated. It is true that when the fullest approval and confirmation of the community of the realm is sought it is to parliament that the king goes, but as yet there is no rule of constitutional law to determine what must be done with such approval and what can be done otherwise. Aid is, and has for long been, increasingly matter for parliament, but the limits of what the king can exact by ways other than commons' grant are barely fixed. Change in the fundamental common law can only be made in parliament, but the restriction is one hard to define when concrete cases arise. War, peace, treaties, matters of state, the descent of the crown, are all matters which will be most fully established if they have been passed upon by lords and commons, but there is no rule that every man would accept, and in times of emergency the king and the Council will act without apology and ask no indemnity afterwards. The value of parliamentary authority is still less that of establishing acts and laws as against the will of the king, or against that of groups or orders of the community, than of giving to any enactment the permanence which was attributed to statute, together with the full publicity and acceptance of national assent. The older feudal dissension between crown and magnates has been fought out and finished; the final clash between crown and commons will not come until the seventeenth century. It is a time when there are few fundamental differences as to the constitution, when king and commons, and the lords also in some measure, proceed upon the assumption of common interest, and can meet without friction in parliament, accepting each other's advice and consent as useful elements in a common decision, without deeply questioning the right from which they proceed. One effect of the absence of constitutional controversy—the reign of Richard II is, of course, a partial exception—is the absence of any historical sense as to the growth and institution of parliament. The commons make statements as to what is the "ancient use and custom of Parliaments" which could be contradicted by the memory of a normal lifetime, and no one cares to correct them.[1] Another is that king or commons make or

<hr>

[1] Thus in 1388 they claimed that impeachment was among the "ancient ordinances and liberties of Parliament". *Rotuli Parliamentorum*, iii. 232. As early as 1376 they believed that the county representation in parliament was *de*

admit from time to time claims which seem to us, from our more experienced view, to presuppose wide principles of autocracy or parliamentary right, but pass them almost without comment. Things are done in one parliament which ought to set the precedent for a radical diversion of the line of constitutional progress, but are done without emphasis or debate and forgotten in the next. It is a time of apparent clashes of principles which produce no explosion and pass without effect, only to be denied the character of an age of constitutional experiment because the variety of practice is the result of indifference to rules which we think essential but which are then made and broken lightly as advantage serves.

In spite of a kind of shared inertia as to fundamentals, there are, of course, repeated dissensions upon minor issues, mainly upon the spending of the revenue and especially that part of it which goes for the royal household. For that reason, the commons of Richard II and Henry IV are constantly trying to control the size, personnel, and expense of the king and queen's households, and, partly from the same motive, they concern themselves in the membership of the Council, though both these interests begin to flag with the reign of Henry V and the renewal of the war upon a great scale. Because of these recurrent disputes, the rule of the house of Lancaster, with its prelude in the unsuccessful attempt of Richard II to rule by prerogative, has acquired the reputation of being a time of constitutional experiment. It would be wrong to deny that habits of parliamentary initiative—especially that of the commons—and a great deal of compliance on the part of Henry IV and Henry V, do give the appearance of a new character to the period. Henry IV is the first king to whom it has happened to say in the face of opposition that he "well understands that that which the Lords and Commons do or ordain is for the welfare of himself and his realm",[1] though he himself can see no reason for their actions. The generalization is, however, a dangerous one if it prepossesses us to interpret every act of parliament and crown in the light of modern constitutionalism. There is a real increase in parliamentary experience, a real improvement in procedure, and at times, as in 1401, 1404, and 1406, a display of new energy in

---

commune droit du Roialme: ibid. ii. 368. The clergy also are ready to assert that their aids never were and ought not to be granted in parliament: *ibid.* iii. 90.

[1] *Rotuli Parliamentorum*, iii. 525.

parliament. On the other hand, a great deal of this was by allowance of the crown, a great deal of initiative remained to king and Council and had not been conceived of as a possible function of parliament, we find little consistent theory, and certainly no general principle of constitutionalism entertained by the crown or urged consistently by the commons. Above all, as we approach the middle of the century, the decay of order begins to affect every aspect of life, and the progress which has been made towards parliamentary government becomes more and more a mere screen for dynastic and party intrigue. As these forces assert themselves there is a decline not only in the independence, but in the energy of parliaments. Those of the late 'thirties and 'forties do little but petition upon commerce and trade, and the requests of individuals. They have almost ceased to grapple with the prevailing lawlessness, and the charges made at the opening of sessions become lifeless and perfunctory. In 1437 they are content to leave a body of unfinished business to the Council, who are asked to dispatch the outstanding petitions and have them inserted in the Parliament Roll;[1] Richard II's requirement of a parliamentary commission to continue such business after the day of dismissal at Shrewsbury had been a principal charge against him, but it was a less serious derogation than this to the competence of parliament. The weakness of the commons is confirmed under the Yorkists, when they seldom moot business of real national importance and when parliamentary legislation is beginning to be made at the initiative of the crown. To sum up the balance of loss and gain in constitutional progress under the Lancastrians is, and must remain, an attempt at generalization which can produce no exhaustive formula, for to do so assumes principles which were only slowly being built up out of the experience of contemporaries. Parliament is strong by allowance when government is strong, weak—and with little courage to assert its rights upon principle—when faction is dividing the nobility and the country is in disorder. From much parliamentary activity little change in the theory of the state emerges and certainly no clear doctrine of a parliamentary crown.

It was inevitable that a further century of practice should

[1] *Rotuli Parliamentorum*, iv. 506.

Structure of parliament

develop and stereotype the procedure and the nominal rights of parliament; apart from a period of success and some formal advances in the first Lancastrian generation, it probably lost rather than gained in power during the fifteenth century, and suffered the same decay as was coming upon all the institutions of a degenerate community. Nevertheless, however unreal the development may have been in apparent parliamentary right, it was capitalized in the later ages of the real power of parliament, and must be studied for its own sake and for our understanding of the future. The most difficult problems still centre upon the structure of parliament, its houses and estates. Already the substance of these divisions had been achieved. They were the product of the formative reign of Edward III working upon an original dualism in function and personnel; but a minority was still sufficient to revive the function of the magnates as a *commune consilium*, the original trustees of the self-government of the nation and in a more ancient right than that of the commons,[1] and official language had not yet been brought into accord with modern developments. The term "estate" was already in use before the end of the fourteenth century, but the commons of 1381 still applied it to denote all the various components of parliament. "The said commons pray, that the Prelates by themselves, the great temporal Lords by themselves, the Knights by themselves, the Justices by themselves, and all the other Estates separately, be charged to treat and consider of their charge".[2] The idea of three estates against the crown has not yet mastered the forms of parliamentary language. The king's judicial officers are still involved among the estates,[3] and in this, if in no other feature, common speech is still determined by the tradition that the

The estates

---

[1] Thus in 1427 Council decided that the king's authority was complete in spite of his nonage "but the execution of the king's said authority . . . belongeth unto the lords spiritual and temporal of this land at such time as they be assembled in parliament, or in great council". H. Nicolas, *Proceedings and Ordinances of the Privy Council*, iii. 233, 238. In 1377 the prelates and commons were addressed together by Richard Scrope without the temporal lords, who had clearly been in council on the minority as the constituent authority of the new reign. *Rotuli Parliamentorum*, iii. 5.

[2] *Ibid*. iii. 100.

[3] This still seems to be so in 1406, when the justices are commanded to make observations upon the ill-government of the country along with the peers and commons. *Ibid*. iii. 579.

Council *ad Parliamenta* is the core of the institution. The parliamentary estates are not yet reduced to three, and are therefore not yet fully accepted as standing for the future three estates of the realm. Indeed, if we replace the term "estate" by the older *gradus* the classification is that of the author of the *Modus Tenendi Parliamentum*. Half a century of change has not yet been assimilated. If the commons of 1382 put too low a value upon the growth of coöperation within the various orders of parliament, those of 1401 carried their acknowledgment of the consolidation of the estates of the realm too far. Blending the clerical and temporal orders into one, they spoke of a realm of king, lords, and commons, "showing how the Estates of the Realm may well be likened to a Trinity, that is to say the person of the King, the Lords Spiritual and Temporal, and the Commons". Clearly language is wavering between several interpretations and reflects a variable parliamentary habit, but it is moving towards its final choice, and in 1421[1] there swore to the Treaty of Tours the *tres status Regni*—the "Prelates and Clergy, the Nobles and Magnates, and the Communities of the said Realm". This also is a mixed conception in which the estates of the realm and the estates of parliament are not clearly differentiated,[2] but it marks the virtual realization of parliament's final form. The completed formula comes with the reign of Henry VI, when "the King and the Three Estates of the Realm" are recorded as the components of parliament.[3] The components of the estates—lords spiritual and temporal on the one hand, and commons on the other—had, of course, long been accomplished fact,[4] but we have to wait until late in Henry VI's reign for the convenient phrase the "two Houses of

[1] *Rotuli Parliamentorum*, iv. 135.

[2] The "Prelates and Clergy" make up the first estate of the *Realm*, while the assent to the treaty can only have been that of the estates of parliament.

[3] *Ibid.* v. 213: *Domino Rege et Tribus Regni Statibus in pleno Parliamento comparentibus.* This quotation shows that the estates of the parliament were still regarded as the estates of the realm in parliament, since by representation they bore their persons. *Report on the Dignity of a Peer*, App. v. p. 213; 11 Hen. VI: *in trium statuum ejusdem Parliamenti presencia*; *Rotuli Parliamentorum*, v. 213: *Domino Rege et Tribus Regni Statibus in pleno Parliamento comparentibus*, 1450.

[4] The last occasion on which the burgesses were treated as a separate order was in 1372, when they were kept back after the knights had gone home, and, "in a room near the White Chamber", made a grant of sixpence on the tun of wine. *Ibid.* ii. 310.

*The
Houses*

Parliament" to denote it. In 1450 "the Speker of the Parlement opened and declared (the charges against the Duke of Suffolk) in the Commen Hous", and "there were sent unto the seid Chanceller certeyn of the seid Hous" to convey the commons' further indictment of the duke.[1] Finally, a gradual realization that the Council and the executive form no part of the parliamentary estates is marked by the admission of the judicial officers themselves, who, consulted by the lords as to the privilege of freedom from arrest in the case of the speaker, Thomas Thorpe, answered in 1454, "that it hath not be used afore tyme that the Justicez should in eny weye determine the Privilegge of this high Court of Parlement".[2]

Membership of parliament: the peers

The personnel of parliament, and the right by which its members attended, is clearer than in the fourteenth century. The quality of peerage is at last being clarified. Bishops, dukes, and earls, and the holders of the new honours of marquess and viscount, presumably sat without question. Their creation had always been by letters patent; for this reason there was no doubt of their title, and peerage of parliament seems to have been assumed to inhere in it.[3] But with the baronage a new procedure has to be recognized. In his eleventh year Richard II made the innovation of creating a baron, John Beauchamp of Holt, by patent,[4] and, though he was only summoned once, in the year of his creation, and nearly half a century elapsed before the next patented barony was made, Henry VI created nine between his eleventh and twenty-seventh years. There is little doubt that the reduction in the number of those who were called to parliament by no higher title than baron was one of the reasons for this departure, and that part of its motive at least was to strengthen parliament[5]; the vital point for the history of peerage is that these patents include among the privileges of the new title a seat and precedence there. This is

[1] *Rotuli Parliamentorum*, v. 177.   [2] *Ibid.* v. 239.
[3] Nevertheless the justices determined that, although the name of earl descended by common law, the right to a seat in parliament was cognizable only by the king and the peers. H. Nicolas, *Proceedings and Ordinances of the Privy Council*, iii. 325 (1429).
[4] *Report on the Dignity of a Peer*, App. v, p. 81.
[5] Among the motives given for the creation of the barony of Lisle in 1436 is "to add to the number of those by whose counsel our realm may be guided". *Ibid.* 466, p. 245.

expressly stated by Richard II of the Beauchamp honour of Kidderminster—*locum . . . in futurum in nostris consiliis et parliamentis*—and in all the patents of Henry VI,[1] and it compels us to enquire whether the fifteenth-century peerage had not already reached its modern basis of a determinate list of honours beyond which the king did not extend the direct writ without formal creation by patent, and all of whose holders might rightly expect a summons to parliament? Had not all the ambiguities of the tenure of baronage and its relation to parliament become things of the past, and were not the peers of parliament a group of the greatest of the tenants by barony who had established a monopoly of the direct writ by prescription or letters patent?

If we go by the text of the letters patent, we shall probably answer "yes" to all these questions. In creating the barony of Sudeley Henry VI granted Ralf Butler "the estate of a baron of our realm of England as well in session in Parliaments and Councils as in other matters",[2] and in this, albeit obliquely, he seems to recognize a parliamentary quality in barony, and a writ *De Veniendo ad Parliamentum* of 27 Henry VI (which, it is true, stands alone) recognizes the modern principle that summons to parliament in itself creates peerage, for to the routine clauses summoning Henry Bromfleet it adds "for we desire that you and your legitimate male heirs shall take rank as barons de Vessy".[3] Prescriptive right by the mere fact of summons and patented creation seem, therefore, to alternate in practice, nor can we doubt that the fact that about a quarter of the barons who sat in the parliaments of Henry's middle years were secured in their parliamentary right by letters patent must have reflected favourably upon the older and more substantial baronial honours, whose titles were by ancient inheritance. If these were beginning to regard their seats as prescriptive and of right, they would be confirmed in their claim when new baronies were being accorded seats in parliament as part of their baronial privilege, and it would become increasingly hard to deny them what was secured to lesser men by royal grant. Certainly

Basis of parlia-mentary baronage: patented right

---

[1] *Report on the Dignity of a Peer*, App. v. 239: *status baronis regni nostri Angliae tam in sessione in parliamentis et consiliis nostris quam alias.*

[2] *Loc. cit.*

[3] *Ibid.* App. i. p. 919: *volumos enim vos et heredes vestros masculos de corpore vestro legitime exeuntes barones de Vessy existere.*

prescription was appealed to with increasing acceptance in other aspects of parliamentary right.

Precedence and prescription

Lords, patented and unpatented, knew their order of precedence and seating in parliament, and guarded it jealously. As early as 1405 the king decided that the earl of Warwick should be "preferred in his seat" in parliament and Council above the earl of Norfolk, and Lord Grey above Lord Beaumont,[1] and in 1425 [2] the earls of Norfolk and Warwick again disputed each other's precedency, and the blood royal of Warwick was set against an alleged prescriptive precedence, going back, it was said, to the reign of Henry III, by which the earls of Norfolk sat above those of Warwick. Parliament evaded a decision by making Norfolk a duke, but during the pleadings an "inheritance of place in Parliament" was acknowledged. Thus prescription was a recognized element in the status of peer; that it should be coming to be so, if only by custom and courtesy, would have been consonant with what was happening even earlier with the order of abbots, and with the boroughs. By the end of Edward III's reign at latest the townsmen considered that the list of parliamentary boroughs had been fixed by custom and that any addition to it was to be petitioned against by the borough affected as a result of the "malice of the sheriff",[3] while as early as 1341 it was asserted that not every abbot or prior who held by barony owed attendance in parliament, but only those whose duty to do so had been established by custom.[4] Prescription, therefore, was becoming a ruling principle in peerage, though the de Vesci writ, which was not used as a precedent, may have been thought to express it too absolutely.

Analogy of the abbacies and boroughs

Practice in issuing writs

In spite, however, of the language of the letters patent with their apparent recognition of a fixed and known body of baronial peers, the practice of Chancery was such as to make us doubt whether the crown yet felt obliged to adhere to an unvarying rule in the issue of writs.[5] Even peers by patent were sometimes not summoned; John Beauchamp sat only once, in the year of his creation,

---

[1] H. Nicolas, *Proceedings and Ordinances of the Privy Council*, ii. 104.
[2] *Rotuli Parliamentorum*, iv. 267.
[3] Cf. the case of Torrington. *Ibid.* ii. 459.
[4] *Report on the Dignity of a Peer*, i. p. 342.
[5] For the facts as to the issue of writs which follow see *Parliamentary Writs* under the years named.

for his patented barony of Kidderminster. John Cornwall, baron of Fanhope by patent of 11 Henry VI, was omitted from the parliaments of the twelfth and twenty-third years; Thomas Percy of Egremont and Thomas Grey were not summoned until two years after their creation. The barons by ancient descent were subject to about the same degree of discrimination in the issue of their writs. Lord Scales sat in the last three parliaments of Richard II and in the first two of Henry IV and in that of Henry's fourth year. He was omitted from those of the third and fifth. Lord Seymour was not called in the third and eleventh years of Henry IV. Thus the parliaments of Richard II and the Henries, except when they were depleted by foreign expedition, continued to give seats to a group of barons which did not alter substantially, but which yet varied from session to session sufficiently to make it likely that the king retained and used a certain discretion with individuals. Richard's parliaments contained about forty temporal peers of baronial rank or below it, Henry IV's thirty-four or thirty-five, Henry VI's barely half this number at first, though they were added to as the reign went on.[1] The solid block of great men whose names come in the first two-thirds of the list of writs vary little, the names which commonly stand in the last third of it vary rather more. It does not seem that party had much effect upon the membership of the upper house. Richard II made no significant changes in the summonses for the parliament of September 1397, which was to try Gloucester, and for which the writs were issued three days after his arrest.[2] Henry VI called almost exactly the same lords to the Lancastrian parliament of Reading in January 1453, as had sat in that of 1450-1451, in which there had been a strong Yorkist interest. Whether all those who were summoned attended these or any other parliaments is, of course, another matter. Thirty-seven lords below the rank of earl were invited to that of 1397, but only twenty-four took the oath

1 The drop in the number of writs under Henry V and Henry VI is no doubt due to attendance upon the king and Bedford in France. It shows, however, that Chancery does not yet summon a full list of peers as a matter of course.

2 Of those who had attended the last parliament, the lords Montacute and Zouche of Harringworth were omitted from that of 1397, while the lord Fitz Walter was added. 1395, when eleven names were suddenly dropped, is the only year when Richard II's parliaments showed a sudden change in personnel. But this is probably to be accounted for by the Irish expedition.

to hold its proceedings irrevocable. It must have been almost impossible for those who were present to avoid doing so, and it is likely that the other thirteen had absented themselves. If we are to assume that these thirteen or some of them were summoned with the clear knowledge that they would not venture to appear, there is the more reason to think that the king was beginning to feel constitutionally bound to accord the direct writ to the forty-odd lords who made up the active parliamentary nobility, and that the peerage was upon the point of becoming a closed body. Whether that obligation was actually binding during our period there must still be room for doubt, but it was coming to be so.

The personnel of the commons had reached what was to be its final form until the reign of Henry VIII, and such progress as there was took the form of definition of privilege and procedure. The commons have forgotten that their summons once depended upon the pleasure of the king, and assert that "by common right of the Realm there are and ought to be two persons elected from every county of England to be in Parliament for the commune of the said counties".[1] They claim favourable points of procedure as "the ancient custom and form of Parliament", though they may be barely a generation old.[2] Especially, since the late fourteenth and the fifteenth centuries saw the first attempts to influence parliamentary election by wrongful means, the forms of election and the right to the franchise were the subject of statute. Throughout the reign of Edward III efforts had been made, by commons' petition and by orders incorporated in the writs, to secure that only good, discreet, or sufficient knights were returned, but in 1376 it still had to be requested that the sheriffs should accord open

Freedom of election, and the request was shelved by the crown. In 1387
election Richard inserted in the writs the requirement that the knights returned should be "indifferent to the present dissensions", and in 1404 Henry forbade the election of lawyers. The commons, however, continued to prefer unfettered election, and in 1406, having protested that sheriffs were used to nominate members without submitting them to the county, obtained a statute by which forthcoming elections were to be proclaimed in every market

---

[1] *Rotuli Parliamentorum*, ii. 368 (Hilary, 1377).
[2] As that the commons should make their petitions before considering supply. Stubbs, *Constitutional History*, ii. 600.

town fifteen days before the poll,[1] and the elections themselves made in full county court. The *plenus comitatus* was, perhaps, as ambiguous in application to contemporaries as it is to us, but the intention was to secure choice by the most substantial elements in the shires, for the act of 1406 required that the names of the representatives should be written in an indenture and sealed with the seals of those who chose them, which indenture should, with the writ, be returned into Chancery. The effect of this, as far as the indentures are a guide, was to reduce the effective voices to a number which rarely exceeded forty, and might fall beneath twelve,[2] but it can hardly be doubted that those who appended their seals did so in the names of many others who had none. The statute of 1430 limiting the right to vote in parliamentary elections to those who held freehold of the annual value of forty shillings, settled the point of right, and became the rule of the constitution until the nineteenth century, but it seems to have done little to secure independence in election.

The estates were approaching their final form, but there can be no more fruitful sources of misunderstanding as to the nature of the fifteenth-century parliament than to seize upon each antici- pation of modern parliamentary practice as it appears as a perman- ent victory for popular government. To do so is to read into the second century of parliamentary history the common will and purpose, the reasoned jealousy for its rights and powers, the fuller sense of its place in the constitution, which only came to parlia- ment after it had fought its way to predominance against the Stuarts. The parliaments of Lancaster and York were still ancillary to the Council, which remained the permanent governing power of the realm, and the commons of the parliament which established the Lancastrian monarchy asked for and received a delimitation of their parliamentary function: "they are petitioners and demanders . . . saving that in making statutes, or for grants and subsidies, or in like matters for the common profit of the realm, the King wishes to have especially their advice and consent".[3] Their sessions were seldom for more than a few weeks, and not in every year, the only function that they discharged with any willingness was that of petition, and, as we shall see, commons' petitions continued

Function of the estates in parliament

[1] *Rotuli Parliamentorum*, iii. 588.   [2] Stubbs, *Constitutional History*, iii. 422.
[3] *Rotuli Parliamentorum*, iii. 427.

to be a force which was only spasmodically effective in legislation.
For the commons at least, the ideal was "plentiful governance" by
King in Council, smooth working of the courts of common law,
a crown which lived of its own and needed little subsidy from
its "poor lieges". They were never conscious of being radical
reformers; two years after the Merciless Parliament they "pray
our Lord King in full Parliament that the royal right and prerogative of our Lord the King and of his Crown be guarded and
maintained in all things . . . and that our said Lord King be as free
in his time as his noble progenitors Kings of England were in
theirs".[1] Parliaments were to secure redress for exceptional hardships and supplement the knowledge of a benevolent government.
For the king, the "four points which belong to every Christian king
to do in his Parliament were first that holy church be governed
in full peace and liberty, second that all his subjects be governed
in justice and peace without oppression, and evil-doers punished
according to their deserts, third to maintain the good laws of the
Realm, and to amend or make new law where the old is lacking,
and lastly to defend the people of his Realm from their enemies
without".[2] The commons' role is a passive one compared with that
of the great legislating parliaments of later days, but the realities
of this age, still essentially medieval in its limitations, have been
obscured, partly by the busy search of the historian for constitutional precedents, and still more by the series of political and
dynastic crises in which parliament was dragged more or less unwillingly into the train of the victorious party and used to give a
colour of popular initiative to what was essentially the legalizing
of successful faction, and this is hardly less true of the lords than
of the knights and burgesses. Except for a few great individuals,
the prelates dissociated themselves from politics and confined their
real activities to the convocations, and the secular lords were a
much depleted body. When, as in 3 Henry V or 2 Henry VI, the
number of the lords was no more than nineteen and twenty-two
respectively, some of whom were also members of the Council,
it is idle to think of the peers in parliament in terms of the great
feudal assemblies of the early thirteenth century. Powerful as
single nobles may have been, the house of lords was too weak not
to have been the prey of the predominant party in the court and

[1] *Rotuli Parliamentorum* iii. 279, 256.   [2] *Ibid.* iii. 337.

the Council, and it was, in fact, in Council that ambitious individuals looked for the political leverage to make good their schemes.

Almost without exception, therefore, parliament appears as the tool rather than the maker of revolutions. The Merciless Parliament of 1388 met under the influence of the Appellants.[1] It sat under the menace of the armed companies of Gloucester, Warwick, and Arundel, and the cause of the Appellants in the country was buttressed by the imposition of oaths of confederacy with the five lords taken in the counties and towns. All subjects were enjoined by sheriff's proclamation to lend no credence to reports or opinions against the tenor of the appeal.[2] It is not surprising that many men of standing in the retinue of certain of the magnates were not to be found when the oath was exacted. The Appellants averred that for some time past the lords of Parliament had been prevented from speaking honestly for fear of their lives. The accusation may well have been true, but the Merciless Parliament was clearly no more independent of Gloucester than earlier parliaments had been of the king. The Shrewsbury parliament of 1397, again, met under the threat of Richard's Cheshire bowmen. Intimidation had, indeed, come to be notorious as the excuse of the peers for their subservience to the predominant faction. The commons of Henry IV's first parliament[3]—who had seen many of the same lords who had judged Vere and the archbishop of York condemn Gloucester, sanction the prerogative rule of Richard, and then depose him and put Henry on his throne—asked that the lords spiritual and temporal and the justices should never again be excused from their past acts by plea of mortal fear, "for they are more bound to stand by their oaths than to fear death or forfeiture".[4]

That the commons should be disillusioned is natural enough, since in most crises, as in 1397,[5] they were driven through a show of initiative which was little more than a cover for the revenge of

Parliament in times of crisis

---

[1] *Rotuli Parliamentorum*, iii. 228. [2] *Ibid.* p. 400.
[3] *Ibid.* iii. 433.
[4] Norfolk's fears of treachery, which he confided to Hereford and thereby secured his own and Hereford's exile, show the atmosphere of suspicion and hatred which prevailed in Richard's court and paralysed all independent action. *Ibid.* iii. 360.
[5] Richard conducted his revenge on Gloucester in the form of a commons' impeachment.

the king or the ambition of a prevailing clique of magnates, for
every revolution was staged in parliament, and the law of parliament was explored desperately to give perpetuity to the statutes
by which it was sought to embody the proscriptions and dis-
herisons of the *coup d'état* in fundamental law.[1] To challenge the
statutes of a crucial parliament was made treason, as in 1397,[2] or,
as in 1387, all and singular were required to swear that they would
never consent to their repeal.[3] But parliament remained variable
as ever. In September 1397 eighteen spiritual and forty temporal
peers swore upon the shrine of the Confessor that they would
"never suffer the judgments, statutes, and ordinances of that year
to be revoked or annulled", and heard the bishops of the two
provinces pronounce excommunication from the high altar of
Westminster upon all who violated the oath;[4] at Michaelmas 1399
the same lords spiritual and temporal, "examined severally in full
Parliament", advised that the said statutes and ordinances and the
whole acts of the parliament that made them, "be altogether
repealed and annulled for ever".[5] It was natural, therefore, that
the commons, who regarded parliament as a means of sober
government, should shrink from the periodic proscriptions of
which it was made the scene. The impeachment of Suffolk in 1450
was, perhaps, the only occasion when they were clearly eager to
press an indictment against the will of a majority of the lords and
the king. In contrast, in 1399 they were careful to put it upon
record that the responsibility for the judgment of great offenders
was with the lords,[6] and in the worst crises the commons feared
to fulfil the duty of knight of the shire.[7]

---

[1] *Rotuli Parliamentorum*, iii. 359 (1397). "The Justices and Sergeants of the
King were questioned by the King whether they knew any other sure way to
confirm and keep perpetually the said judgments, establishments, statutes, and
ordinances; and they said that the very greatest surety that could be is that
which is ordained and affirmed by Parliament". On hearing this Richard had
the peers sworn a second time and meditated writing to the Pope to get papal
confirmation of the statutes.   [2] *Ibid.* iii. 372.
[3] "Then all the said prelates, lords temporal, and commons made publicly the
oath as follows. You shall swear that you will never suffer or consent as far as
in you lies, that any judgment, statute, or ordinance made in the present
parliament, shall be in any way annulled, reversed, or repealed for all time to
come." *Ibid.* iii. 252 (1387).
[4] *Ibid.* iii. 355.   [5] *Ibid.* iii. 425.   [6] *Ibid.* iii. 427.
[7] *Paston Letters* (ed. Gairdner), no. 249: "Sum men holde it right straunge to
be in this Parlement and me thenketh they be wyse men that soo doo" (1455).

No doubt a great deal of the illusion of spontaneity in commons' action was due to packing and intimidation in the counties. This is a common accusation by an angry parliament against its predecessors, and indeed it is hard to see how the interrelation of party connections about the countrysides could have left room for independent elections. A parliament which met within the sphere of influence of one of the great lords might be hardly more than a party convention.[1] In an electioneering letter of 1455 the duchess of Norfolk tells John Paston that "it is right necessary that my Lord have at this tyme in the Parlement suche persones as longe unto him, and be of his menyall servaunts".[2] Richard II is said to have issued his writs to the sheriffs, naming the knights to be returned in 1387 and 1397.[3] Northumberland's rising of 1405 denounced the unlearned parliament of Coventry as a packed one[4] and the parliament of 1460 reflected upon that of 1459 that its members were returned "some of theym without dieu and free election, and some of them withoute any election".[5]

Years like 1387, 1397, 1399, 1450, and 1460, when parliament *Parliament* was called upon to commit itself to the reversal of a régime, were *and the* *crown* exceptional. At such times lords and commons acted automatically in response to external force, and the prelates retired into politic obscurity till the storm was past.[6] On such occasions constitutional theory is not deeply involved, and even the vacating of Richard's throne—in which, indeed, the forms of resignation and the renouncing of homage were carefully preserved—followed by the act of 1404 regulating the succession by statute, left no new or deep mark upon the constitution. The so-called "statutory right" of the Lancastrian throne had so little imaginative hold that in the

---

[1] Thus, Suffolk held the parliament which was to undo Gloucester at Bury St. Edmunds, where his influence was unassailable, "and alle the weyez aboute the said town off Bury, be commaundement of the said duke of Suffolk, were kept with gret multitude of peple of the cuntre, wakyng day and nyghte". *An English Chronicle* (Camden Society), p. 62.

[2] *Paston Letters* (ed. Gairdner), no. 244.

[3] *Rotuli Parliamentorum*, iii. 235 and 420.   [4] Walsingham, ii. 265.

[5] *Rotuli Parliamentorum*, v. 374.

[6] The failure of the prelates to give any political direction is one of the cardinal weaknesses of the parliaments of this age. They made no effort to protect the archbishop of York in 1388, or the archbishop of Canterbury in 1397.

elaborate justification of the Yorkish claim by "Godds Lawe,
Mannys Lawe, and Lawe of Nature", put forward by the commons of 1461,[1] it was not mentioned even to be refuted.[2] That a
bad or incapable reign broke the bond between the king and the
lieges, and that the throne could be claimed and filled with their
assent, was immemorial belief, hardly a formal departure from
constitutional precedent, and certainly not the creation of a new
monarchy. It is true that Richard had offended the constitutionalism of the day, not only in his affront to common law and his
vaunt that "the law was in the King's mouth, and often in the
King's breast", but also by attacking what had come to be
accepted as parliamentary custom, asserting that it was for him to
lay down the order of parliament's business and dismiss it when
he would, and by dictating the personnel of the commons and
continuing full parliament after most of its members had been
dismissed.[3] But, in so far as this motive of opposition was genuine,
the remedy sought was to change the person of the king and not
to restrict the monarchy: "At the request of Richard lately King
of England . . . the Commons of Parliament granted that he
should be in as good liberty as his progenitors before him; by
which grant the said king said that he might turn the laws to his
good pleasure, and turned them against his oath (of coronation).
Now in this present Parliament the Commons, of their own free
and good will, trusting in the nobility, high discretion, and gracious
governance of the King our Lord, have granted him that they
desire that he shall be in as full Royal Liberty as his noble progenitors before him."[4]

Judgment of treason upon the defeated, and statutes revoking
previous judgments against the members of the predominant
party, decreeing the resumption of the former's lands, and in
general comprising the results of the *coup d'état*, were the means
by which revolutions strove after permanence and security, and
these things they could obtain only from the highest court of the
realm, and from the assembly whose assent to statute had become

[1] *Rotuli Parliamentorum*, v. 463.

[2] In dealing with Gloucester's demand for a definition of his powers as Protector in 1427 the lords carefully avoid any positive definition, and content
themselves with saying that Henry V could not dispose of the realm beyond
his own lifetime without the assent of the estates. *Ibid.* iv. 326.

[3] *Ibid.* iii. 417 *et seq.*   [4] *Ibid.* iii. 434.

essential. Thus revolution must pass through parliament before it becomes legitimate, and it was connivance in a legal process, and the permanence and publicity of parliamentary act, rather than the spontaneous judgment of the estates or the nation, that was sought for.

Thus it would be a mistake to think of the fifteenth-century *Parliament* parliament as a power embodying a true national will, controlling *and* *legislation* the destinies of the nation and changing them by a conscious right to revolutionize law. There was, however, greater reality and value in the routine work of parliament, and especially in that of the commons, in normal years of peace, when no revolutionary force was breaking in upon the session from without.[1] Indeed, the best warrant for the reputation of the house of Lancaster for constitutionalism in the modern use of the term lies in the larger share which the commons came to take under them in law-making. There is less difference between statute and ordinance in the fifteenth century than in the past, the terms being used almost indifferently for acts of parliament, but both have come to be referred to lords and commons before they become valid. The commons of 1376 had failed to establish the necessity of their assent to statute, but during and after the reign of Richard II bills which are put forward by the lords are minuted *soit baillés aux communes* as an almost invariable practice. In 1414 the commons are able to assert that "hit hath evere more be thair liberte and fredom that thar sholde no Statute ne Lawe be made oslasse that they yaf therto their assent".[2] At no time is it true, even in the Lancastrian reigns, that all or almost all the petitions of the commons are made good in legislation, but under Henry IV and Henry V more of them are accepted as the basis of statute than at any other time in the Middle Ages. There seems, indeed, to be a fairly consistent relation between the rise and fall of prerogative pretensions in the crown and the commons' parliamentary influence. Beginning with the last four parliaments of Edward III, we find that of 255 articles of petitions presented by the commons only five left any trace on the statute rolls, while in the reign of Richard II the periods during which most petitions were made acts in parliament were those when the king was most closely

[1] For what follows see H. L. Gray, *Commons' Influence on Early Legislation.*
[2] *Rotuli Parliamentorum*, iv. 22.

under control, 1381-83 and 1388-94. The great days of commons'
influence began, however, with the accession of Henry IV.
"Throughout his reign and that of his son practically all legislation
arose from commons petitions",[1] and what is, perhaps, even more
striking than the fact that the response by statute to petition was
continued and accentuated, is the almost complete absence at this
time of legislation by the initiative of the crown. In all Henry IV's
reign only seven statutes originated apart from the commons, and
only one of them, made in favour of foreign merchants, can be
thought to have offended popular feeling, while in that of Henry V
only a single statute was officially inspired. Moreover, in 1414,
perhaps stimulated by certain changes made in their petitions of
1413 before they were put into statute, the commons were able
to secure that in future commons' demands and statute should
correspond textually. In the course of their protest the commons
had asserted that they were "as wel assenters as peticioners",[2] and,
probably in recognition of this, the king's responses of 1414 began
with the new introduction, "the King, with the assent of the
Lords Spiritual and Temporal and of the Commons, wills. . . ."
From this it seems that amendments made in the petitions were
referred back to the commons, and that their assent was now
obtained to the final draft of statute, and at least between 1414 and
1421 this correspondence of petition and statute seems to have
remained the rule.

Up to the outbreak of the Wars of the Roses—specifically until
the parliament of 1453—the predominance of the commons in
legislation was maintained, though not so completely as before
Henry VI's accession, since their bills were more often subject to
amendment. Such amendments, however, seldom affected the
spirit of the enactments. These facts, which are the result of
Mr. H. L. Gray's examination of commons' bills and rolls of
parliament published in 1932, go some way to restoring the
view that the régime of the Lancastrian monarchy was more
"constitutional" than those which preceded and followed it.

True as such a conclusion seems to be of the means by which
statute was made, it still remains the fact that the influence of the
commons was at any period of the Middle Ages strictly limited,

---

[1] H. L. Gray, *Commons' Influence on Early Legislation.*
[2] *Rotuli Parliamentorum*, iv. 22.

and that the real power lay in the king and Council while government was strong, and in the local influence of magnates when it was weak. Even in legislation the commons' power may be flattered by dwelling too exclusively upon what they actually achieved, for the king retained his veto which was from time to time expressly recognized,[1] hardly half of the commons' petitions reached the statute rolls, and those which did dealt on the whole with matters which—as between king and commons at least—were not controversial. The regulation of commerce and trade, and the whole machinery of the Peace in all its aspects, were constantly legislated upon, but there were few great issues such as the religious problems of the following century. In legislation king and commons may be said to have been acting in an alliance under cover of which the real strength or weakness of the latter was not put to the test. When great political factions intruded personal issues into parliament the resistance of both lords and commons was, as we have seen, very easily overcome.

Moreover, in the matter of legislation proper the commons came towards the middle of the fifteenth century to find a serious rival in the crown itself, and in the last quarter of the century their initiative was largely eclipsed. The commons' bill was the principal source of statute until 1453, but the crown was already producing bills which it presented to the two houses and passed into statute.[2] These official bills were, presumably, originated in Council, and there is no sign of challenge or amendment by lords or commons. In form public bills, since they preserved the procedure of consent by both houses, they were in fact legislation by the king in parliament and without petition addressed to him, and, as might be expected, they reflect the personal interest of the crown. Typical of them are an act of 1455 appropriating £3000 to the "expenses of the King's honourable household"[3]—which may be set in

---

[1] As in 1414, when the commons themselves asserted it. *Rotuli Parliamentorum*, iv. 22.

[2] H. L. Gray, *Commons' Influence on Early Legislation*, p. 58.

[3] *Rotuli Parliamentorum*, v. 320. The change in initiative from commons to crown is marked in this case by the changed formula of the introduction—"it pleaseth the Kyng oure Soverayne Lord, by the aide and assent of the Lordes Spirituell and Temporell, and Commyns"—as against the older form of commons' petition, "prayed the Communes in this present Parlement assembled".

contrast to the contrary action of parliament in restricting the
king's domestic expenditure by commons' bills under Henry IV—
grants made to various great persons such as the king's mother
and the duchess of Exeter, bills of attainder against the king's
rebels, such as that upon the duke of York in 1459, and revocation
of patents of privilege and protection exacted from the king by
his enemies, as after St. Albans, Blore Heath, and Ludford.[1] After
1465 the acts of resumption of alienated royal lands, which had
become largely punitive in intention, were also introduced by
official bills. It is clear that the violent nature of the times, and
the need for ruthless action upon the moment, is reviving the
need for executive action clothed in parliamentary form, and the
laborious pretence of popular initiative which concealed the real
nature of the acts of 1388 and 1397 is no longer maintained. It was
to be expected that parliament would not retain in the period of
the Wars of the Roses that initiative which it had obtained in the
more peaceful Lancastrian reigns. The commons seem, however,
to have lost not only the coercive, emergency legislation which
carried on the war in parliament, but much of their constitutional
function as law-makers at large. After 1450 their influence upon
general legislation began to decline. Important commons' bills
were rejected in 1453 and 1455, under Edward IV few acts of
any kind were made, and under Richard III, and still more under
Henry VII, the crown became increasingly active at the expense
of the commons. Thus the end of the Wars of the Roses sees a
change as important as that with which the Lancastrian reigns
began. In Richard III's parliament of 1484 the old preponderance
of commons' over official bills was reversed. Nine statutes of that
year were introduced by the crown as against only four by the
commons.[2]

Parlia-
mentary
privilege

 The reality of parliamentary power in its rise and decline centres
upon the history of legislation. Less fundamental, but still issues
of importance, are those acknowledgments of the privilege and
special standing of parliament and of its members which mark its
growing prestige even if they are not always observed by contem-

[1] H. L. Gray, *Commons' Influence on Early Legislation*, p. 102.
[2] *Ibid.* p. 137.

poraries or given that importance in the constitutional order which is attributed to parliamentary privilege to-day.

"The acceptance of the Speaker completed the constitution of the house of commons".[1] From Thomas Hungerford in 1377 the Speaker of every subsequent parliament is known. He asked at the opening of every session that if he misrepresented the words of the commons unintentionally he might be held guiltless, but this, of course, conferred no general liberty of speech upon the house, and though, in general, the topics chosen for debate and petition by the "poor Commons" were not at this time likely to be resented, a sensitive king might regard any especially hostile attack as seditious and proceed against those who made it. In January 1397 Richard II denounced the attempt of the commons to control his household as against the regality,[2] and ordered the Speaker to reveal the name of the person who had prompted a bill to this end. The commons gave up the name of Sir Thomas Haxey, came before the king "in all humility and obeisance, in great grief, as appeared by their demeanour", "well knowing and acknowledging that such matters at no time pertained to themselves", and submitting themselves to the king's grace and favour right humbly. Parliament then proceeded to adjudge Haxey to death as a traitor, but on the petition of the prelates he was granted his life and committed to their custody "solely by the special grace *Liberty of* and will of the King".[3] In the same parliament [4] the commons had *speech* to make an equally humble disclaimer of any intention to criticize the king's projected voyage into Lombardy, but the events of this session were, of course, quite exceptional, and the interpretation which Richard chose to put upon Haxey's bill was extravagantly harsh. The commons explained that they had meant no more than to commend the state of the king's household for consideration to the lords in the way of humble advice, and upon many occasions the Lancastrian parliaments discussed similar matters, and made their recommendations upon them without rebuke. In fact, though, when the issue was raised formally, the commons did not

---

[1] Stubbs, *Constitutional History*, iii. 473.

[2] *Rotuli Parliamentorum*, iii. 339.

[3] *Ibid.* iii. 341.

[4] *Ibid.* iii. 338. The general charge against the commons of this parliament was that of presenting articles which would infringe "the Royal Right, Estate, and Liberty". *Ibid.* iii. 339.

venture to claim complete freedom as to the matter of their petitions,[1] or as to the terms in which they discussed them. Henry IV began his reign by a promise not to enquire too closely into the commons' debates among themselves,[2] and in 1404 the Speaker asked and received leave to report criticism of the king's own governance without offence,[3] and a very considerable latitude was accorded in practice. The abstract question of liberty of speech was hardly one which presented itself to contemporaries as of any urgency. Upon the only occasion in the Lancastrian period when the claim was made explicitly, it was by an individual, and, though the commons presented the complainant's petition, the king remitted the matter to his Council, and, as far as record goes, the grievance was not pressed further.[4]

Liberty of person   The more tangible matter of the immunity of members from violence to their persons, or from certain kinds of legal process, during the session of parliament, and while going to and coming from it, was pressed more confidently. Since the right of the magnates to judgment by their peers was of long standing, the matter was mainly one for the commons, but certain minor privileges were shared by both houses. Barony excused the lords from service upon juries and assizes, and from 8 Edward II at latest this immunity was shared by the representatives during session.[5] In 1404 the commons raised the question of violence to members of parliament, both lords and others, together with that of their immunity from arrest, in both cases claiming to extend the privilege of the member to his servants, and to those who travelled or resided with him.[6] As to their safety from assault they

[1] Haxey's condemnation was reversed on the accession of Henry IV, but only on the ground of erroneous judgment. The issue of privilege was not raised. *Rotuli Parliamentorum*, iii. 430.   [2] *Ibid*. iii. 456.   [3] *Ibid*. iii. 523.

[4] The case was that of Thomas Young, member for Bristol, who proposed in the parliament of 1451 that the duke of York should be declared heir to the throne, and was subsequently imprisoned in the Tower for his presumption. In 1455 he petitioned for damages alleging "the olde liberte and fredom of the Comyns of this lande . . . for the time that no mynde is, [that] alle suche persones, as for the tyme been assembled in eny Parlement for the same comyn, ought to have theire fredom to speke and sey in the Hous of their assemble, as to theym is thought convenyent or resonable, withoute eny maner chalange, charge or punycion therefore to be leyde to theym in eny wyse". *Ibid*. v. 337.

[5] *Ibid*. i. 450.

[6] *Ibid*. iii. 542. The case was that of Richard Cheddar, who was in the company of Thomas Brook, member for Somerset.

appealed to the special protection of the king over those obeying a royal letter of summons, and the basis of their claim was, for that reason, hardly a special privilege of parliament,[1] but they proceeded to beg that such special privilege should be established; the murder of members and their attendants was in future to be ranked as treason, and lesser assaults were to be punished by a year's imprisonment and fine at the king's mercy. The king refused to make a new crime of violence against members of parliament, and reduced the commons' demands to a stricter process to secure the surrender of the party charged, who, if he failed to present himself for trial, might be attainted in absence, condemned to double damages and amercement at the king's discretion, and this modified security was made statute and governed the law until 1433, when the commons secured the substance of their demands of 1404 while the doubling of the damages and arbitrary amercement was made the penalty, whether the defendant presented himself for judgment or no. The safeguard was, however, restricted to members and was not extended to their servants or companions.[2]

Freedom of arrest for members and their servants seems to have rested upon older principles. In 1314 Edward II issued writs to restrain all action by assize against members of either house during the session,[3] and in 1315 stigmatized the arrest of the prior of Malton on his way from parliament as against the king's peace, and as giving him a claim to damages. In 1393 occurred a curious incident, the bearing of which is doubtful from lack of evidence as to the charges involved, but which at least shows that the commons were at that time more jealous of their status than were the king and the peers. Philip Courtney, a knight of the shire for Devon, "came before the King in full Parliament saying that he had been accused and slandered to the King and the Lords both verbally and by bill of certain heinous matters", and that pending trial he wished to be discharged of his membership of Parliament. The King and the Peers thought this reasonable and "discharged

Freedom from arrest

---

[1] The later statute of 1433, also, did not confine the protection to members of parliament, for the king extended it to lords attending his Council. H. L. Gray, *Commons' Influence on Early Legislation*, p. 300.

[2] *Rotuli Parliamentorum*, iv. 453. The case was that of an assault upon Richard Quartermain, one of the knights for the county of Oxford.

[3] Stubbs, *Constitutional History*, iii. 514.

him in full Parliament". Five days later, however, the commons
asked that he should be returned to his place to take part in business, and "because he had shown himself reasonable, and had lent
himself to a compromise with the complainants" their request
was granted, "and he was restored to his good fame in full Parliament"[1]. In 1404 the commons claimed by ancient custom freedom
from arrest for debt, trespass, or contract,[2] that the freedom
should extend to their servants, and that those who infringed it
should be fined at mercy and pay treble damages. The king
admitted the principle, but said that sufficient remedy was already
available. In 1429 the privilege was defined as covering arrest for
all offences short of treason, felony, or the peace, and commons
asked for it to be put into statute, which was refused, and by the
reign of Edward IV it had become customary when occasion arose
to execute an act of parliament authorizing the chancellor to issue
a writ of release for those imprisoned on process of the crown,
and for those arrested on the suit of subjects to obtain a writ of
privilege and so stay the action till after parliament was over. The
most famous case of this kind, since it arose from party enmities
and left no doubt as to the necessity of parliamentary immunity,
was that of Thomas Thorpe, who was Speaker in the parliament
of 1453.[3] Thorpe had attacked the interest of the duke of York
during the first session of this parliament, and, upon reassembling
after a prorogation, the commons learned that he was in the Fleet
pending payment of a thousand marks damages for trespass and
theft, which the court of the Exchequer had awarded against him
in favour of the duke of York. The case is notable for the failure
of the commons to establish their principle—the only occasion
upon which it was rejected—for, after a protest by the justices
that it was not for them to meddle with privilege of parliament,
and a colourless statement of custom as we have already seen it
applied, the Lords declared without further justification for the
duke, and the commons were ordered to elect a new Speaker.
This they did, apparently without protest, and Thorpe remained
in prison. The declaration of the judges may be taken to prove
that parliamentary privilege in this matter was now firmly
established, while the issue of the case shows how helpless the

---

[1] *Rotuli Parliamentorum*, iii. 301.
[2] *Ibid.* iii. 541.   [3] *Ibid.* v. 239.

commons still were in the face of the lords' prerogative as judges of parliament, and the material power of the predominant Yorkist clique.[1] It is weakness in the face of faction, rather than privilege—unquestioned as that may be in theory—which is the truest character of the fifteenth-century commons, and, in a less degree, of the lords also.

In spite of their subservience to outside influence, the parliaments of the fifteenth century had a secure place in the constitution, and their form did not vary as the power of the king increased or diminished. Parliament met with the same fullness under a strong king as under a weak, and was allowed a greater share in legislation under the powerful Henry V than in the later days of his imbecile son. Matters were very different with the king's Council. Here, where the secrets of the king were known, where he was in daily contact with his counsellors, not as the crowned figure in parliament speaking in formal phrases to the estates, but as a man with weaknesses and prejudices or policies which he pursued behind a screen of deference to opinion, the problem of counsel was as acute as it had been under Henry III, the Council was no less certainly the real centre of government, and its form was no nearer to definition. Thus, while the structure of parliament grew to completion without controversy and almost unnoticed, the Council remained, under Richard II as under Henry III, the target of converging ambitions, the subject of conflicting schemes for its constitution, variable, responsive to the changing fortunes of king, lords, commons, and parties. Through all the controversies and struggles of the fourteenth and fifteenth centuries it was the first stronghold to be attacked by opposition and the last to be surrendered by the king. *A new form of Council*

There is, therefore, no one formula which will characterize Council of the later Middle Ages either in form or function, for both reflected faithfully the temperament, policy, and immediate purposes of the reigning monarch, or, in the times of his weakness, the views of the opposition party of the day. Among other

[1] The privilege of the lords was recognized in the case of a servant of Lord Scales arrested in time of parliament in 1450. H. Nicolas, *Proceedings and Ordinances of the Privy Council*, vi. 103.

generalizations that which sees the Lancastrian councils as parliamentary, controlled by statute, and intended to reproduce the composition and temper of the estates, is misleading, for, though such views were occasionally and imperfectly expressed by opposition under Richard II, the development of the Lancastrian reigns is towards a small but powerful Council of magnates, more strong in relation to both crown and parliament than any which had gone before it. There is, of course, no question that the king's Council was of the utmost concern to the nation and therefore to parliament, and, since the latter expressed popular grievances very freely, Council was often the subject of petition. But, looking back from the modern standpoint, it is easy to misinterpret the desire for an effective Council as a demand for constitutional control—to attribute to the fifteenth-century commons our preoccupation with the form of the constitution, and to believe that when they petitioned for "abundant governance", "wise and sufficient council", and the like, they were asserting a right to dictate the exact form of the king's Council and to control its membership. That this was not so we shall realize if we remember that commons never once presumed to suggest the name of a councillor, and only once went so near to making requirements as to its composition as to ask that it should be made up "of divers estates," that only in two years, 1376 and 1386, were wholesale changes in Council made against the king's will in compliance with parliamentary demands, and that occasional compliance with the request that the name of the councillors should be announced in parliament, and their oath taken there, in no way bound the king not to make subsequent changes as he wished. Indeed, the particular form taken by the Lancastrian Council, that of a small body of great nobles, was promoted as much by the personal policy of Henry IV and Henry V as by external pressure, and after 1423 no statute dealing with Council was passed, nor was Council sworn in parliament, nor, except occasionally, was parliament informed of the names of the councillors.

Two views of Council

But, though we cannot speak of a parliamentary régime in Council, the late fourteenth and early fifteenth centuries were faced with a conciliar problem upon which the commons held very strong views, upon which they constantly petitioned, and as to which they were, if not of the better opinion, at least of that to which Henry IV and his successors finally rallied. We shall probably come nearest to the way of thinking of contemporaries if we say that from the end of Edward III's reign two views held the field, that which desired a "continual" Council—the term appears first in 1376, and carries the implication "unofficial", since councillors who were of the household were without saying continually about the court—one in which certain notables, usually men of standing from the several estates, should be sworn to attend continually upon the king's person and occupy themselves with the national business, and, as against this, the view which accepted the king's sense of what was convenient as final in the selection of councillors, which required no defined or permanent composition for Council, and which was probably indifferent not only to the existence of a formal Council but even to the acknowledgment by individual councillors of the special obligations which were undertaken in the councillor's oath. Usually, though not always, a "continual council" was the constitutional programme of Richard's parliaments, and especially of the commons, while the king preferred to retain freedom of choice and that power to give or withhold his full confidence of which any settled rule would deprive him. In the past, Councils had usually been of the latter sort. Inevitably, the great officers, the chancellor, treasurer, keeper of the Privy Seal, and usually the chamberlain and steward, were in the king's secrets and of his Council. Beyond that official nucleus the range of the Council varied with the personality of the king. Edward I, whose preoccupation with government for its own sake imposed the same impersonal quality upon his relations with every competent minister, worked without friction or discrimination with a large council which included, with the great officers, the justices of both Benches, the chamberlains and barons of the Exchequer, a selection of knights and clerks of the Council of less specialized function, and a sufficient number of prelates and temporal lords. His Council might on occasion rise to seventy. With rather more friction, notably in the year 1341, Edward III continued to exercise his free choice of councillors, and with Richard II it was a point of principle that the king should be "free and unfettered to remove his Officers and Councillors when and as he pleased".[1]

[1] *Rotuli Parliamentorum*, iii. 258.

Under an able king the habit of distributing confidence and responsibility as the various exigencies of government and counsel required worked satisfactorily. The country submitted to thirty years of this sort of government contentedly enough under Edward III. But, because this arbitrary choice of advisers could not create a sense of joint and equal responsibility in the Council, it was essentially the method appropriate to prerogative rule, and could be nothing else. Indeed, the royal Plantagenet Council was devised less to formulate and control policy than to maintain contact with the chief ministries of war and peace, and to bring their holders into personal contact with the king and each other when consultation was necessary. Under Edward III, and, indeed, much later, large meetings of the Council were rare, the members were summoned *ad hoc*, and, if the business were of great moment, were likely to be merged in a *Magnum Consilium* of magnates, while the daily Council about the king might be no more than a handful. Many of the Council—Exchequer officials, justices, an occasional foreigner, provincials, could not give constant attendance; to them the king's confidence could be only at times and partially extended. From such a council there was absent all that sense of equal participation and responsibility which is sought in cabinet government, and for that reason, if for no other, it could never be used to embody the politics of the nation or of a predominant party and to enforce them upon the king; inevitably, it was upon these defects—the need for "continuous" attendance, and equal participation—that parliamentary criticism centred when the crown fell out of favour with the nation. There were, however, defects of a more permanent kind. It is apparent that a Council so informally conducted could not be representative of parliamentary interests, and equally it provided no safeguard against the intrusion of unpopular persons into the king's confidence, or against the monopolizing of it by self-interested groups. It is probable that the councillor's oath was not always exacted, especially from the nobles, and that men were retained of the Council as a mark of honour whom the king no longer employed actively, or whom he only consulted upon the ground of some special qualification and at intervals. Within this large and heterogeneous body the group actively coöperating in the principal concerns of government at any given moment might be kept together by the king's

Defects of Council

favour, and might represent its best or worst elements according as his sympathies lay. The worst effects of this indefiniteness were seen in the last years of Edward III, when the membership of the Council blended imperceptibly into a group of *privez autour le Roi*, some of them, like Nevill and Latimer, councillors, and some, using their influence with Council to forward their own schemes, as did Richard Lyons, who, as the commons complained, "made himself busy about the Palace and the King's Council", and got authority to act "by covin made between him and certain of the King's Privy Councillors". Thus the sovereign authority came to be accessible to private persons, and the commons marked the danger accurately in accusing Lyons of "accroaching to himself royal power",[1] since, not being a councillor himself, he presumed to act by Council's authority, as, indeed, in his defence he claimed to do.[2] Thus the Council's monopoly of counsel was insecure. Walsingham tells us that Richard II was influenced more by the clerks of his chapel than by his nobles,[3] and in 1406 parliament had the king's confessor removed, probably from the same motive.[4] All this was especially dangerous at a time when bribery, maintenance, undue influence, and all kinds of conspiracy were coming to have a strangling hold upon the community, and it was the defects of Council as giving opportunity for financial corruption which most, indeed almost solely at first, engaged the commons. As with Latimer and Nevill, so with Richard's earl of Suffolk, the clearest charges were those of misuse of office to make private profit, and in the first seven years of Henry IV the principal requirement of parliament, that gifts and grants should be made openly in Council, showed that the king's confidence was being abused by his intimates much as that of Richard had been.

The current remedy for this was a reform of Council, sometimes the appointment of a defined and influential body of councillors, sometimes the lodging in Council of the warrants by which all grants must be initiated. The theory behind parliament's petitions was a restricted one, of the infancy of parliamentary control, not of its maturity. Parliament professed, and probably felt, a

---

[1] *Rotuli Parliamentorum*, ii. 323.

[2] *Ibid.* ii. 324: "By the commandment of the King himself and of his Council".

[3] Walsingham, ii. 113.   [4] *Rotuli Parliamentorum*, iii. 525.

very real reverence for the office and prerogative of the king. Four times between 1377 and 1413 it asserted its wish that Richard, or *Efforts at* Henry, should "enjoy the right, power, and prerogative of his *reform* progenitors undiminished". Its action against corrupt councillors was in theory *plus royaliste que le Roi*. The commons' impeachments assumed a kind of ideal monarchy, from which it was treason to divert the king, and to which, as soon as he returned to his senses, parliament would accord all its accustomed prerogative.

The purpose of the agitation was, therefore, to establish conditions under which reputable men could act effectively, and the publishing of names in parliament was mainly, as was so often the case at this time, to bind all the parties to their obligations; such a precaution made clear who were not councillors, and gave those who were a better warrant for insisting on being heard, and did not bind the king not to change them without consent of parliament.[1] It was sometimes required by the councillors themselves as a condition of taking office, and in fact the pressure towards defining and improving the rules of Council did not always come from the commons. Henry IV himself, perhaps in part because he felt criticism of recent alienations could not be staved off any longer, accorded a "bill" of rules for Council in 1406[2] which shows how closely the councillors' difficulties in existing circumstances had been appreciated, and promised them the undivided confidence without which their office would be useless. From 1376 to 1410 parliament continued to approach the problem of the Council in this spirit. It did not claim power to create Councils; but intermittently it presented the crown with the necessity of confining the king's confidence to men of representative standing, and put forward rules by which the ideal of "sufficient counsel" could be realized in face of his desire for free hands and of the nobles' reluctance to serve. It did so with a decent assumption that the king was equally anxious for integrity of Council, and on one occasion, in his bill of 1406, Henry IV lived up to the assumption. Commons' petitions show a very creditable understanding of the difficulties of official councillors to a king who has no great

1 Thus the list of councillors announced in the parliament of May 1406, had been considerably changed before parliament met again in the autumn. H. Nicolas, *Proceedings and Ordinances of the Privy Council*, i. 295.
2 *Rotuli Parliamentorum*, iii. 572.

enthusiasm for their advice, and under a constitution which has not yet incorporated the rules of secrecy, loyalty, and mutual responsibility into its canons of Council. Taken as a whole, they might be consolidated into a treatise in which almost every aspect of the councillor's craft would be illustrated.

Indeed, if the history of the fifteenth century shows no con- *Problems* scious attempt to set up a new constitutional theory by which *of the* parliament might assert a general control of government through *continual* parliamentary Councils, it is, nevertheless, concerned with some- *Council* thing of fundamental importance. Ideal or practice, as they worked their way through the phases of feudalism and monarchical bureaucracy, had lodged government first in the *concilium* of the feudal *curia* and later in the royalist Council of Henry III and his successors, and each of these had demanded a different technique of counsel, different loyalties, a different kind of faith, different skill. With the continual Councils we come to still a third type, whose purpose is to be not a servant of the crown, nor of the feudal magnates, nor a clearing house for the work of the crown offices, but a neutral guardian of the interests of both king and nation. The demands made upon such councillors were in their kind new. The change in function called less for a change in form than for a new political type, almost for a new political morality. If the continual Council was to be what the commons at times desired it to be, an epitome of the estates,[1] it must contain nobles who would lay aside the commitments and interests and jealousies of their rank and devote themselves to conciliar routine for long periods without favour or self-interest, and with them men of the third estate capable of putting aside their commoners' prejudices and understanding and supporting the legitimate needs of the crown. Even when all parties had resigned themselves to govern- ment by a group of nobles, Council could not be true to its en- hanced authority without a break with the bad tradition which made the individual councillor the head of a party connection and brought the ambitions and dissensions of factions into its meetings. There were lacking even those elementary conventions of conduct which would preserve judicial fairness and the rudiments of loyalty between one councillor and another. Council, or at least the con- tinual Council as it was then understood, had, in fact, still to find

[1] *Rotuli Parliamentorum*, iii. 5: *De divers estatz.*

itself. More than for a new political institution, the commons were
petitioning for councillors who should understand the elements of
their own function, loyalty to the crown, to the parliament, and
to each other, disinterestedness, diligence, freedom from factions,
secrecy, and discretion. In short solidarity in the interest of the
king, the nation, and their own—a new technique of counsel.

Various
recom-
mendations
The Good Parliament and the Appellants, self-interested as the
latter were, did something to define current abuses and their
remedy in a continual Council. The admission of external interests
to collaborate in Council business was the substance of the charge
against Nevill, Latimer, and Lyons. In 1386 the grievance was
discrimination in the degree of confidence accorded to individual
councillors, even to the point of the binding of the king by oath
to be guided only by Suffolk, Oxford, and Bishop Nevill. By
their influence the king had "departed from the Council of the
realm".[1] The remedies proposed in 1376 were that the lords of the
continual Council should always be about the king, that no great
matter should be dispatched without the consent of all, that no
report of Council's deliberations should be made save by its
members authorized to do so, and that all officials of state should
act on its warrants without demur.[2] In 1386, when the grant was
made conditional upon a definition of the rights of the continual
Council, it was required that it should remain in London to have
access to records and to be in touch with the Justices, and that no
one not a Councillor should offer advice to the king.[3] In 1390
Council itself adopted a fixed hour of assembly, asserted the principle of payment of wages, and made certain orders as to the
conduct of business.[4] In December 1406 a number of commons'
articles renewed the recommendations of former years,[5] repeated
Articles
of 1406
the request that no one should share the secrets of the Council, and
made the suggestion that its unity should be preserved by those

[1] *Rotuli Parliamentorum*, iii. 230.
[2] *Ibid.* ii. 322. At some time unascertained during the minority of Richard,
Council drew up similar but more stringent rules for the king's conduct towards
itself. H. Nicolas, *Proceedings and Ordinances of the Privy Council*, i. 84.
[3] *Rotuli Parliamentorum*, iii. 220 and 221.
[4] H. Nicolas, *Proceedings and Ordinances of the Privy Council*, i. 18a.
[5] *Rotuli Parliamentorum*, iii. 585. The Council made some reservations on
grounds of expediency. H. Nicolas, *Proceedings and Ordinances of the Privy
Council*, i. 296.

who remained in attendance keeping those who were absent informed of Council business. The king was asked to put equal trust in all the councillors, and to wait for proof by appeal before he let himself be prejudiced against any of them by charges of misconduct. He was required to receive no promptings other than from the Council in any plea, and to refer any who ventured on them to Council to be dealt with. All petitions for offices in the king's gift were to be made and granted in the presence of Council, and no councillor was to give special advocacy to the request of any petitioner, and finally every matter before the Council must be fully considered by each of its members, and absent members were to receive minutes of decisions with the reasons for them, and to signify their assent or dissent by letter.[1] In the previous parliament of this year, in May 1406, the king had, for his part, already insisted on a substantial Council[2]— apparently in part because of his illness, and in part to carry off the routine business of finance and justice and leave him free to attend to affairs of state[3]—and in December he also made his contribution to the right practice of counsel in a series of articles. He will name the councillors in parliament that they may be the more ready to act, he will support them in all things, place all his confidence in them, will suffer no impediment to hinder their task, will make no difficulties for them nor suffer others to do so. He will have all letters touching the matters assigned, whether letters of the chamberlain or under the Signet, and all other mandates addressed to the chancellor, treasurer or keeper of the Privy Seal, endorsed by the advice of the Council. The sphere of the latter's actions is limited by previous usage, excluding charters of pardon and collations to benefices and offices; but the king's rules are a model for the relations of king and Council. Finally, if he found that he was obstructed in carrying out his office, any councillor might resign "without the King's indignation", and Lord Lovell, who had a cause pending before the Council, was careful to

---

1 *Rotuli Parliamentorum*, iii. 623. The parliament of 1410 summed up their demands from the councillors in an oath to give counsel "loyally . . . without favour, fear, affection, or affinity".

2 *Rotuli Parliamentorum*, iii. 572. The names were considered in Council. H. Nicolas, *Proceedings and Ordinances of the Privy Council*, i. 288.

3 "Because he cannot devote himself (to affairs) as much as he would like." *Ibid.* p. 291.

abstain from taking his place until it was settled. The king's "bill" was entered upon the roll of parliament at his own command, and thirty years later it was still thought sufficiently to embody the obligations of Council, and was rehearsed before the then councillors at the assumption of his regal authority by Henry VI.[1]

Council freed from parliamentary criticism

Thus the rules of a new institution of state were elicited from the experience of Henry IV's reign. The Council which was commissioned to govern the minority in 1422 had for the most part served throughout the reign of Henry V, and gave proof that the duties and obligations of their status had come to be much more fully realized. From this time onwards the Council does not receive direction from without as to how to conduct its business. It puts its own procedure in order by articles issued from time to time,[2] and brings them to parliament only for the sake of the permanent record of the parliament roll.

In part these articles were directed to securing the authority of Council against the Protector—offices, benefices, farms, and wardships and escheats were to be at their disposal—but they also show a clearer sense of the unity and stability of Council. Council alone was to know the state of the king's treasure, four or six were always to be present for the conduct of business, and decisions were to be made by the vote of the majority present; in 1423[3] Council had a further schedule of articles placed upon the roll of parliament forbidding the usurpation by single councillors of the right to answer petitions and make grants, announcing its intention of

Articles of 1423 and 1426

calling the judges into consultation where the king's prerogative or freehold were concerned, requiring the ministers present to be unanimous before the Council decided upon suits "touching the weal of the king and of his Realm", and even foreshadowing later doctrines of joint political responsibility by requiring an outward show of unanimity from all councillors in matters of foreign relations: "for as miche as it is to greet a shame, that in to strange Countrees oure soverein Lord shal write his Letters by th' advyce

---

1 J. F. Baldwin, *The King's Council*, p. 186.
2 A contrast with the conduct of the councillors of Henry IV, who refused to swear to the articles of 1406 without an express order from the king. *Rotuli Parliamentorum*, iii. 585.
3 *Ibid.* iv. 201, H. Nicolas, *Proceedings and Ordinances of the Privy Council*, iii. 148, and J. F. Baldwin, *The King's Council*, p. 174, attribute this to 1424, but it is upon the parliament roll of October of the second year.

of his Counsail . . . and singular persons of the Counsail to write the contrarie". In 1426[1] thirty-nine articles record and guard against the friction inevitable when a body so small as the Council has to deal with matters of great interest to its members individually. No councillor is to make himself party to any cause moved before Council,[2] every member is to have full right of speech, due reverence being given to order and estate, and none is to admit grievance against another for words used in Council. Proceedings are to be confidential, for the disclosure of what has been said has caused jealousy between councillors and has put some of them in danger. For this reason no one is to be admitted during the sessions unless upon special summons. No bill is to be passed upon except in the Council chamber, in formal session, and after formal reading. Finally, an important article tries to secure independence from the characteristic danger of the time by enacting that no lord of the king's Council shall be sworn of the Council of any other person. Neglect of this provision was to play a part in the fall of Suffolk twenty years later.

That these precepts were not always carried out in practice *Importance of rules of Council* is a commonplace of Lancastrian history, but their conception is a constitutional fact of the greatest importance, for they mark the emergency of Council from that phase of its history when it was a chaos of conflicting wills with no common policy or loyalty to itself. As a body of conventional procedure the self-imposed rules of Council are of the same importance to itself and to the nation as the procedure of parliament. They enable Council to function as an organic institution, and to rise to the task of government with an impersonal, corporate purpose, and it is not to be forgotten that Council did succeed in the very formidable task of stifling the quarrel of Beaufort and Gloucester and kept the realm in outward unity for over twenty years under a helpless king. Hitherto, the country had always gone to pieces when the leadership of the crown was withheld, and the compromise and firmness shown by the nobles who served on the Lancastrian Council—many of them for long terms of years—is

---

[1] *Rotuli Parliamentorum*, v. 407. H. Nicolas, *Proceedings and Ordinances of the Privy Council*, iii. 214.

[2] "But oonly to answere that the bill shal be seen by all the counsail and the partie suyng to have resonable answere." *Rotuli Parliamentorum*, v. 407.

proof of the effectiveness of what was in all essentials a new branch
of the constitution.

*Function
of
Council*

It is impossible to bring the work of the Council under a single
formula. Its authority as stated in the 8th year of Henry IV[1] and
reasserted in the 16th of Henry VI was to "hear, treat . . . and
determine" all matters brought before it except "charters of
pardon, appointments to benefices and offices and other matters of
grace", "matters of great weight and importance" being referred
to the king that his advice and pleasure might be taken therein.
Being at the centre of the state, it did all that work of government
which had not become appropriated to any of the courts or
ministries. The more any function had been specialized and reduced to routine, the more likely it was to have its acknowledged
official channel and to proceed automatically under its appropriate
seal without Council's intervention. This is clearest in justice.
Council still represents that ultimate fountain of judgment which
comes from the king, but it has become a rule of the constitution—
broken, no doubt, upon occasion by Richard II, and, very infrequently, under his Lancastrian successors—that it cannot judge

In justice in common law. It cannot, that is to say, hear any cause which
already has redress by writ and action in either of the Benches.
From time to time it is suspected of doing so (parliament petitions against the abuse),[2] but precedent is against it.[3] Again,
the chancellor, who has been the presiding officer of Council
justice since the thirteenth century,[4] is beginning, though he has
not completed, a formularized jurisdiction of his own. By the
beginning of the fourteenth century he has been presiding over

[1] *Rotuli Parliamentorum*, iii. 572.
[2] The conclusion of a long controversy is best summarized in the Council's
own articles of 1426: "that all the bills that comprehend matters terminable
at the common law be remitted there to be determined, but if it so be that the
discretion of the Council feel too great might on that one side and unmight on
that other, or else other cause reasonable that shall move them". H. Nicolas,
Proceedings and Ordinances of the Privy Council, iii. 214.
[3] *Rotuli Parliamentorum*, iii. 44, 587.
[4] For a phase of the earlier history of Chancery cf. F. M. Powicke, "Chancery
during the minority of Henry III", *English Historical Review*, vol. xxiii.

special sessions of the Council, or of part of it, to redress those wrongs for which there is no common law remedy, or for which that remedy has proved for some reason ineffective. In 1319 we hear of the "Council of the Chancery,"[1] though the "Council in Chancery" would be a more appropriate phrase. The rise of a chancellor's jurisdiction in such matters was, no doubt, as inevitable as that of the older jurisdiction of the court of the Exchequer.[2] It arose from the discrepancy of a stereotyped system of writs with many of the grievances it was devised to remedy. When the Chancery could not offer an appropriate writ the plaintiff expected informal justice, the king allowed it to be provided, and the Council, deferring to the legal knowledge of the chancellor, acted under his presidency, and, as time went on, was glad that he should choose his own collaborators, who were more and more likely to be taken from the ranks of the justices, serjeants, and others learned in the law. Precedent, moreover, tended to establish procedure, and, like the common law justices before him, the chancellor began to act by rule, to follow set stages *in consimili casu*, and to develop a characteristic procedure of Chancery. Thus, long before the theory that the chancellor's jurisdiction was the jurisdiction of Council in Chancery died, its so-called "common law" or "Latin" side had hardened into routine; appeals against letters patent, petitions of right, claims for recovery of property against the crown, and similar claims, for which no suit at common law lay, might be sued for directly to the chancellor, and carried through by his procedure in a court which came to look less and less like the Council and more and more like one of the Benches in action. In Henry VI's reign we have an account of a session of chancery in which the Chancellor sits with the Master of the Rolls, two other justices, and four Masters in Chancery.[3] On the whole, both parliament and Council seem to have been glad to encourage the passage of Council justice into Chancery. Especially in those cases where the simple fact of violence—fraud, violent maintenance, intimidation, refusal of access to courts, or of remedy by the courts themselves—entered into the grievance, petitioners

Jurisdiction of Chancery

---

[1] J. F. Baldwin, *The King's Council*, p. 238.
[2] Indeed, it seemed for a time that the Treasurer might become the principal judge in equity. *Ibid.* p. 237.
[3] *Ibid.* p. 253.

were referred to the chancellor, and statutes appointed him as the authority to whom grievance must be presented. Where a choice of remedy seemed open, petitioners themselves felt their best choice of address to be the chancellor rather than the king, the Council, or the commons, and towards the end of the fourteenth century—the process is rapid under Richard II—the flood of petitions to Chancery grows and they come to exceed all others in number. We cannot say that a defined, recognized and invariable body of chancery law, nor an unmistakably separate court of Chancery, has been acknowledged within our period, but the jurisdiction is being practised, the Council has been relieved in practice of the greater portion of its judicial preoccupation, and has become free to devote itself to business of state. In Henry IV's reign Council was able to reduce its judicial sessions to two days of the week, and in that of Henry VI to one.[1] Without such a development, the small, continual Council of the nobility would hardly have established its tradition and found leisure to govern England.

Executive   Thus, more exclusively than any Council before it, that of the
functions   Lancastrian kings was a Council of State, and little is gained by trying to analyse and classify what is in effect the whole domestic and external business of English government. Under Henry IV perhaps its most pressing preoccupation was with the inextinguishable unrest of Wales and the threat from the Scotch. The safety of the Welsh and Northern Marches, the pay and provisioning of garrisons, the commissioning of officers, the answering of the perennial complaints of ill-supported captains, take up much of Council's sessions. With the reign of Henry VI the interest shifts to Guienne and Calais. The agenda for November 2, 1401, provide for taking the king's pleasure concerning the terms to be offered to Owen Glendower, and the orders to be sent to the Prince of Wales, then on campaign against the rebels; for considering letters from the English and Scotch Wardens of the March of Scotland, and providing for the security of Roxburgh Castle; for debating the possibilities of action in the event of the French denouncing the truce. It is thought useful, in view of the scarcity

---

[1] H. Nicolas, *Proceedings and Ordinances of the Privy Council*, iii. 214. Even so, judicial sessions were to be postponed to "great and notable causes touching the King's realm and his lordships".

of corn, to consider removing the custom duty for a period of six months. Letters patent of friendship with the Frisian merchants are suggested, and consideration is given to an embassy into Picardy and to the commission of Admirals for an enterprise in the Channel. Finally, it is intended to ask the king to inform Council of the contents of a recent letter from Bayonne, and to ascertain whether he wishes to make public the recent news from Ireland.[1] Such matters, the routine of war and peace, regulations of commerce, were, of course, the constant charge of the Council, and, especially under the minority, they were added to by many considerations of domestic diplomacy which might normally be thought to fall to the king. From 1425 onwards the burden of the dissensions of Gloucester and Beaufort fell upon their shoulders, and, though they invoked the help of Bedford and the parliament, the prolonged crisis necessitated a series of placatory letters, the engineering of conferences, and the devising of conditions of agreement. Besides these high matters of state, there is a daily routine of executive and of the prompting of executive acts by others. New acts of Parliament are rehearsed before the Council by the clerk of parliaments for their necessary action,[2] and upon one occasion the commons actually ask that Council shall deal with all petitions not dispatched at the rising of the session, and have them engrossed upon the roll of parliament.[3] During Henry VI's minority Council appoints the great officers, justices, and barons of the Exchequer,[4] and has all power except alienation of the king's inheritance and annulment of his letters patent. It summons the great duke of Bedford to its presence, and he is "ruled by the lordes of the counsail, and obeyes unto the King and to theim as for the King, as lowely as the leest and poverest subgit that the King has in his land".[5]

The continual Council, embodying such rules of counsel and exercising such powers, established itself slowly over a period of *Parliament and Council*

1 H. Nicolas, *Proceedings and Ordinances of the Privy Council*, i. 173. The decisions arrived at in most of these matters are to be found at p. 177.

2 *Ibid.* iii. 22.

3 *Rotuli Parliamentorum*, iv. 506.

4 H. Nicolas, *Proceedings and Ordinances of the Privy Council*, iii. 70, 121.

5 *Ibid.* iii. 235 (Bedford to the Council).

some thirty years. The demand for it came intermittently from the commons, who, just as they appealed for a commission of peers to advise them at the beginning of every parliament, still believed that the nobility were the natural counsellors of the crown and leaders of the community, but their demands came at such long intervals, and were so far from being informed by any clear design, that it is impossible to attribute to them any constant policy of making council a parliamentary institution, and towards the end of Henry IV's reign such petitions ceased. The commons of the Good Parliament demanded only the strengthening of the ordinary Council by additional lords,[1] the continual Council of 1377 was in fact, though not in name, a regency, and in 1380 the commons, having found its three years of office expensive, petitioned that it should be discharged and that the king should govern with no Council but his five great officers. Between 1380 and 1386 parliament was brought to realize the constitutional problem with which it was faced, and the great and continual Council of nine notables, with the great officers, which was forced upon the king in the latter year, was the first occasion upon which the new constitutional remedy was clearly formulated. It is no discredit to Richard and his supporters that the restriction upon his right of choice of advisers seemed a dangerous and intolerable innovation. It was in effect to reimpose the tutelage of his minority, and the answer which he made, that of appointing additional councillors, withdrawing himself beyond reach of his official Council, and finding an alternative in the advice of Suffolk, Vere, and Alexander Nevill, can only be condemned on grounds of expediency. Nor did the opposition theory justify itself when

Continual Council under Richard II the Merciless Parliament put the policy of the Appellants into action with a free hand. The continual Council of 1388 claimed £20,000 for the salaries of its members. In January 1389 the councillors themselves pleaded for their discharge on the ground of their "great labour and cost", and Richard, in assenting to their reappointment in parliament for a further term, announced that for the future he intended to be free to choose his ministers and councillors and to dismiss them as and when he thought fit,[2] and,

[1] The commons petitioned in 1377, not very precisely, for a Council *de diverses estatz. Rotuli Parliamentorum*, iii. 5.

[2] *Ibid.* iii. 258.

having freed his hands without arousing protest, set himself to restore the normal system of a large Council of diverse elements. By the end of 1390, though its original members were retained, the identity of the continual Council was lost in a body of councillors, of whom thirty-four have been noted from the records of proceedings,[1] and many of whom were knights and clerks of no parliamentary standing. Thus the continual Council was pressed for no more than intermittently by the opposition under Richard, and had very indifferent success in practice. When it was resorted to in the later years of Henry IV it was largely at the proposal of the king.

It is clear, indeed, from his own words in 1399, that Henry *Under* was in a position to use his discretion in the matter of Council: *Henry IV* "it is the King's pleasure to be advised by the wise men of his Council in matters touching his own estate and that of the Realm, saving his liberty".[2] The same politic evasion was repeated in substance to petitions made in 1401 and 1402.[3] Parliament, for its part, contented itself until 1404[4] with asking that alienations of royal lands and revenues should be made with the advice of Council, without seeking to determine its form, and, though the first rising of the Percies revived the old cry that the king should have better advisers about him, it was not until Henry's health began to fail[5] that the continual Council again became essential, and then the initiative was shared by the king; the chancellor made his charge to the parliament of 1406 from the text "in the multitude of counsellors there is wisdom",[6] and Henry himself put forward a bill of conciliar reform. In a sense the history of the continual Council as a permanent institution begins with this action of Henry IV's. At this time it changes its nature, ceasing to be an occasional concession to criticism, becoming a permanent institution fostered by the crown, and drawing the few members

---

[1] J. F. Baldwin, *The King's Council*, p. 132.

[2] *Rotuli Parliamentorum*, iii. 433.   [3] *Ibid*. iii. 473 and 495.

[4] In this year Henry appointed twenty-two councillors, seven of them commoners, and reported their names to parliament. This was in response to "great instances and special requests made to him on several occasions in this Parliament by the Commons". *Ibid*. iii. 530.

[5] Henry fell ill, and was unable to travel, before April 28, 1406 (H. Nicolas, *Proceedings and Ordinances of the Privy Council*, i. 290). The Council was appointed on May 22.

[6] *Rotuli Parliamentorum*, iii. 567.

who are not also peers from knights who hold office in or are attached to the court.[1] Under Henry V and Henry VI the continual Council is a royalist institution. There are independent elements— Savage is one—in the Council of 1406, but it is the first of an unbroken succession. The archbishop of Canterbury, the bishops of Winchester and Exeter, the duke of York, the earl of Somerset, the lords Roos, Burnell, Lovell, and Willoughby, the chancellor, treasurer, keeper of the Privy Seal, chamberlain, and steward, with Hugh Waterton, John Cheyne, and Arnold Savage, were named in the bill. They were allotted substantial salaries, and, though they did not all survive till the next parliament and those who did resigned at the parliament of Gloucester in 1407, a similarly composed Council carried on their work and was succeeded by others, in which the parties of the king and the prince were alternately predominant,[2] until the end of the reign. The commoners were eliminated in 1407, and the nomination of councillors in parliament was only resorted to on one other occasion, in 1410,[3] but it may be said that the crown finally adopted the principle of the continual Council between 1406 and 1413, resigning itself to governing through a small group of magnates who were given a great measure of confidence and authority. No doubt the continual Council was riveted upon the constitution in part by the rivalry between the king and his son, which made it dangerous for either's supporters to relax their attendance, and which, with the payment of salaries, overcame the great men's reluctance. By 1415 the principle had justified itself sufficiently for Henry V to rest his government upon a small but extremely influential Council, which for much of the reign acted under Bedford as custos of the realm with commission to do all things with the consent of the Council,[4] and such a Council governed the country until the rise of Suffolk in 1445 or 1446.

There is, then, a specific constitutional form which may be

[1] Thomas Chaucer (1423) had been four times Speaker, but he was also the king's butler. William Alington was a member of Henry V's Council and Treasurer of Normandy. J. F. Baldwin, *The King's Council*, p. 173 n.

[2] *Rotuli Parliamentorum*, iii. 632.   [3] *Ibid.* iii. 623.

[4] The archbishop of Canterbury, the bishops of Winchester and Durham, the earl of Westmorland, the prior of the Hospital, the lords Grey de Ruthin, Berkeley, Powys, and Morley. The councillors of 1410 were the prince, three bishops, two earls, and lord Burnell. H. Nicolas, *Proceedings and Ordinances of the Privy Council*, ii. 157.

called the Lancastrian Council. It is not wholly the creation of *The Lan-*
either king or parliament, and, though the rise of parliament had *castrian*
made either a wholly feudal or a wholly ministerial council almost *Council*
impossible to maintain, it is not the outcome of a consistent
parliamentary scheme to control the state. More immediately, it
comes into being in response to certain defects which characterize
the age, of which the greatest is the prolonged weakness of the
monarchy, which from 1370 to 1461 never gave the country a
strong king resident in England for more than a few years
together. The degrees in which these defects were realized by
king and parliament varied almost year by year, but every crisis
brought the problem nearer to its solution, and if we recognize, in
the parliamentary view at least, an intermittent desire that the
Council should be drawn from all the estates, we may admit that
when the institution reached its normal shape under Henry V it
represented a compromise, in which the element of strength and
continuity required by parliament was compensated for by the
exclusion of elements of possible opposition and the restriction
of membership to nobles who were the relations or close friends
of the king.[1] A council like that of 1415,[2] which consisted of the
duke of Bedford, the archbishop of Canterbury, the bishops of
Winchester and Durham, the prior of the Hospital, the earl of
Westmorland, and the lords Grey of Ruthin, Berkeley, Powys, and
Morley, and which served till a new commission was issued in 1417,
satisfied the commons' requirements for a continual Council of
great men, but it had no immediate relation to parliament, either
in the nature of its authority, which was by letters patent, or in its
membership.[3] The crises of 1376 and 1377 had fallen upon a crown
which lacked any conciliar system capable of carrying on the
king's government without the decisive leadership of the king.
The death of Henry V showed that this defect had been to a large
degree remedied, and that fifty years of canvassing of the ethics of

[1] Commoners were again admitted under Henry VI—the archbishop's
charge to the first parliament of the reign called for "honorable and discreet
persons and from every estate of the realm"—but they were usually men holding office of the crown. *Rotuli Parliamentorum*, iv. 169.

[2] J. F. Baldwin, *The King's Council*, p. 165. The fact that the magnates attend
only irregularly during these years is an additional failure to carry out the full
conciliar ideal of parliament.

[3] The last occasion on which the commons asked to be informed of the
names of councillors seems to have been in 1423. *Rotuli Parliamentorum*, iv. 201.

the councillor's office, and the habit of action in council formed in the nobility under Henry IV and Henry V, had provided the nation with a Council which could master the offices of state, reduce faction to manageable proportions, and conduct what was, in effect, if not in name, a regency of the peers and great officers.

Minority of Henry VI   This Council sat from 1422-1437. According to the views then held, it was ultimately the creation of the authority of the king exercised by the lords spiritual and temporal in virtue of his minority. Acting with this warrant, the lords initiated the new reign by ordering a parliament by the king's letters patent *de avisamento consilii,*[1] and appointing the duke of Gloucester to act in it *vice Rege*. There the infant king appointed Gloucester Protector and Defender of the Realm and Church and Principal Councillor in the absence of John of Bedford, and, by "the request of the commons" and "the advice and assent of all the Lords", seventeen persons were named *pur Conseillers assistentz a la governanz*.[2] Council, once created, became not assistants to government but the government itself, and its own arbiter. At no time after 1422 does it seem to have been dismissed as a whole, and it had, therefore, a continuous existence, usually filling vacancies by coöption. The only case of the naming of a new councillor in parliament, that of the bishop of Durham in 1426, was "by election by the Council in Parliament", and in 1433 parliament acknowledged the principle that the Council should appoint its own members. In 1430 Council decided that no councillor should be added or removed without Council's consent,[3] and in 1433 Bedford secured parliamentary recognition of the rule as a condition of taking office.[4] It was a somewhat larger Council than that of Henry V, usually something over twenty. By the beginning of the minority it had won itself clear of commons' criticism, become an accepted institution, and had sufficient jealousy for its charge of the king's government to make rules for itself in the common interest and to insist upon a standard of attendance and conduct which was markedly higher than that of any continual Council

[1] *Rotuli Parliamentorum*, iv. 169.   [2] *Ibid*. iv. 175.
[3] H. Nicolas, *Proceedings and Ordinances of the Privy Council*, iv. 38.
[4] *Rotuli Parliamentorum*, iv. 424.

up to the death of Henry IV. The chances of Council holding together were, no doubt, greatly enhanced by the payment of salaries, which the councillors secured for themselves by their own ordinance in 1424 upon a graded scale according to rank from 8000 marks for the duke of Gloucester to 40 marks for the simple esquire. Every day of absence was to be paid for by a fine. But it is probable that the indirect opportunities for influence and patronage were even more attractive, for precisely at the point which the commons of recent reigns had considered the most valuable function of the continual Council—the conservation of the crown's resources and the prevention of too lavish alienations— Henry VI's Council had little conscience, and parliament soon ceased to be an effective critic. "The patent rolls are filled with grants to Lords Cromwell, Hungerford, Tiptoft and others",[1] and the balance of power in the Council came, at least towards the end of the reign, to be watched eagerly by the many clients who were ranked behind each of the lords[2] and sought a point of vantage for preferring their petitions. In Council, as elsewhere, maintenance came to be a danger to justice.[3] Councillors promised to abstain from it, and denounced it in their articles, but with what success we cannot say.

These abuses were inevitable in the England of Henry VI. It is more remarkable that for twenty years of such a reign the Council kept together as a governing body. In this the strength of the institution was seen to rise above that of individuals,[4] and it was

Success of the minority Council

[1] J. F. Baldwin, *The King's Council*, p. 179.

[2] So Margaret Paston, writing to her husband in 1448, concludes that "Daniel is out of the King's good grace, and he shall down with all his men, and all that be their well-willers". *Paston Letters* (ed. Gairdner), no. 56.

[3] An early and fairly unobjectionable instance of maintenance is a letter by the Black Prince to the justices of the Common Bench in which he asks them to be "as favourable and lenient (*cedauntes*) to the poor tenants of ancient demesne at Merton" against the prior of Merton "as they are reasonably able to be". *Stonor Letters* (Camden Society, ed. C. L. Kingsford), no. 4. From 1440 we have the story of a piece of legal chicanery by Suffolk which, since it involved the connivance of the treasurer, and did not need to use violence, is an even better example of a councillor's power to manipulate the law to maintain his men. *Paston Letters* (ed. Gairdner), no. 27. The contrast between the two methods may be taken as a rough measure of the decline in political morality in the first men of the land between 1351 and 1440.

[4] In 1427 they claimed to be "one whole (united) council for the king as they ought to be". H. Nicolas, *Proceedings and Ordinances of the Privy Council*, iii. 232.

not until the king became a rallying point for faction in the late 'forties that Council began to lose its unity, though before that time it was preserved with a difficulty which shows the magnitude of its task, and survived several dangerous crises. An united loyalty was preserved against a threat of treason from the earl of March and his supporter John Mortimer in 1423, and again in 1425, when the quarrel between Warwick and Norfolk threatened to divide the nobility, a number of notables, among whom were most of the councillors, put themselves upon oath to remain impartial and maintain the peace and had their act recorded upon the roll of parliament,[1] and this oath seems to have been first planned in Council.[2] From the outset of the reign there had been growing a still more dangerous force of disunion, the jealousy between Gloucester and the Beauforts, fanned by Gloucester's disappointment with the terms of his Protectorship and by the general dislike for his personal adventure into foreign affairs.[3] By the beginning of 1426 Gloucester was accusing Bishop Beaufort of plotting his own murder and the seizure of the king's person, and it was not until 1427, after Bedford had spent fifteen months in England to secure the peace, that the quarrel was got under control. Throughout this long period of uncertainty, when the formation of parties behind the Beauforts or the duke would have meant civil war, the Council acted with a due sense of their responsibility, and probably with as much firmness as the circumstances would allow. No faction emerged to support Gloucester's Flemish ambitions; in April 1425 power was taken from parliament to invite the arbitration of the queens of France and England, of the duke of Bedford and of the Councils of France and England[4]; in January 1426 Council, by Bedford's advice, urged Gloucester to meet Beaufort at Northampton and promised safe-conduct and mediation,[5] persuaded the bishop to keep his men in hand,[6] and

Crisis of 1426

---

[1] *Rotuli Parliamentorum*, iv. 262.

[2] H. Nicolas, *Proceedings and Ordinances of the Privy Council*, iii. 177.

[3] He married Jacqueline of Hainault in March 1423.

[4] *Rotuli Parliamentorum*, iv. 277.

[5] H. Nicolas, *Proceedings and Ordinances of the Privy Council*, iii. 181; Stubbs *Constitutional History*, iii. 105.

[6] "At the stirring of my said lord of Bedford and my said lords of the consail he is agreed to send from him notable part of his meyne that he is now accompanied with and to content him of such number as shall be thought...reasonable for his estate". H. Nicolas, *Proceedings and Ordinances of the Privy Council*, iii. 184.

in the Leicester parliament of February 1426, together with the lords, forced a settlement. Thenceforward they maintained a strict neutrality as far as Gloucester would permit them to do so, constantly put before him the need of unity in the Council and the realm, and, while they insisted that Bishop Beaufort should offer legal proof of his innocence, constantly resisted Gloucester's claim that he was accountable to no subject for his actions while the king remained a minor and that the powers of the crown, so long as Bedford remained in France, were vested in his hands by right of descent. The final settlement, coming after Beaufort's resignation of the Chancery and followed by his voluntary exile upon pilgrimage—Gloucester withdrawing his charges, and swallowing his failure to make the Protectorship absolute—was a triumph for the Council backed by Bedford and the parliament. That it was made less galling for Gloucester by large loans of money on the security of the Council was probably inevitable. The Council's survival of the prolonged test of its loyalty and firmness which these two perilous years imposed is more striking than any concessions made to the great contestants for power, and the successful proof of its quality may be said to have secured another twenty years of comparative peace for the realm. In 1427 Bedford was able to say that "it was unto him one of the greatest gladnesses that ever fell to his heart to see the King in this tenderness of age to have so sad, so substantial, and so true a council".[1]

As a result of this victory the Council was able to repress a further attempt by Gloucester to convert the Protectorate into a regency in 1427. It was now asserting its capacity to govern without the coöperation either of the princes or of the leader of the Beauforts, and with a neutral lord, the earl of Warwick, as tutor to the king, and basing its authority, as always, upon the undiminished authority of the crown,[2] carried through his coronation in November 1429, when the lords of parliament

---

[1] H. Nicolas, *Proceedings and Ordinances of the Privy Council*, iii. 235.

[2] In 1427 they had told Gloucester that he had no more power in Parliament than he would have had "the King being in Parliament, at yeres of most discretion", and that Henry was "like with the grace of God to occupy his own royal power within few years". *Rotuli Parliamentorum*, iv. 327. "Not in our names, but in our said sovereign lord's name, whose authority we have". H. Nicolas, *Proceedings and Ordinances of the Privy Council*, iii. 239.

declared the Protectorate at an end. Gloucester himself, helped no doubt by the unpopularity which Bishop Beaufort's cardinalate had brought upon him, seems to have extricated himself from his isolated position, and assured the parliament of 1432 that he had no intention of claiming more than an equal voice in Council and parliament,[1] and that "the Lords Spiritual and Temporal were in unanimous and cordial agreement with each other".

Parties in that year seemed ready to subordinate themselves to Council's leadership, and, with the return of Bedford and the king's approach to years of discretion, it might have been expected that the dangerous years were passing and that the Council had brought the nation precariously but without disaster to the safety of active kingly rule again. The year 1433 was, indeed, a turning-point in the history of the nation, for which the cause

Return of Bedford of unity and order was not yet lost. Bedford returned to England, and a few months were enough to show how the mere presence of a great and wise, and, above all, a good prince, was enough to shame and frighten the violence and corruption of all classes into a show of amendment. While he had as yet taken no powers other than those his birth gave him, "the restful rule and governail of this land" had "greatly grown and been increased by his presence by the noble mirror and ensample that he hath given to others".[2] In the parliament of 1433 the king and all the estates petitioned Bedford to regard his work in France as finished, and to devote himself to the saving of peace and law in England, and this he agreed to do "as far as it may goodly be with the weal of the King's lands and lordships beyond the sea" and "unto the time that it shall like my Lord to take the exercize of the governance of this his Realm in his own person". The principles upon which the duke intended to rule are expressed in the articles which he put before parliament[3] "for the good of his Lord", and they are governed by his sense of his own commanding qualities, not questioning that he would receive the loyal coöperation of all those "who will take upon them to be my Lords Councillors", nor asking for the compulsion of law to confirm his leadership. The articles vest the government of the realm, as any statesman

[1] *Rotuli Parliamentorum,* iv. 389.
[2] Commons' address in the parliament of 1433. *Ibid.* iv. 423.
[3] *Ibid.* iv. 424.

of the day would have been compelled to do, in Council, whether in the filling of the great offices and bishop's sees and of vacancies in the Council, or in the calling of parliaments, and they ask no more for Bedford as chief of the Council than that he shall be informed of all its intentions and give his "advice and opinion wherever I am in my lord's service". It can hardly be doubted that, had he lived to the normal term of life, the prestige and wisdom that he brought to Council's action would have carried government securely during his lifetime, and, perhaps, transferred it peacefully to York or to a wiser Gloucester at his death. More than this, his example in life, "restfully governing himself and all his keeping, and obeying the King's peace and his laws",[1] might have turned the disordered forces of society into safer channels, and checked that disintegration of order which made the Wars of the Roses inevitable.

The fine and rather pathetic address in which the commons pleaded for the services of Bedford for England reveals at once their mistrust of such assurances of the unanimity and disinterestedness of the nobility as Gloucester had offered in 1432, their sense of lack of guidance, and their instinctive turning to the leadership of the single person who, as nearly as might be, stood for the accustomed preëminence of the crown.[2] It is, indeed, certain that the diversion of Bedford a second time to France by the worsening of Burgundian relations, and his death at Rouen in 1435, sealed the fate of the Lancastrian dynasty and of the political order of the Middle Ages in so far as it still survived. Gloucester was now heir presumptive, the Beauforts had to face the possibility of a succession which would mean their irreparable ruin, and York was brought within two degrees of the throne. The rise of French nationalism, marked in 1436 by the fall of Paris, committed the government to a losing war with France which swallowed the revenues of the kingdom and the reputation of almost every noble whose rank might have qualified him as Bedford's successor. In so far as any lieutenant of France came out of the test undiscredited, it was York, whose prestige was beyond all others that which it least profited the crown of Lancaster to enhance.

[1] *Rotuli Parliamentorum*, iv. 424.
[2] "The greatest surety that could be thought to the welfare of the King's noble person ... and of this land". *Ibid.* iv. 423.

Beginning
of the
Council's
decline The record of Council had been good up to this time—at least
its standard of political morality was higher than that of the
generality. But for some years there had been signs that this
higher standard had needed an effort to maintain it. As early as
1426[1] the articles of the Council bind its members not to harbour
wrongdoers or maintain parties to suits by intimidating their
adversaries or the justices or officers concerned. The articles of
1430 make the prohibition more explicit and add maintenance by
giving of livery and the intimidation of justices by letter.[2] It is
true that this was by way of "example of restful rule and good
governail to all subjects", but it can hardly have been without
reference to the growth of the Beaufort and Gloucester connections and to the sense of instability which prompted the recall
of Bedford to England. The disruptive forces gained against the
*The king
enters
politics* state. Moreover, the king was ceasing to be a negligible factor. He
had been crowned in 1429, and in 1434 the Council was already
finding it necessary to warn him against being influenced "by
stirrings or motions made to him apart in things of great weight
and substance" and especially any directed against their joint
authority.[3] By 1438 Henry was granting pardons on his own
initiative "to his own great disavail" and in despite of Council's
authority,[4] and had given away the constableship of Chirk Castle
without its advice.[5] In 1437, being then about fifteen years old, he
began himself to sit in Council, and in 1440 Gloucester was attri-
buting his eclipse to Beaufort's hold upon his confidence. The
disorderly state of the country was forcing itself upon the Council
in these years, as far as their records go, for the first time, if the
Lollard rising of 1431 be treated as exceptional. In 1437 a commission at Silsoe in Bedfordshire to repress riots and felonies was
openly defied by Lord Grey and Lord Fanhope, who prevented
their business with armed bands and threatened to hold the king's
sessions themselves. Council apparently swallowed the insult and
did not summon the offenders.[6] At the end of the same year a
general proclamation against riot and breaches of the peace was

[1] H. Nicolas, *Proceedings and Ordinances of the Privy Council*, iii. 217.
[2] *Ibid.* iv. 59: "Maintenance as by word, by deed, or by message, or by
writing to judge, jury, or party, or by gift of his clothing or livery or taking
into his service the party".   [3] *Ibid.* iv. 288.
[4] *Ibid.* v. 88.   [5] *Ibid.* v. 90.   [6] *Ibid.* v. 35, 57.

necessary. Henry's approach to his majority may, perhaps, have played some part in the gradual reëstablishment of Cardinal Beaufort's influence, which was marked by the growth of a peace *Rise of* party in 1439 and introduced into the Council its first serious *the peace* cleavage upon a fundamental matter of policy. Against Glouces- *party* ter's opposition an embassy left England in May 1439 with orders to make large concessions in the cause of peace, even, as the later phases of the negotiations revealed, to the point of relinquishing Henry's title to France. Of the terms of this commission Gloucester later professed ignorance, not only on his own behalf but on that of the Council. Against the release of Orleans, which was carried through by the peace party in 1440, he appealed from Council in a protest to the king that "I never was, am, nor never shall be consenting, counselling, nor agreeing".[1] His protest was followed by a letter of general indictment of Cardinal Beaufort and the archbishop of York, Kemp, whom he charged with gaining an illicit ascendancy over the king and shutting out himself and the duke of York from their proper share of Council. Whether the embassy and the release was the work of a minority of councillors or of Beaufort's influence with the king, it marks the end of that "unity of council" for which Bedford had pleaded, and which had been maintained, however precariously, for seventeen years, and *Council* from about that time the character of Council changes. Clearly *loses its* Gloucester, once he had realized that his antagonism to the treaty *unity* had committed him to permanent opposition, and that his following in the Council was insufficient to make his word of any weight, began to absent himself. From attending assiduously, as he did in the days of his power, he becomes a rare visitor, showing himself only sufficiently to avoid the appearance of a complete abdication. Cardinal Beaufort's influence is said to have predominated from this time until his death in 1447, but as far as Council attendance goes the party of peace for which he stood was represented more often by his supporters, the archbishop of York and the earl of Suffolk. In the early 'forties the most frequent attendants are the chancellor, the cardinal of York, and Suffolk, who may be taken as the working body of the peace faction, Adam Moleyns of the same party, the earl of Huntingdon, who Gloucester said had been

[1] H. Nicolas, *Proceedings and Ordinances of the Privy Council*, v. lxxxiv.; Rymer, *Foedera*, x. 764.

offended at Beaufort's supremacy, and, less regularly, the earls of
Stafford and Northumberland. The attendance of the cardinal of
York and the earl of Suffolk throughout 1442 and 1443 is almost
unbroken, and this must have been the time when the latter was
building up his hold upon the king. Thus, with the less regular
appearances of the cardinal of England, his party had a steady
supremacy.

Supremacy
of
Suffolk

It may be said, therefore, that, after 1440, the government was
in the hands of that one of two bitterly antagonistic parties which
had secured the ear of the king. To this extent Gloucester's
accusations were justified, and the situation was made even more
dangerous as Suffolk's power began to rise above that of the two
cardinals. In 1444, apparently with real reluctance, Suffolk undertook the great embassy which ended with the cession of Maine
and Anjou and the Angevin marriage. The result of this revolution
in foreign and domestic politics was to establish Suffolk in
unquestioned control by his influence with the king and queen,
and to commit the court and the court party to bringing the
French treaty to a conclusion which would satisfy national pride,
silence Gloucester, and prevent the war party from making
capital out of the awkward fact that Suffolk was admittedly close
friends with the king of France and the duke of Orleans. In 1447
Suffolk was left in a still more dangerous eminence by the death
of Cardinal Beaufort and of Humphrey, Duke of Gloucester.

We have very few council records for the period of Suffolk's
unchallenged supremacy, and it has been considered [1] that this in
itself is a proof that its power was failing, and that the favourite
withdrew all but the least important business from its control. The
attendance fell away, leaving such business as was done in the
hands of the archbishop of York, Moleyns, and the state ministers;
Suffolk himself ignored the Council and acted as sole counsellor
with the king and queen. Such, setting aside the childish accusations of the commons—that he "had sold the realm of England to
the King's adversaries of France" and was fortifying the castle
of Wallingford to receive a French invasion [2]—was the main
gravamen against him in 1450. He had monopolized the confidence of the king and used it to carry through an extremely

[1] J. F. Baldwin, *The King's Council*, pp. 191 *et seq.*
[2] *Rotuli Parliamentorum*, v. 176 *et seq.*

hazardous foreign policy which was ending in a resounding disaster. If the accepted opinion of conciliar history between 1445 and 1450 be the right one, Suffolk is deeply responsible for the collapse of the Lancastrian régime, for it depended upon the unity of the Council, and to a less degree on the support of parliament, and here again the holding of parliament in his own countryside at Bury to put Gloucester at his mercy is a breach with the more decent conventions of the past thirty years. The ruthlessness of the commons' attack in 1450 may have been in some measure a revenge for his intimidation of the parliament of 1447.

The impeachment of Suffolk in March 1450 may be taken as a necessary political move if the crown were to be saved, though it *Fall of* *Suffolk* included grotesque charges, and was prompted to a large degree by the mistaken hope that the French possessions might yet be saved. Had the sentence of temporary exile not been darkened by his murder it would have been accepted as a wise and not unduly severe measure to remove a too powerful counsellor. But the events which followed the minister's fall showed that Henry and his remaining councillors could not govern England. Somerset was in France, York in Ireland, Suffolk and Moleyns dead, the latter murdered in January in a riot in the camp at Portsmouth, and in the interval before the need of reconstituting the Council was realised the great revolt of Cade broke out in May 1450. Its political programme was not without wisdom, since *York and* it attacked the exclusion of the great lords from the Council and *Somerset* demanded the return of the duke of York, but it did his cause no good, for it confirmed the court in its belief that he intended treason. Henry, moreover, had been persuaded that the murderers of Moleyns were acting in York's interest. Accordingly, though the leaders of the two parties—Somerset the heir to the connection of the cardinal and Suffolk and to their favour with the court, and York the exponent of a restored conciliar régime—returned to England, they came laden with the hatreds and suspicions bred of recent happenings. Both York and Henry saw the essential need to be "sad and substantial Council",[1] but York was at first denied landing by the king's officers and had to force his way into the king's presence. Angered at this reception, he coupled his demand for a Council and a parliament with one for justice upon those

[1] *Paston Letters* (ed. Gairdner), xcvii.

reputed to be traitors, and the parliament of January 1451—
strongly Yorkist in favour—accordingly petitioned for Somerset's
removal from court. From parliament, also, came the first fatal
reference to the question of the succession. A number of the
commons petitioned for the recognition of York as heir to the
throne in the event, which now seemed likely, of Henry dying
without issue.

The circumstances of this petition show that the Lancastrian
crown—as distinct from the persons and factions who claimed to
be its principal supporters—still had a substantial party behind it.
As the lords of parliament had refused to try Suffolk for treason,
so now they rejected York's claim to recognition as heir, and on
this cleavage between lords and commons the long session of
parliament was dismissed. It is clear that the majority of the
magnates were still independent of party, and that Henry's influence was not exhausted.[1] The year 1451 ended in a dead-lock,
Somerset retaining his place at court, and York remaining in the
country, and for the time being holding his hand. It may be
guessed that at this stage a decisive victory by either party would
have produced a sufficiently compliant parliament and a general
response from the nobility, but the long tension between York
and Somerset, which lasted throughout the rest of the year 1451
and was made the more dangerous by the fall of Bordeaux and
Bayonne in the summer, discredited the cause of compromise.
York's In February 1452 York made his initial act of avowed war,
first rising raised the West Country, and, with the earl of Devon and Lord
Cobham, marched on London. Again the magnates remained
neutral, the rebels were obliged to accept a formal promise of
redress by way of common law—they did not think it worth while
to pursue it—Somerset remained, and York disbanded his forces.
This was the position when, in September 1453, the king first
showed signs of derangement, and by the time of the October
parliament he was clearly incapable of rule. The situation had been
made more difficult by the birth of Prince Edward, but, faced
with a choice between a regency of the queen or the duke of York,
the nobles began to rally to the latter, and he was able to come to

[1] Even as late as February 1458 there was a neutral party of bishops—one of
their rare acts of self-assertion in this age—and nobles, who persuaded the
parties to a brief peace. *English Chronicle* (Camden Society), p. 77.

the parliament of February 1454 supported by the earls of Warwick, Richmond, and Pembroke.[1] It was a parliament in arms;
even Cardinal Kemp armed his retainers for his protection, the
duke of Buckingham had badges for two thousand men preparing,
and the duke of Somerset "had spies in every lord's house, some *Protec-*
as friars, some as shipmen taken on the sea, and some in other *torate*
wise";[2] but it produced a tolerable settlement. Many of the *York*
Council favoured York,[3] the lords chose him as Protector, offices
and benefices were shared fairly evenly between the two parties,
Somerset was put in ward but no motion was made to try him.

At this point, when the country became committed to a civil
war which could only end in the extinction of one or other of
the two parties, it may be well to take stock of those three Lancastrian reigns which have been given the credit of being an
experiment in constitutional rule, and to see how far their own
utterances or the estimate of contemporaries establish their claim
to a distinctive political theory. How far was the constitutional
position of the crown altered by them, and a new and more liberal
view of the constitution evolved? Difference of practice there
certainly was, for the continual Council is a new feature in the *Theory of*
constitution, but it arose less from a new theory than from the *the crown*
necessity created by Henry IV's illness, Henry V's absences abroad,
and Henry VI's long minority and subsequent ineffectiveness. It is
true that the Lancastrian Justice Sir John Fortescue thought of
England as *dominium politicum et regale* as opposed to the autocratic
dominium regale of France, but he wrote his "Governance of England" at the height of Edward IV's power—in 1473—and he did
not claim that his "mixed polity" was a Lancastrian innovation.
Indeed he thought it was the original form of the English state,
the work of Brutus, its first known king.[4] Nor did any parliamentary right of Lancaster figure largely in controversy in the
revolutions which founded the dynasty or brought it to its end.
In so far as the house of Lancaster was committed to a constitutional theory of the crown, it might be expected to be embodied

[1] *Paston Letters* (ed. Gairdner), no. 195.　　　　[2] *Loc. cit.*
[3] Stubbs, *Constitutional History*, iii. 171.
[4] *The Government of England* (ed. C. Plummer), p. 112.

in the indictment of Richard II's reign presented by the parliament which deposed him. This indictment [1] consisted of thirty-three articles—*objectus contra Regem*—and seems to have aimed at stating every grievance against the late king from his claim to pronounce law by his own mouth to his taking the crown jewels out of England. But it is devoid of logical plan, hardly rises to generalities, and presents no doctrine of constitutional monarchy which Richard might be supposed to have violated and from which he was to be deposed. The objections are, indeed, typical of that ill-directed age, in which the catholic-feudal treatises of the scholastics are out of favour and no fresh review of monarchy has yet been made, and they reflect the confused, though still highly practical, mentality of their makers. To this extent they are of value as showing the minds of those peers, knights, burgesses, and justices who had been driven through the reign of Richard, hectored by both parties in turn, till one order of the realm after another confessed that "they feared for their lives to speak honestly". If we look for theory in them, they show a clinging to the familiar safeguards, rather than any hope for a new régime. The centre of the case for Richard's unfitness is the time-worn doctrine of the king's trust for the law and of its sacrosanctity. Sitting in Council to hear the pleas of subjects and instructed by his justices as to the law appropriate to each, he had used to answer "austerely and with anger" that "the law was in the king's mouth, and often in his breast"—"that he could make and change the laws of his kingdom"—and thus many subjects were deterred from seeking their legal remedy. He had so brow-beat his justices in Council that they did not dare speak the truth. Specifically in the Shrewsbury parliament, he had forced them to rule according to his own view of the case against Gloucester and Arundel. He had said that the lives and goods of his subjects were at his mercy—thus intending to "enervate" the primary civil rights—had had men appealed for *lèse majesté* in the military court of the marshal and constable and forced to defend themselves by the duel, and had banished Bolingbroke and archbishop Arundel without trial. He had stayed process in the courts Christian by letters under his signet when the chancellor had refused to issue them under the Great Seal. All this is unquestionably sound defence of the proper

As expressed in the deposition of Richard II

[1] *Rotuli Parliamentorum,* iii. 417.

standing of the king in relation to common law right, and had been written constitutional law since the Great Charter. It is the weightiest part of the indictment. With this traditional matter go certain complaints which reflect the special status which had come to attach to statute law, and this is the most modern element in the articles. Whereas statutes are binding till revoked by statute, Richard induced the commons to petition him to "be as free as any of his progenitors", and on this excuse did many things which were against statutes, ignoring those which prescribed the election of sheriffs and their vacation of office after a year. He had procured the Shrewsbury parliament to commit its authority to certain of its members for the hearing of unanswered petitions only, but upon this pretence had proceeded to certain matters touching the whole parliament. At any time within the past two hundred years similar offences would have called forth, and in many instances had called forth, similar complaints, and the whole of this defence of the law falls within the accepted limits of medieval kingship without new remedy, and, except for the prominence given to statute—itself not new—without any extended views of a constitutional crown.

The same medievalism of outlook is betrayed in the handling of Richard's great political offences by which the Appellants and Bolingbroke and Norfolk had suffered. Even the cancelling of the commission or Council of 1386, which involved the setting aside of parliament's favourite constitutional expedient of a continual Council, was condemned not on constitutional grounds, but on that of unjust proceedings against its individual members and of royal coercion of the justices. Apart from those legal irregularities which we have already mentioned, the king's dealings with Gloucester, Bolingbroke, and the archbishop were handled not so as to bring out any proof of violation of constitutional practice, but to fasten upon him those sins of cruelty, duplicity, and, above all, of perjury, which canonically unfitted a man from legitimate wearing of the crown. In article after article the climax is reached with *et ideo est perjurus*, and the conclusion sums up for deposition upon grounds of moral guilt *attentis perjuribus multiplicibus ac crudelitate aliisque quampluribus criminibus dicti Ricardi*. The sum of all this should make us slow to believe that those who made the revolution of 1399 had any wide constitutional scheme to put forward, still less one that was new. What was out of the accustomed order in the past reign had been upon the side of Richard, who from time to time used words which might have come from a Renaissance prince. Parliament asserted the accustomed rule and little more. Yet such was the change in the times that things were said and done in 1399 that did not suggest themselves in 1327. There was a fuller recognition of parliament and statute, and a complaint against the packing of the commons. The vacating of the throne involved a process which had not been attempted in 1327, judgment upon the king by parliament in the person of a commission of its members, and a formal act of deposition. Richard's own confession of insufficiency for his office was indeed taken into account, but it was not like that of Edward II an abdication, and the commission deposed him "by definitive sentence", and only after this had been pronounced did the members of the estates, interrogated one by one, appoint proctors to renounce their homage. In 1327 the diffidation, though it had followed upon the king's renunciation, had itself been the effective act which broke the reign.

The Lancastrian right

If the deposition had been carried through without the formularization of a constitutional creed, the Lancastrian accession was made with none also. Henry advanced to the throne in parliament and made his claim by virtue of the right blood of Henry III, and as such was accepted, the right of Clarence's heir being neither put forward nor denied and parliament making no other motion than that of the customary acceptance and swearing of allegiance. On his death-bed Henry IV is said to have repented this act of assumption, "only God knows by what right I took the crown".

It is true that in 1404 [1] the estates made an "affirmation" of their loyalty to Henry's reign and reaffirmed their oaths to him and to the succession of the prince, and that this was accepted as a statute, but their intention was clearly to put their own allegiance beyond doubt and to declare the order of the succession rather than to assert the parliamentary basis of Henry's right. It is also true that in Henry IV's first parliament the archbishop announced that the king intended to be "counselled and governed by the honourable, wise, and discreet persons of his Realm", [2] but this is a voluntary statement of policy, though one which, as we have seen, Henry and his successors conformed to in the main. There is no

[1] *Rotuli Parliamentorum*, iii. 525.   [2] *Ibid.* iii. 415.

act or occasion which can be pointed to as explicitly giving to the Lancastrian dynasty a statutory right or as binding them to any specific form of government. In 1460 the defence of the Lancastrian crown was, of course, a forlorn hope, no doubt half-heartedly undertaken. The appeal to Henry himself to "search the chronicles"[1] for a justification of his own case shows that the lords had little hope that much could be got from the rolls of parliament, and the justices, in claiming that the matter of the crown was above all cognisance but that of the "Princes of the King's blood", indirectly admitted the same.[2] There was some tendency upon the part of the lords to assert that a statutory right had been built up in the course of the Lancastrian reigns by "the great and notable Acts of Parliaments . . . of much more authority than any chronicle",[2] but this was not pressed against York's retort that such statutes were neither many nor great but no more than the one statute of 1404 regularising the succession as between Henry IV's sons, and that this would not have been needed had his descent been good. The statute could, indeed, hardly bear the interpretation which it was sought to put upon it, and against the patently superior lineage of the dukes of York the descendants of John of Gaunt, once they were challenged, had nothing better to urge than that their rivals had borne the arms of Edmund of Langley and not of Lionel of Clarence. In 1460 the throne was saved to Henry for his life, not by any constitutional principles admitted, or even asserted, but by the newness of the oaths sworn to him by the nobles at Coventry, and perhaps by some lingering conscience that the oaths of homage ought not to be broken without diffidation, and diffidation not made with more cause of offence than the unfortunate Henry VI had it in his power to give. Thus neither in 1399 nor in 1459 when the Lancastrians had most need to make the dynastic right good, nor in 1460 when Edmund of York assumed the throne by hereditary right almost unopposed, did either party—if we except a faint-hearted offer to plead a statutory claim for Lancaster—formulate a distinctive political theory of its crown.[3] The Yorkists came nearest to doing so when, the way for

---

[1] *Rotuli Parliamentorum*, v. 376.   [2] *Loc. cit.*

[3] A Lancastrian tract of Edward IV's reign put forward the Salic Law as a bar to his claim through Clarence. J. Fortescue, *Government of England* (ed. C. Plummer), p. 354.

*The
Yorkist
crown*

Richard III's accession having been cleared by the denunciation of Edward IV's marriage as invalid, Richard's claim was rehearsed in parliament.[1] His title, it was then said, was perfect by the laws of God, of Nature, and of the realm; but in view of the ignorance of the people, and because of their willingness to put "faith and certainty" in what was rehearsed by the three estates in parliament, it was now declared by statute. It may be suspected that Henry IV's statute of 1404 on the succession was scarcely intended to do more than this.

Edward IV, therefore, took the throne with no new theory of kingly right, but with the same right as that of Henry, though by a better lineage. Nor did he announce any new theory of kingship. The tradition of his house, in so far as his father had had an opportunity to display it, had been the normal, constitutional government of the day, a council of notables, a right course of common law, the king to live of his own. It was the policy of Suffolk's opponents continued against the personal rule of the queen. That Edward IV did not follow it, and, indeed, allowed both parliament and Council to take a far less prominent part than they had done in the early years of Henry VI, is due less to any settled theory of government than to the general failure of confidence in these institutions which had overcome the nation. The change is, however, a marked one, and becomes even more so as the reign goes

*Decline
of the
Continual
Council*

on. The form of the Council changes entirely, reverting back to those large bodies of officials whose joint responsibility was very slightly emphasized, and whose members the king took counsel with or neglected according to his conscience and to the business in hand. No continual Council was appointed in 1461, nor at any subsequent date. The Yorkist lords were careless in attendance— Warwick especially—and even the king made no rule of presiding, and the mass of the council were of the secondary rank of the court, knights of the Household, justices, serjeants, and attorneys predominating, the legal members being so numerous that it has been questioned whether the term King's Counsel had not already acquired its modern, restrictive, legal meaning. In spite of this influx of lawyers, Council was far less active in justice than it had been in the past, and in the first seven years of the reign its judicial function was almost in abeyance, with the result that it largely lost

[1] Stubbs, *Constitutional History*, iii. 235.

its preëminence as the principal authority for redress of grievance. Not only did the chancellor's jurisdiction thrive rapidly upon this change of practice in petition, but petitions to the king in person became common, and Edward, whose intention of strong government was apparently genuine, took the initiative in many cases when the peace was broken, and summoned the culprits to appear before himself or the Council. The drift of events, accentuated after the alienation of the Nevills by the great reduction in the number of the peers who were willing to serve in Council, was thus in the direction of personal government in the literal sense of the term. More frequently than any of his predecessors, it was Edward himself who was responsible for acts of government, and the eclipse of the Council is reflected in the fact that warrants commanding action *per consilium* fell in his reign to something like a twentieth of their accustomed proportion to the whole.

The decline of parliament was hardly less marked. Not only *Decline* were there many years in which no parliament met, but Edward, *of parliament* having tested and approved the temper of any one assembly, tended to retain it in being by prorogation over a series of years. Thus, the parliament of April 1463 sat until 1465, and that of 1472, the first after Edward's restoration, was not dismissed until the spring of 1475. Between January 1478 and January 1483 no parliament was summoned. In this it does not seem that the king was going counter to any strong popular demand, for parliaments did little when summoned, and the stream of commons' petition had run almost dry. To all appearances this tendency was, as has already been said, less a characteristic feature of Yorkist rule than the accentuation of a decline of parliament which had already set in in the later years of Henry VI. From about 1450 the initiative of the commons had become less frequent, fewer commons' petitions were presented, they dealt with less important matters, and the crown was far less ready to accept them;[1] indeed, in the first four years of Edward IV's reign there was even a slight revival of commons' activity and of the king's complaisance towards it. But from 1465 to 1483 only twenty-six such bills were approved in four parliaments, and of these the majority were of little general importance and dealt with the redress of local grievances or gave remedy to groups or individuals at the instance of the commons.

[1] H. L. Gray, *Commons' Influence on Early Legislation*, pp. 98 and 118 *et seq.*

In the last parliament of Edward's reign only four commons' petitions became statutes, and they dealt with minor matters of sumptuary law and trading practice.

Parliament   The crown did not cease to use parliament. Rather, it drew the
as the   lesson of recent years as to its value as an obedient servant of any
king's   power which happened to be predominant, called it when con-
servant   venient, and, keeping it in being over two and three years together, used the publicity and special authority of statute to give effect to its own enactments. The official bill, prompted by the crown, introduced in the lords, but passing through the form of commons' assent, which was a not infrequent device of the last decade of Henry VI's reign, became common in that of Edward IV, and in Richard III's one parliament took in importance the first place in legislation. Richard III's estimate of the value of parliamentary enactment may perhaps be taken to be that of the Yorkist crown at large: its value for the monarch is declaratory as giving "faith and certainty" to the matter enacted.

The same willingness to accord to parliament a part in the task of government, together with much initiative in which the rôle of parliament is not considered, characterizes the haphazard but not unsuccessful conduct of Edward IV's finance. In part Edward relied upon the normal course of parliamentary grant. He took no tax until 1463, but received a Tenth and Fifteenth in that year, tonnage and poundage for life in 1465, two Tenths and Fifteenths in 1468 on the promise of an expedition to France, and single Tenths and Fifteenths in 1473, 1474, 1475, and 1483. But by 1473 he was coercing individual subjects in numbers into "voluntary" gifts of money—benevolences—and this device, together with sharp fines imposed for breaches of the peace, either in his own reign or in that of Henry, together with the use of the crown's shipping upon private trading ventures of the king, made him to an increasing degree self-supporting, and enabled him to go for periods of years without the help of subsidy. There was little tendency to systematize these occasional, though large, sources of revenue into a prerogative taxation like that of France, nor, per-haps, was the revenue vastly augmented in Edward's reign, but the financial policy of the reign is another proof of the comparative independence of the crown and of a new power to ignore the criticism of parliament and the country. It is the lack of apparent system in Edward IV's rule—Richard III's was too brief to have revealed its real trend, but it began with a denunciation of Edward's despotism—which makes it difficult to speak of a new monarchy, or to regard its effects as lasting. Edward acts with great spontaneity and far more effect than Henry, but it is the self-assertion of a powerful individual who governs empirically and does not care to build up institutions for the future. The usurpation of Richard is itself a proof of this, for it was made in the face of what was at best indifference on the part of the people, and a strong Council might well have made it impossible. It was the dwindling of all those forces which habitually surrounded the throne which, as in the earlier tragedy of Margaret and Henry, left the royal family alone to work out their own fate undefended and unimpeded.

Thus time, as it discredited one remedy after another, bringing with it no new inspiration, confirmed the nation in its belief that *Conclusion* salvation must come from the crown, and bred even a sort of indifference. At the end of the fifteenth century the demand was still for "plentiful governance", a king who "gave good lordship", a strong Council. But the ancient means to these ends were almost discredited. It is not a mere seeking to introduce a pattern into history which sees in these last reigns of the fifteenth century the end of the Middle Ages, for the institutions which the medieval community had built, and in which it had flourished, had reached what was probably their fullest expression at a time when the society they had grown up to serve was losing its old beliefs and its original integrity. If there is a single predominant theme in the institutions of the first thousand years of English history it is the supremacy of law and the function of the community to declare, and, if necessary, change it. Given a community of lawful men, these fundamentals were secured century after century, according to the method of each generation, by popular assembly, or by councils really or fictitiously representative of that part of the nation which was politically recognized. Whether, as in the full age of feudalism, through the *commune consilium*, or, as later, by continual council and parliament, this idea did not fail, nor was its realisation entirely frustrated, until the mass of individuals began to lose their vision of the community and to grasp at immediate material interest, until wealth and private power ceased to stand in any organized relation to the state. When this had come to pass medieval constitutionalism in county and parliament could no longer be maintained. Parliaments became rarer than in the past, and more perfunctory when they met. Fortescue, the only articulate theorist in a declining age, no longer believed in the continual Council of the nobles, but looked forward to some such strong, royalist Council as the Tudors made. The problem of order had, indeed, outrun the resources of the medieval state, and the expedients of government in 1485 were as yet medieval. However much our knowledge of the uses to which it was to be put in later days may blind us to the fact, its presumptions were still feudal. Even after two hundred years of parliament, the view—no longer true to facts, but still determining action—was held that the ultimate governing right lay between the king and some body of magnates standing in the place and inheriting the virtue of the *commune consilium regni*. In the final recourse the constituent core of parliament even in the fifteenth century was the king sitting in the Great Council of the peers. It was to these that the royal power lapsed in minority, and, though the commons had secured a more or less firm acceptance of the necessity of their assent to statute, their habits, traditions, and outlook were still those of petitioners. They had no real defence against the packing of their house, they did not react against dictation with any confidence, and they reflected slavishly the political colour of the moment. According as opportunity presented itself, they were either petitioners or critics, never equal and confident participators in the task of government with the king and the lords; they never mastered its difficulties or associated themselves with the crown in its responsibilities. Therefore they wanted the executive power to be strong and successful, and at the same time cheap to the point of carrying on war in France and maintaining peace in England upon those revenues which were derived from the royal demesne and barely sufficed for the upkeep of the king's household. Fortescue is the first writer to recognize clearly that, beyond the ordinary revenue for his person, he needed an extraordinary revenue of state. Not until the restricted medieval view of kingship was enlarged, and the belief in the limitation of the subjects' obligation—derived from the fixed custom of the feudal tenant—was relaxed in a sense of common interest and identity of purpose with the crown, could parliament be more than a place of redress of grievance. No medieval king or parliament could rise to the full implication of an impersonal crown responding to and putting into action the will of parliament, nor, for its part, could parliament accept frankly the directing power of the crown, as it was to do more fully in Tudor times. It was an age when that system of checks and balances, which was to be read into the English constitution of the eighteenth century, was still a reality. Such a system was, indeed, the natural expression of the feudal relation, but in the lawless, faithless, and over-wealthy society of the later Middle Ages it made steadily for the paralysis of all government. In that contraction of the force of all legitimate institutions, and in the freeing of lawless power from its ancient legal restraints, the long history of feudal England was drawing to its close.

BIBLIOGRAPHICAL NOTE

THE following list of books, though not exhaustive, will be found useful in following up the various topics dealt with in this volume.

In spite of the amount of research which has been carried out since the last edition of Bishop Stubbs's *Constitutional History of England,* it still remains incomparably the best study of English medieval history, and there is little probability of its being replaced. In one field only has a wholesale addition been made to the corpus of constitutional history, the investigation by Professor T. F. Tout of all that side of government which was carried on through the domestic offices which is contained in his *Chapters in Administrative History.* With these two general works it is, however, necessary to read such studies of constitutional law and economic history as may be found in F. Pollock and F. W. Maitland's *History of English Law before Edward I,* Professor W. S. Holdsworth's *History of English Law,* and E. Lipson's *An Introduction to the Economic History of England.* Other general works of constitutional history which may be read with profit are R. Gneist's *Englische Verfassungsgeschichte* (translated by P. A. Ashworth), F. W. Maitland's *Constitutional History of England,* and that of Professor G. B. Adams. C. Petit-Dutaillis' *Studies Supplementary to Stubbs's Constitutional History* discusses a number of the more debatable passages in Bishop Stubbs's work in the light of more recent knowledge.

(i) The nature of Teutonic society in general may best be studied in the works of the German scholars of the last century. Of these the most comprehensive is G. Waitz's *Deutsche Verfassungsgeschichte,* while the structure of the kindred may be studied in K. von Amira's *Erbenfolge und Verwandschaftsgliederung nach den altniederdeutschen Rechten* and H. Brunner's *Sippe und Wergeld.* The particular form of such institutions among the Anglo-Saxons is best shown in H. M. Chadwick's *Studies in Anglo-Saxon Institutions,* K. Maurer's *Angelsächsische Rechtsverhältnisse, Essays in Anglo-Saxon Law* (Boston, 1876), and F. Seebohm's *Tribal Custom in Anglo-Saxon Law.*

The economic structure of Saxon England may best be studied in K. Rhamm's *Die Grosshufen der Nordgermanen,* P. Hatschek's *Angelsächsische Verfassungsgeschichte,* Professor P. Vinogradoff's *The Growth of the Manor,* F. W. Maitland's *The Domesday Book and Beyond,* F. Seebohm's *The English Village Community,* and *Customary Acres and their Historical Significance.*

A work of a special general scope, but still bearing upon constitutional history, is H. M. Chadwick's *Origins of the English Nation.*

(ii) The following works bear upon one or other aspect of constitutional or social history in the later centuries of the Saxon era. J. C. H. R. Steenstrup's *Normannerne*, Professor P. Vinogradoff's *English Society in the Eleventh Century*, L. M. Larson's *The King's Household before the Norman Conquest*, H. M. Cam's *Local Government in Francia and England*, W. A. Morris's *The Frankpledge System*, P. Guilhiermoz's *Essai sur l'origine de la noblesse en France au moyen âge*. J. M. Kemble's *The Saxons in England* is still of value. The notes of the Rev. C. Plummer to his *Historia Ecclesiastica* of Bede and to the *Two Saxon Chronicles Parallel*, which he edited together with J. Earle, contain a very great deal of learning, and R. H. Hodgkin's *A History of the Anglo-Saxons*, now re-issued, bring together the results of the studies of the last thirty years and are invaluable surveys of every aspect of Anglo-Saxon life. Professor J. Goebel's *Felony and Misdemeanour* is important for its examination of the growth of Frankish law in relation to that of England and of the development of the Frankish and Norman franchise.

(iii) For the Norman and Angevin reigns the first essential is an understanding of feudal custom, and for this the best general survey is that of Professor F. M. Stenton in *English Feudalism*. Sir Henry Spelman's *Of Feuds and Tenures by Knight Service* is still valuable, as are T. Madox's *Baronia Anglica* and W. Dugdale's *The Baronage of England*. The custom of the Norman Duchy is best studied in C. H. Haskins's *Norman Institutions*, and various incidents of feudal tenure and administration are examined and illustrated in the works of J. H. Round, *Geoffrey de Mandeville*, *Feudal England*, and *The Commune of London*, in Sir Maurice Powicke's *Loss of Normandy*, J. F. Baldwin's *The Scutage and Knight Service of England*, H. Denholm Young's *Seignorial Administration in England*, and Miss H. M. Chew's *English Ecclesiastical Tenants in Chief*. For the history of law, besides the works already cited, there should be read M. M. Bigelow's *History of Procedure in England*, H. Brunner's *Die Entstehung der Schwurgerichte*, E. Jenks's *Law and Politics in the Middle Ages*, J. B. Thayer's *A Preliminary Treatise on the Common Law*, J. W. Jeudwine's *Tort, Crime, and Police in Medieval England*, F. W. Maitland's *Equity*, and *Roman Canon Law in the Church of England*, and Professor P. Vinogradoff's *Roman Law in Medieval Europe*. Legal administration is described in W. A. Morris's *The Frankpledge System*, W. C. Bolland's *The General Eyre*, and in *Self-Government at the King's Command*, by A. B. White. Miss H. M. Cam has made the medieval hundred her special study, and her *Studies in the Hundred Rolls* and *The Hundred and the Hundred Rolls* should be read. The higher branches of the administration are best described in S. B. Chrimes's *Introduction to the Administrative History of Medieval England*, in *The Medieval English Sheriff to 1300* by W. A. Morris, W. Parow's *Compotus Vicecomitis*, and C. A. Beard's *The Office of the Justice of the Peace in England in its Origin and Development*. Much has been written about the boroughs, studies of particular aspects of which may be found in T. Madox's *Firma Burgi*, C. Gross's *The Gild Merchant*, M. Bateson's *Borough Customs*, M. de W. Hemmeon's *Burgess Tenure in Mediaeval England*, F. W. Maitland's *Township and Borough*, A. Ballard's *The Domesday Boroughs*. Professor J. Tait has brought together the existing materials into a volume, *The Medieval English Borough*, which is the only authoritative work upon the subject as a whole.

Of the central government of the Norman and Angevin reigns, the Exchequer has been the subject of studies by T. Madox, *The History and Antiquities of the Exchequer of England*, R. L. Poole, *The Exchequer in the Twelfth Century*, H. Hall, *Antiquities and Curiosities of the Exchequer* and *An Introduction to the Pipe Rolls*, and *Dialogus de Scaccario*, edited by Charles Johnson, and receives constant illustration from the essays of J. H. Round. For the court and household, besides Professor Tout's first volume, there should be read Professor G. B. Adams' *Council and Courts in Anglo-Norman England*, R. W. Eyton's *Court, Household, and Itinerary of Henry II*, and H. Hall's *Court Life under the Plantagenets*. The working of government in practice is best shown in Bishop Stubbs's collected *Historical Introduction to the Rolls Series*.

Professor E. A. Freeman's *History of the Norman Conquest* and *History of the Reign of William Rufus* can still be read with profit if taken with some caution. C. Petit-Dutaillis has recently published a comparison of the growth of the English and French monarchies during the period, *La Monarchie féodale en France et en Angleterre, x^e-xiiie siècle*.

(iv) The constitutional activity of the thirteenth century naturally takes its rise from the Charter. For this there should be read W. S. M'Kechnie's *Magna Carta, Magna Carta Commemoration Essays*, ed. H. E. Maldon, Professor F. M. Powicke's *Stephen Langton*, the introductory matter in C. Bémont's *Chartes de libertés anglaises 1100-1305*, and *The First Century of Magna Carta*, by F. Thompson. The later phases of the conflict are covered by C. Bémont's *Simon de Montfort* (ed. E. F. Jacob), by Professor E. F. Jacob's *Studies in the Period of Baronial Reform and Rebellion (1258-1267)*, Professor R. F. Treharne's *The Baronial Plan of Reform (1258-1263)*, and G. W. Prothero's *The Life of Simon de Montfort*. S. K. Mitchell's *Studies in Taxation under John and Henry III* should also be used, and the history of the revenue may be followed in J. H. Ramsey's *Revenues of the Kings of England*, S. Dowell's *A History of Taxation and Taxes in England*, and H. Hall's *History of the Customs Revenues in England*. Social relations which have their reaction upon political life are dealt with in Professor P. Vinogradoff's *Villainage in England* and *Custom and Right*, H. L. Gray's *English Field Systems*, and F. Mugnier's *Les Savoyards en Angleterre au xiiie siècle*. The political thought of the age is best studied in R. L. Poole's *Illustrations of the History of Medieval Thought and Learning*, C. H. M'Ilwain's *The Growth of Political Thought in the West*, A. J. Carlyle's *A History of Medieval*

Political Thought in the West, and O. Gierke's *Political Theories of the Middle Ages*, translated by F. W. Maitland.

(v) Perhaps the best treatments of the latest phase of constitutional theory and growth is to be found in S. B. Chrimes's *English Constitutional Ideas in the XVth Century*. Various aspects of the origin and development of Parliament are to be studied in the introduction to F. W. Maitland's *Memoranda de Parliamento*, in Professor C. H. M'Ilwain's *High Court of Parliament*, Professor A. F. Pollard's *Evolution of Parliament*, in the Report of the House of Lords' Committee *On the Dignity of a Peer*, L. W. Vernon Harcourt's *His Grace the Steward* and *Trial by Peers*, D. Pasquet's *The Origin of the House of Commons* (translated by R. G. D. Laffan), in H. L. Gray's *Commons Influence on Early Legislation*, L. O. Pike's *A Constitutional History of the House of Lords*, M. V. Clarke's *Medieval Representation and Consent*, M. M'Kisack's *The Parliamentary Representation of the English Boroughs during the Middle Ages*, and in essays by Mr Richardson and Professor Sayles in the *English Historical Review* (vols. xlvi., xlvii.), the *Transactions of the Royal Historical Society*, 4th Series, vol. xi., and the *Bulletin of the Institute of Historical Research*, vols. v., vi., and xi. For the development of legislation T. F. T. Plucknett's *Statutes and their Interpretation in the First Half of the Fourteenth Century* should be read, and for taxation J. F. Willard's *Parliamentary Taxes on Personal Property, 1290–1334*. For the history of the Privy Council the principal authority is J. F. Baldwin's *The King's Council*, and there is a short study of the medieval council in A. V. Dicey's *Privy Council*. The Chancery is dealt with by E. H. Goodwin in *The Equity of the King's Court before the Reign of Edward I* and D. M. Kerly's *An Historical Sketch of the Court of Chancery*. J. E. Morris' *The Welsh Wars of Edward I* is of great value for its account of the decline of feudal obligations in the host. Studies of constitutional movements in individual reigns are Professor T. F. Tout's *The Place of Edward II in English History*, H. Wallon's *Richard II*, and J. H. Wylie's *The History of England under Henry IV*.

A full bibliography of English history, including periodical sources, will be found in C. Gross's *Sources and Literature of English History to 1485*. This was re-edited and revised in 1915, and for the years 1915–1929 the *Short Bibliography of English Constitutional History*, by H. M. Cam and A. S. Turberville, will be found of value. To the dates of their publication the bibliographies of the Cambridge Medieval History, arranged according to the several subjects of its chapters, are full, reliable, and extremely convenient for reference. An article, "Some Recent Advances in English Constitutional History (before 1485)", by Gaillard Lapsley in the *Cambridge Historical Journal*, vol. v., no. 2, discusses recent historical production under the heads of Parliament, Law, and Constitutional Theory.

INDEX

Abacus, calculation by the, 190

Abba, reeve, 16

Abergavenny, 428

Abingdon, Abbot of, 67

Administration and baronage, 150; fusion of English and Danish, 104; Norman, 181

Ælfic, reeve, 126

Æflaeda, the Lady, 79, 123

Ælfred, king: and maintenance, 15; and the law, 28; and the oath, 9; and the witan, 27; ealdormen of, 123; estates bequeathed by, 36; grith of, 114; household of, 131; laws of, 97; monarchy under, 50, 54; political unification at death of, 101; priests at court of, 132; revenue of, 53; seal of, 133; treatment of reeveship, 112

Ælfric, Archbishop, 25

Ælfric Cild, 28

Ælwin, King of Northumbria, 34

Æthelbald, King of Mercia, 14, 31; new dynasty of, 48

Æthelbert, King of Kent, accession of, 31; law of, 11

Æthelflaeda, the Lady, 101

Æthelheah, *pedes sessor*, 26, 132

Æthelred I, King of Wessex, 30, 31,

Æthelred II, 101; and outlawry, 108; ealdormanry under, 123; grith of, 114; king, 127; seal of, 133

Æthelric, *sub-regulus*, 14

Æthelsige, 135

Æthelstan, King, 27, 101, 109, 110; and hundred guild, 117; and the frith, 115; farm in time of, 129

Æthelstan, Half-King, 40

Æthelstan of Sunbury, 27

Æthelwulf, King of Wessex, 29, 31; endowment of king's thegns, 90

Affinities, 424, 428-429

Aid, 154, 308; assessment to, 309; authority for grant of, 241; consent to exceptional, 242; feudal, under

Henry II, 220; in Magna Carta, 257; in Parliament, 355; of 1198, 1204 and 1207, 309; of 1225 and 1232, 310; of 1237 and 1254, 311; *pur fille marier*, 355, 357; resistance to, under John, 241; transition from tallage to, 325

Aids: collectors of, 310; non-Parliamentary, 356; of the boroughs, 326

Albini, William of, 232, 237

Alcuin, 31, 43

Aldermen of London, 319

Ale, Assize of, 239

Alfhun, Abbot, 191

Alod, 7, 74

Aluric, 129

Andred, 36

Angelcynn, 2

Angevin: judiciary, 323; marriage, 482; monarchy, 204, 218, 236, 247, 262, 265, 272

Anglesey, 172

Angyld, 66, 67

Anjou, 482

Annandale, 427

Anselm, Archbishop of Canterbury, 196

Antiqua custuma, 401

Appellants, the, 443, 462, 470, 487

Arches, William des, 192

Ardua negotia regni, 344

Argentien, Richard of, 265

Aristocracy in Saxon history, 72

Arms, assize of, 211, 239, 313

Arosetna, 25

Arrest, freedom of members of Parliament from, 453

Articles: for Council of 1406, 460, 462; for Council of 1423 and 1426, 464; of barons of 1215, 252, 253

Articuli super cartas, 361, 404

Articuli Willelmi, 327

Arundel, Earl of, 238, 486

Asgar the Staller, 141

END OF VOL. I

THE JEWISH EXPERIENCE
IN LATIN AMERICA

Selected Studies From
The Publications of The

AMERICAN JEWISH
HISTORICAL SOCIETY

VOLUME I

Edited with An Introduction By
MARTIN A. COHEN

AMERICAN JEWISH HISTORICAL SOCIETY
WALTHAM, MASSACHUSETTS

KTAV PUBLISHING HOUSE, INC.
NEW YORK

THE JEWISH EXPERIENCE
IN LATIN AMERICA

Selected Studies From
The Publications of The

AMERICAN JEWISH
HISTORICAL SOCIETY

VOLUME I

Edited with An Introduction By
MARTIN A. COHEN

AMERICAN JEWISH HISTORICAL SOCIETY
WALTHAM, MASSACHUSETTS

KTAV PUBLISHING HOUSE, INC.
NEW YORK

Library of Congress Cataloging in Publication Data

Cohen, Martin A   comp.
    The Jewish experience in Latin America.

    Bibliography: p.
    1. Jews in South America--Collections. I. American
Jewish Historical Society. II. Title.
F2239.J5C63   301.451'92408   78-138850
ISBN 0-87068-136-2

SBN ‹ 87068-136-2

Library of Congress Catalog Card Number: 78-138850

Manufactured in the United States of America

To

DR. JACOB RADER MARCUS

Distinguished historian,

Inspiring teacher,

Faithful friend

Contents
VOLUME I

Contents

VOLUME II

Volumes 1-50 (1892-1961) were published as the
*Publications of the American Jewish Historical
Society*. Since 1961 the *Publications* are titled
the *American Jewish Historical Quarterly*.

PREFACE

The Jewish experience in Latin America is known only fragmentarily. A number of books and a host of articles deal with various aspects of this experience, but together they tell only a fraction of the story. The rest remains imbedded in rich stores of manuscript and printed materials. Many of these are readily available, while others are difficult to reach. Some day patient scholars will distill this material into reliable monographs, and then the history of Latin American Jewry can be adequately told.

For anyone interested in Latin American Jewry there is no better starting point than the pages of the *Publications* and *Quarterly* of the American Jewish Historical Society. Since the first appearance of its journals in 1894, the Society has consistently encouraged research on Latin American Jewish themes, and its harvest of studies across the years has been impressively rewarding. Almost all these articles have abiding value, despite occasional corrections necessitated by new information that has become available since the time of their publication.

The circle of scholars producing these studies has been exceedingly small. The same names crop up again and again not only in the journals of the American Jewish Historical Society but in those of other organizations as well. A handful of men are responsible for nearly all the contributions on Spanish American Jewry found in the *Publications* and the *Quarterly*, while two scholars have written all its major studies on the Jews of Brazil. The interests of these men have given the *Publications* and the *Quarterly* a heavy concentration in some areas of Latin American Jewish history and little or no representation in others. Thus the modern period has attracted only one major contribution, a translation of a manuscript written in Russian by a Russian Jew. Colonial Mexico, or New Spain, is well represented, as is Brazil, but the rest of Latin America is only occasionally considered. At the same time it should be noted that this imbalance prevails in Latin American Jewish studies in general. It is the result of a combination of the traditional interests of Jewish scholars in Latin American Jewish history and the accessibility of the materials available for study.

In this anthology are collected most of the contributions on Latin American Jewry found in the pages of the American Jewish Historical Society's *Publications* and *Quarterly*. They include survey articles on entire periods, annotated translations of some of the most significant documents and pioneering investigations of vast caches of indispensable data. The articles on Spanish America precede the studies devoted to Brazil. In the former category the numerous articles on colonial Mexico come first, in the order of the chronology of their subject matter. They are followed by two articles on Peru, one on the Cuban Fray Joseph Diaz Pimienta, and two on nineteenth-century Mexico, which contain a possible link to the Judaism of the colonial period. The section on Brazil is followed by Leo Shpall's translation of David Feinberg's article on the colonization of Russian Jews in Argentina.

Many of these articles, particularly the older ones, are in some measure inadequate and outdated. They occasionally contain errors of commission, some of the more important of which are mentioned in the modest notes on pages lxxi to lxxviii. More often they suffer from errors of omission, due in large measure to insufficient reliance on manuscripts and the nascent state of scholarship in the field. But even if occasionally flawed, the majority of these articles represent seminal achievement. They are far superior in methodology and factual accuracy to many more recent writings on the same subjects. Every reader will find profit in the pages of even the oldest articles. In the hands of a competent teacher the budding scholar will be led to a correctness of detail and an appreciation of the place of each contribution.

The accompanying introduction contains an overview of the history of Latin American Jewry, concentrating, like the articles, on the colonial period. It is intended to provide a framework for the material in these volumes. Regrettably the confines of this anthology do not permit a more comprehensive treatment of the subject or any of its manifold aspects. A fully integrated history of Latin American Jewry, even in one volume, remains a desideratum. Accompanying each volume of articles are brief notes calling attention to major items and in some cases providing new information.

It is hoped that the collection of the studies in these volumes will serve to bring the Latin American Jewish experience to the attention of a wider audience and atract a larger number of scholars to this young and significant field.

A special debt of gratitude is owed to a number of people who have helped in the preparation of this anthology—Mr. Bernard Wax, Director of the American Jewish Historical Society; Dr. Nathan M. Kaganoff, the Society's Librarian and Editor of its *Quarterly;* Dr. Herbert C. Zafren, Director of Libraries, Hebrew Union College-Jewish Institute of Religion; Dr. I. Edward Kiev, Librarian of the New York School of the Hebrew Union College-Jewish Institute of Religion; and Miss Sima Mittman, who prepared the two indexes.

March, 1971

MARTIN A. COHEN
Professor of Jewish History
Hebrew Union College—
Jewish Institute of Religion
New York, New York

INTRODUCTION

1.

The Two Jewries of Latin America

The history of the Jews in Latin America is the record of two successive and radically different populations. The first community took form shortly after the discovery of the New World. It always lived under adverse conditions and disintegrated long before the end of the colonial era. No census of its constituency is available or possible. At no time could it have comprised more than a few thousand individuals, and the likelihood is that for most periods its numbers were appreciably smaller. The second or contemporary settlement dates from the close of the wars of independence. Its beginnings were inauspicious, but a massive immigration at the end of the nineteenth and the beginning of the twentieth centuries injected it with strength and stability. Today Latin America is the home of more than six hundred thousand Jews, divided by national boundaries, but united by their common experiences and the fundamental ties underlying Latin American diversity.

With the fewest of exceptions, the colonial community was composed of Sephardim, or Jews of Spanish and Portuguese descent. The vast majority arrived in the New World directly from the Iberian Peninsula or by way of Holland during the period of Dutch rule in Brazil. The contemporary community consists of Ashkenazim, or Germanic and Eastern European Jews, as well as Sephardim. Its earliest immigrants were Sephardim from the Caribbean islands, while those arriving late in the nineteenth and during the twentieth centuries have included

Sephardim from Syria, Egypt and Morocco and Ashkenazim from Russia, Poland, Hungary, Rumania, Austria and Germany.

Occasionally one reads claims that the first community of Latin American Jewry laid the foundations for the second. This was hardly the case. The first group left no culture for the second to inherit and to the best of scholarly knowledge, there was no contact between the two groups.

Some of the Sephardic immigrants of recent decades may have been distantly related to the early immigrants from Portugal and Spain. Some of the Sephardim who left colonial Latin America for Europe and Asia may have been together with the ancestors of some of the later immigrants. And some of the Jews from Jamaica, Curaçao and other Caribbean islands who settled in Great Colombia shortly after its independence could well have been descendants of the earlier Jewish settlers in Latin America. But enticing though these possibilities are, they lack documentation to remove them from the realm of conjecture.

What made the experience of the two settlements so strikingly divergent were the contradictory attitudes toward Jews and Judaism they confronted on reaching the New World. The Latin America to which the components of the contemporary Jewry came guaranteed them untrammeled religious and cultural freedom. Jews have been able to practice their religion and maintain their separate identity without impediment. To be sure, Jews in Latin America have not been without their problems in the form of sporadic anti-Semitism, restrictions on immigration and curbs on Zionist activity. But on the whole the environment they have found in Latin America has been salutary and supportive.

The experience of the colonial Jewish community was dramatically different. In the sections of America under Spanish and Portuguese control only Catholics and Catholicism were allowed. Jews and Jewish activities were strictly prohibited throughout the colonial period. This means that Jews in colonial Latin America had to go underground in order to survive. Though there were times when some defiantly flaunted their identity, all Jews were engaged in a constant flight from arrest and persecution by the Spanish and Portuguese authorities.

To complicate matters, almost to a man, these Jews had at one time been converted to Christianity or were descendants of such converts. With the conversion of all Jews remaining in Spain at the time of the expulsion of the Spanish Jews in 1492 and with the conversion of the Jews in Portugal in 1497 the entire Iberian Peninsula was officially Catholic. As we shall see, many of the converts continued to regard themselves as Jews, but the ecclesiastical and lay authorities understandably presumed that they and their descendants were Catholics. The only major exception made in Latin America was in the case of the Jews captured in the Dutch territories of Brazil by the Portuguese-Brazilian armies. Most of these Jews were also of Sephardic descent, but since they had lived openly as Jews in Holland and Dutch Brazil, often for several generations, they were not regarded as baptized Catholics. For the people who were so regarded, the practice of Judaism involved more than an ordinary misdemeanor. It was nothing short of the crime of heresy, and heresy was punishable by death.

Thus, the two communities comprising the Jewish experience in Latin America shared the same geographical setting but lived in polar worlds. Their histories, though fortuitously contiguous, must be treated as the separate entities they were, without even the engaging presupposition that the memory of the first group in any way influenced the life of the second.

2.

The New Christians

The roots of the first community hark back to Christian Spain in the last decade of the fourteenth century. In the year 1391 vicious anti-Jewish riots engulfed the entire country and even spread to the Balearic Isles. The riots had all the trappings of spontaneity. But like the Russian pogroms nearly half a millennium later, they had been carefully planned by the ruling classes of Spanish society. Troubled by decades of internal disorder and the mounting threat of revolution, these classes cast about for a scapegoat to absorb the discontent of the mob. They found their targets in the Jewish community, which had been the most comfortable and acculturated of any of the Jewish communities in Christian Europe.

The riots resulted in the confiscation and destruction of untold property and the death of as many as fifty thousand Jews.

The rationale for the persecution was borrowed from the arsenal of Church polemics. It focused sharply on the Jews' implication in the death of Jesus and their purblindness in refusing to accept him as the Messiah. Such arguments had been employed by the lower Spanish clergy for centuries, but only in the last decades of the fourteenth do they appear to have become part of ruling class policy. The highest authorities of the Spanish kingdoms appeared to stand behind them, and no less a personage than Ferrán Martínez, the archdeacon of Ecija, resorted to them to galvanize popular hatred against the Jews.

But regardless of the aims of Spanish statesmen, the ideology of the Church was geared primarily to the destruction of Judaism rather than the Jews. Implicit within it was a plea to the Jews to drop their accursed state and cleanse themselves by conversion to the Church. Thus while the Spanish governments were waging their battle to destroy the Jews, the ecclesiastics during the riots and for decades thereafter were striving to draw them to the bapismal font.

Seeing baptism as an escape hatch for their troubles, thousands of Jews converted to Christianity in the wake of the 1391 riots. By no coincidence, the representation from the wealthy and propertied classes was large. In the subsequent decades countless other Jews succumbed to the relentless onslaught of conversionist preaching. These converts and their descendants came to be known as *conversos* or New Christians; those who were Christian before the riots were known as Old Christians. When coined, the terms *conversos* and New Christians were entirely descriptive; they carried no necessary pejorative connotation. However, the connotation was soon to undergo a rapid change.

Doubtless one consideration which impelled Jews to the baptismal font was the recognition that Jews baptized in Spain in previous decades and centuries were given full Christian privileges and were quickly integrated into Spanish society. If a hope for similar treatment was in the minds of the New Christians, it was not frustrated, at least initially. The New Christians found that conversion magically dissolved all obstacles to their advancement. Within a short time New Christians could be found high in the echelons of government, the universities, the army, and even the hierarchy of the Church. Many Old Christian families eagerly sought to ally themselves with New Christians in marriage. By the end of the fifteenth century New Christian blood ran in the veins of a considerable percentage of the leading families of Spain.

In the last decade of the fifteenth century the Iberian Peninsula witnessed two more periods of mass conversion by Jews to Christianity. The first came in 1492 when the Catholic Sovereigns, Ferdinand and Isabel, offered the Jews of Spain the alternatives of conversion to Christianity or expulsion from the country. Though the majority of the Jews chose to leave the land, large numbers converted to save their positions and property.

The second period came five years later in Portugal. Prior to 1492, the Jews in Portugal were fewer than those in Spain and enjoyed a much more placid history. In that year their numbers swelled with the immigration of many of the refugees from Spain. The new Jewish community soon made itself indispensable to King Manuel, and he was understandably reluctant to expel the Jews when prodded to do so by the Catholic Sovereigns. Manuel tried to persuade the Jews to convert, even before the demands of Ferdinand and Isabel, and he tried at least as hard thereafter, but his efforts were unavailing. The exiles who had rejected conversion in Spain were not prepared to succumb in Portugal. Frustrated, Manuel assembled a large number of Jews in Lisbon in 1497, baptized many by force and declared all of his Jews to be Christians by fiat.

It requires little imagination to realize that few of these conversions could have been sincere. In Spain, it was the desire to protect life and property which impelled Jews to the baptismal font. In Portugal, the Jews as a group were the passive recipients of legislated grace. Under these circumstances, it would have been natural for many New Christians in both countries to continue to regard themselves religiously as Jews, and for at least some to practice Judaism clandestinely, even at the risk of being branded as heretics if discovered. Information on New Christian Judaizing in the first half of the fifteenth century is scant, and the recorded cases of devotion to Judaism are few. But their number increases sharply after 1450, rises with the second group of New Christians and crescendoes with the third. It is likely that the vast majority of the Portuguese New Christians continued to reject Catholicism long after their conversion. So numerous were the Portuguese New Christians practicing Judaism that by the end of the sixteenth century the terms Portuguese and Jew had become synonymous throughout Europe and Latin America.

At the same time, it is a fact that large numbers of New Christians and their descendants, and perhaps even a majority in the case of the first and second groups of converts, severed themselves from all Jewish ties and adjusted to their Catholic status with varying degrees of enthusiasm. The notion current today in some Jewish circles that all or nearly all the New Christians were Jews in disguise derives from an anti-Jewish myth with racist overtones conceived by the enemies of the New Christians.

The myth was a creation of the Old Christian leadership elements in Spain around the middle of the fifteenth century. Beset by mounting internal problems and frightened by the rising prominence of the New Christians, they claimed that the *conversos* as a group were insincere Christians and really Jews at heart. This claim was intended to demean and demote the New Christians, regardless of their proven sincerity to the Church. It was the first instance of racial anti-Semitism used in modern Europe and as such foreshadowed the philosophy of Nazism half a millennium later. Soon after the introduction of this ideology a call was heard to prosecute all the heretics among the New Christians with an Inquisition similar to the one used successfully in the Albigensian crusade.

Many unimpeachable Old Christians denounced this blanket indictment and the motives behind it. Old Christian churchmen came to the defense of the sincerity of the *conversos*. Many Old Christians fought alongside the New Christians in an attempt to prevent the introduction of an Inquisition. Their efforts proved futile. An Inquisition was established in Spain in 1478 and sentenced its first victims three years later in Seville.

In Portugal nearly four decades passed between the general conversion and the introduction of an Inquisition. The authorities at first gave the involuntary New Christians two decades of immunity from any kind of arrest on matters of faith and then made them subject to civil rather than ecclesiastical courts. But they too finally succumbed to the clamors for an Inquisition. An Inquisition like the one in Spain was established in 1536 and the first sentencing took place in Lisbon four years later.

The Inquisition's primary concern was with Christians. It could arrest Jews or Moslems for abetting Christians in their crimes against the Church or otherwise interfering with Church procedure.

There were numerous unconverted Jews in Spain before the expulsion of 1492 and in Portugal before the forced apostasy of 1497. After these dates the only Jews in Spain, Portugal or the territories under their jurisdiction were illegal immigrants. The only possible exception was Dutch Brazil after its recapture by the Portuguese.

Nor were the interests of the Inquisition confined to heresy. The Holy Office dealt with the entire panoply of crimes against the faith, including bigamy, blasphemy, concubinage and immoral suggestions by priests in the confessional. But the alleged heresies of the New Christians provided its most fertile field for action.

The growing insecurity of New Christian life in Spain after the middle of the fifteenth century was instrumental in dissuading large numbers of Jews from adopting Christianity at the time of the Catholic Sovereigns' ultimatum in 1492. And it was doubtless decisive in the Jews' refusal to offer themsleves for conversion in Portugal five years later.

3.

The New Christians in the Americas

New Christians were present in the Americas from the moment of their discovery. Whether Columbus himself was of Jewish descent remains a moot question, but several members of his crew unquestionably were. They included the physicians Marco and Bernal and the interpreter Luis de Torres. Dr. Bernal was once convicted and penanced for practicing Judaism. Luis de Torres was the first member of Columbus' expedition to set foot on American soil. In Brazil, a colorful New Christian and godson of Vasco da Gama named Gaspar da Gama was one of the first two Europeans who together set foot on the soil of Brazil. Among the earliest explorers of Brazil were a group of New Christians headed by Fernando de Noronha or Loronha. Noronha and his company were authorized to explore and exploit a large section of Brazilian territory. Noronha developed the timber industry, stimulated trade and was instrumental in the introduction of the sugar cane industry into Brazil. He also discovered an island off Brazil's northern coast which still bears his name. His work in the sugar cane industry was continued and rationalized by Duarte Coelho. Coelho imported skilled workmen from the islands of Madeira and São Thomé, most of them of Jewish descent. At least one of the five sugar mills in Brazil in the middle of the sixteenth century was headed by New Christians.

For much of the early colonial period, New Christians were prohibited by law from entering the Americas. Not long after Columbus' discovery, the Catholic Sovereigns issued an edict forbidding the emigration of New Christians, and its intention was reinforced by additional pronouncements in subsequent decades. Though the term New Christian was applicable to anyone of Jewish descent, Charles V limited it to converts or convicted Judaizers and two generations of their descendants. In addition, care was usually taken to prevent the emigration of New Christians who were suspect in matters of faith. In Portugal the substance of a pronouncement by King Manuel in 1499 restricting the emigration of New Christians remained in effect through the sixteenth century and part of the early decades of the seventeenth. In 1601, in consideration of the sum of 200,000 ducats, King Philip III granted the New Christians the right to emigrate freely to any of the colonies of the combined kingdoms of Spain and Portugal. Though granted irrevocably, the right was withdrawn in 1610. It was however restored in 1629.

But even in the early colonial period New Christians came over to the Americas in appreciable numbers. Some came openly during times when the prohibitory legislation was suspended or allowed to lapse, and others came over illegally. There were in addition instances where permission was given for Spaniards and Portuguese to leave for the Americas without the customary investigation into their origins and background. Besides, in 1535, the year of one of the renewals of the prohibition in Portugal, the government began sending convicted Judaizers to the New World as punishment.

It is difficult to determine how many New Christians came to the Americas, but two facts are certain: not all the New Christians were Judaizers, and few if any of the Judaizers came over primarily to find a haven for the practice of their secret faith. If faith had been their primary concern, they would have sought to flee, as so many others did, to Moslem lands, Protestant lands, or at least to Catholic territories where Judaism was freely practiced, outside the orbit of Spain and Portugal, there can be little doubt that the primary motivations of most of the Judaizers who came to Latin America were economic and social. They wanted to take advantage of the opportunities for wealth and position which the New World was ready to offer.

A recognition of the Judaizers' order of priorities does not imply that they were tepid in matters of faith. The Judaizers were often intensely devoted to their secret religion. Many were eager to propagate it in the New World, and as a result of their unrelenting efforts, numerous New Christians marginally attached to Judaism became ardent Judaizers. Some of these even became martyrs for their ancestral faith. While the Americas did not offer the safest haven, these Judaizers could not have failed to recognize that the greater distances, the smaller European populations and the comparative weakness of religious investigative agencies in the Americas made them far safer than either Spain or Portugal. Even in the direst persecution of the New Christians, in the Viceroyalties of both New Spain and Peru in the fifth decade of the seventeenth century the chances for the New Christians' safety were still greater in the New World than in the Iberian Peninsula.

4.

The Inquisition

Formal tribunals of the Holy Office of the Inquisition were not established in Latin America until 1570 in Peru and 1571 in New Spain. But Inquisitional activity was very much in evidence from the earliest days of Spanish rule. Inquisitional functions were relegated to bishops and to monks of various orders, particularly the Dominicans and Franciscans. In New Spain the Dominicans and Franciscans exercised such functions from 1522, when the first actions against heretics were taken, to 1532, when they passed into the hands of the newly consecrated bishop Juan de Zumárraga. Three years later Zumárraga became the first Archbishop of Mexico City and was given the title of Apostolic Inquisitor. Although this title was revoked in 1543, Zumárraga's inquisitorial powers remained essentially unchanged until his death in 1548. His duties passed to his successor in the Archbishopric, the Dominican Alonso de Montúfar. A bitter struggle between the episcopacy and the regular clergy over jurisdiction and control of inquisitional matters during Montúfar's administration helped influence the Spanish Crown to introduce the Holy Office into New Spain.

In Peru also an episcopal Inquisition was in force in the early decades of the sixteenth century, with records of its activity going back to the 1530s. In 1548 Lima was the site of an auto-da-fé arranged by its first Archbishop, Gerónimo de Loaisa. Subsequently additional autos-da-fé were celebrated elsewhere in the viceroyalty. The power of this Inquisition grew steadily and when the Holy Office was established in Peru, the bishops relinquished it only when ordered to do so. Eventually, as we shall see, a third tribunal was established at Cartagena at the beginning of the seventeenth century.

The workings of the Inquisition can best be appreciated by an examination of the systematized procedures employed by the Holy Office.

The formal Inquisitional tribunal was everywhere publicly inaugurated with the solemn reading of an Edict of Grace. Within a period of grace, usually thirty days, but only six in New Spain, it required everyone to disclose all knowledge they had of crimes against the faith. The Inquisition promised leniency if people implicated themselves within this period. If they withheld information their penalty would be severe. The evidence accumulated from these confessions and denunciations launched an Inquisition into feverish activity.

The Inquisition usually apprehended its suspects in the quiet of the night. It whisked them off to its jail, where it assigned them to areas corresponding to the seriousness of their crimes. The speed of a suspect's trial depended entirely on the Inquisition. Sometimes there were unavoidable delays, as the Inquisitors waited for new evidence. But on other occasions the Inquisition simply forgot about the prisoner even to the point of letting him die and rot in his cell.

The Inquisition's conception of justice was quite different from the one prevailing in the Western world today. Throughout the trial the prisoner was presumed to be guilty, and he was required to pay for all expenses incurred in the prosecution of his case. Not until well into his trial did the Inquisition inform him of the charges which led to his arrest. When it read these charges and the evidence behind them, it carefully concealed the names of the accusers. The prisoner was never permitted to learn their identity, much less to confront them. The Inquisition permitted a prisoner to have an attorney, provided he chose one from a panel of attorneys in the Inquisition's employ. Prisoners soon learned that the task of the attorney was not to prepare the best possible defense but to urge them to render a full confession, however incriminating it might be.

As a result of such procedures, prisoners generally tried to disclose as little information as possible. They did this both to avoid revealing more about themselves than the Inquisition knew or involving others about whom the Inquisition might as yet have gathered insufficient information. If the Inquisitors suspected a prisoner of withholding evidence, they might submit him to various forms of excruciating torture. Under torture only the most tenacious were able to retain their secrets.

When it was satisfied that it had gathered all pertinent information from a prisoner, the Inquisition proceeded to close its case. Only the fewest escaped without sentence. If the defendant was a first offender and had confessed his guilt, either voluntarily or under the various forms of Inquisitional persuasion, he would be reconciled to the Church and given a threefold sentence, spiritual, financial and occupational. He might be required to attend several special masses or march in a number of religious processions, at all times clad in the humiliating *sambenito*, the long robe of penitence he would first wear on the day of his sentencing. He would have to pay a substantial fine in addition to all costs of his trial. Finally, he would have to complete a period of service, in the galleys, a hospital, monastery or other public place. After the completion of his sentence, he would be a free man again, though he and his descendants would always face certain disabilities, including a prohibition against wearing finery and holding certain jobs. Besides, his *sambenito* might be hung in the cathedral to remind future generations of his misdeed.

If a prisoner suspect of heresy insisted on his innocence, or if a reconciled criminal reverted to his heresy, the Inquisition could label him contumacious and mark him for the stake. Viewing itself as a guardian of life, the Inquisition itself did not do the executing. It adopted the legal fiction of releasing relapsed heretics to the secular authorities, with a recommendation that they be treated mercifully. The secular authorities, too wise to risk suspicion by misunderstanding the Inquisition's intent, invariably proceeded to execute the death penalty. The only mercy a heretic condemned to the stake could expect was the privilege of being garroted before the pyre was lit if he showed any last-minute signs of repentance.

The sentencing took place during a ceremony known as *auto de fe* in Spanish and *auto da fé* in Portuguese. While an auto-da-fé could be simple and private, the Inquisitors liked to turn it into a public spectacle whenever large numbers of malefactors, especially heretics, were involved. Such spectacles strengthened the position of the Inquisition and provided an acceptable public release for mass hostility and frustration. The autos-da-fé were announced well in advance and were usually held in a large public place, such as the town square near the cathedral.

Usually the day's festivities began before dawn with the assembling of a procession that was to march from the Inquisition's building to the site of the auto-da-fé. Heading the procession were the convicts, the lesser offenders first and the relapsed heretics last. Also in the procession were the effigies of fugitives sentenced in absentia and the exhumed remains of the posthumously condemned. After the prisoners came the Inquisitors, the viceroy, members of the Inquisitional tribunal and other ecclesiastical and lay dignitaries, all accompanied by their colors. The populace brought up the rear.

The two high points of the ceremony were the sermon and the sentencing. The sermon was usually delivered by an outstanding guest preacher. It was a demonstration of theological and homiletical virtuosity, bitingly castigating the defendants and exalting the Holy Office. The sentences, stereotyped in form and usually monotonously read, rewarded the patient listeners with the details of each defendant's crimes and punishment.

At the conclusion of the auto-da-fé, the relapsed or impenitent heretics were led away to the *quemadero*, or burning site.

The Inquisition kept meticulous trial records. These reveal the Judaizers' origins, travels, occupations, friends and foes, and above all, their religious attitudes. It is largely on the basis of these accounts that we can today reconstruct the activities and beliefs of the Judaizing New Christians.

5.

The Religion of the Judaizers

The Judaizers appropriately referred to their secret religion as the "Law of Moses," and believed it to be the authentic Jewish faith. But the combination of beliefs and practices of the vast majority stood in sharp contrast to any other form of Judaism ever known. It would have been rejected as spurious in Venice, Ferrara, Lublin, Cracow, Salonika, Amsterdam or any other place where Judaism was permitted to flourish. In the sixteenth century, few aspects in the Judaizers' religion could be called traditional. The quantity of traditional elements increased in the seventeenth century, due primarily to the arrival of appreciable numbers of authentic Jews in Dutch Brazil. The additions of traditional knowledge and practices modified but did not uproot the distinctiveness of the Judaizers' religion, particularly in Spanish America. Throughout Spanish America and in much of Brazil the patterns established from the sixteenth to the early seventeenth century—the "classical period" of crypto-Judaism in America—continued to be visible throughout the colonial period.

The Judaizers' "Law of Moses" was the product of the enforced decadence of Judaism and the isolation of its practitioners. With the expulsion from Spain in 1492 and the forced conversions in Portugal five years later Jewish academies became obsolete and rabbinic learning was banned. For a few decades the Judaizers were able to preserve a fair amount of traditional knowledge, as they met secretly in private homes to study illicitly guarded books under the guidance of men trained in traditional Jewish schools before the catastrophes at the end of the fifteenth century. But as these teachers died and the irreplaceable books were confiscated or worn, the knowledge of traditional Judaism began to decline. The Judaizers' grasp of Hebrew and rabbinic Judaism dwindled precipitately. Soon their only continuing contact with their ancestral faith was the Bible, not in its Hebrew original but in the Vulgate. Since even this text was not readily accessible to laymen, ardent secret Jews would often send a son to study for the priesthood in the hope that he might opt for Judaism and use his knowledge of Bible to teach the Jewish heritage.

By the end of the sixteenth century even the leaders and teachers of the Judaizers, though called "rabbis" by the Inquisition, had no direct knowledge of Talmud, Midrash, Codes, rabbinic commentaries or other aspects of the traditional literature. Biblical or rather Vulgate Judaism, spiced with reminiscences of traditional practice and unmistakable influences of the surrounding Catholic environment, was what now constituted the Judaizers' "Law of Moses." The Inquisitorial trials of the time record recitations of the *Shema* and its liturgical response and a few other Hebrew phrases. The transliteration of these phrases is always garbled, and there is good reason to suspect that the garbling was as much the creation of the Judaizers as of the Inquisitional scribes. The one Hebrew word which almost all Judaizers knew and pronounced correctly was *Adonay*, the traditional appellation for God.

The differences between the "Law of Moses" as it was practiced by the most learned and observant Judaizers in the New World at the end of the sixteenth century and the early decades of the seventeenth and the Judaism of tradition are apparent at every turn. The Judaizers' liturgy, for example, was based almost entirely on the Bible, with only the faintest recollections of the traditional liturgy. Their prayers derived largely from the Psalms, and these were frequently chosen from the liturgy of the Church. These selections, offered in vernacular and occasionally in Latin, when there was a learned man or woman among them, were interspersed with orisons of the Judaizers' own composition. At all times the Judaizers' liturgy bore the marks of improvisation and the influence of the surrounding Catholic environment.

The Judaizers' religious services were usually confined to the Sabbaths and the major holy days. Of these they did not mention Rosh Hashanah at the end of the sixteenth century and there is little evidence of their celebration of either Shavuot or Succot. Of the important minor festivals some knew of Hanukkah, but there is little reason to assume that the holiday enjoyed any significant observance, while the feast of Purim was ignored and the Fast of Esther raised to the status of a major holy occasion. The Judaizers regularly observed only three such holy occasions each year. Yom Kippur, which they called "The Great Day" or "The Day of Kippur," or "the Pure Day," the Fast of Esther, expanded to three days and Passover, usually observed for seven days and occasionally for eight.

The Judaizers tried to celebrate these holy days on the traditional dates, but rarely did, since they lacked the Jewish calendar operative elsewhere and had to devise one of their own.

Each of these occasions sharply reflected the Judaizers' needs and aspirations. Yom Kippur and the Fast of Easther gave them an opportunity to seek forgiveness for their ancestors' apostasy, even if involuntary, and their own continuing official connection with the Church. The Fast of Esther and Passover expressed their hopes for a miraculous deliverance from their plight like those attained by the Jews of Egypt through Moses and the Persian Jews through Queen Esther. Queen Esther came to occupy a position among the secret Jews analogous to that of the Virgin Mary in the Catholic world around them.

In addition to these holy days, some Jews, especially in the seventeenth century, observed Tisha b'Av, and many kept weekly fasts, some on the traditional days of Monday and Thursday, others on different days.

Some of these observances may have been introduced by Judaizers who had lived in centers of authentic Judaism, in Italy and elsewhere. Yet, surprisingly, there is no evidence that crypto-Judaism in New Spain was appreciably influenced by these immigrants or by the other contacts the crypto-Jews were purported to have had with European Jewish communities outside of Spain and Portugal.

Whenever possible, observant secret Jews celebrated the Sabbath from sundown Friday to sunset Saturday. On Friday they cleaned their homes, changed linens, prepared food for the entire Sabbath, pared their nails, bathed and dressed in their finest clothes. They lit a Sabbath lamp or candle and gathered for Sabbath prayers either late on Friday night or Saturday morning. They abstained from work all day, but the ladies generally kept some sewing handy so as not to be caught idle if some unexpected visitor showed up. Throughout the Sabbath day a fire lit on Friday kept the food warm.

The Judaizers also retained some other traditional customs, or at least their version of them. They avoided pork products, slaughtered fowl in the traditional manner, removed the ischiatic nerve from meat, washed a corpse before burial and wherever possible buried it in virgin ground. Many practiced circumcision, frequently circumcising themselves in their adult years. Often these customs were mingled with pagan and Catholic influences. Often a gold coin was given to a corpse as a viaticum.

The Judaizers' theology was simple. They affirmed that God was One, Israel was chosen, the Messiah was coming and the "Law of Moses" was the only avenue to salvation. They also believed in revelation, resurrection, retribution and other biblical concepts. But they lacked acquaintance with rabbinic concepts like Oral Law or Halakhah or the Merit of the Fathers.

Under the influence of their Catholic surroundings, they prayed frequently on their knees. They also gave the great Jewish worthies the title of saint and spoke of Saint Moses, Saint Job and Saint Jeremiah. They believed that the lighting of Sabbath candles was beneficial for the souls of the deceased and accordingly dedicated the candles to their departed relatives and friends. Since their Bible was the Vulgate they were unaware that some of the books it contained were regarded as apocryphal in the Jewish tradition.

Not all Judaizers knew all these details about their distinctive religion or observed them fully. Some were totally ignorant or nearly so. The Jewish practice of some was limited to a single ritual or the abstention from forbidden food. Others were afraid to go even so far and engaged in no Judaizing rituals, their secret identity being revealed in denunciations to the Inquisition by their relatives and friends.

6.

The Crypto-Jews in Mexico

In both the Spanish and Portuguese colonies the history of the Judaizers lends itself conveniently to a fourfold division. The four periods represent the burgeoning, the development, the zenith and the decline of the respective communities.

These periods exhibit nearly identical characteristics in the territories of Spanish America, despite the fact that they were not politically united. In 1535 a centralized authority in the form of a viceroyalty assumed control over New Spain and seven years later a similar office was created for the region of Peru. This division remained intact until the last century of colonial rule, when additional viceroyalties were established at New Granada in 1740 and Buenos Aires in 1776. By that time there were captains general in Guatemala, Venezuela, Cuba and Chile, each with increasing autonomy.

In both New Spain and Peru the early period ends with the establishment of formal Inquisitional tribunals. The second period goes to 1601, when the Portuguese New Christians obtained a general pardon from Philip III, king of the union of Spain and Portugal. The third period continues to the crushing of the "Great Conspiracies" of Judaizers in both viceroyalties around the middle of the seventeenth century. And the final period proceeds to the end of the colonial era.

Much more knowledge is available about the struggles of the New Christians in New Spain than their counterparts in Peru. This is due partly to the preservation of more Inquisitional material from New Spain. Most of this material is presently housed in the Archivo General de la Nación in Mexico City, though some of it has found its way to various libraries in the United States and elsewhere. It is also due to the fact that the authorities in New Spain during the colonial period left more auxiliary documents, in the form of descriptions, letters and reflections on the Inquisition than their counterparts in Peru. Besides, since the Independence, scholars in Mexico have focused more attention on the Inquisition and its predecessors than their counterparts in South America.

The major elements in the history of the Judaizers of New Spain are traced in considerable detail by Arnold Wiznitzer in his excellent two-article summary reprinted in these volumes. Though they are based primarily on printed sources and omit a consideration of the wealth of manuscript material indispensable for an appreciation of the role of the crypto-Jews in New Spain, they nevertheless faithfully limn the major contours of their history.

In New Spain serious concern with the New Christians did not begin until the advent of the Holy Office. It was not that the earlier episcopal Inquisitions were oblivious to the Judaizers. It was simply that the Judaizers did not constitute a major focus of their interest, a phenomenon most plausibly attributable to the paucity of Judaizers—as distinguished from New Christians —and the sparseness of their heretical activities. Of more than six hundred cases begun by the episcopal Inquisition between 1527 and 1571, less than thirty, probably only twenty-five, dealt with Judaizers. The exact charge in five of these cases is uncertain and little is known about the disposition of the rest.

The specific charges brought against the first three Judaizers, all sentenced at an auto-da-fé in 1528, give an idea of the variety of activities lumped together by the Inquisition under the rubric of Judaic practice. The three were Diego de Ocaña, Francisco alias Gonzalo de Morales and Hernando Alonso (not Alonzo, as Wiznitzer has it).

Diego de Ocaña was accused of being a Judaizer on two counts. He was observed eating meat on Fridays and slaughtering chickens in accordance with Jewish practice. Only the second involved an unmistakable Jewish ritual. The tradition of the Judaizers did not demand the consumption of meat on Fridays. The practice may have served as a symbol of defiance of Catholicism, but there is insufficient evidence at present to permit the conclusion that it was consistently practiced by Judaizers or confined to them.

Nor did the charge against Francisco de Morales, namely the disrespectful treatment of a crucifix, involve an intrinsically Jewish practice, although many Judaizers were notoriously guilty of it. At least as important in determining Morales' fate was the fact that Morales' sister had been burned at the stake as a Judaizer in Spain.

So, too, Hernando Alonso, a carpenter and smith who had helped construct the brigantines used by Cortés in his siege of the Aztec capital, was charged on two counts of Judaizing, although, as Wiznitzer correctly states, "Alonso's incriminating activities did not warrant the charge because they were not Jewish at all." (See below, Vol. I, p. 91). Alonso was indicted first for rebaptizing his son in a bizarre private ceremony, and second, for forbidding his wife to attend church during menstruation "because in your condition you might profane the church." The only possible connection between these actions and Judaism comes from the fact that during the ceremony of rebaptism Alonso is reported to have recited a Psalm, probably Psalm 114, recalling God's deliverance of the Israelites from Egypt.

Diego de Ocaña was reconciled to the Church; Morales and Alonso were sentenced to the stake and probably burned alive. The cases of both men are troubling, for both were first offenders and the charges against them were not the gravest. In Alonso's case the sentence is more puzzling. Alonso denied that he was a Judaizer until he was brought into the torture chamber. There he confessed to his "Jewish crimes" and begged the Inquisitors for mercy, apparently expecting to be granted reconciliation. When Fray Vicente Santa María condemned him to the flames, several Christians of immaculate religious reputation protested against the irregularity of the sentence. All of this creates the suspicion that Alonso's death, and perhaps Morales' as well, belong to the category of judicial murders. The occasional attempts, beginning with Conway, to regard Alonso as the first Jew in the Americas, appear to be based more on a desire to exploit the sensational than a careful weighing of the facts at hand.

Among the accused Judaizers during this period, the other one of interest, as Wiznitzer points out, was Francisco Millán.

Heresy in general did not become a major concern until after the introduction of the Holy Office in 1571. Even then, the Inquisition focused more on "heretics of the sect of Luther," as all Protestants were indiscriminately called, than on the secret Jews. Before 1589 only a small number of New Christians were arrested and not all on the charge of Judaizing. One of these, the shoemaker Gonzalo Sánchez from Extremadura, was given two hundred lashes and sentenced to six years at the galleys for trying to trick the Inquisition into commuting the sentences of a number of its prisoners. Another, the learned Pedro de San Lúcar, who was said to have studied in Italy and Russia as well as Spain, was absolved from a charge of Judaizing when it was found that his only crime consisted in his refusal to marry an Old Christian woman on the ground that she might despise him for being a New Christian. Among those convicted for Judaizing were Hernando Alvarez Pliego, reconciled on December 15, 1577, who revealed many others as Judaizers under torture though he later revoked his confession, and Garci González Bermegero—a poor septuaginarian with many children, one of them a monk—who was put to death on October 11, 1579.

But by the middle of the 1580s the Inquisition was engaged in a concentrated effort to ferret out the Judaizers in New Spain. It discovered various enclaves and cells of Judaizing activity and began to make extensive arrests.

The account of its discoveries, outlined by Wiznitzer, centers around two of the leading figures among the New Christians of sixteenth century New Spain. They were an uncle and a nephew known by the same name, Luis de Carvajal.

The older Luis de Carvajal, known also as Luis de Carvajal y de la Cueva, was an admiral, pirate chaser, conquistador, Indian pacifier, rancher, administrator, and the first governor of the vast expanse of territory to the north of Mexico City known as the New Kingdom of Leon. He was also a staunch Catholic throughout his life. His nephew, Luis de Carvajal, the younger, was one of the most sensitive, able, brilliant and creative personalities in the history of Latin America. According to one estimable writer, he is "the most exciting personage in New Spain."

Young Carvajal had studied in a Jesuit school in Spain. In

the New World he worked as a merchant and served effectively as his uncle's apprentice and heir apparent before leaving him to become an intrepid leader of the secret Jews. He was twenty-eight years old when he was arrested for the second time by the Inquisition and only thirty when he died at the stake, a relapsed heretic in the eyes of the church and a martyr for the secret Jews. During his final imprisonment he completed his fascinating memoirs, wrote a learned and impassioned spiritual testament and penned a series of heartrending letters of consolation to his mother and sisters who like him had also been arrested and were facing death. These stirring documents place Luis in the forefront of the creators of Spanish literature in the New World.

Wiznitzer gives an excellent introduction to the Carvajal family, despite his reliance on only three printed trial records—covering the one trial of Governor Carvajal and the two of his nephew—and his preference to present information in the same order as revealed before the Inquisitors rather than chronologically. The trial records still in manuscript of other members of the family and their many associates permit us to add many colorful and important chapters in the history of these unsual Judaizers, including, for example, the account of the religious devotion, madness and pitiable death of young Luis' brilliant sister, Mariana; the frightening experiences of his youngest sister, Anica, in the chambers of the Inquisition; the touching story of the beautiful Justa Méndez, with whom young Luis de Carvajal was apparently deeply in love, and the extraordinary escapades of his two brothers-in-law, the colorful miner and entrepreneur, Jorge de Almeida, and the swashbuckling adventurer, Antonio Díaz de Cáceres, both probably Judaizers and both certainly sympathetic to the cause of the secret Jews. The trial record of Antonio Díaz de Cáceres is even more fascinating than Almeida's. Antonio Díaz de Cáceres had such good connections with the highest circles in New Spain that he managed to learn of the Inquisition's prurient interest in his family in time to escape to Acapulco and then to Manila. His adventures in the Far East and in New Spain on his return rival those of any other adventurer in the New World. His ability to get into difficulty

was matched only by his knack for extricating himself unscathed. Though he was eventually arrested by the Inquisition
and placed under torture, he managed to escape with only a
light penalty at the auto-da-fé of March 25, 1601.

From the manuscripts we also learn of Díaz de Cáceres'
daughter, Leonor, who confessed to her Judaizing and was
reconciled as a teenager in the same auto-da-fé where her father
appeared. After a half century of life as an exemplary New
Christian, she voluntarily came before the Inquisition as an
elderly dowager in 1650 to revoke her adolescent confessions.
She did this primarily to clear her name and remove the usual
disabilities from her descendants. Her efforts failed. She was
arrested by the Inquisition in 1652 and was lucky to get off
with only a reprimand. Two of her descendants, a grandson and
a greatgrandson, picked up where she left off and tried to establish the clearness of their religious descent, but they also failed.

The trials of most of the Carvajal family were completed by
1601. Young Luis' father was sentenced posthumously and two
of his brothers in absentia. Almeida was also sentenced in absentia in 1609. Young Anica, released by the Inquisition into
the custody of devout Catholics, was arrested again decades
later and sent to the stake in 1649.

By the end of the first decade of the seventeenth century the
persecution of the Judaizers in New Spain had all but ceased.
The Judaizers' purchase of the pardon of 1601 was one of the
factors leading to this happier state of affairs, but it was by no
means the only one. No less important was the fact that with
the decimation of the Carvajals and their circles of acquaintances the Inquisition had wiped out all significant Judaizing
activity in New Spain. This often forgotten fact becomes dramatically evident when it is realized that at the time of the
promulgation of the general pardon, only one accused Judaizer,
Francisco López Enríquez, remained in the Inquisition's custody.

But the general pardon provided the New Christians and
the Judaizers among them with an opportunity to replenish their
ranks. Whatever else it may have done, the pardon served as an
open invitation by King Philip III to all New Christians to

migrate to the far-flung colonies of Portugal and Spain. If Philip abandoned the doctrinaire consideration of keeping his colonies clean of New Christians and Judaizers, it was due largely to the increasing economic plight of his nation and his apparent conviction that it could be at least partially alleviated by an injection of New Christian enterprises in the colonies, particularly the Americas.

The fact is that the new New Christian immigrants, most visibly the Judaizers among them, greatly developed the industry and trade of the New World, and soon included some of the wealthiest and most important citizens of both New Spain and Peru. Some of the Judaizers felt so secure that they reduced the caution surrounding their Jewish observance and in a few cases practically flaunted it openly. The mounting importance of the Judaizers was bound to produce a reaction.

The competitors of these newcomers and their longer established Judaizing allies were always seeking pretexts to destroy them. Their stance was shared by the Inquisition, inactive, impoverished and discredited, and lustfully eyeing the Judaizers' enormous wealth. It is far from unlikely that envy of the recent and older arrivals among the New Christians induced their enemies to see them involved in Judaizing to a greater extent than they actually were.

In 1640, as Portugal broke away from its union with Spain, the enemies of the "Portuguese," as the Judaizers were indiscriminately called, began to plan concerted action. Before two and a half years had elapsed, the Inquisition was in hot pursuit of all the Judaizers. The immediate cause for its actions was a conversation between four New Christian men overheard by two boys in the employ of a priest. The New Christians were alleged to have declared that if there were four others in the city who felt the way they did, they would all together set fire "to the Inquisition and its ministers." The priest's report of the conversation to the Inquisition ignited a flood of arrests, beginning on July 13. A contemporary account written in Mexico City leaves a vivid impression of the events that followed:

The incarcerations continued during the following months

that year and the subsequent years. Entire families were seized.
Once between nightfall and the dawn an unusually large number of people were arrested, some of them with a far fairer
reputation than was merited by their depraved customs. This
unexpected event brought great excitement to the country and
general commendation for the Holy Office.

In the city the only thing that people were talking about were
the details of the imprisonments involving so many people, the
sequestration of estates, and the proper and secret manner of
the execution of the arrests by the obedient and punctilious
officials.

The news circulated through the interior of the viceroyalty.
People heard how at that very time the Inquisitors' apostolic
zeal was dealing severely with the perfidious Hebrews, scattered
about and engaged in various businesses and commerce, and
ordering them to be brought to the secret cells. This city received news of events in the remote areas and from there news
flowed to the other places, where the same things were simultaneously going on. As a result all these states and provinces
were filled with rumors of the imprisonment of Hebrews. This
impelled Catholic hearts to a more fervent piety and increased
the faith of all. (Quoted in José Toribio Medina, *Historia . . .
de la Inquisición de Mexico* [Santiago de Chile, 1905] p. 175.

As a result of these imprisonments, the existing penal facilities
of the Inquisition proved inadequate. The Inquisitors found it
necessary to borrow other houses and equip them as jails, and
even then there was not enough room. With the use of all the
makeshift space at their disposal they were finally able to
accommodate the prisoners whom they regarded as the most
dangerous malefactors. By 1643 over seventy had been arrested
as Judaizers. Before the end of the decade the number of
arrests soared to well over two hundred, while numerous others
were indicted in absentia.

The prisoners appeared at various autos-da-fé beginning in
the second half of the decade. The earliest of these trials, in
1646, has especial interest because of the sentencing of Blanca
de Rivera, her three daughters, Margarita, Isabel, and Clara,
and Clara's two sons, Rafael and Gabriel de Granada. Gabriel
de Granada, thirteen years old at the time of his arrest, was so

terrorized by the Inquisitors that he revealed everything he knew and deposed against eighty-nine other Judaizers. Clara de Rivera starved herself to death in jail and was reconciled in effigy.

Despite the cases dispatched in the earlier trials of these Judaizers the Inquisition was preening itself for what was to be its most spectacular auto-da-fé in the history of New Spain. The *auto* took place on April 11, 1649 with a hundred and six prisoners parading in person or in effigy, the vast majority of them Judaizers. Of these twelve were relaxed, or turned over, to the secular authorities to be sent to the stake in person, and a staggering total of fifty-seven were sentenced to the stake in effigy. Those relaxed included, in effigy, Justa Méndez, who had died several years before, and, in person, Ana de León Carvajal, the martyr Luis de Carvajal's youngest sister, who was sent to the stake despite the fact that she was desperately ill with cancer. It also included Leonor Gómez and her family—her son-in-law Duarte de León Jaramillo; her deceased daughter and wife of Duarte de León, Isabel Núñez, relaxed in effigy; her three surviving children, Francisco López Blandón and Ana and María Gómez. María Gómez was the wife of Tomás Treviño de Sobremonte, the most important Judaizer at the auto of 1649, and next to Luis de Carvajal the younger, the most captivating figure among the secret Jews of New Spain. Wealthy and nobly born on his paternal side, he combined the pride of the Spanish *hidalguía* with an unshakable commitment to the Jewish faith. Like the younger Luis de Carvajal, Treviño de Sobremonte was planning an escape to Europe at the time of his arrest and condemnation. As his executioners prepared to light his death pyre, Treviño de Sobremonte is said to have commanded them, "Throw on more wood, you wretches; it is I who am paying for it." Contrary to Wiznitzer's belief, this statement is documented but not necessarily authentic. It is a later legend which comports well with the character of the hero.

Along with Sobremonte and his in-laws were a number of other great Judaizers, including the learned Simón Montero and Antonio Váez. Among the many Judaizers reconciled were Treviño de Sobremonte's daughter and son.

The holocaust of 1649 dealt a lethal blow to the organic community of Judaizers in New Spain. For a while the Inquisitional prison had only two inmates left, the Judaizer Juan Pacheco de León and the remarkable Irishman William Lamport, known in Hispanic circles as Guillén Lombardo de Guzmán. Lamport had been arrested on the charge of plotting to make Mexico an independent kingdom with himself as monarch, though the Inquisition, in order to validate its claim of jurisdiction over him, insisted that he was being held in its jails because he had resorted to a sorcerer and various astrologers to help him achieve his ends. Lamport was sent to the stake on October 8, 1659.

In the meantime the population of the Inquisitional prisons was increasing, though neither the number of suspects nor the quality of their crimes merit protracted attention. The number of prisoners accused of Judaizing greatly declined. There were none among the twelve prisoners at the auto-da-fé of 1652 or the thirty-one sentenced on October 29, 1656. Of the thirty-two appearing in the 1659 *auto* only four were sentenced on charges relating to Judaism. Two of these, Diego Díaz and Francisco Botelho, paid the supreme penalty. From then on, the autos-da-fé rarely involved as many as ten criminals, though sixteen bigamists were paraded in 1676, and the Judaizers are notable by the extreme infrequency of their appearance.

The death at the stake of Fernando de Medina on June 14, 1699, closes the last truly significant case of Judaizing in New Spain. Numerous people, including priests, are known to have been arrested on charges of Judaizing during the course of the eighteenth century, and even the beginning of the nineteenth. Many of the charges are flimsy, and even spurious, as for example in the case of the great Mexican patriot in the war for independence, Miguel Hidalgo y Costilla. There is no evidence for the belief, occasionally articulated by scholars, of massive arrests during this period. The unmistakeable impression left by the trial records is that the manifestations of secret

Judaism in the last century of colonial New Spain were the distorted death gasps of a movement whose fate had been sealed long before.

7.

Crypto-Jews in the Viceroyalty of Peru

The involvement of the New Christians in the development of Spanish South America was no less significant than in Mexico. From the shores of the Caribbean to the banks of the River Plate (Río de la Plata), they fanned out over the entire continent. The presence of the "Portuguese" in the mining regions of upper Peru was an open secret. One of the leading citizens in the Viceroyalty of Peru during the early seventeenth century was a New Christian named Antonio de León Pinelo. He held official positions in the mines of Oruro from 1618 to 1620, but left a more lasting mark on the history of Latin America by codifying the laws of the Indies and becoming the first American bibliographer. His family continued to exercise great influence in the political and intellectual circles of Lima. By the middle of the seventeenth century the Portuguese were perhaps the most important element in the economic life of the Viceroyalty of Peru.

As in Mexico, the Inquisition at first devoted little attention to the Judaizers in the viceroyalty. In 1570 it arrested the physician Juan Álvarez and his brother-in-law Alonso Álvarez and the latter's wife and family on charges of Judaizing, but none of them ever appeared for sentencing. In all probability they were released for want of sufficient evidence. For the first two decades of its existence the Inquisition's major concerns were errant priests, especially solicitors in the confessional, and laymen with parallel peccadillos, and its interest in heresy was confined to the incursions of Protestant thought. No Judaizers are known to have appeared in its first two autos-da-fé, held respectively in 1573 and 1578, while in the third there was only one Judaizer out of twenty people sentenced.

Of the twenty penitents appearing at the auto-da-fé of October

29, 1581, two were Judaizers. Six years later, in November 1587, there were no Judaizers among the thirty-two prisoners sentenced, and in April 1592, there was only one among thirty-eight.

In the early 1590s the Inquisition began to concentrate on identifying secret Jews, and paraded ten of them in the auto-da-fé of December 17, 1595. Five of these Judaizers were reconciled to the Church and four were burned at the stake, at least one of them alive. A tenth, Hernán Jorge, died during the course of his trial and charges against him were apparently dropped. Doubtless because of the Inquisition's new focus on Judaizers, the Inquisitor Ordóñez called this auto-da-fé "the greatest and the one with the most extraordinary cases that has been arranged by this Inquisition."

Five years later, on December 10, 1600, fourteen Judaizers appeared for sentencing. Two of these were turned over to the secular authorities to be burned at the stake. On March 13, 1605, twenty-eight Judaizers were sentenced, nineteen in person and nine in effigy. Of these three were relaxed in person and six in effigy. The great historian of the Latin American inquisitions, José Toribio Medina, records that one of the Judaizers, Antonio Correo, claimed during his trial that he had been converted back to Christianity by divine inspiration. He was reconciled and spent three years working in a monastery as part of his sentence. He then went to Spain, where he became a monk, and acquired fame as a holy man. He has been the subject of several biographies.

After the auto-da-fé of 1605, arrests and convictions of Judaizers fell sharply, due to the general pardon obtained by the Portuguese in 1601. Two suspected Judaizers were even acquitted, Domingo López in 1608 and Manuel Ramos in 1610. Ramos' case is particularly remarkable in that he had been convicted in absentia and burned in effigy on the day of the auto-da-fé of 1605. After reconciling three Judaizers in 1612 and one in 1618, the Inquisition was quiescent until 1625, despite the fact that during the intervening years Judaizers fleeing Brazil in the wake of the visit of the Inquisitional emissary from Lisbon in 1618, were pouring into the Viceroyalty of Peru. On December 21, 1625, twelve Judaizers were sentenced, two to the stake.

By the mid 1630s the number of Judaizers in the Viceroyalty of Peru was considerable. Their ranks had swelled with the arrival of refugees from Brazil. The recent arrivals and the established New Christian community together controlled much of the commerce of South America. As H. C. Lea put it, "from brocade to sack-cloth, from diamonds to cumin-seed, everything passed through their hands; the Castilian who had not a Portuguese partner could look for no success in trade. . . . They would buy cargoes of whole fleets with the fictitious credits which they exchanged, thus rendering capital unnecessary, and would distribute the merchandise throughout the land by their agents, who were likewise Portuguese, and their capacity developed until, in 1634, they negotiated for the framing of the royal customs." (*The Inquisition in the Spanish Dependencies* [New York, 1908] pp. 425 f.)

As in Spain, so too in Spanish South America the increasing prominence and wealth of the New Christians proved to be their undoing. The Old Christian authorities, fearful of their perogatives, determined to destroy the New Christians, regardless of the damage that might result to their society. They could hardly fault the New Christians with impeding the progress of Spanish South America or using business tactics scrupulously avoided by the Old Christians. But they could use the old strategem of impugning their loyalty to the Catholic faith. An indiscretion on the part of a young New Christian from Lima named Antonio Cordero gave them the opportunity they wanted.

The twenty-four year old Cordero was working in the store of his employer, a wholesale merchant, one Saturday when some customers came to make a purchase. Cordero informed them that he could not sell them the goods they wanted because he could not do business on a Saturday. This surprised the prospective customers, and when one of them asked him what was so special about Saturday that he could not make any sales, Cordero, sensing a possible difficulty, simply replied that he would not make any sales on that day or on the next day, Sunday. The puzzled men went away laughing over the fact that the Portuguese refused to do business of a Saturday.

They returned the following week, this time on Friday, and found Cordero lunching on a piece of bread and an apple. One of them, not realizing that it was Friday, suggested that it might be better for Cordero to eat a rasher of bacon. Instead of responding that he would not eat meat on Fridays, Cordero blundered and said, "Should I eat what my parents and grandparents never ate?" The customer, surprised, said, "Do you mean that your parents and grandparents did not eat bacon?" Thereupon Cordero's employer, eager to extricate everyone from a potentially troublesome situation, said, "He meant that they did not eat what he is now eating, and he said that what he is now eating is not bacon but an apple."

The excuse failed, and Cordero was soon arrested by the Inquisition. Cleverly, the Inquisition did not sequester the suspect's possessions, thus giving the impression that he had been arrested by the civil authorities.

Because it was in its interest to do so, the Inquisition immediately brought Cordero to trial and quickly subjected him to torture when he refused to reveal information it believed he was hiding. Within a month the Inquisition had extracted an abundance of data on the identity and activities of the secret Jews in the viceroyalty.

But the Inquisition moved slowly. On May 11, it arrested three suspects, including Cordero's employer. They also were uncooperative until persuaded by torture. As a result of their declarations, the Inquisition made one of the biggest raids of its history on the night of August 11. Within an hour and a half, between half past twelve and two a.m., seventeen arrests were carried out with such precision that few outsiders were aware of what was going on. Before the night was over, more than seventy people were arrested, including entire families. Among them were some of the noblest families in Lima. By August 16 the total number arrested had reached eighty-one. Of these sixty-four were charged with Judaizing. They constitute what has come to be called the Great Conspiracy of colonial Peru.

The suspects included thirty-one merchants, two surgeons, several mine owners, a lapidary, a silk mercer, several salesmen, a cashier, a letter carrier, some petty brokers and some peddlars. All but a handful were of Portuguese descent.

Once word of the arrests got out panic spread throughout the entire viceroyalty. New Christians began to flee for refuge, and the viceroy, acting on the appeal of the Inquisitors, soon closed the borders of Peru for a year to all prospective emigrants except those with special permission. Creditors scurried about trying to collect their debts from New Christians before the Inquisition moved to sequester their property. The Inquisition's letters of October 22 and November 9, 1635, forbidding the surrender of any property that its representatives had taken from the prisoners, did little to alleviate the situation. The arrest or flight of many important New Christians and the confiscation of their property plunged the viceroyalty into economic chaos and filled it with hysteria and despair.

The Inquisition handled the trials of its prisoners with unusual dispatch and within three years had completed them all. To accelerate matters, its officers did not hesitate to appply torture more liberally than was regarded as proper even by the theoreticians of the Holy Office. One prisoner, Antonio de Acuña, had his arms torn to pieces after a three-hour application of torture, while Mencia de Luna died during her ordeal. She received the posthumous solace of having her case temporarily suspended. It was eventually reopened and she was burned in effigy in 1664.

The other sixty-three Judaizers were all convicted, and were sentenced at a spectacular auto-da-fé held on January 23, 1639. Eleven were turned over to the secular authorities to be burned at the stake. A twelfth, Manuel de Paz, who had committed suicide during his trial, was burned in effigy.

Two of the victims of this holocaust were among the most distinguished Judaizers of all time.

One of them, the Sevillian Manuel Bautista Pérez, the wealthiest and most powerful merchant in Lima, and the owner of silver mines and two large plantations, was the leader of the Judaizers. His friends and associates referred to him as El Gran

Capitán, the Great Captain, a title proudly worn a century and a half before by Gonzalo Fernández de Córdova. Bautista Pérez's mansion in Lima was the center of an intricate network of activities linking the secret Jews of the viceroyalty. True to the ideal code of the Judaizers, Bautista Pérez refused to disclose any incriminatory information about himself or any other person, even when subjected to the most excruciating torture. He tried to escape his Inquisitors by attempting suicide. He plunged a knife six times into his stomach and groin and opened several deep gashes, but amazingly survived. In prison he persuaded his brother-in-law, Sebastián Duarte, to revoke his confessions. Sebastián paid with his life for his change of mind, as he was relaxed to the secular authorities.

At the stake Manuel Bautista Pérez embraced his brother-in-law and looked disdainfully upon the members of their family who had confesssed their crimes. When a fellow victim, the surgeon Tomé Cuaresma, cried out for mercy just before fire was set to his body, Bautista Pérez gave him a commanding look of disapproval, and the surgeon suddenly stopped. The Great Captain of the Judaizers went to his death proudly and serenely. The official Inquisitional recorder was sufficiently impressed with his last moments to note that "he heard his sentence with great sedateness and dignity. He died impenitent, asking the executioner to carry out his duty."

Bautista Pérez was so wealthy that, according to his trial record, his sequestered carriage was sold for the staggering sum of 3,800 pesos. His mansion, later known as Pilate's house, was eventually converted into a school for girls.

The most interesting of all the martyrs of 1639 had been arrested in 1627 and was not actually part of the Great Conspiracy. He was the physician Francisco Maldonado de Silva.

Francisco Maldonado de Silva was born in the year 1592 in San Miguel de Tucumán, now in Argentina. His mother was of Old Christian stock, but his father, the physician Diego Núñez de Silva, was a New Christian and a Judaizer. When Francisco was nine years old his father and older brother were arrested by the Inquisition. Shortly after his release from prison, Don

Diego moved to Lima, Peru. There young Francisco, who had received a good grounding in the humanities, appears to have enrolled at the University of San Marcos to pursue studies in medicine and the humanities. Three years later he was appointed surgeon at the hospital in Santiago.

As a youth Francisco had picked up a work entitled *Scrutinium Scripturarum*. It had been written by the Spaniard Pablo de Burgos, a convert from Judaism, to expose the errors of his former faith. But the book had the reverse effect on Francisco. Its references to Judaism set him to questioning the foundations of Christianity. When he queried his father about the book, Don Diego thought the time had come to persuade him to become a secret Jew.

Francisco practiced his Judaism in Chile. He circumcised himself and observed Sabbaths and fast days, especially the Day of Pardon. His life as a secret Jew was uneventful until he tried to convert his two sisters, Isabel and Felipa. Unimpeded by sororal affection, they immediately denounced Francisco to the Inquisition. On April 26, 1627, the agent of the Holy Office tore him away from his pregnant wife and young daughter and deposited him in its secret cells.

Maldonado de Silva did not prove to be a model prisoner. No matter what the Inquisition tried, he refused to repent of his heresy. Embarrassed to have a man of his stature die as an impenitent at the stake, the Inquisitors let him languish in prison for twelve years. On fourteen occasions during this period they sent learned theologians to crack his strong defense of Judaism. But Maldonado de Silva staunchly maintained his faith, and even devised some daring and ingenious ways to propagandize in its behalf. He wrote several apologetical tracts on scraps of paper he accumulated in his cell, using a chicken bone for a quill and coal dust for ink. With a rope made out of ears of corn he lowered himself from his prison window and flitted from cell to cell exhorting other accused Judaizers to remain firm in their faith. To give evidence of his own decision, Maldonado de Silva fasted continually in his cell, breakfasting only occasionally on small quantities of corn pap.

Maldonado de Silva's fasting brought on or aggravated various ailments, and he lived in pain a great deal of the time. But his faith in Judaism did not buckle. To leave no doubt of his devotion, he let the hair of his head and beard grow long in the manner of the biblical Nazirities and began to call himself "Eli the Nazirite (Eli Nazareno), the unworthy servant of the God of Israel, alias Silva."

By the time of the Great Conspiracy he had become deaf, much to the relief of the Inquisitors. They made it a point to note in his trial record that he never found out about the conspiracy because of his deafness. "For with the zeal he had for his faith," they said, "he would have resorted to all kinds of deviltry to encourage so many Jews if he had learned of their arrest."

But on the day of the fateful auto-da-fé Francisco Maldonado de Silva joined the ten other martyrs of the conspiracy at the stake. A number of his tracts, perhaps all of them, were also thrown to the flames.

At the end of the notice of Maldonado de Silva's relaxation, the recording Inquisitor could not refrain from adding the following paragraph:

> It is noteworthy that at the conclusion of the reading of the sentences of those who were to be relaxed, a powerful wind arose. It was so strong that the old inhabitants of the city claim that they have not seen anything like it in many years. It violently ripped off the awning that shaded the stands [erected for the auto-da-fé] at the very spot where this condemned man was standing. He turned his eyes heavenward and said: "This has been ordained by the God of Israel, in order to see me face to face from heaven."

The day after the great auto-da-fé, the crowd remaining in Lima could enjoy the anticlimactic spectacle of the public scourging of twenty-nine of the prisoners who had been reconciled to the Church.

After the great auto-da-fé of 1639 the pursuit of Judaizers by the Peruvian Inquisition declined appreciably. Either the

Inquisition had become inactive or it had cleansed the viceroyalty of Judaizers by terrorizing them into sacrificial flight or Catholic conformity. After 1639 a number of cases pending against Judaizers were dismissed or closed by reconciliation. Three Judaizers were reconciled in an *auto* held in 1641 and another in 1666, the latter convicted of buying fish without scales(!) on Friday and keeping his children out of school on Saturday. There may have been some Judaizers among the three people relaxed, one in person and two in effigy, or those reconciled at the *auto* of 1664. After the 1666 case there are no further known cases involving Judaizers until the eighteenth century.

Even then the arrests and trials of suspected Judaizers were few and far between. They include the case of Alvaro Rodríguez, around 1726 and that of Juan Antonio Pereyra, in 1787 Rodríguez died in prison and his case was apparently discontinued. Pereyra, also known as Juan Ferreira, was reconciled with a stiff penalty.

The records also include two extraordinary cases. One was that of the noblewoman, Doña Ana de Castro, who was burned at the stake as an impenitent Judaizing heretic on December 23, 1736. Though sufficient to force her to martyrdom, her religious offenses were less shocking than her marital infidelities. Among her many lovers was the viceroy himself. There are sufficient inconsistencies in her trial record to foster the suspicion that the authorities found her presence a bit too embarrassing and that her death at the stake was a diplomatic murder. Doña Ana is reported to have accepted her fate with calmness and courage. She even took time to arrange her hair immediately before she was executed. She was, incidentally, the last person to be sent to the stake by the Peruvian Inquisition.

The other case involved a certain Don Teodoro Candioti, a Levantine Christian. He was arrested in the early 1720s because he regarded Moses as a saint and fasted on the day before Christmas. He did both, he said, in accordance with the custom of his land, and insisted that he was an exemplary Christian. From the time of his arrest until his death in prison on May 19, 1726, the Inquisition found no evidence to challenge Candioti's devotion to the Church. He was buried in one of the Inquisition's graves, but eventually his bones were secretly reburied in a parish churchyard and his widow and children were given certificates clearing his name.

The final case involving Judaism before the Peruvian Inquisition was equally pathetic. It was the case of the noble Don Juan de Loyola y Haro, a descendant of the family of Ignatius of Loyola, and a man of stature in Peru. Loyola was arrested as a suspected Judaizer on the testimony of one of his slaves and proceedings against him continued even when evidence appeared showing the testimony to be false and part of a conspiracy by four of his servants. Loyola died during his trial in December, 1745, but his family did not learn of his death for nearly four years. In the meantime, with a change of Inquisitors, his case was brought under review and he was posthumously cleared of guilt. To rectify the mistake of the Holy Office, the Inquisitors arranged for a procession to publicize Don Juan's acquittal. In the procession, held on October 19, 1749, Don Juan's effigy was ceremoniously borne through the streets. In one hand it bore a gold baton, symbolizing the high military rank he held during his lifetime and in the other a palm branch, representing his posthumous victory. On the practical side, Loyola's acquittal returned to his family the right to live without disabilities.

8.

New Granada

In New Granada the number of Judaizers brought before the Inquisition was never very high.

The Inquisition in New Granada was established in 1610, with headquarters at Cartagena. Its jurisdiction extended over all the territories surrounding the Caribbean Sea, except for Central America. It included the bishoprics of Cartagena, Panamá, Santa María, Popayán, Venezuela, Puerto Rico, Santiago de Cuba and the archbishoprics of Santo Domingo and Santa Fe. Although its domain was larger than that of either of the older Inquisitions in Latin America, it was not satisfied and sought to extend its control over Florida.

Its inaugural Edict of Grace was followed by a surprisingly small number of accusations. But then suddenly the voluntary depositions began to pour in. As was to be expected, they covered a wide variety of offenses against the faith and the Inquisitors had to confess that "in matters pertaining to heresy of Judaism there have been very few." The first auto-da-fé was held on February 2, 1614 with pomp and solemnity worthy of the traditions established in Lima and Mexico City. But most of its victims were sentenced for trivial offenses hardly worthy of such a lavish expenditure. In 1613 a Portuguese named Francisco Gómez de León had been arrested on a charge of Judaizing, but he did not appear in an auto-da-fé until June of 1618. He was originally sentenced to die at the stake, but the sentence was later commuted and he was reconciled to the Church.

In 1626 some six Judaizers appeared, and one in 1632. There were several more in 1638, in an auto-da-fé corresponding to the great spectacle in Peru the following year, though the "Great Conspiracy" in Cartagena involved more witches than Judaizers. From then on Judaizers appeared singly or in pairs in a dozen autos-da-fé from 1641 to 1710.

9.

Brazil

In Brazil the four phases of the Judaizers' history displayed different characteristics from their counterparts in Spanish America. This was due in large measure to two factors—on the one hand the conquest of an important section of Brazil by the Dutch and the freedom the Dutch granted for the practice of Judaism, and on the other, the absence throughout the history of Brazil of an inquisitional tribunal on the model of the one in Lisbon or those established in Lima, Mexico City, and Cartagena. Beginning with the Bishop of Bahia in 1580 various churchmen held inquisitorial powers as delegates of the Inquisition in Lisbon and had to send all capital cases and many others to Portugal for trial.

Both sincerely Catholic and Judaizing New Christians were always in greater evidence in Brazil than in Spanish America. From the very beginning, many of Brazil's most important families were of New Christian origin. Their power may well have been instrumental in preventing the introduction of an autonomous Inquisition, with only minimal ties to Portugal.

The life of one man, João Ramalho, one of Brazil's local heroes, epitomizes the greater freedom New Christians enjoyed in Portuguese America. Ramalho had distinguished himself in his battles with the Indians and his ability to make peace with them. He even married the daughter of an Indian chieftain. He never openly professed to be a Judaizer, but he was most liberal in admitting Judaizers to his territory and most emphatic in his rejection of Christianity. He even refused extreme unction when he lay on his deathbed at the age of a hundred. Amazingly he recovered from his illness and lived another twelve years.

In the decades that followed, the Judaizers in Brazil participated in every aspect of the economy. They owned sugar mills and plantations, or administered them. They were prominent in domestic and international trade. Their numbers also included various farmers, masons, teachers, and writers.

It was not until 1591 that the Inquisition's bite was first felt in Brazil. In that year an Inquisitional inspector or *visitador* from Lisbon named Heitor Furtado de Mendoça reached Bahia and began a quest for religious offenders. In the course of the next two years he also established an investigative commission at Olinda and visited Itamaracá and Parahiba. His presence sowed panic among the New Christians and elicited a host of confessions and denunciations involving secret Judaism. Among those denounced were Ambrosio Fernandes Brandão, author of the *Dialogos das grandezas do Brasil,* the first major work in Portuguese on American soil; Bento Teixeira Pinto, author of the *Prosopopea,* the first poem written in Brazil; and the wealthy Diogo Fernandes, owner of one of Brazil's first sugar mills, and his wife Branca. Fernandes and his wife had died some time before, but their crippled daughter Beatriz was paraded in an auto-da-fé held on January 31, 1599. Teixeira was sent to Lisbon for trial while Brandão apparently was not indicted.

In all, Furtado de Mendoça's investigations proved only mildly successful. Most of the evidence he gathered was too inconclusive to warrant further action. As a result, there were few arrests and even fewer convictions. More important, the amount of money the Inquisition made on the project was not commensurate with the efforts it invested. When Furtado de Mendoça left Brazil in 1595 the primary responsibility for ferreting out heretics fell again on the Bishop of Bahia.

In 1618 Lisbon sent another *visitador,* named Marcos Teixeira, to Brazil. The three decades since the departure of Furtado de Mendoça had witnessed a progressive increase in the number of Judaizers in the Portuguese colony, especially in the wake of the pardon extended by Philip III to Portuguese New Christians in 1601. Teixeira quickly rounded up a hundred and thirty-four suspects, ninety of them alleged Judaizers. Many of the denunciations of Judaizers had been made by the learned Melchior de Bragança. A convert from Judaism to Christianity, Bragança held the signal distinction of having taught at both of Spain's great universities, Alcalá de Henares and Salamanca. He later taught at a Jesuit college in Coimbra.

Teixeira's visit proved no more effective than his predecessor's. Its greatest success came indirectly, as New Christians fleeing Brazil fell into the clutches of the Peruvian Inquisition in Buenos Aires and other parts of Latin America. In Brazil the arrests and prosecutions were few, and the community of Judaizers remained essentially unharmed.

The situation of the Judaizers throughout Portuguese America took a dramatic turn for the better with the capture of a portion of Northern Brazil by the Dutch. The Dutch first seized Bahia in 1624 but had to surrender it the following year. In 1630, however, they captured Recife, capital of the province of Pernambuco and established a Dutch enclave that was to endure for a quarter of a century. Participating in this expedition were a number of Dutch Jews, among them Moses Cohen, Antonio Manoel, and a naval cadet named Moses Navarro.

Almost immediately after capturing the Portuguese cities, the Dutch declared religious tolerance for all their residents. In Bahia alone two hundred refugees, apparently all secret Jews, returned to take advantage of this offer. Later, in Pernambuco, throngs of New Christians embraced Judaism. They even boasted that every New Christian had become a Jew. They were joined in their Judaism by numerous Jews arriving from Holland. Most of these were also of Spanish-Portuguese descent, but in the free atmosphere of Holland they had been living openly as Jews and practicing an authentic Judaism.

A new period of prosperity opened for the Jews in the Dutch territories of Brazil. It reached its zenith during the governorship of Johan Maurits (John Maurice) van Nassau. John Maurice brought security and order to his land and carried out the provisions of the Dutch charter protecting Catholics and Jews at the same time that it established the priority of the Dutch Reformed Church. Dutch fanatics repeatedly tried to curtail the religious practice of the Jews and their churchmen sought incessantly to convert them, but Jewish rights were regularly upheld.

The population of the Jews in Brazil grew steadily between 1630 and 1654. It reached its height around 1645, when Brazil could count about a thousand five hundred Jews, approximately as many as there were in Amsterdam. After 1645 the number declined precipitately. There were only seven hundred Jews in Dutch Brazil in 1648 and no more than six hundred and fifty in 1654. Statements occasionally found to the effect that there were over five thousand Jews in Dutch Brazil belong to the category of legend rather than fact.

For several years these Jews held their services in private homes. In 1636 they appear to have established a public synagogue in Recife. A second synagogue was established in Mauricia the following year. A third appears to have been established in Parahiba.

Fortunately the minute books of the major congregations, Zur Israel in Recife and Magen Abraham in Mauricia, have been preserved. They were brought to Amsterdam shortly after the Dutch capitulation in 1654. These precious books cover the last six full years of the community's existence. They reveal a thriving and traditional Jewish community life, with its synagogues, its schools and learning, its communal officers and government. Like the free Jewish communities in Europe, the one in Dutch Brazil was self-regulating. Its leadership, called the Mahamad, ruled oligarchically over every aspect of Jewish life. To enforce its decrees, the Mahamad could invoke an entire panoply of sanctions, ranging from a refusal to admit an offender to the synagogue to his ostracism from Jewish society through excommunication.

The congregation lacked rabbinic leadership until 1642, when Isaac Aboab, one of the four rabbis or *hakhamim* of Amsterdam's Congregation Talmud Torah, came to Brazil. One of the unsuccessful candidates for the position was Isaac Aboab's colleague, the famous Mannaseh ben Israel. The *hakham* Moses Raphael de Aguilar accompanied Isaac Aboab to Brazil, and a number of excellent scholars came in the subsequent years.

The rich spiritual life of the Jews in Dutch Brazil was sustained by a material prosperity unprecedented for the Jews in the New World.

The economic activities of the Jews in Dutch Brazil ranged over a wide spectrum of business enterprises and professions. They could boast the first Jewish physician and pharmacist in the Western Hemisphere in Dr. Abraham de Mercado, the first lawyer in Michael Cardoso and the first bridge builder in the architect Balthasar da Fonseca.

More Jews, of course, were devoted to business than to the trades and professions. Some were active in export and import enterprises, while others were important in large-scale farming and the mining of sugar. Though the erstwhile New Christians owned only a small number of the sugar mills, men like Duarte Saraiva, Pedro Lopes de Vera and the former freebooter Moses Navarro owned some of the most important ones. Ironically the mills continued to display such un-Jewish names as "Good Jesus," "Our Lady of the Rosary," "St. John" and "St. Bartholomew."

Even more important was the role of the Jews in finance, particularly banking and tax farming. In the first capacity they established themselves as middlemen in the slave trade, buying slaves at auction and selling them for credit. So vital was this function of the Jews to the slavers that slave auctions were not held on the Jewish Sabbath or holy days.

The Dutch foothold in Brazil was always precarious. The Portuguese-Brazilians begrudged them their territory, even after Portugal broke away from Spain in 1640 and joined Holland in an anti-Spanish alliance. As early as 1642 the Portuguese-Brazilians began to map plans for a reconquest of the Dutch possessions. Catholics dwelling in Dutch Brazil, like João Fernando Vieira, allied themselves with the Portuguese-Brazilian cause and planned a revolution from within. The Portuguese-Brazilians at all times categorically denied that they were participating in any conspiracy against the Dutch

One of the earliest insurrections resulted in the capture of the town of Maranhão by the Portuguese-Brazilians. The rebels also planned to occupy Recife, but three men, including one Jew, revealed their plot to the Dutch. At Ipojuca, in June, 1645, in the first battle of the rebels' guerrilla war, two Jews were killed.

As the guerilla warfare increased the rebels captured forts and settlements and gradually chewed away at the Dutch possessions. By March, 1648, the Dutch possessions had been reduced to a small strip on the coast, including Recife, Mauricia, Parahiba, Itamaracá and Rio Grande do Norte. Various attempts by the Dutch to break out of these pockets met with disaster, and efforts at a peaceful settlement of the struggle failed time and again. In face of a massive land attack on Recife the Dutch finaly capitulated on January 26, 1654.

That year a hundred and fifty Jewish families left Brazil, most of them returning to Holland. Those who did not included two shiploads captured on the high seas and the group detained by the Spaniards in Jamaica. Of this group twenty-three people, men, women and children, managed to leave, late in the spring or early in the summer of 1654. They headed first for Cuba and then for the North American mainland, reaching New York, or as the Dutch called it, New Amsterdam, early in September, 1654. With their arrival began the history of the North American Jewish community.

During the wars the Jews fought valiantly on the side of the Dutch, financing their defenses and serving in the ranks of their soldiers and sailors. The Jews, particularly the former New Christians among them, knew how indissolubly their fate was bound with that of the Dutch in Brazil.

They were dramatically reminded of this fact on many occasions during the war. In the early phases of the war some Jewish prisoners were hanged as traitors by the Brazilian-Portuguese. Soon Jewish prisoners who spoke Portuguese were sent to Lisbon to be tried by the Inquisition as renegade New Christians. A number of Jews, for example, appeared at the auto-da-fé held in Lisbon on December 13, 1647. After the war, Brazilian Jews of New Christian descent began to appear regularly at the Lisbon autos-da-fé.

Among the first of these was the young and brilliant Isaac de Castro Tartas. Along with a number of other Brazilian Judaizers he was paraded at the auto-da-fé of December 15, 1647. He had come to Dutch Brazil in 1641 and lived as a practicing Jew for three years. He then moved to Catholic Bahia, where he began practicing Catholicism publicly, though he remained a secret Jew. When he was arrested as a Judaizer, De Castro admitted that he had only pretended to be a Christian. He claimed that he had been born a Jew, to Jewish parents, in Avignon, and that the Inquisition therefore could not charge him with heretical Judaizing. Unconvinced by his remonstrations, the authorities at Bahia indicted him as a heretical New Christian and sent him to the Inquisition in Lisbon early in 1645.

In Lisbon Isaac confessed that his parents were Portuguese New Christians from Bragança, but he insisted that he could not be tried because he had never been baptized. He explained that he had come to Bahia despite its obvious dangers because he had killed a man in Pernambuco. But the Inquisition's witnesses contradicted Isaac's story. They testified that he had come to Bahia to spread Judaism among the New Christians, and said that his claim to be a Jew of Jewish descent was a ruse by which he hoped to evade prosecution.

Thus exposed, Isaac de Castro could have saved his life through repentance and reconciliation with the Church. But he chose to die a martyr's death rather than abjure his Judaism. He therefore proceeded to give a full disclosure of his Jewish beliefs and practices and expressed regret at his inability to perform them more meticulously. The Inquisition, embarrassed to have so learned a Judaizer remain unconverted, sent learned theologians to convince him of his errors, but their efforts were in vain. Young De Castro tenaciously clung to his faith and the Inquisition had no alternative but to declare him an impenitent heretic. He appeared at the auto-da-fé on December 14, 1647 and went to the stake later that day. According to one report he died with the words *Ely, Adonai Sebaot* ("My God, the Lord of Hosts") on his lips.

After the conclusion of the war with the Dutch, the bishops of Brazil continued to send Judaizers to Lisbon. In the first half of the seventeenth century, seventeen Judaizers were sent to Lisbon, and in the second half, eight. Most of them came from Bahia, where Judaizers were in evidence through the early part of the eighteenth century.

The sending of Brazilian Judaizers to Portugal continued during the eighteenth century, beginning with the physician Francisco Nuñes de Miranda of Bahia. But during the eighteenth century a steady stream of Judaizers flowed from Rio de Janeiro to Portugal. This was due largely to the intensive search for Judaizers instituted by the bishop of Rio de Janeiro, Francisco de San Jerónimo. Many of these were indicted as a result of denunciations by two people, Francisco Gómez da Silva in 1705 and the young Catherina Soares Brandoa in 1706. Catherina denounced seventy-nine men and women as Judaizers. Many of the unfortunates were paraded at the auto-da-fé held at Lisbon on July 30, 1709. Francisco himself was tried by the Inquisition at Evora. Beginning with 1709, Brazilian Judaizers regularly appeared at Portuguese autos-da-fé for sixty years. Fifty-two were sentenced in 1711, seventy-eight in 1713, twenty-six in 1714, fifteen in 1729, twenty-four in 1732, eighteen in 1735, and smaller numbers in the intervening and subsequent years. Many of the victims belonged to the cream of Brazilian society.

Perhaps the most noteworthy was Antonio José da Silva, a twenty-one year old law student who was to become one of the distinguished playwrights in the history of Portugal. Da Silva's three uncles and three aunts had appeared at the auto-da-fé of

July 9, 1713. Young Antonio was reconciled at the auto-da-fé of October 13, 1726, only to be arrested a decade later and convicted as an impenitent heretic. A last minute expression of repentance granted him the mercy of being garroted before his body was consigned to the flames after the auto-da-fé of October 18, 1739. From this day on Portuguese documents regularly refer to him as "the Jew."

Brazilian Judaizers continued appearing at the autos-da-fé until 1769, when Manoel Abreu de Campos was delivered to the secular authorities and the stake. In all some four hundred Brazilian Judaizers were tried by the Inquisition in Portugal. Of these eighteen made the supreme sacrifice but only one, Isaac de Castro Tartas, was burned alive.

Despite the concerted efforts to uproot it, secret Judaism persisted in Brazil. Persecution may even have strengthened it by compelling prospective victims to band together for safety and mutual help.

On May 25, 1773, King Joseph I of Portugal, responding to the cogent advice of his enlightened Minister of State, José de Carvalho e Mello, the Marquis de Pombal, ordered an end to the distinctions made between Old Christians and New and prohibited the oral and written use of the term "New Christian" under the strictest of penalties.

This law succeeded where persecution had failed. Gradually, with only rare exceptions, the Judaizers disappeared into the dominant Catholic faith and culture of Brazil.

10.

A Word on Jews and Judaism in the Independent Nations of Latin America.

Jewish life in Latin America since the departure of Portugal and Spain has been substantially conditioned by the separate countries of their residence. Yet the composition of the various Jewish communities and the process of their experiences permit a composite introduction to their history.

On achieving their independence the new nations of Latin America adopted the principle of religious freedom. For the first time since the brief period of Dutch rule in Brazil, Judaism was a licit faith, and people openly identifying as Jews were soon present throughout Latin America.

The immigration of Jews into modern Latin America can be divided chronologically into four phases. The first covers most of the nineteenth century.

Sephardic Jews from Jamaica, Curaçao and other Caribbean islands appear to have moved into the territory of Great Colombia shortly after the wars of independence.

Ashkenazic Jews from Central and Eastern Europe and Sephardim from Turkey and Morocco came to Brazil after Emperor Pedro II (1831–1889) opened the doors of his nation to immigration. Around 1860 an unprecedented number of four hundred European Jews are said to have reached Peru. A colorful group of European Jews came to Mexico in the entourage of Emperor Maximilian (1864–1867), among them the Emperor's personal physician, Siegfried or Samuel Basch. By that time Chile and Argentina both had colonies of Jews from Germany, England, and France. At the end of the century it is estimated that there were no more than 10,000 Jews in Latin America, nearly 7,000 of them in Argentina.

The second period began in 1889 and went through World War I. During this time a much larger number of immigrants, including both Sephardim and Ashkenazim, began to arrive from Eastern Europe. By 1917, the Jewish population in Latin America had risen to over 115,000. Of these 110,000 resided in Argentina, another 4,000 in Brazil, and 300 to 500 in each of three other countries, Peru, Uruguay and Venezuela.

The third period ran from the conclusion of World War I until the beginning of the 1930s, when large numbers of additional immigrants arrived in Latin America, principally from Eastern Europe.

The fourth period, beginning around 1933 and continuing to the early years of the next decade, witnessed the admission into Latin America of large numbers of refugees from Hitler's Europe, especially from Germany and Austria.

But by the mid-1930s, ten years after the passage of the restrictive National Origins Act in the United States, a reaction against liberal immigration policies in the Latin American countries began to set in, and the new policies that were established hit hardest at the Jews. As early as 1934, a law included in the Brazilian constitution provided that the number of people of any nationality permitted to enter the country during any year could not exceed two percent of the total of that nationality present in Brazil in the previous fifty years. In 1937 Mexico placed a limit of a hundred immigrants annually from Poland and Rumania. In Argentina a decree of July 28, 1938 required special permission for anyone desiring to enter the country. Soon most countries in Latin America had restrictive legislation. And though exceptions have been made for the immigration of close relatives of people already settled in the Latin American nations and occasionally for other humanitarian reasons, the borders of most Latin American countries have been sealed against further Jewish immigration. At present, over 800,000 Jews live in Latin America. There are 500,000 in Argentina; 140,000 in Brazil; 54,000 in Uruguay; 35,000 in Chile; 30,000 in Mexico; 12,000 in Venezuela; 10,000 in Columbia, 4,000 each in Bolivia and Peru, and smaller numbers scattered throughout the rest of Latin America.

For the most part, the small number of Jews in Latin America during the early and middle part of the nineteenth century were skilled and worldly and occupied important business and professional positions. The Sephardim among them were fully at home in the linguistic and cultural milieu of the native populations, and the Ashkenazim required little time for acclimation.

The history of the Sephardic and Ashkenazic immigrants toward the end of the century can be said to begin with the arrival of the Eastern European Jews who had been persuaded by Jewish philanthropists and offers of land to establish farm communities in Argentina.

This possibility was first considered at a conference convened in Kattowitz, Silesia in 1884 and officially called "The Montefiore Association for the Promotion of Agriculture among Jews and especially for the Support of the Jewish Colonies of Palestine." Although the assemblage was not enthusiastic about emigration to Latin America, it decided to send a delegation to Paris for consultation with the Alliance Israélite Universelle. In Paris they received attractive offers from the Argentine consul, and laid plans to organize an immigration of Eastern European Jews to Argentina. As a result of their efforts, a group of eight hundred and twenty-four Jews left Eastern Europe in the spring of 1889. They experienced many difficulties and delays in Western Europe, some the result of misunderstandings with the Argentine consul, but they finally arrived in the New World.

Here they suffered a new round of troubles. The original lands offered them were no longer available. On the land they were finally able to obtain, in the province of Santa Fe, they faced unbelievable hardships, due in no small measure to the refusal of the local authorities to comply with the terms of their agreement. For two months they lived in unsanitary conditions, with inadequate housing or food. Workers and train-passengers would often throw them food. "In the Jewish colonies," one writer noted without exaggeration, "cemeteries appeared before houses."

Eventually these settlers moved to another locale in Santa Fe and in November, 1899, they established the colony called Moisesville. Thanks to the generosity of Baron Maurice de Hirsch, who interested himself in the Argentinian project shortly after the founding of Moisesville, an entire series of Jewish agricultural communities were established, first through the Baron Hirsch Colonizing Enterprise (Empresa Colonizadora Barón Hirsch) and then, beginning in 1892, through his Jewish Colonization Association (the J.C.A.).

Shortly after its initial successes in Argentina, the J.C.A. established the colony called Philippson in the Brazilian state of Rio Grande do Sul and then in the same state in 1910 the colony of Quatro Irmãos. Colonies founded in later decades included the small settlement of Rezende, in the state of Rio de Janeiro, in 1936.

There were also attempts to establish similar communities in Uruguay. Under the auspices of the J.C.A. the first such community, called the Nineteenth of April (19 de abril) in commemoration of the date of its founding in 1914, was established by some thirty families who had left Quatro Irmãos.

Today small settlements of Jewish farmers exist in various Latin American countries. But Argentina, with more than twenty agricultural communities, and over thirty thousand people producing a wide range of commodities, is the only country where the original settlements have thrived.

Most of these Sephardic and Ashkenazic Jews settled in the cities as did most of the Eastern European immigrants after World War I. Like the immigrant farmers, the vast majority of both groups were poor. Large numbers made their living by peddling, and by the early decades of the twentieth century the itinerant vendor had become as familiar a sight in many parts of Latin America as he had been in the United States and its continental possessions nearly a century before. The Jews roamed through cities, towns and hamlets, carrying a dazzling variety of merchandise, much of it previously unseen by the populace, especially in the remote provincial areas of the various countries.

In order to compete with the established merchants, the Jews extended credit and introduced a system of time payments. In this way they brought countless articles of clothing and furniture within the easy reach of the working classes of society. Many Christian merchants at first regarded the Jews as dread competitors. But they soon realized that they had nothing to fear. The enterprise of the Jews dramatically increased the demand for consumer goods. This in turn spurred manufacturing and created countless jobs. The fuller employment and production of goods contributed to an unprecedented prosperity.

The itinerant merchants shared in this prosperity. Most attained a comfortable standard of living and some acquired considerable wealth. Many invested their savings in businesses of their own, buying stores, opening factories and entering into large-scale shipping.

The fourth wave of immigrants, in the 1930's and 1940s, built upon the patterns of economic opportunity already prepared for them, and in numerous instances, utilized their funds and their manifold talents to create or develop new industries and services.

The extent of Jewish achievement in Latin America has varied from country to country. It has depended largely on the economic and legal conditions of the country and the size and talents of its Jewish population. But on the whole the Jewish communities of Latin America are well integrated into the economic life of their respective countries.

Today Jews are prominent in numerous commercial and industrial enterprises. They are well represented in domestic and international trade and in a wide spectrum of manufacturing enterprises, including furniture and clothing, food and pharmaceuticals, chemicals, metals and electrical products. They have introduced many new industries, like the bakelite industry in Chile and the manufacture of silk stockings in Mexico. In Argentina the Jews have made monumental contributions to agriculture, both in the quality of their multifarious products and in their advancement of technique and administration, including the introduction of harvesters and circular plows and the development of farm-credit funds.

In addition to their participation in these industries, Jews throughout Latin America are well represented in the ranks of skilled workers. A significant number have also entered the liberal professions.

Among the Jewish professionals, physicians are the most numerous, but there are also lawyers, teachers, scientists and writers. In several places various factors restrict the extent of Jewish participation in the professions.

Except for a congregation in Argentina and the synagogue and cemetery of the Sephardim in Panama in the same period, the Jewish settlers in Latin America in the decades immediately following independence made little attempt to develop Jewish communities.

The economic and social position of these early settlers gave them unobstructed entree into the highest echelons of society, with the result that they were frequently lost to Judaism through intermarriage or assimilation. Nowhere did they establish an enduring community. The Sephardic and Ashkenazic Jews of Argentina joined to establish "The Israelite Congregation of the Argentine Republic," in 1862, but the congregation did not long survive. Its spiritual leader, Henry Joseph, was intermarried, and his children were raised as Catholics.

While many of the descendants of these Jews today deny their Jewish origins, there are others who affirm them with pride.

The beginnings of enduring community structures had to wait until the more substantial immigration at the end of the nineteenth century and the beginning of the twentieth. Almost all the immigrants at that time, regardless of their country of origin, were community minded. They "already formed a kehila when they were on the boat," as the noted historian Jacob Shatzky said speaking of the Eastern European Jews on their way to the agricultural communities in Argentina.

Actually, in no Latin American country did all the immigrants join together for the formation of an organic community. Sephardic and Ashkenazic Jews established separate structures, and when there were enough of either group, there was further division based on the place of the immigrants' origins. Thus, for example, in Argentina there were Sephardic synagogues for the Jews of Damascus, Smyrna, Rhodes and Morocco. So, too, German Jews regularly had their own organizations and frequently the Polish, Rumanian and Hungarian Jews as well.

The difficulty in effecting a unity of these people was due not only to the sentimental attachment they felt for their respective places of origin but to the great diversity in their conceptions of Jewish identity. For the Sephardic and German-speaking Ashkenazim the synagogue was the central institution in Judaism. The German and Austrian Jews frequently regarded it as the only necessary Jewish communal body. But the Eastern Europeans held a variety of opinions about the role of the synagogue in Jewish life, some regarding it as central, others as peripheral, and still others as dispensable. For Ashkenazic Jews the boundaries of Jewishness were flexible enough to accommodate secularists, Yiddishists, socialists, Zionists and others without strong ideological leanings but with a nostalgic attachment to Jewish culture. To serve the many needs and interests of so broadly defined a community, a variety of organizations have been established, not infrequently with a duplication of functions. In a number of places one of the first such societies was *Hevra Kadisha*. A *Hevra Kadisha* was established in Argentina as early as 1892. Though the primary function of these organizations was to assist in matters pertaining to the burial of the dead, their scope frequently broadened to include numerous other religious and charitable activities. Ashkenazic and Sephardic Jews established regional associations, as well as their own philanthropic societies, hospitals, sanitaria, athletic clubs and women's groups.

There have been several forces working to bring the various groups of Jews into closer contact. One of the most important of these has been Zionism. With few exceptions, Latin American Jews are intensely Zionistic. Zionism flourishes through numerous active organizations whose success has been measured not only by their outstanding financial contributions but by their deep concern for Jewish life and culture. The rise of the State of Israel has given Latin American Jewry a new dimension of identity, brotherhood and pride. In some places the Zionist federations are the most important organizations in the community. In Chile, for example, the *Federación Sionista* frequently represented the total Jewish community until its functions were transferred to a convention of delegates of the major Jewish organizations.

There have also been natural movements toward federating the variety of organizations in many countries of Latin America. Sometimes an already established organization will become an umbrella for various cultural, philanthropic or religious groups, as happened in the case of the Argentinian *Hevra Kadisha,* which expanded into the pan-Ashkenazic *Asociación Mutual Israelita de Buenos Aires* (AMIA). On other occasions, the separate organizations have created new overhead structures, as in case of Uruguay, where the Ashekenazim formed the *Comunidad Israelita de Montevideo* and the Sephardim the *Comunidad Israelita Sefardí,* both in 1932.

In addition, Jewish leadership throughout Latin America has been sensitive to the need for the complete unification of each community behind an organization that could represent it before the government and take concerted action in behalf of Jewish rights. The need for such organizations became increasingly apparent during the 1930s when anti-Semitism in Latin America, previously sporadic and mostly local, was organized under the Nazis. Anti-Semitic propaganda appeared in almost every country of Latin America during the 1930s and 1940s. Though the menace of this anti-Semitism subsided with the strong action of responsible governments and the defeat of the Axis, it has not been uprooted from Latin America. This has been due primarily to a combination of two factors, the presence in Latin America of many ex-Nazis and their sympathizers, and unstable economic, social and political conditions which afford a fertile soil for anti-Semitic propaganda. Since World War II, Jews in various countries of Latin America have had to face smears in print and mail, from neo-Nazis and Arab sympathizers, as well as instances of vandalism, bombings of synagogues and other community buildings, the defacing of cemeteries and even attacks on persons. These were particularly frequent during the Eichmann trial and after Eichmann's execution. In the first week of June, 1962, Argentina witnessed ten serious anti-Semitic attacks. In September of 1968 a bomb shattered an Israeli fair in Buenos Aires.

In a few places, like Costa Rica in 1952, the government declined to check anti-Semitic agitation on the ground that such action would infringe upon the agitators' right of free speech, and Peronist Argentina allowed oral and printed anti-Semitic salvos to be fired freely. But generally Latin American governments have been quick to condemn all manifestations of anti-Semitism.

An additional blow from another quarter struck the eleven to thirteen thousand Jews of Cuba with the takeover of that country by Fidel Castro in January of 1961. Laws expropriating the property of the rich, and particularly those aimed at expropriating part of the property of the middle class, hit severely at the Jewish population. These facts, coupled with fears of repression of religion and reprisals because of their sympathies with the United States, sowed panic among the Jews, and they began leaving Cuba. Nearly half the total population left within the first year. A large number of these people were admitted to the United States, where they have quickly become acclimated to the life of the country, though for many this has meant adjustment to a new language and new skills.

The representative organizations of the various Jewish communities include the *Delegación de Asociaciones Israelitas Argentinas,* the *Confederaçao Israelita do Brasil* and the *Confederación de Asociaciones Israelitas de Venezuela.*

The synagogue remains a respected institution in Latin American Jewish life, and nuclei of the faithful are to be found in nearly every community. But, in general, Jewish religious life is not intense. The majority of Latin American Jews do not frequent the synagogue. Only a small portion, ranging from some twenty percent in a few places to a handful of families or even less in others, observe the dietary laws. Rabbis and ritual slaughterers are few. Jewish educational facilities, from part-time *heders* to all day schools and teachers' seminaries, are strong in the larger communities. But with few exceptions, notably that of Mexico, the percentage of Jewish children attending the schools is not impressive and the extent of their exposure to Jewish learning is, in the opinion of many communal leaders, inadequate.

Most communities have library facilities, a Jewish press in Yiddish, Hebrew, Spanish, Portuguese or other languages, and some measure of Jewish cultural activity. The larger communities, like Argentina, Brazil, Chile, Uruguay, Mexico and Colombia enjoy a wide range of cultural activities. They publish numerous Jewish books and periodicals in a variety of languages. Yiddish publications in abundance come from Argentina, whose Yiddish press is the largest in the world. In addition, these communities regularly present lectures, symposia and theatre dealing with matters of Jewish interest, and possess numerous talented writers, artists, and sculptors who devote at least part of their time to Jewish themes Particularly noteworthy have been the many contributions of high quality made to Jewish belles-lettres.

Jews have contributed their talents with equal dedication to the general culture of the countries in which they live. Many Jewish artists have worked exclusively with themes derived from

Spanish, Portuguese, or general secular culture, and have achieved impressive results. Equally notable have been the contributions of Jews in the sciences, and, in some countries, in politics. Jews have served as senators, governors, ambassadors, cabinet ministers and members of parliaments, and one, Benjamin Cohen, formerly the Chilean ambassador to Bolivia (1939–1945), and then to Venezuela, came to hold the post of assistant secretary general of the United Nations in charge of the Public Information Department and other positions in the U.N.

There is now little possibility for additional large-scale Jewish immigration into Latin America. As a result, the melting-pot process, now well under way, will soon near completion. As in the case of the Jewish community in the United States several decades earlier, the divisions between Ashkenazim and Sephardim, Germans and Poles, Smyrnans and Berditchevites are beginning to fade, and a new sense of Jewish unity is being forged. At the same time, an alarming tendency toward assimilation has been accompanying the process of acculturation to Latin American life. The use of Yiddish, one of the traditional hallmarks of Eastern European Jewry, is declining; so, too frequently is the interest in the Jewish press and communal activities, Concern for Jewish education is often less deep than it appears. The parents of many children attending Jewish schools too frequently display little interest in the activities or welfare of their Jewish community as a whole. The smaller communities have been particularly vulnerable to stagnation and erosion. Throughout much of Latin America the most pressing long-range problem faced by Jewish leadership is how their constituency can achieve integration into general society without relinquishing the values and pride of the Jewish heritage.

Their ability to provide a successful solution to this dilemma will depend largely upon a combination of three factors: the stability of the Latin American scene, the willingness of the various communities to deal concertedly with this problem and the readiness of North American Jewry to establish even closer ties than heretofore with their coreligionists south of the Río Grande.

Some Notes on the Articles Appearing in Volume I

1. Kohut's "Jewish Martyrs of the Inquisition in South America," (pp. 1–87) is an excellent, if somewhat outdated, introduction to the subject, and is furnished with a series of invaluable appendixes. It contains a number of errors. For example, contrary to the statement on p. 1, the identity of the New Christians was not always discovered, and prisoners of the Inquisition in the New World were not sent to Goa for sentencing. In the sixteenth century there were only two centers of the Inquisition in America, Mexico City and Lima; hence Kohut's statement of autos-da-fé being held in "Lima and other localities of America" (pp. 1 f.) is misleading. Kohut also fails to distinguish between New Christians and Jews (pp. 3, 7, and especially p. 48, for example). King Philip II approved the Inquisition for Latin America not in 1580, as Kohut says (pp. 8 f.) but by a royal decree (*cédula*) dated January 25, 1569. The Inquisition was inaugurated in Peru in 1570 and in New Spain in 1571, as Kohut himself should have recognized when he placed the first auto-da-fé in the New World in 1574 (p. 10). This statement, however, is not quite correct. There were autos-da-fé in the New World during the inquisitions operative prior to the advent of the Holy Office.

Besides, the statements about the auto-da-fé of 1574 are grossly exaggerated. There were some seventy-four people sentenced in all, not one of them for the crime of Judaizing, and only three or four were sent to the stake. The description of the burning is sheer fantasy. Equally incorrect are the statements about Francisco Rodríguez de Matos on p. 22. There is no evidence that any of the Carvajals in 1580 or 1596 were related to Luis del Marmol Carvajal (p. 23).

Kohut also confuses Treviño de Sobremente with Maldonado de Silva (p. 24) and is quite out of date in many of his statements on Brazil (p. 27). He incorrectly assumes Francisco Moyen to have been a Judaizer (p. 51). He also mistakenly regards the garb with the special adornments worn by impenitent heretics to the stake with the garb of all other prisoners sentenced for Judaizing (p. 58). He also confuses the term *auto de fe* with the scaffolds erected for the proceedings or the subsequent executions (p. 32). There are also occasional spelling errors, (v.g. pp. 11, 12, 18, 48).

2. and 3. Arnold Wiznitzer's two articles, "Crypto-Jews in Mexico During the Sixteenth Century," (pp. 18–132) and "Crypto-Jews in Mexico During the Seventeenth Century," (pp. 133–177) form the most balanced and scholarly introduction to the subject of Mexican Judaizing to date (March 1971), this despite the fact that Wiznitzer did not make use of the vast resources of manuscript material without which no adequate history of the subject can be written. A few corrections might be mentioned.

The term New Christians referred originally to the converts in Spain after 1391 (see p. 88). The spelling "Alonso" is preferable to "Alonzo" on p. 90, and the translation "attended' instead of "assisted" should be used for the original "asistieron" at the end of note 27 on p. 101, and on p. 245. Governor Carvajal, arrested in 1589 and dead by the end of 1591, did not languish in prison for several years (p. 184). His nephew and namesake should be called Luis de Carvajal, the Younger (pp. 189 ff) and not "junior." Luis the Younger's father was "relaxed posthumously," not "released as dead," (p. 188). Wiznitzer also is a bit confused about young Carvajal's religious practices (cf. my study, "The Religion of Luis Rodriguez Carvajal," in *American Jewish Archives XX* (1968), pp. 33 ff. Also read "Oaxaca" for "Gauxaca" on p. 141, and "lewdly" instead of "dishonestly" on p. 142.

4. Conway's article is the most thorough of the many written on the subject. It is based largely on documents now available in Alfonso Toro, ed., *Los judíos en la Nueva España, Publicaciones del Archivo General de la Nación*, XX, Mexico City, 1932, especially pp. 20 ff. See also p. 93. Conway's use of the term "Jewish" (v.g. p. 178) and his conclusion (p. 194) are infelicitous (see introduction to these

volumes) and have contributed to much confusion in later writers. For the sake of clarity, an explanation should be added on p. 188 to the effect that the Sunday on which the witness saw Hernando Alonso and Gonzalo de Morales attired in their *sambenitos* was the day of their sentencing. Conway's appendix (pp. 195–200) contains a translation of a very valuable document.

5. and 6. My own translations of the Autobiography (pp. 201–242), and Letters and Last Will and Testament (pp. 243–312) of Luis de Carvajal, the Younger, should be supplemented by a reading of Seymour Liebman's translation, which appeared the following year (*The Enlightened,* Coral Gables, Florida, 1967), Liebman's work contains a long introduction and epilogue, which make some use of the vast manuscript treasures available for the subject in numerous archives, especially the *Archivo General de la Nación* in Mexico City. My translations were part of my work on a full forthcoming biography of Luis de Carvajal based on the material still in manuscript as well as the significant items that have been printed. For a bibliography, see my article, "A Brief Survey of Studies Relating to Luis de Carvajal, the Younger," *The American Sephardi,* III (1969), pp. 89 f.

7. Aside from some misspellings (v.g. genten, p. 313; Manozca, p. 319; Lenor, pp. 325, 344; Nunez, p. 327; Parmco [for Pánuco], pp. 333; Tarco (for Tasco, written Taxco in the manuscript, where the "x" resembles an "r", p. 336), Cyrus Adler's "Trial of Jorge de Almeida by the Inquisition in Mexico," (pp. 313–363) is an excellent summary of the Inquisitional proceedings against the fugitive Almeida in 1607. The note on p. 344 bears correction: the governor in question was indeed Don Luis de Carvajal de la Cueva.

8. David Fergusson's translation of the "Trial of Gabriel de Granada by the Inquisition in Mexico" (pp. 365–497), remains the only translation of an Inquisitional trial to be published in full to date. Translations of other trial records have also been made, notably that of Treviño de Sobremonte, but these remain in manuscript. Gabriel de

Granada's is one of the more interesting cases of the Mexican Inquisition and sheds light on the epoch of the Great Conspiracy of the Judaizers in New Spain. The translation is generally faithful though occasionally infelicitous. The notes by Fergusson and Adler are illuminating but inadequate for the full elucidation of the trial record. Actually, the entire transcript was not published. In an act of questionable scholarly judgment Fergusson chose to omit one of Gabriel de Granda's prayers "it being too long and foolish" (p. 487). He also omitted repetitions of depositions, but here his decision was justified.

Some Notes on the Articles Appearing in Volume II

1. Adler's "Original Unpublished Documents Relating to Thomas [sic!, for Tomas] Tremino [sic for Tremiño or, more appropriately Treviño] de Sobremonte (1638)" (pp. 1–5) contains the translation of two valuable Inquisition documents pertaining to the famous Judaizing martyr of New Spain. Unfortunately, the translation is unaccompanied by notes and the kind of introduction that would place the documents in clearer perspective.

2. Adler's "The Inquisition in Peru" (pp. 6–37) despite its date of publication, remains one of the few articles devoted to the subject containing Inquisitional material in English translation, though the substance and wording of the documents, especially in the case of the Edict of Faith (pp. 21 ff.), are hardly unique. Adler erred in believing that the incriminating activities mentioned on p. 23 constituted the test of an "American Jew" (he too means "Judaizer") in contradistinction to Judaizers elsewhere. The two appendices (pp. 32 ff.) contain useful lists of the autos-da-fé in Lima and Cartagena.

3. "The Trial of Francisco Maldonado da Silva" (pp. 39–55) by Alexander Kohut is a pedestrian but nonetheless valuable article, based largely on the lengthy account in Spanish in José Toribio Medina's *Historia del Tribunal del Santo Oficio de la Inquisición en Chile*, pp. 71–145. There are a number

of infelicities in Kohut's work. Thus for example, he translates "Heli Nazareo" as "Sun of Nazareth," instead of "Eli the Nazirite"; he gives the impression that Maldonado de Silva knew the short prayer mentioned on p. 47 as the beginning of the Eighteen Benedictions and he misleads the reader by claiming that Maldonado de Silva spoke in the spirit of Rabbi Akiba, of whom he did not know, and the later Nathan Hale, whose devotion was directed to his country rather than his faith. (p. 48).

4. Gottheil's article on "Fray Joseph Díaz Pimienta, Alias Abraham Díaz Pimienta," the Cuban martyr (pp. 56–65), is based on material in the archives of Seville. It adds a fascinating chapter to the history of secret Judaism in Latin America.

5. and 6. Martin Zielonka's two articles, "Francisco Rivas" (pp. 66–72) and "A Spanish-American Jewish Periodical" (pp. 73–79), written nearly a quarter of a century earlier, throw light on a baffling phenomenon of Mexican Jewish history. The puzzle is aptly explained in the opening sentence of the second article: "A country without a Jewish congregation, a Jewish charity organization or a Jewish cemetery organization or a Jewish cemetery and yet a country with a Jewish periodical, such was Mexico in 1889." The skimpy and short-lived journal with shifting titles contained a variety of material, ranging from Inquisitional documents to fanciful editorials about the origin and identity of the Mexican Jews (see pp. 66 ff., 74 f.) and naive derivations of various names, including that of Abravanel (pp. 68 ff.). Equally fantastic is Rivas' account of the arrival of the Jews in the New World (pp. 70 f.).

The fact that people doubted that Rivas was a Jew (p. 72) is perfectly understandable, despite his own ardent identification as a Jew, his Jewish library and his concern with matters Jewish. It is impossible to ascertain either Rivas' ancestry or his motivation for creating his journal. It is highly likely that Rivas acquired his rudimentary knowledge of Judaism during his studies in New York City and that his identity as a Jew, like that of many if not all of the so-called Indian Jews of twentieth-century Mexico, resulted from social and perhaps even political ambitions.

7. "A Study of Brazilian Jewish History 1623–1634, Based Chiefly Upon the Findings of the Late Samuel Oppenheim" (pp. 80–162), by Herbert I. Bloom, is a thorough and balanced account shedding important light on many aspects of the history of the Jews in Dutch Brazil. Although Bloom did not handle Portuguese and makes several errors (like his confusion of St. Thomas [p. 93] with the penal colony of São Thomé, off the African coast), the details of the study are for the most part reliable. The appendixes are excellent.

8. Like all of Wiznitzer's studies, his "Jewish Soldiers in Dutch Brazil (1630–1654)" (pp. 163–173) is an accurate and scholarly presentation, based largely on printed and manuscript material of difficult accessibility. In conjunction with Wiznitzer's studies on the Jews in Brazil one should keep in mind Wiznitzer's volume entitled *Jews in Colonial Brazil* (New York, 1960) and Isaac S. Emmanuel's "Seventeenth-Century Brazilian Jewry: A Critical Review," *American Jewish Archives XIV* (1962), pp. 32-68.

9. Wiznitzer's "The Synagogue and Cemetery of the Jewish Community in Recife, Brazil (1630–1654)" is an excellent brief treatment of the subject.

10. Adler's, "A Contemporary Memorial Relating to Damages to Spanish Interests in America Done by Jews of Holland (1634)" (pp. 178–184) contains the translation of an important document found in the general archives of Simancas. There are, however, a number of infelicities in the translation, such as "the first *amente* [!]" and "concealed by *flamenco de amberes*" [sic!] on p. 180 and the rendering of "digo" by "I say" instead of "I mean" on p. 173. In its brief introduction Adler fails to question the credibility of the patently partisan view of the author of the document, and appears to accept his conclusion that the Jews of Holland were decisively active in Brazil.

11. Kayserling's "The Earliest Rabbis and Jewish Writers of

America" (pp. 185–192) is a brief but important contribution by the foremost authority on Spanish and Portuguese Jewry of his time. It does have to be brought up to date bibliographically, chiefly on the basis of Wiznitzer's *Jews in Colonial Brazil* (New York, 1960).

12. Kayserling's "Isaac Aboab, the First Jewish Author in America" (pp. 193–204) contains a brief biographical introduction to Aboab and reproduces several of his Hebrew compositions. Not included is the *Zekher 'Asiti l'Nifl'ot El*. Regrettably, there is little analysis of these compositions and neither translations nor summaries of their contents in English. Like the previous article, this valuable study too should be read in the light of more recent scholarship.

13. Like all the other studies by Arnold Wiznitzer, the article "Isaac de Castro, Brazilian Jewish Martyr" (pp. 205–217) is characterized by meticulous research and cautious reconstruction. The notes and appendix contain two valuable documents in their original languages (Portuguese and French respectively) and in English translation.

14. Wiznitzer's "The Members of the Brazilian Jewish Community (1648–1653)" (pp. 218–226) is based upon a study of the minute book of the Congregations Zur Israel and Magen Abraham. The study would have been enhanced by an alphabetical index of the names of the members of the community, including their often confused variant spellings and biographical details, where available.

15. Wiznitzer's lengthy study "The Minute Book of Congregations Zur Israel of Recife and Magen Abraham of Mauricia, Brazil" (pp. 227–312) represents one of the author's most important contributions to the field of Brazilian Jewish history. It contains an excellent analysis of the major areas of Jewish life supervised by the governing *Mahamad* (pp. 234–262), the minutes of its meetings between 1649 and 1653 (pp. 262–269) a translation of the minute book itself (pp. 270–303) and a glossary of Hebrew and Portuguese words, including selected proper names (pp. 304–312). Here also we lack a much needed

alphabetical index, including the variant spellings appearing for the same name in the document.

16. Wiznitzer's "The Exodus from Brazil and Arrival in New Amsterdam of the Jewish Pilgrim Fathers, 1654" (pp. 313–330) represents a major contribution to the history of both Latin American and North American Jewry. With his characteristic precision of detail the author throws considerable new light on this exodus. Among other original insights, he offers a striking challenge to the current belief that the twenty-three Jews from Brazil who arrived in New Amsterdam late in the summer of 1654 found no other Jew there except the Ashkenazi Jacob Barsimson.

17. David Feinberg's historical survey of the colonization of the Russian Jews in Argentina (pp. 331–363) is the only major contribution to the pages of the American Jewish Historical Society's journals dealing with the modern period in Latin America. The document is one of the most important as well as fascinating sources for the study of the Russian Jews who migrated to Argentina to settle in farming communities there toward the end of the nineteenth century. The translation, in natural and lucid English by Leo Shpall, is accompanied by an excellent, if brief, introduction and notes.

BIBLIOGRAPHY

Although the field of Latin American Jewish studies is young, the bibliography of relevant books and articles is too vast to cite in an introductory essay. The bibliography presented here does not aim for completeness. It is intended to provide readers with an introduction to the various aspects of the field discussed in the text and reliable references to the many problems mentioned there. A fuller bibliography and discussion of these problems must await the expansion to this introductory essay into a fuller study of Latin American Jewry.

Section I: The Colonial Period

Amador de los Ríos, José, *Historia social, política y religiosa de los judíos de España y Portugal*, 3 vols., Madrid, 1875.

Azevedo, João. Lucio d', *Historia dos Christãos Novos portugueses*, Lisbon, 1921.

Baião, Antonio, *Episodios dramaticos da Inquisição portuguesa*, 3 vols., 1919-1937.

Baião, Antonio, *A Inquisição em Portugal e no Brazil*, Lisbon, 1921.

Benardete, Maír José, *Hispanic Culture and Character of the Sephardic Jews*, New York, 1952.

Boxer, C. R., *The Dutch in Brazil 1624-1654*, London, 1957.

Boxer, C. R., *Four Centuries of Portuguese Expansion 1415-1823*, Johannesburg, 1961.

Boxer, C. R., *The Portuguese Seaborne Empire 1415-1825*, London, 1969.

Boxer, C. R., *Salvador de Sa and the Struggle for Brazil and Angola 1602-1686*, London, 1952.

Caro Baroja, Julio, *Los judiós en la España moderna y contemporanea*, 3 vols., Madrid, 1961.

Cohen, Martin A., "Marrano Diaspora," in *Encyclopedia Judaica*, Jerusalem, 1971.

Cohen, Martin A., "The Religion of Luis Rodríguez Carvajal," *American Jewish Archives,* XX (1968), pp. 33-62.

Emmanuel, Isaac S., "Seventeenth-Century Brazilian Jewry: A Critical Review," American Jewish Archives XIV (1962), pp. 32-68.

Encyclopedia Judaica, ed. Cecil Roth, Jerusalem–New York, 1971.

Enciclopedia Judaica Castellana, ed. Eduardo Weinfeld, Mexico D.F. 10 vols., 1948-1951.

Gonçalves Salvador, José *Christãos Novos, Jesuitas e Inquisição,* São Paulo, 1969.

Glaser, Edward, "Invitation to Intolerance: A Study of the Portuguese Sermons Preached at Autos-da-fé," *Hebrew Union College Annual* XXVII (1956), pp. 327-385.

Herculano, Alejandro, *Da origem e estabelecimento da Inquisição em Portugal,* 3 vols., Lisbon, 1864.

Herring, Hubert, *A History of Latin America,* New York, 1963.

Kamens, Henry, *The Spanish Inquisition,* New York, 1965.

Kayserling, Moritz, *Geschichte der Juden in Portugal,* Leipzig, 1867.

Kellenbenz, Hermann, *Sephardim an der Unteren Elbe: Ihre Wirtschaftliche und Politische Bedeutung vom Ende des 16. bis zum Beginn des 18. Jahrhunderts,* Wiesbaden, 1958.

Konetzke, A. Richard, *La emigración española al Río de la Plata durante el siglo XVI,* Madrid, 1952.

Lafuente Machaín, R. de, *Los portugueses en Buenos Aires,* Madrid, 1931.

Lea, Henry C., *A History of the Inquisition in Spain,* 4 vols., New York, 1906-1907.

Lea, Henry C., *The Inquisition in the Spanish Dependencies,* New York, 1908.

Lewin, Boleslao, *El Santo Oficio en América y el más grande proceso inquisitorial,* Buenos Aires, 1950.

Lewin, Boleslao, *Mártires y conquistadores judíos en la America Hispana,* Buenos Aires, 1954.

López Martínez, Nicolás, *Los judaizantes castellanos y la Inquisición en tiempo de Isabel la Católica,* Burgos, 1954.

Mariel de Ibáñez, Yolanda, *La Inquisición en México durante el siglo XVI,* Mexico, 1946.

Medina, José Toribio, *Historia del tribunal del Santo Oficio de la Inquisición de Cartageña de las Indias,* Santiago de Chile, 1899.

Medina, José Toribio, *Historia del tribunal del Santo Oficio de la Inquisicíon en Chile,* Santiago de Chile, 2 vols., 1890, 2nd ed. 1952.

Medina, José Toribio, *Historia del tribunal del Santo Oficio de la Inquisición de Lima*, 2 vols. Santiago de Chile, 1887, 2nd ed. 1956.

Medina, José Toribio, *Historia del tribunal del Santo Oficio de la Inquisición en México*, Santiago de Chile, 1905, 2nd ed. revised Mexico, 1952.

Medina, José Toribio, *La primitiva inquisición americana* (1493-1569), 2 vols., Santiago de Chile, 1914.

Medina, José Toribio, *El tribunal del Santo Oficio de la Inquisición en las Islas Filipinas*, Santiago de Chile, 1889.

Medina, José Toribio de, *El tribunal del Santo Oficio de la Inquisición en las provincias de la Plata*, Santiago de Chile, 1899.

Mendes dos Remedios, Joaquim, *Os judeus em Portugal*, 2 vols., Coimbra, 1895-1928.

Mendes dos Remedios, Joaquim, *Os judeus portugueses em Amsterdam*, Coimbra, 1911.

Netanyahu, B., *The Marranos of Spain from the Late XIVth to the Early XVIth Century*, New York, 1966.

Pallares, Eduardo, *El procedimiento inquisitorial*, Mexico City, 1951.

Palma, Ricardo, *Tradiciones peruanas completas*, Madrid, 1961.

Revah, I., "Les Marranes," *Revue des etudes juives*, CXVIII (1959-1960), pp. 29-77.

Roth, Cecil, *A History of the Marranos*, Philadelphia, 1932, and later reprints.

Roth, Cecil, "The Religion of the Marranos," *Jewish Quarterly Review*, (new series), XX (1931-1932), pp. 1-33.

Roth, Cecil, *The Spanish Inquisition*, London, 1937, reprint New York, 1964.

Saraiva, Antonio José, *Historia da cultura em Portugal*, 3 vols., Lisbon, 1950-1962.

Saraiva, António José, *Inquisiçao e Cristãos-Novos* Porto, 1969.

Sicroff, Albert A., *Les controverses des statuts de pureté de sang en Espagne du XVe au XVIIe siècles* Paris, 1960.

Silva Rosa, J. S. da, *Geschiedenis der Portugeesche Joden te Amsterdam*, Amsterdam, 1925.

Toro, Alfonso, *La familia Carvajal*, 2 vols., Mexico City, 1944.

Wiznitzer, Arnold, *Jews in Colonial Brazil*, New York, 1960.

Zimmels, H. J., *Die Marranen in der rabbinischen Literatur*, Berlin, 1932.

Section II: The Modern Period

American Jewish Year Book
American Jewish Committee. New York, 71 vols. 1899/1900-
1970.

[Argentina]   אַרגענטינע. פופציק יאָר אידישער אישעוו, צוואָנציק יאָר די
Buenos Aires, 1938.   פרעסע.

Argentina   יובל־בוך. סך־הכל'ן פון 50 יאָהר אידיש לעבען אין ארגענטינע.
לכבוד „די אידישע צייטונג" צו איהר 25־יאָהריגען יובילעאום.
Buenos Aires, 1940.

Beller, Jacob, *Jews in Latin America.* New York, 1969.

Beller, Jacob.   איבער צוואָנציק לאַטיין־אַמעריקאַנער לענדער ; באַגעגענישן
Buenos Aires, 1953.   מיט יידן אין וייטע ווינקלען.

Bistritsky, Nathan. על היהדות והציונות באמריקה הלטינית
Jerusalem, 1946-47.

Cohen, Jacob, Xenab, *Jewish Life in South America,* New York,
1941.

Comité Judío Americano
Comunidades judias de Latinoamerica, 3 vols., Buenos Aires,
1966, 1968, 1970.

Emmanuel, Isaac S., *Precious Stones of the Jews of Curacao*
New York, 1957.

Emmanuel, Isaac S. and Suzanne D.
The Jews in the Netherlands Antilles, Cincinnati, 1970.

Fruchter, Nathan. די געשיכטע פון ארגענטינע.
2 vols., Buenos Aires, 1944-45.

Goldman, David   די יודען אין ארגענטינע : אין דער פערגאַנגענהייט און
אין דער געגענווארט : אין וואָרט און אין בילד.
Vol. 1, Buenos Aires, 1914.

Gamzer, Haim   שירת הקיבוץ. רשמי מסע באמריקה הלאטינית.
Tel-Aviv, 1948-1949.

Gotlib, Isaac, 1902   יידן אין לאַטיין אַמעריקע.
New York, 1960.

Kitron, Moshe. הישוב היהודי באמריקה הלטינית.
Jerusalem, 1960.

Lee, Samuel J., *Moses of the New World: The Work of Baron de
Hirsch,* New York, 1970.

Monk, Abraham
Comunidades judías de Latinoamérica,
Buenos Aires, 1968.

Neumann, Gerhardt
"German Jews in Columbia. A Study in Immigrant Adjustment."

Jewish Social Studies, III (1941), pp. 387-398.

Raffalovich, Israel

"The Condition of Jewry and Judaism in South America",
Yearbook of the Central Conference of American Rabbis, vol. 40
(1930), pp. 414-423.

Regalski, M. [ ] ‏די לאַגע פון יידן אין אַרגעטינע.‏
Zukunft, Vol. 47 (1942), pp. 33-35.

Razovsky, Cecilia

"The Jew Rediscovers America. Jewish immigration to Latin
American countries," in *Jewish Social Service Quarterly,* vol. 5
(1929), pp. 119-127.

Rosell, Cesar Garcia

"El aporte económico-comercial de los judíos en la Lima antigua,"
Judaica, vol. 9 (Buenos Aires, 1941), pp. 132-134.

Ruppin, Arthur, 1876-1943

Los judíos en América del sur (Introduction by Boris Vainstock),
Buenos Aires, 1938.

Sapir, Boris

The Jewish Community of Cuba, Settlement and Growth, New
York, 1948.

Schwartz, Ernst

Jews in Latin America, Pan American Union Bulletin
Washington, vol. 74 (1940), pp. 729-736.

Schwartz, Ernst

Jews of Latin America, Inter-American Quarterly, July 1941,
pp. 18-26.

Shatzky, Jacob 1894-1956

Comunidades judías en latinoamérica, Buenos Aires, 1952.

Shore, Maurice

*Notes and Glimpses at Jewish Community Life in Central and
South America.* New York, 1944.

Sobel, Louis

"Jewish community life and organization in Latin America"
Jewish Social Service Quarterly. Vol. 20 (1944), pp. 179-190.

Trotzki, Elijah ‏„די יידן אין אורוגוואַי".‏
Zukunft, Vol. 48 (1943), pp. 687-690.

Vainstock, B. and Feldman, F. eds.

Guía anual israelita de los países latino-americanos, Buenos Aires,
1953-

Weinfeld, Eduardo

"Los judíos de México," *Judaica* vol. 15 (Buenos Aires, 1940),
pp. 3-14.

JEWISH MARTYRS OF THE INQUISITION IN SOUTH AMERICA.

By George Alexander Kohut, *New York*.

Torquemada's sway extended even beyond the Atlantic. There are few decades in the sixteenth, seventeenth and eighteenth centuries which do not deserve a conspicuous place in the annals of history for excess of wanton cruelty and inhuman oppression, and there were few countries exempt from the influence of those barbaric times, when fanatic zeal and holy bigotry were virtue.

Contrary to popular belief, intolerance reigned supreme in America almost immediately after its colonization. Monks and Jesuits who had settled in Mexico, Peru, Central America and the West Indies took particular care not to favor the Marranos or New Christians who fled from Spain and Portugal to escape the tortures of the Inquisition. It is not at all unlikely that they informed against them, and persuaded Queen Johanna, in 1511, to restrict their immigration.* Despite all efforts at concealment, their identity was always discovered, and many victims were snatched away from the New World by agents of the so-called Holy Office, to be consigned to the infernal flames of the *autos de fe* whose fires were kindled in Goa (India),† Lima and other localities

---

*See Dr. M. Kayserling's article, "The Colonization of America by the Jews," *Pub. Am. Jewish Hist. Soc.* No. 2, p. 73; *Christopher Columbus and the participation of the Jews in the Spanish and Portuguese discoveries*, New York, 1894, pp. 126 ff., 169-171 ; George A. Kohut in the *Reform Advocate*, January 19, 1895, p. 354.

† A curious and valuable account of the proceedings of the Inquisition in Goa and other Indian cities, together with various interesting facts in connection with the attempt to establish the Holy Office in Brazil, is found in a duodecimo volume of 250 pages, pub-

1

of America. On the 30th of June, 1567, and again on March 15, 1568, the Cardinal-Infant D. Enrique, as Regent of Portugal, issued an edict forbidding the Marranos to settle in India and Brazil, which was only repealed when a ransom of 1,700,000 cruzados ($714,000) was offered by the New Christians. A law, passed on May 21, 1577, accorded them the privileges of residence and free commerce, and any reproach against the names of Jew, Marrano or New Christian, says Dr. Kayserling, was strictly punishable.* This enormous monetary sacrifice, however, did not purchase lasting peace for the unfortunate *conversos,* for, says Dr. Kayserling,† "the law of March 15, 1568, was renewed, and the captains of ships received peremptory instructions to confiscate for the state treasury all the property of New Christians who should be found in their vessels, and to send them back to Portugal. If no ship happened to be ready to return to Portugal, the New Christians were to be carried to Goa, and were there to be retained in prison by the Inquisition until some ship set sail for the mother-country. The Inquisition was to deal in a similar manner with the Jews and New Christians who had already settled in the colonies; a number of them were to be sent back annually to Portugal, and thus the Indies were gradually to be purged."

It appears from the notes made by a conscientious historian of the Inquisition that the principal objects of persecution

lished in Paris, and reprinted at Amsterdam, 1697, bearing the following title : *Relation de l'Inquisition de Goa : A Paris : Chez Daniel Horthemels, rue Saint Jacques, an Mecoenas. M.DC.LXXXVIII. Avec privilege du roi.* This anonymous book (written by the physician Claude Dellon) on the Inquisition at Goa contains several vivid illustrations (wood-cuts) of the sufferings of those who were accused of heresy and Judaism. An English translation of this book was issued in London in 1688, by Henry Wharton, entitled, *History of the Inquisition as it is exercised at Goa.*

　*Kayserling, *Pub. Am. Jewish Hist. Soc.* No. 2, p. 75 ; *Christopher Columbus,* p. 130.

　† *Christopher Columbus,* p. 132.

at the hands of the Christian clergy in the newly acquired possessions of Hispañola were the various sects of Marranos or New Christians. Already the Spanish Inquisitor-General, Cardinal Ximenes de Cisneros, took heed that none of their number should find refuge in America. On the 7th of May, 1516, he appointed Fray Juan Quevedo, Bishop of Cuba, his delegate for the kingdom of *Terra Firma,* as the mainland of Spanish America was then called, and authorized him to select personally such officials as he needed to hunt down and exterminate the Marranos, who, despite all precautions, had sought the shelter of the new dominion in Hispañola and other places of America. Charles V, with the permission of Cardinal Hadrian, the Dutch Inquisitor and later Pope, issued an edict on May 25, 1520—at the time when bishoprics were few and far between in the New World— whereby he ordained Alonso Manso, Bishop of Porto Rico, and Pedro de Cordova, Vice-Provincial of the Dominicans, as Inquisitors for the Indies and the islands of the ocean.*

The New Christians in America were not only fugitive Jews from Europe, says Hoffmann;† there were among them many heathenish natives, who were forcibly converted by the mighty clerical arm of the Spanish conqueror, but who nevertheless remained at heart loyal to their hereditary belief and practised their idolatrous customs with as much zeal as the fear of discovery and consequent punishment would allow. The rigor and inhumanity of the yet unsystematic Tribunal knew no bounds. The Indians particularly were subject to the ire and cruelty of the newly established Holy Office. The fiendish atrocities com-

---

* Cf. W. H. Rule's *History of the Inquisition,* vol. II, pp. 15–16.

† *Gesch. d. Inquisition,* vol. II, pp. 40–41. After this paper was in type, the writer found that Hoffmann's data on the American Inquisition were largely taken from W. H. Rule's *History of the Inquisition from its establishment in the twelfth century to its extinction in the nineteenth,* London and New York, 1874, vol. II, pp. 13–32. Hoffmann, however, has acknowledged his indebtedness to him and other authorities in the Preface to vol. I, p. iii.

mitted against them in the name of the Christian faith
are vividly recounted in a profusely illustrated Dutch
narrative, whose title is given below in one of the notes,
concerning the Inquisition in the West Indies. The copperplates accompanying that (now exceedingly rare) publication present a ghastly spectacle of the diabolical ingenuity
employed by the divine agency in torturing the bodies of
its victims. This fearful persecution depopulated the
country to such an extent that the tyrants themselves perceived that they must desist for a while, and accordingly
appealed to Charles V, recommending a discontinuance of
the Inquisitorial scourge.* The Emperor also recognized the
danger and issued an edict under date of October 15, 1538,
commanding the Tribunal not to pay any more attention to the
aborigines, but only to European immigrants and their offspring.† It is needless to state that this order was trans-
gressed more than once. In fact many complaints reached
the imperial ears concerning the renewed persecution of the
Indians, and the law of 1538 was again put into force on
October 18, 1549. In order to divert the tide of Inquisitorial
fury, Philip II, who actually had a heart, as Hoffmann
(p. 41) remarks, gave it out on January 25, 1569, that heresy
is being reinforced by the circulation of books and false
dogmas in America, in consequence of which the *Consejo de
la Suprema* was organized.‡ This resulted in the firm establishment of the Holy Office in Mexico and Peru, as will be
shown at length below.

The Marranos appear to have been quite prosperous

---

* Dr. Adler has kindly referred me, in this connection, to Arthur
Helps' *Life of Las Casas, The Apostle of the Indies*, London, 1868,
2d ed., pp. 178–231, where a full history of the conversion of the
Indians, and other matters referred to in the text, are given. See
also his *Spanish Conquest in America* (London, 1855–61), Index, *s. v.*
Indians.

† See Rule, *History of the Inquisition*, p. 16.

‡ *Ibid.*, p. 17.

for a while, so that, secure in their unrevealed identity, they became indiscreet, until the spies of the Holy Office found them out. It is well known that many secret Jews from Spain and Portugal settled very early in the Portuguese Indies, especially in Brazil, whither shiploads of them were exported annually to expiate for some offense or crime.* They are reported to have been scattered along the entire coast of the Portuguese colonies in the New World, and to have carried on an extensive trade in precious stones with Venice, Turkey and other countries. Just as soon as they could do so with impunity, they emerged from obscurity and reavowed the old Mosaic faith, which for a time only they were constrained to discard. We have documentary evidence to prove the patriotism and earnest zeal of the Marranos in the Indies and elsewhere. They were especially attached to the Dutch, under whose protection they enjoyed unqualified peace, and to show their gratitude, enlisted their persons and wealth in the conflict between Holland and Portugal.† King Philip II, in a letter addressed to Martin Affonso de Castro, Viceroy of the Indies, declares that two New Christians in Columbo were in active correspondence with the Dutch, and that several in Malacca reported their military plans to the Dutch. The secret Jews in the Indies sent considerable supplies to the Spanish and Portuguese Jews in Hamburg and Aleppo, who in turn forwarded them to Holland and Zealand. (See Appendix V.) It was this open boast of Jewish loyalty that called forth the edict of March 15, 1568, whose purport was communicated above. Despite the peremptory tone of the various imperial

---

* See Dr. Kayserling's note in his *Geschichte der Juden in Portugal,* Leipzig, 1867, p. 294; *Christopher Columbus,* p. 129 seq. See especially, Appendix VII to this paper.

† Ample evidence for this statement is furnished by the writer in a paper entitled "Sketches of Jewish Loyalty, Bravery and Patriotism in the South American Colonies and the West Indies," in Hon. S. Wolf's *American Jew as Patriot, Soldier and Citizen,* Philadelphia, 1895, pp. 443–484.

commands, it appears that the Marranos came to this country in great numbers, for in the beginning of the seventeenth century another edict was issued by Philip III.

"We command and decree," runs the message, "that no one recently converted to our holy faith, be he Moor or Jew, or the offspring of these, should settle in our Indies without our distinct permission. Furthermore, we forbid most emphatically the immigration into New Spain of any one [who is at the expiration of some prescribed penance] newly reconciled with the church ; of the child or grandchild of any person who has ever worn the *sambenito* publicly; of the child or grandchild of any person who was either burnt as a heretic or otherwise punished for the crime of heresy, through either male or female descent. Should any one [falling under this category] presume to violate this law, his goods will be confiscated in behalf of the royal treasury, and upon him the full measure of our grace or disgrace shall fall, so that under any circumstances and for all times he shall be banished from our Indies. Whosoever does not possess personal effects, however, should atone for his transgression by the public infliction of one hundred lashes."*

There was no end of lashes, says Hoffmann ;† nor were cases of confiscation rare, yet the immigration did not cease. Marranos and other objectionable heretics found a way through all obstacles, for we meet them everywhere, toiling and progressing and prospering. One needed only to understand the art or the trick of procuring a royal license. A merchant who paid a respectable amount of taxes for his commercial privileges was permitted to travel everywhere, regardless of his origin or family history, and even those of the lower classes could at any moment board a ship bound for Hispañola or other American port if they

---

* The original document is printed in *Ordenanzas Reales para la Contratacion de Sevilla*, etc. (Valladolid, 1604). See also Rule's *History of the Inquisition, l. c.*, pp. 18–19.

† Vol. II, p. 43 ; Rule, p. 19.

took care to gild the palms of the inferior officers with as much gold as their means would allow.*

Soon the number of the New Christians among the Spaniards and Americans in the Indies, writes Hoffmann (p. 43), "became considerable, and furnished the Inquisition sufficient material for the trial-chambers and prisons. Authentic memoirs of these cases may yet come to light from the libraries of Mexico and Peru and the archives of Spain and Portugal." In Brazil, where eminent authors and rabbis founded a colony in 1642, and where already in 1624 large numbers of our co-religionists flourished,† almost every ship that landed brought fresh recruits, who were transported thither by imperial order to serve sentence for the crime of heresy. Only the names of very few such culprits are preserved for us in historic annals. For example, at an *auto de fe* held on the 10th of May, 1682, in Lisbon—the grandest and most horrible in the history of the Portuguese Inquisition —many Jews were burnt, among them Pedro Serrão, son of the apothecary Antonio Serrão. A sister of Pedro's, 27 years old, an aged Jewess of 72, named Paula de Crasto, and Simon Henriquez, tenant of the crown-lands, who was twice before accused of Judaism, were exported to Brazil as penitent New Christians.‡ Two other persons

---

* See citation from the *Voyage of Francis Pryard* in *Pub. Am. Jewish Hist. Soc.* No. 2, p. 95. Rule says, p. 19: "Spanish merchants of impure blood might pay their fees of office, and pass without notice beyond the ocean; or, through petty bribery to underlings, persons of inferior class could at any time emigrate; and thus a rapidly increasing multitude of New Christians was mingled with the Spanish-American population. These people brought constant work for the Inquisitors, who not only demanded aid of the secular arm, but were ever encroaching on the jurisdiction of the magistrates."

† See *Pub. Am. Jewish Hist. Soc.* No. 3, pp. 104, 135 ff.; G. A. Kohut's paper in Wolf's *American Jew*, etc , p. 443 ff.

‡ See Michael Geddes, *View of the Court of Inquisition of Portugal*, in his *Miscellaneous Tracts*, London, 1702, pp. 417–448. Geddes was an eye-witness of this *auto*. See also Don Miguel Levi de Barrios,

of Jewish origin met the same fate in another *auto de fe* celebrated at Lisbon, in 1683.   One, a Jewess, 61 years old, who
together with others, was arraigned and lashed for witchcraft,
was sent to Brazil for five years.   The other, Francisco
Manoel Delgado, 43 years old, a merchant, was convicted of
Judaizing.   Fourteen days before, he was reconciled with the
church in the chapel of St. Anna in Triana, the suburb of
Seville, but avoided the heavy penance imposed upon him
by flight.   He was recaptured in Lisbon, but seems to
have bought off his judges with a light sentence, banishment to Brazil for three years, clad in penitential robes, at
the expiration of which time he might resume his commercial pursuits.*   There are no doubt other lists of penance-
doing heretics extant, scattered in various historical sources,
not now accessible.†

It was not long before tribunals of the Holy Office were
established in Mexico, Peru and Lima.   After Cardinal
Enrique's death in 1580, Philip II of Spain assumed control of America, and permitted, if he did not command, the

---

Govierno Popular Judayco, pp. 46, 47 ; Kayserling, *Sephardim,* Leipzig, 1859, p. 305, and note 498 on p. 361 ; his *Geschichte der Juden
in Portugal,* Leipzig, 1867, p. 318.   Fridolin Hoffmann, *Geschichte
der Inquisition,* Bonn, 1878, vol. II, pp. 81, 82, erroneously calls the
first named victim Serraon.   Cf. also Rule's *History of the Inquisition,* vol. II, p. 69.

* See Hoffmann, p. 83.   He says of Delgado : "Auch sein Ur-
theil ist ein verhältnissmässig mildes, weil ein Jüdisch geborener
Kaufmann sich rentabeler erwies zum Scheeren als zum Schlachten.
Wenn Delgado im Busskleide drei Jahre Verbannung in Brasilien
überstanden hatte, konnte er sich den Geschäften wieder zuwenden,
um dann zu gelegener Zeit auf's Neue Wolle zu lassen."   There is
more truth than poetry in this historian's figure, borrowed from
Rule's *History,* vol. II, p. 71 : "This punishment seems comparatively light, but a Jew-born merchant was not a man to be killed.
He could be robbed now and again, and being let loose after the
three years convict life, could return to business and be made prey
of at any convenient occasion."

† In Appendix VII there is given a list of some Marranos who
were sent to Brazil for various crimes in the years 1682 and 1707.

introduction of the Inquisition * into a country yet in the innocence of infancy, upon whose altars strange fires had never

* According to Dr. M. Kayserling, however, *Christopher Columbus*, pp. 128, 129, the above-mentioned decree, dated October 5, 1511 (printed in his book, Appendix XVIII, pp. 169–171), introduced the Spanish Inquisition into the newly discovered lands, and full scope was given to its activity. B. Röse, in his article, *Inquisition*, published in the large Ersch and Gruber *Allgemeine Encyclopaedie*, II Section, vol. XVIII, p. 468, writes : "In der neuen Welt wurde 1516 die Inquisition eingeführt und die Tribunale daselbst unter einen besondern Generalinquisitor gestellt. Blos die getauften Indianer, welche sich in mancher Beziehung wieder dem Heidenthume hingaben wurden anfänglich verfolgt, wodurch grosser Schaden erwuchs und Karl V gebot demnach 1538, dass nicht die Indianer, sondern die Europäer unter Aufsicht der Inquisition gestellt werden sollten. Diese hatten wenig zu thun, ihr Sitz war wandelnd, bis ihr 1569 eine festere Einrichtung gegeben wurde und erst 1571 wurden die beiden Tribunale zu Lima und Mexico für ganz America unter Aufsicht des Grossinquisitors und des grossen Rathes zu Madrid gestellt, und das zu Carthagena erst 1610 errichtet. Man hatte dort Mühe taugliche Subjecte zu diesen Aemtern zu erhalten da sich Niemand gern hierzu hergab." According to Llorente (quoted *l. c.* p. 471), under the jurisdiction of 44 "General-Inquisitors," whose office was abolished in 1808, there were publicly burned 31,912 individuals in person, 17,659 in effigy, and 291,456 were condemned to do penance ; hence 341,021 of both sexes were victims of the Holy Office. From this number are, however, excluded the martyrs who were punished and tortured in Mexico, Lima, Carthagena, Sicily, Sardinia, Naples, Milan, Flanders, Malta, and other places. For other calculations see Röse *in loco* and p. 469 ; Herzog and Plitt's *Real-Encyclopaedie*, etc., *s. v. Inquisition*, vol. VI², Leipzig, 1880, p. 745, and McClintock and Strong's *Theological Cyclopaedia*, vol. IV, p. 605a. Prof. Albert Réville, in his Hibbert Lectures on the *Native Religions of Mexico and Peru*, American ed., New York, 1884, p. 103, states that the Inquisition was established in Mexico in 1571. It is recorded on good authority that one of the first victims of the Holy Office in Española was Diego Caballero of Barrameda, whose mother and father, Juan Caballero, according to the statement of two witnesses, had been persecuted and condemned by the Inquisition in Spain. Cf. *Collecion de Documentos inéditos rel. al descubrimiento, conquista y organizacion de las antiguas posesiones españoles. Segunda Seria*, Madrid, 1885, vol. I, p. 422, cited by Kayserling, *Christopher Columbus*, p. 129. Was Caballero a Jew?

before been burning. In justice to this cruel monarch, who
scrupled not to torture his own son,* we must state that
already, 30 years before, the dread fires of that fiendish agency
were glaring in the rich empire of the Inkas. " Paramus, a
creature like Torquemada and Lucero," writes Dr. Kayserling,† " who is astonished that the Jews in Mexico, notwithstanding all the obstacles put in their way, were able to
sacrifice their Passover offering and celebrate their festival
of freedom, tells us, with great gusto, of the first *auto de fe*
in the New World, which took place in 1574 [not 1554, as
Kayserling has it], the year of Fernando Cortez's death.
Large tribunes were erected in the public place, and eighty
unfortunate Judaizers died at the stake.   The savage
Indians were delighted with the flames, which burned from
six o'clock in the morning till five in the evening; the
festive music, the ringing of bells and the songs of the
priests pleased them, and they burst out in wild rejoicings.
The spectators, who had attended such festivities before,
avowed that this ceremony would have been much finer
than many others if the Court had only been present."‡

---

* *Pub. Am. Jewish Hist. Soc.* No. 2, p. 75.

† Cf. Paramus : *De origine et progressu officii sanctae Inquisitionis, eiusque dignitate et utilitate,* Madrid, 1598 ; Antwerp, 1619, fol.
242 ; cited by Dr. Kayserling in his *Sephardim ; Romanische Poesien
der Juden in Spanien,* Leipzig, 1859, p. 295 ; his article, "Sephardic Jews in America," in *The Occident,* vol. XXVI, 1868, p. 217 ;
S. R. Hirsch's *Jeschurun,* vol. III, 1857, pp. 415, 416 ; Isaac Markens,
The Hebrews in America, New York, 1888, p. 3.

‡ His words, more elaborate in the Latin original, are given in
Appendix I to this paper ; see also Rule's *History,* vol. II, p. 18 :
"It is known that in 1574, the very year that the conqueror of
Mexico, Hernan Cortés, died, the first *auto* was celebrated in the
city of Mexico with great pomp ; and, unless by the absence of
royalty, was not inferior in grandeur to that of Valladolid, where
Philip . . . so rigidly and ostentatiously fulfilled his vow to take
vengeance on the heretics. At this first Mexican *auto,* it is related
that a Frenchman, who had probably escaped the Bartholomew
massacres, and an Englishman, were burnt as impenitent Lutherans.
Eighty penitents were exhibited at the same time, some punished

This pious wish was soon destined to be realized, for almost immediately after the establishment of the Holy Office in 1580 or 1581 (?), a physician named Juan Alvarez of Zafra, who together with his wife, children and nephew, Alonzo Alvarez, lived according to the law of Moses (à la Ley de Moyses), were publicly burned at Lima, as adherents to Judaism. A few years later, in 1582, Manuel (Moses ?) Lopez of Yelves in Portugal, who was also called Luis Coronado, was led to the stake. He openly admitted that he was an Israelite, and proudly declared himself to be a staunch follower of his ancestral faith. In fact, it appeared that he, in company with other co-religionists, worshiped the God of Israel and observed the Mosaic laws in his own house. The same fate was in store for the merchant Duarte Nuñez de Cea, forty-one years of age, who died as bravely as he had lived for his religion. Before ascending the funeral pyre he confessed that as a Jew he had lived, observing the precepts of Judaism, and that it was his simple wish to die a Jew, as his ancestors had done. The learned physician, Alvaro Nuñez of Braganza, who lived in La Plata, Diego Nuñez de Silva, Diego Rodriguez de Silveyra (Silvera ?) of Peru, who settled in Guamanga, and many other unfortunate victims, succeeded him.*

On the 22d of June, 1636, says Don Juan Antonio Llorento,† the secretary of the Inquisition, an *auto de fe* was celebrated at Valladolid, on which occasion ten Judaizers (of the 28 condemned victims) were sacrificed.‡ We cannot ascertain whether a town in Spain is thereby indicated, or some locality of the same name in America. There

for *Judaizing*, and some for holding the opinions of Luther or Calvin . . . And a few others did sore penance for magic and superstition."

* Cf. Kayserling, *Publ. Am. Jewish Hist. Soc.* No. 2, p. 75 ; *Christopher Columbus*, pp. 133, 134.

† *Histoire critique de l'Inquisition d'Espagne*, Paris, 1818, 2d ed , vol. III, p. 466.

‡ Graetz, *Geschichte der Juden*, vol. X², Leipzig, 1882, p. 100.

is in Central America a city now called Comayagua, the capital of Honduras, formerly Valladolid, founded in 1540. The capital of Michoacan (Mexico) was called Valladolid from its foundation by the Spaniards in 1541 until 1828, when it was changed into Morelia, in memory of the revolutionary chief José Maria Morelos. And to this day the name survives in a town of the Mexican Confederation, in Yucatan. It will be remembered that Columbus died in Valladolid on May 20, 1506.*

On January 23, 1639, further narrates Llorente,† there was a great *auto de fe* at Lima, the capital of Peru.‡ Seventy-two were condemned to death, among them sixty-three adherents of Judaism, all Portuguese, and three non-Jews, who facilitated the intercourse between the victims. Eleven§ Mar-

---

*See Kayserling's *Christopher Columbus*, p. 123.

† Vol. III, p. 469; cf. also Kayserling, *Sephardim*, etc., Leipzig, 1859, p. 295; Leeser's *Occident*, vol. XXVI, p. 217; and Moïse Schwab's "Victimes de l'Inquisition au XVIIᵉ siècle," in *Revue des Études Juives*, vol. XXX, 1895, p. 100.

‡ " Le 23 janvier 1639, il y eut à Lima, capitale du Pérou, un *auto de fe* général où parurent soixante-douze condamnés, dont trois comme ayant facilité aux prisonniers les moyens de communiquer les uns avec les autres, et avec des personnes du dehors ; un comme bigamie, cinq pour cause de sorcellerie, et soixante-trois qu'on avait accusés de judaïsme, et qui étaient Portugais ou enfans de Juifs de cette nation ; onze furent livrés au bras seculier, et brûlés vifs comme impénitens ; un autre le fut en effigie pour s'être pendu dans sa prison. Dans cet *auto de fe*, on vit paraître avec honneur, sur un siége élevé, et avec des palmes de chevalier, six individus que de faux témoins avaient fait arrêter, et qui réussirent à prouver qu'on les avait injustement accusés, et qu'ils n'avaient pas cessé d'être bons catholiques. Parmi les Juifs obstinés il s'en trouvait un fort savant dans l'Ecriture sainte ; il demanda à disputer avec des théologiens, et en confondit plusieurs qui n'étaient que d'ignorans scolastiques ; d'autres cependant lui prouvèrent le veritable sens des prophéties, en les rapprochant des évenemens qui étaient arrivés depuis le temps des prophètes."

§ So Kayserling. Graetz, however, says seventeen. Llorente, whose words we have given in a footnote, says eleven also, which undoubtedly is correct. Mackenna, in his *Francisco Moyen* (1869), has twelve.

ranos were openly burned at the stake on that day. Among the prisoners was a very learned physician of Lima, Francisco Meldonado de Silva,* who caused the ignorant scholastics sore travail. He had passed thirteen years in prison ; during all that period he had tasted no meat; a little maize had been his daily food. He permitted his beard and hair to grow, and gave himself the name of Eli Nazareno, as a servant of God. He wrote several works while in prison, which are said to have been subsequently printed. Old leaves artistically tied together served him for paper, ink he prepared from coal, the pointed leg of a hen was his pen, and notwithstanding the poverty of these materials his handwriting resembled print. During his confinement several attempts were made to convert him by illiterate Peruvian priests, who were no match in erudition for the unfortunate scholar, and only argued him into a firmer persuasion of belief in the doctrines of his ancestral creed. After thirteen years of suffering he died, admired even by his enemies. A fearful storm, more terrible than any remembered by the oldest inhabitant, raged over the city while the dread scene was being enacted.†

* Graetz has Maldonad da Silva.

† Llorente, vol. III, p. 469, does not mention his name. Isaac Cardoso : *Excellencias de Israel* (Spanish title : *Las excelencias y calunias de los Hebreos*), Amsterdam, 1679, p. 323, cites a work written in 1640 about this *auto de fe.* Cf. Graetz, *Geschichte,* vol. X, p. 101, n. 1 ; Kayserling, *Sephardim,* and *Occident,* vol. XXVI. See also J. Kohn-Zedek's *Or Thora ; Monatsschrift fuer Exegese, Kritik, Geschichte und Belletristik,* etc., vol. I, Frankfurt a. M., 1874, p. 123, *s. v.*: יאנואר [January 23d] : ובעצם היום ההוא רשנת 1639 הומתו בעיר ליׄמאׄ, אחד עשר אחרי סילוׄוא די הרופא ובתוכם ספרדים עברים בסוהר. שנה עשרה שלש שבתו.

It is interesting to find that both Menasseh ben Israel and Basnage refer to this historical fact. We read in מקוה ישראל, Spanish version, Amsterdam, 1650, p. 100 ; Hebrew edition, Amsterdam, 1697, p. 53a, the following : " A las mismas llamas se entregò en Lima en 23 de Enero, año 1639, Eli Nazareno, despues de 14 años de prision, en todos los quales, ni comio carne, ni quiso immundar su boca, aviendose el mismo circuncidado dentro, y dado este nombre." Menasseh gives the term of his imprisonment as fourteen years, which

Senor Don B. Vicuña Mackenna of Santiago, to whom we are indebted for many important items concerning the doings of the Holy Office in South America,* writes at length of this *auto de fe.* The first at which any one was burnt, says he, took place in Lima, on the 29th of October, 1581, for the purpose of celebrating the entry into that city of the viceroy, Don Martin Enriquez; in it were burnt Juan Bernal (a Jew ?) and other heretics, and the last took place in 1776 ; . . . 29 *autos de fe* were celebrated during the 250 years of the existence of the Inquisition in America (1570–1820). According to Fuentes, during the period of 195 years (1581–1776) fifty-nine were burnt alive, eighteen in effigy, and the bones of nine others, in all eighty-six. Of the butcheries of the Inquisition at Carthagena, which was one of the three in America, I have not been able to obtain any account. "The most solemn and famous of the Peruvian *autos* was that which the Inquisitor Juan de Mañosca celebrated on the 23d of January, 1639, and in which were burnt twelve Portuguese (Jews) merchants, and, as it happened by a

seems to be an error, as all the other authorities reckon only thirteen. Basnage, in his *Histoire des Juifs,* English translation by Taylor, p. 695, writes that "The Jewish Historians make bitter complaints of the Continuance of these Violences at Corduba [Cordova], Lisbon and Coimbra, and even in the Indies, against the women as well as the men. They tell, that a physician call'd Sylva, who had been kept Prisoner thirteen years at Lima, and had led an exemplary Life, was no sooner thrown into the Flames, but an impetuous Wind and dreadful Tempest overturn'd the House where he had been condemned. Even the Indians were astonish'd at this Prodigy, and confess'd they never saw anything like it before." Here he interposes a note in which the date is erroneously given. He says : "An. 1693 at Lima, Sylva was Circumcis'd in his Imprisonment ; he ate no Meat, he turned Nazarene, and was call'd Heli Nazareno indigno Siervo de Dios, alios Sylva." He refers to Cardoso, who must certainly have chronicled the correct date 1639. Not having access to the work at present, I cannot verify this statement.

* Francisco Moyen, or the Inquisition as it was in South America, translated from the Spanish by J. W. Duffy, M. D., London, 1869, pp. 103, 174, 179, 189, 208.

curious coincidence, they were the richest men in Lima. One of these alone, Don Manuel Bautista Perez, owner of the regal residence in Lima which yet bears the name of the house of Pilate, possessed a fortune equivalent to a million dollars at the present day, and it was the sequestration of his effects, held by those who were indebted to him, by the rapacious myrmidons of the spoilers, which gave origin to the disturbances in Santiago and Coquimbo." In other places of his book he refers frequently to "the judaizing millionaire Manuel Bautista Perez and his wealthy (Jewish) companions." Sometimes he erroneously gives the date 1630 (p. 174). He wants to know (on p. 189) "what had become of the confiscated millions of the Judaizing merchants, Manuel Bautista Perez and his companions? What of the 200,000 ducats for which the Conde de Chinchon sold permission of residence to the 6000 Portuguese (also Judaizing because they were rich), and whom, for the purpose of robbing them, he threatened with expulsion? And lastly, what of the annual produce of the 32,000 dollars of Philip II, and of the suppressed canonships of Santiago, Lima and all the capitals of Spanish America south of the equator?"

Another who was burnt in that *auto de fe* (January 23, 1639) was the *judaizing* (for thus they called the Portuguese when they were rich) Don Diego Lopez de Fonseca, whom they accused of having a crucifix placed beneath a stone in the threshold of the door of his shop, and, as his informers asserted, to any one upon entering to purchase goods who would tread upon that stone, he would sell for half the price of what he would sell to another.* Three jailors of the Holy Office, convicted of having permitted some of the prisoners to hold communication with each other, were punished on this occasion.†

---

* Quoted in a monograph by Richard Palma, "Studies relating to the Inquisition of Lima," in the *South American Review*, Valparaiso, 1881; see Mackenna, *Francisco Moyen*, p. 105.

† Llorente reports the same fact, as was shown above.

In the year 1648 a little volume was printed in Mexico, entitled: *Account of the Third Particular auto de fe, celebrated by the Tribunal of the Holy Inquisition of the kingdom and provinces of New Spain, in the cloister-chapel of the Holy Brotherhood of Jesus, March* 13, 1648, *at the time when the most illustrious Sirs Dr. Don Francisco de Estrada y Escovedo, Dr. Don Juan Saenz de Mañozca and Licentiate Don Bernabé de la Higuera y Amarilla officiated as Inquisitors.* This exceedingly scarce work contains the exact transcript of the legal proceedings on that memorable occasion. Hoffmann* tells us that no modern translation could possibly be made of this book written in "antediluvian Castilian style."† From the few facts gleaned by Rule, we learn that in the years 1646 and 1647, two special *autos de fe* were held, on which occasion seventy-one suits, most of them affecting Jews, were settled. In the *auto* of which the volume treats, 28 persons were duly sentenced and punished.

Rule quotes from this curious work the following paragraph in "precisely correspondent English," giving as faithful a version as possible of the original text:

"As indefatigable for vigilance of the care, and awake to the duties of the labour, the upright, just and holy Tribunal of the Inquisition of New Spain, always desiring to manifest to the Christian people, amidst the accustomed piety that is an attribute of their profession, and to make known to the world, in view of the clemency that is the boast of their glories, the necessary punishment and inevitable chastisement that is done on the heretical perfidy and rebellious obstinacy of the cruel and sanguinary enemies of our sacred religion; who, blind to its light, deny it, and deaf to its voice, flee from it. The Lords Inquisitors who act therein, anxious to gain in rich perfection the foreseen toil of their

---

* *Geschichte der Inquisition . . . in Spanien, Portugal, Italien, den Niederlanden, Frankreich, Deutschland, Süd-Amerika, Indien und China*, Bonn, 1878, vol. II, p. 44 seq.

† Rule, p. 20: It is "written in intricate out-of-date Castilian."

wakefulness, and the fruit of their unwearied labour, have celebrated two Particular Acts of Faith in the past years, 1646 and 1647, in which, with all attention and good order, were despatched, and went forth to public theatre, seventy-one causes: the greater part of them Jews, observant of the dead and detestable law of Moses. And now, for particular and convenient ends, not open to the investigation of curiosity, and not without well-advised resolution, this Holy Tribunal determined to celebrate another Particular Act of Faith in the Church of the Professed House of the Sacred Religion of the Company of Jesus, one of the most capacious and convenient for the purpose, that there are in the city, on March 30th, 1648. In which were put to penance and punished (manifesting its severity no less than its clemency and pity) twenty-eight persons, as well men as women, for the atrocious delinquencies and grave crimes by them perpetrated, that in this brief and summary relation shall be told. The guilty penitents going out of the prisons of the Inquisition, each one between two ministers of the Holy Tribunal, at six o'clock in the morning, without any obstruction of the way, or disturbance of good order, from the numerous multitudes of people that were packed close on both sides of the broad streets, but who gave good way to the criminals until they reached the said Church: where after the orderly procession of penitents was brought in, and the Lords Inquisitors were seated in their tribunal, it being then seven o'clock in the morning, the noise of the people that attended being hushed, in good and prescribed order began the reading of the causes, and continued until six o'clock in the evening; and the guilty having abjured, and they with whom that business had to be done being absolved and reconciled, they took them back in the same form and order to the house of the Inquisition, whence they had come by different streets, with the same accompaniment. And the day following the justice of lashes was executed; all this kingdom remaining in hope of another more numerous and General Act, for exaltation and glory of our Holy Catholic faith, punishment and warning of her enemies, edification and instruction of the faithful." So far this barbaric chronicle.

Of the many cases recorded by Rule* (pp. 21–32) we shall relate only one—the story of a Jewess who was in the fullest sense of the word an *Ēshĕth Hāyīl*.

Anna Xuares, described in the Inquisitorial records as 25 years old, a native of Mexico, was one of the victims upon whom the lynx eye of holy suspicion rested. She figured conspicuously in the trial of 1648, of which we have spoken above. Her parents were previously punished as *judaizers* by the Holy Office. About a year before (in 1647) Anna's first marriage was, for some unknown reason, declared invalid. Her husband was still alive and compelled to do penance in the *sambenito*† garb. He was sentenced to the galleys for five years, at the expiration of which term he was to settle down in some specially appointed place. Anna married a second time. Almost immediately afterwards, without the least warning or provocation, they were ruthlessly separated and taken into custody, to await the pleasure of the merciless agency. After spending a few days in prison, Anna appealed to the mercy of the court. She was granted a hearing, and the following confessions, or rather imputations were made. Since her fourteenth year she has rigidly observed the fast days and other ceremonial observances of the Mosaic law. Her maternal grandmother is said to have encouraged and personally attended the secret

---

* See also G. A. Kohut, "Some Jewish Heroines," in *The American Jewess*, October, 1895, vol. II, No. 1, p. 47, No. 67.

† Richard Palmer, in his curious episodes concerning the Inquisition at Lima, published in the *South American Review* (1861), erroneously attributes the name of *sambenito* to the intervention in the first *autos de fe* of certain monks of the Order of San Benito (St. Bennett). But the name is derived from *saco bendito* (blessed sack). In form it was similar to the aprons worn by the friars over their cassock as the scapulary of their order, and was a very essential part in the Inquisitorial celebrations. Cf. Mackenna's work, p. 212.

(religious ?) meetings at the house of one Simon Vaez,* in Seville, where discussions were carried on concerning the dietary laws, the religious usages and kindred topics relating to Jewish ceremonial life. All attendants at those gatherings were in so far guilty of participation in the said proceedings, that they related to each other instances of their unswerving allegiance to the ancient commandments, and exchanged cheerful confidences, whereby their loyalty could only be strengthened.

These Jews, we are told, constituted a sort of *conciliabulum*, a mock council, where the Catholics were consigned to eternal damnation (Rule). Of the pious practices of that holy sect, their processes and processions and the like, they spoke in an insolent, profane manner, " so that the living hate which these miserable and obstinate Jews carried in their perfidious hearts openly manifested itself."

An old Jewess, " the notorious grand-mistress of unbelief," used to preside over this false council, and was wont to boast with arrogance of her children and grandchildren, who were staunch and dauntless champions of their race, having been conscientiously instructed in the path of the Jewish fathers even from infancy. They made rapid progress in sacred things—fasted to perfection—in short, they were esteemed by the entire Jewry (of Mexico?).

One of her special favorites was Anna Xuares, who seemed surcharged with true inspiration for her ancestral faith—an enthusiasm which developed with each succeeding day. She is said to have loved her second husband much more than the first, and it was even rumored that she gave him her hand and heart with greater willingness, not because he was a better Jew, but simply for the reason that the father of her second husband was the victim of an *auto de fe* in Portugal.†

---

* Persons bearing this name lived contemporaneously in Amsterdam and Algiers. See Kayserling's *Sephardim*, p. 258.

† She herself was probably descended from Albert Xuarez, who, with twenty-two other Jews, was burnt at the stake in Murcia, on March 15, 1562. Cf. Llorente, vol. II, p. 340 ; Kayserling, *Sephardim*, p. 152.

While she was in prison she carried on an active correspondence with several of her fellow-sufferers, and knowing full well the deftness of the Inquisitorial spies, she successfully evaded them by signing fictitious names to her epistles. In the billets which she handed to her companions (who were undoubtedly Israelites) she made merry over the *sambenitos* which they all had to wear, saying that they ought to be more elaborately draped, like all garments of honor, for they were actually raiments of honor, not of disgrace, as they were intended. They are ornaments for those who have honestly deserved them. The following sentence was pronounced in punishment of the offence of the Jewess Anna Xuares: She was to appear at the coming *auto,* clad in penitential garb and carrying a green wax candle; confiscation of her property; formal abjuration; life-long confinement to a certain locality as residence; to be forever banished from the West Indies (perhaps her relatives lived there?); and transported to Old Spain on the first imperial vessel leaving from the port of St. Juan de Ulloa; to be forever banished from Seville, the old family seat, and from the royal residence at Madrid; finally, she was in duty bound, upon landing in Old Spain, to present herself immediately before the Holy Office, that she might be known by all and enter at once upon the fulfillment of the duties and penances prescribed and designated, in the place to be there assigned. Should she fail in the performance of any of these injunctions she would be punished, as impenitent, with death.*

There are no doubt many interesting items† concerning

---

* Hoffmann, pp. 45–50, recounts the story of Anna Xuares in a briefer form.

† Besides Llorente and other modern works on the Holy Office above cited, see especially, *A Complete History of the Inquisition in Portugal, Spain, Italy, East Indies and West Indies,* by the Rev. Mr. Baker, M. A., Westminster, 1736; *Memorias para servir á la Historia de las Persecuciones de la Iglesia en America,* Lima, 1821; D. Antonio Puigblanch, *La Inquisicion sin Máscara,* etc., Mexico, 1824, and Fridolin Hoffmann's *Geschichte der Inquisition,* vol. II, pp. 37–56.

the activity of the Inquisition in Mexico, a few of which, affecting our co-religionists, we have succeeded in recovering from oblivion. Puigblanch, in his *Inquisition Unveiled*, p. 106 (Spanish edition, Mexico, 1824), gives a detailed account of an *auto de fe* held in Mexico, in 1659, and mentions among the accused two Jews whose names are given in no other record. His information was derived from a contemporary chronicle written by Rodrigo Ruiz de Zepeda, entitled *Auto general de fe celebrado en Mexico en 1659*. It is said there : " Francisco Botello, dice la citada relacion se hebo tan descaradamente en el tablado, que diciendole uno de los confesores que pretendio convencerle del judaismo, que mirase como verdaderamente era judio, pues su muger estaba alli tambien penitencia por ello, levantó los ojos para verla con tan grande alegria y alborozo, como si fuera el dia de mayor contento para él que en su vida hubiese tenido, é hizo mucha diligencia para hablarla, pero no lo consignio porque le desendieron dos gradas mas abajo.' Los reos pues ya que otra cosa no podian se exhortaban con seuas [señas ?] á mantenerse firmes en la religion que profesaban, ó á seguir en su proposito cuando no profeseban ninguna. Diego Diaz, añade la misma relacion, totalmente se declaró judio en el tablado y asi con los dos reos Aponte (another of the condemned at the same *auto*) y Botello se estaban haciendo señas como animandose para morir en su caduca ley y reprehendido por uno de los religiosos que le asistian respondió ; Pues padre ¿no es bien que nos exhortemos ā morir por Dios ? Y como le replicase que siendo judio no moria por Dios, sino en desgracia suya y ofendiendole, se endureció del todo sin querer como antes la santa cruz en la mano." Both Botello and Diaz were apparently staunch Israelites, who were pronounced impenitent by the Mexican tribunal and condemned accordingly (cf. also Puigblanch p. 59).

The same author refers to one of the greatest of Sephardic poets, Daniel Israel Lopez Laguna, who spent the major portion of his life in Jamaica, where he wrote his famous *Espejo*.* It is of interest to us to know that he was the first and only American Jewish bard to refer to the Inquisition.† We are not yet in possession of even the outlines for a complete history of the Jewish martyrs of the American Inquisition, for the sources are scant and hardly accessible in public libraries. Paramus states in his *Origin and Progress of the Holy Inquisition* (1599), fol. 242, that there was scarcely a year which did not witness a solemn *auto de fe* where *Judaizers* were punished. They must surely have been recorded.‡ Paramus also notes the following curious facts: "In the year 1592, a certain Jewish family, polluted by the pest [of heresy], were publicly announced penitent, and the statue of Franciscus Rodriguez Matos, a Portuguese [Jew], the head of the family and author of these crimes [of heresy?], who was already dead, was consigned to the flames by law, because he was a dogmatist and a Rabbi of the Jewish sect. His wife and four daughters were reconciled openly in the sacred garb of penitence. He had a son who inherited all his crimes, and whose effigy, because he had escaped from the country in the year following, was burnt at a certain *auto de fe* held in the Mexican church."

It must not be omitted, however, that the youngest daughter of this most depraved man, 17 years old (of those four mentioned above), recited the whole Psalter of David without hesitation, so wonderful was her memory. The oration preceding Esther (?) and some other Jewish songs she could recite in inverted order from beginning to end, with equal facility.§

* See *Pub. Am. Jewish Hist. Soc.* No. 3, pp. 110–112 ; 140–141.
† See Appendix III to this paper.
‡ Cf. Appendix I to this paper, and Kayserling's article on "Daniel Israel Lopez Laguna," in S. R. Hirsch's *Jeschurun*, vol. III, Frankf. a. M., 1857, p. 416.
§ See the original, in Appendix I.

The uncle of these four women, Louis de Carvajal,* underwent public penance because he had not denounced the crimes of his family and even concealed them. He was Governor and General of the province of Tampico (in Mexico) and Panucio (?), and was addressed with the title of President. He had now to hear openly his ignominious sentence, was forever deprived of royal offices and reduced to the utmost misery. At last he went the way of all flesh in bitter grief and utter disgust of life.

Was he identical with Luis del Mārmol Carvajal mentioned by Puigblanch ?† It would be interesting to discover in the archives of Mexico the full account of the exposé of this distinguished man, who held a responsible public trust, but who as a secret Jew remained true to his faith and his family, both of which he shielded at any risk.‡ Especially important are the data and facts recorded in the MS material preserved in the British Museum, notably in the so-called Documentos Historicos de Mexico, which contain among other papers an authentic account of a convention of priests —a general council—wherein Emperor Charles V, King of Spain, and representatives of the clergy of Mexico, Guatemala and Oaxaca participated. The date of this congress is given as November, 1537. Soon afterwards, a smaller meeting of divines was held in the " city of Thenuxtillan [Mexico] of New Spain." The first Bishop of Mexico, Don Fray Juan de Zumárraga, with several of his colleagues, was present.

---

* Many of the persons mentioned here and in Appendix I, figure prominently in the "Trial of Jorge de Almeida by the Inquisition in Mexico," printed in this *Publication*, by Dr. Adler.

† See *La Inquisicion sin Máscara*, etc., Mexico, 1824, p. 108. Dr. Adler discusses his identity, p. 60, note, in this *Publication*. See also Helps' *Spanish Conquest of America*, vol. IV, Index, *s. v.* Caravajal and Carvajal.

‡ Other matters in connection with the Mexican Inquisition will be found in Fr. Juan de Torquemada's *Monarchia indiana*, esp. lib. xix, cap. xxix, and *Fragmento de dicha relacion reimpreso en el Diano de México de 6 de Abril de* 1807.

The result of their proceedings was dispatched to the Emperor under date of April 17, 1539.*

Another martyr was put to death seemingly about the same time either in Mexico† or Lima. The conflicting histories leave it in doubt which is the true place. This was the Doctor Thomas (Isaac) Tremiño or Trebiño de Sobremonte,‡ a Marrano from Medina de Rio Seco, which city, on account of its extended commerce, was formerly called Little India. After a confinement of twenty-two years he died in the flames.§

* Hoffmann, *Gesch. d. Inquisition*, vol. II, p. 39 seq., gives some of the details. Rule, p. 14 seq., gives extracts from this report.

† As will be seen from the extracts in Appendix II, some authorities state that Tomas Trebiño was executed in Mexico in 1549, not contemporaneously with the *auto de fe* celebrated in Mexico in 1574, as Kayserling (who in his *Sephardim* has erroneously 1547) would have us believe. This date, however, must be incorrect, for it is assumed that the Inquisition was ordered to be established in America the 7th of February, 1569, by the royal letters patent of Philip the Second. In consequence of which were created the three Grand Inquisitors of Mexico, Carthagena, and Lima, to the last of which was assigned the jurisdiction of Chile. The first appointment was made in Panama, June 20, 1569 : the second in Lima, January 29, 1570 (see Mackenna's *Francisco Moyen*, p. 100 ; Rule, p. 17 ; F. Hoffmann, *Gesch. d. Inquis.*, vol. II, p. 42). According to these historians the first *auto de fe* was held in Mexico in 1574. Hoffmann gives an extensive account of it. Juan Torquemada, whose description of an *auto de fe* is given in Appendix IV, tells us in his *Indian Monarchy*, vol. III, p. 379, that nine *autos de fe* were celebrated from 1574 to 1593.

‡ Dr. A. Jeilinek in his article, "Opfer der Inquisition," in Fuerst's *Litteraturblatt des Orients*, Leipzig, 1847, p. 263, writes : "Nach einer 14 jährigen Kerkerstrafe wurde Thomas Tremiño de Sobremonte in Mejico (Mexico) ein glorreicher Märtyrer." He was in prison 22 years, not 14. In a later article on the same subject, published in S. I. Gräber's *Ozar Hassifruth*, Krakau, 1888, vol. II, p. 204, he repeats his error : אחרי אשר סבל סאמם טערמינא דע זאברעמונטע וישב כ"יד שנה במאסר הכלא נהרג ע"ק השם במעי־יצא [! Mexico]

Prof. Graetz calls him Thomas Trebinjo (Termino de Sobremonte).

§ Cf. Cardoso, *Las Excellencias*; he names him Trebiño and places his death in Mexico. Menasseh ben Israel writes : " Y este año en Mexico, Thomas Terbiño [*sic*], celebro con grande constancia su

As has been shown, the Inquisition was most powerful in Mexico. It was terribly severe in Carthagena and Lima. Whether other American countries were under its tyrannic sway cannot be asserted with any degree of certainty. Some say * that the Spaniards introduced the Holy Office in Brazil simultaneously with its establishment at Goa.† That officers were commissioned to watch in behalf of the Inquisition in Brazil also,‡ even though the torture chamber and the funeral pyre were not actually erected, is attested by the sad stories of Isaac de Castro Tartas and Don Antonio José

Martirio." The Hebrew version has טומ"ש טערב"נא which of course ought to read טערבינא. He also places his death in Mexico. Don Miguel de Barrios, one of the proudest lights of Spanish Jewish literature, speaks of him at length, but does not seem to be quite clear concerning his identity. Indeed, as Drs. Kayserling (*Sephardim*, p. 360, note 489) and Graetz have pointed out, Barrios confused Trebiño with da Silva, called Eli Nazareno (cf. *supra* in the text and notes). He cites him in many of his works and composed two interesting sonnets in his honor, one of which, superscribed with the words "La cuidad de Medina de Rioseco, produjo al insigne Thomas Tremiño de Sobremonte," runs in part thus :

> Que tres cometas brillan en el cielo?
> Que tres nuevos luzeros ví la tierra?
> Que tres milagros den al herror guerra?

See for particulars his works cited in Kayserling's *Sephardim*, his article in the *Occident*, Steinschneider's *Hebräische Bibliographie*, Bd. VII, 1864, p. 40, and especially p. 133.

* Herzog's *Real-Encyclopaedie*, vol. VI, p. 745: "Jene [the Spaniards] führten sie in Amerika bald nach der Entdeckung des Landes ein, wo sie namentlich in Mexico, Cartagena und Lima furchtbar wütete. Diese brachten sie 1560 nach Ostindien, wo sie in Goa ihren Hauptsitz fand; ebenso nach Brasilien. Erst in unserem Jahrhundert ist sie dort aufgehoben worden."

† Cf. *Relation de l'Inquisition de Goa*, Paris, 1688, p. 206 ff.

‡ See B. Röse's article in Ersch and Gruber's *Allgemeine Encyclopaedie*, section II, vol. XVIII, Leipzig, 1840, p. 472, note 18: "Ob die Amerikanischen Besitzungen, Brasilien, wie von einigen bezweifelt wird, auch von Tribunalen der Inquisition bewacht und gequält wurden, dürfte schwerlich bestritten werden können. Besondere Angaben darüber haben sich nicht gefunden."

da Silva. Johann Jacob Schudt, a disciple of Eisenmenger, writes in his celebrated *Memorabilia Judaica** that Jews in Brazil did not suffer from the fear of the Inquisition, partly because they had contributed not a small share to the welfare of Brazil and partly because the introduction of the Holy Office would have ruined trade and commerce. Despite such emphatic denials, however, we have every reason for believing, on the strength of evidence to be adduced later, that the zealous clergy of South America, who, according to Schudt, made strenuous efforts in that direction, did succeed in establishing the dread tribunal in Brazil. Even Dr. Kayserling, who is very conservative on this score, leaves the question open. "Brazil, the most blessed empire on earth," says he,† "was the only portion of the New World where the Jews, for a time at least, were not burned." De Beauchamp and Southey, however, in their respective his-

---

* *Jüdische Merkwuerdigkeiten*, etc., Frankfurt a. M. and Leipzig, 1714–18, 4to, vol. IV, pt. I, pp. 54, 55 : "In Brasilien ist es für solche verstellte Juden nicht ebenso gefährlich | weil da die Inquisition, als die Pest und Verderben der Handlung | nicht gelidten wird | dann weil einige Particuliers, welche bey dess Landes Eroberung viel mit beygetragen | grosse Länder ! und einiger massen an der Regierung mit Theil haben | so leiden sie die Inquisition in Brasilien nicht|wie dann Anonymous im neuesten Staat des Koenigreichs Portugall (Halle, An. 1714 in 8.) p. 284, solches bestättiget | dann die Portugiesen erkennen wohl | dass die Inquisition der Handelschafft grossen Abbruch thue | dahero sie auch niemals zugeben wollen | dass selbige in Brasilien eingeführet wuerde | ohnerachtet aller der Clerisey desswegen angewandter Bemühung. In andern Orten aber der Spanier | und Portugiesen ist es vor solche heimliche Juden gefährlich | Basnage *Hist[oire] de [la religion des]*, *Juifs [dépuis J. Christ jusqu'à present.]*], (Rotterdam, 1707–1711, 8vo ; new ed. 15 vols.: Haage, 1716, 12mo), L. 7, C. 33, §9, p. 2130, bezeuget | dass nur eintzele Juden von den verstellten umb sich in dieser Neuen-Welt zubereichern | dahin gehen | welche aber die Inquisition daselbst verfolget | und die offt ihren Geitz und Liebe zum Reichthum hart genug bestraffet." De Costa, *Israel and the Gentiles*, Germ. ed., 1855, p. 318, says that in Brazil they were not molested by the Inquisition and that great numbers were there.

† *Sephardim*, p. 296 ; Leeser's *Occident*, vol. XXVI, p. 218 ; Markens' *Hebrews in America*, New York, 1888, p. 3.

tories of Brazil,* record that during the Portuguese reconquest of Brazil from the Dutch, brief as that supremacy was,
at least five Jews who had been friendly to the Dutch were
executed.

That our co-religionists did not fare so well in Brazil
as is usually supposed, has been proven by various
writers.† Suffice it here to quote what Watson says, p. 47,
under date of 1644: "At length, however, the time came
when his practices [Fernandes'] could no longer be ignored
by the government, who were set on their guard against him
chiefly by the Jews. These are certainly not to be blamed
for wishing a continuance of the *status quo*; since, in the
event of an outbreak, they were certain to be plundered by
both parties with complete impartiality; whilst in the event
of a victory on the part of the Portuguese, they had before
them the image of the fiendish agents of the Inquisition."
It seems that this surmise was justifiable, for, on the
following page, he informs us that Fernandes could not be
captured and summoned troops. "Many obeyed the call
and fell upon such Dutchmen and Jews as happened to be
within their reach."‡ In another place he says (p. 119):
"Bahia owed its prosperity, amongst other causes, to its
being a place of safety for the New Christians, who were
persecuted with such cruelty in Portugal and Spain. Super-
stitious as were the Brazilians, even they successfully resisted
the establishment of the Inquisition amongst them. If the

* Quoted in *Pub. Am. Jewish Hist. Soc.* No. 1, p. 44; see also the
writer's paper on "Early Jewish Literature in America," in *Pub.
Am. Jewish Hist. Soc.* No. 3, pp. 103, 134 and 135, note 1.

† See Pieter Marinus Netscher's *Les Hollandais au Brésil, Notice
Historique sur les Pays-Bas et le Brésil au XVII siècle*, La Haye,
1853, pp. 14, 20, 35, 94, 128, 142, 145, 153, 154, 197, 202, 204; R. G.
Watson's *Spanish and Portuguese South America during the Colonial
Period*, London, 1884, vol. II, pp. 1, 2, 29, 47, 48, 119 and 242, where
some valuable information is given.

‡ See on this more fully the writer's paper published in Wolf's
American Jew as Soldier, etc., pp. 443 seq.

New Christians were in Brazil a despised race, they could at any rate count on opportunities of gaining wealth and retaining it when gained."* Further on we read the following interesting note (p. 242) : " Happily for Brazil, that country never boasted an establishment of the Inquisition. Nevertheless some of the agents of the Holy Office had found a field for their energies on the other side of the Atlantic. These agents had arrested and sent to Lisbon a large number of New Christians—persons fulfilling every duty of citizenship, but whose crime it was to be wealthy. These unfortunate people, having confessed to being Jews, escaped with their lives at the expense of all their property, which of course went to the informers. In consequence of this profitable practice, many *engenhos* [?] had to be stopped, and widespread ruin ensued. Even Pombal did not venture to proclaim toleration for the Jewish faith, but he made it penal for any person to reproach another for his Jewish origin,† whilst he removed all disabilities attaching to Jewish blood, even if their ancestors had suffered at the hands of the Inquisition. He likewise published an edict decreeing severe chastisement against such persons as should retain lists of persons of Jewish origin."

As we have seen, the sources relating to the establishment of the Sacred Agency in Brazil are conflicting and contradictory. Only in the case of Mexico, Peru and other places of Central and South America are the records clear and unanimous.‡

* See the account of the prosperity and wealth of Brazilian Jews in *Pub. Am. Jewish Hist. Soc.* No. 2, p. 95.

† This is similar to the law passed on May 21, 1577, forbidding under penalty to call them any longer Jews, Marranos or New Christians. (See above, p. 102.)

‡ On the outrages and *autos de fe* enacted at Lima we have authentic material in a volume entitled *Historia del Tribunal del S. Oficio de la Inquisicion de Lima* (1569–1820), compiled by J. T. Medina, to whom we are beholden for preserving to us the names of some Jewish martyrs on this continent.

Antonio de Montezinos, the account of whose travels has been preserved by Menasseh ben Israel in his curious treatise on the identification of the American Indians with the lost Ten Tribes, experienced rough treatment at the hands of the Tribunal in the West Indies,* where, according to a rare and curious volume,† the most barbarous cruelties were perpetrated.‡

And now we shall speak of the martyrdom of a noble Brazilian Jew who deserves a conspicuous place in the

---

* See his *Esperança de Israel*, Amsterdam, 1650, Spanish ed., p. 43; Hebrew ed., Amst., 1697, p. 25a, § xvii, where we read : " Most credible of all is the report made by Montezinos, Portuguese by nationality, Jew by religion, born in Villflor, a city of Portugal, of well-known and humble parents, forty years old, a man of wealth, without ambition, he sailed to the [West] Indies, and was there imprisoned by the Inquisition, as has been the lot of many others in Portugal, descendants of those whom King Don Emanuel made Christians by force. . . . Later on he went to Pernambuco, and died there after two years' residence," etc., etc. We have followed the excellent English translation of Rev. Dr. L. Grossmann, published under the title, " The origin of the American Indians and the lost ten tribes," in *The American Jews' Annual* for 5649 (1889), p. 83. The first English version made by Moses Wall in London, 1651, has become so rare that Dr. Grossmann could not obtain a copy for his work. He did not then know that there is one in Baltimore in private possession. See *Catalogue of a Hebrew Library—being the collection, with a few additions, of the late Joshua I. Cohen, M. D., of Baltimore. Now in possession of Mrs. Harriett Cohen.* Compiled by Cyrus Adler, Ph. D. ; privately printed, Baltimore, 1887, p. 37.

†In a bulky quarto volume in the library of Columbia College, New York, are bound together several curious miscellaneous tracts, dealing chiefly with the Inquisition in Spain, Netherlands and the colonies. The titles are too long to be given here, so we shall content ourselves with copying that of the one which concerns us most, and in whose pages are recounted the greatest conceivable crimes committed in the West Indies by the agents and hirelings of the Holy Office. It runs as follows : *Den Spiegel der Spaensche Tyrannye gheschiet in West Indien. Waer in te sien is de onmenschelycke wreede seyten der Spanjaerde, met t'samen de Beschryvinghe der selver Lande, Volckere aert ende natuere, etc.*, Amsterdam, 1620. The book is illustrated with numerous copperplates.

‡ See also Helps' *Life of Las Casas* and his *Spanish Conquest in America.*

annals of history — Isaac de Castro Tartas. So tragic were his end and career that many authors took occasion to narrate them in prose, poetry and song.* He was a relative of the celebrated court-physician Elias (Eliahu) Montalto,† and of the Amsterdam publisher, David ben Abraham de Castro Tartas,‡ whose press has enriched Jewish literature. He was born in the village of Tartas in the French province of Gascony (Gascogne), which he called his

---

* Cf. Menasseh ben Israel's מקוה ישראל ; Spanish ed., pp. 99, 100 ; (Appendix VI^a) Hebrew, pp. 52b–53a ; Latin version, p. 89 ; Isaac Cardoso, *Las excelencias y calunias de los Hebreos*, Amsterdam, 1679, p. 324 ff. ; Salomon de Oliveyra : שרשת גבלת, Amsterdam, 1765, p. 52b ; Don Miguel Levi de Barrios: *Govierno popular Judayco*, p. 44 ; *Historia da Inquisição*, p. 271 ; Dr. M. Kayserling : " Isaac de Castro Tartas," in Dr. J. Kobak's *Jeschurun, Zeitschrift für die Wissenschaft des Judenthums*, Jahrg. II, Lemberg, 5618, pp. 97–100 ; *Sephardim*, Leipzig, 1859, pp. 204–6 ; 347, nos. 255–256a ; his *Juden in Navarra, den Baskenländern und auf den Balearen*, Berlin, 1861, p. 151 ; *Geschichte der Juden in Portugal*, Leipzig, 1867, pp. 308–310 ; D. Cassel, *Lehrbuch der jüdischen Geschichte und Literatur*, Leipzig, 1879, p. 471. Graetz, *Geschichte der Juden*, vol. X², Leipzig, 1882, pp. 102, 103. Koenen, *Geschiedenis der Joden in Nederland*, Utrecht, 1843, pp. 432–3, calls him simply Isaac de Castro, and refers only to his death.

† See concerning him, *Sephardim*, pp. 176, 201 and notes. We must remember Dr. Montalto with gratitude because he reconverted Rohel (Rëuel) Jeshurun, *alias* Paul de Pina, who in 1599 was sent to him in Livorno, before his promotion as body-physician to Maria de Medici, by his kinsman Diego Gomez Lobato (also named Abraham Cohen Lobato) with the intention of becoming a monk (*Frayle*). After his return to Portugal he repaired, together with his cousin Lobato, to Brazil, whence he returned in the year 1604. Cf. also Barrios, *Casa de Jacob*, p. 18 ; *Relacion de los Poetas Españoles*, p. 54 ; Wolf, *Bibliotheca Hebraea*, vol. I, p. 1014, No. 19(9 [erroneously *Dina*] ; III, p. 909, No. MDCCCXI, c, and p. 988, No. MCMIX, *s. v.* רוהל ישורון and באורום די פינה ; Ad. de Castro, *Protestantes Españoles*, pp. 541 and 628 ; *Sephardim*, p. 340, nn. 189, 190 ; *Revue des Etudes Juives*, vol. XVIII, p. 282; Graetz, *Geschichte der Juden*, vol. IX², p. 499 ; X², p. 4 ; Kayserling, *Geschichte der Juden in Portugal*, Leipzig, 1867, pp. 283, 284.

‡ See *Revue des Etudes Juives*, vol. XVIII, p. 282, note 3, and the references given above.

home, for it was the ancestral seat of his family.* At the time when Brazil was under Dutch supremacy, young Castro went to Bahia and lived for several years in a city of this region—Parahiba. When, one day, heedless of the counsel and warnings of his numerous friends in that town, he visited the capitol da Bahia dos Santos, he was immediately recognized and seized by the vigilant Portuguese spies of the Holy Office and transported to Lisbon, there to await trial before the Tribunal. Already at the first hearing he confessed that he was a Jew, and that he desired to live and die as a faithful professor of that religion. Although the judges knew by past experiences that no logic or learning could convince a Jew condemned by them, especially one so well versed in history, theology and the classical languages as was this young martyr, they gave themselves no end of trouble and pains to convert him, and sent shrewd, sanctimonious and worldly-wise priests to argue him into rejecting his faith and accepting the dogmas of the Church. But he was proof against oily-tongued friars. Conscious of the truth of his divine mission as an Israelite, and nothing daunted by the fearful prospect of a horrible death, he resisted bravely and, with a defiance that is magnificently heroic, he announced his intention of ending his life in glory and praise of Israel's God. He furnished his many friends and relatives an example of fortitude and self-sacrifice of which only a devout believer could be capable. Feeling intuitively the near approach of his end, yet not wishing to apprise them of his sad forebodings, he wrote to his parents in Amsterdam that he proposed going to Rio de Janeiro in order to imbue some of his friends there (who were known as Marranos) with a greater fear of God. At the same time he told them not to expect letters from him for four years to come. Before the expiration of the stated time the dread news of his martyrdom was communicated to his

* See Kayserling in Kobak's *Jeschurun*, Jahrg. II, p. 97.

anxious and sorrowing relatives and friends. He died as he had lived, a hero and a saint.

The *auto de fe* was erected over six persons,* but none were so firm and brave as he. After standing many hours at the stake, when the livid flames were already scorching his skin and licking his face, suffused with a halo brighter than the flaring funeral fire, he suddenly summoned all his remaining strength and cried out for the last time, שמע ישראל יְיָ אלהינו יְיָ אחד (Hear, O Israel, the Lord our God the Lord is One). With the word "One," he, like Rabbi Akiba† of old, expired. This was indeed an *auto de fe* in its literal sense—"an act of faith," hallowed by suffering and pious devotion. We are told‡ that he uttered this sublime confession so touchingly that the witnesses of the dread ceremony, and even the judges themselves, were moved to the soul with pity and remorse. For several days after the execution nothing was heard but the story of his tragic end. It was the general topic of conversation in every circle, and years afterwards the people of Lisbon delighted to recite the thrilling words of the *Sh'mā*, so that the Inquisition was constrained to forbid, under heavy penalty, the indulgence of this pleasure.§ The date of this *auto de fe* is variously given. We shall have to accept the one established by Dr. Kayser-

---

* Among the condemned on that occasion, sixty were otherwise punished, either with lifelong imprisonment or penal servitude. Cf. Dr. Kayserling, *Geschichte der Juden in Portugal,* Leipzig, 1867, p. 308; *Sephardim,* Leipzig, 1859, p. 347, n. 255, and p. 354, n. 371.

† The martyrdom of Hanina ben Theradion and Akiba ben Joseph is chronicled in the Talmud (*Berachoth* 9ª and *Aboda Zarah* 18ª) and is beautifully told in Rev. L. Weiss' *Talmudic and Other Legends,* 2d ed., New York, 1888, pp. 105–108; see also Dr. A. Kohut's article on "R. Akiba ben Josef," in *Menorah Monthly,* vol. III, 1887, pp. 350–1.

‡ Kayserling, *Sephardim,* pp. 205, 206.

§ Cf. Cardoso, *Las excelencias,* p. 325; Kobak's *Jeschurun,* Jahrg. II, p. 98; Kayserling, *Geschichte der Juden in Portugal,* p. 309.

ling and Graetz,* December 15th (22d), 1647.† Great were
the sorrow and mourning of the Jewish congregation in
Amsterdam when the news of the martyrdom of this twenty-
four year old youth came from Lisbon. He was well known
in Amsterdam, and was much esteemed for his learning and
character. The Rabbi Saul Levi Morteira, who was the
teacher and excommunicator of the philosopher Spinoza,
delivered an impressive memorial sermon, and the celebrated
Hebrew poet Salomon ben David Israel de Oliveyra‡ dedicated to him a beautiful Hebrew poem, which we give in

*See the references given above; furthermore, Em. Hecht's
Handbuch d. israel. Geschichte, ed. by Kayserling, Leipzig, 1879, p.
126 ; and also *Revue des Etudes Juives*, vol. XVIII, 1889, p. 285.

† Menasseh ben Israel does not give the date in his *Esperança* ;
Cardoso, *Las excelencias*, p. 324 ff., gives the same date, as does
Oliveyra in the superscription to his Hebrew elegy, in *Sharsh. Gabl.*,
p. 52 seq. Barrios fixes it at the 23d of September, 1647 (*Govierñ*
popular Judayco, p. 44). Zunz, following Barrios, writes in *Synago-*
gale Poesie des Mittelalters, Berlin, 1855, p. 343, "on 13. Sept., 1647,
Isaac de Castro Tartas was burned at Lisbon." This error is repeated by S. L. Grossmann, in his *Môädïm l'Simchah*, etc., Fünf-
kirchen, 1885, p. 250, *ad voc.* Elul 13 : " Wurde 5407 (13 September,
1647) Isak de Castro Tartas in Lissabon durch die Inquisition ge-
tödtet." Of course, 13 is a misprint for 23, as Dr. Kayserling
corrects in his *Sephardim*, p. 347, note 255. Dr. Graetz maintains
against Kayserling, *Geschichte der Juden*, vol. X², p. 102, note 1, that
Oliveyra did not desire to indicate the date of Tartas' martyrdom
in his superscription, which reads : חורש שבט התי״ח (Kayserling
amends ח״ת), but the date of the composition of his poem, for
the beginning of Shebath 5418 is equivalent to January 25th, 1648,
the month when the tidings of his destiny reached Amsterdam.
The *Historia da Inquisição*, p. 271, states that he died at the *auto de*
fe celebrated on December 15, 1647 : "Morreo queimado vivo por
herege un Francez natural da Cascunha." See furthermore, Kayserling, *Sephardim*, p. 347, n. 255 ; *Geschichte der Juden in Portugal*,
p. 308, n. 4. Dr. M. Steinschneider, in his large *Catalogus librorum*
in Bibliotheca Bodleiana, Berlin, 1852–60, pp. 2381–2, n. 6964[10], calls
him Tartaz.

‡ Concerning his life and works, see especially Dr. M. Kayserling's
article, "Zur Literatur der spanisch-portugiesischen Juden," in
Frankel's *Monatsschrift f. d. Gesch. u. Wiss. d. Judth.*, vol. X, 1861,
pp. 432–6.

Appendix VI to this paper. Other poets, among them
Jonas Abravanel (or Abrabanel, Abarbanel), son of Joseph
Abrabanel and a nephew of Menasseh ben Israel, honored his
name in Portuguese and Spanish verses.* So powerful was
the impression which Castro's death made upon the zealous
Inquisitors that they determined not to institute any more
autos de fe. This resolution, however, did not prevent the
tribunals from sacrificing upon the funeral pyre, about five
years after that melancholy event, another Jewish martyr of
Lisbon, named Manuel Fernandes de Villa-Real.†

Rio de Janeiro, it appears from the records, furnished many
victims to the insatiable fury of the Inquisition. Thus we
are told by Dr. Kayserling‡ that it was not unusual to
transport suspected Marranos from the capital of Brazil to
Lisbon, where they were duly arraigned and condemned,
often without trial. At the *auto de fe* held on the 10th of
October, 1723, the following persons, all from Rio de Janeiro,
were sentenced: The miner Diego Lopez Simon, 26 years
old, was executed; the student Joseph Gomez de Paredes,
aged 24, and his elder brother Francisco de Paredes were
condemned to lifelong imprisonment; Catalina Marques,
who already on October 24th, 1712, was punished for her
adherence to Judaism; and, sad to relate, the aged Matheo
de Moura Fogaza, 84 years old, a resident of Rio de Janeiro,
was burned at the stake as an obstinate Jew.

That metropolis was the birthplace and home of other
Jewish martyrs who were ruthlessly tortured by the Inquisi-

* Cf. Kayserling's works already cited; D. Cassel, *Lehrbuch
der jüd. Gesch. und Litteratur*, p. 471, and Graetz, vol. X, p. 103, n. 2;
Wolf, *Bibliotheca Hebraea*, vol. III, p. 370, no. DCCCXXXV, e, *s. v.*:
יונה אברבניר 'ר ; Dr. E. Carmoly's biography of Don Isaac Abarbanel
in *Ozar Nechmad, Briefe und Abhandlungen jüdische Literatur betref-
fend*, etc., II Jahrg., Wien, 1857, pp. 61, 65, no. 67, and especially
Geschichte der Juden in Portugal, Leipzig, 1867, p. 311, and n. 3.

† Cf. Kayserling, *Geschichte der Juden in Portugal*, p. 310.

‡ See his article in Frankel's *Monatsschrift für die Geschichte und
Wissenschaft des Judenthums*, vol. IX, Leipzig, 1860, pp. 334-5.

tion. Foremost among them, by reason of his literary distinction, is Antonio José da Silva, the illustrious Portuguese poet and dramatist, whose fate was indeed cruel, for he, his mother and his wife were publicly burned at Lisbon on the 19th of October, 1739. Many essays and biographies were devoted to this eminent martyr,* so that we are in possession of almost all the facts relating to his ·eventful career.†

Antonio José, the greatest genius among the poets and dramatists of Portugal, whose plays evoked the admiration of two continents and are to this day popular in the land of his birth, belonged to a Marrano family, who, owing to bitter persecution in Spain, were forced to embrace the Christian faith, though remaining loyal at heart to the Mosaic creed, and were transported to Brazil together with the New Christians, as we have seen above, at the time of the reconquest of Brazil from the Dutch—a period of desolation 'for the Jews, who, under the tolerant government of Holland,

* In Appendix XII a full list is given of the works written concerning Antonio. See also Appendix VIII, IX, X and XI.

† Besides the bibliography in Appendix XII to this study, cf. the anonymous *Historia da Inquisição em Portugal*, Lisbon, 1845, p. 285 : Sahio á morrer o Bacharel Antonio José da Silva, auctor dos 4 tomos das operas portuguezas de que ha duas edicoes; e sua mulher de 27 annos de-idade foc penitenciada. He gives the correct date of Antonio's execution as October 19 (18th), 1739, not 13th, as Kayserling in *Monatsschrift*, vol. IX, p. 338, note 5, has it ; and not 1745, as an anonymous reviewer ("π") of *Sephardim*, in the same periodical, vol. VIII (1859), p. 44, records. Dr. Isaac de Costa, of Amsterdam, in his interesting book, *Israel and the Gentiles* (Dutch ed., Amsterdam, 1848 ; English ed., London, 1850 ; German ed., by K. Mann, Frankfort a. M., 1855, p. 220, note), confuses our hero with Antonio Alvarez Soares, who flourished at the beginning of the seventeenth century, hence one hundred years before de Silva. See on him Wolf, *Bibliotheca Hebraea*, vol. III, p. 129, No. CCCXXXIVᶜ, and the authorities cited in *Sephardim*, pp. 175, 340, n. 188. On Antonio José see also Emanuel Hecht's *Handbuch der israelitischen Geschichte*, ed. by Dr. M. Kayserling, Leipzig, 1879, p. 88 ; Dr. Alexander Kohut's Hungarian Jewish History : *A Zsidók Története*, Nagyvárad, 1881, p. 205.

enjoyed the peace and prosperity denied them elsewhere. It was a sad day for Israel when the forces of Portugal were victorious and the thriving band of earnest and devout worshipers were again placed under the ban of expulsion. Then it was that Isaac Aboab de Fonseca and Moses Raphael de Aguilar, the two principal Rabbis of the Brazilian community, were compelled to return to Amsterdam, in order to escape the vengeance of their conquerors, who were well aware that the Jews took an active part in the conflict against them, with a loyalty for which they were also distinguished in Surinam and Jamaica.*

Antonio's family settled in Rio de Janeiro, where they were leading a quiet, unostentatious life, fearing lest their secret adherence to the Jewish faith might be betrayed despite their outward devotion to Catholic Portugal. His father, João Mendes da Silva, was a celebrated jurist, highly esteemed, learned in his profession and endowed with remarkable poetic gifts. He is said to have composed many sonnets and larger pieces on Christological themes, in order to avert suspicion from himself, and even sacred hymns and fables highly praised by some critics, as De Macedo observes,† although almost all biographers of Antonio state that his productions were unpublished and are consequently lost.‡ We know that he was born in Rio de Janeiro in 1656, and that being graduated with honors in the University of Coimbra, he returned to his native city, where he remained until his wife was snatched away by agents of the Holy Office and sent to Lisbon for trial. He followed, fearing the worst, and took up his practice in that city of mediæval horrors, hoping to rescue her from the clutches of the Inquisition, but in vain.

* See on this point the writer's paper on "Early Jewish Literature in America," in *Pub. American Jewish Historical Society*, No. 3, pp. 134–5, notes 1 and 2, and the sources there cited; also his article in Wolf's *American Jew as Soldier*, etc., where fuller details are given.

†*Brazilian Biographical Annual* (Rio de Janeiro, 1876), pp. 441–42, and Appendix IX to this paper.

‡ See Kayserling in *Monatsschrift*, vol. IX, p. 333.

It is a relief to know that he did not witness the wholesale murder of his dear ones, he having died in 1736, although they were already then languishing in prison. We will follow his fortunes in delineating the story of Antonio's career. João's wife, Lourença Coutinho,* bore him three sons, the youngest of whom, the poet, was born in Rio de Janeiro on May 8, 1705. It will be remembered that during that period the influence of the Inquisition was mighty in Brazil and the unfortunate Marranos there settled were in mortal dread of their lives, for any one possessing wealth was soon accused as a *suspicio* and persecuted accordingly, despite avowals of loyalty and proofs of previous concessions. Antonio was baptized in the cradle—a ceremony necessary for the safety of both child and parents; but that fact did not prevent his mother from educating him most rigidly in the Mosaic faith, which she *in petto* esteemed and loved, and subsequently glorified by her heroic end. Antonio's father was fortunate enough to elude the vigilance of the Jew-baiters and heresy-hunters, whose spies were alert in Mexico, Lima, Carthagena, Chili, Brazil and the Indies, and even succeeded, by the deliberate choice of dogmatic themes for his poems, such as the *Messiade* and a *Hymn inscribed to Saint Barbara* (see also Appendix IX), in acquiring a great reputation for piety and patriotism. His wife, however, who was not sufficiently cautious in disguising her real sentiments, fared worse. For a long time suspected of heresy, palpable proofs were at last collected against her at an examination held on October 10, 1712, and finally in the

---

* This is a common Portuguese name, borne by many eminent Jewish families. A certain Manuel Rodriguez Coutinho was punished at Lisbon about 1713 for the third time as an adherent of the Mosaic faith. Cf. Ross, *Dissert. Philos., qua Inquisit. Pontif. iniquitas evincitur,* Marburg, 1737, p. 16, cited by Kayserling, *Monatsschrift,* vol. IX, p. 333, n. 4; and the latter's *Ein Feiertag in Madrid,* Leipzig, 1859, p. 38. Fernando Coutinho, Bishop of Silva, was president of the Supreme Tribunal (*Geschichte der Juden in Portugal,* p. 130 seq.)

year 1713 she was dragged to Lisbon at the instance of the Inquisition and committed to prison, as was many years before the noble martyr Isaac de Castro Tartas. It was in those days not unusual to summon peaceful, law-abiding Jews from American countries to Spain or Portugal to await the judgment of the tribunal, frequently for no other offence save that they were wealthy and prosperous and controlled the financial market. Loth to leave his devoted wife, the tender husband contrived to dispose of his personal effects at a great monetary sacrifice, and with dread forebodings in his heart, followed his unhappy spouse to Lisbon, taking with him his three sons, among them Antonio, then about 8 years of age.* Lourença Coutinho remained in prison until the 9th of July, 1713, when she was released, probably at the earnest solicitation of her husband, who, to achieve his purpose, took up his abode in that city and pursued his calling, and after doing public penance she became reconciled with the Church (*reconciliada*). No wonder then that Antonio, whose tenderest years were marred by the shadows of suffering and fanaticism, early developed a talent for the satirical, which in his hand became a powerful weapon against the Inquisition.

Antonio attended the colleges of Lisbon, where he made an excellent record for himself. After he passed the high-school, his father sent him to the University of Coimbra to study canon law. In a short time he became honor-student of his class, and was graduated at the age of 21 with the degree of bachelor of divinity. During a vacation in 1726 he repaired to Lisbon to visit his mother, and she was in consequence accused of *Judaizing* the second time, for she had been under careful watch since her first escapade. It is true that she was a faithful observer of the Jewish ceremonial laws, in the exercise of which she was detected, so that it did not

---

* The *Brazilian Biographical Annual*, *l. c.*, p. 31–2; Kayserling, *Sephardim*, p. 320, say that Antonio José was 8 years old when his father left Brazil. In *Monatsschrift*, vol. IX, p. 334, and *Geschichte der Juden in Portugal*, p. 330, he is made 2 years younger.

take long for the lynx eye of suspicion to rest on other members of the family. The father was much too politic to betray his secret attachment to the ancestral faith, and upon him the vengeance of the Holy Office did not fall. His two elder sons were also exempt from persecution. Antonio himself was arraigned before the tribunal on the 8th of August, 1726, whose ire he seems to have excited by some satirical poems. He also was taken to task for following the Mosaic commands. On the 16th of August, 1726, the investigation of his case was begun, and as he was yet a minor according to Portuguese law, not having attained the age of 25, a certain Philipp Nery, who was probably a subaltern of the Holy Office, was appointed his guardian. The Inquisitor João Alvarez Soarez asked him to state what his personal effects were, upon which Antonio replied, somewhat sarcastically, that " as a child of his parents, he possessed only linen and the necessary clothing." The penitent confession of his fault did not save him from the torture-rack, and he was so exhausted and crushed after the application of the gibbet (*tratos de polé*) that for quite a while he was not able to sign his name. It was noted with care in the judgment that during the ordeal to which he was subjected he designedly " called upon the only one God, but did not once pronounce the name of the Holy One " (Jesus). After suffering the most excruciating pain he was finally released, having been compelled, however, to openly acknowledge his guilt at an *auto de fe* held in Lisbon on October 13, 1726,* where he solemnly promised to become henceforth a good Catholic and to give up his old associates, whose companionship was

* Grünwald, in his character sketch of Antonio, in Frankel-Graetz's *Monatsschrift*, vol. XXIX, Krotoschin, 1880, p. 242, gives the date October 23, 1726, which we are inclined to dispute, as he does not quote authorities, whilst Dr. Kayserling consulted the best historical sources. In several important details, however, Grünwald is much fuller, and especially valuable in the analysis of De Silva's literary works, of which we give an outline in Appendix XIII to this essay.

fraught with such danger. Any violation of this resolve would entail condign and severe punishment. His mother Lourença did not come off so cheaply, for she was imprisoned three years longer than her son—until October 17, 1729.

Knowing full well the fate that awaited him should he again expose himself to suspicion, Antonio systematically avoided excessive intercourse with Jews and New Christians, and deliberately sought the esteem and friendship of several monks well known for their zeal and piety. It must be added here that immediately after his release Antonio returned to the university at Coimbra, intending to finish his course of studies. Having once obtained the necessary degree and entered his name among the practicing lawyers, he devised plans by which means he could best avoid persecution in the future, and assumed the air of a devout Christian, thinking to hoodwink the spies that were on his track. Nevertheless he neglected not to worship, in the utmost secrecy and retirement, the God of his fathers, with a fervor which is only increased and sanctified by adversity. Already then he conceived a decided predilection for the theatre, and devoted his leisure to the composition of poems and comedies, destined to exert great influence in the education of the masses.*

In 1734 he married Leonore de Carvalho, of Covilhão in Guarda, a secret Jewess, who, strange to say, was condemned by the Inquisition in Valladolid (in her eighteenth year) *in absente* almost simultaneously with her future husband. She, together with several members of her family, had fled to France.† A daughter was born to them in the year following,

---

* Cf. Barbosa, *Bibliotheca Lusitana*, vol. IV, p. 41 (also vol. I, p. 303); Wolf's biography, p. 8; Kayserling, *Monatsschrift*, vol. IX, p. 335; Grünwald, vol. XXIX, p. 243; and Appendix XIII, where a chronological table of his compositions is given.

† It is remarkable that no reference is made to Leonore by the numerous biographers of Antonio. Kayserling, *l. c.*, pp. 334-5 ; *Geschichte der Juden in Portugal*, pp. 330-1, seems to be the only one to mention her. The family is well known in Spain, Portugal, and even

whom he named Lourença, after his suffering and aged mother, just liberated from prison. For a time it seemed as if he would end his days in peace, for prosperity attended him. His office, which since his father's death (on January 9, 1736) he mastered alone, yielded a handsome yearly income; he had almost dared to hope for a life of comfort and plenty. He had a lovely and amiable wife,* and a charming little daughter whom he adored. The mother, whom he loved all the more tenderly since her late trials, was free again, and they could in the secrecy of their household give praise to the God of Israel.

in America, where we meet with the name in Brazil, Jamaica, Barbadoes and Mexico repeatedly. It survives to-day in many Jewish names. Manuel de Carvalho, of Covilhão in Guarda, 48 years old, undoubtedly some near relative of Leonore, was sentenced at an *auto de fe* held in Lisbon on May 10, 1682, to lifelong penal servitude. See M. Geddes, *View of the Court of Inquisition of Portugal*, in his *Miscellaneous Tracts*, London, 1702, p. 432. Another Manuel de Carvalho, perhaps the father of Leonore, was burnt, together with Isabella Mendes, in 1719, on suspicion of breaking a holy wafer to pieces. Cf. Ross, *Dissert. Philos., qua Inquisit. Pontif. iniquitas evincitur*, Marburg, 1737, p. 20. Whether his relatives fled on this account or not, it is known that during their sojourn in France the Tribunal in Valladolid punished with confiscation of property and banished on the 26th of January, 1727, the following persons *in absente:* Miguel Muñes [Nuñes] Carvalho of Covilhão, a merchant, aged 40 years, formerly royal administrator; his sisters Anna, 19 years old, and Leonore, 18 years old, his wife and other relations, altogether 16 in number, hailing from Covilhão and Piyel. On this same occasion the student Joseph Pereyra Cavalho was sentenced *por culpa de Judaismo* to three years' seclusion in a cloister. Cf. Kayserling, *Monatsschrift*, vol. IX, p. 335, n. 7, and *Geschichte der Juden in Portugal*, p. 331, note 1.

* De Lara's statement, repeated by Dr. Kayserling, *Sephardim*, p. 320, that Antonio in his 30th year became a widower and then began to write for the stage, is incorrect, for it is known that his wife, his mother and himself were sacrificed at the same time. The same author reports, without naming the source, that in his 37th year he underwent the Abrahamitic rite, out of devotion to his ancestral faith. This also is unauthentic, for Antonio was executed in 1739 at the age of 34.

But every prosperous man has enemies and every genius foes. Envy and hatred, these twin passions of vice, seized some fanatics, who pretended to read in the comedies of this gifted Portuguese Plautus polemics against the Holy Office. The people laughed at his plays, which they sneeringly called the operas of the Jew; they applauded the sentiment, but reviled its author. The Holy Tribunal became apprised of the insult offered to its cause and only bided its time. It did not escape them that Antonio, despite his outward attachment to Catholicism, remained true to his faith. He appended to each of his operas a sort of confession of faith, assuring us that he does not believe in the deities mentioned in his works—a fact which served as a basis for the accusations of the future. It was not long before the lowering clouds of suspicion, which had gradually gathered over Antonio's home, suddenly burst, and denunciations poured in thick and fast. At last on the 5th of October, 1737, when Antonio, whose palace was his home, was celebrating, in happy unconcern of danger, the second birthday of his infant daughter, he was disturbed by loud and imperative knocks at the door. In strode the familiar figures of the Inquisitorial bailiffs and ruthlessly separated the joyous domestic circle. Both he and his wife were cast into prison and the house of the unfortunate poet was sacked. They only found 75 reis in silver, which of course was duly appropriated for sacred purposes. The informer was a negro slave named Leonore Gomes, of the Cape of Good Hope, in his mother's service, upon whom she desired to wreak vengeance for a recent reprimand received at the hands of her mistress owing to the immoral life she was leading. Prompted by Antonio's enemies, who watched with jealous eyes his growing fame and popularity as jurist, poet and dramatist, the ungrateful negress bore witness to his Jewish loyalty.* She also was

* Grünwald, *Monatsschrift*, vol. XXIX, pp. 249-50, specifies the charges laid at his door by the African slave. She claimed to have seen her mistress's household usually change their linen on Fridays (*sexta feira*), and to feign illness on the Sabbath (Saturday), in order

incarcerated, but a few days after was suddenly seized with terror and remorse and gave up her miserable soul. Just when he was in the zenith of his power and felt himself the most secure from trouble, he was deprived within the briefest possible time of his liberty and effects. On the 3d of October, 1737, the apostolic Inquisitors issued a "warrant against the attorney Antonio José da Silva, residing at Lisbon, near the Church of Succour, for heretical degeneration and apostasy" (*Os inquisidores apostolicos contra a heretica pravidade e apostasia*), ordering him "to be taken into custody wherever he might be found; his property to be confiscated because of the crime charged against him by the *Sanctum Officium;* and his person to be secured in some safe prison." His bed and the barest daily necessaries, with an allowance of 40 milreis (=$1.50 in our money), were accorded to him. The imperial tax-gatherer served this sentence on the luckless poet. It was customary and even a matter of no little pride for persons of high dignity and social standing to volunteer their services in behalf of the Holy Inquisition, who bore the title of *Familiares.* The fear of these officials must have indeed been dreadful, if the bare words, "in the name of the most holy Inquisition," sufficed to cast any one into prison. None dared to dispute its authority. Accordingly Antonio and his wife were imprisoned on October 5, 1737. His mother, Lourença Coutinho, who for a year past was widowed, was also apprehended, for the third time, on October 12th of the same year. Cell No. 6 of the Corrido called *meis-novo* was reserved for the poet. The doors of *Citta dolente* opened for the martyr; he again entered the dreary solitude of the *eterno dolore,* where every hope dies. The Inquisitors knew full well the groundlessness of the charges brought against him by the negress, but they pretended to consider them of the gravest character, and had it not been for the unexpected

to avoid attending mass in church. Furthermore, in Passion Week, the duties incumbent upon every devout Christian were neglected by them.

death of the informer, who was the only witness, they would at once have pronounced the fatal verdict. As it was, however, Antonio being an individual whose genius was enlisted in the public cause, the judges, with great show of clemency and systematic mercy, postponed the decision until more proofs should be forthcoming. Antonio, accused of Judaizing, was quite unmoved by all this—he actually hoped to be set free again in the near future. Did he not have the friendship of pious friars — of Pater Antonio Coutinho, Pater Luis de san Vincete Fereira and José da Camara—all Dominicans, who would testify to his religiousness?

The cell wherein the unfortunate Antonio was locked was perforated with little holes, not visible to the inmate thereof, but through which all his movements could be watched. In order to spy out all his doings, the sly judges committed to the same jail a pseudo-criminal, one José Luiz de Azevedo, who was undoubtedly a hireling, for no record of his offense and arraignment is to be found in the *Torre do Tombo.* In order to divert his monotony, however, Azevedo was discharged in September, 1728, and a soldier named Bento Pereira, who appears to have been no counterfeit, was put in his place. So satisfied were the Inquisitors with his espionage that on the day of Antonio's execution the soldier was set at liberty.

From the proceedings of the trial, the documents of which are preserved in the royal archives of *Torre do Tombo,* and were first extracted by Adolpho de Varnhagen,* we learn the following facts. His beloved wife, who had been cruelly torn away from him, gave birth to a boy in prison, and the thought of her solitary anguish and forlorn hope made his soul shudder and his heart grow sick. No wonder then that he rejected the uninviting food placed before him, little caring to nourish a body whose spirit was crushed and famished. And this

---

* *Florilegio da poesia brasileira,* Lisboā, 1850, 207 seq.; Wolf's biography, p. 10. Dr. M. Grünwald, whom we follow, gives full particulars (pp. 251–7). See also the authorities cited in Appendix XII to this paper, especially the article of De Lara, who popularized his history.

very self-abnegation was the cause of his doom. The refusal to eat was at once interpreted as a contempt for the Christian religion and a desire to observe the Mosaic dietary laws. One of the witnesses, described as No. 4 in the records of the trial, Antonio Gomes Estéres, gives the following details of Antonio's behavior while in the cell. When the eye-witness looked through the watch-hole he observed the prisoner lying on his bed, where he remained till 2 o'clock ; then from 2 to 3 he paced up and down the floor of his dungeon, fixing his eyes constantly upon the sun and burying his hands in his nightgown. After that he again took to his bed until 4 o'clock, at which time he arose and sat down on a bench until the watchman, Antonio Francisco Rodrigues, brought a basket. Seeing him, he got up and received several oranges and eggs. In reciting the *Ave Maria* he knelt down devoutly and crossed himself. That done, he again paced up and down until light was brought to him, and as it was then half-past seven o'clock, he ate some bread, butter and cheese. After his meal he thanked God, crossed himself and arranged his couch. More than this the witness could not report, for he left his post, together with his colleague, at about 8 o'clock.

The witness Maximiliano Gomes da Silva declared, however, that he saw the prisoner receiving nourishment, but that he observed him throwing all the meat into "the unclean vessel " which stood by his bed.

Witness No. 20, Antonio Gomes Prego, stated that Antonio was pale, but in good spirits nevertheless, and that he could have eaten had he been so disposed.

Witness No. 22, João Gomes Da Costa, reports to the same effect, and No. 6, Antonio Baptista, endorses these statements. No. 8 does not mention the grace after meal which he was said to have uttered.

The *familiar*, Antonio Esteves Ribero, as the tenth witness, brought forward the weightiest evidence. According to his deposition, Antonio had the prayer-book in his hand without perusing it, and grace was said long after the proper time.

Witness No. 19, Felippe Rodrigues, said that the prisoner had dragged himself about, kneeling on the ground, which he kissed three times.

Let us conclude these declarations with the evidence furnished by the soldier, Bento Pereira, who was a fellow-captive of Antonio's from September, 1738, to February, 1739. This rascal maintained upon oath that Antonio fasted in accordance with the Jewish law, that he tried to seduce him, and that he did not pray at all. When he chanted the *Ave Maria*, the prisoner did not respond either by voice or gesture, but coughed at the holy portraits hanging on the wall and refused to touch any meat.

These are the only offences with which the worthy judges of faith (*los juizes de fé*) could charge their victim, despite all the espionage of the various witnesses. The evidence thus collected sufficed to sentence him to death. Being asked by the Inquisitor, Theotonio da Fonseca Santo Maior, concerning his property, he replied that at the time of his capture he possessed nothing, his library being his costly furniture, and part of it belonging to his brother, Balthazar Rodrigo.

His personal anguish was heightened by the knowledge that his mother and wife were subjected to the torture. His wife Leonore was arraigned before the Tribunal four months after her imprisonment. From October 5, 1737, to February 28, 1738, she languished in the gloomy dungeon without even being apprised of the cause. Being summoned on the 15th of March anew, she disavowed all knowledge of guilt, in consequence of which she was pronounced heretical, faithless and unbelieving, and on the 10th of October, 1739, scarcely two weeks after the execution of her aged mother-in-law (Sept. 28th), she died at the age of 27.*

* According to Kayserling, *Monatsschrift*, vol. IX, p. 338 ; *Gesch. d. Juden in Portugal*, p. 333, Antonio's mother and sister survived him some time. His mother lived 3 months after his execution. De Macedo makes them all die at the same *auto de fe*, on the 19th of October, 1739.

Antonio also, when put on trial before the Holy Office, stoutly denied the charges brought against him, and proved that since his conversion he had been a constant Catholic, shunning the association of Marranos, as persons of esteem could testify. As the judges themselves saw the contradictory reports in the testimony of the witnesses, they attempted to inveigle him by tricky questions and flattering overtures. But he was no more the careless, inexperienced young student who 13 years before betrayed his parents and friends. Bitter experience and much suffering made him a keen observer. He remained non-committal. All schemes availed nought. At last, forced to the wall, the Inquisitors gave it out that he was seen in company with adherents of the laws of Moses on a certain day and at a certain time. Neither time, place nor persons, however, were specified in fuller detail.

After Antonio heard these accusations, he begged for counsel, which request, as in the trial of 1726, was granted by the hypocritical judges. The Inquisitor selected two licensed practitioners, José Rodriguez Leal and Dr. José da Motta Faria, who, out of consideration for the *Sanctum Officium* and out of charity for the prisoner, pleaded Antonio's cause.

His innocence was as clear as sunlight, and it did not take the lawyers long to establish the fact that our poet, after his apostasy to Judaism, adopted the Christian faith, to whose tenets he remained loyal and whose ceremonials, unless official duties interfered, he carried out most minutely. When these mock formalities were gone through with, the members of the Holy Office called a secret meeting for March 11, 1739, and " after they deliberated on the pros and cons of the case " (as if their verdict had not been premeditated) they unanimously resolved that Antonio José da Silva, heretical and prone to apostasy, be properly punished with the confiscation of his property and with the great ban. For seven months this verdict remained unknown. It was carried into execution despite the painstaking interest of his friends, particu-

larly of D. Mathias Ayres Ramos da Silva Eça, president of
the imperial mint, and Don Francisco Xavier de Menezes,
Count of Ericeiro, himself a talented poet, both of whom
were devotedly attached to him and remained loyal unto
death,* hoping against hope for many weary months that
his innocence would yet be known and his person set at
liberty. It was even rumored that King João V, who
appreciated the genius of his poetry, made many efforts to
save him. But the Inquisition recognized no authority. No
king, no friend, no power of any kind could liberate a
wretched victim about whose neck the brawny arm of fanatic
hatred was once tightening.

At an *auto de fe* held in the Church of St. Dominique, on
the 18th of October, 1739,† Antonio heard his sentence *de
relaçao*. True to the motto of the Inquisition, every word of
which was cant, not to be too severe in judgment and to delay
as long as possible the capital punishment without spilling
blood (*sem procederem a pena de morte, nem effusão de sangue*),
Antonio was convicted to be publicly burnt as an impenitent
Judaizer. He went into the chapel and a confessor was sent
to torture his last hours. In triumph and glory let it be said
that this noble martyr, who had often foreshadowed his
destiny in his inspired verses,‡ offered up his last prayer to
the one only God, to the God of Israel, who was always his
God.

After all, the Inquisitors were right—he was an obstinate,
heretical miscreant, a Jew. His old mother and his wife are
said to have been spectators at the *auto de fe*. In an authentic
document still extant, we read, under the heading, *Pessoas
relaxadas em carne*, the following: "No. 7, 34 years old.
Antonio José da Silva (*christianus novus*), attorney, born at
Rio de Janeiro, lives in Western Lisbon, pronounced free

* See Appendix VII to this paper ; J. M. Pereira de Silva's *Os
varies illustres do Brasil*, Paris, 1858, vol. I, pp. 262, 266.

† Kayserling has the 16th of October, 1739.

‡ Cf. Wolf's *Antonio José da Silva* (see Appendix XII), p. 10 seq.

from the crime of *judaizing* at the *auto de fe* celebrated in
the Church of St. Dominique, October 13, 1726. Newly
accused, lying and relapsing into the old sins."

On the 19th of October, 1739, escorted by a confessor and
the whole brotherhood of mercy (*Irmandad da Misericorda*),
the immense assemblage there gathered beheld advancing a
dark-haired man of middle stature, pale and emaciated from
long confinement in the dingy, unwholesome dungeon; clad
in a yellow *sambenito* (or *san-benito*) which was adorned with
red flames and fantastic devils, holding a green wax-candle
in his hand. It was Antonio José da Silva, the famous poet
and dramatist, one of whose popular *operettas* by a strange
irony of fate was played at the great theatre of Lisbon on the
very evening of the day when he expired on the funeral-pyre.*
He was calm and heroic, a typical martyr. To make his
last moments still more horrible, the humane Holy Office, to
whom everything was holy, invited his aged mother and
youthful wife to watch his dying anguish. His crime being
only that of Judaizing, one sign of grace was shown him,
he was first strangled and then burned. Had he been "a
genuine Jew" he would have been sacrificed alive. How
merciful was that sublime brotherhood! De Lara, and following him, Kayserling, give some romantic episodes of the
final scene which we shall not reproduce, as they can be consulted elsewhere. Suffice it here to repeat a portion of the
last withering denouncement from the lips of the hero-poet:
" I am a follower of a faith God-given according to your own
teachings. God once loved this religion. I believe He still
loves it; but because you maintain that He no longer turns
upon it the light of His countenance, you condemn to death
those convinced that God has not withdrawn His grace from
what He once favored. You demand that we become Chris-

---

* This coincidence has just been pointed out by Dr. Gustav Karpeles, in his new series of studies, issued by the Jewish Publication Society of America, Philadelphia, 1895, entitled, *Jewish Literature and other Essays*, pp. 236–7 (cf. also *ibid.*, p. 100).

tians, yet you are far from being Christians yourselves. Be at least men, and act towards us as reasonably as if you had no religion at all to guide you and no revelation for your enlightenment." Some say that Antonio's last cry was the ancient, glorious *Shema Yisrael.** Hate pursued him even after death. When a collected edition of his operas was spoken of, the Inquisition forbade it. Only five years later, in 1744, did his works appear anonymously, under the title, *Theatro comico portuguez,* edition in 2 vols. by Francisco Luiz Ameno (see Appendix XIII), who, whatever his motives were, deserves full credit for preserving in more permanent form the genial productions of the greatest Portuguese dramatist—the regenerator of the comic opera.

It is a sad consolation for us to know that Antonio was the last Jewish martyr to die at the stake in Portugal. There were several *autos de fe* held, but the torture and funeral-pyre were abolished after the accession to the throne of Don José.† In 1766 the last *auto de fe* was held in Lisbon without victims, and the laws of King Manuel (March 1st, 1507) and João III (December 16th, 1524) affecting New Christians and Marranos, were renewed on the 2d May, 1768. These sects were henceforth to be punished with deportation and the confiscation of property.

And now let us turn back to the Inquisition on native

---

* See Krauskopf's *Jews and Moors in Spain,* Kansas City, 1887, pp. 183–4, where the death-scene is graphically described. Antonio was, however, a young man of 34 years, and not a venerable sage. as the author thinks. Kayserling, *Sephardim,* pp. 321–3, gives the picture as seen by an eye-witness. He followed there De Lara (see Appendix XII, *s. v.*), whose information, owing to the omission of sources, is not at all reliable. Kayserling himself calls it the "artistic elaboration of the truth" (*Monatsschrift,* vol. IX, pp. 331–2). Krauskopf, Kayserling, Karpeles (*Geschichte der jüdischen Literatur,* Berlin, 1866, vol. II, p. 960 ; *Jewish Literature and other Essays,* pp. 236–7), and De Lara give extracts of this stirring and eloquent speech.

† Cf. Kayserling's *Geschichte der Juden in Portugal,* Leipzig, 1867, pp. 333–4.

American soil—in Peru. One more *judaizing* victim, a contemporary of Antonio José da Silva, claims our attention. We refer to Francisco Moyen, the martyr of Lima, who, after nearly twelve years' imprisonment, was exiled from that country, shipped to Spain, and finally perished off Cape Horn.

His story has been exhaustively treated by B. Vicuña Mackenna in his treatise, *Francisco Moyen; or the Inquisition as it was in South America* (London, 1869; 8vo, 230 pp.), written originally in Spanish and translated into English by Dr. James W. Duffy, in answer to the high-strung panegyric of the Holy Office published by the Chilian Prebendary, Señor Saavedra.* It is a highly interesting and valuable compilation, for Mackenna, a just man and an erudite, conscientious historian, investigated all documents extant, and incorporated only what is authentic in his biography. He was not satisfied with merely recording the life and trials of Moyen, but has devoted several pages to a brief survey of the beginning and development of the Sacred Tribunal in South America, particularly in Mexico and Peru. It was he who first brought to light from the dusty archives of Lima the account of " the noble, illustrious and courageous resistance which about the middle of the seventeenth century (1634–40) the ecclesiastical chapter of Santiago, composed entirely of members of the Chilian clergy, made to the encroachments of the Inquisition of Lima, represented by the Dean, Don Tomas de Santiago, acting as its Commissary-General in Chile."†

The writer of this work was residing in Lima in the year 1860, and in one of his visits to the public library of that

* *La Inquisicion : rapida ojeada sobre aquella antiqua institucion, por el prependado Don José Ramon Saavedra.* Santiago, 1867, 4to, 128 pp.

† In a discourse delivered on the 17th of August, 1862, before the Faculty of Humanities of the University of Chile, bearing the title, *What was formerly the State of the Inquisition in Chile,* published in 1862.

city he came by chance upon an immense quantity of law papers which had formerly belonged to the Inquisition, among which were those of the whole of the suit against Moyen. In the public library of Lima was furthermore found a large book of memoranda or records, which had belonged to the archives of the Inquisition of Lima. It is a folio volume, 30 centimetres in length, 21 in width, and 17 in thickness; it is bound in parchment, and has a table on the back on which is written *Penitenciado, No. 78—Don Francisco Moyen, de nacion frances, por proposiciones* (= condemned, No. 78, Don Fr. Moyen, a native of France, for propositions*). This valuable collection, together with others in the same library containing important records of numberless *autos de fe*, was bought for half an ounce of gold by the worthy librarian, Presbyter Don Francisco de Paula Vigil, from a poor woman, to whom it had been bequeathed after the famous sack of the record office of the Inquisition at Lima on the 3d of September, 1813. It contains not only the suit of Moyen, but also those of six others : that of Pedro Fos, likewise a Frenchman, and those of Manuel Galeano, Pascual Estacio Vargas, Juan Pablo Rodriguez de Soto, Fr. Matias Ponce de Leon and José de Medina. That of Moyen alone occupies from 800 to 900 leaves, which is two-thirds of the volume; the writing is very clear and legible; the identity of the signatures, and the impossibility of falsifying so much without motive, removes the least shadow of doubt about it.

The defence of Moyen was written by himself in a character extremely clear and distinct, occupying altogether 100 pages in folio, and although they seemed to be only notes for his advocate, they showed proofs of extraordinary erudition, and his language, though incorrect and even barbarous, was considerably better than the French-Portuguese jargon of his earlier writings. (Mackenna, p. 162, note.)

Francisco Moyen was born in Paris in the year 1720;

---

* Meaning heretical ideas.

most of the members of his family were artists. His father, Nicholas Moyen, and his grandfather of the same name had been musicians belonging to the royal chapel at the French court. His mother was a lady, a native of Burgundy, named Elena Adin. Francisco was a true Parisian—equipped with a liberal education, and by nature with genius, and became a trader. He had a chequered, romantic career, minutely described by his biographer, into the details of which we will not enter here. He was at home in the Orient, in Lisbon, England and America. He journeyed to Rio de Janeiro several times and to the Indies, and at last came to Peru. He was jovial, careless and frivolous; had remarkable talents for music, painting and literature, but was ill-tempered and talkative to excess. Therein lay the secret of his destiny. Mackenna says (pp. 60–61): "On the 18th of December he, with a party of traders, passed by Cordoba, and in the first days of February arrived at Jujui (Jujuy, in the Argentine Republic). The loquaciousness of Moyen, his violin and his animated and cheerful character made him the favorite of the company. As for his heresies against the Popes, the good folks of the road did not hear or else did not listen to them. Only the muleteers were accustomed to say whenever he passed before their mules, ' There goes a Jew.' The truth is that at that time in America there were only known three classes of men: the Chapetones, who were the inhabitants of the Peninsula, or natives of Spain; the Creoles, those born in America, and Jews; to the last category (Jews) belonged all foreigners, and especially the Portuguese, because it is well known that at the expulsion of the Jews from Spain, the greater part of them took refuge at the more tolerant court of Lisbon . . . One day (the 10th or 11th of March, 1749) José Antonio Soto, a native of Galicia in Spain, born in the town of Redondela, was dining with the (other) companions of Moyen at the table of a merchant of Jujui called Juan Tomas Perez, when they commenced a conversation, very common at that time and since

among Spaniards, about the sixth commandment of the law
of God, and between the laughing and drinking it happened
that one of them made the remark that Moyen was a heretic
because he did not attribute very great importance to that
prohibition." At this irreverent remark the Galician withdrew to investigate the previous utterances of the French
Jew during their journey. The muleteers assured him that
Moyen was a consummate heretic, which was endorsed by
Don Rodrigo Palacio, a member of the company. The
curate of Cotagaita, Don Juan Antonio Leon, being advised
beforehand, informed Soto that "he was in the company
of a Jew" (p. 64), so that he began carefully to jot down
every item of their intercourse and conversation, intending
to make good use of it in the future. The agents of the
Holy Office were soon notified of the possibility of procuring
another victim, and his movements were watched and
reported. "Denunciations poured in abundantly from all
who had seen the heretic pass by their door, from all who had
ever heard anything spoken about the Jew" (pp. 74–5).
Finally on the 14th of May, 1749, the Commissary Lizarazu,
Beaumont y Navarra of Potosi, where Moyen lived for two
months, issued a warrant, which is printed in full by Mackenna (pp. 77, 78). He was imprisoned three years in that
city. At length, on the 26th of March, 1752, he was delivered
within the gates of the Holy Office at Lima. "About 3
years before," writes his biographer, "Moyen had arrived at
Potosi, young, gay, brave, full of talent, and fervently glowing with all the passion of gallantry. He was then, according to the description of his own comrades, of well-propor-
tioned stature, stout, round face, a beard full and black,
white skin, Roman nose, thick lips, large, sharp and blue
eyes, and with a mark of a cut across the jaw to the extremity
of the mouth (from an old duel). Now the man behind whose
tottering steps they had drawn the bolts of the Holy Office
was but the shadow of that robust youth of nine and twenty
years—emaciated, cadaverous, his hair tinged with grey . . .

Moyen had lived in three years a whole life of pain and misery. In the prime of his life he had already the signs of premature old age, produced by the combined torture of the flesh and spirit."

The first audience to which Moyen was admitted before the Inquisitors took place on the 4th of May, 1752. Ten sessions, lasting till June 21st, followed. In the first his genealogy was investigated. "Moyen had to give a most prolix history of his grandfathers, brothers and all his relations, to prove the purity of his race, because, according to the constitution of the Inquisition, one may be born a heretic. Judaism, for example, is a heresy constitutional and hereditary. But in this part the Parisian and Burgundy lineage of Moyen came out triumphant; for he proved, so says the respective act, to be of a good race and generation, without any mixture of heresy, Mohammedanism or Judaism."*

The second and third admonitions were made to him four months later, the 13th of October, 1752. The document of condemnation, of which only the conclusion is cited by Mackenna (pp. 112, 113), issued on the 11th of October, 1752, by Bartholomé Lopez Grillo, pronounced said Don Francisco Moyen to be a " heretic, formal, obstinate, and sequacious

---

* Almerico, in his *Directory for Inquisitors*, quoted by Mackenna, pp. 109, 110, says : " The accused is to be asked whether any of his family had been inclined to Judaism, or if any one had been condemned by the Holy Office, because those who have not the pure blood may more likely offend against the faith." Don J. Machena, in his compendium based upon the above *Directory* (published at Montpellier, 1821), says : "Infidels and Jews are subject to the Inquisition, the last when they sin against the articles of their faith, which are the same in both religions, as sacrificing to the devil, this being against the unity of God, an article admitted by Jews and Christians." He reckons as indications of Judaism the following observances : "To put on a clean shirt or clothes on Saturdays ; to remove the fat from the meat which they are going to eat ; to examine if the knife is notched with which they are going to kill a fowl or other animal ; to repeat the Psalms without the *Gloria Patri.*" (Cf. also Mackenna, p. 206.)

of the said sects of Luther, Calvin, Sacramen, Jansenius, Quesnel, Manichoeus, and Mahommed, and most vehemently suspected of Judaism, and approver of other errors and heresies." He was to be put to the torture.

Among the numerous evidences given by his biographer under various systematized paragraphs summing up the crimes he was charged with, we read :

"XXXIX.—*Fatality.*

"The accused, talking with the curate mentioned in the antecedent charge (headed *The Cross*) concerning predestination and of the great number who are lost eternally for not having had a knowledge of the Messiah, said, 'It is a very hard case that so many should be condemned for not having ever heard of the son of a carpenter.'

They said they were agreed that this scandalous proposition was offensive *piarum aurium*, impious, temerarious, erroneous, formally heretical, and approaching to Judaism, which constituted the accused a formal heretic, and suspected of Judaism."

We shall pass over the other audiences and trials concerning Moyen, his tortures and horrible sufferings from disease, so graphically told by his biographer. Suffice it to say in brief that in a deed of February 18, 1761 (pp. 166–9) we read the full account of his sentence. Among other things he had to present himself at a public *auto de fe*, in the form of a penitential, with a *sambenito* on which is half a cross, a cap on his head, a rope round his neck, a gag in his mouth, and a taper of green wax in his hand . . . "We condemn him to the confiscation and loss of half his goods . . . and we banish him perpetually from both the Americas and Islands adjacent . . . and from the city of Madrid . . . for the term of ten years, which time must be passed in one of the garrisons of Africa, Oran, Ceuta or Melilla," etc. etc.

A thorough search in the libraries of Mexico and Peru
and judicious inquiries made among private collections would
reveal an astonishing amount of new material relative to our
topic. Thus Mackenna (p. 9) writes that "several individuals hold in their possession bundles of old papers, the
judicial records of the Inquisition : one friend of mine has
the process of Madam Castro. He was kind enough to show
it to me, and even allowed me to copy it ; he found it by
chance in the great chest which the people could not carry
away in the sack of 1821. These relics are so much the
more valuable on account of their rarity, and therefore should
be completed wherever it is possible."

As we have seen above, printed records of the American
Inquisition in the Indies, Lima and in the wealthy Empire
of Montezinos, are by no means so scarce as our historians
would have us believe. It is true, as José Toribio Polo
remarks in Mackenna's *Francisco Moyen* (p. 9), that many
precious documents were destroyed by fanatical officials of
the *Sanctum Officium*, who "took the atrocious oath of
secrecy never to reveal, either by words, acts or gestures,
the least thing relating to the Holy Office." Of the very
earliest phases of the activity of the Tribunal on this continent we still know very little. Everything in this connection
has been communicated above. We can now accept as true
the fact that from 1548, the year in which the first *auto de fe*
took place, until 1570, three public *autos* were celebrated by
the Archbishop Don Francisco Jeronimo de Loaisa, and it
requires the patient labor of a chronicler to discover any
traces of these acts. Not even Señor Palma succeeded in
finding those records for his *Annals of the Inquisition* (*ib.*,
p. 9).

To the rarities of historical literature belongs a curious
quarto volume of more than 300 pages, printed in Lima in
1737—"a most wonderful production of pedantry and stupid-
ity, of gross adulation and barbarous fanaticism"—whose
title is : *Triumphs of the Peruvian Holy Office ; a Panegyrical,*

*Historical and Political Relation of the public auto de fe
celebrated the* 23rd *of December,* 1736, *by Doctor Don Pedro
José Bermudez de la Torre y Solar.* This book, to which
Mackenna often refers and extracts,* narrates the proceedings at the public *auto de fe,* " which was without doubt the
most famous after that which a century earlier (1639) was
celebrated by the Inquisitor Mañosca to burn the *judaizing*
millionaire Manuel Bautista Perez and his wealthy companions." Its principal attraction was the burning of Madame
Castro, about whom we have spoken, and the punishment
of ten other women, " amongst whom were the Chilian Flea,
and the Little Flea, her daughter, all of them for being
witches."

The Jews appear to have been distinguished from other
offenders on these occasions by the so-called *corozas*, or caps
of derision, generally made of pasteboard. On them were
printed figures of devils and reptiles ; those of the *judaizing*
had tails twisted around them, " and from this," says Mackenna (p. 212, n. 1), " very likely came the vulgar idea (and
which we in our childhood believed as an article of faith) that
the Jews had tails like monkeys."

Even Chile, the brave little kingdom which so successfully resisted the establishment of the Tribunal, did not
remain entirely free from the insult of the *sambenito*,
although she escaped the horrors of the burning pile.

It may truly be said that the Inquisition expired at the
commencement of the age in which we live. Travellers
like Stevenson, Mellet, and others have given vivid illustrations of the Inquisition in South American countries. They
were even witnesses to many private *autos de fe* as late as the
year 1812, in one of which was condemned the celebrated
seaman Urdaneja for heretical propositions and for reading
the works of French philosophers. He made his escape and
died in Mexico. In Peru the Holy Office was abolished on

*Pp. 31, note ; 75, n.; 95, n.; 191 ; 192, n.; Appendix II, pp. 207–
217.

March 9, 1820. Mackenna furnishes us with the exact copies (in English) of the numerous documents relating to the Inquisition and its extermination, in the appendices to his work on *Francisco Moyen.*

Our co-religionists have led a checkered life here in America as everywhere. Many and various were the trials through which Israel had to stride to the higher levels of culture and civilization. It is well to revive his history, if only to show unto the nations the thorn-bush of his heroism ever burning but never consumed—not even by the glaring fires of *autos de fe.*

APPENDIX I.

Ludovico à Paramo on Jewish victims of the first American auto de fe.

[From his work : *De Origine et Progressu Officii Sanctae Inquisitionis, ejusque dignitate et utilitate, de Romani pontificis Potestate et delegata Inquisitorum, etc.*, Matriti, MDXCIX, folio, pp. 241–42. Extracts of the subjoined text are also copied by Philip Limborch in his *Historia Inquisitionis*, etc., Amsterdam, 1692, p. 104.]

" . . . Intra breve temporis spatium ab incunabulis huius sanctae fidei Tribunalis ubi eres fruges, quae ab eo in omnibus Provinciis, ubi illud residet, colliguntur, editae sunt. Nam anno 1574, qui tertius erat post eius initia, actus primus fidei nova ac admirabili celebritate in foro Marchionis (ut vocant) ad latus Ecclesiae maioris habitus est, magno erecto theatro, qui universam prope fori aream occupans, Ecclesiae contiguum erat : ubi astiterunt Prorex ac Regius senatus, Capitulum, ac Religiosorum conventus, Proregis, senatus regii, aliorumq́; pluriū concomitantium caterva stipati, ad forum usque progressi fuere, quippe solennibus supplicationibus, in quibus octoginta poenitentes circiter erant solennis hic fidei actus ab hora sexta de mane usq́; ad quintam vesperi duravit. In quo duo haeretici, alter Anglus, Gallus alter, relaxati sunt, nonnulli *Judaizātes* reconciliati, fueruntque plures polygamia laborātes, sive bis uxorati, illicitis ac maleficis artibus, & praestigiis studētes dediti. Sane Poly-

gamiae crimē in eis Provinciis, ob locorū distantia, ac frequē-
tiores, longinquasq́ ; hominū peregrinationes (opinātibus illis
in tāta distantia haud detegi posse) plerumq ; comittitur.

In
hoc actu Dominus Antonius Morales de Molina sancti Jacobi
Spatiferi Religiosus, ac Episcopus Tlaxalensis (Mexico), con-
cionem habuit, ac tam celebris fuit hominū conventio,
actusque solennitas, ut qui viderat Pincianum famigeratis-
simum fidei actum, habitū 21. Maii, an. 1559, dixerint hunc
illi non maiestate, sed Regiarum personarū, qui in illo inter
venerunt, praesentia esse inferiorem. Ab illis temporibus
quotannis solennes fidei actiones celebrantur, in quibus fre-
quēter sunt *Lusitani Judaizātes*, incaestis ac nefariis nuptiis
polluti strigesque ac lamiae multae.

In hoc fidei actu mulier quedam lamia ostensa est, quae
virum suū Goa timale ducentis leucis Mexico distātis degen-
tem, magicis incantationibus Mexicū, ubi ipsa erat, duorū
dierum spatio venire fecit. Ab hac dum sciscitaretur Inquisitor, quare id effecerat : ut viderem (respondit) ac fruerer
speciosissima viri mei fronte, ac ore, cum tamen hoc ille
spurcus ac foedissimus esset, ac supra modū abominabilis.
Illud autem fuit ab omnibus insigniter demirandum, quod
in una actione contigit, in qua relaxatus est quidam Garcia
Gonzalez Bermejero, qui quinquaginta annis *Mexici Judaicis*
superstitionibus nefariis misere volutabatur : qui tandem
cōvictus, fictus & impoenitens in miserrimum fatum concessit.
Alius Castellanus appellatus, duo de quinquaginta annis,
qui Mexici non detectus *judaizaverat*, misericordia ei concessa fuit reconciliatus : & valde miror, qui fieri potuit, ut
tantū scelus rituū, et caeremoniarum *Judaicarum*, quae
natura sua rumorē ac strepitum prese ferrit, tam lōgo tempo-
rum curriculo, etiam in opulentissima civitate, summaque
hominum frequentia exculta occultū sub tenebris latuerit eo
vel maxime, quod agnum Paschalem comedebant & eius san-
guine domorum umbracula linirent : nec ob id detectum
scelus fuit donec quidam fidei noxius in Hispaniae Inqui-
sitionibus eiusdē criminis reus, praedictū Garciam Gōçalez

cōplicem, qui tunc Mexico degebat, casu hanc ceremoniarum congeriem pateficit.

Anno 1592, familia quedam Judeorum tabe polluta ad poenitentiam est exhibita: & Frɛncisci Rodriguez Matos Lusitani, eius familiae capitis & scelerum autoris, iam demortui statua, igni iure tradita est, quia dogmatizator ac Rabinus Judaeorum sectae fuerat: eius uxor ac filiae quatuor inpoenitētiam publicam saccorum benedictorum reconciliatae sunt. Ille filium universorum scelerū heredē ac successorē habuit, cuius statua (quia aufugerat sequenti anno in quadam publica fidei actione in Ecclesia Mexicana habita), incensa est.

Illud vero praetereundum non est, illius profligatissimi hominis filiam natu minorem, septēdecem annis natam, illarum quatuor, quas supra commemoravimus, David Psalterium universum per insignem memoriam absque haesitatione rececuisse, oratiōnē antē Hesther [?] ac alia nonnulla Judeorum cantica inverso ordine ab ultimo verso usque ad primum repetentem facilitate eadem recitasse: harum quatuor mulierum avunculus Ludovicus de Carvajal in publicam poenitentiam prodiit, quod illius familiae scelera non denunciasset, imo potuis cōtexisset. Is erat Gubernator ac Generalis Dux Provinciae Tampicii ac Panucii ac qui paulo ante Praesidis titulo salutabatur, suam ignominiosam sententiam publice exaudivit, ac perpetuo Regiis officiis privatus est, & in summā miseriam deductus, moerore ac vitae taedio brevi spatio viā universae carnis ingressus est," etc., etc.

APPENDIX II.

The Mexican Jew, Tomas Trebiño's Martyrdom in 1549 (?).

[See *Fragmento de dicha relacion reimpreso en el Diario de México de 6 Abril de* 1807 ; *apud* Don Antonio Puigblanch, *La Inquisicion sin Máscara, ó Disertacion en que se prueban hasta la evidencia los vicios de este Tribunal, etc.*, Mexico, 1824, pp. 104, 105.]

" . . . En la relacion del auto de México de 1549 se lee lo siguiente hablando de la ejecucion de algunos reos *judaizantes*.

'Fueron relajados para el brasero en persona trece, con quienes se usó la piedad de darles garrote antes de ser quemados; menos en Tomas Trebiño de Sobremonte, por su insolente rebeldía y diabòlica furia, con que aun habiendole dado ā sentir en las barbas, antes de ponerle en el cadahalso el fuego que le esperaba, prorumpió en execrables blasfemias, y atrahia con los pies á si los leños de la hoguera, en la cual tambien ardieron cuarenta y siete osamentas con suas estatuas, y de los fugitives diez.''

"En el auto de México de 1549 al llevar al suplicio al mencionado Tomas Trebiño" sucediŏ, sugun dice la la relacion, que montandole los ministros en una bestia de albarda tan ruin, tan floja y tan mansa, como todas las de este gēnero, lo mismo fue sentir esta la carga que sacudirle con furia y partirse ā reparos por entre el concurso. Se trajo otra y sucediò lo mismo. Hasta seis se remudaron echandose mano de aquellas, en que habian caminado algun trecho otros de los relajados sin repugnancia, y como aun los brutos se horrorizaban de aquel monstruo ninguno le admitio en su espalda. Caminó el infeliz á pie algun espacio; mas como lo sucedido era argumento bastante de que el caso era misterioso, deparò la divina providencia un caballo que le admitió sobre si para entregar mas pronto al fuego tan maldita carga.''

Appendix III.

Laguna on the Inquisition.

[Cf. Puigblanch, Spanish ed., p. 108, and n. 261; German ed., Weimar, 1817 (?), p. 153 seq.; Kayserling, *Sephardim*, Leipzig, 1859, pp. 297–303, and notes 494–5; his biography in S. R. Hirsch's *Jeschurun*, vol. III, Frankf. a. M., 1857, pp. 414–20.]

"Entre los escritos que abundan en semejantes aluciones es singular una traduccion castellana de los Salmos en varias especies de metro publicada en Lòndres á principios del siglo pasado. Su autor llamado Daniel Israel Lopez Laguna, el cual segun dice en el prologo habia estado preso por la Inquisicion, la escribió con el fin de auxiliar en la inteligencia de aquel libro ã sus hermanos los judios españoles y portugueses, que de aquì pasaban ã Inglaterra, é ignoraban el hebreo. Merecen con especialidad leerse las dos siguientes octavas sobre el salmo X segun el texto original y IX segun la vulgata ; ellas solas demuestran la idea que tienen los judios del rigor de este tribunal. Dicen pues asì.

Vers. 22. Ut quid, Domine, recessisti longe etc. 23. Dum superbit impius etc. 24. Quonian laudatur peccatur etc.:

"¿ Por qué, Señor, te encubres ã lo lejos
A nuestro ruego en horas del quebranto?
Piadosas nos alumbren tus reflejos
Cuando soberbio el malo causa espanto
Al pobre persiguiendole en consejos
Del *Tribunal*, que infieles llaman *Santo*.
Preso sea el malsin que tal se alaba,
Pues aunque él se bendice, en mal se acaba."

Vers. 29. Sedet in insidiis etc. 30. Oculi ejus in pauperem respiciunt etc. 31. In laqueo suo humiliabit eum etc.:

"Acechador violento en las aldeas
Cual oso ambriento enviste al inocente ;
Sus ojos, sin temer que tu los veas,
Atalayan, cual leon de lo eminente
De su gruta, á las miseras plebeas
Gentes, que asalta audaz cuanto inclemente.
Pues liso geando hipocrita, abatidos
Coge en la red rebaños de afligidos."

(Kayserling, *Sephardim*, quotes only one verse with variations.)

Appendix IV.

Description of a Mexican Auto de fe.

[From B. Vicuña Mackenna's *Francisco Moyen: or the Inquisition as it was in South America*, translated from the Spanish by James W. Duffy, M. D., London, 1869, pp. 102-104.]

". . . . Of the opulent Mexico, which stands first in the category, it is well known that it displayed a greater degree of luxury in its executions than that of the Holy Office of Lima. According to Juan Torquemada (*Indian Monarchy*, vol. III, p. 379), from 1574 to 1593, a term of only 19 years, were celebrated nine *autos de fe*, in the first of which were present 63 penitentials, of whom 5 were burnt alive. In the tenth *auto de fe*, celebrated in honor of the Immaculate Conception of the Virgin, on the 8th of December, 1596, were present 60 penitentials. In another, celebrated 25th of March, 1602, the number exceeded 100.

Juan de Torquemada (we do not know if he was a descendant of the famous Thomas, although both were monks), who published his *Indian Monarchy* in 1723, appears to have been a great enthusiast in the burning of heretics, and the picture he has given of one of those festivities, of which he appears to have been an eye-witness, is so characteristic of his ferocious but ingenuous simplicity that we cannot do less than copy some parts of it as a specimen. He says :

" The place selected was the town-hall, being in the principal square of the city, where was ordered to be erected a sumptuous seat. Its base was on a level with the balustrade of the balcony, which formed a running cornice, with curious mouldings, in the clear of which they placed the seat, raised in form of a dais, with sufficient room for the chairs of the Viceroy, Inquisitors and the Town Council, above which was the canopy of the tribunal, which with its silk curtains and the beautiful worked and rich carpets, spread all over the spaces and flooring of the dais, made a most majestic appearance.

" It was quite a marvelous thing to see the people who crowded to this celebrated and famous *auto ;* they were in the windows, and every place, which they filled, and even to the house and doors of the Holy Office ; and to see the singular procession and accompaniment of the relaxed and penitentials who came out with ropes about their necks and pasteboard caps on their heads, with flames of fire painted on them, in their hands they held a green cross, and each had a monk by his side who exhorted him to die well; they had also familiars of the Holy Office for a guard. The reconciled Jews with *sambenitos*, those twice married with caps, upon which were painted objects signifying their crimes. Those accused of witchcraft with white caps on their heads, candles in their hands, and ropes about their necks. Others for blasphemy, with gags in their mouths, half naked, their heads uncovered, and with candles in their hands, all in order, following one after the other; those for lesser crimes going first, and in the same order the rest, the *relaxed* following behind, and the dogmatists and teachers of the law of Moses as captains or leaders, the last with their trains on their caps, rolled up and twisted to signify the false doctrines they taught, and in this manner they proceeded towards the place erected for them, which was in front of the seats for the tribunal, at the foot of which were also seats in the form of steps, upon which were seated the familiars of the Holy Office, each according to his seniority.

"As for the scaffold, or framework for the seats of the condemned, it was marvellous, because in the middle of it was a half pyramid, surrounded by semicircular steps up to the top; upon these were seated in their order the relaxed, the dogmatists upon the highest steps, and the others in gradation, and in this order also were the effigies of those who were relaxed but who were either dead or absent. The reconciled and other penitentials were seated upon low benches in the open space of the scaffold. The head jailor of the Holy Office had a chair placed for him at the base of the scaffold, a pulpit was also placed upon the right of the Holy Office, from which a sermon was preached by the Archbishop of the Philippine Islands, Don Frai Ignacio de Santivañes, of the order of my glorious father San Francisco. Two other pulpits were placed, one on each side of the tribunal, from which were read by the reporters the sentences of the condemned, but which for the sake of not being too prolix, I will not give here; it will be enough to say that there were many of those obstinate Jews, who each one might have been a Rabbi of a synagogue. All this was celebrated with great majesty, the immense majority of the people not being a little astonished at the rites and ceremonies, as well as at the enormous crimes, an account of which they had just heard read to them, of these judaizing heretics." *

APPENDIX V.

Enterprise of the Marranos in the Indies.

[From *Documentos remittidos da India, publ. da Academia real das sciencias de Lisbôa, p. R. Ant. de Bulhão Pato*, Lisbon, 1880, vol. I, p. 106 (cf. also vol. II, 215 sq.; III, pp. 495, 510 sq., etc.); *apud* Kayserling, *Christopher Columbus and the Participation of the Jews in the Spanish and Portuguese Discoveries*, Engl. ed. by Dr. C. Gross, New York, 1894, p. 131, note.]

". . . . os Christãos-Novos de Portugal e Hispanha ajudavan a D. Manuel para armar alguns navios de guerra junto com os dos mercadores que por todos fizessen copia de trinta velas, e n'ellas ir D. Manuel para que mandavan dinheiro a Hamburgo e Alepo, e d'ahi se passava a Holanda e Gelanda, e que os Christãos-Novos d'esse Estado entravam tamben na dita liga, e que em Columbo havia dous que se carteavam com os Hollandeses, e em Malaca havia quatro ou cinco que os avisavam pelos moços que jam mos portos ende elles estavam por cuja via havia d'ahi muita correspondencia con ellas."

APPENDIX VI.

A) *Menasseh ben Israel on Isaac De Castro Tartas.*

"Ishak de Castro tartas, conocido nuestro, y harto inteligente en las letras Griegas y Latinas, no se por que furtuna, passando daqui a Pernabuco, siendo alli captivo de los Por-

---

* A very similar description of a Mexican *auto de fe* is given in Dr. Cyrus Adler's paper on the "Trial of Jorge de Almeida by the Inquisition in Mexico," in this *Publication*, Appendix.

tuguezes, fue lo mismo que cercado de lobos carniceros.
Embianle a Lixboa, donde tiranicamente preso, de edad de
24. años, es quemado vivo, no por alguna traicion que
hiziesse, que a ley de soldado, estava obligado a defender su
plassa, como hazen los nuestros en aquella provincia, donde
por su fidelidad, les encargan los mas importantes puestos;
mas quien tal imaginara? por que dixo, que no queria creer,
mas que en un solo Dios, de Israel, que avia criado el cielo,
y la tierra."

See *Esperança de Israel,* Spanish ed., Amsterdam, 5410
(1650), pp. 99–100. Both the Hebrew and Latin versions
(Amsterdam, 1697, pp. 52ᵇ–53ᵃ; Amsterdam, 1650, p. 89), the
latter of which is cited in full by Dr. Kayserling, *Geschichte
der Juden in Portugal,* Leipzig, 1867, p. 309, note 1, are
briefer than the above, for which reason the Spanish original is given here.

B) *Salomon de Oliveyra's Elegy.*

אל גויעת איש האלהים הנחמד ונעים יצחק די קאסטרו תארתאס* בחור
כארוזים אשר חי בלעוהו להבות אש לוהט על יחוד קדושת השם ויצאה נשמתו
הקרושה בטהרה קדוש יאמר לו בחדש שבט התי"ח.

אנשי אמונה גברו כארץ
המה ראות ראו וכן תמהו
איש תם לבכו מעריץ אל עריץ
עלה בלבת אש כאליהו.

לפני אלוה יעמוד בפרץ
כי מחשבותיו גדלו גבהו
כל כוכבי אור קדרו, ויעל
על רום שרפים עומדים ממעל.

---

* Graetz, *Geschichte der Juden,* X², p. 102, note 1, has טארתאס;
Jellinek, in his article published in the Hebrew annual *Ozar Hassifruth,* edited by S. I. Gräber, Krakau, 1888, vol. II, p. 204, as also
in Fürst's *Litteraturblatt d. Orient,* 1847, p. 263, has the wrong date,
Sept. 13, 1647. He transcribes his name so: טַאַרתש. On the title-
page of several of Oliveyra's Hebrew books, printed by Isaac's
brother, the name is spelt די קאשטרו תארטס

קמו אריות חרקו שן, ערב
רב פערו פיהם, וחי בלעו
שה שרקו לו, והפכו לערב
יומו, וקדשו עממו בלעו.

אמרו לכה תעבוד שתי וערב
חלקו לשון מרמה והם בלעו
לא ידעו כסלם כאוכלי תבן
מעשה ידי אדם ועץ ואבן.

ענה בקול ערב ולב שמח
מה תענו אותי ומה תבולו
אקום ואתעודד אני נוצח
אתם להבל תכרעו תפולו.

אל חי נשא נס איש בך בוטח
ירדו שאולה צוררים יבולו
ואני בצדק אחזה פניך
אשבע בהקיץ את תמונתך.

אש אהבה תבער בתוך לבך
אש להבות שמך בהשמים
הראה לטין כל אנוש ריבך
רוחך בקרבך נשרפה פעמים.

מחוץ ומבית יקר נפשך
לא יוכלו כבות המוני מים
אהבה רשפיה כאש צרבת
רשפי פלדות יעלו שלהבת.

לך בשלשה שם והוד קנית
באת עדי עדיים הכי נכבדת
הם יצאו לאור אשר בזית
אתה אלי מקום אשר חמדת.

קמת להתרומם ואף עלית
שמה עטרות ראשך ענדת
נפשך טהורה פה בעולת בעל
פשטה לבושה עד שרוך הנעל.

עוז אב המון גוים מלמדך
גם בן זקוניו עד הלום הגיע
עלה עשן כליל כמזבחך
על מוקדה בו רוחך תרגיע.

שוב אל ולא עוד יעשן אפך
צדקת ישרים תזכרה תופיע
קומה ד' למנוחתך
אתה אלהים וארון עוזך.

Translation:

On the demise of the youthful, comely, and God-fearing man, Isaac de Castro Tartas, stately as the cedar, whose life flames of fire did devour [because of his zeal] for the unity and holiness of God. His pure soul left [the body] in innocence. Well may he be called a martyr! It was in the month of Shebat, in the year 5418 [read 5408].

Men of faith prevailed in the land
They saw indeed and were astounded that
A hero, perfect in heart, dreading the fearful God
Ascended in a flame of fire like Elijah.
Firm and unyielding he stood for his God ;
For his thoughts were great and lofty.
All the brightest stars were wrapped in mourning
As he ascended to the height of the Seraphim
That stood on the firmament.
Lions arose and grated their teeth,
The rabble gaped with their mouth,
They swallowed alive the lamb at whom they hissed
And changed to night his day.
They darkened and profaned his holiness (piety).
Go and worship the cross ! said they [the inquisitors]
[As they] smoothed their deceitful tongue [ready] to swallow him.
(Not knowing, like dumb cattle, that their folly
Was the work of the hands of man—wood and stone.)
And he answered in a pleasant tone and joyful heart :
Wherefore do ye annoy and confuse me?
I shall arise and be strengthened, for I triumph
[Whilst] you crouch and fall to naught.
To thee [alone], O living God, man lifts up the standard.
Let my oppressors down into hell and rot
Whilst I shall behold Thy Face in righteousness
And upon reviving, rejoice in Thy Image.*
The fire of love that is kindled within thee,
The glowing flame that has inspired thee (liter.: brought thee into
        heaven)
Made manifest to every eye thy cause.
Thy spirit has been twice burned :
Within and without thy soul did flame
Quantities (liter.: multitudes) of water could not extinguish it !

* Referring to immortality.

Love, her sparks are like the scorching fire,
Thy heroism * has gained thee name and glory.
Thou camest adorned with ornaments (virtues?), aye much
    esteemed.
They went forth to the light which thou didst despise,
Thou wentest to the place whither thou didst desire,
Thou didst arise to be exalted and hast indeed succeeded.
Then thou didst enwreath thy head with crowns,
Thy pure soul was here blended with the body
Her (the soul's) garments stripped off entirely (*i. e.* in its original
    purity.)
The example of Abraham enthused thee,†
Even (thou) his youngest son (his last follower)
Has met his destiny thus (lit. reached hither)
The smoke of the holocaust ascended on thine altar
Upon its hearth thou gavest thy soul repose.
Return, O God, and let no more thy anger rage (smoke),
Remember, I pray, the righteousness of the upright
And cause it to shine forth in splendor.
Arise, O Lord, to thy rest,
Thou and the ark of thy power.

The above is a free yet literal rendering of the poem
which in some places is quite obscure, although the original
text is punctuated throughout. After the 12th line a few lines
were omitted by Dr. M. Kayserling, who published these
verses in Kobak's *Jeschurun,* Jahrg. II, pp. 99-100. The
original was printed in Salomon de Oliveyra's שרשת גבלת
Amsterdam, 1765, p. 52[b]. Four lines, with the introductory dedication, are given in *Sephardim,* Leipzig, 1859, p.
347, note 256[a]. Isaac Cardoso, in *Excelencias,* p. 323 seq.,
reproduced this and other poems in his honor, among them
a Spanish dirge of six lines by Jonas Abarbanel, of which

---

* The meaning is uncertain. It is sometimes used in the sense
given in my rendering, see Fürst's Dictionary, s. v. שָׁרֵשׁ. Cf.
II Samuel xxiii. 19, 23.

† Referring undoubtedly to the legend of Abraham being cast into
a fiery furnace by Nimrod. Cf. *Sefer Hajashar;* Talmud Synhedrin
93a ; other sources are given in Beer's *Leben Abrahams,* Leipzig,
1859, p. 112 ff.; S. B. Gould's *Legends of Patriarchs,* New York,
1872, pp. 158-60.

two are preserved in *Sephardim*, p. 206, note 1. The volume is very rare and difficult of access, hence I could only copy the elegy of the famous Amsterdam Rabbi. R. Saul Levi Morteira's (or Mortera) funeral oration appeared, according to Fuerst, *Bibliotheca Judaica*, vol. I, Leipzig, 1849, p. 149, *s. v.* under the title הֶסְפֵּד [*Sermão funeral?*], in Amsterdam, 1648, in octavo. He calls attention also to Cardoso's notes in his *Excellencias*, p. 324, and in note 3 gives some biographical details.

APPENDIX VII.

Marranos exiled to Brazil by the Inquisition in 1682 *and* 1707.

[Collected from *A View of the Court of Inquisition in Portugal*, etc., in *Miscellaneous Tracts*, edited by Dr. Michael Geddes, vol. I, 1st ed., London, 1702; 2d ed., London, 1714, pp. 389–448, 423–482, 482–519 of both editions. The original orthography is retained throughout this Appendix.]

a. "A List of the Persons who received their Sentences in the Act of the Faith, celebrated in the City of Lisbon, on the 10th of May, 1682.

AGE.	A Person who wore the Habit but did not Abjure.	PUNISHMENT.
48	Joan Alexio, a New Christian, a Merchant, Native of Montemor, in the Kingdom of Castile, an Inhabitant in Sevil, and Resident in this City, reconciled by the Church of Sevil, in the Year 1672 for the Faults of Judaism; and· imprisoned a second time for having relapsed into the same. [The Reason of this person's not having Abjured, was, because he was taken up for having relapsed, and so must have died without Mercy, had he been convicted.]	Prison and Habit perpetual, without remission, and 5 Years in Brasil.
	Abjuration de Leve.	
48	Catherina Baretta, a Maid, the Daughter of Antonio de Crasto, a Native of Villa Franca, and an Inhabitant of this City, for the Faults of Witchcraft.	Prison during pleasure, and to be whipp'd, and 4 Years in Brasil.

AGE.	Abjuration for Judaism *de vehemente.*	PUNISHMENT.
51	Luis de Mattos Couto, a New Christian, who lived upon his own Estate, a Native of this City, and Inhabitant in the Government of *Spirito Santo*, in the State of Brasil. [He must have lived there as a secret Jew.]	Prison during pleasure.
	Fourth Abjuration.	
72	Paula de [or da] Crasto, half a New Christian, married with Antonio Duarte, a Scrivener of the Civil Court, a Native and Inhabitant of this City.*	Perpetual Prison and Habit, and 3 Years in Brasil.
	Persons who did not Abjure.	
46	Magdalena da Cruz, the Wife of Augustino Nuñes, who was *Alcaide* [Alcáyde = jailer] of the secret Prisons of this Inquisition, a Native and Inhabitant of this City, for having co-operated to corrupt certain officers of the Holy Office to give intelligence to persons in the Prisons, and to receive answers from them to Persons that were abroad.	5 Years in the (*sic*) Brasil.
75	Simãon Henriques,† a New Christian, who was a Farmer of the Revenue, Native and Inhabitant of this City, who abjured *de vehemente*, for the Crimes of Judaism, in an Act of the Faith, celebrated therein in the Year 1656: Imprisoned a second time for having relapsed into the same.	5 Years in Brasil.
27	Thereza Maria de Jesus, more than half a New Christian, a Maid, the Daughter of Antonio Serrãon, an Apothecary, who is in the List, a Native and Inhabitant of this City.‡	The same, with the Ensigns of Fire, and 7 Years in Brasil.

* Cf. also Kayserling's *Sephardim*, Leipzig, 1859, p. 305 and notes; and George A. Kohut: "Some Jewish Heroines—A chapter in Martyrology," published in the *American Jewess*, vol. II, No. 1, Chicago, 1895, p. 44, no. 12.

† See *Sephardim, ibid., l. c.*

‡ Many members of this family suffered at the hands of the Inquisition in 1682 and were present at the above *auto de fe*. For further particulars see Kayserling, *Ein Feiertag in Madrid*, Leipzig, 1859, p. 23, note, and G. A. Kohut, "Jewish Victims of the Inquisition in Lisbon in the seventeenth and eighteenth century," in *Revue des Études Juives*, vol. XXXI. On Thereza Maria de Jesus, see also G. A. Kohut in *American Jewess* for October, 1875, p. 45, no. 23.

AGE.	Abjuration de Leve.	PUNISHMENT.
30	Ursula Maria, a Maid, the Daughter of Francisco de Salhas, a Glass Merchant, a Native of the Town of Alhas Vedros, and an Inhabitant of this City for the same Fault.	Prison during pleasure, and five Years in Brasil.
41	Maria Pinheira, married with Goncalo da Gama Volante, a Native and Inhabitant of this City, for the said Fault.	The same.
	Abjuration for Judaism *de vehemente.*	
55	Francisco de Almeida Negrāon, a New Christian, who belonged to the Sea, a Native and Inhabitant of the Town of Pedrenero, for the same fault of Judaism, and for having spoke Propositions with an Heretical Obstinacy after he had been Reproved for 'em."	Prison during pleasure, and Three Years in Brasil.

b. "A List of the Prisoners and of their Condemnation and Sentence who were in the Publick Act of the Faith, celebrated by the Inquisition in the City of Lisbon, on Sunday, the 6th of November, 1707, Consisting of above Threescore Men and Women with some Notes upon it.

AGE.	The second Abjuration in Form for Judaism.	PUNISHMENT.
21	Donna Theresa Barreira,* a New Christian, not marry'd, the Daughter of Andre Barreira, a Merchant, Native of the City of Olinda, in the Bishoprick of Parnamburo [Pernambuco ?] in the State of Brasil and Inhabitant in this city of Lisbon, originally of the Kingdom of Castile (p. 507, no. 16)."	Perpetual Prison and Habit.

c. We also append from the same list, the record of four others punished for various offences. It is probable that these were Jews or Marranos. Their names, though quite familiar, do not give us the slightest clue to their identity.

* Cf. my article on "Jewish Heroines," p. 44, no. 5; and the *Revue des Études Juives, l. c.*

AGE.	Abjuration de Leve.	PUNISHMENT.
45	Antonio Laurenco de Almaida,* a Soldier of the Regiment of Algarves; Native of the City of Faro, and Inhabitánt of Spirito Santo, in the State of Brasil, for having married twice, his first Wife being alive.	Prison during pleasure, Whipping, and 5 Years in the Galleys.
46	Manuel Jorge, a Seaman, Native of the Island of Pico [in the Azores] and Inhabitant of this City for the same fault.	The same.
34	Joan de Conto [Couto?] Toledo, who has no Calling, Native of the Town of Praya, in the Island of Tercera [in the Azores] and Inhabitant of Sanctos, under the Government of the Rio de Janeico [Janeiro?] for the said Fault."	The same.

APPENDIX VIII.

Antonio José Da Silva, the Jew.

[From the *Brazilian Biographical Annual*, ed. by Joaquim Manoel de Macedo, Rio de Janeiro, 1876, pp. 31–34, under date of the 8th of May.]

"The Inquisition, the so-called *Santo Officio*, could in its beginning perhaps excuse itself on the plea of religious zeal and well-intentioned aspirations; but even so, it was plainly subject to abuses and to degenerating into fanatical persecutions, as was shortly the case, when it became a terrible calumny on the holy religion of the Lamb of God and of the pure and undefiled teachings of our Lord Jesus Christ.

The Inquisition, introduced into Portugal and then firmly established by D. John III, increased the number of its agents and spread like a net over the kingdom of Portugal and its possessions. In Brazil it made an abundant harvest of victims, who were burnt at the stake or subjected to horrible tortures by means of infernal machines invented by a cruel and diabolical ingenuity.†

* Marranos of this name are known to have lived in Mexico already in the sixteenth and seventeenth centuries. See the paper by Dr. Cyrus Adler, on "The Trial of Jorge de Almeida by the Inquisition in Mexico," in this *Publication.*

† This corroborates the theory, advanced above, that Brazil was very much under the control of the Inquisition.

Antonio José da Silva was born in Rio de Janeiro on May 8, 1705. He was the legitimate son of the lawyer João Mendes da Silva (see Appendix IX) and Lourença Coutinho. The latter, on a mere suspicion of Judaism, was arrested and sent to Lisbon. João Mendes followed his wife, carrying with him his three children, the youngest of whom, Antonio José, was then eight years of age, and to support his family and defend his wife, commenced the practice of law in Lisbon. Lourença Coutinho was not at that time brought to the stake.

Antonio José was educated in Lisbon. His college career was made brilliant by his talent and vivacity, and at the age of twenty-one he graduated at Coimbra as bachelor of divinity. He returned to Lisbon, and in August of the same year (1726) fell into the hands of the Inquisition, which had renewed its persecutions of the martyr Lourença Coutinho. After being subjected to torture for two months, he was released in October by an *auto de fe*.

He practised law with his father, whom he greatly assisted in his professional labors. He was an author of fables and of humorous and witty poetry, and became known and esteemed. He began to write comedies, which were very successful and drew crowded houses to the theatre of *Bairro Alto*.

Antonio José da Silva married Leonor Maria de Carvalho. The fruit of this union was one daughter, on whom he lavished the whole wealth of a father's love and tenderness. He professed to be an ardent Catholic, either from sincere conviction or from fear of the Inquisition, which had again incarcerated his wretched mother.

João Mendes da Silva died in 1736, probably cursing the diabolical institution which had kept him in constant torment by its cruelty to his wife and by the apprehensions which it excited for his son. Antonio José da Silva, rendered famous by his amusing comedies, so full of wit and originality, was honored by his admirers with the flattering epithet of the Portuguese Plautus. He resuscitated and regenerated the drama at Lisbon and won the friendship of many eminent persons, among whom were Mathias Ayres Ramos da Silva Eça,* director of the mint, a man of considerable literary acquirements, and D. Francisco Xavier de Menezes, Count of Ericeiro, who, like his father, was a poet.

But the people called the comedies of Antonio José da Silva the operas of the Jew. Was this his crime, forsooth?

The wretched poet was again arrested and incarcerated by the Inquisition, together with his young and innocent wife, on the 7th [read 5th] of October, 1737. It is wonderful that his persecutors even spared his infant daughter. Neither the love of the people, which was a crime, nor his literary glory, which was a reproach, nor the faithful friendship of Silva Eça and the Count of Ericeira, could save Antonio José from the doom which awaited him.

The diabolical tribunal, the so-called *Santo Officio*, the notorious calumniator and sacrilegious enemy of Christ's holy religion, in cold blood and with cruel perversity murdered, in the name of the God of pardon, charity and mercy, Antonio José da Silva, his mother Lourença Coutinho, and his wife Leonor Maria de Carvalho! The three victims were publicly burned in Lisbon on October 19, 1739. The Inquisition had roasted and devoured its prey.

The memory of Antonio José da Silva has been perpetuated by his comedies, which are so conspicuous for their wit, elegance and originality that, having been carelessly published with others not written by him, they were easily distinguished from the spurious productions, the difference being apparent to any one of ordinary intelligence on a simple inspection.

---

* See his biography in the same volume, p. 45, where we read that "he was a friend of the unfortunate Antonio José, whom he made every effort to save from the clutches and fire of the Inquisition." That this excellent man with all his influence could not save his friend is very singular indeed.

The number of the genuine comedies is twelve. They would not now be admitted on the stage, as neither would those of Plautus, Terence, Gil Vicente and other classical writers; but the *Guerras do Alecrim e da Mangerona, Escantos de Medéa, Labyrintho de Creta, Vida de D. Queixote, Precipicio de Phaetonte* and others, are works whose merit is more than sufficient to establish the glory of this illustrious Brazilian whose inspired genius was the life and soul of the Portuguese theatre in the eighteenth century.

The Brazilian poet Dr. Domingos Magalhães, now Viscount of Araguaya, has written a tragedy, frequently represented before applauding andiences, of which José Antonio is the hero and which bears his name.

The production and representation of this play has united in one complex, three glorious Brazilian names : that of the hero, Antonio José, and finally that of the actor, João Caetano, who amidst enthusiastic applause represented the character of the illustrious victim of the unhallowed Inquisition."

APPENDIX IX.

João Mendes da Silva.

[*Ibidem*, pp. 441-2.]

" A native of Rio de Janeiro, where he was born in 1656, João Mendes da Silva took his degree in law in the University of Coimbra, and on his return to the country of his birth he worthily followed the profession of Advocate, and married Lourença Coutinho, who, years after, suspected of Judaism, was arrested in Rio de Janeiro by the agents of the Holy Office and sent to Lisbon.

João Mendes abandoned everything to follow and protect his wife, whose fate, as also that of his son, Antonio José da Silva, will be mentioned in the article relating to the latter (cf. previous sketch). Although João Mendes practiced advocacy in Lisbon, and in spite of the friends he made, he could not succeed in snatching his wife from the prisons of the Inquisition; he at least, however, educated his son, and saw him take his degree in canon law in the University of Coimbra, and practiced law with him in his office.

But on the 8th of August, 1726, Antonio José da Silva, his son and his hope, was also seized by the Inquisition under pretext of a *suspicio*, of Judaism! . . . .

Notwithstanding, after two months of torments and ill-treatment with the pulleys, they set free the poor youth. The 8th day of August was for João Mendes a precursor of horrible misfortune, and it remained in his mind as a black shadow and bad omen for the future. The fond father saw on the 8th of August the mark of the implacable Inquisition cast on his son.

Even so, even under the persecution of this ominous fancy, and the fearful martyrdom that threatened his wife, the unfortunate João Mendes, desponding and sorrowful, internally cursing the Inquisition but outwardly feigning to esteem it, lived ten years, dying at length in 1736. God had had mercy on that devoted husband and fond father, who at least saw not the accursed flames of the sacrilegious pile devour his wife and son.

João Mendes da Silva was a lawyer and advocate of much credit and a poet of some merit.

He wrote *A Poem dedicated to our Lord Jesus Christ*, sacred hymns, and fables, and light poems, to which critics of authority give a decided preference."

APPENDIX X.

Brief Biography of Antonio José da Silva.

[From Brockhaus' *Conversations-Lexikon*, XIII ed., vol. XIV, Leipzig, 1886, p. 827b.]

" Silva (Antonio José da) genannt *o Judeu*, ist der Verfasser portugiesischer burlesk-komischer Singspiele von genialer Originalität, welche 1733–38 im Theater des Bairro-Alto von

Lissabon, unter dem rauschenden Beifall der Menge, darge-
stellt wurden. Silva wurde als Sohn eines getauften Juden
8. Mai 1705 in Rio de Janeiro geboren, studierte in Coimbra
die Rechte und wollte eben 1726 seine Thätigkeit als Advokat beginnen, als er mit samt seiner schon früher des
Judäismus verdächtigen Mutter vor das Inquisitionstribunal
gefordert wurde. Schliesslich freigesprochen arbeitete er
als Advokat in Lissabon. Im Jahre 1737 wurde Silva jedoch
von neuem vor die Schranken des Inquisitionstribunals
geladen, nach zweijähriger Gefangenschaft zum Tode verur-
teilt und am 19. Oktober 1739 das Urteil in feierlichem
Auto da Fé vollstreckt.

Das Volk nannte Silva's Singspiele nur "die Opern des
Juden," im Hinblick darauf, dass in den eigenartigen Dramen
die kernige volkstümliche Prosa, welche ihre eigentliche
Sprache ist, häufig durch eingelegte Gesangsstücke unter-
brochen wird. Die Parodie mythologischer Stoffe und alt-
klassischer Fabeln, und der grosse scenische Apparat der
Operas nähert sie den modernen Offenbachiaden; der Humor,
welcher die echt portugiesische Sitten und Zeitbilder adelt,
erhebt sie jedoch zu epochemachenden Erscheinungen. Die
bedeutendsten der Stücke sind: "Amphytrião," "Esopaida,"
"Don Quixote" und "Guerras de Alecrim e Mangerona."
Gedruckt wurden sie erst in Einzelheften (1736–1737), dann
gesammelt im *Theatro comico Portuguez* (4 Bde., Lissabon,
1744, 1747, 1753, 1759 und 1787–92), welches acht Stücke
von Silva enthält. Ein Stück, "O Ocabinho da mão
furada," erschien erst 1860 in der *Revista Brazeleira*. Vgl.
Wolf, *Don Antonio José da Silva, der Verfasser der sogenannten Opern des Juden* (Wien, 1860); David, *Les Opéras du
Juif* (Paris, 1880).*"

---

*In the *Encyclopædia Britannica*, *s. v. Portugal* (9th ed., vol. XIX,
p. 557ᵇ), Antonio José da Silva is barely mentioned.

APPENDIX XI.

Sismondi's Estimate.

[From a *Historical View of the Literature of the South of Europe*, by J. C. L. Simonde de Sismondi, English transl. by Thomas Roscoe, 4th ed., Bohn's Library, London, 1853, vol. II, pp. 590–91.]

"About the epoch of Ericeyra [1673–1744] some promise of a Portuguese drama began to dawn in Lisbon. During the whole seventeenth century that city had to boast only of a Spanish theatre, and such of the Portuguese as cultivated the dramatic art adopted the Castilian tongue. Added to which John V patronized an Italian opera in Lisbon which, supported by his munificence, soon appeared to flourish; and this new example gave rise to another species of mixed spectacle. This consisted of comic operas played without the recitative, and composed probably with borrowed music, in the manner of the vaudevilles, accompanied at the same time with all the attractions and display of the Italian opera. The pieces were written by a Jew of the name of Antonio José, an illiterate and obscure individual, whose coarseness both of style and imagination betrayed the vulgar rank to which he had belonged (*sic!*). A genuine vein of humor and familiar gaiety, however, gave life to the Portuguese stage for the first time; there was a certain vigor as well in the subjects as in the style, and from the period of 1730 to 1740 the people rushed in crowds to the theater. The nation seemed on the point of possessing its own drama, when Antonio José, the Jew, was seized and burnt by order of the Inquisition, at the last *auto de fe*, which took place in the year 1745 [read 1739]. The managers were then, perhaps, alarmed lest their faith should become suspected by continuing the presentation of the unfortunate Jew's productions, and the theater was in consequence closed. There are extant two collections of these Portuguese operas, dated 1746 and 1787, in two volumes octavo, which appeared without the author's name. The eight or ten pieces which they contain are all equally rude in point of language and construction, but are by no means deficient in sprightliness and originality. One of these, of which Esop is made the hero (*Esopaida*), and in which the brilliant exploits of the Persian war are whimsically enough included in order to exhibit battles and evolutions of cavalry upon the stage, gives to the character of Esop all the ridicule and gaiety of a true harlequin.

A Portuguese poet of our own day has addressed some lines to the memory of this victim of the Inquisition, in a style of extreme boldness and severity. After passing in review several other human sacrifices, no less disgraceful and atrocious than those which bathed the altars of Mexico in blood, he exclaims:

> O' Antonio Jose dóce e faceto,
> Tu que fostes o primeiro que pizaste
> Com mais regular sono a scena luza !
> O provo da Lisboa mais sensivel
> Foi no Theatro aos teus jocosos ditos
> Que no Rocio à voz de humanidade,
> Que infame horrenda, pompa, que fogueire
> Te vejo preparada ! ''

(The Rocio is the public place in Lisbon provided for the exhibition of the *autos de fe.*)

Appendix XII.

Bibliography of Works relating to Antonio José da Silva.

1. 1813. The first French edition of J. C. L. Simonde de Sismondi's *Historical View of the Literature of the South of Europe.* English transl. by Thomas Roscoe, 4th ed., Bohn's Library, London, 1853, vol. II, pp. 590, 591.

   [See Appendix XI, where an extract of a poem written in honor of da Silva, by a contemporary poet, is reproduced.]

2. 1826. F. Denis, *Résumé de l'histoire littéraire du Portugal,* Paris, 1826, p. 432 *seq.*

3. 1847. *Portugal Pittoresco*, Lisboa, 1847, vol. III, p. 270.
4. 1850. Adolpho de Varnhagen, *Florilegio da poesia brasileira*, Lisboa, 1850, p. 207 *seq.*
5. 1852. Vegezzi Rusculla, *Il Giudeo Portoghese*, Turin, 1852.
6. 1855. De Lara, *Antonio Joseph, the Portuguese dramatist*, published at first in the American Jewish weekly, *The Asmonean, a Family Journal of Commerce, Politics, Religion and Literature, devoted to the interest of the American Israelite*, edited by Robert Lyon, New York, 1855 ; reprinted in the *Jewish Chronicle*, London, 1855, No. 29; German versions in Samson Raphael Hirsch's *Jeschurun, ein Monatsblatt zur Förderung jüdischen Geistes und jüdischen Lebens in Haus, Gemeinde und Schule*, I Jahrg., 5615, Frankfort a. M., 1855, p. 598 *seq.*; by Dr. M. Wiener, in Dr. Z. Frankel's *Monatsschrift für Geschichte und Wissenschaft des Judenthums*, IV Jahrg., Leipzig, 1855, pp. 328–36.
7. 1856. José Maria da Costa é Silva, *Ensayo biographico-critico sobre os melhores poetas portuguezes*, Lisboa, 1856, vol. X.
8. 1858. Innoc. Franc. da Silva, *Diccion bibl. portuguez*, Lisboa, 1858.
9. 1858. J. M. Pereira da Silva, *Antonio José*, in his *Os varies.illustres do Brasil*, Paris, 1858, vol. I, pp. 259–281.
10. 1859. Dr. M. Kayserling *Sephardim ; Romanische Poesien der Juden in Spanien*, Leipzig, 1859, pp. 320–323 and notes. (See also note 207.)
11. 1860. Ferdinand Wolf, *Don Antonio José da Silva, der Verfasser der sogenannten Opern des Juden*, published in (and afterwards reprinted from) the *Sitzungsberichte der philosoph. histor. Classe der Kaiserl. Akademie der Wissenschaften*, Wien, 1860. See also Kayserling's review of Wolf's book in Steinschneider's *Hebraeische Bibliographie*, vol. III (1860), pp. 111–112.

12. 1860. Dr. M. Kayserling, *Antonio José da Silva*, in Frankel's *Monatsschrift f. d. Gesch. und Wissensch. d. Judenth.*, vol. IX, Leipzig, 1860, pp. 331–38.

13. 1861. Joachim Norberto de Sousa Silva, *A coròa de fogo*, Rio de Janeiro, 1861.

[An epic poem entitled " The diadem of fire," dedicated to Antonio's memory by one of Brazil's modern poets, whose writings rank very high.]

14. 1863. Ferdinand Wolf, *Le Brésil Littéraire*, Berlin, 1863, p. 31 *seq.*

15. 1867. Dr. M. Kayserling, *Geschichte der Juden in Portugal*, Leipzig, 1867, pp. 329–33.

16. 1876. Joaquim Manoel de Macedo, *Antonio José da Silva, the Jew*, in his *Brazilian Biographical Annual*, Rio de Janeiro, 1876, pp. 31–34.

[See Appendix VIII and IX, where Antonio's and his father's biography are given from this valuable record.]

17. 1877. Frederic David Mocatta, *The Jews of Spain and Portugal and the Inquisition*, London, 1877, pp. 88, 89; also in the Hebrew translation by I. H. Barta (באַרטה?) which appeared in an appendix to S. I. Gräber's *Ozar Hassifruth*, Krakau, 1888, vol. II, p. 34.

18. 1878. Fridolin Hoffmann, *Geschichte der Inquisition. Einrichtung und Thätigkeit derselben in Spanien, Portugal, Italien, den Niederlanden, Frankreich, Deutschland, Süd-Amerika, Indien und China*, Bonn, 1878, vol. II, pp. 88, 89.

19. 1880. Ernest David, *Les opéras du Juif Antonio José da Silva*, 1705–1739 (Extrait du *Journal des archives israélites*, Paris, 1880, impr. et libr. Wittersheim in 8vo de 74 p.).

20. 1880. Isidore Loeb in *Revue des Études Juives*, vol. I, 1880, p. 126 (cf. also *ibid.*, vol. III, 1881, p. 157).

[Review of the above cited work of David's.]

21. 1880. Dr. M. Gruenwald, *José da Silva, ein tragisches Opfer der Inquisition im achtzehnten Jahrhundert,* in Frankel-Graetz's *Monatsschrift f. d. Gesch. und Wissensch. d. Judenth.,* vol. XXIX, Krotoschin, 1880, pp. 241–57.

22. 1882. Dr. M. Levin, *Antonio Joseph da Silva,* first published in Dr. Adolph Brüll's *Populär-wissenschaftliche Monatsblätter,* etc., 2 Jahrg., Frankfurt a. M., 1882, pp. 211, 212; reprinted in his *Iberia, Bilder aus der spanisch-jüdischen Geschichte,* Berlin, 1885, and in Rev. Joseph Krauskopf's *The Jews and Moors in Spain,* Kansas City, 1887, pp. 185–188.

    [One of the most vivid and picturesque descriptions, in verse, of the execution of Don Antonio. In Brüll's magazine, *l. c.* p. 211, note, Dr. Levin gives a brief outline of his life. See also *Revue des Études Juives,* vol. XII, 1886, p. 127.]

23. 1886. Brockhaus's *Conversations-Lexikon,* 13th ed., vol. XIV, Leipzig, 1886, p. 827ᵇ, *s. v.*

24. 1886. Dr. Gustav Karpeles, *Geschichte der Jüdischen Literatur,* vol. II, Berlin, 1886, p. 960.

25. 1887. Rev. Joseph Krauskopf, *The Jews and Moors in Spain,* Kansas City, 1887, pp. 183, 184.

26. 1895. Gustav Karpeles, *Jewish Literature and other Essays,* Philad., 1895, Jewish Pub. Soc., pp. 100, 236, 237.

APPENDIX XIII.

Bibliography of Don Antonio's Compositions.

1. 1729. *Os a mantesde escabeche.* (Slyness in love.)
2. 1729–33. *El prodigio de Amarante.* (The wonder of Amarante.)
3. 1729–33. *San-Gonçalo.* (St. Gonzales.)
4. 1729–33. *Amor vincido da Amour.* (Love conquered by Love.)

    [This operette was written in honor of the Crown-Prince of Brazil, afterwards King Don José.]

5. 1729–33. *Vida do grande Don Quixote da Mancha e do gorde Sancho Pansa.* (Life of the great Don Quixote de la Mancha and of the servant Sancho Pansa.)

[Upon this excellent drama his fame chiefly rests. It was performed in October, 1733, upon the stage of Bairro Alto. Of course, Cervantes' famous classic furnished him the material. It is a sharp *critique* of the Portuguese customs and manners in the eighteenth century. It became so popular in Portugal and Brazil, that long after his death, in 1774, it was again reprinted under the title *O grande Governador da Isla dos Lagardos* (The illustrious Governor of the Lizard Islands), and was incorporated in the large collection of comedies called *Intermez de Cordel.* (See, however, the remarks of Ernest David in his *Les opéras du Juif Antonio José da Silva,* Paris, 1880, and Dr. M. Grünwald, in Frankel's *Monatsschrift,* vol. XXIX, 1880, pp. 244–246.)]

6. 1734. *Esopaida.* (The Life of Aesop.)

[Likewise introduced upon the stage of Bairro Alto in 1734.]

7. 1735. *Os encantos de Medea.* (The incantations of Medea.)

8. 1736. *Alma minha gentil, que te pertiste.* (Noble and precious soul, wherefore hast thou forsaken me.)

[A dirge of Camoens lamenting the death of the beautiful Infanta Donna Francisca, of Portugal, to which De Silva has added a gloss. (Grünwald, p. 247.).]

9. 1736. *Amphitriāo.* (Jupiter and Alkmene.)

[A popular comedy directed as a satire against King John V, who in disguise visited the cloister of Ocidellas or the chapel of St. Sacrement.]

10. 1736. (?) *O Labyrintho de Creta.* (The labyrinth of Creta.)

[A polemic against mythology and religion.]

11. 1737. *As guerras do Alecrim e de Mengerona.* (The
battle of Rosmarin and Majoran.)

[The most original and national of his comedies, not
unknown even to-day. A true picture of the customs
of the first half of the eighteenth century. It was
first launched at the time of the Carnival in 1737.]

12. 1737. *Variedades de Protes.* (The metamorphoses of
Proteus.)

[A sort of variety show, written upon popular demand, with numerous tableaux and gorgeous scenery.
First performed in the theatre of Bairro Alto in
1737.]

13. 1737. *O Precipicio de Faetonte.* (The precipice of
Phaeton.)

[This, his last piece, was composed from May till
October, 1737, and was introduced in 1738, when its
author was languishing in the dungeon of the Tribunal.]

14. 1744, 1747, 1753, 1759, 1787, 1792. His collected writings
were published. In 1744 they appeared anonymously
in two volumes, under the title *Theatro comico portuguez,* edited by Franzisco Luiz Ameno. Three different editions were issued subsequently; the best is
entitled *Theatro comico portuguez: Collecção das
operas portuguezes que se representaram na caso do
theatro publico da Bairro Alto e Mouria de Lisboa.*

It is interesting to note that the editor of this
anthology added other compositions by foreign
authors, ascribing them to our Antonio, and only in
1858 was the forgery detected by Innocencio Francisco de Silva in his *Os varies illustres do Brasil,*
Paris, 1858, vol. I, pp. 259–81, who showed that da
Silva, like the ancient Jewish hymnologists (*Payeta-
nim*), affixed his name in the form of an acrostic to
every one of his plays.

15. 1860. *O ocabinho da mão furada.*

[A recently recovered production of Don Joseph's, published in 1860 in the *Revista Braseleira.*]

See also for other important details, beside the authorities given in the last Appendix, the works of David and Gruenwald, who speak more elaborately of his literary achievements. De Macedo, in his biography of Antonio, quoted above (no. 16), says that the Brazilian poet, Dr. Domingos Magalhães, Viscount of Araguaya, " has written a tragedy, frequently represented before applauding audiences, of which José Antonio is the hero and which bears his name," etc. It would be interesting to publish an anthology of poems written in honor of this Portuguese Plautus whom Brazil so proudly claims for her own. In the recently written historical and literary compendiums of that country, this illustrious martyr must surely be accorded a conspicuous place.

Crypto-Jews in Mexico during the Sixteenth Century

By Arnold Wiznitzer*

I

INTRODUCTION

Mexico was originally inhabited by a number of Indian races, who dominated the land until they were subjugated by the Spaniards. Historians date the beginning of the Colonial Period of Mexico as of August 13, 1521, for it was on that day that a Spanish force, commanded by Hernando Cortéz, occupied Tenochtitlán [later called Mexico City], the capital of the Aztec empire. Cortéz accomplished this hard-won conquest after having made his way to the Aztec capital from Cuba via Vera Cruz. Using Mexico City as his base, Cortéz rapidly ramified his military effort, founding the viceroyalty of New Spain. From 1535, this dominion embraced all the territories north of Panama to Taos and Charleston, extending as far west as the Pacific Ocean. It also included the Spanish West Indies and Venezuela; the Philippine Islands, too, between the years 1565 and 1584.

The newly discovered countries had mines of precious metals and vast expanses of arable land; they offered an excellent market for European goods and skills, and the aborigines were pressed into service as slave laborers. It is no wonder, then, that the possibilities of quick enrichment appealed not only to Cortéz' *conquistadores* [conquerors], who were rewarded by him with *encomiendas* [country estates with Indian slaves], but also brought about an influx of other enterprising adventurers. From the beginning, this latter group included a number of "New Christians," a term used to designate those Jews and their descendants who had accepted baptism in order to remain in Spain at the time of the expulsion, following the decree of May 31, 1492; and those Jews who

* Dr. Wiznitzer is Associate Research Professor of Latin American Jewish History at the University of Judaism, Los Angeles, California. He is the author of *The Records of the Earliest Jewish Community in the New World* and *Jews in Colonial Brazil*.

were forcibly converted in Portugal in the year 1497. A small minority of the New Christians became observant and devout Catholics, but a great number of them remained underground Jews for centuries to come. Ostensibly they were Catholics, in that they went to Church and outwardly observed the Catholic ritual, but at the same time they continued to practice Jewish rites and ceremonies in secret. These Jews and their descendants were called *Anusim* in Hebrew [the forcibly converted]; their scorners branded them as *Marranos* [pigs].¹ In the documents of the Inquisition in Mexico, they were called Hebreos Christianos Nuevos Judaizantes [Judaizing Hebrew New Christians]. Hereinafter we shall refer to them as Judaizers. They emigrated to Mexico partly because of economic opportunities already mentioned, but mainly in order to live far away from the suspicious eyes of their Christian neighbors and acquaintances, so that they might be able to follow and to practice secretly the religion of their ancestors. The Spanish authorities, who had justified the expulsion decree of May, 1492, by their fear of Jews corrupting the Christians in their faith, were also suspicious of the new converts to Christianity and did not trust their sincerity. Thus, Queen Isabella the Catholic gave strict orders that only Old Christians, who could prove that their four grandparents had already been converted to the Catholic faith [*por los quatro costados*] might emigrate to the newly-discovered American territories. After her death, King Ferdinand, however, allowed New Christians to do it. King Charles V cancelled this permission in 1518. On September 5, 1522, a decree was published which allowed new Jewish or Moslem converts and their children to emigrate to New Spain only by special permission of the Crown; those who were already settled there were required to re-embark for Spain on the first available ship.² In January, 1523, the first edict against Jews and other heretics was published in Mexico City, and shortly afterwards, *pregoneros* [town criers]

---

1 Attempts to derive the word "Marrano" from the Hebrew, Aramaic, and Arabic, with various meanings, make little sense. Any Spanish dictionary defines the word very clearly: "a swine, a dirty fellow." The Portuguese priest Francisco de Torregoncilho wrote, "Among the marranos or marrones, whenever one grunts and complains, all the others grunt with him, and the Jews lament in the same manner in tune whenever one of them moans; this is why they are called Marranos." Cf. Francisco de Torregoncilho, *Sentinella contra Judeos* (Coimbra, 1730), chapter II.

2 Alfonso Toro in his Introduction to *Los Judios en la Nueva España*, in *Publicaciones del Archivo General de la Nación* [=PAGN] (Mexico, D.F., 1932), vol. XX, pp. xxi-xxiii. Julio Jimenez Rueda, *Herejias y Supersticiones en la Nueva España* (Mexico, D.F., 1946), pp. 83-84.

announced in the streets of the City that the descendants of Jews and Moslems had to leave New Spain within six months.[3] In spite of the decree, New Christians succeeded in migrating from the Iberian Peninsula to Mexico through the use of assumed names, and by employing false documents concerning their ancestors, as well as by resorting to bribery.

The history of the Judaizers in Mexico is a sad one indeed. The omnipotent Inquisition was their pitiless and deadly enemy.

For a long time the Inquisition in Mexico functioned in a primitive manner. The bishops in their respective dioceses acted as agents of the Spanish Inquisition and were charged with inquisitorial powers. All bishops in the newly-discovered territories were empowered by an order of Don Fr.[4] Francisco de Cisneros, Archbishop of Toledo, General Inquisitor of Spain, on July 22, 1517, to investigate, imprison, prosecute, and punish heretics, and also to release them, if necessary to the secular authorities for capital punishment.[5]

The first persecutor of Judaizers in America was Fr. Vicente de Santa María, General Vicar of the Dominican Order, Superior of the Dominican monastery in Mexico City, who arrived in Mexico in the year 1528.[6] The earliest Judaizers in Mexico, who are known to us by name were Hernando Alonzo, Francisco alias Gonzálo de Morales alias Regaton, and Diego Ocaña. These three Judaizers became the first victims of Fr. Vicente de Santa María.[7]

Hernando Alonzo was born in Niebla, Spain, about the year 1460. He emigrated to Cuba where he settled as a carpenter and

---

[3] Bernal Diaz de Castillo, *Historia Verdadera de la Conquista de la Nueva España* (1st ed.: Madrid, 1632). We used the edition printed in Mexico in 1904, vol. II, p. 397.

[4] Fr. is an abbreviation of the word Fray, Friar, a member of a religious order. This word is always written in abbreviation. Cf. *New Revised Velasquez Spanish and English Dictionary* (New York, 1959), first part, p. 346.

[5] José Toribio Medina, *La Primitiva Inquisición Americana (1493-1569)*; *Documentos* (Santiago de Chile, 1914). Cf. Document I, "Inquisitorial Powers to the Bishops of the Indias," dated Madrid, July 22, 1517, pp. 3-5.

[6] Vicente Riva Palacio, Introduction to José Toribio Medina, *Historia del Tribunal del Santa Oficio de la Inquisición en Mexico* (Santiago de Chile, 1905). We used the edition printed in Mexico in 1952, p. 12.

[7] The manuscripts of the trials of 1528 were lost, but many old men who remembered or were witnesses of the events of 1528 made depositions before the Inquisitors in the year 1574 concerning the three trials of 1528. This document, called "Diligencias sobre Sambenitos Antiguos, Renovación de Elles y Postura de los Que se han Relajado y Requerido por este Santo Oficio, 1574 años" is to be found in the Archivo General de la Nación [=AGN], Mexico City, and was published entirely in the *Publicaciones del Archivo General de la Nación*, vol. XI (Mexico, D.F., 1932), pp. 20-44.

blacksmith. In the year 1516, he there met Hernando Cortéz, and in the year 1520, he left Cuba for Mexico and became a member of Cortéz' army. He helped to build the brigantines that Cortéz, needed for the conquest of Tenochtitlán, since that place was situated in a lake region. Later Cortéz sent Alonzo to pacify the Indians of Panúco, and, in 1525-1526, to participate in the conquest of Guanachuato. Finally, Cortéz rewarded him for all his services, as he did other *conquistadores* by giving him an estate, the estate of Actopan, about forty miles distance from Mexico City. Alonzo possessed Indian slaves, raised cattle, and supplied Mexico City with meat.

He was married three times. His first wife Dona Isabel de Ordaz gave birth to a son in Cuba. The name of his second wife was Ana. Both died in Cuba. In Mexico City, Alonzo married Isabel Ruiz de Aguilar, the beautiful daughter of a tailor who bore him a daughter.

In the year 1528, Fr. Vicente de Santa María received a denunciation asserting that Alonzo was a Judaizer. The denunciation stated that Alonzo had twice baptized his son in Porto Real, once in the church and afterwards at his home. In the presence of invited friends, so the report stated, the boy was put into a washbowl, wine was poured over his head and allowed to run down over his genitals; it was then drunk by the parents and guests. Afterwards they danced around the boy singing the psalm *"Dominus Deus Israel Egypto"*[8] which tells of the liberation by God of Israel from Egypt. Another denunciation asserted that Alonzo kept his wife from going to church during her menstrual period. The Inquisitor jailed Alonzo, charging him with Judaizing, although the facts did not warrant the charge because they were not Jewish rites at all. Alonzo, at first, denied all the accusations, but, under torture, he confessed that he was practicing Judaism. He also declared that he was repentant, and asked the Inquisition for mercy. Any regular tribunal of the Inquisition would have taken into account the fact that Alonzo was being tried for the first time in his life and would have considered his confession, penitence, and plea for mercy as sufficient grounds for leniency. He would have probably been condemned to abjuration of his errors and sentenced to confiscation of his possessions, a prison term and expulsion from

8 *Ibid.*, pp. 20-44, G.R.G. Conway, "Hernando Alonso: A Jewish Conquistador with Cortes in Mexico" in *Publications of the American Jewish Historical Society*, no. 31 (New York, 1938), pp. 9-31.

Mexico. Fr. Vicente de Santa María, however, condemned Alonzo to appear at an auto-da-fé [act of faith ceremony] and after hearing the sentence to be delivered to the secular arm. The secular authority condemned Alonzo to be burnt at the stake on the *Plaza* [square] *de Santiago de Thaltelolco* in Mexico City.[9] The sentence was as usual most probably executed on the day of the auto-da-fé.

Francisco alias Gonzálo de Morales alias Regaton was born in Seville. In the year 1528 we find him as a shopkeeper in Mexico City. There he was imprisoned for living in concubinage. While he was in jail, a letter arrived from the Bishop of San Juan, Puerto Rico, where de Morales had formerly lived, informing the Inquisitor that de Morales' sister had been tried there for Judaizing and burnt at the stake. During her trial, she had confessed that she and her brother used to flog a crucifix and that he had also urinated upon it. De Morales admitted that his sister had told the truth, declared himself repentant and pleaded for mercy. In spite of all that, he was condemned to appear at an auto-da-fé (on the same day as Alonzo), was released to the secular arm and burnt at the stake. It is most probable that both had not been granted the indulgence to be first garroted and afterwards burnt, and they were burned alive at the stake.[10]

Diego de Ocaña was born in Seville. De Ocaña emigrated after the death of his wife, Berta Núñez, first to Santo Domingo and then to Mexico City. He brought his son, Garcia Xuares, and his daughter, Leonor Xuares de Ocaña with him. When, in early 1523, the New Christians were instructed to return to Spain, de Ocaña denounced himself, but managed with the payment of a small fine to remain in Mexico.[11]

In the year 1528, de Ocaña was denounced to the Inquisitor as being a Judaizer, who had been prosecuted by the Inquisition in Seville and reconciled to Catholicism. He had been seen in Mexico City eating meat on Fridays and slaughtering chickens in accordance with Jewish ritual. De Ocaña was known to be a descendant of the Spanish Jewish family de Benadeva.[12]

De Ocaña, in his last will, written in the year 1533, relates, that Fr. Vicente de Santa María had thrown him into a dark cell, where

9 *PAGN*, vol. XX, pp. 20-44.
10 *Ibid.*, pp. 20-44. Bernal Diaz de Castillo, *Historia Verdadera*, vol. II, p. 397, Rueda, *Herejias y Supersticiones*, p. 84.
11 *Ibid.*
12 Last will of Diego Ocaña, manuscript in the AGN, published in *PAGN*, vol. VII (Mexico, D.F., 1932), pp. 1-8.

he was tied and tortured, and had behaved like a man "possessed by the Devil," with the intention to have him put to death. He stated further that the other inquisitorial judges did not agree with Santa María.[13]

In 1528, de Ocaña appeared at the same auto-da-fé with Alonzo and de Morales, but he was only condemned to the abjuration of his errors and to wearing the penitential garment [sambenito] during six months. There were rumors that the influence of his important friend Gonzálo de Salazar had saved his life.[14] De Ocaña's last will is a curiously interesting document. Here he asks that his bones shall one day be transferred to Seville and buried near those of his wife Berta Núñez in the same cemetery. He makes his daughter, Leonor, his principal heir, and bequeaths gifts to Catholic priests and other persons in Seville, so that they may pray for his soul. He disinherits his light-minded son, Garcia Xuarez, and also forbids him to gamble at cards or dice before the age of forty, and stipulates that even afterwards he shall not wager more than two or three ducats a day, and this only as a pastime; and he declares that he shall be accursed if he does not heed his injunction. Rumor had it that de Ocaña had disinherited his son because Garcia Xuarez had refused to be on the side of his father after having been accused of Judaizing.[14a] Believing that Anosico, a boy born to his Indian maid, Antonica, was his own son, de Ocaña bequeathed to Antonica ten Castillian sheep and one ram, and a quantity of clothes; he also requested that she marry a Christian Indian.

De Ocaña asserted repeatedly and solemnly in his last will that in spite of having been a sinner he had always been a good Catholic and that he had been unjustly accused of Judaizing. He added that he had petitioned the General Inquisitor in Spain to revise and annul the sentence against him, and exhorted his heirs to continue to seek justice and to clear the family name in the event of his death before the General Inquisitor would render the decision.[15] Reading de Ocaña's will, one gets the impression that he was really a sincere Christian and not a Judaizer at all.

Between the years 1536 and 1539, a number of other indictments were made by Mexican Inquisitors. These included the following:

13 *Ibid.*, vol. XX, pp. 20-44.
14 *Ibid.*
14a *Ibid.*
15 *Ibid.*, vol. VII, pp. 1-8.

Gonzálo Gómez, living in Michocán (1536); Manuel Borallo (1537); Pedro Ruiz alias Hernandez de Alvor (1538); Anton Carmona, Francisco Serrano, Juan Ruiz, Garcia Hernandez, Beatrix Hernandez, Rodrigo de Soria, Juan de Salamanca, Alvaro Mateos and his wife, Beatrix Gómez, and Francisco Millán (all in the year 1539). These fourteen arraigned people became reconciled to Catholicism.[16] The case of the mentioned Francisco Millán is of special interest.

Francisco Millán was born in Utrera, Spain, of Portuguese-Jewish descent, and worked in Mexico City as a tavernkeeper. His Indian girl slave spread the gossip that Millán was a Jew and that she had seen him lashing an image of Christ. After the Inquisitor had jailed him, Millán deposed that his parents were Jewish and that they had died early, when he was four years of age. He did not know whether or not he had been baptized at all, but he had always considered himself a Jew, although he did not have knowledge of or practiced any Jewish rites. Surgeons of the Inquisition verified that Millán was circumcized. Millán deposed further that he had met many Jews while in Lisbon and had observed their ceremonies through an open door of a Synagogue. He had been afraid to be seen inside. A few months before his arraignment he missed some money and suspecting his Indian girl slave to have stolen it, he had lashed her. In his anger, he then also struck two crucifixes in his room, while screaming "Return my money!" and had broken them; a demon must have influenced him to do such a thing. Millán confessed to have eaten meat during the previous Lent, because his health was not good at the time, and to have had sexual relations with a Moorish girl sometime before, an act which he thought was extenuated because she was not Christian. Finally Millán admitted fully that he had practiced Judaism and specified ceremonies and rites. He deposed that the Judaizers in Mexico helped themselves mutually and did not charge any interest for loans to their own people. Millán then denounced about thirty New Christians for Judaizing, showed himself repentant and asked for mercy. Fr. Juan de Zumarraga in the year 1539 Bishop of Mexico and the apostolic Inquisitor there, permitted Millán to be reconciled to Catholicism. Millán's fortune was confiscated and he was also sentenced to wear

---

[16] J. T. Medina, *La Primitiva Inquisición Americana*, document no. XLIV, pp. 212-282; Rueda, *Herejias y Supersticiones*, pp. 85-86; "Lista de Judios procesados por la Inquisicion de Mexico durante el Siglo XVI." Manuscript in the AGN, published in *PAGN*, vol. XX, pp. 9-13.

a penitential garb for a certain period and expulsion from New Spain.[17]

II

THE ESTABLISHMENT OF A HOLY OFFICE IN MEXICO

In the year 1571, the primitive Inquisitorial Tribunals were replaced in New Spain by a regular establishment, in conformity with the decision of the Spanish King Philip II. Don Diego de Espinosa, General Inquisitor of Spain, then appointed Dr. Pedro Moya de Contreras as Inquisitor for New Spain. He arrived on September 12, 1571, to assume his duties. On November 4, 1571, an impressive ceremony in the Cathedral of Mexico City was held in presence of the Viceroy Martin Enriquez, the ecclesiastical and secular authorities, and the entire population of the City. Everyone twelve years of age or over had been summoned the day before by town criers to assist in inaugurating the foundation of a Holy Office in New Spain. All those present agreed under oath not to tolerate heretics among them, to denounce them to the Holy Office, and to help persecute them as "wolves and rabid dogs" [lobos y perros rabiosos]. Otherwise they would suffer major excommunication.[18]

The customary Edict of Grace was proclaimed, admonishing people who were practicing well-known and enumerated Jewish rites and ceremonies to denounce themselves within six days, in which case they would be treated mith mercy. The newly appointed Inquisitor thus departed from the customary term of thirty to forty days.[19] The manuscript of the original Edict of Grace, published in the year 1571 in Mexico, is no longer available, but from

---

17 Manuscript of Millán's trial in AGN, tomo 20, no. 8 of the Ramo de Inquisición. Extract published in PAGN, vol. XX, pp. 20-44. Cf. "Lista de judios...." PAGN, vol. XX, pp. 9-13, and Rueda, Herejias y Supersticiones, pp. 85-86.

18 Vicente Riva Palacio, Mexico a Traves de Los Siglos, vol. II, pp. 401-403, (Barcelona); J. T. Medina, Historia del Tribunal del Santo Oficio, de la Inquisición en Mexico, pp. 33-40; Genaro Garcia y Carlos Pereyra, Documentos ineditos y mui raros para la Historia de Mexico (Mexico, D.F., 1906), tomo V, p. 269. The "Edict of Oath" was proclaimed on November 3, 1571. An excommunimation formula contained many maledictions for the disobedient, that they might be punished by the plague and disasters that came upon Pharoah and Sodom and Gomorrah; their food, bed, and clothing were cursed; their children were to become orphans and to be always in need. All the curses of the Old and New Testament were invoked upon them, etc.

19 Riva Palacio, op. cit., pp. 404.

a later Mexican Edict of Grace, dated March 22, 1621, we can precisely verify which rites and customs were considered in New Spain as Judaizing.[20]

The consequence of the Edict of Grace of November 4, 1571, was a reign of terror and panic. Immediately after the ceremony in the Cathedral, the new Holy Office began receiving denunciations of people suspected of the crimes enumerated in the Edict. Within six months the Holy Office was investigating more than 400 such denunciations. Most of them were without foundation; nonetheless, 127 persons were arrested. Meanwhile the public prosecutor [*fiscal*], the inquisitorial secretaries and other officers of the Tribunal arrived in Mexico City from Spain. Thus, Dr. Contreras was soon enabled to prepare the first regular auto-da-fé.[21]

It should be stated at this point that the assumption that Judaizers were the main problem of the Mexican Holy Office is definitely wrong. During the nearly 300 years from the conquest of Mexico to its independence from Spain, Judaizers represented only about sixteen per cent of all the people tried by the Inquisition there. There was not a single Judaizer among the victims of the first three autos-da-fé, which were celebrated on February 28, 1574, March 6, 1575, and February 19, 1576. About 126 persons were tried, and condemnations were obtained for a variety of offenses: fornication, bigamy, blasphemy, Lutheranism (six Lutherans were condemned to be burnt at the stake and were executed); several Franciscan and Dominican friars were condemned for soliciting sexual favors from people who had come to them to confess their sins.[22]

The basic Law of the Mexican Inquisition was derived from the Constitution of the Spanish Inquisition, which was set forth in the *Instructions of Sevilla* and in the *Instructions of Toledo*. The former had been elaborated upon by the first General Inquisitor of Spain, Fr. Tomás de Torquemada and his assistants, and proclaimed in the year 1484 in Seville. The latter had been developed by the General Inquisitor, Don Fernando de Valdez,

---

20 "Edicto de la Inquisicion expedido par la ciudad de Mexico, estados y provincias de la Nueva España, Nueva Galicia, Guatemala, Nicaragua, las Philipinas y sus cercancias, Mexico, 22 de marzo de 1621". Cf. J. J. Rueda, *Herejias y Supersticiones*, pp. 86-87.

21 Cf. J. T. Medina, *Historia del Tribunal del Santo Oficio*, pp. 47-50.

22 *Ibid.*, pp. 60-74.

and proclaimed in the year 1561. Each trial was a struggle of "the wolf with the sheep."[23]

The procedures at the trials are well known and described in many publications dealing with the Spanish Inquisition.[24]

The methods of torture employed in Mexico were somewhat milder than those used in Spain. They were the cords [cordeles], the rack [potro], combined mith iron rings [garrotilhos] and the water torture [agua].[25] The main objective of the Inquisitors, besides the confiscation of the possessions of the accused heretics, was that the accused should repent and seriously return to the bosom of the Catholic Church, in order that their souls could be saved during their lifetime, and for eternity, since God does not desire the death of the impious, but that he be converted and continue to live ("Nolo mortem impii, sed ut convertatur et vivat").[25a] The great majority of the accused Judaizers in Mexico as elsewhere declared that they were repentant and asked for mercy. Therefore, they were condemned to appear at an auto-da-fé in order to abjure publicly their heretical errors and to hear the recitation of the sentence. They were sentenced to the loss of their possessions through confiscation, to prison terms, to expulsion from Mexico to

23 Fray Tomás de Torquemada, "Instrucciones del Oficio de la Sancta Inquisicion hechas por el muy Reverendo Señor Tomás de Torquemada Prior del monasterio de Sancta Segovia, primero Inquisidor general de los reynos y Senorios de España (Sevilla, October 29, 1481) called Instrucciones de Torquemada, they are to be found in the Publicaciones del Archivo General de la Nación, Ramo de Inquisición (Mexico City, 1519), Exp. 1. The General Inquisitors of Spain who succeeded Torquemada added to the mentioned Instructions with many others, and there exists in the same Archive a "Copilación" of all these complementary Instructions. In order to have these Instructions simplified and uniform, Don Valdez published in the year 1561 the so-called "Ordenanzas de Toledo" with the title: "Copilación de las instrucciones del Oficio del Sancta Inquisicion hechas en Toledo año de mil y quinientos y sesenta y uno." (Granada, 1561.) Besides the mentioned Instructions and compilations of these Instructions, the Mexican Inquisitors used for reference the beginning of the book "Tractatus contra hereticam pravitatem et etiam tractatus de irregularitate" (Salamanca, 1519). There exists also in the Archives a booklet with the title "Cartilla de Comisarios del Santo Oficio de la Inquisición de México" (Mexico; cf. also Riva Palacio, Mexico a Traves de los Siglos, pp. 406-408, and Eduardo Pallares, El Procedimiento Inquisitorial (Mexico, 1951) Appendix, pp. 99-169.

24 Cf. especially Bernard Picart, Ceremonies et Coutûmes Religieuses de tous les Peuples du Monde, vol. II, (Amsterdam, 1739) and Eduardo Pallares, op. cit.

25 Riva Palacio, op. cit., p. 427. He publishes Instructions from the Inquisition Tribunal in Cordoba (1646), from the Tribunal of the Kingdom of Galicia (1662), from Don Gonzálo in Madrid to the Tribunal of Santiago (1662) with elaborated details on how to proceed with and handle the various torture instruments, pp. 415-422.

25a Cf. Ezekiel, chapter 33:11.

Spain and often to public lashing. The majority of the condemned Judaizers were called the reconciled [to Catholicism], the *Reconciliados*. Those expelled were required to return to Spain at their own expenses. Because of their poverty, they could not pay for their trip to Spain and somehow contrived to remain in Mexico illegally. Then they usually again got into trouble with the Holy Office.

The autos-da-fé were celebrated in Mexico with an extraordinary show of splendor and were a great spectacle wherewith the Holy Office impressed the populace and satisfied their cruel instincts. The largest public square of Mexico City was usually chosen for the event. Several large tribunes were erected there for the occasion, some of them decorated with rich carpets and tapestries. On the tribune reserved for the Viceroy, his family, and close friends lunch and refreshments were served. An alcove was even provided for the Viceroy's siesta. Other tribunes were reserved for the members of the Holy Office, guests of honor, the town Council, and other dignitaries. A special pulpit was set up for the eminent guest preacher, invited especially for the occasion, and there were rows of seats for the ordinary people. Those who could not get seats or who sought a better view of the spectacle, climbed up the trees or monuments in the square and adjacent streets.

Those accused who were condemned to be released to the arm of the secular power [for capital punishment] were called the released ones, the *Relajados*. They were visited the evening before the day of the auto-da-fé which also was the day of their execution, by clergymen who spent the night with them, trying by persuasion and even by argument to convert them. They would not desist from their efforts even in the face of the stoniest obstinacy of the heretic and they continued their efforts until the last breath of the heretic at the stake. The clergymen not only spent the night before the auto-da-fé in the prison-cells with the condemned, but also accompanied them during the procession early next morning to the square where the auto-da-fé was celebrated and afterwards to the burning place [*Quemadero*]. The great majority of the *relajados* allowed themselves to be convinced to appear in the procession of the auto-da-fé with a cross in their hands, to kiss a cross publicly, and to recite a Catholic prayer. Even in case the doomed *relajado* agreed to kiss a cross or to say a prayer in the last moments of his life, he gained the easier course of being first strangulated to death by garrotes and burned immediately afterwards, rather than being burned alive. Even so, they were martyrs. In Mexico as elsewhere a few Judaizers were heroes and martyrs. They refused to give in, to kiss a cross, to say a Catholic prayer or to appear at the auto-da-fé carrying a cross in their hands and wished to be burnt alive *al kiddush ha-shem* [for the sanctification of God's name.]

Those condemned to death were mounted after the auto-da-fé on pack animals (donkeys or mules) and were borne through the avenues and streets of Mexico City to the *Quemadero,* where stakes and pyres had been erected. They were closely accompanied by the exhorting priests, by officers of the secular justice and by a company of soldiers. The whole population was on the avenues and streets and on the trees to see the gloomy procession. The condemned were also accompanied by trumpeters and town criers, who publicized the crime of each of the condemned.

In 1528, the *Quemadero* in Mexico City was on the Square of Santiago de Thaltelelco, and later, on the Plaza de Marques. From 1574 on, it was on the square known as Tianguis de San Hipolito, in front of the Convent of San Diego, which is situated to the west of the present-day Avenida de Alameda. The martyrs and heroes who insisted that they be burnt alive were often beaten during the death march to the *Quemadero* by the mob and by the very soldiers who were there to protect them from lynching. Fire was put to their beard and faces after they had been tied to the stake by the executioners, while priests held crosses to their lips begging them to die as Catholics. The executioners fanned the fire, the mob piled on more wood and looked on as the martyr's body was consumed. The ashes were shoveled into the muddy waters of the ditch around the Alameda.

It was considered as a great triumph and victory for the Inquisition and Catholicism to convert a relapsed heretic Jew by having him kiss a cross or saying a Catholic prayer even in the last moments of his life when he obviously was frightened of being burnt at the stake alive. On the other hand, it was considered a crushing defeat of the Inquisition and Catholicism whenever a crypto-Jew insisted on meeting a fiery death for the sanctification of God's name.

III

THE TRIALS OF JUDAIZERS FROM 1579 TO 1596

The first Judaizers tried before the regular Inquisitorial Tribunal, established in 1571, were Hernando Alvarez Pliego and

Garcia Gonzáles Bergemero. Pliego was born in Oporto, Portugal, and lived in Tula, Mexico. He was denounced as a Judaizer, but the court could not come to a decision and instituted inquiries about him in Spain on March 22, 1576. Although the Chief Inquisitor, Dr. Contreras, eventually voted for Pliego's acquittal, he was opposed by the six other members of the court. An elderly, depressed, and very ill man, Pliego appeared at the auto-da-fé of December 15, 1577, as reconciled [*reconciliado*] and was condemned to pay a fine of 500 gold pesos for the expenses of the court.[26]

Bergemero was born in Albuquerque, Portugal, and came to Mexico City in 1559. When the Holy Office made investigations concerning several suspicious immigrants the name of Bergemero was among them. This man was about seventy years of age and the father of several sons, one of whom was an Augustinian monk. On July 6, 1579, a report came from the tribunal of Llerena in Spain that many of Bergemero's near relatives had been tried and condemned by the Inquisition for Judaizing. As a result, Bergemero was imprisoned on the same day. He admitted that two of his brothers and their wives and also his uncle had been burned in Llerena for Judaizing, but he avowed that he was himself a good Christian. The public prosecutor charged Bergemero with being an "apostate and a negative obstinate Judaizer." He demanded capital punishment for Bergemero. The court tried to induce Bergemero to make a clear confession and to become reconciled to Catholicism, but the accused did not co-operate and the defense lawyers conceded him by the court, declined to defend him. The court declared Bergemero "a Judaizing heretic, impenitent, negative, a renegade, and a protector and accomplice of heretics." He appeared at the auto-da-fé of October 11, 1579, as a *relajado,* and consequently was delivered on the same day to the secular arm and condemned to capital punishment. It is not mentioned in the manuscript of the trial, but Bergemero certainly agreed to die as a Catholic (it was sufficient for him, as stated above, to kiss a cross or to recite a Catholic prayer in the last moments of his life), because he was

---

26 Manuscript of Pliego's trial in Archivo General de la Nación, Mexico City, tomo 59, no. 1 of the *Ramo de Inquisición.* Cf. J. T. Medina *Historia del Tribunal del Santa Oficio de la Inquisición en Mexico* (Mexico, 1952), pp. 74-75; *Libro primero de votos de la Inquisición de Mexico,* 1573-1600 (Mexico, 1649), p. 81.

not burnt alive, but first garroted and afterwards burnt at the stake.[27]

IV

LUIS DE CARVAJAL, GOVERNOR OF THE NEW KINGDOM OF LEON

The most prominent victim of the Mexican Inquisition in the sixteenth century was Governor Luis de Carvajal. He was born about 1539 in Mogodorio, Portugal, of New Christian parents, Gaspar de Carvajal and Catalina de Leon. His grandparents on his father's side were Gutierrez Vasquez de la Cueva and Francisca de Carvajal. Luis lived and attended school in Mogodorio until he was eight years old, when his father took him on a trip to visit relatives in Sahagim. They then went to Salamanca, where his father became sick and died. Duarte de Leon, his mother's brother and a factor for the King of Portugal, took the young Luis to Lisbon and raised him. Later he obtained for Luis a post as accountant and cashier to the Crown on the island of Cabo Verde where Luis worked for many years. He subsequently returned to Lisbon and then removed to Seville, where he married Dona Guiomar de Rivera, a native of Lisbon. After having lost a great deal of money as a businessman in Guadalquivir, in order to renew his fortune, he decided to set sail for Mexico with a cargo of wine. He also secured an appointment from the King of Spain as Admiral, without salary, of a fleet that embarked from the island of Palma for New Spain in 1567. He became friendly with the newly appointed Viceroy of New Spain, Don Martín Enríquez, who traveled aboard his vessel. Upon reaching Jamaica he captured three British privateers and handed them over to the Governor of Jamaica without taking any of the booty for himself. After his

---

27 Manuscript of Bergemero's trial in AGN., tomo 59, as above no. 6. The certificate on the last page of the trial concerning Bergemero's execution reads translated into English:

I, Rodrigo Vezerro, public notary of Mexico, certify that immediately and instantly after the order of the Señor Magistrate was given to the Chief Bailiff Don Carlo de Semano, he started to execute the mentioned sentence and the mentioned Garcia González was brought while riding on a beast of burden through the San Francisco street— accompanied by a towncrier who disclosed his delict—to the part of the San Ipolito market where the pyres are located. The mentioned Garcia González was strangled with a cord on the throat until he naturally died. The corpse of the mentioned Garcia González and his bones were burnt by wood and an ardent fire. I was present until the fire stopped at about five in the afternoon—more or less—and at that time no flesh or bones were any more seen and many people assisted [the execution].

arrival in Mexico, he sold the cargo of wine and purchased a cattle ranch in Panúco from Don Lope de Sosa.

Luis soon distinguished himself by another exploit. In 1568, the pirate vessels of Sir John Hawkins [called Joan Aquines] were defeated by the Spaniards off the coast of Mexico. One hundred survivors landed near Tampico, of which city Carvajal was mayor. Frightened by the pirates, the inhabitants of the town were about to run away, when Carvajal went out to meet them with a force of only twenty men. He forced eighty-eight survivors to surrender; the others had already been killed by Indians. Carvajal dispatched the prisoners to the Viceroy of Mexico City, where many of them were later tried and condemned by the Inquisition as Lutheran heretics. Shortly afterwards the Viceroy asked Carvajal to subdue rebellious Indians in Xalpa, Jelitla, and Chapuluacan, where they had destroyed a monastery and churches. Within ten months, Carvajal brought them under control. He then rebuilt with his own money the village of Xalpa, constructed a strong fort, a church, and a monastery, and pacified the whole region. After his return to his ranch in Panúco, he won a hard-fought battle against the Chichimecas Indians. About 1576, the Viceroy requested his aid in fighting the Indians in the country adjoining the Huasteca region and in invading this territory. In the performance of this duty, he opened up the area which was to become the New Kingdom of Leon.

In 1578, Carvajal went to Spain in order to request from the King compensation for his patriotic deeds and to bring his family to Mexico. He was then about forty years old and had been absent from his family for some eleven years. Carvajal bore with him laudatory letters of recommendation from the Viceroy Enríquez and obtained from the King the right to subjugate 40,000 square leagues of territory in Mexico. The King appointed Carvajal as Governor and Captain General of this region during his lifetime and during the lifetime of anyone he might designate as his successor in the event he did not have a son. He was also accorded the privilege of taking with him to Mexico one hundred married or unmarried people without being obligated to ask of them any proof that they were Old Christians. Carvajal undertook to convert the Indians of the region to Catholicism and to build several villages that were settled by Spaniards. Thus far, his trip was successful. However, he was unable to convince his wife Dona Guimar and her family to accompany him, since she had always been a secret

Judaizer, whereas Carvajal was a good Catholic. The others who decided to accompany Carvajal to Mexico were composed partly of Old Christians, partly of New Christians. The New Christian members of his family who were in the party were as follows: Dona Francisca Núñez de Carvajal, his sister, Francisco Rodrigues de Mattos, her husband, who was a businessman and tax collector in the service of the Count de Benavente, and several of their children —Balthazar Rodrigues de Carvajal, Luis de Carvajal, Jr., Miguel [a child], Dona Isabel Rodriguez de Andrade [the widow of Gabriel Herrera], Dona Catalina de la Cueva [the widow of Antonio Dias de Caceras], Dona Mariana de Carvajal, Dona Leonor de Andrade [married later to Jorge de Almeida], and Anica, a young girl. Their son the Dominican friar, Gaspar de Carvajal had come one year earlier to Mexico City.

Before embarking, Francisco Rodrigues de Mattos and his family visited Carvajal in Seville, which was the residence of the Governor's wife, Dona Guiomar. She and Dona Isabel, Francisco's daughter and her niece, were both Judaizers and quickly became good friends. Dona Guiomar took her aside one day and begged her to tell her husband the Governor after they had arrived in Mexico that "he must observe the old Law of Moses, since otherwise nothing could go right." She was to wait for an opportune moment when he was overwhelmed by work and trouble. Isabel promised to do so and to inform her about the Governor's reaction. In the event he was favorable to the idea, she proposed to come to Mexico to live with him. Dona Guiomar also requested that Isabel speak in the same vein to Captain Felipe Núñez, a relative of hers who had fought under the Governor for several years and always accompanied him. Dona Isabel promised under oath to do this favor and to keep everything in strict confidence.

Finally, after purchasing a ship with his own money, the Governor set sail for Mexico with his party and with a full cargo of animals, plants, wine, agricultural implements, and other supplies. The Governor and his relatives first settled in Panúco, where they eked out a living by hard work. Carvajal himself traveled a great deal; discovered a number of silver mines; founded and settled the cities of Leon and Cueva; fought and subjugated many Indians, whom he converted to Christianity; and built a number of churches. There is no doubt but that the Governor was an exceedingly hard worker, a courageous soldier, an excellent administrator, and a highly successful colonizer. His family, however, was unhappy in Panúco and desired to settle elsewhere. His nieces Dona Catalina and Leonor married, his nephews, Luis, Jr. and Balthazar, and their father Francisco Rordigues de Mattos looked for opportunities in Mexico City, though shortly afterwards Francisco took sick there and died.

One day the news came to Panúco that Dona Guiomar, the Governor's wife, had passed away in Seville. Shortly afterwards, Dona Isabel decided that the time had come to keep the promise she had given to her late aunt. She seized her opportunity after the Governor had finished his customary recitation of the Psalms one evening. As he concluded with the *"Gloria Patri et Filio et Spiritui Sancto Dominus nostro Jesu Christo,"* Dona Isabel shouted:

> There is no Christ: How can a wise man like you follow the wrong way of the law of Jesus Christ? It means that you will go to hell.

The Governor became so enraged that he gave her a slap that knocked her to the ground. He said sharply:

> What do you mean by saying that there is no Christ? . . . Oh, that you had never been born.

Her brothers and sisters heard the dispute and rushed in from the next room. The Governor exclaimed: "You should choke this girl." Of course, he realized that the whole family, except for the friar, Gaspar, were Judaizers. Later, Dona Isabel also tried to turn Captain Felipe Núñez against the law of Christ, but he answered that he believed that Christ came into the world, died, and rose from the dead is order to save them.

About the year 1583, the Governor had a serious conflict with the Viceroy Conde de Coruña concerning the jurisdiction over several villages. Now it so happened that the Viceroy possessed information from a priest, who had lived in Huasteca and who disliked the Governor, that Carvajal was a descendent of New Christians. On the strength of this intelligence the Viceroy ordered that Carvajal be arrested and imprisoned in Mexico City. He was left to languish there for several years. In March, 1589, Captain Felipe Núñez denounced Dona Isabel to the Holy Office as a secret Jewess. He also asserted that she had tried to convert him to Judaism. After she had confessed the truth of this charge, the Public Prosecutor immediately suspected the Governor of Judaizing or at least of not denouncing his Judaizing family to the Inquisition. He, therefore, asked the Viceroy to remand the Governor to the secret prison of the Holy Office, which was done on April 14, 1589.

The Governor told the Inquisitors that he was a Catholic, the son of Old Christian parents, and that from his first years he had been brought up in the Catholic faith, for which he had always fought and for which he was ready to die. He made the sign of the cross and knew the catechism and all points of Christian doctrine perfectly. He repeated the Paternoster, Ave Maria, the Credo, Salve Regina, the Ten Commandments, and the text of the general confession. He stated that his sister Dona Francisca had married Francisco de Mattos, who, as he now understood, had converted her to Judaism and that they had brought up their children as Jews. All of them, he said, were his personal enemies. He told of the discussion with his niece and said that he had mentioned the event to his confessor at the time, asking him whether he had committed a sin by not denouncing her to the Holy Office. The confessor, whose name he mentioned, had advised that he was not guilty of any sin. He deposed that he had no time to denounce the family because he was too busy with the war against the Indians. However, he had separated himself from his nephew Luis de Carvajal, Jr. [whom he had previously intended to nominate as governor in his stead] and from his nephew Balthazar, his accountant in Panúco. He detailed the story of his life in a defense writ that he delivered to the court at the request of his lawyer Licenciado Valdes in October, 1589. There can be no doubt but that the Governor was a fervent Catholic and not a secret Jew in any way.

The Public Prosecutor was of a different opinion. He accused Carvajal of having been an accomplice of Jewish apostates and demanded the heaviest punishment. The tribunal voted twice on his case, once on November 8, 1589, and the second time on February 13, 1590, and decided that he was guilty as an accomplice and concealer of Jewish heretics and therefore had to be sentenced. He appeared at the *auto* of February 24, 1590, which was celebrated in the cathedral. He carried the wax candle of a reconciled penitent, was required to abjure his offense *de vehementi*,[28] and was sen-

---

28 The tribunal could condemn to a light abjuration called *"de levi"* or to a vehement abjuration called *"de vehementi."* In the first case, the condemned would in case of a relapse not be liable to capital punishment. In the second case a relapser would under any circumstances be released to the secular arm for capital punishment. Cf. Bernard Picart, *The Religious Ceremonies and Customs of the Several Nations of the Known World* (London, 1731), p. 243.

tenced to expulsion from New Spain for a period of six years. After the *auto* the governor was returned to the Viceroy's prison because of the criminal offense pending against him. This man, who had been so powerful in Mexico only one year before, could not survive this humiliation and died shortly afterwards at the age of fifty-one. The Holy Office gradually exterminated all the members of his Judaizing family except for his nephew the Dominican friar Gaspar de Carvajal and others who fled to Europe.[29]

V

THE TRIALS OF OTHER CARVAJAL FAMILY MEMBERS

At the same *auto* of February 24, 1590, most of the members of Luis de Carvajal's family in Mexico were tried and sentenced for Judaizing. Dona Isabel Rodriguez de Andrade, his niece, was the first of the group to be imprisoned by the Holy Office, after she had been denounced by Captain Felipe Núñez. Her first hearing occurred on March 16, 1589, when she was about thirty years of age. At this hearing she refused to make any confession. Later, however, she admitted that her deceased husband, Gabriel Herrera, and Dona Guiomar, the late wife of Governor Carvajal, had taught her Judaism. She obviously tried to refrain from denouncing living Judaizers in order to spare them the tortures of the Inquisition. In spite of the fact that an enmity existed between her and the Governor, she stated emphatically that her uncle was a good Christian and said that she did not want "the just and innocent to atone for the sinner."

After hearing the confession of Judaizing, the court condemned her to be tortured *in caput alienum* [coerced to accuse others].[29] She was stripped to the waist, to her great humiliation, and her arms were bound with the *cordeles* [cords]. She was now admonished to tell the truth, but she replied that she had nothing further to say. When the cords were twisted, however, she confessed that her

---

[29] The manuscript of the Governor's trial in AGN., vol. II of the Riva Palacio Collection, has been completely published under the title *Processo integro de Luis Carvajal el Viejo, Gobernador del Nueva Reino de Leon, por Judaizante,* in *PAGN,* vol. XX (Mexico, 1932), pp. 207-372. Cf. Alfonso Toro, *La Familia Carvajal,* tomo 1 (Mexico, D.F., 1944). An English translation of the trial manuscript exists in the Cambridge University Library, England, containing 249 pages and 4 photos. Cf. J. Street, "The G.R.G. Conway Collection in Cambridge University Library: A. Checklist" in *The Hispanic American Historical Review,* vol. XXXVII, no. 1, (Durham, February, 1957), p. 74.

mother and her brothers Balthazar and Luis, Jr., were Judaizers and had taught her Judaism. She then avowed that she had told everything. After a second twist of the cords the victim screamed that they were killing her and begged them to stop. Since she could no longer withstand the pain, she denounced her entire family as Judaizers, together with other people living in Mexico. Thus, it was her testimony that led to the arraignment not only of the Governor but also of her mother and most of her blood relatives. Dona Isabel begged the court for mercy, and was sentenced as a *reconciliado* [reconciled] with the usual punishment of confiscation of her possessions, the wearing of the *sambenito*, and a prison term of four years.[30]

Dona Francisca Núñez de Carvajal, the mother of Dona Isabel and of eight other children, was fifty years of age at the time of her trial. As was the case with her daughter, she was ordered to the torture of *in caput alienum* after she had failed to give sufficient information. When she learned that she was to be stripped to the waist in the presence of the court, Dona Francisca screamed:

> Strangle me now, but do not strip me; do not insult me. I prefer a thousand deaths. Remember that I am a woman and an honest widow! I have already told you that I believe in the Law of Moses and not in that of Jesus Christ, and I have nothing more to say!

But her pleas were of no avail. Admonished to tell the truth, she was stripped to the waist, her arms and legs were tied, and she was subjected to the torture of the *cordeles* up to five twists of the rope. Broken by this torment, Dona Francisca told in detail of the Jewish ceremonies and rites she had practiced, saying that she and her daughter Isabel had often recited together the Jewish prayers and hymns. She confessed that she had learned Judaism from the teaching of her late husband, Francisco Rodrigues de Mattos. Not yet satisfied, the court ordered that she be placed on her back and the torture be continued. After three hours, the procedure was stopped when the victim appeared to be in dying condition. The court doctor remained with her while the court recessed for lunch and siesta. When the court reconvened they ordered the torture to begin again. Terror-stricken, Dona Francisca confessed that all her children, with the exception of Fray Gaspar,

30 The article, "La familia Carvajal," in Vicente Riva Palacio Payno, *El Libro Rojo*, (Mexico, 1870 and 1946), pp. 173-200.

had been taught the Jewish rites and ceremonies by her and her husband and that they were all practicing Judaizers. She asked the court for mercy and received the same sentence as her daughter Isabel.[31]

Don Francisco Rodrigues de Mattos, the deceased husband of Dona Francisca, was sentenced *relajado muerto* [released as dead][32] by reason of his widow's confession, and an effigy of him was carried in the same auto-da-fé[33] and his body exhumed and burnt at the stake.

Balthazar Rodrigues de Carvajal, their son, was sentenced *relajado en estatua* [released in effigy] since he had been able to escape to Spain and afterwards to Italy.[34]

Luis de Carvajal, Jr., whose case is doubtless the most interesting of all the Judaizers in Mexico during the sixteenth century, is treated at length in the next chapters.

Dona Catalina de la Cueva, a daughter of Don Francisco and Dona Francisca, and the widow of Antonio Dias de Caceres, was sentenced as a *reconciliada* to appear in the auto-da-fé, to wear the *sambenito,* and to spend one year in prison.[35]

Dona Mariana de Carvajal, another daughter, seventeen years of age, knew the Vulgate Bible almost by heart and recited several passages from it to the Inquisitors. She also repeated certain prayers in Spanish. She was condemned as a *reconciliada* and was sentenced to two years in prison and the wearing of the *sambenito.*[36]

Dona Leonor de Andrade, another daughter, sixteen years of age, married to Jorge de Almeida, was also sentenced as a *reconciliada* to the wearing of the *sambenito* and to a prison term of one year.[37]

Fray Gaspar de Carvajal was charged with failing to denounce his family as Judaizers although he knew of their practices. Probably because of his habit and to his lesser offense he was not required to appear in the auto-da-fé of 1590, but was condemned to abjure *de*

---

[31] Manuscript of Doña Francisca's trial in Archivo General de la Nación, tomo 1488 del Ramo de Inquisición, 12 of the collection Riva Palacio. Cf. J. T. Medina, *Historia del Tribunal,* pp. 125-126.

[32] Those accused who had passed away before the auto-da-fé was held, were released to the secular power and their effigy, carried in the procession, was burnt at the *Quemadero.*

[33] *Ibid.,* p. 108.

[34] *Ibid.*

[35] Cf. Vicente Riva Palacio y Payno, *op. cit.,* pp. 173-220.

[36] *Ibid.*

[37] *Ibid.*

levi in the presence of other Dominican friars. He was also forbidden to perform his priestly duties for six months, during which time he was kept in seclusion in the Dominican Convent in Mexico City.[38]

Other Judaizers who were tried at this time included Dona Catalina de Leon, the cousin of Governor Carvajal, who was reconciled with the usual punishments;[39] and her husband Gonzálo Perez Ferro, who refused to confess at first. He was put to the torture and condemned to abjure *de vehementi,* and was expelled from New Spain.[40] Two other men not related to the Carvajals were also arraigned. Hernando Rodriguez de Herrera, a businessman from Fondon, Portugal, was reconciled with the usual punishments.[41] Tomás de Fonseca Castellanos, another businessman from Portugal, who lived in the mining region of Taxco, was the only accused Judaizer who was acquitted. He received an *absolucion de la instancia* [acquittal of instance] since he was able to prove that he had been denounced falsely by his worst enemy.[42]

VI

LUIS DE CARVAJAL, JUNIOR: THE FIRST TRIAL

On April 18, 1589, the Public Prosecutor of the Holy Office in Mexico City requested that the inquisitorial judges imprison Luis de Carvajal, Jr. This action was taken as a result of the testimony of his uncle, Governor Luis de Carvajal, and of his brother Gaspar de Carvajal, both of whom incriminated the young man as a Judaizer. A further charge against him was based upon his failure to denounce the Judaizing practices of his sister Dona Isabel Rodriguez de Andrade. The Inquisitors signed the warrant of arrest on April 20, 1589. Since Luis could not immediately be found in Mexico City, a search was instituted for him in Taxco, Sultepeque, and other towns of the mining region in which Luis was accustomed to sell goods. He was ultimately found hiding in the house of his mother, Dona Francisca, when she was seized on the night of May 9, 1589. He was brought at once to the secret prison of the Inquisition.

---

38 J. T. Medina, *op. cit.,* p. 108.
39 *Ibid.,* p. 108.
40 *Ibid.*
41 *Ibid.*
42 *Ibid.,* pp. 109f. In case the public prosecutor could not prove the culpability of the accused the case was dismissed by an acquittal of instance (impelling motive) .

Luis' first hearing took place three days afterwards. On this occasion he told the Inquisitors that he was born in Benavente, in the year 1567, and was now a merchant. He recited the names of his parents and of his brothers and sisters. These names are already well known to the reader from the account of the trial of Luis' uncle, the Governor. He stated that his maternal grandparents had been Gaspar de Carvajal and Catalina de Leon, both of Benavente and both of whom were deceased. He also stated in detail that he had been taught reading, writing, and calculation in Benavente, and that he had further studied Latin and rhetoric at the Jesuit school there for three years. His parents, he said, left Benavente for Medina del Campo in Spain when he was eleven years old. He also declared that he had been baptized and confirmed by the Bishop in Benavente, and recited for the judges the Paternoster, the Credo, the Salve Regina, the formula for the general confession—all in Latin—and the Ten Commandments.

Other points in his story were that he later sailed with his family on the vessel of the Governor and landed in Tampico, Mexico. He resided in this place and in Panúco until 1584. In this year he removed to Mexico City and became active as a trader in the mining region. He bought clothes, shoes, food, wine, etc., in the port of Vera Cruz and Mexico City and sold these goods in Taxco, Sultepeque, and Zacualpa. When asked by the Inquisitors whether he knew the reason for his imprisonment, Luis related that there had been family quarrels between him and the Governor. He asserted, too, that the Governor had induced all of them to follow him to Mexico by making deceitful promises, and that the entire family was impoverished and felt lost there. Although he supposed that his uncle had caused his imprisonment by denouncing him, he stated that his conscience was clear and that he had done nothing countrary to Catholic doctrine.

During two further hearings in the months of May and July in the year 1589, Luis confessed that he and his brother Balthazar left Mexico City for Vera Cruz at the time the Governor had been transferred to the prison of the Holy Office, because they feared he would denounce them. While Balthazar remained in Vera Cruz, Luis returned to Mexico City because of his anxiety about the fate of his mother.

At each hearing Luis was admonished to speak the truth in good conscience so that he would be favored by the mercy of the court instead of having to endure its justice. Since he was not yet twenty-five years old, he was represented by a curator nominated by the court, one, Gaspar de Valdes, an advocate attached to the Holy Office. During the proceedings he consistently maintained that he was innocent and that he had nothing to confess

The Public Prosecutor, Dr. Lobo Guerrero, finally read a writ of accusation against him during the hearing of July 27, 1589:

> Luis, a baptized and confirmed Christian, is a heretic and apostate against the Catholic Church. A descendant of Jews, he has returned to Judaism and has practiced the ceremonies and rites of the Law of Moses, believing that he could obtain salvation in that way.

A number of detailed charges were levelled against him, viz.:

> A parent [father] of Luis had asked him while he, the father, lay dying to wash his corpse according to the Jewish rite in order that it should not be buried unclean; Luis had studied the Old Testament and the Prophets in order to be more knowledgeable in his practice of Judaism; he quoted the Prophets habitually; and it was impossible to convince him that the Prophets had predicted that Jesus Christ would come as the Messiah; he had run away to Vera Cruz when his sister, Isabel de Andrade was imprisoned by the Holy Office and finally that he had protected Judaizers by not denouncing them.

In consideration of the charges, the Prosecutor asked that Luis' possessions be confiscated for the King's Treasury and that he be delivered to the secular arm for punishment (execution). If, in the opinion of the court, the charges did not seem to be substantiated, he urged that Luis be tortured in order to induce him to confess the truth. Luis read the bill of indictment and declared that he did not know whether he was a descendant of Jews or of Old Christians. He alleged that he was unaware that the washing of the dead was a Jewish rite and that he had told a Negro slave to wash the corpse of his father only because it needed such attention after the prolonged illness. He asserted that he had told the truth and had no guilt to confess. At another hearing on August 2, 1589, Luis' court-appointed lawyer admonished him to confess the whole truth, but Luis reiterated his denial of guilt and the court adjourned.

On August 7, 1589, Luis appeared *sua sponte* [voluntarily] before the Inquisitors. He went down on his knees, kissed the floor, shed tears, beat his breast, and said: *"Peccavi, misericordia"* ["I have sinned, mercy, mercy."] He was ordered to rise from the floor and be seated. He related to the court that he had endured a terrible combat with the devil [*demonio*] during the past few days. He asserted that it was the devil who had prevented his confessing earlier, but that God had assisted him in his struggle and had inspired and enlightened him, so that he had now decided to speak the truth to the court rather than the lies he had previously told. He then related that his father had told him a few months before his death that the Law of Moses came from the hands of God Himself and that men could obtain salvation only by this Law. Fearing and respecting his father, he had promised that he would adhere to Judaism and had subsequently remained firm in this error, something that he enormously repented. After the death of his father he discovered that his mother, his sister Dona Isabel, and his brother Balthazar were practicing Jews. All of them piously waited for the arrival of the Messiah who would reunite the people of Israel. He exculpated his brother, the friar Gaspar, and the latter had explained to them that the old Law of Moses had been perfected and replaced by the Christian Law of the New Testament.

During the months of August and September, 1589, Luis appeared before the court several times. He mentioned a conversation that he had had with his uncle some six years before. In the course of a trip that they were taking together, the Governor asked him whether he knew that his [Luis'] late father observed the Law of Moses. The Governor added that Francisco had tried to convert him to Judaism! But Governor Carvajal had contended that the evangelical law of Jesus was the true one and that it was observed by kings and wise men the world-over—men who certainly desired to save their souls. Luis recounted the Jewish teachings of his late father: The Law of Moses is the only true law because God himself had inscribed it on the tables and had come down from heaven to give them to Moses; there is but one God, and man must believe in Him and love Him; the worship of images and the eating of pork or of scaleless fish is forbidden. He had set forth reasons for observing the Sabbath, the Passover, and other Jewish holidays, rites, and ceremonies. He had once bought a Bible in Panúco from a priest and used it to acquaint himself with Judaism. He had read especially the prophets Ezekiel and Isaiah and believed that the Messiah had not yet arrived.

Whenever he recited the Psalms, he omitted the words *"Gloria patri, et filio, et spiritui sancto."* During Passover he ate unleavened bread, or in the event there was none to be had, he ate corn tortillas that were made without yeast.

Luis made certain other admissions: On Passover nights, his mother, his sister Dona Isabel, and his brother Balthazar assembled and sang the Psalms, especially those relating to the exodus of the Jews from Egypt. He attributed a statement to his father that the Portuguese physician Morales, who came over from Spain on the same vessel with them, was a Judaizer. [This man had returned to Spain four years previously]. Luis denied knowledge of any other Judaizers, and even those whom he consented to name were either absent from the country, already imprisoned, or dead. Although he admitted that he had practiced Judaism for five years past, he claimed that his heart had been entirely converted to Christianity during the last few days. While he was in prison, he had read in the breviary of a fellow inmate certain epistles of the Popes St. Leo and St. Gregory and this reading moved him to confess.

After having made his depositions, Luis kneeled again and declared that he was a believing Catholic willing to live and die as a good Christian. Following the usual legal procedures of the tribunal, on February 24, 1590, Luis was permitted to be reconciled to the Catholic faith at an auto-da-fé after public abjuration of his errors. He was condemned to wear the penitential cloak [*sambenito*] and to perpetual imprisonment.[43]

43 Manuscript of Luis de Carvajal, Junior's trial in *AGN*, tomo 1489 del Ramo de Inquisición, has been entirely published in the *PAGN*, vol. XXVIII, (Mexico, 1935), pp. 1-111. Alfonso Toro, in his *La Familia Carvajal*, vol. I and II (Mexico, 1944), did not add anything to the facts related in the aforementioned published manuscript of the trial. The famous historian José Toribio Medina of Santiago de Chile, studied for his aforementioned book, *Historia del Tribunal del Santo Oficio de la Inquisición en Mexico* (first edition in Santiago de Chile, 1905), the manuscripts in the General Archives of Simancas in Spain, as he states in the "Advertencias" [advertisements to the reader] and the relations of the autos-da-fé published in the sixteenth and seventeenth centuries (Cf. *Historia*, 1952 edition, p. 28). These manuscripts were mainly *Cartas* [Letters] written by the Holy Office in Mexico City to the Consejo de Inquisición [Council of the Inquisition], their headquarters office in Spain. They were transferred in 1912 from Simancas to the Archivo Historica Nacional [National Historical Archives], Madrid, Calle de Serrano [Serrano Street 15]. Medina did not study the extensive manuscripts of the trials in Mexico, only the short reports of them that he found in Madrid. He also received by request from Mexican historians some information taken from the original trial manuscripts. Unfortunately, Medina confused Luis de Carvajal, the Governor, with his nephew Luis de Carvajal, el Mozo (junior), and thought that they were

Luis was then admonished to respect his abjuration strictly, for otherwise he would incur the penalty of the relapsed and would be delivered without mercy to the secular arm and burnt [*y quemado en llamas de fuego*].[44] Luis agreed to these conditions and

---

one and the same person: the Governor: Cf. J. T. Medina, *Historia, op. cit.,* pp. 108, 127-133, also Alfonso Toro, *La Familia Carvajal, op. cit.,* p. 8. Cecil Roth obviously copied the blunder from Medina but without even mentioning his standard work: *Historia del Tribunal del Santo Oficio de la Inquisición en Mexico.* On the other hand it is incomprehensible that Roth could confound the two Carvajal's in 1932 as Medina did in 1905, because Roth in his Bibliography mentioned the *PAGN,* vol. XX (Mexico, 1932), where the complete trial of the Governor had been published. Cf. Cecil Roth, *A History of the Marranos* (Philadelphia. 1932), pp. 276-277 and 408.

[44] The following represents the most important part of the condemnation by the court, in an abridged form:

> *Christi nomine invocato.* We consider that the Public Prosecutor has well proved his accusation and thus we consider the accused Luis de Carvajal as a heretic, Judaizer, apostate, and as an accomplice and concealer of heretics. He was converted to the dead Law of Moses and to its rites and ceremonies wherefrom he sought to obtain salvation. By so doing he has incurred the sentence of major excommunication and confiscation of his belongings in favor of the King's Treasury. In view of the fact that the accused has confessed, has shown signs of contrition and of repentance, has begged God to forgive him his offenses and has sought from us punishment with mercy, protesting the desire to live henceforth and to die in our Catholic Faith, to fulfill any penalty we shall impose on him and to abjure the aforementioned errors, and in view of the fact that God does not wish the death of the sinner, but that he be converted and continue to live—and provided that Luis de Carvajal return to our holy Catholic Faith with a pure heart and belief free of any simulation and that he has confessed the whole truth, without concealing anything concerning himself and other people, dead or alive,—then we must and we do admit him to Reconciliation. As penance, and punishment he shall appear, in person, at the auto-da-fé on this day, together with the other penitents, wearing no belt or hat, but dressed in a yellow penitential cloak bearing two red St. Andrew's Crosses, and carrying a wax candle in his hands. At the auto-da-fé he shall hear this sentence pronounced and shall abjure his confessed errors, heresy, and apostasy. Having done this he shall be absolved of the excommunication and restored to the bosom of Holy Mother Church and to the participation in the Holy Sacraments and the Communion of the true and Catholic Christians therein. We condemn Luis de Carvajal to perpetual imprisonment and to the wearing of the penitential cloak. He shall spend the term of imprisonment in a monastery, or wherever we shall indicate and there shall serve and be instructed and confirmed in the Catholic Faith. He shall wear the penitential garment in public over his clothes. Moreover, he shall observe all spiritual penances such as we shall prescribe. Further, the condemned may not receive dignities, public offices, or honors, as the Laws of these Kingdoms and the Instructions of the Holy Office of the Inquisition ordain for such disqualified persons.

The above mentioned sentence was officially and publicly pronounced on Saturday, February 24, 1590, during the auto-da-fé celebrated in the Cathedral of Mexico City. Luis de Carvajal abjured in the following words:

> I, Luis de Carvajal, Junior, bachelor, born in the city of Benavente in Castile, son of Francisco Rodrigues de Mattos, deceased, and Dona Francisca Núñes de Carvajal, here present as I am, do abjure, detest,

declared under oath that he would keep everything perfectly secret that he had seen or had heard in the prison of the Holy Office. Certain spiritual penitences were then assigned to him. He was required to fast every Friday of the year, to say the rosary on Fridays, Sundays, and holy days, and to perform devotions of his own free will on other solemn days during the time of his penance.

The Holy Office in Mexico did not have at its disposal a prison similar to the one in Spain for those condemned to a perpetual sentence. Luis, who had already been incarcerated in the prison of the Holy Office from May 9, 1589 to March 5, 1590, was therefore ordered on the latter date (being then twenty-three years of age) to be transferred to San Hipolito Martyr, the convalescent hospital in Mexico City, where he was required to perform any services that the administrator of the hospital might ask of him. Fr. Mateo Garcia was appointed his spiritual advisor, and the jailer of the prison of the Holy Office, Arias de Valdes, was assigned to make frequent visits to Luis in order to verify that his sentence was being carried out in the proper fashion.

Luis' mother and his four sisters, who had been reconciled at the auto-da-fé of 1590 and sentenced to prison, were confined in an isolated house facing the College of the Holy Cross of Tlalte-

---

renounce, and remove from me all heresy whatsoever, especially that one which was charged and proved against me and which I have confessed: adherence to the old Law of Moses, its rites and ceremonies. I vow with my mouth and with a pure and true heart to cleave to the holy Catholic Faith, to what is held and preached, followed, and taught by the Holy Mother Church of Rome. I retain and wish to retain and to follow and to stay with it permanently and to die in it and never separate me from it; and I swear to God our Lord, by the Four Holy Gospels and by the sign of the cross to become and to be obedient to the blessed Saint Peter, Prince of the Apostles and Vicar of our Lord Jesus Christ, and to our Holy Father Sixtus V, who at this time rules and governs the Church, and to his successors; and I will never separate myself from this obedience by any suasion or heresy, especially by that one that defamed me and wherewith I was charged; and I will remain always within the unity and congregation of the Holy Church, and will defend this holy Catholic Faith, and will persecute all who should be or should turn against her, and will disclose and make them public, and I will not unite with them or congregate with them, neither receive, guide, visit, or accompany them, nor give them gifts or presents or favors; and should I at any time act in contradiction to what I say, then shall I fall into and incur the penalty of the impenitent and relapsed and shall be damned and excommunicated; and I beg the secretary present, the signatory of my confession and abjuration, and all the other people here present, to witness; and I have signed [the abjuration] with my name before these same witnesses.

This document, signed by Luis de Carvajal and Pedro de los Rios, is a typical abjuration *de vehementi*.

lolco in Mexico City. The members of the family who had not been arraigned were permitted to live there with the condemned. Luis thus spent two years in the hospital apart from the other members of his family. His duties as sacristan of the church which formed a part of the hospital were a cause of deep distress to him. Not only was he out of touch with his close relatives but he was also constrained to clean the images of the saints in the church and to eat food that was forbidden by Jewish law.

It so happened that one of his brothers-in-law had to travel to Taxco on business, and this man petitioned the Inquisitors to allow Luis to live for a short time with his family, in order that the women should not be left without a man's protection. The Inquisitors acceded to this request and Luis joined his family. He found his mother and sisters completely overcome by their experiences with the Inquisition, but it was not long before he persuaded them again to practice Jewish rites.

Near the end of the time of Luis' leave of absence from the hospital, Fray Pedro de Oroz, a Franciscan who had been designated by the Holy Office as confessor and vigilant of the Carvajal family, paid a visit to Dona Francisca. She was on good terms with this benevolent old man and had won his sympathy. In the course of his visit she begged him to obtain the permission of the Holy Office for Luis to remain with them. He was successful in fulfilling her wish and subsequently arranged for Luis to work during the daytime in the College of the Holy Cross of Tlaltololco. Fr. Pedro was the supervisor of the college, which was dedicated to helping worthy Indians. He assigned Luis a position as a teacher of Latin and as his private secretary. The priest, who was obviously a good-hearted man, helped Luis and his family not only financially but also by supplying them with food, as Luis tells in his autobiography.

He also gave Luis a key to the library of the college, where the young man took a keen interest in studying the Old Testament. Many classical works were also available there, as well as Latin and Spanish dictionaries, including Josephus Flavius' *History of the Jews*. After the students left school, Luis remained in the college studying and translating passages of the Bible into Spanish verse. He was delighted when Father Oroz asked him to extract moral precepts from a book written by Jeronimo Oleaster [Oleastro], a Portuguese Dominican scholar who wrote commentaries on the Pentateuch and on the prophet Isaiah. Luis relates that he discovered in this book the thirteen fundamentals of the Jewish faith, "something unknown and unheard of in the lands of captivity" ["cosa no sabida v. oidas en las tierras de cautiverio"]. Luis obviously meant the Thirteen Fundamentals [ikkarim] set down by Moses Maimonides (1135-1204), the Spanish-Jewish scholar, physician, and philosopher. Of course Maimonides' texts were known to the learned Jews everywhere, but were a novelty to Luis.[45]

Meanwhile, Jorge de Almeida,[46] the husband of Dona Leonor who had escaped from Mexico to Madrid, had been petitioning the Chief Inquisitor there for several years in behalf of the oppressed Carvajals. He finally obtained a letter (June 7, 1594) from that official to the Inquisitors in Mexico City which ordered the release of Luis and his family from all the penalties imposed upon them in 1590. On October 24, 1594, the Inquisitors informed Luis of the good news. He was set free after the payment of 325 Castillian ducats and the imposition of the following spiritual penances: During the next two years he had to fast every Friday, to recite a rosary of 150 Ave Marias and 15 Paternosters, and to perform other similar duties. He was sternly reminded of his abjuration in the auto-da-fé of February 24, 1590, and was told that he must henceforth comfort himself as a good Catholic. He was a free man for only a short time. Slightly more than three months later, on February 1, 1595, the Public Prosecutor of the Holy Office denounced Luis, then twenty-eight years old, as a relapsed heretic, apostate, and Judaizer, and obtained from the Inquisitors an authorization for Luis' arrest, which was executed during the night of February first and early the next morning. When he was searched by the jailer of the secret prison, a leather bag was found on his person which contained three small books

45 The thirteen fundamentals are to be found in Maimonides' Commentary on the Mishnah, chapter 10, in Tractate Sanhedrin of the Talmud Babli (Vilna, 1895) ; also, in prayer-books in abridged form. Luis de Carvajal, Junior, quoted them in a very abridged version, but quite correctly, he only confused the eighth and ninth fundamentals. Alfonso Toro thought that the thirteen fundamentals were a part of the Pentateuch and that Luis had discovered them there. Cf. Toro, La Familia Carvajal, vol. II, p. 25, while Luis had read them in Osorius F. Hieronymus, Commentaria in Mosi Pentateuchum (Antverpiae, 1569) .

46 In 1609, Almeida was condemned in absentia in Mexico City and burnt in effigy. Dr. Cyrus Adler found the manuscript of Almeida's trial in a bookshop in Washington and bought it for the American Jewish Historical Society, New York. Dr. Adler published a summary of the trial. Cf. "Trial of Jorge de Almeida by the Inquisition in Mexico", in PAJHS., no. 4 (New York, 1896) , pp. 28-79.

in black leather and bearing the hand lettered titles *Psalmorum,
Prophets,* and *Genesis.* These books were handed over to the Inquisitors and later formed an important piece of evidence against
him.

VII

LUIS DE CARVAJAL, JUNIOR: THE SECOND TRIAL

The new prosecution of Luis was based upon the testimony of
some seventeen witnesses, all of whom confirmed the fact that
Luis engaged in Judaizing practices after his reconciliation to
Catholicism in 1590; but as it turned out, the most damaging
witness was Luis himself. We shall, therefore, devote the major
part of this chapter to the record of his own statements, with
some brief indication of the remarks of four other important
witnesses.

One, Manuel de Lucena, attributed to Luis the remark that
all religions with the exception of Judaism were a hoax. He also
declared that Luis and his family saluted him in the Jewish
manner with the words: "May God be with you" [*"El Señor sea
con Vd."*]. When he visited Luis on September 10, 1592, the
mother's house was locked; when he was let in, he found Luis,
his mother, and his sisters on their knees facing east, praying and
weeping. Luis was reciting prayers and the family repeated them
after him. This was on the Day of Atonement [Yom Kippur].
Another time, on a Sabbath day, he found them intoning a long
prayer that began, as he remembered, with the words:

> In the name of the Lord *Adonai.*
> May the name of the Lord *Adonai* be blessed forever,
> *Amen.*
> Who brings the light of the morning
> And of the evening to the night
> And from the night to dawn
> And from dawn to the morning.

Another witness was a Catholic priest named Luis Diaz. This
man, an informer who had shared the prison cell with Luis, appeared before the Inquisitors on February 3, 1595, two days after
the victim had been seized. He deposed that his fellow prisoner
[whose name, he said, was unknown to him when they first met]
prayed in the cell for hours. All the while he knelt with his face

to the east and wore a hat.[47] Whenever he pronounced the word *Adonai* he kissed the floor. By questioning Luis de Carvajal, he learned his identity and his whole story. Luis explained that he had learned a great deal about the Jewish faith in the Library of the College of Tlaltololco. He danced in the prison cell for joy that he was about to be burnt for the sake of the ancient Law of Moses. This time he was not afraid of death and proved his fearlessness by saying that one day in Pánuco he had circumcized himself with a pair of scissors. Not realizing that his confidant would betray him, Luis spoke freely about many other Judaizers. The priest asked him many questions about Judaism to which the naïve, mystically inclined, idealistic young Jew readily responded, thinking that he could convert him to Judaism. Luis showed him a small notebook with the title *Lex Adonai* which he had kept hidden in a hat under the lining. The Ten Commandments, with the initials in large gilded letters, were copied out in this book.

The priest further testified that Luis sometimes fasted all day long and in the evening ate only two bananas and a piece of bread. Before sunset he was in the habit of washing his body with drinking water. Luis ventured to tell him that, besides the three books which the jailer had confiscated and the one he had managed to conceal in his hat, there was another book in which he had written the story of his life. This was concealed in a room of the house in Tlaltololco where he had been arrested. He asked the priest to fetch this booklet as soon as he was released from prison and to give it to one Antonio Diaz Marques. This man was to forward it to Fernandez de Pereyra, a rich Portuguese businessman then residing in Seville, with the request that the booklet be sent to his brothers, Balthazar and Miguel de Carvajal, who were in Pisa. The Inquisitors immediately dispatched an investigator to the house and Luis' biography was found. On February 11th, while still in prison, Luis discovered that the priest was an informer. He begged him not to betray his mother and sisters and the names of other Judaizers whom he had mentioned.

At this point Pedro de Fonseca a notary of the Holy Office, was introduced as a witness. On February 3, 1595, at 7 p.m., this man together with two others had eavesdropped at the prison cell door, as ordered by the Inquisitor. The *agent-provacateur*, Luis Dias,

---

[47] *"Sombrero y herreruelo"* is the original. Most probably *herreruelo* refers to phylacteries; even so, it is odd that Luis could have smuggled them into the secret prison. They are not mentioned again in the trial.

asked his cell-mate to tell him about the Law of Moses. Luis [Carvajal] poured out his belief that the Messiah had not yet come and that there was only one God. Dias further stated that Carvajal maligned Jesus and Mary, and that the Pope, the King, the Apostles, the Inquisitors—all Christians, in fact—are doomed to hell. He said, too, that the Jews called the Holy Mary "Maria Hernandes,"[48] and Jesus, "Juan Garrido." The same witness deposed on February 20, 1595, that he had heard Luis de Carvajal answering certain questions of the priest and saying that the tenth day of the moon[49] in September was the Day of Atonement, that February 14th was the fast day of Esther, and that Jews fasted for three consecutive days of the latter fast day.[50] He had further declared that he considered himself a good Jew and was ready to die for his faith.

In May and July of 1595, Dona Leonor de Carvajal, Luis' sister, who was the wife of Jorge de Almeida, was brought before the Inquisitors from the secret prison. She deposed that her brother had again converted her to Judaism after she had been reconciled to Catholicism in 1590. She recited nine poems composed and sung by Luis on Friday evenings when he, together with the family, celebrated the Sabbath in Tlaltololco. These poems and the Ten Commandments she knew by memory and recited them before the court.[51]

During Luis' first trial, he had confessed to heresy and asked for mercy, since he well knew that the Inquisitorial Tribunal was obliged by its own rules to allow anyone, accused for the first time, who showed repentance and asked for mercy, to be reconciled with the church. However, at his second trial Luis understood that as a relapsed apostate—having abjured his heresy *de vehementi* in 1590

---

48 We could not determine the significance of this name.

49 What is meant in the tenth day after the new moon in September. The Day of Atonement is celebrated on the tenth day of the Jewish month Tishri. Since the crypto-Jews had no Jewish calendars available, they either depended on information from new immigrants from Italy, Turkey, and other countries in which Jews practiced their religion freely; or else they worked out their own approximate calendar dates as Luis did.

50 Three days, because the biblical Queen Esther, her servant girls, and all the Jews of Shushan, the capital of Persia, fasted three days before Esther went uninvited to see King Ahasuerus.

51 She knew only the following Hebrew words: *"Shema Israel Adonay Eloin Paro es em que vos Malcuto Eloin Bael,"* a misspelled version of *"Shema Israel, Adonay Elohenu Adonay ehad. Baruch shem kevod malkhuto leolam vaed."* ["Hear, O Israel, the Lord, our God is One. Blessed be the honor of His kingdom forever."] It is quite possible that Doña Leonor quoted the Hebrew correctly and that the court-clerk corrupted it.

izing the rebuilding of the temple of Jerusalem; and Purim,
—he would receive the death penalty. By this time, however, he
was quite a different man from the one who had been tried earlier,
when his Judaism was based only on the rudimentary teachings of
his father. From 1592 to 1594, he had studied the Bible and the
biblical commentaries of Fr. Jeronimo Oleaster. He was now
twenty-eight years old, and an enthusiastic Jewish believer, a mystic
given to fasting and praying and the writing of religious poetry.
Thus, it was understandable that he now made up his mind to
become a martyr for his faith. The following paragraphs summarize
his testimony at a number of hearings from February 11 to June
10, 1595.

One day in Panúco, Mexico, he bought a Latin Bible from a
clergymen and studied it. When he came to the seventeenth chapter
of Genesis he learned everything about circumcision—about the
covenant of God with Abraham, about Abraham's circumcizing himself, at the age of ninety-nine, by the order of God, and about
Abraham's having all of his domestics circumcized. The verse from
Genesis:

> And the man-child the flesh of whose foreskin is not cir-
> cumcized, that soul shall be cut off from his people; he has
> broken my covenant—[17:14]

made such an impression upon him that he took a pair of scissors
and painfully circumcized himself. From then on, he practiced all
the ceremonies ordained by God in the four other books of the
Pentateuch. He had always fasted on *Quipur* [Yom Kippur], the
day on which God forgives sins, and on Mondays and Thursdays.
He observed Jewish ceremonies and rites, and kept the Sabbath
day as holy as possible by changing his undergarments and bed-
linen and by praying and chanting psalms. He celebrated Passover
beginning on the fourteenth day of the new moon in March[52] and
ate unleavened bread while standing and while wearing a belt and
holding a walking stick in his hand. He, also, celebrated Pentecost
in remembrance of the benefits that God bestowed on the people
of Israel by giving them the Holy Law. He mentioned several other
holy days that he kept: the festival of the Tents [*Sukkot*] which
commences on the fifteenth day of the September new moon,[53] in
thanksgiving to God for having given the Promised Land to the
people of Israel; the festival of the Lights [Hanukkah], memorial-

52 Instead of the fourteenth day of the Hebrew month Nisan.
53 Instead of the fifteenth day of the Hebrew month Tishri.

celebrating the liberation of the Jews from the perfidious Haman, and the day before which he was in the habit of keeping the fast of Esther for three days as mentioned above. In addition, he fasted every Monday and Thursday. He ate only meat that was not prohibited in the Bible and that was ritually prepared, and he never partook of pork, since it supposedly makes one lustful.

Some years before, he had visited the ailing Antonio Machado, who showed him a holograph book by the late Licentiate Manuel de Morales wherein the fifth book of the Old Testament was copied out in verses. Machado loaned him this book so that he might translate it [from Latin into Spanish]. He and his brother Balthazar wept when they read about the maledictions of God upon those who do not obey the Jewish Law, especially when they realized that some of these curses had already been visited upon them. Together, they copied from Morales' book many prayers and psalms in verse form in the manner in which Jews recite them in the synagogue; and they made a similar use of them. Luis' influence on Balthazar was made evident in that Balthazar imitated Luis' self-circumcision by cutting his own foreskin with a razor.

At the time before the second arrest by the Holy Office, Luis, and his mother and sisters had decided to flee from Mexico to Spain. He freely admitted that he had duped the Inquisitors during his first trial. It was purely and simply the fear of the death penalty that caused him to pretend to repent and to be converted to Catholicism. The truth was that he had in fact been a Judaizer from the age of fourteen, that he rejected Jesus, and waited for the promised Messiah, and that he believed in the Ten Commandments as he had learned them in the books of *Exodus* and *Deuteronomy*.

When the Inquisitors asked Luis to recite the Ten Commandments, he asked permission to kneel while he did so, because the most Holy Name of God, Who created heaven and the earth, was mentioned in them. This permission was denied. Luis then repeated the Commandments, correctly, except that he mistakenly included the monotheistic formula, the *Shema,* as the very first Commandment.[54]

---

[54] Luis recited in Hebrew, as part of the First Commandment: *"Semha Israel, Alhieno Varocsem que vos malcuto leolam vaed,"* in incorrect version of the *Shema,* and translated it into Spanish: *"Oye Israel Adonay, to Dios uno Solo es, uno bendito nombre de honra de su reino para consigo y siempre."* Since he had recited the *Shema* erroneously as the First Commandment, he, therefore, called what is actually the First Commandment the Second, and so on; at the end, he combined the Ninth and Tenth Commandments.

Luis declared that he accepted the "articles of the Law that God had given to Moses" (mentioned above) and that some of them did not contradict the Christian faith. He then quoted from memory Maimonides' Thirteen Fundamentals [*Ikkarim*], some in an expanded version of his own, others in an abridged form. He added that, besides the Ten Commandments and Thirteen Fundamentals, there were many positive and negative precepts in the Law. (There are indeed 613 such precepts.)

Certain other remarks demonstrated his scrupulous respect for ceremony: Whenever he had a pollution, he went the same night to the river to bathe and purify himself. Also, he often fasted half of the week, eating only during lunchtime to avoid calling attention to himself. The previous September he had been in a small Indian village near Pachuco where he remained to observe the Day of Atonement; but not being sure of the exact date, he fasted completely for forty-eight hours.[55] (Manuel de Lucena, who testified against him, had sent him candles which he had requested for use on that day.)

He told of a dream that he had five years before in the prison of the Inquisition. It seemed that he saw a wooden bottle containing a precious liquor, and God told Solomon to take a spoonful of this liquor and put it into the mouth of this young man; and Solomon did so. When he awoke he felt consoled, so that the prison did not oppress him as before. He interpreted this dream to mean that God wished to illuminate his spirit in order that he might observe the Law of Moses and understand the Holy Scriptures. For this reason he henceforth called himself "Lumbrosso" (the illuminated, or enlightened one) and altered his first name to "Joseph." Although he gave no explanation for the latter, it was probably the Hebrew name which his crypto-Jewish parents had given him secretly after his baptism under the Christian name, Luis. This was an ordinary practice among the crypto-Jews. Luis stated that his brother Balthazar had followed his example and changed his name to David Lumbroso.

The Inquisitors asked whether in the future he desired to follow Judaism, and Luis responded that he wished to live and die observing the Law of Moses. In response to a question, he gave nine reasons for denying the Catholic faith:

[55] Even so, he probably did not fast on the correct day.

1. The chief reason was that God has given the Jewish Law; and that the Christians themselves observe, believe, and preach the Ten Commandments.

2. God said that if a prophet or a dreamer should arise among you, and pretend to have had visions and prove it even with miracles, and induce you to withdraw from My Law to the right or left, do not believe him, but preserve My Law, because this is temptation that I have sent to find out whether or not you love Me. Such a prophet or dreamer shall be put to death by you. (Luis here quoted at length from *Deuteronomy*, chapter XIII.)

3. We can verify that God's maledictions against the Jewish transgressors of His Law as written in *Deuteronomy*, chapter XXVIII, had come true.

4. God also warned the children of Israel as to what would happen to them if they did not respect the Covenant and did not follow the Law, as in the hymn that begins "*Auditis coeli que loquor*," ("Give ear, O ye heavens, and I will speak" [Cf. *Deuteronomy*, chapter XXXII] האזינו השמים ואדברה).

5. All the Psalms of David are evidence, especially the "*Coeli narrant gloriam Dei*" [Psalm 19] השמים מספרים כבוד אל.

6. Likewise, Psalm 118 (correctly, 119), that begins with the words "*Beati immaculati in via*" (אשרי תמימי דרך) is filled with the praise of God and of His Law, in which he, Luis, wishes to live and die.

7. Likewise, Psalm 74, the Psalm of Asaph, which begins with the words "*Ut qui Deus repulisti in perpetuam?*" ("Why, O God, hast Thou cast us off forever?" למה אלהים זנחת לנצח).

8. The prophecies of Ezekiel deal with the coming of the Messiah and the reunion of the people of Israel. The fact that the Jews are still dispersed and that Jerusalem is not yet rebuilt with the foretold glory proves that the prophecies have not yet been fulfilled and that Jesus could not have been the Messiah.

9. All the prophecies of Isaiah, Jeremiah, Ezra, Daniel, and others are further evidence.

The Inquisitors then asked Luis whether he would care to discuss religion with learned Catholic priests who would convince him that he was in a state of blind error and convert him to Christ. Luis answered that he would like to do so, and would be converted if they could convince him, since he wanted above all else to save his soul.[56]

On February 25, 1595, the Inquisitors produced Luis' autobiography, which we have mentioned earlier. This was a holograph booklet covered in black sheepskin. It began with the words: "In the name of the Lord of hosts." Luis recognized the booklet as his and admitted that it contained an account of his life which he wanted to send to his brothers Balthazar and Miguel in order to tell them God's miracles and mercy.

On March 2, 1595, the Inquisitors showed Luis a letter from Madrid, dated November 15, 1590, addressed to him by one Francisco Ramirez. Luis admitted that this had been written by his brother Balthazar. The letter related that he and Diego (a pseudonym for his younger brother Miguel) had arrived safely in Spain and were trying to liberate the whole family in Mexico from the clutches of the Holy Office. Balthazar mentioned that he had found the right man to accomplish their release, and referred to him as "the banker in these dealings." All the names in the document are pseudonyms.

The Mexican Inquisitors Lobo Guerrero and Alonso Peralta reported in a letter dated March 31, 1595, to the Council of the Inquisition in Spain, that a man named Luis de Carvajal, a relapsed Judaizer, imprisoned in Mexico City, and processed, wished to die as a Jew. There were, continued the letter, many *Judios* [Jews] in prison and all of them poor, so that their confiscated belongings do not bring even enough money necessary to feed them in prison. The report tells that the Mexican Judaizers used to read the book *Espejo de Consolación* [mirror of consolation], which contained the Old Testament translated into Spanish [*en lengua vulgar*], and the book *Symbolo de la Fee* [Symbol of the faith] and suggests that the book *Espejo de Consolación* be put on the blacklist.[56a]

At the hearing of June 10, 1595, Luis repeated his willingness to die for his faith, and the Public Prosecutor, Dr. Martos de

[56] Luis, like other crypto-Jews, often spoke of the "salvation of the soul," meaning deliverance from sin and eternal damnation. This conception belongs to Catholic doctrine and not to Judaism.

[56a] We found the manuscript of this letter in the Archivo Historico Nacional in Madrid, volume 1049/762, second book under "*Cartas de la Inquon de la Nueva España, al Consejo de Inqon desde el Año de mil y quinientos y noventa y quatro*" [Letters of the Inquisition of New Spain to the Council of the Inquisition from 1594 on].

Bohorques, presented a bill of indictment against him. The bill consists of twenty-two paragraphs that recapitulate almost everything that Luis had confessed. The document betrays an extreme hostility towards the prisoner. For example, it says that Luis returned to the Law of Moses after his reconciliation of 1590 "as a dog returns to the vomit." It also brings out the fact that Balthazar was living as a Jew in Rome and Miguel as Grand Rabbi in Salonika; that Luis was a great proselytizer of Catholics to Judaism, and that he wished to become a martyr for his faith. Calling Luis a heretical, Judaizing, impenitent, relapsed apostate, it demands that his belongings be confiscated for the King's Treasury and that he be released to the secular arm in order "to be burnt alive in flames of fire."

The accused heard the indictment and agreed generally with its correctness, saying also that he looked forward to dying at the stake and to being taken to heaven in glory. The court then gave Luis the privilege of choosing his defense counsel from among four persons; and he selected Dr. Dionisio de Ribera Florez, Canon of the Cathedral in Mexico City. This man resigned almost immediately, on June 14th, when Luis refused to heed his advice to embrace the Church once again. Some months later (October 30-31 and November 4, 1595), two Jesuit priests, Dr. Pedro Sanchez and Dr. Hortigosa, tried for several hours to convert him before the Inquisitors, but to no avail.

On February 6, 1596, the Inquisitors decided to have the prisoner tortured *in caput alienum*.[57] This decision was made known to Luis on February 8th, but he continued to maintain that he had no information to disclose about other people. He also invoked the Canon Law—"*de complicibus non debeo interrogare,*" ["One should not question the accused about his accomplices"]—in arguing that torture *in caput alienum* was not licit. Nonetheless, the order was given by the court, and he was brought to the torture chamber at 9:30 A.M. of the same day, with the Inquisitors in attendance.

After the usual admonition to speak the truth in order to escape torture, Luis repeated that he had nothing to disclose and exclaimed: "Give me, O God, the strength not to tell lies!" The

---

57 Tortures "*in caput proprium*" had the objective to force the accused to confess his own transgressions. Tortures "*in caput alienum*" had the objective to extract from the accused denunciations against other persons. In the first case, he was asked questions, in the second case the Inquisitors did not ask any questions and listened to eventual denunciations.

black-hooded executioner was summoned to strip the accused of his clothing. When he was naked, except for the *pudenda*,[58] his arms were tied loosely and he was again warned to speak; this time he consented, whereupon the executioner was instructed to withdraw. He began to denounce his family and friends as Judaizers, but the moment he stopped the executioner was recalled and applied the *cordeles* with four twists of the ropes. He then resumed his denunciations until 2 p.m., when the Inquisitors adjourned for lunch. Ironically, they were careful to see to it that Luis dressed, since it was cold in the chamber. He had become such a precious witness that they wanted to be sure his health was protected.

From 3 to 7 P.M. on the same day the questioning and taking of depositions were continued. The same procedure was followed between 8:30 A.M. and 5 P.M. on each of the two days succeeding, Thursday and Friday, February 9 and 10, 1596. After the interruption of the weekend, Luis was placed, fully clothed, on the rack at 9 A.M. on Monday, February 12th, and asked to unburden his conscience. When he claimed that he had nothing more to tell, the executioner was ordered to strip the victim naked. Some difference of opinion ensued between the Inquisitors as to the severity of the torment which should be inflicted: Dr. Lobo Guerrero proposed only two twists of the rope on the arms, but Licenciado Don Alonso de Peralta and Dr. Juan de Cervantes insisted upon six twists. When Luis' arms were tied and the usual threats were made, he again weakened and resumed his denunciation of Judaizers. During lunch time, food was withheld from Luis while he waited in his cell. In the afternoon he was laid fully dressed on the rack and was induced to tell about Jewish ceremonies and rites, besides adding to the list of those he had accused. He was even brought to mention a Judaizer named Manuel Rodriguez Novarro, a Portuguese, who had come to Mexico from China, whither he had returned meanwhile, and who had supplied information about Jewish customs in the Orient. The session ended with Luis asking for paper, ink, and a pen, and the indulgence of a day without meetings in the torture-chamber, in order that he might write down the names of other Judaizers. The Inquisitors agreed. To the hearing of Wednesday, February 14th, Luis brought four sheets of names of secret Jews in Mexico, Cuba, Spain, and elsewhere, written and signed by himself. During the afternoon meeting of a seven-

58 Bernard Picart, *The Religious Ceremonies and Customs of the Several Nations of the Known World* (London, 1731), p. 237.

member court, the status of the trial was discussed. Again, there was a difference of opinion about continuing the torture. Three members voted for halting; one, for three to four twists of the arms; two, for continuation; and one, for merely threatening the victim with new tortures.

The next day, February 15th brought a turn of events. The court held an afternoon session at which the questioning of Luis was resumed. However, Luis had recovered from fear and weakness sufficiently to realize that he would surely lose his soul, by betraying others to misery and death at the hands of the Holy Office. Accordingly, he told the court to recall that a week before he had begged it not to force him to tell falsehoods. His dread of torture had impelled him to fabricate the whole story that he had told about other Judaizers. He had been brought to his senses by a voice that spoke to him in the cell—something he considered to be a divine revelation—and that threatened him with Hell unless he confessed his lies to the court. The hearing was adjourned.

Immediately afterwards, the jailer burst in on the Inquisitors with the news that Luis, on his way back to the cell, had broken free and thrown himself from the gallery. However, he had failed to kill himself and had only injured his right arm. The Inquisitors visited the cell and ordered that his hands be manacled so that he could not attempt suicide again; they also placed two other prisoners in the cell to watch him. Confined to the bed the next day, he sent a message through the jailer to the Inquisitor, Dr. Guerrero, asking him to visit his cell, but without Licenciado Alonso de Peralta, since the very sight of this cruel man made him shudder with fear.

Dr. Guerrero had a surprise in store. Again reversing his story, Luis told him that it was the devil who had persuaded him on the previous day to attempt suicide, the greatest sin, and to revoke his depositions against others. The result was that all the depositions made by Luis in the torture-chamber on February 8th and afterwards were read to him, word for word [verbo ad verbum]. Luis declared that they were true statements, and that neither fear nor any false motive had induced him to make them. Inasmuch as Luis was ill and his life in danger, the Public Prosecutor asked the court to have the denunciations ratified in the presence of two honest and religious persons. On February 19th, Dr. Guerrero, attended by two Dominican friars, Pedro de Galarza and Jeronimo de Araux, caused Luis to listen to the reading of the names of the denounced and the accompanying protocols. After Luis had been advised that he would be used as a witness against all the offenders in the document, he again confirmed and signed the papers.[59]

[59] The names of the denounced Judaizers were:

Balthasar Rodríguez [his absent brother]
Antonio Machado
Manuel de Lucena
Manual Gómez Navarro
Francisco Ruiz de Luna
Francisco Rodríguez
Antonio López
Antonio Nieto
Sebastián Nieto
Juan Rodríguez de Silva
Jorge de Almeida [his absent brother-in-law]
Doña Mariana de Carvajal [his sister],
Miguel de Carvajal [his absent brother]
Fabian Granados
Francisco Vaez
Doña Francisca de Carvajal [his mother]
Doña Isabel de Carvajal [his sister]
Doña Leonor de Carvajal [his sister]
Doña Ana de Carvajal [his sister]
Antonio Díaz Márquez
Justa Méndez
Tomás de Fonseca [living in Taxco]
Doña Catalina de León
Sebastián de la Peña
Clara Enríquez
Ana Lopez
Tomás de Fonseca [living in Talpuxagua]
Héctor de Fonseca [living in Taxco]
Miguel Hernández
Manuel Alvarez
Jorge Alvarez
Diego Enríquez
Pedro Enríquez
Pedro Rodríguez Zas
Leonor Díaz
Manuel Rodríguez
Clara Enríquez
Gabriel Enríquez
Andrés Rodríguez
Manuel Díaz
Catalina Enríquez
Beatriz Enríquez
Sebastian Rodríguez,
Antonio Rodríguez
Tomás Cardosso
Isabel Rodríguez
Christóbal Gómez
Marco Antonio
Gregorio López
Francisco Jorge

Francisco Díaz
Balthazar Rodríguez
Leonor Rodríguez
Ana Vaez
Julián Castellanos
Constanza Rodríguez
Domingo Rodríguez
Jorge Rodríguez
Simón Rodríguez
Domingo Cuello
Ruy Díaz Nieto
Diego Díaz Nieto
Gómez de Acosta
Duarte Rodríguez
Gonzalo Pérez Ferro
Francisco Rodríguez de Mattos [his father]
Matheo Ruiz
García de Quadros
Antonio Conde
a silk manufacturer whose name he did not remember
Enrique Rodríguez
Violante Rodríguez
Benito Baez [from Michoacan]
Hernán Rodríguez de Herrera
Andrés Núñez
Jorge Vaez
Jorge Díaz
Manuel Rodríguez Navarro
Manuel Gil de la Guardia
Juan Méndez [in Havana]
a Vaez in Patzcuaro
a de Silva
Domingo López
Juan Rodríguez
Nuño Alvarez de Riviera
Doña Guiomar de Rivera
Blanca Rodríguez
Francisco Deza
a Rodríguez in Taxco
Vicente Correa
Gaspar Delgado
Felipe Núñez
Felipa López
Gaspal Pereyra
Gonzálo Fernandez
Manuel Gómez
Manuel de Herrera
Paiba [Manuel's uncle]
Simon Payba
Hernán Rodríguez
Diego Rodríguez
Antonio Díaz de Cáceres
Duarte de León
Jorge de León

On February 23, 1596, the court in full session voted unanimously that Luis de Carvajal, *alias* Joseph Lumbroso, should be declared a Judaizing heretic, relapsed, obstinate, and a dogmatist of the dead Law of Moses, and that he should be released to the secular arm and his belongings confiscated. There is some indication that Luis had been very ill since his suicide attempt, in that Dr. Guerrero visited him on March 4th to clarify doubtful points in his depositions. Eight months later, on August 24th, the court brought Luis and two Augustinian theologians before it, who tried to satisfy the prisoner's religious doubts; but after three-and-a-half hours of discussion, he persisted in declaring that he wished to live and die a loyal Jew. On September 12th, he presented a document, written and signed by himself, to the Inquisitors with the request that it be included in the dossier of the trial. It was a statement of his religious beliefs, in which he asked God to accept the sacrifice of his poor life and of his death for God's most holy Name and for the true Law, and to give him the strength of will to die as a Jew! It is a pathetic document, especially in that it shows Luis' uncertainty of himself, his fear that he would accept Christ in the last moments in order not to be burnt alive, just as he had already given way under the fear and pain of torture.

Luis was released to the secular arm on December 8, 1596, the day of the auto-da-fé which was held on the main square of Mexico

Fernán López	Fernando Cardoso
Gaspar de Villafranca	Isabel Machado
Pelayo Alvarez	Antonio Machado
Luis Diáz	Alvara de Carrión
Daniel Benítez	Juan del Casal
Aillón	Lic. Feliciano de Valencia

Luis de Carvajal shortly before his execution, in conversation with Frey Alonso de Contreras withdrew his denunciation against the following: Garcia de Quadros, Antonio, Conde, Antonio Diáz de Caceres, Paiba, Manuel de Herrera, Vicente Correa, Tomás de Fonseca (living in Tlalpujahua, probably the same as Talpuxagua), Hernán Rodríguez de Herrera ["*dijo que habia reincidido, y que le dijo con mal animo porque muriese también*" or "I have said that he had relapsed, and I did it with the bad intention that he, too, should die"], the late Benito Baez, Juan Mendez [from Havana]. Carvajal's original trial appears in *PAGN*, vol. XXVIII (Mexico, 1935), and the list appears *ibid.*, pp. 117-123.

Some of those denounced by Luis de Carvajal, Junior, are mentioned in G.R.G. Conway's "List of the Sambenitos of the Condemned Jews Placed in the Cathedral Church of Mexico between 1528 and 1603," *PAJHS*, vol. XXXI (1928), pp. 26-31. The list was taken from vol. LXXVII, Inquisition Records, AGN.

City.[60] The civil magistrate to whom Luis was delivered pronounced the following sentence at once:

Luis de Carvajal shall be brought riding on a beast of burden through the public streets of the city, accompanied by a town-crier who shall proclaim his crime, to the market of San Hipolito, where he shall be burnt alive in kindled flames of fire, until he turns ashes and nothing remains of him.

The execution of the sentence followed on the same day. On the way from the auto-da-fé to the Square of San Hipolito, Luis was overcome with fear. He took a cross in his hands and said a few words avowing his repentance and conversion. As was customary in such cases, he was first garroted and his corpse was afterwards burnt. The Dominican Fr. Alonso de Contreras handed over a statement to the Inquisitors the next day, declaring that he had succeeded in converting Luis to Catholicism and that before his death Luis had confessed his sins and had professed aloud the ineffable mystery of the most holy Trinity. The friar included in this document, at Luis' request, the names of nine persons whom Luis had previously alleged to be Judaizers but who were actually innocent of such practices.

60 The sentence against Luis de Carvajal, Junior, repeats in its preamble everything we have seen before in his depositions and in the Bill of Indictment. It concludes as follows:

> *Christo nomine invocato.* We declare: In view of the proceedings and merits of the trial, that the Public Prosecutor has well and completely proved his accusation, as he ought to have done; we declare his case to be well proved, and declare that the said Luis de Carvajal to have been to be a Judaizing heretic, an apostate from our holy Catholic Faith, an accomplice and concealer of Judaizing heretics, a false and simulating proselyter, impenitent, relapsed, a pertinacious dogmatist. For these reasons he has become liable to major excommunication and is thereby bound to have all his possessions confiscated. We order that these be applied and we do apply them to the Chamber and Royal Treasury of his Majesty and to his Treasurer, from the day on which he began committing the stated delicts of heresy, which fixation we keep reserved to ourselves. We must and do release the person of the said Luis de Carvajal to the secular justice and power, in particular to Lic. Vasco López de Bibero, magistrate of this city, whom we implore and recommend as strongly as we can do so under the law, to treat him mercifully. We declare that the sons and daughter of said Luis de Carvajal and his grandchildren in the male line are unqualified and incapable, and we disqualify them from holding or obtaining dignities, benefits, or offices, whether ecclesiastical or secular, or other public or honorable offices; we also forbid the wearing about them or on their persons of gold, silver, pearls, precious stones or corals, silk or cambric or fine cloth, or to ride horseback, or to wear arms, or to perform or use other things which by the ordinances and practice of the civil law of these Kingdoms are prohibited to similarly disqualified persons. Because this was our definitive sentence, we have pronounced it and written it. Signed: Dr. Lobo Guerrero, Lic. Don Alonzo de Peralta, Mo. Don Johan de Cervantes.

Luis de Carvajal, *alias* Joseph Lumbroso, was a learned, deeply pious, zealous, young crypto-Jew. It is apparent that he longed to become a saint and a martyr for his religion. A very human fear of bodily suffering prevented him from becoming a heroic figure; a single ordeal of torture caused him to denounce more than one hundred crypto-Jews; and apparently he accepted Christ in the last moments of his life and died as a Catholic. Nonetheless, he was one of the most interesting personalities among the secret Jews of Mexico and a martyr for his faith.

Luis' mother, Dona Francisca and his sisters, Dona Catalina, Dona Isabel, and Dona Leonor, all reconciled in 1590 and again accused as relapsed Judaizers, appeared at the auto-da-fé with their son and brother Luis, on December 8, 1596, and were condemned and executed the same day. They too, were first garroted and afterwards burnt.

The tribunal of the Inquisition in Mexico City between 1577 and 1596, tried sixty-three Judaizers altogether. One of them was set free. Thirty-eight were tried for the first time, repented at least formally, asked for mercy, abjured their heretic errors publicly, *de levi* or *de vehementi,* and became reconciled to Catholicism. They, however, lost their possessions, were condemned to prison, and expelled from Mexico. Fifteen were burnt in effigy because they were absent (dead or escaped). Ten crypto-Jews were condemned to death and burnt at the stake after having been garroted.

The twelve crypto-Jewish Mexican martyrs of the sixteenth century were:

> HERNANDO ALONSO (1528)
> GONZÁLO DE MORALES (1528)
> GARCIA GONZÁLEZ BERMEJERO (1579)
> DONA LEONOR CARVAJAL Y ANDRADE (1596)
> DONA ISABEL RODRIGUES DE ANDRADA (1596)
> LUIS DE CARVAJAL, JUNIOR (1596)
> DONA FRANCISCA NÚÑEZ DE CARVAJAL (1596)
> DONA CATALINA DE LA CUEVA (1596)
> MANUEL DIAZ (1596)
> DIEGO ENRIQUEZ (1596)
> MANUEL DE LUCENA (1596)
> DONA BEATRIX ENRIQUEZ DE LA PAYBA (1596)

Crypto-Jews in Mexico during the Seventeenth Century

By ARNOLD WIZNITZER

I

INTRODUCTION

The beginning of the seventeenth century found only a few dozen Judaizers in the prison of the Holy Office in Mexico City. After trying these prisoners, the Inquisitors prepared a spectacular auto-da-fé for March 25, 1601. One hundred and twenty-three persons indicted for bigamy, blasphemy, witchcraft, Lutheranism, Judaism, and other crimes appeared in the presence of seven hundred clergymen, the Viceroy of New Spain, and the general population of Mexico City. Among the victims were thirty-nine accused of Judaizing.

Twenty-one of the latter group were accused for the first time. These showed repentance, asked for mercy, and abjured their heretical errors. As *reconciliados* they were accepted into the Catholic faith. As a result, instead of being condemned to death they were sentenced to confiscation of their possessions and to variable prison terms, expulsion from New Spain, public lashing, or galley slavery. Such was the mercy conceded to the penitents by the Inquisition.

Among the *reconciliados* was Doña Ana de Leon Carvajal, a nineteen-year-old unmarried sister of the martyr Luis de Carvajal who had been executed in 1596.[1]

Among the Judaizers condemned to death were the following:

1. Doña María Núñez de Carvajal, another unmarried sister of Luis de Carvajal, reconciled in 1596, was again imprisoned on the charge of having relapsed into Judaism. Because she expressed a wish to die as a Catholic, she was executed by the garrote [strangulation],

---

[1] Cf. Luis González Obregón, *Mexico viejo* (Mexico D.F. 1959), p. 686. Cf. José Toribio Medina, *Historia del Tribunal del Santo Oficio de la Inquisición en México* (Mexico D.F., 1952), p. 160.

and her body was immediately afterward burned at the stake. She was twenty-nine-years old.[2]

2. Thomas de Fonseca Castellanos, a native of Portugal, had come to Mexico from Holland. He became a miner in Taxco. Accused of relapsing into Judaism and condemned to death, because he showed a slight intention to die as a Catholic he was garroted and afterward burned.[3]

3. Francisco Rodríguez de Ledesma was accused of Judaizing and condemned to death. At the reading of his sentence at the auto-da-fé he asked for a new hearing and made some confessions. Consequently his execution was suspended, and he was returned to his cell. He died in prison, and his body was burned on April 20, 1603.[4]

Fifteen of the accused crypto-Jews had already left Mexico or had died. Their effigies were burned on March 25, 1601, and the bodies of those who had died in Mexico were exhumed and burned at the same time.[5]

Another auto-da-fé was celebrated on April 20, 1603. At this, Juan Núñez de León was executed by garrote, while Doña Clara Enríquez and Rodrigo del Campo were reconciled.[6] A sick old man, Antonio Gómez, was condemned to death for Judaizing, but he confessed at the last moment and was returned to prison for further investigation. At the March 25, 1605, auto-da-fé he appeared as reconciled.[7]

Diego Dias Nieto, born in Oporto, Portugal, had lived for some time in Ferrara, Italy, where Jews could openly profess their faith. In 1596, he was imprisoned in Mexico City as the result of a denunciation. He served one year in prison and was again imprisoned in 1601. He told the strange story that he had come to Mexico with a *Bulla* of Pope Clement VIII and with a royal license to collect alms. Being very learned in Judaism, he was able to discuss Bible passages and

2 L. G. Obregón, *op. cit.*, p. 690; J. T. Medina, *op. cit.*, pp. 160-161. For the garrote the condemned was placed with his back to a wooden pillar, his neck tied to the pillar (stake) with a thick cord on which an iron tourniquet was twisted, to strangle the condemned gradually. Cf. D. J. Garcia Icazbalceta, *Obras*, vol. I (Mexico, 1896), chapter "Autos da Fé celebrados in Mexico," pp. 271-316.

3 L. G. Obregón, *op. cit.*, p. 689; J. T. Medina, *op. cit.*, p. 160.

4 J. T. Medina, *op. cit.*, pp. 161, 162, 171; L. G. Obregón, *op. cit.*, p. 690.

5 *Ibid.*

6 J. T. Medina, *op. cit.*, p. 171. Juan Núñez de Leon is not mentioned in Obregón's list.

7 J. T. Medina, *op. cit.*, p. 171; L. G. Obregón, *op. cit.*, p. 691.

their interpretations with the scholarly clergymen. He appeared as reconciled during the auto-da-fé of March 25, 1605.[8]

Spain had been left virtually bankrupt at the death of Philip II in 1598. Portugal had been under Spanish rule since 1580 and, in 1605, rich Portuguese New Christians succeeded in buying from King Philip III a General Pardon for Judaizers of Portugese descent at that time indicted or imprisoned by the Holy Office in Spain, Portugal, or the Colonies. For this they paid 2,925,000 cruzados. The king's patent was dated February 1, 1605. When it reached Mexico, the only Judaizer in prison was Francisco López Enríquez, and he was set free.[9]

As a consequence of the trials of 1590, 1596, and 1601, Mexican Judaizers were ruined financially, imprisoned, expelled, or killed. The remnants certainly exercised caution in their observation of Jewish rites. During the subsequent thirty years only nine Judaizers were accused at autos-da-fé. Seven of them were reconciled and two were accused in absentia.[10] At the April 12, 1635, auto-da-fé twelve Judaizers appeared as reconciled and two were in absentia.[11] And in the year 1638 one person was reconciled.[12]

The tapering off of persecutions in Mexico and the economic prospects of the silver rush encouraged many Judaizers to migrate to Mexico from 1606 to 1642. They were active in business, and some became very wealthy. The Holy Office, seeking an opportunity to fill its coffers, in 1642 created such an occasion.

One day a priest reported that his two servants had overheard in the streets of Mexico City a conversation to the effect that certain Portuguese intended to set the Inquisition buildings on fire. Immediately a guard was placed around those buildings and an order was issued that no Portuguese should be allowed to embark at the Port of Vera Cruz.

The moment for the attack on the Portuguese was carefully chosen. Two years earlier Portugal had regained her independence and had crowned the Duke of Braganza as King John IV.

Portuguese all over the world, including Judaizers, were in sympathy with Portugal and thus were considered enemies of Spain.

8 J. T. Medina, op. cit., p. 173.
9 Ibid., pp. 112, 174.
10 L. G. Obregón, op. cit., p. 691; J. T. Medina, op. cit., pp. 170-176.
11 L. G. Obregón, op. cit., pp. 692-693; J. T. Medina, op. cit., pp. 184-185.
12 Ibid., p. 186.

On July 13, 1642, the Mexican Holy Office started a new campaign to exterminate the Judaizers by imprisoning forty of them. This move made a great stir all over Mexico, with the general population discussing the country's concern over the problem of the "perfidious Hebrews." The Holy Office had to arrange for additional space when, in a short time, more than a hundred and fifty prisoners were apprehended. Altogether, two hundred and sixteen Judaizers were tried, some in prison and others absent by death or flight. Between 1646 and 1649, several autos-da-fé were held. The last one, celebrated on April 11, 1649, was called the "Big One" [el auto grande]. On that occasion sixty-seven, who had either escaped in time or had died outside of Mexico, were burned in effigy. The bodies of those who had died in Mexico were exhumed and burned. One hundred and thirty-five of the accused were reconciliados who were punished in the manner explained above.

Fourteen Judaizers were accused of being relapsed heretics, and these perished as martyrs. One of them was burned alive, and thirteen died by the garrote. Here is a report of the fourteen trials, based on the accounts [relaciones del auto-da-fé] published under the auspices of the Holy Office in Mexico, on manuscripts and on other printed sources, which give an insight into social, economic, and religious conditions of the Judaizers of that time.[13]

1. Doña Ana de León Carvajal was a daughter of Francisco Rodríguez de Mattos and Doña Francisca Núñez de Carvajal, a sister of the martyr Luis de Carvajal. In 1601, at the age of nineteen, she had been reconciled. A widow of Cristóbal Miguel, she was very religious, observed holy days and fast days, prayed unceasingly, and was known among fellow Judaizers as a Santa [saint]. Even in prison she was heard to pray, repeating the word ADONAI. She denied all accusations and did not denounce anybody. As the last survivor of the Carvajal family, at the age of sixty-seven she was garroted and her body afterward burned at the stake.

---

13 The sources are Relacion sumaria del Auto particular de Fee ... Ano de 1646. Reprinted in Genaro Garcia y Carlos Pereyra, "Documentos inéditos o muy raros para la Historia de México," vol. XXVIII, p. 94; Breve y Sumaria Relacion de un Auto particular ... Mexico, 1647. Reprinted in "Documentos inéditos," vol. XXVIII, pp. 95-132; Relacion del Tercero Auto Particular de Fee ... treinta del mes de Marzo de 1648 (Mexico, 1648). Reprinted in "Documentos inéditos," vol. XXVIII, pp. 133-269, also in Museo Mexicano, tomo I, pp. 387 ff. (Mexico, 1943); Auto General de la Fee, Celebrado ... en la Ciudad de Mexico ... 11 de Abril, 1649 (Mexico, 1649). Cf. also Obregón, op. cit., pp. 693-709, and J. T. Medina, op. cit., pp. 111-120 and pp. 189-208.

2. Francisco López Blandon (alias Ferrasas) was born in 1619, son of Doña Leonor Núñez, and became a goldsmith in Mexico. Having been reconciled in 1635, he was subsequently imprisoned again on the charge of Judaizing. Blandon belonged to a family of well known Judaizers and was a brother-in-law of Thomas Trebiño de Sobremonte. He was specifically accused of having circumcised his little son born of a mulatto mother. Even in prison he was seen praying on his knees and fasting. He did not admit anything, nor did he denounce anybody during his trial. He was executed by garrote and later his body was burned at the stake.

3. Gonzálo Flores (alias Gonzáles Váez Méndez) was born in 1605 in La Torre de Moncorbo, Portugal, and was given the Hebrew name of Samuel. In Mexico he was a merchant. During his three years in prison, he consistently denied that he was a Judaizer, but later admitted it. Gonzálo behaved like an insane person, but during his incarceration in an asylum the doctors declared he was completely sane and responsible. He was executed by garrote and his body was burned at the stake.

4. Ana Gómez, born in Madrid in 1606, was a daughter of Leonor Núñez and Diego Fernando Cardado, a descendant of a family of martyrs. While in prison she often claimed that she wished to die as a martyr of the Jewish faith. She was executed by strangulation and her body was burned at the stake.

5. María Gómez, born in Madrid in 1617, was a sister of Ana Gómez and was married to Thomas Trebiño de Sobremonte. Having been reconciled in 1625, she was this time condemned for relapsing in Judaism. She was executed by strangulation, and her body was burned at the stake on the same day as her mother, Leonor Gómez Núñez, her sister Ana, and her husband Sobremonte were similarly executed.

6. Duarte de León Jaramillo, a businessman in Mexico, born in 1596 at Casteloblanco, Portugal, was the husband of Isabel Núñez. The Inquisition had always shadowed him. First imprisoned in 1628, his trial was suspended. In 1635 he was reconciled to Catholicism and later imprisoned again as a relapsed Judaizer because he had instructed his three sons, Francisco de León Jamarillo, Simón de León, Iorge Duarte (alias Iorge de León), and his three daughters, Clara Núñez, Antonia Núñez, and Ana Núñez, in the observation of the Jewish rites. He was known to have been very severe with his children. It was claimed that he had beaten them whenever he heard

them pray to the Holy Virgin María but to have treated them well from the moment they began to Judaize. He circumcised his son, Francisco de León. During the hearings his imprisoned daughters testified that he had performed a small operation on them when he initiated them into Judaism: He cut a piece of flesh from the left shoulder of each, roasted it, and ate it. The Tribunal accepted this fantastic story as an example of Jewish cannibalism. Padre Mathias de Bocanegra, who wrote the published report of the auto-da-fé, decided that this was a newly revealed method of circumcision and called Jamarillo "the inhuman Jew." His children further deposed that Jamarillo had often fasted in penance for having broken his vow to migrate to a country where Jews could freely practice their religion. They declared that on Friday evenings he and his wife and many other Jews locked themselves in a warehouse where they uttered shouts of joy. Jamarillo did not confess to anything, and at the auto-da-fé of April 11, 1649, he was condemned to death. He was executed by garrote and on the same day his body was burned at the stake.

7. Simón Montero, born in 1600 in Casteloblanco, Portugal, was a businessman and was married in Seville to Doña Elena Montero. Before migrating to Mexico, he visited Jewish communities in France, Rome, Livorno, and Pisa, studying to be a rabbi and teacher of dogma. In Mexico, he was seen to pray with other Judaizers while wearing *"túnicas judaicas con sus cucuruchos en las Cabezas"* [prayer shawl and phylacteries]. He was first imprisoned in 1635 as the result of a denunciation, on a charge that he had tried to buy a fresh grave for one of his friends. He denied everything when under torture and was set free. Again imprisoned and tried, he was condemned to death. During the auto of April 11, 1649, he was executed by garrote and his body was burned at the stake.

8. Leonor Gómez Núñez, born in Madrid in 1585, was the daughter of Gaspar Fernandes of Portugal. She was married three times. Her first husband was Fernando Cardado, and the children of this marriage were Ana Gómez and Isabel Núñez. Her second husband was Pedro López (alias Simón Fernández), and the children of this marriage were Francisco López Blandon and María Gómez (wife of Sobremonte). Her third husband was Francisco Nieto. Leonor Gómez Núñez was a devoted Jewess and instructed her children accordingly.

9. Simón Rodríguez Núñez, born in Portugal, had come to Mexico from Seville. He was accused of relapsing into Judaism and appeared

at the auto of January 23, 1647, and was condemned to death. He was executed the following day, by being first garroted and then burned at the stake.

10. Doña Catalina de Silva (alias Enríquez) was born in Seville in 1601. She was the wife of Diego Tinoco and sister of Antonio Rodrigues Arias and Blanca Enríquez, all of whom were tried by the Inquisition. She practiced Jewish rites and taught her children, Pedro and Isabel Tinoco, their observance. In Church, she was in the habit of covering her face with a handkerchef in order to avoid seeing the host and the chalice. In prison she fasted regularly and did not confess anything and did not ask for mercy. On April 11, 1649, she appeared at the auto-da-fé as condemned. On the insistence of her children she asked for mercy at the last moment. Because of this she was executed by garrote, and her body was burned at the stake.

11. Isabel Tristán, born in Seville in 1599, was the daughter of Simón López, a Portuguese, and married to her uncle, Luis Fernández Tristán. She was a pious Jewess and was accused of having invited other Judaizers to spend Jewish fast days in her home, where she served them appropriate meals at the completion of the fast. She appeared at the April 11, 1649, auto-da-fé as condemned and was executed the same day by garrote, and her body was burned at the stake.

12. Antonio Váez (alias Tirado, also called Captain de Casteloblanco) was born in Portugal in 1574, a brother of the famous Judaizer Simón Váez Sevilla. In 1625, Antonio appeared for the first time at an auto in Mexico and was reconciled to Catholicism. He boasted that he had not denounced anybody. Immediately after his liberation, he resumed the practice of Judaism and also instructed other New Christians in Judaism at the home of his brother Simón. Antonio told people that he was a descendant of the priestly tribe of Levi. Before couples went to their weddings in the Church, he married them at home in conformity with Jewish custom. He was often asked to visit the sick, when he would lay hands on the ailing part of the body, praying to ADONAI SABAOT. Many of those whom he instructed in Judaism were invited to participate in the *Seder* [home service on Passover eve] in his house and to partake of the Passover meal of lamb and *mazzot* [unleavened bread]. In 1640, he disagreed with Sobremonte concerning the exact date of *Yom Kippur*—as to whether the Judaizers in Mexico should fast during one week or another. While in prison, in 1625, he had circumcised Sobremonte. When the

wave of arrests began in 1642 Antonio Váez admonished his friends to confess to nothing and to denounce no one. During his own trial he behaved accordingly. Called by Padre Bocanegra "the priest of the Jews in this part of the Kingdom," he appeared at the April 11, 1649, auto-da-fé and was condemned. He was garroted and his body was burned at the stake.

13. Gonzálo Váez was born in 1602 at Casteloblanco, Portugal. He was a traveling salesman in the interior of Mexico. He was related as a nephew or cousin to most of the Judaizers in Mexico. Imprisoned and accused of practicing and propagating Judaism, he first admitted everything but later recanted. He also simulated insanity, but the doctors declared him responsible. On April 11, 1649, he appeared at the auto-da-fé, was condemned and, on the same day, was garroted, and his body was burned at the stake.

All these thirteen martyrs had practiced and propagated Judaism in Mexico knowing well the risk involved. As courageous and as strong as some of them were during the torturing by the Inquisition, they could not face being burned alive. That is the reason they appeared in the autos-da-fé procession carrying a green cross, agreeing to say a paternoster or to kiss a crucifix, sometimes at the last moment, and thereby were executed through strangulation, with their bodies being burned immediately afterward.

II

THOMAS TREBIÑO DE SOBREMONTE

Sobremonte was arrested by the Inquisition for the first time on March 1, 1624, and removed from Antequera, Mexico, to Mexico City on November 23, 1624.[14] During his hearings he vouchsafed the following biographical details.

14 The manuscripts of the Sobremonte trials (1625 and 1649) are found in the *Archivo General de la Nación* in Mexico City, vol. 1495. Photocopies of Sobremonte's signature and the sentences of the ecclesiastical and civil authorities have been obtained. The complete trials have been published in the original Spanish in *Boletín del Archivo General de la Nación*, vol. VI (Mexico City, 1935), pp. 99-148, 305-308, 420-464 and 578-620; vol. VII (Mexico City, 1936), pp. 88-142, 757-777; vol. VIII (Mexico City, 1937), pp. 1-172. There exists an English translation of the trials in the Library of the Cambridge University, England. Cf. J. Street, "The G. R. G. Collection in the Cambridge University Library: A Checklist," in the *Hispanic American Historical Review*, vol. XXXVII, no. 1, February, 1957, pp. 60-82.

He was born in the town of Medina de Rioseco in Castile, Spain. At the death of his father, Antonio, his mother, Doña Leonor Martínez de Villagómez, as he was told, was imprisoned by the Holy Office in Valladolid and died there. His brother Francisco was in Peru and his brother Jerónimo in Valladolid. His ancestors on his father's side had been Old Christians and noblemen [hidalgos]: De Sobremontes. He himself was baptized at birth and confirmed at the age of seven or eight.

Sobremonte correctly recited the paternoster and other Catholic prayers.[15] He knew how to read and write in his own language and in Latin because he had attended the College of the Jesuits in Valencia, Spain, for one year and had studied canonical law at the University of Salamanca. He was appointed page of Don Rodrigo Enríquez de Mendoza in Medina de Rioseco. One day another page in the same service called him "Jew" and in anger Sobremonte killed him. Because of this he went into hiding in a neighboring convent and changed his name to Jerónimo de Represa. In the year 1612, he sailed from Cadiz to Mexico and settled as a trader in the town of Guaxaca.

Accused by the Inquisitors of being a Judaizer, Sobremonte averred that when he was about fourteen years old his mother explained to him that Christians adore figures of wood and metal, while Jews adore ADONAI who gave the true law to Moses in the desert; that in order to obtain salvation (deliverance from sin and eternal damnation) he would have to believe in ADONAI, the God of the Jews. Under this influence he accepted ADONAI and the Law of Moses.

His mother had instructed him to keep his Judaism secret in order not to endanger their lives. She taught him several prayers but did not allow him to write them down. In broken Hebrew he recited:

> Sema, Adonai, Beruto, Ceolan, Banel [obviously the Shema prayer: "Shema Israel Adonai Elohenu Adonai Ehad. Baruch Shem Kevod Malchuto leolam Vaed"].

He further quoted a prayer which started with the defective Hebrew words:

> Binuam, Adonai, Maciadeno, [continuing in Spanish:] debajo o a sombra del abastado me adormezo, debajo, o so tu allas

---

[15] The Court usually examined the accused Judaizers, asking them to recite the Paternoster, Ave María, Credo y Salve, and the Doctrina. Cf. Nicolas Lopez Martinez, Los Judaizantes Castellanos y la Inquisición en Tiempo de Isabel la Católica (Burgos, 1954), p. 327.

sede alumbrado y enderezado a tu servicio, no temere, el pavor de la noche, y asi mismo decia, Adarja y escudo, y también no llegara a ti malicia, ni llaga que tralla dice en la prea de tu mano.[16]

Sobremonte then went on to explain that his mother had owned a notebook entitled *"Los Siete Salmos Penitenciales"* [the Seven Penitential Psalms] including psalms in her own handwriting. On the day before *Yom Kippur* the whole family assembled, took baths, and put on fresh linen, and ate fish. The same evening all prayed together while standing until two in the morning, and they also discussed the Law of Moses. They fasted a day and a night, then dined on fishmeal.

Sobremonte confessed that one day while on a business trip in Rio Hondo, Mexico, he had behaved dishonestly [*deshonesto*] with an Indian girl named Juana. When he returned to Rio Hondo a year and a half later he was told that Juana was the mother of twins, but he was not sure whether he was their father. He also admitted having had intercourse with Doña Luisa de Bilona, the wife of Don Alonso de Carriage. She too became pregnant and could not abort the child.

During renewed interrogations about his mother's teachings, Sobremonte deposed that the family rested on *Shabbat* [the Jewish Sabbath] but sometimes had to eat pork in order not to attract attention. He was taught to wash his hands before each meal and to pray:

> *Bendito sea el Poderoso Adonai, que en las enseñanzas me enseñaste el lavar de las manos, boca y ojos te alabrar y servir en loor y honra del Señor y en la Ley de Moisen* [Blessed be the Almighty Adonai, who taught me in his teachings to wash hands, mouth, and eyes in order to glorify and serve in praise and honor of the Lord and the Law of Moses].[17]

Sobremonte told the Court that he relented of having followed his mother's instructions and was willing to return to Catholicism. Even so, on February 1, 1625, the Promoter Fiscal [Ecclesiastic Attorney General] demanded capital punishment for him. The Court condemned him to appear at the March 25th auto-da-fé as a reconciled Catholic wearing the *sambenito* [penitential garment]. He was also sentenced to one year in prison and to confiscation of all his belongings.

---

16 Cf. *Boletin* mentioned above, vol. VI, pp. 426-427.
17 *Ibid.*, p. 435.

Besides, he was required to assist every Sunday and on holy days at High Mass and to attend the sermons in the Convent of the Dominican friars.

How serious Sobremonte's repentance was can be learned from subsequent events. On November 29, 1624, complying with his request, the Court assigned him a cell mate. This companion was Antonio Váez, who circumcised Sobremonte during his incarceration in the prison cell.

After his first condemnation, Sobremonte became seriously ill in the damp cell and was transferred to the hospital for paupers, where he was detained for four months. He was set free on June 16, 1626. He then resumed his business and was successful.

On June 20, 1629, he was again denounced to the Inquisitors by the Attorney General because he was seen horseback riding, publicly wearing arms, and dressed in silk and fine clothes—conduct as such was forbidden to persons reconciled by the Tribunals of the Holy Office. On July 16, 1629, several witnesses confirmed the denunciation. On February 26, 1630, a member of the Holy Office deposed that he had seen Sobremonte elegantly dressed and wearing a sword. Despite all this, Sobremonte was not imprisoned; however, he was frightened. In 1633, he wrote to the Holy Office offering one hundred pesos as a voluntary fine for delaying to present his rehabilitation document dated May 6, 1631, in Madrid, and signed by the Cardinal and General Inquisitor of Spain, Don Antonio Zapata. According to this document Sobremonte was entitled to wear arms and expensive clothes, to ride a horse, and to enjoy other privileges usually forbidden to the *reconciliados*. Inquisitors everywhere were expected to respect this Royal Decree. On April 23, 1633, the Inquisitors in Mexico acquiesced to this document and accepted the one hundred pesos offered by Sobremonte, and decided to use the money for repairs on the Holy Office's building.

Sobremonte was then left in peace by the Inquisition until 1644. Then the Attorney General denounced him on the ground that, since his reconciliation in 1625, he had been practicing Judaism. Information had been obtained that Sobremonte intended to sail from Acapulco to the Philippines, from where it would be easy for him to escape to Portuguese India. Consequently, Sobremonte was imprisoned again on October 11, 1644.

At his hearing on November 11, 1644, he deposed that the name of his grandfather was Pedro de Sobremonte, and that the name of his grandmother was María García Tremiño. One year after his reconciliation, in 1626, he had married Doña María Gómez, the daughter of Leonor Núñez and Pedro López. By 1644, he had five children: Rafael, Leonor, Micaela, Gabriel, and Salvador, their ages ranging from one and a half month to thirteen years. One son, Antonio, had died. From 1626 to 1632, he had lived in Guadalajara, and, since 1632, in Mexico City. He was a businessman and often traveled to Acapulco, Vera Cruz, Zacatecas, and Guadalajara.

Sobremonte did not confess to anything and did not denounce anybody, but many witnesses testified against him. Doña Margarita de Rivera told the Inquisitors about his 1624 circumcision by his cell mate, Antonio Váez. Four surgeons examined him and verified signs of circumcision. Rafael Sobremonte, his son, told the Inquisitors that his father had instructed him in Judaism, first telling him that all the Christians believed was nonsense [patarata], that God has no mother, and that they adored wooden images painted as saints. He was taught to believe in One God who had created heaven and earth. They fasted every Thursday and his father once struck him when he was caught eating on a Thursday. He stated also that his father circumcised him when he was about thirteen years old and taught him to pray daily upon awakening as follows:

> Bendita sea la luz del día, y el Señor que nos lo envía. Alabad al Señor todas las gentes; Alabad al Señor todos los pueblos. Porque ha confirmado sobre nosotros, y la verdad del Señor permanecerá para siempre. [Blessed be the light of the day and the Lord who sends it out. All peoples praise the Lord, all nations praise the Lord, because he has supported us. And the truth of the Lord remains forever.][18]

Many witnesses claimed that when Sobremonte married María Gómez, he celebrated the marriage in conformity with Jewish customs; that he and his family endeavored to eat kasher in accordance with Jewish dietary laws; that he recited psalms in Latin while his head was covered with a cap [montera]; that the crypto-Jewish community in Mexico considered him as a clergyman-rabbi [sacerdote-rabino]; that he calculated the dates of holy days and fast days in conformity with the Jewish calendar; that in the year 1640 he had a long discussion with Antonio Váez concerning the date of Yom Kippur [because an error had been made in observing the appearance of the new moon] as to whether the fast day that year was one week

18 Ibid., vol. VIII, p. 41.

earlier or later; that he and his family in that year fasted for eight days in order not to miss the day of Atonement;[19] that he prayed three times a day and sometimes even at midnight—always with his head covered and a towel tied to the cap for drying his hands after washing; that his family attended Mass and made confession in the Church only to deceive neighbors and authorities, but whenever they did so they fasted previously at home and knelt to ask God to forgive them for this sin.

Other witnesses testified concerning the wealth of Sobremonte, claiming that he had buried a few thousand pesos just before his trial in 1624; that he had always planned to take his family to Flanders, where they could live freely as professing Jews; that he had even made a vow to do so and that as long as he did not fulfill this vow he punished himself by regularly fasting twice a week.

Sobremonte denied everything that he was accused of during this second trial. Orally and in writing he protested that the depositions of his son Rafael and all the other witnesses were pure inventions, especially accusing Margarita de Rivera of having a treacherous tongue. The trial continued for five years. Sobremonte often fasted in prison, and he became emaciated. On February 21, 1649, the Tribunal condemned him to capital punishment.[20] He was required to appear at the auto-da-fé of April 11, 1649, to be burned alive at the stake.

The evening before that auto-da-fé, on April 10, 1649, Sobremonte was visited in his cell by three clergymen who tried to convert him to Catholicism before his death. One of them, Licenciado Francisco Corchero Correño, wrote a report covering the twenty-four hours spent with Sobremonte, and this report, attached to the trial manuscript, was dated April 17th [six days after the execution]. It relates that Correño and the padres Master Fr. Lorenzo Macdonald and Fr. Miguel de Leon, both Dominicans, were chosen to assist Sobremonte during his last twenty-four hours; that they admonished him to prepare himself to die as a Catholic; that Sobremonte became terribly irritated and, when he was asked to kiss a crucifix, he turned his face away and started to blaspheme Christianity, declaring that he was a Jew and wished to die as a Jew. The three clergymen tried all night to convert him, arguing without success. At five A.M., the time to leave the prison for the auto-da-fé procession, Sobremonte told his

19 *Ibid.,* vol. VII, p. 128.
20 See photograph on p. 230.

visitors that they should convert themselves to Judaism, because his God was the true one. Moreover, they asserted:

> No solo ya se contentaba esta bestia con confesar su muerta Ley de Moisés, pero su descaro llegó 'a que decía a voces que la siguiésemos porque su dios era el verdadero. [This beast was not satisfied to confess his dead Law of Moses, but his impudence reached the point of screaming that we should follow his God because he was the true one.]

During the procession to the plaza where the auto-da-fé was to be celebrated, Sobremonte was accompanied by the three clergymen who continued to plead with him for a last-minute conversion. The masses on the streets, says Correño—men, women, and children—begged Sobremonte "with Christian piety," while they were crying aloud and reciting the *Credo* and other prayers, to accept Catholicism before his execution.

When Sobremonte arrived on the stage of the auto-da-fé, priests of all orders tried to persuade him. Though he had been fasting for four days, he refused the food and drink offered him. Correño explained chapter 9 of Daniel to him, in which the appearance of a Messiah was prophesied, and showed him several other Bible passages. Finally Sobremonte answered:

> Do not exert yourself to convince me, for I must die as a Jew. It would be better to convert yourself to Judaism.

Because of the blasphemies Sobremonte had uttered, he was gagged. When other condemned Judaizers were brought upon the stage, Sobremonte tried to give them signs with his eyes that they should remain firm and die as Jews. When his mother-in-law, Leonor Gómez Núñez, her daughter María Gómez [Sobremonte's wife], and her other daughter, Ana Gómez, all condemned to death, appeared on the stage, Sobremonte [obviously not gagged at that time] said:

> Remember the mother of the Maccabeans!

When his sentence was read he said that he believed only in the God of Israel. (*"Como si nosotros lo negáramos"* [as if we others would deny him], adds Correño.)

After Sobremonte was declared *relajado* and released to the civil authorities for punishment, Correño accompanied him to the stage where General Don Jerónimo de Bañuelos, Corregidor of Mexico City, was performing his duties. This official condemned all other *relajados* to be garroted and burned after death. Only Thomas Trebiño de Sobremonte was condemned to be burned alive.

Following the other *relajados* who had to ride on pack animals through the streets of Mexico City from the stage of the auto-da-fé to the square selected for the burning, Sobremonte (the "perfidious") tried to mount a mule. But the mule, otherwise docile, refused to let him mount, leaping and jerking. Other mules acted in the same way. Finally Sobremonte was put on a mule with an Indian behind him to keep him in the saddle. During this ride even, the Indian tried to persuade Sobremonte to accept Catholicism.

The public on the streets along the way to the *Quemadero* was inflamed against Sobremonte and would have lynched him many times [*muchas veces*], says Correño, if he had not intervened, expecting that Sobremonte would show some sign of repentance at the last moment.

When Sobremonte was tied to the stake, the clergymen who surrounded him and also the public made continuous exhortations. When he was set on fire the clergymen begged him to make some sign of accepting Christianity (since this would have still saved him from being burned alive). But brave Sobremonte, not surrendering, asked in a loud voice that they should finish burning him. The report concludes:

> *Irritados los soldados, sacaron las espadas y dándole muchos golpes y los verdugos soplando el fuego y echando de abajo los hombres, mujeres y muchachos, la leña, murió entre las llamas, empezando a sentir su maldito cuerpo el fuego que su descomulgada alma estea y estará sintiendo en el infierno.*
> [The soldiers, irritated, drew their swords and gave him many blows while the executioners fanned the fire and men, women and children threw the wood into the burning flames, and his cursed body began to feel the fire which his excommunicated soul is feeling and will feel in hell.][21]

In Mexico City, the *Quemadero* [the burning place], in 1649, was situated in front of the still existing building of the Convent of San Diego [to the west of the Alemada passageway], on a plaza then called Tianguis de San Hipolito [Saint Hippolyte market square].

Besides the report by Correño there is a description of Sobremonte's execution in the booklet printed in Mexico City in 1649 covering that April 11th auto-da-fé. It explains that Sobremonte's neck and hands

[21] *Ibid.*, vol. VIII, pp. 154-158.

were tied to the stake before the burning began. Everybody hoped that, when he saw the other thirteen executed by strangulation and later burning, he would become frightened and say something that would cause him to die as a Christian and save himself from being burned alive.[22] The semi-official narrative closes with the statement that the following day at noon the flames were still burning. The Corregidor ordered that the ashes be assembled in carts and thrown into a canal behind the San Diego Convent.[23]

In none of the seventeenth century manuscripts or printed documents is there any trace of the claim that Sobremonte at the last moment with his feet drew the burning coals toward his body exclaiming:

> Echen leña, que mi dinero me cuesta [Throw in wood; I pay for it anyway].[24]

The Mexico City house where Sobremonte had lived could still be seen at the end of the nineteenth century and was shown as "La Casa del Judío" [the Jew's house].[25]

III

OTHER INTERESTING VICTIMS OF THE AUTOS-DA-FÉ CELEBRATED IN THE YEARS 1646 TO 1649

Besides the fourteen crypto-Jews who were burned at the stake there were, as mentioned earlier, hundreds of accused Judaizers who were reconciled during the autos-da-fé of the years 1646, 1647, 1648, and 1649. Of these, we shall here discuss the most interesting trials.

22 Don Gregorio Martin de Guijo, "Diario de Sucesos Notables" (1648-1664), in *Documentos para la Historia de México*, vol. I (Mexico, 1863). He calls Sobremonte: Tomás Tremiño de Campos.

23 L. G. Obregón, *op. cit.*, p. 246. "The victim, almost suffocated, but without heaving a scream, or a sigh, or the slightest complaint, contented himself to exclaim remembering his confiscated fortune and drawing with his feet the burning coal *(Echen leña, que mi dinero me cuesta)*." Obregón's unverified story was repeated but not quoted in Cecil Roth's account that Sobremonte's last audible words were, "Pile on the wood! How much money it costs me!" See *A History of the Marranos* (Philadelphia, 1947), p. 163. It was also repeated in Dr. George Alexander Kohut's statement that Sobremonte exclaimed amid the flames, "That's right—burn wood, pile it thick and fast; it costs you nothing; the fire is built with my money," see *PAJHS*, vol. XI, pp. 179, "Trial of Pedro Arias Maldonado."

24 De Guijo, *Diario de Sucesos Notables, op. cit.*

25 Cf. photo of the house in L. G. Obregón, *op. cit.*, p. 243, and in D. Vicente Riva Palacio, *México a través de los Siglos* (Barcelona), vol. II, p. 425.

Esperanza Rodrigues, a mulatto woman, born in Seville, Spain, in 1582, was the daughter of the Negro, Isabel, of Guinea, Africa, and the New Christian, Francisco Rodrigues. She married a German sculptor by the name of Juan Francisco del Bosque, and bore him three daughters: María Rodrigues del Bosque, Isabel Rodrigues del Bosque, and Juana Rodrigues del Bosque, the last marrying the Portuguese Judaizer, Blas López. The mother and the three daughters admitted Judaizing and asked for mercy. They were reconciled to Catholicism during the auto-da-fé of April 16, 1646.[26]

Manuel Carrasco, a native of Villa Flor, Portugal, at this time twenty-six years old, was the manager of a sugar storehouse in Valle das Amilpas. He was accustomed to wearing in a bag on his chest a piece of *mazzah* [unleavened bread] as a relic brought from a *seder* in Madrid. He used it as a remedy for sick people. He was reconciled to Catholicism in 1646.[27]

Captain Francisco Gómez Tejoso Tristán, a fifty-eight-year-old bachelor, born in Valencia del Cid, Spain, and circumcised, captain of infantry in Vera Cruz, son of Pedro Gómez Tejoso Tristán of Lisbon, averred that his grandfather on his mother's side had been baptized in order to avoid persecution. Being very sad [*triste*] because of that, he adopted the name Tristán, which all his descendants used. Tejoso was reconciled in 1646.[28]

Rafael and Gabriel Granada were the sons of Manuel de Granada and Doña María de Rivera. They testified that their mother had instructed them in Judaism when they were thirteen years old. Fast days were observed in their home, and after fasting they ate eggs, fish and vegetables. Gabriel told the court that it was the custom to put some grains of seed pearls into the mouth of a deceased person. His aunt Margarita de Rivera spoke about the "Virgin and her son" with contempt and confided to him that she used to lash a crucifix. While Gabriel was in prison he was visited by five surgeons who, in the presence of an officer of the court and a jailor, separately examined him to see if he had been circumcised. They found signs of circumcision. Both brothers showed repentance, asked for mercy, and became reconciled to Catholicism in 1646. In the sentence, the court

26 Genaro Garcia, *Documentos inéditos, op. cit.,* vol. XXVIII, pp. 47-48; L. G. Obregón, *op. cit.,* p. 693; J. T. Medina, *op. cit.,* pp. 114 and 193.

27 Genaro Garcia, *op. cit.,* pp. 72-73; L. G. Obregón, *op. cit.,* p. 701; J. T. Medina, *op. cit.,* p. 193.

28 Genaro Garcia, *op. cit.,* pp. 51-52; L. G. Obregón, *op. cit.,* p. 695; *Historia,* pp. 114, 193.

quoted from the Bible that "God desires not the death of the sinner but that he should be converted and live."[29]

Margarita de Morera, the thirty-six-year-old wife of Pedro de Castro, had once in Mexico City witnessed the public lashing of a condemned Judaizer and had freely manifested her pity for the sufferer. When an Old Christian once asked her how the Judaizers knew when to congregate for their ceremonies, she said the signal was the beating of a drum by a little Negro boy gaily dressed and going through the streets. She appeared at the 1646 auto as reconciled.[30]

Manuel Rodríguez Núñez, thirty-four years old, born in Casteloblanco, was unemployed and therefore in the documents was called an idle vagrant [vagamundo]. In fear of the Inquisition, he had changed his name to Manuel Méndez (alias Manuel Díaz) and lived in the suburbs of Mexico City. He told the Inquisitors that in the year 1640 there was a great dispute among the secret Jews in Mexico concerning the exact day of Yom Kippur—as to whether it occurred eight days sooner or later in conformity with the Christian calendar. He added that each of the two groups followed the decision of the leader and fasted on different days.[31]

Margarita de Rivera, born in Seville, was the thirty-three-year-old daughter of Blanco de Rivera. She was a dollmaker and was married to Miguel Núñez de Huerta. She was a great faster, and she was accustomed to participating at the washing of corpses and in performing other ceremonies for the dead. Whenever she had a bad dream she went to confession so as to transfer the bad omen to the priest [por echar el mal agüero en el confessor]. She used to say that Judaizers who married Old Christians would go to hell. She was reconciled in the year 1646.[32]

Gaspar Váez Sevilla was the twenty-eight-year-old son of the wealthy and very pious Judaizer, Simón Váez Sevilla, and of Doña Juana Enríquez. While his mother was carrying him, the Mexican Judaizers expected that he would be born the Messiah of the Jews,

29 Genaro Garcia, op. cit., vol. XXVIII, pp. 54, 82, 83; L. G. Obregón, op. cit., p. 696; J. T. Medina, op. cit., pp. 114, 191, 193. The manuscript of Gabriel de Granada's trial was published with a preface and notes by Dr. Cyrus Adler. Cf. "Trial of Gabriel de Granada by the Inquisition of Mexico. 1642-1652," in PAJHS, vol. VII (1899), pp. 1-134.

30 Genaro Garcia, op. cit., vol. XXVIII, pp. 70-71; L. G. Obregón, op. cit., p. 697.

31 Genaro Garcia, op. cit., vol. XXVIII, pp. 73-75; L. G. Obregón, op. cit., p. 694.

32 Genaro Garcia, op. cit., vol. XXVIII, pp. 67-70; L. G. Obregón, op. cit., pp. 695-696; J. T. Medina, op. cit., pp. 113, 115, 191, 193.

and his mother made nine visits to a Saint Moses that a certain woman had painted.[33] He was reconciled in 1646.

Miguel Tinoco, a twenty-three-year-old bachelor, apprenticed to a silversmith, functioned as sexton of the secret Jewish community. Three days before Passover he distributed unleavened bread which had been baked by Blanca Enríquez, the "great Jewess" [la gran Judía]. Miguel became reconciled in 1646.[34]

Pedro López de Morales, having been born in Rodrigo, Spain, was a forty-nine-year-old miner in Ixtan, Mexico. He was the son of Morales de Mercado of Portugal. It was proven that he had intended to send his little daughter [mestizuela, since her mother was a Mexican Indian], to Spain to be instructed in Judaism by relatives there. Morales was reconciled in 1647.[35]

Pedro Fernández de Castro, born in Valladolid, Spain, and bearing signs of circumcision, was a thirty-four-year-old peddler in Santiago de los Valles, Mexico. He was the son of the lawyer, Ignacio de Aguado, of Portuguese descent. Pedro had previously lived in Ferrara, Italy, as a freely professing Jew and had also visited the synagogues in Genoa and in Livorno, Italy. He arrived in Mexico in 1640 in order to cash the promised dowry from his rich father-in-law, Simón Váez Sevilla. Pedro had married Simón's daughter, Leonor Váez, in Pisa, where she was living with a sister and nieces. When he fell into the hands of the Inquisition he declared that in the house of his father-in-law in Mexico City he met crypto-Jews from Spain, Peru, and the Philippines, and that they observed fast days together. He became reconciled in 1647.[36]

Francisco de León Jaramillo, born in Mexico in 1626 and unmarried, was the son of Duarte de León Jaramillo (burned at the stake in 1649) and Isabel Núñez. He deposed that his father had circumcised him in the presence of his mother and grandmother, Justa Mendes, and that he had learned the common prayers of Judaizers in his father's home. He became reconciled in 1647.[37]

33 Genaro Garcia, op. cit., pp. 52-53; L. G. Obregón, op. cit., p. 696; J. T. Medina, op. cit., 114, 193.
34 Genaro Garcia, op. cit., pp. 76-77; L.G. Obregón, op. cit., p. 698; J. T. Medina, op. cit., p. 193.
35 Genaro Garcia, op cit., pp. 124-125; L. G. Obregón, op. cit., p. 696; J. T. Medina, op. cit., p. 117.
36 Genaro Garcia, op. cit., pp. 125-128; L. G. Obregón, op. cit., p. 697; J. T. Medina, op. cit., pp. 117, 194.
37 Genaro Garcia, op. cit., pp. 109-111; Anonimo, Autos-de-Fe (Mexico, 1953), pp. 7-14; L. G. Obregón, op. cit., p. 697; J. T. Medina, op. cit., pp. 116, 195; Misterios de la Inquisición y otras Sociedades Secretas de España (traducido del francés, México, 1850), p. 25.

Jorge Jacinto Bazan (alias Baca), of Portuguese Jewish descent, had been born in Malaga, Spain, in 1610. He was married to Doña Blanca Juárez, a niece of Juana Enríquez (wife of Simón Váez Sevilla), and was a merchant in Mexico City. At the age of thirteen, he had been circumcised in Marseilles, France, by a surgeon from Florence, Italy. He migrated to Mexico in the year 1637, bringing a letter of recommendation to Simón Váez Sevilla. Sevilla sent him as a salesman on trips to the interior of Mexico. Once in Sevilla's house he met a famous rabbi recently arrived from Spain who was acquainted with his Jewish parents in Italy. Bazan himself had been in Pisa, Livorno, Salonika, and Marseilles. The famous rabbi advised him that, in case of interrogation by the Inquisition, he should say he was a circumcised Jew from Pisa. Bazan was considered a fine Jew [un Judío fino], and his pretty wife was very religious too. He was reconciled in 1648.[38]

Francisco Lopes Dias [nicknamed el chato], was born in the year 1608 in Casteloblanco, Portugal, and at this time lived in Zacatecas, Mexico. He and his family had left Portugal because of severe persecutions of crypto-Jews and had first settled in Seville. They prayed and fasted there together with many other Portuguese Judaizers. On Yom Kippur one of them recited prayers from a Hebrew prayer book. In 1637, Dias migrated to Mexico City and continued to observe Judaism with Mexican Judaizers. He advised them as to what they should do and say in case of persecution by the Inquisition. Dias was reconciled in 1648.[39]

Beatriz Enríquez, twenty-nine years old, was the daughter of Antonio Rodrigues Arias and Blanca Enríquez of Seville, and married to Tomás Núñez de Peralta. She told the Court that at the age of twelve she was instructed in Judaism by her mother. The whole night before the Day of Atonement she prayed with her parents, standing without shoes. She had married Peralta because he was known to be a pious Jew. Good Jews like Peralta, and especially children of martyrs, were considered as being aristocrats and highly eligible for marriage. Judaizers used to assemble in the house of Simón Váez Sevilla who often told the guests that in case of imprisonment and persecution by the Inquisition they should not, even under torture, admit anything or denounce anybody. He used to boast that his arms were strong

[38] Genaro Garcia, op cit., pp. 133-269; L. G .Obregón, op. cit., p. 699; Misterios, pp. 46-48; J. T. Medina, op. cit., pp. 118-195.

[39] Anonimo, pp. 11-22; Misterios, pp. 43-48; Relacion del Tercero Auto particular Mexico, 1648); L. G. Obregón, op. cit., p. 699; J. T. Medina, op. cit., p. 195.

enough to endure tortures. Blanca Enríquez said that after the burial of a Judaizer visitors brought hardboiled eggs (which had to be eaten without salt). Such a visit of mourners was considered a very good deed and called *Aveluz*.[40] After a death, the water from all pitchers in the house was poured out, because it was believed that the departing soul had washed away all his sins in this water. Whenever there was no rabbi present to perform a marriage ceremony, the Judaizers would marry by giving each other their word of honor and then go to the Church for the required Catholic marriage. In case a rabbi [*sacerdote de su ley*] was available, he offered the benedictions over a glass of wine; the married couple and the guests then drank of the wine, and the glass was thrown upward and broken. Beatriz Enríquez was reconciled in 1648.[41]

Micaela Enríquez, the thirty-four-year-old sister of this Beatriz Enríquez, was married to Sebastián Cardoso. She repeated the same charges to the court as her sister and added that on Friday evenings her mother used to light oil lamps instead of the usual candles. In order not to attract the attention of the slave-girl servants, the lamps were hidden in an empty wooden box. Her mother used to call the Old Christians "*Orcos*"[42] and instructed the children neither to eat pork nor any meat at the same time with butter. After the death of her grandmother, so many Judaizers came to their house for the *Aveluz* ceremony, that it looked like a public synagogue. Doña Micaela was called a witch [*hechizera*] because she carried on her body certain roots and the teeth of dead people. She was reconciled in 1648.[43]

Doña Rafaela Enríquez, another daughter of Doña Blanca Enríquez and Antonio Rodríguez, was married to Gaspar Juárez. She deposed that when she was twelve or thirteen her parents sent her to a relative for instruction in Judaism. The whole family in Mexico practiced Judaism almost as openly as they had done in Amsterdam, Livorno, and Pisa. They married only crypto-Jews and were categorically opposed to intermarriage with Old Christians because they knew that the offspring not receiving a Jewish education would be lost to Judaism. Before the Day of Atonement, everybody took warm baths and lighted

---

40 Even though the word *Aveluz* sounds Spanish, there is no such word in the Spanish language. It is obviously the Hebrew word *Avelut* (mourning).

41 *Misterios*, pp. 34-38; *Anonimo*, vol. IV, pp. 15-35; Genaro Garcia, vol. XXVIII, pp. 203-212; L. G. Obregón, *op. cit.*, p. 699; J. T. Medina, *op. cit.*, pp. 112, 116, 117 and 195.

42 *Orcos* most probably is an abbreviation of *porcos* (hogs).

43 *Misterios*, pp. 53-54; L. G. Obregón, *op. cit.*, p. 699; J. T. Medina, *op. cit.*, pp. 119, 195, 218.

about eighty wax candles for the souls of the living and the dead. In Simón's house meetings were held for discussions of Judaism. When the wave of arrests began, the leaders distributed among the crypto-Jews notes concerning the Catholic doctrines in order that everybody could learn them by heart and recite them in case of arrest, because prisoners were usually asked to prove that they were good Catholics by reciting the *Paternoster*, the *Ave María*, the *Credo*, and the *Salve Regina*. Besides, everybody was instructed not to confess anything and was threatened in case they denounced others. Doña Rafaela Enríquez was reconciled in 1648.[44]

Doña Blanca Juárez, a native of Mexico, was the twenty-two-year-old daughter of Rafaela Enríquez. She was very religious and was considered a *Santa* [holy woman]. She was married to Jorge Jacinto Bazan, and it was expected that she would give birth to the Messiah. Her family dressed her in a tunic of silver cloth and seated her in the center of visitors who prayed that she should give birth to the Messiah. She could speak the African language of Angola and used that language in speaking to the Negro servants in prison. She told the Inquisitors that her grandmother, Doña Blanca Enríquez, on the Day of Atonement used to put her hands on her head while she was kneeling, to bless her in the name of Abraham, Isaac, and Jacob. She became reconciled in 1648.[45]

Doña Violante Juárez, born in Lima, Peru, was the thirty-six-year-old illegitimate daughter of Gaspar Juárez and was married to Manuel de Mello. Their house in Guadalajara was a prayer center for Judaizers. She became reconciled in 1648.[46]

Leonor Martínez, the fourteen-year-old daughter of the martyr Sobremonte, told the Court that her parentts and grandparents had instructed her in Judaism. She had assisted at a Jewish marriage which was afterwards celebrated in the Church. Whenever her father left on a journey he first assembled his children, put his hands on their heads, and gave them his blessing. Leonor was a very religious girl and was considered by the Mexican Judaizers as being a little *Santa*.[47]

[44] *Relacion del Tercero Auto particular* (Mexico, 1648); *Misterios*, pp. 55-58; L. G. Obregón, *op. cit.*, pp. 698-699; J. T. Medina, *op. cit.*, pp. 119, 195, 218.
[45] Cf. *Relacion del Tercero Auto particular* (Mexico, 1648); L. G. Obregón, *op. cit.*, p. 699; J. T. Medina, *op. cit.*, pp. 118, 195.
[46] *Relacion, op. cit.; Misterios*, pp. 63-65; L. G. Obregón, *op. cit.*, p. 699; J. T. Medina, *op. cit.*, p. 195.
[47] *Relacion, op. cit., Misterios*, pp. 48-49; L. G. Obregón, *op. cit.*, p. 699; J. T. Medina, *op. cit.*, pp. 118, 120, 195.

Manuel de Mello arrived in Mexico in 1624 where he worked as a silver- and goldsmith and was known as one of the finest Jews who had ever migrated from Spain. He instructed many people in Judaism and married a pious girl, Violante Juárez, daughter of Gaspar Juárez. In order to be less exposed, they left Mexico City and went to Guadalajara, where their house became the center [*sinagoga*] for secret Jews, and where, whenever necessary, the secret Jews could get food and help. He was reconciled in 1648.[48]

Ana Núñez, Antonio Núñez, and Clara Núñez were the daughters of León Jaramillo who was burned at the stake in 1649. All three of them had told the Inquisition the strange story mentioned earlier that their father, when starting to instruct them in Judaism, had cut a piece of flesh from the left shoulder of each, roasted and eaten it. Ana also said that her father beat her cruelly whenever he heard her tell her rosary beads. Antonia said her father loved her more than the other children and gave her nice dresses because she used to fast and pray and observe Jewish rites. She further deposed that her father had prayed with his face to the East while wearing a cap on his head and a Jewish prayer shawl and phylacteries (*una vestidura colorada de bombazi con su cucurucho y capirote*). Clara deposed that her family had forbidden her to fraternize with Old Christians; that the night after her mother was imprisoned she saw her father and brothers bury silver money, ingots and other valuable things. After her father's imprisonment, because she had been called Clara, the Jewess, she changed her name to Josefa de Alzate and told people she was a Moorish girl [*Morisca*]. All three sisters were reconciled in 1648.[49]

Rafael de Sobremonte was the young son of the martyr, Thomas Trebiño de Sobremonte, who was burned alive in 1649. Rafael, born in Guadalajara, Mexico, in 1648 was only seventeen years old. He told the Inquisitors that his father had circumcised him while his mother, Doña María Gómez, and his grandmother held him in their laps. Until he was healed a wax candle was burned nightly in his room and his father prayed until dawn. After his convalescence he was bathed and neatly dressed for the family's festivities. He was brought up to be very religious. In 1643 and 1644, he accompanied his father on a business trip to Zacatacas and Guadalajara, and they did

48 *Relacion, op. cit., Misterios,* pp. 51-52; L. G. Obregón, *op. cit.,* p. 699.
49 *Relacion, op. cit., Antonimo,* vol. IV, pp. 7-13 and 39-49, 46-55; *Misterios,* pp. 30-34, 40-42; Genaro Garcia, *op. cit.,* vol. XXVIII, pp. 201-203; J. T. Medina, *op. cit.,* pp. 117-119, 195.

not eat on Thursdays, sometimes not even on Mondays. His father instructed him in Jewish prayers and in Judaism generally. When he returned to Mexico City his mother, grandmother and aunt were very proud of the "new Judaizer."

Rafael further said that when he was traveling with his father they were one day caught by a heavy rain shower. When his father then heard him praying to the Queen of the Angels, he scolded him and told him that God does not have a mother and that there exists only one God who created heaven and earth. His father had also confided in him his intention of soon taking the whole family away from Mexico to a country where they could worship freely. Rafael was reconciled in 1648.[50]

Doña Ana Enríquez, born in Seville, Spain, had already been reconciled in Seville, and it was known that she had been very brave and had not denounced anybody under torture. In Mexico City, she was a fervent Judaizer and instructed others in Jewish rites and ceremonies. People came to her to be cured by her prayers from the consequences of an evil eye and bewitchment. In the case of a death among the Judaizers she gave instructions on the rites to be observed. She passed away in Mexico City before she could be apprehended. Nevertheless, she was indicted and burned in effigy on April 11, 1649.[51]

Doña Blanca Enríquez, born in Lisbon, Portugal was the daughter of Diego Núñez Batoca and Juana Rodríguez, both persecuted and reconciled by the Inquisition in Granada, Spain. She was married to Antonio Rodrigues Arias. The teachings of her mother Juana had made her a very religious person and an instructor of Judaism in Mexico. She educated her children—Beatrix, Micaela, and Rafaela mentioned above—to practice Judaism and to teach it to her grandchildren. She saw to it that they did not marry Old Christians whom she always called enemies. All crypto-Jews in Mexico considered her as the master-teacher [maestra] of Jewish prayers and ceremonies. She believed the year 1642 to 1643 was the date of the arrival of the Messiah who would liberate all of them from the persecutions by the Inquisition. Doña Blanca Enríquez died in prison. Her body was

50 Relacion, op. cit., Misterios, pp. 58-60; L. G. Obregón, op. cit., p. 699; J. T. Medina, op. cit., pp. 119, 120, 195.
51 Cf. P. Mathias de Bocanegra, Auto General de la Fee 1649 (Mexico, 1649); L. G. Obregón, op. cit., p. 705; J. T. Medina, op. cit., p. 206.

exhumed and delivered to the secular powers for burning at the stake on April 11, 1649.[52]

Juana Enríquez, born in Seville, as mentioned above, was the wife of Simón Váez Sevilla and the mother of Gaspar and Leonor Váez Sevilla. Juana was a very religious woman, observing *Shabbat*, fast and holy days and ritual baths, and giving generously for charity. Being the wife of a rich businessman she also attracted attention by her elegant ways, her fine dresses, luxurious carriages, servants, etc. She was considered a *Santa* because she prayed very often. She was expected to bring the Messiah into the world. As mentioned earlier, her house was a center for Mexican Jews. In her home Saturday meals were cooked on Friday, and Judaizers celebrated *Shabbat* there.

Padre Bocanegra, who wrote the report on the auto-da-fé in which she appeared, declares that the Mexican Jews expected that María Gómez, wife of Sobremonte, or Juana Enríquez, wife of Simón Váez Sevilla, would give birth to the Messiah. He adds with obvious pleasure that both these mothers were publicly lashed.

The Inquisitors had sentenced Juana not only to become reconciled, but also to confiscation of her possessions, to the wearing of the penitential cloak, to expulsion from the West Indies, to permanent imprisonment, and also to 200 lashes in the streets of Mexico City.[53]

Matias Rodrigues de Olivera, a fifty-one-year-old bachelor from Portugal, was known as a very religious Judaizer. He wore a gold medal with a Hebrew letter on it, which was suspended from a golden chain. He did not permit his slaves to be baptized. He was reconciled in 1649.[54]

Doña María de Rivera, the daughter of Diego López, had come from Casteloblanco, Portugal. She was the mother of Gabriel and Rafael de Granada who were circumcised by Alvaro de Acuña in San Luis Potosí, Mexico. She refused food in prison and died of hunger. Her corpse was exhumed and burned on April 11, 1649.[55]

Juana Rodríguez, born in Lisbon, was considered a holy person among the crypto-Jews in Mexico because of her way of life. She was the daughter of Rodrigo Rodríguez (alias Núñez) and Ysabel Rodríguez and was married to Diego Núñez Batoca. She had four

52 Mathias de Bocanegra, *op. cit.;* L. G. Obregón, *op. cit.,* p. 707; J. T. Medina, *op. cit.,* pp. 205, 408.
53 Mathias de Bocanegra, *op. cit.;* L. G. Obregón, *op. cit.,* pp. 700-701; J. T. Medina, *op. cit.,* pp. 203-204.
54 Mathias de Bocanegra, *op. cit.*
55 Mathias de Bocanegra, *op. cit.;* L. G. Obregón, *op. cit.,* p. 707.

daughters—Juana Enríquez, Clara de Silva, Ysabel de Silva, Gerónima Esperança—and a son named Gabriel Rodríguez Arias. She had raised them in the Jewish faith. When she died her children buried her in a separate virgin grave prepared only for her, her children, and her grandchildren. She was already dead in 1649, and therefore her body was exhumed and burned.

The above-mentioned Padre Bocanegra calls her the "root and the trunk of the great number of Judaizers" [raíz y tronco de la multitud de Judaizantes].[56]

Gonzálo Díaz Santillán, born in Casteloblanco, Portugal, was murdered by fellow crypto-Jews because he had extorted money from them by threatening to denounce them to the Holy Office.[57] The informer has always been considered an outlaw by the Jews.

> The most dangerous offenders, informers, were subject to the extreme penalty wherever the community could exercise capital jurisdiction.[58]

In the twelfth century an informer was stoned to death at the most solemn hour of Yom Kippur.[59] The medieval rabbis proclaimed it a good deed to kill an informer. Santillán was exhumed and burned by the Inquisitors on April 11, 1649.

Simón Váez Sevilla (alias Simon Soburro), born in Casteloblanco, Portugal, in the year 1598, was the son of Gaspar Gonçález (alias Soburro) and Leonor Váez, both of whom were prosecuted, tried, and reconciled by the Inquisition in Lisbon. Simón was a businessman in Mexico City, married to Doña Juana Enríquez and the father of Gaspar Váez Sevilla and Leonor Váez Sevilla, all tried by the Inquisition in Mexico. His brother was Antonio Váez (alias Antonio Tirado) who had been burned at the stake as a relapsed Judaizer. His sister, Doña Elena de Silva (alias Elena López), was tried and reconciled. He was an uncle of Isabel de Silva (alias Isabel Correa) who was tried and reconciled, and of Leonor Váez and Gonzálo Váez, who was burned at the stake as a relapsed Judaizer. His

---

56 Mathias de Bocanegra, op. cit., L. G. Obregón, op. cit., p. 702; J. T. Medina, op. cit., pp. 205, 409.

57 Mathias de Bocanegra, op. cit.; L. G. Obregón, op. cit., p. 702; J. T. Medina, op. cit., p. 408.

58 Cf. Salo Wittmayer Baron, The Jewish Community, vol. I, (Philadelphia, 1948), p. 169.

59 Cf. Abraham A. Neuman, The Jews in Spain, vol. I (Philadelphia, 1948), p. 132.

daughter, Leonor Váez Sevilla, and his sister, María, lived as freely professing Jews in Pisa, Italy.

The Inquisitors imprisoned Simón Váez as a leader of the Judaizers in Mexico. He was one of the richest, and his house was the center for those who came from Portugal, Spain, Italy, or the Philippines with letters of recommendation. Simón helped them to get started by giving them merchandise which they peddled in the interior of Mexico. Externally he lived as a Catholic, keeping good relations with the authorities. His house was not only a prayer center but also a forum of discussion. Everybody was instructed in case of imprisonment not to confess anything and not to denounce anybody, even under torture. It was known that Simón belonged to the tribe of Levi, and also that because of this the Mexican Judaizers considered him their leader. In view of the fact that he was now tried for the first time, he became reconciled to Catholicism, declaring to the Inquisitors that he was repentant and asking for mercy. At the auto-da-fé of April 11, 1649, he was sentenced to wear the penitential garment, to prison, to confiscation of his fortune, and to expulsion from Mexico.[60]

Pedro Tinoco, twenty-nine and unmarried, a native of Mexico, was a Bachelor of Philosophy and Medicine. In Mexico City he practiced as a physician. He was the son of Diego Tinoco and Doña Catalina de Silva (alias Enríquez). His mother was burned at the stake on April 11, 1649, as mentioned above. The Inquisitors considered Pedro one of the most skilled and dangerous Judaizers and were afraid that he, like Sobremonte, could become another martyr for Judaism. His first instruction in Judaism he had received from his grandmother, Blanca Enríquez. Later, he had studied the Bible, Jewish history, customs and rites, and had explained them to other Judaizers who consulted him. He observed Passover, as well as the fast days of *Yom Kippur, Esther,* and *Tishah be-'Ab.* In prison, he was at first stubborn; then he asked for mercy and was reconciled on April 11, 1649. He had to abjure his heretical errors, wear the penitential garment, and be deported to Spain. In addition, his academic diplomas were canceled and he was given 200 lashes in public.[61]

The impoverished Holy Office in Mexico City grew rich in 1640 as a result of the persecutions *en masse* of the Marranos and the

60 Mathias de Bocanegra, *op. cit.;* J. T. Medina, *op. cit.,* pp. 116, 203.
61 Mathias de Bocanegra, *op. cit.;* L. G. Obregón, *op. cit.,* p. 703; J. T. Medina, *op. cit.,* pp. 203-204.

confiscation of their fortunes—cash, goods, real estate, etc. The value
of the confiscations from 1640 to 1646 amounted to 429,389 pesos.[62]
Confiscations in 1646 amounted to 38,732 pesos; and, in 1647, to
109,930 pesos.[63] Most of the confiscated three million pesos (1640-
1649) was pocketed by the Judges-Inquisitors in the form of loans.
Besides, they purchased for themselves at very advantageous prices
the properties of the imprisoned crypto-Jews put up for sale by the
Holy Office—that is, by themselves.[64]

The crypto-Jewish community in Mexico was completely destroyed
by the trials, condemnations, and executions during the years 1646 to
1649. In the subsequent fifty years—up to the last trial of a Judaizer
in Mexico—only ten were tried.[64a] Seven of them were Juan Pacheco
de León, Luis Pérez Roldán, María de Zárate, Diego de Alvarado
[who died in prison], Manuel de León, Domingo Rodrigues, and

[62] Cf. J. T. Medina, op. cit., p. 210.
[63] The list of the confiscations for the years 1646 and 1647, found in manuscript
in the Archivo Histórico Nacional, Madrid (vol. 1054/768, folio 493) shows:

1646

Francisco Núñez Navarro	922
Francisco Gómez Texosso	3,353
Doña Juana Tinoco	1,884
Luis de Amesquita Sarmiento	8,827
Doña Leonor Núñez	268
Doña Margarita de Rivera	1,239
Doña Margarita de Morera	9,827
Manuel Dias de Castilla	1,320
D. Nuño Pereyra	1,324
Simón Feruz de Torres	8,796
Thomas Nunes de Peralta	972
Total	38,732 pesos

1647

Antonio Mendes Chillon	25,087
Da. Beatriz Enriques	105
Fernando Rodríguez	9,997
Francisco Franco de Morera	35,081
Gerónimo Fernández Correa	106
Juan Méndez de Villaniciosa	36,319
Juan Juárez	102
Juan Cardosso	1,498
Pedro López de Morales	492
Thomas Méndez	1,143
Total	109,930 pesos

This is the correct addition of the figures. In the manuscript, however, the
figures are erroneously given as 14,862 instead of 148,662. Medina, on the
other hand, did not check the figures and gives the amount in 1646 as
38,732 and in 1647 as 148,562. Cf. J. T. Medina, op. cit., p. 210. There are
no figures available concerning the years 1648 and 1649.
[64] Cf., J. T. Medina, op. cit., p. 210.
[64a] Cf. Trial manuscripts in the Archivo General de la Nación in Mexico City.

Luis de Burgos. Three others—Francisco Botello, Diego Dias, and Fernando de Medina—became martyrs.[64b]

The manuscripts covering the trials of the last three have never been published; a summary of them follows.

IV

THE TRIAL OF FRANCISCO BOTELLO

Francisco Botello was born in Priego, Andalucia, Spain, a descendant of Portuguese Judaizers who were persecuted and punished by different Inquisition tribunals. Botello became a mason and lived in Tacubaya, a suburb of Mexico City, and married María de Zárate.

The first time he was arrested by the Inquisitors was in 1642, and never during his seven years of imprisonment did he admit that he was a Judaizer. Neither did he denounce other Judaizers, despite cruel tortures. He was condemned to appear at the auto-da-fé of April 11, 1649, to abjure his errors de vehementi, to suffer 200 lashings, and to be deported to Spain. As in the case of most Judaizers condemned to expulsion, he did not leave Mexico, because he did not have the means to pay for a trip to Spain.

Subsequently, Botello was denounced to the Holy Office for not having obeyed the expulsion order. He was also accused of having displayed his hand crippled by tortures and of having said, "This has cost me five thousand pesos; one day they will have to repay me."

This time Botello was imprisoned for nine years. Even then he did not admit to Judaism and did not denounce anybody else. Botello often asked for a hearing, and during any hearing given him he made reports such as, for instance, that a mysterious Indian visited him in his cell to strike him, or that somebody often entered his cell to sing and play the guitar, or that he spent thirty-six sleepless nights while the Indian spoke through his [Botello's] mouth. Botello claimed he was being visited by the devil.

After observing Botello in his cell, the authorities were informed that he ate and slept well and that his stories were pure fiction. No doubt, Botello invented these stories in order to simulate madness.

[64b] Manuscripts in the Archivo Histórico Nacional in Madrid also quoted by J. T. Medina, op. cit., pp. 110, 113, 138, 193, 203, 205, 193, 243, 247, 248, 249, 266, 278, 279 and 415.

Witnesses deposed that, before and after his trial, Botello was a
Judaizer who tried to win converts; that he owned parchment-bound
booklets containing Jewish prayers; that he never mentioned or
invoked the name of Jesus or the Virgin Mary or any Catholic saint
and did not possess an image of any of them. When he wanted to
thank God for something, he said in the Jewish style:

> Praised be the most Holy God of Israel, or the most Holy
> God of the Hosts [*Y cuando se ofrecía dar gracia a Dios, lo
> hacía al estilo judaico, diciendo: loado sea el Santísimo Dios
> de Israel, o el Santísimo Dios de los Exercitos*].

The testimony continued that he rose early every morning and, after
having washed his hands before eating, he retired with his wife, the
Mexican María de Zárate, to a room from where the sky could be
seen, and on their knees they recited penitential psalms. Botello did
not eat pork and observed Jewish fast days. After having been released
from prison in 1649, he lived on the San Juan marketplace with four
others who had appeared as reconciled to Catholicism at the auto
of 1649. Because of this the Court claimed that he was continuing his
affection for those who "observed and followed the dead Law of
Moyses" [*guardado y seguido la muerta ley de Moyses*]. If he had
been truly converted to Catholicism in 1649, it was claimed, he would
have avoided any further social life with crypto-Jews.

Botello was further accused of having boasted to friends that, in
case of a new trial against him and condemnation to be burned, he
would when brought to the stake act even worse than Thomas Trebiño
—he would loudly announce the error of the Christians and urge them
to convert to Judaism. He told his wife that it would be a mistake
not to teach their children Judaism, because they would be lost without it. On that occasion he told her a story about a Judaizer who had
made this mistake and later saw his son become a Bishop in Spain.

While in prison, Botello refused food for three days in September,
because he did not know the exact date of the tenth of Tishri, the
Day of Atonement.

The public prosecutor asked the Court to release Botello to the
secular authorities as a relapsed Judaizer. In other words, he recommended capital punishment. Botello, in his defense, declared that he
had always been and still remained a true Christian and a Catholic.
He explained that the only reason he had not complied with the
expulsion order was that he did not have the price of passage to
Spain. Beyond that he denied everything he was accused of.

Nevertheless, Botello was condemned as a heretic Judaizer [*hereje Judaizante*], an apostate of the holy Catholic faith. He was sentenced to have all his possessions confiscated and to be released to the secular arm—specifically to the Corregidor of Mexico City and his first officer, whom the Church urgently asked to treat the condemned benevolently and mercifully. This was the customary formula of the Inquisitors in cases of capital punishment.

Botello appeared on November 19, 1659, at an auto-da-fé celebrated on the main square [*Plaza Mayor*] of the city. He was handed over to the Corregidor Don Juan Altamirano y Velasco, Conde de Santiago, who pronounced the following sentence: Botello was to ride a pack animal through the streets of Mexico City to the San Hipólito Square, there to be burned "in vivid flames of fire until he turned to ashes with no memory of him left."

The last page of the trial manuscript reports that Botello was immediately brought to the *Quemadero* where he was garroted, and that after his death his body was burned [*le fue dado garrote y después de muerto fue quemado su cuerpo en vibas llamas de fuego*].[65]

Considering this official version, it would seem that Botello must have shown some sign of repentance at the last moment, for otherwise he would not have been garroted first. But there is another and contradictory version.

Rodrigo Ruiz de Zepeda Martínez, author of the booklet, *Auto General de la Fee ... celebrado a los 19 de Noviembre de 1659 Años* (*En la Imprensa del Secreto del Santo Officio*), reports differently. He says that the Jesuit, Padre Bartolomé Castão, and the Franciscan friar, Juan de Zurita, tried without success to convince the sixty-five-year-old Botello that he ought to make a confession in the last hours of his life. When Botello adamantly refused to mention even the name of Jesus or Mary, the clergymen were extremely disconsolate at his letting himself be burned alive [*se dexo bresar viuo*].[66]

65 Cf. the manuscript of the trial found in the Archivo General de la Nación, Mexico City, Inquisición, vol. 412. "Proceso contra Francisco Botello, Natural de la Villa de Priego." Cf. also manuscript in the Archivo Histórico Nacional, Madrid, vol. no. 1065/779, "Relaciones de causas de fee desde Año 1615 a de 1669," folios 419-426.

66 Rodriguez Ruiz de Zepeda Martínez, *Auto General de la Fee ... celebrado a los 19 de Noviembre de 1659 años* (Mexico, 1660); L. G. Obregón, *op. cit.*, p. 710; J. T. Medina, *op. cit.*, pp. 203, 247, 248ff. Cf. also manuscript in Madrid, vol. 1065/779, folios 426-429. D. J. Garcia Icazbalceta, *Obras*, vol. I (Mexico, 1896), chapter, "Autos da Fe celebrados in Mexico," pp. 298-299, accepts the version that Botello was burned alive.

Botello's wife, María de Zárate, appeared at the same auto-da-fé as reconciled to Catholicism. She was fined a thousand pesos and was interned as a hospital nurse for four years.[67]

V

THE TRIAL OF DIEGO DIAS

Diego Dias was born in Ameda, Portugal, and became a farmer in Tacubaya, Mexico. His wife, Doña Ana Gómez, was executed as a relapsed Judaizer in 1649. Dias also had appeared at the auto-da-fé, April 11, 1649, as reconciled to Catholicism. He had abjured his errors *de vehementi* and was condemned to expulsion from Mexico. Remaining in Mexico, he moved from one place to another in order not to be discovered. In 1652, when he was almost seventy years old, he was again imprisoned as a relapsed Judaizer.

Witnesses presented by the prosecution deposed that Dias had in conversation with them expressed great joy that Sobremonte had resisted all endeavors to convert him to Catholicism and had chosen the death of a hero by letting himself be burned alive. The prosecutor saw in this the proof that Dias was "a Jew at heart," because it was an established fact that Judaizers rejoiced whenever one of them became a martyr in dying as a Jew.

It was further deposed that Dias called his former wife, Ana Gómez, a *Santa*. Moreover, Dias never mentioned the name Jesus but, when speaking of God, said, "the Holy God [*Santo Dios*]," or "the Creator." Despite the fact that he had lived near a church, he was never seen attending Mass there. He often ate hardboiled eggs, cheese, bread and honey, and whenever he was invited out for a meal he refused to eat meat but carried his own provisions, such as the aforementioned victuals.

The public prosecutor finally accused Dias of being an impenitent, relapsed apostate to Catholicism and asked capital punishment for him. It was recommended that the Court should release the condemned to the secular arm after confiscation of his fortune, so that his penalty might serve as an example for others.

Dias' reply to the writ of indictment was that its content was constructed in malice and that he had always been a Roman Catholic Christian. And he added ironically:

---

[67] Rodriguez Ruiz de Zepeda Martínez, *op. cit.;* L. G. Obregón, *op. cit.*, p. 711; J. T. Medina, *op. cit.*, p. 247.

How could he be a Jew in a country where so many Bishops, clerks, and religious persons preached and taught the truth? [*Y cómo había de ser Judío en tierra donde hay tantos Obispos clérigos y religiosos que predican y enseñan la verdad?*]

He denied ever having been a Judaizer and admitted none of the charges against him.

The Court did not credit his assertions and on October 27, 1659, condemned him to appear at the auto-da-fé of November 19, 1659, there to be released to the secular authorities. After the sentence was read to him, he was handed over to the Corregidor Don Juan Altamirano y Velasco, Conde de Santiago, who pronounced the death sentence: he was to ride through the streets of the city on a pack animal to the square of San Hipólito, accompanied by the town crier announcing the delict of the condemned. At the designated spot on the square the condemned would be burned "in vivid flames of fire until turned into ashes and no memory is left of him."

The manuscript of the trial closes with the following certificate:

And immediately incontinently on the mentioned day, month, and year at about 5 p.m., the mentioned Diego Dias, riding a pack animal and accompanied by Don Marcos Rodrigues de Sulvara, the major bailiff of this city and a town crier and trumpeter, was brought through the usual streets to the post and part and spot selected for this purpose where the executioner put him to a stake, garroted him, and his body was burned in vivid flames of fire until he turned into ashes. All this happened in my presence which I certify.—Witnesses: Marcos de Bobadilla and Diego Flores, Citizens of Mexico.[68]

From this certificate it appears that Diego Dias was burned at the stake after having been strangulated, in contradiction to the sentence.

We find the explanation of this discrepancy in the 1660 printed booklet describing the auto celebrated in 1659. The author, Rodrigo Ruiz de Zepeda Martínez, states that on the day of the auto the avenues and streets of Mexico City were jammed with 40,000 spectators. Diego Dias was accompanied by the clergymen, Fr. Miguel de Aguilera, and Fr. Augustín de la Madre de Dios, who had spent the previous night and day with him. While Dias had during the whole

---

68 The manuscript of the trial is to be found in the Archivo General de la Nación, Mexico City, Inquisición, vols. 390 and 394. "Processo contra Diego Dias, Portugues, por Judaizante" (1642 and 1656). Cf. also manuscript in the Archivo Histórico Nacional, Madrid, vol. 1065/779, folios 430-437.

trial denied that he had been a Judaizer and had pretended to be a good Catholic, he could even now not be persuaded to make a confession. He "insulted" the Inquisition and refused to kiss a cross. During the procession to the *Quemadero* the friars told him that the kissing of the cross would be "the source of his remedy and the instrument of his salvation," and they held a crucifix near his mouth. Dias pushed it away, declaring,

> Take it away, Padre, because a piece of timber does not bring salvation to anybody! [*Quite, Padre, que un palo a nadie salva.*]

All further endeavors of the clergymen to make Dias die as a Christian were in vain. The executioners then started in error to apply the garrote instead of burning him alive. The major bailiff called their attention to the error and, when Dias was half dead, they set him on fire.[69]

VI

THE TRIAL OF FERNANDO DE MEDINA

Fernando de Medina, alias de Merida, alias Moisés Gómez y Dias, born in Peña Orada, Diocese of Bordeaux, France, in the year 1656, was of Portuguese Jewish descent. At the age of twelve he went to Spain to help his uncle in the tobacco business, assuming the name of Fernando de Medina. At the same time his two brothers adopted the name Medina.

Medina remained in Madrid for about six years and then spent nine years in the tobacco business at Osuña, Spain. Later he became a traveling salesman in Seville and other Spanish cities. In Luzena and Puente de Gonzálo he was in business for himself for a year and a half, then entered into a partnership in Seville, where he went bankrupt. He was imprisoned until a friend bailed him out fourteen months later. In 1687, after eleven months' residence in Estepa Malaga, Santa María, Spain, he migrated to Mexico on a vessel in the fleet of General Don Joseph de Santillán. He again changed his name, this time to Merida. In Mexico he made his living by peddling goods or selling from his own tent in Mexico City.

[69] *Ibid.*, p. 298; Zepeda Martínez, *op. cit.*; L. G. Obregón, *op. cit.*, p. 710; J. T. Medina, *op. cit.*, pp. 203, 249.

The Inquisitional Court had received information that Medina had been a lifelong Judaizer. He was imprisoned on April 24, 1691, when he was about thirty-three years old and unmarried. Witnesses accused him of being circumcised and of having cohabited with other Judaizers in Seville and Porcuña. It was said that he had a prayer book with prayers for morning, afternoon, and evening services; that he was observed fasting on *Yom Kippur* and on the day of the fast of Esther. In several Spanish cities he had been heard to recite the *Shema-Israel* prayer when alone and also when in company; and he was known to have observed Jewish ceremonies and rites.

At his first hearing Medina was, as was usual, examined in Catholicism. He knew only how to make the sign of the cross and could not recite any Catholic prayers. His defense was confused and contradictory and, though he simulated insanity, the Court doctor pronounced him sane.

Medina told the Court that in his youth he had been taught the principles of Judaism as a means to attain salvation but that later he had oscillated. In Mexico, upon hearing sermons and reading books concerning the Catholic doctrine, he contemplated going to Rome to throw himself at the mercy of the Pope and to ask for reconciliation to Catholicism. He asked the Holy Office for pardon, mercy, and reconciliation.

Asked by the Court about details concerning the Jewish ceremonies he had once observed, Medina deposed that, when he was a young boy in France, with his father, brothers, and other Jews, he used to visit a synagogue where the book of the Law [Bible] was recited and explained from a pulpit. On Saturdays no work was done and no fire lighted, the meals having been prepared on Friday afternoon. They did not eat pork or fish without scales. The animals were slaughtered in a ritual way. They visited the synagogue for prayer in the morning, at three in the afternoon, and in the evening for about half an hour each session. Everyone had a prayer book in the language he understood—his own in Spanish—while the rabbi recited it in Hebrew. Certain holy days were observed. He had not been circumcised at the age of eight days but only when he was seven or eight years old, and then in the synagogue. Upon his arrival in Spain at the age of twelve he ceased to observe Jewish ceremonies, although he had fasted a few times, probably not on the correct days since he could not ascertain the exact dates of the fast days. He further declared that he did not know anybody whom he could denounce as a Judaizer; that he regretted having followed Jewish ceremonies and would like to have a book from which he could learn Catholicism. The Court gave him a catechism book.

During many hearings, the Inquisitors encouraged Medina to unburden his conscience by denouncing his Judaizing friends in Spain and promised him mercy if he complied. He finally denounced many people in France (whom the arm of the Inquisition could not reach) and some people in Spain who were already dead. On the other hand, he named as Spanish Judaizers certain ones whom he suspected of having denounced him.

Medina's defense tactics were to confuse the Inquisitors. He often revoked what he had admitted earlier and refused to sign statements of his oral depositions. As punishment for this chains were applied to his hands and feet for a certain period.

One day the jailors saw him dressed with a white shirt over his prison garment. Questioned about the meaning of this, Medina explained that it was a Jewish custom which showed that the Law of Moses was the better and cleaner one and that he was not a Christian but a Jew. The same day he asked for a new hearing. Brought before the Inquisitors, he told them that he did not feel as a delinquent at all; that he was only doing what his mother and father had taught him to do in case he should ever be imprisoned in Spain, for in such a case the Inquisitors there would have liberated him; that he thought the court in Mexico should do the same.

In this way Medina changed his tactics. At first he claimed to be repentant, wanting to be reconciled to Catholicism, hoping that, since this was the first accusation against him, he would be released from prison and expelled with confiscation of his fortune [if any]. Then, he remembered [or else had received advice while in jail] that people born as Jews and never baptized were not subject to the jurisdiction of the Inquisition, because those authorities only persecuted apostates.

Often during Medina's years in prison clergymen tried to obtain his full confession and to convert him, but they finally reached the conclusion that this was impossible. Even the defense lawyer provided him by the court desisted from defending him.

The public prosecutor formulated the bill of indictment against "Fernando de Medina, alias Don Fernando de Medina y Merida, alias Moisés Gómez," a heretic, Judaizer, apostate of the Holy Catholic faith, a pertinacious and stubborn perjurer, confessing and

revoking, and simulating insanity. The Court was asked to release
Medina to the secular arm for punishment as a heretic and a Judaizing, obstinate Jew.

When this bill of indictment was read to Medina, he answered
that he was not forty-one but thirty-four years old; that he was of
the Jewish nation, an observer of the Law of Moses [*que era de
nación judía, observante de la Ley de Moisés*] as so many others
in Spain and in other parts of the world; that he had always admitted
that he was baptized and confirmed a Catholic; that he had declared
to the qualified priests of the court visiting him in prison [*padres
calificadores*] that he wished henceforth to live in conformity with
the Law of Jesus Christ. Medina protested against the prosecutor's
demand for his release to the secular authorities because such a procedure was not according to custom; that, in view of the fact that this
Court was an ecclesiastical body and he a confessed defendant reduced
to the practice of the Law of Jesus Christ, he should not be delivered
to secular justice but only to the jail warden for penitence. He requested the Court to act accordingly.

The Court gave Medina another chance to discuss his religious
beliefs with a learned and competent Inquisition lawyer and with
qualified priests. Their report to the Court was that Medina continued
to talk in a confusing manner. Medina finally persisted in these
discussions that his salvation could be obtained only through the Law
of Moses, and that he would die for it if necessary [*persistía con toda
expresión y claridad en que se podía salvar y se salvaba en la ley de
Moisés, y que era buena y que moriría por ella si fuese menester*].

The Court released Medina to the secular arm, asking the Corregidor of Mexico City, Don Carlos Tristán de el Pozo, to treat the
condemned kindly. On Sunday, June 14, 1699, Medina appeared at
an auto-da-fé celebrated in the patio of the Dominican Convent in
Mexico City, which was crowded with ecclesiastical and secular officers as well as with spectators. The sentence was read aloud, and
the Corregidor condemned him to death at the stake.

Medina was afterward brought riding a pack animal, accompanied
by a town crier who published his delict to the people on the streets.
At the place of burning (this time called in the manuscript *brazero*
instead of *Quemadero*), he was put to the stake. Friars of different
religious fraternities and qualified priests of the Holy Office admonished him to die as a Catholic, but in vain. The executors tied him to

the stake and burned him alive. The ashes of his body were thrown into the nearby canal at nine p.m.[70]

Besides the manuscript of the trial from which we have related the story of the martyr Moisés Gómez (alias Fernando de Medina y Merida), there exists a printed source of the year 1699: the report of the auto-da-fé of June 14, 1699, during which Fr. Domingo de Soussa delivered the sermon. Here we find more details concerning the last twenty-four hours of Medina's life. During the previous night he was visited in his cell every hour by a different priest who tried to convert him to Catholicism. Medina refused to argue and repeatedly answered, "Yes" [*Si*], with the result that the visitors could not ascertain his true intentions. Also during the next day's procession, Medina behaved with composure, kept his serenity while the sentences were read to him, and ignored all supplications concerning a last-minute conversion. To the very end he remained calm until his body was turned to ashes.[71]

On the other hand, Antonio de Robles wrote in his diary that Medina (whom he also called "Alberto" Moisen Gómez) seated himself at the stake and behaved with much effrontery before he was burned alive on June 15[?], 1699.[72] There is also a report from the Tribunal in Mexico City, addressed to the Head Office of the Spanish Inquisition and dated March 9, 1700, on the trial of Medina and his execution by burning alive at the stake.[73]

Judaism was thus exterminated in Mexico at the end of the seventeenth century.

In the year 1788, Don Rafael Gil Rodríguez, a clergyman, native of Granada, Spain, but living in Guatemala, was accused of Judaism, taken to Mexico, and imprisoned. On February 9, 1792, he was sentenced to be released to the secular arm. As a repentant he asked for mercy and appeared at the auto of August 9, 1795, as reconciled.[74]

---

[70] The manuscript of the trial is in the Archivo General de la Nación, Mexico City. *Inquisición,* vols. 681 and 704. "Causa contra Fernando de Medina y Merida, alias Moisés Gómez, por judaizante. Sentencia con méritos de este reo."

[71] *Sermón en el Auto Público de Fee que el Tribunal de El Santo Oficio de Nueva España, celebró el día quatorze de Junio de 1699, en el Real Convento de N.P.S. Domingo de México. Dixolo el M. Fr. Domingo de Soussa* (Mexico, 1699).

[72] Antonio de Robles, *Diario de Sucesos Notables,* tomo III (Mexico, 1946), p. 79.

[73] Cf. J. T. Medina, *op. cit.,* p. 415; note 45; *ibid.,* pp. 278, 279, 415; L. G. Obregón, *op. cit.,* p. 713.

[74] Cf. J. T. Medina, *op. cit.,* p. 306. Cf. also Ybáñez, as in note 75.

The nineteen crypto-Jewish martyrs of the seventeenth century were:

Doña María Núñez de Carvajal (1601)
Thomas de Fonseca Castellanos (1601)
Simón Rodríguez Núñez (1648)
Francisco Lópes Blandon (1649)
Doña Ana de León Carvajal (1649)
Gonzálo Flores (1649)
Ana Gómez (1649)
María Gómez (1649)
Duarte de León Jamarillo (1649)
Simón Montero (1649)
Leonor Gómez Núñez (1649)
Doña Catalina de Silva (1649)
Thomas Trebiño de Sobremonte (1649)
Antonio Váez Tirado (1649)
Isabel Tristán (1649)
Gonzálo Váez (1649)
Francisco Botello (1659)
Diego Dias (1659)
Fernando de Medina (1699)

By a decree dated Feebruary 22, 1813, the *Cortes* (the senate and congress of deputies) in Spain abolished the tribunals of the Inquisition for Spain and New Spain. They were re-established by King Ferdinand VII's decree of July 21, 1814, and were again suppressed in the year 1820 (this time permanently).[75]

VII

SOCIAL, ECONOMIC, AND RELIGIOUS CONDITIONS AMONG THE CRYPTO-JEWS IN COLONIAL MEXICO

Some of the Jews who had been forcefully converted to Catholicism in Spain and in Portugal were with Christopher Columbus when he discovered America, with Pedro Alvares Cabral when he discovered Brazil, and also with Hernando Cortéz when in 1521 he conquered Tenochtitlán (Mexico City), the capital of the Aztec empire. Other Jews followed them to the newly opened hemisphere.

75 Cf. Yolanda Mariel de Ybáñez, *La Inquisición de México durante el Siglo XVI* (Mexico, D.F., 1945), p. 368.

These New Christians (as they were called) were officially Catholics, but the majority of them secretly observed Jewish rites. Those who risked a voyage of several months on a sailing vessel to reach a land inhabited by savages were adventurers attracted by reports of gold, silver, and precious stones to be obtained, as well as by business prospects. But many were crypto-Jews escaping persecution. These were descendants of Spanish and Portuguese Jews. Some who had been expelled from Spain in 1492 followed the land route from Spain to Portugal, returning to Spain later with changed names as New Christians. They then migrated to the Americas and were known as "Portugals."

Between 1580 and 1630 several hundred crypto-Jews settled in Mexico. They had to adjust to the climate of Mexico City (elevation 7,347 feet) and to the completely different population. They encountered the following ethnical and social conditions:

1. Native Indians cultivated *manioc* or *yucca* (source of tapioca), did the hard work in the mines, and transported loads on their backs.

2. African Negroes who were slave laborers.

3. *Gachupins,* Spanish-born government officials.

4. Catholic clergymen.

5. *Creoles* (white Spaniards born in Mexico, mostly heirs of Cortéz' *conquistadores*) who owned big estates, slaves, gold and silver mines, or held well-paid Church or government positions, and who lived in luxury, occupied themselves mostly with gambling, courtesans, bullfights, and cockfights.

6. *Mestizos* (offspring of Europeans and Indians), energetic and enterprising, who built up the country.

7. *Sambos* (offspring of Indians and Negroes).

8. *Mulattoes* (offspring of whites and Negroes).

It is easy to see that the crypto-Jews could hardly be assimilated by any of these ethnic entities. Naturally they clustered together, intermarried, and remained bound together by their common secret. They were mostly merchants, with tents or stores in the cities, or peddlers traveling throughout the country to distribute merchandise imported from Europe.

Mexico was then, as now, the leading silver producer of the world. This enormous production enriched the Creoles who created a silver nobility by purchasing Spanish titles of *Conde* (Count) and *Marqués.*[76]

[76] Cf. Lesly Byrd Simpson, *Many Mexicos* (Los Angeles, 1959), pp. 127-135.

These new aristocrats needed wine, silk, spices, and other delicacies. They were good customers for the goods the New Christians imported from the Far East via Acapulco and from Europe via Vera Cruz. Simón Váez Sevilla and Thomas Trebiño de Sobremonte were known as the wealthiest crypto-Jews in seventeenth-century Mexico. The value of the liquidated wealth of all crypto-Jews, as appraised by the Inquisition in the years 1642 to 1649, was more than three million pesos.[77] The real value of this confiscated wealth must have been several times that amount.

Most of these crypto-Jews arrived in Mexico without means but with letters of recommendation to the already established crypto-Jews who received them as guests in their homes, supplied them with merchandise, and sent them to the interior on sales trips. Those who had success opened their own tents or stores. Some of them became miners, some gold- or silversmiths. The best recommendation for a new immigrant was his knowledge of Judaism, his practice of Jewish rites, and his connection with the families of persecuted crypto-Jews. Such immigrants eventually married the prettiest and most religious daughters of the richest crypto-Jews in Mexico.

The manuscripts of the inquisitorial trials tell us of very few Negro and Indian children born to Jewish fathers. Francisco Lópes Blandon, garroted in 1649 for Judaizing, had been accused of circumcising his son born to a mulatto woman. Esperanza Rodrigues, a mulatto, was the daughter of the New Christian Francisco Rodriguez and the Negro Isabel who came from African Guinea. Esperanza and her three daughters observed Jewish rites. Pedro López de Morales was accused, during his trial for Judaizing, of having intended to send his *mestizuela* daughter (born to an Indian woman) to relatives in Spain for instruction in Judaism.

A fantastic story was told to the Inquisitors during the trial of the martyr Duarte de León Jamarillo by his young daughters, Ana, Antonia, and Clara Núñez. They deposed that when they were about twelve years old their father instructed them in Judaism, cut a piece of flesh from their left shoulders (in the presence of their mother), roasted it and ate it. The Inquisitors claimed to have thus discovered a new kind of circumcision.

---

[77] J. T. Medina, *op. cit.*, p. 210, based on a letter of the visitor, Don Pedro de Medina Rico, dated July 10, 1656, to the Council of the Inquisition in Spain.

The trial manuscripts also reveal that a Judaizer, Manuel Carrasco, carried a piece of *mazzah* [unleavened bread] brought from Madrid in a small bag on his chest, and that he used it for healing sick people; that Gonzálo Díaz Santillán was murdered by fellow Judaizers because he extorted money from them by threatening to report them to the Holy Office.

Besides many such eccentric stories, the trial manuscripts and *relaciones* [printed reports] give other clues to the religion practiced by the Mexican crypto-Jews. They lived as Judaizing Catholics. From time to time they had to attend Mass, to make confession, and to obtain sacramental absolution. They had to celebrate Catholic saints' days and to observe Catholic fast days, to baptize newborn children, to marry in the Church, to bury their dead in the Catholic cemetery. At the same time they observed *Shabbat* [the Jewish sabbath]. Meals were prepared on Friday for Saturday, because the Jewish law prohibits the kindling of a fire and work on *Shabbat*. Oil lamps instead of candles were lighted on Friday evenings and hidden in wooden boxes (in order not to be seen by servants) until they burnt out.

In many homes in Mexico City the crypto-Jews gathered on Friday evenings and other holidays to pray, to eat, to fast, and, last but not least, to discuss their problems with the Holy Office—that is, how to behave in case of imprisonment and torture. The general instruction was not to admit anything and not to denounce anybody even under the cruelest tortures. Very, very few were strong enough to follow this rule.

Circumcision of sons was rarely performed in Mexico on the eighth day after birth, as ordered by the Jewish law, because the danger of discovery was too great. The children until the age of thirteen were raised as Catholics. Only then the boys were circumcised. Boys and girls both were then told their parents' secret and initiated into Judaism. They were also told that in observing Judaism they were risking their lives and the lives of their relatives and friends.

Boys who for some reason could not be circumcised at the age of thirteen often circumcised themselves or were circumcised later in life. It seems that there was usually some specialist available for this rite, and sometimes the expert was a guest from Europe whom the Inquisitors called *famoso Rabbino* [a famous rabbi]. There is no proof that all newborn children were given, besides a Christian first name, also a secret Hebrew name, but there is proof enough that some of them did receive Hebrew names.

It seems that the Mexican crypto-Jews did not know how to read Hebrew but that they knew by heart a few Hebrew words, such as ADONAI (my Lord), ADONAI SABAOT (the Lord of the Hosts), *Shema* (Hear, the first word of the *Shema Yisrael* prayer), and *Aveluz* (mourning). Some of them could recite a prayer in imperfect Hebrew. Their prayers and psalms were in Spanish. Those who knew Latin learned Judaism from the Latin Bible and from ecclesiastical books. For instance, Luis de Carvajal, Jr., in this way learned the ten commandments and Maimonides' thirteen fundamentals of the Jewish creed.

It is hard to say whether the crypto-Jews in seventeenth-century Mexico were organized in a kind of community, but we know they assembled for prayer in the homes of Simón Váez Sevilla, Thomas Trebiño de Sobremonte in Mexico City, and Manuel de Mello in Guadalajara. The Inquisitors called these men rabbis or dogmatists and their homes synagogues.

In the trial records woman are often mentioned as specialists in baking and distributing unleavened bread for Passover and in treating corpses in conformity with Jewish customs. The families of the deceased always tried to bury them in virgin soil. The mourning families were visited by other crypto-Jews, who brought them cold eggs for their first meal. Such a visit was called *Aveluz* (mourning) and was considered as a good deed.

Some Judaizers, such as Simón Montero and Duarte de León Jamarillo, are mentioned as having been seen praying in *tallit* [prayer shawl] and *tefillin* [phylacteries] while wearing caps brought from Europe. Mention is also made of *Yom Kippur* [Day of Atonement], the fast day of Esther, and *Tishah be-'Ab* [day of commemorating the destruction of the Temple]. Many Judaizers fasted also every Monday and Thursday. Duarte de León Jamarillo explained that, before coming to Mexico, he had vowed to take his family from the Iberian Peninsula to a country where Jews could practice Judaism freely. He felt guilty at not having kept his vow and therefore fasted Mondays and Thursdays in penance.

Because of the variation between the Christian and Jewish calendars, it was not easy to know the exact days of the Jewish holidays and fast days. Luis de Carvajal and other Judaizers who lived in Mexico in the sixteenth century simplified the problem by celebrating Passover on the fourteenth day after the new moon observed in March, the Day of Atonement on the tenth day after the new moon of September, and so forth. On the other hand, it seems that the seventeenth-century Judaizers did not use the Christian calendar based on the lunisolar system as a medium for a simplified lunar calculation. They most probably learned the exact dates from new immigrants every year, though without such vital information they observed the appearance of the new moon and calculated when *Yom Kippur* and other holidays were due. In 1640 the two most important leaders, Antonio Váez and Thomas Trebiño de Sobremonte, disagreed concerning the proper day of *Yom Kippur*. Sobremonte, and certainly all his followers, in that year fasted not less than eight days in order not to miss the correct date.

Meat is never mentioned as the food of the Mexican Judaizers (certainly because it was impossible for them to have animals slaughtered ritually), but fish, eggs, vegetables, honey, and cheese are often mentioned. On Fridays and the eves of holidays people took baths, changed underwear, and replaced bed linen. On the eve of *Yom Kippur* wax candles were lighted for the souls of the departed and the living also. Some Judaizers used to spend the whole night before the Day of Atonement praying while standing.

Crypto-Jews in Mexico as in other countries avoided marriage with bona fide Christians and intermarried. Usually the marriages were celebrated at home in conformity with Jewish tradition and only later in the Church, and children were blessed in the Jewish way, hands on the children's heads during the recitation of the blessing.

Always afraid of being discovered and tried by the Inquisition, the Mexican Judaizers expected that the Messiah was already born or would be born in Mexico to liberate them. Their hopes concentrated on the sons of especially religious young women. It was expected that Gaspar Váez Sevilla, son of the very religious Doña Juana Enríquez (considered a *Santa*) and Simón Váez Sevilla, would turn out to be the Messiah. Some expected that Rafael de Sobremonte, son of the *Santa* María Gómez and Thomas Trebiño de Sobremonte, would be the Messiah. Others expected that other devoted women, such as Doña Blanca Juárez or Ynés Pereira, would give birth to the Messiah.

Under the influence of Catholicism some of the crypto-Jews prayed to ADONAI on their knees, a Catholic and not a Jewish method. Most of them believed that Judaism would save their souls from the spiritual consequences of sin—that is, from eternal damnation—a concept strange to Judaism.

Much superstition prevailed, especially among some women who were inclined to believe in witchcraft. Doña Micaela Enríquez, for instance, used to carry certain roots and the teeth of deceased. Doña Ana Enríquez used to cure people from the consequences of the Evil Eye. Doña Margarita de Rivera, on days following a bad dream, used to visit the Padre confessor in order to transfer the bad omen upon him. Isabel de Rivera told people that the Jewish law did not permit the eating of pork because pigs were metamorphosed human beings. But no crypto-Jewish woman was ever processed by the Inquisition on a charge of witchcraft, while many Gentile women in Mexico were so prosecuted and condemned.

The Judaizing women, in Mexico as in other countries of the dispersion, played an enormous part in holding the torch of Judaism for centuries after the forced conversion to Catholicism at the end of the fifteenth century. They taught their children Jewish rites and prayers, and often they endured tortures in the prisons of the Inquisition with greater fortitude than men. Eleven of the thirty-one Judaizers executed in Mexico were women.

There are no statistics on the crypto-Jewish population of Colonial Mexico, for the Inquisition documents record only those who were apprehended. Among 2,281 trials of the Mexican Holy Office, 351 concerned crypto-Jews, including many who had left Mexico in time and many who were already dead or who died in prison during the trials. Twenty-seven of the condemned were executed by garrote (strangulation), and their bodies burnt at the stake. Four were burnt alive: the martyrs Thomas Trebiño de Sobremonte, in 1649, Francisco Botello and Diego Dias, in 1659, and Fernando de Medina, in 1699.

The crypto-Jews had come to Mexico full of hope that they would make their fortunes in the New World and that, far away from Spain and Portugal, they would be able to serve their God. A few did become rich but, poor or rich, none of them could avoid the persecutions of the Holy Office, so they lived in constant terror.

By the end of the seventeenth century the whole crypto-Jewish community in Mexico had been destroyed.

HERNANDO ALONSO, A JEWISH CONQUISTADOR
WITH CORTES IN MEXICO.

By G. R. G. Conway.

I.

In the City of Mexico on August 12, 1574, the inquisitors of the newly established tribunal in New Spain,[1] Dr. Don Pedro Moya de Contreras, archbishop-elect, and his colleague, the Licentiate Alonso Fernandez de Bonilla, in their afternoon audience, reviewed the proceedings that had been taken by the Holy Office against certain persons who in the past had been condemned to the stake or had been " reconciled " for the offence of heresy. They duly considered the authority for the former proceedings whether apostolic or secular and investigated what *sambenitos* (penitential garments) in the previous forty-six years had been set up in the cathedral church of the city. As a result of careful enquiry, which had extended over the previous two months, in which many witnesses were examined, the inquisitors ordered the setting up in the cathedral church of twenty-two *sambenitos;* upon each of these was to be written the name and nationality of the prisoner and the year of his condemnation and punishment. The different

---

[1] The regular tribunal of the inquisition was authorized in the Spanish colonies by a decree of Philip II, dated January 25, 1569, and established in Mexico by a supplementary decree dated Madrid, August 16, 1570. Dr. Don Pedro de Moya de Contreras, who had been inquisitor at Murcia, was the first chief inquisitor. He became archbishop of Mexico in 1574, viceroy in 1583, and in 1586 he returned to Spain and was appointed president of the Council of the Indies, but died a few months after he had taken office. See J. T. Medina, *Historia del Tribunal del Santo Oficio de la Inquisición en México,* Santiago de Chile, 1905; H. C. Lea, " The Inquisition in the Spanish Dependencies," New York, 1922.

sambenitos were to be set up in two rows in the public part of the church, one row on the Gospel side and the other on that of the Epistles. The first three names were as follows:

(1) Hernando Alonso, smith, born in the Condado de Niebla, inhabitant of Mexico, Jewish heretic, burnt at the stake, year 1528.

(2) Gonzalo de Morales, trader, born in Seville, inhabitant of Mexico, of Jewish descent, heretic, burnt at the stake for Jewish practices, year 1528.

(3) Diego de Ocaña, scrivener, born in Seville, inhabitant of Mexico, of Jewish descent, heretic, condemned for Jewish beliefs, reconciled, year 1528.

Upon other *sambenitos* there was recorded the punishment of a Lutheran called Andres Moral, a lapidary, who was reconciled in 1536; Francisco Millan, a Jew, reconciled in 1539; and that of Robert Tomson² an Englishman and Agustin Bocacio, a Genoese,³ who were both reconciled in 1560. The remaining fifteen *sambenitos* were those of the recent victims of the first great *auto de fe* of the newly established tribunal, held on February 28, 1574, twelve of whom were sailors captured from the fleet of Captain John Hawkins, after the epoch-making disaster at San Juan de Ulua in 1568.⁴

In the present paper an endeavor will be made to throw some further light, from the fragmentary information that has been preserved, on the fate of Hernando Alonso. J. T. Medina⁵ has already recorded some brief particulars of his trial, and the writer has discovered a few additional facts in examining some original documents to be found among the

---

² See Hakluyt's " Principal Navigations," 1589 edition, pp. 580-587; *Archivo General de la Nacion,* Mexico, Inquisition Records, vol. xxxii; G. R. G. Conway, " An Englishman and the Mexican Inquisition, 1556-1560," Mexico, 1927.

³ A. G. N. Mexico; Inquisition Records, vol. xxxi.

⁴ See Julian S. Corbett, " Drake and the Tudor Navy," London, 1899, vol. i, chap. iii; J. A. Williamson, " Sir John Hawkins, Oxford, 1927, pp. 184-202.

⁵ *La Primitiva Inquisición Americana,* Santiago de Chile, 1914, pp. 121-124.

inquisition records in the Mexican National Archives and from other sources in Mexico City.[6]

Hernando Alonso was a smith, or iron-worker, who came to Mexico from Cuba with Panfilo de Narvaez in 1520. He was then a man of over sixty years of age and married to Beatriz, the sister (?) of Diego de Ordaz,[7] and had been acquainted with Hernando Cortes since 1516.

In the course of a suit that was brought by Juan Tirado against Cortés in April, 1529,[8] during the presidency of Nuño de Guzman, and in the presence of the judges, Ortiz de Matienzo and Diego Delgadillo, there was incorporated the earlier evidence against Cortes taken in 1526, evidence which was submitted when the famous *Residencia* was held.[9] Among the witnesses called at the earlier date were Diego de Ocaña[10] and Hernando Alonso. To various questions asked at this

[6] Particularly a MS. volume entitled: *Autos y diligencias hechas . . . . Sambenitos Antiguos y re . . . . y postura de los que sean relaxado por este Santo Oficio hasta el año de 1632 que se renovaron y pusieron de Nuevo." Inquisición correspondencia, Siglo xvi. Tomo lxxvii.* A. G. N., Mexico.

[7] See Bernal Diaz del Castillo, " The Conquest of New Spain," London, 1908, references to Diego de Ordaz in index, vol. i, p. 387.

[8] *Documentos para la Historia de México,. Archivo Mexicano,* Mexico, 1852, vol. ii, pp. 377-499.

[9] *Documentos, supra,* vols. i and ii.

[10] Diego de Ocaña was a native of Seville, of reputed Jewish descent. He arrived in Mexico from Santo Domingo, in June, 1525, and was authorized by the city council to exercise his profession of notary the same month. He was the author of several violent letters against Cortes written to the *Casa de Contractación* in Seville. See *Documentos Ineditos del Archivo de Indias,* Madrid, 1870, vol. xiii, pp. 348-356, 393-406. For his evidence against Cortes see *Documentos para la Historia de Mexico, supra,* vol. lxxvii, Inquisition Records, A. G. N., Mexico, gives some account of his trial and further light is thrown upon this extraordinary man by his will, made in 1533, a transcript of which is published in *La Vida Colonial, Publicaciones del Archivo General de la Nacion,* Mexico, 1923, vol. vii.

enquiry [11] regarding the authority and intentions of Narvaez, and Cortes's action in consequence of the arrival of Narvaez, we find Alonso giving specific answers showing that his sympathies were with his former commander. He had, he said, seen the warrants which Narvaez had brought to New Spain and had heard them proclaimed in the Port of San Juan de Ulua as soon as he had landed. Describing the famous attack by Cortes against Narvaez at Zempoala [12] he said that

Narvaez was a resolute man who, if he had been animated by the intentions which had been attributed to him, would have sought out Hernando Cortes because, in addition to being a capable leader, his men were more numerous and better equipped and who, on the night of the fight, even though taken by surprise, showed himself to be a brave man.

After Cortes had captured Narvaez and all his equipment and men, he returned to Tenoxtitlan, Mexico and

re-entered it with more than eight hundred men between horse and foot.

From Hernando Alonso's statement it is evident that he was also present during the Spaniards' retreat on the famous *Noche Triste,* as he was familiar with the great loss of gold, silver and jewels which the Spaniards suffered. During the latter part of 1520 and the beginning of 1521 he was engaged on the construction of the thirteen brigantines which Cortes ordered Martin Lopez to build at Texcoco, a fact which was confirmed by a surviving *conquistador* named Bartolomé Gonzalez, who told the Inquisitor Bonilla in 1574 that Alonso

had hammered many nails into the brigantines that served to recapture the City of Mexico,

and that he had seen the old man taking part in the attack.

Alonso, too, was present in Mexico when the humiliated Francisco de Garay [13] returned from Panuco, and when the

---

[11] The full evidence of Hernando Alonso, forming part of this enquiry, is contained in a fragment of an unpublished MS. in the archives of the *Hospitál de Jesús* in Mexico.

[12] " The Conquest of New Spain," *supra,* vol. ii, p. 207.

[13] H. H. Bancroft, " History of Mexico," vol. ii, chapters vi and vii.

Indians had arisen in that territory and Gonzalo de Sandoval
had been dispatched by Cortes in 1523 to quell the disturbances, Alonso was one of his force, which included one
hundred and fifty Spaniards and thirty thousand natives.
When asked about the failure of Cortes to make a proper
distribution of the spoils of war, he said the accusation was
true because, had they been distributed fairly, he would have
been informed of it and, as a *conquistador,* he would have
received his share. He also stated that he had seen

the said Hernando Cortes wearing a belt of refined gold which he had
exacted from the natives,

and added that Cortes had kept for himself the best and
richest land in all the country, this being common knowledge.
Alonso

believed that he had retained three-quarters of such land and distributed less than one-quarter, the allotments given to the *conquistadores* and other inhabitants being insufficient for their support.

Alonso appears to have been familiar with all the stirring
activities of 1525 and 1526. He had also been present in
Mexico City on the arrival of Ponce de Leon,[14] whom Charles V
sent to take the *Residencia* of Cortes. Questioned on this
subject, he replied that

he had seen, on the day when the Licentiate Luis Ponce died and
before he was buried, that the alcaldes and city councillors assembled in the church of this city and started to shout, and that Juan
de Valdivieso, procurator of Guatiqualco, in the chapter cried out
that Don Hernando Cortes was their governor and captain-general,
and the community wanted to have him back; that the witness was
in the chapter house and saw Don Hernando Cortes enter looking
very haughty.

Alonso's evidence, although given against Cortes, is moderate in expression and not marked with the virulence and
hatred shown by Diego de Ocaña and other witnesses. He had
fought for Cortes in many an arduous campaign for five years,
and although he had been awarded an *encomienda* at Acto-

[14] Bancroft, *supra,* chap. xii.

4

pan [15] and was called its lord, apparently it was insufficient for his support, and from many *conquistadores* hard things were heard against the captain-general during those times when his star appeared to be declining. Sometime towards the end of 1525, or the beginning of 1526, Alonso had been on an expedition to Guanajuato, but we have no information regarding under whom he served or for how long he was away from Mexico.

Between March 15, 1524, and March 9, 1528, we find frequent references to Hernando Alonso in the first book of the *Actas de Cabildo* [16] of the newly-formed city council of Mexico City. That he was a respected and trusted citizen there is no doubt. He was granted by the city council several ground plots, and apparently on his property at Actopan he raised cattle for the supply of meat to Mexico City. On March 15, 1524, he appeared before the mayor and aldermen and stated that, whereas Pedro de Maya, who had the butcher's shop of the city, sold the *arrelde* (four pounds) of pork at six *reales,* he would sell the same weight for four *reales,* and asked them to accept his bid. The aldermen gave orders that the same bid should be proclaimed by the city crier so that, if within nine days any other person wished to make a lower bid, he should be favored. On October 3, 1525, Rodrigo de Paz, in the name of the governor, appeared before the city council and offered to sell the *arrelde* of pork for two *reales.* Hernando Alonso agreed, on certain conditions, to lower his price to one and a half *reales.* A notification was then sent to Hernan Lopez de Avila, who, in the absence of the governor, represented him, asking if he was willing to sell at one and a half *reales* the *arrelde,* otherwise the bid of Hernando Alonso would be accepted. On May 7, 1527, he again appeared with an offer to sell mutton and beef at five *reales* the *arrelde* and one gold *real* for pork.

[15] Actopan is about sixty miles north of Mexico City.
[16] In the archives of the municipality of Mexico.

The last reference to Alonso in the *Actas de Cabildo* is on March 9, 1528, when he appeared in partnership with Bartolomé de Morales and gave the mayor and aldermen the prices at which they were willing to sell meat from Easter of that year until *Carnestolendas* (three days before Ash Wednesday) of 1529, as follows:

Mutton at 4 *reales* the *arrelde*. Beef at 4 *reales* the *arrelde*. Pork at 28 *maravedis* the *arrelde*.

The aldermen received the bid apparently without further question, as they ordered it to be proclaimed by the city crier. The minutes of this meeting of the city council are signed among others by Alonso de Estrada, the governor.

II.

The events and reasons which led to the martyrdom of the old *conquistador* are very difficult to understand. Between March, 1528, when he appears to have been in the favor of Alonso de Estrada, the acting governor of New Spain, and his persecution only a few months later by the Dominican inquisitors, there was a stormy and unsettled period, full of rivalries and bitter jealousies, and one of virulent partisanship. Cortes was, at that time, practically exiled and had gone to Spain to lay his own merits and services before the emperor, and it was not until the end of the year that Nuño de Guzman, as president of the first *audiencia,* arrived, accompanied by Friar Juan Zumárraga, the newly-appointed bishop of Mexico.

There are no contemporary documents available recording the first *auto de fe* in 1528, and, but for the zeal and thoroughness of Inquisitor Bonilla in 1574, all knowledge of many interesting facts regarding the primitive inquisition in Mexico would have been lost. Fortunately, the documents relating to Bonilla's enquiry are preserved in the Mexican National Archives,[17] and from these we are able to obtain fairly reliable

[17] A. G. N., Mexico, Inquisition Records, vol. lxxvii.

information regarding the first victims of the inquisition in New Spain.

For a proper understanding of the authority assumed and wielded by the friars in cases of heresy in the early days after the conquest, it is necessary to briefly review the early history of inquisitorial authority in North America.

It was many years after the colonization of the West Indian territories had been considerably advanced before Spain introduced the formal tribunal of the inquisition in Mexico. According to Las Casas,[18] Friar Pedro de Cordoba was the founder of the Dominican order in the New World. He arrived in Hispaniola in September, 1510, but, due to his fervent preaching on behalf of the native Indians, the Spanish settlers grew angry, and he returned to Spain to lay the matter before his provincial. Pedro de Cordoba returned to Hispaniola some years later. Cardinal Tortosa, the inquisitor general in Spain, on January 7, 1519, appointed as apostolic inquisitors in the Indies, Alonso Manso, bishop of San Juan de Puerto Rico, and Friar Pedro de Cordoba, the vice-provincial of the Order of St. Dominic.[19] Apparently the only official act of Friar Cordoba, who died at Santo Domingo in June, 1525, was to grant a commission to Friar Martin de Valencia of the Franciscan order, who passed through Hispaniola in 1524 on the way to Mexico. Under this commission Friar Martin was appointed commissary for the whole of New Spain, with limited authority to punish delinquents. By virtue of two papal bulls,[20] one granted by Leo X, dated April 25, 1521, and another by Adrian VI, dated May 9, 1522, the Franciscan friars were granted far-reaching authority in religious matters, although no specific reference is made to inquisitorial powers. With the authority of these papal bulls, Friar Martin de Valencia, on his arrival in Mexico in 1524, was sufficiently authorized to

[18] *Historia de las Indias,* Madrid 1875, vol. iii, pp. 273-274.
[19] Medina, *La Primitiva Inquisición Americana,* vol. ii, p. 5.
[20] Medina, *supra,* vol. i, p 99.

act as inquisitor, an authority which he apparently limited
to curbing the hardy *conquistadores'* habit of blasphemous
swearing. In this connection it is interesting to note that
Hernando Cortes, some years earlier, a month or two after
his retreat from Mexico in June, 1520, had himself issued a
decree imposing heavy penalties for blasphemy and gambling.[21]

When the Dominicans passed over to New Spain in 1526,
the judges of the *audiencia* of Hispaniola decided that Friar
Martin de Valencia's commission should only hold good until
their arrival in Mexico. The appointment of commissary was
held soon after their arrival by Friar Domingo de Betanzos,
who exercised the office until July, 1528, and during this
period no serious cases, other than blasphemy, came before
him.

About that date there arrived in Mexico Friar Vicente
de Santa Maria, the founder of the Dominican monastery,
and Friar Betanzos was relieved of the office of commissary.
Friar Santa Maria had first come to Mexico two years before,
but left for Spain soon afterwards. On his return he came
with the title of vicar general, and in the first chapter of his
order celebrated in New Spain he was elected superior of the
monastery and, as such, became commissary of the Holy
Office. The authority with which he was endowed made him
the first persecutor of the Jews in America, and the first to
condemn to the stake two reputable citizens for judaical
practices. Friar Santa Maria does not appear to have exercised any authority after 1528, and Medina suggests that his
relentless conduct probably led to his removal from Mexico.

Don Sebastian Ramirez de Fuenleal, the president of the
second *audiencia,* writing to the emperor in 1532,[22] indicated
that the conduct of the friars was not approved in higher
quarters; the letter read in part as follows:

The friars of these orders of St. Dominic and St. Francis hold an
apostolic brief from Adrian, given at the request of Your Majesty,

[21] *Documentos Ineditos, supra,* vol. xxvi, pp. 16-18.
[22] *Documentos Ineditos, supra,* vol. xiii, p. 211.

in virtue of which the friars of both orders have arrogated to themselves episcopal and even pontifical functions . . . . and by virtue of the same brief they have instituted proceedings in cases of heresy, and have appointed constables with the wand and title of constable of the inquisition, and employed notaries, and have sentenced some offenders to the flames, and others to public reconciliation and penitence, and it appears to me that what was granted to them to effect the conversion of the Indians, they have turned into a stumbling block and a pretext for invading the jurisdiction of others. . . . .

From the time of Friar Santa Maria there are few cases of importance dealt with by the Dominican or episcopal authorities until the appointment of Bishop Zumárraga in 1535 as apostolic inquisitor, and in 1536 he proceeded to establish a tribunal, nominating as secretary Miguel Lopez de Legazpi, famous afterwards as the conquerer of the Philippines. Bishop Zumárraga as an inquisitor is chiefly remembered for his trial of the Indian chief, Don Carlos, whom he condemned to the stake in 1539. In 1543 Zumárraga was superseded as inquisitor by the *Visitador* Francisco Tello de Sandoval.[23] Sandoval does not appear to have been active as an inquisitor, and after his return to Spain in 1546 the inquisitorial proceedings were in the hands of the episcopal authorities, until the arrival, in 1571, of Dr. Pedro Moya de Contreras, with the Licentiate Alonso Hernandez de Bonilla as fiscal. At this time the regular tribunal of the inquisition was established under the decree of Philip II, dated at Madrid, August 16, 1570. The authority of this tribunal extended not only over the whole of New Spain, but also to Guatemala, Nicaragua and Honduras.

The new tribunal began its active work at the beginning of 1572, and an examination of many *procesos* prior to that time shows that they were carefully annotated by the fiscal, Bonilla, who appears to have shown amazing energy and thoroughness in his new position. Bonilla discovered in examining the old documents that many of the *procesos* were

[23] *Cedulario de Puga*, Mexico, 1563, fol. 97.

missing and that the *sambenitos* of some former heretics were no longer hanging in the cathedral church.

With the new inquisitors' first great onslaught against heresy, which culminated in the *auto de fe* of February 28, 1574, Bonilla, who had succeeded Pedro Moya de Contreras as chief inquisitor, determined to keep the record of heresy straight from the time Spain had colonized the new territories, now under the inquisition's jurisdiction. He examined all those who might be in a position to inform him of the past, and opened an enquiry by calling before him, at his afternoon audience on June 16, 1574, Friar Vicente de las Casas of the Dominican order. Friar Vicente was a native of Seville, seventy-five years of age, and had arrived in Mexico a few years after the conquest.

When questioned as to whether he knew the number of *sambenitos* there had been in the cathedral church in past times, who were the people who had worn them, and under what authority they had been condemned, he replied that during 1528, more or less, when Friar Vicente de Santa Maria of the order of Santo Domingo came to this country, the Franciscan friars, who had come out previously and had been entrusted with apostolic authority under the bull of Adrian VI to take cognizance of matters relating to heresy, by mutual agreement handed over the said charge to Friar Vicente de Santa Maria, who at once commenced to punish blasphemies as had previously been done by Friar Domingo de Betanzos of the same order. In the same year Friar Santa Maria proceeded against a certain Hernando Alonso, a smith, and another man called Gonzalo de Morales. The witness one Sunday saw Hernando Alonso and Gonzalo de Morales garmented with *sambenitos* having devices of flames upon them. These two were handed over to the secular authorities to be burnt at the stake in virtue of the sentence passed upon them, which sentence the witness believed was carried out near

Santiago,[24] the sentence having been pronounced in the cathedral church, where two scaffolds had been erected, on one of which were the condemned and on the other the said Friar Santa Maria, the Licentiate Altamirano and Alonso de Estrada, governor of the City, and a number of other religious and prominent personages.

He was further questioned as to whether the *sambenitos* of the two prisoners were hung up in the cathedral church, to which he answered that he had seen them a number of times but did not remember when they were removed. He also said that the *sambenitos* had flames of fire upon them and each bore the name of the offender.

The witness was questioned as to the offences committed by Hernando Alonso and Gonzalo de Morales, and he replied that he understood that Alonso was thrown into prison for having twice baptised a child, it being at first believed that he had done it through ignorance, but later he confessed that the second baptism was according to the ritual of the law of Moses. The witness said he had heard Friar Santa Maria and the Dominican friar, Pedro de Contreras, remark that they had found that the baptismal ceremony appertained to the law of Moses. The witness also said that Gonzalo de Morales was imprisoned as the result of a dispatch which the bishop of San Juan de Puerto Rico had sent to the monastery of Santo Domingo in this city, in which the bishop, who was named Manso,[25] said he had condemned to the stake as a Jewess a sister of Morales, who had inculpated her brother, saying that the two of them had beaten a crucifix, hanging it on a latch, and in the course of the trial Morales had confessed and had been burnt as a Jew. The witness said he had seen the *proceso* on the case, and had heard Friar Pedro de Contreras preach a sermon in the cathedral church recounting the

[24] Santiago was situated at the northern boundary of what is now the present city of Mexico. It was there that the Franciscans founded a monastery in 1529, near the site of the famous temple of Tlaltetolco.

[25] Medina, *supra*, vol. ii, p. 5.

offences of the accused. The witness also told the inquisitor that Hernando Alonso had two or three children, already advanced in years, living at that time in the City of Mexico.

The witness was asked how it came about that Hernando Alonso and Gonzalo de Morales had been turned over to the secular authorities to be burnt at the stake, seeing that they had confessed their offences, and whether it was that they had relapsed or recanted, and he replied that he had understood from Friar Pedro de Contreras that Morales had confessed too late, but that he did not know why they had burnt Hernando Alonso.

Two days later the Inquisitor Bonilla called before him the pious and erudite Friar Bartolomé Ledesma, the prior of the monastery of Santo Domingo, and formerly *administrador* of the archbishopric. Ledesma could not throw any light on the missing *sambenitos;* he had been in Mexico twenty-two years, and the only persons whom he had seen punished with a *sambenito* were Robert Tomson, an Englishman, and Agustin Bocacio, a Genoese, who had been punished fourteen years previously by the ordinary inquisition in the time of Archbishop Don Alonso de Montufar.

Maria de Cuenca, an old resident, was asked about Hernando Alonso's relatives. She told the inquisitors that he had left a widow, Isabel de Aguilar, who, being very beautiful, afterwards married Juan Perez de Gama, a *conquistador,* who took her to Spain, together with a daughter of hers by Hernando Alonso, whom they married in Seville to an official scrivener. Isabel de Aguilar again became a widow and married a certain Rodriguez, who was employed in the mint at Seville.

Another witness, Pedro Vasquez de Vergara, a resident of Mexico, seventy years of age, said that in 1528 he had been present in the cathedral church at an *auto de fe* presided over by Friar Vicente de Santa Maria, who had come out with the functions of an inquisitor and was issuing edicts in the same manner as the inquisition, and that at the ceremony he had seen Hernando Alonso, whom he had heard had come from the

Condado de Niebla, and Gonzalo de Morales, sentenced to be burnt at the stake; and later in the same day he had seen them burnt at Santiago. Hernando Alonso, he said, was condemned because he had performed a Jewish ceremony and because he had in accordance with the Mosaic law forbidden his wife, Isabel de Aguilar, to go to church during her menstrual period, of which fact witness was aware because six or seven months before Hernando Alonso was arrested, and before Friar Vicente de Santa Maria had come to Mexico, the witness himself had heard Alonso say to his wife in the presence of Anton Ruiz Maldonado, when she expressed her desire to go to Mass on the following day, Sunday:

Señora, thou must not go to Mass,

and on her enquiring why not, he had answered:

Because in your present condition thou wouldst profane the church.

Whereupon the witness remarked to him:

These are old ceremonies of the Jews which are not observed now we have adopted the law of evangelical grace.

To this Alonso made no reply, and the witness thought no more of the matter; but Anton Ruiz took the matter seriously and denounced it to Friar Santa Maria when he came to Mexico. Pedro Vasquez also remembered that Friar Santa Maria, in delivering sentence, had said that Hernando Alonso had confessed to this, and said it was a ceremony of the Jewish law. And then the witness went on to tell Inquisitor Bonilla that the sentence also recounted how in the Port known as *Real Puerto* (Port Royal) of the island of Española (Santo Domingo) Hernando Alonso and another man named Palma, and others, had taken an infant of two years of age and placed it in a basin and poured water on its head from a jar and the water that ran down from the body of the child and what dripped from its organ they gathered in a cup and drank. On Hernando Alonso, during the course of his trial, being asked why this had been done, he confessed and admitted that it was done in mockery of the sacrament of baptism. This witness also remembered that Hernando Alonso having a child baptized by Friar Diego Campanero,[26] a Franciscan, one of the three friars that took part in the conquest of Mexico, caused the child to be again baptized by a priest of the cathedral church of Mexico whom witness believed was named Juan Diaz,[27] on the ground that the baptism of the friar was worthless. These facts, said the witness, were related to him by Friar Pedro de Contreras, who was a friend of his, and who had also told him that Alonso when sworn had denied everything, but when threatened with the rack and other instruments for applying the torture had confessed and besought mercy; but this he had done when it was too late to grant it to him and there was nothing to do but to burn him at the stake. Pedro Vasquez told Bonilla that on his remarking to Friar Pedro de Contreras that it seemed a hard thing not to concede mercy to him because he sought it only a few days, not more than fifteen, after his denial, the friar had said that it had to be done.

On Pedro Vasquez asking Friar Pedro de Contreras how Gonzalo de Morales had behaved during his imprisonment, he had replied:

Leave him alone; he is a dog, and only confessed out of dread of the torture the same as Hernando Alonso.

Pedro Vasquez also told that in 1530 or thereabouts there came to the city, as president of the royal *audiencia,* Don Sebastian Ramirez de Fuenleal, Archbishop of Santo Domingo, and that the archbishop had remarked that the procedure in the trials of Hernando Alonso and Gonzalo de Morales had

[26] The present writer has been unable to trace this name among the early friars.

[27] The licentiate, Juan Diaz, was one of the two religious men who accompanied Cortes to Mexico; his companion was Bartolomé de Olmedo. Juan Diaz was the author of the *Itinerario de Grijalva;* see J. Garcia Icazbalceta, *Documentos para la Historia de Mexico,* Mexico, 1858, vol. i, pp. 281-308.

been irregular and that they had been wronged by being denied the mercy they had implored, the which he (Fuenleal) knew from his experience as an inquisitor in Spain.

This witness further told the inquisitor that Hernando Alonso and he were intimate friends, and on account of their great friendship they called each other *compadre*.

Among other witnesses was the treasurer of the royal exchequer, Bernardino de Albornoz, who confirmed the evidence of Pedro Vasquez de Vergara.

In the course of the enquiry it was elicited that two old residents, both *conquistadores,* could perhaps give additional evidence. Bonilla therefore authorized Pedro de los Rios, the secretary of the inquisition, to go to their houses and examine them. The first old *conquistador* examined was named Diego Valdes, eighty years of age and very infirm. He remembered that when the Marquis del Valle, Don Hernando Cortes, came back to Mexico from his expedition to Honduras and shortly after his return, he saw, wearing the *sambenito* of a reconciled person, a certain Ocaña, a tall old man who had come to Mexico from the island of Santo Domingo. He also said that Hernando Alonso was a *conquistador* of the country, and the old man remembered the story of the baptism of the child and that Hernando Alonso was married to Isabel de Aguilar.

Bartolomé Gonzalez, the other witness, who was a native of Portugal, stated he was a *conquistador* and seventy-four years of age. He told how he had taken part in the siege of Mexico fifty-three years before, and how, between forty-five and fifty years ago, he had seen Hernando Alonso, a *conquistador,* and a certain Gonzalo de Morales, a trader, condemned to the stake, and he confirmed the evidence of other witnesses. He also said he believed that Hernando Alonso came from Lope or Moguer in the Condado de Niebla, and that he had been married to Isabel de Ordaz (Beatriz de Ordaz), who must have been buried in Cholula or Tepeaca, as she died during the conquest before the siege of Mexico; and the second time he married in Coyoacan a woman called Ana, who died in Mexico; and a third time Isabel de Aguilar, the beautiful daughter of a one-eyed tailor called Aguilar, who, when a widow, married Juan Perez de Gama, a *conquistador*. This witness was asked if he was certain that Hernando Alonso had been one of the *conquistadores,* and he replied that he

knew it very well, because he had seen him in the conquest, when he had hammered many nails into the brigantines which had been built to recapture Mexico, and he and others were lords of Actopan, which was now owned by Juan Guerrero.

The last witness called by Inquisitor Bonilla on August 5, 1574, was Melchor de Legazpi, the accountant of the royal exchequer, at that time thirty years of age. This witness was the son of Miguel Lopez de Legazpi, the conqueror of the Philippines, and he was asked if he knew of the whereabouts of the various *procesos* of the early heretics. He told the inquisitor that his father had had in his possession certain papers connected with the past trials, but that when he went to the western isles he had left them in the house of Pedro de Salzedo, a brother-in-law, who was now dead, which papers he had understood had all been taken to the Holy Office. The inquisitor told him to make further search, because there were many papers lacking on matters pertaining to the Inquisition, not only in the times of Bishop Friar Juan Zumárraga, but also in those of Friar Vicente de Santa Maria. Melchor de Legazpi promised to make further search, and with that the audience terminated and the enquiry closed.

The foregoing is all that the writer has so far found regarding the trial of Hernando Alonso; but the evidence seems to prove that he was a Jew, or of Jewish descent, and undoubtedly one of the first to suffer for his race and ancestral religion on the mainland of North America.

APPENDIX.

LIST OF THE SAMBENITOS OF THE CONDEMNED JEWS PLACED IN THE
CATHEDRAL CHURCH OF MEXICO BETWEEN 1528 AND 1603.[1]

In the City of Mexico on Thursday, the 16th, and Friday, the 17th
of February, 1606, in fulfillment of what had been provided and
ordered by the worshipful inquisitors, Licenciados Don Alfonso de
Peralta and Gutierre Bernardo de Quiros in the official act of yesterday, Wednesday, the 15th of this present month and year, I placed
the *sambenitos* of the condemned and reconciled offenders of this
Holy Office, both the ones renovated and those newly painted, upon
the wall which begins at the principal door of the cathedral church
which faces the palace and ends at the altar of San Miguel, in the
customary form and in the following manner:

1. Hernando Alonso, smith; born in the County of Niebla; resident of Mexico; Jewish heretic; condemned to the stake and burnt,
year 1528.

2. Gonzalo de Morales, trader; born in Seville; resident of Mexico;
of Jewish descent; Judaic heretic; condemned to the stake, year 1528.

3. Diego de Ocaña; scrivener; born in Seville; resident of Mexico;
of Jewish descent; Judaic heretic; reconciled year 1528.

5. Francisco Millan; tavern-keeper; born in Utrera; inhabitant of
Mexico; of Jewish descent; Judaic heretic; reconciled year 1539.

35. Garcia Gonzalez Bermegero; born in the town of Albuquerque;
resident of Mexico; of Jewish descent; Judaic heretic; condemned
to the stake year 1579.

38. Francisco Rodriguez Matos; Portuguese; native of Benavente;
resident of Panuco; of Jewish descent; Judaic heretic; dogmatist;
deceased;' condemned year 1590.

39. Baltasar Rodriguez de Caravajal; son of Francisco Rodriguez
Matos; born in Benavente; a youth; unmarried; resident of Mexico;
of Jewish descent; Judaic heretic; dogmatist; a fugitive.

40. Doña Francisca Nuñez de Caravajal; wife of Francisco Rodriguez de Matos; Portuguese; native of Benavente; of Jewish descent;
Judaic heretic; reconciled year 1590.

41. Doña Catalina de Leon; daughter of the aforesaid (Francisco
Rodriguez de Matos); born in Benavente; resident of Mexico; of
Jewish descent; Judaic heretic; reconciled year 1590.

---

[1] Vol. lxxvii, Inquisition Records, A. G. N. The names of other persons punished by the inquisition during this period have been
omitted.

42. Doña Mariana Nuñez; maiden, likewise daughter of the aforesaid (Francisco Rodriguez de Matos); born in Benavente; resident of Mexico; of Jewish descent; Judaic heretic; reconciled year 1590.

43. Doña Leonor de Andrada; likewise daughter of the aforesaid (Francisco Rodriguez de Matos); born in Benavente; inhabitant of Mexico; of Jewish descent; Judaic heretic; reconciled year 1590.

44. Luis de Caravajal; youth; unmarried; son of the aforesaid (Francisco Rodriguez de Matos); born in Benavente; resident of Mexico; of Jewish descent; Judaic heretic; reconciled year 1590.

45. Doña Catalina de Leon; wife of Gonzalo Perez Ferro; resident of Mexico; Portuguese; Judaic heretic; reconciled year 1590.

46. Doña Isabel de Andrada; widow; daughter of the said Francisco Rodriguez de Matos and Doña Francisca Nuñez de Caravajal; Judaic heretic; reconciled year 1590.

47. Gabriel Rodriguez; born in Cercedas in Portugal; trader in Zacatecas; of Jewish descent; Judaic heretic; reconciled year 1591.

48. Francisco Ruiz de Luna; born in Cordoba; residing in this New Spain; Judaic heretic; reconciled year 1591.

50. Julian Castellanos Obragero; resident of Mexico; Judaic heretic; reconciled year 1591.

51. Licenciado Manuel de Morales; Portuguese; doctor; resident of Mexico; of Jewish descent; Judaic heretic; condemned to the stake year 1593.

53. Doña Francisca Nuñez de Caravajal; wife of Francisco Rodriguez de Matos; born in Benavente; reconciled in the year 1590 but relapsing into Jewish practices was burnt at the stake in the year 1596.

54. Doña Isabel de Andrada; born in Benavente; daughter of the aforesaid Francisco Rodriguez de Matos and his wife; burnt at the stake for persistence in Jewish practices in the year 1596.

55. Doña Catalina de Leon; daughter of the aforesaid (Francisco Rodriguez de Matos) and wife of Antonio Diaz de Cazeres; burnt at the stake for persistence in Jewish practices in the year 1596.

56. Luis de Caravajal; a son of the aforesaid (Francisco Rodriguez de Matos) a youth; unmarried; a persistent dogmatist and Judaic heretic; burnt at the stake in the year 1596.[2]

---

[2] The second *sambenito;* see No. 44. This youth has often been confused with his uncle, Luis de Caravajal, the Governor of Nuevo Leon, who was condemned by the Inquisition in February 1590 to be banished for six years from New Spain. See A. G. N. Inquisition Records, vol. mcccclxxxvii. Transcript in possession of the present writer.

57. Miguel Rodriguez; brother of the last-named, and son of the aforesaid Francisco Rodriguez de Matos and Doña Francisca Nuñez; Judaic heretic; burnt in effigy in the year 1596.

58. Doña Leonor de Andrada; daughter of the aforesaid Francisco Rodriguez de Matos and Doña Francisca Nuñez de Caravajal and wife of Jorge de Almeida; resident of Mexico; incorrigible Judaic heretic; burnt at the stake in the year 1596.

59. Manuel de Lucena; Portuguese; born in San Vicente; resident of the mines of Pachuca; Judaic heretic; dogmatist; burnt at the stake in the year 1596.

60. Catalina Enriquez; wife of the said Manuel de Lucena; Judaic heretic; reconciled year 1596.

61. Leonor Diaz; born in Seville; wife of Francisco Rodriguez de Sa; Portuguese; resident of Mexico; Judaic heretic; reconciled year 1596.

62. Andres Rodriguez; born in Fondon in Portugal; trader; resident of Texcoco; Judaic heretic; reconciled year 1596.

63. Antonio de Morales; Portuguese; nephew of Licenciado Manuel de Morales, doctor, who was burnt in effigy; also burnt in effigy for Judaic heresy in the year 1596.

64. Doña Isabel Perez; wife of the aforesaid Manuel de Morales; Judaic heretic; burnt in effigy in the year 1596.

65. Antonio Rodriguez; deceased; Portuguese; youth; unmarried; born in San Vicente; Judaic heretic; burnt in effigy in the year 1596.

66. Antonio Lopez; Portuguese; born in Celorico; resident of Mexico; Judaic heretic; burnt in effigy in the year 1596.

67. Beatriz Enriquez la Payba, wife of Simon Payba; Portuguese; resident of Mexico; Judaic heretic; burnt at the stake in the year 1596.

68. Diego Enriquez, son of the aforesaid; Judaic heretic; reconciled, but lapsing into the same offence is burnt at the stake in the year 1596.

69. Pedro Enriquez, a youth; unmarried; brother of the last-named and son of the said Simon Payba and Beatriz Enriquez; Judaic heretic; reconciled year 1596.

70. Diego Lopez; born in the town of San Vicente in Portugal; youth; unmarried; Judaic heretic; reconciled in the year 1596.

71. Domingo Cuello; Portuguese; born in the City of Braga; Judaic heretic; reconciled year 1596.

72. Domingo Rodriguez; Portuguese; resident of Mexico; reconciled as a Jewish heretic but relapsing into the same offence was burnt in effigy in the year 1596.

73. Francisco Jorge; blind of one eye; born in Benavente; resident of Taxco; Judaic heretic; burnt in effigy in the year 1596.

74. Fabian Granados; born in Lamego in Portugal; Judaic heretic; burnt in effigy in the year 1596.

75. Francisco Vaez; Portuguese; youth; unmarried; servant of the aforesaid Manuel de Lucena; Judaic heretic; burnt in effigy in the year 1596.

76. Francisco Rodriguez; youth; unmarried; born in San Vicente in Portugal; Judaic heretic. Burnt in effigy in the year 1596.

77. Francisco Rodriguez, silversmith, alias Francisco Rodriguez de Cea; Portuguese; resident of Mexico; Judaic heretic; burnt in effigy in the year 1596.

78. Justa Mendez, daughter of Clara Enriquez; Portuguese; resident of Mexico; reconciled for Judaism; again reconciled for the same offence in the year 1596.

79. Juan Rodriguez de Silva; Portuguese; youth; unmarried; a resident of Mexico; Judaic heretic; burnt in effigy in the year 1596.

80. Jorge Alvarez, son of Manuel Alvarez; trader; a resident of Mexico; born in Fondon in Portugal; Judaic heretic; reconciled year 1596.

81. Jorge Vaez; Portuguese; born in San Vicente; reconciled as Judaic heretic; year 1596.

82. Manuel Gomez Navarro; born in San Martin de Trevejos in Portugal; a youth; unmarried; Judaic heretic; reconciled year 1596.

83. Manuel Francisco de Belmonte; born in the town of Cuicillana in Portugal; resident of the mines of Sultepec; Judaic heretic; reconciled year 1596.

84. Violante Rodriguez, widow of Simon Gonzalez; born in the town of La Salceda in Portugal; Judaic heretic; reconciled year 1596.

85. Manuel Diaz; merchant; Portuguese, son-in-law of the aforesaid Violante Rodriguez; resident of Mexico. Burnt at the stake for persistency in his errors as Judaic heretic year 1596.

86. Manuel Rodriguez; born in Fondon in Portugal; Judaic heretic; reconciled year 1596.

87. Miguel Hernandez; Portuguese; unmarried; born in the City of Viesco; Judaic heretic; burnt in effigy in the year 1596.

88. Pedro Rodriguez; born in Fondon, in Portugal; Judaic heretic; reconciled year 1596.

89. Doña Mariana Nuñez; maiden; born in Benavente; daughter of the aforesaid Francisco Rodriguez de Matos and his wife, Doña Francisca Nuñez de Caravajal. Reconciled for Judaism, but relapsing into the same offence was burnt at the stake in the year 1601.

5

91. Andres Nuñez, a youth; unmarried; Portuguese; born in Mogodoric; resident of Mexico; Judaic heretic; burnt at the stake in the year 1601.

92. Antonio Machado; tailor; deceased; born in the City of Lisbon; resident of Mexico; Judaic heretic and dogmatist; burnt in effigy in the year 1601.

93. Alvaro de Carrion; born in Cervera de Rio Pisuegra in Castille. Judaic heretic; reconciled year 1601.

94. Alvaro Rodriguez Achocado; Portuguese; resident of Mexico; Judaic heretic; burnt in effigy in the year 1601.

95. Antonio Diaz Marquez; trader; native of Alvala, near Lisbon. Judaic heretic; reconciled year 1601.

96. Alvaro Gonzalez; born in Fondon; resident of Mexico; Judaic heretic; burnt in effigy in the year 1601.

98. Blanca de Morales, wife of Pedro Hernandez; Portuguese and sister of the aforesaid Manuel de Morales; Judaic heretic; burnt in effigy in the year 1601.

99. Cristobal Gomez; born in the village of Escarigo in Portugal; resident of Mexico; Judaic heretic; burnt in effigy in year 1601.

102. Jorge Rodriguez; Portuguese; born in Seville; Judaic heretic; reconciled year 1601.

103. Diego Lopez Regalon; born in Fondon in Portugal; resident of Mexico; Judaic heretic; burnt in effigy in the year 1601.

104. Doña Ana de Caravajal, maiden; daughter of the aforesaid Francisco Rodriguez de Matos and Doña Francisca de Caravajal his wife; Judaic heretic; reconciled year 1601.

106. Francisco Rodriguez; shoemaker; resident of Mexico; born in the town of Certan in Portugal; Judaic heretic; reconciled year 1601.

109. Gonzalo Perez Ferro; Portuguese; born in the town of Villaflor; resident of Mexico; Judaic heretic; reconciled year 1601.

110. Isabel Clara; Portuguese; wife of Francisco Hernandez, brother of the aforesaid Licenciado Manuel de Morales, doctor; Judaic heretic; burnt in effigy in the year 1601.

119. Ines Fernandez, wife of Francisco Alvarez and sister of the aforesaid Manuel de Morales; Judaic heretic; burnt in effigy in the year 1601.

120. Jorge Diaz; silversmith; Portuguese; resident of Mexico; Judaic heretic; burnt in effigy in the year 1601.

121. Juan Rodriguez; soapmaker; Portuguese; inhabitant of Mexico; Judaic heretic; burnt in effigy in the year 1601.

125. Leonor de Cazeres, Portuguese; daughter of the aforesaid Antonio Diaz de Cazeres and of Doña Catalina de Leon his wife. Accused of persistence in Judaic practices; reconciled year 1601.

127. Luis Diaz, silversmith; Portuguese; resident of Mexico; Judaic heretic; burnt in effigy in the year 1601.

129. Manuel Tavares; Portuguese; born in the town of Cuvillana; resident of Mexico; Judaic heretic; reconciled year 1601.

130. Manuel Alvarez; merchant; Portuguese; born in Fondon; inhabitant of Mexico; Judaic heretic; reconciled year 1601.

131. Manuel Gomez Silberna; Portuguese; born in Moron; resident of the mines of Sultepec; Judaic heretic; reconciled year 1601.

134. Pelayo Alvarez; Portuguese; born in Freixo de Espada Cinta; Judaic heretic; reconciled in effigy year 1601.

137. Simon Payba, deceased; Portuguese; husband of the aforesaid Beatriz Enriquez la Payba; resident of Mexico; Judaic heretic; burnt in effigy in the year 1601.

138. Simon Rodriguez, trader; native of La Salzeda in Portugal; resident of Mexico; Judaic heretic; reconciled year 1601.

139. Tomas de Fonseca; native of Viesco de Espada Cinta in Portugal; resident in the mines of Tlalpujahua; Judaic heretic; reconciled year 1601.

140. Tomas de Fonseca; a native of Viesco in Portugal; inhabitant of and miner in the mines of Taxco; Judaic heretic; burnt at the stake in the year 1601.

142. Clara Enriquez, a maiden; daughter of Manuel de Lucena; burnt at the stake for Judaism, and Catalina Enriquez, reconciled for Judaism. Reconciled for the same offence, year 1603.

144. Francisco Rodriguez de Ledesma; native of the town of Berrueco Pardo in the Bishopric of Salamanca; Judaic heretic; reconciled year 1603.

146. Rodrigo del Campo; public scrivener on the roll of Mexico; a native of the town of Quintanar; Judaic heretic; reconciled year 1603.

The witnesses were Don Alonso Alvarez de Caldas, Chief *Alguacil* of this Holy Office; Pedro de Fonseca, Notary of the Secret Chamber; Juan Salzedo, master carpenter, who hung the said *sambenitos;* and many other persons, to which I certify.

Pedro de Manozca [Rubric].

The Autobiography of Luis De Carvajal, the Younger

Translated by MARTIN A. COHEN

INTRODUCTION

The autobiography of Luis de Carvajal, the younger, which is here translated from its original Spanish for the first time, is one of the most interesting and valuable documents written by any Judaizer of colonial Mexico. Its author, who met an untimely death at the stake when he was only thirty years old, had been for a decade the leader of the community, or rather, the communities of Judaizers in New Spain. Born in Benavente, Spain, in the year 1566, Luis emigrated to the New World, or, as he calls it, Occidental India, fourteen years later. He came in the company of his parents, his siblings and his famous uncle and namesake, Don Luis de Carvajal, called the older. For the older Luis de Carvajal this was the second trip. He had first come around 1569 and had achieved fame as a conquistador and pacifier of Indians. Shortly before his 1580 trip, he had been designated governor of an expansive province, impressively named the New Kingdom of Leon.

The Governor was Luis' maternal uncle. Luis had not been born a Carvajal, but a Rodríguez, though in proper Spanish style he could combine patronymic and metronymic and call himself Rodríguez Carvajal. The fact that not only he but other members of his family stressed their mother's name to the frequent exclusion of their father's may well manifest the Governor's influence. The Governor was indeed solicitous for his family's welfare. He persuaded his sister and brother-in-law to emigrate to New Spain and seems to have made them attractive promises for the improvement of their material well-being.

In bringing his relatives over to the New World the Governor, however, may well have been motivated by more than fraternal love. A staunch Catholic, he had heard that his sister's family was secretly practicing Judaism. This, to be sure, could not have failed to jar his religious sensibilities. Nor could it have failed to open his mind to the realization that if knowledge of his family's Judaizing reached the wrong people, the taint of suspicion might be attached to him and his soaring career jeopardized.

The Governor had never told anyone that he and his family were descended from Jews in Spain and Portugal who, during the previous two centuries, had converted to Christianity under pressure or force, and who in large numbers continued clandestinely to practice the Jewish religion. He told everyone that he was an Old Christian. Even if they were devout Catholics, New Christians could easily become suspect of practicing Judaism and as such could be subject to social disabilities and even to prosecution by the Inquisition.

Under these circumstances it would have been folly for Don Luis to leave his family in Spain right under the Inquisitors' noses. It would have been equally prejudicial to allow his brother-in-law to go through with his plans to escape to one of the Jewish communities in France or in Italy. Mexico, that is New Spain, was not exactly the safest place to bring them. Since 1570 it had an Inquisition of its own. But New Spain was a huge and virgin land. The Inquisition had a vast territory to cover. Its sights so far had been trained on Protestants and the usual assortment of comparatively petty offenders such as bigamists, blasphemers and clerics who abused the confessional. Besides, in the New World the Governor could keep an eye on his errant family and at least contain them if he failed to convert them.

If the Governor entertained such dreams, they soon turned to nightmares. In the New World his family Judaized even more than before. Young Luis, whom the Governor at one time loved so much that he designated him his heir and successor, and whom he thought to be an exemplary Catholic, disillusioned him when he openly came out as a Judaizer and set as his life's task the leading of others to the truth of the God whom he knew as Adonay.

Luis was arrested by the Inquisition in April, 1589. In his cell he began to reflect on the meaning and purpose of his life and, he tells us, to receive messages from on high that gave him courage and determination to continue as a leader of the Judaizers. He was tried by the Inquisition and found guilty, but feigned repentance and was reconciled to the Church. As part of his penance he was sent to serve as an orderly at the Convalescent Hospital of Mexico City. Soon, by a stroke of good fortune, which he narrates in his Autobiography,[1] he was transferred to a school for Indians, where

---

[1] See *infra*, pp. 300–301.

he became teacher of grammar to the students and private secretary to the rector. Here he not only had leisure time to reflect on his Judaism and to plan future activities, but he also had at his disposal the rector's well-stocked library, where he increased his knowledge of his ancestral heritage.

When he was reconciled to the Church, Luis knew that if he were rearrested, he would be indicted as an impenitent heretic. This meant that he would be burned at the stake. If he begged for reconciliation, he would attain the mercy of being garroted before the burning, but this would be as much as he could hope for. Yet Luis had determined to continue Judaizing and to encourage others to follow his example. He began to regard himself as another Joseph of the Bible, destined to sustain his people during the darkness of their enslavement that was certain to be followed by a miraculous deliverance. He felt that this was the mission for which his entire life had prepared him. He even adopted the name Joseph and later the surname "Lumbroso," meaning "enlightened" or "illumined." As he looked back on the varied and often terrifying experiences that had been his, he saw in each of them the hand of God, now rewarding, now punishing, but always dealing with mercy and always guiding him toward what Luis was convinced was his mission and goal. Aureoled with this faith, the events of Luis-Joseph's life, often drab and commonplace, often unfortunate and damaging, began to form themselves into a skein of miracles.

It was these miracles which Luis-Joseph wished to record in his autobiography, written in the third person with occasional lapses into the first. He may well have been interested in preserving them for posterity, but we must accept at face value his word that he wished that through them other New Christian Judaizers would take heart and remain steadfast in their faith. He began the autobiography in 1591 or early in 1592. Its final entry, dealing with events that occurred on the last day of October, 1594, was made three months or less before he was rearrested and charged with impenitent heresy. The Inquisition sequestered the document, had it transcribed, and, thanks to its obsession for conserving all in-

---

[2] The original document is not available. We have used the Inquisition's transcript, published at the end of the *Procesos de Luis de Carvajal* (*El Mozo*), in the *Publicaciones del Archivo General de la Nación*, Vol. XXVIII (Mexico, 1935), pp. 463–496. The publication was under the directorship of Rafael López. The documents were collated by Rodolfo Gómez and arranged and selected by Luis González Obregón.

It should be noted that all citations from the Spanish text, including page numbers in brackets, appearing below in the footnotes, refer to the aforementioned Spanish edition of the transcript.

criminating evidence, appended its text to the transcript of the proceedings of Luis-Joseph's two trials.

The autobiography reveals better than a thousand pieces of circumstantial evidence the spirit of this leader of Mexican Judaism. It gives proof of his ability to lead men, his linguistic power and the sensitivity and imagination with which he confronted life. It reveals his hopes, his frustrations, his fears, his dreams, his predilections and his prejudices. Luis-Joseph tells his story with consummate skill. Few will forget the vividness of his descriptions — the tropical storm, his brother's close call with the Inquisition, his sister's madness, and many others. They will provide a reservoir of emotion to be tapped whenever a book dealing with the New Christian Judaizers is read.

The autobiography is the first and by far the most important of the three literary bequests which young Luis-Joseph, with the assistance of the Inquisition, unwittingly made to posterity. During his second confinement, he used his genius to compose a series of letters to his mother and sisters which are more striking for their history than for their content. As a prisoner, Luis-Joseph was permitted no contact with the outside and none with other prisoners. His mother and his sisters were in the Inquisitional jail and Luis was determined to communicate with them. He wanted to send them words of encouragement and cheer and finally found a way to do it. He inscribed a message on the core of an alligator pear, hid it in a melon and asked the jailer to bring the fruit to one of his sisters for her solace. The jailer suspected a message, found the one Luis-Joseph had written and immediately informed his superiors. They told him to say nothing but to continue to supply Luis-Joseph with alligator pears, other fruits and even paper that he might continue what he thought were secret messages and perhaps thereby reveal incriminating information to the Inquisitors. The jailer did as he was told, and Luis-Joseph, considering as miraculous every opportunity to send a letter, continued to pen them. The Inquisitors, however, obtained nothing for their efforts. All that . Luis-Joseph revealed was his ability to write beautiful and inspiring epistles.

Finally, in the last months of his second trial, Luis-Joseph prepared his Last Will and Testament, which turns out to be a learned statement of his beliefs. There is little originality in this composition, except perhaps the idea of calling it a will; yet as a formal expression of the theology of the Judaizers, its historical value is not slight.[3]

---

[3] The reader may also wish to consult my study entitled, "The Religion of Luis

Regrettably, the text of the autobiography as it appears in the trial records of Luis de Carvajal, the younger, is corrupt. Words are misspelled, omitted or exchanged for others similarly spelled, perhaps carelessly copied from Luis' manuscript, but making no sense in their present context. Occasionally parts of sentences are omitted and sentences and even paragraphs are not to be found in their logical sequence. It is likely that the sad state of our present text is wholly due to a hurried and careless transcription of Luis-Joseph's manuscript by an indifferent and doubtless far from learned Inquisitional scribe. Fortunately, in most cases it is not difficult conservatively to reconstruct the text, and this has been done in the translation. In the cases where entire sections are omitted, the loss is irretrievable and the hiatus is accordingly marked.

The translation seeks faithfully to impart the concepts and tone of Luis de Carvajal's writing across the barriers of time and culture. The criteria of readability and precision of thought have not resulted, it is hoped, in loose, or, as it is often called, free translation. Syntactical and connotational changes have been made when necessitated by the English idiom, but these have been kept to a minimum. Brackets in the translation call attention to words added for clarity, and the notes include transcriptions of portions of the text containing many of the salient problems with which the translator must cope. The text as it appears in these notes faithfully preserves the orthography, punctuation, word divisions and, of course, errors found in the text that was used.

The other notes have been limited to biblical references, elucidations of unusual statements and identifications of individuals whose identity Luis, in his desire not to implicate others, tries to conceal in his text. The translator urges the reader interested in fuller material on Luis de Carvajal, the younger, to look for his book on this subject which will be forthcoming in the not too distant future, and which he hopes will be worthy of the reader's patience.

Rodríguez Carvajal: Glimpses into the Passion of a Mexican Judaizer," to be published in the near future in the *American Jewish Archives*.

THE AUTOBIOGRAPHY OF LUIS DE CARVAJAL, THE YOUNGER

[Written in][1] Mexico City, New Spain, [by] Joseph Lumbroso, of the Hebrew nation, a pilgrim in Occidental India,[2] in devoted recognition[3] of the favors and boons received from the hand of the Most High, who freed him from the gravest perils, in order that they may be known to all who believe in the Most Holy One and await the great mercies that He employs with sinners.[4]

Awakened by the Spirit Divine, Joseph committed these to writing, along with [the story of] his life until the twenty-fifth year of his wandering, in the form of a brief history.

Before beginning he kneels on the ground before the universal God, the Lord of all mercy, and promises, with the God of truth always before him,[5] to portray accurately everything that he writes below.

In the name of God, Adonay Sevaoth,[6] the Lord of Hosts: Joseph begins his life at the beginning. It should be mentioned that he was born and raised at Benavente, a city in Spain[7] where he lived until the age of twelve or thirteen. There he began to receive instruction in the rudiments of Christianity from a relative,[8] and he completed these studies in Medina del Campo [to which his family moved from Benavente]. There it pleased God's mercy to shed upon him the light by which he recognized His holiness. [It happened] on a special day, which we call the Day of Pardon, a holy and solemn occasion for us, [which falls] on the tenth day of the seventh month.[9] Since God's truth is so clear and pleasant,

---

[1] Text: *De Mexico*, etc. An introductory note in the text indicates that the material beginning here was originally written in the margin of the copy. The autobiography proper begins below. The Inquisition's transcript commences with the words, "In the name of God, Adonay Sevaoth," etc., which belong before the autobiography proper and are accordingly so placed in the translation.

[2] That is, the New World, the "India" of the West.

[3] Text: *y de los captivos en reconocimiento . . .* [p. 463].

[4] Text: *para que sean notorias a todos los que en el santo de los santos creen y esperan sus grandes misericordias . . .* [p. 463].

[5] Text: *trayendo por to. al sr. de las verdades . . .* [p. 463].

[6] The Hebrew *Adonay Sebaoth* [for *Adonay Tsev[b]aoth* (the Lord of Hosts)], or, more simply and frequently *Adonay* [the Lord] was the name which the New Christians, following biblical tradition, called God.

[7] The text reads *"villa de la europa."* [p. 463].

[8] This was his brother Baltasar [Balthasar], who was several years Luis' senior.

[9] The day, better known as the Yom Ha-Kippurim, or the Day of Atonement, falls on the tenth day of the seventh month [Tishri] in the traditional Jewish calendar. On the holidays celebrated by Luis and his group in New Spain and on the calendar which they had to follow, see my article, "The Religion of Luis Rodríguez Carvajal: Glimpses into the Passion of a Mexican Judaizer," referred to *supra*, p. 280, note 3.

all that his mother, his older brother, his older sister, and his cousin from that city had to do was to make mention of it to him [and he understood].

Joseph's father and his entire family emigrated to this land of New Spain, though they first planned[10] to cross over into Italy, where all could better serve, worship and love the true God.[11] But God's judgments are incomprehensible and just, and the change of plans bringing them to this land must have been God's punishment for one of [his father's] sins, a punishment meted out to his children by God's justice, though not without great compassion,[12] as we shall presently see.

Joseph [who had become] very ill [aboard ship] was removed [when the ship docked] at the port of Tampico. At the same time [another passenger] disembarked, who was best known for his fear of the Lord, our God. He was [also] a famous doctor, and, with God's guidance,[13] he treated Joseph in Tampico until he was cured.[14]

One night, while Joseph and his older brother were sleeping in a small shed, housing certain wares that they had brought from Castile, the Lord lashed the port with a hurricane. Its strong and terrible winds uprooted trees and razed most of the buildings to the ground. The building in which Joseph and his brother were sleeping began to shake. The violent wind ripped some of the beams from the roof with such terrible fury that Joseph and his brother instinctively huddled in fear under the delusive protection of their bedclothes.[15] At length, realizing that the collapse of the building was imminent, they arose, drenched and windlashed,[16] [and groped their way to the door]. But the wind blew so strongly against the door that, try as they might, they could not open it until God permitted them to pry it partially open by pulling it in the opposite direction. They opened it enough to leave the building before it tumbled to the ground. [In this way] the Holy One came forth in the sight of men to free

---

[10] Text: *intentado y deseado* ... [p. 463].

[11] Text: *conocido* ... [p. 463].

[12] Luis is aware of the rabbinic ideas (including those of the mystical schools, as represented for example in the *Zohar*) regarding the tension between God's justice and mercy, the *middath ha-din* and the *middath ha-raḥamim*. In this tension, the rabbis felt, and the mystics among them stressed, God's justice was regularly tempered if not overcome by His mercy.

[13] Text: *el qual y D. primero* ... [p. 464].

[14] This was the renowned Licentiate Manuel de Morales, who had taught Judaism to Luis' father.

[15] Text: *que caian con toda que les hazia meter debajo de la ropa engañosa defensa del gran miedo* ... [p. 464].

[16] Text: *llobiendo y ventando horriblemente* ... [p. 464].

them from death. Blessed be His most holy name. They went to recuperate in the home of their parents [who] feared that they were dead. On hearing their voices, their loving father received them with tears, thanking and praising the Lord a thousand times.

Shortly thereafter Joseph accompanied his father to Mexico City, leaving his mother, five sisters and two brothers domiciled — or rather disconsolately exiled — in Panuco, for they lived in penury in this mosquito-infested and heat-plagued town. When God took his father from this life, Joseph returned to Panuco.

Here God provided him with a holy Bible, which a priest sold him for six pesos. He read it assiduously in that forsaken land and came to learn many divine mysteries.

One day he came to the seventeenth chapter of [the *Book of*] *Genesis*, where the Lord commands[17] our holy father, Abraham, to circumcise himself. The words which say "The soul which is uncircumcised shall be blotted out from the Book of the Living"[18] caught Joseph's eye and struck his heart with terror. Without delay and with the inspiration of the Most High and His good angel, he got up, put the Bible down without even stopping to close it, left the hall in his house where he had been reading, took a pair of blunted and worn shears and went to the ravine at the Panuco River. Burning with desire to fulfill this holy sacrament,[19] without which one cannot be inscribed in the Book of Life, he placed its seal upon his flesh. The shears worked so well[20] that he cut off nearly the entire prepuce and left only a little flesh. Yet, despite this imperfection, Joseph had no reason to doubt that our Lord would accept his intention. This can be inferred from the *Second Book of Chronicles*, in the chapter where [Solomon] the wise king of Israel, speaks of his saintly father David's worthy desire, fulfilled by Solomon, to build a temple to the Lord.[21] On the day of its holy dedication, Solomon praised the excellence[22] of the Lord and said that though His supreme Majesty had, through revelation and Nathan's message, forbidden David to build the holy Temple, He accepted David's good intention in place of the deed.

---

[17] Text: *mando* . . . [p. 464].

[18] The quotation, from *Genesis* XVII:14 is not quite accurate. The verse reads, "And the uncircumcised male, who is not circumcised in the flesh of his foreskin, that soul shall be cut off from his people." (Translation: Jewish Publication Society of America [1917]).

[19] As will be seen in my article on the religion of Luis Rodríguez Carvajal, the New Christians, influenced by the theology and concepts of their Catholic environment, found within Judaism sacraments, saints, salvation and other elements of Catholic faith and worship.

[20] Text: *por so tambien las tijeras* . . . [p. 465].

[21] *II Chronicles* VI:8.   [22] Text: *las verdades* . . . [p. 465].

It is worth noting that once Joseph received the seal of this holy sacrament upon his flesh, it served as a bulwark against lust and an aid to chastity. Prior to this he had been a weak sinner, who often merited the stroke of death, which the Lord God sent upon a son[23] of our patriarch Judah and his consort Tamar,[24] for committing the same sin.[25] [Now] God's mercy was upon him, and, with the holy sacrament of circumcision, he was henceforth delivered from [the perversity of] this sin. The Lord helped him so much that, though he kept looking [for trouble,] like a sick man who always longs for the forbidden, and occasions were not lacking in which he could offend God, it seems that God's hand removed the dangers, because of His boundless mercy. Let us therefore give our thanks to God, for He is good, for His mercy endures forever.[26]

A year after his circumcision [Joseph had a strange adventure]. He [had] accompanied a wretched, blind uncle of his,[27] who was governor, in the name of the King of Spain, of the province called the New Kingdom of Leon, to some mines recently discovered within that province. He carried with him a small book, containing a transcription of the *Fourth Book of Ezra*,[28] the holy and pure priest and prophet. Joseph's devoted reading of this book had been one of the chief inspirations for his conversion. [And now,] since he did not have the Holy Bible with him in that land of savage Chichimecs,[29] the reading of this book absorbed his leisure hours.

One [September] day — it was the seventh month [according to the Jewish calendar] — his pack horse broke away. Joseph, carrying only harquebus, sword and dagger, took a brawny horse and pursued it. Two leagues out of town, the horse tired. It was in the midst of a dangerous area; several soldiers had been killed by the Chichimecs there, even near [Spaniards'] houses. When the horse tired and refused to budge, Joseph left its saddle at the foot of a tree, [put fresh priming in the pan,] slid the cover forward, shouldered the gun[30] and started to town on foot.

Night fell on the hilly and pathless terrain before he could determine where he was. He was not a little afraid that some barbarous Indian might chance by and with a single arrow take his life. He

---

[23] Text: *a una hija* ... [p. 465].   [24] Text: *marido de tomar* ... [p. 465].

[25] *Genesis* XXXVIII:10.   [26] *Psalms* CXVIII:1.

[27] This was Don Luis de Carvajal, the older.

[28] *Fourth Ezra, Second Ezra [Esdras]* of the official *Apocrypha*, was considered canonical by Luis, for whom the Bible was the Vulgate.

[29] Technically, the Chichimecs were Indians of the Nahuatlan or Piman tribes. The term Chichimecs, however, was used to describe any of the groups of hostile Indians in the northern regions of New Spain.

[30] Text: *puesto el freno e la coz del arcabuz que llebaba, sobre el hombro* ... [p. 466].

was a defenseless target, though he clung for defense to the hope of God's mercy.

Joseph had not breakfasted that day, and though he was not bothered by hunger, he had become terribly thirsty from traveling on foot in the heat of the day without a drop of water. Frenzied with thirst, he had taken his dagger, and cut some leaves of the prickly pear, called *nopal* in the Indian language. Since they are naturally moist, they soothed him for a while, but he was so insatiably thirsty that [he took too many] and his mouth and tongue were sore for a week.

Night thus enveloped him. Lost, hungry, thirsty and defenseless in the land of the hostile Chichimecs, he not unnaturally[31] began to fear a horrible death.

By this time he was missed in the town, and his uncle had sent a soldier to a small settlement a half league away to see if he had gone there. When the soldier returned and said no, everyone, especially his uncle, was alarmed, for they feared that he had been killed by [their] enemies. They immediately sent out a search party, composed of a captain and ten men, divided into two groups, each with a trumpet and each moving in a different direction. Those who remained in the town, where Joseph was greatly loved, tried to be of help to him in every possible way. One man, who went to string a lantern on a tall tree in the town, fell and broke his legs. It was a gratuitous gesture of affection, for the terrain was so mountainous that the lantern could not be seen [where Joseph was].

Since, as has been said, Joseph was so terrified and anguished, he committed himself to God with heart and soul. As the darkness thickened, his despair and his cries increased. [Then] he heard the blasts of a trumpet echoing loudly through that entire craggy valley. When he realized by this signal that they were looking for him, he fell to the ground and worshiped and thanked the Lord God. Then he got up buoyantly, listened for the sounds and began to walk in their direction. Soon he heard the trumpet of the second group, but he continued toward the sound of the first trumpet until he could hear his friends talking.[32] Joyously he called to them and they answered. They halted their horses and dismounted, surrounding him and embracing him repeatedly. They put him on a sprightly horse and shot their guns to signal their success. Not long thereafter the entire party assembled and returned to town to an equally joyous reception from the men who had remained behind with Joseph's uncle. Let us give thanks to the Lord of the

---

[31] Text: *como es advno. al hoe. . . .* [p. 466].

[32] Text: *ollo hablar a los compañeros . . .* [p. 467].

universe, for He is good, for His mercy with men endures forever. As Saint David said, He is the one who restores to the right path those who have gone astray. He says that when [the children of Israel] lost their way in the wilderness and could not find the road to their dwelling place, and were in addition afflicted with hunger and thirst to the point of death, they cried to the Lord in their distress, and He heard them: He showed them the road and led them to safety.[33] Let us give thanks to Adonay for His goodness and for the miracles He performs for the children of men.

Joseph remained in that region for two years, after leaving his family in the exile of Panuco. His mother and sisters were clad in mourning and [his brothers were] garbed in sadness at the death of their father, who, as has already been said, had died a short while before.

During their father's lifetime,[34] their blind uncle had been introducing his sisters to refined soldiers and officers in an attempt to help them marry well. But their father, who greatly feared the Lord, had opposed such matches and heeded the Lord's most holy commandment prohibiting them. [Now their uncle,] recognizing that as orphans their marital prospects were diminished, [tried all the harder even] before they had removed their mourning garb. The girls endured such poverty that they[35] went about shabby and barefoot a good part of the time. [Yet] they led a chaste and secluded life and virtuously helped their mother.

One day when their minds were far from marriage,[36] they suddenly heard clarions and trumpets at their door. The reason was that the two men whom the Lord had designated as husbands for the orphans,[37] both fearers of the Lord and part of His people, were now arriving. They were rich and prosperous, well-dressed and wearing golden chains around their necks. Spurred to come for this good deed by the Lord of heaven, they had come the seventy leagues separating Panuco from Mexico City expressly to marry the girls and to bring clothes and other gifts to them and their mother. They returned to Mexico City after the wedding, which was celebrated with delight by family and friends. As they congratulated

---

[33] *Psalms* CVII:4 ff.

[34] This paragraph in the original provides a good example of clauses illogically arranged, with the obvious omission of connecting ideas.

[35] Text: *algunas dellas* ... [p. 468].

[36] Text: *estando* ... *bien descuidadas* ... [p. 468].

[37] These were Jorge de Almeyda, who was to marry Leonor, and Antonio Díaz de Cáceres, who was to marry Catalina (Catherine). Cf. Cyrus Adler, "Trial of Jorge del Almeida by the Inquisition in Mexico," *Publication of the American Jewish Historical Society*, vol. IV (1896), pp. 29–77.

the fortunate mother, many Gentile women, marveling at what had happened, said to her, "What good prayer did you utter [to bring all of this about]?" Like the saintly Sarah, she [answered humbly and] said, "God's mercy is hardly proportional to man's merits, which are always few or none." To the grooms they gave a similar compliment, declaring[38] that they had come to pluck roses from amidst the thorns — roses, indeed, not so much for their beauty, which was slight, as for the virtue and chastity which the Lord had given them. A few days later they all left for Mexico City together, praising the Lord with much joy and gladness: *"Orphano tu eris adiutor"* ["You have been the helper of the fatherless"], says [David to God in a Psalm] and in another *"Pupillum et viduam suscipiet"* ["He upholds the fatherless and the widow"]. Blessed be the Protector of orphans forever.[39]

The news of all this reached Joseph in the battle[-scarred] land he spoke of, [where] his life [was] in great danger because the savage and hostile Chichimecs around him[40] were many and the soldiers with him few. His eyes welled with tears of joy as he thanked the Most High for the good news. As soon as he heard it, he resolved to go to Mexico City at the first opportunity. When the soldiers and the mayor of the town heard of his intentions, they were greatly disturbed and said that if he went away the whole area would be depopulated.[41]

But since His strength surpasses human power, God provided miraculous circumstances for Joseph to leave. The inhabitants of the region, as is usual for battle zones, relied on imports of provisions. [They now] found themselves in dire need of supplies[42] and [were happy that there was] a lull in the fighting and that they had silver to trade.[43] Relying first on God's help [they entrusted Joseph with the mission].

It seemed on the day that Joseph left that the Most High had extricated him from the confinement of [hopeless] chains. And so it was, for in a few short days the Chichimecs flayed and then killed the mayor, in whose house he stayed. Doubtless Joseph would have

[38] Text: *y a ellos menos les dezian* . . . [p. 468].

[39] *Psalms* X:14 and CXLVI:9. The text reads: . . . *orphanotueris adiutos dize el sr. cantos pa. que y en otro pupillum et viduam suscipi et* . . . [p. 468].

[40] Text: *en aquella villa* . . . [p. 468].

[41] Text: *y dezian que avian [los chichimecos?] de despoblar la tierra* . . . [p. 469].

[42] This section is especially corrupt. The text reads: *alegaban aquellos vezinos y gte. [urgente] falta de sentimientos [mantenimientos] porque se sustentaban de los traidos de otras partes* . . . [p. 469].

[43] Text: *apaziguados con dexarles una plancha de plata con que ymbiasen a comprarlos* . . . [p. 469].

met a [similar] end had the Lord, in His lovingkindness, not freed him and removed him from that town. Exalted be His holy name forever.

Joseph arrived safely in Mexico City with God's help. He received his mother's blessing and saw his orphaned sisters protected by God. When he had seen them last, they were wearing tattered skirts; now, in their husband's homes, he saw them clad in silk and velvet and bedecked with golden jewels. [And his sisters' husbands] divided the rest of the family[44] between them and gave them shelter. May they be sheltered by the Lord, and may His most holy name be extolled alone forever and ever.

But because of their heavy expenditures for the weddings and their subsequent support of so many people, Joseph's brothers-in-law were at the brink ǒf ruin in less than a year. But they never rejected their in-laws. [Yet] as was proper, Joseph and his older brother wished to earn a living for their poor mother and unmarried sisters. The realization that they were poor and without resources grieved them greatly. Despite their outwardly respectable appearance their necessities were so great that when his brothers-in-law and their wives left for Tasco, Joseph had to take a job as a merchant's bookkeeper in order to make both ends meet. With God's kindness things soon improved a little.

When Joseph and his older brother[45] were in Mexico City they heard of an old Hebrew cripple who had been bed-ridden for thirteen years with suffering and its attendant problems. [They went to visit him.] To demonstrate that everyone should love works of charity, God abundantly rewarded their visit, for the cripple presented them with a book which the good Licentiate Morales, who was mentioned earlier, had left for his consolation. Licentiate Morales had kept this cripple in his house for many days and tried to cure him, but when he saw the impossibility of a physical cure, he prepared a book to serve as a salve for his spiritual health. In it, he included a Spanish translation for the holy [Book of] Deuteronomy in the Law of the Most High and also an anthology of a thousand beautiful selections in verse, culled [and translated] from the rich garden of Sacred Writ. [Joseph and his brother proceeded] to make a copy.[46]

One day Joseph and his brother were reading together the chapter containing the curses of the most holy Law when they saw how those

---

[44] Text: *las demas viudas y huerfanas* . . . [p. 469]. The widows referred to are Luis' mother and older sister, Isabel (for whom see *infra*, p. 294, note 73).

[45] This was Baltasar.

[46] Text: *el qual trasladaron* . . . [p. 470].

true and holy prophecies had been carried out to the letter [among their people] and realized that their way of life was removed from the true path. As they clutched the book of the Law of the Lord they began to lament like a compassionate mother over the dead body of her beloved son.

A few days later, after leaving their mother and sisters with their in-laws in Tasco, Joseph and his brother returned to Mexico City, yearning for the Lord like earth for water.[47] Joseph's brother, who had ardently desired for some time to circumcise himself, carried out his wish during the solemn Passover season. Inspired by God, the brothers went to a barber on one Passover day and rented a razor. Joseph's brother took it, fell on his knees and began to cut off his foreskin, but wounded himself severely. At first the wound did not bleed. The brothers consecrated the act to the Lord their God, sang praises to Him and recited Psalms of His servant, David. A short while later, Joseph's brother sensed the flow of blood. The brothers therefore went to a house which they had rented from an uncle of theirs[48] in a sparsely inhabited area outside the city and there very cautiously completed the circumcision, all the while fearing that they might be discovered by their hapless uncle, who was blind [in matters of faith].

The house of their refuge was solitary[49] and it contained nothing with which they could stop the [flow of] blood. Without knowing what he was doing, Joseph [decided to] treat it with wine and salt.

When he went to a neighbor and asked for salt to cure a wounded man he got into another serious predicament, because the neighbor said that out of love for God, he wanted to administer it personally to the patient. [Finally he let Joseph have it,] but it did not stop the poor patient's bleeding. It only increased his pain.[50]

Seeing the danger that confronted them, they went to the nearby house of a young man who feared the Lord. When they explained their plight — the situation of the patient with the dripping wound — he graciously welcomed them. Soon, with God's pleasure, the bleeding stopped, but since the wound was large and the cure not administered by a physician, the patient suffered greatly before he recovered, though this furnished him with no small merit to counterweigh his past sins.

---

[47] Text: *que en el sor. se amaban como el agua y la tierra)* [*sic!*] . . . [p. 470].

[48] Text: *de la de un tio suyo* . . . [p. 470].

[49] The next section of the text is found below in the translation, in its logical sequence, in the paragraphs beginning respectively "When their uncle" and "When a sister of their uncle."

[50] Note that this sentence, appearing earlier in the original text, is out of place there.

When their uncle came to take them to his house and discovered blood-stained cloths, the brothers were terrified. But since it was the Lenten season,[51] they distracted him by saying that they had scourged themselves in penitence and this had brought forth the blood.

When a sister of their uncle,[52] who knew and loved the Lord,[53] learned of this circumcision, she spoke tenderly to Joseph and remonstrated with him because in the time of their need, when they had to cure the wound,[54] they had gone elsewhere [and not come to her].

After removing them from the solitude and mosquitos of Panuco, the Lord showed them further kindness by providing them with many of the holy and devout prayers by which the wise and chosen people of the Lord's ecclesia[55] invoke and praise Him in Jewish synagogues.

This was the way in which the Lord in His holiness took this blessing that is found in the lands where our brothers freely and unobstructedly practice their faith[56] and brought it to the lands of Jewish captivity:

In the Diaspora, in Italy, there lived a servant of the Lord who was extremely poor. Having no trade or occupation by which to support himself[57] or his family, he engaged himself in spiritual affairs and translated the holy prayers I mentioned into the Spanish and Portuguese tongues. He emigrated alone to the New World. An Israelite brother of ours, who at the time was a merchant in Mexico City, told us that this newcomer greatly revered the Lord and abhorred idolatry. He often saw the immigrant running toward his store so fast that he thought something terrible had happened to him.[58] And when he looked for a hiding-place, he thought surely he was fleeing from the police. But the reason for these flights was that he had perceived the most abominable idolatry ever heard of or imagined in the world. When he heard the bell that is sounded as [the image of] the crucified one is carried through the streets, he ran to his hiding-place to avoid having to kneel down before it.

When this good man returned to Italy he left behind [the book] containing the holy prayers which Joseph and his brother obtained.[59]

[51] Text: *como el tiempo era desso* . . . [p. 470].
[52] This was Joseph's mother, Francisca de Carvajal.
[53] Text: *al que sor.* [for *q.(uien) al sor.(señor)*] *conozia y amaba* . . . [p. 471].
[54] Text: *al herido,* "the wounded man" [p. 471].
[55] Text: *iglesia* . . . [p. 471] in its sense of "congregation."
[56] Text: *la ley del muy alto D.* [p. 471].
[57] Text: *que no tenia rmo. pa. sustentarse* . . . [p. 471].
[58] Text: *pensaba verles sucedido alguna desgra.* . . . [p. 471].
[59] Text: *de quien el y su mayor hermano las* [correct form] *obieron* . . . [p. 472].

After the Lord's boundless mercy had satisfied their most essential need, the spiritual need, His divine providence did not fail to repair the material deprivations they suffered. Though they had neither funds nor business knowledge nor acumen, within a year the Lord had given them property worth more than seven thousand pesos. Blessed be He forever and ever who thus provides for the hungry.

In this dilemma the brothers determined to go in the first fleet to Italy in order there to serve the Lord. But it seemed a pity to leave behind a blind brother of theirs who was a Dominican, a preaching friar,[60] and already a master in his order. Wherefore, with determination and concern for him, the two brothers paid him a visit in his monastery, located near the Inquisition's jail, and where at the time he was a teacher of novitiates, to see if they could bring him to the recognition of God's truth and His holy Law.

After the three had sat down in the friar's cell and conversed for a while, Joseph asked, as if randomly: "Is it really true, as it seems to me I have sometimes heard,[61] that when Saint Moses was holding the tablets of the Law, the Lord God wrote His most holy commandments upon them?" The monk replied. "It is as you say." As he said this, he took the Holy Bible from his bookshelf,[62] found the exact chapter in Exodus and gave it to Joseph to read. After he had read it, Joseph exclaimed, "As I live, this is — this is really the Law that must be kept."

At this point the hapless friar got up and uttered a great blasphemy. He said that it was good to read the Law but not to keep it, and that although it had been the Law of God, it was superseded. He supported his folly and lie with the very frivolous simile of a king donning a cloak, and then, as it wore out, casting it away and giving it to a page.

He was answered by Joseph's brother, who was older than Joseph but younger than the monk. It should be mentioned here that the three brothers were looking out of a window in the cell that faced the orchard and through it they could see the sky and the sunset with its brilliant rays.

Said Joseph's brother, "This cloak of the heavens, and this shining sun which God created, have they changed, have they perchance grown old?"[63]

"No," replied the monk.

---

[60] His name was Gaspar (Jasper). His blindness, according to Luis, was a blindness in matters of faith.

[61] Text: *lo que algas. vezes me pareze que a* [sic!], *oido* . . . [p. 472].

[62] Text: *tomo la biblia sacra que tenia entre sus libros* . . . [p. 472].

[63] Text: *ase por ventura envejecido?* . . . [p. 473].

"So," he retorted, "much less change has there been in God's incorruptible and holy Law and His word, and even less will there be. We hear this affirmed by your own preachers and scholars and in the Gospel itself you declare that your crucified one said, 'Do not think that I am come[64] to remove the Law or the Prophets, for their prophecies are holy and true.' Rather he said this: 'It is certainly easier for heaven and earth to be lacking than for one jot or tittle of this holy Law to be lacking or change.' "

Realizing he must acknowledge the truth of their claim, the benighted priest retreated,[65] saying, "Let's not talk about this any more," and adding "Blessed be God, who took me out from among you." To which his brothers on either side responded, "Be Thou glorified, our God and Lord,[66] who hast not left us in blindness and perdition like this wretch." The monk said that he deemed his lot happier than theirs and concluded by quoting the Psalms,[67] "Non fecit taliter omni nationi"[68] etc. ["He had not dealt in such a way with any other nation"].[69] Thus, seeing the truth and unable to deny or contradict it, the miserable, sightless friar was frustrated. And with this the brothers parted.

On another occasion, at Joseph's suggestion,[70] his two older brothers agreed to study for several days and then meet for a discussion of their respective faiths with the condition that whoever was defeated by the truth of the other's religion must accept it. Though he had said yes, the monk refused to go through with the discussion because he was a cleric, giving the excuse that his law forbade him to investigate or discuss matters of faith. Those wretches think that by shielding their eyes from the light, they can keep from falling into the pits of hell. Rightly did Saint Isaiah marvel at them when he said [in the name of God], "They are not inclined to stop and say, 'Maybe what I believe is a lie,'. I make all men alike,[71] but their sin keeps some blinded."[72]

The fleet was scheduled to depart shortly and the brothers began to look to their affairs. But for the good of the entire family, God

---

[64] Text: no penseis que viene . . . [p. 473]. Cf. Matthew V:17.

[65] Text: a esto cayo el triste ciego, y dixoles viendose convencido . . . [p. 473].

[66] Text: glorificado sea ntro. D. y Sr. . . . [p. 473].

[67] Text: concluyo yo con lo del po. s. [sic!] . . . [p. 473].

[68] Text: non fecit talliter omni nationi, ety. . . . [p. 473].

[69] Psalms CXLVII:20. The monk seems to have been referring to the fact of the stupendous success of Christianity.

[70] Text: en sus — [sic!] de joseph . . . [p. 473].

[71] Text: y hago tambien a todos . . . [p. 473].

[72] This is not a direct quotation from Isaiah, but a paraphrase, possibly of Isaiah XXVII:9 ff.

in His infinite and divine wisdom and mercy ordained that the Inquisition should now arrest a widowed sister of theirs.[73] She had been accused [of practicing Judaism] by a heretic who was one of our own people and whom a year before she had tried to indoctrinate into the truth of God. On learning of this, the brothers, struck with fright, decided to flee with their mother and [remaining] sisters, but some God-fearing [Israelite] friends, with whom they discussed the matter, convinced them that it was impossible for them [to take the women along]. After a painful separation which is beyond the power of my words to describe, the brothers therefore went off alone leaving their family exposed to danger, and wending their way to the cadence of their bitter cries and howls. [But] when they reached port, loaded their ship and were ready to embark, the thought of their mother and sisters exposed to mounting dangers overwhelmed them and made them change their plans. Joseph decided to return home and see what was going on, while his brother would remain behind and await word from him.

Two or three days after arriving home, Joseph went to visit his mother in the evening hours. By day they did not dare to be together, because of what they feared might happen. They were about to sit down to dinner when the constables and notaries of the Inquisition knocked on the door. When they opened it the Inquisitional officials set guards there, raised ladders, mounted them and came into the house to arrest Joseph's mother. Though wounded with this cruel enemy's fierce stroke, she donned the garb of modesty,[74] bemoaning her troubles, yet praising the Lord who had sent them. She was then brought to the pitch-black prison by those ministers of malediction and executioners of our lives.

When her two maiden daughters saw their beloved mother sighing with such pain and sadness that she even moved to compassion the cruel and beastly enemies who were taking her away, they anxiously rushed toward her and cried, "Where are they taking you?"[75] We leave to the prudent reader's imagination the feelings of their lamenting mother as she heard these words.

After she was taken away her son Joseph was arrested. They found him behind a door, where he had run for refuge out of fear of the atrocious tyrants. They pounced on him, seized him and carried him to the gloomy, black prison. Joseph uttered nothing except the words, "O God, reveal the truth."

---

[73] This was Isabel. Her husband, Gabriel de Herrera, had died in Astorga, Spain, where he had been a merchant. Cf. *Procesos de Luis de Carvajal (El Mozo)*, p. 14.

[74] Text: *cubrio su manto con mansedumbre . . .* [p. 474].

[75] Text: *a donde nos la* [correct form] *lleban?* [p. 474].

The next day one of his maiden sisters got word to their mother that Joseph had been arrested. A prisoner of the Inquisition was permitted to receive neither visitors nor letters from outside. What his sister did was to put some of Joseph's shirts among the clothes she sent her mother; and as soon as she saw them, she understood. This doubled her affliction, but also her merit.

The night that Joseph was arrested, his older brother returned to Mexico City and sent for him that the two might get together with a younger brother.[76] Then he learned that Joseph had been arrested.[77] This was a severe blow to Joseph's older brother, but he took it like a [true] servant of the Lord God: He prostrated himself on the ground and accepted the divine decree.

With half his family arrested, he was advised to flee the storm. He thought it over and decided to stay. He found a room [which became] his voluntary jail, and remained in it for a full year, waiting to see what the Lord would decree for his family. His companions were the Holy Bible and other sacred tomes which the Lord provided for him, and their assiduous reading absorbed his time.

Nor was Joseph in his prison forgotten by the Lord, his God. Exemplary gifts and favors did he receive from God's most merciful hand.

The Lord is witness that many times in that lonely and dark prison cell, Joseph would think longingly, "Would that in this solitude I were given the companionship of the Psalms of the saintly prophet David. If I read them, I would feel better." He believed that this desire was impossible of fulfillment by human means.

But since for the omnipotent God nothing is impossible, it was fulfilled by His holy decree. At the very time Joseph entertained these thoughts, a Franciscan friar was arrested [by the Inquisition] and brought to his jail. On a Saturday afternoon, when the savage judges of the Inquisition generally visit the prisoners to comfort them and to minister to their needs (not that this benevolence originates within them, for they are cruel and inhuman, but rather because the Lord our God and Father is pleased to bring the prisoners the solace that comes from sweeping and cleaning[78] their cells for the visit), they came first to the monk. They asked him if he needed anything, and he answered that he would like only a breviary to find consolation in his cell by reciting his customary Divine Office. Then they visited Joseph, and finding him emaciated and depressed, they assigned the monk to him as his cellmate. They brought the

[76] This was Miguel [Michael].
[77] Text: *que ya los abian llebado presos* ... [p. 475].
[78] Text: *es seruido de dar aquel solaz el rato que tardan en barrer* ... [p. 475].

monk to Joseph's cell on that very Sabbath afternoon and enjoined him not to reveal that he was a monk.

The two prisoners talked for a while, rejoicing that they had met and would now be together. At dusk the jailer came, opened the cell door and presented Joseph's companion with a breviary. Joseph was overcome with joy and gladness, for he recognized that this was the way in which the Lord his God satisfied his longing, which was to give him a book from which to recite[79] the Psalms as he used to do. He, therefore, gave thanks to God most High for this signal kindness. Let us [all] give thanks to the Lord Adonay, for He is good and supreme and His mercy endures forever. For with one hand He punishes yet [with the other] shows us lovingkindness a thousandfold.

Indeed, through one event we can clearly see what Saint[80] David realized from his learning[81] and travels: *"Secundum multitudinem dolorum meorum in corde meo consolationes tuae laetificaverunt animam meam"*[82] ["When many cares are within me, Your comforts delight my soul"].[83]

It happened in the following way:

When Joseph's long confinement in his cell of agony had made him anxious and depressed, he began to receive special consolations from the eternal God, which for the most part were communicated to him in dreams at night. Once, after a day of fasting and prayer, he no sooner lay down and fell asleep when he heard a voice in his dreams saying, "Be strong and take comfort, for saints Job and Jeremiah are most effectively interceding for you." For a few days he felt better. Then he had another dream, which, judging from what later happened, seems to have been a true and divine revelation. He saw a glass vial, tightly stopped and wrapped outside. It was filled with the sweetest liquid, divine wisdom itself, which is dispensed only in small quantities. Then he heard the Lord commanding Saint Solomon. He said, "Take a spoon, fill it with this liquid and give it to this boy to drink." The wise king began to execute the command. He took a spoonful of that sweet liquid and put it to Joseph's mouth; and as Joseph drank it, he felt greatly

[79] Text: *por donde rezar* . . . [p. 476].

[80] Text: *sor* [*señor*], a probable error for *so.*, or more likely *sto.* [*santo*] [p. 476].

[81] Text: *conimtos* . . . [p. 476].

[82] Text: *secundum multitudinendo loxmeox consolationes tuaelaetificaueuont animan meam* . . . (p. 476). Here is an excellent example of the scribe's ignorance or carelessness or both. It should be recalled that Luis was considered sufficiently learned in Latin to teach it and, in his capacity as secretary to the monk who was the rector of the school for Indians where he taught, to use it for official purposes. See *infra*, pp. 301–303 and 310–313.

[83] *Psalms* XCIV:19.

consoled. Later, as the reader will be able to observe, this consolation was to come to him again in the world of reality.[84]

Since the imprisonment of Joseph and his mother dragged on and they remained in the hands of such cruel beasts, their fear made them hide their true identity, and they refrained from confessing publicly that they were keepers of the Lord God's most holy Law. For our affliction and travail has reached such a state that if anyone confesses and affirms [this fact] he is subjected by these heretics to exquisite torture and is [then] burned alive. And fear of this is responsible for their denial of their true identity.

One Friday morning, the Inquisitors, in order to determine whether Joseph and his family were practicing Judaism,[85] summoned Joseph's mother for a hearing, as they had done on many previous occasions. Through a small hole which he and his companion had carved with two sheep bones at the threshold of his cell door, Joseph could watch his mother being led to the court of audience.

When the tyrants saw that she continued to deny [that her family practiced Judaism], they decided to subject her to torture. Preceded by the judges, notary, jailer and constable, she was therefore led to the torture chamber, where the torturer was standing, covered from head to toe with a shroud and white hood.

They immediately ordered the patient sheep to disrobe. They stretched her chaste flesh on the instrument of torture known as the donkey and tied her arms and legs. Then they cruelly twisted the ropes in its iron rings. As the ropes grated her flesh, she heaved the most pitiful sighs, which could be heard by all [the prisoners].

Joseph, on his knees in his cell, heard it all, and that day brought him[86] greater affliction and bitterness than any that had gone before. But he was not without the divine consolation that comes from the hand of the Lord. Blessed be His holy name forever. In the midst of that day of affliction, the Lord permitted him to doze off by the door of his cell. On other days, if he fell asleep for a moment, he awoke melancholy and faint, but not that day.

As soon as he fell asleep, he saw the Lord sending him a man who was a paragon of virtue and patience. He was a fearer of God, one of his own people.[87] In his hands he carried a large and beautiful yam. He showed it to Joseph and said, "Look! What a handsome and beautiful fruit!"

---

[84] This doubtless refers to the events narrated *infra.*, pp. 301–303.

[85] Text: *y pa. averiguar esto* . . . [p. 477].

[86] Text: *que [fue] para el el día* . . . [p. 477].

[87] It is difficult to determine who is meant. It may be Luis' own father, Francisco Rodríguez [or Rodrigues] de Mattos, or the Licentiate Morales, or perhaps someone else.

To this Joseph replied, "Indeed."

He gave it to Joseph to smell. Joseph blessed the Lord, creator of all, and said to the man, "Indeed, it smells good, indeed." The man then cut the yam in two and said to him, "Now it smells better." The man then gave Joseph the interpretation. He said, "Before being imprisoned and racked with torture, your mother was whole and she smelled sweet; she was a fruit of sweet savor before the Lord. But now, when she is cut with torture, she exudes the superior fragrance of patience before the Lord."

With this Joseph awoke and was consoled. May the Most High God, who brings consolation to the afflicted, likewise be adored and extolled.

Joseph suffered even more in his cell because his companion's presence prevented him from praying and fasting as he used to. But in that very cell his companion, with the help of the Lord God,[88] was enlightened and converted to the truth of His holy Law.[89]

This was the way in which, for Joseph's benefit and consolation, the Lord brought healing to his companion:

In their cell stood a wooden cross, before which the poor wretch would kneel and offer his prayers. Once, as the two of them were sitting near their candle, the monk took up the cross or gallows, approached it to the flame and said, "By God, if I should put the cross in the fire, it would burn like any other stick." To which Joseph replied, "Now you see in what you place your trust."

Then they began to converse at length [about matters of religion]. They spoke continually for a week and more, until Joseph's hapless companion came to the recognition of God's truth. Then he rejoiced and sang hymns and praises to the Lord, especially the *Magnus Dominus et laudabilis nimis*[90] which means in Spanish "Great is the Lord and worthy to be praised."[91] [The monk went on to say:] "Because He deigned to enlighten a sinner like me." And the monk danced and thanked the Creator for having shown him such signal kindness in permitting him to recognize His sacred truth.[92]

All this was ordained by God not only for the salvation of that poor soul but also for Joseph's consolation and relief, because [henceforth] they both kept the Law of Almighty God insofar as they could and they commended themselves to His divine majesty.

---

[88] Text: *del Sr. D. suyo* . . . [p. 478].

[89] Text: *alumbrado y convertido al verdadero D. y a su sta. ley* . . . [p. 478].

[90] Text: *mas nus Dns. ey laudabilis nimis* . . . [p. 478].

[91] *Psalms* XCVI:4. Cf. *I Chronicles* XVI:25.

[92] Text: *de darle su smo. conozimiento* . . . [p. 478].

One day, when his companion was eagerly and devoutly listening to Joseph tell some of the stories of the Bible, he said, "I wish I had had the opportunity to be enlightened by God's truth before I came to this cell. I wish I had chanced upon it in one of the monasteries where I lived, where they have open libraries with Bibles and many good books."

Joseph's reply was, "Do they keep their libraries open for everyone?"

The monk said, "Yes, and they keep the books out so that anyone may consult them and read them."

Joseph said, "I wish I were put in one of them." Let this be noted in advance for the praise of the Most High and His sacred mercy, for the Lord fulfilled this wish with an extraordinary miracle, as will be seen below.

Once the Most High had enlightened his companion, Joseph lived contentedly in his confinement. He spent his time telling Bible stories to his companion, who listened with rapt attention and devotion. Soon God's truth[93] became so impressed upon this good Gentile's soul that it seemed as if he had been nurtured on it all his life and taught by believing parents. Though he had but so recently been converted, he loathed bacon and lard and the other foods forbidden by the Most High's holy Law. [He and Joseph adhered] so faithfully [to the dietary commands] that when bacon or sausage or any other forbidden food was served them they agreed to bury it. They would say, "Let us offer the sacrifice," which meant to bury such food and abstain from eating it. As a result they not infrequently suffered hunger in their harsh cell, but when they did they commended it to the Lord and uttered the Psalmist's prayer, "*Miserere mei*" ["Have mercy upon me"].[94]

This happened most often at midday on Friday, for at that time the heretics' entire meal was contaminated.

In short, Joseph's companion comported himself in such a way that he earned the right to be a witness of the true God and his most holy Law and received the crown of martyrdom [in public when he was burned at the stake], as I shall narrate below.[95]

When Joseph and his family left their prison [duly] penanced and cloaked in the distinctive garb which the enemies of the Law of God require for those who have been convicted of keeping it, the

[93] Text: *la berdad del a la diuina* . . . [p. 479].

[94] *Psalms* LI:3.

[95] See *infra*, pp. 307–308. It does not, however describe the death of this monk, whose name was Francisco Ruiz de Luna. See *Procesos de Luis de Carvajal (el Mozo)*, pp. 136 and 352.

Inquisitors wished to separate the family. They wanted to put each of the women in a different room of a convent that in the company of its idolators they might suffer twice as much as before. But the Lord in His infinite mercy frustrated this plan. He moved the Inquisitor himself to mention it to Jorge de Almeyda, one of Joseph's brothers-in-law, in whose mouth the Lord put the following reply:[96]

"Sir, the action you are contemplating should be well considered[97] before you put it into effect. Do not forget that women are extremely curious and impressionable. The [damaging] influence [of these women] upon the nuns might be very difficult to counteract."[98]

This made quite an impression on the enemy. At the Lord's prompting the Inquisitor changed his mind, and instead of such confinement for life, which is the standard punishment for penitents, he arranged for the women to be given a house where they could all live together — for the sake of the Lord.

Joseph was separated from them and assigned to a hospital, where he was made keeper of the idols — which afflicted him not a little — and employed in other tasks, such as sweeping the floors, which he did after he had moistened them with his tears. But the Lord his God came to his rescue again as He had in all his previous difficulties.

When Joseph despaired of returning to the company of his mother and sisters — he did not even know how he could ask for such a thing — God on High, who was even more grieved, provided a remedy. He ordained that one of Joseph's brothers-in-law find it necessary to take a trip to Tasco and leave Joseph's mother and sisters alone.[99] He [therefore] went to ask the Inquisitor the favor of allowing Joseph to stay with them while he traveled. This was the first step taken by the Most High to remove Joseph from [what he regarded as] his second captivity, where he sat and wept disconsolately[100] because he was forced to eat forbidden foods. Highly exalted be the Most High, who thus came to Joseph's aid in all his difficulties.

When he returned to his mother and sisters, Joseph found that their enemies' threats and some friends' evil counsel had persuaded them to buy and eat Gentile foods,[101] forbidden by the Law of God.

---

[96] Text: *en cuya boca el sr. se puso para que le dixese* ... [p. 479].

[97] Text: *mirese bien esso* [p. 479].

[98] Text: *que podria venir un daño notable a todas las monjas* ... [pp. 479–480].

[99] Text: *y quedar solas su me. y hermanas* ... [p. 480].

[100] The allusion is to *Psalms* CXXXVII:1. Text: *que ... vivia muy lloroso y desconsolado* ... [p. 480].

[101] Text: *que las gres. [de las gentes?]* ... [p. 480].

With divine inspiration Joseph changed this. He set before them the example of the saints who preferred to be torn to shreds by cruel tortures rather than eat forbidden foods or even pretend to eat them. But since their hearts were steadfast with their God and Lord[102] — the family had been acting out of fright — little was needed to convince them of their wrongdoing.[103] With many tears and affirmations of their reverence of heaven, they turned again to their God and Lord and added to their merit by rejecting all filthy foods.

As the time drew near for Joseph to return to the hospital where he served, an old monk, a man of great virtue, came to see his mother. The Inquisitor had asked him to be the family's confessor and guardian.

Joseph's mother importuned the monk to secure permission for Joseph to remain on with her and the family. And Joseph received this permission with the requirement that he spend his daytime hours working in a school for Indians which the monk directed. Joseph was given the responsibility of teaching grammar to some of the Indians and helping the monk with his letters and sermons. The Lord his God gave Joseph such favor [in the eyes of] this man that he loved him dearly and cherished him, and not only he, but all his staff as well.

Since the carnivorous wolves had confiscated the family's property and left them destitute, the Lord maintained them in their affliction[104] for four and a half years by having the monk support them from his own pocket and from charities of the Church that was so hostile to them.[105] The Lord's performing a miracle for such sinful and wretched people [as Joseph and his family] is even more striking than His performance of a miracle with the innocent and saintly Daniel.[106]

Let us now observe how the Lord in His mercy fulfilled the desire which Joseph expressed to his cellmate when he said, "I wish I were put into one of those libraries." The Lord induced the monk to give Joseph a key to his [private] room in the school,[107] where he kept all his books, a privilege he extended to none of his fellow monks at the school. This kindness from the Lord was soon sur-

---

[102] See the examples of the saintly scribe Eleazar in *II Maccabees* VI:18 ff. and Hannah's seven sons, *ibid.* VII:1 ff.

[103] Text: *para estorbarles* . . . [p. 480].   [104] Text: *en el lago* . . . [p. 481].

[105] Text: *y ansi por su mano como por la de los enemigos los sustento el sr.* . . . [p. 481].

[106] See *infra*, pp. 317–318. The reference to Daniel derives from the story of Bel and the Dragon in the *Apocrypha*.

[107] The text adds *quedandose el con la otra*, which is omitted in the translation.

passed by another from His munificent hand. Joseph had been in the school for less than four months when God ordained that the same monk should purchase [Nicholas] de Lyra's *Glosses*, a commentary to the Holy Bible, in four large tomes,[108] from the estate of a great preacher of his order who had [recently] passed away. When they were delivered, he went to Joseph, as if looking for compliments and said, "What precious things we are bringing to our school."

With great caution Joseph availed himself of these gifts of God on high. When the monk and all the collegians would go to their quarters to eat, Joseph would remain behind within the [classroom] compound [and steal into the library]. There, by reading the Holy Bible and translating many of its sections into Spanish, he would nourish his spirit, troubled as it was by the thought of [a repetition of the] imprisonment and affliction from which the Lord had so miraculously extricated him.[109]

In his hours of duty, whatever time Joseph had left after teaching his students was consigned by the monk to the arrangement of Oleaster's moralities on the Pentateuch[110] into alphabetical order. This work was so suited to Joseph's temperament and interests that [he realized that] were it not for God's help he could not have

---

[108] Nicholas of Lyra (1270–1340), rumored in the fifteenth century to have been of Jewish descent, was a master of Hebrew and utilized Hebrew sources, especially Rashi's commentary, for his own great commentary, the *Postillae*. Nicholas de Lyra's commentary was the first Bible commentary to be printed. On this, see Herman Hailperin, *Rashi and the Christian Scholars* (Pittsburgh, 1963), pp. 137 ff.

[109] Such study was forbidden to a non-cleric, not to speak of a person suspect in matters of faith.

[110] Jerome Oleaster [Oleastro] (d. 1563) was a Portuguese Dominican scholar and biblical commentator who likewise utilized Hebrew sources and may well have obtained the Thirteen Articles of the Faith directly from Maimonides [*Commentary to the Mishnah, Sanhedrin* X:1 (*Perek Ḥelek*)]. His commentary on the Pentateuch, originally published in parts between 1556 and 1558, was first published in its entirety in Antwerp, 1569, with the title *Reverendi Patris Fratris Hieronymi ab Oleastro [sic!] Lusitani, Praedicatorij Ordinis . . . Commentaria in Mósi Pentateuchum . . .* The Thirteen Articles, from which Carvajal quotes almost verbatim, are found on f. 251 v. col. b., as part of the comment of *Deut*. VI:4 [*Audi Israel Dominus noster. Deus vnus*]. They read as follows:

Habent Iehudaei. 13. articulos fidei; quos tredecim vocant fundamenta: quorum primus est creatorem esse absolutae & perfectae essentiae, causam omnium: a quo pendet & deriuatur omnium rerum virtus. Secundus Deum esse vnum. Tertius non esse corporeum. Quartus quod sit primus inter omnia. Quintus omni laude sit dignus, & nihil aliud. Sextus esse affluentiam diuinam in aliquot hominibus, & fuisse prophetiam. Septimo vt credas Moseh patrem omniũ prophetarũ & quod fuerit omnibus excellentior. Octauo quod lex è coelis data est Moseh à deo. Nono quod lex nõ abolebitur neq; mutabitur, neq; alia proficiscetur à creatore, neq; addetur aut minuetur. Decimo quod deus cognoscit opera hominũ & curat ea. Vndecimo quod benefacit servãtibus legẽ & frangẽtes punit. Duodecimo credas tẽpus Messię etiã si tardet. Tertiodecimo est credere mortuorum resurrectionẽ.

obtained it even if he were willing to pay for it with all his blood. Blessed and extolled be the Lord, who satisfies worthy desires.

In this book [of Oleaster's] the Lord revealed to Joseph the holy Thirteen Articles which are the principles of our faith and religion and which are unknown in the lands of our captivity.

One day as Joseph was about to open the door of the monk's room with his key as he had so often done, in order to continue with his translation of the Bible's holy prophecies, he had a presentiment that the monk was coming. The Lord seems to have been warning him. With this premonotion he closed the door [and hid himself nearby], thinking, "If the monk comes now, it is a certain sign that the Lord has warned me and is with me." No sooner had this thought crossed his mind when he saw the monk entering his room. Blessed and praised be the Lord!

Joseph longed to find a spring or fountain of water in which to bathe. He thought, "If I had such a privilege in this school, I would lack none other." And the blessed Lord in His infinite mercy satisfied this desire. He ordained that a lay-friar who worked as a gardener in the orchard of that convent, and who was more scrupulous [about his cleanliness] than the rest, should also feel the need of such water for bathing. At this very time the Lord moved him to approach his superior and ask him for permission [— which was granted —] to bring a conduit into the school compound — and to the area where Joseph wanted it! Blessed be the Lord, who alone is good, for His mercy endures forever.

When Joseph, his mother and his sisters left prison, his older brother, who had been carefully following their fortunes, decided [that it was time for him] to be on his way. Before he left the house which served as his voluntary jail[111] the Lord performed an extraordinary miracle for him.

In that house lived an Israelite friend who could move about freely. He had the key to the door where Joseph's brother was hiding and he brought him food and drink.

One day the Inquisition sent out an alarm for a concubinary, and when it heard that he might be living next door to the Israelite, it sent to the area a bailiff, whom the Israelite knew well, to arrest the suspect. [The bailiff looked for the suspect in the house next door], and when he could not find him, he thought that he might have jumped over the wall to the house where Joseph's brother was hiding. The bailiff therefore asked the Israelite to open his

---

[111] Text: *antes que saliese de la casa donde estaban* [*sic!*] . . . The words *carzel voluntaria* are translated from the following clause [p. 482].

door that he might come in and look for the fugitive. The Israelite tried to dissuade him from entering, swearing again and again that the suspect was not there, but to no avail. Fortunately, because it usually took some time to open the door and it was night, the Israelite could stop in Joseph's brother's room and tell him[112] to get out and hide under a staircase. This he did. The bailiff then entered[113] the house to look for his suspect.

After looking all over for him, the bailiff and his party were about to leave when the Lord God worked another of his miracles to demonstrate that a man protected by God is really protected. As the bailiff approached the staircase under which Joseph's brother was hiding, one of his deputies said to him, "Sir, let us look underneath this staircase." But, moved by the Lord [the bailiff answered], "Forget it, that fellow wouldn't be hiding there." And with this they left, and Joseph's brother came out from under the staircase and went to hide in a room which had already been searched.

He had no sooner done this when the bailiff, who had reached the gate of the house, had a change of heart. He came back and said, "I'll wager that our man is underneath the staircase where I wouldn't look before. I have come back to inspect it." He came in, looked [under the staircase] and was satisfied [that no one was there], and the man protected and freed by the Lord of the world remained free, thanks to His great lovingkindness. May the Lord be extolled forever and ever.[114]

So Joseph's older brother left Mexico City one night. He was accompanied by a younger brother.[115] [Both were] frightened at the prospect of being apprehended by the Inquisition, and determined to die for the Lord if they were. The [Israelite] friend whom we mentioned [above] went with them.

Shortly after they left, word reached Joseph that they had been arrested. He broke into bitter tears and a pall of sadness and melancholy fell over him, his mother and his sisters. But the report was false: Their good God and Lord was preserving and guiding the fugitives. They traveled about four hundred leagues overland in peace and safety until they reached the so-called Port of Horses.[115a]

---

[112] Text: *mas que por el sr. que no fue tan brebe que primo. no tubiese lugar de entrar el compañero por ser de noche a avisar al hermo. mayor* ... [p. 483].

[113] Text: *puesto alli, entro el alguazil* ... [p. 483].

[114] Text: *se a su sma. me. pa. siempre de siempre ensalsado* ... [p. 483].

[115] This, of course, was Miguel [Michael].

[115a] Text: *puerto de los caballos.* This appears to be identical with the modern Puerto Cortés in northwestern Honduras. See the *Columbia Lippincott Gazetteer of the World* (New York, 1962), p. 1528.

Here by no small miracle they came upon an anchored ship, whose captain was also a Hebrew and a cousin of the Israelite who accompanied Joseph's brothers. He took them aboard, showered them with presents, and transported them to Spain.

After Joseph had spent several days in tearful sorrow, the Lord sent him the happy news that his brothers had not been arrested and that their precious cargo had arrived at a safe port. Let us again give praise to Adonay, for He is good and supreme. Let us give glory to His holy name, for His mercy endures forever.

When the family was imprisoned, one of Joseph's brothers-in-law left for China but the other remained in Mexico City.[116] After the family had left prison, this brother-in-law[117] continued to help them as he had when they were in jail,[118] and he was always a very obedient son to Joseph's mother. Because God is good and leaves no good work unrewarded, He performed an exemplary miracle for Joseph's brother-in-law, not only to help him but even more [to help] Joseph's mother and sisters.

It seems that after the family had left prison, the Inquisition began to look for Joseph's brother-in-law. The Inquisition's constable called on him, but he refused to go with him and ran away [to Tasco]. Incensed, the Inquisitors sent a warrant for his arrest to a constable in Tasco, who very arrogantly went out to search for him. At this moment the Lord God sent one of the [wild] bulls that roamed in the area against the constable. The bull savagely attacked him, gored him to death, and dragged his body back to his own doorstep.

In this manner, the Lord, God of Israel, permitted Joseph's brother-in-law to remain free. He then stirred his heart to go to Spain to seek liberty for Joseph and his family. He accepted God's mandate with such strong resolve that he spent three and a half years in Spain in quest of this liberty. Finally, with God's help, he attained the necessary document and sent it on [to New Spain], again inspired and aided by the Lord.

I understand now that when Joseph and his family were imprisoned his other brother-in-law left for China, from whence the Lord brought him back miraculously, for the sake of his wife and infant daughter.

In the Orient, Joseph's brother-in-law was often in prison or in danger. The governor of China, moved by personal hatred but even

---

[116] Antonio Díaz de Cáceres left for China; Jorge de Almeyda remained behind in New Spain, as is seen from the record of Luis' second trial, *passim*.

[117] Text: *el cura* [*el cuña.*] . . . [p. 484].

[118] Text: *les hizo no menos regalos que a ella les embiado que fueron muchos* . . . [p. 484].

more so by God's design, sent him in his ship to Macao. Since trade there was controlled by the Spanish crown, which had circulated a warrant for the arrest of Joseph's brother-in-law in New Spain, he was apprehended. His ship and all his merchandise were sequestered, and he was bound in chains and sent toward India by ship.[118a]

It seems impossible that anyone in such straits could be seen by his wife again. But for the Lord nothing is impossible. One night, in His holy kindness,[119] He suggested to Joseph's brother-in-law that he file away his chains and take refuge in the ship. Here a friend of his hid him under the deck and brought him food until the day when the departing fleet set sail. And though Joseph's brother-in-law was later arrested and harassed, God soon extricated him from this difficulty and even from the greater ones that he experienced in Manila.

These were occasioned by the enmity which the governor of that Island conceived for him. I cannot now go into the reasons for this hatred, because I want to make this story short, since my purpose is to confine myself to the signal benefits and favors which the Lord God of Israel did for Joseph and his entire family.

In order that Joseph's brother-in-law might come back to care for his wife and daughter, the Lord freed him from the governor, who in his capacity as judge, would have unjustly taken his life. And He brought him and his ship to a safe port [in New Spain] at the time when Joseph and his family were still in prison. The news of this unexpected arrival brought great consolation, coming from God's hand, to the entire family, particularly to the man's wife and daughter. For this and for all other consolations may the Lord God of Israel be greatly blessed and adored.

As has been stated above, Joseph's fears that his unmarried sisters would yet be arrested by the Inquisition [proved well-founded] . . .[120] and they put the younger one in a building of maximum confinement, where for His glory, the Lord so instructed her that nothing, not even threats of torture, could extract from her any information that would benefit the Inquisitors and hurt her family. From the mouths of sucklings the Lord brings forth praises to confound the enemy and avenger![121]

[118a] Portugal at the time (1580–1640) was united with Spain; hence its Indian territories in Asia were part of the Hispanic empire.

[119] Text: *cuya sanctisima mde. [sic!]* . . . [p. 485]. See also *supra*, p. 304, note 114.

[120] Our text makes no mention of Joseph's fears [see *supra*, p. 294], and omits an explanation of what was done to Joseph's older unmarried sister.

[121] *Psalms* VIII:3.

Joseph's sister spent more than two years in that building, removed from the companionship of her mother and sisters, who grieved with heavy hearts. Pitiful indeed was the dejection felt by her sisters and especially her loving mother on the occasions when the female warden would bring her to see them and would then take her away. They fervently prayed to the Lord their God to deign to free her and restore her to them.

Adored be His most holy name. He heard them at an auspicious moment with His infinite mercy. At the end of two years, when the sentences of Joseph's married sister and the older unmarried one were completed and they were permitted to remove their penitential garb, the God of heaven gave them favor in the eyes of the Inquisitors; they delivered his younger, unmarried sister[122] into their custody, at the moment when the girl, as her mother told her to, was about to kneel and pray for this very thing. Thus, God the most liberal Provider returned all three in freedom and joy to their mother. As their home rang with the happiness of all, so may there ring blessings and praises of the Lord of the heavens, whom the entire family thanked again and again for such favors.

A year after Joseph's captivity, the jailer of the Inquisition told him that the monk who was his cellmate had been rearrested and arraigned on the charge of shattering an idol in the galleys where he was serving his sentence. Joseph was terrified. He was afraid that the monk would try to hurt him — though he had great confidence that with the Lord's help he would be left unscathed. And God, our Lord, immediately performed such a miracle for Joseph that it cannot in all fairness be passed over in silence. Nor can one keep from uttering the praises due to the lofty and sovereign God who protected him.

One night His exalted Majesty revealed to Joseph's mother in a dream what was later to come to pass in reality!

She saw the Inquisitor thrusting a sword at Joseph, but the sword was sheathed. It had been sheathed by the Lord, exalted be His most holy name. And this is exactly what happened. When the monk, Joseph's former cellmate, was asked who had taught him, he told the Inquisitors that it was someone who had been his companion in that jail several years before, making it clear by such testimony that he had no intention of letting Joseph get away unharmed. But Joseph's blessed God and Lord saved him. He put the sword in a sheath: When the monk was asked whether he had been taught [Judaism] by his companion before or after the latter's

---

[122] Text: *la hermana mayor [menor] donzella* . . . [p. 486].

confession, the Lord ordained that the monk should say before.[123] And with this the Lord saved Joseph from the harsh and dark prison. May His most Holy name be eternally exalted. Amen.

At the same time, Joseph's former cellmate, in the presence of those tryants, so valiantly professed a belief in the God of heaven that the like of it has not been seen with any other Gentile in our time. He told them of the mighty acts of the Lord God and [the greatness] of His most holy Law, and then he said, "The Law which I believe[124] and accept is the true faith and the others are frauds and deceptions of the devil. The king understands this well and so do the filthy Inquisitors, but the Lord hardens their hearts as he did Pharaoh's for He is determined to take full vengeance upon them when the day of His most holy judgment comes." Though because of this he was subjected to severe trials and afflictions, our God permitted him to pass through them with exemplary patience and faith. Blessed be His most holy name forever. Amen.

Three and a half years after Joseph, his mother and his sisters entered into captivity, an unfortunate event took place, involving one of Joseph's unmarried sisters, who was particularly hostile to the idols and idolatries of her hapless, blind neighbors. On a Sabbath of the Lord when they celebrated a festival, she asked her brother Joseph, for the love of God, to take her to the home of a God-fearing Israelite sister. She did this that they might spend the day in the service of the Lord God and might avoid the offense [to God] that would come [by their remaining home, where they did not dare to observe the holy day properly].

She took along a book containing an anthology of passages from Sacred Scripture, which Joseph and his older brother had carefully culled and translated, and other writings attesting to the truth of the Lord our God and His holy Law. It also included a translation of the Psalms and other holy prayers. This treasure was highly prized by Joseph and his sisters.

On that holy day Joseph's sister put the book in her bosom and took it along for prayer. They left at dawn, happy and singing praises to the Lord God. As evidence of His holy Majesty's loving-kindness, God permitted the book to slip down unnoticed from her bosom and fall on a well traveled public thoroughfare. When the young girl discovered that the book was missing she was shocked and dispirited and her grief was uncontrollable. She retraced her

---

[123] This was the truth. Luis might have regarded as a miracle the fact that Francisco Ruiz de Luna did not lie in order to get Luis into trouble.

[124] Text: *estas que yo creo* . . . [p. 486].

steps in search of the lost gem, but no trace of it was to be found. Joseph and his two sisters returned home and the rest of the family shared their consternation. Their pain and fright were understandable, since at stake for all of them was nothing less than their lives and what they treasured most in life.[125] They began to regard themselves as arrested and even dead. So great was their fright that were it not for the danger of damning their souls they would have taken their own lives rather than risk falling into the cruel hands of their terrible enemies.[126] In short, every hour they fearfully and bitterly expected the moment of their imprisonment. But, blessed and exalted be the infinite and true Lord God, for He helped them in this difficulty with His accustomed kindness.

Whenever anyone knocked, they thought that the Inquisition's nefarious ministers were at the door to arrest them, and as a result they were in a continuous state of anxiety and trepidation. They purchased only half their usual amounts of oil and other necessities, thinking they would not even be able to finish these.

At the time of these anxieties their Father on high deigned to show His greatness. The mayor of the city was making an inspection tour of bakers and bakeries, when, in one of the bakeries he discovered bread that lacked the required weight [and proceeded to confiscate all the loaves]. Since he knew that Joseph's mother and sisters lived in need, he sent an inspector, staff in hand, to bring them two baskets of bread. Joseph's family lived in such terror that when the Indian maid, who served them,[127] announced that the authorities were at the door, they were stunned and shaken beyond description. No one[128] dared go down to open the door, for they all feared the blow — a blow which the Lord God turned into mercy.

In short, when they did go down, not a little afraid and expecting imminent imprisonment, they discovered that the mayor, or rather the Lord God Almighty, had sent them his deputy with two baskets full of bread as alms. In this way the Lord filled their houses with His blessing, for they had bread for more than a week. And all their other fears were to be dispelled in a similar manner as the Lord is witness.

In this state of constant anxiety, Joseph used to bore holes in the walls of his house in the middle of the night, and planned to slip

---

[125] This most probably refers to their practice of Judaism.
[126] Text: *por no venir a tan crueles manos como las de los enemigos* . . . [p. 487].
[127] Text: *la yndia que los sabia* . . . [p. 488]!
[128] Text: *ninguna* . . . [p. 488].

out through them[129] and escape when they came to arrest him. But here we can see how vain are the plans of man, if the Lord God does not confirm them; and if His divine majesty does not protect a city, in vain does he labor who would protect it.[130]

At the same time Joseph had another terrifying experience. By the will of God most high the officers of the Crown and the chief constable of the Inquisition happened to clash in the port of Ulua[131] over the question of institutional priorities. In connection with this the commissary of the Inquisition for that region came to Mexico City. The commissary at the time was a Franciscan friar and, when he came to Mexico, he naturally went to lodge in the monastery of Santiago, belonging to his order, while he awaited the start of the discussions.

This Inquisitor had a brother [a Dominican monk] who knew that Joseph used to write and transcribe sermons and other ordinary materials for the Franciscan friars. He asked his brother to get the old monk of the school, in whose care Joseph had been entrusted, to have Joseph copy over a notebook which had been lent him by a fellow monk of his Dominican order.[132] The commissary said he would look into the matter. The Inquisitor agreed to send his brother a note written in Joseph's hand in order to see whether Joseph's handwriting was to his liking.

Joseph [of course], was unaware of what was going on. One day, when Joseph's fears were at their height, the Inquisitor sent for Joseph with one of the monks of the monastery, with whom Joseph was not particularly familiar, though he was loved and esteemed by all the monks and all were very friendly toward him. Not without fear and great misgiving Joseph asked the young man, "Who is that with Brother Christopher, our superior?"

He answered, "Brother Christopher is now with the commissary of the Inquisition, on whose errand I have come."[133]

When Joseph heard this, his heart skipped a beat. He suspected that through the commissary the Inquisition was sending for him. You can imagine the fright and panic he was in when he finally resigned himself to going.[134]

He found Brother Christopher and the commissary standing at

---

[129] Text: *imaginando escapar por ellos o salirse* . . . [p. 488].

[130] *Psalms* CXXVII:1. Cf. *infra*, p. 311, note 141, related text.

[131] This refers to San Juan de Ulúa, an island fortress, a mile from Vera Cruz, Mexico.

[132] Text: *un cartapacio de un fraile dado de su orden dominico* . . . [p. 489].

[133] Text: *que es mi sr.* . . . [p. 489].

[134] Text: *en fin hubo de yr y sabe el sr. D. como y cuan cercado de temores* . . . [p. 489].

the convent door. When Brother Christopher saw Joseph he said to the commissary, "Here he is," and even this seemed to confirm Joseph's fears.[135]

The commissary then said, "Let us go up to [my] room." They did, and Joseph's fears received further confirmation when the commissary told him to take pen and paper and write a personal note. Joseph, who knew how well he could write, was terrified, for he not unnaturally suspected that they wanted the note to compare his handwriting with that of the book which his sister had lost.[136] As a result he was plummeted into indescribable distress and anxiety.

Having written this note,[137] Joseph was dismissed. He went home in trepidation — for which the Lord [later] repaid him —[138] and began to think of fleeing for safety. But on this occasion as on others, he experienced the truth of the prophet David's statement[139] that if the Lord does not protect a city,[140] in vain does he wake who would protect it, and if the Lord does not build a city, in vain does he labor who would build it.[141]

A short while later Joseph learned why the commissary of the Inquisition had had him write the note which had induced the anxiety. It was because the monk, who was the Inquisitor's brother, had learned that Joseph was copying papers and sermons for the Franciscan friars. A great preacher in his order had lent the monk a notebook and the latter eagerly wished to have it copied. In order to determine whether Joseph should do the copying for him,[142] he asked the commissary to have Joseph write a note so that he could see his handwriting. When he saw it, he asked his brother the Inquisitor to have Joseph proceed; and the notebook accordingly was forwarded to the old monk who supervised Joseph.[143]

When Joseph realized that his suspicions were groundless, he gave thanks to the Lord. Yet he was perturbed by the fact that the time involved in copying that book reduced the time he could devote to prayer and the service of the Lord his God. But this unbearable situation was turned by the Lord into a means for

---

[135] Text: *sus temores y ymaginacion* . . . [p. 489].
[136] Text: *con la del libro que se les habia perdido* . . . [p. 489].
[137] Text: *al fin despues del billete escrito* . . . [p. 489].
[138] Text: *que el sr. D. remedio* . . . [p. 489].
[139] Text: *el dicho verdadero del propheta Dauid* . . . [p. 489].
[140] Text: *si el Senor no guarda la cifra* [*cibda.*, for *cibdad* (= *ciudad*)] . . . [p. 489].
[141] *Psalms* CXXVII:1, with part *b* of the verse somewhat altered. See *supra*, p. 310, note 130.
[142] Text: *para hazer que se lo trasladase* . . . [p. 490].
[143] Text: *el fraile viejo con quien estaba* . . . [p. 490].

Joseph's consolation and eventual freedom. For in the very midst of Joseph's anxieties, when he did not even know how to go about seeking his freedom, the Lord was pleased to begin to give it to him. But before I explain how, I shall relate a miracle which the Lord most high performed concerning the notebook [Joseph was copying].

During this time Joseph received word in letters from his brother-in-law [in Spain], informing him that his liberty, mentioned above, had been attained, but for lack of funds,[144] which had to be paid in Madrid, the documents could not yet be [released and] forwarded.

Rather to be freed from a situation that brought anxiety upon him than to obtain these documents [of liberty for himself and his family], Joseph asked the Inquisitor's brother, for whom he was copying the notebook to help him get permission to move about freely in order to obtain alms [to pay] for his liberty. By command of the omnipotent Lord God, Joseph was given six months' leave.

When Joseph was about to take advantage of this [freedom] he was prevented from so doing by the fact that he had not finished copying the book.[145] He had already arranged with the old monk, his confessor and the school's rector,[146] to pay four Indian scribes to finish it.[147] However — if you want more evidence of the mercies of the Most High, God permitted the old monk to change his mind and for the first time to harden his heart against Joseph. The day after making these arrangements, the rector said to him, with agitation and annoyance, "You must not go. It is unfair for you to leave before finishing the Inquisitor's notebook. A fine thing it is that now that they have given you liberty you scorn them and abandon your work."

Now if Joseph were to finish the notebook by himself, he would need more than his six months' leave which had been given to him. But since he was a captive, he said nothing. He humbly bemoaned his troubles and the fact that they delayed his going into hiding.

On the very day and at the very hour when the monk displayed such hostility and Joseph found himself in that plight, the Lord God sent two of the pages of the Inquisitor on behalf of his brother to pick up the notebook, unfinished though it was, because the preacher who had let the Inquisitor's brother examine it,[148] was

---

144 Text: *por falta de qntos.* . . . [p. 490].

145 Text: *estorbabaselo el libro que trasladaba* . . . [p. 490].

146 Text: *redor del colegio* . . . [p. 490].

147 Omitted from the translation is the additional clause *el qual le prometio el lo haria ansi* [p. 490].

148 Text: *se yba el predicador que se lo avia prestado para la puebla* . . . [p. 491].

going away.[149] When the [monk who was the] rector of the school saw this he was astonished [at Joseph's good fortune], and, inspired by the Lord God, he again favored Joseph as before.

When the Provincial of the Franciscan friars learned that Joseph had been granted permission to seek alms, the Lord God touched his heart, and without a word from Joseph, he told his monks to inform Joseph that if he wished he would give him a very favorable letter-patent for the entire province, which would facilitate his being accorded a friendly reception in all the monasteries. Joseph said yes and received the letter as promised.

Then the Lord God moved the heart of the Vicar General, and by God's decree, he gave Joseph fifty favorable letters [of introduction]. The Lord God also gave Joseph favor in the sight of the Governor of the Archbishopric, who granted an indefinite extension of Joseph's leave. And since everything was being decreed by God's hand, He moved the Provincial of the Augustinian friars to give Joseph yet another letter that would serve him well in all the monasteries of his order.

Joseph also applied for a letter from the Viceroy, but believed that it would be impossible to obtain. Since nothing is impossible for the Almighty God who was guiding him, no sooner did Joseph's confessor ask it on behalf of Joseph, his mother and his sisters, than he was given not one letter, but twenty-five.

Taking these letters and the favor of the Lord his God with him, Joseph left his confinement in Mexico City after four years of anguish and affliction. Yet in the midst of it, he was abundantly aided by the Most High. [Now] wherever he went, God's divine majesty gave him grace. It was no small miracle that he moved his very enemies to shower him with their gifts of money, hens, cheese, corn and other items. Laden with these, he would return to the house of his penance, where his mother and sisters still lived.

Whenever Joseph came to a monastery, he was provided with lodging and offered food; but ever mindful of the Law and commandment of his Lord God, he refused the food to avoid defiling himself, saying that he had already eaten. It often happened, when he left the company and board of these men whom he loathed, that he went to eat his bread among the beasts, thinking it better to eat among horses in cleanliness than in uncleanliness at the tables of his well-bred enemies.

Two months after he first left, Joseph returned to the home of

---

[149] Omitted from the translation is the additional clause *al fin lo llebaron* . . . [p. 491].

his mother and sisters sound [but not secure], for his heart was still agitated by the fear that his lost book would turn up and lead to an [Inquisitional] warrant for his arrest. He, therefore, first decided to find out whether it was safe for him to return to his mother's house. He first went to the older of his married sisters, who lived in a separate house with her husband and daughter, and asked her if there was anything new. Since the mercy of the Most High was guiding Joseph along this road of [his] fears, He permitted an occasion to come up in which Joseph would experience fears for his greater good. At his sister's [home] he learned that shortly after he had left, a man had come to his mother's house asking for him and saying that he was a page of the Inquisition's high constable. This had greatly alarmed his mother and sisters and now caused him not a little fright. He debated with himself whether or not he should go into hiding, but the Lord gave him courage to face anything, even death, and he went to his mother's house. It was soon evident that all this had been the prompting of fear, permitted and decreed, like everything else, by God on high, that Joseph might recall all His mercies and be able the better to appreciate the gift of liberty that the Lord was about to grant him.

Joseph collected more than eight hundred and fifty pesos in alms from the hands of the barbarous Gentiles. May the Lord God of Israel enlighten them and bring them to a recognition of His holiness, that He may be adored and served by all His creatures. His mighty hand moved them to give Joseph these alms so willingly in most places that it was clear that the alms were coming from the Lord. Then Joseph and his mother received word that the brother-in-law who miraculously escaped from [Mexico City] for this purpose — with God's help — as I have already narrated,[150] had succeeded, with the favor of the Most High, in obtaining the family's restoration to liberty.[151] Again, this news arrived in time to serve as celestial medicine for Joseph's mother, for with its joy the Lord revived her from an illness that had her at the brink of death.

The decrees of liberty came in the first fleet, the one that arrived in this [land of] New Spain around September, 1594. When they came the Lord had already provided Joseph with sufficient alms to pay for them. But before I tell how, by the Lord's hand and kind-

---

[150] Text: *que ya dire* . . . [p. 493].

[151] Almeyda in the meantime had apparently collected the funds required to release the document. See *supra*, p. 312. When the documents reached the New World more payments were necessary. See *infra*, pp. 316–317. This was part of the process piously called "the redemption of the penitential garb."

ness, their penitential garb was removed, it is only proper that I mention two remarkable illnesses that the Lord God inflicted upon Joseph's two unmarried sisters as a most merciful atonement for the entire family, for, like sinning monks, we always need in this life bread and the rod. This is what our holy prophet gave thanks to God for when he said, *"Virga tua et baculus tuus ipsa me consolata sunt"*[152] ["Your rod and your staff, they comfort me"].[153]

The Lord gave the younger girl[154] a throat ailment like quinsy, which lasted more than eight months. The Lord [finally] freed her from that illness by having her throat lanced in several places, but left her with another malady. She was left crippled, and as a result of her treatment, her speech was so impaired that for a few months she could barely make herself understood. But even then the patient girl did not lack divine aid and consolation, because it pleased the Lord to open the understanding of his sister, the one who married Jorge de Almeyda, to everything that the sick girl said. The physician and the surgeon and everyone else, therefore, relied on her to interpret the speech of the sick girl. May the infinite mercy of the Lord God heal her, for she is still an invalid.[155]

To the older unmarried sister,[156] our God, the Lord on High, then gave another very serious and equally perilous illness. Following severe depressions, the girl became mad, and as a result would have endangered not only her own life,[157] but the lives of all the rest of the family were it not for the providence of the One who has never abandoned them in their straits and hopefully never will. For in her madness, she has taken the idols in the homes of her heathen neighbors and before their very eyes thrown them out of their windows to be shattered down below. And on top of this she has done things and said things which have brought upon us such fright and danger that only our God and Lord can deliver us, for the glory of His sweet name.

The madness of this poor maiden is such that she babbles ceaselessly, day and night; yet in the course of her occasional gibberish, she utters many bald and lucid truths to the monks and idolatrous nuns who visit her in an attempt to cure her of her sickness.

Two doctors gave her ten stomach cauteries which brought on such pain and fury that she threw things at her mother and sisters

[152] Text: *Virgo tua et bacubustus ipsame consolata sunt* . . . [p. 493].
[153] *Psalms* XXIII:4.
[154] This was Anica [or Ana].
[155] Text: *a quien sano la infinita mya. del sr. D. pues todavia lo esta.* . . . [p. 493].
[156] This was Mariana.
[157] Text: *y esta sy en muy temido peligro su vida* . . . [p. 493].

and would have killed them, were it not for the grace of God. They have had such a difficult time with the girl that even strangers are moved to pity and compassion and they cry over the family's misfortune as if they were their kith and kin. But they [the members of the family] hope that God on high will extricate them in peace from these crises and bring them to the place where, in recognition of all His kindness and mercy, they may offer a sacrifice of praise in the midst of his servants,[158] for the honor and glory of His most holy name.

The documents freeing Joseph, his mother and sisters had arrived with the fleet that entered the port of New Spain around September, 1594. Since God our Lord has always led them on the road reserved for His special servants, He ordained that on a Thursday afternoon, on the sixth of October of that year, four days before the news of their liberty reached them, the constable of the Inquisition should come to summon them.[159] This plunged them into the worst predicament imaginable. They bemoaned their lot as if they were already arrested and delivered over to the cruel enemy. But the Lord God, in His great mercy, had decreed that the purpose of the summons was to have them ratify[160] their previous testimony before the Inquisition to the effect that Jacob Lumbroso, Joseph's younger brother[161] [who had escaped from New Spain and] whom the Inquisitors were planning to burn in effigy, studied and kept the holy Law of the Most High.[162] When they had done so, they were sent home, where they joyously celebrated God's merciful deliverance with sacred hymns and songs.

Four days later, which was Monday, October 10th, they received the writ of liberty. This was one of the greatest mercies and blessings that [our] wandering and sinning people have ever received from the Lord. So great was the joy it brought that even their non-Jewish acquaintances rejoiced at their cheer, praising God and saying, "Blessed be the Lord God, who [has] had compassion upon you and [has] delivered you from such great travail and affliction."

And because this best suited [God's purpose] they could not [afford

---

[158] Text: *a donde . . . le offrescan entre sus ciervos sacrificio de alabanzas* . . . [p. 494].

[159] Text: *de mandado de los inquisidores* . . . [p. 494].

[160] Text: *redificarlas* . . . [p. 494].

[161] As Luis changed his name to Joseph Lumbroso, so Miguel changed his to Jacob Lumbroso.

[162] Miguel had escaped from New Spain and was at the time in Salonika, safely out of the reach of the Inquisition. The family did not mind at all giving evidence that could in no way hurt him.

immediately to] redeem their penitential garb.[163] Soon God moved a wealthy neighbor of theirs to bond them for eight hundred and fifty pesos.[164] They immediately paid four hundred and twenty of these from the alms that Joseph had collected and took eight months to accumulate the balance. On Monday, October 24, 1594, on the command of God Most High, their penitential garb was removed.

On the same day the Lord performed a great miracle for Joseph. It happened that, at the very moment Joseph went to have his penitential garb removed, a heretic of our own people went before the Inquisitors to accuse one of his [Israelite] brothers [of Judaizing] and also to accuse Manuel de Lucena for having tried to enlighten him and direct him to the knowledge of the Lord God. At that time Joseph was in Lucena's house, though he was not together with him.

Joseph next went to Pachuca to gather some more alms. A week went by after the [heretic's] accusation when the Lord ordained that the Inquisition arrest the men he had accused. Though the heretic had stated that Joseph was in the same house as Lucena, the Inquisition did not arrest him, because God on High, God Almighty had decided to deliver him with an extraordinary miracle. . . .[165] May His holy name[166] be eternally glorified and praised. Amen.

And because the road along which the Lord God has been leading them has been full of mercies, and His rod has been only the soft scourge of fear, He decreed that on the following Monday, a week after [they had taken off their penitential garb], they should suffer a new blow, one of the most severe yet — though they never suffered any from which the Lord God, in His infinite mercy, did not deliver them in two hours. What this blow was and how it came about are not being recorded for the time being, because the writer is still in lands of captivity, though with the help and favor of the Omnipotent[167] and Almighty Adonay, the God of Israel, he is on the verge of leaving one of the greatest and most dangerous captivities which members of our nation have suffered.[168] Here by the singular kind-

---

[163] Text: *no se les quitaron luego los habitos* . . . [p. 495].

[164] See *supra*, p. 314. There Joseph is said to have collected more than eight hundred and fifty pesos. What happened to the balance we are not told.

[165] The miracle is not narrated here.

[166] Text: *a su santisima madre* [sic!] *sea dada eterna gloria y alabanza amen* . . . [p. 495]. See *supra*, p. 306, note 119.

[167] Text: *altisimo* . . . [p. 495].

[168] Luis may have been referring to his escape to the Old World through a miracle; more likely he was alluding to the escape of his soul from New Spain, by way of the stake, to the Paradise he was awaiting.

ness of the Lord our God he and his family have been living in a danger no less great than the one which confronted Saint Daniel when he was thrown into the lions' den. The Almighty very miraculously shut the cruel mouths of the [enemies] surrounding him,[169] for had not the Lord our God intervened, he would have immediately been torn to pieces.

Wherefore I humble my heart, worship and glorify God's most holy name and declare that He is good and very great and His mercy is eternal. May it help us[170] and all Israel. Amen.[171]

---

[169] Text: *a estos que los cercan* ... [p. 496].

[170] Text: *la qual no valga* ... [p. 496].

[171] Supplementing Carvajal's autobiography, the next issue of the *American Jewish Historical Quarterly* will contain Carvajal's last will and testament and his letters to his mother and sisters during their second incarceration by the Inquisition.

The Letters and Last Will and Testament of Luis De Carvajal, the Younger

Translated by MARTIN A. COHEN

I

THE LETTERS

INTRODUCTION

Although the Inquisition strictly forbade its prisoners to communicate with one another, the younger Luis de Carvajal and his family decided to circumvent this interdict when they were jailed by the Inquisition for a second time early in 1595. Since they were apparently permitted to send objects other than messages from one cell to another, the family devised an ingenious system of communication in which cloths, raisins, olive pits and other items in sundry combinations conveyed a wide variety of information.

However, as Luis apparently soon recognized, the best of such signals could not equal the written word. He consequently decided to find a way to send written messages to his mother and sisters. Paper was difficult to come by, and Luis soon realized that if he were to send messages, he would have to scratch them on pears or on the pits of avocados. This he proceeded to do. In order to insure their delivery, he would wrap his messages in bands of cloth, if available. He would then hide them in a plantain or a melon and would ask his guard or warden to take the fruit to his mother or one of his sisters.

We do not know how many such letters were written. That Luis' family was receiving some is inferable from the fact that letters, doubtless in reply to his,[1] were delivered to Luis. We do know that a considerable number — at least thirty-nine — did not reach their destination as planned. These were the letters intercepted and preserved by the Inquisition.[2]

---

[1] See Section A, *infra*, p. 482, note 175.

[2] The Inquisition apparently had some of the messages it intercepted and transcribed sent on to their intended destination to see what reply they might elicit. See *Procesos de Luis de Carvajal (el Mozo)*, p. 181.

The first such letter was discovered on May 13, 1595 by the Inquisition's warden, Gaspar de los Reyes Plata, in a melon that Luis had asked him to deliver to his favorite sister, Leonor.[3] Dutifully, and one might imagine, excitedly, Gaspar spirited the strange fruit to his superiors. He made several more such interceptions before the Inquisitors, realizing that such letters might reveal intimate information which they could use to condemn Luis' family and friends, advised Gaspar de los Reyes unobtrusively to leave occasional pieces of paper and supplies of ink in Luis' cell.[4] Seemingly unaware of what was transpiring, Luis attributed the felicitous turn of events to a miracle of God and proceeded to compose letter after letter. Between May 22 and June 3, 1595, he handed a total of twenty-one letters to Gaspar de los Reyes for delivery to his mother and sisters. The warden obligingly accepted them, collected them and formally presented them, singly or in groups, to his masters, the Inquisitors.

Eventually the Inquisitors ordered a transcript of these letters to be appended to the testimony of Luis' trial. The appendix is now found on pages 499 to 534 of the published *Procesos de Luis de Carvajal (el Mozo)*. The translation of these letters will be found in Section A below [see *infra*, pp. 457–501].

In section B [see *infra*, pp. 501–509] we include the translation of the messages Luis etched on pears and avocado pits. Since these messages were difficult to preserve, Gaspar de los Reyes read them into the testimony of Luis' trial, and they now appear on pages 171–183 of the aforementioned *Procesos*. As he had them recorded, Gaspar de los Reyes indicated how they were wrapped, in what fruit they were hidden, and the date when he received them, which we can assume to have been the date of composition. In the translation below all this information appears in brackets.

Together with these perishable letters, Gaspar de los Reyes also read into the testimony two that were written on paper and were handed to him together by Luis on May 23, 1595. These are to be found in Section B, below, under nos. 38 and 39. Gaspar did not give a reason for his inclusion of these letters in the testimony. Perhaps the reason might lie in Luis' attitude of contempt for the Inquisitors which he so clearly and forcefully expressed in both.

In addition, Gaspar de los Reyes alluded to a third letter written on paper, which he did not have recorded, and whose existence we acknowledge in Section B below by designating it no. 37.

In total, Gaspar read twelve letters into the testimony and alluded

---

[3] *Ibid.*, pp. 171–172.
[4] *Ibid.*, p. 176.

to six others which he did not record, perhaps because they were impossible to decipher.[5] Even the letters he did read into the testimony were in a poor state of preservation, as the reader can observe from their many lacunae. It is because of these that we present the translation of the letters in the testimony [Section B], after those in the appendix [Section A] although the former were for the most part composed earlier. After perusing the letters found in Section A, the reader will better be able to appreciate those in Section B and even to imagine their missing contents.

* * *

As one reads the letters, it appears clear that one of Luis' major aims is to buoy the spirits of his mother and sisters who, like him, faced conviction as impenitent heretics and the automatic penalty of death at the stake. However, while Luis looked to the future with unswerving faith in his Judaism and trust in God's promises of Paradise, the women sank into despair. In the letters Luis, therefore tries to convince his mother and sisters that they should rejoice at their lot, for, he says, God has imprisoned them and confronted them with death in order the more quickly to bring them to Paradise and their promised reward. Of course, they are experiencing suffering and hardship, but faith can help them surmount all this precisely as it had helped other great women in Jewish tradition to overcome their obstacles, women like the biblical Sarah and Rachel, Jael and Esther; or women like Susanna and Judith, who appear in the Apocrypha, which Luis, using the Vulgate as his Bible, considered canonical; or women like Asenath, the wife of Joseph in the Bible and a model of piety in the Jewish — and Christian — traditions. Similarly the staff of faith helped great male worthies, like Tobit (of the Apocrypha) or Abraham and Isaac, to meet their trials. In two of his extant letters Luis dwells on the narrative of the binding of Isaac to demonstrate that faith in God, even when His demands seem exorbitant and unjust, is ultimately rewarded; for God's purpose, however inscrutable and unfathomable, is nevertheless always just and benign.

More than any other source, the letters reveal Luis' sensitivity and concern for his family. He understood quite accurately the psychology of his young, maiden sisters, who, as they faced death,

[5] These are letters found in Section B, *infra*, letters nos. 25, 30, 31, 32, 33 and 37.

could look back only upon a dark and barren life. In his letters, he therefore tries to compensate for the disappointments and agonies they have suffered on earth by painting glowing pictures of the heavenly bliss that awaits them. In Paradise, he tells them, they will tread soft fields, luxuriate in scented orchards, and thrill to the thrum of the harp and the click of castanets. They will be queens, elegantly attired by command of God Himself, who will summon His angels and say:

> Angels, bring My daughters, bring My betrothed some of those rich robes I have told you to make. Exchange their skirts of ordinary cloth for skirts of white satin; their plain jackets for new ones that have seven layers of brocade. Set their hair beautifully and put rich headdresses and garlands on their heads. Leave no finger without a ring, for they have suffered so much on My behalf. And before you dress them, be sure to bathe them in luxurious, scented waters, for they have to eat at My table.[6]

And there in heaven they will be married — to none other than the King of the angels Himself.

For all these reasons, Luis tells his family, especially his younger sisters, that they are wrong to spend their time in idle moping. While yet on earth they should rather busy themselves preparing a bridal bouquet worthy of their heavenly groom. This bouquet should be composed of the motley-hued spiritual flowers called faith and hope and charity and patience and humility and meekness and innocence and chastity and perseverance.

Recognizing also the youth of his unmarried sisters and the regression induced by their desperate situation, Luis paints another touching picture. He tells them that when they reach heaven, God, their Father, will rush to greet them with an embrace. Observing their tears, He will take the kerchief of consolations from His pocket and solicitously wipe them away. Then, nestling His daughters in the security of His lap, He will say to them, "Come, My darling ewes. Show Me, show Me, where did the dog bite you?" And then they, relishing the joy of that supreme moment of release, will each cry out with happy tears:

> Father, the bite cut to our souls. And [do You know] why [he bit me] — a curse be upon him? He attacked me and bit me a thousand times because I was calling Your name, because I was going to perform Your commandment, [because I was about] to fulfill Your Law.[7]

*   *   *

[6] See *infra*, p. 487.
[7] *Ibid.*

On reading these letters, it is difficult to repress wonderment at Luis' apparent unawareness that many, if not most of them, were not reaching their destination. Questions he was posing were obviously going unanswered. Bold statements he was making were understandably eliciting no reaction. Yet at no time does Luis give voice to any suspicion that something might be amiss. Was he so naïve as to be unaware of what was going on? Could he have failed to realize the possibility that his letters might be intercepted?

There are other facts which are puzzling. First, these letters are highly repetitious. To be sure, their themes bore repetition, but the extent of the repetition and the lack of variation are little short of amazing.

Second, the Inquisition, as we have seen, facilitated Luis' writing of these letters in the hope that he might reveal data about his family and friends that could be employed to incriminate them. To our surprise and doubtless to the Inquisition's dismay, these letters contain not one shred of information that could incriminate anyone except Luis himself. However, since Luis had already confessed his guilt, such data possessed no practical value for the Inquisitors.

Third, many of Luis' letters contain an incredible statement. Repeatedly Luis insists that his mother and sisters are wholly innocent of the charges of Judaizing on which they were arrested. Acknowledging that he is guilty and that the evidence on which he was indicted was solid and substantial, Luis proceeds to remind his mother and sisters that they were arrested only on the basis of suspicion, which he then implies was unfounded. He furthermore states that in his desire to give accurate evidence before the Inquisitional tribunal, he has stoutly defended their innocence.[8]

Now if anyone was aware of the incorrectness of such statements, it was Luis himself; for it was he who had led his family in their Judaizing practices before their first arrest; it was he who had encouraged them to return wholeheartedly to Judaism after their release from the Inquisitional jail following their first trial; and it was he who inspired them and led them in their Judaizing in the years immediately preceding their second arrest. Obviously, he could not have believed his own statements, nor could his family. Why, then, did he make them?

There is a way to explain these anomalies that suggests itself to someone who studies the entire life of Luis de Carvajal, the younger. From such a study it appears that Luis was anything but naïve; that

[8] See *infra*, pp. 458, 468–469, 482–483, 491 and 498.

he could not have failed to realize the dangers inherent in his fruited correspondence; that he must have known that some, if not all, of his letters could easily fall into the Inquisition's hands; and that he must even have realized that the Inquisitors had something to do with the miracle from God by which he was provided with material for writing.

Nor could Luis have been oblivious to an even more important fact, namely, that by feigning naïveté and unawareness of what was happening to the letters, he might be able to deceive the Inquisitors into believing the information he volunteered in them. If in these letters he regularly cast doubt upon his family's Judaizing, those that were intercepted might lead the Inquisitors to delay the prosecution of his family, and, though this possibility was remote, even to restore them to liberty.

Such a hypothesis, perfectly consistent with the personality and attitudes of young Luis, would explain the four perplexing characteristics we have observed in these letters — first, Luis' repetitiousness; second, his omission of all useful incriminating information; third, his insistence on his family's innocence; and, of course, fourth, for these letters that did get through, his attempt to buoy the faith of his mother and sisters and prepare them for the eventuality of martyrdom. And as for the intensely and militantly Jewish terms in which this message was couched, it is obvious that only Luis, and not his family, could be held responsible for them.

The hypothesis that Luis was, or became aware of the Inquisitors' machinations is further buttressed by the fact that in none of his eartly letters — those written on pears or avocado pits — does Luis mention anything about his family's innocence. He does once state that he has made a confession of guilt about himself alone,[9] but such statements were usual for Judaizers who were determined not to implicate anyone else. Luis' mention of his family's innocence did not appear until he began receiving the special paper and ink from Gaspar de los Reyes, and then it appeared in his very first letter. It would not be unreasonable to suppose that Luis, never a dullard, saw through the Inquisition's strategy from the very beginning and decided then and there on the counter-strategem of professing his family's innocence.

*   *   *

---

[9] See Section B, *infra*, letter no. 23, p. 502.

As has been mentioned, the text of the letters in Section B is full of lacunae; that of Section A is nearly free of errors. There are occasional unimportant errors of orthography, with which we chose not to burden the notes. Nor did we include in them simple variations of translation, such as our use of adjective and noun for cases of hendiadys, of which Luis was so fond. Like those to the "Autobiography," the notes to this section identify important individuals, explain important concepts and allusions and call attention to the more noteworthy problems and challenges confronting the translator.

Brackets indicate our insertions; parentheses, Carvajal's asides or his comments on biblical verses.

SECTION A

THE LETTERS OF LUIS DE CARVAJAL, THE YOUNGER
FOUND IN THE APPENDIX TO HIS TRIAL RECORDS

[The Inquisition prefaced the letters with the following note:]

Included in this document are all the papers which the warden [of the Inquisitional prison], Gaspar de los Reyes, presented as evidence before the [Inquisitional] Tribunal, relative to Luis de Carvajal, his mother and sisters. These papers and [the pits of the] avocados, likewise delivered[10] *by the said warden, are mentioned in his aforesaid [depositions], which are to be found above.*[11]

[The following are the] first papers presented, on May 22, 1595. The first [is] for Doña Leonor and Doña Isabel, the second for Doña Leonor.[12]

[1]

[To Doña Leonor and Doña Isabel]:

My precious ones, by a miracle I was given an ink-well today and a pen, [obviously so] that I might send this note to you [for you are] the apple of my eye. Whoever[13] should receive it first can very circumspectly wrap it in something and send it on to my other dear sisters.

---

[10] Text: *hizo preson.* . . . [p. 499].

[11] *Procesos de Luis de Carvajal (el Mozo)*, pp. 171–183.

[12] Doña Leonor was the wife of Jorge de Almeyda. See "Autobiography," *supra,* p. 287, note 37. On Isabel, see *ibid.*, p. 294, note 73.

[13] Text: *que; [for quien ?]* . . . [p. 499].

I was arrested by the express will and judgment of the Most High
and through an accusation [made] by Manuel de Lucena.[14] In order
not to implicate anyone else[15] I have confessed the truth about myself alone, expecting God's certain reward, of which I have had substantial and sure promise during my incarceration.[16]

My darlings, my angels, my dears, you were arrested on suspicion
alone. I [have] defended your innocence; may my soul be similarly
defended against Satan and his agents by the holy angel of my Lord,
God.

I can tell you that when I was alone [in jail][17] I spent my time
rejoicing.[18] But from the time I was shown my little red book[19]
and my letters[20] and learned of your imprisonment, I have been extremely grieved. With hot tears and bended knees I have sighed
and cried to my Lord God, asking help from His merciful hand —
which I very confidently await — for the salvation of [our] souls.
This is what matters most.

Dear ones, this [imprisonment] was the will of the Most High,
and His lash was less than our sins [demanded]. Let us accept it
wholeheartedly,[21] for God can bring good out of evil [and] water,
honey and oil from hard rocks.

I hear that there may be more than thirty people [in this jail]
whom that poor Manuel de Lucena and others have implicated [as
Judaizers]. May our Lord, as the Father of mercy, come to our rescue, even though our faithlessness[22] makes us unworthy.

I am [now] in shackles, but neither these nor [the prospect of]
burning alive[23] will divert my spirit from [clinging to] the sweetness
of the Lord my God.[24]

---

[14] Manuel de Lucena, a Judaizer, was a friend of Luis and his family. He was arrested
by the Inquisition and some of his testimony was used against Luis. See *Procesos de Luis
de Carvajal (el Mozo)*, pp. 125–135.

[15] See "Introduction" to these letters, *supra*, pp. 455–456.

[16] These apparently are the visions to which Luis repeatedly refers below and those
he mentions in his "Autobiography," *supra*, pp. 296–298 and 307–308.

[17] That is, before his family was rearrested.

[18] This conviction resulted from Luis' belief that after his death at the stake his soul
would ascend to Paradise. This was all that he could look forward to; he knew that he
had no chance of escaping death.

[19] This was the booklet which Mariana had lost. See "Autobiography," *supra*, pp.
308–309.

[20] This doubtless refers to the letters sent to his sisters prior to his incarceration.

[21] Text: *postremonos a ella con almas y corazones . . .* [p. 499].

[22] Luis may be referring to the occasions where wittingly or unwittingly he and his
family failed fully to adhere to what they believed to be the requirements of the Jewish
religion.

[23] Text: *ni el fuego vivo . . .* [p. 500].

[24] Text: *de mi dulcissimo señor y Dios . . .* [p. 500].

Since I have trust in Him, my Creator has often mercifully revealed Himself here to me.[25]

One day, as my poor mind was sweetly absorbed in petition to my Lord God, I said[26] to Him: "Why, O Lord, would You show so much mercy to a worm like me? And how can it be that I will have a greater crown in Your kingdom than my father?" [Then] this answer was revealed and given to me: "Do you know how this will be? — As it was when Joseph stood before his father as Prince of Egypt, and the saintly Jacob greatly rejoiced on seeing his son's honor and fame."[27]

I think I have already told you that in Tasco, a few days before my arrest, our good father appeared to me [in a dream] one night. He was all dressed in white and was kneeling in a green field [and] praying to the Lord, my God. And when I reached the field he came toward me with open arms and gave me his blessing. And then the earth on which I stood suddenly rose toward heaven.

My good Lord God [now] wishes to turn this dream into reality, my dearest ones, and I will try to do nothing to obstruct His plans. God's truth is witness [to the fact] that I write [these words] not out of vainglory, for I know that I deserve Hell because of my sins, but in order to bring joy and solace to your dejected spirits, which have touched my heart [with compassion]. Yet I trust in my good Lord God that since He shows such kindness to a sinner like me, His mercy and comfort will not be lacking for you, my dear ones.

Remember the sacrifice of the saintly Isaac.[28] When he was bound, how obediently he awaited the thrust of the knife! [Remember] the faith of his saintly father, our patriarch, Abraham. [Remember] what the Lord did with Joseph's imprisonment,[29] [or] the dangers confronting the saintly Moses, [or] the wanderings of our holy father, Israel [-Jacob], or of David and all the [later] saints.

This [imprisonment given by God] is the road to the glory of Paradise, where we are awaited, and there is no other road [open to us]. And such a journey is preferable to a journey to Castile.[30] And since our good God is opening the door for us, let us not obstruct Him.

---

[25] Text: *ame revelado mi criador aqui muchas misericordias suyas* . . . [p. 500].

[26] Text: *dire* [for *dixe*] . . . [p. 500].

[27] *Genesis* XLVI–XLVII.

[28] *Genesis* XXII:1–19. The *Akedah* ("The Binding [of Isaac]") as an atonement for Jews of subsequent generations was a concept stressed by Jews in the Medieval and Renaissance worlds. According to some this concept shows the influence of the Christian dogma of vicarious atonement. See Max Landsberg, "Akedah," *The Jewish Encyclopedia*, vol. I, p. 303. Cf. also *infra*, pp. 488–490 and 495–498.

[29] *Genesis* XXXIX:20–XLI:45.

[30] New Christian Judaizers dreamed of returning to the Old World. They would often

In [times of] temptation, have faith, have faith like Tobit.[31]   Be humble [and] patient like Job. Boldly cry out, cry out[32] to the Lord, who has not changed [in His affection toward us and ask] that He deny us not the mercy with which He raises the dead, heals [the] sick, looses [the] bound, etc. May that mercy help you, my precious ones, my darlings, dear companions of my captivity. Though buckling under afflictions and hardships, I entreat Adonay, my great God, that we may [yet] be bent [in thanksgiving] in the glory of His holy kingdom.[33] Amen. Amen. Amen. Amen. Amen. Amen. Amen.

For three weeks I lived in darkness in a dungeon. They brought me food by candlelight[34] [and this was the only light I saw]. But then my blessed Lord God took me out. (Blessed be His holy name.) And He brought me to a cell in this courtyard with a window through which day and night I can see the sky.

And what more shall I tell you about God's mercy? For a week there was a honeycomb near me, [a Bible,][35] full of the sweetest honey from the lips of the Most High.[36]   I tasted the honey and my eyes have been opened, though not fully.[37]   I saw [the meaning of] great

---

go to Spain, either to stay there and help their relatives who might be in difficulty with the Inquisition in Latin America, as Jorge de Almeyda did (see "Autobiography," *supra*, pp. 305 and 312), or go on from there to other areas of Europe or Asia where they could practice Judaism more freely.

[31] See *Tobit* I:9–15; III:2–6; XI:14–15, etc.

[32] Text: *clamar, clamar . . . ya osadas . . .* [p. 500].

[33] Text: *en su Sto. reyno y gloria . . .* [p. 501].

[34] Text: *en un calabozo en tinieblas do me llebaban de comer con candela . . .* [p. 501].

[35] Text: *tuve una colmena . . .* [p. 501]. That this was a Bible is apparent from another letter. See *infra*, p. 502. Luis nowhere explains how he happened to have a Bible in his cell. It is not unreasonable to assume that he came by it in a way analogous to his obtaining the breviary from which he recited Psalms during his first incarceration. (See "Autobiography," *supra*, pp. 295–296). There he had as a cellmate a Franciscan friar, Francisco de Luna, who had been arrested by the Inquisition and then requested the breviary. During his second incarceration he had a priest, Luis Díaz, as a cellmate. Luis Díaz, however, was a spy who had been placed in Luis' cell by the Inquisition. See *Procesos de Luis de Carvajal (el Mozo)*, p. 136 and A. Toro, *La Familia Carvajal*, vol. II (Mexico, 1944), p. 149. It is quite possible that Díaz gave Carvajal a Bible to read to see what unusual interpretation he might come up with, especially after Díaz heard Luis proudly recount how he had converted the Franciscan friar to Judaism. This Bible had commentaries as is evidenced by the presence within it of the Midrash found in letter no. 39, *infra*, p. 508, and the explanations of the *ceci* or *zizit* found *infra*, pp. 461 and 477.

[36] This honey was celestial wisdom. See "Autobiography," *supra*, p. 296.

[37] See *Numbers* XXIV:3–4. Luis appears to be saying that he has seen enough to be convinced of the glories that await all the martyrs for Judaism, but not enough to be able to describe the bliss of Paradise in detail.

and incomparable mysteries[38] and the great joys which await us in Paradise.

Rejoice! Rejoice! Let sobbing and sighing stop, for great is the joy that will be placed upon our heads through all eternity.

Leonor, my dearest — whom I love, as I do all [my sisters] like darling Rachels[39] — since you are nearby, send me signs [to let me know] whether you are alone. The two cloths they gave you yesterday to hem are mine.[40] If they come back [to me] together, I will understand that there is someone with you. If they come back separately I will know that you are alone. May the holy angel who visited Asenath[41] go with you. May he visit you and bless you and me on behalf of God most High.

Our dear mother is in one of the rooms near you.

How I wish I could go to see you and to greet you [and be with you] for a while. I ask my Lord God for permission to do this; perhaps He will grant it to me.[42] If it can not be done, I am [at least]

[38] It almost certainly is the Hebrew word ציצת, a word fitting perfectly within the context of the narrative on pp. 477 and 494 infra. Here, clearly, the word "fringe" or "fringes" presents some difficulty. It may be that in his Bible or biblical commentary, Luis saw a picture or read a description of a man wearing fringes, and, above him, the heavens filled with wondrous objects. These mysteries appear to have included the explanations of the Akedah, found infra, pp. 488 and 495; the description of the bliss awaiting the martyred in Paradise (infra, passim) and the like.

[39] Text: como aracheles de mys contentos . . . [p. 501].

[40] The cloths were one of the objects used for secret communication. See supra, p. 451.

[41] Text: Asenec . . . [p. 501]. Amazingly, it seems that Luis was aware of the Greek tract known as "The Life and Confession of Asenath," or "The Prayer of Asenath," which, insofar as is known, was available in Luis' day only in an abridged Latin translation found in Vincent of Beauvais' Speculum Historiale. Luis knew Latin and could therefore have read the story in some form in the library of the old monk (see "Autobiography," supra, pp. 301-303). Asenath, of course, was the daughter of the priest of On, Poti-pherah, and the wife of the biblical Joseph (Genesis XLI:45). In the "Confession of Asenath," she is depicted as a model proselyte to Judaism. Repenting of her idolatrous practices, she spends her days in fasting and penance, hoping in this way to join those whom God has chosen for life everlasting. She is finally visited by the angel Michael, who gives her the assurance of immortality.

Any doubts that Luis was aware of the contents of this tract are dispelled by the fact that this account contains the image of the honeycomb, which played so important a rôle in Luis' life and which is repeated frequently in his letters. In the "Confession of Asenath," the angel puts some honey in Asenath's mouth and announces that she has thereby attained immortality. In Luis' "Autobiography" (supra, p. 296) it is Solomon who spoon-feeds the honey and it brings wisdom rather than immortality (which is assured anyway), but the ingredients of the image remain the same. And, above all, after eating the honey Luis is convinced that he is Joseph, the provider for his people. On the "Confession of Asenath," see Kaufmann Kohler "Asenath, Life and Confession or Prayer of," The Jewish Encyclopedia, vol. I, pp. 172-176.

[42] Luis believed that God was controlling every event in his life. He could therefore miraculously arrange for a meeting between Luis and his family.

consoled [by the fact] that we shall see each other [first, at the stake] before we die, and then, eternally, in the glorious inheritance [which awaits us in Paradise] among the surpassingly handsome angels and saints. O, what a delicious expectation! You will live! You will survive your death![43] Hallelujah!

What do you suppose my Lord God has done with our little [sister] Anica[44] and [Mariana,] the poor little lunatic[45] and [our sister Isabel,] the poor widow?[46] O, my darling flock, who are so dispersed!

"Be consoled, be consoled," says the Lord, "for I will free you[47] from the wolves and in green pastures shall I put you, [the] sheep and [their] mother."[48]

I was near Ana Lopez[49] for a few days and she gave me some news about you.

If I am not mistaken, either of you or my [dear sister] Doña Catalina was standing with her daughter in the other court when I sent you my pillowcase.[50]

One night [in my dreams] I was shown some tortillas, made of corn flour and the size of shields. And through them I was given to understand the fulness of the joy that awaits us.

[If there is someone else in your cell,] put the first two letters of her name on the cloths [you will be returning to me].

When you pass by my cell, I can tell it is you from the sound of your clogs,[51] and as I kneel, I ask you to help me. I shall always keep a cloth in my little window for you to see when you pass by.

As children of Adam we are all born to die. Happy is the man who leaves the lingering death of this life to enter into the true life of eternity.

You sent me a pen and raisins: I understood what you wanted.[52]

* * *

[43] Text: *vivireis muertos mios* . . . [p. 501].

[44] Anica was approximately fifteen years old at the time. See "Autobiography," *supra*, p. 315, and *Procesos de Luis de Carvajal (el Mozo)*, p. 14.

[45] This was Mariana, then approximately twenty-four years old. See "Autobiography," *supra*, p. 315, and *Procesos de Luis de Carvajal (el Mozo)*, p. 14.

[46] This was Isabel. See *supra*, p. 457, note 12.

[47] Text: *yo lo librare de los lobos* . . . [p. 501].

[48] *Isaiah* XXX:23–24. Cf. *Ezekiel* XXXIV:11–12. Carvajal paraphrases the Bible here, as he frequently does below.

[49] Ana López, mother of the actor Antonio López, was one of the numerous people whom Luis, in the agony of the Inquisition's torture chamber, implicated as Judaizers. See *Procesos de Luis de Carvajal (el Mozo)*, p. 309.

[50] See *supra*, p. 461, note 40.

[51] Apparently Luis would kneel at the threshold of his room and perhaps peer through an opening such as the one he had once carved in the door of his cell (Cf. "Autobiography," *supra*, p. 297) whenever he heard someone passing by.

[52] See *supra*, p. 461, note 40, and p. 462, note 50.

[2]

[To] D[oña] Leonor:

Dearest sister, I cannot begin to tell you the comfort I felt when I saw in my hand the banana which you, whom I so love and cherish, had held in yours.[53]

Believe me, darling, if you think, as you seem to, that I was a good son and brother when the occasion demanded it during our life [of freedom] — though I grieve when I think of how little I helped and assisted you — with the help of my Lord God I shall be a better [son and brother] in the greater need [you are now experiencing]. And when God on high, with His goodness, gives me more strength than I presently have, as I deeply trust He will, I shall lovingly give my mother and darling sisters [the benefit of this strength, which is] the wheat that I will have, just as the good Joseph shared his [wheat] with his saintly father and brothers. Though you remain in Egypt and I find myself in the Promised Land,[54] I shall answer your request with action, my angel, in every way I can.

Just believe what you say — "You shall love God above all else," and what follows.[55] Thus I bend my knee to the ground and raise my right hand to heaven, swearing by the everliving God that I shall do nothing and say nothing to offend Him, though I find myself in the furnace like Azariah.[56] May God be favorable to me and grant me His help and grace that things may be so.

I was born to die sooner or later. It would be folly for me to relinquish the life eternal which my God offers me for the sake of gaining two [additional] moments of weary life [on earth].[57]

Note, my sister, that mercy is cruelty if it goes counter to God['s will] and [hurts] the soul.[58]

---

[53] *Ibid.* The bananas to which Carvajal refers were actually plantains. In this translation the word "banana" is used.

[54] It is unlikely that Luis could have hoped for any kind of promised land on earth. His promised land was Paradise. What he seems to be saying, therefore, is that when he leaves this world and goes to Paradise, he will not forget the family he has left behind in prison — which he calls Egypt. See *supra*, p. 458, note 18, and "Autobiography," *supra*, p. 317, note 168.

[55] *Deuteronomy* VI:5 and following. Cf. *Procesos de Luis de Carvajal (el Mozo)*, p. 203.

[56] *Daniel* I:7 and III:13–30.

[57] This statement is intended solely to emphasize the value of the life that awaits Luis in Paradise and not to intimate that there is any chance for life on earth to be spared. See *supra*, p. 463, note 54.

[58] This is another one of those statements by which Luis tries to get his family to accept the possibility of martyrdom with confidence that since God wills their martyrdom, it is in their best interest and will assure them Paradise; while any alteration of this decree, which might seem to be merciful in their eyes, might actually prejudice their chances for eternal bliss.

I can tell you that you have consoled me by telling me that these gentlemen [of the Inquisition][59] have shown you mercy.

Because the Lord God does not oblige anyone, young or old,[60] to do anything not within his power, I am in many ways obliged to die for His holy faith rather than deny it. And let no one who likes me be troubled by this.

I assure you that you are mentioned more than I in my tearful prayers; and my tears are so many that, except for God's mercy, I would be blind. For every moment here I picture you, my wounded darlings, and your grief is always before me. May my God give you patience and [extend to you] His helping hand.

I tell you that if you are grieved by the anguish of our dear and beloved mother, my heart is so pierced by her [anguish] and yours that were it not for my Lord God's comfort, I would have died a thousand times. But if His supreme goodness chooses the way of anguish to take her and [the rest of] us to His glory as His favored [children], I shall thank Him endlessly.

The Lord God loved Jacob dearly, yet He let him suffer anguish that his joy might be increased. He permitted Jacob to hear that his [son] Joseph had been devoured by wild beasts. However, [at that very time] the Lord was taking Joseph to Egypt that he might become a prince. He thus repaid Jacob's weeping with many consolations.[61]

I can tell you honestly, my darling, that I do not feel sad about my imprisonment, but about yours. I bemoan not my shackles and solitude, but your sighs, groans and cries. Alas! How they pierce my heart! What help can I give you, my shelterless [darlings]? Turn your eyes to the One who hurt you so that He might better heal you. Alas! I commend you to Him with my cries. May his [angels] see your abandonment. Alas! Alas! No pain in the liver[62] ever hurt as much as the thrust of your tears. What can I, without resources, do to assist you except to ask alms on your behalf, my darlings, from your most wealthy and compassionate Father? Alas, my captive ones! Would that I could remain [forever] captive in exchange for your freedom! Alas, my darlings! Would that I could give all my blood to free you.[63] But what am I saying? If I love you, then God,

---

[59] Luis seems to be saying that the Inquisitors have shown some kindness to his family, doubtless in the hope of eliciting information from them which would be prejudicial to others.

[60] Text: *ni al niño atanto como al viejo* . . . [p. 503].

[61] See *supra*, p. 459, note 27.

[62] Text: *dolor de hijada* . . . [p. 503].

[63] Text: *quien pudiera libertaros con toda su sangre* . . . [p. 503].

our Lord, loves you much more, for He is your Father, and He knows what He is doing. I shall commend you to Him incessantly. There now. There now. Everything is for the best; and let no one be so ignorant, foolish or blind [as not to realize this]. Woe betide those who live and die carefree, without passing through such adversity; and blessed be those who [do] pass through them unsullied in their faith![64]

You of course know, my sister, how throughout my life I have been an enemy of the devil. You can imagine whether I will relish hearing about him or even the mention of his name at the time of my death.[65] May the living God deliver me from his claws and deceits, and may He shelter you and console you and strengthen you and protect you.

I am comforted to learn of your determination [to remain steadfast in your faith]. Since these gentlemen [of the Inquisition] are very kindly[66] and God, our Lord, sees that we are [made] of flesh and that even the righteous man falls seven times a day, He gives His hands to those sinners who want to rise. May He who can [be of help] extend His [hand] to you. Amen.

You were remiss in not informing me that someone else was in your cell — and any other news you may have [had]. Since the Lord God has done me the kindness of showing me your writing, I ask you, for heaven's sake, to let me know, if possible, who is with you and whatever else you can — even if you have to get down on your knees again [and beg them] to give me the banana.[67]

Now calm yourself, my darling, sleep and eat, for God is great. [Look at] Jonah. He was in a greater danger and in a worse prison, yet God brought him to safety. Hezekiah had given up all hope [of life]; yet the Supreme Physician granted him fifteen more years.[68]

And observe that the soul which sincerely acknowledges and laments its guilt and repents receives God's chastisement with loving devotion, as the blessed David did when he went about barefoot and weeping, though he was king, at the time when his son [Absalom] was pursuing him.[69]

O, my dearest delight, I drenched your present[70] with my tears.

---

[64] Text: *y dichosos los que en ellos no desfallezen* . . . [p. 503].

[65] Luis is stating that even at the stake he will not profess Christianity in order to avoid being burned alive.

[66] See *supra*, p. 464, note 59.

[67] See *supra*, p. 461, note 40; p. 462, note 50; p. 462, note 52, and p. 463, note 53.

[68] *II Kings* XX:6.

[69] *II Samuel* XV:30.

[70] That is, the cloth which Leonor had sent.

And though I lack an inkstand, my God has been providing me with ink with which to write you. Praised be His holy name. Amen.

I refuse to touch meat or broth. I get along without them, [managing] with fruit,[71] cheese and tears.

* * *

Second Papers. Presented on May 26, 1595.

[3]

[To] D[oña] Leonor:

My dear, may my God send you days and hours of salvation, Amen.

O, mother of mine, would that I could give you a consolation [such as you need]. My darlings, let us ask the Lord God to give it to her from His hand. For we were borne by her and we owe so much to her. May the Lord gladden her for His sake and cover her with His holy blessings.

Lacking time and paper I was briefer yesterday than I might have wished. I therefore am [now] letting you know, my angel, that from the time when I [first] tasted the sweet honey from the honeycomb[72] I wrote to you about, I have felt[73] the pearly dew of [the knowledge] of divine mysteries falling into my soul. They are the eleemosynary gifts of God's hands.

Since the Lord has given you good manna,[74] use it all for my sake, in [devotion to] Him and His marvels and miracles. Love God dearly and set the rich, golden crown of His love upon your will. Ask him to kindle and open the light[75] of your understanding that you might see and note His marvelous deeds. Consider that everything the eye sees and the ear hears and the nose smells and the palate tastes are all gifts of His kindness. Use these rich gifts from God to express your love for Him. O, how this will enrich your spirit! How rich is the creature that devotes all its love to the One who gave it being and life!

[My] very saintly one, remember yesterday's banana and send it on for my darling Anica's sake to comfort her excruciating pains. And [do it] without fail, for the love of heaven, for God orders us to share His gifts with our kin.

---

[71] Text: *con fruta, con fruta* . . . [p. 504].

[72] See *supra*, p. 460, note 35.

[73] Text: *veo caer en mi anyma* . . . [p. 504].

[74] That is, gifts and favors.

[75] Text: *pidele que abra y sople la candela de* . . . [p. 505].

And though I would wish to [write and] console you daily, I cannot fulfill my desire, because [although] I have been obtaining paper I am constantly afraid that the jailer will ask me for it and we will be left without this [source of our] refreshment, which comes to my soul when I write to you and to yours when you read what I write and compose.[76]

This morning I heard our poor sister Justa [Mendez][77] pass by. O, if I were only [in the same section] with you, for she is there; and I imagine that she is [in a cell] with my [sister] Anica or one of my other sisters. To know that you had this comfort would be a great consolation for me.

O, Shepherd of ours, have pity on Your flock. We have been ungrateful sheep, but Your righteousness outweighs our ingratitude.

It has struck twelve. Goodbye, my darlings.

[To] Leonor.

*   *   *

[4]

[To] D[oña] Isabel:

My dear, may the mighty God be with you and all His believing children. Amen.

Do not fear or allow your heart to lose courage, for God lives and is omnipotent, and He will save us from the mouth of the mighty who now possess us; for He can prevail over them and over all. It was He who in Egypt, in defense of His beloved [people], clothed the heavens in darkness to confound their pursuers.[78] Soon, soon [indeed], He will redeem us. He will pick up His zealous sword and His great might will perform miracles. Revered be He and [revered be] His holy name. He has performed many [miracles] for me in this abyss. I tell you this that you may be comforted.

For a week I had a honeycomb here [in my cell], filled with the sweetest honey from the lips of the Most High. I tasted it and my eyes have been opened, though not fully.[79] There I saw great and amazing mysteries above the horizon. Trusting in God, I hope to tell you about these soon in triumph and joy.

---

[76] Apparently Luis always kept some paper in his cell, just in case the warden should ask him what happened to all the paper that was left for him.

[77] Justa Méndez, Luis' sweetheart and later wife of Francisco Núñez, was one of the most active Judaizers of the period. For a summary of biographical data on her, see S. B. Liebman, *A Guide to Jewish References in the Mexican Colonial Era 1521–1821* (Philadelphia, 1964), p. 105.

[78] *Exodus* X:21. Cf. *Psalms* CV:28.

[79] See *supra*, p. 460.

Have faith in temptation[80] like Abraham, our holy father and his descendant, Tobit, and the Lord will reveal His great miracles to you. Pray, pray; submit to God and humble yourselves. Wait for Him, wait, and He will show you favors, befitting a wealthy Lord who is liberal and charitable to His poor people. Ask Him. Ask Him. Cry out endlessly, "We are in need,"[81] and His most holy majesty will respond.

I have been suffering for His truth and I unequivocally confess it regarding myself alone,[82] in order not to lie. May this truth be a mighty shield for us in this battle [we are waging] against infidelity [to our faith].

O blessed daughters of the living God, have patience and fight on, for you shall certainly have the crown, the crown of olives,[83] [the crown] of everlasting salvation. May the Lord of hosts place it upon our heads.

Look at Tobit, the captive.[84] He was blind; [yet God enabled him] to see his joys. Joseph [spent] thirteen years in prison before he became a prince. Have courage. Have courage, for you cannot achieve anything unless you are willing to take a chance.[85]

About six nights ago [I,] Joseph, [dreamt] that I was walking in the midst of the ocean without wetting more than my feet.[86] [I] also [saw] hunters with guns trying to kill ducks, but without success, for the ducks were flying [too] high. Then a mighty voice,[87] a revelation from the Most High, said to me: "The sea is this jail of temptations;[88] [the] hunters [are] the bustards who are the tonsured [Inquisitors];[89] the guns [are] deceits; the live ducks [are] souls who believe in your God; their flight [is] the holy prayer [you offer]."

Fly [then], fly with prayer to the mighty God, that He may defend us. Amen. Amen. Amen. Amen. Amen. Amen. Amen.

*   *   *

[80] Temptation meant not only a weakening of faith in Judaism but a possible attempt to re-embrace Christianity in the hope of thereby saving their lives.

[81] Text: *clama sin cesar padezcamos* . . . [p. 506]. Cf. *Isaiah* LXII:6-7.

[82] See *supra*, pp. 455 and 458.

[83] Cf. *Judith* XV:13.

[84] *Tobit* I:3.

[85] The Spanish proverb goes *"No se cogen truchas a bragas enjutas,"* meaning literally "You cannot catch trout with dry breeches."

[86] This is reminiscent of Jesus' walking on the sea. See *Matthew* XIV:25, *Mark* VI:48 and *John* VI:19.

[87] Text: *es mi dicho por su ge: voz* . . . [p. 506].

[88] That is, where he is tempted to eat foods that are ritually unclean, to implicate others as Judaizers and even to recant his faith.

[89] Text: *cazadores gallalin* [sic!] *que son los tres quisados* . . . [p. 506].

Third [group of] papers, presented on May 26.
Addresssed to Isabel, his sister.

[5]

[To Doña] Isabel:

May the *Shekinah*[90] [of] Adonay be upon us.
You shall live, my martyrs. Rejoice! Rejoice, blessed martyr
of the living God. May God in His lovingkindness visit you and
strengthen you.

By a miracle of His I received ink today and this piece of paper
on which to write you. Though this [means of] communication is
[at times] lacking, because of my sins, I always keep you foremost
in my mind. My eyes often fill with tears because of your afflictions;
[yet] as often my heart wells with joy when the Most High opens
my eyes to consider and see that this [suffering of ours] is the road
to glory. You are being led along it by God's goodness alone. And
since on the right and on the left lie the dangers of fire and deep
water,[91] which you have read about in the [*Fourth Book of*] the holy
Ezra,[92] let us not depart from our God through unfaithfulness or
impatience. Let us rather give infinite thanks to Him, that He takes
notice of us tiny worms and tries us as He tried our saintly fathers.

By His goodness I have been giving witness to His truth, which
is so strong a shield to me that neither [the] jails nor [the] dungeons
in which [I have] been, nor the shackles I wear [can] divert me one
whit from it. Rather every hour they reconfirm [His truth] within
me.

But [remember!] You were arrested on suspicion only.[93] And
since you patently see that it was the will of the Most High to lead
you through these prison cells to His Paradise and glory without
the circuity and waste of [the journey to] Castile,[94] which we desired
[to take], let us not block His will with ours. For the road [we are
taking] is far superior, despite this hill [of our troubles which stands]
in its midst. And since we have such a good staff for climbing —
the support of God's promises — let none [of us] grow faint. And

---

[90] Text: *Sequina* . . . [p. 506]. The term *Shekinah* refers to God's Holy Presence, which
comes "to dwell" in the world of men.

[91] Note how Luis, in speaking of his family's deliverance from its present bondage,
conjures up the imagery of the Exodus.

[92] *II Ezra* VII:6–8.

[93] See *supra*, p. 455.

[94] Text: *los rodeos, y debaneos de castilla* . . . [p. 507]. His family had dreamt of escaping
to Spain, and thence possibly to other areas of Europe, where they could safely practice
their Judaism. Cf. *supra*, pp. 459–460, note 30.

when you feel weary and fatigued, as has [at times] happened to me, fall to your knees, literally and figuratively,[95] and ask the God of might for strength. Through [the prophet] Isaiah, He promises it to His weary and afflicted [people], saying that just as it is true that His exalted holiness lives in eternity and in His sanctuary and glory, so does He dwell with His [people], to quicken the hearts of the afflicted and to gladden the spirit of the humble.[96] "I myself, I myself," He says, "shall comfort them as one who can so do; and I shall have mercy upon my poor and fearful children."[97] "The heaven," He says, "is the throne of My glory, and the earth My footstool large. Upon whom shall the eyes of My great holiness look, if not at the wounded, the humbled and the broken, those who fear my words."[98]

"Do not fear, My children," He says, "children of Abraham, My friend,[99] who know Me, in whose hearts is My holy Law.[100] Fear not the injury or insults of men, for the worm and the moth shall devour them like a garment of wool, but over you shall come My everlasting salvation. The heavens shall dissolve like smoke and the earth shall grow old and disintegrate like a worn garment, but the salvation I have promised you will not fail; it will be forever over you throughout all generations."[101] Thus says the One who gave laws to the sun, to the heavens, [the] nights [and the] days, whose arm dried the sea, the water of the impetuous abyss, the One who made roads in the deep to lead His freed [people] across.[102]

There now, there now, be happy and glad. Stop your sobbing and sighing, for God Himself has promised us salvation. He will fill us with eternal joy and gladness. He will make pretty crowns of gladness to set upon the heads of His darling children, those who believe in Him and hope in Him and have reverence for Him.

There now, there now, blessed martyrs. Rejoice and be consoled. Be glad. Be glad. I send you felicitations, for you, my queens, shall travel from this sad and lonely earth like the Queen of Sheba to see the consummately wise and handsome King of the angels, who fashioned heaven and earth.

What rich and holy palaces you shall see, what delightful gardens

---

[95] Text: con el cn. [corazón] y cuerpo ... [p. 507]. Cf. infra, p. 499, note 214.

[96] Isaiah LVII:15.

[97] Ibid., LI:12, a radical paraphrase.

[98] Ibid., LXVI:1-2.

[99] Ibid., XLI:8.

[100] Ibid., LI:7.

[101] Ibid., LI:8.

[102] Ibid., LI:10.

[there will be] in that Paradise! There stands the Tree of Life, a life of bliss everlasting, which will be yours to enjoy. There you shall eat in supreme holiness at the table of your true Father, who gave you life in this [nether] world. How He will embrace you! He will take the kerchief of comfort from His pocket. He will wipe away your tears with favors. He will say to you, "Let them flow no more."

Do you know how He will embrace you? As a doting mother embraces the child she loves and cherishes even more than her very life. When he utters a clever word, she seizes him, smothers him with kisses and feels like devouring him with love. So will God embrace you. He will say, "Come, my darling daughters, who endured so much for My sake though you were so small." He will call out, "Angels of mine! Clothe them in brocade."

O, what garlands of glory He will place upon you. What dances and parties there will be on the day of your heavenly espousals. Then all of us will sing [the Psalm], "Let us sing for joy," and the saintly David will play for us with his harp and we shall dance [to the Psalm], "Let my soul bless the Lord."

There now, there now, be consoled. Deck yourselves in joy and gladness.

There now, be penitent, my Asenaths. Pray, my Hannahs and Esthers. There now, my beautiful Rachels, chaste Susannas, strong Jaels, Judiths and Salomes. Sing victoriously with Deborah and Miriam.[103]

---

[103] Rachel, the symbol of tenderness, (*Jeremiah* XXX:14) was the patriarch Jacob's favorite wife (*Genesis* XXIX: 18 and 26–28; XXXIII:2 and 7); Susanna, the heroine of the narrative in the *Apocrypha* that bears her name, was sentenced to death for adultery, but was miraculously saved at the last minute by the young Daniel, who showed the testimony against her to be false; Jael, wife of Heber the Kenite (*Judges* IV:17) courageously lured the Canaanite Sisera into her tent and killed him, thereby saving the Israelites; the widow Judith, another heroine in the *Apocrypha*, saved her city, Bethulia, from an Assyrian army by charming its general Holofernes, and then cutting off his head (*Judith* X:20–XIII:10); Deborah was the judge (*Judges* IV and V) under whose guidance Israel was saved from the Canaanites; Miriam, sister of Moses and Aaron, was instrumental in saving Moses when he was left on the river and in getting Moses' mother to be chosen by Pharaoh's daughter as Moses' nurse (*Exodus* II:4–8); Asenath, in the Bible (*Genesis* XLI:45) was the daughter of Poti-pherah, priest of On and became the wife of Joseph. Cf. *supra*, p. 461, note 41. Salome's presence in this and other lists in Luis' letters is not as easy to explain. There were three important Salomes in the Judeo-Christian heritage of the Second Commonwealth, Salome Alexandra, queen of Judea from 76–67 B.C.E.; Salome, Antipater's daughter, later in the first century B.C.E.; and Salome, wife of the tetrarch Herod Antipas, living in the first century C. E., and though not mentioned by name in the New Testament, reputed by Christian tradition to have been the daughter of Herodias responsible for Herod's beheading of John the Baptist (*Matthew* XIV:6, *Mark* VI:22). Judging from the sources available to Carvajal, the chances are he had the latter Salome in mind.

May my Lord, [the] God of mercy, send you good days, days of rest [and] days of salvation, my blessed ones, my lonely ones, my afflicted ones.

May my Lord God, send you good days, happy days, days of eternal rest and salvation, my blessed ones, my lonely ones, my afflicted ones.

May my Lord God send you good days, happy days of eternal rest, days of salvation, my blessed ones, my darlings.[104]

* * *

Four papers. [For]
Doña Francisca,
Doña Catalina,
Doña Anica,
[Doña Leonor].
The part concerning Leonor was taken out and collated and appears separately below.[105]
Presented on May 28, 1595.

[6]

[To] D[oña] Cata[lina]:

My dearest, may God Most High strengthen you and accompany you. When I do not write to you[106] I become depressed. Alas! The empty space [on the sheet] is being used up. But blessed be my God, who made pears and avocados [for us to use for messages]. [I write to you] although it makes me postpone and [even] omit some of my [spiritual] exercises and prayer[s], in which I ask the rich, merciful and liberal God to grant alms to us all. And I trust that He will give it to us in His usual way, so that all [of us], [yes, you] widows and orphans [too], will have enough to eat for the entire year.[107]

---

[104] This three-fold benediction, Messianic in character, may well have formed part of the Judaizers' liturgy. It is interesting to note the identity in content and the differences in form in the three sections.

[105] There were actually four letters for Leonor [nos. 9-12] written on the back of the sheets Luis used for letters to his other sisters. Luis could not afford the luxury of blank spaces and doubtless hoped that if the letters reached his other sisters, they could somehow get them forwarded to Leonor.

[106] Text: *el rato que no hago esto* . . . [p. 509].

[107] The allusion is not clear.

Yesterday a poor woman prisoner passed by. [She was] a Portuguese,[108] and from her voice I would guess that she was Manuel Diaz' wife.

May the Lord remember [us] all for His sake, even though we do not deserve it.

See if you can send me an olive pit;[109] I shall [then] understand that the woman with you [in your cell] is Portuguese. And if, in your name, you send me the pit of anything [else] I shall understand that she is Spanish. May the Shekinah[110] be with you and with all of us. Amen.

Look, dearest, when the [Messiah, the] Prince of Peace [comes],[111] — and it will be very soon — all the souls of the saints[112] — Abraham, Isaac, Jacob and Moses — will return to their bodies, and all of us will see each other then. O what marvels we shall see in Jerusalem!

*   *   *

[7]

For his mother:

Alas, my darling mother. May the Shekinah be with you. Alas, my scattered flock that are so dispersed.[113] May the mighty God protect you. Alas, my darling mother. May Adonay comfort you. (Alas, my dearest sisters. May the Father of orphans shelter you.) Alas, my beloved mother. May my Lord, God, see your affliction and be with you and bring you deliverance. May He cloak you and all your children[114] with His holy benediction. Alas, my wounded ones. May the Lord of the world heal you. Alas, my captive ones. May the Almighty free you from prison and sin, from confinement and hell. Amen. Amen. Amen. Amen. Amen. Amen. Amen.

*   *   *

[108] That is, a Portuguese New Christian Judaizer, or Marrano. By this time the term "Portuguese" had become synonymous in Spanish lands with the words "Judaizer" and "Jew." Cf. B. Lewin, El Santo Oficio en América (Buenos Aires, 1950), pp. 43–44. See also the notes to my translation of Samuel Usque's Consolation for the Tribulations of Israel (Philadelphia, 1965), p. 299, notes 1 and 16 to "Dedication and Prologue."

[109] See supra, p. 451.

[110] See supra, p. 469, note 90.

[111] Cf. Isaiah IX:5.

[112] Text: todas las almas santas . . . [p. 509].

[113] The flock, of course, is the family, scattered throughout the Inquisitional jail. Cf. supra, p. 451.

[114] Text: a todo tu fructo . . . [p. 510].

[8]

[To] D[oña] Anna [Anica]:

My dear girl, my tiny girl, my sick girl,[115] may the holy God, who holds healing in His hand, visit you and cure you. Amen. May His holiness provide me with some of this healing power that I may strengthen you; and you will thereby see how much your Lord and Father loves and cherishes you.

Since He now gives me an order to do so, I am letting you know, my angel, that the Lord has been showering endless favors upon me here in this cell. Blessed be His holy name. For seven days I had a honeycomb [full] of the sweetest honey, from the lips of the Most High. I tasted of it and ate of it and my eyes were almost [fully] opened. Then I saw [the meaning of] great mysteries which I did not know before, and joy entered my heart.

Take comfort, my darling, for you [too] shall taste of this joy. O, what delights [and] what sweetness the Lord has in store for you! Happy [are] you, happy your illness, happy your imprisonment, my innocent one, for you shall enjoy five garments of glory. [You shall be favored] like Benjamin was, over all the others, my little one.[116]

Be strong, and of good courage, apple of my eye, for this is what my Lord God says to you: "Your reward is being held in My hand. You were born in a happy hour. Fear not the insults of men." (Let neither prisons nor afflictions make you afraid.) "For the worm shall eat them like wool, and the moth shall devour them like a cloth."[117] (In vain do they dress the dead in a shroud, for the worms break through and eat its flesh.[118]) "So, My children," says God, "shall those who afflict you be, while the salvation which I will give you will endure forever.[119] I, [even] I shall console you, my tearful ones. Because of your sins[120] I was angry with you, but My quarrel

[115] See "Autobiography," *supra*, p. 315.

[116] Anica was the youngest of Luis' siblings as Benjamin was of Joseph's. Since Luis regarded himself as Joseph, the analogy was natural.

[117] *Isaiah* LI:7-8.

[118] This statement, not found in the biblical verse, was added by Joseph, quite clearly to depreciate the normal, peaceful burial which he, and in all probability, his mother and sisters could not look forward to. In all likelihood, no one in the family would rest in a shroud, Luis believed; they would all burn at the stake.

[119] The biblical quotation thus far is from *Isaiah* LI:6.

[120] The allusion is not only to the usual shortcomings of the family, common to all human beings, but also to its failure to uphold the ideals of Judaism. Perhaps it also alludes to the fact that, as titular Christians, they still bore the taint of the sin which, from the Jewish point of view, attached to their forbears who willingly or otherwise had converted to Catholicism.

with you is only for a moment; your peace will be everlasting.[121] Be glad and rejoice, for I have had compassion upon you, like a most loving and compassionate father.[122]

"There now. There now. That is enough. For I shall wipe away your tears.[123] I shall turn each one into a thousand joys. There will be no more deluge, no more imprisonment, no more illness. I swear it to you by My holy name. I, [even] I shall bring times of peace, in which I will be angry no more. My darlings, who [now] walk on sharp brambles along rough and arduous roads, I shall in recompense delight you in My orchards and gardens. O, My hungry and thirsty [daughters], I shall satisfy you with my sweetest manna. I shall give you waters of consolation [to repay] seven-fold for what was taken from you.[124]

"Hush, for if I put you in prison cells, it is because when you roam free, you are enticed by the world and are not sufficiently mindful of Me. I [therefore] place these thorns on the road which you are taking to [your] destruction, not to hurt you, but only to get you to turn to Me. Turn and come back to your Father, my daughters, for I [alone] am [the] living [God], and [the] Lord of life and death. Call me, and I shall come to your side, My afflicted daughters. Do not be dismayed, for I am near you; [and], My humble ones, I am the one who will save you. If I give you these purges, it is for your soul to emit the distempers which would destroy you — the sins, the acts of disobedience, the animosities, the passions of anger and envy. Let them come out, for I am the physician who cures you. I wounded you in order to heal you."

O darling, how I envy you for what you have suffered! How great a reward you will enjoy as a result! Patience, my angel.

*   *   *

[9]

[To Doña] Leonor:

May [the *Shekinah* of] Adonay be upon us. Amen.

My darling Rachel,[125] the Most High sent me ink again today. This is a miracle, for it is the second time I have received it [immediately] after receiving the paper containing the letter and the raisins

---

[121] *Isaiah* LIV:8.

[122] Text: *como padre amorosisimo apiadador vro. . . .* [p. 511].

[123] Cf. *Isaiah* XXV:8.

[124] Cf. *Isaiah* XII:3.

[125] Since Rachel was the patriarch Jacob's favorite wife, Luis, who was unmarried, conferred her name as a term of endearment, upon his favorite sister, Leonor.

you sent me. May the Lord's holy hand send you the consolations for which I humbly implore Him.

I have already heard you pass by [my cell today]. When you pass by [next time], turn your eyes toward my door. May your Creator turn His compassionate eyes toward you. Amen.

From your failure to write me, I gather that you cannot help it. Do not feel bad, and believe that when I stop my writing, it is for the same reason — and [also at times] to avoid being discovered and losing[126] the great privilege which the Lord my God gives us because of His goodness.

Today I sent a banana to [our] dear [sister] Catalina. I do not know whether you have tried to contact her[127] with your pears and avocados. When you do so, let it be very circumspectly, please.[128]

The pleasure which my God gives us in enabling us to communicate is a great joy for my spirit. Blessed be His holy name, for He moves the jailer [to provide me with the necessary materials]. Express your thanks to Him as I do.

Rejoice and be glad, my darlings, for there awaits you a banquet as splendid as the one I described to you. How can I begin to tell you about the delicious meals of your heavenly wedding feasts[129] — the rose-colored candy, the delicious appetizers and desserts? If a puny little earthly king like Ahasuerus[130] could make the kind of banquet you have read about, you can imagine what the banquet of the King of Kings will be like. What music [there] will [be]! What dancing! After eating that delicious food, that milk sweetened with God's love and wisdom, we shall all dance together with our saintly mother to the [words of the Psalm] "Let us sing for joy."[131] How we shall jump for joy! We shall be happier than the lamb or [fatted] calf.[132] What delightful castanets [we shall hear]! And the most blessed David will provide the music with his pleasant songs.[133] And we will all join the chorus of the angels and saints[134] and will dance to the words [of the Psalm] "Bless [the Lord], O my soul."[135]

O, how the Lord will move our tongues! What expressions of love we shall utter [to] that sweetest Lover of chaste and pure souls.

[126] Text: y por que no . . . nos quiten . . . [p. 512].
[127] Text: si las as combydado . . . [p. 512].
[128] Text: por cd. [caridad] . . . [p. 512].
[129] Text: aquella boda sancta . . . [p. 512].
[130] Esther I:3–8.
[131] Psalms XCVIII, especially v. 4.
[132] Text: no ay cordero ny bezerro harto que ansi brinque . . . [p. 512].
[133] Text: David donoso en sus cantares . . . [p. 512].
[134] Text: y todos en coro en compañya de los angeles y santos . . . [p. 512].
[135] Psalms CIII:1–2; CIV:1 and 35.

Now, in anticipation of such delight, who can be sad? Who need fear men and worms of flesh if he has the Creator of the world as his defender? What if we are imprisoned! What if we die! What if we are burned! For the fire of God's love will quench all [fires] and overcome all [obstacles]. He has given us His word through the saintly Isaiah, saying, "Fear not, My children, the seed of Jacob, My servant, My people, in whose hearts is My Law.[136] When you pass through the waters, I will be with you; and the seas [of your imprisonments and temptations] will not overwhelm you. When you pass through the fire, I will take you by the hand and the flame will not burn you."[137]

Be brave, be brave, for Zamora was not won without a long struggle,[138] and you get only what you pay for.[139] Woe betide him who is going to suffer in the next world! Happy he who suffers here for a [fleeting] moment that he might rest in the eternal years.

Look, my dearest. In the honeycomb[140] I saw that the *ẓiẓi[t]*[141] are each composed of four threads, representing the four seasons of the year — spring, winter, fall and summer. Each thread was folded to indicate the days and nights of all these seasons.

Throughout the seasons the soul enamored of its Creator must go about with His blessed Law in its heart and thoughts and words.[142]

Running through the lower part of the threads were four strands. Three of them each had three knots, separated one from the other. These represented the three ages [of man] — childhood, youth and old age —, in each of which the righteous soul must be occupied with God's blessed Law. The other two strands each had two little knots, one representing the world where we live, which has now lasted five thousand three hundred and forty-six years from the

---

[136] *Isaiah* XLI:8 and LI:7.

[137] *Ibid.*, XLIII:2.

[138] Text: *no se gano Zamora en una hora* . . . [p. 512], an old Spanish proverb denoting the difficulty involved in acquiring anything that is precious, and referring to the bitter struggles between Christians and Moslems for control of this strategic city during the period of the Christian Reconquest of Spain. See *Enciclopedia Universal Ilustrada (Espasa-Calpe)*, vol. LXX (Bilbao-Madrid-Barcelona, n.d. [193?], p. 940 [no author].

[139] See *supra*, p. 468, note 85.

[140] See *supra*, p. 460, note 35.

[141] Text: *ceci* . . . [p. 512], a word which does not occur in Latin or Nahuatl, or in Spanish with the connotation called for here. The context makes it clear that what is intended is the Hebrew word [ציצית] which Luis somehow learned, perhaps in the library of the monk (Pedro de Oroz). See *supra*, p. 461, note 38 and "Autobiography," *supra*, p. 301. For lack of better evidence, we have to posit that Luis' conception of the four threads derived from a combination of *Numbers* XVI:38 and *Deuteronomy* XXII:12, rather than from the rabbinic literature.

[142] *Deuteronomy* VI:5–7.

time when Adonay most high created it;[143] and the other little knot representing the happy world of King Messiah, the true Christ,[144] at whose coming the faithful among our dead will revive and will be taken along with those living at the time, to the Holy Land there to see and enjoy great marvels. Then the glorious Jerusalem will be rebuilt and the Temple of the Lord will be wondrously [constructed], for, as the angel showed Ezekiel, the city will be more than ten thousand leagues in space and size.[145]

How we shall dance there and sing! We were born in an auspicious hour. Blessed be Adonay forever. This is the portion of the servants of God, the heirs of His holy kingdom and glory.[146] These are the [people] sung [in the Psalm] "Happy are the righteous, etc."[147] These are the trees which will be transplanted from the earth below to the glory where [please God] may we find ourselves soon.[148] Be glad! Be glad! Felicitations! Felicitations! [We have] good tidings. Hallelujah! Amen.

Send me paper, dearest, if you have it, for the blessed Adonay has been providing me with ink; but do not send me what you need, for I will be angry.

I also saw wonders as I studied the saintly Elijah [sic!].[149] Some day I shall tell them to you, because I trust in my blessed God that I will be able to visit you one evening.

Please take what I first wrote you, and send it in your name to our dear sisters — very cautiously [and] at night. Wrap it in something first. Alas, mother of mine! Would that I could comfort you. May God, who can, do it for us.

Look! Our dear [sister], Mariana, is now well,[150] for I hear her pass by here untied and calm with Catalina. They are in your section. May Adonay be with [us] all.

* * *

---

[143] According to the traditional Jewish reckoning, Luis' calculations were a decade off. May, 1595 corresponded to the Hebrew year 5355.

[144] The word "Christ" is found in the form "Christus" [=Spanish "Cristo"] in the Vulgate, which was Luis' Bible.

[145] *Ezekiel* XL.

[146] Text: *esta es la encomienda* [sic!] *de los siervos de D.* . . . [p. 513].

[147] Cf. *Psalms* I; V:12; XXXIII:1; XXXIV:16; XCII; CXVIII:20; and *passim*.

[148] Cf. *ibid.*, XCII:13–15.

[149] Text: *del estudio del sto. Elias* [sic!] . . . [p. 513].

[150] See *supra*, p. 462, note 45 and "Autobiography," *supra*, p. 315.

[10]

[To] D[oña] L[eonor]:

My dear, may the Lord God send days of deliverance and comfort to you and all [our] poor people here.[151] Amen. They finally took my inkwell today. And although I have some ink, I cannot write well with it since it is made without gum. I therefore cannot write you as much as my heart would have wished. But I shall take comfort in being able to say hello [and] wish you a good day. Woe is me! May my Lord God give you the good days that I pray for on your behalf. Amen.

O, if you could only let me know whether Leonor Diaz[152] is still with you for your companionship. It would be a source of comfort for me to know that you two Leonors are together. Look! If it is so, why do you not send me a pin, and I shall know;[153] if not, take one of the olive pits I sent you, wrap it in something and send it on to me, and I shall understand [that she is] not [with you].

Do not be racked by imprisonment or fears, for whoever has the fear of God, the blessed Lord, who made the world, the heaven, the sea and the earth and all that is seen and unseen within them — if he truly believes in Him — he will not fear[154] [the] maggot.

The [kind of] person to whom the living [God] will give [true] death He tells us about through His spokesman, Isaiah, when He says: "Hear Me, My children, who know Me, children who love Me. Give ear to what I tell you, My servants, in whose hearts is My Law. Look at the heavens above and observe the earth here below. For the heavens shall vanish like smoke, and the earth like a torn garment, but the salvation which I shall give you will be eternal. Be consoled, for the reward of your righteousness is held in good hands, which are Mine.[155]

"My children, do not fear the insult[s] men have hurled upon you because of [your faithfulness to] My Law. Do not be afraid of their revilings, for the moth shall eat them up like a garment and the worm shall devour them like wool. (In vain is a corpse clothed in a shroud, for the worms break through it to devour its flesh.)[156] So, My children, shall they be who afflict you and revile Me. And My

[151] Text: *a toda la pobre compañia* . . . [p. 514].
[152] Text: *Dias* . . . [p. 514]. Cf. *supra*, p. 473.
[153] Text: *creerelo* . . . [p. 514].
[154] Text: *no teme* . . . [p. 514].
[155] Text: *que en buena mano, que es la mya esta* . . . [p. 514].
[156] See *supra*, p. 474, note 118.

salvation, which I shall give you, will be upon you forever and ever.[157] I, [even] I shall console you, my sorrowful [children]. Because of your sins I was angry with you and gave you this punishment. But rejoice, My children, for as your most loving Father, the One who pities you, I have had compassion upon you.[158] I, [even] I shall make peace with you, a peace[159] in which I will become angry no more. I shall direct My anger and punishment upon the heads of your oppressors. O, My hungry [children], hungry for [the] bread of My words, I shall satisfy you with [the] very sweet manna of My Law. O, My thirsty and afflicted [children], hush, for I shall repay you sevenfold for the waters of consolation which were taken from you.[160] Hush, for if I place you in prisons, it is because you are enticed by the world when you roam free [and] are not sufficiently mindful of Me. [Therefore] I place these thorns in your road — which you are taking to your destruction — not to hurt you, but in order that you might return to Me. Turn, My children. Return to your Father, for I am [the] living [God] and Lord of life and death. I wounded you in order to heal you.[161] I gave you purges to cleanse the soul of the distempers which threatened to destroy it. I bled you to cast out the angers, the envies, the grudges. Hush! Hush!, for I am your physician, a physician who, since He is your Father, gives you medicine from His own home, a physician who wounds and then heals. Hush, for I will heal you." Amen.

Send this to our dear [sister] Isabel.

*　　*　　*

[11]

[To] D[oña] Leonor:

Dearest, may the Lord of the world accompany you. My heart is afflicted with your[162] afflictions. [But] they are the road to heaven. May my God give you patience like Job's to bear with love whatever His divine majesty ordains.

My afflicted one, commend yourself well to our God and you will find comfort and relief. May He remove your yoke. Woe is me! May He give you His hand and help you carry your burden. And may He unburden you as I beg Him with my cries and tears. Amen.

---

[157] *Isaiah* LI:4–6.
[158] *Ibid.* LX:10. Cf. *ibid.*, LIV:8.
[159] Text: *pazes* . . . [p. 514].
[160] Cf. *Isaiah* XII:3 and *supra*, p. 475, note 124.
[161] Cf. *Jeremiah* XXX:17 and *Isaiah* XXX:26.
[162] Text: *sus* . . . [p. 515].

Dearest, if you send me a pin, I shall understand that you are not alone.[163] And if it comes stuck in a pear or anything else you happen to have around, I shall understand that you are pleased with your companion. I would be happy to know this for my own consolation. If you send it to me, ask the jailer, for the love of God, to give it to me in your name,[164] — like the salad [he gave me], which seemed as if it came from your hand. May My God and Lord give you eternal pleasure. Amen.

* * *

[12]

[To] Doña Leonor:

Have faith in God and pray[165] to Him, for the God of Israel lives, who freed Hananiah, Mishael and Azariah from the midst of the fire[166] and Daniel from the [lions'] den.[167]

I cannot determine from whom this note [I have received] comes. Alas, My darlings! Alas, My flock! Alas, My companions! May God, who can, protect you! If it is from my Anica [let me tell you that] you are not to blame [for her troubles] nor [are] any of you, for you have already atoned for [what happened in] the past.[168] In a word this [imprisonment] has been the will of the Most High, who wishes to take us to heaven and not to Castile. I regard this journey preferable to remaining [here, where we are] dying a thousand deaths each day and offending God.[169]

Woe is me! May He come to your rescue, as I entreat Him to. Let us not do evil and God will shower good things upon us. Patience,

---

[163] Text: *que estas con compañia* . . . [p. 515].

[164] Otherwise he would be unable to determine the sender: He would not know whether the pin came from her or one of his other sisters or even his mother.

[165] Text: *y oron.* . . . [p. 515].

[166] *Daniel* I:7 and III:19.

[167] See, in the *Apocrypha*, the *Story of Bel and the Dragon*, verses 31–42.

[168] Luis' older sisters apparently regarded their imprisonment and Anica's illness — and doubtless Mariana's as well — as punishments meted out by God for their failure to adhere zealously to Judaism in the past, particularly after they were first tried and released by the Inquisition. See "Autobiography," *supra*, pp. 300–301.

[169] That is, they are suffering excruciating physical and mental torture in their confinement, where, unable to practice Judaism fully, they are not fulfilling the will of God and are hence offending Him.

my angels. May the true God who guided Susanna[170] guide and deliver you.[171] Amen. Amen. Amen. Amen. Amen. Amen. Amen.

My cherished sister, may the Lord Most High guide you and save your soul and [your] life for His sake. Amen.

I have confessed the truth of God about myself alone, expecting the reward of Paradise and eternal glory. You, my darlings, were arrested only on suspicion. Thanks to the Lord, God, I have implicated no one falsely, for you are not at fault.[172]

[Yet] I do not really know what to tell you [to do]. I know that [for you] to deny [everything] is useless. If you ask for clemency, I think they will grant it to you a second time,[173] [that is] if you do not dare to jump into heaven across the passage of death, which must come sooner or later, at home or through the court. For this reason, with the help of my Lord God — may He be favorable to us — I have chosen to die for His holy Law in order to live eternally. I commend you to the guidance of the Lord God [Al]mighty. Amen.

If in her madness the little [sister of ours] has not uttered any lies about you,[174] there is no witness who can hurt you.

*   *   *

Fifth bundle of papers, presented by the jailer on May 30, 1595, in the afternoon, or rather, in the morning, [the] first [for] Doña Catalina and Doña Leonor, and two from Doña Leonor for her brother, Luis de Carvajal.[175]

[13]

[To Doña] Catalina:

Dear one, my life's pleasure, may God in His sweetness visit you and comfort you with one of His miracles. It would not be the first that I have seen [God do] for me, poor sinner that I am.

I received ink, and I can write to you.

---

[170] See the *Story of Susanna* in the *Apocrypha*. Susanna found herself in a situation where she could easily have committed the grave sin of adultery, but she staunchly resisted. Similarly, Luis counsels his sisters to resist the even greater sin of unfaithfulness to God.

[171] Text: *aconsejo . . . aconseje . . .* [p. 516].

[172] See *supra*, p. 455.

[173] See *supra*, p. 456.

[174] Actually these would not be lies but bald truths which Mariana did not hesitate to utter. See "Autobiography," *supra*, p. 315.

[175] From an editorial note by the Inquisition's scribe, we learn that the last two letters were taken out of the bundle.

I was arrested by the express will of the Most High and the accusation of the good Lucena.[176] Although in front of you, my darlings, I feigned to be something else, the truth is that my heart never departed from the Law of its God. I have been confessing this about myself alone, because to say otherwise would be to give false testimony.

You, my angels, were arrested on suspicion only. I have been defending your innocence, like a true brother. When I was down here [in this jail] alone, I spent my time rejoicing. [However], since I heard of your imprisonment, my spirit has been exceedingly troubled. Yet if I knew that you are bearing it with patience and love of God, I would jump for joy. For happy is the one who suffers in this evanescent life in order to enjoy the eternal contentment of the heavens which can be reached only by the road of hardships. And if anyone lacks them here on earth, let him say goodbye to [eternal] glory.

So, my angel, remember [this] in order to gain courage, for all the saints that are yonder awaiting us [once] passed through this world. And since our most gentle God and Lord wants to do so much good for us, let us not obstruct Him with [our] impatience. Abraham, our holy father, bound his son hand and foot, and the blessed Isaac, marvelously obedient, awaited the knife's blow. Courage, courage, my beloved, for at that very moment the angel of the Lord was approaching, carrying the ram that was [to be] offered in Isaac's stead. It is not God's will, no, that Isaac should die;[177] rather [it is His will] to give you this [same] merit by putting you to the test in order to bestow upon you the prize of life eternal, for this [life] is nothing but one long death and torment.

[Have] faith like Sarah, who gave birth in old age. (What power God has to bring forth laughter from weeping!)[178] Fall down at God's feet with holy penitence like Asenath; He will not deny you His consolation. Pray, pray, like Hannah and Esther [when they were] in danger. [Have] courage, like the blessed Judith and Salome. O blessed martyr, nail the seductive enemy in his temples, as Jael did to Sisera. And when you have left your imprisonment in Egypt you will sing victoriously with Miriam and Deborah in Paradise, where they await you to dance in chorus when you are crowned by the Lord.

There now, there now, my tearful ones, be consoled, be consoled;

---

[176] See *supra*, p. 458.
[177] Isaac in this context refers to Luis' sisters.
[178] This is a play on the pun in *Genesis* XXI:3-6.

for you will be going like the Queen of Sheba to visit the most hand-some and wise King of the angels, to see His sumptuous palaces and gardens of Paradise [and] to eat His savory meals.

What pretty skirts He will give you, [and] jackets [and] head-dress [and] garlands of heaven's fine gold! What fragrant waters you will be bathed in! How great [will be] your joy as you all dance together [to] the [Psalm] "Let us sing with joy!"[179] What dances [there will be and how we shall] dance and leap for [joy]! O, how you will be embraced by that most blessed Father [of yours], in whom you have believed and trusted.

There now. There now. If you would [but] raise the eyes of faith to those joys, everything down here [on earth] would appear like filth swept by the wind. May my good Lord God and His good angel open your eyes as He opened [those of] Tobit [the] saint.[180] May He heal you and free you as [He freed] Sarah.[181] Joseph was in prison for thirteen years but then became a prince. There now. There now. The God who freed Daniel from the [lions'] den and the three saints from the fire is [the] living [God]. There now. He has given us His word of faith that He will deliver us if we have faith and patience. May the Lord give you and [all of] us the faith and patience he gave Job. Amen.

I wish I could detail for you what the blessed God has done for me. On account of His truth [which I professed] I was kept in a dungeon where [I saw light only when] I was brought food by the light of a candle. Now His holy hand has taken me out of there and I am [in a cell] where day and night I can look out a little window and see the sky. I shall put a cloth in the window for you to see when you pass by, my dear.

What shall I tell you about? For a week I had a honeycomb full of the sweetest honey from the lips of the Most High.[182] I ate of it and I have seen and enjoyed [the secret of] great mysteries. I wish I could tell you all about them.

I trust that the Lord will take me to see you one evening that I might console you.[183]

I am [now] in shackles; they are removed once a week — by my God — so that I can bathe. [But] irons[184] cannot separate me from

---

[179] Cf. *Psalms* XCV:1; XCVI:1, XCVIII:1, CXLIX:1.

[180] *Tobit* XI:10-15.

[181] *Genesis* XX:14.

[182] See *supra*, p. 460, note 35.

[183] That is, God will make it possible. It seems that such secret visits, if rare, did take place.

[184] Text: *yerros* [for *hierros*] . . . [p. 518].

my sweetest delight, my Father, for He has bound my soul with the links and pretty gems of the rich chain of His affection.

Patience, my dear, for our reward is coming soon. I have great assurance of our [coming] glory, in the words[185] of the true God.

There now. There now. For once we have scaled the hill of this jail, we shall behold our glory!

There now. Our God is waiting for us. What delightful jousts and tournaments there will be on our arrival in the true kingdom!

Happy the day on which you were born. [Happy] the bread you have eaten and the water you have drunk.

And since you are going to see your God and King, do not go empty-handed. Bring Him a present, a fragrant bouquet of fresh flowers — faith and patience and prayer — [nurtured] in these [very] prison cells. May He who created us give us favor to do so, as I entreat [Him] in my cries. Amen.

* * *

[14]

[To] D[oña] Leonor:

My darling, if you have blank paper and can write me a note, put a dish to [the flame of] your candle [and let soot accumulate. Then] take a feather and write with the soot like ink. And let me know if you are alone or not and if you have any news about our gentle mother who is near you; for when I sent her the raisins you had sent me, they took it [all] upstairs [to the Inquisitors' chambers]. The edge of my [makeshift] pen hurt my fingers greatly, though it brought great consolation to my spirit. For, since we have been companions in affliction, I realized that for the price of a moment of death,[186] we shall be companions in Paradise.

I thought I would write only until I touched the feather of the pen, but since our good God and Lord has been showing us such abundant kindness [and permitted me to use the little that is left], let us show Him many thanks, faith and patience for the sake of His name.

There now, there now, you warriors of the Lord. [Have] courage in your battle, like Judah and Salome. [Have] confidence like Susanna, when she was unjustly being led to her death. [Show] repen-

---

[185] See *supra*, p. 458, note 16.

[186] Text: *un memento* [*sic!*] *de muerte* . . . [p. 519], a fascinating error, clearly scribal.

tance like Asenath, and humbly [utter a] prayer[187] like Hannah [and] Esther. [Have] faith like your saintly mother, Sarah, who conceived in old age. For out of danger and struggle the Lord draws forth victory. Pierce Satan and his temptations in both temples, as Jael [did] to Sisera. Then when you have escaped from the flood and swells of Egypt you shall join Miriam and Deborah in singing songs to the Most High in Paradise, where they await you to take you [to your heavenly coronation] with delightful singing and with charming dances and fiestas. They will don new crowns on the day of your coronation, when you receive yours with honor and blessing from the Most High. May they be granted to you for His name's sake.

O, how little is our suffering on earth when compared to the reward that awaits us! Whenever a new knight, [meaning] a new faithful soul, comes to that splendid city ruled by the King and Emperor of the angels, to profess the holy religion through which one ___ find the blessed Father,[188] the angels and saints prepare elaborate jousts, splendid dances, concerts and tournaments.

There now, there now, my crowned queens. Happy the day when you were born! [Happy] the bread you have eaten! [Happy] the earth you have trodden! [Happy] the torments you have endured! [Happy] the womb where you were formed! For like the Queen [of] Sheba you will be traveling from this lowly Earth to the holy court and [heavenly] city of Jerusalem. [You will be going] to see the King of Kings and Lord of Lords, to see His sumptuous palaces, His orchards [and] gardens of Paradise, to delight in His wisdom and beauty, to see the numberless angels and saints who are His handsome pages.

There now, there now. Prepare presents to give Him when you kneel down at His feet. In your cells [preserve] the charm of patience: it is more fragrant than myrrh and it brings immortality to the soul. Prepare a bouquet for His holiness to smell. And, my dear girls, be sure that it is properly arranged, for our Father, to whom you will be offering it, is most holy. Let it be composed of all kinds of flowers and of all the colors of marigold — of faith, hope, charity, patience, humility, meekness, innocence, chastity and perseverance, for these are the flowers of Paradise. For flowers [like these], never wither; they exude a rich fragrance before the Lord Most High, even [though they grow] amidst thorns and troubles.

How God will reward you for your present! He will say to you — it seems my ears can hear it now — "[Let] My blessing [fall] upon such daughters, a blessing of eternal glory, a blessing of life and peace." How I would envy you if I had to remain here [on earth].

---

[187] Text: *y oración y humilde* . . . [p. 519].
[188] Text: *prelado* [for *pdre. (padre)*] . . . [p. 519].

There now, my little girls, the Lord has not forgotten your sackcloth [or] your cilices [or] your prayers [or your] fasts and penances. He brought you here [to this jail] for that reason — in order to give you your full reward. He remembers well how you went about barefoot on the cold earth bringing alms to the poorhouses.[188a] Do you know how He will reward you for it — according to what I have been told? Like a doting parent who, on hearing his little child utter a clever word, rushes to him [and] smothers him with hugs and kisses, [so will He reward you].

There now, there now, my tearful and afflicted [darlings]. You have a good Father. He will take the kerchief of His consolations from His pocket and will wipe away your tears. O, how He will embrace you! He will say to you, "Weep no more, weep no more, my daughters." O! My shepherd, the shepherd of Israel, who has my soul aflame for His love, will say to you, "Come, come, my darling ewes. Show [Me], show [Me], where did the dog bite you? O! And how you will [each] answer joyously, "Father, the bite cut to our souls. And [do You know] why [he bit me] — a curse be upon him? He attacked me and bit me a thousand times because I was calling Your name, because I was going to perform Your commandment, [because I was about] to fulfill Your Law."

"So, my daughters," [God will answer] — and with a thousand embraces and as many kisses — "[do not worry], for this will pass. Hush, for I shall avenge you. Now take this rich chain; let it bind you for ever in love of Me." (How fortunate you were born! How happy your lot!) "Angels," [He will say], "bring My daughters, bring My betrothed some of those rich robes I have told you to make. Exchange their skirts of ordinary cloth for skirts of white satin; their plain jackets for new ones that have seven layers of brocade. Set their hair beautifully and put rich headdresses and garlands on their heads. Leave no finger without a ring, for they have suffered so much on My behalf. And before you dress them, be sure to bathe them in luxurious, scented waters, for they have to eat at My table." Amen.

I am out of ink. Hallelujah.

* * *

Sixth paper.

(In the audience of the afternoon of the first of June, 1595, the jailer made presentation of this paper, which had been given to him by Luis de Carvajal for his sister, Doña Leonor.)

[188a] This may be a veiled allusion to their proselytizing activities on behalf of Judaism.

[15]

[To] D[oña] Leonor:

May the *Shekinah* be upon us. Amen.

May my God give you and all our poor and afflicted family days of favor, comfort and salvation. Amen.

The great love I have for you does not let me allow a day to go by without my greeting you. Blessed [be] Adonay for ever, who miraculously gives us such great refreshment in this abyss.

Yesterday was not one of those good and holy days: therefore there was no special banana [in which to enclose a message] for you.

I think that since most of the abundance of my affection is for you, it is well for you to be jealous, for jealousy is the smoke of the fire of love. May the [love] of the most blessed Adonay ever burn in our souls. Amen.

My pilgrim and holy wayfarer, [who is] destined to go to Paradise, where dwells the Source of all goodness, I have thought [it would be] proper, in the name of my Lord God, Adonay, to send you a staff on which you can lean and support yourself in on your ascent [to Paradise], [a staff] cut from the tree of life, from Sacred Scripture [itself]. Take it in the hand of your memory and grasp it every day, and with the favor of the Lord, you will not fall into this temptation.[189]

[Remember that] the Lord God tried Abraham and said to him, "Abraham, Abraham, take your beloved son, Isaac, and come and offer him in sacrifice to Me upon one of the mountains which I shall show you." On hearing the divine command, our holy father Abraham arose early in the morning, before dawn, saddled his ass, cut firewood for the sacrifice and took along Isaac, his son, and two servants of his house; and he went as, the Lord had commanded him, toward the holy mountain, Moriah, where the holy Temple was later erected.[190]

When he drew near, he said to his servants, "Wait for me here, while I and my son climb to the summit of the mountain: and after we have worshiped the Lord God, we shall return to you." And he took the firewood and put it on the shoulders of his beloved son;

[189] By temptation, Luis again seems to mean despair or religious doubt. Cf. *supra*, p. 468, note 80 and note 88.

[190] These details stem from the rabbinic tradition of which Luis became aware by reading the Latin commentaries based on Hebrew sources in the library of the monk, whose name was Pedro de Oroz. See "Autobiography," *supra*, pp. 301–303.

and he took the fire in one hand and the knife in the other, the two of them walked on together.

(Alas! For [the sake of] those devout and faithful steps may the Lord accompany us in ours.)

Then Isaac said to his father, "My father?" [And] Abraham answered him, "What is it, my darling son?" He said to him, "We are carrying firewood, a knife and fire. What about the sacrifice which is to be offered as a whole offering to the Lord, our God? I do not see any, father." Abraham replied, "The Lord God will provide a victim for us to offer Him in sacrifice, my son."

(Alas! Just as the Lord provided [one] at that time, so, Holy Father, for Your sake, provide for us now a sacrifice of faith and patience and obedience. Amen.)

When they arrived at the top, Abraham took his son, bound him hand and foot, placed him upon the firewood on the altar, took the knife and was about to strike the [lethal] blow when an angel of the Lord stopped him, calling out and saying [to him in the name of the Lord], "Abraham, Abraham, do not touch the child. My will is not that Isaac die, no, but only to give you the wages of eternal merit with Me. You have shown how much you love Me and revere Me, because for My sake you did not even spare your child."

Then Abraham saw the ram which the Lord had prepared, and he offered it in place of his son. And after he had offered it, the angel of the Lord called to Abraham a second time and said to him [in the name of the Lord], "By Myself do I swear," says the Lord, "because you have done this, you will not be without an abundant reward. [Because] you have not spared a son for My sake, therefore I swear by My name that I will give you more sons than there are stars in the heavens or sands on the shore of the sea. Your offspring shall possess the gates of their enemies and in your progeny (that is, in the King Messiah) may all the generations of the earth be blessed."

Abraham worshiped the Lord and believed in Him.

And the Lord said to Isaac, "Because you have obeyed My commandment and the voice of your father, I shall fulfill all My benedictions through you." Blessed [be] Adonay. Amen.

I wanted to explain to you some of the deep implications of this subject, dear, but, alas, it is already twelve o'clock and even many sheets of paper would be insufficient. Suffice for now those that fit [on the sheet I am now sending you]:

Consider that God leads his loved ones through temptations, and through their struggle with them, to the victory of [heavenly] glory. After curing Tobit, who, [though] blind, had been occupied in such good works [the holy angel explained to him,] "Because God loved you greatly and you were pleasing to His majesty, He ordained, and it became necessary, that you be tested with temptation."[191]

My burdened [darlings], when the burdens of imprisonment and affliction constrain you, kneel down before the Lord and entreat Him for the sake of the burden which the blessed, innocent Isaac bore, that He aid you to bear yours, and give you faith and obedience that you do not fall. And [ask] this not for yourselves alone, but for everyone close to you. For the Lord is most compassionate, and He orders us in His holy Law to help [even] the animal [that has] fallen under its load. Tell Him all this in your humble prayer. Ask Him for His hand, for He will give it to you. Consider the devotion and faith of these saints [Abraham and Isaac] and their obedience. Had Abraham been someone else, he would have said, "So, Lord, did You give me a son in my old age to show me this pain?" No, [he said] nothing of the kind. [Instead] he said, "Let faith always abide with God, for everything is for [one's] greater merit." Just realize that while Abraham was binding his blessed son, the angel of the Lord was busily preparing and tying the ram which was [to be] sacrificed in his stead.

Just consider the great reward [Abraham attained] for [offering] one child — [the promise to have] as many as the sands and the stars. [How much greater will our reward be!] O my dear, how little it is that we are suffering and how great [is] the reward which the Lord God will give us.

I swear to you that the other night [in my dreams] I saw you wearing a splendid robe, studded with golden loops, and a golden chain, with big and pretty beads around your neck. I therefore trust in God — if you have faith — to see your holy soul all decked in glory. Amen. Amen.

* * *

Seventh Paper.
(On the third of June, in the morning, the jailer presented this paper given to him by Luis de Carvajal for his sister, Doña Anica.)

[16]

D[oña] Anica[192]

[To] Doña Anica:

My Ana, apple of my eye, darling of my heart, may my mighty God and Lord visit you. May He strengthen you and our entire

---

[191] *Tobit* XII:6–15 and 17–20, paraphrased.
[192] The text mentions Doña Anica twice, in the positions seen above.

holy family, as I, poor sinner, entreat Him day and night with my continuous cries and tears.

By a miracle of God, I received ink and this little bit of paper on which to write to you. Although, due to my sins, you are [all] removed from my sight, you are always standing before the eyes of my imagination — especially you, my little wounded girl, my little orphan girl, [who is] favored by my God. May you be protected by His mercies.

My dearest, I was arrested by the express will of my God and through the accusation of the good Lucena,[193] for the great[er] good of my soul. [But] you, my angels, [were arrested] on suspicion only; and if your innocence is put to pain, consider it a most certain sign, not of [the] dislike, but rather of the great love which my Lord God, your celestial Father, has for you.

Be glad and rejoice, dear child, for this is the road to Paradise and [the] glory which awaits you. This is the way trodden by all the saints who are now flourishing there. O, martyr of mine, God will see to it that pretty strands of pearls and Ophir's gold — such pretty chains, such [pretty] jewels — are put around your afflicted neck, in recompense for [all] that you have suffered inside it.

There now, there now, innocent one, [have] patience, for I will soon be asking a reward from you for giving you this good news.

Be glad in anticipation of the glory which awaits you. [Show] repentance, my angel, like Asenath, and the [angel] of the Most High will come to bring you honeycombs of sweet honey and consolation [taken] from the honey of Paradise.

There, my child, virtuous like Ruth, the wings of the Father of orphans will [surely] shelter you. Fight, fight your troubles and afflictions like the saints Deborah, Judith and Salome, O blessed martyr, and you will be blessed by God Most High.

There now, there now, beautiful one, beautify your soul and you will be beloved [of God] like Rachel, and fertile like Leah — in the bearing of virtues — and faithful like Sarah.

There now, my little one, for the medicine of the mighty God in the guise of His holy angel Raphael, will come to heal us, as [he came] to Sarah and Tobit.

Cry out. Cry out and pray with Hannah and Esther. Wait for God with the saintly Susanna, for He will free you from false testimony.

There now, my beloved, [do not cry]; for all these saints will dance in Paradise at your wedding, when the sovereign King of glory takes your soul as His bride.

---

[193] See *supra*, p. 458, note 14 and p. 455, note 8.

There now, there now, my Queen [of] Sheba. Get ready, for you are about to go to the holy, [heavenly] city of Jerusalem, to see the most handsome King of the angels, a king full of wisdom. What beautiful things He is going to show you — the groves and orchards and gardens and vineyards and muscats; the flowers and scented springs; the mountains covered with lilies; the brooks flowing with milk and honey! There now; your troubles and imprisonment are the road [to all this]. [Therefore], my dearest, in faithful devotion, prepare a bouquet on this lowly earth to bring as a present to your Lord and Father, a bouquet of all flowers — of patience, faith, hope, chastity and obedience — for these [are] the flowers of Paradise, [the] blooms which never die. How fragrant the scent of these marigolds before God! Do not worry, for He will reward you for your present with the payment of eternal bliss. What pretty clothes He will give you to wear — skirts of pretty silk; jackets woven of rich brocade; pretty, embroidered headdress and garlands of fresh flowers! What festivities [there will be for you], with dancing and lavish entertainment! You will delight to music [played] by saintly cherubim and you will hear angels [sing], if you would [now but] humble yourselves and pray to God, and have [true] patience. For, with such hope, who can be afflicted? Who will not [rather] dance in his prison cell?

There now, there now. Felicitations, felicitations. [Be] glad. [Be] glad. Let [your] anxieties and sighing cease, for my Lord God has revealed some of His great wonders to me here. To Him I commend you, my angels. May He visit you and deliver you. Amen.

Though unworthy, I am a servant of the Most High.

*   *   *

(The following letters are found without any designation [as to addressee] in the original.)

[17]

May the *Shekinah* be upon us.

Dearest, may my God grant you a good night and days of deliverance. Unless my heart deceives me, I understand from the tokens you sent me that your cellmate is a Negress or a mulatto. If she [really] is a mulatto, as I imagine, I am a good guesser.

May my Lord God provide [for] all your needs and ours. But whenever one's spirit is accompanied by the recollection of its most handsome Creator, it has nothing more to want. May He be with you and with all of us. Amen.

I laughed heartily at your prediction.[194] May good prophecies come to you.

Consider, angel, in the honeycomb I saw, that all the kingdoms and wealth of this life do not amount to a sixtieth of what the holy [and] blessed God will give us. This sea of [our] imprisonment will [surely] lead to a good port!

[Be] glad, [for] in the kingdom of the Prince of Peace, you women [now childless] will bear righteous sons until the number [of the righteous] is filled.

And consider [that there] the birds will come to our call and the fish and wild animals will obey what[ever] we tell them. What a great glory awaits those who believe and trust in the God of truth! May He enable us to reach this truth. Amen.

* * *

[18]

Look, beloved of God. May [the] *Shekinah*, which is His supreme Presence, be with you and all [of us]. Amen.

You should know that His most holy majesty has been showing me abundant mercies here. Trust in Him and call upon Him and submit to Him, and you will see that He will give you[195] gifts worthy of His hand.

He took me out of a dungeon where I [had] spent three weeks. Blessed be He and [blessed be] His name. Now I can see the sky day and night through a little window.

For a week I had [before me] a honeycomb with the sweetest honey from the lips of the Most High.[196] I ate of it and my eyes have been almost [completely] opened. There I saw [the meaning of] great mysteries. I saw part of this in marvelous announcements of times to come and [the] redemption which awaits us. At the coming of the star of Jacob[197] all our dead, that is those who have kept living faith with the living God in this life, the foundation of life eternal, will resurrect to enjoy His kingdom. Those who [now] have knowledge of Him in their hearts shall [in the meantime] be transferred [when they die] from this lowly earth to heaven.

---

[194] The prediction seems to have been made in a letter his sister had sent him.
[195] Text: *que os dara daraos dadivas* . . . [p. 526].
[196] Cf. *supra*, p. 460, note 35.
[197] That is, the Messiah. See *Numbers* XXIV:17.

I also saw that the *ẓiẓi[t]* signifies the domain of the children of the Most High, and [I saw] the wonders its parts represent. I can now tell you those that are pertinent [to you]:

(Be consoled, my martyrs, for we shall soon see each other [in Paradise]. Earnestly entreat the Lord to open your eyes, and you will behold hidden wonders, which are the sweetness He gives His children to taste)."

I saw that the *ẓiẓi[t]* is composed of four threads,[198] each of them folded over. The threads themselves represent the four seasons of the year — spring, winter, fall and summer. The folds represent the days and nights of all these seasons: in all of these a man, when working, speaking and meditating [should have his mind fixed] upon the blessed Law of his God.

These threads had five strands crossing over them below. Three of these had three knots each, representing three ages. [The first stood for the three ages] of the righteous man — childhood, youth and old age — in all of which man should be absorbed in this blessed exercise [of God's Law] and ruminate, like a clean animal, on its most fragrant and savory anise. Then, the second of the three, with its three knots, signifies the [three] epochs of the blessed Law of Nature written on the holy tablets, and [culminating] in the coming of the Messiah, the true Christ,[199] by the grace of the Lord, God, which He will bring into our inmost hearts. [The thread with] the other three symbolized the three ages of the synagogue, that is, the ecclesia of the holy blessed God. It is now in the [period of its] old age, when it will be renewed like the eagle, because it is now five thousand, three hundred and forty-six years since Adonay Most High created the world.[200]

The other [strands had] two knots. They [symbolized] the present world and the coming world of grace.

This is the representation of the children of the holy God, concerning whom we sing "Happy is the man"[201] and "Blessed are the righteous."[202] Blessed [is] the tree — the soul — which is truly planted by this river. It will always be green and luxuriant, bearing fruit and flowers in the springtime of prosperity and [weathering] the winter of troubles and adversity with holy patience, faith, obedience and prayers.[203]

---

[198] See *supra*, p. 477, for the parallel to this passage.

[199] See *supra*, p. 478, note 144.

[200] See *supra*, p. 478, note 143.

[201] *Psalms* I:1. Carvajal gives the Latin, *"Beatus vir."*

[202] Cf. *supra*, p. 478, note 147.

[203] Cf. *Jeremiah* XVII:8.

How sweet is the scent of these marigolds before the Most High! They [can] secure favors from Him [as] great as those obtained through Noah's sacrifice.[204] Look! When you read the *Shema* and come to [the words] "You shall love [the Lord your God with all your heart, all your soul and all your might]," recite all the Ten most holy Commandments and then [continue] with "And these words shall be . . ."[205]

I received this revelation when I was in the dungeon. It is a revelation of the Most High.

Pray, pray, for our God lives and will live forever.

* * *

[19]

[To Doña] Catalina:

Dear one of the living God, may the shield of His truth be around you and shelter you and our entire sad family in this [time of] temptation. Since my Lord God has not unmiraculously given me the wherewithal in this abyss, it seems proper[206] that I should send you a staff cut from the tree of His sacred writ so that, by resting your weakened spirit upon it,[207] you can better climb the difficult slope of solitude and imprisonment to the summit [of the mountain of] the glory of Paradise. Through His kindness He holds out [this goal] to those souls seeking to climb to its enjoyment by grasping His holy mercy with faith and patience.

Here, then, is the staff. Take it daily in the hand of your memory so that you will not [slip and] fall.

The Lord tried Abraham and said to him, "Abraham, Abraham, take your beloved son, Isaac, and come to offer him as a sacrifice to Me upon one of the mountains which I shall show you."

Hearing the divine command, our holy father Abraham arose early in the morning, before dawn, saddled his ass and cut the firewood for the sacrifice. And he took along his son, Isaac, and two servants of his and went, as the Lord had commanded him, toward the holy mountain Moriah, where the holy Temple was later erected.[208]

(Alas! May the Lord, God, for [the sake of] the merit of those

---

[204] *Genesis* VIII:20–22.
[205] *Deuteronomy* VI:4–6.
[206] Text: *cosa de vida* . . . [p. 527].
[207] Text: *animada [arrimada] a el la flaqueza de tu espiritu* . . . [p. 527].
[208] See *supra*, p. 488, note 190.

sacred steps, so faithful[ly] and diligent[ly taken], accompany us in all the steps of our tribulation. Amen.)

So, when they arrived near [Mount Moriah], Abraham said to his servants, "Wait for us here, while my son and I go to the top of the mountain [to worship]; and as soon as we have finished worshiping the Lord, we shall return. And he took the firewood and put it on his son's shoulders, while he took the fire in the one hand and the knife in the other. And the two of them walked along together.

(Alas! For [the sake of] that burden which our holy and innocent father [Isaac] bore [upon his shoulders], may the Lord aid you to bear your burdens; and may He give you His helping hand. And when you fall from exhaustion, may He raise you [to your feet].)

And the blessed Isaac said to his father, "My father?" Abraham answered, "What is it, my son?" Said Isaac, "We are carrying firewood, a knife and fire, but, father, where is the sacrificial animal that is to be offered to the Lord, our God, for I do not see it?"

Abraham answered him, "My darling son, the Lord will provide an animal for His sacrifice."

(Alas! Just as God provided then and regularly provides in our greatest needs, so, for your sake, our holy father, [Isaac], may He now provide and come to our rescue in our trouble and distress. Amen.)

When they arrived at the crest of the mountain, Abraham said to his son, "You should know, my son, that the Lord our God has commanded me to offer you as a sacrifice to His divine majesty. Blessed and fortunate are you, for since dying is [the] certain [fate] of all the children of Adam, you are dying in a noble way by being offered to the God most high, the Lord of life eternal. I am not angry at you, my son, but rather envious, for you are being sacrificed to a good Lord."

The saintly Isaac answered like a [worthy] son of such a blessed father (O holy people, O holy conquistadors of the Kingdom of Heaven which awaits us!) "Certainly, my father, since the Lord so commands it, let His will be fulfilled, for here I am, obedient and prepared. I entreat you only that you put a band in front of the eyes of my fragile flesh that I should not see the knife as you deal the blow, in order that I should not [try to] flee. Since my soul and will are so obedient, let not [the flesh] stand in their way."

Father and son embraced and said good-bye with copious tears of faithfulness. Another father might have said, "So, O Lord, was it for this purpose that You gave me a son in my old age, to show me such great pain? It would have been better had You not given him to me."

No, there was none of this lack of trust in our holy father, but only a living faith in the Lord, that He would fulfill the promises which He had made to him, and that although he sacrificed his son, God could revive him.

Therefore Abraham took his son and bound him hand and foot.

(Alas! For [the sake of] that saintly [lad who was] bound and, for [the sake of] his faithful father, may my Lord God give us patience, faith and obedience with which to imitate them by offering ourselves all to His holiness. Amen.)

Then Abraham put Isaac upon the firewood on the altar he had prepared. And he raised the knife in his hand to cut his throat.

(With what humility did the saintly one, [Isaac,] await it.)

And as the blow was coming down, the angel of the most blessed God called to Abraham and stayed his arm with a powerful word. He said to him, "Abraham, Abraham, do not dare to touch the child, for no, it is not My will, says God, that Isaac die, but [it is] rather [My will] to give you this [way of attaining] eternal merit for My glorious reward."

([Have] courage; [have] courage, my imprisoned [darlings], for God does not wish your death, but rather, by way of your present path, to give you the true [life, the] life eternal.)

Then the angel said [in the name of God]: "You have shown how you love Me, because for My sake you did not hold back your own son. Since you have done this, you shall not be without ample reward."

(O, how little is what we are able to do, and how great [is] the glorious reward which the Lord promises and gives if we have faith in Him.)

Then Abraham saw a ram which the Lord had prepared, which was caught in the thicket; and he offered it to the Lord in place of his son. And when he had made the offering, the angel of the Lord called to him a second time and said, "By Myself have I sworn, says the Lord; because you have done this, because, for My sake, you have not held back your son whom I gave you, I shall give you [not only] him, but, in addition, as many children as there are stars and sands; and your seed shall possess the gates of its enemies; and in it, that is, in Christ[209] the true Messiah, shall all the nations of the earth be blessed and led to a knowledge of Me."

Abraham worshiped the Lord and [he and his party] went homeward in great joy.

There now, there now, my martyrs. [Have] faith in temptation,

[209] See *supra*, p. 478, note 144, and p. 494, note 199.

and you will not die. [Just] consider, my darlings, that while the
saintly Abraham was binding his son, the angel of the Lord was going
about preparing the ram which was [to be] sacrificed in [Isaac's]
stead. [Therefore,] bend the knee to God. Ask for His helping hand,
for He will give it to us, for it is the wont of His great mercy to come
to His people's aid in their greatest danger. May He come to your
aid [as well]. Amen.[210]

*   *   *

[20]

[To Doña] Mariana:

May the *Shekinah* of Adonay be upon [all of] you and me.
You shall live. You shall live, [all] my loved ones who are destined
to die.[211]

[Be] glad, [be] glad, blessed martyr of the living God. May He
visit you with His mercy and strengthen you.

By a miracle of His I received ink today and this little piece of
paper to write you. For though I am deprived of your presence and
sweet company because of my sins, I always see you before my eyes;
and these are bathed in tears for your afflictions as often as my heart
wells with joy; for the Most High opens my eyes to consider and
see that ours is the sure road to glory, and that He is bringing you
there through His goodness alone. And since to the right and to the
left are the dangers of fire and deep water, which you heard about
in [the book of] the holy Ezra,[212] let us not depart from [the narrow
path] through lack of faithfulness or impatience. Rather let us give
infinite thanks to the Lord, our God, for He takes note of small
worms like us and tries us like our holy patriarchs.

I have confessed [to the keeping of] His truth in my own case
alone in order not to give false testimony about anyone [else].

Now this truth [of God] is a strong shield in the chains of my imprisonment, and with it I await the day of my glory, when, with the
help of my Lord, God, I shall see myself at His feet.

You were arrested on suspicion only. And since we see clearly
that it is the will of the Most High to bring you through these cells
to His glorious Paradise without the meaningless circuities of

---

[210] Text: *amen ansi* . . . [p. 530].
[211] Text: *vivireis muertos mios* . . . [p. 530].
[212] *II Ezra* [=*IV Esdras*] VII:6–8. Cf. *supra*, p. 469, note 92.

Castile,[213] where we were planning to go, let our will not thwart His, for the exchange is so beneficial, despite the fact that the slope and loneliness of this jail are in the middle of our road. But since we possess the excellent staff of divine promises to climb [this hill], let none [of us] be dejected. And when you feel that you[r spirits] are tired and fatigued, as has happened to me, bend your knees literally and figuratively[214] and ask the most mighty God for courage; for He gives it and promises it with marvelous words through His servant Isaiah. "You tired and wounded ones of His," he [Isaiah] says, "Just as it is true that His exalted holiness dwells in eternity and in His glorious sanctuary, so does He dwell with the afflicted, to quicken the hearts of His humble ones and to animate their spirits."[215]

"I, even I," He [God] says, "I Myself will comfort them, as One who can; and I shall have compassion upon My poor and timorous children. The heaven is the seat of My glory and the earth My footstool large. Upon whom shall the eyes of My greatness look if not upon the wounded [and the] humbled, and the crushed who fear My words."[216]

He says, "My children, children of Abraham, My friend, who acknowledge Me, children of My chosen one, Israel, in whose hearts is My holy Law, do not fear the injury of men, or their revilings; for the worm shall devour them like a garment and the moth shall consume them like wool; but upon you shall come My eternal salvation. The heavens shall vanish like smoke and the earth shall grow old and crumble like a worn garment, but the salvation which I have promised you shall not fail: it shall be forever upon you."[217]

So says He who gave laws to the sun, skies, nights and days, whose arm dried the sea and the water of the impetuous abyss, the One who made roads in the deep to take his freed [children] across.[218]

There now, there now. [Be] glad, [be] glad. Rejoice and be happy. Skip and jump like well-fed lambs, for God Himself promises to save us and fill us with eternal joy and gladness.[219]

Out of these He will make pretty crowns to place upon the heads of His beloved children — those who believe and trust [in Him] and revere Him.

---

[213] See *supra*, pp. 459–460, note 30.

[214] Text: *hinca las rodillas del corazón y cuerpo* . . . [p. 530]. Cf. *supra*, p. 470, note 95.

[215] *Isaiah* LVII:15, paraphrased.

[216] *Ibid.* LXVI:1–2, 13.

[217] *Ibid.* LI:6–7.

[218] *Ibid.* LI:10.

[219] Cf. *Psalms* CXIV:4.

Be comforted. Be comforted my, blessed martyrs, for you will be going like [the Queen of] Sheba, my queens, from this sad and lowly earth to see the King of the angels, handsome, glorious and consummately wise, who rules heaven and earth.

What rich and sacred palaces you are going to see — [and] the pretty orchards of Paradise and the gardens where stands the tree of life! O, [how splendid] the vineyards [you will see], the muscats, the orange blossoms, the roses, the trees with all kinds of fruit, the rivulets of milk and honey!

There your most loving Father who permitted you to be born into this world will invite you to His table, a table of sweetness and glory. How He will embrace you! He will send His blessing upon you. He will take out the kerchief of His consolations from His pocket. He will solicitously wipe away your tears. He will say to you, "Let there be no more." He will embrace you like the loving mother [embraces] the child whom she adores. When he is very small and says something clever, she rushes to him, showers him with a thousand hugs[220] and kisses and wants to devour him. In the same way God will embrace you and say, "Come, My little ones, who have suffered so much for My honor and My Law."

O, what rich clothing he will put on you — seven layers of brocade, garlands, headdress of fine gold, chains [for your necks], jewels and rings [for your fingers], and crowns of laurel that victors wear. What dancing there will be [in your honor], what entertainment on the day of your [heavenly] nuptials! How we shall dance there [to the words of] the [Psalm], "Let us sing with joy!"[221] And the saintly David will accompany us on the harp, so that we can dance with the angels and saints.

With what great joy God awaits us! "Bless [the Lord], O my soul."[222]

With such hope, who need fear imprisonment, or death, or fire?

There now. Be comforted, be comforted. Victory, victory [is near]. Cloak yourselves in joy and gladness. There now, my Asenaths, repent. Pray, my Hannahs and Esthers. There now, my beautiful Rachels [and] faithful Sarahs. There now, chaste Susannas! There now, strong Jaels and Judiths. There now, blessed Salomes! Sing! Sing [a song of] victory with Deborah and Miriam.

Hallelujah! Hallelujah!

*   *   *

[220] See *supra*, pp. 471 and 487.
[221] See *supra*, p. 484, note 179.
[222] See *supra*, p. 476, note 135.

[21]

Dearest . . .:

May Adonay, my Lord, [the mighty] God, be with you. Amen.
They no longer want to take anything from me [to be delivered
to any of you]. I do not know why. Perhaps they have suspected
you. Or maybe your cellmate said something in her audience
[before the Inquisition.]

I dedicate the following potpourri to God. By chance the Lord
may perhaps wish it to be delivered to you for comfort in your loneliness. My heart has sent [it] to you. Commend it to the Lord God
for me.

[There follows a transcript of what appears to have been a poetic
composition, written in five columns on the two sides of a single
sheet of paper. All that remains of the piece are stray words and
phrases, poorly transcribed].

*   *   *

SECTION B

THE LETTERS READ INTO THE RECORD OF THE SECOND
TRIAL OF LUIS DE CARVAJAL, THE YOUNGER[223]

[22]

[Saturday, May 13, 1595]

[For Doña Leonor. Letter written on an avocado pit, wrapped in
a piece of taffeta and hidden in a melon].

[Have] patience like Job . . .
My darlings, may Adonay, our Lord, visit you.
I have it.[224] Glory to God.
I am in chains for my God.

*   *   *

[23]

[Sunday, May 14, 1595].

[Addressee unknown. Letter written on an avocado pit, wrapped
in taffeta and hidden in a banana].

Congratulations, for Adonay's angels and saints are awaiting us

[223] These are found in the *Procesos de Luis de Carvajal* (*el Mozo*), pp. 171–183. The
translation follow the order of the letters as they appear in these pages. The reader will
note that the last four letters are not in chronological order.

[224] There is, of course, no way of knowing what is referred to, but chances are that
Leonor has secretly sent him something.

in Paradise, my martyrs, blessed ones of Adonay. I thought I would go alone [to see you (?)], my dear; send me some indication as to whether you are alone or not.

May Adonay remember our saintly mother. She and you and all [the rest of my sisters] are so close to my heart . . .

I have been confessing the truth of Adonay about myself alone.

*   *   *

[24]

[Tuesday, May 16, 1595]

[For Doña Leonor. Letter written on an avocado pit, wrapped in a ribbon resembling a hat band and hidden in a banana].

Congratulations, my angel, for the trip to Paradise is better than a trip to Castile.[225] Happy the bread you have eaten and the water you have drunk and the earth you have trodden and the womb in which we were borne, for in a little while we shall go to profess the sacred religion of the angels and saints and to see the very land of Adonay. O! What sumptuous gardens [and] music and entertainment await us! What wonderful tournaments will be held in heaven when Adonay crowns us for [our] firm [allegiance to] His faith.[226]

[Therefore] let none [of us] be dispirited, for with the help of my Lord, God, Adonay, the life [of every one of us] will be saved;[227] for us the glory [of heaven] is [on the other side of] the hill of this jail.

Who could [begin to] tell you everything that the Lord has shown me? But with His help we shall see each other soon.

I spent three weeks in a dungeon. Now Adonay, my Lord, has taken me out and put me [in a place] where I can see the sky day and night. [And] miraculously, I had a Bible here for a week.

Darlings of Adonay, I commend you to Him; [and] when I remember you, I forget myself. He has revealed [the secret of] many mysteries to me [here]. So do not fear these worms,[228] for we have a good Lord and God and we believe in a holy and true Law.

---

[225] Cf. *supra*, pp. 459–460, note 30.
[226] Text: *por su firme fe* . . . [p. 173].
[227] Text: *que su vida, con ayuda de A. mi Señor Dios* . . . [p. 173].
[228] That is, the Inquisitors.

One night God secretly showed me tortillas [made] of flour-meal . . .[229]

Listen, my angel, do not let them[230] confuse you. Adonay, our God, is One and there is no other.

* * *

[25]

[Wednesday, May 17, 1595]

For Doña Leonor

* * *

[26]

[Thursday, May 18, 1595]

[For Doña Leonor. Letter written on an avocado pit and hidden in a banana].

Look, angel, the night before last I dreamt that I was walking on the broad [expanse of the] sea, wetting only my feet — which represent the body [and not the soul]. And I saw hunters, who [really] are the three tonsured [Inquisitors], with their guns — which, I am told, stand for their deceits. [They were trying] to kill live ducks, which, my dears, mean those [people] who acknowledge Adonay, the living God. But they could kill none, because the ducks were flying on the light wings of prayer toward the mighty God who was defending us.

Courage. Courage. Felicitations! Rejoice, my saintly Rachel. May the *Shekinah* — which is the name of the Almighty[231] — be with you and all [the rest of you].

I am not always in a position to communicate. If you can, wrap this in something and send it on by night to my dear and darling sisters.

* * *

[229] Cf. *supra*, p. 462.
[230] That is, the Inquisitors.
[231] Cf. *supra*, p. 469, note 90.

[27]

[Friday, May 19, 1595]

[Two letters, each scratched on a pear].

[First pear, for Doña Leonor].

My dearest Rachel.[232] Adonay, my Lord, has given me instruction to comfort you and gives me this paper and ink.[233] My angel, send me news on another pear. Write with a needle and send it by night, [letting me know] how you are and feel and who your cellmate is, or if you are alone.

Oh, how you will relish the preserves of these pears,[234] my soul. If you can, share it with your dear sisters and mother.[235] Realize also that the night before last there was rotten fish[236] in the sea of this jail.

Let us cry out [to God]. Let us cry out [to God]. Let us cry out [to God], my darling martyrs, that it be none of us or those near to us. Justa [Mendez][237] has confessed already; I know it.

*   *   *

[28]

[Second Pear: To be delivered to his mother, for his mother and other sisters].

Apples of my eye, darlings of Adonay, My God:

May He visit you and comfort you in [your] tribulation. And [have] courage; [have] courage like Deborah, Jael and Judith; faith like Sarah, your holy matriarch; devotion like the holy martyr, Salome.[238] Pray, pray, [for] they await you in Paradise with a crown. Be glad. Rejoice! Felicitations! Felicitations! Rejoice! For you are going like [the Queen of] Sheba to see the King of the Angels, to delight in His wisdom and beauty. Be glad. Hallelujah!

*   *   *

[232] Cf. *supra*, p. 475, note 125.

[233] This clearly does not refer to actual paper and ink. It simply means the pear, Luis' strange writing material. Gaspar de los Reyes specifically states that this letter "*venía escrito en la una de las dichas peras*" [p. 176].

[234] That is, the messages.

[235] Text: *si pudieres, convida a tus almas* . . . [p. 176].

[236] This seems to refer to Judaizers who have testified against others before the Inquisition.

[237] Cf. *supra*, p. 467, note 77.

[238] Cf. *supra*, p. 471, note 103.

[29]

[Saturday, May 20, 1595].

[For Doña Catalina: Letter written on a banana [peel?] and hidden in a banana].

Felicitations! Felicitations! Be glad! Be glad! For Paradise awaits us.

Last night Joseph[239] saw that we were all walking on the expanse of the sea and only our feet — representing our bodies in this jail [but not our souls] — got wet; and that hunters were chasing live ducks but missing them all, because they were flying with wings of prayer to the mighty God, who defended them. The guns [of the hunters] represented deceits. The live ducks [represented] those who believe in the living God. [And] the hunters [themselves represented] the tonsured [Inquisitors]. This was revealed to me, darlings of my Adonay. May He visit you and comfort you in your tribulation.[240]

Courage, courage, my Judith, my dear. Pray. Pray.

*   *   *

[30]

[Sunday, May 21, 1595]

[For Doña Catalina]

[31]

[For Doña Leonor]

[32]

[For Doña Mariana]

[33]

[For Doña Isabel]

*   *   *

[239] Cf. "Autobiography," *supra*, p. 279.
[240] See *supra*, p. 468.

[34]

[Tuesday, May 23, 15195].

[Two pears, hidden in bananas]
[The larger pear was intended for Doña Mariana].

Beloved of my God: May He send[241] blessed and happy nights, and days of consolation, to you and to all my darlings who are in despair.[242] Amen.

[I have] good news. Be glad, for your agony will be turned to joy.

My darling, if you can, let me hear from you. If you can, be sure to write on a pear with a needle, and send it on by night, telling me how you feel and who your cellmate is, please. And have faith, for the God of Israel is good toward His children who trust in Him.

* * *

[35]

[The smaller pear was intended for Doña Ana].

Martyr, martyr of . . . [the living God, pray that you might(?)] die like a saint, which is what I, sinner that I am, ask and beg [Him for].

My darling, may my God [give you good] nights and days. Rejoice . . .

[There were also four sheets of paper written in a very fine hand. We assume that they were also intended for Mariana and Leonor].

* * *

[36]

[Thursday, May 25, 1595]

[For Doña Catalina. Letter written on half of an avocado pit and hidden in a banana].

May my God give you nights of gladness. May the Almighty accompany you and strengthen you, darling of God, sister of my heart.

* * *

[241] Text: *El te envía* . . . [p. 179].
[242] Text: *y a todas mis almas y tristes* . . . [p. 179].

[37]

[A paper for Doña Ana]²⁴³
My darling Ana . . .

* * *

[38]

[Tuesday, May 23, 1595].
[Two papers, given to the warden along with fruit, to be delivered to Doña Leonor].
[The smaller paper was intended for Doña Leonor].
My darling, may the mighty God give good days to you and to all [of you]. Amen.
Remember, when you go upstairs [to your audience before the Inquisitors] be sure to say this²⁴⁴ [to them]: "Your mother will be ashamed; the one who bore you will soon be repudiated, for you will end up as worms, while the *Shekinah* of Adonay²⁴⁵ will be upon us and His eternal salvation [will be] upon our heads."²⁴⁶
I saw this in the honeycomb²⁴⁷ and that is all I can tell you [now], for it has already struck twelve.
I could not write to you [before] because they were keeping my little window barred [and I therefore had no light].
Our dear [sister] Catalina is the one who went to her audience today. I think [so], because I thought I could make out her voice when she passed by.
May Adonay be with all of us. Amen.

* * *

[39]

[The larger paper, whose destination could not be determined].
Darling,
May Adonay be with you. I heard you pass by. Why didn't you turn your face toward my cell?

---

²⁴³ See *supra*, p. 452.
²⁴⁴ Text: *aprende esto* . . . [p. 181].
²⁴⁵ Text: *A. Sequina* . . . [p. 182].
²⁴⁶ If, as is posited in my introduction to these letters, Luis recognized the possibility of their interception, we can regard statements like these as attempts by Luis to direct the Inquisitors' ire against his own heresies, to which he had already confessed.
²⁴⁷ Cf. *supra*, p. 460, note 35.

The day has twelve hours. In the first hour of Friday [the sixth day of Creation] the dust of which Adam was [to be] formed was assembled. In the second [hour], his limbs were fashioned. In the third, the breath of life was breathed into him by my Lord God, Adonay. In the fourth, he rose to his feet. In the fifth, he gave a name to all the animals. In the sixth, the holy Adonay sent him a blessed sleep and took out his rib. In the seventh, Eve was formed. In the eighth, husband and wife united and Eve conceived Cain and a sister of his. In the ninth they were taken to Paradise and enjoined not to eat from the forbidden tree. In the tenth, they sinned by eating from it. In the eleventh, they were judged. In the twelfth, they were ejected from Paradise.[248]

I saw this in the honeycomb[249] which I told you about. And so that you will understand [the reckoning of] these hours and this [kind of] day, remember that at six in the morning, the first hour begins, at seven the second, and so on, and the twelfth hour comes [or ends] at six at night.

Look, my little angel. [You must] have living faith, and [if you do] my holy and blessed God will reveal great mysteries to you. He will open your eyes. Entreat Him earnestly to do this, for our eyes are shut; then you will see great marvels. And those who do not [behold and] enjoy them, see like the beasts, for although they have sight, they do not know what they see.

Look, you are all [going to be] there [in heaven] above.

O, *Shekinah!*

Look. Yesterday I invited all [my sisters and my mother] to banana preserves[250] — except for my little angel, Anica. You invite her — which means, may the presence of the Most High be with you.[251]

Remember! When you say the *Shema,* and you reach [the point] where you say, "You shall love [the Lord your God with all your heart] say immediately "because I took you out from Egypt" and [then recite] all the Ten Commandments; and when you finish these

---

[248] This legend has roots in early rabbinic thought and derived parallels in the Church Fathers. See L. Ginzberg, *The Legends of the Jews* (Philadelphia, 1909), vol. I, p. 82 and vol. V, pp. 106–107, note 97, and *Die Haggada bei den Kirchenvätern und in der apokryphischen Litteratur* (Berlin, 1900), pp. 48–49.

[249] Cf. *supra*, p. 460, note 35.

[250] Cf. *supra*, p. 504, note 234.

[251] This statement appears to be another deliberate effort by Luis to divert the Inquisitors' attention — this time from the fact that his family was exchanging letters. The preserves were the messages being sent; the word "invite" is calculatedly confusing.

[then] you will say, "And these words [which I command you this day] shall be etc.[252]

Look! When I was in the dungeon, I hèard [all] this in a daughter of a voice,[253] which means a revelation of the Most High.

Today the warden, on coming down from upstairs, said to me, "Blessed and praised *seija Deus* [be God]."[254] I understand who told him to say this.[255] Amen. Amen. Amen. Amen. Amen. Amen. Amen. For God never abandons *aos seus* [His own].

I now know that you have someone else [in your cell], but [that your companion is] not to your liking. May the holy, blessed God look to it. For this reason I am delighted to be alone; and the two weeks that I did have companions, I did[256] in their presence what the Lord God commands to the extent that was possible for me. May His goodness compensate for my deficiencies and yours. Amen.

Look, dearest. Try to get along well with them[257] so that they do not afflict you, for right now they are our masters. Soon, soon [however, they shall be] our slaves.

Remember. Learn this for the day of your glory: It is better to be the criers of Adonay than kings over all that there is in all of a hundred thousand worlds. And there are other [things to be remembered] for such time. May He accompany us until [the day of our] death. Amen. Amen.

---

[252] Cf. *supra*, p. 495, note 205.

[253] Text: *hija de vos*, the Spanish version of what ultimately goes back to the Hebrew *bat kol*. Luis did not know the denotation of the term, and my English attempts to render his understanding of the expression.

[254] The words are Portuguese, as are the concluding words of Luis' remark that appear below.

[255] The chances are that it was the Inquisitors who so instructed the warden, apparently in an effort to make him appear a New Christian himself, and perhaps a Judaizer. In this way he might hope to get Luis to reveal additional information about his family and friends.

[256] Text: *hago* . . . [p. 183]. That is, he practiced Judaism.

[257] That is, the Inquisitors.

II

THE LAST WILL AND TESTAMENT OF
LUIS DE CARVAJAL, THE YOUNGER

INTRODUCTION

On September 12, 1596, Luis de Carvajal, the Younger, facing death at the stake, presented to the Inquisitors a paper containing a transcription of the Ten Commandments and another precious document which he called his last will and testament.

Since the Inquisition had sequestered all of Luis' material possessions, his will dealt solely with the spiritual goods that he cherished. All were derived from the Jewish faith as he understood it from the Bible.

In his will Luis detailed the ideals of his Judaism, to let the world know the principles by which he sought to live his life and for which he was prepared to relinquish it.

The will discloses a learned mind, trained in Bible, theology and polemics. It reveals as well a spirit unbent by persecution and torture and upheld to the very end by the pinions of faith.

The notes to the translation which follows will evidence the extent to which the Inquisition's scribe or scribes garbled the text. Within the translation, brackets are used for editorial additions. These include the English equivalent of the biblical quotations that Luis de Carvajal gives in Latin. They include also the location of biblical quotations in the Hebrew Bible, and where there is a difference, for the Vulgate as well. The Vulgate is identified by a *V*.

*   *   *

THE TESTAMENT OF LUIS DE CARVAJAL
BY WHICH HE SAYS[1] HE WISHES TO DIE

O most high and sovereign Creator of heaven and earth, not one of Your countless creatures can resist Your will. Without it neither men nor birds nor brutish beasts[2] could live upon the earth. Unless Your desire and will sustained them and ordered the elements [of the world], the heavens would become confused; their natural orbits

---

[1] Text: *debajo del cual dijo* . . . [p. 412].
[2] Text: *brutos y animales* . . . [p. 412].

would vanish;[3] the whole earth would shake; the peaks of the lofty hills[4] would tumble; the waters of the sea would cover the land and no living thing would have a chance of surviving.

But by Your infinite goodness and mercy You give order and sustenance to all, not that this is necessary for You, but for the sake of the common good and benefit of men.

And since You employ such kindness and boundless mercy with them, I, the poorest and most wretched among them all, ask and beg of You not to abandon me in the perilous entry into death, where I have elected to go for the sake of Your most holy name and true Law. Accept as a sacrifice this poor life which You have given me. Look not at my countless sins, but rather at Your lovingkindness and upon my immortal soul which You have created in Your own likeness for life eternal. I beg You to pardon it and receive it when it has left my mortal frame.

Wherefore, having prepared my last and final will and testament and given it its final form, I write and affix my signature to the religious truths in which I believe and in which I profess to die in Your presence.

First, I believe in a single God, omnipotent and true, the creator, of the sky, earth and sea and all things visible and invisible therein and I repudiate the devil and all his lies.

Second, I believe that God, our Lord and universal Creator, is one and not many. *Deuteronomy* VI:[4][5]: "Hear, O Israel, the Lord your God, the Lord is One," and no more. He, even He, is the very God of the heavens above and of the earth beneath. He is the one God alone, and there is none besides. This is confirmed in *Deuteronomy* XXXII:[39]: *Videte quod ego sim solus* ["See that I am alone"], etc.

Third, I believe that the Law of God, our Lord, which the Christians call the dead Law of Moses, is living and infinite, as is evident from the entire holy Pentateuch. Here, in a thousand places, God signs His name, *Ego Dominus* ["I, the Lord"] etc. He says and commands that the Law be kept *in sempiternas generationes*, that is, forever and ever. This is certified by the saintly David in *Psalms* [V] CX [:8 = CXI:8], where he says, "All His commandments are sure; they are established forever, and are made endlessly in truth and uprightness,"[6] etc. In the same place it says [verse 9] *Mandavit in*

---

[3] Text: *perderian sus cursos y naturales movimientos* . . . [p. 412].

[4] Text: *las cumbres y grandes collados* . . . [p. 412].

[5] Text: *Deuteronomio 4* . . . [p. 413].

[6] The Vulgate here reads: *Fidelia omnia mandata eius; confirmata in saeculum saeculi, facta in veritate et aequitate.*

aeternum testamentum suum,[7] ["He commanded His covenant forever,"] etc. And in many other places [Scripture says the same thing]: *Malachi* [III:6] *Ego enim Dominus et non mutor*[8] ["I am the Lord and do not change"]; *Numbers* [XXIII:19] *Non est Deus quasi homo . . . ut mutetur*[9] ["The Lord is not a man . . . that He should change"], etc.; *Psalms* [V XXXII:11 = XXXIII:11] *Cogitationes cordis eius*[10] [*in generatione et generationem*] ["The counsel of the Lord stands forever; the thoughts of His heart (are to all generations)"], etc. and *Psalms* CXIX[11] throughout [the Psalm].

And as to the Christians' claim that the ceremonial and legal precepts have already expired and are dead, this is contrary to one of their Gospels. There it says [*Matthew* V:17] *Nolite putare*[12] etc. ["Think not (that I am come to destroy the law, or the prophets: I am not come to destroy, but to fulfil)"]; because in truth and reality [Luke XVI:17] *Facilius est autem caelum et terram praeterire quam de lege unum apicem cadere.*[13] ["It is easier for heaven and earth to pass than one tittle of the Law to fail."] And it is a great impudence of men to wish to change the commandments of God our Lord because this redounds to the dishonor of the Lawgiver. This is seen in . . .[14] [*Deuteronomy* XII:32]: *nec addas quidquam nec minuas*[15] "We cannot add anything to them or take away anything," etc. And this is the express command of the Lord our God in *Deuteronomy*, where He says [*Deuteronomy* IV:2] *Non addetis ad verbum*[16] [*quod vobis loquor*] ["You shall not add to the word which I command you, neither shall you diminish from it"], etc.

Fourth, I believe that to make any kind of sculpture or icon of a god and to worship them is a mortal sin, for it is something directly contrary to the commandment of the Lord our God in *Exodus* [XX:4–5] and *Deuteronomy* [V:8–9], where it says *Non facies tibi sculptile, neque omnem similitudinem*[17] ["You shall not make for your-

---

[7] Text: *mandauit in eternum testamentum suu* (for *suū*) [p. 413].

[8] Text: *Ego Dns, etnomutur* [p. 413].

[9] Text: *non es homo deg ut mutetur* [p. 413].

[10] Text: *cogitationes cordie eig* [p. 413].

[11] The quotation is from *Psalms* CXVIII in the Vulgate, which Luis used; it is *Psalms* CXIX in the Hebrew Bible.

[12] Text: *noliteputare* [p. 413].

[13] Text: *facilius est coelis et terra transfire quan iota unum autapex alegeperire* [p. 413].

[14] Text: *constant Eccles.* [p. 413]. Is this *Ecclesiastes, Ecclesiasticus,* or perhaps even "Evangelia" [the Gospels]? (Cf. *Matthew* V:17–20). The verse quoted by Carvajal (see following note) is closest to *Deuteronomy* XII:32.

[15] Text: *non posumus eis sadere nec auscne*(?) *quid qz.* [p. 413].

[16] Text: *Nonades adberbum* [p. 413].

[17] Text: *Nonfaciestibi sculptile aut aliquid similitudinen* [p. 413]. The text of the Bible

self a graven image, nor any manner of likeness (of anything that is in heaven above, or that is in the earth beneath, or that is in the water under the earth. You shall not bow down unto them, or serve them.)"] Jeremiah X[:15] confirms it, *Vana sunt, et opus risu dignum*[18] ["They are vanity, a work of delusion"]. Isaiah [XLIV:20] says *Cor insipiens adoravit illud*[19] ["A deceived heart has turned him aside"] and [XLIV:19] *Non recogitant in mente sua*[20] ["And none considers in his heart"]. Likewise Psalms [V CXIII B:4 = CXV:4][21] *simulacra gentium argentum et aurum* ["Their idols are silver and gold (the work of men's hands)"] and *Psalms* [V XCVI:7 = XCVII:7] *Confundantur omnes [qui adorant sculptilia]* ["Ashamed be all they (that serve graven images)"] and *Psalms* [V XCV:5 = XCVI:5] *[Quoniam] omnes dii gentium daemonia*[22] ["For all the gods of the peoples are things of naught"].

And what Christians say contrary to this is heresy; and if I were to believe it, the Lord would make me repay dearly because He has already informed me what I must believe. [*Deuteronomy* XXXII:17] *Immolaverunt daemoniis et non Deo, diis quos ignorabant*[23] ["They sacrificed to demons, gods that they knew not"], etc.

For His sake, may He guide me by His holy hand: [according to] *Deuteronomy* [XXIX:17] "Lest there not be among you any man or woman whose heart departs from the Lord our God, which is a root that engenders gall and bitterness or makes or worships any idol, for the Lord's ire and fury will arise" etc.

Likewise I say that if any man in the guise of an angel of light should tell me that the keeping of the holy Sabbath day, so emphasized in so many parts of the Law by God our Lord, has ceased, and that it is not a sin to eat blood, suet and pork, which is not only contrary to the Law of Scripture, but contrary to natural law as well, I will not believe it, even though at the same time he told me many holy things, but I shall remain firm in my faith in the Lord's true word during such temptation, as His divine majesty informs me and commands me. *Deuteronomy* XIII:[1] *Si surrexerit [in medio tui prophetes*[24] ["If there should arise in your midst a prophet . . ."], etc.

I quote is that of *Exodus*. The parallel in *Deuteronomy* reads *Non facies tibi sculptile nec similitudinem omnium*.

[18] Text: *opus risidignum* [p. 413].

[19] Text: *corinsipiens adorabitil* [p. 413].

[20] Text: *Non recogitate* [p. 413].

[21] Text: *salmo 112* [p. 413].

[22] Text: *omnes gentium dem°* [pp. 413–414].

[23] Text: *Inmolaucrum doemoniis, & non Deo diis quos ignorabant* [p. 414].

[24] Text: *Si surregerite* [p. 414] in the Hebrew Bible, *Deuteronomy* XIII:2.

Sixth, I believe that the holy sacrament of circumcision is eternal, as God our Lord told the saintly Abraham and afterwards the saintly Moses in the Law: "The soul of any man who is not circumcised shall be erased from the roll of the living." Genesis XVII:[14].[25]

Seventh, I believe that the Messiah,[26] the true father of the future world, [the] Prince of Peace, [the] righteous son of David, [the] possessor of the scepter of Judah, [the] light of the nations and [the] greatly beloved of God most high, has not come. And even supposing he had been born,[27] I believe and feel that the redemption of God's people and the world has not been accomplished, for, as is patent from all the holy prophets and especially from the thirty-ninth[28] chapter of Ezekiel, "All the faithful dead of Israel, [now] living in the Lord our God by a great miracle of His, will be resurrected, and the scattered Jews who are then living will be gathered from the four corners of the earth."

Jeremiah says [XVI:14] [Propterea ecce dies veniunt, dicit Dominus, et] non dicetur ultra: "Vivit Dominus [qui eduxit filios Israel de terra Aegypti," sed "Vivit Dominus qui eduxit filios Israel de terra aquilonis, et de universis terris ad quas eieci eos, et reducam eos in terram suam, quam dedi patribus eorum." ["Therefore, behold, the days come, says the Lord, that it shall no more be said: 'As the Lord lives, that brought up the children of Israel out of the land of Egypt,' but 'As the Lord lives, that brought up the children of Israel from the land of the north, and from all the countries whither He had driven them'; and I will bring them back into their land that I gave unto their fathers."]

And this will take place with greater miracles than the ones the Lord performed when He redeemed us from Egypt or at any other time. He will bring them to Zion and He will rebuild the glorious city of Jerusalem, according to Isaiah and Jeremiah,[29] and [He will rebuild] the marvelous Temple of God, which will endure throughout all ages and eras.

Says Haggai [V II:7 = II:6]: Adhuc unum modicum est,[30] [et ego commovebo caelum, et terram, et mare, et aridam. Et movebo omnes gentes, et veniet desideratus cunctis gentibus; et implebo domum istam

---

[25] Cf. Luis' "Autobiography," supra, p. 284.

[26] Text: Cristo . . . [p. 414], translating the Vulgate's rendition of the Hebrew Mašiaḥ.

[27] See Lamentations Rabbah I:51. This text was often used by Christian polemics. For an example, see Martin A. Cohen, "Reflections on the Text and Context of the Disputations of Barcelona," Hebrew Union College Annual, vol. XXXV (1964), pp. 171 f.

[28] Ezekiel XXXVII, especially verses 12 and 21, not Ezekiel, XXXIX.

[29] Cf. for example Isaiah XXVII:13, XXXIII:20, XLIV:26–28, LII:7–12, LXII, LXV:18–19, LXVI:10–14 and Jeremiah XXXIII.

[30] Text: Ad huepusillum [p. 415].

LUIS DE CARVAJAL, THE YOUNGER　　　307

gloria, dicit Dominus exercituum.] ["Yet once, it is a little while, and I
will shake the heavens, and the earth, and the sea, and the dry land;
and I will shake all nations, and the choicest things of all nations
shall come, and I will fill this house with glory, says the Lord of
hosts."], and Israel will be captive no more. *Lamentations* [IV:22]:
Non addet ultra ut transmigret te[31] ["He will no more carry you
away into captivity."]

Baruch [II:35] *Et non movebo amplius populum meum, filios Israel,
a terra quam dedi illis.*[32] ["And I will never again remove my people
Israel from the land which I have given them."]

Warfare, sin and idolatry will [then] cease from the world, according to Isaiah, David, Daniel and Ezekiel.

All parts of the world will be converted to the knowledge of the
true God, and man will be restored to his primal state of innocence,
according to Isaiah, Micah, Joel and Obadiah.

And finally, this is evident from all the prophets, in almost all
their chapters and statements. And when the benighted say that
all this has already been accomplished, it is like trying to prove that
the snow is not white and that there are no longer any nights, but
only days.

May the immense God, for His own sake, grieve for those who
live in darkness and bring them out to the road of his light. Amen.

Eighth, I believe in the interpretation of the mysterious vision of
the saintly Daniel,[33] which I have been accused of believing in this
trial.[34] I believe in the following interpretation of the three beasts
he saw: First, the lion represented Chaldean Empire, which was
cruel and brutal like a lion against the ecclesia of the Lord our God,
which is His beloved people Israel. And [second], the bear[35] was the
representation of the Persians and the Medes, who were less brutal
toward it, for from them came Cyrus, who in Isaiah was called
Messiah,[36] that is, the anointed of the Lord. In his days God our
Lord delivered His people from their Babylonian captivity. And
[third,] the leopard with wings and motley colors was a representation
of the empire of the Greeks and of Alexander, with his conquests and
diverse victories.

So, too, the fourth beast, frightful and [even] more savage, which
bit everything with its teeth and trampled everything with its feet,

---

[31] Text: *Non adiiciet ut transmigret te ultra* [p. 415].
[32] Text: *Non conmovebo amplius filius Israel a terra quan dabo illis* [p. 415].
[33] *Daniel* VII.
[34] *Procesos de Luis de Carvajal (el Mozo)*, p. 238.
[35] Text: *el ojo* . . . [p. 415].
[36] *Isaiah* XLV:1.

represented the fourth monarchy, [that of Christendom,] which has lasted until today. The ten horns, as is clearly evident from the words of the angel, Saint Gabriel, who showed them to Daniel, were ten kings who reigned during this period. Finally from their midst a small horn came forth on the head of that beast, a horn with two eyes and a mouth that greatly blasphemed the exalted Lord. It said that God is subject to passion, though He has no passion. Though God is one, [it said] that He is three and that the Law of God is dead. [It said] that the infinite became finite, the eternal temporal, that cause is effect, that the Lord is a servant and that God is a man, [all of] which is of course impossible as well as contrary to what our Lord teaches in His most holy Law. And this is what the holy prophet Asaph complains about [in the *Psalms*] when he says: [*Psalms V* LXXIII:18 = LXXIV:18] *Memor esto huius inimicus improperavit Domino*[37] ["Remember this, how the enemy has reproached the Lord."] And also the holy David [in the] Psalm [*V* CXIX:3 = CXX:3] *Quid detur tibi [aut quid apponatur tibi ad linguam dolosam]?*[38] ["What shall be given to you (and what shall be done to you, you deceitful tongue)?"] [He responds]: [*Psalms V* CXIX:4 = CXX:4]: *Sagittae potentis acutae, cum carbonibus desolatoriis*[39] ["Sharp arrows of the mighty, with coals of broom."], etc.

And God our Lord speaks of the horns and dominions of this monarchy when He says through the Psalmist: [*Psalms V* LXXIV:11 = LXXV:11] *Omnia cornua peccatorum confringam*[40] ["All the horns of the wicked will I also cut off"], etc. [He will do this] when he exalts the horn of His people: [*Psalms* CXLVIII:14], *Exaltavit cornu populi sui*[41] ["He will lift up the horn of His people"] and [*Psalms V* LXXIV:11 = LXXV:11] *Et exaltabantur cornua iusti*[42] ["And the horns of the righteous shall be lifted up"], where He promises to judge the wicked[43] with the dreadful punishment of the Judgment Day.

And the Lord explains himself in some detail through Joel, when He says [*Joel V* III:2 = IV:2]: *Congregabo omnes gentes et deducam eas in vallem Iosaphat*[44] ["I will gather all nations and will bring them down into the valley of Jehoshaphat"], etc., and there I shall

---

[37] Text: *memt° improperio tuo* [p. 416].
[38] Text: *quid Davitur tibi* [p. 416].
[39] Text: *sagitte potentis acutae cun carbonibg de sola toriis* [p. 416].
[40] Text: *omnia conua peccato confringan* [p. 416].
[41] Text: *Exaltabi conu populi sui* [p. 416].
[42] Text: *et exaltaban cornua justi* [p. 416].
[43] Text: *do . . . promete juzgarlos . . .* [p. 416].
[44] Text: *congregato omnes gentes in valle Josaphat* [p. 416].

enter into judgment concerning the evil which they have done to My people.

And in chapters forty-nine[45] and sixty-six of [the Book of] *Isaiah* He says [*Isaiah* LXVI:24], *Et ignis eorum non extinguetur*[46] ["And their fire shall not be quenched"], because they have loved and chosen all that the Lord forbade and abhorred.

And then the kingdom shall be restored to the Messiah[47] and to the saints of the Lord Most High. As Daniel says [*Daniel* VII:13], *Aspiciebam (ergo in visione noctis, et ecce) cum nubibus caeli (quasi filius hominis veniebat)*[48] ["I saw (in the vision of the night and lo! one in the likeness of a human being was coming) with the clouds of heaven"]. Their permanent reign, represented in Nebuchadnezzar's dream[49] by the stone uncut by human hands which fell from the mountain, will fall upon the empire, represented by the statue in the dream, and will quickly destroy it, because [like the statue] it [now] stands on feet of clay and iron. These [substances] do not go well together, as can be seen in the [religious] divisions of these heretics: Englishmen, Frenchmen, and the others all used to belong to one religion, [symbolized by] the feet of this statue.[50] Now they no longer get on very well together, and this foreshadows the great fall they will all soon have. This [fact] is likewise evident from *Deuteronomy* XXXII[:32], *De vinea Sodomorum*[51] ["For their vine is the vine of Sodom"], etc. and [verse 35] *Mea est ultio, et ego retribuam in tempore, ut labatur pes eorum.*[52] ["Vengeance is Mine and recompense, against the time when their foot shall slip."]

Tenth, I believe that the mighty king[53] Antiochus, whom Sacred Writ calls the root of sin[54] because he was a persecutor of God's people and of His holy Law, was a representation of the kings of Spain and Portugal. These have ever been the root [of the tree] whose branches of inquisitions and persecutions, have spread over the people of God, our Lord, and His holy Law.[55] [And they have also been responsible for the death of] the blessed martyrs — the faithful and

[45] This seems to be a reference to verses 25–26.
[46] Text: *igniseo- non extinguetur* [p. 416].
[47] See *supra*, p. 514, note 26.
[48] Text: *Conbalcebat cun nubq coeli* [p. 416].
[49] *Daniel* II:34.
[50] Text: *que solían ser todos unos mismos pies de esta estatua . . .* [p. 416].
[51] Text: *devite, sedon, &a.* [p. 416].
[52] Text: *Vsque ego retribuan ei sinten pore quo lebatur peseo* [p. 416].
[53] Text: *aquel rey Antioco . . .* [p. 416].
[54] Cf. *II Maccabees* VII:31 *et passim*.
[55] Text: *los cuales han sido y son la raiz de que han procedido y proceden los ramos de las inquisiciones y persecuciones del pueblo de Dios . . .* [p. 416].

true Jews who have died[56] out of allegiance to this Law. The princes have persecuted[57] them without cause, calling them Judaizing heretics [and] unjustly [so], for the practice of Judaism is not heresy: it is the fulfillment of the will of God our Lord.

This is evident from the angel Saint Gabriel's instruction [in the Book of *Daniel*]: [*Daniel* VIII:26]: "This vision, Daniel, of the evening[s] and the morning[s], is true."[58] There he deals with Antiochus' persecution [foreshadowing Israel's present straits], and he explains it when he says: " 'in the morning[s]' [refers to the days of the Messiah] and 'in the evening[s]' refers to our own time." He mentions the evenings first because [the darkness of night] was destined to be greater and much longer, [for] now Israel is in the [darkness of the] final captivity from which, please God, it will be redeemed[59] as Isaiah promised [*Isaiah* LI:11]: *Et nunc qui redempti sunt a Domino revertentur; et venient in Sion laudantes, et laetitia sempiterna super capita eorum*[60] ["And the ransomed of the Lord shall return, and come with singing unto Zion, and everlasting joy shall be upon their heads"], etc.

Furthermore, I confess and declare that if I gave my consent for theologians and [religious] pundits[61] [to come to talk to me] on two occasions, it was not because I ever doubted these sovereign and certain truths.[62] Indeed, I trust them more than I do my own human existence. I did it merely to be able to acknowledge them more fully, as is confirmed by the last chapter of [the Book of] *Tobit*:[63] [*Tobit* XIII:3], "Acknowledge the Lord, O children of Israel, and praise Him before the nations, because He has scattered you among them for this purpose, that you might tell strangers of His wonders and inform them that besides Him there is no (other) god omnipotent and true," etc.[64] [I also did it] to see if I could convert them and even the chief Inquisitors themselves because they showed a sincere desire for my salvation, although Holy Scripture, in *Second*

---

[56] Text: *mueren* . . . [p. 416].

[57] Text: *persiguen* . . . [p. 416].

[58] Text: *esta vision Daniel en la tarde y en la mañana es verdadera* . . . [p. 417].

[59] Text: *de que Dios Nuestro Señor lo redima* . . . [p. 417].

[60] Text: *& nunc qu redemtio sunta Bn° verentinsion laudantes et latitia sempiterna super capitalo &a* [p. 417].

[61] Text: *sátrapas* . . . [p. 417].

[62] For the record of Luis' talks with these theologians see the *Procesos de Luis de Carvajal* (*el Mozo*), pp. 395 and 453.

[63] Text: *urta illub Thob. ult°* [p. 417]. It is, of course, not the last chapter.

[64] The Vulgate, used by Carvajal, reads: *Confitemini Domino filii Israel, et in conspectu gentium laudate eum: quoniam ideo dispersit vos inter gentes, quae ignorant eum, ut vos enarretis mirabilia eius, et faciatis scire eos, quia non est alius Deus omnipotens praeter eum.* Carvajal gives only his Spanish translation, which is quite accurate.

Maccabees, states that any mercy which is contrary to the Law of the Lord our God is not good.[65]

By God's most exalted name, I again swear that I will live and die in this faith. May God favor me that I may imitate the holy zeal of Hananiah, Azariah, Mishael[66] and Mattathiah,[67] and joyously give up my soul for the faith of the holy covenant in which they died. [As the Book of *Deuteronomy* says:] *Et si omnes obediant* ["And if all obey... (the Lord will make you abundant in all the work of your hand)"].[68] And these holy truths are so evident that, as our Lord God said in His own words[69] in the song which He taught Moses, *Audite caeli*[70] ["Give ear, you heavens"], His very enemies acknowledge it and are unable to deny it: [*Deuteronomy* XXXII:31]: *Non enim est Deus noster ut dii eorum; et inimici nostri sunt iudices*[71] ["For our God is not like their gods, even when our enemies are judging"].[72]

And thus it is my desire and will to die for God's holy faith and true Law. I look to the Lord for strength, lacking all confidence in my own, for after all I am flesh born of fragile seed. And if instead of five sisters — in addition to my mother — who are now in danger because of their trust in God's Law[73] I had a thousand, I would give them all up for my faith in each one of God's holy commandments.

In witness whereof I have written and signed this testament of mine, and with this final deposition,[74] in which I [re]affirm and [re]confirm my faith, I [hereby] conclude the process of my trial.

My God and Lord, give me grace in the eyes of my captors that it may be seen and known in this kingdom and in all kingdoms of the earth that You are our God and that You, O most high and sanctified God, named Adonay,[75] are correctly invoked by Israel and his descendants.

---

[65] This appears to be a paraphrase of what Luis considers to be the essence of Eleazar's refusal to pretend to eat forbidden food in *II Maccabees* VI:18–28, or that of *II Maccabees* VII:24–25, which deal with Antiochus' offer of mercy to the youngest of Hannah's seven sons.

[66] *Daniel* I:6–7 and III:8–30.

[67] *I Maccabees* II:1–70.

[68] Luis seems to have been thinking of *Deuteronomy* XXX:2(–9). The Vulgate's text reads: (*Cum . . .*) *obedieris eius imperiis . . .* The word *omnes* is found in verse 1.

[69] Text: *por su boca . . .* [p. 417].

[70] Text: *Audite Cœli, &c. [sic!]* [p. 417].

[71] Text: *Non enim et Deus noster ut dii eo So ini mici nostri sunt judices* [p. 417].

[72] This translation represents my attempt to render the verse as Luis appears to have understood it.

[73] Text: *puestas en peligro por ella . . .* [p. 417].

[74] Text: *con esta postrera respuesta . . .* [p. 418].

[75] Text: *tu Altísimo y sanctificado nombre Adonaí . . .* [p. 418].

I commend this soul which You have given me to Your most holy hands, solemnly declaring that I will not change my faith until I die, nor when I die.[76] I happily bring to an end the course of my present life, bearing a living faith in Your divine promise[77] of salvation through Your infinite mercy, and when Your holy will is fulfilled, of resurrection in the company of our saintly patriarchs, Abraham, Isaac and Jacob, and their faithful children. For the sake of their holiness[78] I very humbly entreat You to admit me to your love[79] and not to abandon me, and to deign send to my succor and aid that saintly angel, Michael, our prince, with his saintly and angelical soldiery,[80] to help me persevere and die in Your holy faith, and to free me from the Adversary's hands and temptations.

My good God and Lord, have mercy upon the glory of Your name, [Your] Law and [Your] people, and upon the world which You have created. Fill it with Your light and with the true knowledge of Your name, that heaven and earth may be filled with praise of Your glory.[81] Amen. Amen.

Dated in Purgatory[82] this fifth month of the year of our creation, five thousand three hundred and fifty seven.[83]

---

[76] Text: *en tus manos . . . hasta la muerte, ni en ella con tu ayuda . . .* [p. 418]. He is referring to death at the stake, where, for abandoning this faith, he could be spared the agony of being burned alive, and could instead be garroted before being consigned to the flames.

[77] Text: *en tu divina esperanza . . .* [p. 418].

[78] Text: *por cuyo santo amor . . .* [p. 418].

[79] Text: *te suplico muy humildemente me lo confirmes . . .* [p. 418].

[80] *Daniel* X:13 and 21. Cf. *ibid.*, XII:1.

[81] Text: *sean llenas de tu gloria y alabanza . . .* [p. 418].

[82] That is, the Inquisition's jail.

[83] Actually, the year 5356. On Luis' calendar, see my article dealing with his religion mentioned *supra*, p. 280, note 3.

TRIAL OF JORGE DE ALMEIDA BY THE INQUISITION IN MEXICO.

By Dr. Cyrus Adler, *Washington, D. C.*

Some time since the President of the Society, the Honorable Oscar S. Straus, and the writer, while engaged in the pleasant task of searching among the book-shops of Washington, happened upon a manuscript which relates to the trial in Mexico by the Inquisition, of a certain Jorge de Almeida, a Jew,* and incidentally to the Marrano colony in Mexico at the end of the sixteenth and beginning of the seventeenth century.

The Inquisition was established in Spain in 1480; it was soon transplanted to all of the Spanish dominions, and set up in America shortly after the discovery of this continent. In Mexico no less than in South America has it left its trail of horror. Its establishment in Mexico dates back to 1571, for the purpose, in the words of Torquemada, of freeing the land, " que estaba contaminadisima de Judios y Hereges en especial de genten Portuguesa."† The general history of

---

* The name is frequent among Portuguese Jews. See Kayserling, *Sephardim, Romanische Poesien der Juden in Spanien,* Leipzig, 1859, pp. 251, 299 ; *Geschichte der Juden in Portugal,* Leipzig, 1867 ; *Biblioteca Española-Portugueza-Judaica,* Strassbourg, 1890, p. 10. Joseph Jacobs, *An Inquiry into the sources of the History of the Jews in Spain,* London, 1894, p. 2, records a Dona Maria de Almeida who suffered from the Inquisition at Toledo, 1651-1661. The exact name has survived to modern times ; see *Les Mimes d'Hérondas, traduction Française,* par Georges Dalmeyda, Professeur de Rhétorique au Lycée d'Alger ; Paris, Hachette, 1893. The name is derived from Almeida, a town in the province of Beira, Portugal, of some importance in the Napoleonic wars ; it is variously spelled in the MS Almeyda or Almeida ; to avoid confusion, the form Almeida has been adopted throughout.

† *La Monarquia Indiana,* Madrid, 1723, vol. I, p. 648.

this tribunal and its acts must be sought elsewhere. Here there is given but the record of a single trial, of particular interest because of the side-lights it casts on the doings of the Inquisition at the end of the sixteenth and the beginning of the seventeenth centuries. The summary is given at greater length than might at first seem necessary, because perfect records of trials by the Inquisition (such as this one is) are rare, and for the further reason that to the writer's knowledge but one relating to this continent has been published with any degree of fulness.

It is hoped that this summary may prove useful to students of Jewish history, and of interest to those who are concerned with the methods and processes of the Inquisition. No attempt is made to draw any general conclusions with regard to the size or condition of the Marrano community. But the bare recital indicates the dangers and trials to which these unfortunate people were exposed, the chicanery and even deceit to which they were forced, and the depraving influence, both mental and moral, which the cruel Holy Office exercised.*

The MS has been purchased for the Society's collections. It is written in the Spanish language, measures 12⅛ inches by 8½ inches, and numbers 55 leaves exclusive of blank leaves.† Some of the documents are written in a beautifully clear hand, while others are somewhat obscure. With the exception of being slightly worm-eaten, the MS is in a perfect state of preservation.

The cover reads: "Mexico, 1607. Proceedings against Jorge de Almeida, a Portuguese domiciled in this city of Mexico, husband of Dona Lenor de Andrada, convicted of being a Jewess. The Jew absent." This is followed by the table of contents, which includes: "The information; order of arrest; not found; summoned by edicts; returns

---

* For general facts concerning the Inquisition in Mexico see Mr. G. A. Kohut's paper on "Jewish Martyrs of the Inquisition in South America," in this *Publication*.

† The MS is marked No. 149, letter J, file 7.

1, 2 and 3 of his failure to appear ; adjudged to be in default ; formal accusation ; communication thereof to the accused ; notice served by publication ; period for filing evidence opened ; publication of the testimony ; sentence."

The original complaint or information was filed March 8, 1607, and is here given in full :

COMPLAINT.

" Most Illustrious Sir :

I, Doctor Martos de Boorques, prosecuting attorney for the Holy Office of the Inquisition of this City of Mexico, in the states and provinces of New Spain, do come before you, and in the most proper and solemn manner of law, do make and enter a complaint against Jorge de Almeida, a Portuguese, domiciled in this city, whose wife, Dona Lenor de Andrada,* was convicted of observing the Mosaic Law, and therefore surrendered to the secular arm, and say : That according to evidence on file in this Holy Office, and submitted with this bill, the above-named Almeida, after having kept and believed all that Our Holy Catholic Evangelical Law keeps, believes, preaches and teaches, did become a convert to the dead Law of Moses, and an observer of the rites and ceremonies of the same, thinking that salvation can be secured for him through the said observance, and not through the Evangelical Law of grace of Jesus Christ our Redeemer, in whom he does not believe. For all of this he must be punished.

Therefore I do hereby pray Your Honor to be pleased to issue an order for the arrest of the said Jorge de Almeida and his commitment to one of the secret jails of this Holy Office, and furthermore, for the sequestration of his property. I promise to file in due time the formal accusation or in-

* She is sometimes called Caravajal, her family name, but, strangely enough, never Almeida. The name Andrada, or D'Andrada, was common among the Marranos of Brazil and the West Indies in the 17th century. Many members of this Portuguese stock are mentioned in a list of Jews who lived in Martinique in 1683.

dictment. What I ask is justice, and this I do in the name of the Holy Office.

[Signed]   I, DOCTOR MARTOS BOORQUES."

This statement was filed by the attorney in person on Thursday, March 8, 1607, at the morning session, while the Inquisitor Licentiate Gutierre Bernado de Quirros was holding court.

He and the Inquisitor Licentiate Don Alonzo de Peralta* having examined the complaint and the testimony filed with it, issued orders that Almeida be arrested and committed to the secret jails of the Holy Office, that his property be sequestered, that the proper proceedings be instituted against him, and that, as his whereabouts were unknown, steps be taken to insure his capture. This decree was attested by Pedro de Manozca, secretary of the Tribunal.

The capture of Almeida was entrusted to Pedro de Fonseca, "a clerk for the secret affairs of the Holy Office," who was ordered to report the result of his search. This clerk was again summoned and directed to be diligent, and further ordered that "if it were impossible for him to arrest the said Almeida, his efforts must then be directed to finding out where he is. By so doing, the purposes of the good service of God, Our Lord, and of the rightful administration of justice will be promoted." On March 12th he was obliged to report his failure, adding that "it was generally reported that the said Almeida, shortly before the imprisonment of his wife, Dona Lenor de Caravajal,† by order of the Holy Office, had left for Spain and had never returned to Mexico. No person knew to what part of Spain" he had gone.

The next portion of the MS is devoted to the testimony which was on file in the Holy Office and was submitted with the original accusation. While all bearing directly on the

---

* Subsequently Bishop of Charcas. See Appendix.
† The same as Lenor de Andrada. Caravajal or Carvajal was her family name.

case of Almeida, it incidentally yet clearly proves the existence of a considerable Marrano colony in Mexico.*

TESTIMONY I.

The first testimony is an extract from the records of the case against Manuel de Lucena. It reads as follows :

" In the City of Mexico, on Thursday the 3d of November, 1594, the Inquisitor Doctor Lobo Guerrero† being present and holding the morning session of the court, the said Inquisitor ordered a prisoner to be brought from the secret jails of the Holy Office into his presence, and the said prisoner after having been duly sworn to tell the truth, both now and in all other subsequent examinations, and to keep everything he may see, or hear, or understand, or that may be said to him, strictly secret, gave the following testimony :

" His name is Manuel de Lucena.‡ He is a native of the town of San Vicente, in the Archbishopric of La Guardia,§ in Portugal. He is thirty years old, and a merchant by occupation. He has been engaged in trade between the mines of Pachuca‖ and this City of Mexico. He was arrested about six days ago, and brought and committed to one of the secret jails of this Holy Office."

Following this the MS summarizes Lucena's case, stating that " this witness was arrested on suspicion of being a

---

* That such a colony did exist in Mexico towards the end of the XVI century is proven by Paramo in his work *De origine et progressu Inquisitionis*, published about that time, in which he declaims against the observance of the Passover by Mexican Jews, etc. See on this point, G. A. Kohut, in this *Publication*, Appendix I.

† His full name was Bartolome Lobo Guerrero, and he is no doubt the same who afterwards became Archbishop of Lima and published in 1613 *Constituciones Synodales del Arcobispado de Los Reyes en el Peru;* a second edition appeared in 1636 and a third in 1754.

‡ This name is frequent in the early colonial records, as may be seen from the index to Judge Daly's *Settlement of the Jews in North America* and in the previous numbers of this Society's *Publications.*

§ Sometimes written Laguardia.

‖ The mines at this place are still the most valuable in Mexico.

judaizante (Judaizer), founded on the fact that he had aided or assisted other *judaizantes,* and also on certain allegations respecting his own beliefs. In the testimony on file against him it appears that according to his own admissions he had gone to certain mines and talked there with a Jew against whom analogous charges had been made. During his trial he made a confession and acknowledged to be a Jew, and to observe and to have observed the Law of Moses. He said also that he had taught the Jewish doctrines to other people, and that it was his intention to teach them. The court adjudged him guilty, passed sentence against him, and turned him over for proper punishment to the secular authorities."

This account of de Lucena's case being given, the MS now returns to those portions of his testimony which relate to Almeida. At a session of the court held Thursday, February 16, 1595, " He said, further, that Antonio Lopez* told him that Jorge de Almeida's mother, who died in this country, and whose name the prisoner did not remember, was a Jewess, and a strict observer of the Mosaic Law to such an extent as to fast during the whole week, and eat only once every third day.† The prisoner said also that Jorge de Almeida, the husband of Dona Lenor de Caravajal, who was convicted by this Holy Office of being a Jewess, and Francisco Rodriguez,‡ a brother of Jorge de Almeida, were also observers of the Law of Moses. Both brothers are now in Spain, but the prisoner does not know in what part. Antonio Lopez told the prisoner that Francisco Rodriguez had

---

* A contemporary of the same name is said to have left Spain in 1590 for London. He might have journeyed to Mexico. See De Barrios, quoted by Kayserling, *Sephardim,* etc., p. 167 and note 177.

† The Marranos imposed these penances upon themselves to expiate their sin of outward adherence to the Roman Catholic Church.

‡ Persons of the same name flourished about this time in Spain, whence they were driven by the Inquisition. See Kayserling, *Sephardim,* p. 167.

married in Spain a true Christian woman, by whom he had
a son, whom he had taken to Italy, and that there he had
married a Jewess, although his Christian wife was still
living."

This testimony being read to Lucena was pronounced
correct and was signed by him and by the secretary, Manozca.
The revelations thus made seem to have had the effect of
preserving de Lucena's life, for on September 26, 1596, he
was again brought from jail before the Inquisitor Alonso de
Peralta. On this occasion he presented a statement signed
by himself, " covering five double sheets of paper," which
contained the following relating to Jorge de Almeida :

" Further, I say that Antonio Lopez told me that Christoval Gomez, his cousin, was a Jew, and that the said Gomez
had told this fact to the Licentiate Manuel de Morales, and
to Jorge de Almeida, owing to the circumstance that a negro
woman who belonged to him had called him a Jew." The
object of the consultation was to decide what was to be done
to the negro woman. " That then, while the said Christoval
Gomez was in his store, the above-named Licentiate and
Jorge de Almeida strangled the poor negro woman . . . .
That while they were killing her she cried imploringly
'Sancta Maria,' and that they said to her 'Let her help
you.' . . . . I also say that I suspect that Jorge de
Almeida is a Jew, and found my suspicion on the fact of his
participation in the death of the negro woman belonging to
Christoval Gomez . . . . and also on the fact he is of Jew-
ish descent and is married to a Jewess." This testimony
was duly signed, and a few months later, Thursday, Novem-
ber 21, 1596, as well as on the following day, the Inquisitor
Peralta holding court, and the Dominicans Fray Hernando
de Almansa and Fray Pedro de Mendieta being present,
Lucena repeated his testimony. All of this is attested by
Manozca, the secretary of the tribunal.

TESTIMONY II.

The second piece of testimony is derived from the records of the case against Luis de Caravajal.* He was brought before the tribunal on the 9th of February, 1595, Doctor Lobo Guerrero holding court. He describes himself as a native of the city of Benavente in Castille, but now a resident of Mexico, a bachelor; " he is the son of Francisco Rodriguez Matos,† convicted and turned over by this Holy Office to the secular power and punished in effigy, and of Dona Francisca de Caravajal, the wife of said Rodriguez, who was charged with being an observer of the Mosaic Law, but who was reconciled by this Holy Office. His age is about thirty years. He has no special occupation. He was arrested nine days ago and was committed to the secret jails of this Holy Office."

The MS then summarizes the case of Luis de Caravajal as follows: " This man was arrested by this Holy Office, the first time upon the charge that he observed the Mosaic Law and its rites and ceremonies, but he was admitted to reconciliation at the *auto de fe* which took place on February 24, 1590. Subsequently he was arrested again, on information that he had fallen anew into his former habits and practices. When first examined he did not acknowledge his guilt, but at subsequent examinations, made at his own request, he testified against himself and against his mother and sisters, and said that although he had endeavored to make others believe that he had been converted to the Law of Our Lord Jesus Christ, he always had held the Law of Moses to be true, and had believed in it ever since it was taught to him at the

---

* A family of this name was prominent in the Marrano colony in England at the time of Cromwell. See Lucien Wolf, " Crypto-Jews under the Commonwealth," *Trans. Jewish Hist. Soc. of England,* vol. I, 1895.

† He was burned in effigy in 1592. This *auto de fe* is described by Paramo, quoted by Mr. G. A. Kohut, " Jewish Martyrs of the Inquisition in South America," Appendix I, in this *Publication.*

town of Medina del Campo.   He said also that he expected
to obtain salvation through that law."

On February 25, 1595, the prisoner was again brought
before the tribunal, and after the usual preliminaries he "was
shown a small manuscript book, bound in black leather,
which begins with the words, ' In the name of the Lord of
Hosts,' and was asked whether he recognized it. He
answered that the book was in his own handwriting, and
that it contained a narrative of his life, which he had written
in commemoration of the miracles performed in his favor
and of the mercies shown to him by God.* The book had
been written to be sent, as a letter, to the prisoner's brothers
Balthasar Rodrigues de Çaravajal† and Miguel Rodrigues."
Then follows an examination based on statements contained
in the book which refer to Jorge de Almeida.

"*Question.*   Who is the person mentioned in the said book
who was riding on horseback and took flight when the janitor
of the Inquisition called him, thus refusing to obey the
orders of the Inquisition, and who afterwards, when ordered
to be arrested, made his escape and went to Spain to work
for the release of the prisoner, and of his mother and sisters.

Answer.   That man was Jorge de Almeida, a brother-in-
law of deponent, who was afraid that the Inquisition would
imprison him in order to take possession of the property of
his wife Dona Lenor de Andrada, the sister of deponent,
reconciled by this Holy Office."

The court now adjourned and Luis de Caravajal was
remanded to jail. There he seems to have been kept for
almost a year, when the following action is recorded: " This
prisoner was made acquainted with the testimony given
against him by three witnesses, and was ordered to be tortured
in caput alienum so as to extort from him the confession of

* This appears to be the earliest reference to a book written by a
Jew on the American continent.
† A person of this name (possibly the same) was in Mexico in
1604. See Torquemada, *La Monarquia Indiana,* vol. I, p. 730.

the truth in regard to the persons known by him to be observers of the Law of Moses. This order was given on Thursday, the 8th of February, 1596, but before it was carried into execution the prisoner was admonished and urged, as is the custom in this Holy Office, not to conceal the truth. But as he refused to say anything, he was taken to the torture-chamber, where the same admonition and advice was repeated. The prisoner insisting on his denials, the executioner stripped him of his clothes, leaving him with only his linen drawers. He was again admonished and urged to tell the truth and avoid the torture, but refused to answer. Then the arms of the prisoner were bound together loosely, by means of a rope, and he began to name some persons, saying that they observed the Law of Moses. But as his answers were not satisfactory, the rope was ordered to be twisted four times,* the examination and the torture continuing in this way from half-past nine in the morning until about two o'clock in the afternoon, at which time they suspended because it was dinner-time. The prisoner was left in the torture-chamber, but was allowed to put on his clothes, because it was cold. When dinner was over, at about half-past three, the examination continued."

This occasion was deemed so important that " the Inquisitors Doctor Lobo Guerrero and Licentiate Don Alonso de Peralta . . . . associated themselves to Doctor Don Juan de Cervantes, the Archdeacon of the Cathedral of this city, and Governor of the diocese, in the absence of the Archbishop."

The torture seems to have had the desired effect, for at half-past three, when the court, having dined, resumed its sitting, Luis de Caravajal began to testify as follows :

"And now he remembers that the said Jorge de Almeida, his brother-in-law, and the brother of Miguel Hernandez and

---

* Numerous pictorial representations of the torture exist. See *e. g.* Bernard Picart, *Ceremonies et Coutumes Religieuses de tous les Peuples du Monde*, vol. II, pl. 29 (Amsterdam, 1739).

Hector de Fonseca, believes in the Law which God gave to Moses.* That deponent, after having been reconciled by this Holy Office, and while living at Santiago Hatilulco, with Dona Francisca his mother, and with his sisters, knew that the said Jorge de Almeida was concealed in a house at Santiago because he had been informed that the Holy Office wished to arrest him, and that then when deponent took to the said Jorge de Almeida the book of Fray Luis de Granada entitled ' El Simbolo de la Fé,' wherein many quotations were made from the Law which God gave to Moses, Almeida laughed a great deal at the said Fray Luis, and said that Fray Luis, when writing on these things which he did not understand, must have been drunk.† On that occasion the said Jorge de Almeida confessed to deponent that he was a believer in the Law of Moses and was a Jew."

The prisoner was now asked whether any other person was present at this conversation, and responded specifically : " No other person was present. When the said Jorge de Almeida read in ' El Simbolo de la Fé,' in the presence of deponent, the quotations made therein from the Prophecies of Ezekiel and Zecharias, and noted the words ' There shall be no more than òne flock and one Shepherd,' and 'the Law shall be one,' and ' Israel shall never again be captive,' he laughed and remarked ' How well this has been fulfilled ! ' meaning, as in fact he said, that Christ the Messiah, promised by the Law, had not come." Being again pressed as to whether any one else was present at this interview, he replied that Almeida spoke " only in the presence of deponent and of Miguel Hernandez, who was hidden in the same house." . . . A man named Thomas de Fonseca sent their meals to

* This form is used throughout by the witness.
† Francisco Moyen, a Frenchman who suffered greatly at the hands of the Inquisition in Peru, about a century and a half later, and who was accused of *Judaizing*, had to defend himself against similar charges of irreverently criticising books and dogmas. See Mackenna's work on the *Inquisition as it was in South America* (London, 1869).

the two fugitives and kept watch for their protection. "The said Jorge de Almeida read sometimes from 'El Simbolo' in the presence of deponent and Thomas de Fonseca, but he never spoke of the Law of Moses or declared his belief except when he was with deponent alone or with Miguel Hernandez, his brother.

Question. Whether the said Thomas de Fonseca knew that Jorge de Almeida and Miguel Hernandez were hidden for fear of being arrested by the Inquisition.

Answer. Deponent suspects that he ought to have been acquainted with the fact, but neither Fonseca, nor Almeida, nor Hernandez told deponent that he was so acquainted. The reason why he suspects it is because the said Thomas de Fonseca sent them their meals, and because Jorge de Almeida objected to having the said meals sent from the house of his wife Dona Lenor, who is deponent's sister, on the ground, as said Jorge de Almeida told the said Thomas Fonseca, that he was afraid the Holy Office wanted to arrest him."

The hour of seven P. M. having arrived, the court adjourned, and the prisoner was taken from the torture-chamber to his cell. One week was allowed to elapse, most of it being spent in examinations in the torture-chamber, and on Thursday, Feb. 15, 1596, Luis de Caravajal was again brought before the court, and being asked "whether he remembered anything else in regard to his case, answered: That previous to his having been subjected to torture he had requested for the love of God not to be compelled to tell lies, and that everything he said from the moment at which he began to be tortured until the end of the act was a lie. He said further that he made the present declaration in discharge of his conscience, as he would rather die at the torture than go to hell."

He was then asked what had "induced him to say that all that he had said in the torture-chamber was a lie, when it appears that he said it all of his own will, and with little more than a simple threat, in the torture-chamber on Thursday the 8th, Friday the 9th, Saturday the 10th, Monday the 12th, and Wednesday the 14th of the present month of February, 1596.

Answer. He said it all to avoid being again submitted to torture.

Question. Whether his mother Dona Francisca de Caravajal, and Dona Isabel, Dona Catalina, Dona Mariana,* Dona Lenor, and Anna, Balthasar Rodrigues de Caravajal, his brother Miguel, the two Thomas de Fonseca, Sebastian Rodrigues, Sebastian de la Pena,† Manuel de Lucena,‡ Manuel Gomez Navarro,§ Andres Rodrigues, Manuel Rodrigues, Anna Lopez and her daughter Lenor Diaz, Constanca Rodrigues, Clara Henriquez, Justa Mendez, Beatriz Enriquez la Payba,‖ and her daughter Catalina Enriquez, and Diego and Pedro Enriquez, observe the Law of Moses, and are Jews, or whether deponent has borne false witness against them.

Answer. That his mother Dona Francisca, and Dona Isabel, Dona Mariana, Dona Lenor, Balthasar Rodrigues, Miguel, Justa Mendez, Manuel de Lucena and Manuel Gomez Navarro are Jews and keep and observe the Law which God gave to Moses. In regard to all the other persons mentioned he has borne false witness against them for fear of the torture. He heard in jail that if he did not retract

---

* See her testimony below.

† In the seventeenth century several persons bearing this name suffered martyrdom. Some are mentioned in Kayserling's *Ein Feiertag in Madrid* (Leipzig, 1859), pp. 38, 43. The name is uncommon even in Spain.

‡ See his testimony above.

§ Three persons of this name are mentioned as settled in Barbados, 1670. *Pub. Am. Jewish Hist. Soc.* No. 1, pp. 105–107.

‖ The name Payba occurs in the list of *Judaizantes* of the Inquisition of Toledo, 1654. See Joseph Jacobs, *An Inquiry into the sources of the History of the Jews in Spain*, London, 1894, p. 1, No. 6. This name is undoubtedly identical with Paiva, often met with in Jewish history and literature. See Kayserling's *Sephardim*, p. 285.

and withdraw all the false testimony given by him he would go to hell."

Being asked from whom he heard this, the prisoner replied that " he did not hear any voice, but that it was an inner voice, in the manner of a revelation, which is heard the same as a voice."

This testimony was read over to the prisoner and pronounced by him to be correct.

That the combined torture and examination joined to the horror of his situation rendered Luis de Caravajal desperate is shown by the next entry. "As soon as the prisoner left the court-room he threw himself from the windows of the hall into the yard below, and in consequence thereof the said Luis de Caravajal was hurt."

The next day, Friday the 16th of February, 1596, " the Inquisitor Doctor Lobo Guerrero having come down to the cell of Luis de Caravajal, where the latter was lying in bed in consequence of the fall of yesterday, His Honor told the said Luis de Caravajal that the warden of the jail had reported that he (the prisoner) wished to say something to the court, and that in compliance with that request he (the Inquisitor) had come to hear what he desired to state. Then the prisoner said that it was true that he had requested to be granted this audience, and also had begged that the Inquisitor Don Alonso de Peralta should not be present, because the mere sight of him made his flesh creep, such was the terror with which his rigor inspired him. He said all this to the Warden and asked him to request the Inquisitor Doctor Lobo Guerrero to do him the favor to come down alone, in order to ratify all that deponent had stated in the torture-chamber on the different occasions of his examination there. What he said there is the truth; and if deponent yesterday retracted the said statement it was only because the demon had tempted him so to do by making him believe that he would go to eternal damnation if he did not take back all he had said, and also for the fear he feels of the anger of the Inquisitor Licentiate Don Alonso de Peralta. In his opinion the best evidence of the fact that he was tempted by the demon, as aforesaid, is to be found in the event which took place yesterday evening, when deponent left the court-room and threw himself down into the yard below, because the attempt of any one to kill himself is a far graver sin than bearing false witness against another. That the latter was not the case with him, because what he said in the torture-chamber is the truth."

The various depositions made by the prisoner in the torture-chamber were now read to him, and declaring them to be true, he affixed his signature to the record.

On the 19th of February, 1596, the Inquisitor Doctor Lobo Guerrero, accompanied by Fray Pedro de Galanza and Fray Geronimo de Araux, priests of the religious order of St. Dominic, " who promised under oath to keep the matter secret," and Doctor Martos de Boorques, the prosecuting attorney of the Holy Office, visited Luis de Caravajal in his cell and there obtained a ratification from him of all his testimony against Jorge de Almeida.

TESTIMONY III.

The third testimony is derived from a member of the same family, the sister of the previous witness. On May 29th, 1600, a woman was brought before the court, Alonso de Peralta holding the evening session. In answer to a question she stated " her name is Dona Mariana Nunez de Caravajal ; her age 29 years; she is the daughter of Francisco Rodrigues, convicted of being a Jew, and condemned and executed in effigy, and of Dona Francisca Nunez de Caravajal, also convicted of being a *judaizante*, both natives of the city of Benavente in the kingdom of Castille ; she is not married ; she has lived during the last three years in this city of Mexico, in the house of Dona Maria de Peralta, the mother of Bernadino Vasquez de Tapia,* a familiar of this Holy Office. In the first year she suffered much from a disease which she contracted in her mother's house, and lost her mind. She suffered from great melancholy brought about by the troubles she had and by her sins. At the expiration of the said three years," in 1599, this unfortunate young woman stated that she recovered her reason, which was signalized by her becoming a true convert to the Catholic Church. She had had lucid intervals, she stated, during this period, and had gone to confession to Fray Juan de Santiago, a Franciscan. From him she received absolution. She had confessed to Fray Alonso de Contreras and to Fernando de Bustamente, but had not mentioned to them the facts described to the first-named priest. Not satisfied with this confession, she told Juan de Santiago that she felt it necessary, in order to clear her conscience, to make confession before the Holy Office. The priest told her "that to speak as she was speaking was insanity." She told him that she was forced to confess that she had relapsed into Jewish practices after having been given absolution and admitted to reconciliation, and that her confession had to be made in the Holy Office and nowhere else. This priest, Juan de Santiago, tried to dissuade her and told her that she could be saved without going before the Inquisition. She asserts, however, that she asked to be brought there, and expresses her pleasure at being brought. This, however, she immediately denies, stating that she had come of her own free will,† "in company with Pedro de Fonseca."

"Her object in coming to this tribunal was to request the

---

*A person of this name was in the train of Fernando Cortez; he held the office of *Fator del Rei*. See Torquemada, *La Monarquia Indiana*, vol. I, p. 486. The Marrano Pedro Vasquez of Madrid is mentioned among the victims of the Inquisition at an *auto de fe* held there in 1680. See Kayserling, *Ein Feiertag in Madrid* (1859), p. 27.

† It will be noticed below that in the summary of the case it is stated that she was arrested.

arrest of her niece Dona Lenor de Caceres, the daughter of
Antonio Diaz de Caceres and Dona Catalina de la Cueva,*
who is deponent's sister. . . . . She declared that, thinking
the Law of Moses to be the good Law, and the one through
which she could be saved, she had returned to it and to its
practices. And it is not right to say that she had returned
to that Law, because in reality she had never abandoned it,
although when imprisoned and tried for the first time, she
testified that she had relinquished it.

Deponent was admitted to reconciliation, the ceremony
taking place on the festival of St. Mathias, she abjuring all
her errors and saying that she detested them and not less all
other kinds of heresy. That on that occasion she appeared
at the *auto de fe* wearing the penitential robe. On the day
following she was brought to the court-room, and then she
made the abjuration and signed it. But all of this was
merely *pro forma*, because truly and really she never gave up,
as has already been stated, the Mosaic Law, until the day of
the festival of the Immaculate Conception in 1596, when a
public *auto de fe* took place.† That during the whole time
aforesaid deponent continued to observe the Law of Moses,
and to keep Saturdays as holy days, the festivities beginning
on Fridays after sunset, to read the Psalms without adding
to them the words *gloria patri*,‡ and in fact to do all the
things which she had confessed and of which she had been
accused when first imprisoned and tried.

She also kept the festivals of the Passover and of the
unleavened bread and the lamb, which are one and the same
thing, and coincided with the Holy Week, and also the festi-

* The same as Catalina de Caravajal, wife of Antonio Diaz de
Caceres. A person of this name was in Pizarro's camp, 1547. See
Helps, *Spanish Conquest of America*, vol. IV, p. 227.

† For an account of this *auto de fe*, the tenth in Mexico, see
Appendix.

‡ Francisco Moyen was charged with the same offence of omitting
the words *gloria patri* by the Inquisition at Lima in the middle of
the eighteenth century. See Mackenna's work, *l. c.*

val of the giving of the Law of Moses which takes place forty* days afterwards. She fasted from sunrise to sunset on all Sundays in the week, and ordinarily on Mondays and Thursdays. On some occasions she also fasted on Fridays. The fast of Queen Esther, which lasts three days, was also observed by her. She does not remember now at what part of the year this latter fast occurs, but she remembers distinctly to have kept it two years in succession and to have done so for purposes of penance. During these three days deponent ate nothing, and employed her time in reading the Psalms and saying some prayers which she does not remember now. Other years the said fast was kept by her only in part, as deponent used to take, once every day, after dark, some lenten food, and even meat, when she was told that she could do so.

She also kept the fast of the great day of the Lord, which occurs on the tenth day of the September moon; and then deponent ate nothing from sunset on the eve of the holy day until the rising of the star on the day following. When she took any supper during those fasts she only had lenten food. She never worked during those festivals, and she employed her time in reciting psalms without the *gloria patri*, also saying certain prayers which Licentiate Manuel de Morales had given to Luis de Caravajal and Balthasar Rodrigues, brothers of deponent. When she felt tired at night deponent used to lie down for a while on her bed, and then she got up again and continued her prayers and exercises throughout the following day until supper-time.

She does not remember any particular ceremony to have taken place in addition to those fasts and prayers. On Saturdays they never did any work, but they dressed better than during the rest of the week. When possible, the meals eaten that day were cooked the day before. Deponent did and observed all this in company with her mother Dona Francisca de Caravajal, and her brother and sisters Luis

* Fifty.

de Caravajal and Dona Isabel, Dona Lenor, Dona Catalina
and Dona Anna."

The court was now adjourned and the witness admonished
"to keep quiet in her prison, without communicating with
any one, and to keep all she had heard, said or seen, in strict
secrecy."

Then a summary of the case follows, whose divergence
from the testimony above given will be noticed.

"This deponent was arrested on the charge of having
relapsed into the observation of the dead law of Moses, a
charge to which she pleaded guilty, giving full testimony both
against herself and against other persons who were guilty of
the same offence. In addition to the declaration made by
her that she had recovered entirely and was again fully of
sound mind and understanding, the proper investigation on
the subject was made previous to her arrest, and it was found
that the deponent had been indeed restored to reason,* and
had been of sound mind for some time and had gone to confession and communion as a person of good judgment."

On the next day, May 30, 1600, Dona Mariana was again
brought before the court and testified as follows:

"That Antonio Diaz de Caceres, Jorge de Almeida,
Hector de Fonseca, Thomas de Fonseca (the latter a resident
of Las Minas de Tarco), Isabel Machado† and her father
Antonio Machado, Clara Enriquez, Justa Mendez, Con-
stanca Rodriguez and her brother Domingo Rodriguez, Jorge
Rodriguez, Antonio Diaz Marquez,‡ Sebastian de la Pena,

---

*This statement is contradicted by the evident incoherence of the
testimony.

† Francisco Machado fled from the Inquisition in Portugal in
1680. See Kayserling, *Ein Feiertag in Madrid*, p. 33. Another,
Abraham de Macado, is mentioned as living in Martinique in 1680.
Revue des Études Juives, vol. II, p. 102. Mr. N. Taylor Phillips
published in this Society's *Publications* No. 2 some interesting
notes on the Machado family in New York.

‡ In 1680 several persons bearing this name were condemned by
the tribunal at Madrid. See Kayserling, *Ein Feiertag*, etc., p. 24.

Lenor Rodriguez wife of Manuel Alvarez,* her son George Alvarez, and Anna Lopez and her daughter Lenor Diaz, are Jews and observe the Law of Moses.

What she knows about Antonio Diaz Caceres is that he fasted on the great day of the Lord when he was living at the house of Hernando de Avila in San Juan in this city of Mexico, about twelve years ago, in company with deponent and Dona Catalina de la Cueva his wife and the sister of the deponent, a certain Francisco Jorge who had just arrived from Spain and is now dead, and Dona Anna his sister, who, although at that time a mere girl, fasted like the others. No other persons were present at those fastings, as Dona Francisca, deponent's mother, and her other brothers lived at that time at Tarco. The said fasting was kept in obedience to the Law of Moses, and lasted from the sunset of the day before until the rising of the evening star on the day of the fast itself, and then they had for their supper fish and other things which deponent does not remember now.

Deponent used to recite on that day some of the prayers in the book left to her brother by Licentiate Morales, and the said Antonio Diaz de Caceres and Dona Catalina and Dona Anna listened to what she read, standing up and looking toward the east. About an hour was consumed in reading the said prayers. Immediately afterwards Antonio Diaz de Caceres went out to attend to his business and did not come back until supper-time. Deponent and Dona Catalina and Dona Anna remained together the whole day and employed their time in reciting some other prayers from the book aforesaid and in confessing their sins to God in a general way. Antonio Diaz Caceres afterwards did the same thing by reading the formula of confession given by that book, which deponent does not remember now in the least. The said Antonio Diaz de Caceres was allowed to marry Dona

---

* Concerning Juan Alvarez who fell a victim to the Inquisition see *Pub. Am. Jewish Hist. Soc.* No. 2, p. 75.

Catalina because he was a Jew and an observer of the Law of Moses.

Deponent said further that upon information given to Antonio Diaz de Caceres that deponent's father was a Jew, he attended the funeral of the latter and was one of the pallbearers. He also made arrangements with deponent's brother Luis de Caravajal to marry the said Dona Catalina and to cause Jorge de Almeida to marry Don Lenor. Luis de Carvajal himself wrote to deponent's mother Dona Francisca Nunez de Carvajal, saying that Antonio Diaz de Caceres and Jorge de Almeida desired to marry the above-named sisters of deponent, and vouching for their respectability and other qualities which made them worthy of the young ladies' hands. Dona Francisca gave her consent to the marriages, but nothing about the arrangements was reported to the Governor."

The two marriages were solemnized at the city of Parmco,* and two days later the newly wedded couples, accompanied by Dona Francisca and Donna Anna, sailed for Spain. They returned in six months, and together with Balthasar Rodriguez and Dona Isabel, brother and sister of deponent, moved to the San Paolo ward in this City of Mexico, and occupied the houses of Dona Anna de Alcaçar.

"Two days afterwards deponent was sent to the college for young ladies, where she remained for nine months. Soon after she had left the college, Jorge de Almeida sent for her, and for her mother and sisters, asking them to go and stay with him for some time at his estates in Tarco, which they did. Subsequently they came back to the City of Mexico, to the house of Antonio Diaz de Caceres, in the district named San Juan. . . . It was there that they acknowledged for the first time that they were Jews and observed the Law of Moses, and fasted (as the deponent has said) on the great day of the Lord. Francisco Jorge was a relative of deponent, who used to lead Dona Catalina by the hand when she went

*In Mexico.

to hear mass, and he often came to the house to see Antonio
Diaz de Caceres and the rest of the family. Deponent understands that he also fasted on the said great day of the Lord
and acknowledged to be a Jew. . . . Soon after that fasting the
arrest of deponent and of her mother and brothers, by order
of this Holy Office, took place. Antonio Diaz de Caceres,
seeing what had happened, went to China, where he lived
three years, at the end of which time he came back and
stayed at the home of Antonio de los Cobos, feigning not to
live with his wife, on the ground that her reconciliation by
this Holy Office proved that she had professed the Jewish
religion. He did this for fear he himself might be taken
for a Jew. When they were again together, because he
at last made pretence to yield to the entreaties of several
religious persons who pleaded for his wife, they began at
once to practice the religion of Moses and to observe all its
rites. And deponent used to read to them from the book which
she has said was given to her family by Licentiate Morales,
and to recite with them some Psalms without the *gloria
patri.* . . . She also used to read to them some canticles
taken from the sacred Scriptures, in regard to the keeping of
the Sabbath-day. They often came on Saturdays, for the
purpose of enjoying rest and pleasure. . . . The said Antonio
Diaz de Caceres advised them always to be very cautious,
because if arrested again and convicted of having relapsed
into the practice of the Law of Moses they would be punished
by death. That deponent's mother and her sons and daughters
were very imprudent in this respect, and did not guard
themselves against an Indian woman whom they had in the
house, and before whom they sang their canticles, without
thinking that she might accuse them. He tried always to
persuade deponent's mother and her sisters and brothers to
wear patiently, for the love of God, their penitential garments,
and explained to them why he had apparently refused to take
back Dona Catalina as his wife. Sometimes deponent herself
went to the home of Antonio Diaz de Caceres to spend there

the Sabbath-day, and keep it with him and his wife. Her brother Luis de Caravajal used also to go there and to read . . . some of the precepts of the Law of Moses, which in the said book were written in verse, and also some of the canticles which have been mentioned before. Antonio Diaz de Caceres thought that all these things were very appropriate to keep the Sabbath-day in due form. Otherwise he never kept it publicly as a holy day, and was particular in going on Saturdays to his place of business, and in never wearing on that day a better dress, or even a clean shirt, and in not refusing to eat pork. He did all these things carefully because he was very prudent."

At this time Dona Mariana fell sick and was obliged to take to her bed. She asserts that from this time on her family began to grow suspicious of her. She "saw them all eating a meal at noon, on the great day of the Lord, and as she expressed her surprise at such a thing, Dona Catalina replied that she did not know the reason why they could not take a meal at that time. Deponent understood that they distrusted her and said nothing more."

The testimony was now read to the witness, and upon her signing it she was taken back to her cell.

On Friday, June 2, 1600, Dona Mariana was again brought before the court, and stated in reply to a question that she remembered that "Gabriel Enriquez, a brother of Justa Mendez, is a Jew and an observer of the Mosaic Law."

To the question "How deponent knows that Jorge de Almeida is a Jew and observes the Law of Moses," she summarized her testimony before given and adds these statements : "That he observed the Law of Moses because he believed the said Law to be good, and the only one through which they could be saved. He also said that he awaited the coming of the Messiah—that Christ our Redeemer had not been the Messiah, and that he thought that the people who threw stones at him when he wanted to act as God, had been blessed." She then repeats the account of his fasting, and

adds, " This fasting took place one or two years before Dona
Isabel was arrested for the first time by this Holy Office.
. . . Antonio Diaz de Caceres was not present at the Tarco
fasting, because he happened to be then in the City of Mexico,
temporarily, on account of certain lawsuits in which he was
engaged at that time. When Dona Isabel was arrested the
first time, by order of this Holy Office, Jorge de Almeida
came to deponent's house and informed her mother and her
brothers and sisters of what had happened. He was afraid
that they would also be arrested, and that they would, after
arrest, depose against him and against Antonio Diaz de
Caceres, in which case, he said, they would have no one to
protect them." . . .

Again asked for further testimony against Jorge de
Almeida, " she remembers to have heard him say that his
mother, whose name he did not mention, was a Jewess and
observed the Law of Moses."

On Tuesday afternoon, June 6, 1600, the Inquisitor
Peralta holding court, and " two honorable and religious
persons, Fray Diego and Fray Pedro de Carranca of the
order of St. Dominic" being present, Dona Mariana de
Caravajal was brought in, and upon motion of the prosecuting
attorney ratified all her testimony.

But the court was not yet finished with Dona Mariana, and
on Tuesday, June 13, 1600, she was again summoned. She
now introduces a most astonishing narrative, the truth of
which is difficult to believe. Thirteen years before the
present time (when she was 16 years old) she was engaged to
be married to Jorge de Leon, a cousin of Jorge de Almeida.
That though Almeida was already married to her sister
Dona Lenor, he proposed to marry her as well. That
Almeida objected to Jorge de Leon because the latter did
not observe the Law of Moses. That on this ground she
broke her engagement, and with the consent of Dona Lenor
became engaged to Jorge de Almeida. That this marriage

was objected to by Gonçalo Perez Ferro* on the ground of its unwisdom, as well as because Jorge de Leon was a brother of his wife Dona Catalina de Leon. According to her statement, Ferro advised that she marry Hector de Fonseca, "a brother of Jorge de Almeida," who was himself married to a Christian woman and whose marriage was therefore null and void. To this plan she says she agreed, and finally married Hector de Fonseca "in the Jewish way." She did not, however, live with Fonseca, it being understood that their actual union was to be postponed until they could go to some Jewish community and keep the Law of Moses with entire freedom. When Almeida heard this he protested to such a degree that Fonseca gave up the idea, he being afraid of Jorge de Almeida. "It was even said that Jorge de Almeida had challenged him to a duel." At this time, the witness said, she lost her reason.

Her next piece of testimony is to the effect that " Jorge de Almeida, Luis de Caravajal, Balthasar Rodriguez and Cristoval Gomez had a counterfeited mark or seal to be stamped on silver bullion, so as to make it appear that the fifth due to the treasury on that particular amount of silver had been paid . . . . the stamp was kept in the possession of the said Jorge de Almeida, deponent's husband.

Question. How long is it since Hector de Fonseca acknowledged to deponent that he was a Jew, and observed the Law of Moses, and whether he had told deponent who had taught him the said Law.

Answer. It was about the time at which the said Hector de Fonseca married deponent,† which was, she thinks, about twelve years or more. . . . . He had a book all written in verse, which contained prayers and explanations of the

* This is a very rare name among the Spanish-Portuguese Jews. One Manuel Ferro is spoken of as a martyr in Kayserling's *Sephardim*, p. 264.

† It will be noted that at first Dona Mariana stated that she was unmarried ; above she states that Jorge de Almeida was her husband, and now mentions Hector de Fonseca in the same capacity.

Mosaic Law, for which he expressed great admiration. He
said also that he regretted very much being married to a
staunch Christian, because he had no liberty to practice his
own religion, and had to live as a martyr, for which reason
he often climbed to the top of the mountains and wandered
alone through the wilderness, crying aloud and asking God
to pardon him for his sins. From all of these statements
deponent inferred that Hector de Fonseca ought to have
learned the Law of Moses from his own parents when he
reached the age of reason. He was older than his brother
Jorge de Almeida, and the latter was a great Jew.". . . .
Then follow some further questions and answers concerning
her marriage complications, but as they brought out nothing
new, the prisoner was taken back to her cell.

On Thursday, June 15, 1600, the examination of Dona
Mariana was continued. The only fact elicited was "that
one Miguel Hernandez, who is a brother of Jorge de
Almeida, is a Jew and a follower of the Law of Moses,
and that she knows it because she heard Jorge de Almeida
himself say so. Deponent heard the same thing from Dona
Lenor her sister. The said Miguel Hernandez went to
Spain together with his brother Jorge de Almeida."

More than one month was allowed to elapse, and on Sunday, July 16, 1600 (for no day was too good for this holy
work) the Inquisitor Peralta held the morning session of the
court, assisted by the Dominicans Fray Pedro de Galança
and Fray Diego de Carrança. Dona Mariana was asked
" whether she remembers to have testified in this Holy Office
in regard to matters connected with the Faith." Her answer
is significant of the state of her reason, for she only remembers to have testified against Antonio Diaz de Caceres. She
is then informed that she has testified against Antonio Diaz
de Caceres, Antonio Diaz Marquez, Sebastian de la Pena,
Justa Mendez, Clara Enriquez, Thomas de Fonseca of Tarco,
Hector de Fonseca, Jorge de Almeida, Miguel Hernandez,
Marco Antonio, and Gonzalo Perez Ferro. The testimony
was then read to her, and she ratified it.

Testimony IV.

The fourth and last piece of testimony was derived from one Diego Diaz Nieto. He was brought before the court on Wednesday, January 3, 1601, and stated in reply to a question that "he is a native of Oporto in the kingdom of Portugal; he is the son of Ruy Diaz Nieto and Ines Nunez; he is 25 or 26 years old and is a merchant engaged in trade between the City of Mexico and the neighboring towns. Deponent said that he had served a term of imprisonment in jail for one year, wearing the reconciliation garments, under a sentence passed against him on December 8, 1596. He said also that he was admitted to reconciliation upon his having abjured, and protested to detest, all the errors he had committed by observing the Law of Moses, or by holding any other tenet whatever which might be construed as heresy or apostasy against the Holy Catholic Evangelical Church of our Redeemer and Saviour Jesus Christ, and against the Holy See and the Roman Church; and that the said abjuration was made in writing and signed by him, as the record of his first trial must show." The record was brought and he declared his signature genuine.

"Deponent further said that he was arrested last Saturday at Tescuco,* and brought here and committed to prison in one of the secret jails." The following summary of his case is given: "This man was arrested again on the charge that he had relapsed into the observance of the dead law of Moses and its rites and ceremonies, in spite of his abjuration and reconciliation at the end of his first trial. He denied the charge."

On January 16, 1601, he was brought before the court and arraigned: "For having entered into discussion with several Jews, with whom he was in friendly relations, about several matters concerning the Law of Moses, and stating that the said Law was good, and that men should be saved

* A town in Mexico; also written Tezcuco and Texcoco.

through it and not through the Law of Jesus Christ, which was mockery, which statements were approved by a person who was very close to him.

Also for having kept the Sabbath-day on Saturdays, on which day he was particular in wearing a clean shirt, and reciting several prayers, particularly the great prayer called *Amida,* which the prisoner knew by heart, which begins 'Adonay, Adonay, thou shalt open my lips' and which is made up out of many Psalms.

The prisoner then said that there is something in these statements which is correct, and that as in the end everything will be found out, he has determined to tell the truth as follows: He was born and brought up in the city of Ferrara in Italy, where there are three Jewish communities, the Portuguese, the Italian and the German. The prisoner was brought up in the Portuguese, to which his father Ruy Diaz Nieto belonged. The real name of deponent is Isaac Nieto, and that of his father Jacob Nieto.* In the year 1590, or a little before or afterwards, deponent came with his father to this country, bringing with them a rescript or bull which his father had succeeded in obtaining from Pope Clement VIII,† on the pretence that he was to engage in the redemption of captives. His father went to Rome for the bull, and when he had obtained it he and deponent made a trip to Spain for the purpose of making some money out of that document. While in Madrid they met Jorge de Almeida, with whom they were acquainted, because he had been in the Jewish community aforesaid about 17 years

* About this famous family, a member of which was Rabbi in Surinam, see Dr. Kayserling in *Pub. Am. Jewish Hist. Soc.*, No. 3, p. 18; G. A. Kohut, *ibid.*, pp. 112, 119.

† A search through the *Bullarum privilegiorum ac diplomatum Romanorum pontificium amplissima collectio* (Rome, 1753) has failed to reveal this bull. Nieto's memory must have been wrong either with regard to the date or the name of the Pope, as Clement VIII was not made a Pope until January 30, 1592. His predecessor, Sixtus V, issued two bulls with relation to the redemption of captives in 1589, but no mention has been found of Ruy Diaz Nieto. No light is cast on this subject by Berliner's *Gesch. d. Juden in Rom,* 1893.

ago, if not more, having left the said community to come
to this country. Almeida then advised deponent and his
father to come to New Spain, and said that he would obtain
from His Majesty, as he indeed obtained, the proper permission to collect in this country the alms which the said
bull authorized deponent's father to ask. He charged for his
services 100 or 150 ducats, and he gave deponent and his
father some letters of recommendation for Luis de Caravajal
and his mother and sisters, and also, if deponent remembers
aright, for his brother-in-law Antonio Diaz de Caceres.
This was the way in which they happened to decide to come to
this country of New Spain. Neither deponent nor his father
brought any letter from the brothers of Luis de Caravajal, who
went to Europe from here and resided in the aforesaid Jewish
community, namely Joseph Lumbrosso, who is the eldest, and
is married not to Esther, as stated in the indictment, but to
Anna, and Jacob Lumbrosso,* who is a bachelor. But they
gave information about them to Luis de Caravajal and to his
mother and sisters, and reported how the said brothers were in
the said Jewish community and practiced the Jewish religion.
This was said in the presence of Antonio Diaz de Caceres,
who . . . tried to stop them and change the subject of the
conversation. He is very guarded, and was afraid that some
harm might come to him out of that conversation. Domingo
Cuello, who it is rumored died in Guastepec† after having been
reconciled by this Holy Office, took deponent and his father,
as soon as they arrived in this country, to the house of Luis
de Caravajal and his mother and sisters. The said Domingo
Cuello came with deponent and his father from Seville, in
the fleet of General Luis Alfonso Flores, but did not stop at

---

* The occurrence of this name in the present MS is of much
interest, in view of the presence of an individual of the same name
in Maryland 50 years later. See Hollander, *Pub. Am. Jewish Hist.
Soc.*, No. 1, p. 25 ff. A Jacob Lumbroso was a physician and Rabbi
and writer at Venice about the period of this MS. See Kayserling,
Biblioteca Española-Portugueza Judaica, p. 64.

† A town in Mexico.

the port of San Juan de Ulua,* as deponent and his father did, but continued his voyage to this city. Deponent and his father stayed a while at the inn called Del Volador, and then started for this city. Shortly after their arrival they met Domingo Cuello at the door of Manuel Alvarez, and, as deponent has stated, Cuello took him and his father, or rather deponent alone, to the home of Luis de Caravajal, which was very far from there. Deponent remembers now very well that his father decided not to go when he heard of the long distance to be traversed to reach that house, and that he remained at the store of Antonio Fernandez and of Beatriz Rodriguez, his wife, which was opposite to the house of Don Geronimo de Carcamo, near the cathedral of this city. When deponent reached the house of Luis de Caravajal and delivered to him the letter of which he was the bearer, Domingo Cuello told the said Caravajal and his mother and sisters that deponent and his father had come from a Jewish community and were acquainted with the Lumbrosso brothers, and then they all acknowledged to each other to be Jews, and followers and observers of the Law of Moses. The same mutual recognition took place afterwards in deponent's presence in regard to his father. At 5 o'clock in the afternoon deponent took leave of the said Dona Francisca de Caravajal and her daughters Dona Isabel, Dona Lenor, Dona Mariana and Dona Anna, and returned accompanied by Luis de Caravajal and Domingo Cuello to the store of Antonio Fernandez, where his father was waiting for him. Then the said Luis de Caravajal took deponent and his father to the house of Antonio de Caceres, where, at the invitation of the latter and of his wife Dona Catalina, they all took supper. Before sitting at the table the conversation turned on the subject of the Jewish community whence they came and where Antonio Diaz's brothers-in-law had been left; but the said Antonio Diaz cut short the conversation by saying 'let that matter alone and come on to supper.' Antonio Diaz de Caceres gave

* The fort guarding the harbor of Vera Cruz.

rooms in his house, which is near the church of Santa Catalina, to deponent and to his father, and his wife Dona Catalina treated them with great kindness. Deponent and his father said to Diaz that they had in their possession the bull before mentioned, and that Jorge de Almeida, his brother-in-law, was left by them in Seville when he had delivered to them the permits necessary to carry on the redemption of the captives."

It was now time to adjourn the court, but before this was done the prisoner stated that he was a Jew and had never been baptized. He had, however, some doubts, and asked that a copy of the Hebrew Bible be given him; if his doubts could be removed he would ask for the waters of baptism. This testimony is witnessed by Juan de la Pavia, notary.

His doubts were settled and he was baptized. On the 17th of January, 1601, he again appeared before the court and testified as follows: "That while deponent was in Madrid he became acquainted there with one Juan Rodriguez Silva, a native of some place in Portugal which deponent does not know, who had been in the Jewish community at Ceronique,* in the land of the Great Turk, and knew something of the Hebrew language, ... that he was living in the house of Jorge de Almeida, a brother-in-law of Luis de Caravajal. Said house was near the main post office." . . . . Rodriguez Silva was also a Jew. The witness then repeats his statement made about Jorge de Almeida and the Papal bull, and continues: "One day while deponent was walking through the streets with Jorge de Almeida alone, it happened that they saw the Most Holy Sacrament coming down from San Felipe toward the Square. And the said Jorge de Almeida told him, ' Let us turn back and go the other way, so as not to be obliged to take off our hats before this,' meaning the Most Holy Sacrament, 'because it is just as good to keep the hat on as to take it off.' Then he declared to deponent that he was a Jew, that he

* Salonica.

observed the Law of Moses, that he had been at the Jewish community at Ferrara, that he had married in this City of Mexico Dona Lenor de Caravajal, who was a niece of a Governor,* and a sister of Luis de Caravajal and of the two Jews who lived at Ferrara. . . . Deponent left the said Jorge de Almeida and Juan Rodriguez de Silva at Seville in the house of Blanca Lorenço, the sister of one Petayo Alvarez, who was in this country. Another brother of Almeida, Miguel Hernandez, was living in the house, and these two, as well as the two Nietos, confessed to one another that they were Jews in the presence of Rodriguez de Silva and Domingo Cuello, the latter having been 'reconciled.'"

He relates other instances which show that they were all Jews and indulged in mockery at the expense of Catholic ceremonies, and speaks of a rich "captain" in Lisbon, whose name he forgets, but who is a Jew, who had given Rodriguez de Silva a hundred ducats. "Deponent understands that the said Blanca Lorenço is also a Jewess and observes the Law of Moses, and he holds this opinion because of the fact that she admits Jews to her house, and also that he has seen her cut off the heads of chickens, and clean the meat and put it in water so as to take away from it all the blood; but she never told deponent or any one else that she was a Jewess, nor has deponent heard any one say so. The said Jorge de Almeida and Miguel Hernandez told deponent that they had in this country a brother who called himself Francisco Rodriguez, and is known also by another name which deponent does not recollect, and deponent remembers to have seen the said Francisco Rodriguez in the Jewish community at Ferrara, whence he went

---

*The governor was also named Luis de Caravajal. See G. A. Kohut, Appendix I, in this *Publication*. It is barely possible, however, that the uncle here referred to was Luis de Carabajal y de la Cueva who planted the colony of New Leon, 1580-5, and died 1595. Bancroft, *Mexico*, vol. II, pp. 777-9. It will be remembered that Dona Catalina de Carvajal is called de la Cueva in this MS.

to Venice, in which city he married a Jewess whose name deponent has forgotten. From Venice he went with his wife to Ceronique, and from there both came to this country. Deponent has heard from Marco Antonio, who was reconciled by this Holy Office, that the said Francisco Rodriguez is now in Sonçonate." . . . .

In answer to a question he says: " Jorge de Almeida is of medium height and dark complexion; he has a peculiar mark on his face, and his head is hairless in several places, caused, in deponent's opinion, by ulcers; his age must be from 35 to 40 years.

Deponent further said that when the fleet was about to start for New Spain, Jorge de Almeida came from Madrid, and took rooms at the house of Blanca Lorenço, whom he called a cousin; he had in his possession three letters to be delivered in this city, one to Luis de Caravajal, another to this Holy Office, and a third to some one now forgotten by deponent. Said letters were relative to relieving the said Luis de Caravajal and his sisters from the necessity of wearing the penitential garments." After taking this testimony the court adjourned.

On January 26, 1601, Diego Diaz Nieto was again summoned and subjected to a cross-examination. He reiterated some of his former statements, but nothing new was elicited.

On the 10th of March, 1601, the Inquisitor Don Alonso de Peralta held court assisted by Fray Luis de Vallejo, a *quali- ficador* of the Holy Office, and Fray Pedro de Galanca, a Dominican. Diego Diaz Nieto was then summoned and informed that " owing to the fact that he had accepted baptism " he had at previous hearings been sworn in the Christian way " by making with his right hand the sign of the cross," but for greater safety it was decided to examine him again upon oath administered in the Jewish way, as follows :* " Do

---

* For a somewhat similar oath administered to Jews in France in the thirteenth century, see Hannah Adams, *History of the Jews,* vol. I, p. 287.

you swear by the Creator who made heaven and earth and the sea, and the sands, and wrote his name in four letters *Jot, He, Vav, He,* and took the children of Israel out from the land of Egypt and parted the sea, and gave the Law to Moses on Mt. Sinai, and brought the children of Israel through the desert and gave them the manna, and afterwards took them to the promised land, to tell the truth in answer to the questions which may be propounded to you by this Holy Office—all other oaths which you may have taken to the contrary notwithstanding,—whether the said questions refer to persons now living, and are either present or absent, or to persons who have departed this life?" "I do." "If you so do, may the Creator have mercy on you, and grant you, and confer upon you all the promises made by the Prophets to the people of Israel. But if you fail so to do, may the Creator destroy you as he destroyed the people of the Flood in the time of Noah, and Sodom and Gomorrah in the time of Abraham, and may you be confounded like Korah and his companions Dathan and Abiram were confounded in the desert, and may all the curses set forth in the fifth book of the Law of Moses, and in the Psalms of David, in the fifth book of Elohete and Laçiategras, fall upon you; and may no son who inherits your name be born in your house. You must state the truth, without adding to it or taking from it anything at all, and must not fail so to do, either because of love, or kinship, or for the sake of peace, or because of gifts given you, or interest of any kind. All that you may say must be said and explained in such a way as to permit its being put down in writing, and understood, and confirmed and ratified at all times as the expression of the truth. And you must not pay any attention to any threat, or any consideration of fear, because Our Lord will deliver you from all evil if you say the truth and nothing but the truth *baruthie sino aruthie.* And the said Diego Diaz said then 'Amen.'

Whereupon the prisoner was informed that the prosecuting attorney for this Holy Office has produced him as a witness against the persons here below named, and has caused all that deponent said against them in his testimony in his own case to be recorded here, namely: against his father Ruy Diaz, and against Antonio de Fonseca, Pedro Fernandez the servant of Antonio de Fonseca, Benito Mendez, Juan Rodriguez de Silva, Gomez de Acosta, the employer of said Gomez de Acosta, Jorge de Almeida, Diego Diaz, Antonio Diaz de Caceres, Dona Mariana de Caravajal, Dona Anna de Leon Caravajal, Lenor de Caceres, Domingo Cuello, Francisco de Fonseca of Murcia, and his brothers, sisters, mother, brother- and sister-in-law, uncles, aunts and cousins of both sexes, Basco Perez and his parents, Miguel Hernandez the brother of Jorge de Almeida, Blanca Lorenço, Francisco Rodriguez the brother of Jorge de Almeida, Miguel Hernandez, Manuel Castaño,* and Fernan Mendez de Sossa. And the prisoner is now required, therefore, to ratify and affirm in such manner as may be valid according to the Jewish rites, all that he stated in the said testimony, and say it and depose it again upon oath made in the Jewish fashion, without bearing false witness against any one."

The record of his two trials in 1596 and 1601 was now read to the prisoner and "he ratified and affirmed it, and stated again, if necessary, all that is set forth in said testimony, against the said Ruy Diaz Nieto, his father, and against Antonio de Fonseca, who did not teach to deponent the Law of Moses, because deponent, as stated by him in his second trial, already knew that law, but taught deponent the prayer which begins 'O High God of Abraham,' and all the other things stated in the testimony, and against Pedro Fernandez, the servant of the above-named Antonio de Fonseca, and Benito Mendez, and Juan Rodriguez de Silva, and against Gomez de Acosta, in regard to whom deponent adds

---

*A Gaspar de Castaño was lieutenant-governor of New Leon under Luis de Carabajal in 1591.

that he (Gomez de Acosta) knew deponent and his father Ruy Diaz Nieto to be Jews, because they acknowledged the fact to each other, and all went together to the synagogue at Ferrara, where they worshipped according to the rites and ceremonies of the Law of Moses." He then recited the names given in the above list without adding any further particulars and subscribed his name to the testimony. The correctness of the transcript is attested by Pedro de Manozca.

This completes the testimony offered by the prosecuting attorney against Jorge de Almeida. On March 12, 1607, the former appeared before the court. He recites the testimony offered, the only new statement being that the accused was "a native of the city of Almeida in the kingdom of Portugal." He then continues: "The efforts thus far made to arrest him have failed, because of his having absented himself, but as it is proper and necessary that such grave crimes as those of which Jorge de Almeida is guilty should not remain unpunished, I move respectfully that the present prosecution and trial of Jorge de Almeida should not be stopped, but on the contrary be allowed to proceed *in contumaciam.* And to this effect I pray your Honor to cause the usual proclamation or edict to be issued, summoning the said Jorge de Almeida to appear before this Holy Office, and ordering the sequestration of his property, if he should happen to own any, inasmuch as the conviction of guilt of the crimes of heresy and apostasy carries with it *ipso jure* the confiscation of his property, said property passing to the State from the date at which the crime was first committed."

The court granted the petition in part and "ordered and decreed that the said Jorge de Almeida be summoned by edicts or proclamations, in the usual form of this Holy Office, to appear before the same, within the period of sixty days."

SUMMONS.

The following is the text of the summons; a transcript properly signed and sealed is given, and there is inserted as well the original summons.

"We the Inquisitors against heretical wickedness and apostasy in the city and archbishopric of Mexico, in the states and provinces of New Spain, and the district thereof, by apostolical authority, &c. &c.

To you Jorge de Almeida, Portuguese by nationality, residing in Mexico, the husband of Dona Lenor de Andrada, who was convicted by this Holy Office of having kept and observed the dead Law of Moses, greeting:

Know you that we wish you to enjoy health in Our Lord Jesus Christ, who is the true health, and to obey and faithfully comply with our commands, which most truly might be called apostolic; and we do hereby inform you that the prosecuting attorney for this Holy Office appeared before us and gave us information that you, as it appears from the records of this Holy Office, and from the testimony given in the same against you, are guilty of the crimes of heresy and apostasy, consisting in having relapsed into the observance of the dead Law of Moses and its rites and ceremonies, and furthermore that you, for fear of being arrested and punished for the said crimes, had absented yourself from this district and country; that the said prosecuting attorney urged us to consider that the crimes of heresy and apostasy would be suffered to go on unpunished if the present prosecution was not continued, for which reason he prayed us to cause you to be summoned by edict or proclamation to appear before this Tribunal within a certain time, to answer to the charges preferred against you, and to adjudge you, if you should happen to fail to obey this summons, guilty of antagonizing our Holy Catholic Faith, and to then deal with you with all the rigor of the law. And whereas we have deemed the said petition to be just and proper, and have examined the testimony on file against you, relative to your being guilty of the crime of heresy for having relapsed into the observance of the Law of Moses and of its rites and ceremonies, and are aware, furthermore, of your absence,—we have therefore decided, and ordered and decreed to summon you to appear

before this Tribunal within the term of sixty days, to be
counted from the day on which this warrant may be served
on you, if you are found, or from the day on which a copy
of it is left at your residence in the presence of some of the
neighbors, or of its being read and published in the Cathedral
Church of this city at High Mass on any Sunday or holy day
of obligation, in the presence of the people congregated to
attend divine service, this being done in order that information of the said summons shall not fail to reach you. And
we have decided that this edict or proclamation should be
published and repeated three times, at intervals of twenty
days. You are therefore called to come and personally
appear before us and listen and answer to what the said
prosecuting attorney may say and state, and be provided
with copies of the charge or charges and specifications filed
against you, and say and allege whatever you may deem
advisable for you to say and allege. Should you come and
appear personally before us as ordered, we shall hear all that
you say, and will deal with you justly and properly. But if
you fail to obey, we shall only hear what the prosecuting
attorneys may say or state, and will allow the case to go on
and be decided in your absence and without your defense,
the service of all papers and writs being made, as is usual in
those cases, *in contumaciam*, but as firmly and validly as if
personally served on you. And we do hereby command a
copy of this proclamation or edict to be engrossed and posted
on one of the principal doors of the Cathedral aforesaid, and
declare that any person who may dare to remove it thence,
or deface it, shall be guilty of a grave offence and shall be
punished with the penalty of excommunication, and a fine
of five hundred dollars for the benefit of this Holy Office,
in addition to any other penalties to be imposed upon said
person as abettor of heresy, and opposed to the free action
of this Holy Office. In testimony of which we have hereunto subscribed our names and affixed the seal of this

Holy Office, at the City of Mexico, this 17th day of March, 1607.

[Signed] LICENTIATE DON ALONSO DE PERALTA.
[Signed] LICENTIATE GUTIERRE BERNADO DE QUIROS.
By command of the Holy Office.
[Seal] [Signed] P? DE MANOZCA."

The document is endorsed as follows: "The above was posted on the main door of the Cathedral, and remained there from March 18th, 1607, to April 10th of the same year."

"In the City of Mexico, on the third Sunday in Lent, the 18th of March, 1607, the Inquisitor Licentiate Don Alonso de Peralta and Licentiate Gutierre Bernado de Quiros, the Marquis of Monteclaros, Viceroy of this New Spain,* and a large number of people having come to the Cathedral to attend divine services and hear high mass, the foregoing edict and proclamation was read *de verbo ad verbum* from the pulpit, immediately before Fray Diego de Contreras,† Rector of Saint Paul and a Qualifier (*qualificador*) of the Holy Office, began his sermon. A copy of the same edict was subsequently posted at the door of the church, as witnessed by several persons, both ecclesiastical and lay, prominent among whom the following may be cited: Don Garcia Lopez del Espinar, Mayor of this city, Doctor Garcia de Carvajal, a lawyer admitted to the bar in this Holy Office, Francisco de Irarracanal, an officer of the Royal Treasury in this city, and others."

On Saturday, April 7th, 1607, the prosecuting attorney moved that Jorge de Almeida be adjudged *in contumaciam*. This motion was put on record by order of the court.

---

* Tenth Viceroy, appointed 1603. See Bancroft's *Mexico*, vol. III, p. 5.

† Afterwards Archbishop of St. Domingo. See Torquemada, *La Monarquia Indiana*, vol. III, p. 296.

On Friday, April 27th, 1607, the prosecuting attorney renewed this motion, which renewal was also placed on the record by order of the court.

On Thursday, the 17th of May, 1607, the prosecuting attorney made the same motion for a third time, but the Inquisitors, "upon consideration of the antecedents of the case, and wishing to give the said Jorge de Almeida a further proof of kindness and benignity, decided to grant him sixty days more, during which he may come and appear in obedience to the summons." But Almeida did not take advantage of this "kindness," as appears from the following:

PROCLAMATION.

"We the Inquisitors against heretical wickedness and apostasy in this city and archbishopric of Mexico, in the States and Provinces of New Spain, and the district thereof, by Apostolic authority, etc., etc., do hereby inform you all Vicars, Curates, Canons, Clergy, and Chaplains, in all the cities, towns and villages, within and without our district and jurisdiction, that on motion of the prosecuting attorney for this Holy Office an edict or proclamation was issued by us, summoning in due form Jorge de Almeida, the husband of Dona Lenor de Andrada who was convicted by this Holy Office of keeping the dead Law of Moses, a resident of Mexico, but now a fugitive from justice, to come and appear before our court within the period of time therein provided for, to answer to the charges of heresy, made against him, as appears more fully from the text of the proclamation itself; and that the said proclamation was read from the pulpit, at high mass, in the Cathedral in this city, of which he was a resident, and was also posted at the door of the said Cathedral, —and that the said prosecuting attorney has moved three times that the said Jorge de Almeida be adjudged to be *in contumaciam* and subject to excommunication. Whereupon we deeming the said petition to be just, and considering that the said Jorge de Almeida has not obeyed the summons, and taken no advantage of the two periods which were granted him, do hereby declare and adjudge the said Jorge de Almeida to be *in contumaciam* and subject to all the consequences of the sentence of excommunication which we pass against him. And you all are hereby commanded to publicly denounce at your respective churches the said Jorge de Almeida as one who has been excommunicated, and to treat him as such if you should ever happen to meet him,—all of this to be done and repeated as long as he remains absent and refuses to obey the summons issued by us. Given in the City of Mexico this 6th day of September, 1608.

[Signed] LICENTIATE DON ALONSO DE PERALTA.

[Signed] LICENTIATE GUTIERRE BERNADO DE QUIROS.

By command of the Holy Office.

[Seal]   [Signed] P. DE MANOZCA."

This document is endorsed with the statement by Manozca that he published it from the pulpit at the Cathedral in the presence of Pedro de Fonseca, an arrest clerk, Diego de Espinossa, warden of the jail, Clemente de Valdes, a familiar of the Holy Office, and many other persons. A copy was posted at the principal door of the Cathedral from the 9th to the 19th of the month.

On the 19th of January, 1609, the prosecuting attorney appeared before the court and petitioned that Jorge de Almeida be adjudged in default "a heretic and an apostate, convicted of being a *judaizante,* who forsook Our Holy Catholic Faith, and incurred all the censures and penalties established by law. I ask further that the said Jorge de Almeida be surrendered to the secular authorities, either in person, when caught, or in effigy, if not caught, in order that he may be dealt with according to law. And I ask finally that the whole of the property of the said Jorge de Almeida be confiscated."

On the same day the petition was placed on file by order of the court. On Saturday, January 31, 1609, the prose-

cuting attorney presented a written argument against Jorge
de Almeida as a fugitive from justice, and this was also filed
by order of the court. A copy of this formal indictment
follows, but is not here given, inasmuch as it merely contains a repetition of the statements already made. It is in
nine counts, and the attorney promises to present further
charges at the trial. The indictment was then read and a
copy served on Jorge de Almeida, "by publishing the same
outside the court-room, as is usual in those cases where the
party concerned is absent and a fugitive from justice."

Prior to this, on January 26th, the prosecuting attorney
had already moved for a judgment in default, but the Inquisitors refused, and decided "to leave the case open, and
allow both parties thereto to file evidence, provided it be
pertinent and admissible."

On January 29th the prosecuting attorney requested that
the testimony against Jorge de Almeida be published,
together with the names of the witnesses. The Inquisitors
ordered the publication of the testimony, but directed that the
names of the witnesses be withheld as well as "certain necessary circumstances, to avoid ill-feeling between the parties
concerned in said testimony."

On March 4, 1609, Ash Wednesday, the prosecuting
attorney appeared before the court, and after reciting the
charges and Jorge de Almeida's refusal to obey the summons,
stated that "the next step to be taken is to declare the case
closed and terminated, and pass the proper sentence. He
prayed the court so to do. And the Inquisitors, upon due
consideration of this petition, decided to grant it."

Immediately after this the Inquisitors, having associated
with themselves the following-named officials, to wit:
"Licentiate Alonso Lopez de Cardenas, the senior canon of the
Cathedral of this city and now head of this diocese, Licen-
tiate Pedro Suarez de Longozia and Doctor Don Marcos
Guerrero, both of them associate justices of the Supreme
Court or *Audiencia* of the dominions, and Doctor Antonio

de Morga, judge (*Alcade*) of this city; these officials held a meeting in the court-room of this Holy Office, in order to consult about the case against Jorge de Almeida, ... and upon due consideration of the facts of the case the aforesaid Inquisition and officials unanimously expressed the opinion that the said Jorge de Almeida must be publicly declared and proclaimed in a public *auto de fe* to be a heretic and a *judaizante*, and also an abettor of other heretics and *judaizantes*, and that he must then be delivered in effigy to the secular justice, and have his property confiscated. And in order to fix the date on which the said confiscation should take effect, their Honors said that as Jorge de Almeida was adjudged to be *in contumaciam* on the 7th day of September, 1608, that date is the one to be fixed."

On March 22, 1609, the following sentence was read and published. Although abounding in repetitions of matters already stated, it is given in full, as being of interest in connection with the legal procedure of the Inquisition.

" SENTENCE

passed in the case of Jorge de Almeida, a Portuguese, born in the town of Almeida in the kingdom of Portugal, domiciled in this City of Mexico, but now absent and a fugitive from justice, who was married to Dona Lenor de Andrada, convicted by this Holy Office of being a Jewess and surrendered to the secular courts.

Whereas, we the Inquisitors against heretical wickedness and apostasy in this City of Mexico, in the States and Provinces of New Spain, and the district thereof, by apostolic and ordinary authority, have examined the record of the criminal proceedings instituted and prosecuted before us, between parties, on the one side Doctor Martos de Boorques, the prosecuting attorney for this Holy Office, and on the other Jorge de Almeida, absent, but whose statue or effigy is now in the presence of the court, charged with the crimes

of heresy and apostasy: and whereas the said prosecuting
attorney stated in due form before us, that according to
evidence on file in the records and books of this Holy Office,
transcripts of which he presented, the said Jorge de Almeida
appeared to be a heretic and an apostate, because he had forsaken Our Holy Catholic Faith and relapsed into the observance of the dead Law of Moses,* awaiting the coming of the
Messiah promised by the said Law, and keeping and observing all the rites and ceremonies of the same,—and further,
that the said Jorge de Almeida, for fear of being arrested and
tried and punished for the said crimes, had fled from this City
of Mexico, where he had his residence, and had left these
provinces for parts unknown;—and whereas the said prosecuting attorney stated further that if the said Jorge de Almeida
was not proceeded against and prosecuted in his absence,
such grave crimes as heresy and apostasy would appear to
be left unnoticed and unpunished, for which reason he prayed
us to cause the said Jorge de Almeida to be summoned by
means of edicts or proclamations, and commanded to appear
before us, and answer to the charges made against him, and
supported by the evidence already on file;—and whereas the
said petition of the prosecuting attorney and the evidence
to which he referred were duly considered by us and granted,
and the proper edicts or proclamations were issued by us,
commanding the said Jorge de Almeida to appear before us
and answer to the charges of heresy and other crimes, resulting
from the evidence on file, he being informed that by doing as
commanded, a full hearing would be given to him, and that
by failing to obey the summons he would incur the penalty
of excommunication, and would be adjudged *in contumaciam,*

---

*It is curious to notice that the designation "dead law of Moses"
is peculiar to the tribunals of Mexico, as has been pointed out by
G. A. Kohut in his paper on the "Jewish Martyrs of the South
American Inquisition," in this *Publication*. A very rare book on
the Mexican *autos de fe* is preserved in the British Museum, the
only copy known to be extant, which abounds with references to
the "dead law of Moses."

the proceedings to be continued and sentence passed against him by default; and whereas the said edicts and proclamations were published and a copy of the same was posted at the principal door of the Cathedral of this city;—and whereas the said Jorge de Almeida did not obey the summons, and we through mercy and benignity decided, in spite of the representations of the prosecuting attorney, to grant him a further period of time within which he might make his appearance;—and whereas the said second period elapsed in vain, and the prosecuting attorney prayed us, in view of this fact, to adjudge the said Jorge de Almeida to be *in contumaciam*, and to have incurred the penalty of excommunication in its highest degree, the proceedings against him to be continued by default, according to law;—and whereas we, upon consideration of the facts, as shown by the evidence on file, decided to grant the aforesaid request of the prosecuting attorney, and made the proper decree to that effect, which was published and proclaimed in due form of law: and whereas the said prosecuting attorney represented to us that one year had passed without the said Jorge de Almeida having made his appearance voluntarily, or having been arrested, and that the sentence of excommunication passed against him for his disobedience had been standing for more than one year, for which reasons he was persuaded that the circumstances of the case warranted the declaration by the court that Jorge de Almeida was guilty, as indicted, of the crimes of heresy and apostasy, and the surrendering of his person in effigy to the secular authority for the proper action, as well as the confiscation of his property, from the date of his first committing the above-named crimes;— and whereas full and attentive consideration has been given by us to all the facts and merits of the case, and a consultation was held by us with persons of learning and righteous conscience, who might aid us with their prudent advice in reaching the proper decision :

The name of Christ having been invoked :

We have, therefore, ordered, adjudged and decreed, and by these presents do order, adjudge and decree, that the case as presented and made by the prosecuting attorney for this Holy Office has been well made and substantiated and proved, and that the said Jorge de Almeida is, and must be declared, as we do hereby declare him, to be a heretic and a *judaizante*, and an apostate against Our Holy Catholic Faith, subject therefore to all the censures and penalties to which heretics and apostates are subject under the law. And we do hereby command that his person and his property be seized, the former to be surrendered to the secular authority for the punishment which may be provided by law, and the latter to be confiscated. And as the said Jorge de Almeida has not been arrested, we have also commanded the statue, or effigy representing his person, which has been brought before us, to be dressed with a *sanbenito* and armed with a *corona** and clothed with all the other garments and insignia of convicted and condemned criminals, and also that a card bearing the name of Jorge de Almeida and a statement of the present sentence be attached or affixed or pasted on the said statue, which shall then be delivered to the secular authority, namely, the Mayor of this city, in order that the said authority may cause the said effigy to be publicly burned and reduced to ashes. And we do further command that the whole property of Jorge de Almeida be confiscated and appropriated to the Crown, the said confiscation and appropriation to take effect from the date on which the said Jorge de Almeida first committed the crimes of which he has been convicted. And the sons and daughters, if any, of the said Jorge de Almeida are hereby disqualified from serving in any public office, or occupying any public position of honor or trust, whether in the secular or ecclesiastical branches of the government; and they are also forbidden to wear about their persons any ornament or

---

*The ordinary form of the rosary, although in reality it is but one third or five decades.

jewel of gold or silver, or precious stones, or coral, or to dress in silk or fine cloth, or any other fine material of any kind.

In witness whereof we have hereunto subscribed our names.

[Signed] LICENTIATE DON ALONSO DE PERALTA.

[Signed] LICENTIATE GUTIERRE BERNADO DE QUIROS.

[Signed] LICENTIATE ALONSO LOPEZ DE CARDENAS.

The above sentence was given out and published by the Inquisition and the Governor of the diocese, who signed their names to it, in the Cathedral Church of this City of Mexico, on the 3d Sunday in Lent, the 22nd day of March, 1609, after the Gospel of the day was read at High Mass. Immediately after the reading and publication of the sentence the general edict of the Faith was also read, and then the Reverend Doctor P? de Morales, of the Society of Jesus, preached a sermon. The ceremony was attended up to the conclusion of the mass by Senor Don Luis de Velasco, Viceroy of this New Spain,* and by Doctor Martos de Boorques, prosecuting attorney for this Holy Office, as well as by the said Jorge de Almeida represented by his effigy, bearing the garments and insignia ordered to be put on it by the sentence. The act was witnessed also by Don Juan Altamirano, a knight of the order of Santiago, his son Don Fernando Altamirano,† a captain in the guard of the Viceroy, Don Garcia Lopez del Espinar, the Mayor of this City of Mexico, Don Pedro Altamirano, Don Juan de Samano, and many other persons both secular and lay.

All passed before me.

[Signed] P? DE MANOZCA."

The work of the Inquisition was now done and the few remaining documents relate to the formal announcement of

---

* Eighth Viceroy; appointed 1589, reappointed 1607.

† The Altamiranos were a distinguished family in Mexico. See Torquemada, *La Monarquia Indiana*, vol. I, p. 344; Bancroft, *Mexico*, vol. III, p. 70. Don Juan Altamirano is mentioned anno 1590, Torquemada, vol. I, p. 652. Dr. Herman Carrillo Altamirano was the legal adviser of the *audiencia* in 1624.

the sentence to the secular authorities and to its execution by them.

Immediately after service the Inquisitors convened in the church officially, " and it was ordered by their Honors that the foregoing record, as well as the sentence passed against Jorge de Almeida, should be read in full. . . . .

And when the reading of the said record and sentence was finished, Senor Don Garcia Lopez del Espinar, the Mayor of this city, in behalf of His Majesty, to whom, in his capacity of superior secular authority, the case was referred, and the effigy of the convict surrendered for final action, said that upon the consideration of all the facts and evidence it was incumbent upon him to pass sentence as follows :

Whereas the said Jorge de Almeida, a Portuguese by nationality, convicted by the Holy Office of the crimes imputed to him, and surrendered to me as the secular authority, for the proper action, was adjudged by the said Holy Office to be guilty as indicted. I, therefore, have decided to condemn the said Jorge de Almeida, as I do hereby condemn him, to suffer the penalty established by law in such cases ; and I do, hereby, further order and command that the effigy which represents the person of the convict be taken from this place and carried processionally through the principal streets of this city to the usual place of execution; that the procession be attended by a crier who shall announce in a loud voice to all persons present the crimes of Jorge de Almeida and the punishment to be suffered by him; and that upon the arrival of the said effigy at the said place of execution, it is to be fixed to the stake and burned and destroyed by fire and reduced to ashes, so that no memory be left of it. So I have ordered, adjudged and decreed by this my final sentence, which shall be executed at once.

[Signed]   Don Garcia Lopez del Espinar."

This sentence was at once proclaimed, the fact being attested by B. S. Campos de Rivera, notary.

The final act is the

EXECUTION.

" In the City of Mexico, on Sunday the 22nd of March, the third Sunday in Lent, 1609, Francisco Velez de Gurvara, a bailiff of the Holy Office, accompanied by me, the undersigned notary, proceeded, in compliance with the foregoing sentence, to carry the statue of Jorge de Almeida, a Portuguese, convicted of heresy and apostasy, processionally to the place of execution, stopping from time to time to read and proclaim aloud the sentence by which the said criminal was condemned. All of this was done in the forenoon, and before a great concourse of people. When the place of execution was reached, the bailiff tied the effigy to the stake, and publicly burned it and reduced it to ashes as commanded. The act was witnessed by P? Herran, Diego de Anaya, P? Mejia* and many other persons.

In testimony of which I have hereunto subscribed my name.

> [Signed]   B. S. CAMPOS DE RIVERA,
> Notary Public,
> And familiar of the Holy Office."

APPENDIX.

[Extract from Bancroft's Works, vol. X, p. 679 (History of Mexico, vol. II), San Francisco, 1882.]

" The tenth *auto de fe* occurred on the 8th of December, 1596, and of this I will give a description. Preparations on a grand scale were made to present to the authorities and people a spectacle worthy of the cause. To increase the solemnity of the occasion the day fixed upon was that of the immaculate conception; and the place, the chief plaza with its

---

* The names Anaya and Mejia are still common family names in Mexico.

extensive appointments of railings covered with platforms, and thousands of seats or benches arranged as in an amphitheatre, which was used after the celebration as a bull-ring.

The time having arrived, the viceroy, Conde de Monterey, accompanied by the justices and officers of the audiencia, the royal treasury officials, military officers, and other members of his suite repaired to the inquisition building, where the inquisitors Bartolome Lobo Guerrero, an archbishop elect, and Alonso de Peralta, subsequently bishop of Charcas, awaited them. Sixty-seven penitents were then led forth from the dungeons, and the procession marched to the plaza. A great concourse of people, from far and near, followed the procession and occupied windows and squares to the very gate and houses of the holy office.

The prisoners appeared, wearing ropes round their necks, and conical hats on which were painted hellish flames, and with green candles in their hands, each with a priest at his side exhorting him to Christian fortitude. They were marched under a guard of the holy office. Among those doomed to suffer were persons convicted of the following offences : Those who had become reconciled with the church and afterwards relapsed into Judaism, in sambenitos, and with familiars of the inquisition at their side; bigamists, with similar hats descriptive of their crime; sorceresses, with white hats of the same kind, candles and ropes; blasphemers with gags to their tongues, marching together, one after the other, with heads uncovered and candles in their hands. First among them came those convicted of petty offences, followed in regular order of criminality by the rest, the last being the relapsed, the dogmatists, the teachers of the Mosaic law, who wore the tails of their sambenitos rolled up and wrapped round their caps to signify the falsity of their doctrine. On arriving at their platform the prisoners were made to sit down, the relapsed, the readers of the Mosaic law, the dogmatists occupying the higher seats; the others according to their offences, last being the statues of the dead and absent relapsed ones. The reconciled and other penitents occupied benches in the plaza. On the right side of the holy office was a pulpit from which preached the Franciscan friar Ignacio de Santibanez, archbishop of the Philippines. Then followed the usual admonitions, opportunities to recant, to repent, and finally the fierce flames, the foretaste of eternal torments."

See also *Francisco Moyen, or the Inquisition as it was in South America*, by B. Vicuña Mackenna, translated by James W. Duffy, M. D.; London, 1869, pp. 102–103.

TRIAL OF GABRIEL DE GRANADA BY THE INQUISITION IN MEXICO 1642-1645

TRANSLATED FROM THE ORIGINAL

BY

DAVID FERGUSSON

OF SEATTLE, WASHINGTON

EDITED WITH NOTES

BY

CYRUS ADLER

PREFACE.

At the third meeting of the Society, held in Washington in December, 1894, I presented an abstract of the trial of Jorge De Almeida by the Inquisition in Mexico in 1607. This was printed in No. 4 of the *Publications*, and of the reprints I sent the first copy to Mr. Henry C. Lea, the distinguished historian. In acknowledging it Mr. Lea suggested that I send a copy to Colonel David Fergusson of Seattle, Washington, adding: "There is no one who knows more than he about the Mexican Inquisition or takes more interest in it." To this suggestion the present volume is due, and it is hoped that much more that is important for the history of the Jews in Mexico may follow in these *Publications* from the same generous sources.

Colonel David Fergusson was born in Scotland in 1824 and came to America while a young man. He was Colonel of the First California Volunteer Cavalry in the Civil War, and, with a portion of his command, went over the border and into the interior of Mexico in quest of some Federal cannon that had found their way into the hands of the authorities of a Mexican city. He was also for a time in command of the Department of Arizona. Resigning his commission some time later, Colonel Fergusson took up his residence in the neighboring Republic and resided over twenty years in different parts of the country. He was prominent in mining, banking and railway enterprises, and secured the concessions for the two first roads built by American capital. While residing in the City of Mexico, from 1872 to 1883, he became interested in the collection of rare manuscripts, books and paintings, and was much sought after by antiquarians. He gathered together hundreds of original manuscripts of the Inquisition in New Granada, now the Republic of Colombia, and in Mexico. Moving to the City of Washington late in 1883, he resided there until 1888, when he went to Seattle, Washington, where he has established his home on the shores of Lake Washington. While his household goods, library and rare manuscripts were stored in Knox's warehouse in the City of Washington it was completely destroyed by fire, and some twelve boxes containing Inquisition records were reduced to ashes. Colonel Fergusson had translated thousands of pages of these records into English and had sent them to Mr. Lea, so that a portion of this interesting material has been preserved.

I have selected the present trial to print from among a number, because while not particularly interesting in itself the record is practically a complete one, and gives a very good idea of the formalities and details of the Inquisitorial Courts.

Students of American Jewish history will no doubt be interested to notice the new references to Thomas Tremino de Sobremonte. I have purposely avoided giving any notes about him, as the amount of material concerning this interesting man now in my possession deserves a separate paper.

It is also worth noting that Jews were in the Philippine Islands as early as 1593, and that, dating from 1590, these Islands were governed through the Viceroy and Audiencia of Mexico, so that the endeavor to rule the Philippines from the American continent is not a novel one.

As indicated above, the original of this trial was destroyed, and not being able to refer to it I have faithfully followed the translation of Colonel Fergusson even to spelling and capitalization. The notes signed D. F. are his, and the remainder I have added.

This and similar trials cannot fail to have an interest for the general student of Jewish history and of religious ceremonies, since the minute testimony occasionally reveals among the Marranos (secret Jews) the development of new customs plainly influenced by their outward allegiance to the Catholic Church.

CYRUS ADLER.

PROCESS (OR TRIAL) OF GABRIEL DE GRANADA Mexico.
1642 (13 YEARS OLD), OBSERVER OF THE LAW OF MOSES, 1642 TO 1645.

Process and Criminal Cause against

Gabriel de Granada,* native of this city. Observer of the Age 13 to 14 years. Law of Moses.

Petition, Information. Votes of Arrest

Mandate, execution thereof July 12th, 1642.

Audiences

Monitibus 1. 2. 3.

Appointment of guardian.

Accusation. His answer and Communication.

Publication of Witnesses depositions

His answer, Communication and

Definitive Conclusion

Ratifications

Inspection of Circumcision. He is circum^d.

Advocate & Guardian

D JUAN BAUTISTA MARTINEZ.

Confined July 12th, 1642.

---

* The following brief summary of the case is obtained from the List of the Heretics posted in the Cathedral at Mexico: "Gabriel Granados, native and citizen of this city of Mexico, son of Gabriel Granados, deceased, and Maria Ribera, Hebrew new Christians, Judaizing heretic, Reconciled 1646" (p. 361). This is derived from a most valuable work frequently cited in these notes: "Época Colonial; México Viejo; Noticias Históricas, Tradiciones, Leyendas y Costumbres, por Luis González Obregón; Segunda Serie; Mexico, Oficina tip. de la Secretaría de Fomento, 1895."

Witnesses who depose against this culprit:

Ratified RAPHAEL DE GRANADA, accomplice. age 15.

Ratified JULIANA, a Negress (a slave) age 27.

Ratified DOÑA MARIA DE RIVERA,* accomplice. age 35.

Ratified DOÑA CATALINA DE RIVERA, accomplice. age 24.

Ratified DOÑA CLARA DE RIVERA, accomplice. age 24.

Ratified DOÑA BEATRICE HENRIQUEZ, accomplice. age 23.

Ratified DOÑA BLANCA XUAREZ, accomplice. age 16.

Ratified DOÑA MARGARITA DE RIVERA, accomplice. age 28.

Ratified DOÑA JUANA TINOCO, accomplice. age 16.

Ratified DOÑA ISABEL TINOCO, accomplice. age 16.

Ratified DOÑA ANA XUAREZ,† accomplice. age 19.

Ratified DOÑA ELENA DE SILVA, accomplice. age 45.

Ratified DOÑA MICAELA HENRIQUEZ, accomplice. age 28.

Ratified DOÑA ISABEL DE RIVERA, accomplice. age 20.

Ratified DOÑA ISABEL DE SYLVA, wife of Caravallo, accomplice. age 21.

Ratified ANTO. LOPEZ DE ORDUÑA, accomplice. age 23.

Ratified ESPERANZA RODRIGUEZ, a mulatto woman, accomplice. age 60.

Feigned madness Ratified DIEGO CORREA, accomplice. age 28.

DOÑA BLANCA DE RIVERA, accomplice. age 50.

Ratified GASPAR DE ROBLES, accomplice. age 32.

Ratified JUANA RODRIGUEZ DEL BOSQUE, accomplice. age 26.

Persons against whom this culprit deposes:

DOÑA BLANCA MENDEZ DE RIVERA

DOÑA MARGARITA DE RIVERA

---

*For the Rivera family in North America see Max Kohler, *Pub. Am. Jewish Hist. Soc.*, No. 2, p. 101 ff.

†It is very important to find additional information concerning this interesting woman. There are six references to her in this MS. What was heretofore known of Ana Xuarez was summarized by G. A. Kohut, *Pub. Am. Jewish Hist. Soc.*, No. 4, pp. 118–120.

Doña Maria de Rivera, died in prison
Doña Catalina de Rivera, died in prison
Doña Clara de Rivera
Doña Isabel de Rivera
Raphael de Granada
Francisco Home, *alias* Vicente Henriquez, died in prison
Juan Pacheco de Leon, *alias* Solomon Machorro
Doña Juana Enriquez
Simon Vaez Sevilla
Gaspar Vaez Sevilla
Doña Catalina Henriquez or Tinoco
Doña Raphaela Henriquez
Doña Micaela Henriquez
Doña Beatrice Henriquez
Doña Blanca Henriquez, died in Mexico, tortured in the Inquisition of Seville
Doña Isabede (sic) Sylva, She of Espinosa
Francisco Lopez Diaz
Diego Antunez, died in Mexico
Doña Isabel Duarte, Antunez's wife
Manuel Antunez
Luis Nuñez Perez
Pedro de Espinosa
Doña Isabel Henriquez, *alias* She of Huerta
Antonio Lopez de Orduña
Doña Isabel Tristan
Manuel Nuñez, or Rodriguez Caravalla
Juana Tinoco
Isabel Tinoco
Pedro Tinoco
Diego de Campos*

---

*Diego de Campos Segobia, Portuguese, trader of Campeche, in Vera Cruz, son of Hebrew new Christian, brother of one who was executed, Judaizing heretic, executed in effigy, 1649 (Obregon, p. 369).

ISABEL DE SEGOVIA, *alias* de Campos, died in Mex.*
THOMAS NUÑEZ DE PERALTA
SIMON XUAREZ de ESPINOSA
DIEGO CORREA
MANUEL DIAZ CASTILLA
ESPERANZA RODRIGUEZ INALATTA
ISABEL DEL BOSQUE
MARIA DEL BOSQUE
GASPAR DE ROBLES
PEDRO FERNANDEZ DE CASTRO†
MANUEL DE ACOSTA
GASPAR JUAREZ, died in prison
DOÑA ANA XUAREZ
DOÑA BLANCA XUAREZ
FRANCISCO LOPEZ DE FONSECA
JORGE JACINTO BAZAN‡
MIGUEL TINOCO
SIMON FERNANDEZ DE TORRES§

---

* For the name see *Relaçion Histórica del Auto general de fe que se celebró en Madrid en el año de* 1680 *con asistencia del Rey don Carlos II*, Madrid, 1820, a reprint of a contemporary pamphlet by Jose del Olmo. This reprint has a copy of the original title page, and 3 separate paginations, viz., I–XIX + 1–76 + 1–83. The present reference is to p. 39 of the third pagination. See also Kayserling *Ein Feiertag in Madrid* p. 26. A Mrs. Leah de Campos was in Barbadoes in 1680, see Adler, *Pub. Am. Jewish Hist. Soc.*, No. 1, p. 106, and Kayserling, *Ibid.*, No. 2, p. 76 note. Several persons of this name were naturalized in Jamaica shortly after 1740; see Hollander, *Ibid.*, No. 5, pp. 112, 114 and 115.

† Pedro Ferandez de Castro, *alias* Julio Fernandez de Castro, native of the city of Valladolid, in Castille, residing in the town of los Valles, of this Archbishopric, descendant of new Christians, Judaizing heretic, reconciled 1647 (Obregon, pp. 361, 362).

‡ Jeorge Jacinto Basan or Basa, native of Malaga in Andalusia, citizen of Mexico, merchant, son of Portuguese new Christians, Judaizing heretic, reconciled 1648 (Obregon, pp. 364, 365).

§ For the well known Luis de Torres see Kayserling's *Columbus*; Judieah Torez was in Barbadoes in 1680. Adler. *Pub. Am. Jewish Hist. Soc.*, No. 1, p. 106. Jacobe de Torres was made a denizen in Jamaica in 1671, see Friedenwald *Ibid.* No. 5, p. 51, note.

HENRIQUE FERNANDEZ, died in prison
NUÑO DE SYLVA *alias* Xuarez
DON NUÑO PEREA *alias* de Figueroa
GOMEZ DE SYLVA
DOÑA ELENA DE SYLVA
DOÑA ISABEL DE SYLVA
ANTONIO CARABALLO
DOÑA CLARA DE SYLVA. Died in Mexico
DOÑA ESPERANZA GERONIMA. Died in Mexico
MARIA GOMEZ. Relapse. Reconciled by this Inquisition
THOMAS TREMIÑO DE SOBREMONTE. Relapse. Reconciled by this Inquisition
INEZ PEREIRA
ANTONIO VAEZ CASTELO BLANCO. Relapse. Reconciled by this Holy office
LEONOR NUÑEZ. Relapse. Reconciled by this Inqn
ISABEL NUÑEZ. Relapse. Reconciled by this Inqon
ANA GOMEZ. Relapse. Reconciled by this Inq.
LUIS PEREZ ROLDAN
BALTAZAR DIAZ
FRANCISCO LOPEZ BLANDON. Relapse. Reconciled by this Inquisition
FRANCISCO NIETO or NETO
DUARTE DE LEON XARAMILLO, who abjured *de Vehementi* in this Inquisition
SIMON LOPEZ DE AGUARDA
SIMON LOPEZ *alias* RAMIREZ. Absent in Seville
THOMAS LOPEZ MONFORTE
THOINÉ GOMEZ
DIEGO MENDEZ DE SYLVA
JULIAN DE ARBOLAEZ or ALOALAEZ.
ELVIRA, a Negress who served in these prisons. She died
SEBASTIAN ROMAN
FRANCISCO FEBO
MATHIAS RODRIGUEZ DE OLIVEIRA
LUIS DE AMEZQUITA SARMIENTO

Fugitive.   PEDRO DE GUEVARA
JUANA DEL BOSQUE
MANUEL ALVAREZ DE ARELLANO
ISABEL NUÑEZ DUARTE DE LEON, Xaramillo's wife

Presented on the 18th of June, 1642.

Most Illustrious Lords:

I, Doctor Don Juan Saenz de Mañozca, Apostolical Inquisitor and Promotor-Fiscal of this Inquisition, in the most favorable manner and form permitted by law, the legal solemnities having preceded, appear before your Lordships and denounce Gabriel de Granada, a native of this city of Mexico, son of Manuel de Granada* and of Maria de Rivera,† new Christians, and I say that he, the above-named, being a baptized and confirmed Christian, has committed many and grievous crimes against our holy catholic faith, he having apostatized therefrom and passed over to the dead law of Moses, in the keeping and observance of which he has lived and does live, as is set forth by the proofs which I present, in consideration of which I pray and supplicate Your Lordships to be pleased to command that the said Gabriel de Granada be arrested and his goods sequestrated, and that he be brought to the secret prisons of this Holy Office, where being imprisoned, I solemnly declare that I will accuse him more in form; I pray for justice, and I swear, &c.

[Signed]   DR. DON JUAN SAENZ DE MAÑOZCA

*Manuel de Granada *alias* Granado, native of the city of Seville, merchant and citizen of this city of Mexico, resident in the Phillipines where he died; son of Hebrew new Christians, Judaizing heretic; executed in effigy 1649 (Obregon, p. 371).

† Maria Ribera, native of the city of Seville, citizen of the city of Mexico, wife of Manuel Granado or Granados; daughter, sister, aunt and cousin of many who were executed; Judaizing heretic; executed in effigy, with her bones 1649 (Obregon, p. 377).

In the city of Mexico, Wednesday, the 18th of June, 1642, Presentation the Inquisitors Domingo Velez de Assas y Argos and D^{or} Don Francisco de Estrado y Escobedo, D. D., being in their morning audience, Don Juan Saenz de Mañozca presented himself, Inquisitor Fiscal of this Holy Office, and presented the foregoing petition and asked for what is therein contained and for justice.

The said Inquisitors said that they admitted it, and that on his presenting proofs of what is therein alleged they were ready to decree justice.

The said Inquisitor Fiscal said that in evidence of what was contained in his Information, he made presentation of the following proofs:

Before me

[Signed]   Lic. THOMAS LOPEZ DE ERENCHUN

In the city of Mexico, 19th June, 1642, the Inquisitors Do- Votes for mingo Velez de Assas y Argos and Don Francisco de Estra- arrest of Gabriel da y Escobedo [D. D.] being in their afternoon audience in Granada review and examination of Processes, together with Christobal Sanchez de Guevara, Canon of this Cathedral, as Ordinary, he holding powers from the Cathedral Chapter *in sede vacante,* and from the other Bishops, to which I certify: the testifications there are in this Holy office against Gabriel de Granada, a native of this city, and son of Manuel de Granada and Doña Maria de Rivera, having been examined, in which he is testified against as an observer of the Law of Moses, and of performing its rites and ceremonies and having fasted as such an observer, they were unanimous, and agreed in their votes and opinions, that he should be confined in the secret prisons of this Holy office and that his goods be sequestrated and his trial proceeded with according to law and the practice of this Holy office; and the said Inquisitors affixed their rubrics.

This agrees with its original which more exclusively is in

the Book of prison Votes* at folio thirteen, to which I certify.

[Signed]   Lic. THOMAS LOPEZ DE ERENCHUN

In the city of Mexico, 20th of June, 1642, the said Inquisitors† being in their morning audience and having examined this process and Information concerning the said Gabriel de Granada and what has been voted upon in regard to it : They said : that they ordered and did order their mandate of arrest, to be made out, directed to Captain Thomas de Suasnabar y Aguirre, head Alguacil of this Holy Office in order that he may arrest the said Gabriel de Granada and bring him as a prisoner to these prisons, and deliver him to the Alcaide and sequestrate all his property, which was made out and given in due form, to which I certify.

[Signd]   Lic. THOMAS LOPEZ DE ERENCHUN

Delivery of the Mandate of Arrest In the city of Mexico, Saturday the 12th day of the month of July, 1642, the said Inquisitors (naming them) being in their afternoon audience, they ordered Captain Thomas de Suasnabar y Aguirre, head alguacil of this Holy office to enter and he being in his accustomed seat, a Mandate of arrest against Gabriel de Granada was given to him, which he was commanded to execute immediately, and he having promised so to do and comply, he was ordered to leave the audience, to which I certify.

(Signed)   Lic. THOMAS LOPEZ DE ERENCHUN

Mandate of Arrest and Sequestration of property against Gabriel de Granada We, the Apostolic Inquisitors against heretical pravity and apostasy in all the Kingdoms and dominions of His Majesty, in this New Spain, &c. Command you, Captain

* Or, votes for arrests.   D. F.   † Here are their names.   D. F.

Thomas de Suasnabar y Aguirre, head alguacil of this Holy office, that immediately after this our Mandate shall have been delivered to you, ye shall go to the house and habitation, and to any other parts or places whatsoever that may be necessary and ye shall seize the body of Gabriel de Granada, a resident of this city of Mexico wheresoever ye may find him, although it may be in a church, monastery or other consecrated, fortified or privileged place; and thus arrested and in safe custody ye shall bring him to the secret prisons of this Holy office; and ye shall deliver him to the alcayde thereof, to whom we give our commands to receive him from you, before one of the Notaries of the secret chamber, and to keep him as a prisoner under safe custody and not to let him loose, nor out on bail without our permission and order; and ye shall sequestrate all his property, real and personal, wheresoever ye may find it, in the presence and with the assistance of the Receiver General of this Holy office, and before Michael de Almonazir, Notary of Sequestrations, and ye shall deposit them in possession of solvent and legally qualified persons to the satisfaction of the said Receiver General, to which said persons, in whose power ye shall deposit them, we give our commands that they keep them in faithful custody under sequestration and subject to delivery on demand, and not to deliver any part or thing thereof without our licence and command under penalty of paying for them with their persons and goods besides the other pains that ye, on our part, may impose; and for which purpose they shall give an obligation in due form at the end of the said Inventory of Sequestration and deposit; and, if, in the said sequestration, there should be any money ye shall bring with you for the food and maintenance of the above-named One hundred dollars, in dollars of eight rials each, and should there be no money ye shall sell goods whose sale shall be the least detrimental, to the above sum, at public auction, in the presence of and with the assistance of the said Receiver, and before the aforesaid notary of sequestrations, before whom and in our presence ye shall deliver them to the said Alcayde, in order that from that sum he may feed him, and thus likewise ye shall bring from the said sequestration a bed with bedding in which the above-named may sleep, and the clothing and linen under clothing that he may require for the use of his person, which shall be delivered to the Alcayde before the said Notary of Sequestrations. And if for complying with and executing what is contained in this our Mandate ye should require aid and assistance, we exhort, and request, and if necessary, in virtue of holy obedience and under pain of the greater excommunication *latæ sententiæ trina Canonica monitione premissa* and a fine of five hundred ducats of Castile for the extraordinary expenses of this Holy office, We Command all and each and every judge and justice whatsoever, ecclesiastical as well as secular, of these Kingdoms and dominions of his Majesty that, on being by you requested, they give and cause to be given to you all the aid and assistance that ye may ask of them and which ye may need. Given in our Audience Chamber in Mexico on the twenty-first day of the month of June, Sixteen-hundred and Forty-two.

The Lic. DOMINGO VELEZ   Don FRANCISCO DE ESTRADA
    DE ASSAS Y ARGOS   Y ESCOBEDO D. D.

By Command of the Holy office.

[Signed]   EUGENIO DE SARAVIA.*

Delivery of the prisoner to the alcaide   On the 12th of July, 1642, Captain Thomas de Suasnabar y Aguirre, head alguacil of the Holy office, delivered as a prisoner thereof Gabriel de Granada, mentioned in this Mandate, and Francisco Ruiz Marañon, Alcayde of the Secret prisons of this Holy office received him and acknow-

*The foregoing signature of the Inquisitor Velez de Assas y Argos and his rubric were stamped, and consequently illegal.
            D. F.

ledged that the said prisoner was given into his charge; and
he searched him and examined him in my presence for what   Examination
he may have on his person, he being in cell number three   and Search
where he was confined; and no money, arms or any other
prohibited things were found on him; and what is above
related was done at seven o'clock at night of this day and ojo
the said Alcayde signed it with his name.

[Signed]   FRAN^{CO} RUIZ MARAÑON.

                 Before me,

[Signed]   THOMAS LOPEZ DE ERENCHUN.

In the city of Mexico, Monday 14th of July, 1642, the In-   Ration
quisitors (naming them) being in their morning Audience of
this day, they designated as an ordinary daily ration for the
sustenance of this culprit two rials and a half.*

                     Before me,

[Signed]   Lic. THOMAS LOPEZ DE ERENCHUN.

In the city of Mexico, Monday, Fourteenth day of July   First Audience
                                                        to Gabriel
Sixteen hundred and forty-two, the Inquisitor Don Francisco Granada.
de Estrada y Escobedo (D. D.), who at present attends alone, asked for
on account of the indisposition of the Inquisitor Licentiate
Don Domingo Velez de Assas y Argos, being in his morning
audience, there appeared therein Francisco Ruiz Marañon,
alcaide of the secret prisons, and made a statement that
Gabriel de Granada, a prisoner in the secret prisons of this
Holy Office prayed for an audience, and being ordered to be
brought there, he being present, an oath in due form of law
was received from him, under which he promised to speak
the truth as well in this audience as in all the rest that may
be had with him; and to keep and observe secrecy about all

*Thirty-one and one-quarter cents. D. F.

that he may see and hear and all that may come to pass to him until the determination of his cause;—Being asked why he has asked the audience, that he is in it, and told to say why he has asked it and in all to speak the truth.

He Said that he asked it for unburdening his conscience and in all to tell the truth, and that in comformity with

Against Dᵃ Maria de Rivera, his mother Dᵃ Margarita Dᵃ Clara Dᵃ Catalina Dᵃ Isabel Dᵃ Blanca, his grandmother.

which he declares : *that about six or seven months ago, more or less,* when this confessant was at the age of thirteen years, Doña Maria de Rivera, his mother, called him and when alone with him in the house in which they then lived in the Alcayceria, she told him how the law of our Lord Jesus Christ which he followed was not good, nor true, but that of Moses, that she and her mother Doña Blanca de Rivera* and his aunts Doña Margarita, Doña Catalina† Doña Clara and Doña Isabel de Rivera‡ observed and followed, and because he was her son, and for the love she bore him, she wanted to bring him out of the error and deception in which he was and teach him the said law of Moses, because it alone is the good, true and necessary law for his salvation ; and this confessant as a child and of scant capacity believed what his said mother told him; and from that instant he left the law of our Lord Jesus Christ and passed over to the faith and belief of the said law of Moses, believing and holding for certain, as his mother told him, that it was the good and the true and the one in which he must be saved, and not that of our

---

* Doña Blanca Mendes *alias* Blanca de Ribera, native of the city of Seville, citizen of this [city] of Mexico, descendant of new Christians, Judaizing heretic, reconciled 1646 (Obregon p. 357.)

† Catalina Rribera, native of the city of Seville, citizen of this [city] of Mexico, deceased, wife that was of Diego Correa de Silba, reconciled, daughter of persons executed & reconciled, sister, aunt & cousin of persons reconciled, Judaizing heretic, executed in effigy with her bones 1649 (Obregon p. 375).

‡ Isabel de Ribera, spinster, native of the city of Seville, citizen of this [city] of Mexico, by employment a nursery maid, daughter of Diego Lopez de Ribera and of Blanca de Ribera, new Christians, Judaizing heretic, reconciled 1646 (Obregon p. 358).

Lord Jesus Christ, knowing that it was contrary to and different from the said law of Moses; and he answered unto his mother that he would observe it if there were whom would teach it to him; and on this occasion and on many others his said mother told him and taught him how in the month of September the fast of the great day must be kept in observance of the said law, bathing on the eve of the day previous and putting on clean clothing and supping on fish and vegetables, and not flesh (meat) and that wax candles must be lighted and put on a clean cloth, and that on that night the prayers of the said law must be recited without going to sleep until after midnight; and that all the following day they had to go without eating until night when the evening star came forth; and that then they must sup on fish and vegetables and not meat; and that they must ask forgiveness one of another, and those who had quarreled become friends again. And in conformity with this, this confessant made the said fast of the great day in the month of September of last year with his said mother Doña Maria de Rivera and with his grandmother Doña Blanca and his aunts Margaret, Catherine, Clara* and Isabella de Rivera and with his brother Raphael† de Granada; and on the eve thereof all the above-named concerted with this confessant and his brother how they were going to keep it, and they (the women) all bathed in his room and this confessant in another and his brother Raphael in another, and they all put on clean clothes that they had ready; and at night they all supped together on eggs, fish and vegetables and afterwards they lighted four or five wax candles and they put them on the floor of a bedroom, on a

Dª Blanca, his grandmother
Dª Maria, his mother.
Dª Margarita
Dª Catalina
Dª Clara and Dª Isabel his aunts.
Raphael his brother.

---

*Clara de Ribera native of the city of Seville, citizen of this [city] of Mexico, nursery maid by employment, wife of Felipe Lopez de Noroña, new Christians, Judaizing heretic, reconciled 1646 (Obregon p. 358).

†Rafael de Granada, unmarried, student, native and citizen of this city of Mexico, son of Manuel de Granada Portuguese and of Maria Ribera, Hebrew new Christians, Judaizing heretic, reconciled 1646 (Obregon p. 361).

clean towel; and afterwards his said mother, grandmother, and aunts recited some prayers of the said law; and this confessant one which he knows and was taught him by his said mother; and his brother Raphael also recited those he knows and were taught him by his said mother; and they all embraced each other and asked each other's forgiveness, and this confessant and his brother Raphael kissed their mother's and their grandmother's hands and they gave them their blessing, saying to them, God bless you and make you good, and he does not remember if they said any other words to them; and that night his said grandmother Doña Blanca and his aunt Margaret became friends for they had quarreled, and the said Margaret asked her forgiveness and kissed her hand; and after midnight they went to sleep, and they left the candles lighted until they should be burnt out; and in the morning his mother said unto this confessant to go out and play and spend the day wherever he pleased without eating or drinking, because if he did he would break the said fast, and to return at night to supper. And this confessant did thus do, and he went that said day to the Alameda and to other places, spending the day, and he did not eat or drink anything whatsoever; and after vespers he returned to his house, where he found all the above-named persons assembled together, and his brother Raphael, and they supped all the things mentioned, upon which they concluded the said fast; and he remembers that there was no outside person, either the first or the second night, at supper with his said mother, grandmother and aunts and this confessant and his brother Raphael; for Diego Correa* and Felipe Lopez de Noroña

Marginal notes: Dª Blanca his grandmother · Dª Margarita his aunt · Dª Maria, his mother · Raphael.

---

* Compare the name of the well-known Spanish-Jewish poetess Isabella Correa, *Relacion* &c. (cited in full p. 4) p. 40, Kayserling, *Ein Feiertag in Madrid*, p. 22, note 15. *Sephardim*, p. 246 ff. Graetz, *History of the Jews* (American edition), vol. 5, p. 114. Blanca Correa was burned at the stake in 1680, *Relacion* &c., p. 37. Moses Alvarez Correa was naturalized in Jamaica in 1743. Hollander *Pub. Am. Jewish Hist. Soc.*, No. 5, p. 113.

they cooked some albondiguillas (round balls of chopped-up meat) of meat which they took to them in their rooms.

And that she also told him how they must keep Saturdays as feastdays without working on them, in observance of the said Law of Moses, and this confessant although he observed them did not leave off going to school to learn to write and to read.

And that his said mother did likewise teach him that other fasts had to be kept in observance of the law of Moses on Mondays and Thursdays, as well for the living as for the dead, supping on the evening previous on fish and vegetables and keeping the following day as a fast without eating until night, after the evening star came forth, when they must eat the aforesaid things and no meat without any more ceremonies; and that keeping these fasts was voluntary on the part of those who were willing to keep them; and that so this confessant kept six or seven of these fasts referred to, on Mondays and Thursdays, for himself and others, for the soul of his grandfather, Diego Lopez Rivera,* because his said mother, grandmother and aunts told him on different occasions to keep them, to the end that God would make him good, and also for the soul of his grandfather, as he did in the manner related; and that two or three of them this confessant kept alone, and they gave him eggs, fish and vegetables for supper, and the others were kept by his said mother, grandmother and aunts, supping the said things in company with this confessant; and although the other two or three fasts of which he has spoken they did not keep with him and they ate meat those days at dinner and supper, they knew and understood how this confessant had kept them.

He fasted for the Soul of Diego Lopez Rivera

And that his said brother, Raphael de Granada, has kept six or seven of these ordinary Monday and Thursday fasts of

Against Raphael, his grandmother, his mother and his aunts.

* Diego Lopez Ribero, native of Casteloblanco in Portugal, citizen of this city of Mexico, where he died, husband of Blanca Ribera alias Mendes, reconciled, children of Hebrew new Christians, Judaizing heretic, executed in effigy 1649 (Obregon, p. 378).

the said law, and one of them in company with this confessant and his mother, grandmother and aunts, and others alone, and he said so to this confessant as they are voluntary fasts they did not always keep them together. And that he does not know if his brother has kept more fasts than those he mentioned.

Doña Maria, his mother   And that his said mother taught and told him that there are other fasts of the said law of Moses, and especially those of Queen Esther, which they kept by eating, the previous evening at supper, fish and vegetables and going the three following days without eating or drinking anything, until the night of the last day when they again supped off the same things upon which they finished the said fasts, and that these were kept by such observers of the said law as pleased ; and that this confessant has never kept them ; and that he remembers that these fasts of Queen Esther were kept one time by his said mother, Doña Maria, and his grandmother, Doña Blanca, and his two aunts, Margaret and Isabella, and they did not keep the three together without eating during the whole of the three days, but some of them the first day, and others the second and others the third, supping on fish and vegetables the first and second night of the days on which they kept the said fasts, and that his aunts, Catherine and Clara, did not keep them because they were sick, nor did his brother Raphael keep them, because he did not want to.

Against his mother, grandmother and aunts.

Against Doña Maria his mother   And that his said mother also told him and taught this confessant that there are other passovers and solemn feasts of the said law of Moses, the names of which he does not remember, more than that she told him that at their due time she would teach them to him ; and unto the present time she has neither told him about them or taught them to him.

And that she likewise told and taught him that in the observance of the said law of Moses fowls that were to be eaten must have their heads cut off with a knife, and also that it is forbidden to eat bacon, and fish without scales ; and that this confessant never beheaded hens nor does he know

whether his mother, grandmother and aunts beheaded them
or ordered Juliana, the negress, who cooked them for them to *Juliana the negress*
behead them; and that this confessant and his mother,
grandmother and aunts and his brother have always eaten
bacon in the stew (olla) and in other ways, although it was
contrary to what the said law teaches. And that he has
never paid any attention to whether the fish that he has
eaten had scales or not.

And that his said mother taught him and told him how
there were prayers of the said law of Moses that must be
said and recited in the morning and at night for the living
and for the dead, and that she did not teach him more than
one prayer to recite when he wanted to pray, and it is the
following :

Lord, my soul calleth upon thee to deliver me from the *Prayer.*
fire and the flame that I may not be burnt or scorched. Here
am I in this desert, turned into a servato (a plant), where
great trouble shall overtake me. Into thick darkness shall
they cast me where nor brother nor cousin can aught avail
me, but only the works of my hands can save me. One
thing, My God, shall I ask of thee, that thou remember my
soul and deliver it at the mouth of a cave and going out at a
door, and that I may not amuse myself except in counting
the Stars of Heaven or throwing water in the Sea.* And
that with this the said prayer ends.

And that this confessant has recited it sometimes in observance of the said law but not frequently or usually.

And that his said brother Raphael has told this confessant at *Raphael.*
different times how his mother, Maria de Rivera, had taught
him the said law of Moses, although he did not tell him so fully
that she taught him all the things which he has related, but he
presumes and he holds it for certain that she did teach them to
him in detail as unto this confessant; for he kept with him and

* This is written in the original as if it were rhyme or poetry, but
it is not. D. F.

2

His mother, grandmother and aunts. with the aforesaid his mother, grandmother and aunts, the fasts of the said law which he has mentioned.

And that last night, about eleven o'clock, this confessant Prison communications against Dᵃ Isabel, his aunt, and Dᵃ Maria, his mother. heard a voice, by which he knew that it was that of his aunt, who called him and his brother Raphael by their names, asking them if it were they and when did they bring them as prisoners, and both answered that it was they and that they had brought them as prisoners the preceding Saturday night; and his said aunt, Doña Maria, very weepingly said unto them to be careful what they did and not to give testimony against any person whatsoever without naming any Raphael one, and this confessant and his brother Raphael answered that they would do as she said. And then his mother, Doña Maria, who it seemed to him was near, heard what was said to them by their aunt Isabella and she asked them the same as their aunt, charging them not to depose against any one, and this confessant and his brother Raphael told her they would do as she wished and they have not spoken any more. And this confessant is determined not to answer even tho' his said mother and aunt call him and he has thus admonished his said brother Raphael, who has come to the same determination.

The said Inquisitor told him and admonished him thus to do, because it is expedient for him for unburdening his conscience and for the quicker and better dispatch of his business, who said he would comply as he was commanded.

Interrogated what is his name, of what place is he a native, what is his age and what occupation has he, and how long is it since he came as a prisoner

He said that his name is Gabriel de Granada, and that he is a native of this city of Mexico, thirteen and a half years Age 13 years of age, and that he has no occupation (trade, calling, &c.) but that he has been at school writing and reading, until last ojo Saturday about midnight on the twelfth day of this month and year they brought him as a prisoner to this Holy office, and he declares his genealogy in the following form :

Parents.

Manuel de Granada, defunct, who died in China* about two years ago ; and he was a native of Seville, by occupation a merchant ; and Doña Maria de Rivera, his mother, a native of Seville, a prisoner in this Holy office.

Paternal Grandparents.

That he does not know them nor has he heard them mentioned.

Maternal Grandparents.

Diego Lopez Rivera, Portuguese, defunct, and he does not know of what place in Portugal he was a native ; and Doña Blanca de Rivera, a native of Seville, and a prisoner in this Holy office.

Paternal Uncles and Aunts.

That he neither knows or heard of any.

Maternal Uncles and Aunts.

Doña Margarita de Rivera, engaged to be married to a cousin of hers called Miguel Nuñez† said to be in Havana.‡ ojo and they have no children.

Doña Catalina de Rivera, wife of Diego Correa, merchant, a native of Portugal, and she has a son four years old called Luis.

Doña Clara de Rivera wife of Philip Lopez de Noroña ; he does not know where he is from and she has no children.

---

*This is undoubtedly an error on the part of the boy ; his father died in the Phillipine Islands, see above, p. 6 foot note.

† Miguel Nuñez de Guerta alias Huerto, native of Cubillana in Portugal, merchant, son of Hebrew new Christians, Judaizing heretic, deceased, executed in effigy with his bones 1649 (Obregon, p. 373).

‡ This would indicate the presence of Marranos in Cuba ; see *Settlement of the Jews in North America.* Daly-Kohler, pp. xiii and xvii and Kayserling's *Christopher Columbus*, pp. 93 and 95.

Dᵃ Isabel de Rivera, who is not married and has no children, and all his said aunts are natives of Seville and they are prisoners in this Holy office, and he has no uncle.

Wife and Children.

That he is not married and has no children.

Brothers and Sisters.

Raphael de Granada, a native of this said city, who is about fourteen and a half years old and he is a student of rhetoric.

Interrogated about what caste and generation his said parents and grandparents are and the other transverse and collateral relations about whom he has declared, and if they or any of them or this confessant have been imprisoned, penanced, reconciled or condemned by the Holy office of the Inquisition

Quality. He said that he considered his father, Manuel de Granada, as a good Catholic Christian and also his maternal grandfather, Diego Lopez Rivera; but his said maternal grandmother, Doña Blanca de Rivera, and his mother and his aunts, he considers and holds them, as he has declared, as observers of the Law of Moses, and he does not know of what race and caste they are; and that he does not know and he has not been told that any of them have been chastised by the Holy office, and that he only knows that within the last few days his said grandmother, mother and his aunts and this confessant and his brother, Raphael de Granada, have been brought as prisoners to this Inquisition, and also his uncle, Diego Correa, whom he believes to be an old Christian, and likewise his uncle, Philip Lopez de Noroña, because he does not know that they are observers of the said law of Moses, nor has he seen them keep any fast nor any other thing of the said law, nor has this confessant declared himself to them nor they to him, nor does he know that his grandmother, his mother and aunts and his brother Raphael have declared themselves to them or they to them: that they are able to tell.

Interrogated if he is a baptized and confirmed Christian, if he hears mass, confesses and takes the holy communion when the holy mother church commands, and if he has the bull of the holy Crusade.

He said that he is a Christian, baptized and confirmed in the Cathedral Church of this city, and that his Sponsor in baptism was Gabriel ybañez, separator of gold and silver in the mines of San Luis, and the archbishop Don Francisco Manso confirmed him in the said Cathedral, and his godfather was Don Felipe de Chagoia, an advocate in this city, and that he has a bull of the holy crusade; and he confesses and takes communion in Lent, and the last time he went to confession was in holy week of this last Lent with a clergyman called Don Gaspar de la Paz, a servant of the archbishop Don Feliciano de Vega, and he took communion in the Sagrario of the said Cathedral, and they gave him a communion ticket which his said mother keeps with the others; and that he has a bull of the holy crusade in order to gain the Indulgences thereof. He crossed himself and said the Lord's Prayer, Hail Mary, the Creed, Salve Regina, the articles of faith, the Commandments of the Law of God and of the church and the general confession all in Spanish, very well recited, and he said he knew the rest of the Christian doctrine as contained in the catechism.

Interrogated if he knows how to write and to read and if he has studied for any profession

He said that he knew how to read and write and that he was taught in this city; the first master being Peter de Sepulveda, deceased; and the second Pedro de Vizcarra, a priest, defunct, and the third Francisco Ortiz de Rivera, schoolmaster; that they likewise taught him the christian doctrine which he has repeated, and he has not studied any profession.

Interrogated if he has left these Kingdoms of His Majesty, and with what persons, and for the course of his life. ^{Course of his life.}

He said that he was born, as he has already said, in this city

whence he was taken by his parents when a little over one
year old to the mines of San Luis because of the inundation
of this city, where they were about two years, and they
brought him back to this city, where they brought him up
until the present time.without his having again left this city
nor has he treated with or had intercourse with anyone but
his parents, grandmother, his aunts and their husbands and
his brother Raphael, and he does not know nor has he had
any dealings with any other persons whatsoever nor does he
know that they are observers of the said law of Moses except those he has declared, because he is a child and he associated only with the school children.

Interrogated if he knows, presumes or suspects the cause
why he has been arrested and brought to the Secret prisons
of this Holy office.

He said he knows it well, and that it is for what he has
confessed of his being an observer of the law of Moses as
his said mother, grandmother, aunts and his brother are, who
are prisoners for this same.

1st Monition   He was told that in this Holy office it is not customary to
arrest any person without sufficient sworn information of
having said, done and committed, or having seen or heard
other persons do, say or commit something that is or appears
to be contrary to our holy Catholic faith and evangelical law
(or religion) which the holy mother Roman Catholic church
holds, preaches and teaches, or contrary to the right and free
exercise of the Holy office, and so he should believe that
upon this information he has been brought as a prisoner,
that from reverence to God our Lord and his glorious and
blessed mother, our Lady, the Virgin Mary, he is admonished and charged to search his memory and to tell and entirely
confess the whole truth of all that about which he feels himself guilty, and what he knows about other persons who may
be guilty without concealing anything about himself or about
them, or raising false testimony against himself or against
others, because in so doing he will unburden his conscience

as a catholic christian and save his soul, and his cause shall
be despatched with all the celerity and mercy that by law
may be permitted; otherwise justice shall be done.

He said that he has told and declared the whole truth
about all that he has done and committed in offense of God
our Lord and of our Holy Catholic faith, and about all that
he has seen done, heard said and committed by the aforesaid
his mother, grandmother, aunts and brother, without his
knowing of anything else or heard said about any other person whatsoever, because if he did know it he would declare
it fully and plainly. And that he is heartily sorry for what
he has done, as God knows, and he truly repents of having
left the true law of our Lord Jesus Christ and passed over
to the Law of Moses, believing, as a child, his mother, and
that he begs, for the love of God, that he be treated with mercy
for he is truly repentant, and that his tender years be taken
into consideration. And that he has told and declared the
truth as he will do whenever and wherever he may recollect
anything which he ought to tell and declare; and he solemnly
promises that he will pray for an audience for this purpose,
and that he is very sorry that he did not come voluntarily
to this Holy office to make a confession and beg for mercy;
and many times he was determined upon doing it and that
from fear and fright he, as a child without experience, failed
to do it; and that at present he has nothing more to say.

Interrogated as to what moved him to ask for this said
audience and to confess therein the crimes that he has committed

He said that God has moved him thereto, and considering
that he was deceived and that the said law of Moses was not
good which his said mother had taught him, for she and his
grandmother and his aunts and his brother were prisoners
for the same crime, and that what his mother had taught
him could not be good and true, and so from this day forward
he has made up his mind and is determined to follow the law
of our Lord Jesus Christ as good and true and to separate

himself from the said law of Moses as false and deceitful; and that he begs and prays, for the love of God, this Holy office to direct him in the way of his salvation, leading him away from his errors and teaching him all that he ought to hold and believe as a christian, because he wants to be one and live and die as such in the faith and belief of our holy catholic faith; and having read to him what he has declared in this Audience he said that he had declared it and that it was true and that there was nothing in it to correct, and if necessary he would declare it anew; and straitly admonished to think it over well again and tell the truth, and warned how he must behave or conduct himself in his cell he was ordered to be taken back thereto, and he signed it with his name.

[Signed]   GABRIEL DE GRANADA

Before me,

[Sigd.]   Lic. THOMAS LOPEZ DE ERENCHUN,
(the notary of the Secret Chamber)

I accept these confessions in so far as they favor me. Said day, month and year.

[Signed]   Dr. MAÑOZCA   (the fiscal)

2nd Audience to Gabriel de Granada.   In the city of Mexico, Thursday, 17th day of the month of July, 1642, the Inquisitor Licentiate Don Domingo Velez de Assas y Argos being in his morning audience, he ordered Gabriel de Granada to be brought thereto; and he being present he was asked if he remembered anything about his business to tell it and speak the truth in all things on the oath which he has taken,

He said that he does not remember anything, and if he did that he would declare it as he did in his first audience, to which and to his confession he refers.

He was told how in the past audience he was admonished 2nd Monition.
on the part of God our Lord, &c.*

He said that God well knows that he has told the whole truth
and unburdened his conscience, and that he again solemnly
promises to tell anything that he may remember or know or
believe about any other persons whatsoever, because he has
confessed against himself and against his mother, his brother,
his grandmother and his aunts, and about all he has done in
company with them; if he knew of any other persons he would
say and declare against them, for it would be of less importance to him; and because he is a boy he has not communicated or treated with others about the said law of Moses, as
he has said, more than with the said his mother, grandmother, aunts and brother; and that he has nothing more to
say. And straitly admonished still to think well of it he
was ordered back to his cell. And he signed it:

GABRIEL DE GRANADOS

Before me,

[Signed]   Lic. THOMAS LOPEZ DE ERENCHUN

In the city of Mexico, Monday, 28th day of July, 1642, 2nd Voluntary Audience
the Inquisitor Lic. Domingo Velez de Assas y Argos, who
attends alone because the Inquisitor Francisco de Estrada y
Escobedo is attending at the new prison, being in his afternoon Audience, there appeared therein Francisco Ruiz Marañon, alcaide of the Secret prisons and stated that Gabriel de
Granada asks for an audience; and he being brought and
being there present he was told that the alcaide said that he
prays for an audience that he is in it: to say why he wants
it and in all to speak the truth on the oath he has taken

He said that he asked for it and he wishes it in order to

---

*The monitions are all alike and it is useless to repeat them,
although they are always repeated in full in every process. D. F.

Against his mother, his grandmother and aunts. Dᵃ Catalina Tinoco Dᵃ Rafaela Dᵃ Juana Dᵃ Micaela† Dᵃ Beatriz Henriquez, sisters.

declare that he has remembered that after they perverted him from the law of our Lord Jesus Christ he sometimes heard his mother, his grandmother and aunts say that the daughters of Doña Blanca Enriques,* Doña Catalina Tinoco, and Doña Rafaela and Doña Juana, Doña Micaela and Doña Beatriz Enriquez were observers of the Law of Moses, but this confessant did not see them do anything of the said law nor did he declare himself to them nor they to him as such observers, and perhaps from his mother, his grandmother and aunts some of them may have heard that he is an observer of the law of Moses, but by no means does any one know such a thing directly from his own mouth except his mother, grandmother and aunts as being such near relations who lived inside of the same door; and that he does not remember anything else to declare, that whenever he does he will ask for an audience in order to make it manifest with the desire to merit the mercy which this Holy office is accustomed to extend to those who well and truly confess. And very straitly admonished to think it well over again and tell the truth he was ordered back to his cell. And he signed it.

GABRIEL DE GRANADA.

Before me [Sig'd] EUGENIO DE SARAVIA.

I acept this confession in so much as it does in my favor and no more. Said day, month and year.

[Signed] Doctor MAÑOZCA—(Fiscal).

* Blanca Enrriquez, native of the city of Lisbon, in Portugal, citizen of New Veracruz, daughter of Hebrew new Christians, wife of Fernando Rios, reconciled, Judaizing heretic, deceased, executed in effigy with her bones, 1649 (Obregon, p. 376).

A Joshua Mordekay En Riques was in New York December, 1656, and Jacob Cohen Henriques, in 1655; see Max Kohler, *Pub. Am. Jewish Hist. Soc.*, No. 2, p. 80; Jacob Jeosua Bueno Enriques was in Jamaica about 1655, see Herbert Friedenwald, *Ibid.*, No. 5, pp. 67 and 68.

† Micaela Enrriquez, native of Mexico, daughter of Antonio Rodriguez Arias and of Blanca Enrriquez, married to Sebastian Cardoso, reconciled, Judaizing heretic, reconciled 1648 (Obregon, p. 365).

In Mexico, Tuesday, the 9th day of September, 1642, the 3rd Audience.
Inquisitors Lic. Domingo Velez de Assas y Argos and Don
Francisco de Estrada y Escobedo being in their afternoon
audience, they ordered Gabriel de Granada to be brought
thereto, to whom, he being present, it was said that the
alcaide said he wanted an audience that he is in it: to say
why he wants it and speak the truth on the oath he has
taken*

He said that he asked for it in order to declare what he
has remembered, which is that he heard it said in his house,
he does not recollect well whether by his grandmother, Dᵃ   Dᵃ Blanca de
Blanca de Rivera or his mother, Dᵃ Maria, or which one of   Rivera and her daughters.
his aunts, Dᵃ Margarita, Dᵃ Catalina, Dᵃ Isabel de Rivera,
that a Portuguese named Francisco Ome, who is away from   Franco Home.
this city, he does not know where,† is an observer of the law   Raphael.
of Moses whom he has never seen nor does he know him or
anything more about him than having heard what he has
stated, and that he remembers that his brother was present
and heard it and it is possible he may remember which of
the said persons said it; and that to make this declaration he
has asked this audience and that at present he does not
remember anything else; that should he remember anything
he solemnly promises to tell it and ask an audience for the purpose; and that what he has now told is the truth on the oath
he has taken; and it having been read to him he said it was
well written; and very straitly admonished to think over it
well he was ordered back to his cell. And he signed it.

GABRIEL DE GRANADA.

Before me [Sᵈ·] THOMAS LOPEZ DE ERENCHUN.

I accept this confession in so far as it is in my favor and
not in more. Said day, month and year.

[Signed]   DR. MAÑOZCA

---

* Hereafter this long heading of the audiences will be condensed
to merely giving the place, date and names of the Inquisitors. D. F.

† The Holy office soon discovered where he was and he was
arrested. D. F.

4th Audience.   Mexico, Tuesday, 16th day of September, 1642. Inquisitors Argos and Estrada. Afternoon.

He said that he has asked the audience for unburdening his conscience and to declare what he has remembered, which is that after she taught this confesssant the law of Moses his mother, Doña Maria de Rivera, was heard by him to say, and also his grandmother, Dᵃ Blanca and his aunts, Dᵃ Margarita Dᵃ Catalina, Doña Clara and Doña Isabel de Rivera, that a young man named Juan Pacheco de Leon, who has been absent for two years, he does not know where, and Captain Simon Baez Sevilla* and his son Gaspar Baez† are observers of the law of Moses, which *he heard them say at different times,* and that this confessant has never declared himself to them nor they to him, and although he lived in the house of the said Simon Baez, the said Baez and his wife and his son Gaspar considered him as a good Christian and they kept aloof from him and he thinks that for this and his being a boy although they may be observers of the said law, they did not declare themselves to him and he did not see them do or say anything of the said law more than he heard his mother, grandmother and aunts say about them and the said Juan Pacheco de Leon who he knows used to live in the said Simon Baez Sevilla's house before he left the city; and that he has asked the audience to declare this and that it is true on the oath he has taken. And he signed it with his name; and very straitly

---

*Simon Baez Sebilla, *alias* Soburto, native of Castelo blanco, husband of Doña Enrriquez, reconciled, son of Gaspar Gonsalez Soburto, inn-keeper and butcher, who performed the function of executioner, Judaizing heretic, reconciled 1649 (Obregon, p. 366).

See also Wm. Harris Rule, *History of the Inquisition.* London and New York, 1884, p. 24 ff. quoted by G. A. Kohut. *Pub. Am. Jewish Hist. Soc.* No. 4, p. 119.

† Gaspar baes Sebilla, unmarried, native and citizen of this city of Mexico, son of Simon Baes Soburto *alias* Sebilla, and of Juana Enrriquez. Hebrews, all of whose ancestors were executed, Judaizing heretic, reconciled 1646 (Obregon p. 360).

admonished to think well over it again he was ordered back
to his cell.
[Signed] GABRIEL GRANADA.

Before me [S^{d·}] EUGENIO DE SARAVIA.

I accept this confession in so much as it makes in my favor
and no more. Said day, month and year.
DR. MAÑOZCA.

Mexico, Wednesday, Sept. 17th, 1642. Inquisitors Argos 5th Audience
and Estrada. Morning.

He was ordered t·· appear at this audience and 3rd Monition
He said that he does not remember anything at present
which he ought to declare as he has already done so.*

He said he has nothing more to say than he has already
declared and that if he had remembered anything he would
say it with all truth; that he has confessed all his crimes in
order to deserve the mercy which he has begged for and
he hopes for from this Holy office.

He was told that he has declared that he is a minor under
twenty-five years of age and that in order that his process be
well substantiated, according to law, it is necessary that he be
provided with a guardian and a lawyer with whose counsel,
advice and assistance he can proceed with this suit; and Doc-
ors (D. Ds.) Francisco Lopez de Solis and Juan Bautista de
Martinez and the Licentiates Matheo de Cisnercs and Nicholas de Escobar prisoners' advocates of this Holy office
having been named to him to see which of these he wants to
choose as such.

He said that he named and he did name as his guardian Appointment
and counsel Dr. Juan Baptista Martinez Scotus, Professor in of Guardian
this Royal University; and that now he remembers that after and Counsel.
this Holy office had arrested Doña Maria Rivera, his mother,

---

* This monition is precisely like the two previous ones. D. F.

and Doña Blanca, his grandmother, and his aunts, Margaret, Catherine, Clara and Isabella, he went one night in about a Against Doña uana Enriques fortnight, a little more or less, to see Doña Juana Enriquez,* wife of Simon Vaez Sevilla, who being alone earnestly entreated him because she had been good to him that in case he were arrested by this Holy office not to declare anything against her or against any of her sisters; and this confessant so promised her without anything else having passed; and he presumes that this caution on the part of Doña Juana was because she thought that he knew, from being told by his mother, grandmother and aunts, that she was an observer of the law, as he has already confessed, and that he has nothing more to declare.

Guardian and Advocate And the said Inquisitors ordered the said Doctor Juan Baptista Martinez to enter into the audience, and he having said that he would accept the guardianship of the said Ga- Guardian's oath briel de Granada, his oath was received in due form, under the solemnity of which he promised that he would well, faithfully and diligently defend his said ward in the progress of his cause, and that where he saw anything to his advantage he would allege and plead it in his favor and shield him from loss and injury and not leave him defenseless, and that in all things, he will act as a good, loyal and diligent guardian and advocate is bound to do for his ward; and he binds himself that if from his fault negligence or bad legal advice and defense his said ward should suffer any loss or damage he will make it good with his person and his property; and he gave as a surety in the said guardianship Juan Ramos de Zuñiga a resident of this city, who is here present, who said that he would be his surety and he did bind himself as such surety for the said Dr. Don Baptista Martinez in

---

* Juana Enrriquez, native of the city of Seville, wife of Simon Baez Sebilla, reconciled, daughter of the Rabbinical dogmatists Antonio Rios Arias and of Doña Blanca Enrriquez, executed, mother of reconciled persons, Judaizing heretic, reconciled 1649 (Obregon, p. 367).

the said guardianship, and he took upon himself the obligation to do, comply with and pay what in the matter had been sworn and promised if he did not do and comply with, that he as his surety would pay for him; and to effect which the said Dr. Juan Baptista Martinez as such guardian and counsel and Juan Ramos Zuñiga as his surety, jointly and severally, and held and bound *insolidum* for the whole amount, renouncing as they do renounce the laws of mancomunidad obliging their persons and their property real and personal now held or to be held or acquired by them; and they empowered the Inquisitors at present being or who may hereafter succeed them in this Holy office to whose jurisdiction they submitted themselves and they renounced their proper privileges (fueros) and jurisdiction and the law *si convenerit de jurisdictione omnium judicum* in order that they may compel them to comply as if it were a definitive Sentence passed in *res adjudicata* and they renounced the laws in their favor and they gave a power of attorney in due form, Francisco Murillo Criales, Gonzalo de Estrada and Diego de Almonacir, assistant in the Secret Chamber, being witnesses, and they signed it.

Mancomunidad.

[Signed]   Don Jn^{O.} Bap^{A.} Mrz. de Cep^{DA.}

[Signed]   Jn^{O.} Ramos de Zuñiga.
          Before me,

[Signed]   Lic. Thomas Lopez de Erenchun.

I accept this confession in so far as it favors me and no farther, said month, day and year.

Dr. Mañozca.*

And then forthwith an oath in due form of law was received from the said Gabriel de Granada in presence of the said

Oath of the Minor in presence of his guardian

* Here follows the appointment by the Tribunal of the Guardian, which is similar to the same formality in other courts. D. F.

Doctor Juan Bautista Martinez, his guardian, under the solemnity of which he promised to speak (or tell) the truth. And then in presence of the said guardian and counsel the confessions which he has made in this Holy Office from the Audience that was held with him on the 14th day of last July of this present year until to-day 17th of September, were read to the said Gabriel de Granada, word for word, the said Gabriel de Granada said that these were his confessions, that he had declared them as they were read to him, and that what was written in them was correctly recorded because they are thus true, which he affirms and ratifies, and if necessary he would declare them anew in presence of and with the assistance of his said guardian and counsel; and that for the present he has nothing else to declare, for if he knew anything more he would declare it, and that he solemnly promises that whenever and wherever anything comes to his memory he will declare it. And the said guardian and counsel advised him so to do. And straitly admonished to think well over it again he was ordered back to his cell, and he signed it with the said Guardian & Counsel.

GABRIEL DE GRANADA.   Don J$\text{N}^{\text{o.}}$ BAP$^{\text{a.}}$ MRZ DE CEP$^{\text{da.}}$

Before me,

[Signed] Lic. THOMAS LOPEZ DE ERENCHUN.

Ratification before the Respectable persons   In the city of Mexico, Wednesday, 17th day of September, 1642, the Inquisitors Argos, Estrada and Juan Saenz de Mañozca being in their afternoon audience, they commanded to enter therein, as respectable and religious persons who have sworn to observe secrecy, Father Miguel de Santtanna and Diego de Moedano, presbyters, and they being present, Gabriel de Granada was brought, from whom was received an oath in due form of law under which he promised to tell the truth.

He was told that it is hereby made known unto him

that the Fiscal of this Holy Office presents him as a witness against Doña Blanca Mendez de Rivera, his grandmother; Margaret, Mary, Catherine, Clara and Isabel de Rivera, her daughters; Raphael de Granada, her grandson; Francisco Home, Juan de Leon, Doña Juana Enriquez, Simon Baez, Gaspar Baez his son, Doña Catalina Tinoco,* Da. Rafaela,† Da. Micaela Enriquez and Doña Beatriz Enriquez‡ and Doña Blanca Enriquez, to be attentive, that his depositions shall be read to him, and that if in them there should be anything to alter, to add or amend to do so in such a manner that they may in all things state the truth, and to confirm and ratify them, because what he may now say will stand to the prejudice of all the persons above named, and forthwith what he had said and deposed against the said persons in the audiences had with him from the 14th of July until the 17th of Sept^r· of the year 1642 were read to him; and they having been read to him *de verbo ad verbum*, and the said Gabriel de Granada having said that he had heard it and understood it all, he said that that was his declaration, and he had said it just as it was read to him and it was correctly written and recorded and there was nothing to alter, to add or to amend, because it was true just as it was written, and he adheres to and affirms and ratifies it, and it being necessary he would depose it anew, and he did not declare it from hatred but for unburdening his conscience, and he signed it

---

* Catalina de Silba, *alias* Enrriques, native of the city of Seville, citizen of this city of Mexico, wife of Diego Tinoco, daughter of Antonio Rrios Arias and of Blanca Enrriques, executed, Judaizing heretic, executed in person 1649 (Obregon, p. 368).

† Rafaela Enrriquez, native of Seville, citizen of Mexico, married to Gaspar Juares, daughter of Antonio Rodriguez Arias and of Blanca Enrriquez, Judaizing heretic, reconciled 1648 (Obregon, p. 364).

‡ Beatris Enrriquez, native of and citizen of this city of Mexico, daughter of Antonio Rodriguez and of Doña Blanca Enrriquez, Rabbinïtes, wife of Thomas Nuñes de Peralta, reconciled, Judaizing heretic, reconciled 1648 (Obregon, p. 364).

3

with his name, and admonished still to think it over well he
was ordered back to his cell.

[Signed] GABRIEL DE GRANADA.

Before me,

[Sign'd] EUGENIO DE SARAVIA.

6th Audience,
which he vol-
untarily asked
for.

D ͣ Maria and
D ͣ Catalina de
Rivera want to
present them-
selves in this
Holy Office,
and they fail
to do it on the
advice of D ͣ
Juana Enri-
quez.

Against D ͣ
Juana En-
riquez.

D ͣ Micaela
Enriquez
and D ͣ Isabel
Enriquez.

Mexico, Monday, 13 of October, 1643.
Inquisitors, Argos and Estrada, afternoon.

He said that he has asked this audience to declare what he
has remembered, and it is that one day after the arrest of D ͣ
Blanca de Rivera, his grandmother; and of his aunts Margaret, Clara and Isabella de Rivera; his mother, D ͣ Maria
de Rivera, sent this confessant to the house of D ͣ Juana
Enriquez, wife of Simon Baez Sevilla, who already knew of
the said arrests, and she ordered him to ask the said Doña
Juana if she thought that she the said Doña Maria and her
sister Doña Catalina de Rivera and this confessant ought to
come and present themselves to this Holy office and beg for
mercy; and he remembers that it was on a Sunday morning
and he found the said Doña Juana Enriquez on her dais with
her sister, Doña Micaela Enriquez, and her aunt, Doña Isabel
Enriquez,* wife of Pedro de Espinosa, and in their presence
this confessant gave the said message to the said Juana
Enriquez, who with the two others mentioned were weeping
and greatly distressed because of the said arrest; and having
heard the said message the said Doña Juana answered and
said to this confessant to tell Doña Maria de Rivera, his said
mother, why did she want to go with her said sister, D ͣ Catalina, to present herself? for peradventure her mother, Doña
Blanca, and her three daughters might get out free from
prison, and the said Doña Isabel Enriquez, hearing these

---

*Isabel Enrriquez, *alias* Isabel de Huerta, native of the city of
Malaga, in Spain, citizen of Los Angeles, Judaizing heretic, reconciled 1647 (Obregon, pp. 363-364).

words, said to this confessant to ask his mother why she wanted to put herself into that row and go and present herself, for they knew the risk they were running, and likewise the said Doña Isabel, Doña Juana, Doña Micaela Enriquez and all the relations said the same, and this confessant went home and he gave the said answer to his mother and aunt in the same manner as it was given to him by the said Doña Juana and Doña Isabel Enriquez; and they answered him nothing and they remained very sorrowful and with great fear; and notwithstanding this this confessant knows that they wanted to come but there was no time because on the next Monday night they were arrested.

And likewise he remembers that the day they arrested his said grandmother and aunts, his mother, Dª Maria Rivera, went that same night to the house of Dª Juana Enriquez, with her son Rafael de Granada, brother of this confessant, and they shut themselves up in the saloon where were Simon Vaez Sevilla, Gaspar Vaez, his son, and Francisco Lopez Diaz,* with the said Doña Juana Enriquez, and the mother of this confessant who was in the corridor with his said brother, Rafael de Granada, and this confessant wishing to go into the saloon to hear what they said, the said Gaspar Vaez impeded him, telling him not to go in and to remain in the corridor, and he went in and closed the door; and within an hour, more or less, his said mother came out; and because it had rained, the said Francisco Lopez Diaz took her home behind him on mule-back; and this confessant went home on foot with his said brother, and he has never known what it was that was spoken of and communicated

Against his mother,
Dª Maria de Rivera
Dª Juana Enriquez
Rafael de Granada
Simon Vaez de Sevilla
Gaspar Vaez
Francisco Lopez Diaz

---

*Francisco Lopez Dias, called El Chato, unmarried, resident of Zacatecas, merchant, native of Casteloblanco, in Portugal, son of new Christians, Judaizing heretic, reconciled, 1648 (Obregon, p. 364).

A Lewis Dias was in Barbadoes in 1680. Adler, *Pub. Am. Jewish Hist. Soc.* No. 1 p. 105. Diego Diaz was condemned by the Inquisition of Mexico in 1659. G. A. Kohut, *Ibid.*, No. 4, p. 121.

about by his said mother and the said Doña Juan Enriquez,
and her husband and son, Simon and Gasper Vaez, and
Francisco Lopez Diaz, although from the noise this confessant heard in the corridor, he felt sure there were more persons than those he has mentioned; he does not know who
they were for not having seen the said persons when they
left the house of the said Simon Vaez Sevilla, and for the
purpose of declaring the above, he asked for this audience,
and it having been read to him, he said it was well written
and it was the truth; and straitly admonished, &c., he was
ordered back to his cell and he signed it.

GABRIEL DE GRANADA.

Before me,

[Signed]   Lic. THOMAS LOPEZ DE ERENCHUN.

I accept this confession in so far as it favors me and no
more, said day, month and year.

7th Audience.   Mexico, Monday, 24th of November, 1642.   Inquisitors
Argos and Estrada, morning.

He said that he asked the audience to declare what
he has remembered, and it is that seven days after the

Against   death of Doña Blanca Enriquez, this confessant was in
Dª Blanca
Enriquez   the house of Doña Beatriz Enriquez,* her daughter, in
Dª Beatriz
Enriquez   company with Doña Blanca de Rivera, his grandmother,
Dª Blanca
Rivera   who gave him two dollars and told him to take them to
Dª Isabel
de Rivera.   his aunt, Doña Isabel de Rivera, in order that she might
keep two fasts for the soul of the said Doña Blanca Enriquez,
that her daughter, Doña Beatriz, who gave her those two
dollars so ordered it done for this purpose, and she gave
those two dollars to Blanca de Rivera in presence of this

---

*Beatriz Enrriquez, native of New Veracruz, daughter of Fer-
nando Rios and of Blanca Enrriquez, Judaizing heretic, reconciled
1647 (Obregon, p. 363).

confessant and that of Doña Catalina Rivera, his aunt, who was present; and this confessant took the said two dollars to his said aunt, Doña Isabel, in order that she might keep the said two fasts, and she received them and she said she would fast them, but he does not know if she kept those fasts.

And he also remembers that when Diego Antunes* died, this confessant was that same day in the house of Doña Isabel Duarte,† his wife, in company with Doña Blanca de Rivera, his grandmother, who ordered him to go to her house and ask Doña Catalina de Rivera, his aunt, for some grains of seed pearls, and he went to her house to ask for them in the name of his said grandmother, and the said Doña Catalina gave him wrapped up in a piece of paper, two or three small pearls, which this confessant took and gave to the said Doña Isabel Duarte, and as he has heard it said that when some observer of the law dies, they put gold or pearls in his mouth to be interred with him, a ceremony of the said law, he presumes that the said Doña Isabel Duarte as well as her said husband, Diego Antunes, were observers of the law of Moses.

(margin: Against Diego Antunes deceased Isabel Duarte Blanca de Rivera and Dᵃ Catalina de Rivera.)

And that he remembers when they arrested Thomas Nuñez de Peralta‡ this confessant being in the house of Doña Juana Enriquez and Doña Beatriz Enriquez, the wife of the said Nuñez, they said to this confessant, the said Doña Juana

(margin: Against Dᵃ Juana de Enriquez Dᵃ Beatriz Enriquez)

---

* Diego Antunes, citizen and merchant, Portuguese, of this city of Mexico, where he died, husband of Doña Ysabel Duarte, Judaizing heretic, executed in effigy 1649 (Obregon, p. 376).

Gabrielle Antunes was in Barbadoes in 1680. See Adler, *Pub. Am. Jewish Hist. Soc.*, No. 1, p. 106.

† Isabel Duarte, *alias* she of Antunes, native of the city of Seville, citizen of that of Mexico, juggler by trade, daughter of Marcos Rios Tristan and of Anna Enrriquez, Hebrew new Christians, Judaizing heretic, reconciled, 1646 (Obregon, p. 359.)

‡ Thomas Nuñez de Peralta, native of Cubillina, in Portugal, citizen and merchant of this city of Mexico, son of Jeorge Baes Alcaiceria, tanner by trade, and of Isabel Rios, Portuguese, new Christians, husband of Beatriz Enrriques, Hebrew, Judaizing heretic, reconciled, 1646 (Obregon, pp. 360, 361).

and Doña Beatriz Enriquez, that his mother Doña Maria and his aunts and grandmother had sent the said Thomas Nuñez to the Inquisition, and that they were the cause of his arrest and that if they were to accuse the said Doña Juana and Doña Beatriz and the other sisters and relations that they would revenge themselves on the daughters of the sons of the said Margaret, and this confessant believes that they meant Diego Correa; and that they have made grave depositions against him in this Holy office, and in order that he may not suffer for it at any time by reason of the said Doña Juana and Doña Beatriz Enriquez he has made this declaration in justification of and in favor of the said Diego Correa, his uncle, who has had him in his house and company for six years, and during that time he has never seen or *felt* that he was an observer of the law of Moses, but rather he considered him as a very good christian; and that for this he has asked this audience and that if anything else occurs to him he will ask for an audience to declare it; and strictly admonished still to think well over it he was ordered back to his cell, and it having been read to him he said it was well written and he signed it.

GABRIEL DE GRANADA.

Before me,
[Signed]   Lic. MELCHOR DE ARASUS.

I accept this confession in so far as it favors me and no more. Said day, month and year.

Dr. GAVIOLA (Fiscal).

Ratification before his Guardian   In the city of Mexico, Monday, 23d day of the month of March, 1643, the Inquisitors Argos, Mañozca and Estrada being in their afternoon audience they ordered Gabriel de Granada to be brought, and he being present, he was asked if he remembered anything about his business and if so to declare it and in all things speak the truth. He said he has nothing which he ought to say about his business. And forthwith the said Inquisitors commanded Dr. Juan Bautista Martinez, guardian and counsel of the said Gabriel de Granada, to enter, to which minor there were read in presence of his said guardian and Counsel the confessions which he made in this Holy office on Monday the 13th of last October and Monday, 24th of November of 1642, and having read them to him word for word the said Gabriel de Granada said that those were his confessions and he had declared them according as they were read to him and that they were well written and were true and that he adhered to them and ratified them, and if it were necessary he would repeat them in presence of his said Guardian and Counsel. And he signed it. GABRIEL DE GRANADA.

[Signed] Dr. JUAN BAPT^A MRZ. DE CEP^DA

Before me,

[Signed] MELCHOR ARASUS.

He ratified all his confessions this same day in the afternoon before the respectable and religious persons, father Diego de Segura, of the order of St. Dominick, and the Licentiate Juan de Suvielaga, presbyter and he was told that the Fiscal would present him as a witness against all the persons —mentioning their names—against whom he had made depositions, and he said that there was nothing to alter, add or amend, etc., and signed

GABRIEL DE GRANADA.

Before me,

Lic. MELCHOR DE ARASUS.

In the city of Mexico, Tuesday, 24th day of March, 1643. Inquisitors Argos, Mañozca and Estrada.

He said that he has nothing to say. He was told that the Fiscal of this Holy office wants to present an accusation

Audience in which the accusation was given to him

against him, and that it would be very well for him as well
for unburdening his conscience as for the prompt and favorable despatch of his business that before the accusation is
presented he should declare the truth as he has been admonished and he is now again admonished because there will be
liberty to extend the mercy to him which this Holy office is
accustomed to extend to those who truly confess, otherwise he
is warned that the Fiscal shall be heard and justice shall be done.

He said that he has already told the whole truth in his
confessions, to which he refers, and immediately Dr. Gaviola,
the Promotor Fiscal of this Holy office made his appearance
and presented an accusation signed by his name against the
said Gabriel de Granada, and he swore in due form that he
was not actuated by malice in putting it, the tenor of which
is as follows :—

Very Illustrious Lords :

I, Doctor Don Antonio de Gaviola, Promotor Fiscal of this
Inquisition in the best way and most favorable form allowed
by law, the necessary legal formalities having preceded,
appear before your Lordships and criminally accuse Gabriel
de Granada, a native and resident of this city, son of Manuel
de Granada, deceased, and of Doña Maria de Rivera, prisoner
in the Secret prisons of this Holy office and say :

That he, the above named being a baptised and confirmed
christian, and as such enjoying the graces, privileges and
exemptions that the faithful and catholic christians enjoy
and ought to enjoy, in contravention of the profession made
in holy baptism, has done, said and committed, seen done,
heard said and committed many and grave crimes against
what our holy mother Roman Catholic church and evangelical law believes, holds, preaches and teaches, apostatizing
from her and passing over to the dead law of Moses which
he observed and does observe with all its rites and ceremonies, believing with all his heart that it is the good and true,
and in which he must be saved, feigning and simulating to

be a true and catholic christian, all of which he has done and committed, seen done and committed in the parts and places and at the time set forth by my sworn informations, to which I refer, of which I accuse him in general and in particular of the following :

That in the month of September, of the year 1641, he kept Chapter 1st. the fast of the great day in company with certain persons, his nearest relations, they having concerted together to keep it in guarding and observance of [the law of] Moses, bathing himself for the purpose on the previous evening, putting on himself clean clothing, lighting candles, supping things made of fish, and being the most of the night on foot and reciting in company with certain persons prayers of the said law ; and the said Gabriel de Granada recited the following prayer, which was taught to him by a certain person, his very near relation,* and the following day until the night when the evening star appeared, on which he took the second supper on fish in company with the said certain persons, his very near relations.

And that he has likewise kept six or seven ordinary fasts of 2. the said law of Moses on Mondays and Thursdays for himself and for the soul of a certain person, his very near relation, deceased, supping on fish the previous evenings, and going all those days without eating until night when he ate the same food.

And that being with a certain person, his near relation, in 3. the house of another certain person, an observer of the law of Moses, the said certain person, his near relation, gave two dollars to the said Gabriel de Granada to take them to another person, his near relation, in order to keep two ordinary fasts of the law of Moses for the soul of a certain person, an observer of the said law.

And that a certain person, his very near relative, being in 4. the house of another certain person, deceased, an observer of

* This prayer has been given on page 17.

the law of Moses, the said certain person, his very near relative, sent the said Gabriel de Granada to ask from a certain person, his near relative, some small pearls to put in the mouth of the said deceased as a ceremony of the said law of Moses, which pearls he brought and gave for this purpose to another certain person, likewise an observer of the law of Moses.

5. And that after the arrest by this Holy office of certain persons, his very near relations, a certain person, an observer of the law of Moses, sent for the said Gabriel de Granada and entreated him that in case he should be arrested by this Holy office not to discover her from which it ought to be presumed, that the said Gabriel de Granada has not entirely confessed the whole truth, keeping silent and concealing many accomplices whom he has seen commit many and grave crimes against our holy catholic faith.

6. And that having been admonished of the modesty and silence with which they ought to behave in their cells and the grave penalties which those incur who violate it, he has communicated in prison with a certain other person, his very near relation, inducing him not to expose the persons with whom she had communicated as an observer of the law of Foot. Moses.- Besides which it is to be presumed and believed that the said Gabriel de Granada has done, said and committed many other and grave crimes against our holy catholic faith, and seen them done, said and committed by many other persons, about all of which he keeps silent and maliciously conceals them, of which I solemnly declare that I will accuse him in the prosecution of his cause and every time it comes to my knowledge, and if necessary I accuse him of being a Judaizing heretic, an apostate from our holy catholic faith and that he wants to live and die in the false belief of the reprobated dead law of Moses in which he lives and has lived, and as a perjurer, favorer, aider, abettor and concealer of Judaizing heretics.

Wherefore, accepting his confessions in so far as they act in my favor and not in any more, and protesting not to be obliged to furnish too many proofs

I pray and supplicate your Lordships, that accepting my recital as true in so far as may be sufficient, and to pronounce by your definitive sentence my intent as well proved, and the said Gabriel Granada as a doer and perpetrator of the crimes of which he is by me accused, and as a Judaizing heretic, an apostate from our holy catholic faith, a denier, favorer, aider, abettor and concealer of heretics, and having for this reason incurred the sentence of major excommunication and to be bound and held thereby, condemning him in the gravest and severest penalties established by law, relaxing his person to the secular arm and justice, declaring his goods as confiscated and to belong to the Chamber and exchequer of His Majesty, in order that it may serve to him as a punishment and to others as a warning example.

And in case of necessity and that my intent be not considered as well proved, I pray and entreat that the said Gabriel de Granada be put to the question of torture in which he may be kept and made to persevere until he tells the whole truth, and if it should suit me to petition for more and in a better manner, I so petition; and above all that justice be entirely and fully done according to my petition, and for which, &c., I swear in due form that I do not put this accusation from malicious motives.

[Signed] Dr. Don ANTONIO DE GAVIOLA (Fiscal).

And the said accusation having been presented and read, an oath was received from the said Gabriel de Granada in due form of law, in presence of his guardian and counsel, under the solemnity of which he promised to speak and answer the truth about the contents of the said accusation, and it having been read over to him again, chapter by chapter, he answered thereto in the following manner:

To the caption of the said accusation

Oath of the culprit in presence of his guardian

He said that he is the one referred to in it, and that his name is Gabriel de Granada, a native of this city and a son of the said Manuel de Granada, now deceased, and of Doña Maria de Rivera, and that he is a prisoner in the Secret prisons of this Holy office because of his sins and the evil teachings of his said mother and his aunt, Doña Margaret he left the faith of our Lord Jesus Christ and passed over to the reprobated law of Moses, for which he grieves with all his heart, and he promises not to return thereto because he desires to live and die as a Catholic christian.

Chap 1.   To the first Chapter

He said that what is contained in the chapter is true as he confessed in his confessions from the time that he entered as a prisoner in these prisons, and if necessary, he will again confess it.

Chap 2.   To the second chapter

He said that what the chapter recites is true and that he has so confessed.

Chap 3.   To the third chapter

He said that what the chapter says is true and he has confessed it.

Chap 4.   To the fourth chapter

He said that what the Chapter contains is true and he has confessed very particularly and specifically in his confessions.

Chap 5.   To the fifth chapter

He said that all contained in the Chapter has been confessed by him in his confessions, to which he refers, but that he does not keep silent about or conceal other accomplices, because if he knew of more people than those against whom he has declared he would wholly confess all he knew about them, because he has desired to unburden his conscience entirely and not to remain excommunicated.

Chap 6.   To the sixth chapter

Da Isabel de Rivera.
He said that he has already confessed what took place in the cells the first night that he entered into them in regard to his aunt, Doña Isabel, and that nothing else has taken place in the said cells about communications.

To the *foot* of the said accusation—   To the foot.

He said that he has no more to declare than he has confessed, because his wishes are to live and to die in the law of our Lord Jesus Christ, to which this Holy Tribunal has converted him, and that as a child he was perverted by his said mother and aunt, and that he begs and prays His Lordship to be compassionate and merciful towards him, considering that he is only between thirteen and fourteen years old, and that he has made a spontaneous confession of all his faults and crimes even before he was admonished the first time, and he has gone on confessing whenever he remembers anything that he has done, heard or seen done, said and committed by other persons that may be or appear to be contrary to our holy catholic faith, and that this is the truth on the oath that he has taken, and he signed it.

GABRIEL DE GRANADA.

Before me,

Lic. MELCHOR DE ARASUS.

The said Inquisitors ordered that a transcript be given him of the said accusation, and that on the third day he make his answer in defense, alleging his rights against it, and what in the opinion of the said Dr. Juan Martinez, his guardian and counsel, may be expedient for him to plead; and straitly admonished to think it over well and tell the truth, he was ordered back to his cell. A transcript is ordered to be given him

It passed before me,

[Signed] Lic. MELCHOR DE ARASUS.

I accept this confession in so far as it makes in my favor and in no more.

Dr. GAVIOLA.

Audience to which he was ordered to be brought, and in which he communicated with his advocate about the accusation
In the City of Mexico, Thursday, March 26th, 1643. Inquisitors Argos, Mañozca and Estrada.

He said that he does not remember anything new that he ought to declare in this, his cause, unless it be that the night that he has confessed he went to the house of Dª Juana Enriquez, after his grandmother, Doña Blanca de Rivera, and his aunts, Margaret, Clara and Isabel, were arrested, he saw that Dª Micaela Enriquez also went to that house and went in and was shut in with the persons whom he has declared in his confessions.

He was told that Dr. Juan Bautista Martinez Cepeda, whom he had chosen as his guardian and lawyer, is present to say and communicate to him what he pleases and may be expedient in this, his business and cause, and with his opinion and advice plead his rights, that for this purpose he was ordered to be brought to the audience, and the said Dr. Don Juan Martinez de Cepeda swore in due form of law that well and faithfully and with all care and diligence will he defend the said Gabriel de Granada, his minor ward, in this cause, in so far as the law permits and allows, and if he should not have justice on his side he will undeceive him and that in all things he will do and perform what a good and faithful advocate ought and should do and perform, and that he will observe secrecy about all that takes place and comes to his knowledge.

Communication with the advocate
And then forthwith the confessions of the said Gabriel de Granada were read, and also the accusation and what he replied thereto, and he spoke to and communicated what he pleased about this business and cause with his said advocate and guardian, who said to him and advised him what was expedient for the unburdening of his conscience and rapid and favorable dispatch of his business, and to declare and confess the truth without raising false testimony against himself or others, and if he were guilty to pray for penance, because for this it would be given him with mercy. And the said Gabriel de Granada with the advice of his said counsel and guardian

Said that he has declared and confessed the whole truth, as is evident from the confessions to which he refers, and he denies the rest contained in the said accusation, and that on the publication of witnesses' depositions being given him, he solemnly promises to allege and plead more formally what may be expedient for his rights and defense, and that he closed and did close for the next question, (articulo) coming before the tribunal according to law in his cause. Closing of the culprit

The said Inquisitors said that they ordered and they did order, a transcript to be given to the said promotor fiscal of this Holy office, who said that adhering to and reaffirming what he has said, and accepting the confessions made by the said Gabriel de Granada, so far as they make in his favor and no farther, denying what is against and prejudicial to him, he closes and he did close, and he asked to be admitted to proofs. The Fiscal closes.

The said Inquisitors said that they considered and de- clared this cause as closed, and they decided that they ought to receive and they did admit both parties to proofs, *salvo jure impertinentium et non admitendorum,* according to the style and practice of this Holy office, which was notified to both parties. Sentence to proofs without fixing a term

And then the said Promotor fiscal said that he made a re- production and presentation of the witnesses and proofs which against the said Gabriel de Granada are received, as well in the process as in the Registers and documents of the Holy office, and he asked that the concurring witnesses be examined, and that the witnesses ratify their depositions in the form prescribed by law, and that the other necessary legal measures to know and ascertain the truth be taken, and that this being done, the publication be made of the depositions of witnesses in this cause. Notification to the parties.

The said Inquisitors said that justice shall be done, and all else which may be done in accordance with law; and straitly admonished still to think it over well, he was ordered back to his cell and he and his said guardian and counsel signed it.

[Signed]   Dr. Juan Bap^{ta} Mrz de Cep^{da.}

[Signed]   Gabriel de Granada.

                    Before me,

                              Lic. M. de Arasus.

8th Audience voluntarily asked for.

Isabel, wife of Antunes and her son Manuel.†

Luis Nuñez Perez.

Margarita

Pedro de Espinosa

Mexico, Friday, October 9th, 1643. Morning. Inquisitors Argos, Estrada Mañozca and Higura.*

He said that a week after his mother, grandmother and aunts were arrested Isabel, wife of Antunes, called him, and in her house in presence of her son, she asked him if he had any news from his grandmother, mother and aunts; he answered no, and not to be afraid; to which she replied that neither had they heard anything on her part. And that about four months ago his mother and his aunt Margaret being talking at the grand door (of the Inq.) Luis Nuñez Perez‡ recognized her from his cell and said : "It is an illusion or thou art Margaret", from which it came to pass that they saluted each other, and Pedro de Espinosa asked if they knew how his wife was, and they answered that they did not, but that they suspected she was in the prison, in Picazo's house, as this confessant and his brother had told them. And that about this time they also communicated with a

---

* This and the following audiences are condensed and abbreviated as the verbose jargon in which they are recorded *in extenso* is intolerable. D. F.

† Manuel Antunes, unmarried, vagrant, native and citizen of this city of Mexico, son of Diego Antunes, Portuguese, citizen and merchant of this city, Hebrew; and of Doña Isabel Duarte *alias* de Antunes, reconciled, Judaizing heretic, reconciled 1646 (Obregon, p. 359).

‡ Possibly the same as Luis Muños Perez, native of Samameda, near Lisbon, resident in this [city of] Mexico, peanut-vender, son of Manuel de Abeña, and of Batola Dias Silba, Hebrew new Christians, Judaizing heretic, reconciled, 1646 (Obregon, pp. 359–360).

woman who he suspects is Isabel de Huerta, called by *Isabel de Huerta the Rose.* another name, the Rose, and that the beginning of the com- munication was that she thrust her hand out of a window or door, which was seen by the said Espinosa and Nuñez, and *Pedro de Espinosa and Luis Nuñez* they asked her her name, which she did not tell, feigning first that she was from Zacatecas and then from Celaya. And that after they changed Antonio Orduña's* cell and put him with Espinosa and Luis Nuñez Perez, the said woman, to play a trick on a tame black and white cat, stuck a tooth-pick in his hair, and as they must have made a pet of him in the cell of the said Espinosa he went there, and Orduña took the tooth-pick away from his hair and showed it to the said Isabel and she recognized it, and he said to her that he *Isabel de Huerta* would keep it until he were released to give it to her then; and they spoke of many things touching amours, and that by means of the said cat they carried on a correspondence, the said woman sending them sweetmeats and snuff, and the men whatever they had, tying them to the cat's neck; and that the said woman gave them to understand that her cell-mate was Doña Isabel Tristan, who had been tortured, and she *Doña Isabel Tristan* saluted the said prisoners on the part of the said Dª Isabel Tristan. And that a few days before this confessant's aunt died, the said woman sent by the said cat to Pedro Espinosa *Pedro de Espinosa* something that ran the risk of being broken, because she said to look out that it did not break, etc.

And they being all afraid of the alcaide and his assistant, they dare not speak at all hours, and Espinosa said that *Pedro de Espinosa Isabel de Huerta* when they came and he heard the doors opening and shut, he would give a sign, giving three blows with a small stick on the bars of his window, which he did, &c.†

---

*Antonio Lopez Orduña, native of the city of Seville, merchant by trade, and deputy of the principal Alcalde in the mines of Chichicapa, unmarried, descendant of Hebrew new Christians, reconciled for Judaizing heresy, 1646 (Obregon, p. 356).

† And he goes on giving minute details of trifling conversations held by different prisoners, one of whom was Goys, for which his *Goys*

4

D^a Blanca de Rivera.

And that after they moved him with his grandmother to another cell, in order that they should not be recognized by the adjoining prisoners, they made use of false names, she calling herself D^a Paula, and he Don Jacinto * and the said his grandmother complained that she having been a good confessant, they had moved her away from her daughters; and that the scribes and pharisees, the demons, left off everything as soon as the clock struck and went away, and that it looked as if they would not escape with their lives, and that she was going to ask for her grandson, little Lewis, in order to find out how her daughters were, and that he and his grandmother cursed the Inquisitors for their slowness, (the phlegm with which they proceeded), and they cursed the alcaides with many maledictions; and that being in a state of desperation, he swore many oaths and said other foolish things, and his grandmother said that the witnesses had deposed against her about some money belonging to Duarte de Leon† about which she did not recollect anything, and that they afflicted her, and other details, and that she replied to all of it with great spirit and courage ; and that his grandmother told him to tell Ubiedo to take him to get his hair cut, and when they were cutting it to cough and speak in a

P^o Espinosa Margarita de Rivera

name was put on the margin, a sign that he would be charged with it as a grave crime, and that Espinosa also communicated about this time with Margarita de Rivera ; and he goes on for pages detailing trifling conversations between prisoners, involving no charge beyond the mere violation of the rules to preserve absolute silence. It is quite evident that this wretched boy had orders to act as a spy and eavesdropper, under the false hope of getting off free. (See Gaspar Alfar's prison communications.) D. F.

*See the prison communications reported by Gaspar Alfar. D. F.

†Duarte Leon Xaramillo, native of Casteloblanco in Portugal, citizen of this city of Mexico, husband of Isabel Nuñes, reconciled, son of Hebrew new Christians, Judaizing heretic, relapsed, executed in person, 1649 (Obregon, p. 377).

Francisco de Leon Xaramillo, native and citizen of this city of Mexico, son of Duarte de Leon Xaramillo and of Isabel Nuñes, Judaizing heretic, reconciled 1647 (Obregon, p. 362).

loud voice, so that his mother and aunts should know that he was there, and that on coming down from the audience, she said that the Inquisitor Argos had pressed her very hard, she mocking him, and that he must be possessed of the devil; and that Philip (de Amesqueta, Notary), was an infamous traitor, and that all had conspired against her, and she also complained of the witnesses and that she would consume them with maledictions and make them bite the dust, and that it would be better to put her to the torture than to be tormented by these executioners, meaning the ministers of this Holy office; for this confessant to beware and lookout what he did; and that on another occasion he had great fun with his grandmother, annoying and tiring out Ubiedo, asking him for a great many things to molest him; and one night they maliciously put out the candle and called for the Alcaide until they came to light it, and that altho, another time the same night they put it out again and called the Alcaide, he did not come though they gave a great many knocks on the door; and his grandmother said, cursing Ubiedo with many curses, that she would like to see him wallowing in his blood and that she would drink it; and she said that they spoke to her of some fasts that she did not understand, and that the Inquisitor Argos was a devil (a satan), and this confessant, boy-like, let her say during this occasion other nonsense or foolish things.

And that his grandmother told him that they brought Against D^a Blanca de Rivera. great pressure upon her, and that she did not know what to do with so many witnesses, and that the worst of it was that they wanted her to say one thing and she another, and this was on the occasion that the witnesses said she had taught the Texosso women * which was not true.

* Four women of this name are found in the Mexican Inquisition records: Francisca Texoso, spinster, native of the city of Seville, citizen of New Veracruz, baker by trade, descendant of new Christains, Judaizing heretic, reconciled 1646 (Obregon, p. 360).
Clara Texoso, native of the city of Lima, in Peru, and citizen of

And this confessant, saying that he liked minced meat (or hash), his said grandmother said that she would eat it very well if it were made of the body of Ubiedo, and she sent Against Dᵃ Blanca de Rivera many other maledictions after these gentlemen. And that his grandmother told him that she found herself surrounded by traitors, like a captain amongst his enemies; and she wished that they were so wretched and persecuted as she was, and that she having found him weeping, she said that those traitors, meaning the Inquisitors, having robbed her of all they wanted, they now treated her in this manner; that those Against Dᵃ Maria de Rivera might trust them who would, and believe in them; and he said to her that his mother had well said not to trust them; that all should not be told to the judges, and this he said because he heard his mother say so when she was in the lane (of the prison).

Against Dᵃ Blanca de Rivera. And his grandmother told him to keep his senses about him, and to follow her in all things, and to be careful, because the Inquisitors were such that if you changed a word or a phrase they could catch him and do what they liked with them, that they had them *down,* and he answered that she had nothing to advise him about, and much afflicted and complainingly she said, let them revenge themselves, these traitors, who hated her so much, and that they wanted her, in all that they asked her, to say "Yes, sir, it is so," "I know it:" or "I did it," that they would not see themselves in that mirror, for only what I know, that ye know, and is the truth

that of New Veracruz, in this New Spain, descendant of Hebrew new Christians, Judaizing heretic, reconciled 1646.

Isabel Texoso, native of the city of Seville, and citizen of that of New Veracruz, spinster, baker by trade, daughter of Pedro Gomez Texoso, and of Violante Rios, Portuguese, Hebrew new Christians, Judaizing heretic, reconciled 1646.

Violante Texoso, native of the city of Lima, in Peru, and citizen of that of New Veracruz, spinster, seamstress, and daughter, legitimate, of Rafael Gomez Texoso, merchant, deceased, in this city of Mexico, Judaizing heretic, reconciled 1646 (Obregon, pp. 358, 359).

shall I tell, and the rest I am going to deny, and what could
they do with her?—put her to the torture; that they could not
in justice do it, and that if they should torture her she had
the spirit to suffer it; and he answered her that the rope always broke at the weakest point, and she said that were she
to please them and confess, they would like her, and not address her with obscene, indecent words.* And he tried to
soothe her, and he asked her if much remained to be done,
and she answered but little, that their evil intentions were
oozing from their eyes and mouths; that she was watching
their actions, and that they maltreated a woman like her, and
when he was trying to console her, she said that their hearts
were harder than marble, and that they had no compassion on
her, and that if she wept they would think she was an im-
postor, and he told her to have patience.† And nothing
else occurs to him to declare, that whenever he remembers
anything, he will come to make it manifest with the desire
to unburden his conscience, and he signed it with his
name; and straitly admonished to think it over well, he was
ordered back to his cell.

[Signed]   GABRIEL DE GRANADA.

Before me,

[Signed] THOMAS LOPEZ DE ERUNCHUN.‡

---

* Here she illustrates their language with one of their obscene
proverbs. D. F.

† And then he relates the incident of the shells as declared by
Gaspar Alfar § in his audience on this very day, in the morning,
before this one was given to Gabriel de Granada. It is evident that
the Inquisitors told this boy of Alfar's depositions about him and
his grandmother on the 5th, 6th, 7th, 8th, and 9th of this month,
and so compelled him to testify, and thus they got two witnesses
against Doña Blanca de Rivera. D. F.

‡ This is the fourth audience which the Secretary omitted to read
over, as he ought, to the culprit, as is strictly enjoined by Instructions and accorded letters. D. F.

§ The name occurs in the Archives de Aragon in 1273. See *An Inquiry into
the Sources of the History of the Jews in Spain,* by Joseph Jacobs, London, 1894,
p. 33, no. 535.

I accept this confession in so far as it makes in my favor and no farther.   Said day, month and year.

[Signed] Dr. GAVIOLA.

9th Audience asked of his own volition Mexico, Monday, October 12th, 1643, morning.   Inquisitor Estrada.

He said that in conformity with what he was ordered about advising his grandmother wholly to unburden her conscience, Dª Blanca says she will not confess anything he has done so with great earnestness, and she answered him to let her alone, that she does not want to speak or declare what she does not know and what is not the truth, and she told this confessant that they had accused her of what had passed in that prison, in regard to the conversations that passed between her and him, and the affair of the candle and the mince-meat, or hash, made of Ubiedo, and other things they had spoken against him; and this confessant answering her that they also charged him with it, and he had confessed She became furiously angry with this one because he confessed the communications. it she became furiously angry against him, and asked him why he had confessed it, that she had denied it, and to take notice that she was no longer his grandmother, and that he had neither mother nor aunts; she was enraged because he had declared all that had taken place in the cell in which they are, as it was against the Inquisitors; and that with regard to the cat and other matters that passed in the other cell he had done very well in declaring it because he had related the whole of it to her notwithstanding that they warned him not to mention it, but moved by the love which he ought to feel for his grandmother, and with the desire that she should wholly unburden her conscience, he told her all that passed in the audience, telling her that he had done it to relieve his conscience, and that she ought to do the same, and knowing that he had done wrong in this, and revealed the secrecy which he was under obligations to observe, he repented immediately, and so he has asked this audience to confess his fault, with the deepest sense of repentance, solemnly promising that he will not repeat it nor commit such an offense any more, but that he will be very obedient to what this Holy office may command him.

And that his grandmother has decided to come up to the audience and confess the affair of the cat and prison commu-. nications, but that she will not do it right away in order Cunning of the that it may not be imagined that this confessant has informed Blanca old woman her of it and they have thus concerted together; and to the end that the good faith with which he proceeds should be known, he has declared this circumstance, and he does not recollect any others in particular; that whenever any light is thrown upon them for him he will declare them with all truth ; and that all that he has declared is true on the oath which he had taken, and it having been read to him, he said that it was well written; and very straitly admonished still to think well over it, he was ordered back to his cell, and he signed it.   GABRIEL DE GRANADA.

Before me, [Signed] PHELIPE DE ZAVALZA AMESQUETA.

I accept this confession in so far as it makes in my favor and no farther. Said day, month and year.

[Signed] Dr. GAVIOLA.*

Mexico, Thursday, 5th November, 1643, afterooon. In- 10th Audience quisitor Estrada y Escobedo. . . .   asked by him voluntarily

* Two things are observable in this audience that are prohibited by the Instructions and accorded letters: First, that Gabriel de Granada was ordered to influence his grandmother to make a confession without the fact being recorded in the audience, and that his grandmother should be verbally accused of any offense without its being recorded, and even then it is irregular and illegal, for the accusations should be preferred by the Promotor Fiscal, either in his accusation or the publication of the depositions of witnesses. Here is proof evident of illegal methods practiced by these judges, for every word said should be recorded by the Notary, using the very words uttered, whether by the culprit or by the Inquisitors. D. F.

He said he asked the audience for unburdening his conscience, and it is that he being one day with Diego Correa,
his uncle, he sent him with a message to Manuel Diaz Castillo, whom he found in his house (he then living in Eagle
Street) with a cap on his head, with his hands washed and
raised towards the East, praying, and these being customary
ceremonies of the law of Moses according to what his aunt
Margaret told him when she taught it to him, and because
he is a Portuguese he suspects that the said Manuel Diaz is
an observer of the said law, but he never communicated
anything to him on this matter, although on this point he
remembers that Doña Juana Enriquez told his aunt Margaret
that the said Manuel Diaz observed the said law.

And that some days before Doña Blanca Enriquez died,
this confessant entered into her house, where he found Doña
Juana Enriquez, who gave him a dollar, in order that he
should keep a fast for the health of her said mother; which
this confessant did, and when the said Doña Juana gave
him the dollar Isabel del Bosque* was present, who asked
her mother, Esperanza Rodriguez, why they gave the dollar
to this confessant, and the mother answered her, saying, in
order that he should fast it, to which the said Dᵃ Isabel
replied to give it to her, that she would fast it, to which her
mother said, what sort of fasts did she keep!—that they were
worth nothing; and the daughter answered saying, what other
kind of fasts did she want her to keep? to which the mother
said that she would teach them to her; and she began to
teach them, both of them talking, and afterwards she communicated with this confessant as an observer of the law,
and he with her, one day that the said Isabel went to his
house on an occasion when she fasted.

And that his mother and aunts told him that Gaspar de

Margin notes: Diego Correa / Manuel Diaz Castillo / Dᵃ Margarita de Rivera / Dᵃ Blanca Enriquez / Dᵃ Juana Enriquez. / Dᵃ Juana Enriquez. / Isabel del Bosque. / Esperanza Rodriquez.

---

*Isabel del Bosque, sister of the father and mother of Juana del
Bosque, spinster, seamstress by trade, native and citizen of this city
of Mexico, Judaizing heretic, reconciled 1646 (Obregon, p. 357).

Robles* observes the law of Moses; and that of the money that Doña Blanca Enriques left for fasts for her soul, Doña Beatriz Enriquez gave him ten dollars with which he redeemed from pawn a black dress; and although he has not communicated with the said Gaspar de Robles, he ought to know, and he knows well, that this confessant observed the law, seeing that he used to talk to his mother and aunts about some things concerning it in his presence without any suspicion. *[margin: The Blancas (Thus did the Inquisitors call Blanca de Rivera and all her family) Dª Blanca Enriquez Dª Beatriz Enriquez Gaspar de Robles.]*

And that he has heard all the above-named persons say, at divers times, that Pedro de Castro, son-in-law of Simon Vaez, observed the law of Moses, and that he came from a country where those who observed it did so freely. *[margin: Pedro de Castro]*

Item.—He heard all the above-named say that Manuel de Acosta, Thomas Nuñez de Peralta, Gaspar Xuarez† and his two daughters, Anna and Blanca (Blanche), Sebastian Cardosa,‡ Francisco Lopez de Fonseca,§ Jorge Jacinto, Diego Tinoco and Pedro ‖ and Miguel, Juana and Isabel *[margin: Manuel de Acosta Thomas Nuñez de Peralta Gaspar Xuarez Anna and Blanca Xuarez Franco Lopez de Fonseca Jorge Xacinto, Diego, Pedro, Miguel, Juana and Isabel Tinoco his children. Simon de Espinosa Francisco Lopez, the flat-nosed. Manuel de Acosta. Simon Fernandez Henrique Fernandez Anto. de Orduña Nuño de Silva D. Nuño de Figueroa, Po. de Espinosa Dª Isabel de Silva his wife]*

* Antonio Robles, a Marrano, was in England in 1657 : Graetz, *History of the Jews* (American ed.), Vol. v, p. 49. Six persons of this name suffered martyrdom in Madrid in 1680; see *Relacion*, etc., pp. 41–43; Kayserling, *Ein Feiertag in Madrid*, p. 37. A David Robbles was in New York in 1696; see Max Kohler, *Pub. Am. Jewish Hist. Soc.*, No. 2, p. 80.

† Gasper Xuarez, native of Mego, in Portugal, citizen and merchant of this City of Mexico, husband of Rafaela Enrriquez, reconciled, daughter of Hebrew new Christians, Judaizing heretic, reconciled 1649 (Obregon, p. 378).

‡ Sebastian Cardoso, native of Seville, citizen and merchant of Mexico, son of Diego Cardoso Aseitero and of Antonio (sic) Gomez his wife, native of Marchena in Andalusia, descendant of Hebrew new Christians, married to Micaela Enrriquez, reconciled, Judaizing heretic, reconciled 1648 (Obregon, p. 366).

§ Reverend Abraham Haim Lopez de Fonseca was buried in Curaçao in 1671; see Corcos, *Jews of Curaçao*, p. 10. Joseph Nuñez de Fonseca was in Curaçao in 1652; see G. A. Kohut, *Pub. Am. Jewish Hist. Soc.*, No. 3, p. 118.

‖ Pedro Tinoco, unmarried, native and citizen of this City of Mexico, son of Diego Tinoco and of Catalina Silba, *alias* Enrriquez,

Tinoco, his children, and Simon de Espinosa observed the law of Moses, and to this last-named person it was taught by Francisco Lopez Chato (Snub or Flat Nose),and Manuel de Acosta,* out in the fields, since when he has observed it.

Item.—He heard the same person say that Simon Fernandez † and Henrique Fernandez, Antonio de Orduña and Nuña de Silva ‡ are likewise observers of the said law, and also that Don Nuño de Figueroa § and Pedro de Espinosa and his wife, Doña Isabel de Silva, observed it.

Gomez de Silva
Dᵃ Elena and Dᵃ Isabel de Silva
Antonio Caraballo.

Item.—The same persons told him that Gomez de Silva, his wife Dᵃ Elena, and his daughter Dᵃ Isabel de Silva and her husband, Antonio Caraballo, are observers of the said law, and that just now he does not remember anything else which he ought to declare, and this is the truth on the oath which he has taken; and straitly admonished, still to

executed, and descendants of such, Judaizing heretic, reconciled 1649 (Obregon, p. 370).

Miguel Tinoco, unmarried, apprentice to a silversmith, citizen and native of Mexico, son of Diego Tinoco, Portuguese, and of Catalina Enrriquez, native of Seville, new Christians, Judaizing heretic, reconciled 1647 (Obregon, p. 363.)

* A Joseph D'Acosta was in New York in 1657. See *Pub. Am. Jewish Hist. Soc.*, No. 6, p. 88.

† Simon Fernandez, unmarried, of the trade of merchant, native of Gobea in Portugal, citizen of the city of Guadalaxara in these kingdoms, son of Diego Antunes de Torres and of Isabel Nunes; Hebrew new Christians, Judaizing heretic, reconciled 1647 (Obregon, p. 363).

‡ Nuño de Silba, native and citizen of this City of Mexico, descendant of new Christians, Judaizing heretic, reconciled 1647 (Obregon, p. 363).

§ Nuño de Figueroa, *alias* Nuño de Pereira or Peredo, native of the city of Lisbon, citizen and merchant of the city of Guadalaxara in these kingdoms, son of Antonio Jabeira and of Isabel de Figueroa, Portuguese, Hebrew new Christians, Judaizing heretic, reconciled 1646 (Obregon, p. 361).

think it over well, he was ordered back to his cell, and he
signed it.

[Signed]   GABRIEL DE GRANADA.
       Before me,
[Signed]   LIC. M. DE ARASUS.*

I accept this confession in so far as it makes in my favor
and no farther.

[Signed]   DR. GAVIOLA.

Mexico, Thursday, 5th of Novr, 1643. Afternoon. In- *4th Audience voluntarily asked for.*
quisitor Estrada y Escobedo.

He said that he has asked the audience to declare what
he has remembered since yesterday,† and it is that he has
heard Doña Blanca de Rivera, his grandmother, and his *Dᵃ Blanca de Rivera and her*
aunts say several times that Doña Clara de Silva, Esper- *daughters Dᵃ Clara*
anza, Geronima and Sebastian Roman—all three dead— *de Silva Esperanza*
used to observe the law of Moses. *Geronima and Sebⁿ Roman.*

And that Maria Gomez, wife of Tremiño, a few days before *Mari Gomez*
they arrested her, told him, this confessant being in her house,
chatting in a window of Inez Pereira's ‡ room, that Antonio *Inez Pereyra Antᵒ Vaez*

* Here again they failed to read over his deposition to this boy,
and this omission ought to have been observed by the Fiscal Gaviola before he signed it. D. F.

† His last audience, No. 10, was on this same morning, before the
same Inquisitor, and the same Notary, and both are recorded in
the handwriting of this Notary Arasus; and his previous audience,
No. 9, was held on the 12th of October, before this same Inquisitor,
but a different Notary, viz., Phelipe de Zavalza y Amezqueta,
which makes it quite clear that the audience of *yesterday* was not
recorded; but one of those *strategic* audiences referred to by Eym-
eric and other Inquisitorial authors. D. F.

‡ Ines Pereira, native of Esmiquipan in this archbishopric, wife
of Baltasar Dias Santillano, daughter of Portuguese, of one executed
in person, Judaizing heretic, reconciled 1649 (Obregon, p. 368).
A family of this name settled in Curaçao about 1650; see Corcos,
p. 7. Isaac Perera was in Barbadoes in 1680; Adler, *Pub.Am. Jewish
Hist. Soc.*, No. 1, pp. 105, 106.

Vaez said that since the Inquisition had arrested the Blancas—meaning his grandmother and his mother and aunts—every one ought to look out for himself, because they would not be like him, who said that all the witnesses against him lied, although they had put him to the question of torture, and that she answered him telling him to hush and not to say such things.

Maria Gomez. Thomas Tremiño de Sobremonte.* * He of the two windows. The Blancas.
And that this said Maria Gomez and her husband, Thomas Tremiño de Sobremonte, are, in his opinion, observers of the law of Moses, because he has so heard it said in his house, by his mother, Maria de Rivera, his grandmother, Doña Blanca, and his aunts, Margaret, Catherine and Isabelle de Rivera, and that the above-named run great risks if they were to be arrested again by this Holy office, because they had been already chastised in it,* and that he heard his said

The Blancas Thomas Tremiño Leonor Nuñez Isabel Nunez Ana Gomez her daughters.
mother, grandmother and aunts say the same thing about Leonor Nuñez,† Isabel Nuñez, and Ana Gomez, her daughters, as they said about Thomas Tremiño, and his wife, but that this confessant has never spoken to, or communicated with any of these persons referred to about this matter, more

The Blancas Luis Perez Roldan Franco Blandon
than what took place with the said Maria Gomez. And that he has often heard his mother, grandmother, and aunts say that Luis Perez Roldan,‡ kept the law of Moses, and that Francisco Blandon,§ also observed it, but that with neither

* See the second prison communications of Gaspar Alfar.

† Leonor Nuñes, native of the city of Seville, citizen of that of New Veracruz, widow of Manuel Coronel, broker by trade in this Veracruz, new Christian, legitimate daughter of Gaspar de Agart, and of Maria Nuñes, Judaizing heretic, reconciled 1646 (Obregon, p. 359).

‡ Luis Peres Roldan, native and citizen of this city of Mexico, merchant, husband of Isabel Nuñes, executed, son, cousin, and uncle of reconciled, executed and penitent persons, Judaizer, reconciled 1649 (Obregon, p. 370).

§ Francisco Lopez Blandon, *alias* Terrasas, unmarried, native of this city of Mexico, gilder by trade, son of executed persons, Judaizing heretic, relapsed, executed in person 1649 (Obregon, p. 368).

of the two has he communicated.   And that he has also heard them say that Inez Pereira, Balthazar Diaz, her husband, and her brother, Manuel Diaz Santillan, and Francisco Nietto,* observed the said law, but that neither has he communicated with them.

And that after his said mother, grandmother and aunts were arrested, this confessant went to see Esperanza Rodriguez, who told him that she had lately taught her daughter, Maria del Bosque,† the law, and that the only one now wanting was the Fleming, meaning her son John, but that he would soon fall, (be caught or cave in), and that being in the prison in company with her said mother, grandmother and aunts, he heard his said mother say, that before they had apprehended her, she had been with Duarte de Leon, and that he said to her, that it was better not to talk, (confess or declare), that four turns of the rope on the rack did not signify; (and here he relates about his mother, asking Duarte about a slave of the alcaide, who used to carry messages from him to his wife, &c.)

And that he also heard his said mother say that by means of this same negro slave Luis Perez Roldan used to communicate with his wife, Isabel Nuñez; and all this that he has related, he heard her say in the prison; speaking to his grandmother and his aunts, and that just now he does not

(margin notes: The Blancas / Inez Pereyra / Balthr Diaz / M. D. Santillan / Franco Nietto / Esperanza Rodriguez / Maria del Bosque / The Blancas / Duarte de Leon / Luis Perez Roldan / Isabel Nuñez / Leonor Nuñez)

---

* Francisco Nieto, *alias* Neto, native of Casteloblanco, in Portugual, citizen and merchant of this city of Mexico, son of Hebrew new Christians, married first in Seville to Clara Fernandez, and second in this city to Leonor Nuñes, Judaizing heretic, reconciled 1649 (Obregon, p. 371).

† Maria del Bosque, native of Guadalaxara, spinster, seamstress by trade, daughter of Esperanza Rodriguez, reconciled, and of Juan Baptista del Bosque, German, Judaizing heretic, reconciled 1649 (Obregon, p. 357).

This may be the same name as Bosch, mentioned by Max Kohler, *Pub. Am. Jewish Hist. Soc.*, No. 2, p. 83.

remember anything more, and it is the truth on the oath
which he has taken, and straitly admolished, &c.,* . . . .
and he signed it.

GABRIEL DE GRANADA.

Before me, (Signed), Lic. M^OR. DE ARASUS.

I accept this confession in so far as it makes in my favor,
and no farther.

[Signed]   DR. GAVIOLA.

12th Audience
Voluntarily   Mexico, Friday, 6th Nov., 1643. Afternoon. Inquisitor,
asked for   Estrada y Escobedo. . . . .

He said that two or three months before they were arrested,
as it appears to him, that he does not remember well, his
aunt, Margaret, told him, they being alone, they two, when
speaking about the Virgin and her precious son, she speaking of them both with contempt, how they used some nights
to flog a small wooden crucifix they had there *unnailed*, (or
unscrewed), from a cross from which it had fallen, that she
lashed him with a scourge, and that he was held between
(by) her grandmother, and her aunt, Isabelle, for her to do
this. And that his said aunt, Margaret, had burnt in the
kitchen fireplace of her house, an arm of the holy Christ,
which had dropped from him, because as the Christ was
rolling about without the arm, and the arm without the
Christ, on account of the negress who saw it, they said it
would be better to burn it, but is clear that the intention was
wicked, for they being jewesses, and abhorring and flogging
the effigy of Christ, she would burn the said arm with the
same abhorrence; and although he did not see the said arm
being burnt, his said aunt told him of it; neither did he see
when they flogged the holy Christ, nor could such a thing
enter in his imagination, though two or three nights he

*The reading over of the deposition was again omitted. D. F.

heard in his bedroom, as if they were giving blows in the saloon or in the room where they made the dolls, and not paying attention to what might cause the noise, after his aunt told him of it, he understood then that those blows and noise, as if of flogging, happened on the occasions of committing such a grave and atrocious crime, which this confessant not only did not vituperate, but as a jew, which he was, he applauded his said aunts act and because he thought by doing so he would please her.

This fellow felt a complacency and applauded the enormous sacrilege of flogging the holy Christ and the other vituperations they made with his Most holy Image.

And that he heard his said aunt say that Simon Lopez de Aguarda and Simon Lopez Ramirez and Thomas Lopez Monforte* his brother, Thomas Gomez and Diego Mendez de Silva, Manuel Nuñez Caravallo and Julian de Albalaez were observers of the law of Moses, but this confessant does not know them, except Caravallo and Diego Mendez ; but he has not treated with any of them about this matter.

Margª de Ribera
Simon Lopez de Aguarda
Simon Lopez Ramirez
Thomas Lopez Monforte
Thomé Gomez Diego Mendez de Silva
Man'l Nuñez Caravallo
Julian de Alvalaez

And the Lord Inquisitor showed him a crucifix of wood, a quarter of a yard long, minus an arm, and a scourge (cat) of five tails, of gray ixtle (maguey hemp) with its handle of spool thread ; and the said Gabriel de Granada having seen the said crucifix and held it in his hands, kissing it with all reverence

He said that he recognized the holy Christ very well, because he saw him many times in his house, where he held him in great devotion, on an altar before his said aunt had perverted him to the law of Moses ; and because his arms used to drop off sometimes he used to stick them on again with wax. And that the arm that is missing is the one that his aunt told him she had burnt, and the holy Christ the one she told him she used to flog, and that the scourge, *he does not even know it*, [this was written and then the pen drawn through it thus *"Yque el açote ni ni lo conosse* and then they made him say as follows:] he saw it in his house, and he thinks it was

He recognized the holy Christ that was shown him in this audience Margarita de Rivera

---

*Thomas Lopez de Monforte, native of Monforte in Portugal vagrant, son of Francsisco Gonzales, merchant, and of Constanza Lopez, Portuguese, Hebrew new Christians, Judaizing heretic, reconciled 1646 (Obregon p. 360).

That this scourge was made by Diego Correa to flog the negro
made by his uncle Diego Correa for the purpose of flogging the little nigger, but he does not know that they flogged the holy Christ with it, nor did his said aunt tell with what they flogged him : that if he knew this as having seen it or with a better foundation he is so desirous of unburdening his conscience that with all precision he would declare it; and that this is the truth on the oath which he has taken, and straitly admonished still to think it over well he was ordered back to his cell, and he signed it.*

[Sig'd] GABRIEL DE GRANADA.

Before me, [Sig'd] Lic. M^or DE ARASUS.

I accept these confessions in so far as they favor me and no farther   Said day month and year.

[Signed] Dr GAVIOLA.

13th Audience of his own volition.
Mexico Friday 13th Novr 1643.   Afternoon.   Inquisitor Estrada y Escovedo.

He said that he asked for this audience to declare that he has remembered that the Monday before he was arrested he was with Maria Gomez in her house in a window of Inez Pereira's room, and the said Maria Gomez told him that the Sunday before Antonia, the daughter of Elvira, from the house of the Alcaide Marañon, had been to see her and had told her how they had taken up on Saturday night, to the Alcaide's room, a woman with a blue overskirt, and a white jacket (jubon) who had a little boy dressed in blue; and that the boy held the candle in his hands while the mother was dressing her running sores, and that the Inquisitor, Don Francisco [de Estrada y Escobedo] had sent her up, and that for this good news she had given to the said Antonia a dollar and a chinese mantilla with point lace ; and when the said Maria Gomez told this to this confessant she reasoned

Maria Gomez she of Tremiño

* The reading over again omitted.   D. F.

that seeing that they had sent her upstairs she must have confessed, about which this confessant gave an account to Diego Correa, just as the said Maria Gomez, she of Tremiño, Against Diego Correa had told him, in presence of the said Inez Pereira; and that Inez Pereira a month before he was arrested he went to the foliseo* to see a comedy, and he went to the room where Luis Perez Roldan lived, retired in that hospital, where he found Eleanor Against Eleañor Nuñez, who was there with her daughter, Isabella Nuñez, Nuñez Isabel Nuñez and her son-in-law, the said Luis Perez Roldan, and speak- her daughter Luis Perez ing of the imprisonment of the grandmother, mother and Roldan aunts of this confessant and the privations that he must suffer without them the said Eleañor Nuñez said accursed be the soul who was the cause of their arrest and of those who arrested them also: that they are there now under-going the same sufferings that we underwent when we were there.

And that the night they arrested him before the arrest Witness Raphael de took place, his brother, Raphael de Granada, told him that Granada. against he had just been with Doña Juana Enriquez who told him Dᵃ Juna Enriquez that Elvira, the old negress belonging to the Alcaide, had Elvira the Negress been with her and informed her that his aunt Margaret had oh ho! been the previous Tuesday in the audience, from eight o'clock in the morning until eight o'clock at night, and that that evening, at vespers, which was a Saturday, 12th of July, they had arrested Simon de Espinosa,† from which it was infallible that his aunt Margaret had accused him. And Against Dᵃ Beatriz that Raphael de Granada, his brother told him, that Dᵃ Enriquez Luis Perez Beatriz Enriquez, being sick, had given him twenty dollars Roldan Isabel Nuñez, for Luis Perez Roldan and his wife and Isabel Nuñez, and his wife

---

* This is the oldest theatre in Mexico, now called El Teatro Prin-cipal. D. F.

† Simon Xuares de Espinosa, native and citizen of this city of Mexico, sugar hawker by trade, married to Juana Tinoco, reconciled, son of Julio Xuares de Fegueroa, Portuguese new Christian, and of Anna Espinosa, of this city, daughter of Simon Rios reconciled for Judaizing heresy, reconciled 1646 (Obregon p. 357).

5

Francisco Febo　one dollar for Francisco Febo, who was sick in the Hospital of Our Lady, to whom she sent to commend her to God, and that just now he does not recollect other things, and that this is the Truth on the oath which he has taken, and straitly admonished still to think it well over he was ordered back to his cell* and he signed it

GABRIEL DE GRANADA.

Before me. [Signed] Lic. M^{or} DE ARASUS.

I accept these confessions in so far as they make in my favor and no farther. Said day month and year.

[Signed] Dr GAVIOLA.

Audience in which the publication of Witnesses　Mexico, Friday 20th of Novr 1643, afternoon. Inquisitor Juan Saenz de Mañozca. . . . . .

He was asked what has he remembered about his business, and on the oath he has taken to tell the whole truth.

He said he has confessed all he knows, that if he should recollect anything at any time he will declare it. He was told that he is notified that the Fiscal of this Holy Office is going to request the publication of the witnesses who have deposed against him, and that, before he is informed of what they declare it will be very well for him to declare the whole truth, and he is admonished to do so because there will be more liberty to despatch his cause quickly and extend mercy towards him.

The Fiscal prays for the publication　And forthwith Dr Don Antonio de Gaviola, Promotor Fiscal of this Holy office, appeared present, and said that he prayed, and he did pray, for the publication of the Witnesses who deposed against the said Gabriel de Granada, according to the practice of this Holy office. The said Ordered to be done.　Inquisitor commanded the said publication to be done, omitting the names and surnames and other circumstances

---

*The reading of the deposition was again omitted. D. F.

by which he could arrive at a knowledge of the persons of the witnesses, according to the Instructions and practice of the Holy Office. Which was done in the following form and manner.

+

Publication of the witnesses who deposed against Gabriel de Granada judaizing Jew resident of this city of Mexico.

A witness sworn and ratified in due time and form, who ^{1st Witness.
Chap. 1st} deposed in this city one day of the month of July 1642 ^{Rafael de
Granada}

Said that he knows, saw and heard that the said Gabriel de Granada said to a certain person his very near relation that another person, also his very near relation, whom he named, had taught him the law of Moses, saying to him that it behooves him in order to be saved to depart from and leave the law of our Lord Jesus Christ, because it was not the good and the true law, but the said law of Moses which was the one necessary for his salvation, and that in its observance he must keep some fasts, in the keeping of which he must on the preceding eve sup on fish and vegetables and the following day he must not eat during the whole day until night after the evening star appeared when he must again eat the things mentioned and not meat, and that on the eve of the said fasts he must bathe and put on clean clothes.

And that in conformity with this the said Gabriel kept ^{Chapter 2nd} six fasts of the Law of Moses, on Mondays and Thursdays in company with seven persons his very near relations whom he named, supping the night before on fish and vegetables and going the next day without eating until night after the evening star appeared, when he again supped the aforesaid things and not meat

And that the said Gabriel being a prisoner in this prison ^{Chapter 3rd} of the Inquisition in company with a certain person his very near relation two other persons their very near relations whom he named called (hailed) them and told them to be careful what they did and not to give evidence (testimony) against any one, and the said Gabriel and his said very near relation answered that they would do as they asked.

Chapter 4th   The same witness sworn and ratified in due time and form in another deposition

Said on a day of the said month and year that he knows, saw and heard that in the past year of 1641 in the month of Septr six persons whom he named very near relations of the said Gabriel, notified him and another certain person his very near relation that the fast of the Great Day would fall on the next day and that they and all of them would have to keep it in conformity with which the previous afternoon the said Gabriel and all the before-mentioned persons his very near relations bathed themselves although not altogether, and they put on clean clothes and that night they all supped together fish and vegetables, and not meat. And afterwards they lighted four or five candles, and they placed them on a clean cloth on the floor of the bedroom where they slept and they remained up until near midnight sometimes on foot and sometimes seated. And the said Gabriel and the said his very near relation had their hats on, because they were warned by the said persons that they must not uncover their heads, and each one recited apart by himself the prayers that he knew of the law of Moses, and about midnight they went to bed, and the following night the said Gabriel and all of the aforesaid persons his very near relations at the hour of supper again supped the same eatables of fish and vegetables, and not meat, with which the fast ended

Chapter 5th   And that on the eve of the fast mentioned the said Gabriel and the said his very near relation kissed the hand of their mother and their grandmother who gave them their blessing saying to them May God make ye good and they all embraced each other and asked forgiveness of each other.

Chapter 6th   And that the said Gabriel and his said very near relation saw and knew that six persons their very near relations whom he named when living in the Alcaeceria kept the three days of the fast of Queen Esther and that some kept one day and others another.

The same witness sworn and ratified in due time and form in another deposition that he made — Chapter 7.

Said that one day in the month of January of the year forty-three, that he knows saw and heard that the news came of the death of Manuel de Granada, father of the said Gabriel, he and seven persons his very near relations whom he named : did on the seventh day after receiving the news fast for the soul of the said Manuel de Granada, and they supped on fish and vegetables the night before and the night after having been the whole day without eating; and that the six preceding days the said Gabriel with a person very nearly related to him staid in the house retired without going out as a ceremony of the law of Moses because he was so told to do by both the said persons his near relations, and that on the eve of the second day a certain person whom he named sent the supper in order that the said Gabriel and the aforesaid persons should keep the fast

And that the said six days preceding the seventh of the said fast five persons whom he named sent things to eat to the said Gabriel and his near relations, one of which five persons used to dine some days with the said Gabriel and with his very near relations, and that the said dinners were of fish because on such days the jews eat fish for the sake of their dead—and that this is the truth and he does not declare it from hatred — Chapter 8.

Another witness sworn and ratified in due time and form who deposed in this city on one day of the month of June of the year '42 Said that she knows saw and heard that when this Holy office arrested the grandmother and three aunts of the said Gabriel as soon as they brought them the said Gabriel and two persons his very near relatives whom she named went to the house of a certain person whom she also named and they returned at ten o'clock at night; and very — 2nd Witness. Only Chapter — Juliana the Negress early next morning the said Gabriel and the two said persons his very near relations, went out again, and on a certain person asking the said Gabriel what they were running about for he answered that they were going to the house of certain persons in order that they should entreat the Lords Inquisitors to release his said grandmother and aunts, and that this is the truth and that she does not say it from hatred.

3rd Witness.
Chap. 1.
Another witness sworn and ratified in due time and form who deposed in this city of Mexico one day of the month of

Da Maria de Rivera (this was his mother who starved herself to death in her cell)
July of '42 said that she knows saw and heard that a certain person very nearly related to the said Gabriel about a year ago taught the law of Moses to the said Gabriel and afterwards taught it to another person very nearly related to the said Gabriel, to each one alone telling him that in order to be saved it was necessary to follow it and leave that of our Lord Jesus Christ, and that only the law of Moses was the good the true and the necessary one for salvation and not the other one of Jesus Christ our Lord, and that other persons very nearly related to the said Gabriel observed it, naming them by their names

Chap. 2.
And that likewise the said person very nearly related to the said Gabriel taught him the fasts which in observance of the said law of Moses had to be kept especially that of the great day which fell in the month of September, the rites and ceremonies which on its eve had to be observed and performed bathing themselves and putting on clean clothes, and supping on fish and vegetables that night and not meat, passing the following day without eating or drinking until the evening star came forth when they had to sup on the things mentioned and not on others: asking forgiveness the one from the other and the parents giving their blessing to their children all in observance of the law. And that the said Gabriel for this persuasion left from that time the faith of Jesus Christ and was converted to the Law of Moses, and that they have lived therein until this time, the said person his very near relation telling the said Gabriel that other

persons very nearly related to him, naming them by their
names kept the said law

The same witness sworn and ratified in due time and form Chapter 3rd
in another deposition that he (she) made in this same city
one day in the month of August of '42 Said that he (she)
knows saw and heard that the day that this Holy office
arrested his grandmother and three aunts of his, the said
Gabriel with two persons his very near relations went to
the house of a certain person, whom he (she) named, to whom
one of the persons with whom the said Gabriel had gone
said in presence of another person whom he (she) named that
he wanted to come and present himself in this Holy office,
and that the person to whose house they went told him not
to do it offering him five hundred or one thousand dollars
to give to the Alcaide of this Inquisition to let him speak to
a certain person (female) confined in those prisons very nearly
related to the said Gabriel in order to intimate to and
admonish her not to declare anything against the person in
whose house they were nor against some others who he
named and that this person very nearly related to the said
Gabriel answered that he would thus do.

And that while they were in this conference in the dark, a Chapter 4.
person entered who was the owner of the house with three
others whom he (she) named and upon his asking why the
person very nearly related to Gabriel did weep he was
answered that on account of the arrests made by the Holy
office of the said grandmother and aunts of the said Gabriel
and that he (or she) wanted to speak to one of them and of
the offer that was made of the five hundred or one thousand
dollars for effecting that purpose; and the said person, owner
of the house, approved saying that the said sum of the
thousand dollars should be so promised, and the person very
nearly related to the said Gabriel said to them not to be
troubled that though they should arrest her she would not
expose them, there being present at all this two other persons
whom he named besides those above mentioned

<small>Chap. 5.</small>　　The same witness sworn and ratified in due time and form in another deposition

Said one day in the month of August of the year '42 that he knows saw and heard that the said Gabriel being a prisoner the night that a person a very near relation of his felt that he was arrested said to him from another cell that in no manner should he declare anything about the persons there outside, that it was enough that he should confess his own fault without confessing that of others, and in particular he, (she) said to the said Gabriel not to do harm to a person related to the said Gabriel nor to another whom he, (she) also named and that this is the truth and he (she, his mother), does not declare it from hatred.

<small>4th Witness
Chap. 1st
Dᵃ Catalina
de Rivera
(his aunt)</small>　And another witness sworn and ratified in due time and form who deposed in this city of Mexico on a day of the month of June of 1642 Said that she* knows saw and heard that the said Gabriel is an observer of the law of Moses, and that it had been taught to him by a person very nearly related to the said Gabriel, and that the said Gabriel as such an observer was present at the fasts of the great day of the past years of '40 and '41 other persons also being present whom she named, very near relations to the said Gabriel, and that she is in doubt whether he fasted or not some day of the fast of Queen Esther with the said persons very near relations of his who did hold that fast. And that likewise she is in doubt if the said Gabriel the day of the great fast of the year forty was found in the house of a person very nearly related to him, whom she named, in presence of four other persons, his near relations, whom she also named, when two persons, whom she named, entered into the said house who said that they came very tired from the Alameda, where they had been to dissimulate the fast of the said great day.

*The masculine pronoun is used throughout to deceive the culprit. D. F.

And that in the fast of the great day of the past year of '41 Chap. 2nd the said Gabriel being present the night before the fast a person very nearly related to the said Gabriel lighted six candles and placed them on a clean towel on the floor in observance of the law of Moses, six persons very nearly related to the said Gabriel being present all of whom kept the said fast.

And that when a certain person, whom she named, died, Chap. 3 a certain person, whom she named, very nearly related to the said deceased having retired to her house there went to visit her at her house a person nearly related to Gabriel with another person also very nearly related to him, whom she named; and that they supped with the person very nearly related to the deceased on eggs, fish and vegetables with two other persons whom she named; and that evening the person very nearly related to the said deceased gave certain pieces of money to a person very nearly related to the said Gabriel, to send them to another person, a very near relation of the said Gabriel, who, with another relation of his had staid in his house, in order that he should buy eggs, fish and vegetables because the following day was the seventh after the death of the said defunct so that they might fast for him (or her) in conformity with the observance of the law of Moses when there dies some observer thereof. And this person very nearly related to the said Gabriel who received the money sent it by the said Gabriel who she understands kept the same fast with the person his very near relation to whom he took the money.

The same witness sworn and ratified in due time and form Chap. 4th who deposed in this city on a day of the month of June '42 Said that she knows, saw and heard that the said deceased person having charged a person very nearly related to her (or him) with the manner in which a distribution had to be made of three hundred dollars which he (or she) left; and the manner was that every Wednesday seven fasts of the said law of Moses had to be made, and that an alms of one dol-

lar should be given to the person who kept the fast, and that
if there should be more than three hundred dollars they
should be distributed amongst some of the poor observers of
the law of Moses after they had kept the said fasts for his
(or her) soul for the supper of that day, and that this is
known to the said Gabriel and the rest of the persons his
very near relations, and that the said Gabriel fasted some of
those days, a person very nearly related to said Gabriel
ordering him to do so to which person and to another very
nearly related person they gave some money for this purpose.

Chapter 5th   And that the said Gabriel with the said persons his very
near relations used to read and recite certain prayers and
psalms (which she mentioned) in observance of the law of
Moses on the eve of the great day, and that each one separately lighted candles, and that to a certain person very
nearly related to the said Gabriel, whom she named, who does
not know how to read another person also very nearly
related to the said Gabriel, whom she also named, used to
read the prayers to him (or her).

Chap. 6th   The same witness sworn and ratified in due time and in
another deposition Said on one day of the month of July of
'42 she said that she knows saw and heard that on the
news having arrived of the death of a certain person very
nearly related to the said Gabriel, as a ceremony of the law
of Moses and for the soul of the said defunct (his father)
the said Gabriel ate fish for seven days, fasting on the last
of them, all the rest of the persons very nearly related to
the said Gabriel doing the same except one who did not
fast for a certain cause which she declared.

Chap. 7th   The same witness sworn and ratified in due time and
form in another deposition Said one day of the month of
July of '42 that she knows, saw and heard that this Holy
office having arrested some persons very near relations of
the said Gabriel a person a very near relation of the said
Gabriel taking the said Gabriel in company with him and
another person a very near relation of his went to the house

of a certain person, whom she named, to visit a certain person, whom she also named, to advise him (or her) of the arrest made, the said person returning the said same night with the said Gabriel and the other person his very near relation, who said to another person likewise very nearly related to him that the person to whose house they went together with another who was with that person, naming them both, were afraid and suspicious that one of the said prisoners would expose them in this Holy office.

Item that when a certain person, whom she named, died in Chap. 8th this city, an observer of the said law of Moses, two persons very closely related to the said Gabriel sent some small pearls, that she does not remember how many, in order that they should be put in the mouth of the said defunct and she does not quite recollect if they sent them by the said Gabriel or by another person a very near relation of his.

The same witness sworn and ratified in due time and form Chapter 9th in another deposition she made one day in the month of February of '43 Said that she knows, saw and heard that a certain person, whom she named, having died another person very nearly related to the said Gabriel sent with the said Gabriel or with another person very nearly related to him three hard boiled eggs in order that the other three persons, whom she named, should eat them as soon as they took the said defunct away to be buried, and that this is the truth and she does not declare it from hatred.

Another Witness sworn and ratified in due time and form 5th Witness who deposed in this city on a day of the month of June of Chapter 1st Dª Clara de Rivera. '42 Said that she knows, saw and heard that the said Gabriel observes the law of Moses which was taught to him by a very near relation of his about two years ago, and that a certain person, whom she named, had the said Gabriel in his (or her) house about three months and. that he (or she) had seen him fast twice in that time, the day of the great fast not eating meat at supper and going the whole day without eating until the evening star appeared, supping after-

ward in company with certain persons very near relations of
the said Gabriel and after supper reciting a certain prayer
which he (or she) declared and it was : Holy Consistories,
divine and holy, lift up your voices and clamor to the God
of Israel for me!

Chapter 2nd   Item that a certain person, whom she named, an
observer of the law of Moses, having died and left another
person, whom she also named, a certain sum of money in
order that for her should be kept the fasts of the said law of
Moses a person very closely related to the said Gabriel
received twenty-five dollars and that the said Gabriel and
another person very nearly related to him were making those
fasts some Mondays, Wednesdays, and Thursdays when they
were able, for the soul of the deceased person.

Chapter 3rd   And that on having received news of the death of a
certain person, very nearly related to the said Gabriel, the
said Gabriel with five other persons, very near relations of
his, fasted for the soul of the said defunct according to the
observance of the Law of Moses and that this is the truth
and she does not declare from hatred.

Sixth Witness   Another witness* sworn and ratified in due time and form
Chap. 1st
Dª Beatriz who deposed in this city on one day of the month of August
Henriquez
of '42 Said that he (she) knows saw and heard that the said
Gabriel with another person very nearly related to him
observed the law of Moses which was taught to him by
another person his very near relation.

Chap. 2nd   The same witness sworn and ratified in due time and form
in another deposition that he (she) made one day in the
month of November of '42 Said that she knows, saw and
heard that news having been brought of the death of a person
very nearly related to the said Gabriel, who observed the law
of Moses; on the third day after the said news was known
a certain person, whom she named, sent a supper of fish to a

---

* His reverence puts her in the masculine gender again as he did
with all the female witnesses.   D. F.

certain person very nearly related to the said Gabriel from which six persons, whom she mentioned, took their suppers, all of them very near relations to the said Gabriel and five other persons whom she named, and although this supper which consisted of fish was eaten in the time of lent it was done as ceremony of the law of Moses and that this is the truth and she does not declare it from hatred.

Another witness* sworn and ratified in due time and form who deposed in this city on one day of the month of November of '42 Said that he (she) knows, saw and heard that the said Gabriel and another person a very near relation of his were observers of the law of Moses, and that a certain person his very near relation had taught it to him and that this is the truth and she does not say it from hatred.

Seventh Witness Dᵃ Blanca Suarez†

Another witness ‡ sworn and ratified in due time and form, who deposed in this city on one day of the month of July '42 Said that he (she) knows, saw and heard that the said Gabriel is an observer of the law of Moses, and that a certain person very nearly related to the said Gabriel, whom she named, taught it to him when they were alone about a year and a half ago, and that he should keep in its observance the fast of the great day and that the said Gabriel did so in the Month of September of the past year of 1641 in company with four persons, whom she named, very near relations of his, bathing themselves on the eve of the said fast and putting on themselves clean clothes and going without eating all the following day until night when the evening star had appeared, when they supped on fish and vegetables and other things and not meat, in observance of

8ᵗʰ Witness Chap. 1ˢᵗ Dᵃ Margarita de Rivera

---

* Masculine again. D. F.

† Blanca Xuares, native and citizen of Mexico, wife of Jeorge Jacinto Basan or Basa, reconciled, daughter of Gaspar Xuares and of Rafaela Enrriquez, Judaizing heretic, reconciled 1648 (Obregon p. 365)

‡ Masc. again. D. F.

the said law, and that five other persons very nearly related to the said Gabriel know that he is an observer of the said law and that he kept the fast of the great day. And that the said Gabriel kept two other fasts of the ordinary ones of the law of Moses when a certain person whom she named died.

Chapter 2nd And that a certain person, whom she named, very nearly related to the said Gabriel tried to teach him three prayers of the said law of Moses, two of which are recited in the morning and at night, and the other when some defunct of the law of Moses dies (sic), and that she is in doubt whether the said Gabriel learned them [or not] and that the first morning and evening prayer that the said person very nearly related to the said Gabriel endeavored to teach commences thus : . . . .

9th Witness only chapter Another witness* Sworn and ratified in due time and form who deposed in this city one day in the month of May of the

Doña Juana† Tinoco year 1643 Said that he (she) knows, saw and heard that a certain person, whom she named, being in the house of a certain person, whom she named, very nearly related to the said Gabriel, the said Gabriel entered and the said person his very near relation said to her who was in her house that the said Gabriel was fasting that day, and she put by chocolate and fruit in order that he might sup on them and that she had taught him the law of Moses. And that this is the truth and she does not declare it from odium.

10th Witness Chap. 1st Another witness sworn and ratified in due time and form

Dª Isabel‡ Tinoco who deposed in this city one day in the month of Novr '642

---

* Masc. again. D. F.

† Juana Tinoco native and citizen of this city of Mexico, wife of Simon Xuares Espinosa, sugar merchant, descendant of Hebrew new Christians, Judaizing heretic, reconciled 1647 (Obregon p. 363).

‡ Isabel Tinoco, native of the city of Zacatecas, citizen of that of Mexico, wife of Manuel de Acosta alias Francisco de Torres, reconciled, daughter of Diego Tinoco and of Isabel Silba, executed, Judaizing heretic, reconciled 1649 (Obregon p. 378).

Said that she knows, saw and heard that a certain person whom she named, being in the house of a certain person, whom she named, a certain person, a very near relation of the said Gabriel went there one Saturday night and being alone with this person very nearly related to the said Gabriel she told her that she wanted to teach her a prayer, and she made signs for her to hush because the said Gabriel was there, the said person his very near relative said that it did not matter because the said Gabriel was already instructed in the law of Moses and catching hold of him the said person his very near relative She embraced him and affectionately caressed him, the said person so nearly related to the said Gabriel saying that another person, a very near relation of his, whom she named, had taught him, and that the said Gabriel asked the said person his very near relative who had taught him why they had concealed it from him, and likewise the person very nearly related to the said Gabriel said to the person with whom she was that the said Gabriel had already kept many fasts of his law

And that so likewise what confirms that the said Gabriel Chap. 2nd is an observer of the law of Moses is that one day after last St. Dominic's day, a certain person, whom she named, being a prisoner in the cells of this Holy office, about 10 o'clock in the forenoon she heard from her cell a certain person very nearly related to the said Gabriel, whom she recognized by her voice, speak, in another cell very near hers, and call another person a very near relation of the said Gabriel who answered apparently from another cell to whom the said person very nearly related to the said Gabriel told not to declare in the audience that she had taught the said Gabriel, and to another person her very near relative because she had already declared it, taking upon herself all the blame, to which the said very nearly related person answered that she would so do.

And that the day after the death of a certain person, whom Chapter 3rd she named, she saw that a certain person very nearly related

to the said Gabriel sent to her house, she does not well remember whether with the said Gabriel or with another person very nearly related to her, some wet clothes and asking
what clothes were those she said some clothes with which he
had washed the body of the said defunct as soon as he (or
she) died

Chapter 4th   And that a certain person, an observer of the law of
Moses, whom she named, having died and having left some
money to be distributed in alms and for keeping some fasts
for his (or her) soul, the person with whom this money was
left whom she named, gave alms to the said Gabriel to the
end that he should fast and to some other persons very nearly related to the said Gabriel, and that this is the truth and
she does not declare it from hatred

11th Witness
only chapter
Doña Ana
Xuarez

Another witness sworn and ratified in due time and form,
who deposed one day in the month of August 1642 Said that
she knows, saw and heard that a person very nearly related
to the said Gabriel, whom she named, who said to another
person, whom she named, that she had taught the said Gabriel the law of Moses, and that this is the truth and she
does not declare it from hatred.

12th Witness
Chap. 1st

*Dª Elena
de Silva

Another witness sworn and ratified in due time and form
who deposed one day of the month of January 1643 Said that
she knows, saw and heard that a certain person, whom she
named, going to the house of another person, whom she
named, to see him (or her) found there seventeen other persons, whom she named, and the person whom she visited giving chocolate to this person she asked her why she did not
give it to the others to which she answered that they [of both
sexes] were all fasting and so they would not drink it, and
at this time, the said Gabriel arrived there with another

*Elena Silba, alias Elena Lopez, native of Casteloblanco in Portu-
gal, daughter of Gaspar Voncalbos Soburto innkeeper and butcher
and of Leonor Baez, Judaizing heretics, Judaizing heretic, reconciled 1648 (Obregon p. 366).

person, a very near relative of his, whom she named, who
whispered to the said person of the house, and that from this
and because the said Gabriel and the other person his very
near relation who came with him are very near relations of
the observer of the said law they also must observe it.

And that three years ago, a little more or less, a person Chap. 2nd
very nearly related to the said Gabriel, whom she named,
went to the house of another person, whom she named, to
whom and to a daughter of the said person, whom he named,
he (or she) asked if they wanted to fast because soon a day of
obligation to fast would come, and they told her yes, to which
the person very nearly related to the said Gabriel responded
that she would come on the eve of the said fast, which was
within eight or nine days, and she went and said that it was
the eve of the day that they must fast, and that that night
they supped on salad, eggs and chocolate. And she remembers that the said person very nearly related to the said
Gabriel took with her either Gabriel or another and that the
said Gabriel or the other person his very near relation kept
there the said fast; because although the said Gabriel or the
other person, his very near relation did not sleep there next
day at four o'clock in the afternoon he came for the person his
very near relation who had gone there to fast and had staid
there that night, and asked how she got along with the said
fast

And being at supper on the eve of the said fast a person Chapter 3rd
very nearly related to the said Gabriel, whom she named,
said that it would have been better for her to have gone to
supper to the house of a certain person, whom she named,
who had many presents prepared because a certain person,
whom she named, was at supper there with another, whom
she named, very nearly related to the said Gabriel and the
said Gabriel or another person his very near relation whom
she named.

And that when a certain person, whom she named, died, Chapter 4th
on another person, whom she named, going to make a visit
6

of condolence to a certain person very nearly related to the deceased there was with her thirteen persons, whom she named, and the defunct was in the middle of the parlor covered with a new cloth and she who went to condole noticing it asked those present why they had put a covering over the defunct for she had remained beautiful and with her natural features as they said to which a person very nearly related to the said Gabriel who was with the rest with another person very nearly related to him, whom she named, answered it is because we put a little gold in her mouth and that if she should empty it that they could not see it. And she saw that after they took away the said defunct to be buried the said Gabriel or another person very nearly related to him she does not remember well which of the two it was, brought some eggs boiled hard and a very nearly related person, whom she named, taking them from the said Gabriel she got up from where she was sitting and she went around giving to each one of the persons very nearly related to the defunct every one his egg and at the same time expressing her condolences standing up on foot, and then she did the same with the persons related to the deceased, and having finished giving the said eggs the said person very nearly related to the said Gabriel took her own turning up her eyes towards heaven and giving her own self the condolence saying, it is certain that her soul is enjoying God, for the number of eggs came so exact to the persons who are connected by blood with the defunct, that it appears that such a one counted all of them, naming a person very nearly related to her, who had sent the eggs by the said Gabriel or the other person his very near relation and she does not remember well which of the two it was, and that this is the truth and she does not declare it from hatred

13th Witness
Chap. 1st
Doña Michaela
Henriquez.   Another witness sworn and ratified in due time and form who deposed one day in the month of April 1643 Said that she knows, saw and heard that a person very nearly related to the said Gabriel, whom she named, said to another, whom

she named, how she and seven other persons very near relations of hers, whom she named, amongst whom she mentioned
the said Gabriel, fasted some times on week-days observing
the fasts of the law of Moses.

And that a certain person, whom she named, having died Chap. 2nd
and having left a certain person three hundred dollars to the
end that he (or she) should distribute them amongst poor observers of the said law, the said person distributed a sum of
this money to the said Gabriel and to seven other persons
very near relations of the said Gabriel that they might fast
according to their observance for the soul of the defunct, and
that is the truth, and she does not declare it from hatred.

Another witness sworn and ratified in due time and form 14th Witness
Chap. 1st
who deposed one day of the month of July 1642 Said that Dᵃ Isabel de
Rivera
she knows, saw and heard that a certain person whom she
named declared himself (or herself) as an observer of the law
of Moses with seven persons very near relations of the said
Gabriel, and with Gabriel himself, the said Gabriel living
with with the said person his very near relations in a room
in the house of Hernando de Peñalosa in front of the houses
of Simon Vaez Sevilla.

And that she knows that the said Gabriel is an observer Chap. 2nd
of the law of Moses which was taught him by a certain
person very nearly related to him, whom she named, and he
has declared himself as such with other persons very near
relations of his, whom she named, and that this is the truth
and she does not declare it from odium.

Another witness sworn and ratified in due time and form 15th Witness
Chap. 1st
who deposed one day in the month of June 1643 Said that
she knows, saw and heard that a certain person, whom she *Dᵃ Isabel
de Silva.
named, kept a fast on the great day in the month of September although she does not remember of what year in

---

* Isabel de Silba alias Correa, native of Casteloblanco in Portugual, citizen of this city of Mexico, married to Antonio Carabajal,
reconciled, daughter of reconciled [persons] Judaizing heretic,
reconciled 1649 (Obregon p. 378).

company with two persons his very near relations, whom she named, and of another person very nearly related to the said Gabriel, whom she named, and the said Gabriel or another person a very near relation of his, whom she mentioned, she does not remember which of the two it was, and in company also with two other persons, whom she named.

Chapter 2nd   The same witness sworn and ratified in due time and form in another deposition which she made one day in the month of June 1643 Said that she knows, saw and heard that a certain person, whom she named, having died and left a sum of money with another person very nearly related to him (or her), whom she named, to be distributed among poor observers of the law of Moses to the end that they would do good to his soul the said person sent a certain amount of that money for certain persons very near relations of the said Gabriel and to the said Gabriel in order that they should fast for the soul of the defunct, and that this is the truth and she does not declare it from hatred.

16th Witness only chap.
ntonio Lopez de Orduña.   Another witness sworn and ratified in due time and form who deposed one day in the month of September 1642 Said that he knows, saw and heard that the said Gabriel is a Jew, an observer of the law of Moses, because a person very nearly related to the said Gabriel told him so, and that the said Gabriel fasted for the soul of a certain defunct, whom he named, every time that the said person his very near relation ordered him, and heard the same from two other persons very near relations of the said Gabriel, whom he named, from which he feels sure that the said Gabriel is an observer of the said law of Moses, and because another person, whom he named, and a very near relation of the said Gabriel told him so, and that this is the truth, and he does not declare it from hatred.

The Witness Added.
chap. 2nd   The same witness sworn and ratified in due time and form in another deposition which he made one day in the month of October 1643 Said that he knows, saw and heard that the said Gabriel said to his grandmother, mother and aunts and

his brother that a certain person whom he named had told
him when they were brought as prisoners and he staid out
that his said grandmother, mother and aunts used to flog a
holy christ because the said person lived under the parlor
where they used to flog him, and he heard the blows of the
lashes and he also related, the said Gabriel did, that a certain
person whom he named had told him that the said person
who lived under the parlor had told him the same thing and
that he had heard the said blows, and that this is the truth
and he does not say it from hatred

Another witness sworn and ratified in due time and form _{17th Witness only Chapter.}
who deposed one day in the month of April 1643 Said that *Esperanza Rodriguez.
she knows saw and heard that the said Gabriel de Granada
is a Jew and as such he declared himself to a certain person,
whom she named, and that she thinks a certain person very
nearly related to him, whom she named, taught the law of
Moses to the said Gabriel. And that a certain person very
nearly related to the said Gabriel, whom she named, went to
the house of a certain person, whom she named, to keep the
fast of the great day taking with her the said Gabriel she does
not remember what year it was, and both of them staid there
all day in that house without eating, and that this is the
truth and she does not say it from hatred.†

18th Witness Only Chap.

Another witness sworn and ratified in due time and form
who deposed one day in the month of August 1642 Said that 18th Witness
he knows, saw and heard that a certain person very nearly Diego Correa.
related to the said Gabriel, whom he named, said to another
person, whom he named, that the said Gabriel was an

* Esperanza Rodriguez native of the city of Seville and citizen of
that of Mexico widow and daughter of Hebrew New Christians,
Judaizing heretic, reconciled 1646 (Obregon p. 358).

† Here his Reverence got muddled and repeated a former chapter
as we find by a marginal note in the hand writing of the smart Inquisitor Dr Don Juan Saenz de Mañozca, in these words: "this witness is repeated twice and he is the 16th in order and so he is
passed over." D. F.

observer of the law of Moses and that a person very nearly related to the said Gabriel had taught it to him although he does not remember positively who it was, tho' he understands that all his very near relations may have taught it to him.

Chap. 2nd   The same witness sworn and ratified in due time and form in another deposition that he made one day in the month of December '642 Said that he knows, saw and heard that certain persons, whom he named, told a certain person related to the said Gabriel to tell and instruct the said Gabriel and to two other persons his very near relations not to declare what they all followed which was the law of Moses, altho' they put the knife to their throats.

Chap. 3rd   And that the said persons whom he named, told the said person related to the said Gabriel that when he went to his (or her) house to go at night without any ruff (golilla) and disguised and to change his name calling himself *Don Pedro*, changing his voice and taking with him the said Gabriel with another person very nearly related to him, and that this is the truth and he does not declare it from hatred.

19th Witness Da Blanca de Enriquez.   Another witness sworn and ratified in due time and form who deposed one day in the month of November 1642 Said that she knows, saw and heard that a person very nearly related to the said Gabriel, whom she named, said to another person, whom she named, that the said Gabriel was an observer of the law of Moses and that two persons very nearly related to him had taught it to him and that they must have taught him the said law about a year ago since when the said Gabriel has kept six or seven ordinary fasts, and one of them was for the soul of a certain defunct whom she named the said Gabriel having received the alms therefor

Chap. 2nd   And that a certain person, whom she named, having died a person very nearly related to the said defunct, whom she named, gave to a certain person very nearly related to the said Gabriel in presence of two other persons very near relations of his two dollars to give them to another person a very near relation of the said Gabriel in order that he should keep two fasts for the soul of the said defunct, and the said person very nearly related to the said Gabriel having received them gave them to the said Gabriel who was present to the end that he should give them to the said person his very near relation, and to tell him, that the said person very nearly related to the defunct had sent them to him in order that he should keep those fasts, which the said Gabriel did.

And that a certain person, whom she named, having died Chap. 3rd in this city another person very nearly related to the defunct said to another person very nearly related to the said Gabriel that the defunct person had been an observer of the law of Moses and on his having just expired the said person his very near relation sent to a certain person a very near relation of the said Gabriel asking him (or her) to send him (or her) something made of gold or some pearls to put them in the mouth of the defunct as a ceremony of the said law of Moses, and the said person very nearly related to the said Gabriel sent with the said Gabriel three or four small pearls wrapped up in a small piece of paper and he gave them to the said person very nearly related to the defunct a certain person very nearly related to the said Gabriel being present when he gave them to him (or her)

And that a certain person a very near relation of Gabriel Chap. 4th having died, on the seventh day after the news of the death arrived the said Gabriel with seven other persons his very near relations fasted for the soul of the said defunct: and a certain person, whom she named, sent them their dinners on the Friday and Saturday which fell on those seven days, who said to one of the persons very nearly related to the said Gabriel that he (or she) did not send fish dinners on meat days for the fear in which she lived on account of the harm it might cause them by sending them fish dinners on meat days.*

Witness 20th
only Chap.
This witness
is repeated
and he is the
eleventh in
order "and
so let him be
passed over."
Witness 20th
Chap. 1st
Gaspar de
Robles.
Another witness sworn and ratified in due time and form who deposed on one of the days of the month of August 1641 Said that he knows, saw and heard that a certain person, whom he named, being in the house of a certain person, whom he named, where there was a certain person a very near relation of the said Gabriel they said to him (or to her) that the said Gabriel and five other persons very near relations to the said Gabriel were good people and observed the fasts of the law of Moses, *altho' of the said Gabriel he (or she) did not say that he kept them but that he was good*, and that this is the truth and he does not say it from hatred

Chapter 2nd   The same witness n° 20 sworn and ratified in due time and form in a deposition he made on one of the days of the month of September 1643 Said that he knows, saw and heard that the said Gabriel is an observer of the law of Moses, and as such in the keeping and observance thereof he fasted on the great day in the month of September of the past year of 1641, going without eating all the following day until night after the evening star came forth; when he supped on fish, vegetables and other things and not meat in observance of the said law, putting on himself clean clothes, and he does not remember if he bathed.

Chaptr 3rd   The same witness sworn and ratified in due time and form in another deposition he made on one of the days of the month of October 1643 Said that he knows, saw and heard that a certain person, whom he named, a very near relation of the said Gabriel called the said Gabriel about six or seven months ago and speaking to him alone, said to him that the law of our Lord Jesus Christ which he followed was not

---

* The Reverend gentleman got entangled in his own meshes again, in repeating the 11th "Witness" here as we find in the margin, the discovery having been made by the "Chiquito"—Inq. Saenz de Mañozca. D. F.

good nor true but the law of Moses, which she and another person very nearly related to the said Gabriel observed and followed, and that for the love she bore him she wanted to deliver him from the deception in which he was and teach him the said law of Moses, that the said Gabriel believed the said person very nearly related to him and from that instant he departed from the law of our Lord Jesus Christ and passed over to the faith and belief of the said law of Moses believing and holding it for certain that it was the ood and the true in which he must be saved and not that of our Lord Jesus Christ as the said person his very near relation told him, to whom the said Gabriel answered that he would guard and keep what she would teach him.

And that on this occasion the said person very nearly re- Chap. 4th lated to the said Gabriel told him and taught him that in the month of September the fast of the great day must be kept in observance of the said law bathing the previous evening and putting on clean clothes and supping on fish and vegetables and not meat, and that candles must be lit and put on a clean cloth, and that the prayer of the said law must be recited that night without sleeping until after midnight and that the whole of the next day must be passed without eating until night after the evening star is visible and that then they must again sup on fish and vegetables and not meat and that they must ask forgiveness of each other and those who had quarreled become friends.

And that conforming to this in the month of September Chapter 5th 1641 the said Gabriel fasted the fast of the great day in company with the same persons his very near relations and on the eve of the said fast they all concerted how they had to observe it, and that these persons his very near relations bathed themselves in his room, and the said Gabriel with another person his very near relation bathed each in a different room, and the said Gabriel with the rest of his very near relatives put on them the clean clothes they had, and at night they supped on fish, eggs and vegetables, after which they

lighted four or five wax candles and they put them on the
floor of a bedroom on a clean towel and afterwards the said
persons very near relations of the said Gabriel recited some
prayers of the said law and the said Gabriel also recited one
that he knows which the said person his very near relation
had taught him, and the said persons his very near relations
embraced each other and asked forgiveness of each other, and
the said Gabriel and another person his very near relation
kissed the hands of a person very nearly related to them, who,
with other persons their very near relations gave them their
blessing saying, May God make ye good.

Chapter 6th   And that next morning the said Gabriel was told by his
very near relation to go and play and spend the day where-
ever he pleased without eating or drinking because if he did
he would break the said fast, and to return at night to supper, and the said Gabriel did thus do, and he went the said
day to the Alameda and other places spending the day and he
did neither eat or drink anything, and after vespers he returned home and found his said near relations assembled
together and they supped all the things mentioned, upon
which they ended the said fast.

Chapter 7th   And that the said Gabriel kept six or seven of the ordinary
fasts of the law of Moses some for himself and others for the
soul of a certain defunct person, whom he named, his very
near relation, because the said persons his very near relations
had told him on different occasions to do so telling him to do
so to the end that God would make him good, and that the
said Gabriel kept two or three of these fasts alone and they
gave him eggs, fish and vegetables for supper, and the others
he kept in company with his said very near relations, and all
supped together.

Chap. 8th   And that a certain person a very near relation to the said
Gabriel and the rest of his very near relations said to the
said Gabriel that five persons, whom he named, very near
relations daughters of another person whom he likewise
named were observers of the law of Moses.

And that the said persons his very relations said to the
said Gabriel that a certain person, whom she named, who
has been absent from this city for two years and he does not
know where, and another certain person, whom he also
named, and a son of his, are observers of the said law of
Moses.

The same witness sworn and ratified in due time and form
in another deposition that he made on one of the days of the
month of October 1643 Said that he knows, saw and heard
that a certain person a very near relation to the said Gabriel
and his very near relation said to the said Gabriel that a
certain person whom he named, an old Portuguese who is in
the city of Vera Cruz is an observer of the said law of Moses.

And that a certain person, very nearly related to the
said Gabriel, living in the house of Peñalosa, two persons,
whom he named, entered into her house and being in a conversation with the said person a very near relation to the
said Gabriel and the rest of his very near relations, the
said Gabriel or another person very nearly related to him
asked the said very near relations what people these were to
which all of them responded that the said two persons were
observers of the law of Moses.

And that when a certain person whom he named died,
which was in January 1642, a person whom he named, a
daughter of the defunct, gave to a person very nearly related
to the said Gabriel some dollars in order that his said very
near relations should keep as many fasts as there were dollars
of the said law for the soul of the said defunct, and that the
said person very nearly related to the said Gabriel gave to
the said Gabriel three dollars to the end that he should keep
three fasts, as he did on three different Wednesdays because
they are kept on such days for the dead.

And that a certain person, a very near relation of the said
Gabriel, who was a prisoner in the prison of this Holy office
said (as it appears to him) to the said Gabriel and to the rest
of his very near relations that he was afraid they would

inflict some chastisement on them for having deposed against three persons whom he named ; because altho' the said three persons were Jews they would deny it in order that they should not strip them of their property, to which all of them replied that as they could not deny it neither would the said persons because the Lords Inquisitors knew that all who came to these prisons were Jews.

Chap. 14th   The same Witness sworn and ratified in due time and form in another deposition that he made on one day in the said month of October '43 said that he knows, saw and heard that the said Gabriel being in the cell of his prison with the persons his very near relatives he heard on a certain day that a certain person whom he named imprisoned in another cell asked for some snuff from a certain person very nearly related to the said Gabriel, whom he named, and the said person answering him that he (or she) did not have any person by whom to send them, the said person who asked for it said that there was a tame cat going about there by whom he (or she) could send it to him because a certain person, whom he named, had sent him many things by him, that upon this the said person very nearly related to the said Gabriel called the cat which is a tame black and white one to which they tied some snuff wrapped in paper from the [illegible] of the said Gabriel tying them by a strip of cloth around the cat's neck and sent him with the snuff, and afterwards the said person who asked it said that he had received the snuff and all in the cell saw it with the said Gabriel and this is the truth and he does not declare it from hatred.

Witness 21st   Another witness sworn and ratified in due time and form
Chap. 1st
Juana   who deposed in this city of Mexico one day in the month of
Rodriguez
a mulatto   September 1642 Said that she knows, saw and heard that
woman   going to the house of a certain person, whom she named, a certain person very nearly related to the said Gabriel to keep two fasts of the law took with him (or her) one time the said Gabriel and the other time another certain person whom she also named his very near relation, and at both fasts the

person their very near relation who took them said to the
person to whose house they went that the said Gabriel and
the other person his very near relation also kept the said
fasts and that they observed the said law of Moses and they
told it to the said person declaring themselves to her and she
to them that is, with the said Gabriel and the other person
his very near relation and that this is the truth and he does
not declare it from hatred.

The same witness sworn and ratified in due time and form Chap. 2nd
in another deposition that she made one day in the month of
October 1642 Said that she knows, saw and heard that a
certain person, whom she named, an observer of the law of
Moses having died and it is a ceremony of the law of Moses
when an observer thereof dies to send something to eat to the
widower or widow his greatest friend or nearest relation and
as certain persons very closely related to the said Gabriel
were such great friends of the widow of the defunct, whom
she named, the said person a very near relation to the said
Gabriel sent to her the hard boiled eggs and chocolate which
was eaten by the said widow and her children, whom she
named, and as it is likewise a ceremony of the law of Moses
to spill the water there is in the house of the defunct the
said persons very near relations of the said Gabriel sent a
jar of water which with the eggs and chocolate were taken to
the said widow by the said Gabriel and another person his
very near relation, and that this is the truth and she does
not say it from hatred.

The same witness sworn and ratified in due time and form Chap. 3rd
in another deposition that she made in this same city on one
day of the month of January 1643 Said that she knows, saw
and heard that two certain persons, whom she named, his
very near relations have declared themselves to the said
Gabriel and another person his very near relation in presence
of a certain person, whom she named, as observers of the said
law of Moses, and that this is the truth and she does not
declare it from hatred.

Here is the Inquisitor ⎱
Mañozca's rubric ⎰

Oath of the culprit before his guardian And the said publication having been made an oath in due form of law was received from the said Gabriel de Granada in presence of Dr Juan Martinez de Cespeda his guardian and lawyer under the solemnity of which he promised to tell the truth and answer it in reply to what these witnesses who are given him in publication declare against him, and the said publication being read to him he replied thereto in the following form :

1st Witness Chap. 1 Raphael de Granada. Doña Margarita de Rivera To the first Witness Chapter first

He said that he told his brother Raphael that his aunt Doña Margarita had taught him the law of Moses, and the rest contained in the chapter he has already confessed it.

Chap. 2d His mother granny and aunts To the second chapter

He said that it is true that he kept those fasts in company with his mother and grandmother and aunts as he has already confessed.

Chap. 3rd Raphael Dª Maria & Isabel de Rivera To the third chapter

He said that it is true and passed with this confessant and his brother Raphael and his mother Doña Maria and his aunt Doña Isabel and that he has already confessed it.

Chap. 4th His brother, mother, grandmother, & aunts. To the fourth chapter

He said that he has already confessed what passed at this fast of the great day which he kept in company with his grandmother, mother, aunts and brothers.

Chap. 5th To the fifth chapter

He said that he has already confessed it and it is true.

Chap. 6th His mother grandmother and aunts. To the sixth Chapter

He said it is true that these fasts of Queen Esther were kept by his mother, grandmother and aunts as he has already confessed.

Chap. 7th against Rafael De Granada D^a Juana To the seventh Chapter

He said that he had not confessed what is contained in this chapter because he did not remember it and that is true and happened thus: that when the news came about his father Manuel de Granada who died in the city of Manilla* this confessant and his brother Raphael de Granada fasted the seventh day after receiving the said news which was on Monday, Christmas eve, and that Dª Juana Enriquez wife of Captain Simon Vaez sent some fried eggs and other vegetables in order that they should sup and likewise the grandmother, mother and aunts and the said brother of this confessant fasted to both of whom their aunt Margaret told that they must not go out of the house for those seven days, as a ceremony of the law of Moses, when some relation dies.

To the eighth Chapter

He said that the six days preceding the said seventh Doña Catalina Enriquez and her sisters Rafaela, Micaela, Juana and Beatriz and Doña Ana Suarez and he thinks Doña Elena de Silva sent chocolate one day of the said six, and that who staid there to sup with them was Isabel, she of Antunes, Doña Juana Enriquez and Doña Micaela and that he had forgotten all this and not from malice.

To the second Witness only chapter

He said that who went with his mother Dª Maria was his brother Rafael and that he has already confessed what passed and took place in this matter.

To the third Witness first chapter

He said that he has already confessed that his aunt Margaret taught him the law of Moses and to his brother Rafael and all that took place in this matter.

To the second Chapter

He said that he has already confessed that this confessant and his brother Rafael went with his mother Doña Maria to the house of Doña Juana Enriquez and all that this chapter contains.

To the fourth chapter

Side notes:

Enriquez
Dª Blanca
Dª Margarita
Dª Catalina
Dª Isabel
Dª Clara de Rivera
*He added when ratifying before his guardian that Dª Beatriz Enriquez also sent something for supper, to which I certify Phe de A.

Chap. 8th
Dª Catalina Enriquez
Dª Rafael
Dª Micaela
Dª Juana
Dª Beatriz Enriquez.
Dª Ana Suarez
Dª Elena de Silva
Dª Isabel Duarte

2nd Witness Only chapter
Dª Mª de Rivera
Rafael de Granada

3rd Witness Chap. 1st
Margarita de Rivera
Rafael de Granada

Chap. 2nd
Rafael
Dª Maria de Rivera and
Dª Juana Enriquez.

Chap. 4th

*Indicates the presence of Jews in the Phillipine Islands at this early date.

Chap. 5th He said that it is true and he has already confessed it, and it occurred in the house of Simon Vaez Sevilla.

To the fifth chapter

4th Witness Chap. 1st He said that all that this chapter contains is true and that he has already confessed it.

To the fourth witness first chapter

Chap. 2nd He said that he had already confessed all contained in this chapter with great minuteness.

To the second chapter

He said that he has already confessed what this chapter says.

Chap. 3rd To the third chapter

He says that he has already confessed all contained in this chapter, but that he did not keep the fast with his aunt Doña Isabel, and it is easily seen because the Witness says he thinks or understands that this confessant did it.

Chap. 4th Doña Blanca and Doña Beatriz Enriquez To the fourth chapter

He said that he has already confessed what took place about the fasts kept for the money left by Doña Blanca Enriquez and distributed by Doña Beatriz Enriquez.

Chap. 5th To the fifth Chapter

He said that he had already confessed all that is contained in this chapter.

Chap. 6th To the sixth chapter

He said that he has already confessed what this chapter says in reply to what another witness said because he had forgotten it.

Chap. 7th To the seventh chapter

He said that he has already confessed it.

Chap. 8th To the eighth chapter

He said that he has already confessed this about the pearls.

Chap. 9th against Da. Isabel Duarte Raphael de Granada his brother To the ninth chapter

He said that he who took those eggs to Doña Isabel, she of Antunes, was his brother Raphael and that this he just now remembered.

To the fifth Witness, first chapter

5th Witness
Chap. 1st

He says that it is true and he has already confessed it.

To the second chapter

Chap. 2nd

He says that he has already confessed what this chapter contains.

To the third chapter

Chap. 3rd

He said that he has already confessed what this chapter contains.

To the Sixth Witness first Chapter

6th Witness
Chap. 1st

He said that he had already confessed what this chapter contains.

To the second chapter

Chap. 2nd
against Dᵃ
Beatriz
Enriquez

He said that the person who sent this supper was Dᵃ Beatriz Enriquez, but that the news of the death of his father did not come in Lent but seven days before Christmas, and the witness is mistaken in saying that it came in Lent.

To the Seventh Witness, only chapter

7th Witness
Only Chapter.

He said that some of his aunts, his mother or his grandmother may have told some of the many Jewish persons with whom they are in communication that to this confessant and his brother Raphael the law of Moses had been taught by his aunt Margaret and that he observed it.

To the eighth Witness first chapter

8th Witness
Chap. 1st

He said that all that this chapter contains is true and that he has already confessed it.

To the second chapter

Chap. 2nd
Dᵃ Margarita
de Rivera

He said that his aunt Margaret tried to teach him these three prayers but he was not able to learn them all.

To the ninth Witness, only chapter

9th Witness,
only chap.
against Dᵃ
Juana Tinoco
Maria de
Rivera

He said that it is true and it took place in this confessant's house when Dᵃ Juana Tinoco was there on a visit and that who kept chocolate and fruit for her was his mother Dᵃ Maria, and that he forgot to declare it in his confessions although he has deposed other things against the said Doña Juana.

To the tenth Witness first chapter

10th Witness
Chap. 1st

7

He says that what this chapter says is true and that it
happened with Isabel, she of Acosta, to whom his aunt Doña
Isabel de Rivera was teaching a prayer in the corridor of
Doña Ana Suarez's house when she told the said Isabel, she
of Acosta, that this confessant was now a Jew and that he
kept fasts and that she embraced this confessant rejoicing in
that he was like unto her.

To the second chapter

He said that he has already confessed what this chapter
relates and it happened with his aunt Isabel and his mother
Doña Maria, and that it is very possible that the said
Isabel, she of Acosta, may have heard it, and that it may
have confirmed her in the belief that this confessant was a
Jew.

Chapter 3rd
against
Esperanza
Rodriguez
Isabel, she of
Antunes.

To the third chapter

He said that what this chapter contains is false testimony
and a lie, because neither his mother nor his aunt Margarita
nor his grandmother washed the body of Dᵃ Blanca Enriquez, but Esperanza Rodriguez and so they could not send
the wet cloths of which this witness speaks. And that this
confessant saw that the said Esperanza Rodriguez went into
the parlor where the corpse of the said Doña Blanca was on
her bed with some wet cloths to wash her, and that Doña
Isabel, she of Antunes, was in the said room.

To the fourth Chapter

He said that he has already declared about these fasts
which were kept by Doña Blanca Enriquez.

11th Witness,
only chapter.
Margarita de
Rivera
Rafael de
Granada

To the eleventh witness, only chapter

He said what fault is it of his that his aunt Margarita
should say that she had taught the said law to him and to
his brother Rafael.

12th Witness.
Chap. 1st
against Dᵃ
Juana
Enriquez and
all her
relations and
the relations of
Simon Vaez.
Dᵃ Maria de
Rivera

To the twelfth Witness, chapter first

He said it is true that this confessant and his brother went
into the parlor of the house of Doña Juana Enriquez where
were all her relations and those of her husband and amongst
them his mother Doña Maria to whom both of them went to

speak to give her a message but that this confessant does not Rafael de Granada. know for certain if they were fasting, but that he thinks they were for such meetings are only held for the purpose of fasting, and more so they being so shortly after the death of the said Doña BlancaEnriquez and that his said mother did not say so to him but he conjectures it.

To the second chapter Chapter 2nd against Margarita de Rivera

He said that who went with his aunt Doña Margarita to Dª Elena de Silva the house of Doña Elena de Silva to keep the said fast of the great day with her and with her daughter Doña Isabel Doña Isabel, Antº Caravallo and Don Antonio Caravallo was his brother Raphael, Rafael de Granada and that he does not know how witness can say that his said aunt went to advise the said Doña Elena to keep the said fast because she is an exceedingly great Jewess and fled from the Inquisition of Portugal, as he was told by his mother, grandmother and his aunts.

To the third chapter Chap. 3rd

He said that seeing that he did not go to the house of the said Doña Elena, but his brother he cannot answer what the witness says.

To the fourth chapter Chap. 4th against Raphael de Granada.

He said that who took the hard boiled eggs to the said Doña Blanca's house was his brother Rafael and so he can give no information about what this chapter states, that his brother as a good confessant will confess it or has already done so.

To the thirteenth witness, first chapter 13th Witness Chap. 1

He said that his grandmother, his mother or some one of his aunts may have told what this chapter contains to some Jew, and that he has confessed the fasts he kept and those he saw kept.

To the second chapter Chapter 2nd Dª Blanca Enriquez.

He said that he has already declared about the money left by Doña Blanca Enriquez for keeping fasts for her soul.

To the fourteenth Witness, first Chapter Chap. 14th against Juan de Leon his

He said that this is Juan de Leon and he declared himself

mother his
grandmother with this confessant, his grandmother, his mother and his
aunt and aunts and brother when they were living in Peñalosa's
brother houses as he has already declared.

Chap. 2nd To the second chapter

He said that he has already confessed all that is contained
in this chapter and that it is true.

15th Witness To the fifteenth Witness, first chapter
Chap. 1st
Dª Elena de He said that it refers to the fast that was kept in the
Silva Rafael de
Granada house of Doña Elena de Silva where his brother Rafael
went and which he has confessed.

Chap. 2nd To the second chapter
Dª Blanca
Enriquez. He said that he has already confessed several times this
of the fasts kept for the said Doña Blanca Enriquez.

16th Witness To the sixteenth Witness, only chapter
Only Chapter
His mother his He said that he holds it for certain that his mother, his
grandmother
and his aunts grandmother and his aunts told many Jewish persons that
this confessant and his brother were Jews because they were
very ready to declare themselves to every one.

The 5th Witness To the fourth chapter of what was added by the fifth
Chap. 4th adds
Rafael de witness
Granada
He said that who told this confessant of what this chapter
relates was his brother Rafael, and it is true and he has con-
fessed it.

17th Witness To the seventeenth Witness, only chapter
only Chap.
against He said that although it is true that he declared himself as
Esperanza
Rodriguez. a Jew to Esperanza Rodriguez and her daughters he does
Juana, Maria
Isabel del not remember having gone with any of his aunts to keep any
Bosque.
fast in the house of the said Esperanza Rodriguez and so
this witness lies.

18th Witness To the eighteenth Witness, first chapter
Chap. 1st
His mother He said that although it is true that his aunt Margaret
grandmother
and aunts. taught the law of Moses to him and to his brother, his
mother, grandmother and aunts also taught it to him sometimes.

Chap. 2nd To the second chapter

He said that it is true and he has confessed that before

they were arrested this confessant, his brother, his mother, against His mother his grandmother, and his aunts and his uncle Diego Correa grandmother and brother. were determined not to confess. Diego Correa.

To the third Chapter

He said he has already confessed that his uncle Diego Chap. 3rd Correa used to go to the house of Simon Vaez Savilla at night after the first arrests of his grandmother and uncle and that it is true that Doña Juana Enriquez told his said uncle to change his name and call himself Don Pedro so as not to be recognized by the negroes and also to change his voice as he did sometimes when he went with this confessant and at other times with his brother Rafael.

To the nineteenth Witness first chapter 19th Witness, Chap. 1

He said that he has already confessed what is contained in this chapter.

To the second chapter Chap. 2nd

He said that he also confessed it.

To the third chapter Chap. 3rd

He said that he had already confessed what this chapter says.

To the fourth chapter Chap. 4th

He said that he has already confessed it.

To the twentieth witness, first chapter 20th Witness ap. 1 His

He said that this chapter speaks of his mother, grand- mother his grandmother mother & aunts and his uncle Diego Correa and that what Aunts and Diego Correa. it states is true because it took place with them.

To the second chapter Chap. 2nd

He said that he has already confessed what came to pass in this fast of the year '41.

To the third chapter Chap. 3rd

He said that he has confessed it.

To the fourth chapter Chap. 4th Rafael de

He said that he confessed that his aunt Margaret taught Granada Margarita de the law of Moses to him and to his brother and likewise Rivera. what this chapter contains.

To the fifth chapter Chap. 5th

He said that he has confessed it.

Chap. 6th To the sixth chapter

He says that he has already confessed it.

Chap. 7th To the seventh chapter

He said that he has already confessed all the fasts that he kept and that what this chapter says is true.

Chap. 8th His mother grandmother aunts Da Blanca Enriquez. & all her daughters To the eighth chapter

He said that he has already confessed that his mother grandmother and aunts had told him that Doña Blanca Enriquez and all her daughters were Jews.

Chap. 9th Juan de Leon Simon Vaez Gaspar Vaez To the ninth chapter

He said that this chapter speaks of Juan de Leon, Simon Vaez and Gaspar Vaez and that he has already confessed it.

Chapter 10th Franco Home To the tenth chapter

He said that this chapter speaks of Francisco Ome, that he has already confessed it.

Chap. 11th To the eleventh chapter

He said that he cannot imagine who these two perssons can be, that undoubtedly they must be some persons against whom he has made confessions, that they are Jews because his mother, grandmother and aunts having told him that they were.

Chap. 12th To the twelfth chapter

He said that it is and he has confessed it.

Chap. 13th Matias Rodriguez de Olvera Luis de Amesqueta Pedro de Guevara To the thirteenth chapter

He said that what the chapter contained is true and that his grandmother was suspicious of Matias Rodriguez de Olvera * and Luis de Amesqueta † and Pedro de

---

* A family of the name settled in Curaçoa in 1650. See Corcos, p. 7.

† Luis de Mesquita alias de Amesquita Sarmiento, unmarried, native of the city of Segobia in Castille, citizen and merchant of that of Mexico, son of Lope de Amesquita and of Isabel Gomez, native of that city, Hebrew new Christians, Judaizing heretic, reconciled 1646. (Obregon p. 357).

This is no doubt the same name which appears under the form

Guevara* that they being Jews they would deny what the chapter says, and this took place in the cell where this confessant and his brother were with his mother, grandmother and aunts.

To the fourteenth chapter   Chap. 14th

He said that he has already confessed this about the cat.

To the twenty first witness first chapter   21st Witness Chap. 1st

He said that he has already confessed that who went with his aunt Margaret to Esperaza Rodriguez's house was his brother Raphael and that if this confessant had gone he would have confessed it like a good penitent as he has been.   Esperanza Rodriguez Margarita de Rivera Rafael de Granada.

To the second chapter   Chap. 2nd

He said that it speaks of the death of Diego Autunes and he has already confessed it with all precision and truth.

To the third chapter   Chap. 3rd †Juana Maria, Isabel Rodriguez del Bosque.

He said that the persons of whom this chapter speaks are the daughters of Esperanza Rodriguez and he has already confessed it with all truth and precision and that is the truth on his oath which he has sworn.

The said Inquistor ordered that a copy and transcript of the said publication be given to him and that on the third day he respond thereto and allege against it,   allege

Mesquita. The oldest Jewish gravestone now remaining in New York is that of Benjamin Bueno de Mesquita who was buried in 1683. See N. T. Phillips *Pub. Am. Jewish Hist. Soc.*, No. 1, pp. 91 and 92. David Bueno de Mesquita was a well-known resident of Amsterdam in the beginning of the 18th century. See Graetz, *History of the Jews* (American edition), Vol. V, p. 205. The family Bueno de Mesquita still exists in England.

*Pedro Guebara, Portuguese, merchant and citizen of this city of Mexico, Judaizing heretic, fugitive, executed in effigy 1649 (Obregon p. 375).

† Juana del Bosque native of the city Carthegena of the Indies, resident in this [city] of Mexico, wife of Blas Lopez, Portuguese, fugitive, daughter of Esperanza Rodriguez, reconciled, and Juan Baptista, German, Judaizing heretic, reconciled 1640 (Obregon p. 357).

by and with the opinion and advice of his advocate and guardian what may be expedient in his defence, and very strictly admonished still to think over it well and declare the truth he was ordered back to his cell, and he signed it.*

GABRIEL DE GRANADA.

Before me [Signed] GONZALO DE ESTRADA.

I accept these confessions in so far as they make in my favor and no farther. Said day month and year.

[Signed]　Dr GAVIOLA.

14th Audience.　Mexico, Saturday 18th December 1643. Inquisitor Estraday Escobedo. Morning.

He said that he has asked this audience in order to declare that he has remembered that after his mother, grandmother and aunts were prisoners in this Holy Office Maria Gomez She of Tremiño he went to see Maria Gomez she of Tremiño to give her a dollar that she had sent him for some shoes and having gone to her house which was in San Francisco Street he found them in company with the said Maria Gomez, her Eleanor Nuñez mother Eleanor Nuñez who was sitting down on a bench in the wide corridor near to the door of her said daughter's room, she said to this confessant and to her said daughter Maria Gomez who was standing up with her son Raphael in her arms speaking of the arrest of the said mother, grandmother and aunts of this confessant, what would they not make them suffer in this Tribunal what would they not say to them and charge them with ? that when she was a prisoner, they charged her in the publication of Witnesses that she had flogged a holy christ, and that although she denied it they read it in the auto all of which was heard by this confessant and by the said

---

* The reading over of these answers was omitted.　D. F.

Maria Gomez. And proceeding with her chat with the
two the said Eleanor Nuñez told that shortly after she Eleanor Nuñez
went out in the auto she was making a visit to Doña
Isabel de Espinoza who asked why Isabel Cardado,* she
of Balthazar del Valle,† who had put a holy christ into
a *servicio* (a night-stool) and that she answered that only
those who had been and are prisoners in this Holy office
knew why they confessed, saying all this with a peculiar
look and significant tone giving it to be understood that
they forced them in this Holy office to confess.

Item he remembers that before and after what he has
related he heard the said Eleanor Nuñez telling several Eleanor Nuñez
times that her imprisonment in this Holy office had been
strewn with flowers on account of her having got so well
and so quickly over it.

And that by means of the negro, Manuel, who served in the The Negro
secret prison, they were able to communicate by writing and Manuel
had her daughters Maria and Isabel come and present themselves.

Item. He remembered having heard his aunt Margaret Margarita de
de Rivera (one day in the morning that she sent to Luis Rivera.
Nuñez a cross which was that of the Holy Christ shown him
in this Tribunal) say the following words : what a bad day
Luis Nuñez will pass to-day, for the first thing that
enters his doors will be a cross, and although some of his
aunts were present when she said it he does not remember
which of them.

And that sometimes likewise he heard his said aunt

* Isabel Lopez Cardado, native of Med na del Campos, citizen of
the mines of Pachuca, wife of Baltasar del Balle, reconciled, Judaizing heretic, reconciled 1635 (Obregon p. 355f).

† Baltasar del Balle, Portuguese, or Baltasar Diaz native of the city
of Samora in Castille, citizen of the mines in Pachuca, Judaizing
heretic, reconciled 1635 (Obregon p. 355). Jacob Fonceco Vale was
in Barbadoes in 1680. Adler, *Pub. Am. Jewish Hist. Soc.* No. 1, p.
107 ; Isabella de Valle perished in the flames in Lisbon, May 10,
1682, Kayserling, *Sephardim.*

Margarita de Rivera Margaret when the most holy sacrament happened to pass
near her house when the bell would ring say *there goes the*
!= Oh ho! = *dishevelled* (or the unkempt or the bald-head) meaning the
most holy Sacrament, and at other times he heard her say
when our Lady would be mentioned call her *Doña Maria*,
saying both things about Chrst our Lord and his Most Holy
Mother with scorn and contempt.

And that this kind of language was commonly used by
Dᵃ Catalina Tinoco Isabel Antunes Catalina Tinoca and Isabel, she of Antunes, which this confessant heard several times, in scorn of our Lord Jesus
Christ and his most Holy Mother. And that just now he
does not remember any thing else, and that it is the truth
on the oath he has sworn.

And very straitly admonished to think over it well he
was ordered back to his cell* and he signed it.

GABRIEL DE GRANADA.
Before me
[Signed] LIC. Mᵒʳ DE ARASUS.

I accept this confession in so far as it makes in my
favor and no farther.

Dʳ GAVIOLA.

15th Audience Mexico, Tuesday 22ⁿᵈ November 1643 Inquisitor Higuera
y Amarilla. Afternoon.

He said . . . that he remembers that three or four months
before his grandmother, mother and aunts were arrested . . .
Matias Rodriguez de Olivera Margª de Rivera Dᵃ Rafaela Enriquez Dᵃ Blanca Enriquez. Mathias Rodriguez the daughters of Dᵃ Blanca Enriquez his aunt Margaret said that Mathias Rodriguez de
Olivera was an observer of the law of Moses, that Doña
Raphaela Henriquez had told her so. And that when Doña
Blanca Henriquez died the said Mathias Rodriguez de
Olivera sent a fish supper to the daughters of Doña Blanca,
that he heard his aunt Margarita de Rivera say this on

* Not read over as it ought have been. D. F.

the occasion above referred to, and that so he presumes that the said Mathias Rodriguez de Olivera is an observer of the law of Moses because it is a ceremony of the law of Moses to send the said suppers and dinners of fish to the children and near relations of the dead person who has been an observer of the law on such occasions.

And that six or seven months before they arrested this confesant, his mother aunts and grandmother he heard them say on several occasions sometimes to one and sometimes to others that Manuel Alvarez de Arellano* was an observer of the law of Moses because Doña Raphaela Enriquez had told it to his mother grandmother & aunts. And that three or four months before the arrest of this confessant his mother, grandmother and aunts when they were all talking about Duarte de Leon and his wife Isabel Nuñez his aunts said that the said Duarte de Leon and his said wife Isabel Nuñez were observers of the said law, and that the said Duarte de Leon observed it after he was released from this Holy office, and his aunt Margaret said that the said Isabel Nuñez wife of the said Duarte de Leon told her so. *(margin: Manuel Alvarez de Arellano. Doña Raphaela. Duarte de Leon Isabel Nuñez Marga de Rivera)*

And that now he remembers that a year before he was arrested this confessant went to the house of Doña Juana Enriquez to see her and she gave him two dollars to keep two fasts of the law of Moses for her health, which he kept, and that to declare this he has asked this audience and he solemnly promises that whenever he remembers anything altho' he may be out of these prisons he will ask for an audience and declare it with all precision and truth and this that he has declared is the truth and straitly admonished still to think it over well he was ordered back to his cell† and he signed it. *(margin: Doña Juana Enriquez)*

GABRIEL DE GRANADA.

* Manuel Albarez de Arellano, native of Jelbes in Portugal, unmarried and merchant of Spain in these kingdoms, descendant of new Christians, Judaizing heretic, reconciled 1647 (Obregon p. 362).

† The reading over omitted.   D. F.

Before me.

[Sig^d]   FRANCISCO MURILLO CRIALES.*

I accept this confession as far as it makes in my favor and no farther.

[Signed]   D^{or} GAVIOLA.

<table>
<tr><td>16th Audience
at which he
communicated
the publication
with his
lawyer</td><td>Mexico, Saturday, January 9th 1644 Inquisitors Agros, and Saenz de Mañozca
He said that what he remembers is that less than two years ago this confessant being one Sunday afternoon in the house of Simon Vaez Sevilla sitting down on a bench in the corridor he saw Gaspar Vaez aud his uncle Antonio Vaez Casteloblanco† walking up and down there for a long time,</td></tr>
</table>

and after the said Antonio Vaez had gone away this confessant asked the said Gaspar Vaez what he and his uncle had been talking about, and he answered that he had been teaching a prayer of the law of Moses, and he asking him again if he did not know some prayers of the law of Moses he answered that because of his occupations in his father's service, Simon Vaez Sevilla, he did not have time to learn them, and that his mother Doña Juana Enriquez, when he allowed her could not teach them to him, and that this is what he remembered and had to say.

Gaspar Vaez

Consultation with the advocate He was told that Dr Juan Baptista Martinez his guardian and advocate is present to treat with him and consult with him about the publication of the Witnesses who depose against him the said Gabriel de Granada and what he has answered thereto and so likewise the confessions he has made at audiences voluntarily asked for by him since Friday the

---

* This man Criales was the Secretary of the Archbishop of Mexico and was afterwards Mayor of the city. D. F.

† Antonio Baez and by others called Captain Casteloblanco Portuguese, native of Casteloblanco in Portugal, Judaizing heretic, reconciled 1625 (Obregon p. 354).

ninth day of the month of October of the year 1643 until
Tuesday the 22nd day of December of the said year '43, and
that which he made to-day in the audience had with him the
said Gabriel de Granada with all the rest that was necessary
and he ratified the said confessions and said they were his
and he had made them according to and as they were read
to him, and that they were true and he adhered to, affirmed
and reaffirmed them and ratified and did ratify them and if
necessary he would repeat them and in the presence of and
with the assistance of his said guardian, in whose presence
he had previously sworn to speak the truth and having conferred and consulted what he pleased with his said guardian
and advocate about his business and cause and with his
opinion counsel and advice

Ratification of his confessions in presence of his guardian

He said that as is set forth and evident in and from his
said confessions he has wholly confessed the entire truth
about the crimes which he has committed against our holy
catholic faith in which he solemnly promises to live and die
as a faithful and catholic christian, believing as he well and
faithfully believes all that our holy Roman Catholic mother
church believes, holds and teaches, he being sorrowful and
repentant of the evil deed, in feeling complacent at such a
great iniquity, when he knew that his grandmother, mother
and aunts had flogged the holy christ, and that the reason he
did not confess it instantly, forthwith, was the shame and
terror which put themselves before his eyes, and that these
two things in those of his age even in smaller crimes and in
very light faults are what prevents them from telling the
truth because he is scarcely fifteen years old, for all of which
he humbly begs forgiveness from this Holy Tribunal, as its
custom is to grant to good penitents, as he has been ; and
deceived and persuaded by his own mother, grandmother
and aunts to whom as an incapable boy he believed, and
that all that can be said in his favor on account of his age
and incapacity he begs that it be considered as herein alleged
in his favor and seeing that he is truly repentant he prays

for mercy and firmly purposes to amend his conduct and he begs and implores most humbly that he be absolved from the censures in which he has incurred and incorporated into the bosom of our holy Roman Catholic apostolic mother church and to the communion of the faithful, and he definitively closed by and with the advice and consent of his advocate.

Definitive conclusion.

Referred to the Fiscal

The said Lords Inquisitors commanded that the said Fiscal be served with a notice and that he close at the first audience ; and then straitly admonished he was ordered back to his cell, and he signed it together with his guardian and lawyer.

He answers that he hears it.

(Sig^d)   D^{on} Juan Bapt^a de Cepd^a

(Signed)   Gabriel de Granada.

Before me (Signd) Ph^e de Cabalça Amezqueta.

I accept these confessions in so far as they favor me and no farther.   Do^r Gaviola.

Answer of the Fiscal

And forthwith what was decreed by the Lords Inquisitors was by me the present Notary notified to the said Fiscal who said that he heard it, to which I certify.

(Sig^d)   Ph^e Cabalça Amezqueta.

Ratification in plenary procedure before the respectable persons

And forthwith incontinently the said guardian and advocate having been commanded to leave, there being present as respectable religious persons Father friar Diego de Segura and the Lic. Mohedano presbyters who have sworn the oath of secrecy, in due form of law there was received from the said Gabriel de Granada an oath on which he promised to tell the truth.

He was told that the Fiscal of this Holy Office presents him as a witness against Isabel de Antunes (and 85 other persons, as per list at the beginning of the process) to pay attention and that his confessions shall be read to him and if in them there should be anything to alter to add or amend to do so in such a manner as wholly to tell the truth and to affirm and ratify it because what he now says will stand to the prejudice of the aforesaid persons and then what he declared and deposed against the said persons since the audience of Friday the 9th of October 1643 until to day Saturday 9th of January 1644, all having been read to him word for word,* and the said Gabriel de Granada having said that he had heard and understood it, he declared that those were his depositions and that he had declared them just as they were read to him, and that they were well recorded, and written and he had nothing to alter to add or to amend because they are the truth just as they are written and he adhered to and affirmed and reaffirmed them, that he ratified and did ratify them, and it being necessary he would declare them anew against the above-mentioned persons and not from hatred but for unburdening his conscience and he signed it, and straitly admonished he was ordered back to his cell.

(Signed) GABRIEL DE GRANADA

Before me

PH⁸ DE ÇABALZA AMEZQUETA

In the city of Mexico first day of the month of September of 1645† the Inquisitors Lic. Domingo Velez de Assas y Argos Doctors (D. Dˢ) Don Francisco de Estrada y Escobedo, Don Juan Saenz de Mañozca and the Lic. Don Bernabé de la Higuera y Amarilla being in their afternoon audience They said that in conformity with what is prescribed in the accorded letter of the Lords of the Council of His Majesty, of the Holy and general Inquisition of the 31st of January

Decree for Inspection

---

* De *berbo ad berbum*, as the " present notary " has it. D. F.

† Twenty months after the last audience. D. F.

of the past year of 1635 and which is in the seventh volume
of Letters from the said Lords, folio sixty, Urbano Martinez,
Juan Correa, Pedro and Sebastian del Castillo, Surgeons of
this Holy Office proceed to make an inspection and examine
the said Gabriel de Granada and ascertain if he is cut
around or circumcised and let them declare it under oath in
this Tribunal taking the said oath before all things to exercise faithfully and well their office and to observe secrecy
about all they may see and hear and in their presence should
come to pass, and they affixed their rubrics

[Here are the four rubrics of the Inq.]

Before me (Sig^d) EUGENIO DE SARAVIA

And then the said Inquisitors commanded the said Urbano
Martinez, Juan Correa, Pedro and Sebastian del Castillo to
enter into the audience for the said purpose, from whom,
they being present, was received an oath in due form on
which they promised well and faithfully to perform their
office and to observe secrecy in all that they may see and
hear and in their presence come to pass.

And they were commanded by the said Inquisitors that
with me the present secretary of the secret chamber of this
Holy office and with Francisco Ruiz Marañon alcaide of the
secret prisons thereof they proceed, to the cell where the said
Gabriel de Granada is confined, and to inspect and examine
him with all care according to their art and profession to
ascertain if he is circumcised according to the custom of the
Jews, and they having promised so to do and comply they
went down to the cell where the said Gabriel de Granada is
confined and each one separately having seen him and examined him and gone up to the Audience where the said
Inquisitors were they Declared that having inspected the
said Gabriel de Granada they found a mark . . . . running
longitudinally and with a cicatrix, made apparently with a

cutting instrument, and that it is not a natural mark, and that they remember having inspected and found another culprit with the same mark who they think is Simon Montero,* and that perchance it may be a mark of circumcision amongst the Jews, who have various rites and ceremonies, and that this is what according to the best of their loyal knowledge and belief they are able to declare on the oath which they have sworn, and they signed it   (Signed)

URBANO MARTINEZ SEBASTIAN DEL CASTILLA JOHAN

DE CORREA FRAN^{co} DEL CASTILLO† P° DEL CASTILLO   † Not named in the order

Before me (Sig^d) EUGENIO DE SARAVIA

In the city of Mexico, Saturday 2nd of September 1645 the Inquisitor Doctor Don Juan Saenz de Mañozca being in his morning audience he ordered Gabriel de Granada to be brought there from the secret cells and he being present he was asked if he remembers anything about his business to tell it . . . .   He said that he does not recollect anything that he ought to declare.   He was told that yesterday afternoon as he is aware, he was inspected by five Surgeons of this Holy office and they found on him a mark . . . . and not to be a natural mark which must have been made a few years ago, and that they judged and pronounced it to be a mark of circumcision such as the Jews make use of: that he is admonished and charged to say and confess clearly and openly what he knows about that mark and who made it on him, for it is not likely nor can it be believed that he has not observed it, and tried to find out the purpose for which it

Confession of the culprit about the Circumcision

---

* Simon Montero, native of Casteloblanco in Portugal, citizen and merchant of this city of Mexico, married in Seville to Doña Elena Montero, daughter of Hebrew new Christians, Judaizing heretic, feigned confessor and impenitent, executed in person 1649 (Obregon p. 375).

8

was done; because by so doing he will relieve his conscience and all mercy shall be extended to him

He said that since he entered as a prisoner in this Holy office he has tried to speak the truth and unburden his conscience, with a solemn promise to do so whenever and wherever he would remember anything or aught should be asked him, and that about what he is interrogated he can only say that since the use of reason dawned on him he found himself with that said mark and he believed that it was natural to him and common to all men, and that as he has always acted in these matters so much like a boy that even yesterday when the Surgeons inspected him he did not fall into the suspicion of circumcision nor has he any suspicion of any one but his mother Doña Maria de Rivera who perchance caused him to be circumcised when he was so small that he does not remember the pain or the rest that may have taken place. And that when he was arrested three months had passed since he had left school, and that he had read some books in Spanish about the old law which treats of circumcision comparing it with holy baptism, and that it said that circumcision was a cutting . . . . and as he had no mark around he did not suspect that the mark he has was one of circumcision, for he had neither heard nor read that any other mark would serve for circumcision; and that being in San Luis Potosi when he was a year and a half old he has heard his grandmother his mother and his aunts say that there lived there one Alvaro de Acuña* a great Jew a relation of Manuel de Granada, father of this confessant and that perhaps he may have done him the harm that he to-day has, and that it would not be a miracle that moved by reason of the relationship he may have marked him believing that

---

* Albaro de Aquña, Portuguese, resident in this city of Mexico, drowned at sea, merchant, Judaizing heretic, dogmatist, executed in effigy 1649 (Obregon p. 375).

For the name see Kayserling *Ein Feiertag in Madrid*, p. 33.

this confessant would be as great a Jew as he in which he deceived himself for although they perverted him he acknowledges that he cannot be saved except in the faith and belief of our Lord Jesus Christ because His Divine Majesty has enlightened him, and that this is what he can declare and the truth on the oath that he has sworn, and admonished still to think it well over he was ordered to his cell and he Signed it. GABRIEL DE GRANADA

Before me (S^d) EUGENIO DE SARAVIA*

I accept this confession in so far as it favors me and no farther (S^d) Dr GAVIOLA.†

Gabriel de Granada + No. 26.

Reviewed and Examined [literally *seen*] by Us the Apostolic Inquisitors against heretical pravity and apostasy, by Apostolic authority in this city, and Archbishopric of Mexico, States and provinces of New Spain &c. jointly with the ordinary, a process and criminal cause which before us has pended and is pending between parties litigant; of the one part the Fiscal of this Holy Office Accusing plaintiff, and of the other part a defendant culprit Gabriel de Granada, native of this city and resident therein, who is present, a son of Manuel de Granada defunct in the Phillipine Islands,‡ and

* There are no votes by the Inq. Consultors or Doc. as req^d by law. D. F.

† This deposition was neither read over to him nor ratified by him as absolutely necessary to make it valid. D. F.

‡ See p. 95, where it is stated that he died in Manilla. It is especially interesting to note at this time the early relation between the American continent and the Phillipine Islands; from 1590 the Phillipines were dependent on the viceroy and audiencia of Mexico : *The Establishment of Spanish Rule in America* by Bernard Moses, Ph. D. Putnam, New York and London, 1898, pp. 70, 71.

I found in addition to the above the following entries of Jews

of Doña Maria de Rivera : about and for the reason that the said Gabriel de Granada being a baptized and confirmed Christian and as such enjoying the graces, privileges and exemptions which faithful and catholic Christians enjoy and ought to enjoy, in contravention of the profession made in the holy baptism, had done said and committed, seen done, said, and committed many and heinous crimes, against what our holy mother the Roman catholic church and evangelical law believes, holds, preaches and teaches, apostatising from her and going over to the observance and belief of the dead law of Moses, keeping it with all its rites and ceremonies, believing with all his heart that it was the good and true one, and that one in which he must be saved, he feigning to be a true and catholic Christian, and that the law of our Redeemer Jesus Christ was not the good and the true one, having himself circumcised as a sign of the Judaic profession, as it was evident that he was so circumcised by the hand of a famous Rabbi who had been in these kingdoms and who was a relative of the said Manuel de Granada his father. And that in the past year of Sixteen hundred and forty-one, a certain person very nearly related to the said Gabriel de Granada catching him when alone had said to him, that in order that he should be saved he must follow the law of Moses, which alone was the good and the true and necessary one for salvation, and not that of our Lord Jesus Christ, because she and other persons likewise his very near relations

tried by the Inquisition in Mexico who resided in the Phillipine Islands.

Jeorge Rios, Portuguese, unmarried, native of the city of Seville, resident of Manilla, Phillipine Islands, Judaizing heretic, reconciled 1593 (Obregon, p. 340).

Domingo Rios, Portuguese, brother of Jeorge Rios, native of Fondon in Portugal; resident of Manila, Phillipine Islands, Judaizing heretic, reconciled 1593 (Obregon, p. 340).

Manuel Gil de la Guarda, native of the city of La Guarda in Portugal, citizen of Manilla, Judaizing heretic, reconciled 1601 (Obregon, p. 350).

observed it. Whereupon from that instant he departed from and left the law of our Lord Jesus Christ, and passed over to the Faith, and belief of the said Law of Moses, saying to the said person his very near relation, that he would observe it and do what she would teach him, such as the fasts that he had to keep, especially that of the great day which falls in the month of September, the rites and ceremonies which must be observed on the eve thereof, bathing, putting on clean clothes, supping on fish and vegetables and not on other things on the said eve and day after the evening star came forth, going without eating or drinking the whole day, asking forgiveness the one from the other, those who had quarelled becoming friends, and the parents giving their blessing to their children, lighting wax candles and placing them on a clean cloth, and on the night of the said fast reciting the prayers of the law without sleeping until past midnight. And that the said Gabriel de Granada had asked her why they had concealed from him what has been related.

And that conforming to this in the month of September of the said year of 1641 the said Gabriel de Granada kept a fast of the great day, with the said persons his very near relations they having concerted it between themselves before-hand, bathing himself the previous eve, putting on clean clothes, supping fish, eggs, and vegetables lighting four or five wax candles which they put on the floor of a bedroom on a clean towel, and there they staid until near midnight, some-times on foot and at other times sitting down, and afterwards the said Gabriel de Granada recited the following prayer, his head covered with his hat on according to the custom of the Jews,* and they embraced each other and prayed for forgiveness from each other, and they kissed the hand of the oldest of their said very near relations who gave her blessing to all of them saying : May God make ye good. And in the morning he went to amuse himself and spend the day, and

* The prayer is omitted it being too long and foolish. D. F.

at night he returned to sup on the things mentioned; and
that he also kept many other ordinary fasts of the said Law
of Moses to the end that God would make him good, and he
kept others for the soul of a certain Judaising person, receiving money for them and fasting them on Mondays, Wednesdays and Thursdays. And that a certain person an observer
of the said law having died, as a ceremony thereof, the said
persons very nearly related to the said Gabriel de Granada
for being friends of the widow of the said defunct, sent by
him to the said widow three hard boiled eggs and a vessel
full of water, because she had spilt that of her house as a
ceremony of the said law. And upon the said person having
expired; the said widow, his wife, by means of the said
Gabriel de Granada, sent to ask another certain person, likewise a Judaizer, something made of gold or pearls to put
them in the mouth of the said defunct as a ceremony of the
said law: and the said Gabriel de Granada brought three
or four grains of pearls wrapped in a small piece of paper,
and he gave them to the said widow. And that a certain
person very nearly related to the said Gabriel Granada
having died, on the seventh day after the arrival of the news
he with the said persons his very near relations, fasted for
the soul of the said Defunct, eating things made of fish and
vegetables the other six days, keeping himself retired in his
house without going out therefrom as a ceremony of the said
Law. And that the day that this Holy office arrested certain persons very near relations to the said Manuel de
Granada, he and two other persons likewise his very near
relations went to the house of certain persons who offered one
of the said persons his very near relations five hundred or
one thousand dollars to give them to the Alcaide of this Inquisition to the end that he would let him speak to another
person who was a prisoner to tell her and admonish her not
to declare anything against the people of the said house. And
the said person very nearly related to the said Gabriel de
Granada promised that although they should arrest her she

would not expose them, and that the said Gabriel and his brother should they arrest them would not declare what they knew although they should put knives to their throats. And that the said persons of the said house said to the said person very nearly related to the said Gabriel de Granada that when another certain person should go to her house at night to go without a ruff and disguised changing his name to that of Don Pedro and imitating his voice, and in company with the said Gabriel de Granada and that the said Gabriel de Granada being a prisoner, a certain person also his very near relation exhorted him from her cell not in any manner to declare aught against people outside, that it was enough for him to confess his own faults without confessing those of others. And she continued these prison communications from another cell where she was, by means of a tame cat tying what she sent to his neck, infringing the modesty and silence with which she was admonished to conduct herself in her cell, and of the serious pains [2] incurred by those who act to the contrary. And that it is to be presumed and believed that the said Gabriel de Granada had done said and committed many other and heinous crimes against our holy catholic faith, and seen them done said and committed by many other persons about which he kept silent, maliciously concealing them, of which he solemnly declared that he [The Fiscal] would accuse him in the prosecution of his cause when and where they came to his knowledge and if necessary he from that moment accused him of being a Judaizing heretic an apostate from our holy catholic faith, and that he desired to live and die in the false belief of the reprobated law of Moses, in which he has lived : and of being a perjurer, favorer, aider, abettor and concealer of Judaizing heretics ; and that therefore accepting his confessions in so far as they made in his favor and no farther, protesting against being compelled to too many proofs he begged and prayed us that we should admit his relations as true and his intent as well proved, and that we declare the said Gabriel de Granada to be a doer and perpetrator of the crimes of which he accused him, and a Judaizing heretic, an apostate from our holy catholic faith; and to have incurred a sentence of the greater excommunication and to be held and bound thereby ; and that we should condemn him to the greatest and severest penalties established by Common law, by the laws and pragmatics of these kingdoms Proper Motives of his Holiness and Instructions of the Holy Office, relaxing his person to the secular arm and Justice, declaring all his goods to belong to the Royal Exchequer of this Holy office, from the day that he commenced to commit the said crime to the end that he should suffer condign punishment and to serve for the Christian people as an example and a warning.

And he asked us that if it were necessary the said Gabriel de Granada should be put to the question of the torture and to have it repeated on his person until he should wholly confess the truth ; and that full justice should be given him ; And he swore that he did not make the said accusation from malice; and the said Gabriel de Granada having been arrested on sufficient information [3] and confined in the secret prisons of this Holy office, on the third day he asked for an Audience of his own free will, and he continued them before the said accusation was put against him and also afterwards. And he confessed that about six or seven months before a little more or less, he being about thirteen years old his mother Doña Maria de Rivera called him when alone and said to him that the Law of our Lord Jesus Christ which he followed was not the good or the true but the law of Moses which she, his mother, and her sisters observed and followed. And that because he was her son and the love she bore him she wished to take him out of the deception in which he was and teach him the said law of Moses, because that alone was the good and necessary law for his salvation : and that as a boy of scant capacity he believed what his said mother told him : and that from that instant he had departed from the law of our Lord Jesus Christ and passed over to the Faith and belief of the said law of Moses; believing and holding it for certain (as his said mother told him) that it was the good and the true law and in which he must be saved, and not that of our Lord Jesus Christ, knowing that it was contrary to and different from the said law of Moses. And that he had answered his said mother that he would observe it and do what she might teach him. And that on the said occasion and on many others she had told him and taught him that in observance of the said law, in the month of September, the fast of the great day must be kept, bathing on the eve preceding and putting on clean clothes, supping on fish & vegetable and not meat, and that wax candles must be lighted and put on a clean cloth, and that they must recite until after midnight without sleeping the prayers of the said law; and the following day he must go without eating until the evening star appeared, again supping on fish and vegetables and not meat: and that they must ask forgiveness the one from the other, those who had quarreled becoming friends; and that they must observe Saturdays as feast days not working on them: and that although he observed them, not for that did he fail to go to school to read and write. And that she had taught him that he must keep other fasts in observance of the said law on Mondays and Thursdays as well for the living as for the dead, supping on the eve fish and vegetables going the whole of the next day without eating until night after the evening star appeared, and that he must sup on the said things and not on meat, without doing any more ceremonies. And that there were other fasts of the said law such as that of Queen Esther eating the eve thereof fish and vegetables and going the three following days without eating or drinking all this time until the night of the last when they again supped on the aforesaid things, upon which they finished these fasts which were voluntary. And that there were other passovers and solemn feasts of the said law which she would teach him at the proper time. And that fowls which were to be eaten must be beheaded with a knife, and that bacon must not be eaten nor fish without scales. And that he must recite the prayers of the said law morning and night for the living and the dead and she taught him the said prayer: Lord, My soul calleth upon Thee &c. which he sometimes recited in observance of the said Law. And that in conformity with what his said mother had told him and taught him, he kept with her and with all the said persons his very near relations the fast of the grand day on the past year of 1641 with the said ceremonies bathing themselves in different rooms, putting on clean clothes, supping together on fish and vegetables and other things afterwards lighting four or five wax candles and putting them on the floor of a bedroom on a clean towel, and they recited such prayers of the said law as they knew, and they embraced each other and asked forgiveness of each other; and he and his brother Raphael de Granada kissed their grandmother's hand and that of their mother who gave them their blessing saying unto them, May God make ye good; and they went to sleep after midnight leaving the candles lighted until they burnt out. And that he went to Alameda the Alameda the day of the said fast and to other places to spend the day upon which he did neither eat or drink anything whatever, returning home after vespers where he supped with the persons mentioned the same as the preceding night. And that he had kept six or seven ordinary fasts on Mondays and Thursdays: some for himself and others for the soul of a certain person his very near relation supping on fish and vegetables after the evening star appeared. And he confessed that his name is Gabriel de Granada, a native of this city of Mexico thirteen and a half years of age and that he had no occupation and that he went to school learning to read and to write; and that they had arrested him on the ojo twelfth of July 1642 at twelve o'clock at night[4]. And having declared his genealogy he said he did not know of what caste or generation he is.

And that his said Mother, grandmother and aunts were

prisoners in this Holy office; and that he was baptized and confirmed in the Cathedral of this said city, and that he confessed and took communion at Lent and the last time in the said Cathedral with a certain clergyman, and that he took the communion in the Sacrarium and that he has always had a bull of the Holy Crusade in order to gain the Indulgences and he crossed himself and repeated the christian doctrine as contained in the Catechism. And that he had learned to read and to write in this said city of Catholic Masters, and that he had not studied any profession. And that at the age of one year his parents had taken him to San Luis Potosi from whence he returned at the age of three years to this said city from which he has not gone away nor had intercourse with more persons than his relations and his school fellows. And that he knew that for what he had confessed as being an observer of the said law of Moses like his mother grandmother, aunts and brother who were prisoners they had arrested him. And having been admonished three times to confess the truth and to unburden his conscience, he answered that he had declared and confessed what he remembered and that he solemnly promised that whenever and wherever he should remember anything else that is, or appears to be in offense of God our Lord and of his holy catholic faith to ask for an audience and to confess it. And in order to substantiate this his cause in conformity with the law he was provided with a guardian in whose presences he ratified his confessions and swore to answer the truth to the said accusation which being put he answered it saying that he is the person contained therein and fully satisfying all its chapters; and a transcript of the said accusation having been given to him and he having named an advocate with his advice and opinion he alleged what suited him in his defense and he closed for the question which by law might occur:

And the cause being by US received or admitted to proofs the said Fiscal made a reproduction of the witnesses of the Summary[5] requesting publication of them, and that the witnesses should ratify their depositions and that the concurring witnesses should be examined and they being ratified and the said publication being made he answered on oath which he swore in presence of his said guardian fully satisfying (i. e. confessing) all that they had deposed against him, and a transcript having been given him, by and with the advice and consent of his lawyer he alleged and definitively closed, of which a transcript was given to the said Fiscal. And the said cause being at this stage the said Gabriel de Granada asked of his own free will different audiences and in them he confessed what came to his memory as having done, seen done and heard as being done against our holy catholic faith especially some atrocious deeds at which he was found present and at which as a Jew he felt a peculiar complacency, and likewise the prison communications, the tricks and artifices which for accomplishing them were used, principally the one mentioned of the tame cat. Begging that the mercy which this Holy office is accustomed to exercise towards those who truly repent and voluntarily confess their crimes should be extended to him. And that although he did not remember who had put the mark of circumcision on him which he had he presumed that his said mother had ordered it done by the hand of a certain Jew his relation believing that he would be as great a Jew as himself in which he was deceived. And that at school he had read some books in Romance (Spanish) which treated of Circumcision comparing it with holy baptism. And the cause being at this stage to examine it and determine it, having had our accord and consultation with persons of learning and upright consciences(·)

(*Christi nomine invocato*)

THE NAME OF CHRIST INVOKING

WE decide considering the interlocutory decrees and merits of the said process, that the said Promotor Fiscal proved well and fully his accusation and complaint as well by witnesses as by the confessions of the said Gabriel de Granada, WE Give and pronounce his intent as well proven (his case as well made out, or sustained, by proofs &c.) Wherefore we ought to declare and we do declare the said Gabriel de Granada to have been a Heretical Judaizing apostate a favorer and abettor and concealer of Heretics, and of having passed over to the accursed, perverse and dead law of Moses and his followers, believing he would be saved in it and by it. To have fallen into and incurred in a Sentence of the greater excommunication and in all the other pains and disabilities in which heretics who under the name and title of Christians do and commit similar crimes fall and incur, and in confiscation and loss of his goods which we apply to the chamber and Exchequer of His Majesty and to his Receiver in his name, from the day and time that he commenced to commit the said crimes, the declaration of which we reserve to US. And although with a good conscience we could condemn him to suffer the pains by law established against such heretics but considering that the said Gabriel de Granada in the confessions he made before US showed signs of contrition and repentance, begging from God our Lord pardon for his crimes, and from us penance with mercy, solemnly promising that from henceforth he would live and die in our holy Catholic Faith, and that he was ready to fulfil and comply with any penance which we might impose upon him, and to abjure the said errors and do every other thing by Us commanded (considering that God desires not the death of the sinner but that he should be converted and live) if it so be that the said Gabriel de Granada becomes converted to our holy Catholic faith from a pure heart and faith unfeigned and that he has wholly confessed the truth naught concealing about himself or other persons dead or alive anything whatsoever Willing to extend mercy towards him we ought to

admit him and we do admit him to reconciliation, and We
Command that in pain and penance for what has been by
him done said and committed he shall go forth on the day
of the Auto to the scaffold with the other penitents, in person, without a waist-band and bonnet, and with a penitential
habit of yellow cloth with two red bars in the form of St.
Andrew's cross, and carrying a green wax candle in his
hands where this our sentence shall be read to him, and
publicly abjure his said errors which before us he hath confessed, and all species whatsoever of heresy and apostasy;
And the said abjuration being made WE command the said
Gabriel de Granada to be absolved and we do absolve him
from whatever sentence of excommunication into which for
the above cause he may have fallen and incurred, and we
unite and incorporate him into the bosom of the holy catholic mother church and we reinstate him to the participation
of the holy Sacraments and communion of the faithful and
Catholic christians thereof and we condemn him to imprisonment with a penitential habit for one year; and that he
wear the said habit over his vestments, and keep and observe
seclusion in the perpetual prison of this city, and that every
Sunday and feast day he go to hear high mass, and sermon
where there is any in the Cathedral church, with the other
penitents and on Saturdays go in pilgrimage to the church
which may be designated to him where on his knees and
with great devotion he shall recite the paternoster five times
with the Ave Maria creed and Salve Regina, and that he
confess and receive the Most holy Sacrament of the Altar
pasches the three pasches of each year (Christmas, Epiphany and
Easter) all the days of his life, and to perpetual and precise
banishment from all these Western Indies and from the çity
of Seville and town of Madrid, His Majestys Court, and
that he embark to fulfil it, in the first fleet leaving the port
of San Juan de Ulua (Vera Cruz) on its return to the Kingdoms of Spain, and that as soon as he arrives in the said
Kingdoms, within one month, he present himself in the

Tribunal of the Holy office of the Inquisition of Seville, in order that he may be known and a description taken of his person, and that a part and place be designated to him where he shall finish what may remain unexpired of his imprisonment and habit; and in order that in case of contravention the said Gabriel de Granada may be proceeded against as against an impenitent a relation of this his sentence and condemnation shall be sent with his description and age to the Most Illustrious and Most Reverend Lord Inquisitor General and Lords of the Council of His Majesty of the Holy and General Inquisition and to the Tribunals of the said Inquisition of Seville and of the Cities of Lima and Carthagena in these said Western Indies; and we pronounce the said Gabriel de Granada to be disabled and we disable him from holding and obtaining dignities benefices Ecclesiastical or secular offices which may be public or of honor nor to wear on his person gold, silver, pearls or precious stones nor silk camelot, nor fine cloth, nor go on horseback, nor carry arms nor exercise or use any of the other things which by common right, laws and pragmatics of these Kingdoms and Instructions of the Holy office of the Inquisition are prohibited to those similarly disabled, and to his descendants in the designated grade all of which we Command him so to do and fulfil under pain of relapsed impenitency; and by this our sentence definitively adjudged we thus pronounce and command in and by these writings.

D$^{or}_{OMINGO}$ VELEZ   D$^{or}_{ON}$ FRANCISCO

DE ASSAS Y ARGOS   DE ESTRADA Y ESCOBEDO

The Lic^{do} Don BERNABE   D$^{or}_{on}$ P^o DE BARRIENTOS LOMELIN

DE LA HIG^{A}Y AMARILLA.